Dictionary of Literary Biography • Volume Seventeen

Twentieth-Century American Historians

Dictionary of Literary Biography

1: *The American Renaissance in New England*, edited by Joel Myerson (1978)

2: *American Novelists Since World War II*, edited by Jeffrey Helterman and Richard Layman (1978)

3: *Antebellum Writers in New York and the South*, edited by Joel Myerson (1979)

4: *American Writers in Paris, 1920-1939*, edited by Karen Lane Rood (1980)

5: *American Poets Since World War II*, 2 volumes, edited by Donald J. Greiner (1980)

6: *American Novelists Since World War II*, Second Series, edited by James E. Kibler, Jr. (1980)

7: *Twentieth-Century American Dramatists*, 2 volumes, edited by John MacNicholas (1981)

8: *Twentieth-Century American Science-Fiction Writers*, 2 volumes, edited by David Cowart and Thomas L. Wymer (1981)

9: *American Novelists, 1910-1945*, 3 volumes, edited by James J. Martine (1981)

10: *Modern British Dramatists, 1900-1945*, 2 volumes, edited by Stanley Weintraub (1982)

11: *American Humorists, 1800-1950*, 2 volumes, edited by Stanley Trachtenberg (1982)

12: *American Realists and Naturalists*, edited by Donald Pizer and Earl N. Harbert (1982)

13: *British Dramatists Since World War II*, 2 volumes, edited by Stanley Weintraub (1982)

14: *British Novelists Since 1960*, 2 volumes, edited by Jay L. Halio (1983)

15: *British Novelists, 1930-1959*, 2 volumes, edited by Bernard Oldsey (1983)

16: *The Beats: Literary Bohemians in Postwar America*, 2 volumes, edited by Ann Charters (1983)

17: *Twentieth-Century American Historians*, edited by Clyde N. Wilson (1983)

Yearbook: 1980, edited by Karen L. Rood, Jean W. Ross, and Richard Ziegfeld (1981)

Yearbook: 1981, edited by Karen L. Rood, Jean W. Ross, and Richard Ziegfeld (1982)

Documentary Series, volume 1, edited by Margaret A. Van Antwerp (1982)

Documentary Series, volume 2, edited by Margaret A. Van Antwerp (1982)

Documentary Series, volume 3, edited by Mary Bruccoli (1983)

Dictionary of Literary Biography • Volume Seventeen

Twentieth-Century American Historians

Edited by Clyde N. Wilson
University of South Carolina

A Bruccoli Clark Book
Gale Research Company • Book Tower • Detroit, Michigan 48226
1983

Manufactured by Edwards Brothers, Inc.
Ann Arbor, Michigan
Printed in the United States of America

Copyright © 1983
GALE RESEARCH COMPANY

Library of Congress Cataloging in Publication Data
Main entry under title:

Twentieth-century American historians.

(Dictionary of literary biography; v. 17)
"A Bruccoli Clark Book."
Includes index.
1. Historians—United States—Biography. I. Wilson, Clyde
Norman. II. Series.
E175.45.T85   1983   907'.2022 [B]   82-24210
ISBN 0-8103-1144-5

For Ruby Smith Wilson

Contents

Foreword...ix

Permissions and Acknowledgments....................xi

James Truslow Adams (1878-1949).....................3
  C. James Taylor

Charles M. Andrews (1863-1943).....................9
  Jessica Kross

Bernard Bailyn (1922-   )...................................19
  A. Roger Ekirch

John Spencer Bassett (1867-1928).....................26
  Herbert J. Doherty, Jr.

Howard K. Beale (1899-1959).......................32
  Allan D. Charles

Charles A. Beard (1874-1948).........................38
  John Braeman

Carl Becker (1873-1945)...............................57
  Milton M. Klein

Samuel Flagg Bemis (1891-1973).....................64
  Kendrick A. Clements

Albert J. Beveridge (1862-1927).......................70
  Herbert A. Johnson

Herbert E. Bolton (1870-1953).......................74
  Amy Bushnell

Daniel J. Boorstin (1914-   )..............................79
  Frank Annunziata

Claude G. Bowers (1878-1958).........................86
  Michael Bordelon

Gamaliel Bradford (1863-1932).......................92
  Marion Edmonds

Bruce Catton (1899-1978).............................98
  Carol Reardon

Edward Channing (1856-1931)........................103
  George D. Terry

Thomas C. Cochran (1902-   )........................109
  Steven P. Gietschier

Henry Steele Commager (1902-   )..................117
  Lawrence Wells Cobb

Avery Craven (1885-1980).............................126
  John David Smith

Merle E. Curti (1897-   )...............................131
  David L. Carlton

William E. Dodd (1869-1940).........................135
  Wayne Mixon

David H. Donald (1920-   )............................141
  John McCardell

William A. Dunning (1857-1922).....................148
  Anne W. Chapman

Shelby Foote (1916-   )................................154
  Clyde N. Wilson

Douglas Southall Freeman (1886-1953)...........157
  John L. Gignilliat

John A. Garraty (1920-   )............................170
  Justus D. Doenecke

Eugene D. Genovese (1930-   ).......................178
  Michael Bordelon

Lawrence Henry Gipson (1880-1971)..............187
  J. Barton Starr

Oscar Handlin (1915-   )...............................191
  Arnold Shankman

Albert Bushnell Hart (1854-1943)....................198
  Shirley A. Hickson

Robert Selph Henry (1889-1970).....................207
  Thomas Fleming

Richard Hofstadter (1916-1970)......................211
  Paula S. Fass

J. Franklin Jameson (1859-1937)......................230
  Richard A. Shrader

Merrill Jensen (1905-1980).............................236
  Michael E. Stevens

Arthur S. Link (1920-   )...............................241
  Marcia G. Synnott

Dumas Malone (1892-   )..............................250
  Paul A. Horne, Jr.

Forrest McDonald (1927-   )..........................257
  Justus D. Doenecke

Contents

Perry Miller (1905-1963)....................................272
   Robert M. Calhoon

Edmund S. Morgan (1916-).........................285
   William D. Liddle

Samuel Eliot Morison (1887-1976)..................296
   B. D. Bargar

Richard B. Morris (1904-)..........................307
   Peter A. Coclanis

Allan Nevins (1890-1971)..............................315
   Richard M. McMurry

Roy F. Nichols (1896-1973)............................328
   Carol Reardon

Reinhold Niebuhr (1892-1971)......................333
   David L. Carlton

Frank L. Owsley (1890-1956)..........................336
   M. E. Bradford

Vernon L. Parrington (1871-1929)..................342
   Michael O'Brien

Ulrich B. Phillips (1877-1934).......................350
   Kirk Wood

David M. Potter (1910-1971)..........................364
   Mark T. Carleton

James G. Randall (1881-1953) 373
   John David Smith

Carl Sandburg (1878-1967)............................378
   Mark E. Neely, Jr.

Arthur M. Schlesinger, Jr. (1917-)................382
   Edwin A. Miles

Kenneth M. Stampp (1912-).........................401
   John G. Sproat

Frederick Jackson Turner (1861-1932)............407
   Odie B. Faulk

Walter Prescott Webb (1888-1963)..................418
   Thomas L. Connelly

Bell Irvin Wiley (1906-1980)..........................423
   John Barnwell

T. Harry Williams (1909-1979)........................431
   Joseph G. Dawson III

William Appleman Williams (1921-).............450
   William Marina

Carter G. Woodson (1875-1950)......................458
   Edward L. Cox

C. Vann Woodward (1908-) 465
   Elisabeth Muhlenfeld

Louis B. Wright (1899-   ).............................483
   Suzanne Krebsbach

Supplementary Reading List...........................489

Contributors...493

Cumulative Index 497

Foreword

This volume contains literary biographies of fifty-nine historical writers. To be eligible for inclusion, writers had to meet three criteria. They had to be American; their historical writings had to be concentrated chiefly upon the United States; and their most important work had to fall within the twentieth century.

The historians selected for inclusion are primarily but not exclusively academic and professional ones, a preponderance which merely reflects the way most historical literature has been produced in this century. "Popular" historians have by no means been neglected. Though there has been a tension since the late nineteenth century between popular and academic historians, when dealing with the best of either sort, the distinction tends to break down. Allan Nevins, one of the greatest historians of the period, began life as a journalist and was admitted to the fraternity of academic historians at a late date. Another great historian, Douglas Southall Freeman, was academically trained but spent most of his life as a journalist. If most of the figures included herein were academic professors of history, many were not. Shelby Foote is primarily a novelist and Arthur M. Schlesinger, Jr., primarily a political publicist. Carl Sandburg was a poet and Robert Selph Henry, a railroad executive.

If historical literature has been broadly construed to include both scholarly and nonscholarly writers, the selection of figures has been narrowed in other ways. The writers represented have been limited to those writing primarily on American history because American history itself is a large enough and a clearly enough defined field or "genre" to merit distinct treatment. Thus, the numerous distinguished Americans who have contributed to the history of lands and peoples other than those of North America have not been considered for this particular volume.

If there is another obvious bias in the selection, it is in favor of the earlier years of the twentieth century against the later, of the older against the younger. Only twenty of the fifty-nine figures treated are still living, and all but a few of those have probably completed their major work. There are many historians now in mid-career who will perhaps deserve inclusion in any final accounting of the best of the twentieth century, but it seemed better in making selections of subjects for this volume to err on the side of certainty and to leave as many such decisions as possible for a later and more historical perspective.

Selecting the best historians, even within the limits defined, is a risky business. Two distinguished scholars, Robin W. Winks and Marcus Cunliffe, who edited an excellent book of essays on American historians (*Pastmasters: Some Essays on American Historians*, 1969), expended five pages of introduction defending their selection of figures for treatment and another page defending the contributors selected for the sketches. Since *Twentieth-Century American Historians* is larger and more inclusive than their volume, possibly less of a defense is needed.

Perhaps there will be substantial if not unanimous agreement on the fourteen major figures selected for extended treatment—Charles M. Andrews, Charles A. Beard, Daniel Boorstin, Douglas Southall Freeman, Richard Hofstadter, Perry Miller, Samuel Eliot Morison, Allan Nevins, Vernon L. Parrington, Ulrich B. Phillips, David M. Potter, Frederick Jackson Turner, T. Harry Williams, and C. Vann Woodward. For the remainder of the fifty-nine, the selection may be contested. Since American historians do not agree on methodology, interpretation, or ideological allegiance, there is not likely to be perfect agreement among them on the "important" figures. It would, indeed, be easy to draw up another list of writers as numerous as those in this volume and arguably as important as some of those included herein. Rather than fault the omissions herein, however, the reader is invited to enjoy the unprecedented breadth of ground covered and to recognize that the *Dictionary of Literary Biography* is a lively and flexible enterprise that has not necessarily exhausted with this volume all it has to say about American historical literature.

History is both a branch of literature and a scholarly discipline. As a field of literature, history is perhaps more formal and institutionalized and changes more slowly than fiction or poetry. To speak of schools only in the broadest categories, American history in the early part of the century was dominated by New Englanders of Federalist and patrician heritage, with a strong opposition provided by frontier-oriented or "Progressive" Middle Westerners. Since World War I, "liberal" writers and themes have predominated, though with a continuing, strong, and often subtle counterpoint by Southern and other "conservative" writers. The 1960s and 1970s created other movements and schools that are not yet fully developed. And this is to treat only the largest of observable categories.

But while it is true that most historians fall into "schools," it is also true that each one's encounter with the raw stuff of the human past is highly individual and that the best historians develop over time, the time often being a quite long career. As in the case of Supreme Court nominees, one cannot always predict from a historian's antecedents, training, or previous work which way his research and thought will lead him. An effort has been made to select the best individual historians, from the point of view of published books, without regard to schools. Had the volume focused on teachers, collectors, or researchers, rather than writers, the list would have been slightly, though not greatly, different.

There is no avoiding the fact that historians differ in ideological allegiance, that they debate over methodology and interpretation, and that they compete for professional accolades. They also often leave behind them students, colleagues, and competitors who have vested interests in increasing or lessening their reputations. And there is no universal critical authority that can be appealed to to settle questions of merit and precedence. An effort has been made to give every figure treated herein a generally sympathetic biographer, who has, of course, been urged to give a balanced treatment and to take account of criticism. While there are some risks in this approach, they are not nearly as great as the risk of turning the treatment of important and gifted writers over to their enemies.

American historical writing has produced a number of memorable works and a very respectable body of literature. Nevertheless, history as a whole has suffered in the twentieth century from a considerable disarray—doubt about its philosophical underpinnings and its "relevance," methodological controversy, gaps between profession and practice, uncertainty as to the position of history in the cultural domain. There have been rather few attempts at critical assessment of American historical literature as a body, and the few that exist are not notably successful. An adequate history of American historical writing, strangely, is yet to be written, the few that exist being either catalogues or interpretations based on a limited sample. It could be that the collective biography represented by *Twentieth-Century American Historians* may make, as one of its side effects, a contribution toward that overarching account of American historical literature that remains to be written.

For that reason and many others, the opportunity to treat historians once more as a part of American literature has been very pleasing. Whatever else may be said about them, the greatest historians are also literary artists, and it is nearly impossible to imagine a good historian who is not also a good writer. It may be, too, as has been suggested in a number of quarters, that history, having swung as far as possible toward "science," is in the process of swinging back and rapidly eliminating the gap between itself and "art." If that is the case, this survey by means of literary biography of the accomplishments of Americans writing about their own history in the twentieth century stands a chance to be both timely and enduring.

—*Clyde N. Wilson*

Permissions

The following people and institutions generously permitted the reproduction of photographs and other illustrative materials: The Granger Collection, pp. 3, 70, 79, 198; Yale University Archives, pp. 10, 12, 16, 17, 64; Harvard University News Office, p. 20; Duke University Archives, p. 27; DePauw University Archives, pp. 39, 52; Culver Pictures, pp. 53, 157, 167, 315, 407; Department of Manuscripts and University Archives, Cornell University, p. 57; Mimi Levine, pp. 81, 82; Doris Ulmann, p. 92; Harvard University Archives, pp. 103, 272; University of Chicago Library, p. 126; The Bettmann Archive, pp. 135, 383; Columbia University Public Information Office, p. 170; Stanley Lichens, p. 178; Lehigh University, p. 187; Bachrach, p. 191; Manuscript Division, Library of Congress, p. 231; Firestone Library, Princeton University, p. 241; Studio 350, Boston, p. 297; University of Washington, p. 344; Bentley Historical Library, University of Michigan, p. 350; News and Publications Service, Stanford University, p. 364; University of Illinois, p. 374; Saxon Donnelly, p. 401; Delmont Wilson, p. 424; Louisiana State University Office of Public Relations, p. 445; Lafayette, p. 466; National Endowment for the Humanities, p. 480; Robert S. Oakes, p. 483.

Acknowledgments

This book was produced by BC Research. Karen L. Rood is senior editor for the *Dictionary of Literary Biography* series. Judith S. Baughman and Robert H. Griffin were the in-house editors.

The production staff included Mary Betts, Joseph Caldwell, Patricia Coate, Angela Dixon, Lynn Felder, Joyce Fowler, Nancy L. Houghton, Sharon K. Kirkland, Cynthia D. Lybrand, Alice A. Parsons, Jean W. Ross, Joycelyn R. Smith, Debra D. Straw, Robin A. Sumner, Meredith Walker, and Lynne C. Zeigler. Charles L. Wentworth is photography editor.

Walter W. Ross and Anne Dixon did the library research with the assistance of the staff at the Thomas Cooper Library of the University of South Carolina: Michael Freeman, Gary Geer, Alexander M. Gilchrist, W. Michael Havener, David Lincove, Donna Nance, Harriet B. Oglesbee, Jean Rhyne, Paula Swope, Jane Thesing, Ellen Tillett, and Beth S. Woodard.

The following people were especially helpful in providing illustrations for this volume: Anna Marie Alexander, Emerson University; Donna Latrelle, Organization of American Historians; and Judith Schiff, Yale University Library.

Special thanks are due to Joel Myerson, Carol Reardon, and Robert Weir for their help in launching this project.

Dictionary of Literary Biography • Volume Seventeen

Twentieth-Century American Historians

Dictionary of Literary Biography

James Truslow Adams
(18 October 1878-18 May 1949)

C. James Taylor
University of South Carolina

SELECTED BOOKS: *Some Notes on Currency Problems* (New York: Lindley, 1908);

Speculation and the Reform of the New York Stock Exchange (Summit, N.J.: Privately printed, 1913);

Memorials of Old Bridgehampton (Bridgehampton, N.Y.: Privately printed, 1916);

History of the Town of Southampton, East of Canoe Place (Bridgehampton, N.Y.: Hampton Press, 1918);

The Founding of New England (Boston: Atlantic Monthly Press, 1921);

Revolutionary New England, 1691-1776 (Boston: Atlantic Monthly Press, 1923);

New England in the Republic, 1776-1850 (Boston: Little, Brown, 1926);

Provincial Society, 1690-1763 (New York: Macmillan, 1927);

Our Business Civilization: Some Aspects of American Culture (New York: A. & C. Boni, 1929); republished as *A Searchlight on America* (London: Routledge, 1930);

The Adams Family (Boston: Little, Brown, 1930; London: Oxford University Press, 1930);

The Epic of America (Boston: Little, Brown, 1931; London: Routledge, 1932);

The Tempo of Modern Life (New York: A. & C. Boni, 1931);

The March of Democracy, volumes 1 and 2 (New York & London: Scribners, 1932-1933); republished as *History of the American People* (London: Routledge, 1933);

Henry Adams (New York: A. & C. Boni, 1933; London: Routledge, 1933);

America's Tragedy (New York & London: Scribners, 1934);

The Record of America, by Adams and Charles Garrett

Vannest (New York: Scribners, 1935);

The Living Jefferson (New York & London: Scribners, 1936);

Building the British Empire, to the End of the First Empire (New York & London: Scribners, 1938);

Empire on the Seven Seas: The British Empire, 1784-

James Truslow Adams

3

1939 (New York & London: Scribners, 1940);

An American Looks at the British Empire (New York & Toronto: Farrar & Rinehart, 1940); republished as *America Faces the War* and *An American Looks at the British Empire (America Faces the War, No. 2)* (London: Oxford University Press, 1941);

The American: The Making of a New Man (New York: Scribners, 1943);

Frontiers of American Culture: A Study of Adult Education in a Democracy (New York: Scribners, 1944);

Big Business in a Democracy (New York: Scribners, 1945).

James Truslow Adams, a businessman turned scholar, wrote largely interpretative histories notable for their style and scope. His career spanned the world wars, and he produced scores of volumes and articles, most notably the studies he wrote during the 1920s about early New England.

Adams, a Brooklyn-born member of a business-oriented family, endured an unexceptional childhood during which his training and education better suited him to the world of commerce and investments than to scholarship. His mother, Elizabeth Truslow Adams, was an invalid, and his father, William Newton Adams, was a dour man dissatisfied with his lot in life as a moderately successful employee of a Wall Street brokerage firm. A bookish youth, Adams seldom participated in the games, sports, or other endeavors normally associated with American boys. Aside from an addiction to reading and his success in school, little in his educational background suggested that he would leave a lasting impression on the historical and literary worlds. Rather than attending a well-known college or major university after high-school graduation from Brooklyn Polytechnic, he continued at that institution, where he obtained a bachelor of arts degree in 1898. During his final year there, he edited the school paper and was class president, valedictorian, and poet. He dreamed of a career in law or as an engineer—each, however, was beyond what he believed he could achieve. Lawyers frequently had to declaim, and Adams was painfully shy—too shy to consider the bar seriously. Engineering necessitated advanced study in math and science, areas in which he felt lacking. After dismissing his first career choices for the shortcomings that he perceived in himself, he enrolled at Yale to study philosophy. It did not prove satisfactory to him. Within a year he left the university and returned to New York, where he took employment as a messenger at the firm for which his father worked. The Yale M.A. frequently mentioned among his accomplishments was obtained by a simple application through the mail in 1900, before that institution established standards which necessitated formalized instruction for the degree. A few years later he made a final attempt at graduate study when he began to take history courses at Columbia University. He dropped out after only six weeks, however, believing his classmates too unsophisticated. At this point his association with the academic world came to an end. Invitations extended later to enter the scholastic realm at Columbia, Wesleyan, and elsewhere were dismissed by Adams, who believed himself unfit for teaching or lecturing.

Until 1912 Adams confined his talents to the world of business. He was employed as the secretary of the Jamestown & Chautauqua Railroad and in 1907 became a partner in the Wall Street firm of Henderson, Lindley and Company. Even then he was fearful that the vicissitudes of the stock market might someday financially ruin him. This unwarranted specter of financial failure haunted him during both his business and literary careers. To guard against this possibility, which he suspected was a real likelihood for all Wall Streeters, Adams established a goal for himself whereby he determined to retire from the brokerage business upon reaching the age of thirty-five or when he amassed $100,000 in savings. As it happened, in 1912, when he turned thirty-four, he had accumulated the $100,000, and—as he had promised himself—he retired from Wall Street.

Shortly after taking this new direction, Adams built a house at Bridgehampton, Long Island, where he settled to research and write history. Prior to this time his literary exercises had dealt exclusively with economic affairs. In 1908 he had published *Some Notes on Currency Problems* and in 1913 had completed *Speculation and the Reform of the New York Stock Exchange*. His first historical work, *Memorials of Old Bridgehampton*, a study concerning his adopted Long Island home, was published in 1916 by a local newspaper company. It sold out quickly and immediately became a local favorite. Within two years Adams noted that the $1.50 volume was fetching $75.00 in Boston bookstores.

His next effort, *History of the Town of Southampton, East of Canoe Place* (1918), local history like his first work, treated a larger geographical area and attracted a wider audience, including professional historians, who noted the author's thoroughness of research and literary skill. Assessing as well as chronicling the settlement, society, and commerce of the southeastern Long Island communities, Adams won acclaim for his incisiveness, just as he did for his precise scholarship. Especially noteworthy to the scholarly reviewers was the fact that the book was good local history free from the common filiopietistic burdens. Both of his early works have stood the test of time and were republished in 1962.

By the time Adams had completed the *History of the Town of Southampton*, the United States had entered World War I. At the age of forty he joined the army as an officer in the Military Intelligence Service. He assisted in the accumulation and distillation of historical, geographical, and cultural data about various countries and regions around the globe. With these findings he participated in the writing of officers' handbooks. In 1919 he sailed to France as archivist of the American delegation to the peace conference and was charged with the care of classified maps.

Adams's wartime and peace-conference service introduced him to renowned persons in numerous fields, including history, politics, diplomacy, and journalism. This experience, built upon the years he spent in business, he termed "mixing with the world," which he considered as "important for a Historian as forever poking over sources in a library." In the essay "Is History Science?," collected in *The Tempo of Modern Life* (1931), he came to the "conclusion that too long an academic training and career is rather a detriment than a benefit to a historian." And he continued to express his belief that any professionally trained scholar should have his academic understanding "supplemented by some years of an active career in affairs among men."

Upon his return to America, he embarked upon a new study of New England in which he attempted to correct the hagiographic sentiments that had crept into the works of many nineteenth-century scholars. Adams claimed that he was moved to attempt his New England trilogy by inadequacies in John Gorham Palfrey's highly laudatory and patriotic multivolume *History of New England* (1859-1890). Certainly not the first historian to question the unqualified adoration heaped on the New England founding fathers, Adams found, after an immersion in the primary and secondary sources, that the Puritans were motivated by a whole range of factors more often selfish than selfless. Furthermore, he concluded, the search for religious liberty often associated with their colonization was exaggerated if not entirely inaccurate. The "old conception of New England history" had that section "set-

tled by persecuted religious refugees, devoted to liberty of conscience, who, in the disputes with the mother-country, formed a united mass of liberty-loving patriots unanimously opposed to an unmitigated tyranny." In the first volume, *The Founding of New England* (1921), he did not deify the Puritan leaders nor did he attempt to canonize entire generations of New Englanders. Instead, he contended, his experience "mixing with the world" necessitated a broader critical interpretation.

Perhaps because he believed he was correcting long-standing inaccuracies and misconceptions, Adams went beyond the balanced interpretation he sought to present. Although he attempted to demonstrate that the New England Puritans were moved by multiple influences, the one factor he constantly repeated was economic. Their desire for acquisition of place and property, he wrote, far exceeded their desire to live democratically and humanely. This resulted not in the unbiased history that he insisted he was writing but, in fact, in a work so vehemently anti-Puritan that it was a good balance only for the extreme views presented in nineteenth-century studies such as Palfrey's.

According to Adams the founders of Massachusetts were bigoted, mercenary, undemocratic, and bloodthirsty. What enduring good that developed in and around the Bay Colony evolved in spite of them. Consequently, the heroes were the individuals, families, factions, and congregations who thwarted the minority's leadership. The population, Adams insisted, was overwhelmingly non-Puritan. He estimated that only one in five of the adult males who came to Massachusetts during the height of Puritan influence was in sympathy with the ruling oligarchy.

Adams's unorthodox conclusions alienated some scholars, but most, including the New England establishment, accepted the work for its research and literary value. Samuel Eliot Morison, who disagreed with Adams's violent treatment of the Puritans and felt obliged to answer some of Adams's particular attacks, concluded in 1930 that despite the interpretation "it is still the best general survey of seventeenth-century Massachusetts." And as late as 1962 Richard Schlatter ranked *The Founding of New England* "still the best one-volume synthesis of New England history in the seventeenth century," regardless of its interpretive faults. *The Founding of New England* was Adams's outstanding single work. For it he received a Pulitzer Prize in 1922. It immediately established him as a major authority in American colonial history.

The second volume of his New England trilogy, *Revolutionary New England, 1691-1776*, published in 1923, was also immediately acclaimed by both scholars and popular reviewers. Because he had acquired a reputation as a readable and stimulating author, the sales of this volume surpassed those of *The Founding of New England*. Adams sifted through mainly printed sources to trace the internal social and economic movements as well as the development of political revolution in New England. Reviewers praised the breadth of the work, which included views of the late colonial world from both provincial and English perspectives. As in the first volume, however, his description of bigoted and mercenary Puritans whose influence impeded the development of democracy and liberty distracted from an otherwise first-rate history.

Adams's final volume of the history, *New England in the Republic, 1776-1850*, published in 1926, continued his thesis but proved to be much less successful with critics than were the first two. As in the previous volumes, economics remained the basic interpretative theme. The main thrust of the work was to demonstrate that by the middle of the nineteenth century the common man in New England, who had long been held in the lower class by the dominance of the wealthy patricians, had elevated himself to fulfill the promise of the Revolution. As a minor theme, Adams reviewed New England's contributions to the growth of sectionalism. The period covered in this volume was too long and beyond the scope of his greatest expertise. With less original research, the result was merely a work of sweeping generalizations.

As the New England trilogy unfolded, it presaged the direction that Adams's historical writing would take for the rest of his career. His early writings exhibited traditional scholarly archival research complemented by a firm grasp of the secondary sources. The result, once his fine literary style was added, was a complete history composed of provocative interpretation and resting on a solid foundation of documentation. This formula permitted him to excel in both scholarly and popular realms. Unfortunately, his study of *New England in the Republic* lacked one of the essential ingredients. With a few exceptions his work as a historian after this study was to have little impact in academic circles and was regarded lightly by most scholars. He emerged from the 1920s as one of the most popular and widely read American historians, and while he continued to deal with historical topics, he became more of an essayist than a scholar.

Even before he completed the trilogy, he had started a volume for the History of American Life series, a pioneer multivolume treatment of American social history. *Provincial Society, 1690-1763*, published in 1927 as the third volume of the series, was vastly superior to *New England in the Republic*. Based largely on secondary materials, the work was buttressed by generous extracts from diaries and newspapers—two of his favorite colonial sources. Among his constant concerns were the increasing disparity between the rich and the poor and the growth of sectionalism which resulted in an East-West dichotomy. *Provincial Society, 1690-1763* was the ideal vehicle in which to display his literary style and skill for generalization and interpretation. Furthermore, the book was the most widely and favorably reviewed of all his works and marked the high point of his career as a historian.

Unfortunately, *Provincial Society, 1690-1763* did not sell well initially and proved to be a source of irritation for Adams. He was disappointed that he received only $1,000 for it and at various times blamed the editors (Dixon Ryan Fox and Arthur M. Schlesinger, Sr.) or Macmillan Company, the publisher. As the entire series sold well over the years, he complained privately and in print that he had been abused. Regardless of where the fault, if any existed, lay, his concern over the small return on this literary investment reveals an ironic influence upon his own work. Just as he found the early settlers of New England activated by the desire to improve their economic lot rather than by more praiseworthy religious or ideological motives, his career as a historian was propelled by a desire to write volumes or articles that would be popular and return a profit on the time he invested.

For several reasons Adams became increasingly concerned about the profit his work would return. Before he became a scholar he had made and saved so much money that the return he obtained from his writing often seemed insignificant in comparison. Later, however, holding no academic position, he depended upon his writing for his livelihood. He married Kathryn M. Seely in 1927, which created additional financial burdens for the former bachelor of forty-eight years. This change in his attitude, which saw him become as concerned with receipts as with reviews, generally coincided with the stock market crash and the following Depression. Much of his personal correspondence and some of his essays reveal the remunerative preoccupation of his literary activities.

Beginning in 1927 he wrote ninety-eight sketches for the *Dictionary of American Biography*. It was a task he readily accepted for two reasons: he did not have to leave his home to do research and, as he termed it, the work "comes in handily as a pot boiler." The essays were for the most part biographies of colonial figures, but he did some on nineteenth-century historians as well. Interestingly, he wrote sketches both of his favorite historian Francis Parkman and of John Gorham Palfrey, whose shortcomings led Adams to launch his New England trilogy. In these biographies, as in much of his later work, he revealed as much about himself as he did about his subjects. Parkman offered Adams an opportunity to discuss his own feelings concerning the nature of historical scholarship. The great student of the French and Indian War came off well because he epitomized what Adams believed a historian should do and be. "In the conception and execution of his work," Adams wrote, "Parkman was primarily an artist, with the result that his history has an enduring place in literature." Consequently, the sketch reads like a highly laudatory review emphasizing those things in Parkman's personality and work that resembled Adams's own career. Palfrey, however, whose work he found wanting, was attacked as a person as well as a scholar. Instead of remarking favorably on the wide experience Palfrey had because of his multifaceted career, Adams took an opposite approach and concluded that "his curious career . . . indicates a certain lack of definite purpose and aim, a weakness of some sort in his character."

While the association with the *Dictionary of American Biography* certainly did nothing to diminish his reputation and may have helped to sustain it, the fact that he looked upon his contributions as potboilers suggests that as early as 1927 his desire to be financially successful as a historian had become uppermost in his mind. Allan Nevins, his friend and biographer, attempted to treat this remarkable alteration by noting that Adams became more conservative in his outlook and at the same time increasingly concerned about changes in American life caused by such things as inflation, income tax, and social welfare. Nevins explained that, because "his outlook changed," the subjects of his writing did as well, and "he sought broader themes, and took less interest in precise scholarship."

In April 1929 Adams wrote an article, "Morituri Te Salutamus," for the *Saturday Review*, in which he discussed the low esteem and pay which the nation gave its intellectuals. He detailed problems an American scholar faced in attempting to live and provide for a family in a manner befitting a professional person. Adams went so far as to indicate that the scholar might have to adapt his work to methods employed by modern business and indus-

try, where production and sales relied on mass consumption to turn huge profits. As an example he gave the illustration of an author who might "try to learn the trick of writing for those [magazines] with circulations in millions," and significantly increase his "income or even amass a fortune." He understood that there would be a tradeoff in pursuing that popular path, which he succinctly recognized to be "a serious degeneration in his intellectual quality and character." About the time he wrote this article his work was going through the very transformation he described.

Between 1929 and 1936 Adams spent most of his time in London. He considered it the most civilized and important city in the world and the most comfortable place for him to live and work. There he applied himself in a workmanlike fashion to pounding out six volumes and a flood of over fifty articles for journals and magazines ranging from the *Yale Review* to the *Woman's Home Companion*. These shorter pieces provided a steady income and a forum for his didactic comments about what was occurring in American politics, business, and society. Two collections of his essays were published in book form by Albert and Charles Boni: *Our Business Civilization: Some Aspects of American Culture* (1929) and *The Tempo of Modern Life* (1931). For each he received a handsome advance.

During these years he produced, in rapid succession, studies like *The Adams Family* (1930), a collective biography of four generations of New England's greatest family beginning with John Adams. Reviews were mixed, but thanks to the book's selection by the Literary Guild, it became one of his most profitable works, returning an estimated $30,000. In 1931 *The Epic of America*, his one-volume interpretation of the nation's history, was published and proved to be his most financially successful endeavor. It sold 75,000 copies the first year and was the Book-of-the-Month Club selection for October 1931. Adams later estimated that it had been translated into a dozen languages, sold more than 500,000 copies, and returned an income of $80,000. The central theme of this highly interpretative and selective work was that a guiding dream to improve and grow had vitalized Americans from the earliest colonial settlements.

He followed with *Henry Adams* (1933), his last book published by a company other than Charles Scribner's Sons. This biography is typical of the work of the latter part of his career. Bernard DeVoto described it as "a series of generalizations . . . mostly unsupported, frequently unjustified, and always superficial." He concluded unkindly, but correctly, that Adams "has merely produced one of the pot-boilers which, he feels American scholars usually produce as soon as they achieve eminence." Adams's other books were still accepted by the public and reviewed favorably by the popular press. Historians, however, found most of the publications well below his earlier standards and criticized some of his work to the point of ridicule. Despite the urgings of his friends, he decided that he could not afford to return to the more scholarly but less profitable writing that had won him recognition during the 1920s. In 1932 he signed a long-term contract with Charles Scribner's Sons which guaranteed a basic $5,000 annual income to act as an advisory member of their staff. Scribners, in return, had first call on any book he wrote, for which he would be given a $5,000 advance and a fifteen percent royalty. This relieved him of some fears concerning financial security, but it reduced him to near hack status.

Some of the works he produced for Scribners enjoyed commercial success. His two-volume history of America, *The March of Democracy* (1932-1933), eventually returned almost $80,000, the amount he had earned from *The Epic of America*. A heavily illustrated set, *The March of Democracy* was eventually expanded by other authors and also appeared in a condensed textbook form. In 1934 Adams completed a study of sectionalism and the coming of the Civil War entitled *America's Tragedy*. The book resulted from his renewed interest in sectionalism, which he had developed as a minor theme in the New England trilogy. Because he had researched its subject in some detail earlier, *America's Tragedy* was probably the best history he wrote during the latter part of his career. Some historians reviewed it favorably; however, it was not a commercial success.

Adams decided in 1934 to return to the United States and in 1936 moved permanently from London to Stamford, Connecticut. His reputation among historians continued to decline with the publication of his 1936 study, *The Living Jefferson*. During Franklin Roosevelt's first term (1933-1937), Adams came to despise the New Deal and fought to have Roosevelt defeated in his first reelection bid. In this biography Adams depicted Jefferson as the greatest American liberal and then employed him as a standard to demonstrate how the Roosevelt administration was moving America toward a totalitarian state. The volume degenerated into a partisan attack on the administration, and

Adams was castigated in the journals.

He continued to write about America and the American character and produced several more volumes and numerous popular articles. Much of his energy after the 1930s was devoted to editing reference works to aid in the study of American history. Adams oversaw the preparation of the *Dictionary of American History* (1940), the *Atlas of American History* (1943), and the *Album of American History* (1944-1948).

James Truslow Adams's last years were busy ones with his numerous editorial duties, writing, and political activities. He stopped writing for publication, except for some continuing obligations to Scribners, in 1946, claiming he decided to quit "while I still have a reputation." Indeed, his place as an author, synthesizer, and critic of America and Americans remained intact. Unfortunately, Adams's distinction as a historian did not. The consideration he retained in historical circles was greatly diminished by almost two decades of work that did not live up to the promise of his first histories of New England and provincial society.

Other:

Hamiltonian Principles, edited by Adams (Boston: Little, Brown, 1928);

Jeffersonian Principles, edited by Adams (Boston: Little, Brown, 1928);

New England's Prospect, by Adams, Henry S. Graves, Edward A. Filene, and others (New York: American Geographic Society, 1933);

Dictionary of American History, six volumes, edited by Adams and others (New York: Scribners, 1940; revised, 1942);

James Montgomery Beck, *The Constitution of the United States*, revised and enlarged by Adams (Garden City & Toronto: Doubleday, Doran, 1941);

Atlas of American History (New York: Scribners, 1943);

Album of American History, volumes 1-4, edited by Adams (New York: Scribners, 1944-1948).

Biography:

Allan Nevins, *James Truslow Adams: Historian of the American Dream* (Urbana: University of Illinois Press, 1968).

Papers:

The James Truslow Adams Papers are at Butler Library, Columbia University.

Charles M. Andrews

Jessica Kross
University of South Carolina

BIRTH: Wethersfield, Connecticut, 22 February 1863, to William Watson and Elizabeth Byrne Williams Andrews.

EDUCATION: A.B., Trinity College, Hartford, 1884; Ph. D., Johns Hopkins, 1889.

MARRIAGE: 19 June 1895 to Evangeline Holcombe Walker; children: Ethel, John.

AWARDS AND HONORS: Pulitzer Prize in history for *The Colonial Period of American History: The Settlements*, volume 1, 1935; The Gold Medal for history and biography from the National Institute of Arts and Letters, 1937.

DEATH: East Dover, Vermont, 9 September 1943.

SELECTED BOOKS: *The River Towns of Connecticut. A Study of Wethersfield, Hartford and Windsor* (Baltimore: Johns Hopkins University Press, 1889);

The Old English Manor. A Study in English Economic History (Baltimore: Johns Hopkins University Press, 1892);

The Historical Development of Modern Europe, from the Congress of Vienna to the Present Time, 2 volumes (New York & London: Putnam's, 1896-1898);

Contemporary Europe, Asia, and Africa (Philadelphia & New York: Lea Brothers, 1902);

A History of England (Boston: Allyn & Bacon, 1903; revised, 1921);

Colonial Self Government, 1652-1689, volume 5 of *The American Nation: A History* (New York & London: Harper, 1904);

British Committees, Commissions, and Councils of Trade and Plantations, 1622-1675 (Baltimore: Johns Hopkins University Press, 1908);

Guide to the Manuscript Materials for the History of the United States to 1783, in the British Museum, in Minor London Archives, and in the Libraries of Oxford and Cambridge, by Andrews and Frances G. Davenport (Washington: Carnegie Institution of Washington, 1908);

The Colonial Period (New York: Holt, 1912);

The State Papers, volume 1 of *Guide to the Materials for American History, to 1783, in the Public Record Office of Great Britain* (Washington: Carnegie

Institution of Washington, 1912);

Departmental and Miscellaneous Papers, volume 2 of *Guide to the Materials for American History, to 1783, in the Public Record Office of Great Britain* (Washington: Carnegie Institution of Washington, 1914);

Colonial Folkways: A Chronicle of American Life in the Reign of the Georges (New Haven: Yale University Press, 1919);

The Colonial Background of the American Revolution: Four Essays in American Colonial History (New Haven: Yale University Press, 1924; London: Oxford University Press, 1931);

Our Earliest Colonial Settlements: Their Diversities of Origin and Later Characteristics (New York: New York University Press, 1933; London: Oxford University Press, 1933);

The Colonial Period of American History, 4 volumes (New Haven: Yale University Press, 1934-1938).

Charles McLean Andrews, called the dean of America's colonial historians during his lifetime, was an author, teacher and active member of the organized historical profession. His articles and books, marked by detailed analysis of institutional structures, primary source research, and a sense of the American colonies as only one part of the British colonial empire, set new directions and standards. His guides to the British manuscript repositories remain invaluable research tools for colonial history. Andrews believed that history was a science and that facts were its raw materials. With Herbert Levi Osgood and George L. Beer he "founded" the "imperial school" of American colonial history. In his teaching career Andrews directed graduate studies first at Johns Hopkins University and then for twenty years at Yale. His students, including Leonard W. Labaree and Lawrence Henry Gipson, made invaluable contributions to colonial scholarship. As a working member of the American Historical Association, Andrews presided over the group as acting president after the death of Woodrow Wilson in 1924 and as president in his own right in 1925.

Charles M. Andrews came from old-line Yankee stock, his earliest ancestor having helped to found New Haven in 1638 and Andrewses having

Charles M. Andrews

been in Connecticut ever since. His father, William Watson Andrews, was a minister of the Catholic Apostolic Church who had two sons and a daughter by his first marriage and by his second had Charles and two younger daughters. This large household was presided over by Andrews's mother, Elizabeth Byrne Williams Andrews, who influenced him perhaps more than his father. Andrews's father wanted him to become a minister, while Andrews wanted to drop out of college to pursue a business career. Only his mother's insistence that he finish college kept him there. He graduated from Hartford's Trinity College in 1884 without scholarly distinction but was chosen class poet and recognized for his skills at public speaking.

Upon graduation Andrews stayed close to home and served as principal of West Hartford High School. Two years at West Hartford showed him that he liked teaching but disliked the discipline problems and large classes of a public secondary school. In 1886 an aunt offered to help finance graduate training and Andrews left the safety of Connecticut for the new and challenging world of Johns Hopkins University. He would not return for a quarter of a century.

Johns Hopkins was only ten years old when

Charles Andrews enrolled, but its impact on historical research and writing had already begun. The history curriculum at Johns Hopkins under Herbert Baxter Adams was designed to train research scholars, and following that curriculum Andrews acquired the strict methodical approach to research which characterized his published work and graduate teaching. Herbert Adams, trained in Germany, taught his students in graduate seminars, where they learned to test rigorously both sources and ideas. Out of the seminars came graduate theses, the best of which Adams published in the Johns Hopkins University Studies in Historical and Political Science, which was begun in 1882. Andrews, as editor of the Yale Historical Series, would later do the same for his students.

Andrews's endeavors flourished under the intellectual stimuli of Johns Hopkins and the personal attention granted him by Herbert Baxter Adams. Adams not only taught him in courses but also helped Andrews obtain a fellowship. He also accepted Andrews's dissertation for publication. *The River Towns of Connecticut. A Study of Wethersfield, Hartford, and Windsor* appeared as volumes 7-9 of the Johns Hopkins University Studies in Historical and Political Science, Seventh Series, 1889. *The River Towns of Connecticut* is a treatise on the founding of three early settlements, detailing their land systems and political structures, and it indicates the bent of Andrews's later work on colonial institutions. In researching the monograph, Andrews relied upon both primary and secondary sources and used town meeting minutes and colonial records as well as scholarly and popular published sources. He painstakingly details how lands were divided and includes maps showing the land systems, and chronicles the elections of town officers. He is careful to note that his three towns were different in some respects and to give data on each. Placing the towns in a larger context, he shows how they were subordinate to Connecticut's General Court and how province and town worked together, and he challenged the current historical wisdom about town origins and autonomy by denying the theory of the German *tun.* This notion, popular in the late nineteenth century, traced the origins of American democratic institutions to Germanic tribal organization. This "germ" of democratic government was said to have been carried by Anglo-Saxons and embodied in the newly created New England towns. Andrews argued that this theory was unproved. He reiterated this position in "The Theory of the Village Community," a paper delivered before the American Historical Association in 1891. Andrews mistrusted the theory, asserting that "the support is certainly inadequate to the structure raised thereon." This skepticism would remain part of his own intellectual "structure."

In 1889, Andrews left Johns Hopkins and began teaching at Bryn Mawr College. He also turned his scholarly attention to Europe, and, following his interest in the locality, he published *The Old English Manor* (1892). In the next eleven years he also produced two textbooks and a popular history which studied respectively modern Europe; England; and contemporary Europe, Asia and Africa. Of these four works only the first was an important piece of scholarship. Andrews's chief contributions would be to American colonial history, not English or Continental studies, and his prodigious energies would become confined to that arena. However, Andrews's work on England showed him that American colonial history had to be studied within the context of the British Empire. His first trip to England in 1893 also introduced him to the little-used materials in the Public Record Office, and he was later to build upon these raw materials.

In 1894, in an address to the National Education Association, Andrews spoke on the importance of the study of history. At that time he distinguished between history and literature: literature looks at ideals and moral standards, history at facts and actual behavior; literature records single voices, history the masses. To Andrews the study of history was important because it is "the telescope and microscope of social man" and teaches us to be humble, to be practical. History teaches that no nation develops in isolation; that institutions grow from historical roots. It gives perspective and proportion and in the end makes us less jingoistic, judgmental, and intolerant. Historians have a special burden. History, like the other sciences, searches for truth, but since that truth is seldom self-evident, the historian must be especially thorough, impartial, and sympathetic to all. Historians are not lawyers, said Andrews, but judges "hearing all the evidence."

If Charles Andrews had a theory of scholarship, its foundation was evidence. History was a discipline which answered questions, but the posing of those questions was determined by the sources. Andrews told the American Historical Association in 1898, "To my mind it is not essential that we should know what subjects to study beforehand, but rather it is important that we should know what material is available and let that guide our thoughts."

The 1898 American Historical Association meeting not only heard Andrews give his views on scholarship but also witnessed the foundation of a new school of historical thinking. Andrews's paper, "American Colonial History, 1690-1750," argued that to look at colonial history merely from the vantage point of the colonies is too parochial. Instead, historians must keep in mind "that the colonists were members of a great colonial empire, [and] were subject to an elaborate colonial administration that existed, as it were, outside of themselves. . . ." This colonial administration, often cumbersome and slow, evolved for the benefit of the mother country and encompassed not only the thirteen mainland colonies but also the West Indies and later Canada. Andrews insisted that the empire was a whole and needed to be seen that way. Anything less was incomplete by definition. His own work reflected this bias, and so did that of some of his contemporaries.

Andrews shared the 1898 American Historical Association program with Herbert Levi Osgood, who also called for a broad-based institutional approach which focused on the period before the Seven Years' War. Together Andrews, Osgood, and their students would form the "imperial school" of colonial history. Their impact on what was studied and how it was studied set the tone for colonial history for the next generation.

Andrews's thinking about the direction which scholarship should take was honed in the 1890's, but perhaps as important to his later career and certainly to his well-being was his marriage in 1895 to Evangeline Holcombe Walker, an 1893 graduate of Bryn Mawr who had studied English and Latin. She would henceforth read and correct his manuscripts, run his household, and in general free him to pursue his scholarship. A. S. Eisenstadt, in his biography of Andrews, quoted Evangeline Andrews as noting, "At our home we did nothing else but write the history books." Andrews's ambition was to be a full-time scholar, and in time he would cut back teaching and speaking commitments to devote his time to his writing.

Evangeline Andrews took care of the daily chores, and she also saw to much of the family's social life since by 1890 Charles Andrews was growing deaf. This disability made social gatherings less attractive and the solitary confines of archive and study more appealing. Andrews was shielded from the twentieth-century world both by choice and by accident, and unlike many historians, he remained aloof from politics, confining his pro-British and larger anti-isolationist sentiments to academic or otherwise specialized audiences.

Andrews (left) and friends in his room at Bryn Mawr, 1891

In 1904 Andrews produced his first major work of colonial history, *Colonial Self Government 1652-1689*, volume 5 of Albert Bushnell Hart's *The American Nation* series. This volume is a good readable survey of the political history of those colonies established before 1689. As in all his works, Andrews explains which British institutions were important to the colonies and how they worked. If some of his comments about popular uprisings, such as Bacon's and Leisler's Rebellions, are dated, his clear explanation of how government worked is not. *Colonial Self Government, 1652-1689* could still be used as a basic text in seventeenth-century American history. It was republished in 1969.

Andrews's concern with the way that institutions operated and his conviction that understanding basic institutional structures could only proceed from a firm grasp of the manuscript sources led him

to accept the task of searching through the British depositories and preparing extensive guides to them, a project undertaken at the behest of J. Franklin Jameson, the leading figure of the American Historical Association and a pioneer in professionalizing history. Jameson also found support from both the American Antiquarian Society and the Carnegie Institution of Washington. To prepare the guides Andrews spent November 1903 to September 1904 in England and returned in the summers of 1905 and 1907.

The first set of the *Guide to the Manuscript Materials for the History of the United States to 1783, in the British Museum, in Minor London Archives, and in the Libraries of Oxford and Cambridge*, compiled and annotated by Andrews and Frances G. Davenport, was published by the Carnegie Institution in 1908. It is a prodigious work which gives detailed information on how to get into the various archives, what letters a researcher needs, what the hours and forms are, and what the rules permit. Andrews also noted what aids to research were available at each repository. His compiling this information attests to Andrews's concern for the working scholar with limited time. He prefaced each section on a major collection with a description and analysis of the institution reflected in the documents and how it functioned. These essays are still valuable to anyone studying the first British Empire.

Andrews's and Davenport's guide omitted Great Britain's major manuscript repository, the Public Record Office, which was recataloguing its holdings even as the guide to it was in galley. Andrews redid this section and the first volume of *Guide to the Materials for American History, to 1783, in the Public Record Office of Great Britain* appeared in 1912, the second in 1914. The first volume, *The State Papers*, stated that it was "a book that might serve as an introduction to the system of British administration, particularly in the eighteenth century." As in the earlier guide, Andrews told researchers not only how to get into the building but what they would find there and what it meant. Volume 2, *Departmental and Miscellaneous Papers*, completed the survey. Andrews's own judgment, repeated a few months before his death, was that the guides were his most enduring contribution. He is probably right. All three volumes were republished in 1965.

In 1906 Andrews was offered the chair of his mentor, Herbert B. Adams, at Johns Hopkins. He took up his duties in 1907 and three years later, in 1910, Yale University offered Andrews the Farnam Professorship. Andrews moved again, completing a circuit which had taken him from Connecticut to Baltimore to Bryn Mawr and then back to Baltimore and Connecticut. Along with his position at Yale went the editorship of the new Yale Historical Series, similar to the series edited by Herbert Adams at Johns Hopkins. Andrews's first volume appeared in 1912, and he continued to supervise the series until 1933. While most of his duties at Bryn Mawr had been teaching undergraduates, at Johns Hopkins and then at Yale, he shifted his attention to training historians. At Yale, Andrews could finally control his academic environment. He eschewed committee work; taught only graduate students, never more than fifteen a semester; and even dispensed with an office on campus where he might be disturbed.

In 1912 he had published *The Colonial Period*, a work in which he treated all the British colonies and which was republished in 1964. He also turned out

various overviews of colonial society, such as the now outdated *Colonial Folkways: A Chronicle of American Life in the Reign of the Georges* (1919). In 1921 he and his wife edited *Journal of a Lady of Quality*, which, aside from its intrinsic interest as the journal of a Scottish gentlewoman's journey to the West Indies and North Carolina on the eve of the Revolution, is a model of editorial detail. The footnotes and appendices provide additional information which is both useful and amusing. They revised the journal in 1934 and 1939.

Andrews's most important work during his Yale years was *The Colonial Background of the American Revolution: Four Essays in American Colonial History* (1924). In these well-shaped essays, Andrews sets the colonies in an imperial perspective, noting that England was unprepared to administer an empire and could only see her own short-term self-interests. Ignorant of America or a growing American maturity, those in charge pursued a course which could only end in estrangement. By 1770 it was too late: "The American Revolution, like nearly all revolutions in history, was an uprising not against a king and his ministers, but against a system and a state of mind." Andrews closed *The Colonial Background of the American Revolution* with a plea for toleration and objectivity. As Andrews saw it, the historian has a responsibility to keep history from becoming the property of hero-worshipers, propagandists, and patriots. The proper way to study American history, and by implication America, is in an international context. Andrews believed that humanity moved toward a better future and that American history, unembellished by jingoism or skewed by isolationism, showed that evolution. Addressing his contemporaries about the relevance of the Revolution, Andrews wrote: "A nation's attitude toward its own history is like a window into its own soul and the men and women of such a nation cannot be expected to meet the great obligations of the present if they refuse to exhibit honesty, charity, open-mindedness, and a free and growing intelligence toward the past that has made them what they are." *The Colonial Background of the American Revolution* was revised in 1931 and has gone through fifteen printings.

In addition to *The Colonial Background of the American Revolution*, Andrews also wrote numerous articles, some for lay and some for scholarly audiences, about colonial history and the Revolution, in which he looked at commerce and various parts of imperial organization. His 1926 "The American Revolution: An Interpretation," which appeared in the *American Historical Review*, reiterates a faith in the cumulative nature of knowledge by observing that no historian's judgment was final, even on major events such as the American Revolution. In Andrews's view the Revolution was the explosive result of long-accumulated divergences between mother country and colony. Complex economic, social, political, and legal forces ruled statesmen and political agitators alike, and England and America had evolved different attitudes and convictions based on different experiences and needs. England's responses were reactionary, brutal, formal, and narrow; the government represented privilege resistant to change. America, on the other hand, quickly shed feudal and proprietary elements which conflicted with the needs of a frontier society. To Andrews, the major development in colonial history was the rise of legislative assemblies and England's inability to curb their assertiveness. In America sovereignty resided in the people who created a society without caste or privilege. "Primarily, the American Revolution was a political and constitutional movement and only secondarily one that was either financial, commercial or social." The colonies represented the new order, England the old. Progress lay on the side of the Americans.

In his graduate seminars Andrews developed the perspective for his writings and helped his students develop the skills they would need to elaborate and test their own hypotheses. Former students such as Lawrence Henry Gipson, Leonard W. Labaree, and Dumas Malone mention Andrews's patience, his critical eye, and his knowledge, which he willingly shared. Andrews by example and by the attention he gave his students forced them to do their best. Indeed his interest was almost paternal. When chided by his wife that he devoted more time to his students than to his children, he supposedly replied, "my children have you to look after them, but my students have no one but me." During all but his last years at Yale, Andrews allowed only one doctoral degree per year. He thus kept the quality of dissertations high by lavishing attention on one a year. The best of these dissertations were published in the Yale Historical Series, but only after they were completely rewritten.

In addition to guiding his students and writing, Andrews undertook numerous other responsibilities and pursuits while at Yale. He was active in the American Historical Association during its early years and in the academic historical profession at large. For the AHA he served on the Winsor Prize Committee, the Public Archives Commission, the Committee on Legal History, and the Executive Council. He became acting president of the associa-

tion upon the death of Woodrow Wilson in 1924, and in 1925 he assumed the presidency for a full term. Perhaps most lasting of his contributions to the organization are the large number of book reviews he wrote for the *American Historical Review*, including regular comments upon published editions of primary sources and research guides. Andrews was a regular contributor to the AHA *Annual Reports*, and in one of these contributions, in 1913, he made a plea for the careful preservation of local, state, and federal records by government appropriation. No first-class nation, he said, would ignore or jeopardize its historical record.

In looking back upon the American Historical Association in his 1924 presidential address, "These Forty Years," Andrews stated the major problem he saw facing historians—they were in low repute with a general public which was incapable of distinguishing between a George Bancroft (Andrews's usual example of an unscientific and undisciplined popular mythologizer) and the best-trained minds of the better graduate schools. In a brief historiographic overview showing little of the sympathetic nonjudgmental relativism which he called for as the mark of a professional and which he exercised in his own best work, Andrews maintained that eighteenth-century historians were "credulous, careless, and childish, blinded by their partialities and hatreds," and that they wrote to entertain and indoctrinate, using gossip, diaries, letters, and the unverified memories of those who might have seen the event. Historians of the nineteenth century were wiser, more doubting and skeptical. During late 1880 to 1900 there had been an awakening of historical wisdom, claimed Andrews. The theories of such evolutionists as Darwin and Lecky brought substance and method to history, and events such as the founding of Johns Hopkins and the influence of the German-trained Herbert Baxter Adams at Johns Hopkins and John W. Burgess at Columbia gave America her own training ground. This professionalization resulted in books less popular with the general public, yet it permitted cooperation and cumulative knowledge in history as in the sciences: "The monograph in history corresponds to the experiment in the laboratory. . . ." Research is the first step, then comes interpretation. And interpretation should avoid colorful language and other such pandering to the uneducated reader.

"These Forty Years" goes on to address Andrews's ideas of what is good and bad history. It shows Andrews to be a passionate elitist striving for as value free a history as culture-bound mortals can render. Indeed, Andrews was caught in a dilemma.

A believer in "progress," in the broadening of intelligence within the mass of the people, he also recognized, as he had not earlier in his life, that history has never been a steady march toward the better nor all change for the good. In his 1924 address he asserted that terms such as progress, development, and evolution were inexact, that the only laws of history were those of impermanence. Refusal to see those laws and readjust to new conditions leads to revolution "and to the eventual disappearance of the more conservative elements of society."

In 1931, when Andrews retired, in his honor his former students from Bryn Mawr, Johns Hopkins, and Yale contributed essays to a festschrift, *Essays in Colonial History Presented to Charles McLean Andrews by his Students*, which includes essays by Stanley M. Pargellis, Leonard W. Labaree, Dora Mae Clark, and Lawrence Henry Gipson. Two years later, in 1933, Andrews stepped down as director of historical publications at Yale. That same year he had published *Our Earliest Colonial Settlements: Their Diversities of Origin and Later Characteristics*, an overview of England's colonizing activities and the consequent founding of Virginia, Massachusetts Bay, Rhode Island, Connecticut, and Maryland. The book, comprised of lectures written from Andrews's imperial perspective, is readable, detailed, and gives a good précis of the politics and problems of the first years of settlement. Like all of Andrews's work, it uses official documents as its major sources and so presents a history from the vantage point of each colony's political leaders, revealing their relationships with both England and their own domestic malcontents. The volume has gone through five printings.

In 1934, when Andrews was far past the age when most men do their best work, he produced volume 1 of his four-volume magnum opus, *The Colonial Period of American History*; volumes 2 and 3 were published in 1936 and 1937 respectively. In these first three volumes, subtitled *The Settlements*, Andrews painstakingly and with considerable bibliographic detail chronicles all English settlements in the New World, successful and unsuccessful, through the founding of Pennsylvania. In volume 4, published in 1938 and subtitled *England's Commercial and Colonial Policy*, he details both the thinking behind England's commercial and colonial policy and the structures such as the Customs Service, Vice-Admiralty Courts, and the Board of Trade through which England tried to implement that policy. Taken together, these four volumes are a veritable encyclopedia, and while there are more recent studies of various aspects of the colonial

bureaucracy, there is not and probably will not be another synthesis like Andrews's. If only as a reference work, it is invaluable.

Verner W. Crane's reviews of *The Colonial Period of American History* in the *American Historical Review* were laudatory, although Crane suggests in his look at volume 4 that institutional studies have inherent limitations. In 1935 Andrews received the Pulitzer Prize for volume 1, and that same year his foremost student, Lawrence Henry Gipson, wrote a long article entitled "Charles McLean Andrews and the Re-Orientation of the Study of American Colonial History" in which he traced Andrews's career and then summarized volume 1, concluding by asking if a "finer piece of historical exposition has issued from an American study. . . ." All four volumes have gone through eight printings. In 1937 the National Institute of Arts and Letters awarded Andrews their gold medal for history and biography.

These awards marked the peak of Andrews's career. By 1938, attacks on his work were underway by a new generation raised in a new economic and cultural environment. Samuel Eliot Morison noted that what Andrews said in 1934 was hardly new and Carl Bridenbaugh and others, including Crane, suggested that institutions were only part of the colonial world, hence only part of colonial history. Louis M. Hacker, an economic determinist, was less polite. In a review-essay in the *New Republic* he accused Andrews of allying himself with the ruling class. Moreover, he charged that Andrews was unwilling to follow his own materialist argument to the logical conclusion that economic oppression as a by-product of mercantilism led to the American Revolution.

Andrews realized that his intellectual framework was being undermined. His long concluding note to volume 4 of *The Colonial Period of American History* is an attack on economic determinists in general and Hacker in particular. Their view, he thought, interpreted the past in the light of the present and so was by definition unsound. His reply to Hacker's *New Republic* review is more personal and self-pitying. He was hurt that anyone could accuse him of class bias. "I am, I believe, entirely devoid of class-consciousness . . .," he noted. "As a historian I am neither conservative, liberal nor radical, but possessed of sufficient flexibility of mind to go wherever the evidence leads and to accept the truth where I find it. Can Mr. Hacker say the same of himself?"

In 1938, while volume 4 was in galley, Andrews's health broke, and he was unable to correct

4.

Holland, England, and France — states bordering on the Atlantic Ocean and

the North Sea — were attaining to a political unity and self-conscious-

ness each of its own; and ~~each~~ in its own way and in its own time *Each* was to

take advantage of the opportunities that its maritime location offered.

As local practices and interests *gradually were subordinated to* ~~more or before~~ the larger welfare

of the state as a whole, certain other impulses became effective. Habits

and customs underwent important changes as the earlier feudal provincial-

ism, bred of an agricultural and farming environment, with its limited

supply of the luxuries of life, was broken in upon by the influx of the

products and ideas of other civilizations and other climes. Trading activi-

ties with the East had begun with the Crusades, and in the thirteenth and

fourteenth centuries there had been brought to the West commodities and

usages that were destined to influence, in a constantly accelerating degree,

the daily existence of the western European peoples. The lust for trade had

been growing for two centuries and a half, and through the intermediation

of the Venetians and the ~~mariners~~ *leaguers* of the Hanseatic ~~League~~ *towns* and by routes

partly overland and partly by water, there had been distributed through the

West a more or less regular supply of tropical and semi-tropical goods and

merchandize. The western states bordering on the Atlantic developed no

Page from the typescript for The Colonial Period of American History, *volume 1*

Chapter I
The Beginnings of England's Commercial Policy

The British colonies in America, whether on mainland or island, in proprietary hands or under corporate charter, were not independent, self-sufficient communities, maintaining a separate existence and free from all outside control. Though at the beginning of their careers they were settled under private auspices, without the interfering hand of king or statesman or military head and so were compelled to live largely by their own effort and of their own resources they were still outlying parts of the mother state and indirectly at least subordinate, both as a matter of law and as a matter of policy, to the higher sovereign power across the seas at Whitehall and Westminster. As private colonies, far away beyond the horizon, they lay outside any immediate concern of king and ministers, but they were recognized from an early date as assets of no little importance to the realm itself, legally the king's colonies and subject to his will and pleasure. As far as they could contribute to England's stock in trade and and add to her strength and prosperity they were expected to

Page from the manuscript for The Colonial Period of American History, *volume 4*

final proofs. This debility marked the end of his scholarship, although he did write a few short articles and deliver a speech at the Fiftieth Reunion Dinner, Class of 1893, at Bryn Mawr. His last work of substance, a retrospective article probably written in the late 1930s, appeared posthumously, as he had wished, in the January 1944 *William and Mary Quarterly*. "On the Writing of Colonial History" is both apologia and guide. Andrews notes that he has finished the first four volumes of his most important work on the colonial period. These four volumes represent an attempt to come to grips with the problems which he had always been concerned about—structure and context— and took care of imperial institutions and the Anglo-American context. Andrews then goes on to outline what should be done next. His prescription shows a major shift in emphasis. A projected fifth volume would look at the years 1700-1750 from an American standpoint. The best way to do this would be to treat the materials, which should include everything not political, institutional, or military (and might be labeled social), as an integrated whole. Andrews concedes that this task would involve "perplexing problems of organization and interpretation." Another projected volume would look at political trends in the eighteenth century, especially the rise of the colonial assembly, while volume 7 would examine the period 1763-1776. Andrews's blueprint is still useful, an unexpected gift laying out the task for the next generation.

Charles Andrews died in 1943 at the Vermont farmhouse which he and his wife had enjoyed as a vacation home. He was the last of the important historians of his generation, George Beer, Herbert Levi Osgood, Frederick Jackson Turner, and J. Franklin Jameson having predeceased him. His output was enormous: a bibliography of Andrews's work by Leonard W. Labaree and George Wilson Pierson lists 102 major books, articles, and addresses, and while some of these are republications of earlier works, most are not. Andrews himself had tallied another 360 book reviews, newspaper articles, and short notices between 1888 and 1930.

Charles Andrews's reputation had reached its zenith in the 1920s. By the 1930s a new school was attacking his work much the same way that he had attacked his elders Geroge Bancroft, William H. Prescott, Edward Augustus Freeman, and Sir Henry Maine. A. S. Eisenstadt's biography of Andrews, published in 1956, shares these attitudes. Eisenstadt, while recognizing and appreciating Andrews's discipline and depth, cannot forgive him his imprisonment in his own time: "That he had not

builded better than he knew, nor perhaps even as well, revealed not so much the limited attainments of Andrews himself as the limitations that had been imposed by his age." Others have been kinder. The wheel of fortune, always turning, has again brought Andrews and the Imperial School into favor. Wesley Frank Craven, writing in 1962, noted that the Imperial School's hard work made it possible to see the American Revolution in a new and broader framework. George Athan Billias that same year credited Andrews with recognizing British shortcomings and understanding the evolutionary nature of revolutions. John Higham, writing in 1965, placed Andrews's work in perspective as a manifestation of nineteenth-century rationalism. In Higham's judgment colonial history withstood the onslaught of the so-called New History as long as it did because of the "massive, undeviating strength" of Charles McLean Andrews.

Andrews's shortcomings and his strengths seem obvious. His was probably not a great mind, but it was an educated, disciplined, tenacious, and intellectually honest one. His intangible legacy is twofold. First is his insistence that all history be based on facts and that the evidence be found, organized, and weighed. Second is his injunction that colonial America can never be understood without taking into account England. Scholars such as Sumner Chilton Powell and, more recently, David Grayson Allen have shown how crucial such a perspective is. Andrews's tangible contributions include the guides to British manuscripts and a host of articles and books which explain in painstaking detail how British colonial structures operated. Nobody writing about the colonial period can afford to overlook Andrews. He will be required reading in graduate seminars as long as that institution, which he helped to popularize, exists.

Other:

Journal of a Lady of Quality; Being the Narrative of a Journey from Scotland to the West Indies, North Carolina, and Portugal in the Years 1774 to 1776, edited by Andrews and Evangeline Walker Andrews (New Haven: Yale University Press, 1921).

Periodical Publications:

"American Colonial History, 1690-1750," *1898 Annual Report of the American Historical Association*: 47-60;

"Materials in British Archives for American Colonial History," *American Historical Review*, 10 (January 1905): 325-349;

"These Forty Years," *American Historical Review*, (30 January 1925): 225-250;

"The American Revolution: An Interpretation," *American Historical Review*, 31 (January 1926): 219-232;

"On the Writing of Colonial History," *William and Mary Quarterly*, third series, 1 (January 1944): 27-48.

Bibliography:

Leonard W. Labaree and George Wilson Pierson, "Charles McLean Andrews: A Bibliography," *William and Mary Quarterly*, third series, 1 (January 1944): 15-26.

References:

A. S. Eisenstadt, *Charles McLean Andrews: A Study in American Historical Writing* (New York: Columbia University Press, 1956);

Lawrence Henry Gipson, "Charles McLean Andrews and the Re-Orientation of the Study of American Colonial History," *Pennsylvania Magazine of History and Biography*, 59 (July 1935): 209-222;

Leonard W. Labaree, "Charles McLean Andrews: Historian 1863-1943," *William and Mary Quarterly*, third series, 1 (January 1944): 3-14.

Papers:

Andrews's papers are at the Yale University Library.

Bernard Bailyn

(10 September 1922-)

A. Roger Ekirch
*Virginia Polytechnic Institute
and State University*

SELECTED BOOKS: *The New England Merchants in the Seventeenth Century* (Cambridge, Mass.: Harvard University Press, 1955; London: Oxford University Press, 1955);

Massachusetts Shipping, 1697-1714: A Statistical Study, by Bailyn and Lotte Bailyn (Cambridge, Mass.: Harvard University Press, 1959; London: Oxford University Press, 1959);

Education in the Forming of American Society: Needs and Opportunities for Study (Chapel Hill: University of North Carolina Press, 1960);

The Ideological Origins of the American Revolution (Cambridge, Mass.: Harvard University Press, 1967);

The Origins of American Politics (New York: Knopf, 1968);

The Ordeal of Thomas Hutchinson (Cambridge, Mass.: Harvard University Press, 1974; London: Allen Lane, 1975).

Bernard Bailyn has strongly influenced the study of early American history with his powerful monographs ranging in subject from seventeenth-century New England merchants to the origins of the American Revolution. In his writings, which include economic, social, intellectual, and political history, Bailyn has been a persistent innovator in the application of new research methods, particularly in the use of quantitative techniques, kinship analysis, and collective biography.

Bailyn was born on 10 September 1922 in Hartford, Connecticut, to Charles M. and Esther Schloss Bailyn. He discovered early an interest in history while attending Williams College, where he also studied literature and philosophy. Before receiving an A.B. in 1945, his college years were interrupted by service in the Army Security Agency and the Army Signal Corps during World War II. He later pursued his studies at Harvard and received his M.A. in 1947. In his doctoral research at Harvard, Bailyn came under the influence of several gifted historians: Oscar Handlin and Charles Taylor, who emphasized the importance of social and institutional history, and Samuel Eliot Morison, whose finely crafted narratives set a standard in American historiography. Two books, Marc Bloch's *Feudal Society* and Ronald Syme's *The Roman Revolution*, were also influential. Sweeping in scope and

Bernard Bailyn

fundamentally from medieval and Renaissance merchants in Europe, who were neither propelled nor constrained by spiritual imperatives.

Bailyn expanded upon these early interests when he joined with John Clive, a Harvard friend, to write "England's Cultural Provinces: Scotland and America." Appearing in the *William and Mary Quarterly* in 1954, the article traced and compared the origins of the Scottish Enlightenment and America's Revolutionary literature. As did "The Apologia of Robert Keayne," this article emphasized the strong interplay between intellectual activity and social phenomena. Because Scotland and the American colonies were provincial outposts in the English-speaking world, socially conscious individuals in both felt a deep sense of cultural inferiority, which encouraged either direct imitation of English manners or ardent expressions of local patriotism. A bifurcated self-image resulted, fostering a sense of alienation and rootlessness and leading men ultimately "to the interstices of common thought where were found new views and new approaches to the old."

Having been appointed a Harvard instructor in 1949, Bailyn received his Ph.D. in 1953 and was made assistant professor at Harvard. Drawing on his dissertation research, he wrote a series of articles on merchants and their role in colonial society which established several key points: 1) overseas commerce was uncertain during the seventeenth century; 2) merchants achieved a degree of commercial stability only by placing family and friends as agents in foreign ports; 3) local merchants faced a sharp threat from a growing influx of English merchants and imperial officials after 1660; 4) though merchants were important social leaders, they did not form a coherent class, but only shared a common economic activity; and 5) commerce was a prime means of social mobility during the colonial era.

Nowhere were these patterns clearer than in New England, the principal commercial zone of British North America and the focus of Bailyn's dissertation, revised and published in 1955 as *The New England Merchants in the Seventeenth Century*. In addition to providing a spirited narrative of Massachusetts's rising merchant group, Bailyn explored the growing tensions arising from conflict between entrepreneurial interests and Puritan culture. Merchants were crucial agents of social change, he argued, because they undermined the isolation and religious zeal of early New England. After 1660, however, they became victims of a rapidly changing world, as events in England increasingly impinged

synthesis, they afforded models of how narrative history could transcend the task of description. He found Syme's work especially impressive for its skillful blending of analytical and narrative history. To study past events within a narrative framework became a guiding objective early in Bailyn's career.

As a graduate student, he developed a variety of complementary interests. Two of the most important—the relationship between Europe and the New World and the interplay between social and intellectual history—found expression in doctoral research on New England merchants in the seventeenth century. An offshoot of this research, "The Apologia of Robert Keayne," published in the *William and Mary Quarterly* in 1950, deals with the tribulations of a Puritan merchant in early Massachusetts Bay. Accused on several occasions of greed, Robert Keayne continually sought to achieve a proper balance between profit making and the ethical dictates of Puritanism. Keayne and other New England traders, according to Bailyn, differed upon their dominance.

In *The New England Merchants in the Seventeenth Century*, Bailyn broke new ground in ways that went beyond the originality of his major conclusions. In showing how commercial growth helped to undermine the Puritan commonwealth, he encouraged later historians to pay less attention to the preachings of Puritan divines and, instead, to study broader forces affecting the entire society. Further, at a time when social history was still a fledgling field of research, he subjected a select social group to systematic examination and traced the interconnections between family ties and economic, social, and political currents—all within a narrative format. Bailyn also used such evidence as notarial and family business records in fresh ways, though one reviewer criticized *The New England Merchants in the Seventeenth Century* for its lack of hard statistical data.

Bailyn's next work was not susceptible to such criticism. Aware of a Massachusetts shipping registry for the years 1697-1714, which offered an invaluable source of information for vessels using the port of Boston (owners, size, and place of construction), Bailyn, with the aid of his wife, Lotte, assembled the list and added a lengthy introduction. *Massachusetts Shipping, 1697-1714: A Statistical Study* (1959), marked a departure from Bailyn's earlier studies. By its very nature, it was not so much a narrative as an exhaustive analysis of statistical data. One of several important findings was that Boston's merchant ships by the late seventeenth century formed the third largest fleet in the British Empire, second only to those of London and Bristol, and resident colonists, not absentee Englishmen, owned most of the vessels. Equally important, by studying patterns up to 1714, the Bailyns discovered clear indications of an increasingly mature and sophisticated economy.

As in his other early work, the book both anticipated and encouraged later trends in social history. It was a local study concerned primarily with analyzing changes over time from concrete statistical evidence. "Conceptions of early American social development," the Bailyns noted, "have lacked the anchorage of even approximate quantities." *Massachusetts Shipping, 1697-1714: A Statistical Study* was one of the first books of historical scholarship to use processing machines and Hollerith (IBM) cards in assembling data.

In the same year that *Massachusetts Shipping, 1697-1714* appeared, Bailyn had published his essay "Politics and Social Structure in Virginia," in which he took much the same approach as he had in

The New England Merchants in the Seventeenth Century. Despite its brevity, the article became widely influential for its analysis of seventeenth-century Virginia. (It has been printed in seventeen different anthologies.) The focus was Virginia's colonial elite and how it passed through several stages before finally flowering into the homogenous aristocracy of the eighteenth century. In Virginia, as in Massachusetts, social and political developments were inextricably intertwined, and kinship ties were of vital importance, particularly in later years. Much as in Massachusetts, an influx of English adventurers into Virginia after 1660 bred deep resentments among local leaders. Worse still, no one group had the necessary wealth and position to establish a firm claim to political authority. The upshot, in large measure, was Bacon's Rebellion. Indeed, this same clash between outs and ins, argued Bailyn, occurred in still other American colonies where "the social basis of public life had become uncertain and insecure." More than any other historian, except perhaps Edmund S. Morgan, Bailyn established the family as a valuable area of study in early American history. Kinship, in his view, impinged on nearly every sphere of human activity, from economic relations to politics. In "Politics and Social Structure in Virginia," he even argued that a distinctly American system of partible inheritance contributed to political stability in eighteenth-century Virginia.

No less immune from familial influences was colonial education, as Bailyn showed in *Education in the Forming of American Society: Needs and Opportunities for Study* (1960). Combining an interpretive essay with a bibliographical assessment of available resources, the book grew out of a 1959 Williamsburg conference on early American education. It represented a considerable achievement, both for its insightful hypotheses and original approach. Breaking from previous studies, Bailyn defined education as "the entire process by which a culture transmits itself across the generations," encompassing considerably more than formal institutions of learning. Of key importance during the early years of colonization was the family, which Bailyn discusses in detail, pointing out that, like their European forebears, early colonists relied on the family, not formal schooling, to provide educational instruction. Assisting the family were other institutions, notably apprenticeship, the church, and the community. Before long, however, all these institutions fell victim to the effect of the New World. A shortage of labor, land abundance, and religious pluralism so weakened their effectiveness that, as a consequence, a variety of schools began to grow rapidly during the 1700s.

These and other insights in *Education in the Forming of American Society* confirmed Bailyn as a leading social historian of early America. The book also placed him in the company of a growing body of scholars who, in the years since World War II, had begun to reassert the uniqueness of America's past. Much like Frederick Jackson Turner, they viewed the wilderness environment as a corrosive agent capable of undermining some of the most durable European institutions. Though other circumstances, such as cultural heterogeneity and England's distance, worked in much the same direction, none was so powerful as America's vast and bountiful resources.

Bailyn, in earlier work, had frequently noted emerging distinctions between England and North America, but not until the early 1960s did his views acquire a sharper focus. He presented his most forceful conclusions on the distinctions in "Political Experience and Enlightenment Ideas in Eighteenth-Century America" (1962). The article inaugurated an intimate involvement with the Revolution that established him as one of its principal interpreters.

"Political Experience and Enlightenment Ideas in Eighteenth-Century America" advanced a number of much broader points than several review essays he had already written on the Revolution. Bailyn considered the revolt as primarily a contest of ideas in which the revolutionaries did not seek social upheaval but were instead committed to political and ideological priorities. The relative absence of internal conflict stemmed from the fact that the colonies had long experienced major social and political changes. Americans already enjoyed a considerably freer way of life than their European contemporaries, because of such "mundane exigencies" as distance, religious pluralism, and the wide distribution of property. With all of its emphasis on Enlightenment liberalism, the Revolution's special contribution was to complete and formalize these reforms, and thereby add a vital measure of legitimacy which many innovations had lacked in colonial times. In the space of a reasonably brief article, Bailyn put forth a sweeping hypothesis that achieved considerable popularity. In the twenty years after publication, "Political Experience and Enlightenment Ideas in Eighteenth-Century America" was republished in over twenty collections.

In the early 1960s Bailyn also agreed to edit a mammoth collection of Revolutionary pamphlets for the John Harvard Library. The project potentially encompassed over four hundred pamphlets relating to the period 1750 to 1776. For publication, he was able to narrow the number to seventy-two which had special importance, fourteen of which were included in the first volume, *Pamphlets of the American Revolution, 1750-1776*, which appeared in 1965. Bailyn wrote a lengthy introduction for the volume, in addition to providing editorial notes and describing the context of each document and its author. It is arguably his most impressive work, for he attached new meaning to a set of beliefs variously known in English history as Radical Whig, Country, or Opposition thought. Other historians, such as Caroline Robbins and J. G. A. Pocock, had described this ideology, with its exaggerated fear of government authority, in the context of British politics. Bailyn, through a close examination of the Revolution's pamphlet literature, fully grasped its implications for the American colonies. As he later recalled, "I began to see a new meaning in phrases that I, like most historians, had readily dismissed as mere rhetoric and propaganda: 'slavery,' 'corruption,' 'conspiracy.'"

From his study of the pamphlets, Bailyn concluded that a widespread commitment to the values and ideals of Radical Whig thought predisposed Americans to view the events of the 1760s and 1770s in an especially sinister and menacing light. So extreme was the emphasis this ideology attached to preserving civil and political liberties from governmental tyranny that fearful colonists came to suspect England was engaged in a diabolical conspiracy to rob them of their most basic rights. The Revolution, in the minds of Americans, was fundamentally a struggle to preserve traditional English liberties from the hands of power-hungry officials.

But if the Revolution had conservative underpinnings, its consequences, Bailyn asserted, were decidedly more radical. Convinced that the Revolution served to legitimize long-made reforms, he also believed that the antiauthoritarianism of Revolutionary ideology challenged and, in some cases, transformed a number of institutions ranging from slavery to established religion. The Revolution's radicalism stemmed neither from economic distress nor from social despair but from a mounting hostility to all structures that seemed to restrict human freedom.

Close on the heels of volume one of the *Pamphlets of the American Revolution, 1750-1776*, which received the Faculty Prize of the Harvard University Press, the book's introduction was published separately in 1967 as *The Ideological Origins of the American Revolution*. The introduction was bolstered with additional annotation and was augmented by several newly rewritten sections, including its foreword, in which Bailyn now claimed to have found evidence of Radical Whig ideology as far back as the 1730s.

He elaborated on this assertion in a closely related work, *The Origins of American Politics* (1968). Originally delivered as Charles K. Colver lectures at Brown University, the book analyzed the historical context of Radical Whig thought in the colonies. It also provided a novel analysis of colonial politics, for, in Bailyn's opinion, the peculiar configuration of eighteenth-century politics was crucial to the widespread appeal of this ideology in America. Colonial governors, who held extensive executive powers on paper, nonetheless lacked the vital sources of informal influence, such as patronage, that ministers normally wielded in England. The result was an extremely volatile combination of "swollen claims and shrunken powers." "Conflict," concluded Bailyn, "was inevitable: conflict between a presumptuous prerogative and an overgreat democracy, conflict that had no easy resolution and that raised in minds steeped in the political culture of eighteenth-century Britain the specter of catastrophe."

Taken together, Bailyn's works form a composite and influential interpretation of the Revolution, from its conservative origins, rooted in ideology and the colonial political structure, to its far more radical consequences. Central to this interpretation has been the conviction that ideas lay at the heart of American independence and were to a great degree determinative of men's actions during the Revolutionary era.

The Ideological Origins of the American Revolution and *The Origins of American Politics* earned Bailyn an avalanche of praise. The former received both the Pulitzer and Bancroft Prizes and has been republished at least fifteen times. Not the least of their virtues is Bailyn's vivid, yet elegant, prose. Interspersed through his writing are colorful images and especially powerful metaphors. In one important passage, he likened Radical Whig thought in the colonies to an "intellectual switchboard wired so that certain combinations of events would activate a distinct set of signals—danger signals, indicating hidden impulses and the likely trajectory of events impelled by them."

Both books also provoked sharp debate over the role of ideology in the coming of the Revolution. Almost single-handedly, they revived a scholarly dispute that was nearly as old as the Revolution itself. Although many historians found Bailyn's

claims convincing, several labeled him an "idealist" who did not give sufficient attention to material influences. Others complained that he failed to credit ideological currents other than Radical Whig thought. Still greater opposition arose among historians who charged Bailyn with an elitist bias in examining only upper-class expressions of discontent with Great Britain. Just as important, they argued, was the influence of less affluent colonists who did not always share the views of wealthy men.

In 1962, Bailyn had been named editor-in-chief of the John Harvard Library and in 1967 became a founding coeditor of the journal *Perspectives in American History*, published by the Charles Warren Center at Harvard. Together with his colleague Donald Fleming, he edited two special volumes of the journal, *The Intellectual Migration: Europe and America, 1930-1960* (1969) and *Law in American History* (1972), which appeared separately as books. In their introduction to *The Intellectual Migration*, they returned to the topic of intellectual creativity, which Bailyn and John Clive had earlier explored in their study of Scotland and America. Much like Scottish and American intellectuals in the eighteenth century, the intellectuals who fled Hitler's Europe before World War II were "marginal men" experiencing the tensions of being caught between two different cultures.

Bailyn became a full professor on the Harvard faculty in 1961 and was named Winthrop Professor in 1966. He declined the offer of a position at the Institute of Advanced Study in Princeton because he would have missed teaching and the opportunities it afforded to learn from students. A popular undergraduate lecturer, he also became one of the Harvard history department's most active graduate mentors. By the late 1960s, he had directed a number of doctoral students, many of whom, such as Michael Kammen and Gordon Wood, quickly achieved considerable prominence in their own right. His seminars were widely known for their intellectual excitement and rigor. After class, students commonly continued their discussions in a nearby bar, for as one recalled, "Bailyn had given us a head of steam only time and beer could dissipate."

To his graduate students he has normally emphasized two special aspects of historical study. One has been the proper framing of questions in the formulation of research topics. "Precise, orderly thought applied to this question," he wrote at one point, "would be more valuable to the working historian than volumes of speculation on whether it is conceivable to know the past, or what is the nature of a fact." He has also spent considerable time on writing skills. An excellent literary craftsman, he has typically set aside seminar sessions to discuss the strategy and mechanics of good historical writing.

During the early 1970s, Bailyn wrote several articles dealing with different aspects of American independence: "Religion and Revolution" assessed the influence, or lack of influence, that religion had on American protests; "Common Sense" probed the English origins of Thomas Paine's angry radicalism; "The Central Themes of the American Revolution" provided a forceful restatement of his earlier conclusions and an analysis of the Revolution's implications for later generations; and, no doubt in response to critics, "The Index and Commentaries of Harbottle Dorr" showed how Revolutionary ideology had a strong impact on a rather ordinary Boston shopkeeper. His chief project, however, was a biography, published in 1974, of the arch-Loyalist Thomas Hutchinson. He had first presented some of his findings at New York University and at Cambridge University, where he was Trevelyan Lecturer in 1971. Hutchinson, who served as royal governor of his native Massachusetts from 1771 to 1774, was a central figure during the Revolutionary era. Widely attacked as a corrupt conspirator against American liberties, he left in 1774 for England, where he died an embittered exile six years later. In *The Ordeal of Thomas Hutchinson*, Bailyn provided a sympathetic but balanced narrative. Though a full-length biography, the bulk of the book concentrated on Hutchinson's role in the Revolutionary era, with only a single chapter devoted to his first fifty-four years. His principal frailty was neither avarice nor a lust for power, as his critics alleged, but a moral obtuseness to the Revolutionary protests that ultimately overwhelmed him. He was so enmeshed in the "Anglo-American political world of privilege and patronage," contended Bailyn, that "he could not respond to the aroused moral passion and the optimistic and idealist impulses that gripped the minds of the Revolutionaries."

Bailyn sought to account for more in Hutchinson's biography than just the tragic downfall of one of Massachusetts's most illustrious sons. He also hoped to provide new insights into the Loyalist mind and thereby distinguish it from that of American Whigs. (Some critics of *The Ideological Origins of the American Revolution* had asserted that significant differences did not exist between the two.) If Hutchinson was atypical in his many achievements, he did share with other Loyalists, Bailyn suggested, many of the same assumptions and values about government power and the men who wielded it. As a consequence, they too failed to comprehend the frantic protests of their antagonists, finding instead "only persistent irrationality" in their arguments.

The Ordeal of Thomas Hutchinson provoked more criticism than Bailyn's earlier works. Some reviewers thought it too favorable to Hutchinson, while others again felt Bailyn was inordinately wedded to an ideological interpretation of the Revolution. One commentator even argued that Bailyn's sympathetic portrait stemmed from his own alleged opposition to the antiauthoritarianism of Harvard student protests during the late 1960s. Still, the book received a National Book Award in addition to considerable praise. Even Bailyn's critics applauded his ability to capture the drama and torment of Hutchinson's later life.

Since the Hutchinson biography, Bailyn has generally moved away from the Revolution. In the midst of America's bicentennial, he published "1776: A Year of Challenge—A World Transformed," but this work went beyond the question of American independence. Concerned with the effect of rapid growth in the colonies on Anglo-American relations, the article mostly analyzed long-term economic and demographic trends during the eighteenth century. About the same time, he wrote the colonial portion of *The Great Republic*, an American history textbook which appeared in 1977. In it, Bailyn reaffirmed many of his earlier points about colonial society, the most important being that America's first years witnessed the gradual transformation of European institutions, which the Revolution both legitimized and accelerated. He also included new material which, like that in "1776," was heavily demographic. Currently Bailyn is at work on a study of colonial society tentatively titled *The Peopling of America*, which will examine the recruitment, settlement, and social development of the early American population. It is to be a synthesis incorporating his own research and many of the "local studies" social historians have produced about colonial communities.

Bailyn has remained committed to writing history as an essential blend of narrative and analysis. Although much of his later work, aside from the Hutchinson biography and *The Great Republic*, has lacked the narrative framework which characterized *The New England Merchants in the Seventeenth Century*, still virtually all of his principal writings have possessed a strong temporal dimension. For him history must remain the study of growth, process, and change. His fear is that historians have become both so specialized and so analytical that they no longer produce major syntheses which address the hows as well as the whys of the past. Though a pioneer in the application of statistical methods, he has similarly opposed overreliance on social science techniques. The writing of history remains, in his view, an art that should never forsake its essential narrative character. "In the end," he has written, "historians must be, not analysts of isolated technical problems abstracted from the past, but narrators of worlds in motion—worlds as complex, unpredictable, and transient as our own."

In 1981, Bailyn became Adams University Professor at Harvard and served as president of the American Historical Association. Among other recent distinctions, he has received honorary degrees from numerous universities, including Yale, Rutgers, and Clark. Certainly he has explored the interdynamics of social, political, and intellectual history with considerable brilliance, and his methodological innovations have established trends that historians still follow. His interpretations, if not always fully accepted, have often set the terms of historical debate. He has powerfully reshaped the landscape of early American history, and the aftershocks show few signs of subsiding.

Other:

"Politics and Social Structure in Virginia," in *Seventeenth-Century America*, edited by James M. Smith (Chapel Hill: University of North Carolina Press, 1959), pp. 90-115;

"The Problems of the Working Historian: A Comment," in *Philosophy and History: A Symposium*, edited by Sidney Hook (New York: New York University Press, 1963), pp. 92-101;

"Education as a Discipline: Some Historical Notes," in *The Discipline of Education*, edited by John Walton and James L. Kuethe (Madison: University of Wisconsin Press, 1963), pp. 125-139;

The Apologia of Robert Keayne, edited by Bailyn (New York: Harper & Row, 1965);

Pamphlets of the American Revolution, 1750-1776, volume 1, edited by Bailyn (Cambridge, Mass.: Harvard University Press, 1965);

Perspectives in American History, volumes 1-10, edited by Bailyn and Donald Fleming (Cambridge, Mass.: The Charles Warren Center, Harvard University, 1967-1976);

The Intellectual Migration: Europe and America, 1930-1960, edited by Bailyn and Fleming (Cambridge, Mass.: Harvard University Press, 1969);

Law in American History, edited by Bailyn and Donald Fleming (Boston: Little, Brown, 1972);

"The Central Themes of the American Revolution: An Interpretation," in *Essays on the American Revolution*, edited by Stephen G. Kurtz and James H. Hutson (Chapel Hill: University of North Carolina Press, 1973), pp. 3-31;

"Common Sense," in *Fundamental Testaments of the American Revolution* (Washington, D.C.: Library of Congress, 1973), pp. 7-22;

"Lines of Force in Recent Writings on the American Revolution" (San Francisco: International Congress of Historical Sciences, 1975);

The Great Republic, by Bailyn and others (Lexington, Mass.: D. C. Heath, 1977; revised, 1981);

The Press & the American Revolution, edited by Bailyn and John B. Hench (Worcester, Mass.: American Antiquarian Society, 1980).

Periodical Publications:

"The Apologia of Robert Keayne," *William and Mary Quarterly*, third series, 7 (October 1950): 568-587;

"Communications and Trade: The Atlantic in the Seventeenth Century," *Journal of Economic History*, 13 (Fall 1953): 378-387;

"Blount Papers: Notes on the Merchant 'Class' in the Revolutionary Period," *William and Mary Quarterly*, third series, 11 (January 1954): 98-104;

"England's Cultural Provinces: Scotland and America," by Bailyn and John Clive, *William and Mary Quarterly*, third series, 11 (April 1954): 200-213;

"Kinship and Trade in Seventeenth Century New England," *Explorations in Entrepreneurial History*, 6 (May 1954): 197-205;

"Becker, Andrews, and the Image of Colonial Origins," *New England Quarterly*, 29 (December 1956): 522-534;

"Beekmans of New York," *William and Mary Quarterly*, third series, 14 (October 1957): 598-608;

"Boyd's Jefferson: Notes for a Sketch," *New England Quarterly*, 33 (September 1960): 380-400;

"Political Experience and Enlightenment Ideas in Eighteenth-Century America," *American Historical Review*, 67 (January 1962): 339-351;

"Butterfield's Adams: Notes for a Sketch," *William and Mary Quarterly*, third series, 19 (April 1962): 238-256;

"Religion and Revolution: Three Biographical Studies," *Perspectives in American History*, 4 (1970): 85-139;

"The Index and Commentaries of Harbottle Dorr,"

Proceedings of the Massachusetts Historical Society, 85 (1973): 21-35;

"A Dialogue between an American and a European Englishman by Thomas Hutchinson, [1768]," *Perspectives in American History*, 9 (1975): 341-410;

"1776: A Year of Challenge—A World Transformed," *Journal of Law & Economics*, 19 (October 1976): 437-466;

"Morison: An Appreciation," *Proceedings of the Massachusetts Historical Society*, 89 (1977): 112-123;

"The Challenge of Modern Historiography,"

American Historical Review, 87 (February 1982): 1-24.

Interviews:

John A. Garraty, "Bernard Bailyn: The American Revolution," *Interpreting American History: Conversations with Historians* (New York: Macmillan, 1970; London: Collier-Macmillan, 1970), I: 63-91;

Karen J. Winkler, "Wanted: A History that Pulls Things Together—An Interview with Bernard Bailyn," *Chronicle of Higher Education*, 20 (7 July 1980): 3.

John Spencer Bassett

(10 September 1867-27 January 1928)

Herbert J. Doherty, Jr.
University of Florida

SELECTED BOOKS: *The Constitutional Beginnings of North Carolina, 1663-1729* (Baltimore: Johns Hopkins University Press, 1894);

The Regulators of North Carolina, 1765-1771, in *1894 Annual Report of the American Historical Association* (Washington: U.S. Government Printing Office, 1895);

Suffrage in the State of North Carolina, 1776-1861, in *1895 Annual Report of the American Historical Association* (Washington: U.S. Government Printing Office, 1896);

Slavery and Servitude in the Colony of North Carolina (Baltimore: Johns Hopkins University Press, 1896);

Anti-Slavery Leaders of North Carolina (Baltimore: Johns Hopkins University Press, 1898);

Slavery in the State of North Carolina (Baltimore: Johns Hopkins University Press, 1899);

The Relation between the Virginia Planter and the London Merchant, in *1901 Annual Report of the American Historical Association* (Washington: U.S. Government Printing Office, 1902);

The Federalist System, 1789-1801, volume 11 of *The American Nation: A History* (New York & London: Harper, 1906);

Life of Andrew Jackson, 2 volumes (Garden City: Doubleday, Page, 1911; revised edition, New York: Macmillan, 1916);

A Short History of the United States (New York: Mac-

millan, 1913; revised, 1921);

The Plain Story of American History (New York: Macmillan, 1916);

The Middle Group of American Historians (New York: Macmillan, 1917);

The Lost Fruits of Waterloo (New York: Macmillan, 1918);

Our War with Germany: A History (New York: Knopf, 1919);

Expansion and Reform, 1889-1926, in Epochs of American History series (New York & London: Longmans, Green, 1926);

Makers of a New Nation (New Haven: Yale University Press, 1928);

The League of Nations: A Chapter in World Politics (New York & London: Longmans, Green, 1928).

John Spencer Bassett was the author of the first scholarly biography of Andrew Jackson and editor of the seven-volume *Correspondence of Andrew Jackson* (1926-1935). Among historians he is often noted as the central figure in an academic freedom struggle in North Carolina in the early twentieth century. He was one of the first generation of professionally trained historians who, imbued with "scientific" methods of investigation, were to bring about a revolution in the field of historical inquiry in the South. The careful objectivity and even-handed

John Spencer Bassett

fairness that he brought to his work made *A Short History of the United States* (1913), which went through three revisions and numerous republications, a standard American-history college text for over thirty years.

Bassett was born in Tarboro, North Carolina, and was the second child of Richard Baxter and Mary Jane Wilson Bassett. His father and paternal grandfather were Methodists and Virginians who had earned their livelihoods as carpenter-contractors. They had been small slaveholders who were uneasy with the institution of slavery but were not involved in opposing it. Bassett's father had moved to North Carolina just prior to the Civil War and had served in the Commissary Department of the Confederate army during that conflict. Bassett attended the Graded School of Goldsboro and the Jefferson Davis Military Academy at LaGrange, North Carolina, before entering Trinity College (which became Duke University in 1924). Located at that time in Randolph County, Trinity was a fairly ordinary backwoods Methodist institution. Enter-

ing as a junior in 1886, Bassett was graduated in 1888. Thereafter, he taught for two years in the Durham Graded School, then returned to Trinity in 1890 as an instructor of English. During his year at Trinity he organized the 9019, a secret society which was the institution's first scholarship organization and the predecessor of the Duke University Phi Beta Kappa chapter.

In 1891 Bassett went to Baltimore to pursue his graduate education at Johns Hopkins University and to study under the direction of Herbert Baxter Adams. Already known as a major force in the development of scientific historical scholarship in the United States, Adams had gotten his doctorate at Heidelberg in 1876 and was applying the methods of the German universities to American higher education. Bassett was profoundly impressed with those methods and thereafter insisted upon the necessity of factual history based on primary sources and of fair, truthful assessment of all sides of an issue. Though his dissertation was done in the field of political history, his studies included economics and sociology. He emerged from Johns Hopkins in 1894 as a well-rounded scholar burning to take on the cultural, political, and social problems of his state and region.

Bassett went back to Trinity as professor of history with not only a Ph.D. but also a wife. In 1892 he had married Jessie Lewellyn of Durham, and ultimately they had two children, Richard Horace and Margaret Byrd. During Bassett's graduate study, Trinity College had been moved to Durham with the financial assistance of tobacco millionaire Washington Duke. Bassett and his wife settled in at their new home in Durham, and he was soon deeply involved in the many scholarly and civic activities which were to be characteristic of his life.

Though he entered upon his career at Trinity with enthusiasm, Bassett was disturbed by the financial and intellectual poverty of both his institution and the South. He early attained a reputation as a resourceful and able teacher, but teaching alone did not content him, for the young Bassett wanted to do something to ameliorate the conditions which surrounded him. The paucity of historical and literary resources at Trinity motivated him to crusade for the collection and preservation of source materials and for the building up of the library. His students, friends, and the public were recruited to search their attics and trunks and those of their relatives to find rare books, manuscripts, journals, old newspapers, and pamphlets. In this way the foundation was laid for Duke's valuable historical collection of Southern Americana. Bassett's efforts for the library eventuated in an endowment from the Duke family. After six years he was named manager of the library in addition to his other duties.

In his first year Bassett revitalized the Trinity College Historical Society. He induced the student magazine, the *Archive*, to publish historical essays by some of the students. He arranged for reprints and bound them together as *Trinity Historical Papers*. The college administrators were so impressed that they assumed the publication expense, and the *Trinity Historical Papers* became a regular annual publication in 1897, carrying essays by Bassett as well as by students.

During his Trinity years Bassett was active in research and publication, for the most part writing about North Carolina topics. A source of heavy reliance in his monographs was the ten-volume *Colonial Records of North Carolina* (1886-1890), which had been compiled and published by the state. Its importance to his early writing led him to the recognition that there had to be two kinds of history books: "They are designed to serve as storehouses of information out of which other writers mine precious metals, or they are written to supply to serious-minded men interesting and informing reading that ministers to the culture of the individual and the promotion of a general knowledge of the experience of the men of the past."

Bassett's dissertation, *The Constitutional Beginnings of North Carolina, 1663-1729* (1894), was published in the Johns Hopkins *Studies in Historical and Political Science*, as were three later monographs: *Slavery and Servitude in the Colony of North Carolina* (1896), *Anti-Slavery Leaders of North Carolina* (1898), and *Slavery in the State of North Carolina* (1899). During his Trinity period he also wrote three other books which were published in numbers of the *Annual Report of the American Historical Association*: *The Regulators of North Carolina, 1765-1771* (1895), *Suffrage in the State of North Carolina, 1776-1861* (1896), and *The Relation between the Virginia Planter and the London Merchant* (1902). These were all journeyman works that marked his progress to scholarly maturity. Each was written from a few sources and was narrow in focus. The best of them is that on the Regulators, which anticipated later scholars in viewing the Regulator movement as a justifiable protest of small farmers against political and economic grievances.

As the new century dawned, Bassett was not content. Appalled by political intolerance and the exploitation of racial passions which had marked the 1890s in North Carolina, he feared their corrosive effect on the mind of his region. He wanted an organ in which, as a social critic, he could expose provincialism and religious and political bigotry and promote toleration and independent critical thinking. Patterning their effort after the *Sewanee Review*, Bassett and his 9019 society founded the *South Atlantic Quarterly* in 1901 to provide a forum for liberal thought and advance "the literary, historical, and social development of the South." Bassett and his socially aware friends had their vehicle.

Critics of Bassett and of Trinity held their fire until a particularly stinging article came from Bassett's pen in the October 1903 number of the quarterly. "Stirring up the Fires of Race Antipathy" criticized the racism that was being fanned by Democratic politicians and newspaper editors. The same people had been assailed in earlier articles with no result, but this time they took notice when Bassett observed of Booker T. Washington, "Now Washington is a great and good man, a Christian statesman, and take him all in all the greatest man, save General Lee, born in the South in a hundred years; but he is not a typical negro." Though Bassett specifically denied desiring social equality of the races, he wrote that the only solution to the race problem was to adopt black people into American life. "In spite of our race feeling, of which this writer has his share, they will win equality at some time."

The opposition which had been accumulating against Bassett's ideas now became crystallized. Josephus Daniels, editor of the *Raleigh News and Observer*, led a cacophony of raucous newspaper attacks upon both Bassett and Trinity College, lasting through the spring and summer of 1904 and culminating in demands that Bassett be removed from his post. Though often overlooked, an article by John C. Kilgo, president of Trinity, in the same number of the *South Atlantic Quarterly* is almost as strong as Bassett's in decrying Negrophobia, saying that failure to bring racial harmony would be "the defeat of the Christian religion and the American civilization."

What might superficially appear to be a clearcut issue of academic freedom was, in fact, a complex of issues. Daniels was a rabidly partisan Democratic editor and a devoted alumnus of the state university at Chapel Hill. He had been party to the anti-Negro campaign with which the Democratic party had checked Republican and Populist political gains. Friction between church and public colleges was also part of the picture, and some church college leaders, including Kilgo, had attempted to discourage legislative appropriations for Chapel Hill. Antitrust sentiment was running strong and Daniels played upon churchmen who were furious about "tobacco-trust" financial support for Trinity; tobacco magnate Washington Duke was also a Republican. Bassett appears to have made himself a symbol of much which was anathema to an important segment of state leadership.

President Kilgo recognized that the best course of action in the circumstances was to defend Bassett upon the principles of freedom of inquiry and expression, not to defend what he had written. He believed that if the conflict could be guided so as to result in a victory over irrationalism, it might give his college an enduring tradition. When the trustees met in a lengthy session, Kilgo, with the support of Washington Duke, made that defense, and by a vote of 18-7 the trustees refused to accept Bassett's already proffered resignation. The faculty, prominent alumni, and the students—who burned Daniels in effigy—had already come to his defense.

Bassett himself explicitly repudiated social equality of the races and called blacks "a child race," but his offense was considered grave and the public was given to believe that no one at Trinity agreed with what he had said. The victory, however, was for freedom of expression, and that was impressive in North Carolina in 1904. Though Bassett gave up the editorship of the *South Atlantic Quarterly* in 1905, it was not directly because of the controversy which he had precipitated. He told his readers that he was satisfied that the literary life of the South was being advanced but that he was compelled to resign "because of an accumulation of other labors."

The "other labors" included an invitation to write a volume in *The American Nation* series, a pioneer multivolume collaboration. Albert Bushnell Hart had asked him in October 1904 to write the volume on *The Federalist System, 1789-1801* (1906). His deadline was 1 August 1905, allowing only nine months to research and write the book. The manuscript was completed on time, required few revisions, and was published in January 1906—an amazing accomplishment, typical, however, of the speed and dedication with which Bassett could work. *The Federalist System, 1789-1801* was highly praised by Hart. It is a careful and clearly written presentation which emphasizes political and diplomatic history. The chapters on society and economic conditions are the weakest. Bassett slightly favors the Federalists because he approved of the system they established, but some historians detected a subtle shift of interpretation toward Jefferson's wary view of governmental power. It remains a good general survey of the period covered.

Bassett, who was named to the General Committee of the American Historical Association in 1902, lobbied unsuccessfully to have the 1902 annual meeting in Nashville but did succeed in getting a session on Southern history put into the program and read a paper for it. When the 1903 meeting was scheduled for New Orleans, he was gratified but was too ill to attend. As a result of the Negrophobia controversy of 1904, his repute had spread beyond narrow professional circles, while publication of *The Federalist System, 1789-1801* solidified his professional recognition. By 1906 Bassett was well known within historical circles, and this new status in the world of higher education provided an opportunity to satisfy long-smoldering ambitions.

Bassett had begun his career at Trinity in 1894 with high hopes and youthful energy, but the controversies, the pressures of public conformity, the schedule of publication which he had maintained, and his activity in student and professional organizations and civic life had wearied him. He was discouraged by the poor salary Trinity was able to pay, the paucity of research facilities in North Carolina, and his teaching load, which often amounted to fifteen or eighteen hours a week. He taught a wide variety of history courses and some in other disciplines—even French. Little wonder that by the turn of the century weariness should be a characteristic of his letters. As early as 1896 his complaints had led his old mentor, Adams, to promise to be on the lookout for a new job for him. In that year he had told Adams that it was "uninspiring to live in this State just now. If my salary were larger I could go North every summer and remedy this deficiency." In 1898 he told Adams he could foresee clashes with churchmen on the issue of orthodoxy and declared that North Carolina had its share of fools. If "fool-killing" were to go on, he wanted to stay there to enjoy the fun. The South, he wrote, did not appreciate truthful historians but preferred Confederate veterans, who had fought bravely with the sword "but make *asses* of themselves with the pen."

The coveted new post came when Charles D. Hazen of the Smith College history department in the spring of 1906 invited him to join the faculty in Northampton, Massachusetts. The temptation of better library facilities, the leisure to write, and respite from public dissensions was great, and after negotiating a better salary Bassett accepted the offer. At Smith he taught only three days a week and was paid well enough to travel to libraries, archives, and historical meetings. The years at Smith College were productive ones and were to see the creation of Bassett's most enduring works.

The book for which Bassett will be remembered longest is undoubtedly his two-volume *Life of Andrew Jackson* (1911), which was largely a product of his early years at Smith. Research was undertaken as early as 1902, but his other activities delayed the progress of the work. Based almost exclusively upon manuscript sources, it was the first scholarly, balanced biography of Jackson. Bassett saw Jackson as a product of the western frontier which had conditioned his military and political abilities. Though warmly sympathetic to Jacksonian policies and purposes, Bassett recognized that Jackson had massive shortcomings, all of which gave way, however, before his bravery, his frankness, and his masterful leadership of the democratic movement. A one-volume revision was published in 1916. No major changes were made, but Bassett took the opportunity to respond to critics who had faulted him for not having written a "life and times." The book was not history, he asserted, it was biography, and in biography the subject should be kept in the forefront. The revised edition was reissued four times, the last being in 1967. Scholars have praised Bassett's diligence in working the sources for *Life of Andrew Jackson*, as well as his fairness and accuracy, but his style has come under fire. Wendell H. Stephenson commented that "the author's heavy style was devoid of literary artistry." Marquis James, a later Jackson biographer, wrote of Bassett's volumes, "alas, as reading they are saltless fare." Bassett maintained that he had tried to be dignified and clear rather than "sparkling or highly frivolous." No subsequent biography of Jackson has yet entirely replaced Bassett's.

Within two years after the publication of the Jackson volumes, Bassett produced a work which popularized his name among college students and which brought him substantial royalties. *A Short History of the United States* (1913) was a standard college text for more than thirty years. It was revised by Bassett in 1921, by Allan Nevins in 1929, and by Bassett's son, Richard, in 1939. Each revision went through many printings. As might be expected of a text, it is not great historical literature but is an accurate, objective, systematic catalogue—a classic of utility rather than literature.

Bassett had taken an immediate liking to the town of Northampton and to Smith after arriving in 1906. Few of his writings after the move dealt with the South, and he told his friends that the New England atmosphere, both intellectual and physical, was too stimulating for him to think of permanently returning to the South. As at Trinity, Bassett soon attracted a circle of students who formed a

club to seek out old letters and manuscripts which might be hidden away in family attics, and in 1915, as an avenue of publication for these items, he established the *Smith College Studies in History*, a book series. As his research productivity grew, his social life blossomed. On Sunday afternoons he and his family entertained little groups of students, faculty, and townspeople around their fireside. These pleasant gatherings were marked by good conversation enhanced by Bassett's genial presence.

After *A Short History of the United States*, Bassett's most important work was *The Middle Group of American Historians*, published in 1917. This book features sketches of the literary careers of Jared Sparks, George Bancroft, William H. Trescot, John L. Motley, and Peter Force and reveals the quality of scholarship unique to each. An introductory chapter gives brief notice to earlier historians and a concluding chapter dwells upon the relations between historians and their publishers. In the same year he used the *Smith College Studies in History* to publish *The Correspondence of George Bancroft and Jared Sparks, 1823-1832*.

Meanwhile, World War I was turning Bassett's scholarly interests toward Europe, and his writings during the war years were focused upon the war, its origins, and its aftermath. *The Lost Fruits of Waterloo* (1918), which depicts the breakdown of the Concert of Europe and its replacement by a balance-of-power system as the root of the war, argues that the hope of the future is international organization, a federation of states united to promote world community. Bassett calls for treating the Germans as leniently after the war as were Southerners after the Civil War, a view which did not sit well with contemporary reviewers. *Our War with Germany: A History* (1919) is another exercise in putting together facts in a balanced way and was considered at the time the best one-volume history of the war. It is so dispassionate, however, that one reviewer called it "placid" and lacking in flesh-and-blood characters. A few days before his death in 1928 Bassett had read proofs of his last book to grow out of the war, *The League of Nations: A Chapter in World Politics* (1928). (He had been given a leave of absence the previous year to observe the league in operation.) Though it was judged to be well-written, the book was not well received. It was criticized for using unreliable, incomplete, or inadequate sources and for having ignored much of the rich literature available. International lawyer Manley O. Hudson wrote that Bassett appeared to have "little appreciation of the new conditions which have changed the character of world politics." None of the three war-related books has stood the test of time.

With the exception of *Expansion and Reform, 1889-1926* (1926) and *Makers of a New Nation* (1928), both of which are fairly conventional reference volumes in two larger series, Epochs of American History and Pageant of America, respectively, most of Bassett's publications in the last eight years of his life are compilations of letters or documents. In the *Smith College Studies in History* he published the journals of John A. Selden, Esquire, and Major Howell Tatum (1921, 1922), some letters of Francis Parkman to Pierre Margry (1923), and *The Southern Plantation Overseer as Revealed in His Letters* (1925). The last is by far the most important work of the group and is one of Bassett's most important publications. He used nearly 200 letters, which came from the overseers of two of James K. Polk's Mississippi plantations over a twenty-five year period, to give an insight into conditions surrounding slavery. They reveal the overseers as poorly educated human beings whose job was to get the work done under difficult circumstances. Plantation life is revealed as neither romantic nor barbarous but as an everyday business venture in farming. Though limited in scope, *The Southern Plantation Overseer as Revealed in His Letters* remained the standard work on plantation overseers until the publication of William K. Scarborough's work in 1966.

Without question, the most significant collection of papers which Bassett edited is the *Correspondence of Andrew Jackson* (1926-1935), which appeared in seven volumes under the imprint of the Carnegie Institution of Washington. As the acknowledged expert on Jackson, Bassett was the obvious choice to edit the series. He edited and annotated all the volumes and wrote the informative prefaces as each volume went to press. Bassett died after the third volume had been prepared, and the prefaces to volumes four through six were written by J. Franklin Jameson. (The seventh volume is a general index.) Jameson's prefaces are not founded in as detailed knowledge of the era and are less valuable than Bassett's.

Bassett had been increasingly active in the governing circles of the American Historical Association since his election to the General Committee in 1902. In 1919 he was elected secretary of the association, and its affairs consumed much of his attention. Beyond his scholarly accomplishments, Bassett had a reputation as a good businessman, managing his own financial affairs well, investing profitably, and deriving comfortable income from his textbooks. His shrewd management of the *South Atlantic Quarterly* had led it to financial independence within a few years of its genesis, and it and the *Historical Papers* of the Trinity College Historical Society became the germ of the Duke University Press.

He brought to his new office business talents which served the association well. He appreciated the importance of endowments for cultural organizations and had with considerable success gotten most of those with which he was associated to establish such funds. He conceived and planned the American Historical Association endowment, and at his death the fund had reached $300,000. An anonymous eulogist wrote in the *American Historical Review*, "To him the Association, with its annual meetings, owes much of its success in recent years."

Bassett's death came in the service of the American Historical Association. On 27 January 1928, he was to attend a meeting of the American Council of Learned Societies in Washington to represent the association. Arriving at the club where he was to stay, he dismounted from his trolley car and was crossing the tracks when he was struck by a car passing in the opposite direction. Taken to a hospital in a passing motor truck, he died two hours later.

Bassett was among the early group of "scientific" historians who emerged from the Herbert Baxter Adams seminars at Johns Hopkins having learned that the unvarnished record and the precise facts were all important and that style and form were secondary. Literary historians have faulted this school, terming its adherents "Professors Dryasdust." Scrupulous about truth and fairness and devoted to the principle of no conclusions without the facts, Bassett risked that fault.

Bassett's place among American historians is near, but not in, the first rank. Much of his work is now obsolete. Of his books, *Life of Andrew Jackson* and *The Middle Group of American Historians* may have the longest useful lives. The books he edited, especially *Correspondence of Andrew Jackson*, will be valuable to scholars for years to come. Less tangible are the strength of character which he brought to his profession, the generous liberal enthusiasms which he spread about him among his students and colleagues, the impact upon scholars of his demand for truth and hard facts, and the example which he set of tireless industry in all endeavors to which he laid his hand.

Other:
The Writings of "Colonel William Byrd, of Westover, in Virginia, Esqr," edited by Bassett (Garden City: Doubleday, Page, 1901);
The Correspondence of George Bancroft and Jared

Sparks, 1823-1832, edited by Bassett (Northampton, Mass.: Smith College, 1917);

The Westover Journal of John A. Selden, Esqr., edited by Bassett (Northampton, Mass.: Smith College, 1921);

Major Howell Tatum's Journal while Acting Topographical Engineer (1814) to General Jackson, edited by Bassett (Northampton, Mass.: Smith College, 1922);

Letters of Francis Parkman to Pierre Margry, edited by Bassett (Northampton, Mass.: Smith College, 1923);

The Southern Plantation Overseer as Revealed in His Letters, edited by Bassett (Northampton, Mass.: Smith College, 1925);

Correspondence of Andrew Jackson, 7 volumes, edited by Bassett (Washington: Carnegie Institution of Washington, 1926-1935).

Periodical Publications:

"Character of the Early Virginia Slave Trade," *South Atlantic Quarterly*, 1 (January 1902): 73-81;

"The Bottom of the Matter," *South Atlantic Quarterly*, 1 (April 1902): 99-106;

"The Problems of the Author in the South," *South Atlantic Quarterly*, 1 (July 1902): 201-208;

"The Reign of Passion," *South Atlantic Quarterly*, 1 (October 1902): 301-309;

"The Industrial Decay of the Southern Planter," *South Atlantic Quarterly*, 2 (April 1903): 107-113;

"Two Negro Leaders," *South Atlantic Quarterly*, 2 (July 1903): 267-272;

"Stirring up the Fires of Race Antipathy," *South Atlantic Quarterly*, 2 (October 1903): 297-305;

"The Task of the Critic," *South Atlantic Quarterly*, 3 (October 1904): 297-301.

References:

William B. Hamilton, ed., *Fifty Years of the South Atlantic Quarterly* (Durham: Duke University Press, 1952);

W. Stull Holt, ed., *Historical Scholarship in the United States, 1876-1901: As Revealed in the Correspondence of Herbert B. Adams* (Baltimore: Johns Hopkins University Press, 1938);

"In Memoriam," *South Atlantic Quarterly*, 27 (April 1928): 113-116;

Wendell H. Stephenson, "John Spencer Bassett as a Historian of the South," *North Carolina Historical Review*, 25 (July 1948): 289-317.

Papers:

A small collection of Bassett's papers is in the Duke University Archives.

Howard K. Beale
(8 April 1899-27 December 1959)

Allan D. Charles
University of South Carolina at Union

BOOKS: *The Critical Year: A Study of Andrew Johnson and Reconstruction* (New York: Harcourt, Brace, 1930);

Are American Teachers Free? An Analysis of Restraints upon the Freedom of Teaching in American Schools, part 12 of the Report of the American Historical Association's Commission on Social Studies (New York: Scribners, 1936);

A History of Freedom of Teaching in American Schools, part 16 of the Report of the American Historical Association's Commission on Social Studies (New York: Scribners, 1941);

Theodore Roosevelt and the Rise of America to World Power (Baltimore: Johns Hopkins University Press, 1956).

Howard Kennedy Beale, specialist in nineteenth- and twentieth-century American history, was the leader of a revisionist school which worked to rehabilitate the Reconstruction administration of Andrew Johnson. A close friend of Charles A. Beard, he favored the economic interpretation of history, wrote on Theodore Roosevelt's presidency and, before he died, was preparing a definitive biography of Roosevelt. He was an authority on and a tireless crusader for

Howard K. Beale at The Library of Congress, circa 1940

academic freedom, a subject on which he wrote two books, and he was a strong advocate of peace, freedom, and civil rights.

The son of Frank A. and Nellie Kennedy Beale, Howard K. Beale was born in Chicago as the nineteenth century ended. Twenty-two years later, as a member of Phi Beta Kappa, he completed his undergraduate work at the University of Chicago and headed east to study at Harvard University, an institution which had awarded him a fellowship. Harvard's faith in the potential of the young Midwesterner was maintained when Beale completed his M.A. in 1922, so the university granted him a second fellowship to launch him on his doctoral program.

Edward Channing, an American colonial specialist, urged Beale, who was working under him, to tackle for a dissertation the extensive and thorny historical problem of Andrew Johnson's presidency. When the Chicagoan pleaded his youth and inexperience, his gruff old mentor admonished

him that one would never amount to anything by sticking to limited and pedestrian topics such as the history of sugar-beet culture in a Utah county.

Thus Beale spent many months in the National Archives and other depositories researching Johnson's administration. While poring over the diary of Gideon Welles, Lincoln's and Johnson's secretary of the navy, he noticed discrepancies between the original manuscript and the later printed diary. That observation led to Beale's first publication, an article entitled "Is the Printed Diary of Gideon Welles Reliable?," which appeared in the *American Historical Review* in April 1925. Beale's conclusion, of course, was that the printed version differed significantly from the original. Beale's own edition of the Welles diary, in which he compared the original and modified versions, did not appear until 1960, a few months after his death.

Before Beale's first article appeared in 1925, however, he had the previous year completed his dissertation on Johnson's presidency and was making a fourteen-month grand tour of Europe, courtesy of a Harvard traveling fellowship. It was not until 1927 that Beale actually defended his dissertation and received his Ph.D. When Harcourt, Brace finally published Beale's revised dissertation in 1930 as *The Critical Year: A Study of Andrew Johnson and Reconstruction*, it was six years old. In 1927 Charles A. and Mary Beard had published a brief statement of their economic interpretation of Reconstruction, and their apparent priority led many people to consider Beale a disciple of the Beards. Beale later was at pains to claim priority, but he cheerfully admitted that he had subsequently become a good friend and disciple of Charles Beard, adding, however, that the relationship was not as old as some had imagined.

By 1930 other scholars were also taking new looks at Reconstruction. Beale had to admit that his work was not unique in rehabilitating Johnson and the moderates but was part of an overall revisionist movement. Nevertheless, he was generally and justifiably hailed as the leader of the movement, and Johnson-era revisionism was even referred to by some as the "Beale Thesis." The importance of Beale's *The Critical Year* was evidenced in 1958 when Frederick Ungar published a new edition.

The Critical Year was the most significant effort of Beale's career, and it embodied a thesis that was not seriously challenged in the author's lifetime. Beale contended that during Reconstruction a Radical Republican faction in Congress became dominant by early 1867 and "subjugation came to supersede conciliation." Led by the "vindictive fury" of Pennsylvanian Thaddeus Stevens and the "misguided idealism" of Charles Sumner of Massachusetts, the Congress undertook to chasten the defeated South. That, however, was only the superficial explanation. Beale delved deeper and concluded that unspoken economic motives lay behind the anti-Southern attitude of many of the Radical Republicans. The industrial Northeast was attempting to consolidate its grip on the nation, and the West, only beginning to industrialize, was still a natural ally of the agrarian South. A South readmitted to Congress, moreover, would see its power in the House of Representatives greatly and ironically augmented by the abolition of slavery, as the "Three-fifths Compromise" was no longer in effect. (Formerly only three-fifths of the slaves were counted in the population when calculating the number of representatives, but after 1865 all blacks were freedmen and Southern representation would have to be increased proportionately.) Furthermore, Southerners appeared to be unregenerate

and unrepentant, and it was inevitable that old-line Southern leaders would be sent to Washington unless the radicals moved quickly to seize effective power. The Southerners were low-tariff men, opposed to internal improvements, federal aid to railroads, and central banking. Republican industrialists, therefore, had good cause to fear the loss of wartime high tariffs, enacted when Southerners were absent and in rebellion, and doubted that Southern assistance could be expected for active federal support for transportation and central banking. Beale labeled as "claptrap" the ostensible Northern interest in the welfare of the freedmen, noting that the North abandoned the blacks cheerfully enough in 1876 when the new economic order was firmly entrenched in power.

In *The Critical Year* Beale went on to accuse the Radical Republicans of consciously attempting to create a virtual parliamentary system where chief power lay with the legislature and only an executive who commanded a legislative majority could rule. When Johnson resisted this constitutional revolution, he was impeached and only failed to be convicted by a narrow margin. A successful impeachment of President Johnson would have, according to Beale, not merely set a precedent for political removal of the executive but would have destroyed the principle of separation of powers.

Beale had spent one year (1925-1926) on the faculty at Grinnell College in Iowa and had then returned to New England, where he taught at Bowdoin College in Maine for four years. The following year in the *American Historical Review* his "Tariff and Reconstruction," an article which also grew out of his dissertation, was published.

With the onset of the Great Depression, Beale left Bowdoin and went to Washington, D.C. Working in the manuscript section of the Library of Congress, Beale transcribed and edited the five diary volumes of Edward Bates, who was Lincoln's attorney general from 1861 to 1863. Beale's work was concluded by 1932, and the U.S. Government Printing Office published it the following year as *The Diary of Edward Bates, 1859-1866*. The work ran 685 pages. Beale had had to decipher large numbers of abbreviations, provide summaries of numerous newspaper clippings, and add explanatory notes.

Beale probably found Bates a congenial figure, as Bates had been an antislavery, Virginia-born Missouri Whig placed in Lincoln's cabinet mainly to conciliate pro-Union elements in border states. Bates himself had been a contender for the Republican nomination in 1860, and Beale found it quite significant, in regard to Lincoln's rapid rise from obscurity, that in Bates's speculation-filled diary Abraham Lincoln was first mentioned as a possible nominee only twenty days prior to the convention.

Teaching posts, even for Harvard Ph.D's, were not easily come by during the Depression. After several years of making a living writing, Beale spent the spring semester of 1934 as a visiting associate professor of history at his old alma mater, the University of Chicago. The fall of that year found him at New York University, where he was a lecturer for an academic year. Then, in the fall of 1935, he was called to the University of North Carolina. He was to remain at Chapel Hill until 1948.

After completing his work on Bates, Beale had plunged into a new and broad topic, academic freedom, a subject that was to consume his writing activities for the rest of the decade of the 1930s. An article in *Harper's Magazine* in 1934, "Forces that Control the Schools," was his first publication in his new area. Beale's research was supported by the American Historical Association's Commission on Social Studies in the Schools, and his labors eventually resulted in a book of 856 pages, *Are American Teachers Free? An Analysis of Restraints upon the Freedom of Teaching in American Schools*, published by Scribners in 1936 as part twelve of the report of the AHA's Commission on Social Studies. The book deals with secondary schools and is based upon interviews and questionnaires. The material is arranged in topical chapters, such as "Tenure Rules," "Patriotism," "Politics," "War Problems," black education in the North and in the South (including an indictment of segregation), and other chapters on freedom in various academic disciplines. Even with a guarantee of anonymity, many respondents refused to allow their comments to be put into print. Such fearfulness, Beale concluded, hardly spoke well for freedom in teaching. Beale's zeal for academic freedom was evident in the book, but his tone was scholarly and judicious and had no flavor of polemic.

Continuing his work on freedom, academic and otherwise, Beale in 1936 had published an article in *Independent Woman* entitled "The Truth Shall Make You Free," followed in 1938 by "Freedom for the School Teacher," which appeared in the *Annals of the American Academy of Political and Social Science*. *Educational Freedom and Democracy*, a volume to which he had contributed, was also published in 1938. Not until 1940 did Beale return to his initial subject, producing a twenty-page article, "On Rewriting Reconstruction History," which was published in *American Historical Review*.

Beale's main project at Chapel Hill in the late 1930s was a historical study of academic freedom. In 1941 his 343-page monograph, *A History of Freedom of Teaching in American Schools*, was published by Scribners under the aegis of the AHA's Commission on Social Studies, just as Beale's previous volume on academic freedom had been. The second book, however, was no mere examination of a current situation but a history of academic freedom in American schools below the college level. Its continuing appeal was manifested when Octagon Books republished the work in 1968 and 1974.

Beale's central conclusion was that teachers everywhere and in all time periods were allowed perfect freedom to discuss subjects on which there was no current controversy but were denied freedom to consider issues with which people were emotionally involved. One of Beale's most interesting observations was that not only were schools rather scarce in the middle and Southern colonies, but there were even fewer in New England than had been generally supposed. He was further surprised to discover that some colonial teachers had been indentured servants.

Beale's life changed drastically in 1942, when he married Georgia Robison, a union eventually blessed with three sons. Despite the demands of a growing family, he continued to be quite devoted to his teaching as well as his writing. He was reported to have demanded high achievement from his students, and he attracted many of considerable ability and great promise, including such later notable historians as C. Vann Woodward and George B. Tindall. Woodward later said of his teacher at Chapel Hill: "Howard Beale always made himself available to serious students, socially as well as professionally. That seemed especially so in his unmarried years when he was my teacher. He took an interest in our extra-curricular and political activities as well as our scholarship. As a teacher he was a scrupulous, exacting, and conscientious critic. I remember with special gratitude his postponing his vacation at the end of term in order to read and criticize a draft of my dissertation so that I could finish up and look for a job—and get married."

The war year 1942, in which Beale got married, also saw the professor dividing his time between Chapel Hill and Washington, where he served on the Japanese-American Student Relocation Council and attended a conference of the Social Science Research Council (which had awarded him grants in the late 1930s). The conference's Committee on Historiography decided that Charles A.

Beard, assisted by Beale, John H. Randall, and Merle Curti, should write a book on historiography, and in 1944 appeared *Theory and Practice in Historical Study: A Report of the Committee on Historiography*. Beard wrote one and a half chapters, and Beale wrote one, "What Historians Have Said about the Causes of the Civil War." Beale's contribution constituted what historiographical writer Harvey Wish in 1960 termed one of the two best surveys of Civil War historiography. Beale, by then an old friend and admirer of Beard's, cited the older historian in the first paragraph of his essay. He then gave an objective and succinct account of historians' views on the Civil War, starting with the immediate postwar writers of Northern and Southern polemics and ending with the latest scholarship of his own era.

While Chapel Hill's relative closeness to the nation's capital had facilitated Beale's contribution to the war effort and had made it easier to attend historical meetings in Washington, Beale longed to return to his native Midwest. His outspokenness in behalf of various political causes had alienated some of his colleagues at North Carolina, and consequently it was not too difficult for him to accept a call to the University of Wisconsin when it was offered in 1948.

Other colleagues of Beale's found out why he could sometimes be irritating when, in 1952, he read before the Mississippi Valley Historical Association a paper entitled "The Professional Historian: His Theory and Practice." Published the following year by the relatively obscure *Pacific Historical Review*, the paper reflected Beale's lengthy experience as a teacher of graduate students but was such a bombshell indictment of graduate history teaching that one can understand why some journals might have found it too inflammatory to publish. In the published version much of the documentation was based on confidential sources, and some names were deliberately withheld to avoid embarrassment to colleagues.

In his article Beale asserted that the humanities were neglected vis-à-vis the sciences in terms of government support, and support for history was declining even more than that for other liberal arts. Reflecting his training at Harvard, where he had been encouraged to look at the broad picture, he maintained that most graduate schools tended to stultify young scholars by shunting them off onto trivial topics. He added that the arts of writing and public speaking were neglected and that many professors were too busy or too indifferent to guide graduate students. Ph.D. requirements, he argued, should be overhauled and less

emphasis placed on memorizing facts and bibliographies and more stress placed on research and writing. He also declared that higher degrees from weak institutions should not be recognized by the profession. The Midwesterner in Beale surfaced when he decried the "monopoly" of a small group of book reviewers "centering in the northeast" who exercised excessive power to grant or withhold popularity and claimed that reviewers were slipshod or prejudiced.

One motive for Beale's diatribe against critics was apparently the harsh reviews written of Charles A. Beard's 1948 revisionist *Roosevelt and the Coming of War, 1941*, which Beale felt was attacked emotionally and not judged on its merits. Many historians, Beale was convinced, had long opposed Beard because they did not admire his economic frame of reference, while they failed to admit that they wrote within frames of reference of their own. Beale rebuked Samuel Eliot Morison in particular. Morison had differed with Beard's economic interpretations, but also, according to Beale, they differed in that Beard condemned most wars as futile while Morison viewed America's wars as noble crusades.

After delivering this shotgun blast at academic historians, Beale paused only to write an article appropriately entitled "Teacher as Rebel," published in 1953 also, before buckling down to what was then consuming him, the defense of the recently deceased Charles A. Beard. Beale and others had planned a festschrift in Beard's honor as early as 1939 or 1940, but wartime shortages and dispersal of contributors had precluded it. After the war, it was agreed that Beard himself would be the subject of all the essays, but he died before the book could be completed, perhaps intensifying Beale's desire to defend his friend. Finally, in 1954, *Charles A. Beard: An Appraisal* appeared. Beale edited the work and contributed two of the twelve essays.

He presented a thorough account of Beard's historical philosophy and a well-reasoned defense of it, adding that Beard never contended, a la Marx, that economics was the sole determinant in history and that, after observing the rise of fascism, Beard had even revised his views to give increased emphasis to noneconomic factors in historical causation. In the same volume, Beale also ably summarized Beard's vast writings.

Beale took a leave of absence from Wisconsin in 1955 and 1956 and served as a Fulbright professor at Munich. During that interlude he may have found time to put the final touches on *Theodore Roosevelt and the Rise of America to World Power*, which appeared in 1956. The book ran 600 pages and grew out of the Albert Shaw lectures on diplomatic history, which Beale had delivered at Johns Hopkins in 1953. The Roosevelt book was a product of the most thorough scholarship. Beale interviewed a number of friends and relatives of the president, including Roosevelt's widow and sons, various cabinet members, and senators, and he sifted through all available diplomatic records. He ascertained how Roosevelt was viewed in foreign capitals as well as how foreign diplomatic efforts were seen in Washington.

Beale, like Beard, questioned the value of America's entrance into World War I and sought in the Roosevelt presidency the key to the break with traditional American neutrality that eventuated in the declaration of war in 1917. He also searched for answers to such profound questions as whether blind forces or great leaders are the determinants of history. The result was a book that married intellectual history and biography in a context of diplomatic history.

Beale, whose personal views contrasted greatly with the interventionist imperialism of Roosevelt, came through his researches to admire the president more than he had perhaps believed possible. Roosevelt had, Beale decided, a remarkable comprehension of international problems, superior indeed to most other presidents or secretaries of state. His reputation for snap judgments was undeserved, and he never resorted to idle threats or bombast. Beale faulted Roosevelt for an ambiguous attitude on racial issues, for tying America too closely to British imperialism, and for failing to appreciate Chinese nationalism. Beale exposed the president's pro-Japanese stance in the Russo-Japanese War of 1904-1905 as having been much more pronounced than most people realized then or later.

Beale spent most of his last years researching and compiling material for a definitive biography of Theodore Roosevelt, but the hard-driving historian died of a heart attack before he could write it. The coronary occurred two days after Christmas 1959 as Beale was making preparations to go down to Chicago for the convention of the American Historical Association. A premonitory stroke a few months earlier had failed to convince the sexagenarian to slacken his pace.

In 1960 Beale's three-volume *The Diary of Gideon Welles, Secretary of the Navy under Lincoln and Johnson* was published posthumously. Before his demise, Beale had completed editing the diary, a piece of work which he had in mind to perform ever

since his graduate student years at Harvard when his first published article had challenged the diary's reliability. Reviewers praised the Beale edition as an excellent achievement and a useful aid to scholarship, while differing only as to whether the essential Welles came through even in the earlier doctored version or whether only Beale's corrected diary, based on the original manuscript, permitted the true Welles to be seen. Editing the diary had been a huge task; the completed three-volume set ran 1,942 pages.

The magnitude of Beale's total published work appears even more extraordinary when one considers the amount of time he spent as a political activist and social crusader. He was an active member of the American Association of University Professors, the National Education Association, the American Federation of Teachers (an actual labor union), the American Civil Liberties Union, and the National Association for the Advancement of Colored People. His books and articles continued to be popular into the 1960s, but in the 1970s Beale was largely neglected or rejected by a counterrevisionist school of Reconstruction historians who, apparently motivated by the civil rights crusade, took a harsher view of the South and a kinder one toward such ancient Southern nemeses as Thaddeus Stevens and Charles Sumner. Beale would not have been surprised at the fall from popularity of his views of Reconstruction. His "What Historians Have Said About the Causes of the Civil War" is a classic study of how each generation rewrites history in reflection of its own particular interests and perspectives. However, Beale avowed in that study that historical knowledge did approach, though slowly and unevenly, closer and closer to truth. Further, he wrote: "Writers with a determined philosophy of life of which they are fully conscious and which they make clear to the reader stand a better chance of approaching 'objectivity' than did the older writers who, if they used 'scientific tools,' thought themselves completely objective."

Other:

The Diary of Edward Bates, 1859-1866, edited by Beale, volume 4 of the *1930 Annual Report of the American Historical Association* (Washington: U.S. Government Printing Office, 1933);

"The Present Status of Freedom in the Schools," in *Educational Freedom and Democracy* (New York: Appleton-Century, 1938);

"What Historians Have Said about the Causes of the Civil War," in *Theory and Practice in Historical Study: A Report of the Committee on Historiography*

(New York: Social Science Research Council, 1944);

Charles A. Beard: An Appraisal, edited by Beale (Lexington: University of Kentucky Press, 1954);

The Diary of Gideon Welles, Secretary of the Navy under Lincoln and Johnson, edited by Beale (New York: Norton, 1960).

Periodical Publications:

"Is the Printed Diary of Gideon Welles Reliable?," *American Historical Review*, 30 (April 1925): 547-552;

"Tariff and Reconstruction," *American Historical Review*, 35 (January 1930): 276-294;

"Forces that Control the Schools," *Harper's Magazine*, 169 (October 1934): 603-615;

"The Truth Shall Make You Free," *Independent Woman*, 15 (November 1936): 347-348;

"Freedom for the School Teacher," *Annals of the American Academy of Political and Social Science*, 45 (November 1938): 119-143;

"On Rewriting Reconstruction History," *American Historical Review*, 45 (July 1940): 807-827;

"Teacher as Rebel," *Nation*, 176 (May 1953): 412-414;

"The Professional Historian: His Theory and Practice," *Pacific Historical Review*, 22 (August 1953): 227-255.

Papers:

Beale's research notes and materials in regard to Theodore Roosevelt are at Princeton University.

Charles A. Beard

John Braeman
University of Nebraska-Lincoln

BIRTH: Near Knightstown, Indiana, 27 November 1874, to William Henry Harrison and Mary J. Payne Beard.

EDUCATION: Ph.B., DePauw University, 1898; A.M. Columbia University, 1903; Ph.D., Columbia University, 1904.

MARRIAGE: 8 March 1900 to Mary Ritter; children: Miriam, William.

AWARDS AND HONORS: President, American Political Science Association, 1926; President, American Historical Association, 1933; The Gold Medal for "distinguished achievement," National Institute of Arts and Letters, 1948.

DEATH: New Haven, Connecticut, 1 September 1948.

SELECTED BOOKS: *The Industrial Revolution* (London: Sonnenschein, 1901; New York: Macmillan, 1906);

The Office of Justice of the Peace in England: In Its Origin and Development (New York: Columbia University Press, 1904; London: King, 1904);

The Development of Modern Europe: An Introduction to the Study of Current History, 2 volumes, by Beard and James Harvey Robinson (Boston: Ginn, 1907-1908);

Politics (New York: Columbia University Press, 1908);

American Government and Politics (New York: Macmillan, 1910);

The Supreme Court and the Constitution (New York: Macmillan, 1912);

American City Government: A Survey of Newer Tendencies (New York: Century, 1912);

An Economic Interpretation of the Constitution of the United States (New York: Macmillan, 1913);

Contemporary American History 1877-1913 (New York: Macmillan, 1914);

Economic Origins of Jeffersonian Democracy (New York: Macmillan, 1915);

Cross Currents in Europe To-Day (Boston: Marshall Jones, 1922; London: Harrap, 1923);

The Economic Basis of Politics (New York: Knopf, 1922; London: Allen & Unwin, 1935; revised edition, New York: Knopf, 1945);

The Administration and Politics of Tokyo: A Survey and Opinions (New York: Macmillan, 1923);

The Rise of American Civilization, 2 volumes, by Beard

and Mary R. Beard (New York: Macmillan, 1927);

The American Party Battle (New York: Macmillan, 1928);

The Balkan Pivot: Yugoslavia, A Study in Government and Administration, by Beard and George Radin (New York: Macmillan, 1929);

The American Leviathan: The Republic in the Machine Age, by Beard and William Beard (New York: Macmillan, 1930);

The Navy: Defense or Portent? (New York & London: Harper, 1932);

A Charter for the Social Sciences in the Schools (New York: Scribners, 1932);

The Future Comes: A Study of the New Deal, by Beard and George H. E. Smith (New York: Macmillan, 1933);

The Nature of the Social Sciences in Relation to Objectives of Instruction (New York: Scribners, 1934);

The Idea of National Interest: An Analytical Study in American Foreign Policy, by Beard and Smith (New York: Macmillan, 1934);

The Open Door at Home: A Trial Philosophy of National Interest, by Beard and Smith (New York: Macmillan, 1934);

The Discussion of Human Affairs: An Inquiry into the Nature of the Statements, Assertions, Allegations, Claims, Heats, Tempers, Distempers, Dogmas, and Contentions Which Appear When Human Affairs Are Discussed and into the Possibility of Putting

Some Rhyme and Reason into Processes of Discussion (New York: Macmillan, 1936);

The Devil Theory of War: An Inquiry into the Nature of History and the Possibility of Keeping Out of War (New York: Vanguard, 1936);

Giddy Minds and Foreign Quarrels: An Estimate of American Foreign Policy (New York: Macmillan, 1939);

America in Midpassage, 2 volumes, by Beard and Mary R. Beard (New York: Macmillan, 1939; London: Cape, 1939);

A Foreign Policy for America (New York & London: Knopf, 1940);

The Old Deal and the New, by Beard and Smith (New York: Macmillan, 1940);

Public Policy and the General Welfare (New York: Farrar & Rinehart, 1941);

The American Spirit: A Study of the Idea of Civilization in the United States, by Beard and Mary R. Beard (New York: Macmillan, 1942);

The Republic: Conversations on Fundamentals (New York: Viking, 1943);

A Basic History of the United States, by Beard and Mary R. Beard (New York: New Home Library, 1944);

American Foreign Policy in the Making 1932-1940: A Study in Responsibilities (New Haven: Yale University Press, 1946);

President Roosevelt and the Coming of the War 1941: A Study in Appearances and Realities (New Haven: Yale University Press, 1948).

Charles A. Beard

Few, if any, of his contemporaries matched Charles Austin Beard in his far-reaching impact upon twentieth-century American intellectual and cultural life. He was a major contributor to the reorientation of political science from formalistic description to realistic analysis, one of the progressive era's top experts on municipal government, an apostle of the gospel of efficiency, a pioneer in the establishment of public administration as a field of study, and a leading figure in the revamping of the nation's educational system to make the schools more relevant to current needs and problems. As a historian, he is most familiarly known for his pathbreaking application of an economic interpretation to the American past. At the same time, he was the preeminent exponent-practitioner of a "New History" that aimed not simply at broadening the scope of historical study beyond politics to encompass the full range of human experience but at using knowledge of the past as an instrument for improving the present and shaping the future. If the profession did not fully accept his own radical brand of historical relativism, Beard's agitation had a catalytic role in sensitizing his colleagues to the importance of the historian's attitudes and values in historical interpretation. John Higham has written that during the years between the two world wars, "he came close to dominating the study of American history."

No ivory tower scholar, Beard was during his life and after his death a controversial figure who evoked widely differing reactions. An unsympathetic Allan Nevins dismissed him as the exponent of a "smart, hard materialism." His former student and longtime friend Raymond Moley regarded him as the exemplar of a "hard-bitten realism": a realism heavily laced with skepticism toward "orthodoxy—even his own earlier orthodoxies." His "real spirit," the "essential 'style' of the man," his friend and neighbor Matthew Josephson wrote, "was realistic, skeptical, pragmatic." There was a streak of the gadfly, the irreverent, the iconoclast in Beard, a delight in deflating pretensions, in startling his audience, in puncturing the conventional wisdom. There was an inner restlessness, an impatience with the routine, an ongoing striving to conquer new frontiers. His commitment to what he called "the Socratic elenchus"—"new facts . . . constantly challenging old mental patterns and imagery"—was a lifelong passion. "When I come to the end," he confessed, "my mind will still be beating its wings against the bars of thought's prison." Yet there was another more romantic, even utopian, streak in Beard: a passion for good works, for extending a helping hand to the less favored, for social uplift. Beard, his distinguished fellow historian Carl L. Becker saw, was "a hard-headed idealist"—"too sophisticated not to delight in dispelling illusions; yet too humanely sympathetic to fall back into the easy cynicism of one who is content merely to observe the tragic comedy of existence."

A key to understanding Beard's complex personality lies in his family legacy, a mixture of entrepreneurial acumen with a restless searching for spiritual certitude. He was born 27 November 1874 on a farm near Knightstown, Indiana, the younger of two sons of William Henry Harrison and Mary J. Payne Beard. His maternal grandfather, one of the pioneer settlers of Henry County, Indiana, had amassed for the time and place a substantial fortune. At the same time, he and even more so his wife were strongly attracted to spiritualism. On the Beard side, Charles's forebears had been Quakers who had settled in Guilford County, North Carolina. His paternal grandfather, Nathan Beard, had been read out of the Society of Friends for

marrying out of the fellowship. And thereafter, as he would boast, he ran "a one-man church, in which there can be no dissent." Charles's father, William, had left North Carolina for Indiana after the beginning of the Civil War because of his pro-Union views. After a stint as a schoolteacher, William became a successful farmer, building contractor, and land speculator. A loyal Republican, he was an enthusiastic booster of the United States as the land of opportunity. But he was simultaneously an admirer of the famous late-nineteenth-century atheist Robert Ingersoll and took pride in his reputation as the village skeptic. While Mary Beard's horizons remained limited to home and family, William was an avid reader with an extensive library and wide-ranging interests who encouraged and supported his younger son's intellectual aspirations.

Shortly after Charles was born, the family moved to a farm near the straight-laced Quaker enclave of Spiceland, Indiana. Despite his father's freethinking views, Charles was sent to Quaker services. His youthful exposure to the Quaker ethos would leave its lasting mark in his lifelong belief in the innate dignity of all human beings, his sympathy for the unfortunate and oppressed, and his unswerving courage in standing up for convictions. Charles attended the highly regarded local Friends academy, but left before finishing and was graduated in 1891 from Knightstown High School. After his graduation, his father purchased for Charles and his older brother Clarence the weekly *Knightstown Sun*. While the youthful publishers upgraded the quality and scope of the news coverage, their editorial policy reflected the accepted GOP attitudes of the time. Influenced by a local Methodist minister, Charles abandoned journalism and, in the fall of 1895, entered Methodist-affiliated DePauw University at Greencastle, Indiana. A young man in a hurry, he finished in three years with an impressive academic record culminating in his election to Phi Beta Kappa. He played an active role in campus affairs as a fraternity leader, debater, and editor of the student newspaper. He met and fell in love with his future wife, Mary Ritter of Indianapolis. The DePauw years may have been critical in his intellectual development: "Old DePauw," Beard later told an interviewer, "did more for me than I could ever tell."

Although Beard had started out with the goal of studying for the Methodist ministry, his religious enthusiasm faded in the face of new interests. A history major, he was strongly influenced by Professor Andrew Stephenson, a Johns Hopkins-trained Ph.D. who inculcated his students not to accept any

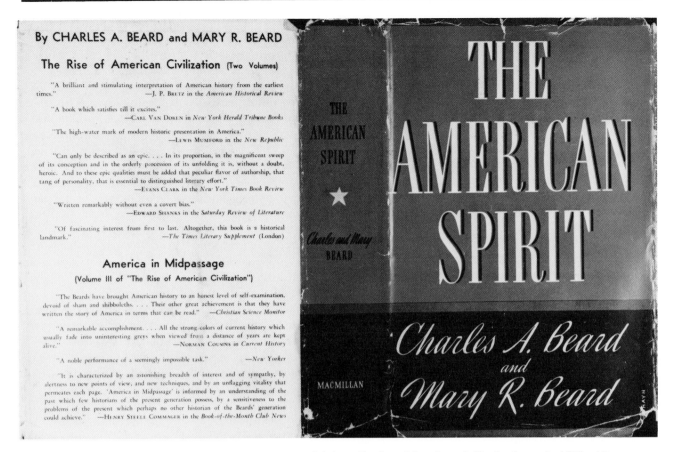

By CHARLES A. BEARD and MARY R. BEARD

The Rise of American Civilization (Two Volumes)

"A brilliant and stimulating interpretation of American history from the earliest times."
—J. P. BRETZ in the *American Historical Review*

"A book which satisfies till it excites."
—CARL VAN DOREN in *New York Herald Tribune Books*

"The high-water mark of modern historic presentation in America."
—LEWIS MUMFORD in the *New Republic*

"Can only be described as an epic. . . . In its proportion, in the magnificent sweep of its conception and in the orderly procession of its unfolding it is, without a doubt, heroic. And to these epic qualities must be added that peculiar flavor of authorship, that tang of personality, that is essential to distinguished literary effort."
—EVANS CLARK in the *New York Times Book Review*

"Written remarkably without even a covert bias."
—EDWARD SHANKS in the *Saturday Review of Literature*

"Of fascinating interest from first to last. Altogether, this book is a historical landmark."
—*The Times Literary Supplement* (London)

America in Midpassage
(Volume III of "The Rise of American Civilization")

"The Beards have brought American history to an honest level of self-examination, devoid of sham and shibboleths. . . . Their other great achievement is that they have written the story of America in terms that can be read." —*Christian Science Monitor*

"A remarkable accomplishment. . . . All the strong colors of current history which usually fade into uninteresting greys when viewed from a distance of years are kept alive." —NORMAN COUSINS in *Current History*

"A noble performance of a seemingly impossible task." —*New Yorker*

"It is characterized by an astonishing breadth of interest and of sympathy, by alertness to new points of view, and new techniques, and by an unflagging vitality that permeates each page. 'America in Midpassage' is informed by an understanding of the past which few historians of the present generation possess, by a sensitiveness to the problems of the present which perhaps no other historian of the Beards' generation could achieve." —HENRY STEELE COMMAGER in the *Book-of-the-Month Club News*

Dust jacket for the Beards' 1942 book, the capstone of their explication of American civilization begun in 1927 with
The Rise of American Civilization

statement without checking the sources. Although an adherent of the dominant "Teutonic-germ theory" (which postulated that Anglo-American institutions grew out of ancient Germanic tribal organization), Stephenson gave more weight to the role of social, economic, and cultural forces than was typical of the school. Col. James R. Weaver exerted even a stronger impact. While listed as professor of political science, Weaver defined his subject broadly to encompass all of what has become known as the social sciences. He had his students read the leading classic and contemporary political and social thinkers—including Marx. Himself an admirer of the reform-minded newer economists and social gospelers, Weaver required his students to supplement their reading with firsthand experience in the field. Accordingly, Beard spent part of the summer of 1896 in Chicago where he saw, and was shocked by, the poverty in the slums of the metropolis. And visiting Jane Addams's Hull House, one of the first settlement houses in the country, he came into touch with the political and intellectual ferment at work there. The result was a

shift away from his father's Republicanism to a sympathy—if still vague and ill-defined—for "reform." Most important, he took as his personal credo, as set forth in his final editorial in the student newspaper, that "the truth that makes men free . . . only will be known when men cease to swallow the capsules of ancient doctors of divinity and politics."

After being graduated from DePauw in 1898, Beard went to Oxford University for further work in history. A "non-collegiate" student, he engaged in independent study and research primarily under the supervision of Regius Professor of Modern History Frederick York Powell. Although sharing the reigning positivist belief in history as a science, Powell gave that faith a reformist twist that made knowledge of the past a tool for improving the present and shaping the future. Powell had close personal and professional ties with the Oxford school of English constitutional history founded by Bishop Stubbs, but, influenced by John R. Green's pioneering *A Short History of the English People*, he was an apostle of a "New History" that would include within its compass the full range of human experience. As his research project, Beard took as his topic the evolution of the office of justice of the peace. But he was diverted from his academic studies by another young American studying at Oxford, Walter Vrooman. Reflecting his own and his family's social consciousness, Vrooman sketched out plans for establishing a workingmen's college at Oxford that caught Beard's imagination. Beard, who had read with admiration John Ruskin's *Unto This Last* while at DePauw, suggested the name Ruskin Hall. Vrooman's wife provided the financing, and, since Vrooman's enthusiasm outran his organizing ability, Beard took over the responsibility for handling the practical details required for the institution's opening in February 1899. And in his enthusiasm, Beard spoke in glowing terms about the time when "the workers who bore upon their shoulders the burden of the world should realise the identity of their own interests and rise to take possession of the means of life."

In the spring of 1899, Beard returned to the United States and that fall enrolled for graduate work in history at Cornell University. Although an impressed professor, Moses Coit Tyler, arranged for a fellowship, Beard left after one semester to resume his work for the Ruskin Hall movement. Before departing, he married his college sweetheart, Mary Ritter. The newlyweds set up their base at Manchester, from which Beard traveled over England's industrial heartland delivering lectures before workingmen's and cooperative society groups. In those lectures and in articles written for *Young Oxford*, the movement's unofficial journal, he paid homage to those prophets—such as William Cobbett, William Morris, Robert Owen, and Thomas Carlyle—who had striven to awaken men's consciences to injustice and exploitation. But the major thrust of his talks—and the theme of his first book, *The Industrial Revolution* (1901)—was an exaltation of the liberating role played by advances in science and technology in bettering the lot of mankind and paving "the way to higher forms of industrial methods in which the people, instead of a few capitalists, will reap the benefits." Although these activities brought Beard increasing prominence in British labor and radical circles, he abruptly—without even a formal resignation—abandoned his position as Ruskin Hall extension secretary in the spring of 1902 and returned to the United States. In part, he was discouraged by what appeared the lagging progress of his workingmen's education efforts. In part, he had increased family responsibilities with the birth in November 1901 of his daughter, Miriam. Most important, he was

torn—as he would remain throughout his life—between political activism and scholarship.

Winning a fellowship, Beard resumed his graduate work in the fall of 1902 at Columbia's Faculty of Political Science. He received his master's degree in the spring of 1903, submitting as his thesis "The Present Status of Civil Service Reform in the United States," and the following year he received his Ph.D. His major professor was John W. Burgess, the school's founder and longtime dean. With his eye for talent, Burgess recognized Beard's brilliance and promise. Beard—at least judged by his later remarks—was not so impressed with Burgess. Burgess regarded history as the working out of the Hegelian world spirit. And he was probably the leading spokesman of the view that the American Constitution sanctified property rights against legislative interference. But there were others on the faculty who would influence Beard's thinking along more innovative lines. He much admired and became a personal friend of Frank J. Goodnow, a leading figure in redirecting political scientists' attention from description of the formal structure of government to analysis of its actual functioning. He forged similarly close ties with James Harvey Robinson, who was then feeling his way toward what he would term the "New History." For his Ph.D. dissertation, Beard did a hurried revision and expansion of the study begun at Oxford on the evolution of the office of justice of the peace in England. Although the work—published in 1904 in the Columbia University *Studies in History, Economics and Public Law*—remained within the institutionalist approach of the Oxford historical school, there was a harbinger of the future in Beard's emphasis on how changes in the "administrative system" reflected "new conditions arising from the natural development of the social and industrial life of the people."

After receiving his Ph.D., Beard was kept on as a lecturer in the history department to teach the Western European survey and English history. Three years later, he was appointed an adjunct professor in the Department of Public Law with the responsibility of inaugurating a new undergraduate program in "Politics." In 1909, when Burgess withdrew from teaching because of his administrative responsibilities, Beard took over his course in American constitutional history. In 1910, he was promoted to associate professor; five years later he was awarded his full professorship. He offered a wide range of different courses: introductory American government, comparative politics and government, "Party Government in the United

States," American state government, and "Municipal Functions." Beard was a highly popular and effective teacher. "There was no one at Columbia," a fellow faculty member observed, "who could rival Beard as an orator." His realistic approach, a graduate student recalled, "was like a salty breeze blowing out the stuffiness from the room." Because of the short time he held senior rank before his resignation, Beard supervised relatively few Ph.D. candidates, and those were all in political science. But they included such future luminaries as FDR brain-truster Raymond Moley, Cornell University's constitutional law expert Robert E. Cushman, and Luther H. Gulick and Arthur W. Macmahon, two of the country's top public administration specialists. And though not formally their mentor, he exerted a major influence upon the elder Arthur M. Schlesinger's dissertation *The Colonial Merchants and the American Revolution* and Dixon Ryan Fox's *The Decline of Aristocracy in the Politics of New York*, long a major interpretation of Jacksonian-era history.

Perhaps even more impressive was Beard's scholarly productivity. During his years on the Columbia faculty, he turned out almost a book a year, plus an imposing roster of articles and reviews. His earliest publications grew directly out of his teaching. He joined with his colleague James Harvey Robinson to prepare a two-volume text, *The Development of Modern Europe* (1907-1908), with an accompanying two volumes of source readings. The authors' breadth of scope—their attention to the role of social, economic, and intellectual developments—was in striking contrast with the narrowly political focus of most competing works. At the same time, their approach was consciously present-minded, with the aim of using the past to illuminate the roots of contemporary problems. Similarly innovative was Beard's *American Government and Politics* (1910), with its supplementary volume of source readings, which was based upon his introductory American government course. His purpose, he explained to his publisher, was to look beneath the formal structure of government "to the great problem of how things are actually done." The book was an immediate success and, repeatedly revised and updated, remained for many years the standard college-level basic American government textbook, going through ten editions. There followed a series of articles and books dealing with current political issues and governmental problems—including *Loose Leaf Digest of Short Ballot Charters* (1911), *American City Government* (1912), and *Documents on the State-Wide Initiative, Referendum and Recall* (1912).

As a student of American government, Beard focused upon two major themes. One was how to make government more responsive to the popular will. He did not share the enthusiasm felt by many reformers of the time for the initiative and referendum, and he shrewdly perceived that the direct primary would be manipulated by, rather than destroy, the political machine. His own favored solution was to reduce the number of elective offices—the so-called short ballot—to concentrate the voters' attention. The reverse side was to improve public administration, first by centralizing responsibility for management of government operations, second by upgrading the quality of governmental personnel. These concerns led him into involvement with the New York Bureau of Municipal Research, the nation's first and leading research organization devoted to improving the efficiency of city government. In 1915, he became supervisor of the bureau's Training School for Public Service, which aimed at preparing young men and women for careers in government. In 1919, he was named director of the bureau. Whereas many of the Progressive era's good-government advocates had the limited goals of economy and of keeping taxes down, Beard saw more efficient administration as the indispensable prerequisite for an activist government regulating business and providing a wide range of social services. Accordingly, he pushed to expand the scope of the bureau's work beyond the local level. He was the primary author of the report of New York's Reconstruction Commission on Retrenchment and Reorganization in the State Government, which laid down the rationale and guidelines for the sweeping revamping of the state's administrative structure carried out by Governor Al Smith. And he was instrumental in the 1921 reorganization of the bureau into the more broadly gauged National Institute of Public Administration.

Beard's work in political science was distinguished not simply by its realistic account of the functioning of American governmental institutions but by its attention to their historical evolution as well. And the contemporary debate over the legitimacy of judicial review led him to undertake a reexamination of the purpose of the framers of the constitution. *The Supreme Court and the Constitution* (1912) gave a strongly affirmative answer to the question of whether or not the framers had intended the Supreme Court to have the power to pass on the constitutionality of acts of Congress. One of his graduate students recalled that Beard had started out expecting to prove the contrary, but found the evidence in support overwhelming. Yet his data were not that conclusive. Much of the evidence for his claim that at a minimum twenty-five of the fifty-five delegates—including the bulk of the more influential—"favored or at least accepted some form of judicial control" came from statements and actions that postdated the Constitutional Convention. Worse, he blurred the differences existing among the delegates about the scope of judicial review. The exaggeration of his case is the more puzzling because Beard, unlike the conservatives who would find in the work ammunition for the defense of the Supreme Court, was not an admirer of the judicial apotheosis of laissez-faire. The answer to this paradox was his wish to emphasize how "the intention of the framers of the Constitution to establish judicial control of legislation" was linked with their anxiety "above everything else to safeguard the rights of private property against any levelling tendencies on the part of the propertyless masses." That dual motivation of the framers became the central theme of his highly controversial *An Economic Interpretation of the Constitution of the United States* (1913)—a work that stands as a landmark in the development of American historiography.

An Economic Interpretation of the Constitution represented a confluence of a complex of intellectual influences. Beard's more vituperative critics claimed Karl Marx was sitting over Beard's shoulder guiding his pen. Though acquainted with Marxist-inspired European historiography, he owed more to his Columbia colleague E. R. A. Seligman's pioneering attempt, in *The Economic Interpretation of History* (1902), to apply the Marxian perspective minus its socialist message. While Beard probably exaggerated his debt to James Madison's *Federalist*, number ten, the founding fathers were not shy about talking about the role of economic conflicts in politics. More proximate influences included Frederick Jackson Turner's exposition of "the influence of the material circumstances of the frontier on American politics," Arthur F. Bentley's classic statement of the interest-group approach to politics in *The Process of Government* (1908), and the emphasis upon the social context of law by the so-called social utilitarian school of German jurisprudence founded by Rudolph von Jhering and such American exponents of "sociological jurisprudence" as Oliver Wendell Holmes, Jr., and Roscoe Pound. Even his application of an economic interpretation to the framing and adoption of the Constitution was not novel. Beard found a forerunner in the nineteenth-century Whig historian Richard Hildreth. And the thesis that the Constitu-

tion was the handiwork of the propertied few designed to safeguard their economic interests had been advanced by J. Allen Smith of the University of Washington in *The Spirit of American Government* (1907) and by socialist activist Algie M. Simons in *Social Forces in American History* (1911). Beard's most significant new contribution lay in his methodology: the book was the first attempt to apply the prosopographical, or collective biography, approach to a major historical problem.

Beard's conclusions in *An Economic Interpretation of the Constitution* can be summarized under five main propositions. First was that the major line of division in the politics of the time lay between what he termed "realty" and "personalty." The realty class was made up primarily of the largely debt-ridden "small farmers" of the interior; the personalty consisted of "money at interest or capital seeking investment," "the holders of state and continental securities," "manufacturing, shipping, trading, and commercial interests," and speculators in western lands. Second was that "personalty" was adversely affected by the conditions existing under the Articles of Confederation. Third was that the leaders of the movement culminating in the 1787 Constitutional Convention, the majority of the delegates to that gathering, and the supporters of ratification came from that interest group. Fourth was that the Constitution was "an economic document" aimed at safeguarding property rights generally—and above all, the interests of "personalty"—against "the attacks of levelling democracy." And fifth was that "no more than one-fourth or one-fifth" of even the adult white males participated in the voting for delegates to the ratifying conventions, with the rest disenfranchised because of property qualifications or "apathy," and success was achieved in many states only through high-pressure, even "irregular," tactics. Although much of his supporting evidence came from published materials, Beard drew upon long-forgotten Treasury Department records for the public securities holdings of those involved in adoption of the Constitution. Yet the prominence given this data was as much a source of difficulty as of strength because of the accompanying imputation that the framers were animated by motives of personal financial gain. In part, Beard's blurring of the distinction between group interest and individual self-seeking was due to what he privately admitted was deliberate exaggeration to underscore his point. But much of the problem was fuzziness in his own thinking about the causal role of economic factors in history.

As a work of historical scholarship, *An Economic Interpretation of the Constitution* has not stood well the test of time. Its more astute contemporary critics—such as the Princeton constitutional historian Edward S. Corwin—pointed out its evidentiary and conceptual shortcomings: its exaggeration of the importance of the delegates' public securities holdings, its assumption of a large propertyless mass barred from voting, and its neglect of noneconomic factors. Since World War II the work has undergone a largely critical reexamination; even those sympathetic to an interest-group approach have found Beard's "realty" versus "personalty" dichotomy oversimplistic. But what is striking is the extent to which Beard's interpretation has defined, and continues to define, the parameters within which the bulk of the subsequent research and writing on the period has been carried on. More immediately important, Beard's skeptical and debunking treatment of the founding fathers exercised a profoundly liberating influence upon the next generation of historians. Nor was its liberating impact limited to the historiographical realm. To knock the framers from their Olympian pedestal by showing their economic motivation was to demythologize the Constitution as a bulwark for the status quo. Despite his disclaimers that such was his purpose, there is no question that Beard knew what he was doing. As he confided to a younger colleague while working on *An Economic Interpretation of the Constitution*, he could hardly restrain his anger at "the dreary drivel on 'Constitutionality' " put forth by "the logic choppers of law." "I do not think," he wrote a leading Senate Progressive, "that it is a question of 'restoring' the government to the people; it is a question of getting possession of it for them for the first time. . . . If you find time to read my book on the Constitution, I think you will see why I believe that we did not have 'a government of the people' to start with."

Beard envisaged *An Economic Interpretation of the Constitution* as the first in a series of studies that would apply the economic interpretation over the full span of American history. He drew upon his research in the Treasury Department records to write an article published in the January 1914 issue of the *American Historical Review* on the role played by the holders of public securities in the adoption of the Hamiltonian fiscal program. That article served as the linchpin of his larger study of the political conflicts of the 1790s that appeared in 1915 under the title *Economic Origins of Jeffersonian Democracy*. Stylistically the volume compares unfavorably with its predecessor. Whereas *An Economic Interpretation*

of the Constitution moves briskly and purposefully toward its final conclusions, *Economic Origins of Jeffersonian Democracy* is less sharply focused, more oblique in its points. Rather than a traditional narrative history, the work is a collection of loosely linked essays on different topics. What provides the unifying thread is a two-pronged thesis: first, that the Federalist-Republican division represented a continuation of the struggle over the Constitution; second, that struggle involved the ongoing contest between "capitalistic and agrarian interests." At times, Beard had to strain to fit his own evidence into his conceptual framework, and later research has required substantial qualifications of his conclusions. But *Economic Origins of Jeffersonian Democracy* was, of Beard's historical work, the most solidly based upon research in primary sources. Most important, he largely avoided the confusion between individual gain and class interest that had marred the Constitution book. The Jefferson/Hamilton conflict was, he emphasized, "a clear case of a collision of economic interests: fluid capital versus agrarianism. The representation of one interest was as legitimate as the other. . . ."

Far from sympathizing with Jefferson, Beard pictured the Virginian as a shifty politician whose democratic rhetoric was not matched in practice by himself or his followers and who, when in power, made his peace with the "capitalistic interests." The explanation for its surprising animus toward Jeffersonian Democracy was that the study—like the Constitution book—had its implications for the contemporary political scene. The implication was that the Jeffersonian vision of a laissez-faire paradise of small producers—which Beard identified with Woodrow Wilson—had scant relevance for dealing with the problems of modern industrial America. What those problems were, and their evolution, was the subject of his 1914 survey, *Contemporary American History 1877-1913*, which focuses upon the political and social changes wrought by the triumph of industrial capitalism in the years since the Civil War. His aim, Beard explained to his research assistant, was "to give the economic interpretation without calling it such" while simultaneously writing a tract for the times. "The important thing is that college students should not go out without some understanding of the new and tremendous economic forces which are now transforming the very world under our eyes and rendering obsolete old moralities and 'principles.' " Given the accelerating pace of business concentration, Beard underlined in his text, "the theories about competition written down in the books on political economy were hopelessly at variance with the facts of business management." Worse was the accompanying "lack of correspondence between the political system and the economic system." Despite the rise of "a national system of manufacturing, transportation, capital, and organized labor," the national government remained "powerless . . . to regulate . . . nearly all of the great national interests."

Although *Contemporary American History* never attracted as much attention as *An Economic Interpretation of the Constitution* or *Economic Origins of Jeffersonian Democracy*, its interpretation of late nineteenth- and early twentieth-century developments—repeated for a much larger audience in Beard and his wife's *The Rise of American Civilization* (1927)—has exerted a lasting influence upon how Americans have viewed that period. Influenced by Thorstein Veblen, Beard traced how with the triumph of big business the "literary and professional dependents of the ruling groups naturally came to the defense of the new order." His most striking chapter is his account of how the federal courts made the due process clause of the Fourteenth Amendment "into a real restraining force . . . to check the assaults of state legislatures on vested rights." And with the champions of "the new capitalism" ascendant in the two major parties, the Republican-Democrat battles of the post-Reconstruction decades were empty shadow-boxing. Such opposition to the hegemony of big business and its allies as there was came from the debt-ridden small farmers of the West in a continuation of the "old contest between agrarianism and capitalism." But after the turn of the century, there emerged a new and more dangerous challenge from the rapidly multiplying urban "proletariat." This threat from below spurred the rise of a middle-class-based reform movement of small property holders, professional men, and intellectuals. "Just as the Protestant Reformation during the sixteenth century was followed by a counter-reformation in the Catholic Church which swept away many abuses, while retaining and fortifying the essential principles of the faith, so the widespread and radical discontent of the working classes with the capitalist system hitherto obtaining produced a counter-reformation on the part of those who wish to preserve its essentials while curtailing some of its excesses."

Although his overall plan for an economic reinterpretation of American history included a fourth volume, dealing with the years from Jefferson's election through the Civil War and Reconstruction, Beard shifted his focus in his 1916 lectures at Amherst College to formulate a fuller and more explicit explanation for the relationship between economics and politics, and the lectures came out in book form as *The Economic Basis of Politics* in 1922. But his treatment highlighted, rather than resolved, the most troublesome ambiguity in his approach: his failure to differentiate between "an economic interpretation" and "the hypothesis of economic determinism." Beard's starting point was that "the fundamental factors with which the statesman has to deal are the forms and distribution of property and the sentiments and views arising from the possession of different degrees and kinds of property." The difficulty arose when he simultaneously affirmed that the "form of a government is determined (except where the sword rules) by the nature and distribution of property." As even those reviewers sympathetic to an economic interest-group approach asked, what did he mean by "determined"? Or, in other words, what was the exact causal role of "the nature and distribution of property"? Beard found the question difficult to answer. Referring to the title of his book, he replied that the dictionary "defines 'basis' as a fundamental ingredient in a compound." Yet he recognized that this answer begged the question. In the end, he had to take refuge in agnosticism: "As to 'how' economics even influences"—much less "determines"—"politics," he admitted, "I cannot make answer, any more than the physicist can explain 'how' a dynamo makes electricity. . . . I do not think that economics determines or even explains politics in the philosophic sense. Neither does anything else that I have yet stumbled across in this vale of tears."

As productive as the Columbia years were, Beard grew increasingly restive with the passage of time. In part, he temperamentally chafed at the routines and conventions of academic life. More important, he rebelled at what he felt was the growing pressure for political conformity. While he largely avoided direct involvement in political affairs except for his and his wife's championship of woman's suffrage, his Columbia colleagues regarded him as a radical, even Socialist. And there is no question that Beard was intellectually and, even more, emotionally attracted to socialism. Although he was too much a maverick to join the Socialist party, he was sufficiently sympathetic to take an active role in the planning for, administration of, and teaching at its Rand School for Social Science. *An Economic Interpretation of the Constitution* reinforced the suspicions of the powers-that-were at Columbia. The resulting tensions came to a head in October 1917, when he dramatically resigned his professorship in protest against the nonreappointment of one faculty member and the firing of two others because of their antiwar stance. Although Beard was, and had been since the sinking of the *Lusitania*, a supporter of United States intervention, he saw the affair as the climax of an effort by a group of trustees, "reactionary and visionless in politics, and narrow and mediaeval in religion"— "unhindered, if not aided," by President Nicholas Murray Butler—to "drive out or humiliate or terrorize every man who held progressive, liberal, or unconventional views."

Because of his family responsibilities—a son, named William after Beard's father, had been born in 1907—Beard accepted the directorship of the New York Bureau of Municipal Research to tide himself over. He joined with a group of intellectuals and disgruntled academicians, including James Harvey Robinson, Herbert Croly of the *New Republic*, and economists Wesley C. Mitchell and Alvin Johnson, to launch in 1919 the New School for Social Research. But finding his administrative responsibilities more and more irksome, he resigned from the Bureau of Municipal Research in 1920. And disappointed in his hopes of making the New School for Social Research a major independent research center, he withdrew from active involvement. Thereafter, he would act—in the phrase of an admiring sketch—as a "Free Lance Among the Historians." An inheritance from his father had enabled him to purchase a large, rambling house at New Milford, Connecticut, which would remain his base for the rest of his life, while his writing brought him growing financial independence. He was a regular contributor to the *New Republic* and *Nation*, and a lengthening list of articles and reviews appeared in a wide range of magazines. *American Government and Politics* brought in a steady flow of royalties. Sales of textbooks spun off from his and Robinson's *The Development of Modern Europe* surpassed a million copies. High-school and elementary-school texts written in collaboration with William C. Bagley of Columbia's Teachers College captured an important share of that lucrative market. In all, his history textbooks sold over five-and-a-half-million copies.

The post-World War I decade saw Beard involved in a kaleidoscope of activities and projects. In 1921, he visited Europe to learn firsthand the changes wrought by the conflict. In *Cross Currents in Europe To-Day* (1922), he tacked on to his analysis of the current situation—which he found depressing—a pioneering revisionist reexamination of the war guilt question. In 1922, he went to

Japan at the invitation of the Tokyo Institute for Municipal Research to study and report on Japanese municipal government. His findings and recommendations were published the following year as *The Administration and Politics of Tokyo*. He so impressed his hosts that after the devastating Tokyo earthquake he was called back to advise on the reconstruction of the city. Elected president of the American Political Science Association in 1926, he took the lead in establishing the Committee on Policy to make a thoroughgoing review of the present status of the discipline and to lay down guidelines for new areas of research. In 1927 and 1928, he was in Yugoslavia on an investigatory trip under the sponsorship of the America-Yugoslav Society of New York: his appraisal of the new nation's governmental and administrative structure appeared under the title *The Balkan Pivot* (1929). And as he would remain throughout his life, he was quick to raise his voice or lift his pen in defense of civil liberties. All progress, he declared in his political science association presidential address, depends upon "the widest freedom to inquire and expound. . . . It is in silence, denial, evasion, and suppression that danger really lies, not in open and free analysis and discussion. Surely if any political lesson is taught by the marvelous history of English-speaking peoples it is this."

The high point of the decade in Beard's writing career was the publication in 1927 of his and his wife's landmark *The Rise of American Civilization*. The work was the outgrowth of Beard's planned follow-up volume to the Jeffersonian Democracy study that would apply the economic interpretation to the years from Jefferson's election through the Civil War and Reconstruction. He appears to have done at least a first draft before deciding to incorporate its substance as part of a more ambitious undertaking. Taking as his model John R. Green's *A Short History of the English People*—a work he had admired since his undergraduate days—he expanded the work to cover the period from settlement to present. Consciously aiming to reach a mass audience, Beard dropped the flat, monographic-like style of *An Economic Interpretation of the Constitution*, writing instead in a luxuriant, even at times lush, prose. More important, he broadened his scope beyond politics to include the wide range and variety of the American experience: political, social, and economic thought, religion, literature, education, science, art and architecture, and even music. What appears the decisive turning point in the shaping of the project came with his visits to the Far East, which had sharply underlined the wide gap dividing different cultures. And probably his growing unhappiness over the European situation reinforced his conviction that the United States constituted a distinct, indeed unique, civilization. No definitive answer can be given about Mary Beard's contribution, yet there is no question that she played a major catalytic role. "In reality," Charles wrote his publisher, complaining about advertisements that pictured the work as exclusively his, "the scope of the book outside of the politics is due to Mrs. Beard's interest and her labors. The grand plan I should not have thought of or attempted to execute alone."

The aspect of *The Rise of American Civilization* that most influenced historians was Beard's view of the Civil War as the "Second American Revolution" marking and consolidating the triumph of Northern capitalism. But what underlay the book's tremendous popular appeal was how it subsumed the totality of the national experience within a single overarching explanatory framework. Its portrayal of the clash of rival economic interests as the dominant shaping factor in American history—along with Vernon L. Parrington's almost concurrently published *Main Currents in American Thought*—exercised a pervasive influence upon the generation coming to maturity in the 1930s. Beard was much taken with *Main Currents in American Thought*: "It," he exclaimed enthusiastically, "yanks Miss Beautiful Letters down from her pedestal and drags her by the hair of the head into the Market Place." And he recognized its affinity with *The Rise of American Civilization*. "It is," he confided to his publisher, "a God's send that we printed this Spring for he has paralleled us in many places and in interpretation. We seem to be on the edge of a new synthesis." Beneath the similarity in approach, however, there was a major difference. Parrington was a latter-day Jeffersonian bewailing the loss of agrarian Eden. By contrast, Beard saw the triumph of industrial capitalism as inevitable and a force in the long run for progress. Although he painted in grim terms the ills and abuses accompanying its ascendancy, the dominant motif was optimism for the future—an optimism resting upon his faith in the continued vitality of the democratic ideal, in the good sense and intelligence of the mass of the American people, and, what most buoyed his hopes, "in the efficacy of that new and mysterious instrument of the modern mind, 'the invention of invention,' moving from one technological triumph to another."

This mood of technological utopianism—with its accompanying confidence in "unlimited progress"—suffused Beard's writings in the latter 1920s. Advancing technology had brought the American people to a level of material well-being unequaled in the world and promised to bring about "an ever wider distribution of the blessings of civilization—health, security, material goods, knowledge, leisure, and aesthetic appreciation." More important, the machine age had its own inner logic: its hallmarks were cooperation, order, and control. By "understanding more clearly the processes of science and the machine," Beard wrote in a symposium that he edited on *Whither Mankind* (1928), "mankind may subject the scattered and perplexing things of this world to a more ordered dominion of the spirit." Progress was thus not simply unlimited, but certain, inevitable, even automatic. "By inherent necessity," he affirmed in a follow-up symposium by a group of reform-minded engineers on *Toward Civilization* (1930), the machine process "forces upon society an ever larger planned area of conduct." The key factor in this process was the expanding role of government. In a calculated twisting of symbolism, Beard borrowed from Thomas Hobbes the title for a survey, written with his son, detailing the functions and activities of the federal government, *The American Leviathan: The Republic in the Machine Age*, which was published in late 1930. His Leviathan—"a half-mythical giant uniting in one person a whole multitude"—is a liberating, not repressive force. "Natural science and machinery," he explained, "have set a new and complex stage for the operations of government, imposed additional functions upon it, and lifted it to a new rôle in the process of civilization."

The worsening economic crisis reinforced Beard's allegiance to what he termed "national planning" to coordinate and rationalize the economy. He was hazy about the details, but unlike many Depression-era intellectuals, he remained confident that such planning was possible within the framework of representative democracy. Although he was briefly attracted by Mussolini's corporatism, his enthusiasm for the Italian Fascist state was short-lived. He never had any illusions about Nazism, which he pictured as "government by irresponsible brute force, by unquestioned and unchallenged berserker rage." Nor did he find the totalitarianism of the left any more appealing. Even in the heyday of the "popular front," Beard scornfully dismissed the American Communists as puppets and agents of the Soviet tyranny. His rereading of Marx and Engels convinced him that the Stalinist regime was not the betrayal but the fulfillment of their ideas. "The essence of Marxism," he underlined, was "violence"—and hence Marxism repudiated all that was valuable "in the idea of civilization: freedom of press, liberty of conscience, personal rights, democracy, the settlement of social conflicts by rational processes." Beard pinned his own hopes upon Franklin D. Roosevelt's New Deal. Roosevelt, he wrote enthusiastically in his appraisal of the first one hundred days of his presidency, *The Future Comes* (1933), "accepts the inexorable collectivism of American economy in fact, and seeks to work out a policy based on recognition of the main course of our economic history." The result was "a break with the historic past and the coming of a future collectivist in character."

At the same time, the Depression—and the accompanying totalitarian challenges—had shattered Beard's faith in inevitable and automatic progress. Does "the idea of progress," he asked in his introduction to the 1932 reissue of J. B. Bury's classic study of the topic, "take on the validity of a law of nature—the law of gravitation, for instance? Is it a conclusion drawn from the facts of history that imposes itself upon us as inescapable?" The answer, he replied, "must be in the negative." Beard had not abandoned his hopes for the future, but thought what was required was "immense efforts of will and intelligence": men acting consciously and purposefully to shape a future that was still in the making. Such action demanded "some standard . . . to furnish a guide for determining directions." His ambition to supply that guide led Beard to undertake an analysis of the meaning of that much used, and much abused, term "national interest." *The Idea of National Interest* (1934)—written with the research assistance of George H. E. Smith—is a lengthy, and at times even plodding, review of the multifarious definitions that had been advanced. The companion work, *The Open Door at Home* (1934), spells out Beard's own definition. One side is a renewed call for overall planning—or what he termed "applied engineering rationality"—to give "effect to the potentialities of the industrial arts, technology, and resources in the United States." The reverse side—signaling what would become of Beard's increasing preoccupation—is a call for the insulation of the United States from international trade conflicts and power rivalries through a policy aimed at national autarky.

At a broader philosophical level, *The Open Door at Home* is a rebuttal of any deterministic system—including by implication his own earlier economic interpretation—that denied the role of men's "ethical and esthetic values" in shaping history. This new approach was inextricably intertwined with Beard's

championship of historical relativism, and strictly intellectual influences played their part. He had been much impressed by the findings of the "new physics" showing the relativity and subjectivity of knowledge even in the physical sciences. His reading—or what many critics have charged was his misreading—of such European philosophers of history and sociologists of knowledge as Karl Heussi, Kurt Riezler, Hans Vaihinger, Karl Mannheim, and Benedetto Croce contributed to reshaping his thinking. But what was decisive was the wish to provide a rationale for his lifelong commitment to the utility of history as a tool for social betterment. The historian, he emphasized in his December 1933 presidential address to the American Historical Association, like the statesman dealing with public affairs, was subject to "the verdict of history yet to come." Thus, the historian must make a judgment about the "nature or direction" of the historical process. There were only three possible alternatives: history as flux or chaos; history as a process of cyclical recurrence; or history as a progressive development "on an upward gradient toward a more ideal order." There was no objective way of choosing; appeal to the facts would be inconclusive. The historian must make an "act of faith." Beard's personal "act of faith" was that history—at least in the United States—was moving forward to "a collectivist democracy."

Beard's attack on "the conception that it is possible to describe the past as it actually was" roused sharp and continuing controversy among historians. The furor was not so much over his denial of the possibility of discovering historical laws having predictive value; the more sophisticated traditionalists could even accept the impossibility of comprehending the totality of "history as past actuality." The problem was his appearing to strike at the basis of the historians' claim to professional status: the ideal of objectivity. While acknowledging the existence of verifiable "facts," Beard underlined that facts did not "select themselves or force themselves automatically" on the mind of the historian. Their selection and arrangement was "an act of choice" reflecting the historian's "frame of reference"—his values and interests, his political, social, and economic beliefs, his conception of "things deemed necessary, things deemed possible, and things deemed desirable." When the debate petered out in the early 1950s, the outcome was a qualified triumph of historical relativism. Beard played a key role in this result through the Social Science Research Council's Committee on Historiography. His more cautious fellow members balked at Beard's rejection of "cause" and "causality." And the committee's final report, *Theory and Practice in Historical Study* (1946), appealed for as much objectivity as possible. But its statement of "Basic Premises" gave the imprimatur of establishment approval to Beard's dictum that all written history "is ordered or organized under the influence of some scheme of reference, interest, or emphasis—avowed or unavowed—in the thought of the author."

But if relativism carried the field, Beard eventually suffered the bitter fate of seeing his own vision of the direction in which history was moving—toward "a collectivist democracy"—proved false, despite his own active involvement in seeking to promote that goal. As the dominant figure on the American Historical Association's Commission on the Social Studies, he was the moving spirit behind its call for a revision of school practices and curricula to prepare students for the "new age of collectivism." The same message—only substituting the not so emotively charged phrase "Associational Life"—ran through *The Unique Function of Education in American Democracy* (1937), a report drafted by Beard for the Educational Policies Commission of the National Education Association. He spent part of each year in Washington to keep in touch with administration officials and influential congressmen. He accepted appointment to the consumer's advisory board of the New Deal National Recovery Administration and organized a committee of fellow small bondholders of the bankrupt Missouri Pacific Railroad to fight what he attacked as banker manipulation of the line's finances. Worried about the rising influence of the neo-Brandeisians with their deep-seated belief in "the curse of bigness," he kept up a drumfire of attack in the popular magazines against "the cult of littleness and Federal impotence." His major contribution—and the most appreciated by the White House—was his defense of the constitutionality of the New Deal measures. And when Roosevelt put forth his "court-packing" plan, Beard delivered a nationwide radio address defending the proposal as a justified and "constitutional" means of bringing "the Court back within the Constitution."

After his first burst of enthusiasm, Beard's attitude toward Roosevelt oscillated between doubt and hope as the master prestidigitator in the White House zigged and zagged. As late as the winter of 1938, when he and Mary finished writing *America in Midpassage* (1939), sequel to *The Rise of American Civilization* surveying developments over the preceding decade, they sympathetically portrayed how

"the major measures of the Roosevelt regime, however open to criticism in details or in execution, looked in the direction of strengthening the economic foundations of democracy." In his final summing up on the eve of the 1940 election, however, the minuses outweighed the pluses. Roosevelt, ran the indictment in *The Old Deal and the New*, had not followed through with a "cooperative, concerted plan for industrial order and progress." The New Deal had failed to restore prosperity, to put the nation's productive capacity and labor force fully back to work, or to solve "the major problem of concentration in private ownership of the greater part of the country's resources and productive plants, with its consequent private control over production and prices." With national planning abandoned, and with "direct government ownership of industrial properties along socialistic lines" not even contemplated, the administration had come to rely upon a continuing high level of government spending to keep the economy "running at even a moderate tempo." Such government spending could supply no more than a temporary and artificial fillip, while the growing national debt portended a new and graver crisis. "At some point in time," Beard concluded gloomily, "the growing debts and costs of the Government cannot be met and must end in a serious explosion. . . ."

Beard's worsening disillusionment with the New Deal fueled, and was simultaneously exacerbated by, his alarm that Roosevelt's foreign policies were threatening to lead the country into war. His response was a flood of articles and books against American involvement. Reflecting the intensity of his feelings, the tone became more and more emotionally strident and historical analysis became more and more subordinated to polemical urgency. Nowhere is this process more strikingly revealed than in his turnabout upon the question of foreign policy motivation. In *The Idea of National Interest* and *The Open Door at Home*—works that would exert a seminal influence upon the New Left historians of the cold war era—Beard had identified as the primary determinant of American expansionism the quest for new markets and investment opportunities and had warned that given the depression-heightened rivalries among the powers, the pursuit of trade and profits abroad must lead to war. Accordingly, his plea was for the Roosevelt administration to deal with the problem of the "so-called surpluses" by domestic reforms that would promote "a large increase in the buying and purchasing power of the American people" through "an *efficient* distribution of wealth within the United States." As

Charles A. Beard

late as 1936, in his *The Devil Theory of War*, he had cautioned against blaming "wicked men" for American involvement in World War I. The fault lay with all those Americans, high and low, who saw in trade with the Allies the way to keep the economy prosperous. But Beard himself shifted to make Roosevelt his own personal "devil." By the latter thirties, he was accusing FDR of taking up "world lecturing and interventionism" as a calculated gambit to distract the country from his failure to restore prosperity.

Beard was no pacifist, nor did he have any illusions about Hitler's aggressive ambitions. Still, he saw hardly more virtue on the other side. The Soviet Union was a totalitarian despotism no different from Nazi Germany, while Britain and France were the most "ruthless" of imperialist powers. Remembering the attacks upon civil liberties, academic freedom, and political dissent accompanying American involvement in World War I, he worried if democracy could survive another such conflict. And war would blast any hope for further domestic reform. More important, he was convinced that whatever happened in Europe and Asia could not threaten United States security given this country's high degree of economic self-sufficiency and geographical position. What most fundamentally underlay his isolationism, however, was his deep, one might say visceral, feeling that the New World and the Old were separated by more than simply the oceans. Their histories, traditions, and values were diametrically opposed: America was a distinctive and unique civilization without the feudal past, class bitterness, and time-encrusted hatreds of the Old World. As the foreign policy battle waxed, Beard threw himself into the struggle. He kept in touch with, advised, and supported leading isolationists in and out of Congress; he championed mandatory neutrality legislation; he testified before congressional committees against Roosevelt's naval expansion program and Lend-Lease. While his temperamental antipathy to organization affiliations kept him from joining the America First Committee, he publicly endorsed its aims.

The consequences of the war confirmed Beard's forebodings. American participation had disrupted and diverted reform while saddling the country with a "stupendous" national debt and "grinding" taxes. The conflict had given further impetus to the shift of power from Congress to the executive, accelerated the growth of a gigantic bureaucracy, and, perhaps most alarming, dangerously increased the influence of the military in American life. The result was an ever more powerful, and now not so benevolent, Leviathan. Nor had the defeat of the Axis powers assured United States security. An even more hostile and dangerous Soviet Union had emerged as the dominant power in Europe and Asia. "The sky," he exclaimed privately in July 1945, "is clear and ominous: only two mighty armed powers are on the horizon. What impends and with what portents? Day and night, I wonder and tremble for the future of my country and mankind." And he was haunted by the specter of the atomic bomb with its threat of world destruction. Whereas the war had converted many of the isolationists of the 1930s into supporters of collective security, not so Beard. He continued to pour his scorn upon the quixotic dreams of the one-worlders. At the same time, he reacted instinctively against the Truman administration's containment policies; he went so far as to accuse the chief executive of plotting another "Pearl Harbor." In his depression he even came to question what had been the fundamental premise of his own intellectual life: man's essential rationality. "Man," he confessed to a friend, "seems bound to have a berserk rage every so often—a senseless berserk rage, and I regard it as a mistake to gloss that fact over."

Nevertheless, Beard refused to succumb to despair. In the aftermath of Pearl Harbor, he threw himself into a new effort to lay down the principles that should guide "our government and economy . . . in the years ahead." The most ambitious work, his and his wife's *The American Spirit* (1942), was intended as the capstone of their explication of America as a distinctive and unique civilization begun with *The Rise of American Civilization*. But whereas the latter portrays men's beliefs as a reflection of their economic interests, *The American Spirit* elevates ideas—or at least those ideas with which Beard sympathized—as an independent shaping force. *The American Spirit* pictures American history in Manichaean terms as a struggle between the forces of light and the representatives of darkness: the champions of a secular, democratic, collectivist America versus the selfish and self-interested defenders of an outmoded individualism and status quo. *The Republic* (1943) is a series of Platonic-style dialogues about the nature of American political institutions and values. More than 180,000 copies were sold, and extracts were serialized in *Life* magazine. *A Basic History of the United States* (1944)—like *The American Spirit*, written with Mary—is a survey of American history written for the general reader, and Beard saw it as their "last will and testament to the American people."

Natural Rights.

The conception of universal humanity and the of rights for all individuals. which forms a central point in all theories of natural rights, stemming from Stoicism and reenforced by Christian teachings, by logic and by inferences leads to democracy as a source of political power and an expression of the liberty accorded to human beings and has been in fact closely associated with the theory and practice of democracy in the United States from the beginning

Page from the manuscript for an essay on natural rights

The regular edition sold approximately 300,000 copies; the Book-of-the-Month Club distributed roughly the same number; and revised and updated by his son, the book remains in print.

A set of common themes runs through these later works. The first is a profound admiration for the virtues of the American system of "constitutional goverment"—with its balance between majority rule and "fundamental rights," between centralization and local autonomy—as "in eternal contradiction to the principle of authoritarian, totalitarian, dictatorial government." The reverse side is a paean of praise—most strikingly found in his introduction to selections from *The Federalist Papers*, *The Enduring Federalist* (1948)—for the realism, practical wisdom, and far-sighted genius of the framers of the Constitution. A second major theme is his exaltation of what he saw as the essential features of the American "idea of civilization": "respect for life, for human worth, for the utmost liberty compatible with the social principle, for equality of rights and opportunities, for the dignity and utility of labor, for the rule of universal participation in the work and benefits of society." Most important, Beard presented a message of hope for the future, a reaffirmation of the ability of human will and action to shape events, a call for a new "co-operative" effort to deal with the nation's problems. "There are," he assured his readers, "immense and varied opportunities in which we can work for the good, the true, the useful, and the beautiful. . . .The little that the strongest of us can do may seem small, but surely the unresting spirit of Americans will endlessly strive to carry on the values in their heritage, to improve upon them, to create new arts and sciences of living, to sustain and make better the Republic."

Beard took as his own contribution to "sustain and make better the Republic" the demolition of the Roosevelt myth—a cause that became an obsession with him. He was convinced that Roosevelt had deceived and misled the American people by promising peace while plotting war, and he was further convinced that in so doing Roosevelt had brought the republic to the verge of Caesarism. The first of his two studies of Roosevelt's foreign policies, *American Foreign Policy in the Making 1932-1940* (1946), aimed to underline Roosevelt's duplicity by showing how the chief executive had up through the 1940 election assured the public "that his foreign policy meant peace for the United States." The second, *President Roosevelt and the Coming of the War 1941* (1948)—focusing upon the critical year 1941—showed how Roosevelt, while still playing the peace game, was engaged in a "series of complicated moves" to provoke a "real war" in the Atlantic. When that effort "fizzled out," Roosevelt embarked upon a course of action deliberately intended at "maneuvering the Japanese into firing the first shot." Beard went so far as to suggest that the chief executive "was not surprised by the Japanese attack when it came on December 7." The volumes provoked an avalanche of angry denunciation from pro-Roosevelt sympathizers—including many of Beard's former admirers and friends, whose attacks stung him sharply. The works do suffer from Beard's bitter animus against "the Saint," and even more from lack of access to the full record. But later research has amply documented Roosevelt's deviousness, and later events have stimulated fuller appreciation of Beard's warnings about the dangers of unrestrained presidential authority in foreign affairs.

At an age when most people were looking forward to retirement, Beard had lost none of his zest for not simply controversy but inquiry. In the fall of 1940, he had accepted for the first time since his resignation from Columbia a regular academic position, a professorship of history at Johns Hopkins University, with the hope of establishing there a center for the interdisciplinary study of American civilization. When the project fell through—partly because the approach of the war dimmed the prospects of obtaining outside funding, partly because his isolationist views antagonized much of the faculty—he left after one year. His work on the Social Science Research Council's Committee on Historiography had stimulated his interest in writing a large-scale study of the development of historical scholarship in the United States. But given the pressure of his other undertakings, the only published result was the reexamination of Henry and Brooks Adams in his introduction to the reissue of Brooks's *The Law of Civilization and Decay* (1943). Immediately after finishing the second Roosevelt foreign policy volume, Beard began research for a third dealing with wartime diplomacy. "I have written two books about this war," he told a friend. "I will write more, if I live." He had suffered a serious illness in 1945, and although he had recovered, the labors on the Roosevelt volumes further sapped his formerly robust constitution. He died 1 September 1948, "a victim," his friend Raymond Moley eulogized, "of hard work induced by a passionate drive to tell the truth as he saw it . . . his frail body literally charred and killed by the drive of his burning mind."

Although a 1938 survey by the *New Republic* of

liberal intellectuals ranked Beard second only to Thorstein Veblen among those whose work had influenced their thinking, Beard's reputation at his death was at a low ebb because of his isolationism and bitter attacks on Roosevelt. The fading of the passions of that time, however, allows a later generation to recognize Beard for the giant he was. A poll of editors, educators, and public figures by *Survey* magazine shortly after Beard's death gave first place to *The Rise of American Civilization* as the book that best explained American democracy. Even the unsympathetic acknowledge the extent of his influence, a hostile Lewis Mumford complaining that Beard "is the most powerful single figure in the teaching of American history." No one had a more exalted view of the historian's calling. The historian, Beard wrote in 1919, "endures only in so far as he succeeds in casting through the warp of the past the weft of the future—a future which he can behold only by prophetic discernment." Judged by that standard, he himself failed. Yet no one made a more valiant attempt. In his life, as in his writings, Beard was the personification of what Merle Curti called "a great democratic humanist." Beneath the shifts in his thinking runs as a unifying thread his vision of the United States as a land "without the degradation of poverty and unemployment on the one side or the degradation of luxury, rivalry, and conspicuous waste on the other . . . a beautiful country—homes beautiful; communities and farms beautiful; stores and workshops beautiful." "Sheer Utopianism," he admitted, but then added in what may stand as his own epitaph, "Without vision men and women perish, nations perish."

Other:

Loose Leaf Digest of Short Ballot Charters: A Documentary History of the Commission Form of Municipal Government, edited by Beard (New York: Short Ballot Organization, 1911);

Documents on the State-Wide Initiative, Referendum and Recall, edited by Beard and Birl E. Schultz (New York: Macmillan, 1912);

New York State Reconstruction Commission, *Report . . . on Retrenchment and Reorganization in the State Government*, written primarily by Beard (Albany: J. B. Lyon, 1919);

Whither Mankind: A Panorama of Modern Civilization, edited by Beard (New York: Longmans, Green, 1928);

"Political Science," in *Research in the Social Sciences: Its Fundamental Methods and Objectives*, edited by Wilson Gee (New York: Macmillan, 1929);

Toward Civilization, edited by Beard (London: Longmans, Green, 1930);

America Faces the Future, edited by Beard (Boston: Houghton Mifflin, 1932);

A Century of Progress, edited by Beard (Chicago: Harper, 1932);

J. B. Bury, *The Idea of Progress: An Inquiry into Its Origin and Growth*, introduction by Beard (New York: Macmillan, 1932);

American Historical Association, Commission on the Social Studies, *Conclusions and Recommendations of the Commission*, written primarily by Beard (New York: Scribners, 1934);

National Education Association, Educational Policies Commission, *The Unique Function of Education in American Democracy*, written primarily by Beard (Washington, D.C.: National Education Association, 1937);

"Historiography and the Constitution," in *The Constitution Reconsidered*, edited by Conyers Read (New York: Columbia University Press, 1938);

Brooks Adams, *The Law of Civilization and Decay: An Essay in History*, introduction by Beard (New York: Knopf, 1943);

"Propositions," in *Theory and Practice in Historical Study: A Report of the Committee on Historiography* edited by Merle Curti (New York: Social Science Research Council, 1946);

"Grounds for a Reconsideration of Historiography" and "Problems of Terminology in Historical Writing: The Need for Greater Precision in the Use of Historical Terms," by Sidney Hook with Beard, in *Theory and Practice in Historical Study: A Report of the Committee on Historiography*;

The Enduring Federalist, edited by Beard (Garden City: Doubleday, 1948).

Periodical Publications:

"Memorandum Relative to the Reconstruction of Tokyo. . . ," *Far Eastern Review*, 21 (June-July 1925): 252-256;

"Time, Technology, and the Creative Spirit in Political Science," *American Political Science Review*, 21 (February 1927):1-111;

"Conditions Favorable to Creative Work in Political Science," *American Political Science Review*, 24 (February 1930, Supplement): 25-32;

"A 'Five-Year Plan' for America," *Forum*, 86 (July 1931): 1-11;

"The Teutonic Origins of Representative Government," *American Political Science Review*, 26 (February 1932): 28-44;

"Representative Government in Evolution," by

Beard and John D. Lewis, *American Political Science Review*, 26 (April 1932): 223-240;

"Written History as an Act of Faith," *American Historical Review*, 39 (January 1934): 219-231;

"The World as I Want It," *Forum and Century*, 91 (June 1934): 332-334;

"That Noble Dream," *American Historical Review*, 41 (October 1935): 74-87;

"Currents of Thought in Historiography," by Beard and Alfred Vagts, *American Historical Review*, 42 (April 1937): 460-483.

References:

Howard K. Beale, ed., *Charles A. Beard: A Reappraisal* (Lexington: University of Kentucky Press, 1954);

Lee Benson, *Turner and Beard: American Historical Writing Reconsidered* (Glencoe, Ill.: Free Press, 1960);

Elias Berg, *The Historical Thinking of Charles A. Beard* (Stockholm: Almqvist & Wicksell, 1957);

Maurice Blinkoff, *The Influence of Charles A. Beard upon American Historiography* (Buffalo: Committee on Publications on the Roswell Park Publication Fund, 1936);

Bernard C. Borning, *The Political and Social Thought of Charles A. Beard* (Seattle: University of Washington Press, 1962);

John Braeman, "Charles A. Beard: The English Experience," *Journal of American Studies*, 15 (August 1981): 165-189;

Braeman, "The Historian as Activist: Charles A. Beard and the New Deal," *South Atlantic Quarterly*, 79 (Autumn 1980): 364-374;

Robert E. Brown, *Charles Beard and the Constitution: A Critical Analysis of "An Economic Interpretation of the Constitution,"* (Princeton: Princeton University Press, 1956);

Warren I. Cohen, *The American Revisionists: The Lessons of Intervention in World War I* (Chicago: University of Chicago Press, 1967);

Jane S. Dahlberg, *The New York Bureau of Municipal Research: Pioneer in Government Administration* (New York: New York University Press, 1966);

James Henderson, "The First Party System," in Alden T. Vaughan and George A. Billias, eds., *Perspectives on Early American History: Essays in Honor of Richard B. Morris* (New York: Harper & Row, 1973), pp. 325-371;

John Higham, Leonard Krieger, and Felix Gilbert, *History* (Englewood Cliffs, N.J.: Prentice-Hall, 1965);

Richard Hofstadter, *The Progressive Historians: Turner, Beard, Parrington* (New York: Knopf, 1968);

Thomas C. Kennedy, *Charles A. Beard and American Foreign Policy* (Gainesville: University Presses of Florida, 1975);

Cecelia M. Kenyon, " 'An Economic Interpretation of the Constitution' after Fifty Years," *Centennial Review*, 7 (Summer 1963): 327-352;

David W. Marcell, *Progress and Pragmatism: James, Dewey, Beard, and the American Idea of Progress* (Westport, Conn.: Greenwood Press, 1974);

Frederick C. Mosher, ed., *American Public Administration: Past, Present, Future* (University: University of Alabama Press, 1975);

Ellen Nore, "Charles A. Beard's Act of Faith: Context and Content," *Journal of American History*, 66 (March 1980): 850-866;

J. R. Pole, "The New History and the Sense of Social Purpose in American Historical Writing," *Transactions of the Royal Historical Society*, fifth series, 23 (1973): 220-242;

Thomas J. Pressly, *Americans Interpret Their Civil War* (Princeton: Princeton University Press, 1954);

Ronald Radosh, *Prophets on the Right: Profiles of Conservative Critics of American Globalism* (New York: Simon & Schuster, 1975);

Robert A. Skotheim, *American Intellectual Histories and Historians* (Princeton: Princeton University Press, 1966);

Lloyd R. Sorenson, "Charles A. Beard and German Historiographical Thought," *Mississippi Valley Historical Review*, 42 (September 1955): 274-287;

Gerald Stourzh, "Charles A. Beard's Interpretations of Foreign Policy," *World Affairs Quarterly*, 28 (July 1957): 111-148;

Cushing Strout, *The Pragmatic Revolt in American History: Carl Becker and Charles Beard* (New Haven: Yale University Press, 1958);

Morton G. White, *Social Thought in America: The Revolt against Formalism* (New York: Viking, 1949).

Papers:

Beard and his wife destroyed the bulk of their manuscripts and private papers shortly before their deaths. Many of the papers that survived are in the Beard collection, DePauw University Archives. There is a substantial quantity of Beard correspondence in different collections in the Butler Library, Columbia University. Additional manuscript collections containing significant Beard correspondence include: Harry Elmer Barnes Papers (Archive of Contemporary History, University of Wyoming); George S. Counts Papers (Southern Illinois University Library); Merle Curti Papers (State Historical Society of Wisconsin); A. C. Krey Papers (University of Minnesota Archives); Macmillan Company Records (New York Public Library); Arthur M. Schlesinger, Sr., Papers (Harvard University Archives); and Oswald Garrison Villard Papers (Houghton Library, Harvard University).

Carl Becker
(7 September 1873-10 April 1945)

Milton M. Klein
University of Tennessee

SELECTED BOOKS: *The History of Political Parties in the Province of New York, 1760-1776* (Madison: University of Wisconsin, 1909);

The Beginnings of the American People (Boston: Houghton Mifflin, 1915);

The Eve of the Revolution: A Chronicle of the Breach with England (New Haven: Yale University Press, 1918; London: Oxford University Press, 1920);

The United States: An Experiment in Democracy (New York & London: Harper, 1920);

The Declaration of Independence: A Study in the History of Political Ideas (New York: Harcourt, Brace, 1922);

Modern History; the Rise of a Democratic, Scientific, and Industrialized Civilization (New York: Silver, Burdett, 1931);

The Heavenly City of the Eighteenth-Century Philosophers (New Haven: Yale University Press, 1932);

Everyman His Own Historian (New York: F. S. Crofts, 1935);

Progress and Power (Palo Alto: Stanford University Press, 1936; London: Oxford University Press, 1936);

The Story of Civilization, by Becker and Frederic Duncalf (New York: Silver, Burdett, 1938);

Modern Democracy (New Haven: Yale University Press, 1941; London: Oxford University Press, 1941);

New Liberties for Old (New Haven: Yale University Press, 1941; London: Oxford University Press, 1941);

Cornell University: Founders and the Founding (Ithaca: Cornell University Press, 1943);

How New Will the Better World Be? (New York: Knopf, 1944);

Freedom and Responsibility in the American Way of Life (New York: Knopf, 1945);

Carl Becker, early 1930s

Detachment and the Writing of History: Essays and Letters of Carl L. Becker, edited by Phil L. Snyder (Ithaca: Cornell University Press, 1958).

Carl Becker was a historian of history as well as a historian of the United States, and his place in American history rests as much on his capacity to raise provocative questions about the nature of historical study as on the history he produced. He preferred to regard himself as a thinker about history and historians rather than as a historian. His forte, he once remarked, consisted "in having thought a good deal about the meaning of history rather than in having achieved erudition in it." The remark was not entirely an expression of false modesty; he seemed never quite sure of his own knowledge. His attitude led him to pursue courses of conduct that are somewhat baffling to later observers. In 1928, while in the midst of writing what was to become an extraordinarily successful high school textbook, *Modern History*, Becker declined an invitation to speak at an American Historical Association session on the social studies because he had "no ideas on the subject of history teaching in the schools" and had never thought much about it. And in 1935, at a time when his distinction as an American historian was widely recognized, he declined nomination for the prestigious Harmsworth visiting professorship of American history at Oxford University on the ground that he had never taught American history and did not think he knew enough of its details to be able to teach it! These incidents reveal as well as anything the somewhat enigmatic character of Carl Becker as an American historian.

Becker was born on a farm in Black Hawk County about fifteen miles from Waterloo, Iowa. His parents, Charles DeWitt and Almeda Sarvay Becker, had moved there from Carthage, New York, in 1868, after his father had served in the Civil War. Like others, the elder Becker was seeking a better life for himself and his family. He originally purchased eighty acres of good farm land; by the time Carl was born, it had been enlarged threefold by additional purchases. Christened Lotus Carl after a maternal uncle, Becker changed his name when in college because his classmates thought it odd and unusual and because Becker himself decided it connoted too much "somnolence." Carl's mother was of English and Irish descent while his father had German and Dutch ancestry, but Carl's father—born in New York—spoke only English, and his son never managed to master German, even in graduate school.

Little is known of Becker's early life. He attended a rural school near the family homestead, but by the time he was eleven, the Beckers had rented their farm and moved to Waterloo, where the elder Becker was active as a Union veteran, a Republican, a Methodist, and a Mason. At the West Side High School in Waterloo, Carl Becker was recognized by his teachers as an exceptional student; one commented to Charles Becker, "Your son is by far the best student in school and we'll hear from him some day."

In the fall of 1892, Becker entered a Methodist school, Cornell College, at Mt. Vernon, Iowa. A year there convinced him that its atmosphere was too stifling, and the next year he enrolled at the University of Wisconsin. The change connoted a rejection of the Becker family's denominational affiliation, which Carl referred to later as "the Methodist menace," and which he found "respectable," "platitudinous," and suffocating. Carl was attracted instead to the rationalist Enlightenment thinkers of the eighteenth century, and they remained the center of his intellectual interests for the rest of his life. The assertion of his own identity took other forms as well: his first presidential ballot was cast for a Republican, McKinley, but he became an independent in politics as he grew older and even cast his vote twice for Socialists—Eugene Debs and Norman Thomas; he chose history as his career, rather than law, which his father preferred; and instead of a young, "gracious and talented" Waterloo girl whom his family expected he would marry, he chose a New York widow, Maude Hepworth Ranney, seven years his senior with a seven-year-old daughter.

At Wisconsin, Becker came under the influence of Frederick Jackson Turner, historian of the frontier. It was not his reputation which made Turner such an inspirational figure for Becker—the famous Turner thesis, written in 1893, had gone virtually unnoticed as yet—but his enthusiasm for history and his ability to communicate it to his students; and it was not what he taught but how he taught it, Becker recalled in a portrait of his mentor which he wrote in 1927. Becker never became as good a teacher as Turner, but he learned from the Wisconsin professor to challenge, to probe, to question, and "in this happy way," he "got a new idea of history," namely, that it was a never-ending adventure into the human past rather than a series of conventions agreed upon and "to be learned by rote." From Turner, too, Becker secured the idea that each age rewrote history to suit its own needs, and this was to become the foundation of Becker's own belief that "everyman" was his own historian, shaped by the contemporary climate of opinion and studying history for answers to questions that seem important in the present.

Upon receipt of his baccalaureate degree in 1896, Becker spent an additional year at Wisconsin and then went to Columbia University with a fellowship for graduate study and high recommendations from Turner and Charles Homer Haskins, a distinguished medievalist and another of Becker's teachers at Madison. At Columbia, Becker was influenced by John W. Burgess, James Harvey Robinson, and Herbert Levi Osgood. From Osgood, Becker acquired his interest in the colonial and revolutionary period of American history (his doctoral dissertation was on the history of political parties in colonial New York); Robinson's seminar turned him toward the eighteenth century, also, as well as to intellectual history. But Becker never completed his graduate studies at Columbia. After only a year there, in 1899, he began teaching, briefly at Pennsylvania State College and at Dartmouth, and in 1902 at the University of Kansas, where he remained for the next fourteen years.

Becker began his prolific writing career at Kansas; he does not appear to have made much of an impression on students there as an exciting teacher. He had already published three scholarly articles in the *American Historical Review* and one in the *Annals of the American Academy of Political and Social Sciences*. They were all somewhat pedantic in style; two were on constitutional history, the others dealt with material drawn from his yet uncompleted doctoral dissertation, which was finished in 1907 and earned him his degree from Wisconsin and a promotion to the rank of associate professor. Written clearly but scarcely gracefully, the dissertation, published two years later as *The History of Political Parties in the Province of New York, 1760-1776*, was not a foretaste of the writing style which was to make Becker so widely read. It was rather in the numerous book reviews he wrote in the pre-World War I era for nonscholarly journals like the *Nation* and the *Dial* that he first demonstrated his flair for writing the urbane, ironic, elegant, witty, and, above all, lucid prose that was to make him so popular as a historian. The first full-length book expressive of his new style was an interpretative overview of American history to 1783, *The Beginnings of the American People* (1915), which emphasized the European background of American colonization, reflecting Becker's teaching of European history rather than American. Perhaps it was the favorable attention accorded this textbook which secured him

a call to the University of Minnesota as professor of European history in 1916. Before he had even completed his first semester at Minnesota, Becker was offered a position as professor of modern history at Cornell, whose history faculty were impressed with his doctoral dissertation, an essay on Kansas he had written in 1910, and his services on the editorial board of the *American Historical Review*, which he had joined in 1914. In the fall of 1917, Becker moved to Cornell University, where he remained until his retirement in 1941. While at Cornell he wrote eleven more books, one of which was published posthumously, and earned the array of honors that marked him as one of the most distinguished historians of his time: election to the Royal Historical Society, the American Academy of Arts and Sciences, the American Antiquarian Society, the National Institute of Arts and Letters, and the American Philosophical Society; honorary doctorates from Yale, Rochester, and Columbia; and the presidency of the American Historical Association in 1931.

Becker's literary output was prodigious: 16 books (9 of which are still in print), 75 articles, and almost 200 book reviews. The range of his interests was catholic and the forms into which he cast his historical knowledge varied. He wrote political history, intellectual history, biographies, college and high school textbooks, historiographical essays, essays of contemporary opinion, reviews, and review essays. He taught European history and wrote numerous essays, book reviews, and one interpretative book, probably his most popular (*The Heavenly City of the Eighteenth-Century Philosophers*, 1932) in that field, but he wrote even more in American history and historiography. Words seemed to come easily to him; his style was as "felicitous" as the language of the Declaration of Independence which he so described; he had a beautiful gift for the apt phrase, an uncanny feeling for mood, and a flair for epigrammatic phrases and sentences which were tantalizing but often mystifying and in which he neatly juxtaposed opposites, used clichés turned upside down, and artfully employed circular reasoning. Of the philosophes, he commented, "having denatured God, they deified nature"; on Jefferson, where he "got his ideas is hardly so much a question as where he could have got away from them"; on the colonists' views on parliamentary taxation, they "would determine the nature of an act by the intention of the framers, and the intention of the framers by the nature of the act"; on Einstein, he was guilty of a slight error in saying that "God is probably a mathematician. . . [.]

he meant to say that a mathematician is probably God"; on the causes of war, "in the last analysis, it is not munitions makers that make war, but the institutions of war that make munitions makers," and "if we could avoid war it would be much easier to resolve our social discords, and . . . if we could resolve our social discords it would be much easier to avoid war"; on the New Deal, "the pre-war New Deal failed to cure unemployment because it tried to cure it, whereas the wartime New Deal succeeded in curing unemployment because it didn't try to"; on progress, if "the idea of progress emerges from progress itself, progress is in turn reinforced by the idea of progress that is in men's minds"; and on human intelligence, man could not "have developed the intelligence he has without the implements of power his intelligence has devised, or . . . have devised the implements of power he has without an intelligence adequate to devise them."

Not all of Becker's writings display this beguiling style, nor does his felicity with words provide the only measure of his work. Becker's reputation among American historians rests heavily on two books, his doctoral dissertation and his extended essay on the Declaration of Independence. In *The History of Political Parties in the Province of New York, 1760-1776* (1909), Becker offered an interpretation of the American Revolution that has had enduring impact and over which debate still continues. The "Becker thesis," as it came to be known, was that the Revolution involved more than a struggle between the colonies and the mother country over "home rule"; alongside it was fought a contest among the colonists over the issue of "who should rule at home." As he described the emergence of these two issues in provincial New York, upper-class merchants and landowners who had controlled the colony's politics before 1776 were pressured by lower-class artisans and workers for a share of political power. The war itself opened the gates for the admission of these "radicals" into the political arena, initiating a movement for the democratization of American government and society. The "dual-revolution" thesis seemed to capture the spirit of the Progressive era in which it appeared, and it rapidly became an accepted interpretation of the character of the Revolution. Becker did no further scholarly research on the two-revolutions idea, but he reiterated the theme in subsequent books, articles, and reviews. In his *The Beginnings of the American People*, which appeared six years later, Becker extended the thesis from New York to all the colonies; he repeated the assertion in a survey of American history he prepared as part of

the public information effort in World War I, *The United States: An Experiment in Democracy* (1920); and in his last book, *Freedom and Responsibility in the American Way of Life* (1945), the idea appeared in only slightly modified language: "the American Revolution . . . was as much an uprising of the populace against the better sort as it was an uprising of the better sort against British control."

The Declaration of Independence: A Study in the History of Political Ideas appeared in 1922. Although it contained a chapter on the evolution of the text of the document and an analysis of its literary quality, the study is chiefly an intellectual history. Becker's remarks on Jefferson's style are remarkably reminiscent of Becker's own literary art: he thought the Declaration was written with "grace and felicity," yet with coolness and detachment. Jefferson's words were "calm and quiescent," since he "felt with the mind, as some people think with the heart." But Becker was less concerned with the Declaration as a literary work than as a political document, as indicated by the book's subtitle. The document's transcendent importance, Becker believed, was as a statement of the political thought of the American revolutionaries, and at the core of this political philosophy was the theory of natural rights. His purpose, he explained to his friend William E. Dodd, was "to show where the Natural Rights philosophy came from and where it went to and why," which Becker did with characteristic lucidity, claiming that Jefferson's ideas were not new, they did not stem from the French philosophes, and they died in the nineteenth century. According to Becker, the sources of the natural rights theory were thoroughly English, derived largely from Locke and other English writers who had participated in the seventeenth-century struggles with the Crown, and Jefferson did not so much invent them as merely reflect a widely held contemporary opinion of their validity. By incorporating these ideas in the document, Jefferson had provided a theory of government that justified the Revolution and gave it a high moral character, making it "respectable and virtuous." Becker thought it was important to understand the natural rights theory because it had been prerequisite to the Revolution, which "was accomplished in men's minds before they made it the work of their hands." (The latter phrase Becker used unchanged as an explanation of the French Revolution in the high school text, *Modern History*, 1931, which he wrote ten years later.)

The Declaration of Independence received almost immediate acclaim, and it has been regarded as the definitive work on the subject until recently. A poll of historians in 1952 rated the book as the sixth best work on American history to appear during the years 1920-1935, and like Becker's volume on New York provincial politics, it is still in print. If the latter volume appealed to the Progressive mood because of its stress on socioeconomic forces and class struggle, the former struck a responsive note among those historians who were concerned with the force of ideas. Another of Becker's books, on European history, confirmed his stature as an intellectual historian. *The Heavenly City of the Eighteenth-Century Philosophers*, which appeared in 1932, was written in the same urbane, elegant, and artful style as *The Declaration of Independence* and dealt with the ideas that provided the underpinning of the French Revolution. In this book, Becker analyzed the rationalist thinkers of the Enlightenment. He startled readers by suggesting that the philosophes were more in tune with the medieval scholastics than with modern rationalists and that faith and reason both, rather than reason alone, characterized eighteenth-century figures like Voltaire, Diderot, and de Condorcet. In fact, Becker seemed to be arguing, the Enlightenment, rather than being an emancipation from the preceding age of faith, only existed on the inherited moral capital of Christianity. Twenty-five years after the appearance of *The Heavenly City of the Eighteenth-Century Philosophers*, a symposium of scholars convened to "revisit" the volume and to test its major premise that the Enlightenment looked backward perhaps more than forward.

Despite the success of *The Declaration of Independence* and *The Heavenly City*, Becker cannot be easily typed as an intellectual historian or as any other kind. He himself eschewed labels: "I don't claim to be old or new or anything that a label can be attached to." Nor did he care to indulge in categorization as a historiographer: "To say of any historian . . . that he is scientific, or literary, or patriotic tells me little that I care to know." His heterodoxy is amply reflected in his other writings in early American history. His interest in the force of ideas on human behavior became matched by his concern for the social and personal determinants of individual conduct, the theme of *The Eve of the Revolution*, which had been published in 1918. It is a speculative work which takes liberties with historical facts and which he admitted was "an enterprise of questionable orthodoxy." Again employing his familiar impressionistic and eminently lucid prose style, he sought to demonstrate through individuals such as Sam Adams and Thomas Hutchinson the state of mind of American radicals and conserva-

tives during the years from 1763 to 1776. The same interest in the psychological roots of behavior appeared in an essay contrasting the positions of the patriot John Jay and the Tory Peter Van Schaack which appeared in the New York State Historical Association's *Quarterly Journal* in 1919; it was reiterated in an imaginatively fictionalized essay on "The Spirit of '76" given as a lecture at the Brookings Institute in 1926; and it reappeared in his biographical sketches of Benjamin Franklin, Sam Adams, Thomas Hutchinson, and Henry Adams published in the *Dictionary of American Biography* and the *Encyclopedia of the Social Sciences*. Denying that this new approach had turned him into a psychological historian, Becker nevertheless responded appreciatively to Merle Curti's compliment that he had enlisted psychology in the service of historical writing without "any borrowing of strange terms."

By 1931, Becker had become recognized as one of the most preeminent American historians and, in the opinion of Charles A. Beard, a distinguished "man of letters" as well. His presidential address that year to the American Historical Association, "Everyman His Own Historian," has come to be viewed as a classic manifesto of one school of modern historians—the relativists who reject the notion of objective truth, abandon the search for a science of history, and boldly proclaim that the historian's account of the past is no more than an imaginative reconstruction expressing his own contemporary milieu, the "dominant ideas of his own age," its "climate of opinion." Becker had been warning historians for years that they could not hope to achieve objectivity by "mental detachment" from their subject, having learned from his teacher Turner that "Each age writes the history of the past anew with reference to the conditions uppermost in its own time." He had expressed similar sentiments in book reviews and articles during the intervening years, but the relativist position was given fullest and most articulate expression in his presidential address, in which he declared that the "facts" of history do not speak for themselves and are indeed mental constructs of the historian. Becker further stated that history written without the intrusion of the historian is an impossibility; if it were possible, it would produce few worthwhile histories, "for the really detached mind is a dead mind." History is, he added, a "useful myth," serving the generation that creates it, "an imaginative creation . . . which each one of us, Mr. Everyman, fashions out of his individual experience," and it need not, indeed, cannot be complete, since memories are indistinct; but it serves its purpose if it is "useful to Mr. Everyman." According to Becker, the best the professional historian can do is to enlarge present memories with as much care and scholarly effort as possible and to keep them in harmony with contemporary social needs.

Becker's address received an ovation at the time it was delivered, but among academic historians it created shock waves that have not yet entirely abated. Traditionalists denounced Becker for denying the validity of history as an intellectual discipline; philosophers of history charged him with leaving history in a state of nihilistic anarchy; but what Becker did was merely give full theoretical expression to a crisis in American historiography that had been long in the making. Two years later, Charles A. Beard in his own presidential address urged that history be deliberately employed as a tool for creating a better future, reiterating that objective history was a chimera. Becker never went that far; he believed that the acquisition of objective historical knowledge was desirable and was content to caution historians that the effort was fraught with hazards. In his "Everyman" pronouncement he insisted that historians were "surely under bond to be as honest and as intelligent as human frailty permits."

Becker's tendency toward relativism, toward judgments that give the appearance of seeking to be on both sides of a question, is reflected also in the third body of his writings—his essays on contemporary affairs. (He had concluded *The Declaration of Independence* with a gloomy assessment that the faith of the eighteenth century in reason, enlightenment, and progress could not survive the harsh realities of the modern world; but when he wrote an introduction to a new edition published in 1942, he reaffirmed his own faith in Jefferson's glittering generalities.) No activist, Becker was nevertheless an acute and sensitive observer of world affairs. World Wars I and II, the rise of Nazism, the Russian Revolution, all led him to think about the Enlightenment faith in progress that he had found so intellectually attractive in his historical studies. Between 1935 and 1944, Becker wrote numerous essays in journals such as the *Yale Review* and gave several public lectures—at Stanford, the University of Virginia, and the University of Michigan—which found their way into print as books: *Progress and Power* (1936), *Modern Democracy* (1941), *New Liberties for Old* (1941), *How New Will the Better World Be?* (1944), and *Freedom and Responsibility in the American Way of Life* (1945). The idea that emerges in all these writings, sometimes hesitantly and at times un-

equivocally, is that despite its limitations the free use of intelligence is the surest guarantor of that humane society to which the eighteenth-century philosophes aspired. Yet Becker was always troubled by doubts as to man's ability to achieve the goal. To him, the impersonal forces of nature seemed to present a perpetual obstacle to human aspirations, and despite his progress, man ultimately recognizes that "in an indifferent universe which alone endures, he alone aspires, endeavors to attain, and attains only to be defeated in the end." Intelligence, Becker thought, was man's only hope, but he was not sure that intelligence was adequate to the task, and he was distrustful of a "mass intelligence that functions at the level of primitive fears and tabus." Having expressed his concern that technology had overwhelmed mankind and that social progress lagged behind scientific advancement, Becker still returned to his belief in those glittering generalities which comprised democratic philosophy.

Becker's reputation rests less on his substantive contributions to American history than on his challenges to those who wrote it. His dual-revolution thesis has been criticized for oversimplification and inaccuracies. His forays into intellectual history have been characterized as superficial. Even Becker's uncanny felicity of language, however captivating, often cloaked some hollow generalizations. One of his own students said that he had the feeling that Becker's words often ran away with his thoughts, and his ideas, however intriguing, seem always to move within a limited circle and to recur again and again with unashamed repetitiveness. Withal, there comes through in all of Becker's writings a distrust of orthodoxies, a persistent search for knowledge, and a humane faith in the power of the unfettered mind to promote the advancement of knowledge and human happiness. Perhaps his greatest contribution to American historiography is his insistence that the quest for truth remain a continuing one. He once told a class of freshmen at Cornell that the chief virtue of any course was to raise questions, not to answer them. And he prefaced his last scholarly work, a history of Cornell University, with a quotation from Abelard: "By doubting we are led to questioning, and by questioning we arrive at truth."

Other:
"John Jay and Peter Van Schaack," *New York State Historical Association Quarterly Journal*, 1 (October 1919): 1-12;
"Frederick Jackson Turner," in *American Masters of Social Science*, edited by Howard W. Odum

(New York: Holt, 1927), 273-318;

The Spirit of '76 and Other Essays, by Becker, J. M. Clark, and William E. Dodd (Washington, D.C.: Brookings Graduate School, 1927);

"Benjamin Franklin," in *Dictionary of American Biography*, edited by Allen Johnson and Dumas Malone (New York: Scribners, 1928-1944), VI: 585-598;

"Samuel Adams," in *Dictionary of American Biography*, I: 95-101;

"Thomas Hutchinson," in *Dictionary of American Biography*, IX: 439-443;

"Henry Adams," in *Encyclopedia of the Social Sciences*, edited by Edwin R. A. Seligman and Alvin Johnson (New York: Macmillan, 1930-1935), I: 431-432;

"Samuel Adams," in *Encyclopedia of the Social Sciences*, I: 435;

"Benjamin Franklin," in *Encyclopedia of the Social Sciences*, VI: 420-422;

"Progress," in *Encyclopedia of the Social Sciences*, XII: 495-499.

References:

Bernard Bailyn, "Becker, Andrews, and the Image of Colonial Origins," *New England Quarterly*, 29 (1956): 522-534;

Harold Bauman, "The Historiography of Carl L. Becker," Ph.D. dissertation, Iowa State University, 1964;

John Braeman and John C. Rule, "Carl Becker: Twentieth Century *Philosophe*," *American Quarterly*, 13 (1961): 534-539;

Robert E. Brown, *Carl Becker on History and the American Revolution* (East Lansing, Mich.: Spartan Press, 1970);

John C. Cairns, "Carl Becker: An American Liberal," *Journal of Politics*, 16 (1954): 623-644;

Milton Gold, "In Search of a Historian," *Centennial Review*, 7 (1963): 282-305;

Louis Gottschalk, "Carl Becker: Skeptic or Humanist?," *Journal of Modern History*, 18 (1946): 160-162;

Peter T. Harstad and Michael D. Gibson, "An Iowa-Born Historian and the American Revolution: Carl Becker and 'The Spirit of '76,' " *Palimpsest*, 17 (1976): 174-192;

David F. Hawke, "Carl L. Becker," M.A. thesis, University of Wisconsin, 1950;

Michael Kammen, ed., *"What is the Good of History?" Selected Letters of Carl L. Becker, 1900-1945* (Ithaca: Cornell University Press, 1973);

Milton M. Klein, "Detachment and the Writing of American History: The Dilemma of Carl Becker," in *Perspectives on Early American History: Essays in Honor of Richard B. Morris*, edited by Alden T. Vaughan and George A. Billias (New York: Harper & Row, 1973);

Klein, "Progressive History's Curmudgeon: The Enigmatic Carl Becker," *Reviews in American History*, 2 (1974): 293-299;

Bernard Mason, "The Heritage of Carl Becker: The Historiography of the Revolution in New York," *New York Historical Society Quarterly*, 53 (1969): 127-147;

David W. Noble, "Carl Becker: Science, Relativism, and the Dilemma of Diderot," *Ethics*, 67 (1957): 233-248;

James L. Penick, "Carl Becker and the Jewel of Consistency," *Antioch Review*, 26 (1966): 235-246;

Raymond O. Rockwood, ed., *Carl Becker's Heavenly City Revisited* (Ithaca: Cornell University Press, 1958);

Charlotte Watkins Smith, *Carl Becker: On History and the Climate of Opinion* (Ithaca: Cornell University Press, 1956);

Phil L. Snyder, "Carl L. Becker and the Great War: A Crisis for a Humane Intelligence," *Western Political Quarterly*, 9 (1956): 1-10;

Cushing Strout, *The Pragmatic Revolt in American History: Carl Becker and Charles Beard* (New Haven: Yale University Press, 1958);

Burleigh T. Wilkins, *Carl Becker: A Biographical Study in American Intellectual History* (Cambridge, Mass.: M.I.T. Press, 1961).

Papers:

Becker's papers are in the Cornell University Library. They include photocopies of originals in the papers of Frederick Jackson Turner, William E. Dodd, Felix Frankfurter, and other correspondents of Becker's.

Samuel Flagg Bemis

(20 October 1891-26 September 1973)

Kendrick A. Clements
University of South Carolina

BOOKS: *Jay's Treaty: A Study in Commerce and Diplomacy* (New York: Macmillan, 1923; revised, New Haven: Yale University Press, 1962);

Pinckney's Treaty: A Study of America's Advantage from Europe's Distress, 1783-1800 (Baltimore: Johns Hopkins University Press, 1926; revised, New Haven: Yale University Press, 1960);

The Hussey-Cumberland Mission and American Independence: An Essay in the Diplomacy of the American Revolution (Princeton: Princeton University Press, 1931);

Guide to the Diplomatic History of the United States, 1775-1921, by Bemis and Grace Gardner Griffin (Washington, D.C.: U.S. Government Printing Office, 1935);

The Diplomacy of the American Revolution (New York & London: Appleton-Century, 1935);

A Diplomatic History of the United States (New York: Holt, 1936; London: Cape, 1937);

La Política internacional de los Estados Unidos: interpretaciones (Lancaster, Pa.: Lancaster Press, 1939);

The Latin American Policy of the United States: An Historical Interpretation (New York: Harcourt, Brace, 1943);

John Quincy Adams and the Foundations of American Foreign Policy (New York: Knopf, 1949);

John Quincy Adams and the Union (New York: Knopf, 1956);

A Short History of American Foreign Policy and Diplomacy (New York: Holt, 1959);

American Foreign Policy and the Blessings of Liberty and Other Essays (New Haven: Yale University Press, 1962).

Samuel Flagg Bemis was a pioneer in America of the idea that to understand the history of international relations one must study the archives of every participating nation, weaving a narrative from the multiple points of view. Almost sixty years after the first of his books was published, and nearly twenty-five years after the last appeared, his works remain standard accounts supplemented but not superseded by the work of other scholars.

Bemis was born in 1891 in Worcester, Mas-

Samuel Flagg Bemis

sachusetts, where he and his two younger brothers were the seventh New England generation of his family. When Bemis was still a child the family moved from Worcester to the 145-acre family farm at Alum Pond near the village of Sturbridge. There Bemis's most vivid childhood memories were formed. Almost seventy years later he recalled that time fondly: "How good to have had in the nineteenth century—that happiest century in the history of mankind—a peaceful Walden or a tranquil Alum behind the tensions of life in this our tumultuous twentieth century." As a young man he had a recurring nightmare of Alum Pond almost dried up, with nothing left but exposed mud and stagnant pools. Throughout his life Thoreau's *Wal-*

den was always on his bedside table.

During Bemis's happy years at Alum, farm chores—swilling the pigs, driving the hay rake, delivering milk in the nearby village, cutting ice on the pond—blended with recreational activities like fishing, berrying, and attending the Sturbridge fair each September. In 1902, however, his grandfather died, and the farm began to deteriorate. Bemis's father went back to work in Worcester as night copy editor of the local newspaper and tried to run the farm during the days, but the struggle was too much. Three years later the farm was sold at auction, and the family moved back to Worcester. For Samuel it was the end of a golden period whose glow would warm his memories for the rest of his life. For Bemis the historian the virtues of childhood at Alum Pond—hard work, integrity, the warmth of family, the pleasures of an outdoor life lived close to the soil—were also the strengths of a nineteenth-century America whose international triumphs he assessed in books and articles. Small wonder that his finest work, a two-volume biography of John Quincy Adams, was a sympathetic study of a man whose life had many parallels to his own.

Bemis attended the public schools in Worcester and was a "middling" student. After graduation from high school he entered Worcester's Clark College, where students completed a condensed program in three years. The first year's tuition of eighty dollars was paid by his father, but thereafter Samuel earned his own way. Clark's excellent faculty included such figures as G. Stanley Hall, who brought Sigmund Freud to the United States in 1907, and George H. Blakeslee, who introduced Bemis to the study of international relations and later became an adviser to the State Department and a founder of the *Journal of International Relations*, which in 1922 became *Foreign Affairs*.

Graduating from Clark in 1912 with an A.B., Bemis moved the next autumn to another part of the college, known grandiloquently as Clark University, and received an M.A. in history in 1913. His thesis, "The Settlement of the Yazoo Boundary Dispute: The First Step in Southern Expansion," was based on archival research at a local institution, the American Antiquarian Society. The experience inspired Bemis's enthusiasm for research, but he later declared the thesis an embarrassment because it was supported by no research in Spanish archives. Nevertheless, it was good enough to receive publication in the *Magazine of History* in the autumn of 1913 and to lead his adviser, a young Harvard Ph.D. named Norman S. B. Gras, to urge Bemis to attempt a doctorate in history at Harvard. Securing a

tuition scholarship, Bemis traveled in September 1913 the forty-five miles from Worcester to Cambridge.

When Bemis went to Harvard, no such field as "diplomatic history" existed. He enrolled to study modern political history, but even then he vaguely determined to unite American history and diplomacy with international law, which was how he subsequently defined diplomatic history. His first practical experience in the study of American foreign relations came when he enrolled in Edward Channing's seminar. Channing was then at work on volume four of his six-volume *History of the United States*, and he assigned his students to write papers on aspects of the history of the early national period. He assigned to Bemis a paper on Jay's Treaty of 1794. Meeting with students for half-hour sessions in the library stacks, Channing stressed the importance of primary research but offered little instruction. He answered questions, but students had to define problems themselves and formulate their own approaches. For a country boy intimidated by Harvard, it was a frightening yet stimulating experience, and it shaped Bemis's own teaching methods, though he was always careful to see that his own students had closer supervision than Channing had given him. Profiting by Channing's scholarly example if not receiving much instruction from him, Bemis worked hard, and after a year of not knowing how his performance measured up, the doubt was at last removed when Channing sent his seminar grade on a postcard reading "A,—the best."

The other major figure in American history at Harvard during Bemis's graduate career was Frederick Jackson Turner, whose thesis that the frontier had determined the course of American development was already well known. Bemis eventually took Turner's undergraduate course but found its lectures "cut and dried." With Turner himself Bemis had only slight personal contact, and a course paper on the Canadian-American frontier and the Anglo-American war crisis of 1794 was "moulded" on what Bemis "understood, second-hand, to be his type of research." Based in part on a week's work in the Canadian archives in Ottawa, which Bemis visited while en route to a summer job as a counselor at a camp in northern Ontario, Bemis's paper was an outgrowth of his work with Channing rather than a reflection of any Turnerian conviction about the importance of the West. As Bemis's subsequent debate with Turner's student Arthur Preston Whitaker about the origins of Pinckney's Treaty showed, Bemis believed that America's diplomatic triumphs were more the result of its ability to exploit the troubles of the European nations than of what happened on its frontier. "America's advantage from Europe's distress" (a phrase he later used in the subtitle for a book on Pinckney's Treaty) seemed to him the central theme of early nineteenth-century diplomatic history.

A traveling fellowship enabled Bemis to go to England and France in October 1915 to trace the history of Jay's Treaty in the archives. Having finished a draft of his dissertation on the treaty in March 1916, he sent it off to Harvard and boarded a channel steamer to return to France to follow up on some last points in the French archives. On 24 March his ship, the *Sussex*, was torpedoed. Bemis, who saw the wake of the approaching torpedo, was subsequently able to give a deposition that helped to establish that the ship had not struck a mine as the Germans at first alleged. President Wilson's protest to the German government, based in part on the deposition, made Bemis a participant in history as well as a recorder of it, but the part he played cost him a cold, frightening night spent on a makeshift raft in the icy Channel waters, after which he contracted tuberculosis and, some people thought, an enduring prejudice against the Germans.

Returning to the United States in the spring of 1916, Bemis breezed through his final examination at Harvard and received his Ph.D. that same year, but his health did not improve. Warned by his doctor to seek a drier, warmer climate, he borrowed $200 from his father and set out for Santa Fe. There his tuberculosis cleared up, but academic opportunities were scarce. In 1917 he found a job at Colorado College in Colorado Springs, where he remained four years. While at Colorado he married Ruth Steele, whom he had courted since high school, on 20 June 1919. They had one daughter, Barbara, and remained happily married until Ruth's death on 30 October 1967. In 1921 the couple moved to Walla Walla, Washington, where Bemis taught for two years at Whitman College.

Bemis's Western experience did not mute his Massachusetts accent, nor did it persuade him that the mainsprings of American culture lay in the West. But it did awaken an appreciation of a great theme in American history—the triumph of American diplomats in envisioning and securing a vast empire in the West. His sketch of Thomas Jefferson in *The American Secretaries of State* series touched on that theme, but he developed it most fully in his study of that quintessential New Englander, John Quincy Adams, whose diplomatic triumphs in Europe and Washington were devoted to securing a

West he had never seen. In the Monroe Doctrine of 1823, and above all in the Adams-Onis Treaty of 1819 (which Bemis rechristened the "Transcontinental Treaty"), Adams had used diplomacy to secure space for the advance of the frontier that Turner called the determinant of American development.

Despite the remoteness of Colorado and Washington State from centers of research, Bemis continued to study and write. He delivered a paper on Hamilton's foreign policy at the American Historical Association meeting at Cleveland in 1919, and he published almost a dozen articles on contemporary issues and on topics relating to Jay's Treaty. In 1923 he submitted his revised dissertation on the treaty to a Knights of Columbus competition. The manuscript won the contest and a $3,000 prize and was declared the best American history book by an American college professor that year. Published by Macmillan, *Jay's Treaty: A Study in Commerce and Diplomacy* (1923) established Bemis as an important scholar and became the standard account of its subject.

Bemis's friendship with one of the great figures of American historical scholarship, J. Franklin Jameson, brought a gladly accepted opportunity to return to the East in 1923. As editor of the *American Historical Review*, Jameson had read Bemis's articles, and he offered the young man a position as associate director of historical research for the Carnegie Institution of Washington. Four years later, when Jameson became chief of the manuscripts division of the Library of Congress, he appointed Bemis to oversee an enormous project of copying documents on American history in European archives. As director of what was known as "Project A," Bemis worked from 1927 to 1929 supervising copying at the British Museum and the Public Record Office in London. He also helped negotiate the opening of the French diplomatic archives for copying of documents dated up to 1830, and he laid the groundwork for the opening of the Spanish archives so that documents for the years prior to 1870 could be copied.

Bemis's work for Project A in Europe gave great opportunities for research of his own, and an appointment to the Department of History of George Washington University (1925-1935) enabled him to exploit the rich American resources in Washington, D.C. A diligent and efficient worker, he produced several remarkable scholarly works. In 1926 he revised his Albert Shaw lectures, which he had delivered as a visiting lecturer at Johns Hopkins University, into *Pinckney's Treaty: A Study of America's*

Advantage from Europe's Distress, 1783-1800 (1926), which won the Pulitzer Prize for history in 1927. Between 1927 and 1929, Alfred A. Knopf published ten volumes of *The American Secretaries of State and Their Diplomacy*, for which Bemis was general editor and the author of the essays on John Jay and Thomas Jefferson. This work contained expert studies of the administrations of each of the U.S. secretaries of state by a variety of writers and was the culmination of scholarly research up to that time in American diplomatic history. In 1935 he had published *The Diplomacy of the American Revolution*, dedicating it to his friend and patron Jameson, whom he regarded as "the greatest man I ever knew personally. . . , a teacher to historians rather than a writer of great history." In the spirit of Jamesonian obligation to other scholars he worked with Grace Gardner Griffin to compile the massive, annotated *Guide to the Diplomatic History of the United States, 1775-1921*, published in 1935 by the U.S. Government Printing Office. His last major publication of this decade was *A Diplomatic History of the United States* (1936), which went through five editions over the next thirty years. The first text on American diplomatic history based on wide research in archives as well as secondary accounts, the book set a standard of accuracy and comprehensiveness for all subsequent textbooks in the field.

For all the strengths of Bemis's textbook and monographs, they, of course, had limitations. A friendly rival in the authorship of diplomatic history texts, Thomas A. Bailey, pointed out that Bemis's work was "history in the traditional style, from the vantage point of the foreign offices and chancelleries." It made little effort to explore public opinion or to analyze the great currents of economics and psychology that lie behind the actions of nations. Public opinion in foreign policy, Bemis replied, was "an interesting subject but not always significant, and often exaggerated."

Bailey's criticism is slightly unfair, for when Bemis began his work such a subdiscipline as American diplomatic history hardly existed. Without the precision of his accounts of *what* was done, subsequent historians would hardly have been able to speculate on *why* events proceeded as they did. Moreover, Bemis's work was not without a philosophical base. He recognized what many other historians who write from the perspective of a single nation often failed to see—that no one nation controls international events. The course of events proceeds from the interaction of states with differing aims and values, and what happens may be the random result of chance collisions rather than any-

one's choice. To understand this process the historian has to look at each participant's actions from that country's viewpoint, grasping the limitations and special interests that determined each government's course. Understanding, therefore, could only come from a multiarchival approach.

Another criticism of Bemis frequently voiced by students assigned his books is that his style is dull. One of Bailey's students lamented that there was "only one joke" in all of Bemis's *A Diplomatic History of the United States*, and others were surprised to hear there was even one. The "joke" is buried midway through the book in a discussion of the obscure Anglo-American controversy over fur seals in the late nineteenth century: "Amphibious is the fur seal, ubiquitous and carnivorous, uniparous, gregarious and withal polygamous," a statement conveying information about the seal that, although perfectly accurate, is entirely irrelevant to the discussion at hand. Such dry New England humor mocks the very erudition it conveys. Yet for many readers, Bemis's style, which Bailey called "prim," is more difficult than entertaining.

At times, however, Bemis's style is both accessible and charming. His description of the roles of Washington and Hamilton in drafting the famous Farewell Address is wonderfully evocative: "Of Washington were the trunk and branches of the sturdy tree. The shimmering foliage dancing and shining in the sunlight was Hamilton's." In such writing, with a combination of attractive style and precise content, Bemis showed that, for him, no fact was too minor to be checked, no thought was too unimportant to be expressed with the right word. And in that concern with precision could be a subtle, double pleasure—the sensuous roll of a perfect but obscure word ("accouplement," "irenic," "oppugnation," "lucubrations," "ominations," "estoppel") was heightened by knowing that most of those who read such words did not know their meaning.

Bemis was the unchallenged major figure in American diplomatic history by the mid-1930s, and his achievement was recognized by an invitation to join the faculty at Yale, where he taught from 1935 to 1945 as Farnam Professor of Diplomatic History, and from 1945 to retirement in 1961 as Sterling Professor of Diplomatic History and International Relations. He was an impressive teacher, his undergraduate lectures carefully staged formal performances crammed with facts but conveying broad points and moral generalizations about American foreign policy. His seminars for graduate students demanded mastery of facts and required good writing. When classes were not meeting, Bemis wrote steadily in his book-filled office, the hall door open but his ears stopped with rubber earplugs. If a student came in with a question, he would look up, remove the earplugs, listen carefully, answer the question directly, replace the earplugs, and return to work. He could be charming and warm with friends, but he was shy with strangers and had little time for small talk, especially during working hours.

At Yale Bemis broadened his approach to diplomatic history by studying naval strategy and Latin American history. For several years he served on the board of historical advisers for the navy and lectured at the National War College, the Air War College, and the Staff and Command College at Maxwell Field. After World War II he wrote a classified study, "Submarine Warfare and the State of American Defense and Diplomacy, 1915-1945." In 1937 and 1938 he traveled to several Latin American universities as Carnegie visiting professor and on his return published his lectures under the title *La Política internacional de los Estados Unidos: interpretaciones* (1939). Four years later, in 1943, he published a historical survey, *The Latin American Policy of the United States*. Although widely used, the book was often criticized by Latin American specialists as too uncritical of American policies judged as imperialistic in Latin America.

Indeed, the charge of nationalistic bias is the most serious criticism of Bemis's work in general. Undergraduates at Yale frequently referred to him as Samuel "Wave-the-Flag" Bemis, and the revisionist scholars of the 1960s often dismissed his work out of hand. Bemis was not disturbed by such attacks. He believed that when American foreign policy was measured by the same standards that scholars applied to the foreign policies of other nations, the record of the United States stood up well. American expansionism in the nineteenth century, sometimes attacked by historians as unbridled greed, he interpreted as the result of maneuvering by American diplomats among the policies of nations which were no less rapacious than the United States and whose methods frequently were less honorable. Along with preservation of the Union, he wrote, "the greatest achievement of American nationality during the nineteenth century was expansion of the nation across the empty continent. . . . It established the territorial basis of the United States as a world power and a bastion of freedom today."

Preservation of the Union and expansion of the nation were the themes of his two-volume biography of John Quincy Adams, appropriately titled *John Quincy Adams and the Foundations of American Foreign Policy* (1949), and *John Quincy Adams and the Union* (1956). He received a second Pulitzer Prize for the first volume, though he always regarded the second as his best work. His treatment of Adams's life was more topical than chronological and while extensive was not exhaustive. Bemis was one of the first scholars to have access to unpublished papers of the Adams family, and he managed to make John Quincy Adams human—no easy task. While sympathetic, Bemis's portrayal was not unreservedly flattering to the second president from Massachusetts, the man whom Bemis undoubtedly considered America's greatest secretary of state. The biography was readable and remains the best available.

Bemis always tried to be provocative in his writing, and occasionally he overstated his case. Unimpressed by arguments that the United States was constantly driven by economic pressure to expand, he dismissed the imperialism of the Spanish-American War period as "a great aberration" from the nineteenth-century American tradition which had been one of expanding the area of freedom. In the nineteenth century, he wrote, the United States had been fortunate. At its founding it had exploited the conflicts among the major European powers, and thereafter it enjoyed decades of security behind the shield of the British fleet. By the end of the nineteenth century, however, the rise of three new world powers—Germany, Japan, and the United States itself—"upset the older calculations of diplomatic astrologers and gave forth new signs and portents of great omination for the daily welfare, indeed for life and death, of hundreds of millions of people on this earth." In this new era America lost its geographical security, while its size, wealth, and strength made it the only real champion of liberty in a dangerous world. Bemis feared the nation would be unequal to this challenge, that Americans would prefer the illusory security of isolationism and the "crooning softness" of "massive self-indulgence" to the "stern discipline" required to meet communism. The dilemma, he admitted, was terrible—to stand fast in defense of liberty and perhaps lose everything in a nuclear war, or to avoid war at the risk of slavery—but "the unchanging value of our inheritance of freedom," he was convinced, must be defended.

In his work on nineteenth-century diplomacy Bemis rightly stressed issues of international law, and his explanations of these complex matters have become standard for many of the great controversies of that period. As his own experience during the torpedoing of the *Sussex* demonstrated, however, international law was less and less a restraint on nations in the twentieth century, and it was perhaps a sense of this international breakdown, together with fears about the decay of American moral fiber and his own declining health, that inclined Bemis to pessimism in his last years. In his presidential address to the American Historical Association in 1961 he urged Americans to renew their allegiance to traditional values and to reassert their "determination as a people to preserve them," but he did not seem to have much faith they would do so.

Like those of many people growing old, Bemis's attitudes became more extreme with the years. A Republican and an interpreter of present-day issues from the perspective of the nineteenth century, his attitudes were shaped by his background. A long, hard climb out of the obscurity of Alum and Worcester, up through Clark and Harvard, out to the West and back to Washington, and at last to Yale with its wealthy, sometimes superficially sophisticated students whom he did not quite understand or, as he would have put it, understood too well, all left indelible marks. Like many self-made men, he sometimes feared that leaders who had not struggled as he had would not share his fortitude in the face of adversity. His was the judgment of a man molded in a time and a nation very different from that of the mid-twentieth century. And so he feared the nation would falter; he worried that communism would win; he believed that Fidel Castro's Cuba was a threat to the huge northern republic. Vietnam came too late to concern him greatly, but there can be little doubt that he would have supported intervention as an obligation of America's leadership of the free world.

Bemis never had any doubt that history should be useful—that it ought to teach lessons to the present. But despite his growing conservatism as he aged, his most important message was not simplistically reactionary. Historians, he believed, must judge tolerantly on the basis of clear and broad moral principles applied equally to all who come under their scrutiny. It is important, he held, to do the research that would enable historians to know why other people acted as they did, but it is even more important to judge resulting national actions fairly, not holding up for the United States impossible standards of morality not expected in other nations. If he erred on the side of charity in interpreting his country's behavior, his error sprang from the same generosity that led him to accept every graduate student who ever applied for his guidance. He examined every document in every archive he could find, scrutinized every word in a student paper, demanded excellence in both national and student performance, but in the end, was charitable to all.

Other:

The American Secretaries of State and Their Diplomacy, 10 volumes, edited by Bemis (New York: Knopf, 1927-1929);

"John Jay," in *The American Secretaries of State and Their Diplomacy*, 1: 191-285;

"Thomas Jefferson," in *The American Secretaries of State and Their Diplomacy*, 2: 1-93;

Periodical Publications:

"Relations between the Vermont Separatists and Great Britain, 1789-1791," *American Historical Review*, 21 (April 1916): 547-560;

"The United States and the Abortive Armed Neutrality of 1794," *American Historical Review*, 24 (October 1918): 26-47;

"Jay's Treaty and the Northwest Boundary Gap," *American Historical Review*, 27 (April 1922): 465-484;

"The London Mission of Thomas Pinckney," *American Historical Review*, 28 (January 1923): 228-247;

"The Background of Washington's Foreign Policy," *Yale Review*, 16 (January 1927): 316-336;

"Fields for Research in the Diplomatic History of the United States to 1900," *American Historical Review*, 36 (October 1930): 68-75;

"Canada and the Peace Settlement of 1782-1783," *Canadian Historical Review*, 14 (September 1933): 265-284;

"Washington's Farewell Address: A Foreign Policy of Independence," *American Historical Review*, 39 (January 1934): 250-268;

"Franklin's Red-Line Map Was a Mitchell," by Bemis and Lawrence Martin, *New England Quarterly*, 10 (March 1937): 105-111;

"The Shifting Strategy of American Defense and Diplomacy," *Virginia Quarterly Review*, 24 (Summer 1948): 321-335;

"American Foreign Policy and the Blessings of Liberty," *American Historical Review*, 67 (January 1962): 291-305.

"Alum Pond and Walden," in *New England Galaxy*, 10 (Summer 1968): 12-18;

"Alum Pond and Walden, Part II," in *New England Galaxy*, 10 (Fall 1968): 9-13;

"Alum Pond and Walden, Part III," in *New England Galaxy*, 10 (Winter 1969): 25-36;

"The Worcester Years," in *New England Galaxy*, 11

(Fall 1969): 8-16;
"Harvard, 1913-1916," in *New England Galaxy*, 11 (Winter 1970): 10-19;
"A Worcester County Student in Wartime London and Paris," in *New England Galaxy*, 11 (Spring 1970): 15-25.

References:

Thomas A. Bailey, "The Friendly Rivals: Bemis and Bailey," *Society for Historians of American Foreign*

Relations Newsletter, 10 (March 1979): 12-17;
Russell H. Bostert and John A. DeNovo, "Samuel Flagg Bemis," *Proceedings of the Massachusetts Historical Society*, 85 (1973), pp. 117-129.

Papers:

Bemis's papers are found in the Manuscripts and Archives section of the Yale University Libraries and in the library of Albertus Magnus College, New Haven.

Albert J. Beveridge

(6 October 1862-27 April 1927)

Herbert A. Johnson
University of South Carolina

SELECTED BOOKS: *The Philippine Situation* (Washington: Government Printing Office, 1902);
The Russian Advance (New York & London: Harper & Brothers, 1903);
What is Back of the War (Indianapolis: Bobbs-Merrill, 1915);
The Life of John Marshall, 4 volumes (Boston & New York: Houghton Mifflin, 1916-1919); 2 volumes (Boston & New York: Houghton Mifflin, 1929);
Abraham Lincoln, 1809-1858, 2 volumes (Boston & New York: Houghton Mifflin, 1928; London: Gollancz, 1928); 4 volumes (Boston & New York: Houghton Mifflin, 1928).

Many Progressive era leaders combined active political careers with literary pursuits, but few met with the national acclaim that rewarded Sen. Albert Jeremiah Beveridge of Indiana. His four-volume biography of John Marshall not only won the Pulitzer Prize for biography in 1920 but has stood the test of time and remains the best biographical treatment of the chief justice.

Beveridge brought to his literary tasks a rich and varied background that served to sharpen his perceptions and grasp of life situations. Born into a Highland County, Ohio, family much "reduced in circumstances," Beveridge moved to Illinois at the age of three. He entered the work force at an early age and served in a variety of menial tasks until at fifteen he was placed in charge of a logging crew.

Before he was sixteen, however, he entered high school, and in 1881 friends lent him money to further his formal education at Asbury College (later DePauw University) in Greencastle, Indiana,

Albert J. Beveridge

where he developed talents in oratory, completed his undergraduate studies, and met the young lady, Katherine Maude Langsdale, who was to become his first wife in 1887. Even before he graduated from DePauw in 1885, Beveridge had become an active campaigner for the Republican party; he supported himself during a law clerkship through work as a reading clerk in the Republican-controlled Indiana legislature and was admitted to practice in December 1887. Presaging his interest in John Marshall, Beveridge's reputation was first established in constitutional law.

Even a busy and highly successful law practice did not dissuade Beveridge from literary activity. A member of the Indianapolis Literary Club, along with Lew Wallace, Booth Tarkington, and James Whitcomb Riley, he delivered a paper asserting that Sir Walter Raleigh had been the author of Shakespeare's plays and a subsequent paper on the materialism in Honoré de Balzac's plays. His first European trip in 1894 produced a series of articles for the *Indianapolis News*, and on occasion he was an anonymous drama critic for the same newspaper. Yet despite these literary accomplishments, it was Beveridge's oratorical and political abilities that first placed him in the public eye—at first throughout Indiana, and after 1898 all over the country—as the "prophet of imperialism."

Elected to the U.S. Senate in 1899, Beveridge was thirty-six when he began his public career, which was marked from the beginning by a deft combination of political campaigning, legislative business, and professional writing. Forced to terminate his law practice by the extended absences required by official duties, the senator found writing to be a lucrative source of financial support, and his travels and his political thought provided him with materials for popular articles and books. An investigative trip to the Philippines to explore the independence movement there, taken just prior to his assuming his duties as senator, resulted in a series of articles in the *Saturday Evening Post*. Edited by George H. Lorimer, who would thereafter become a close personal friend, the articles called for American control of the Philippines and argued that the Filipinos were incapable of self-government.

After their Philippines trip, his wife's health declined, and she died in the summer of 1900. In May 1901 he set sail for Europe, stopping briefly in Britain and Germany but traveling extensively in European and Siberian Russia. His observations were published in *The Russian Advance*, syndicated in the *Saturday Evening Post*, and published in book form in 1903. Favorably impressed with the autocratic regime in Russia and oblivious to the signs of forthcoming revolution, the senator continued his journey from Siberia into Manchuria, where he reported that Russian influence had a "civilizing" impact on the former Chinese province. In *The Russian Advance* he predicted that war would break out between Russia and Japan, but incorrectly surmised that victory would lie with the Russian Empire. Although the Manchurian portion of his journey was not to form the subject of a book, it did provide material for a series of informative articles in the *Saturday Evening Post* in 1901 and 1902.

A dozen years after the appearance of *The Russian Advance*, Beveridge turned once more to the format of political commentary and travelogue to produce *What is Back of the War* (1915), also the product of an investigatory journey, undertaken at the urging of Mark Sullivan of *Collier's* magazine. The discipline and valor of the German troops made a favorable impression on Beveridge, as did the intelligence and judgment of the political leaders of Germany and the emperor's granting him a private interview. The French authorities were less cooperative with his request for information, but he nevertheless gained access to the major figures in the French war effort and formed a favorable opinion concerning the French army. On the other hand, Beveridge was repelled by the lack of vigor displayed by the British army and its leaders and affronted by his difficulties in obtaining interviews in London. These experiences resulted in a book that was held by many to be "pro-German" in orientation, and *What is Back of the War* declined in popularity as the U.S. moved inexorably toward war with the German Empire.

After his political alignment with the Republican insurgents—Progressive Republicans who supported Roosevelt's policies—in the 1910 national party convention, Beveridge found himself increasingly at odds with his party's leadership, and he was defeated for reelection to the Senate in that year. Turning from the U.S. Senate to private life, he decided to expand his literary activities and chose as his first major project the task of writing a biography of Chief Justice John Marshall, a job made easier by his national reputation and political stature. Archivists and librarians were anxious to be of assistance; professional historians were flattered to cooperate in the former senator's research and to critique his chapter drafts. Obsessed with a fear of inaccuracy, Beveridge was meticulous in citing his sources and rechecking his references after writing was completed. His control of the scattered body of extant Marshall materials was remarkable, and his writing practices insured that the best minds in the nation were given an opportunity to comment on his drafts. His critics included constitutional historians Edward S. Corwin of Princeton and Max Farrand of Yale and early American history specialists Samuel Eliot Morison of Harvard, William E. Dodd of the University of Chicago, Charles A. Beard of Columbia, and J. Franklin Jameson of the Carnegie Institution of Washington.

Although Beveridge benefited greatly from the suggestions of these academic readers, his biography retains the undeniable mark of his original approach to biographical writing. Striving to portray Marshall's character, he wove into his narrative a mass of information concerning the personality of the chief justice; at the same time he felt it essential that Marshall be presented to readers against the historical background necessary to explain his jurisprudence and career. Against the advice of Jameson and other draft critics he included an extensive discussion of the French Revolution in his second-volume treatment of the XYZ affair. On the other hand, the chapter on the case of *Marbury* v. *Madison*, vitally important in enunciating the doctrine of judicial review, was rewritten following the suggestions of Corwin and others.

Completing the first two volumes of the Marshall biography in 1916, Beveridge had them published under a contract secured in part by the recommendation of William E. Dodd. Although Dodd had been repelled by the senator's anti-Jefferson bias and frustrated when Beveridge failed to take corrective steps when this was pointed out to him, Dodd nevertheless thought so highly of the two volumes that he recommended to Houghton Mifflin that they undertake publication of the full four-volume set. On the other hand, Dodd declined to participate in Beveridge's writing ventures after the appearance of the last Marshall volume, and his name does not appear among the prepublication readers of the Lincoln biography.

The first two volumes of the Marshall biography and their companion pair published in 1919 received reviews ranging from sharply critical to wildly adulatory. The senator was pleased with the unanticipated volume of sales, which he aided through public appearances and various promotional activities; the ultimate mark of his success was being awarded the 1920 Pulitzer Prize for biography. On the other hand, adverse criticism troubled him and strained certain relationships. A review by Princeton historian Thomas Jefferson Wertenbaker, accusing him of tailoring events of the past to accord with his own preconceived ideas and prejudices, unnerved Beveridge, and he suspected constitutional historian Edward S. Corwin of having urged his junior colleague to make the attack. He was less suspicious of the adverse review by the University of Chicago's constitutional historian, Andrew C. McLaughlin, who had harsh comments to make about Beveridge's treatment of constitutional cases and his blatant anti-Jeffersonian bias. In this instance Beveridge contented himself with writing McLaughlin's senior colleague, William E. Dodd, and expressing the opinion that McLaughlin's review would do more harm to the reviewer's reputation than it would to the status of the author.

An adverse interpretation of Jefferson is by no means the only mark of Beveridge's personality and firmly held opinions. The extended essay on the French Revolution, inserted in the second volume to provide "background" by the author, serves also to show the desirability of neutrality in American foreign relations. Like John Marshall in his biography of George Washington, Beveridge used the vehicle of biography to state his political opinions; also like the chief justice, he was inclined to extensive diversion from the narrative into a heavy interlarding of "background" material. Despite numerous suggestions that this extraneous detail be eliminated, Beveridge clung to the position that readers who were unskilled in history and constitutional law would require more than mere biographical detail if they were to truly understand the chief justice. Because of Beveridge's insistence on this approach, the biography is an invaluable guide to the constitutional development of the U.S. from 1801 through 1835; on the other hand, the "times" of Chief Justice Marshall often tend to overshadow his "life."

A theme that predominates throughout the biography is Marshall's nationalism; in retrospect it seems quite clear that Beveridge's own broad view of American imperial destiny and his fervent dedication to national greatness sharply altered his views concerning Marshall. Despite his service in the American Revolution and his work with George Washington and other Federalists to form a stronger central government, Marshall retained a Virginian's deep affection for his state and its people. Those emotional ties to his native state were reflected in his jurisprudence, which always maintained a respectful balance between the newly established powers of the federal government and the more extensive reserved powers of the states. Marshall's nationalism, unlike that of Beveridge, was the result of a sober judgment that coordination among the states was the only sound basis for economic prosperity and national survival. By way of contrast Beveridge's nationalist sentiments were derived from an expanded view of the place of the American republic in world affairs, and its goals extended well beyond the modest aim of the chief justice.

Another noteworthy but questionable emphasis in the Marshall biography is the stress on Marshall as the product of the frontier. Fauquier County, Virginia, was sparsely settled during the chief justice's boyhood, but the Marshall family was among the leading gentry of that county, as evidenced by Marshall's father's serving as sheriff. It was his father, Col. Thomas Marshall, who moved to Kentucky after the Revolution, leaving his lawyer son in Richmond to handle the family transactions in Kentucky land grants and military half-pay certificates. By way of contrast to his pioneer father, John Marshall developed a taste for dancing assemblies, fine wines, and social clubs. His Richmond residence was well decorated and staffed with about ten Negro house slaves. While it is true that Marshall's mannerisms were simple and unassuming, it is assuming too much to attribute this to "frontier influence."

Despite these interjections of Senator Beveridge's individual preferences into the character of the chief justice, his Marshall biography remains the definitive one. Leonard Baker's 1975 effort lacks the political perception that Beveridge brought to his study, and the analysis of the constitutional law decisions is not as sharp and cogent as it is in Beveridge's study. By way of contrast, Edward Corwin's study of Marshall's constitutional thought appears to be a disembodied intellectual sketch of the great chief justice, as does the definitive monograph on Marshall's jurisprudence written by Robert K. Faulkner and published in 1973. For balance, comprehensiveness, and empathetic biographical treatment, Beveridge's work is yet to be surpassed.

The sweep of international events and domestic politics gradually drew Beveridge back into the whirlpool of public life, particularly after rejoining the Republican party in 1916. Yet political preferment eluded him, and in 1922 he began work on a biography of Abraham Lincoln, his boyhood hero. In dealing with the life of the Great Emancipator, Beveridge was both blessed and plagued by a superabundance of material. Unlike the very small amount of original Marshall material, there was a vast quantity of documentation on Lincoln. And of course he had decided to follow the pattern

of the Marshall biography, setting Lincoln against the background of his times and providing readers with enough detail of local, national, and world history that they might bring the right perceptions to bear upon the career of the president. For Beveridge, the book may well have afforded an opportunity to look back on his own colorful and varied career. For example, he spends some time in a pleasant retelling of Lincoln's Springfield literary circle that seems to parallel Beveridge's early literary contacts and activities in Indianapolis.

If the Lincoln biography shared the strengths of the Marshall work, it also suffered from the same lack of focus that caused critics to complain of the Marshall study. Overarching these literary shortcomings, the principal reaction to the first half of the Lincoln biography, published posthumously in 1928, was strong objection to its "pro-southern" viewpoint. In retrospect, it is clear that Beveridge was strongly influenced by the "plantation school" of Southern historians of slavery. Led by Ulrich B. Phillips, these writers viewed the institution of slavery as a benign and necessary labor system, stressing its humanitarianism and deemphasizing its brutality. In addition, Beveridge's acceptance of Abraham Lincoln's attitude toward matters of race and his rejection of the extremism of the abolitionists led him into what might well be considered a "pro-southern" interpretation. His admiration for the courage and determination of the South, hinted at in the first half of the Lincoln biography, might also have led him to an undue sympathy for the Southern cause. On the other hand, the book as published is certainly neither an apologia for slavery nor an argument for sectionalism.

Unfortunately, Senator Beveridge did not live to complete his monumental biography of Abraham Lincoln. The first half of the text was being completed at the time of his death in April 1927. While it reads well and doubtless indicates his views at that particular stage in the development of the manuscript, we can never be certain that some further work might not have modified Beveridge's views or resulted in a shortening of some of the tangential passages. What is patently clear is that even in its unfinished version, the Lincoln biography is a worthy sequel to the great biography of Chief Justice Marshall.

Without the intervention of an active political career, Albert J. Beveridge might well have become one of the foremost men of letters in his day. Yet it was the conjunction of his experience as a practical politician and his perceptions as a research scholar that brought distinction to his pen. For example, his deft discussion of Lincoln's melancholia is well balanced and nonjudgmental. A lesser writer might well have treated the psychological aspects of the Lincoln biography in a more flamboyant manner. Long experience had taught Beveridge that statesmen were to be judged by their accomplishments and not to be belabored for their human frailties. The senator wrote biography as he had lived his political career, with a sense of pride and satisfaction in the progress of his nation, and with a deep love and affection for the American people and their leaders.

References:

Claude G. Bowers, *Beveridge and the Progressive Era* (Boston: Houghton Mifflin, 1932);

John Braeman, *Albert J. Beveridge: American Nationalist* (Chicago & London: University of Chicago Press, 1971).

Papers:

The major collection of Senator Beveridge's papers is at the Manuscript Division, Library of Congress, Washington, D.C.

Herbert E. Bolton
(20 July 1870-30 January 1953)

Amy Bushnell
Historic St. Augustine Preservation Board

SELECTED BOOKS: *Guide to Materials for the History of the United States in the Principal Archives of Mexico* (Washington, D.C.: Carnegie Institution of Washington, 1913);

Texas in the Middle Eighteenth Century: Studies in Spanish Colonial History and Administration (Berkeley: University of California Press, 1915);

The Colonization of North America, 1492-1783, by Bolton and Thomas Maitland Marshall (New York: Macmillan, 1920);

The Spanish Borderlands: A Chronicle of Old Florida and the Southwest (New Haven: Yale University Press, 1921);

California's Story, by Bolton and Ephraim Douglass Adams (Boston & New York: Allyn & Bacon, 1922);

The Debatable Land: A Sketch of the Anglo-Spanish Contest for the Georgia Country, by Bolton and Mary Ross (Berkeley: University of California Press, 1925);

Palóu and His Writings (Berkeley: University of California Press, 1926);

History of the Americas: A Syllabus with Maps (Boston & New York: Ginn, 1928);

Outpost of Empire: The Story of the Founding of San Francisco (New York: Knopf, 1931);

The Padre on Horseback: A Sketch of Eusebio Francisco Kino, S.J., Apostle to the Pimas (San Francisco: Sonora Press, 1932);

Cross, Sword, and Gold Pan (Los Angeles: Primavera Press, 1936);

Rim of Christendom: A Biography of Eusebio Francisco

Herbert E. Bolton, late 1930s

Kino, Pacific Coast Pioneer (New York: Macmillan, 1936);

Wider Horizons of American History (New York & London: Appleton-Century, 1939);

Coronado on the Turquoise Trail, Knight of Pueblos and Plains (Albuquerque: University of New Mexico Press, 1949); published simultaneously as *Coronado, Knight of Pueblos and Plains* (New York: Whittlesey House, 1949);

Bolton and the Spanish Borderlands, edited by John Francis Bannon (Norman: University of Oklahoma Press, 1964).

Herbert Eugene Bolton's chief contributions to historical literature were in a field of his own making: the "Spanish Borderlands" of Northern New Spain and Florida, which had been neglected by United States and Latin American historians alike. Frequently ranked with Frederick Jackson Turner and Walter Prescott Webb as a historian of the American frontier, Bolton was equally at home on the Spanish-American one and believed that a complete history of either hemisphere must investigate Spain's empire in North America.

Herbert Eugene Bolton was born to Edwin L. and Rosaline Cady Bolton on a farm in Wisconsin, a background to which he credited his hardy constitution. At the University of Wisconsin, where he received his bachelor of letters degree in 1895, he studied under Frederick Jackson Turner but did not find his own métier. He did not find it at the University of Pennsylvania either, where his dissertation topic was "The Free Negro in the South before the Civil War" and where he received the Ph.D. degree in 1899. Nor did he discover his calling at Milwaukee State Teachers College, where he did his first two years of teaching.

It was at the University of Texas (to which he moved in 1901), while editing the state historical quarterly, that Bolton discovered his own frontier and set himself to learn Spanish in order to explore it. It was a happy discovery, and he spent the next half-century engrossed in work: supervising copyists during the summers in Mexican archives, lecturing to large classes, writing or translating until midnight nearly every night, and then going to bed with his work on the nightstand. For Bolton, as for his conquistadores and mission-founding friars, only heroic effort was good enough. Even his holidays were strenuous, and likely to be spent on muleback, document in hand, retracing some long-lost trail. One wonders how Gertrude Janes Bolton, whom he had married in 1895, coped with her single-minded scholar as she ran a house and raised seven children.

Bolton's first published translations, in Emma Blair and James Robertson's collection *The Philippine Islands, 1493-1803* (1903-1909), gave him practice in Spanish and welcome supplements to a small salary, as did his first book, *With the Makers of Texas: A Source Reader in Texas History* (1904), a high-school work coedited with his friend Eugene C. Barker. In 1908 in the *American Historical Review* he had published the papers Spanish authorities had seized from the American officer and explorer Zebulon Montgomery Pike. He also wrote and was paid for more than a hundred short articles on Indian tribes of Texas and Louisiana for the *Handbook of American Indians North of Mexico* (1907-1910). Meanwhile, Bolton reported his archival findings steadily to the *Texas State Historical Association Quarterly* and its successor, the *Southwestern Historical Quarterly*, in articles he would later round up as *Texas in the Middle Eighteenth Century: Studies in Spanish Colonial History and Administration* (1915).

His pioneering work in Mexico received national recognition when the Department of Historical Research of the Carnegie Institution asked Bolton to calendar certain materials in the Mexican archives with the object of preparing a guide. The year 1907-1908 was a splendid one for Bolton, on leave from Texas and with a commission from the institution to compile the guide; it was perhaps less so for Gertrude, living on Avenida Tabasco in Mexico City with five active little girls, none in school. *Guide to Materials for the History of the United States in the Principal Archives of Mexico* (1913) is a monumental work, wider in scope than its title, and nearly seventy years after its publication, it has yet to be superseded. But Bolton did not confine his interests to the guide. In Mexico he was uncovering important documents, and one of his chief concerns was to get those unknown "relaciones" translated and published. With the Arthur H. Clark Company, which was publishing the Philippine series, he projected an ambitious, multivolume "Documentary Sources of American History from the Spanish and Mexican Archives." He found it easier to plan than to complete it. Pressured by other commitments, Bolton sent his publisher only two completed "relaciones" in ten years: *Athanase de Mézières and the Louisiana-Texas Frontier, 1768-1780* (two volumes, 1914) and *Kino's Historical Memoir of Pimería Alta* (two volumes, 1919).

Shortly after his return from Mexico, Bolton agreed to move to Stanford University in California, where he would be able to teach courses in Western America and the Spanish Southwest. During his two years at Stanford (1909-1911), he devoted himself to course preparations and books already in progress. There was only one new commitment, to the Scribners series "Original Narratives of Early American History" to supply a companion to their 1907 volume of readings from the narratives of Cabeza de Vaca, Coronado and de Soto. Bolton's *Spanish Exploration in the Southwest, 1542-1706* (1916), with readings from the narratives of Oñate, Vizcaíno, Kino, and other little-known explorers, received admiring reviews.

There was a gentlemen's agreement between the California universities in the early 1900s not to pirate each other's professors, but it was becoming obvious that Berkeley, home of the Bancroft Collection of Spanish documentary materials, was Bolton's proper place. In a candid letter to his brother Frederick he explained why he was going there: "Stanford is a comfortable place, but Stanford has no policy." He believed the professorship in American history at Berkeley to be "the academic position in history of most influence west of the Mississippi." Bolton went to Berkeley in 1911 and entered his full scholarly stride, which was an energetic, uncompromising one. "Unless I use my vacations for work I will never get anything done," he wrote to a friend who had looked for him at a convention. "The whole profession makes a great mistake by too much 'associating.'. . . This is one of the reasons why American scholars do not produce more work." To this rule he would make an exception if the Southwest were on the program. When the American Historical Association met in San Francisco, Bolton not only read two papers but coedited the proceedings of the meeting with Henry Morse Stephens as *The Pacific Ocean in History* (1917). The next year he was elected to the AHA Council, a position which he used to help launch the *Hispanic American Historical Review*, known to three generations of Latin Americanists as "the Ha-Har."

At Berkeley, Bolton received a good deal of recognition. In 1916 he was made curator of the Bancroft Library. The next year the Academic Senate chose him to give the annual Charter Day lecture in which he presented one of his most enduring studies, "The Mission as a Frontier Institution in the Spanish-American Colonies." That same year Bolton assumed chairmanship of the history department. In spite of these responsibilities, he did not reduce his teaching schedule nor his publications; for Bolton, the two were synergistic. His upper-division course in Western America resulted in a text, *The Colonization of North America, 1492-1783* (1920), written with Thomas Maitland Marshall, the first of his "boys" to finish a doctorate. They meant to write two volumes, but the second was never finished. Bolton's most popular course, "History of the Americas," was not merely continental in scope, but hemispheric. It treated the Americas as a whole, the way one studied the history of Europe. He was urged to write a textbook, and meant to, but all that reached publication were his syllabus and invaluable maps in 1928. Another spin-off from his courses was the text *California's Story* (1922), written with an old Stanford colleague, Ephraim Douglass Adams.

Bolton was proud of his narrative style; he dreamed of popularizing the Spanish presence in North America the way Parkman had the French, and with this in mind he volunteered a volume for the Yale Chronicles of America series oriented to the general reader. He was chagrined when an editor was assigned to remove some of the detail and liven his style. The title chosen, *The Spanish Borderlands: A Chronicle of Old Florida and the Southwest* (1921), marks the first application of the term "Borderlands" to areas once Spanish. He used it again in the reflective essay "Defensive Spanish Expansion and the Significance of the Borderlands."

Bolton followed up his first foray into the Florida-Georgia region with *Arredondo's Historical Proof of Spain's Title to Georgia* (1925), a translation, and *The Debatable Land: A Sketch of the Anglo-Spanish Contest for the Georgia Country* (1925), written with Mary Ross, one of his "girls" (though he generally discouraged women from becoming historians since there were so few teaching positions in women's colleges). Bolton was semiapologetic about extending his range into the Southeast. To his old mentor Frederick Jackson Turner he wrote: "Some persons might get the impression that in this book I have roamed a long way from my proper habitat. But you, of course, will know that just as your American frontier ran north and south as a unit, so my Spanish frontier ran east and west, from ocean to ocean, and was a unit."

In theory this was true; in fact, Bolton was not greatly interested in the eastern end of his long frontier and soon turned his attention back to the West Coast. A San Francisco attorney, Sidney Ehrman, underwrote the expense of a series of translations: *Historical Memoirs of New California, By Fray Francisco Palóu, O.F.M.* (four volumes, 1926), with an introduction separately published as *Palóu and His Writings* (1926); *Fray Juan Crespi, Missionary Explorer on the Pacific Coast, 1769-1774* (1927); and *Anza's California Expeditions* (five volumes, 1930), part of which was separately published as *Font's Complete Diary* (1931). The introduction to *Anza's*

California Expeditions, published as *Outpost of Empire* (1931), was chosen by the Commonwealth Club of San Francisco as the finest book of the year by a California author. While doing the California translations, Bolton published short pieces of general appeal in the magazine *Touring Topics*, pieces later gathered in *Cross, Sword, and Gold Pan* (1936).

Of all the explorers whose paths Bolton had followed, he was most attracted to Father Kino. A trip Bolton took to Europe in 1931 was like a pilgrimage: he journeyed to Tyrol, where Kino was born; to Bavaria, where he received his training; to Holland to find more of his letters. Bolton first wrote a short sketch of his favorite Jesuit, *The Padre on Horseback: A Sketch of Eusebio Francisco Kino, S.J., Apostle to the Pimas* (1932). He went from him to other Jesuits, writing "The Black Robes of New Spain" in 1934 for presentation to the American Catholic Historical Association. Then he returned to Kino for a full-length study, *Rim of Christendom: A Biography of Eusebio Francisco Kino, Pacific Coast Pioneer* (1936), in many ways Bolton's finest piece of work. The research and writing of it were described in a delightful short article, "Archives and Trails." *Rim of Christendom*, like *Outpost of Empire*, was honored by the Commonwealth Club.

Bolton eventually reaped the fruits of a long and diligent career. The king of Spain knighted him in 1925; universities gave him honorary degrees; at Berkeley he was named to the history department's only endowed chair, the Sather Professorship, in 1931. His graduates, the "Bolton school," numbered in the hundreds. The earlier ones presented him with one festschrift, or *homenaje, New Spain and the Anglo-American West* (1932), and the later ones with another, *Greater America* (1945). In 1932 the historical profession honored him with the presidency of the Amerian Historical Association.

For his presidential address in Toronto, Bolton read "The Epic of Greater America," a condensed version of the History of the Americas course he had been teaching for years. It has been reprinted often, notably with his more thoughtful essays, "The Mission as a Frontier Institution," "Defensive Spanish Expansion," and "The Black Robes of New Spain," as *Wider Horizons of American History* (1939). It has been translated into Spanish, and most recently it was reprinted along with less available articles by Bolton's biographer John Francis Bannon in *Bolton and the Spanish Borderlands* (1964). The two themes of "The Epic of Greater America" are, as in most of Bolton's works, that the Spanish past is an essential part of U.S. history and that it is useful to take a broad look at the hemisphere. Bol-

ton was often imagined to be saying that the two Americas have a common history—something he did not propose, but which was roundly rejected nevertheless by U.S. and Latin American historians alike as the "Bolton thesis."

At the age of seventy Bolton was mandatorily retired. Lecture tours and other projects occupied him for awhile; still, he was not sorry to be called back to Berkeley when war broke out. Teaching, he said, had always been his favorite sport. He was retired again in 1944 and busied himself tracing the Coronado and Escalante routes for the National Park Service—a strenuous form of research, done largely on horseback. Two final books were the outcome: a translation, *Pageant in the Wilderness: The Story of the Escalante Expedition to the Interior Basin* (1950), and a narrative history, *Coronado on the Turquoise Trail, Knight of Pueblos and Plains* (1949). The Coronado story, pleasantly readable, won the George Bancroft Prize in 1950 and was also a History Club selection for that year.

In 1952 Bolton suffered a stroke; the twentieth century faded about him, and in his mind he lived among his beloved Spaniards until his death months later. His dream of integrating the Spanish Borderlands with American colonial history has not come about. In elementary schools, high schools, and colleges across the nation, the history of the United States continues to be taught as the "Advance of the Anglos." The successors to Bolton have divided into historians of the Southwest and the Southeast, rarely looking across the Mississippi to the other end of the Borderlands and utterly renouncing Bolton's quixotic effort to see both American continents at once.

Other:

With the Makers of Texas: A Source Reader in Texas History, edited by Bolton and Eugene C. Barker (New York: American Book, 1904);

Contributions to *Handbook of American Indians North of Mexico*, edited by Frederick Webb Hodge, 2 parts (Washington, D.C.: U.S. Government Printing Office, 1907-1910);

Spanish Exploration in the Southwest, 1542-1706, edited by Bolton (New York: Scribners, 1916);

The Pacific Ocean in History, edited by Bolton and Henry Morse Stephens (New York: Macmillan, 1917);

"Defensive Spanish Expansion and the Significance of the Borderlands," in *The Trans-Mississippi West*, edited by James Field Willard and Colin Brummitt Goodykoontz (Boulder: University of Colorado, 1930), pp. 1-42.

Translations:

Translations in volumes 5, 6, 18, and 19 of *The Philippine Islands, 1493-1803*, edited by Emma Helen Blair and James Alexander Robertson, 55 volumes (Cleveland: Arthur H. Clark, 1903-1909);

Athanase de Mézières and the Louisiana-Texas Frontier, 1768-1780, 2 volumes (Cleveland: Arthur H. Clark, 1914);

Kino's Historical Memoir of Pimería Alta: A Contemporary Account of the Beginnings of California, Sonora, and Arizona, by Father Eusebio Francisco Kino, S.J., Pioneer Missionary, Explorer, Cartographer, and Ranchman, 1683-1711, 2 volumes (Cleveland: Arthur H. Clark, 1919);

Arredondo's Historical Proof of Spain's Title to Georgia: A Contribution to the History of One of the Spanish Borderlands (Berkeley: University of California Press, 1925);

Historical Memoirs of New California, By Fray Francisco Palóu, O.F.M., 4 volumes (Berkeley: University of California Press, 1926);

Fray Juan Crespi, Missionary Explorer on the Pacific Coast, 1769-1774 (Berkeley: University of California Press, 1927);

Anza's California Expeditions, 5 volumes (Berkeley: University of California Press, 1930);

Font's Complete Diary: A Chronicle of the Founding of San Francisco (Berkeley: University of California Press, 1931);

Pageant in the Wilderness: The Story of the Escalante Expedition to the Interior Basin, Including the Diary and Itinerary of Father Escalante (Salt Lake City: Utah State Historical Society, 1950).

Periodical Publications:

"Papers of Zebulon M. Pike, 1806-1807," *American Historical Review*, 13 (July 1908): 798-827;

"The Mission as a Frontier Institution in the Spanish American Colonies," *American Historical Review*, 23 (October 1917): 42-61;

"The Epic of Greater America," *American Historical Review*, 38 (April 1933): 448-474;

"The Black Robes of New Spain," *Catholic Historical Review*, 21 (October 1935): 257-282;

"Archives and Trails," *California Monthly*, 37 (October 1936): 19, 40-42.

References:

John Francis Bannon, *Herbert Eugene Bolton: The Historian and the Man, 1870-1953* (Tucson: University of Arizona Press, 1978);

John W. Caughey, "Herbert Eugene Bolton," in *Turner, Bolton, and Webb: Three Historians of the American Frontier*, by Wilbur R. Jacobs, John W. Caughey, and Joe B. Frantz (Seattle & London: University of Washington Press, 1965);

George P. Hammond, ed., *New Spain and the Anglo-American West: Historical Contributions Presented to Herbert Eugene Bolton*, 2 volumes (Los Angeles: Privately printed, 1932);

Lewis Hanke, ed., *Do the Americas Have a Common History? A Critique of the Bolton Theory* (New York: Knopf, 1964);

Adele Ogden, ed., *Greater America: Essays in Honor of Herbert Eugene Bolton* (Berkeley: University of California Press, 1945).

Papers:

Bolton's papers are at the Bancroft Library of the University of California at Berkeley.

Daniel J. Boorstin

Frank Annunziata
Rochester Institute of Technology

BIRTH: Atlanta, Georgia, 1 October 1914, to Samuel Aaron and Dora Olsan Boorstin.

EDUCATION: A.B., Harvard University, 1934; B.A., Oxford University, 1936; B.C.L., Oxford University, 1937; J.S.D., Yale University, 1940.

MARRIAGE: 9 April 1941 to Ruth Carolyn Frankel; children: Paul Terry, Jonathan, David West.

AWARDS AND HONORS: Bancroft Prize for *The Americans: The Colonial Experience*, 1959; Francis Parkman Prize for *The Americans: The National Experience*, 1966; Litt.D., Cambridge University, 1968; Pulitzer Prize for History for *The Americans: The Democratic Experience*, 1974.

SELECTED BOOKS: *The Mysterious Science of the Law* (Cambridge, Mass.: Harvard University Press, 1941);
The Lost World of Thomas Jefferson (New York: Holt, 1948);
The Genius of American Politics (Chicago: University of Chicago Press, 1953);
The Americans: The Colonial Experience (New York: Random House, 1958; Harmondsworth, U.K.: Penguin, 1965);
America and the Image of Europe: Reflections on American Thought (Cleveland: World, 1960);
The Image, or What Happened to the American Dream (New York: Atheneum, 1962; London: Weidenfeld & Nicolson, 1962); republished as *The Image: A Guide to Pseudo-events in America* (New York: Harper & Row, 1964);
The Americans: The National Experience (New York: Random House, 1965; London: Weidenfeld & Nicolson, 1966);
The Decline of Radicalism: Reflections on America Today (New York: Random House, 1969);
The Americans: The Democratic Experience (New York: Random House, 1973);
Democracy and Its Discontents: Reflections on Everyday America (New York: Random House, 1974);
The Exploring Spirit: America and the World, Then and Now (New York: Random House, 1976; London: BBC, 1976).

Daniel J. Boorstin

Daniel Joseph Boorstin, leading exponent of the "consensus" view of American history and institutions, was born on 1 October 1914 in Atlanta, Georgia. By the time he was two his father, Samuel Aaron Boorstin, a lawyer, and his mother, Dora Olsan Boorstin, had moved to Tulsa, Oklahoma. In this burgeoning Southwestern city still redolent of frontier experiences, his family prospered. His father, who had been brought to America as a child by his Russian-Jewish parents, was a self-made man who worked his way through the University of Georgia, practiced law in Atlanta, and then became a "booster" of Tulsa.

After graduating first in his class at age fifteen from Tulsa Central High School in 1930, Boorstin enrolled as a liberal arts undergraduate at Harvard University. There he majored in English history and literature (one of his teachers being F. O. Matthiessen) and was an editor of the undergraduate

79

daily the *Crimson*. His senior honors essay on Edward Gibbon's *History of the Decline and Fall of the Roman Empire* won the Bowdoin Prize. In 1934 he received his B.A. degree summa cum laude and accepted a Rhodes Scholarship to study law at Balliol College, Oxford University. During the next three and a half years, he read law at the Inner Temple in London and earned Oxford's most prestigious academic accolade—a double first—when awarded a B.A. in jurisprudence in 1936 and a B.C.L. (bachelor of civil laws) in 1937. Boorstin was called to the English bar in 1937 as a barrister-at-law. "My three and a half years abroad were divided equally between trying to fit into the aristocratic life of Oxford and on vacation enjoying the bohemian vagrancy of the Continental Left Banks," he has recalled. For a time he considered settling in England but decided to return to the United States.

Upon returning, Boorstin spent the 1937-1938 academic year on a Sterling Fellowship at the Yale Law School and the next four years teaching a course in legal history at Harvard and courses in American history and literature at Radcliffe and Harvard. Yale awarded him a doctor of juridical science (J.S.D.) in 1940, and the next year Harvard University Press published his first book, *The Mysterious Science of the Law*. In 1942 he was admitted to the Massachusetts bar.

During World War II Boorstin worked briefly for the lend-lease administration and then taught at Swarthmore College. In October of 1944 President Robert Maynard Hutchins of the University of Chicago hired him for a new interdisciplinary social sciences program. For the next twenty-five years, until his appointment in 1969 as director of the National Museum of History and Technology of the Smithsonian Institution in Washington, Boorstin was on the Chicago faculty. In 1966 he was appointed to an endowed chair, the Morton Professorship of History, and in 1968 he was designated a distinguished service professor, the university's highest honor.

To understand the historical writing of Daniel J. Boorstin, one must begin with Europe. It was the émigré experiences of his four Russian-Jewish grandparents and his own study and living in Europe which made a heavy impress upon his intellectual temperament and orientation. Indeed, Boorstin's eloquent and compelling descriptions and celebrations of the distinctive features of American life have emerged from a single, original animating question—how has our image of Europe affected Americans' conceptions of themselves? For Boorstin the key to understanding America involves a consideration of our relationship with Europe: "the image of Europe has given us our bearings, and yet how un-European is the framework of our life and the pattern of our history: for example, the way we think of neighboring countries, the role of our intellectuals, the style of our historical monuments, the character of our political leadership, and the sources of our discontent. I have been surprised to discover how difficult it still is to describe our uniqueness except by reference to Europe."

Boorstin's first book, *The Mysterious Science of the Law* (1941), is an in-depth analysis of the background of Sir William Blackstone's *Commentaries on the Laws of England* (1765-1769). Boorstin maintains that England, guided by experience and cautiously adjusting reason and values to custom, evolved into a nation with a harmonious balance between apposite actual law and natural law—an organic relationship fusing what was with what ought to be, the real with the ideal.

In his next book, *The Lost World of Thomas Jefferson* (1948), a study of Jefferson's intellectual environment, Boorstin asserted that a juxtaposition of culture and barbarism—the Bible in the wilderness—was crucial to understanding American experiences, attitudes, and way of life. Eighteenth-century Americans, with Jefferson as prototype, had forged a practical, nonperfectionist philosophy. Their legacy to future generations was not a new philosophical conception or metaphysical system or political theory, but rather a habitual subordination of reflection, speculation, and contemplation to the intuitive, the practical, and the concrete, as was demanded by the necessities of the New World environment: "By admiring the universe as the complete and perfected work of divine artifice, by idealizing process and activity as themselves the end of life, the Jeffersonian was insisting that the values by which the universe was to be assessed were somehow implicit in nature. All facts were endowed with an ambiguous quality: they became normative as well as descriptive."

Although its direction was anticipated in earlier works, *The Genius of American Politics* (1953) was the first Boorstin book with an expansive thesis on the American experience. The animating insight he had offered in his two earlier books was compressed to a formulaic expression: "givenness." "Givenness is the belief [of Americans] that values in America are in some way or other automatically defined: given by certain facts of geography or history peculiar to us." "Givenness" contains three ideas: our values are "a gift from the past"; they are also "from the present"; and "a belief in the continuity or homogeneity of our history. It is the quality of our experience which makes us see our national past as an uninterrupted continuum of similar events so that our past merges indistinguishably into our present." Therefore, "the American is . . . prepared to find in all experience—in his history and his geography, in his past and his present— proof for his conviction that he is equipped with a hierarchy of values, a political theory." Boorstin submitted that "givenness" reveals America's belief that we can find the normative in the descriptive

Boorstin in the study at his Cleveland Park home

rather than in the theoretical, which is why there is the recurrent tendency in American history to identify the "is" with the "ought," to think of values and a theory of society as implicit in facts about society. This "givenness" of belief is in contrast to the a priori ideologies of Europe and is hostile to conflict and conducive to accommodation. American political parties refused to divide on class or ideological lines—they gravitated toward the center, they modulated rather than emphasized divisive issues, a virtue in a world torn apart by ideology. America possessed "a sense for the 'seamlessness' of experience. Aspects of experience which are elsewhere sharply distinguished here seem to merge into each other: the private and the public, the religious and the political, even . . . the 'is' and the 'ought,' the world of fact and the world of fancy, of science and of morals." Seamlessness has both a spatial and a temporal dimension because "to us institutions have appeared as a natural continuum with the non-institutional environment and the historical past."

The Genius of American Politics contains virtually all of the ideas which inform Boorstin's subsequent work. One of the predominant themes is praise for our American avoidance of "extravagant and presumptuous speculations," for the "marvelous success and vitality of our institutions," and for the amazing poverty and inarticulateness of our theorizing about politics." Having no blueprints for remaking society, we had an unrevolutionary "revolution without dogma," according to Boorstin, and a Civil War which, paradoxically, signified continuity because it did not result in any substantive recasting of our institutions.

"Givenness" explained our traditionalism, pragmatism, and adaptiveness. Linked with the concepts of space and security, economic abundance, national character, and moderate two-party politics, it came to be seen as a persuasive case for the existence of a Lockean liberal consensus in America. Boorstin's judgments on the "implicitness" or self-evident character of American ideals cast him as de Tocqueville redivivus—a proponent of the theme of "American exceptionalism" to the common pattern of history. Seen in world perspective, the conflicts in American history shrunk to insignificance and the important aspect was the overwhelming continuity and consensus.

Some historians attacked Boorstin for having contrived an artificial unity and an excessively cheerful and frustratingly complacent characterization of American life. Where were the poverty and oppression, tension and conflict, dissent and

Daniel and Ruth Boorstin

dissatisfaction, angry and alienated intellectuals? Boorstin's history, said John P. Diggins, had "no wise and courageous losers, no agonizing second thoughts about might-have-beens, no brooding over historical alternatives to the given. What happened, happened; those who survived, survived."

In 1958 the first volume of Boorstin's trilogy appeared. *The Americans: The Colonial Experience* aspired to discern and describe the distinctive features of the American past. It reflected an elegant and erudite historical intelligence, a captivating narrative style, a provocative set of theses, and a daring and original exploration of everyday life in America. In its use of aphorism, telling detail, compelling anecdotes, and reflective generalization, *The Colonial Experience* demonstrated that Boorstin's view of the American past encompassed a decided shift in accepted historical assessments. With imaginative conclusions and ingenious illustrations he depicted the essential lineaments of colonial civilization. "The colonies were a disproving ground for utopias. . . . Dreams made in Europe . . . were dissipated or transformed by the American reality. A new civilization was being born less out of plans and purposes than out of the· unsettlement which the New World brought to the ways of the Old." The Puritans of Massachusetts and the planters of Virginia were equally characterized by realistic alteration of their European preconceptions to the environmental constraints of the "howling wilderness." Throughout his account Boorstin linked the

colonists' unreflective, unplanned, anti-ideological mastery of their challenges with their maturity as self-confident settlers ultimately transformed into responsible revolutionaries claiming their new place in a new world. The book was awarded Columbia University's Bancroft Prize for books in American history, diplomacy, and international relations in 1959.

The Americans: The National Experience (1965) introduced some new illustrations of the American theme—technological innovators; upstart boosters endlessly promoting their growth schemes; the varied forms of American community; and the special, non-European features of American speech, law, architecture, and government. Boorstin eschewed conventional history for the significant, previously unremarked social adaptations. His heroes were the New Englanders who figured out how to ship and sell ice to Europe and Asia, the promoters who turned wildernesses into boom towns, the inventors of condensed milk and the Pullman car. America prospered, in Boorstin's judgment, "not from the perfection of its ways but from their fluidity. It lived with the constant belief that something else or something better might turn up. A by-product of looking for ways of living together was a new civilization whose strength was less an idealism than a willingness to be satisfied with less than the ideal. Americans were glad enough to keep things growing and moving. When before had men put so much faith in the unexpected?"

Boorstin viewed America as an indivisible entity containing many diverse particularistic cultures, which is why our definition of nationality has been civic rather than cultural. In reconciling the one and the many, America is one of the few multiethnic countries which has demonstrated the ability to absorb newcomers to a universalizing creed of civic homogenization: "Ethnic pluralism was a way of allowing people to keep as much as they wanted of their Old World language, religion and cuisine—to live among themselves as they wished. The immigrant was not compelled either to keep or to abandon his Old World identity."

In John Higham's critical judgment of the first volume of *The Americans*—"it selects waywardly—even willfully—an assortment of topics for the illustration of a thesis which is both too simple and too elusive to embrace the complex experience of a nation"—we are given what has since become an oft-repeated historiographical verdict. Other critics derided Boorstin's work as nationalistic, conservative, and as uncritically celebrating the American past; they claimed that it minimized class conflict, slighted contradictions and complexities, and was strewn with patriotic banalities befitting the conservative climate of opinion of the Eisenhower era. These critics found Boorstin's analysis unconcerned with the malign aspects of American history. This characterization of Boorstin's work probably explains why, despite his being a preeminent expositor of national ideas and institutions in post-World War II America, Boorstin has never been elected to the presidency of either the Organization of American Historians or the American Historical Association. He has, however, been a State Department lecturer in the Far East; been American history editor of the *Encyclopaedia Britannica*; served on the American Revolution Bicentennial Commission; held visiting-scholar posts at Cambridge University, the Sorbonne, and the Universities of Geneva, Rome, Kyoto, and Puerto Rico; received more than twenty honorary degrees; and had numerous other public honors.

Despite its unpopularity with advocates of conflict and reformist versions of American history, Boorstin's consensus portrayal has not stood alone. Post-World War II American social thought was dominated by Reinhold Niebuhr's theological proposition that the decisive seat of evil in this world resided neither in social nor political institutions but in the weaknesses and imperfections of the human soul. Linked with this revived Christian sense of original sin was the conclusion by many leading American Jewish intellectuals (like Richard Hofstadter and Daniel Bell) that the Holocaust had aroused the Judaic *chayim*—the fear of the animal. These intellectual movements helped to renew an appreciation of American society's accomplishments—especially its principles of comity and civility—and had a striking coincidence with Boorstin's scholarship. Coming to history from a study of law, stressing a comparative historical methodology, and able to see achievements where other historians found deficiencies and inadequacies, Boorstin became an early leader of the emerging "consensus" school of historiography.

As a Harvard radical during the 1930s, Boorstin, along with many other intellectuals, had been temporarily impressed by Marxian analyses and in 1938-1939 was a member of the Communist party. The events in Europe from 1939 on caused a reassessment. Given his formative years in Oklahoma and his generation's experiences with two national disasters—the Great Depression and World War II—it is unsurprising that Boorstin, and other historians of the post-1945 era, would be willing to look favorably on America's achievements. Where earlier historians had focused upon conflict, division, and social reform, Boorstin posed a different series of questions: How had America so successfully reconciled change and continuity? How had a consensus rooted in the common life of Americans forged their resilient institutions? How had our habits and impulses been shaped by the "pragmatic actualities of American life"? How had a special conception of community especially conducive to moderation arisen?

In executing his historical interpretations Boorstin began with a salient assumption: "Perhaps never before has there been a society with such remarkable continuity in its ways of thought from the time of its first settlement. The success criterion, the implicitness, the concern for institutions—all these have prevented abrupt breaks in the direction of our thought. For the chain of circumstances is not casually broken as the chain of ideas can be. A philosopher in his study can think up a new and sometimes attractive frame of ideas; he can propose an anarchy, a revolution, or a new beginning; he is free as the air. But circumstances hold within them certain limits; every event somehow grows out of its predecessors. And American empiricism has tied our thinking to the slow organic growth of institutions. . . . If ever the circumstances of a culture have suited a people to think institutionally, American history has done so. For us, fortunately, it is impossible to distinguish the history of our thought from the history of our institutions."

Those who considered Boorstin an uncritical booster of technology and mass culture have to reckon with *The Image, or What Happened to the American Dream* (1962). The subtitle of the paperback edition of this work is *A Guide to Pseudo-Events in America*. The book is an acerbic attack on the American mass media. Boorstin argues that the media have given Americans a fabricated world in which pseudoevents and illusions substituted for the reality of natural and spontaneous experience.

In *The Americans: The Democratic Experience* (1973), the highly-praised last volume of his trilogy, published eight years after the second volume, Boorstin traced the rise of the idiosyncratic features of our mass society. Here a manifest technological emphasis, arising directly from his experience as director of the National Museum of History and Technology of the Smithsonian, informed his thesis. Statistical communities, the average man, inventions, advertising, entrepreneurship, and consumption communities were the major themes. Once again his angle of vision was the popular, or folk, or broadly social aspect of our everyday lives. The analysis did not ignore technology's unsettling effects, maintaining that if technology had enriched and expanded America's material existence by creating a community of shared experiences, it had also invented artificial needs and isolated and uprooted us. By bringing us both obsolescence and convergence and by attenuating experiences, technology rendered Americans unable to differentiate the pseudo from the real. It imprisoned us in the present and gave us information in the place of knowledge. Where other analysts decried malign tendencies in the America of the 1960s, Boorstin submitted that we were in a "paroxysm of self-abasement" and were becoming a nation of "short-term doomsayers" because we were using only "abstractions," only "baseless utopias to compare ourselves with."

This "national hypochondria" was complicated by peculiarly American traits: "The American belief in speed, which led us to build railroads farther and faster than any other nation, to invent 'quick-lunch' and self-service to save that terrible ten-minute wait, to build automobiles and highways so we can commute at 70 miles an hour, which made us a nation of instant cities, instant coffee, TV-dinners, and instant everything, has bred in us a colossal impatience." To Americans instant solutions to social problems seem essential: "Our appliances and our buildings and our very lives seem out of date even before they are ready for occupancy. What can't be done right now seems hardly worth doing at all." Indeed, Boorstin allowed, our presentist techniques had eroded our sense of history and even in schools "the story of our nation has been displaced by 'social studies'—which is the story of what ails us."

Daniel Boorstin's interpretation represents a shift away from Progressive historiography's emphasis upon economic and class conflicts. Replacing the dichotomies of aristocracy and democracy, capitalists and agrarians, business and labor, he portrayed an America living in essential harmony within a framework of substantive agreement upon democratic capitalism. No ancien régime constrained America's democratic development, and neither socialism nor reaction had ever seriously challenged our enduring eighteenth-century consensus.

During the 1960s, even before he left Chicago, Boorstin was an outspoken critic of violent political and social dissent. Dissent he characterized as "secession from society," in contrast with disagreement, which may lead to reform. Disagreement, he held, is "the life blood of society, dissension is its cancer."

His most recent work, *The Exploring Spirit: America and the World, Then and Now* (1976), consists of lectures given for the BBC in 1975. The lectures returned to the origins of American society. America was shaped by the experience of "whole communities" leaping across the sea into new worlds intact and "uncontaminated" by that contact with strange cultures experienced by overland travelers. The new nation possessed the "therapy of distance," which allowed it to refashion its cultural legacies into inventive new patterns.

In 1975 President Gerald Ford appointed Daniel Boorstin Librarian of Congress. Despite opposition and reservations from individuals and groups who believed him unsuited for the position because he lacked acceptable progressive political opinions or professional librarians' credentials, Boorstin won the unanimous support of the Senate Committee on Rules and Administration. His leadership of the Library of Congress has been marked by imaginative administrative leadership and an enhanced visibility for the library in American institutional and intellectual life. And in the spirit of the title of *The Exploring Spirit*, Boorstin is writing a one-volume world history. Given Boorstin's formidable historical intelligence and captivating narrative and analytical skills, it is likely to have significant influence and perhaps move the consideration of his importance away from divisive debates about the validity of his consensus history of the United States.

Other:

An American Primer, 2 volumes, edited by Boorstin (Chicago: University of Chicago Press, 1966);

The Chicago History of American Civilization, 27 volumes to date, edited by Boorstin (Chicago: University of Chicago Press, 1967-   ).

Periodical Publications:

"The Elusiveness of Mr. Justice Holmes," *New England Quarterly*, 14 (September 1941): 478-487;

"A Dialogue of Two Histories," *Commentary*, 8 (October 1949); 311-315;

"Our Unspoken National Faith: Why Americans Need No Ideology," *Commentary*, 15 (April 1953): 327-337;

"Facade of Our Founding Financiers," *Saturday Review of Literature*, 42 (21 November 1955): 42-43;

"New View of American Reform," *Commentary*, 21 (April 1956): 396-398;

"The Puritan Tradition: Community Above Ideology," *Commentary*, 26 (October 1958): 288-299;

"Eggheads Are Their Own Worst Enemies," *New York Times Magazine*, 26 April 1959, p. 5;

"We, the People, in Quest of Ourselves," *New York Times Magazine*, 26 April 1959, pp. 30, 32, 34;

"Welcome to the Consumption Community," *Fortune*, 76 (1 September 1967): 118-120, 131-138;

"The New Barbarians," *Esquire*, 70 (October 1968): 159-162, 260-262;

"The Spirit of '70," *Newsweek* (4 July 1970): 27-29;

"Gresham's Law: Knowledge or Information," *The American Bookman* (22 February 1982): 1379-1384.

References:

John P. Diggins, "The Perils of Naturalism: Some Reflections on Daniel J. Boorstin's Approach to American History," *American Quarterly*, 23 (1971): 153-180;

John Higham, "Beyond Consensus: The Historian as Moral Critic," *American Historical Review*, 67 (April 1962): 609-625;

Higham, "The Cult of the American Consensus: Homogenizing American History," *Commentary*, 27 (February 1959): 93-100;

J. Rogers Hollingsworth, "Consensus and Continuity in Recent American Historical Writing," *South Atlantic Quarterly*, 61 (Winter 1962): 40-50;

J. R. Pole, "Daniel J. Boorstin," in *Pastmasters: Some Essays on American Historians*, edited by Marcus Cunliffe and Robin W. Winks (New York: Harper & Row, 1969), pp. 210-238;

Robert A. Skotheim, *American Intellectual Histories and Historians* (Princeton: Princeton University Press, 1966);

Larry Van Dyne, "Daniel Boorstin Remembers," *Washingtonian* (June 1982): 129-133, 208-211.

Claude G. Bowers

(20 November 1878-21 January 1958)

Michael Bordelon
St. Thomas Episcopal School, Houston

SELECTED BOOKS: *The Party Battles of the Jackson Period* (Boston & New York: Houghton Mifflin, 1922);

Jefferson and Hamilton: The Struggle for Democracy in America (Boston: Houghton Mifflin, 1925);

Founders of the Republic (Chicago: American Library Association, 1927);

The Tragic Era: The Revolution After Lincoln (Boston: Houghton Mifflin, 1929);

John Tyler; Address of Honorable Claude G. Bowers of New York at the Unveiling of the Bust of President Tyler in the State Capitol, Richmond, Virginia, June 16, 1931 (Richmond: Richmond Press, 1932);

Beveridge and the Progressive Era (Boston: Houghton Mifflin, 1932);

Jefferson in Power: The Death Struggle of the Federalists (Boston: Houghton Mifflin, 1936);

Spanish Adventures of Washington Irving (Boston: Houghton Mifflin, 1940);

The Young Jefferson, 1743-1789 (Boston: Houghton Mifflin, 1945);

Pierre Vergniaud, Voice of the French Revolution (New York: Macmillan, 1950);

Making Democracy a Reality: Jefferson, Jackson, and Polk (Memphis: Memphis State College Press, 1954);

My Mission to Spain: Watching the Rehearsal for World War II (New York: Simon & Schuster, 1954; London: Gollancz, 1954);

Chile Through Embassy Windows (New York: Simon & Schuster, 1958);

My Life: The Memoirs of Claude Bowers (New York: Simon & Schuster, 1962);

Indianapolis in the "Gay Nineties": High School Diaries of Claude G. Bowers, edited by Holman Hamilton and Gayle Thornbrough (Indianapolis: Indiana Historical Society, 1964).

"There has always been a disposition in some quarters to dismiss the Middle West as drab and uninteresting, and yet I think the Midwesterner especially typifies the American way of life." This opening sentence from Claude Gernade Bowers's autobiography suggests qualities of both his life and work. Revolutionary, shocking, and colorful he was not, but hard-working, patriotic, and popular he was in the extreme. Not self-righteously Yankee, not strictly Southern partisan, not radical, not profound, but diligent, orthodox, and supremely democratic, Bowers was the workingman's historian.

Bowers was born in 1878 in Indiana and his Hoosier background exercised an uncommon influence on his works. Born to Lewis and Juliet Bowers, Claude Gernade Bowers was a true son of his boyhood hometown of Whitestown, a community he once described as "overwhelmingly Democratic." His high-school diary is merely the first of his writings to reveal his ardor for democracy, and he remained a Democrat in every sense of the term throughout his life. In fact, scarcely any of his early political views were repudiated or even substantially

Claude G. Bowers

modified in his years of maturity; his works display amazingly little development of thought. From first to last he maintained his faith in the popular judgment, and it was therefore only natural that he should devote himself wholeheartedly to serving the Democratic party, a commitment he himself dated as beginning in 1896 when William Jennings Bryan delivered one of his electrifying speeches in Indianapolis and stirred the blood of every Indiana Democrat.

After graduating from high school in Indianapolis, Bowers embarked upon a journalism career that eventually included service with several Indiana newspapers and the *New York [Evening] World*. Many observers have noted that his historical scholarship was much influenced by his journalistic orientation. Bowers's prolific production, his flair for the dramatic, his eminently readable writing style, and his penchant for biographical detail all reflect the newspaper qualities he acquired in the early years of his career. His histories have the pace and flavor of novels, with both the advantages and disadvantages implied in a narrative approach to history.

Bowers himself clearly recognized his propensity to emphasize action over thought, as he indicated by his frequent comments characterizing his works as "drama." Given the dramatic action of such efforts as *The Tragic Era: The Revolution After Lincoln* (1929) and *Jefferson and Hamilton: The Struggle for Democracy in America* (1925), it would have been almost fitting for Bowers to have listed his "characters" as "dramatis personae." In fact, on several occasions Bowers painted chapter-length verbal "portraits" of some of the more prominent "actors" who starred in his epic productions. In addition, he also provided numerous shorter sketches of secondary figures, including some very fine descriptions of the social queens who figured prominently in the times he described. In some cases his portraits are brilliant; his portrayal of Thaddeus Stevens, for example, is superb. The mixture of personal description and anecdotal detail is often so skillfully done that at times the reader is reminded of Plutarch, a reminder reinforced by the fact that Bowers himself occasionally mentions Plutarch as one of his models.

Bowers's fascination with biographical detail is not difficult to fathom. It accords well with his approach to his discipline: his melodramas routinely present American history as the interplay between democratic and antidemocratic (generally aristocratic) forces, and invariably from his perspective the leaders of democracy are the heroes of their

day. Thus Bowers depicted Jefferson and Andrew Johnson as paragons of personal as well as public virtue, but represented their antagonists— Hamilton, John Adams, and Thaddeus Stevens—as flawed in character, even tragically so. And, not surprisingly, in these tales of conflict the supporting casts reflect the quality of their leadership: Jefferson's subordinates, like Robin Hood's merry men, are consistently honorable in their proceedings, while many of the lesser Federalists and Republicans are unmasked as thoroughly disreputable villains. In fact, summarizing the entire American political tradition from the Claude Bowers perspective is not difficult: in his view the forces of democracy have had both justice and virtue on their side without exception in their never-ending battle against privilege.

Thus in addition to being admired for a writing style which was geared to the popular level, Bowers further enhanced his popularity by interpreting American history in a style so simple (or simplistic) that the lay reader could comprehend it with ease and interest. Bowers had an unwavering faith in the people if they were not led astray by poor leadership. This faith in turn led him naturally to his party preferences, and he regularly favored the party and politics of Jefferson, Jackson, Andrew Johnson, Woodrow Wilson, and Franklin Roosevelt. The following passage from *Making Democracy a Reality: Jefferson, Jackson, and Polk* (1954) reveals the depth of his devotion to those heroes who led America through a series of epic struggles between democracy and aristocracy (often called "plutocracy" by Bowers) in a perennial American saga of conflict between good and evil: "in our country they who disdain the politicians wear blinders to the fact that the greatest of our statesmen from Jefferson down through Jackson, Lincoln, and Franklin Roosevelt have been the most consummate politicians of their generation."

Bowers seems to have been incapable of writing history outside of a political party context, and his various works tend to divide American history into neat little segments, each being a drama of its own. In perhaps his best-known work, *Jefferson and Hamilton*, he describes his version of America's primordial political conflict, the twelve-year power struggle between the popular and the oligarchic forces which began to form and operate as parties during the Washington and Adams administrations. When the common people gradually became disillusioned with the Federalist efforts to form what Bowers called an "aristocratic republic," they shifted their allegiance to their true friend and leader, Jefferson, "the greatest of all Americans, the architect of American ideals." Even though Hamilton receives equal billing in the book's title, Bowers made no serious attempt to describe him in equally sympathetic terms. While the Federalist leader receives credit for his brilliance, political acumen, and financial integrity, he is more vividly portrayed as unfeeling, ambitious, and duplicitous. In like manner, John Adams is also conceded certain good qualities, notably his honesty and patriotism, but even these virtues do not prevent him from being represented as fatally handicapped by his pompous manner and lack of political talent. The real villains of the era, however, are the conniving Federalists in Adams's cabinet who attempt to undermine his administration, the will of the people, and the good of the country. Not surprisingly, the conspiracy fails, and the story ends on a happy note when the people realize their heart's desire by electing Jefferson president in "the Revolution of 1800."

The Federalist conspirators are still plotting mischief, however, in the history's sequel, the reign of Jefferson chronicled in *Jefferson in Power: The Death Struggle of the Federalists* (1936). Although more than a decade had elapsed since the publication of *Jefferson and Hamilton*, the later book offered no fundamental changes in viewpoint: Jefferson is as guileless as ever, while the new set of Federalist villains stoops to such low tactics as "their treasonable attack on the acquisition of Louisiana . . . their bitter battle against a new and necessary constitutional amendment. . . . [and] their conspiracy to raise Aaron Burr to gubernatorial honors." With Washington and Hamilton removed from this stage of history, Bowers made no attempt to credit the Federalist high command with even the semblance of respectability: "The most scintillating of the congressional leaders of the [Federalist] party were as insects crawling upon the earth, compared with Jefferson." Given such an introduction, the trusting reader of *Jefferson in Power* will be relieved to find that Jefferson managed to overcome such scurrilous opposition and give his country two terms which "were, on the whole, eight remarkably brilliant years." Entirely missing from Bowers's version is any account of the negative aspects of Jefferson's presidency, such as the extent of bitterness felt by New England when it seemed that the Embargo Act sponsored by Jefferson might punish the Northeast as surely as Yankee misrule later punished the South during Reconstruction.

After Jefferson's retirement from office, sixteen years of political domination by his party culminated in the period generally known as the Era of Good Feelings, a misnomer according to Bowers since he saw it as a time of stagnation and decay. On several occasions he expressed his conviction that the reign of King Caucus was damaging to the republic because the government was not responsive to popular opinion. Jackson's rise to power was accordingly regarded by Bowers as a healthy return of political parties to playing their proper roles in American politics since they gave the people a chance to make fundamental choices in both programs and leadership. Bowers obviously felt little embarrassment at defending as salutary the Jacksonian emphasis on party discipline and party rule. To Bowers the matter was simple: "In a democracy there must be political parties or there is chaos, and if there are parties there must be politicians to lead them." This point is stressed repeatedly in Bowers's two books on the Jacksonian era, his lengthy 1922 *The Party Battles of the Jackson Period*, and his shorter *Making Democracy a Reality*. Although a quarter of a century separated the writing of the two books, both portrayed Jackson in substantially the same terms. *The Party Battles of the Jackson Period* had portrayed a dramatic struggle of good and evil much like that between Jefferson and Hamilton. *Making Democracy a Reality* merely reiterated the older argument and stressed that it was not Jackson and his camp following who were self-serving, but their lusty antagonists. Thus, Henry Clay is vilified as "an unscrupulous, selfish, scheming politician," John C. Calhoun as "petty in his personal hates and spites and in his resentment over the failure of personal ambitions," and Daniel Webster as the "defender of the Bank from which, at the beginning of the fight, he bluntly solicited a 'refreshment' of his retainer." Fortunately, Bowers tells us, Jackson, the democratic paladin of the day, championed the cause of the common man, thwarted the designs of the aristocratic Whigs and big-money powers, and fundamentally changed the system for the better. "It was not until the Jacksonian epoch," wrote Bowers, "that we became a democracy in fact."

Since Bowers stoutly defended the roles that political parties, party politics, and party leaders came to occupy in the American system, one might suppose that he would have been somewhat neutral in his descriptions of political warfare, carefully noting the virtues and vices of the various contending factions. Such is rarely the case. In the period just mentioned, for instance, the Jacksonians are without blemish, while the nullifiers and "conspirators" are correspondingly without virtue. Admirable and vulgar figures can be found in each stage of American history, but not on both sides of the two political lines of conflict: invariably the pure of heart are the Jeffersonians and their descendants, while the blackguards are their Federalist-Whig-Republican antagonists.

Thus, in *The Tragic Era: The Revolution After Lincoln*, the circumstances vary, but the story line remains the same. In this well-known account of Reconstruction, the power-hungry, rapacious, vengeful leaders of the Republican party misuse the power entrusted to them by a gullible Northern public to prevent reputable Southerners (especially the heroically virtuous Andrew Johnson) from restoring order to their ruined homeland. With considerable skill Bowers defends the vanquished Civil War survivors as good Democrats rather than unreconstructed guardians of the Southern Old Order. And once again the Jeffersonian clan emerges from the conflict with virtue intact, although another set of historians would of course claim that those recalcitrant Southern Democrats represented the Jeffersonian tradition at its worst. Be that as it may, *The Tragic Era* is nonetheless a highly sympathetic account of the problems of unreconstructed white Democrats, and it was one of the chief reasons for the popularity Bowers enjoyed in Dixieland, both in and out of academic circles. Many Southerners clearly appreciated his understanding of the miseries of Reconstruction and the problems their post-Civil War ancestors had in having their honest grievances fairly considered. In fact, scarcely any form of pre-New Deal Democrat found any reason to quarrel with the thrust of Bowers's works, and *The Tragic Era* merely solidified another following for him and his party.

Although *The Tragic Era* served well as a propaganda piece for the Democratic party, it would be unfair to Bowers to suggest that it was written for that purpose. The book is clearly written from conviction. Previous to writing the book Bowers acquired access to numerous contemporary documents made available to him by the Daughters of the Confederacy, with the result that he read "scores of intimate family letters reflecting the fears and feelings of the time, and diaries, some written by young girls, all throwing a white light on the actual living and thinking of the people. Reading these, I really lived as a contemporary through those tragic days." For a historian from Indiana whose chief asset was an imagination which could reproduce the "feel" of a period, such an abundance of material revealing the souls of the participants of the drama of those trying times must have been a revelation, all the more because the materials were unquestionably written from the

hearts of their various authors.

Of his own century Bowers wrote only one major work, a biography of Albert Beveridge, the Republican-turned-Progressive-turned-Republican senator. Since Beveridge clearly does not belong in a gallery of famous Democratic political leaders, the biography seems at first glance to be an uncharacteristic effort for Bowers, but his interest in Beveridge is not really too difficult to explain. Both were from Indiana and they knew and liked each other well. In fact, Beveridge seems to have been one of only a very few Republicans Bowers respected at all. Beveridge was sincerely interested in reform and was not merely a Big Business Republican, and this, together with his Hoosier background, made him of special interest to Bowers. Beveridge's Progressive affiliations also made him an attractive figure for Bowers to study, thus giving the book its full title, *Beveridge and the Progressive Era* (1932). In addition, the two Hoosiers also enjoyed a kind of parallel in careers. Besides satisfying the demands of a highly active political life, Beveridge also devoted himself to historical research, writing lengthy biographies of John Marshall and Abraham Lincoln. Similarly, Bowers conducted an active political and journalistic career simultaneously with his continual historical researches over almost four decades. It must have been a matter of some pride to them both that they managed to maintain their scholarly activities without the benefits and encouragement received from working in a formal academic environment; neither was ever closely associated with any college or university.

In fact, Bowers never even attended college as a student. In the early twentieth century he sandwiched his career as an editorial columnist around a six-year tour of duty as Democratic Sen. John W. Kern's personal secretary in Washington, D.C., from 1910 to 1916. Both his literary efforts and his political activities were undertaken to serve the forces of democracy in America, and in this respect all of his life's work is marked by an admirable unity. During those years he met numerous political figures and eventually he became well known to many important Democrats, including Franklin Roosevelt. Bowers's understanding of the Democratic tradition was admirably suited to the political views of nearly all the Democrats of his time, and he quickly proceeded to become the party's favorite historian, so much so that he was invited to give the party's keynote address at the national convention held in Houston, Texas, in 1928, an invitation which he accepted. He was also frequently asked to speak at various dedication and college ceremonies, and Democrats of both the New Deal and the Southern variety felt at home with him. Although there must have been some exceptions, there is hardly a hint in his autobiography that he ever met a Democrat he did not like. He not only admired the Democrats of the past, such as Jefferson, Jackson, and Andrew Johnson, he genuinely felt that the party leaders of the twentieth century were Jefferson's legitimate descendants. He referred to Harry Truman as one of the nation's "great" presidents, and he commented on the death of Roosevelt with extravagant praise: "The greatest human being I had ever known, and one of the greatest in all our time, had passed into history."

The sincerity of Bowers in his defense of the Democratic tradition cannot be seriously questioned. There is no reason to believe that he wrote to flatter political figures in order to feather his own nest. Nevertheless, the mere fact that his work was of such value to his party almost guaranteed that Democratic administrations would find for him a position of some kind, and during the Roosevelt years he served as ambassador to Spain from 1933 to 1939. His firsthand observations of the Spanish civil war were recorded in *My Mission to Spain* (1954). He served in the same capacity in Chile from 1939 to 1953. His term as ambassador to Chile for fourteen years was especially distinguished, and on his departure from that country he was honored by many of those he had known there. He subsequently recorded his experiences in *Chile Through Embassy Windows* (1958).

During the twenty years he lived away from his native country Bowers's mind turned to considering the democratic movements or absence thereof in other lands, and he took up the study of one of his boyhood heroes, Pierre Vergniaud, the Girondin leader who was executed during the frenzies of the French Revolution. The subject was tailor-made for Bowers, considering the drama of the revolution and his interest in the human element in politics. Both his studies and his official duties led him to ponder the feasibility of democracy in foreign countries, but his conclusions were no different from those he had reached in researching American history. In *Pierre Vergniaud, Voice of the French Revolution* (1950), Bowers said of the Frenchman that "like Jefferson again, he believed that the sound functioning of democracy depends on trained leadership." As the quotation suggests, the admiration Bowers felt for Vergniaud was comparable to his esteem for Jefferson, largely because he perceived striking parallels in political philosophy between the two revolutionaries. Such a comparison was the highest compliment Bowers felt he could pay a political figure. Even when he attempted to broaden his vision, Bowers remained American to the core.

After his return home from Chile in 1953, Bowers did not produce any further major works, although in 1954 he did publish *Making Democracy a Reality*, a small book with only three chapters, one each on Jefferson, Jackson, and James K. Polk. None of the material differed to any significant degree from the essential Claude Bowers; his work remained uniform in theme and tone until his death in 1958. Unlike some of his more radical associates, his democratic propensities never led him to overlook the faults of Stalinism, or totalitarianism in any form, nor was he inclined to drum Southern conservatives out of the Democratic camp. Bowers's democratic ideas were as inclusive and simple as the Democratic party itself during his prime. Whether he could have maintained such a broad tolerance through the party divisions and ideological tensions of the hectic 1960s we can only guess, but he was ideally suited for his own time. He and the Democratic party were made for each other while he lived.

Recent scholars have not been kind to Claude Bowers the historian. His weaknesses as a scholar are only too apparent, especially to a generation of specialists who prefer more detachment in tone if not fact and who frequently view mere political history as too narrow in scope. It requires little insight to observe that Bowers was partial in his judgment, dramatic or even melodramatic in his presentation, and popular or journalistic in his style, and various critics have stated the obvious. Thus far, however, no major study has been produced analyzing the Bowers histories as works of enduring value. As the following comments indicate, the various minor assessments made in recent decades invariably designate Bowers as a scholar of little importance. In *The Writing of American History*, for instance, Michael Kraus gave a balanced estimate when he wrote, "Although Bowers did not present much that was novel, he did accent familiar episodes in a manner that gave them new vitality." Others have applied to his works such appropriate adjectives as "partisan" and "lively," terms which imply both his weaknesses and his strengths. Less kind have been such scholars as Morton Borden, who wrote in a selected bibliography to *Parties and Politics in the Early Republic, 1789-1815* that "Students generally enjoy reading Bowers for his color and fast pace, but the volumes contain innumerable errors of fact and dubious interpretations." Few today defend Bowers as a first-rate historian or protest that his works have unjustly sunk beneath the consciousness of today's authorities.

That Bowers had serious shortcomings as a historian is obvious. His writings contain some quite noticeable factual errors, and he is vulnerable on another score as well: he is regarded as unreliable as much for his "dubious interpretations" as for his misstatements of fact. But Bowers also has his virtues; the vices are simply more easily noted than the virtues. That Bowers can be faulted for his incorrect statements, slanted interpretations, melodramatic descriptions, and uncritical selection of materials, is all true enough. But an assessment of Bowers's worth as a historian by simply accenting the negative is as one-sided as were some of his own accounts of historic battles between the American democrats and "plutocrats."

Scarcely noticed any longer are Bowers's strengths as a historian, strengths that are inextricably interwoven with his weaknesses. More than anything else, Bowers had a gift for recreating the "feel" of a period, prompting the reader to experience for himself the passions, the hopes and the fears, the rage and outrage, the sense of betrayal, and all the other sentiments experienced by the various actors in his "dramas." The characters in his narratives are men of flesh and blood, and because Bowers wished his readers to feel what they felt, he masterfully restored life to many of the actors in the scenes he described. Not the least of his contributions to American history is the skillful manner in which he revivified the women—the queens and their ladies-in-waiting—as well. Such artful introductions frequently induce the reader to feel that he has moved well beyond the "get-acquainted" stage in understanding the figures who shaped our history.

Because Bowers was primarily interested in capturing the flavor of a period, he relied extensively on the writings of the participants themselves, and while this may have unduly influenced his judgment at times, it also made it possible for the reader to see and feel the events of the day as did those who lived through them. Thus one of his finest efforts is *The Tragic Era*, a work influenced strongly by the hundreds of personal documents made available to him by the Daughters of the Confederacy. But the virtue of *The Tragic Era* lies not in the extent to which it is factually accurate, important as that might be. *The Tragic Era*'s chief strength is that it enables the reader to understand and even to experience the problems and the feelings of outrage and helplessness and hopelessness of the in-

habitants of the postbellum South, and for this the book should be remembered and should continue to be read. To appreciate the merits of the book it is not necessary to read it carefully; it is enough to read it quickly. And in reading it, however quickly, the reader will learn something that would probably escape him in reading a more carefully detailed account: he will learn something of what it was like to have lived in the South in her darkest days.

Unfortunately for Bowers, he not only used contemporary newspapers and private correspondence to capture the flavor of a period, he frequently accepted them at face value, particularly when they supported his own preferences, and for this he can be justly criticized. Being a journalist himself, he had perhaps too intimate an acquaintance with newspaper sources, and apparently too high an opinion of their reliability, even when he was well aware that they were frankly partisan. Had Bowers written simply to bring a period to life and have his readers experience the dramatic events of the past, and had he selected and used his source material more judiciously, he would have been a fine historian.

Bowers's chief fault was that he would not let history tell itself. He selected, edited, and interpreted his sources to suit his own purposes. Thus he ably presented the perspectives of Jefferson, Jackson, and Andrew Johnson, but simultaneously diminished the stature of their antagonists. Although Bowers made token efforts to present the alternative points of view, the attempt was clearly half-hearted. The greatness of Hamilton, Adams, Clay, Calhoun, and Webster (and Washington, too, for that matter) is not to be found in the works of Bowers. They are too much the villains or unwitting dupes who are destined to be thwarted by the heroes of democracy.

Bowers weighted his materials in favor of the forces of democracy for a reason—he sought to make history as he was writing it. That is, his purpose was largely didactic. He wanted America to continue to be democratic and to become even more democratic than it was. But in seeking to make history as he was writing it, he was unaware that the whole process was more complicated than he imagined. He did indeed "make" history, even more so than he intended. At his best he made history by making it live again. At his worst he made history by inventing it, mainly through his own slanted judgments and excessive reliance on biased materials. To some degree he made history by presenting it as it never was—the Jeffersonian heritage was never so pure as he presented it nor were their opponents without their redeeming qualities.

But Bowers was more intent on making history from still another perspective. By having the democratic tradition represent all that is best about America, his aim was to incline his readers to become good democrats themselves, even partisan Democrats. Thus he hoped to give history a boost, to ensure that democracy would not only survive but that it would prevail. In a word, he wanted America's future to resemble its past as described by himself. He moved with the democratic Zeitgeist, all the while thinking he was to some degree in advance of it. Admittedly liberal, he did indeed do his part to shape America's liberal democratic future.

Other:

The Diary of Elbridge Gerry, Jr., edited by Bowers (New York: Brentano's, 1927).

Gamaliel Bradford
(9 October 1863 - 11 April 1932)

Marion Edmonds
South Carolina Department of Parks, Recreation and Tourism

SELECTED BOOKS: *Types of American Character* (New York & London: Macmillan, 1895);

A Pageant of Life (Boston: R.G. Badger, 1904);

The Private Tutor (Boston & New York: Houghton Mifflin, 1904);

Between Two Masters (Boston & New York: Houghton Mifflin, 1906);

Matthew Porter, A Story of Today (Boston: L.C. Page, 1908);

Lee the American (Boston & New York: Houghton Mifflin, 1912; London: Constable, 1912);

Confederate Portraits (Boston: Houghton Mifflin, 1912);

Union Portraits (Boston & New York: Houghton Mifflin, 1916);

Portraits of Women (Boston & New York: Houghton Mifflin, 1916);

Portraits of American Women (Boston: Houghton Mifflin, 1917);

A Naturalist of Souls: Studies in Psychography (New York: Dodd, Mead, 1917);

Unmade in Heaven; a Play in Four Acts (New York: Dodd, Mead, 1917);

A Prophet of Joy (Boston & New York: Houghton Mifflin, 1920);

Shadow Verses (New Haven: Yale University Press, 1920);

American Portraits, 1875-1900 (Boston & New York: Houghton Mifflin, 1922; London: National Institute for the Blind, 1939);

Damaged Souls (Boston & New York: Houghton Mifflin, 1923; London: Cape, 1925);

Bare Souls (New York & London: Harper, 1924; London: Cape, 1925);

The Soul of Samuel Pepys (Boston & New York: Houghton Mifflin, 1924; London: Cape, 1924);

Gamaliel Bradford

Wives (New York & London: Harper, 1925);
Darwin (Boston & New York: Houghton Mifflin, 1926);
D. L. Moody, a Worker in Souls (New York: Doran, 1927);
Life and I, an Autobiography of Humanity (Boston & New York: Houghton Mifflin, 1928);
Daughters of Eve (Boston: Houghton Mifflin, 1928);
As God Made Them: Portraits of Some Nineteenth Century Americans (Boston & New York: Houghton Mifflin, 1929);
The Quick and the Dead (Boston & New York: Houghton Mifflin, 1929);
Saints and Sinners (Boston & New York: Houghton Mifflin, 1932);
Biography and the Human Heart (Boston & New York: Houghton Mifflin, 1932);
The Journal of Gamaliel Bradford, 1883-1932, edited by Van Wyck Brooks (Boston & New York: Houghton Mifflin, 1933);
Portraits and Personalities, edited by Mabel A. Bessey (Boston & New York: Houghton Mifflin, 1933);
Elizabethan Women, edited by Harold Ogden White (Boston: Houghton Mifflin, 1936).

During the period from 1912 to 1932, Gamaliel Bradford produced biographical sketches of no fewer than 114 individuals. His subjects were as varied as Daniel Webster and P. T. Barnum, Calvin Coolidge and Casanova. With a few notable exceptions, Bradford employed an essay format to examine his subjects and chose to ignore traditional chronological biography in favor of what he termed "psychography," the profiling of character by sketches comprised of a potpourri of anecdote and quotation he believed revealed a subject's essential personality. While his collections of biographies were initially quite popular with the general public, and although Bradford's books were usually well received by critics, his work has become increasingly less influential.

Gamaliel Bradford, a direct descendant of Governor Bradford of Plymouth, was born in Boston on 9 October 1863. He was the son of Gamaliel Bradford, a successful banker, publicist, and political reformer, and Clara Crowninshield Kinsman, daughter of a prominent Massachusetts lawyer. Bradford's mother, from whom he inherited chronic poor health, died of tuberculosis when he was two, after which father and sons moved to Wellesley Hills, Massachusetts, where Gamaliel led a sheltered and bookish childhood.

Although Bradford learned French, German, and Italian during months spent in Europe in 1878, his formal education, because of ill health, was irregular. To bring Gamaliel up to college level, Prof. M. L. Perrin was hired as a private tutor, and by 1882 Bradford was admitted to Harvard College. Unable to face the crowds and physical demands of college life, Gamaliel withdrew from school during the Thanksgiving recess of his freshman year and returned home to study privately for three more years with Perrin.

On 30 October 1886 Bradford married his closest childhood friend, Helen Hubbard Ford, the daughter of Rev. Lucian Collins Ford. After a honeymoon tour of Europe, Bradford attempted for a time to work in his father's banking concern but by 1890 had given up business to concentrate on writing.

His first published work, *Types of American Character* (1895), consisted of seven essays, each of which dealt with a different personality trait as expressed through the "American" experience. The chapters were on the pessimist, idealist, epicurean, philanthropist, man of letters, outdoorsman, and scholar, and while anecdotal illustration was sometimes employed, the essays were general and speculative rather than biographical. As in most of his later works, the chapters in this book were first published as periodical articles.

Despite the fact that his success would come from writing biography, Bradford always considered poetry and drama as the highest forms of literary expression. After *Types of American Character* was published, he spent more than fifteen years attempting to establish himself as a "creative" writer. Bradford initially turned to poetry, and his second published book was a volume of verse entitled *A Pageant of Life* (1904). Two more books of poetry were published in 1920—*A Prophet of Joy* and *Shadow Verses*— but all three books contained only a small fraction of the estimated 2,000 poems Bradford produced.

In addition to poetry, Bradford published three novels, *The Private Tutor* (1904), *Between Two Masters* (1906), and *Matthew Porter, A Story of Today* (1908). These novels did not receive either the critical or commercial success Bradford hoped for, but even more disappointing was his failure to get several other novels published at all.

Having failed at poetry and novels, Bradford doggedly tried his hand at drama, writing some fifteen plays, of which only one, *Unmade in Heaven* (1917), was published. As Bradford himself wrote, none of his plays ever came "within speaking distance of the stage." By 1910 Gamaliel Bradford's professional future appeared rather bleak. He was in his late forties, in poor health, and by his own admission unable to support himself by writing, depending instead on his inherited wealth and that of his wife.

Lee the American (1912) abruptly changed Bradford's fortunes and revealed a form of literary expression well matched to his talents. The book was not a chronological, formal biography but a group of chapters under such titles as "Lee Before the War," "Lee and his Army," "Lee in Battle," and so forth. Each chapter was made up of quotations and anecdotes bearing on the central theme of that particular chapter. Bradford called this form of biographical writing "psychography," and it became the style for nearly all his subsequent writing.

Bradford's psychography eschewed the use of a consecutive narrative aimed at revealing character development and instead presented incidents and quotations drawn from throughout the subject's life, all brought to bear to define character, or, as Bradford put it, to draw a "portrait" of a soul. This method evolved from Bradford's conception of character not as a plastic quality constantly evolving but as a largely predetermined substance which remains constant throughout a person's life. The basic characteristics of psychography emerged almost complete in *Lee the American* and were little changed in Bradford's work over the next twenty years. Indeed, the concept of soul "portraits" and of himself as a "naturalist of souls," which figure prominently in later works, are all referred to in this initial attempt at biography.

Bradford's concept of the static personality created an almost faultless Lee who emerged as a tragic hero not because of any internal darkness or wavering but as a result of the swirl of history as it washed past him. "As grandeur came upon him, he did not change his manner in the least, but what had before seemed coldness, seemed now dignity, and the austerity of the lieutenant appeared only a proper self-respect in the commanding general."

Lee the American was an immediate commercial success, and in the South it was considered a sign of long-awaited Northern understanding. Washington and Lee University awarded Bradford an honorary doctorate in 1912, and Wake Forest College followed suit seven years later. Most reviews of the work approved Bradford's assessments of Lee, but critics were generally more intrigued with the methodology of psychography than with the content of the book. A number of reviewers speculated

that Bradford's mosaic or composite approach might be better suited to essay rather than book-length treatment.

Bradford reached the same conclusion, and his next eight biographical works were all collections of essays. Each book revolved around a common theme but examined the uniqueness of six to ten dissimilar individuals associated with it. The first of these eight books was *Confederate Portraits* (1912), a logical outgrowth of his research for *Lee the American*. The individuals examined in the work were Joseph E. Johnston, J. E. B. Stuart, James Longstreet, P. G. T. Beauregard, Judah P. Benjamin, Alexander H. Stephens, Robert Toombs, and Raphael Semmes. In each essay Bradford judged the various strengths and weaknesses of his characters primarily as he saw them revealed through their recorded utterances and writings. While little emphasis was placed on their military conduct, success, and failure, there was also less attempt to either condemn or excuse these men than was typical in contemporary works on the Civil War. Although Bradford obviously rated some of his characters, like Stuart, far higher as moral creatures than he did others, like Benjamin, he made clear that all were human and none were monstrous, and that none were the equal of Lee. Critical and public reception of the book, though not as unequivocally positive as for *Lee the American*, demonstrated that Bradford had found his literary niche.

After *Confederate Portraits* came *Union Portraits* in 1916. The subjects of this work were George B. McClellan, Joseph Hooker, George G. Meade, George H. Thomas, William T. Sherman, Edwin M. Stanton, William H. Seward, Charles Sumner, and Samuel Bowles. In style and quality this work was little different from its predecessor, although some reviewers noted that Bradford, a New Englander, was less sympathetic with the foibles of those from his own region than he had been with those of Southerners. While there is some truth in this observation, particularly as it related to Bradford's assessment of Sumner, generally his essays were sympathetic toward the humanity he recognized in each of his subjects. Indeed, as Nathaniel W. Stephenson pointed out, Bradford's Sherman was so endowed with admirable qualities as to be unrecognizable to the Southerners who had relished *Lee the American* and *Confederate Portraits*.

Union Portraits ended Bradford's involvement with the Civil War as a theme, and his next work, *Portraits of Women* (1916), first revealed his considerable sympathy with and interest in women as biographical subjects. Lady Mary Wortley Montagu, Lady Holland, Madame du Deffand, Madame de Choiseul, Madame de Sévigné, Madame d'Arblay, Jane Austen, Eugenie de Guerin, and Mrs. Samuel Pepys at first glance appear to have little other than their sex to serve as a common thread. The cumulative effect of discussing them together, however, is to disclose the high value Bradford placed on feminine charm, culture, grace, and spirituality. Though critically well received, the book was less commercially popular than his three previous psychographical works.

Portraits of American Women (1917), which followed *Portraits of Women*, was an Americanized version of the earlier Continental work. It looks at Abigail Adams, Sarah Alden Ripley, Mary Lyon, Harriet Beecher Stowe, Margaret Fuller Ossoli, Louisa May Alcott, Frances Elizabeth Willard, and Emily Dickinson. It might have been, as Bradford admitted, more appropriately entitled "Portraits of New England Women." As in *Portraits of Women*, Bradford demonstrated through his treatment those qualities he found most desirable in women. Chiefly these were wit tempered by decorum and intelligence mixed with spirituality. Bradford sensed that his ideal for womanliness was of a bygone era and referred rather wistfully to those ages "when there was no offense in saying that women differed from men in their hearts as in their garments."

A Naturalist of Souls: Studies in Psychography, which appeared in the same year as *Portraits of American Women*, is essentially a work of literary criticism employing the techniques of psychography. The subjects of the essays are John Donne, Giacomo Leopardi, Anthony Trollope, Alexandre Dumas, Jules Lemaître, Edward Hyde, Xenophon, Pliny the Younger, Ovid, and Francis of Sales. Perhaps the appendix contained the most important part of this work, for in it Bradford acknowledged Charles Augustin Sainte-Beuve as his stylistic mentor and described the concept of "naturalist of souls," which inspired his own work. The "naturalist of souls" noted and classified the phenomena he observed in the same way that a scientist observed and classified natural objects.

After *A Naturalist of Souls* Bradford spent five years attempting once again to establish himself as a "creative" writer. His attempts all proved to be failures, and so in 1922 he returned to his area of specialty and produced *American Portraits, 1875-1900*, which examines Mark Twain, Henry Adams, Sidney Lanier, James McNeill Whistler, James G. Blaine, Grover Cleveland, Henry James, and Joseph Jefferson. It was Bradford's intention, never

fulfilled, that the volume would be the first in a seven-part series which would stretch back to the origins of European-American history, looking at representatives of the arts, business, and science. *American Portraits, 1875-1900* was extremely well received both critically and commercially and went through no fewer than six editions. Of the eight sketches in the book, most critical attention was directed to his assessment of Mark Twain and the conclusion that he was too dangerous for the masses. "I lived for ten years with the soul of Robert E. Lee and it really made a little better man of me. Six months of Mark Twain made me a worse. . . . And I am fifty-six years old and not over-susceptible to infection. What can he not do to children of sixteen."

Bradford's next two works, *Damaged Souls* (1923) and *Bare Souls* (1924), complemented each other in much the way that his military portraits (Confederate/Union) and sketches of women (European/American) had. In *Damaged Souls* Bradford delved into the tragic flaws of an odd assortment of American characters. Benedict Arnold, P. T. Barnum, John Brown, Aaron Burr, Benjamin F. Butler, Thomas Paine, and John Randolph were all subjected to humane, yet disapproving analysis. In *Bare Souls* the Europeans took the stage, with Voltaire, Thomas Gray, Horace Walpole, William Cowper, Charles Lamb, John Keats, Gustave Flaubert, and Edward Fitzgerald receiving a far more sympathetic treatment than their American counterparts. By the time these two works appeared, Bradford's psychographs had been appearing for more than a decade and the first serious criticisms of his work began to emerge. Arthur M. Schlesinger, Sr., in a review for the *Mississippi Valley Historical Review* in 1924, argued that Bradford, despite his claims, had failed to discover the essential truth concerning the complex characters with which he dealt. In addition, Schlesinger contended that Bradford had failed properly to investigate the climate in which his subjects operated or to take advantage of the rapidly evolving techniques of psychiatry in producing his psychographs.

Perhaps in partial response to such criticism, Bradford's next work was his first biography of a single individual since *Lee the American*. *The Soul of Samuel Pepys* (1924) was primarily an edited and annotated version of Pepys's famous diary, but one in which Bradford rearranged the entries in such a way as to reveal the "soul" of their author. As with *Lee the American*, each chapter illuminated a different aspect of the subject's existence, such as his relationship to office, wife, or God. To accomplish this purpose, excerpts often penned a decade apart were placed together in the text. (While this juxtaposition was seldom pointed out in the text, all such quotations were footnoted and dated at the end of the work.)

In Bradford's next work, *Wives* (1925), he returned to his standard psychographical essay style, and with the exception of Mrs. Abraham Lincoln and Mrs. James Madison, all the other subjects— Mrs. Benedict Arnold, Theodosia Burr, Mrs. Jefferson Davis, Mrs. Benjamin F. Butler, and Mrs. James G. Blaine—were related to previous subjects of Bradford essays. After *Wives*, Bradford produced his last three single-individual biographies, the first two of which were *Darwin* (1926) and *D. L. Moody, a Worker in Souls* (1927). At first glance they seem a strange combination, the scientist and the evangelist, but in his handling of the two, Bradford, by stressing their spirituality rather than their occupations, made them both seem mystical. Indeed, Darwin, whom Bradford unabashedly declared was "one of the simplest, purest, noblest, most candid, most lovable, most Christian souls that ever lived . . .," seems to have rated far higher on the author's moral scale than did Moody, that thoroughly American, aggressive, businesslike "worker in souls." Bradford's last "biography" was unique in that its subject was humanity itself. *Life and I, an Autobiography of Humanity* (1928) applies Bradford's psychographical and literary methods to an examination of the beliefs and attitudes of the human species as a whole. In many ways it is a revision and expansion of his first work, *Types of American Character*.

The rest of Bradford's career was spent producing collections of psychographic essays. *Daughters of Eve*, also published in 1928, examines seven famous and diverse women ranging from Ninon de Lenclos in the seventeenth century to Sarah Bernhardt in the twentieth. Between these two glittering baubles Bradford strung essays on Madame de Maintenon, Madame Guyon, Mademoiselle de Lespinasse, Catherine the Great, and George Sand. After *Daughters of Eve* came *As God Made Them: Portraits of Some Nineteenth Century Americans* (1929), which included a trio of important essays on Daniel Webster, Henry Clay, and John C. Calhoun. In each, Bradford examined the political arguments and positions of the individual protagonists and tried to show how their ethnic heritage and early training locked them into certain opinions and how there was a grain of truth and a portion of folly in each of their stances. There were also essays on Horace Greeley, Edwin Booth, Fran-

cis James Child, and Asa Gray.

Published in the same year as *As God Made Them* was *The Quick and the Dead*, Bradford's only book-length attempt to use psychography on his contemporaries. His letters and journal reveal a certain apprehension on his part about writing on living subjects, for, as he noted in his preface, "living persons may do something to-morrow that will throw your study quite out of joint. . . ." *The Quick and the Dead* presents Theodore Roosevelt, Woodrow Wilson, Thomas Alva Edison, Henry Ford, Nikolai Lenin, Benito Mussolini, and Calvin Coolidge, and the consequences of the actions of the last three certainly proved the wisdom of his fears.

In his next book, *Saints and Sinners* (1932), Bradford stayed well clear of contemporary figures, venturing no further into modern times than 1838. The book deals with saints, Francis of Assisi, Thomas a Kempis, and Fenelon, and sinners, Caesar Borgia, Casanova, Talleyrand, and Byron. As in his earlier works, Bradford concluded that the saints were saintly and the sinners were still human, though flawed.

It is appropriate that the last of his books published during his lifetime, *Biography and the Human Heart* (1932), deals primarily with individuals who achieved literary success in areas where Bradford had striven in vain. Longfellow, Whitman, Charlotte Cushman, William Morris Hunt, John Beauchamp Jones, Jones Very, and Horace Walpole are the subjects of the work, and in its opening chapter Bradford provided one of his clearest statements regarding the efficacy of biography: "Biography is, or should be, or might be, the yeast, the ferment, of the human spirit, which should stir and rouse it to the highest sense of its own achievement and its own powers."

In the winter of 1931 Gamaliel Bradford's health, never good, began a slow deterioration. After four months of illness he died 11 April 1932 at his home of sixty-six years in Wellesley Hills. Little need be said of his personal life during the years his books were written because it was in many ways uneventful. Poor health and chronic vertigo left him a semi-invalid, and in his letters one finds a regret over a "lack of contact with the surface of life." However, what Bradford lacked in physical strength was more than compensated for in determination. He forced himself to write every day, even if only for twenty or thirty minutes. Throughout his adult life he kept a journal, which at his death contained more than 1.4 million words. From 1918 on, he kept a complete and accurate record of all his correspondence, which by 1932 totaled fifty-four volumes. From Bradford's letters and from his journal, Van Wyck Brooks was able to compile and edit two volumes, *The Journal of Gamaliel Bradford, 1883-1932* (1933) and *The Letters of Gamaliel Bradford, 1918-1931* (1934), which have become, in the final analysis, Bradford's most complete psychography. Another work of Bradford's appeared posthumously. Edited by Harold Ogden White, *Elizabethan Women* (1936) contains Bradford's thoughts on the daily lives of women in the sixteenth century and on how they were portrayed in the literature of the day.

At the time of his death, Bradford was referred to as the "Dean of American Biographers" and was credited, along with Lytton Strachey, with establishing a new style of biographical writing. He personally rejected comparisons of his work with Strachey's, preferring instead to refer to his intellectual mentor Sainte-Beuve. Bradford coined the term pschography for the biographical sketches he prepared, and there are similarities between his work and that of later psychohistorians and "new-wave" journalists. The similarities are largely superficial, however, for Bradford's work is firmly grounded in a code of morality, ethics, and propriety that has largely vanished from later biographical writing.

The years following his death have witnessed a slow but steady decline in the popularity of Bradford's works. Historians found that their lack of chronology rendered them of limited value as research tools and looked to them mainly as a stimulus for their own subjective thinking on particular individuals. Popular audiences have felt increasingly uncomfortable with a literary style too strongly rooted in the genteel outlook of a previous generation. At the present time Bradford's work is of value chiefly in offering a speculative and thought-provoking overview of a remarkable number of remarkable people.

Periodical Publications:

"Idealism in Literature," *Andover Review*, 8 (November 1887): 461-468;

"Emerson," *The New Princeton Review*, 63 (March 1888): 145-163;

"An Elizabethan Mystic," *Andover Review*, 19 (September 1893): 550-564;

"The serpent of old Nile! a study of the Cleopatra of tragedy," *Poet-Lore*, 10 (October-December 1898);

"Books new and old, the mission of the literary critic," *Atlantic Monthly*, 94 (October 1904): 537-544;

"Mid-nineteenth-century realism," *The Reader, an illustrated monthly magazine* (September 1906): 450-455;

"A French critic of old imperialism," *Atlantic Monthly*, 96 (December 1906): 805-811;

"Browning and Sainte-Beuve," *North American Review*, 191 (April 1910): 488-500;

"Journalism and Permanence," *North American Review*, 202 (June 1915): 239-241;

"Fiction as Historical material," *Proceedings of the Massachusetts Historical Society*, 48 (1915): 326-332;

"Diversions of a lost soul," *Atlantic Monthly*, 134 (September 1924): 361-370;

"Glimpses of great people, a series of imaginary dialogues," *Forum*, 73 (April 1925): 545-551;

"Early days in Wellesley; being casual recollections of boyhood and later years—1867 to 1881," *Wellesley Historical Society* (1928): 1-43.

Letters:

The Letters of Gamaliel Bradford, 1918-1931, edited by Van Wyck Brooks (Boston & New York: Houghton Mifflin, 1934).

References:

C. K. Bolton, "Gamaliel Bradford: A Memoir," *Proceedings of the Massachusetts Historical Society*, 65 (1940): 81-91;

Gamaliel Bradford, "The Fight for Glory," *Harper's Magazine* (August 1929): 307-315;

Dale Warren, "Gamaliel Bradford: A Personal Sketch," *South Atlantic Quarterly*, 32 (January 1933): 9-18.

Papers:

One hundred twenty-one volumes of Bradford's papers are at Harvard University.

Bruce Catton

(9 October 1899-28 August 1978)

Carol Reardon
University of Kentucky

SELECTED BOOKS: *The War Lords of Washington* (New York: Harcourt, Brace, 1948);

Mr. Lincoln's Army, volume 1 of The Army of the Potomac trilogy (Garden City: Doubleday, 1951; London: White Lion, 1976);

Glory Road, volume 2 of The Army of the Potomac trilogy (Garden City: Doubleday, 1952; London: White Lion, 1977);

A Stillness at Appomattox, volume 3 of The Army of the Potomac trilogy (Garden City: Doubleday, 1953);

U. S. Grant and the American Military Tradition (Boston: Little, Brown, 1954);

This Hallowed Ground: The Story of the Union Side of the Civil War (Garden City: Doubleday, 1956; London: Gollancz, 1957);

America Goes to War (Middletown, Conn.: Wesleyan University Press, 1958);

The American Heritage Picture History of the Civil War, narrative by Catton, edited by Richard H. Ketchum (New York: American Heritage Publishing, 1960); republished as *The Penguin Book of the American Civil War* (Harmondsworth, U.K.: Penguin, 1966);

Grant Moves South (Boston: Little, Brown, 1960);

The Coming Fury, volume 1 of The Centennial History of the Civil War (Garden City: Doubleday, 1961);

Terrible Swift Sword, volume 2 of The Centennial History of the Civil War (Garden City: Doubleday, 1963);

Two Roads to Sumter, by Catton and William B. Catton (New York: McGraw-Hill, 1963);

Never Call Retreat, volume 3 of The Centennial History of the Civil War (Garden City: Doubleday, 1965);

Grant Takes Command (Boston: Little, Brown, 1969);

Prefaces to History (Garden City: Doubleday, 1970);

Waiting for the Morning Train: An American Boyhood (Garden City: Doubleday, 1972);

Michigan: A Bicentennial History (New York: Norton, 1976);

The Bold and Magnificent Dream: America's Founding Years, 1492-1815, by Catton and William B. Catton (Garden City: Doubleday, 1978);

Reflections on the Civil War, edited by John Leekley (Garden City: Doubleday, 1981).

Bruce Catton, Civil War historian and longtime editor of *American Heritage* magazine, ranks as one of the most successful proponents of "popular" history, attracting the general as well as the professional reader. Combining a lively and readable prose style with contemporary reflections and reminiscences, Catton specialized in producing both thrilling and historically accurate narratives of the Civil War years.

Charles Bruce Catton was born in Petoskey, a northern Michigan lumber town, to George Robert and Adella Maude Patten Catton. His family moved to nearby Benzonia several years later, where Catton's father, a Congregationalist minister, became principal of struggling Benzonia Academy, which closed its doors soon after the younger Catton's graduation in 1916. By his own admission, Catton's childhood was a happy, if disciplined, one, instilling values that were as influential to his writings as they were important to his life.

Benzonia had been founded in the 1850s by a

Bruce Catton

group of Congregationalists from Oberlin, Ohio, and their religious intensity still persisted at the turn of the century. Catton remarked in later years that growing up in Benzonia was like living next to the Twelve Apostles. Catton's writings often reflect this religious influence on his upbringing. He always remained optimistic about man's progress and ability to better himself. He firmly believed that all men were put on earth for a purpose and that each person had a destiny to fulfill, sometimes greater than the individual himself. These personal beliefs helped give Catton's Union soldiers an aura of grandeur and righteousness of purpose that transcended the horror of battle, the exhaustion of the march, or the boredom of camp life.

Growing up in the rural Midwest, before industrialization radically changed the tempo of life there, Catton also adopted some of the spirit of the pioneers. He prized individuality. He advocated practicality and honesty in dealings with other individuals and with the government. He preferred the upright to the petty, the plain to the complex, and the progressive, nationalistic spirit of the frontier Midwest over what he saw as the divisive or self-serving attitudes of the East and South. It was no accident that the most prominent individuals in Catton's Civil War histories were fellow Midwesterners Abraham Lincoln, William T. Sherman, and especially Ulysses S. Grant.

Catton left Michigan in 1916 to attend Oberlin College. His academic career ended with World War I when he served briefly in the U.S. Navy. He never completed his course work at Oberlin. Instead, after the war, he turned to newspaper work, becoming a reporter, editorial writer, and reviewer for the *Cleveland News*, the *Cleveland Plain Dealer*, and the *Boston American*. He married Hazel Cherry in 1925, and their only child, William Bruce Catton, was born the next year. Catton remained in the newspaper business until the outbreak of World War II.

In 1943 Catton became information director for the War Production Board in Washington. His experiences there, observing clashes between the civilian government and military planners, with their blunders, their follies, and their wasted opportunities, inspired Catton's first book, *The War Lords of Washington* (1948). The book attracted little notice at the time, but the writing experience changed Catton's future. In 1948 he left government service to write history.

Catton's first major project, his trilogy on the Army of the Potomac, stands high among his most notable works. After initial difficulties in finding a publisher, *Mr. Lincoln's Army* (1951) and *Glory Road* (1952) gained Catton some popular recognition. But it was the third volume, *A Stillness at Appomattox* (1953), which firmly established Catton's reputation as a first-rank Civil War writer. That work won both the National Book Award and the Pulitzer Prize for history in 1954.

In these three volumes, Catton departed from other Civil War historians in both his attitude toward the four-year struggle and in his refusal to adhere to the methodology of the academic world. He avoided formal studies of battle tactics and lengthy discourses on narrow or obscure topics of organizational history. He preferred a wide-ranging narrative approach, based largely on the observations of the soldiers themselves, rather than retrospective evaluations of generalship. In doing so, he reduced the war, with all its complexities, to a more human and consequently more personal level.

Catton made extensive use of regimental histories, wartime newspapers, and contemporary diaries to impart an immediacy to the soldiers' everyday existence. Skillfully culling these sources for colorful personal experiences, Catton successfully gave new life to the individual soldiers who reminded him of the old veterans he remembered from Grand Army of the Republic reunions back in Benzonia. They were not all heroes to be sure, but their behavior as men caught up in something much bigger than themselves was genuine. "Here is war as soldiers saw it . . . cruel, bestial, yet not without moments of decency and even grandeur," one reviewer raved. Even the generals lost some of their gilt and glamour in Catton's prose; they too became human beings with their vanities, envies, and moments of indecision. These were men burdened with the conflicting moral responsibilities of carrying on a war while protecting human lives; there could be little pompousness in these soldiers.

If Catton's popular recognition skyrocketed with *A Stillness at Appomattox*, he was not always so well accepted by the historical profession, in which initially Catton, the newspaperman, was an unwelcome intruder. In an early review for the popular press, historian Bell I. Wiley, whose *The Life of Billy Yank* echoed many of Catton's sentiments about the Northern soldier in the ranks, described the trilogy as "a landmark in Civil War literature, and an outstanding contribution to military history." However, early reviewers for professional historical journals too often dismissed the volumes in Catton's trilogy with less than enthusiasm, although they approved of Catton's refreshing writing style.

Academic historians' complaints were many

and varied. Reviewers noted with some displeasure that Catton's work failed to conform strictly to accepted research methods; he had used no manuscript sources, his research of secondary literature was far from exhaustive, and his objectivity was suspect. One reviewer observed that it was seldom clear where Catton's footnoted references ended and his imagination took over. Further, Catton's understanding and interpretation of the motives and the mind of the South were labeled as derisive and condescending. Catton had added little that was new in the way of interpretation, and some reviewers quibbled with apparently unsupported generalities and Catton's tendency toward hero worship. An early review of *Mr. Lincoln's Army* even questioned the propriety of the title of the volume, noting that in 1862, the time frame of the book, the Army of the Potomac was much more General McClellan's than the president's in the devotion of the soldiers.

Catton countered the professional historians' criticisms of his work not by arguing their charges but by carefully stating his own beliefs about the uses and role of history. Catton believed the historian who wrote only for himself or for a specialized group of colleagues cheated both himself and his calling. He thought that the historian's true mission was to write for those outside the profession, to expand readers' horizons, and to appeal to their sensibilities through portraying their fellow man's daily struggles. The historian had an obligation to be true to the facts as far as they could be ascertained, but beyond that, his role was that of an artist. In presenting his own understanding of man's follies and achievements, a historian should try to strengthen a reader's empathy with those who had gone before him. Catton saw history as a voyage into the shadows of human motivations and thought it the historian's greatest challenge and responsibility to portray those motivations to his readers. Anything less was a refusal to accept the full obligations of historianship. Catton believed that his own manner of approaching the past accomplished this goal, an achievement not guaranteed by academic credentials. The debate between Catton and some academic historians who begrudged him a place in their field never really ended; when *Grant Takes Command*, his last major Civil War work, appeared in 1969, some historians chastised Catton not only for being oversympathetic toward his subject but also for his continuing failure to analyze and evaluate the general's career. Generally, however, Catton's later treatment by professional historians was far more positive than the reviews which

greeted his early works. One of Catton's last works elicited the comment from an admiring reviewer that even "after producing so many books about the Civil War, he shows no sign of battle fatigue or war weariness."

With his rise to national literary prominence in 1954, when some publicists of *A Stillness at Appomattox* were touting Catton as the "Ernie Pyle of the War between the States," he became the editor of *American Heritage*, then a struggling hardcover popular magazine of history. Such a step suited Catton's philosophy of history well. In his preface to the first issue of the newly reorganized magazine, Catton announced the editorial policy of *American Heritage*: "We believe that we do not always need to go to what are supposed to be the great moments of history in order to show American history in the making. The fearful climax of Gettysburg compels the attention, to be sure. But Gettysburg would not have been what it was if there had not been generations of plain folk beforehand, laying out farms and working in shops and stores, quite unaware that they were on the high road to destiny but somehow living and working in such a way that when destiny came along they could meet it without batting an eye."

Until 1959, when he became senior editor of the magazine and freed his schedule from routine duties, he was a prolific writer and reviewer as well as editor for *American Heritage*. Catton's was a quick and versatile mind whose interests stretched far beyond the confines of the four-year struggle between North and South. Whether considering the building of a birchbark canoe or the generalship on the eastern front in World War I, his observations always caught the human element. His connection with *American Heritage* lasted until his death. During his tenure as editor, the magazine flourished and even expanded to take on such special projects as highly praised pictorial histories of the American Revolution and the Civil War. Catton wrote the narrative for *The American Heritage Picture History of the Civil War* (1960), winning a Pulitzer citation in 1961 for his work. And despite academicians' distrust of "popular" history, Catton enticed such prominent historians as Allan Nevins, Henry Steele Commager, Walter Prescott Webb, Arthur M. Schlesinger, Jr., and Eugene Genovese to serve on the advisory board of *American Heritage*.

Despite editorial responsibilities, the pace Catton set for producing books continued unabated. With *This Hallowed Ground* (1956), Catton expanded his view of the war from the military exploits of the Army of the Potomac to a much wider scope to include political, economic, and social matters. In *America Goes to War* (1958), he warned his readers that portrayals of the military aspects of the war years, replete with beating drums and resounding charges, were becoming too romanticized—so much so that modern perceptions of the 1860s differed greatly from the realities of the day. The Civil War was a bloody extension of American politics, not just a military adventure, and Catton urged a retreat from overdramatic battle narratives to more far-reaching accounts of how the war touched everyday lives. The role of the citizen-soldier in a democracy at war, the people's distrust of the professional soldier, and the interplay between professionals and the civilians who controlled the purse strings were all subjects that Catton saw as having relevance not only in the 1860s but at any time in the life of the United States.

With the approach of the Civil War centennial, Catton began work on his second major trilogy of the war. The Centennial History of the Civil War was planned as a comprehensive modern history of the war years based on the most complete and far-reaching research of contemporary sources. With the unflagging aid of his chief researcher, E. B. Long, Catton's second trilogy received the same rave reviews in the popular press as his first. An additional by-product was the publication of Long's own book, *The Civil War Day by Day* (1971), a chronological listing of events plus a summary of statistical studies, manuscript collections, and bibliographies, all originally prepared for Catton's use in writing the Centennial History of the Civil War.

The Coming Fury (1961), *Terrible Swift Sword* (1963), and *Never Call Retreat* (1965) tell the story of the war in all its many shades and colors—again, a blend of the political and the military, the social and the economic. Still using war reminiscences but greatly increasing his use of unpublished sources, Catton's primary focus, as usual, is how the individual soldier or his family back home felt about the confusing and awe-inspiring times through which they lived. It was his way of making a century-old war enlighten a modern audience.

Catton's early fascination with the ordinary individual was not lost as his interest in the broader aspects of the war emerged. He wrote the foreword for a 1958 paperback edition of Frank A. Haskell's *The Battle of Gettysburg* primarily because the Northern lieutenant told an unadulterated story of what he saw on the battlefield and then was articulate and intelligent enough to realize that the fight had had implications and importance far beyond what it had been his fortune to observe there. In a similar vein, Catton and his son, William, by then a professor of

history, collaborated on *Two Roads to Sumter* (1963), about the different paths two young Kentuckians, Abraham Lincoln and Jefferson Davis, had followed which brought them to that crucial day in the nation's history, 12 April 1861, when Fort Sumter was bombarded by Confederate troops.

Catton's undoubted personal favorite of the war leaders was the Union army commander, Lt. Gen. Ulysses S. Grant. In *U. S. Grant and the American Military Tradition* (1954), Catton portrayed his fellow Midwesterner in a quietly heroic style. His was a sympathetic treatment, depicting Grant as an unwilling soldier who happened to be very good at his job, as a lonely man who found great strength in his family, and as a nonpolitical general trying to cope with both Washington politicians and their appointees in uniform. When Lloyd Lewis died in 1949, having completed only *Captain Sam Grant*, the first book of a planned three-volume biography of the general, Catton was the natural choice to take up the task. In *Grant Moves South* (1960) and *Grant Takes Command* (1969), Catton finished Lewis's work, completing a reassessment of the general's character and achievements which he had begun in his own brief attempt to capture the essence of the man.

Catton was in great demand as a speaker and writer during the centennial years. He served on the National Civil War Centennial Committee, by appointment of President Eisenhower. Catton quickly became a noted spokesman on the importance of the celebrations the nation was undertaking, always professing his own belief that history is a continuous process that influences our daily lives, and that, additionally, it is as fascinating a story as one could hope to find. The ground swell of popular interest in the Civil War bore out his statement. In one survey, readers were asked to list Civil War books they had actually read; they ranked four of Bruce Catton's books in the top six of a lengthy list.

Catton's popularity, certainly enhanced by the centennial, surpassed and outlasted that of most of the multitude of Civil War writers of the 1950s and 1960s. At the time of his death in 1978, all of Catton's major works were still in print. Many of these, including both of his trilogies, had also been published in paperback editions, invariably going through several printings. A number of Catton's works were published in England; some were translated into French. Catton's books, while not best-sellers by industry standards, consistently sold well enough that even his unheralded first effort, *The War Lords of Washington*, was reprinted in 1970.

After the fanfare of the centennial faded and Catton's wife died in 1969, he became more reflective about his life and the forces which had shaped it. If he loved the values of the old Midwest, he held a special fondness for his home state of Michigan. He still preferred the small towns of his boyhood; his hometown of Petoskey had declared Bruce Catton Day in 1965 to honor their own son who had made good. He enjoyed frequent trips to the land of his youth, putting down his early memories in *Waiting for the Morning Train: An American Boyhood* (1972), a happy look at days gone by. Again, he felt that one man's experiences were important to understanding the varied texture of American life, and Catton reflected that the memory of something so simple as the unbridled joy of fishing in a clean stream jogs the emotional appreciation of our national heritage as much as a gory narrative of brothers locked in battle to the death a century ago. His pride in his home state was further apparent in *Michigan: A Bicentennial History* (1976), written for the States and the Nation Bicentennial History Series.

Catton's work never ceased to express the value of human experience, and he remained active with several projects for *American Heritage* until he died in Frankfort, Michigan, near his boyhood home. Shortly after his death, his final work appeared, *The Bold and Magnificent Dream: America's Founding Years, 1492-1815* (1978), on which he had again collaborated with his son, William. The title of that last volume again expressed Catton's view of America's past as an inspiration for Americans of any generation.

Bruce Catton, journalist and editor, succeeded in doing what many professional historians could not do. His easy style and vivid characterizations attracted readers who might otherwise never have picked up a history book. The following passage is representative of Catton at his best, describing the armies in battle at the Bloody Angle at Spotsylvania: "it was precisely here that the war came down to its darkest cockpit. It could never be any worse than this because men could not possibly imagine or do anything worse. This fighting was not planned or ordered or directed. It was formless, monstrous, something no general could will. It grew out of what these men were and what the war had taught them—cruel knowledge of killing, wild brief contempt for death, furious unspeakable ferocity that could transcend every limitation of whipped nerves and beaten flesh. There was a frenzy on both armies, and as they grappled in the driving rain with the smoke and the wild shouting and the great shock of gunfire all about them this one muddy ditch with a log wall running down the middle became the center of the whole world. Nothing mattered except to possess it utterly or to clog it breast-high with corpses."

Bruce Catton strove to make the people of the 1860s speak to modern generations, and to make modern readers understand the hopes, dreams, and fears of their forebears. Catton remained true to his belief that good history is also fine literature—a combination of thorough spadework for factual accuracy and the skill of an artist to make it meaningful to others. In producing histories of the American people for the American people, Catton secured a place as one of the major Civil War writers of the twentieth century.

Periodical Publication:
"What They Did There," *American Heritage*, 6 (December 1954): 3-4.

Reference:
Oliver Jensen, "Working with Bruce Catton," *American Heritage*, 30 (February-March 1979): 44-51.

Papers:
Most of Catton's surviving papers are in the Archive of Contemporary History at the University of Wyoming.

Edward Channing

(15 June 1856-7 January 1931)

George D. Terry
University of South Carolina

SELECTED BOOKS: *Town and County Government in the English Colonies of North America* (Baltimore: Johns Hopkins University, 1884);

The Narragansett Planters: A Study of Causes (Baltimore: Johns Hopkins University, 1886);

English History for American Readers, by Channing and Thomas Wentworth Higginson (New York: Longmans, Green, 1893);

The United States of America, 1765-1865 (New York & London: Macmillan, 1896);

Guide to the Study of American History, by Channing and Albert Bushnell Hart (Cambridge: Harvard University Press, 1896; Boston & London: Ginn, 1896);

Student's History of the United States (New York & London: Macmillan, 1898);

The Planting of a Nation in the New World, 1000-1660, volume 1 of *A History of the United States* (New York & London: Macmillan, 1905);

The Jeffersonian System, 1801-1811, volume 12 of *The American Nation: A History*, edited by Hart (New York & London: Harper, 1906);

A Century of Colonial History,1660-1760, volume 2 of *A History of the United States* (New York & London: Macmillan, 1908);

The American Revolution, 1761-1789, volume 3 of *A History of the United States* (New York & London: Macmillan, 1912);

Federalists and Republicans, 1789-1815, volume 4 of *A History of the United States* (New York & London: Macmillan, 1917);

The Period of Transition, 1815-1848, volume 5 of *A History of the United States* (New York & London: Macmillan, 1921);

The War for Southern Independence, volume 6 of *A History of the United States* (New York & London: Macmillan, 1925).

Edward Channing's *A History of the United States* has provided him with a secure place in historical literature. He was the last of the historians, such as George Bancroft and John Bach McMaster, who attempted to write a comprehensive history of the United States, and his project stands as the only such work which even came close to completion.

A product of New England, Channing never

Edward Channing

left his beloved Harvard and was renowned as both a scholar and teacher. Born in Dorchester, Massachusetts, in June 1856, Edward Perkins Channing descended from an illustrious New England family which traced its lineage far back into New England history. His father, William Ellery Channing, was a well-known poet of the Concord School. Channing's mother, Ellen Fuller Channing, a sister of Margaret Fuller, died when he was seven months old. Shortly after his mother's death, he was turned over to a nurse and later to his grandfather to be raised. Channing later recalled that he only remembered seeing his wandering father once during his life. It was perhaps this abandonment by his father which was responsible for his strong dislike of poetry and of the myths about the founding fathers of New England.

Just barely passing his entrance examinations,

Channing entered Harvard in 1874. During the first two years, there was some question as to whether he would ever graduate from college. In his junior year, however, he took his first advanced history course under Henry Adams, and the experience changed his life. Adams's influence on the student was both profound and lasting. Fifty years after this course Channing commented, "I cannot express, no words of mine could, the debt that I owe to Henry Adams. He was the greatest teacher that I ever encountered. He could draw out from a man the very best that was in him." Channing decided to become a historian, and after graduating in 1878 he began work on his Ph.D. at Harvard. During this time he developed a lifelong interest in the sea and began sailing as a hobby; his interest in sailing and the ocean was to surface in several of his works. As a graduate student at Harvard, Channing assisted Henry Adams in gathering research materials for Adams's history of the administrations of Thomas Jefferson and chose as his dissertation topic a history of the Louisiana Purchase.

After completing his Ph.D. in 1880, Channing applied to Harvard for a position teaching American history but was informed that no such job existed and furthermore that such positions were rare in the United States. Instead of concentrating upon teaching American history, he was encouraged to expand his expertise. "History," he was told, "is generally taught by a master who has several other subjects on his hands." With this disappointing news Channing began a grand tour of Europe and returned to the Harvard campus in 1881 to become a "Resident Graduate." Supported by a small independent income from his grandfather's estate, he began a brief career of writing articles and book reviews for such periodicals as *Nation*, *Literary World*, and *Science*. Two years later Channing got his first opportunity to teach when he shared a course at Harvard with the aging senior history professor, Henry Torrey. After establishing himself at Harvard, Channing married Alice Thatcher in 1886. They had two daughters. In 1887 Channing was promoted to assistant professor and ten years later became a full professor.

Channing acquired a reputation as one of the best teachers at Harvard. His classes were so popular that they had to be moved into a larger hall and even then were usually filled to capacity. One reason he was a popular lecturer was that he never used notes during his talks and took great delight in destroying popular myths about New England history. Perhaps his favorite endeavor in this regard was to illustrate through contemporary sources,

maps, and geographical evidence that the first settlers could not have possibly landed at Plymouth Rock. Channing's graduate seminars were restricted to no more than ten students and were usually conducted at his kitchen table. In these seminars students were encouraged to develop their research and teaching skills equally. Among the best students to study under Channing were such diverse writers as Evarts B. Greene, William Garrott Brown, and W. E. B. DuBois.

In 1884 Channing met with a group of other historians in Saratoga, New York, to found the American Historical Association. Despite the fact that he stopped attending the association's annual meetings in 1909 to devote more time to writing *A History of the United States*, Channing was elected president of the association in 1919. The same year the American Historical Association was founded, Channing was elected to membership in the Massachusetts Historical Society. Years later he would still fondly remember being warmly greeted by Francis Parkman at the first society meeting he attended.

Channing's first important piece of historical writing was the essay "Town and County Government in the North American Colonies," an investigation into the evolution of local governmental institutions in the colonies. Channing argued that the town and county governmental systems were "not so unlike as is commonly supposed; that they were *both* the survival of the English common law parish of 1600." He also concluded that the "exact form which the local organization of each colony should assume depended on, (1) the economic conditions of the colony; (2) the experience in the management of local concerns, which its founders brought from the mother-country; and (3) the form of church government and land system which should be found expedient." The essay, written in 1883, won the Toppan Prize at Harvard and the following year was published as *Town and County Government in the English Colonies of North America* in the Johns Hopkins University Studies in Historical and Political Science. An abstract of the essay was the first paper read at the first meeting of the American Historical Association.

In 1886 Channing's second work was published in the Johns Hopkins series. *The Narragansett Planters: A Study of Causes* examines the social and economic foundations of a community situated in the southern part of Rhode Island. Channing found that the inhabitants living in this area differed from most persons living in Rhode Island because they did not owe their wealth to mercantile activities. Instead, those living in Narragansett relied upon raising sheep and the success of their dairy farms. Channing argued that these activities were made possible through the extension of both African and Indian slavery in the area. Although the work was brief, it was important as an early attempt to learn more about the economic and social structure of early America by concentrating on a particular community.

Between 1892 and 1893 Channing, in collaboration with Thomas Wentworth Higginson, wrote the useful textbook *English History for American Readers (1893)*. In 1896 he had published *The United States of America, 1765-1865*, written for the Cambridge Historical Series. A short volume intended primarily for readers in England, the book never received much attention. In 1896 also, Channing and his Harvard colleague Albert Bushnell Hart published the first edition of a *Guide to the Study of American History*, a work which, after many revisions by succeeding authorities, is still in use in graduate schools. Channing's next textbook for the American market, *Student's History of the United States*, was published in 1898 and was the most successful textbook to be written up to that time.

Channing in 1906 completed *The Jeffersonian System, 1801-1811* for the multivolume *The American Nation: A History*, edited by Hart. Channing's was the twelfth volume in the series and received much critical acclaim within the historical profession. In writing the book he was able to utilize much of the research he had collected in assisting Henry Adams's work on the same period. He was also able to use the work done on his Ph.D. dissertation for the first time. In fact, Channing devoted three chapters to the Louisiana Purchase, and his treatment of that subject in particular drew a great deal of praise. "In taking Louisiana," Channing concluded, "we were the accomplices of the greatest highwayman of modern history and the goods which we received were those which he compelled his unwilling victim to disgorge." The chapter dealing with the Yazoo land claims also was pointed to as breaking new ground. The only criticism the book received was of its organization, some reviewers referring to the author's tendency to include unrelated and nonessential topics which weakened "the interest in the narrative and breaks its continuity."

By far Channing's most important work was *A History of the United States*, which was initially planned as an eight-volume project which would extend from the colonial period to the first decades of the twentieth century. It was an enormous undertaking which, considering the fact that the first volume was not published until Channing was nearly fifty, he had little chance of seeing completed. Acutely aware of this, Channing set out to alter his lifestyle to provide as much additional time for writing as possible. He wrote few articles and rarely attended professional meetings. According to one friend he even gave up church attendance in order to free Sundays for additional work. Because of writer's cramp developed early in his career, Channing was forced to dictate most of his work to a secretary, who then typed several revisions of each chapter. As a result, in some instances Channing's narrative seems rambling and disorganized. For the most part, however, his style is clear and concise. Although he lived to complete only six volumes of his work, Channing carried his history further than any of the other great multivolume comprehensive histories of the United States.

Channing believed American history was marked by evolutionary development, and in the preface to the first volume of his history, he contends that "the guiding idea in the present work is to review the subject as the record of an evolution, and to trace the growth of the nation from the standpoint of that which preceded rather than from that which followed." The "most important single fact" in the development of American history, according to Channing, "has been the victory of the forces of union over those of particularism." These concepts of evolutionary progress and the superiority of the forces of unionism over those of particularism are not surprising when considering the time period Channing was writing in. The turn of the century in the United States witnessed an intense surge of nationalism. Because of the scope of the work, however, one of the chief criticisms of his history was Channing's inability to tie it all together with a unifying theme. When he did attempt to integrate his narrative, he was criticized for ignoring key factors. The adoption of the United States Constitution, for instance, was viewed by Channing as just another victory for unionism. Reviews of the book, however, argued that Channing had ignored the economic and social forces which precipitated the sectional struggle over the question of ratification.

The first three volumes of *A History of the United States* were published between 1905 and 1912. It was in these volumes, which covered the colonial period, that Channing did his best work. According to Charles M. Andrews these volumes presented the best "account of the colonies prior to 1765." In these, Channing established himself as a member of what was soon to be termed the "imperial school" of early American history. His portrayal of the American colonies as a part of the English imperial system was an attempt to avoid the prevailing tendency to view the colonies as developing in a vacuum. Early in the first volume, *The Planting of a Nation in the New World, 1000-1660* (1905), Channing wrote, "I have considered the colonies as part of the English empire, as having sprung from that political fabric, and as having simply pursued a course of institutional evolution unlike that of the branch of the English race which remained behind in the old homeland across the Atlantic." In order to place the settlement and settlers into an imperial context he provided an in-depth description of the Tudor and Stuart periods of England. Up to 1660, according to Channing, the new settlers were still English "in their feelings and prejudices, in their virtues and in their vices. Contact with the wilderness and freedom from the constitutional restraints which held down Englishmen in England . . . had not yet resulted in making the colonists Americans." During the next century the colonies developed without much interference from the English government. This development was the theme of the second volume of Channing's U.S. history, *A Century of Colonial History, 1660-1760* (1908), in which he showed that, while England was occupied with other concerns, social and political institutions in America were reshaped to fit local conditions. Royal governors and other officials were hopelessly incompetent or corrupt and were unable to prevent these changes. Thus, by the end of the century, Channing concluded, "in all that constitutes nationality, two nations now owed allegiance to the British crown."

Reviewers of the second volume, however, began to point out some of the pitfalls of attempting to cover as vast a topic as did *A History of the United States*. The criticisms of the volume were in general the same ones which were to be repeated with the publication of each subsequent volume. For a historian who prided himself on objectivity, probably the most painful criticism was the revealing of the unconscious prejudices which were manifested in his work. Channing's New England background and bias were continually pointed to as a handicap the author failed to overcome. Although he admitted at the outset of volume one that "the time and place of one's birth and breeding affect the judgment" of historians, he worked hard to temper his prejudices. Reviewers of *A Century of Colonial History, 1660-1760*, however, found the book "not free from

prejudice." One reviewer, writing for the *American Historical Review*, pointed out that Channing's treatment of the Council for Foreign Plantations of 1660 betrayed a "sympathy with the prejudices of Massachusetts. . . ." A second criticism, which had been levied against the first volume as well and which was to appear frequently as *A History of the United States* progressed, was that the author failed to consider certain key events or important topics in a particular period. The second volume was also criticized for lack of attention to the mechanisms of British colonial control in the seventeenth century. Other reviewers pointed out his failure to examine the origins of British legislation affecting America. Moreover, despite ignoring a number of important subjects in this period, Channing seems to have placed too much attention on topics of little relevance, such as the history of the Quakers before they came to America. Yet, despite these criticisms, most scholars agreed that this second volume was "a book of first importance," covering a period of American history which had up to that time been for the most part neglected. His use of then obscure colonial records in England was praised as was his utilization of contemporary maps. Channing's command of secondary sources and other reference material was also commended.

The third volume, *The American Revolution, 1761-1789*, was published in 1912 and carried the history through the adoption of the Constitution of the United States. In this volume he argued that "commercialism, the desire for advantage and profit in trade and industry, was at the bottom of the struggle between England and America. . . . The governing classes of the old country wished to exploit the American colonists for their own use and behoof." As the American colonists drifted further from England, encroachments by the British government for commercial gain provided more cause for them to revolt. Royal officials from George III to the lowest-ranking placeman in the colonies were portrayed as intent upon enforcing this exploitation of commercialism at any cost. There is also a detailed discussion of the struggle between the British and American armies. The adoption of the Constitution is treated by Channing as just another step in the evolution of the United States as a nation.

Despite its portrayal by some reviewers as "a permanent monument to American scholarship," the third volume came under attack by a number of his contemporaries. The old charge of interpreting American history with a New England bias cropped up again. This time, however, Channing's prejudices were linked to what was to become another recurring criticism—his rejection of Frederick Jackson Turner's frontier thesis. Although Channing never directly challenged the thesis, he did ignore it. In addition, he displayed a tendency to play down or ignore most issues relating to the western frontier. In volume three, for example, the author was criticized on the grounds that "the historical account rarely leaves the Atlantic coast." C. H. Van Tyne pointed out that the "interesting and important history of the West . . . receives the most meager treatment" and asked "what will the historians of the West say to a history of the Revolution which mentions Lord Dunmore's War only in a footnote, and does not contain even the names of Andrew Lewis, Daniel Boone, Sevier, or Robertson?" Other reviewers once again complained of what they felt were serious omissions in Channing's coverage of the period. Very little attention was given, for instance, to the issues relating to the entrance of France into the war and how that affected the Mississippi Valley.

Federalists and Republicans, 1789-1815 (1917), the fourth volume of *A History of the United States*, covered the period from the formation of the new federal government to the end of the War of 1812. Channing's treatment of this period added little to the work by his former mentor Henry Adams. His critics, however, were silenced by his treatment of the coming of the War of 1812, which was described as being "singularly impartial." Channing once again drew praise for his coverage of the Louisiana Purchase, and his work was lauded for providing new light on social and economic conditions in this period.

Four years later Channing published the fifth volume of his history, *The Period of Transition*, which covered the middle period from 1815 to 1848. He departed from his usual chronological narrative of political and constitutional developments to some degree. Possibly responding to earlier criticism that he was slighting social and economic developments, Channing devoted the first half of the volume to addressing those subjects topically. In the second section he reverted to his discussion of political events.

The first half of *The Period of Transition* deals with such diverse topics as religion, education, labor, and literature. Perhaps the most controversial chapter of the work is the one dealing with the revolution in transportation after 1815. Channing wrote that the most important element in the country's growth was the improvement in transporta-

tion and communication. He believed that these improvements facilitated the "transmission of intelligence and of administrative orders from one part of the country to another." To Channing this development had a much more profound effect upon the history of the United States than any other event—including the settlement of the western frontier. He wrote that improvements in transportation quickened the growth of democracy and direct government "by making practicable the working together of human beings in larger units. . . ." By emphasizing the development of a transportation network, Channing was indirectly attacking the frontier thesis of Turner. In fact, when referring to the frontier directly, he seemed to be dismissing its importance out of hand: "It is remarkable how evanescent has been the influence of these new conditions, for the American people is now and has been for some years among the most conservative of the nations of the earth."

Channing's departure from his primarily chronological approach and concentration upon political developments received mixed reviews from his colleagues. While some praised this approach as a new departure in historical writing, others pointed to the confused organization of the subject matter. Because the second half of the volume deals with political events occurring during the same period, there is a great deal of repetition in the volume. In addition to confused organization, Channing's fifth volume was also criticized by some for his nonrecognition of the frontier thesis. Others attacked Channing for some of his conclusions, such as the one declaring that during this period "the United States in poetry, in fiction, and in history stands apart—it is without an equal since the days of Shakespeare, Francis Bacon, and John Milton."

In the sixth volume, *The War for Southern Independence* (1925), which follows the course of American history from the end of the Mexican War to the close of the Civil War, Channing reverted to dealing primarily with political and constitutional issues. Little space was devoted to the social and economic factors which brought about the conflict. In fact, a little more than half of the work was devoted to the military conflict between 1861 and 1865. Channing ended his last volume with the first historical event he was aware of as a child—the assassination of Abraham Lincoln. The events surrounding secession of the South provided Channing with the opportunity to graphically illustrate what he regarded as the most important factor in the country's development—that the forces of unity, in the form of the North and particularly Abraham Lincoln, triumphed over the forces of provincialism in the South. According to Channing, the particularism of the South continually denied that region victory in the struggle over the nature of the Union.

Although some of the reviewers of this final volume of the "Great Work," as the history was known to Harvard students, maintained that they could still discern a New England bias, the majority did not. As Jonas Viles noted, "throughout there is the attitude of mind of a detached contemporary observer, seeking underneath the turmoil the real currents of public opinion and their bases." Despite his efforts to meet critics regarding his inherent biases, Channing was unable to improve on other flaws in his work which had been pointed out in other volumes. For instance, he continued to omit important events from his narrative. The most glaring example of this in volume six was the Wilmot Proviso, which was not even mentioned. Channing was also criticized in some reviews for what he did include in his history. In this regard his love for the sea and sailing was probably responsible for at least one episode which was cited as being overemphasized, the construction of the Monitor and Merrimac, which he elaborately described, and the battle between the two ironclads. One reviewer suggested that this was an "illustration of the tendency in Professor Channing, quite at variance with his usual succinctness, to indulge rather unexpectedly at times in detailed and minute discussion of some topic which enlists his special interest."

Channing did not live to finish the last two volumes of his work. At the end of 1930 he completed the first draft of the seventh volume and was working on revisions when he left his office on 6 January 1931. That night he suffered a cerebral hemorrhage and died the next morning. Although he did not finish his history, Channing covered more ground than any of the other comprehensive historians of America. More important, however, Channing's entire academic career reflects the changes occurring within the historical profession at the end of the nineteenth century. With a background similar to many of the gentleman historians of the nineteenth century, he produced a history which could legitimately be labeled the culminating work of that group. At the same time he trained a new generation of professional historians, and his own work exhibited many of the characteristics of the new professionalism. Channing's career straddled two distinct periods in American historical writing.

Other:

American History Leaflets: Colonial and Constitutional, edited by Channing and Albert Bushnell Hart (New York: Lovell, 1892-1910);

The Virginia and Kentucky Resolutions, with the Alien, Sedition, and other Acts, edited by Channing and Hart (New York: Lovell, 1894);

The Barrington-Bernard Correspondence and Illustrative Matter, 1760-1770, edited by Channing and Archibald Cary Coolidge (Cambridge: Harvard University, 1912).

Periodical Publications:

"Colonel Thomas Dongan, Governor of New York," *Proceedings of the American Antiquarian Society*, 18 (1906): 336-354;

"The Present State of Historical Writing in America," *Proceedings of the American Antiquarian Society*, 20 (1910): 427-434;

"The American Board of the Commission of the Customs," *Proceedings of the Massachusetts Historical Society*, 43 (1910): 477-490;

"Commerce During the Revolutionary Epoch," *Proceedings of the Massachusetts Historical Society*, 44 (1911): 364-376;

"Washington and Parties, 1789-1797," *Proceedings of the Massachusetts Historical Society*, 47 (1913): 35-44;

"Memoir of Thomas Wentworth Higginson," *Proceedings of the Massachusetts Historical Society*, 47 (1914): 348-355;

"Kentucky Resolutions of 1798," *American Historical Review*, 20 (1915): 333-336.

Bibliography:

George W. Robinson, *Bibliography of Edward Channing* (Cambridge: Harvard University Press, 1932).

References:

John A. DeNovo, "Edward Channing's 'Great Work' Twenty Years After," *Mississippi Valley Historical Review*, 39 (1952): 257-274;

Ralph Ray Fahrney, "Edward Channing," *Mississippi Valley Historical Review*, 18 (1931-1932): 53-59;

Fahrney, "Edward Channing," in *The Marcus W. Jernegan Essays in American Historiography*, edited by William T. Hutchinson (New York: Russell & Russell, 1958), pp. 294-312;

Michael Kraus, *The Writing of American History* (Norman: University of Oklahoma Press, 1953), pp. 232-241;

Samuel Eliot Morison, "Edward Channing: A Memoir," *Proceedings of the Massachusetts Historical Society*, 64 (1932): 250-284.

Papers:
Channing's papers are at Harvard University's Houghton Library.

Thomas C. Cochran
(29 April 1902-   )

Steven P. Gietschier
South Carolina Department of Archives and History

SELECTED BOOKS: *New York in the Confederation: An Economic Study* (Philadelphia: University of Pennsylvania Press, 1932; London: Oxford University Press, 1932);

The Age of Enterprise: A Social History of Industrial America, by Cochran and William Miller (New York & London: Macmillan, 1942);

The Pabst Brewing Company: The History of an American Business (New York: New York University Press, 1948; London: Oxford University Press, 1948);

Railroad Leaders, 1845-1890: The Business Mind in Action (Cambridge: Harvard University Press, 1953);

The American Business System: A Historical Perspective, 1900-1955 (Cambridge: Harvard University Press, 1957; London: Oxford University Press, 1957); revised and expanded as *American Business in the Twentieth Century* (Cambridge: Harvard University Press, 1972);

Basic History of American Business (Princeton & London: Van Nostrand, 1959);

The Puerto Rican Businessman: A Study in Cultural Change (Philadelphia: University of Pennsylvania Press, 1959; London: Oxford University Press, 1959);

Entrepreneurship in Argentine Culture: Torcuato Di Tella and S.I.A.M., by Cochran and Ruben E. Reina (Philadelphia: University of Pennsylvania Press, 1962; London: Oxford University Press, 1962);

The Inner Revolution: Essays on the Social Sciences in History (New York & London: Harper & Row, 1964);

Business in American Life: A History (New York & London: McGraw-Hill, 1972);

Social Change in Industrial Society (London: Allen & Unwin, 1972); republished as *Social Change in America: The Twentieth Century* (New York:

Thomas C. Cochran

Harper & Row, 1972);

The Uses of History (Wilmington, Del. & London: Scholarly Resources, 1973);

200 Years of American Business (New York: Basic Books, 1977);

Pennsylvania: A Bicentennial History (New York: Norton, 1978);

Frontiers of Change: Early Industrialism in America
(New York & London: Oxford University
Press, 1981).

Thomas Cochran's enduring contribution to
the study of American history is his careful delineation of business history as a distinct portion of the
discipline. He earned the sobriquet dean of business
history for his steady insistence, over the better part
of a career spanning a half-century, that this field
was rightly separate from economic history.
Moreover, he is credited with the concept that business history is truly an ally of social history because
business is the single institution which has, since
colonial times, most influenced the course of
American social change.

Cochran reasoned that history, to be successful, must be useful and attractive to a general audience. He urged historians to challenge the traditional reliance on narrative and the continual search
for new facts as the essence of their quest, suggesting instead that scholars probe the level beneath
unique events and seek out relationships, patterns,
and generalizations. He sought to take advantage of
the methodological tools generally associated with
the social sciences as a way of enabling history to
speak on current social problems to academics and
the public alike.

Born in 1902 in his paternal grandfather's
house in the Brooklyn Heights section of New York,
Thomas Childs Cochran spent most of his formative years in and around New York City. By his own
account in a frank, unpublished memoir, his family
was a textbook example of downward social mobility, increasingly unable in the inflationary economy
of the early twentieth century to afford the life to
which its members felt accustomed. His father,
Thomas Cochran, failed in business and turned to
teaching mathematics, first at Brooklyn Polytechnic
Institute and later in the city's public school system.
His resourceful mother, Ethel Childs Cochran, led
the family on a steady procession from one residence to another, often boarding with more
affluent relatives.

Cochran's early education can best be described as idiosyncratic. His father believed that
grammar schools were ineffective and kept his son
at home until age eight. Cochran remembers
spending a boring year in second grade, being
skipped to fourth grade the next fall, and not attending school again until he was twelve. Subjected
to this haphazard schedule, Cochran's primary
learning proceeded at his father's whim: a bit of

Greek and Norse mythology, English novels about
the Middle Ages, and astronomy. He picked up
mathematics by himself, did not read until he was
seven, and, perhaps most important, never grasped
the intricacies of good grammar or the ability to
write with style.

Despite his family's economic retrenchment,
Cochran, when he did go to school, was able to
attend a private academy, Adelphi, where he developed an interest in naval architecture. Looking
forward to a life spent designing commercial boats,
he was persuaded by his father to enter college and
study the more practical chemical engineering instead. He enrolled at New York University in 1919
because the chancellor, his father's first cousin, offered him a scholarship. By the middle of his
sophomore year, the long hours in the laboratories
had turned him away from engineering. He flirted
briefly with theoretical physics and then settled on
history as a discipline and teaching as a career.
Cochran recalls being inspired to choose history
after seeing Douglas Fairbanks in the film *The Three
Musketeers*. Taking three history courses in his
senior year allowed him to graduate with a double
major, history and chemistry.

Throughout his schooling, Cochran attended
class only enough to meet basic requirements. From
childhood, he favored reading and learning by himself and grew to dislike lectures so much that even
in graduate school no teacher had much of an influence on him. In lieu of class, he filled his days with a
wide range of other activities, including boxing,
tennis, golf, and the mandolin. He won a prize from
Yachting Magazine for his design of a ship and in his
senior year, 1923, published the first of two short
books on auction bridge. Despite his own financial
constraints, he somehow always managed to consort
with relatives and school friends possessing considerable wealth. Thus, he spent several adolescent
summers at Saratoga Springs, New York, and Old
Lyme, Connecticut, luxuriating in the company of
people bent solely on amusing themselves. During
senior year at NYU, he studied hardly at all, preferring instead to preside over his fraternity house,
socialize heavily in the style of the time, and court
Elizabeth Paul, whom he secretly married in June
1923 just after graduation.

Even with Cochran's penchant for subjugating
studying to alternative pursuits, he was still somehow offered graduate teaching assistantships in
history at both NYU and Princeton. He chose the
former, preferring to remain in New York, and
earned a master's degree in 1925. The Cochrans

celebrated with a summer trip to Europe paid for by a loan from his mother-in-law. Their two months abroad began in the British Isles and concluded in Paris where, Cochran remembers, he had no trouble developing a love of French cuisine that was to last a lifetime.

The NYU history department chairman, John Musser, persuaded Cochran to pursue a doctorate where Musser himself had studied, the University of Pennsylvania, then considered by many to be one of the finest institutions for graduate training in the country. Cochran won a fellowship and enrolled in two seminars which he said failed to light his historical imagination but taught him the basics of sound scholarship. He decided to turn one of his seminar papers, done for St. George L. Sioussat, into a dissertation primarily because the balance of the research could be done back in New York City. The thesis, *New York in the Confederation: An Economic Study*, earned him his degree in 1930 and was published two years later to mixed reviews. In it, Cochran examined wartime finance, land as a factor in economic relations between the states, and economic problems under the Articles of Confederation. He attempted to show that during this period the states themselves were very weak and that the Confederation government suffered primarily because of the unwillingness of people, especially agrarian interests, to pay taxes. As a book, the study is marred by weaknesses often associated with dissertations and by poor editing and proofreading.

While carrying on his doctoral research, Cochran returned to NYU as an instructor and became part of the fine department being recruited by Musser. Besides Cochran, Musser was able to attract to Washington Square during these Depression years a host of fine young historians including Geoffrey Bruun, Wallace Ferguson, Wesley Frank Craven, and Henry Steele Commager. While the scholarly company was undoubtedly stimulating, Cochran pursued the unrestrained social and sexual life of Greenwich Village with greater diligence. The Cochrans were divorced in 1931, and his second marriage, to Marian Moyer in 1935, ended when she died of cirrhosis of the liver in 1937.

Cochran partied several times a week and resumed his enthusiasm for bridge. Yet, at about this time, he met the woman who eventually provided him with the quiet companionship and steadying influence that allowed his scholarship to blossom. It was the good judgment of Rosamond Beebe that truly launched Cochran's career. Within a few years

after their marriage in 1937, she became Cochran's research assistant and, as he tells it, coauthor, though she steadfastly refused to have her name listed on any title page. She provided domestic stability, and he in turn drew her to his passions, especially tennis and golf, albeit in reasonable doses.

Most immediately, Ro, as she was known to friends, recognized that the sprawling manuscript on which her husband had been working intermittently for several years would require some tight editorial work and rewriting if it were ever to be published. She suggested that William Miller, a University of Pennsylvania graduate student who had studied with Cochran as an NYU undergraduate, be engaged for the task. The job forever stopped Miller's progress toward the Ph.D., but the result of their labors, *The Age of Enterprise: A Social History of Industrial America* (1942), has proved to be a durable and stimulating work. In it, the authors took their first preliminary steps in the field of business history. The book is not only a survey of the history of American industry but also Cochran's first attempt to assess the impact of industrial change and particularly business practices upon other American institutions.

Scholars generally agree that the formal study of business history began in 1927 when the Harvard Graduate School of Business Administration created an endowed position, first occupied by Norman S. B. Gras. Under his leadership, business history grew away from muckraking exposés and company apologias and gained respectability as an impartial discipline. Cochran seems not to have known Gras but rather to have come to business history through his own disquietude with the bulk of the eclectic history being produced. Spurred by feelings which would a few years later burst forth into one of his most famous articles, Cochran was drawn into wide reading in the social sciences and into continual arguments with Commager over the nature of the muse they had chosen to serve. The result of these endeavors was Cochran's twofold conviction which henceforth guided his career: that business itself was a worthy subject for historical study and that historians had for too long neglected the importance of business as a social institution.

Cochran's exploration of the social sciences was encouraged by Merle Curti, then a professor at Columbia. Curti arranged for Cochran to read a paper, "The Social History of the Corporation," at the 1939 meeting of the American Historical Association (AHA). He selected him as coeditor, along with Jesse Clarkson, of a collection of papers from the 1940 AHA meeting, published as *War as a Social Institution: the Historian's Perspective* (1941). And in addition, he had Cochran appointed to the Committee on Historiography of the Social Science Research Council (SSRC).

Perhaps even more important than Curti was Cochran's association with Arthur Cole, one of Gras's colleagues at Harvard. In 1940, Cole received a grant of $300,000 from the Rockefeller Foundation for the SSRC to promote a ten-year study of economic history. Cole not only chaired the new committee on research but he also included both the corporation and the entrepreneur as areas to be studied. Selecting the entrepreneur, the business decision maker, as a key element in economic change brought Cole closer to historians and particularly to Cochran, who had pointed out the importance of human attitudes and behavior to the economic process in *The Age of Enterprise*. Later in the 1940s, Cole assembled the informal "East Coast Group in Entrepreneurial History" and invited Cochran to join. Another Rockefeller grant transformed the group into the Research Center in Entrepreneurial History, whose faculty included the internationally famous economist Joseph Schumpeter. Taken together, all of these activities allowed Cochran to hit his stride as a scholar. Coupled with his wife's devotion, they provided the milieu in which he began to produce the work which brought him renown.

Publication of *The Age of Enterprise* led to other job offers for Cochran, which he parlayed into promotions to associate professor in 1943 and full professor a year later. Then, in an attempt to show that the social science approach to business history could yield significant scholarly results, he accepted a grant from the NYU Graduate School of Business Administration to inaugurate a business history series with a study of the Pabst Brewing Company. In preparing this book, published as *The Pabst Brewing Company: The History of an American Business* (1948), Cochran deliberately solicited advice from Cole and other social scientists in order to formulate questions and investigate areas which might not ordinarily occur to the traditional historian. The Cochrans moved to Milwaukee to do their research, aided by a research assistant, Ferdinand Schultz, and by William Miller, who again polished the final draft.

Working in the Pabst records convinced Cochran of the need to urge business executives to keep company records in usable form, and when still another Rockefeller grant led to the creation of the National Records Management Council, of which Cochran became chairman in 1949, the council engaged a staff to teach companies, for a fee, how to reduce the bulk of their records while preserving materials of value to historians and management alike. The council was dissolved when the Internal Revenue Service successfully questioned its nonprofit status. Under New York law, the assets could quite properly be divided among the board members, and Cochran's share provided a stipend to him and his wife for life.

Despite this emerging dedication to his work, Cochran did not turn his back entirely on former pleasures. The Cochrans took weekends and long summer vacations in the New Jersey countryside. He kept up his friendship with other Greenwich Village denizens, including Matthew Josephson and the man he calls his best friend, labor lawyer David Mandel. He served as advisory editor for *Direction*, a radical journal on the arts, for five years, and, while not politically active, sympathized with socialist opposition to the New Deal and to American entrance into World War II. These continuing predilections led to further impatience with his profession, which seemed wedded to outdated and useless concepts. A Greenwich Village New Year's Eve party immediately after the 1946 AHA meeting provided a forum to voice his frustrations, which he transformed on New Year's Day into the rough draft of an article with the working title "The Failure of History." Guy Stanton Ford, editor of the *American History Review*, liked the idea and published a revised version as "The 'Presidential Synthesis' in American History."

So powerful is the argument of this paper that, since its publication in 1948, it seems to have become the jumping-off point for anyone interested in suggesting a new approach to the study of American history. Yet, the article's thesis is really quite simple. Cochran asserted that the traditional organization of American history into a parade of presidential administrations and political movements is inadequate for dealing with the types of problems which concern social scientists and the general public. Picking up where he left off in *The Age of Enterprise*, he called for a more realistic examination of the American past, penetrating beyond the events so prominent in traditional historical narrative. He suggested research to expose the ordinary rather than the unique and urged historians to prowl through source materials that could help build a new synthesis, incorporating changes in factors such as family life, choice of occupations, patterns of mobility, and social beliefs.

With his career now firmly established, the

University of Pennsylvania beckoned in 1949 with the offer of a new chair named for John Bach McMaster. Although Cochran had an ideal situation at NYU, he agreed to the appointment primarily to seek out more able graduate students. The Cochrans regretted leaving New York, but they soon found that Philadelphia could provide a life similar to the one they left behind. Academically, Pennsylvania quickly proved its worth to Cochran. He associated with a growing group of faculty members exploring the new field of American studies in which he had experimented at NYU. He continued his interdisciplinary work by contributing to an investigation of social change and adjustment in Norristown, an industrial center west of Philadelphia (*The Norristown Study*, 1961, edited by Sidney Goldstein). Cochran remained at Pennsylvania for the balance of his academic career with a great deal of satisfaction. He served the history department as chairman and turned down several offers to go elsewhere, including a bid from Columbia University to return to New York. As a graduate professor he attracted students of the highest caliber and became known for his generous spirit and unfailing good humor and for his endless search for new ways to attack problems of historical development.

Research for the Pabst study had focused Cochran's attention on one of the themes being considered by Cole Research Center in Entrepreneurial History at Harvard, the role of the entrepreneur in economic change. Cochran rejected the narrow definition of entrepreneur as one who risks capital and broadened the concept to make it nearly synonymous with business executive. His interest in writing an intellectual history of entrepreneurship became possible when he discovered the existence of the business correspondence of several dozen nineteenth-century railroad leaders. Cochran and his colleagues devised sixty or so categories for examining the thought of these men, but Rosamond Cochran did the bulk of the research in this pioneering work in quantification. In all, she pored over and sorted more than 100,000 letters from sixty-one individuals and allowed her husband to produce *Railroad Leaders, 1845-1890: The Business Mind in Action* (1953). Given the fragmentary nature of the existing evidence, Cochran was understandably tentative in his conclusions about the characteristics of these men, but he still was able to suggest how commonly held opinions and attitudes on such issues as innovation, competition, and government control could lead to the definition of the railroad executive as a distinctive social type.

The role of business as a social institution in American life was now firmly fixed as the dominant theme in Cochran's work. Yet, he knew that the complete examination of this subject would have to be preceded by some comparative study of the place of business in other cultures. Two opportunities arose enabling him to undertake this work. The first was an invitation in 1954 from the Social Science Research Center of the University of Puerto Rico to study business culture there. So tempting was the offer that Cochran actually postponed an appointment to be Pitt Professor at Cambridge University in order to go to Puerto Rico. Once there, the Cochrans had the good fortune to find unusually suitable housing and to establish friendships which allowed them to exchange homes at Christmas over the next few years. The research proceeded speedily, and in *The Puerto Rican Businessman: A Study in Cultural Change* (1959), Cochran explored business attitudes and behavior in an environment where business was not nearly so entrenched as on the mainland. He argued that the Spanish heritage—aristocratic, agrarian, nonmobile, and family centered— strongly influenced Puerto Rican business. Progress often took a back seat to nepotism and an unwillingness to modernize operations.

The second opportunity for cross-cultural research came from a request by Argentinian Guido Di Tella to do a history of his family's firm, S.I.A.M. Di Tella, a manufacturer of heavy steel equipment and durable goods. The language barrier was surmounted when Cochran recruited Ruben Reina to the project. Reina was especially qualified in that he was a native Argentinian, an anthropologist interested in modern history, and a faculty member at the University of Pennsylvania. The Cochrans spent a whirlwind two weeks in South America, inspecting factories, conducting interviews, and being entertained, but the real research was done back in Philadelphia after company records had been shipped there. Cochran credits his later election as president of the AHA to the favorable reception given *Entrepreneurship in Argentine Culture: Torcuato Di Tella and S.I.A.M.* (1962), in which Cochran and Reina broke new ground exploring entrepreneurship in a Latin American context for the first time. The analysis runs chronologically and documents the firm's evolution from a small company under the control of a paternalistic and benevolent owner to a multimillion dollar corporation moving toward impersonalization and the United States industrial model.

After *Railroad Leaders, 1845-1890*, *The Puerto Rican Businessman*, and *Entrepreneurship in Argentine*

Culture, Cochran's scholarship reached a turning point, an end to the study of individual firms and industries and a new concentration on the importance of business in American culture. This broad interest culminated in Cochran's most profound and stimulating work, *Business in American Life: A History* (1972). While this book was germinating over the course of many years, Cochran's star shone so brightly that he was able to engage in several projects open to him as one of his profession's most distinguished practitioners. He revised and had republished a short book which had originally appeared as *The American Business System: A Historical Perspective, 1900-1955* (1957). Cochran thought the first version had been marred by the publisher's insistence that he cover both business and economic history. More than a decade later, the book was substantially reorganized and reformulated, with new material added, as *American Business in the Twentieth Century* (1972).

Cochran also had published two collections of essays, most of which were reprints from other sources. The first, *The Inner Revolution: Essays on the Social Sciences in History* (1964), includes his 1961 essay "Did the Civil War Retard Industrialization?" Published first in the *Mississippi Valley Historical Review*, this article examines the popular belief that the Civil War played a major role in the industrialization of America. Cochran looked at the long-term statistical evidence and concluded that the war had, in fact, retarded growth. This argument, despite absorbing its share of criticism, has had enough force to become known simply as the Cochran thesis.

A second collection, *The Uses of History* (1973), contains an original essay, "Forecasting From History," in which Cochran argues afresh that history must be useful to prosper and that social science methods can transform the discipline from one which emphasizes the discovery of new facts to one which seeks to use primary and secondary sources to understand deeper relationships and to shed light on social problems.

Cochran's delayed appointment at Cambridge materialized in 1965. He found Cambridge to be appealing but did not enjoy the endless array of males-only receptions or the restricted conversation of English "high table." Over the long Cambridge winter vacation, the Cochrans flew to India to fulfill an agreement between the University of Pennsylvania, the State Department, and the University of Bombay. There he delivered seven lectures, and she did paid bibliographic work in the university library. Together they faced the intriguing challenge

of selecting a substantial number of domestic goods for purchase and shipment home since their salaries could not be taken out of the country. In 1970, Cochran returned to England, this time to St. Antony's College, Oxford. He gave a series of eight lectures which were published in London as *Social Change in Industrial Society* (1972) and in the United States as *Social Change in America* (1972). Perhaps the ultimate honor from a university came in 1968 when Cochran was named by his own university Benjamin Franklin Professor of the History of the American People, a special endowed position which carried with it a teaching load of only two hours a week.

The idea for the 1972 work climaxing his study of the importance of business in American culture, *Business in American Life*, had originated at least as early as 1961 when the McGraw-Hill Company had offered to fund a multivolume business history of the United States. Discussions and negotiations eventually brought the number of proposed volumes down to three, one each by Cochran, Arthur Cole, and Alfred Chandler of Harvard, but only Cochran's manuscript ever reached the printer. In presenting this interpretation of American history synthesized around the institution of business rather than politics, Cochran attempted to redress the wrongs he had first pointed out in "The 'Presidential Synthesis' in American History." Instead of the presidential approach, he divided his material into four periods: Heritage, 1607-1775; Transition, 1775-1850; Industrialism, 1850-1915; and Affluence, 1915-1970. For each period, Cochran first analyzed the continuities and changes in the structure of business. He then proceeded to examine the impact of business behavior upon other institutions, including family life, education, religion, law, politics, conditions of employment, and the general social structure. An unusual topical index referred to many other aspects of national life which have influenced or been influenced by business. In sum, the book is a monumental achievement, a suitable demonstration of Cochran's years of reading, the breadth of his knowledge, and, as Stuart Bruchey noted in the *Journal of American History*, his "awareness of the endless interconnectedness of things."

Nearly as significant as Cochran's substantive contribution in this major work was his acknowledgment here and elsewhere that attempts at new syntheses must be tentative and suggestive. Even as far back as 1942, in *The Age of Enterprise*, he had displayed no hesitancy in writing whole sections solely from secondary sources. So much work remained to be done at the monographic level in both pure business history and its social implications that Cochran felt he had no choice but to build on the limited amount of good work by others and to advance his conclusions with some degree of hesitancy. He has recalled always possessing an inbred skepticism and a reluctance to generalize too broadly or forcefully. Thus it is that he presented even those ideas developed over a lifetime with more than a touch of scholarly humility.

The University of Pennsylvania formally retired Cochran in May 1972, awarding him an honorary doctor of laws degree and granting him emeritus status. Relief from academic duties allowed Cochran to concentrate on his term as president of the American Historical Association. He had previously served as president of the Organization of American Historians and delivered an address to the 1967 annual meeting in Chicago, "The History of a Business Society," in which he sketched his business synthesis and showed how an awareness of business influence could significantly alter the interpretation of various periods in American history. Now, as president of the AHA, Cochran felt bound to represent both United States and Latin American historians. He also had to deal with some financial difficulties and worked to postpone the enlargement of the association's bureaucracy to include vice presidents for teaching and research. In his December 1972 presidential address, "History and Cultural Crisis," Cochran sought to reaffirm the relevance of history as a way to explain and deal with the dislocations of the 1960s. America had developed economically, he said, because of the existence of bureaucratic hierarchies erected under a shared value system which allowed a certain amount of autocracy in a democratic society. By the 1960s, these hierarchies had grown too large and impersonal while support for them had diminished. He pointed to business as an institution where the crisis was quite apparent. Once, the nation had permitted a wide variety of business behavior, but more recently, general affluence had allowed the emergence of a concern for the environment and an end to business's claim to moral virtue.

After his retirement, Cochran spent one year as guest editor of the *American Historical Review* and two years as Thomas Lee Bailey Professor at the University of North Carolina, Charlotte. He accepted a pair of two-year terms as senior scholar in residence at the Eleutherian Mills-Hagley Foundation and agreed to serve as director, largely a sinecure, of University of Pennsylvania's special Bicentennial College. He and his wife traveled to Mexico

in 1973, to Japan in 1975, and to Harvard that same year to eulogize Arthur Cole. The exertions of the Japanese trip proved to be severely damaging to his wife, who had already experienced ill health. She suffered a heart attack in Kyoto and died in late 1976.

In 1977, Cochran finished *200 Years of American Business*, which reexamined areas originally probed in *The American Business System* and provided a fuller synthesis of the development of business. In particular, Cochran advanced the idea that the period before 1840 was most crucial to American industrial growth. The business practices pioneered then, he said, were a necessary precursor to the development that followed. Cochran also agreed to supply a volume on the state of Pennsylvania for the American Association for State and Local History's Bicentennial series of state histories. The book, not surprisingly, homed in on Pennsylvania's contributions in business and manufacturing. Throughout, Cochran made a case for the importance of regional economic development, focusing on the Lower Delaware Valley. He contended that up until about 1900, Pennsylvania developed much on its own, but that in the twentieth century, the state merged into the rest of the nation.

Cochran's latest book is *Frontiers of Change: Early Industrialism in America* (1981), a work abetted by his years at the Eleutherian Mills-Hagley Foundation. In this extended essay about the roots of industrialization, he adopts what he calls a geocultural approach to this oft-examined question. He argues with great facility that the technological and business advances which put the United States on the frontier of industrial change depended on resources, geography, culture, and perhaps most especially on Americans' willingness to innovate. Furthermore, he suggests that the turn toward industrialization was firmly set before 1820 and that by 1840 the nation was industrialized. Throughout the book, Cochran buttresses his thesis by frequent references to the fine scholarship of others who have explored questions of regional economic growth. In addition, he eagerly proposes that his study be viewed not only as history but also as another exploration in the social sciences, specifically into the general question of how societies evolve new structures, beliefs, and patterns of action.

Thomas Cochran's writing often lacked the style and grace associated with those historians who have elevated their craft into literary art. But the power of his vision shines through nonetheless. He succeeded beyond question in helping to illuminate and refine a field of history previously undeveloped, and he sought out the common ground between his discipline and its relatives. He has been instrumental in shaping the course of business history and establishing its importance.

Other:

War as a Social Institution: The Historian's Perspective, edited by Cochran and Jesse D. Clarkson (New York: Columbia University Press, 1941; London: Oxford University Press, 1941);

"The City's Business," in *The Greater City: New York, 1898-1948*, edited by Allan Nevins and John Allen Kraut (New York: Columbia University Press, 1948);

"Walter Chrysler: '. . . personality and good practical judgment,' " in *The Unforgettable Americans*, edited by John Garraty (Great Neck, N.Y.: Channel Press, 1960);

"The Social Scientists," in *American Perspectives: the National Self-Image in the Twentieth Century*, edited by Robert E. Spiller and Eric Larrabee (Cambridge: Harvard University Press, 1961; London: Oxford University Press, 1961);

"The Sons of the Trust Busters: the Corporation and the American Dream, 1897-1958," in *Twentieth-Century Pessimism and the American Dream*, edited by Raymond C. Miller (Detroit: Wayne State University Press, 1961).

Periodical Publications:

"The 'Presidential Synthesis' in American History," *American Historical Review*, 53 (July 1948): 748-759;

"A Decade of American Histories," *Pennsylvania Magazine of History and Biography*, 73 (April 1949): 143-190;

"The Legend of the Robber Barons," *Pennsylvania Magazine of History and Biography*, 74 (July 1950): 307-321;

"Entrepreneurial History," *Business History Society Bulletin*, 24 (September 1950): 113-135;

"The American-Hawaiian Steamship Company, 1899-1919," by Cochran and Ray Ginger, *Business History Review*, 28 (December 1954): 343-365;

"Business History in the Social Sciences," *Publications of the American Jewish Historical Society*, 46 (March 1957): 210-220;

"The Organization Man in Historical Perspective," *Pennsylvania History*, 25 (January 1958): 9-24;

"Did the Civil War Retard Industrialization?," *Mississippi Valley Historical Review*, 48 (September 1961): 197-210;

"The Middle Atlantic Area in the Economic History of the United States," *Proceedings of the American Philosophical Society*, 108 (April 1964): 156-157;

"The Entrepreneur in Economic Change," *Explorations in Entrepreneurial History*, 3 (Fall 1965): 25-38;

"The History of a Business Society," *Journal of American History*, 54 (June 1967): 5-18;

"Economic History, Old and New," *American Historical Review*, 74 (June 1969): 1561-1572;

"Toward a Model for Social Change," *Proceedings of the American Philosophical Society*, 114 (October 1970): 366-370;

"History and Cultural Crisis," *American Historical Review*, 78 (February 1973): 1-10;

"The Business Revolution," *American Historical Review*, 79 (December 1974): 1449-1466;

"The Paradox of American Economic Growth," *Journal of American History*, 61 (March 1975): 925-942;

"The Value of Company History: A Review Article," *Business History Review*, 53 (Spring 1979): 79-84.

Papers:

Cochran's papers, including a sixty-page memoir, are in the University of Pennsylvania Archives.

Henry Steele Commager

(25 October 1902-   )

Lawrence Wells Cobb
Oklahoma City University

SELECTED BOOKS: *The Growth of the American Republic*, by Commager and Samuel Eliot Morison (New York & London: Oxford University Press, 1930);

Theodore Parker (Boston: Little, Brown, 1936);

Our Nation, by Commager and Eugene C. Barker (New York: Row, Peterson, 1941);

America: The Story of a Free People, by Commager and Allan Nevins (Boston: Little, Brown, 1942);

Majority Rule and Minority Rights: A Study in Jeffersonian Democracy and Judicial Review (New York & London: Oxford University Press, 1943);

A Short History of the United States, by Commager and Nevins (New York: Modern Library, 1945);

The American Mind: An Interpretation of American Thought and Character Since the 1880's (New Haven: Yale University Press, 1950; London: Oxford University Press, 1950);

America's Robert E. Lee, by Commager and Lynd Ward (Boston: Houghton Mifflin, 1951);

Civil Liberties Under Attack, by Commager and others (Philadelphia: University of Pennsylvania Press, 1951);

Europe and America Since 1492, by Commager and Geoffrey Brunn (Boston: Houghton Mifflin, 1954);

Freedom, Loyalty, Dissent (New York & London: Oxford University Press, 1954);

The Great Declaration (Indianapolis: Bobbs-Merrill, 1958);

The Great Proclamation (Indianapolis: Bobbs-Merrill, 1960);

Education in a Free Society, by Commager, R. W. McEwen, and B. Blanshard (Pittsburgh: University of Pittsburgh Press, 1960);

The Great Constitution (Indianapolis: Bobbs-Merrill, 1961);

Crusaders for Freedom (Garden City: Doubleday, 1962);

Our Schools Have Kept Us Free (Washington: National School Public Relations Association, 1962);

The Nature and the Study of History (Columbus: C. E. Merrill, 1965);

Freedom and Order: A Commentary on the Political Scene (New York: Braziller, 1966);

Was America a Mistake?: An Eighteenth Century Controversy, by Commager and E. Giordonetti (New York: Harper & Row, 1967);

The Search for a Usable Past, and Other Essays in Historiography (New York: Knopf, 1967);

Colonies in Transition, by Commager and Richard B. Morris (New York: Harper & Row, 1968);

Commonwealth of Learning (New York: Harper & Row, 1968);

Jefferson, Nationalism and the Enlightenment (New York: Braziller, 1975);

The Empire of Reason: How Europe Imagined and America Realized the Enlightenment (Garden City: Doubleday, 1978; London: Weidenfeld & Nicolson, 1978).

Henry Steele Commager

For over half a century Henry Steele Commager has devoted his energies to making it easier for scholars and lay readers both to "get at" the sources of the American historical record and to understand their heritage more fully. He has undertaken these tasks so that his readers might become more informed and responsible participants in the great experiment launched in the eighteenth century to make a free, democratic, and bountiful society a reality on the North American continent.

117

His efforts have included the publication of textbooks for youth and university students, the editing of volumes of original source material, the writing of biographies of prominent Americans, the exploration of the American character, and the hectoring of the reading public in numerous popular articles demanding that Americans live responsibly and prove worthy of their heritage. He proudly calls himself a Jeffersonian, and his sprightly style, his eye for the illuminating vignette, his catholic knowledge, and his optimistic perspective have served him well in bringing his insights to generations of readers.

Commager was born in Pittsburgh in 1902, the son of James Williams and Anna Elizabeth Dan Commager, and moved as a child to Chicago. He received his Ph.B., M.A., and Ph.D. degrees at the University of Chicago and did further study at Copenhagen, Cambridge, and Oxford universities. His teaching career began at New York University (1926-1938), but the bulk of it was spent at Columbia University (1939-1956) and Amherst College (1956-1972). During World War II Commager served as a historian with the army and the Office of War Information. He became a visiting lecturer at a dozen foreign universities over the next thirty years and interpreted America to students from Oxford to Santiago to Jerusalem, and he also found time to lecture at American universities, including Duke, Virginia, Harvard, California, Indiana, and Brandeis.

A central interest of Commager's has always been to reach the widest possible audience with an optimistic and didactic story of America, complete with its ideas, ideals, foibles, and personalities. For the college student, this purpose was accomplished in 1930 when Commager collaborated with Samuel Eliot Morison to produce *The Growth of the American Republic*, a revision of the New Englander Morison's 1927 *The Oxford History of the United States, 1783-1917*. According to James Truslow Adams, the collaboration had the great advantage of balancing New England biases with the Midwesterner Commager's Southern leanings. For half a century the supple style and tolerant, balanced judgment of this standard text served to bring pleasure and enlightenment to generations of survey students. Allan Nevins pronounced the original version of *The Growth of the American Republic* "the most entertaining, stimulating, and instructive single-volume history . . . that meets a demand for all the principal facts. . . ." What Commager helped to do for the college student with *The Growth of the American Republic*, he did for the high-school reader in 1941

with *Our Nation* and for the layman with *America: The Story of a Free People*, written with Allan Nevins in 1942. His aim was always to provide the facts within the matrix of an unobtrusive liberal interpretation and to provoke thought on the part of the reader.

While at Columbia, Commager compiled his most valuable work to date, *Documents of American History* (1934), which has gone through several editions and has remained the best single-volume source book in its field. It was the first volume (followed in 1939 by his and Allan Nevins's *The Heritage of America*; *The Blue and the Gray*, 1950; *Living Ideas in America*, 1951; and *The Spirit of 'Seventy-Six*, written with Richard B. Morris, 1958) in a series of massive editions of original sources and earned him the *Nation*'s description of "our most prolific anthologizer." Such collections were intended to put the words and ideas that shaped America within easy reach of both the generalist and interested layman. As editor, his choices were dictated by his experience in the classroom, personal interest, and availability. The generations of survey students weaned on Morison and Commager's text often developed a love of history and then turned to *Documents of American History* as a vital reference equipped with brief introductory notes and bibliography.

In 1936 Commager had published his first monograph, *Theodore Parker*, a biography of the New England preacher and abolitionist hailed as "the best hated man of his generation." Parker was an appealing subject because, like Commager, he was an intellectual who used history to fashion moral lessons for the present. Throughout his career Commager "applied" history cautiously, but he was always omnivorous and drew on any evidence from his massive knowledge of American history to buttress his views. In the Parker biography, Commager intended to see men and events through Parker's eyes, but he never judged the *use* to which "America's Savonarola" put his energies. The *Nation* saw the book as succeeding as art and failing as criticism because the *man* Parker came alive on the page, but questions of value were avoided; judgment was never passed on the abolitionists, the Higher Law, or the Inner Light. Other present-oriented critics faulted Commager for not distilling parallels for the present from the past: they thought fascism and communism, as the twin imperialisms of 1936, should have been echoed in a book touching on the prelude to conflict between the expanding imperialisms of the slavocracy and Northern capitalism. That was not Commager's intention, and he did not succumb to the temptation of the facile, presentist analogy.

In Parker, Commager saw part of America in microcosm: Parker voiced convictions derived from his Inner Light, then tried to prove them objectively; he loved facts, but he was more interested in results than in principles. For Commager, Parker's transcendentalist dilemma mirrored a problem in America's history: how to prove the validity of innately felt ideals such as democracy, equality, and liberty. As always in Commager's books, the reader's task of assessing the working out of this dilemma was made easier by a pleasing style and the reassuring soundness of Commager's research.

In 1943, amid a world war between alliances of massive governments, Commager delivered his first exposition of another great theme—that Thomas Jefferson's philosophy and practice were timeless and highly appropriate for twentieth-century America. *Majority Rule and Minority Rights* was a cogent historical and philosophical pleading that independent power was by definition subject to abuse. Subtitled *A Study in Jeffersonian Democracy and Judicial Review*, the series of lectures (originally delivered at the University of Virginia) was primarily an attack on the Supreme Court. For Commager the Supreme Court's protection of civil liberties had always been more theory than fact. He flirted with advocating the end of judicial review because it was undemocratic, and he argued that the potential tyranny of the majority would be limited by the realities of politics.

In the light of the experience of the civil rights crusade of the 1960s, Commager's view that the rights of minorities and individuals should best be left to the wisdom of legislators might seem naive. Nevertheless, Commager made a strong case that a responsible legislature elected by an informed and involved people should be a more supple, responsible, and wise medium for deciding public questions than any bench of wise and impartial jurists. He pointed out that the courts have intervened to thwart Congress in efforts to free the slaves, guarantee Negroes' civil rights, protect workers, outlaw child labor, assist poor farmers, and establish a democratic tax system. He wrote before the 1954 *Brown* case and the Warren era that provoked civil libertarians to look to the Court as a friend, and his writings pleaded that final trust could never be placed in a wise elite and that citizens' responsibilities could never be abdicated. Commager's books were dedicated to producing that informed electorate and provoking them to the necessary involvement.

Commager has always trusted the good sense of Americans and believed that the majority would not trifle with the minorities' rights. On the basis of the historical record, he did not trust the courts to protect minorities' rights and argued that if the majority could not be trusted to protect the individual's rights, then neither could any minority. This did not mean that the majority was always right, only that the democratic *method* of arriving at a decision was right.

Jefferson's means to avoid the tyranny of the majority were education and self-government: let the people experiment and make mistakes because mistakes teach wisdom. Do not let judicial review become a crutch or excuse that allows the sovereign people to avoid their responsibility and their right of good government. Commager knew judicial review was here to stay, but he argued to keep it in its historical function—preserving the Federal system.

In addition to producing books, during the 1930s and 1940s Commager also developed a habit of writing articles for the general audience interested in history and current events. His examples were different, but his theses always revolved around Jeffersonian liberalism: give the public the maximum amount of information and the people can be trusted to make the right decisions in the long run. He argued from the record of the past that a government created by the people should be trusted rather than feared, but that the distrust of government, "a curious anachronism," was still a vibrant psychological fact of American life. He approved of the New Deal in 1938 as a "natural and spontaneous expression of American democracy" which was consonant with the Founding Fathers' ideals, and he objected to Republican opposition as a repudiation of the GOP's heritage.

As America's interdependence with the rest of the world became more obvious, Commager devoted more effort to writing for the informed lay audience that read such magazines as *Harper's*, the *Atlantic*, and the *Saturday Review of Literature*. In February 1946 he asserted that the nation had no coherent security policy and that Americans did not understand that the atom bomb made war, sovereignty, and even security obsolete. America's reliance on the bomb for security was simply admitting the bankruptcy of its statesmanship. He argued that there was no American security outside the United Nations and that the United States probably could not win an arms race with the Soviets because the American public would not tolerate the garrison state which would be required. He proposed internationalizing the atom bomb, working out American military plans in the UN Security Council, and avoiding meddling in other nations' affairs. To some, this blueprint sounded irresponsibly naive, but Commager, aware that the nuclear age was radically different from any past epoch, sought new, appropriate solutions.

Once the Cold War was underway, Commager struck a theme to which he returned often in the next decades: the pernicious effects and "un-American" nature of an insistence on "loyalty." He based his arguments on historical experience as well as "bottom line" practical grounds. He railed against the conformity demanded by defenders of "Americanism," whom he portrayed as uncritically accepting the status quo, abandoning the idea of progress, and perceiving America as finished and complete. For Commager these attitudes denied the essence of America. The distinctively American philosophies were transcendentalism (which extolled the higher law) and pragmatism (which exalted experiment and pluralism), which were contrary to the "Loyalists'" impulse to confine Americanism to a single pattern and to reject free inquiry. He also warned against defining loyalty as attachment to capitalism, because he feared that if that economic system failed, then America would be discredited too. He reminded his readers, after they had read the headlines in 1947 on Truman's Loyalty Oath, that America had always been a rebellious nation, that its tradition was one of protest and revolt, and that to demand a puny, formal loyalty oath was worse than useless. If readers were not convinced by appeals to the American heritage, Commager also had practical objections to witch-hunting: if an orthodoxy were proclaimed, first-rate minds would rebel and refuse to work, and America would lose its leadership in research. Commager was adamant that there was no conflict between freedom and loyalty, an idea to which he returned later.

While he was telling Americans that their own heritage held the principles for their Cold War conduct, Commager brought out another anthology in 1947, *America in Perspective: The United States Through Foreign Eyes*, a book marked by cogent biographical sketches of those foreign visitors who were both curious about America and literate. But Commager gave no yardstick to enable the reader to evaluate the hodgepodge of judgments. The "perspective" in the title was not delivered. Howard Mumford Jones accurately criticized the book as being too cozy; there was no dirt or brutality, no underside of American history. Cromwell's "warts

and all" admonition was not adhered to. The volume was a fine bedside table "dipper," but it was more superficial than it needed to be.

Between 1948 and 1952 Commager turned his pen to a variety of tasks. He edited an anthology of children's stories from the *St. Nicholas* magazine, which had brightened his childhood. He wrote a youth's biography of Robert E. Lee that did not talk down to children but told fairly (although it indulged in a forgivable degree of romanticism) a dramatic story and kindled a love for the spectacle of history and personality in thousands of young minds. Further juvenile works—on the Declaration of Independence, the Constitution, the Emancipation Proclamation, and other subjects—appeared in subsequent years. On a harsher mission, he lectured *New Republic* readers on the folly of red-baiting on college campuses. As in his criticism of the Loyalty Oath, in this matter his reasoning was pragmatic: the meager benefit derived from ferreting out a few Communist party members was not worth the cost in time to the hunters, and, most crucially, the effort poisoned the fragile atmosphere of free inquiry so necessary on a campus. He advised that free inquiry *is* a fragile thing and that it is the first casualty in the effort to impose orthodoxy.

Commager's Jeffersonian trust of the people showed in his critique of a 1949 case involving the firing of three tenured University of Washington professors accused of Communist affiliations. Commager argued that college students were not idiots, that they could judge for themselves when they heard the views of the small number of Red professors that they had. There was no compelling need to protect the students' minds. The impulse to exorcise threatening ideas worried Commager: the nation *feared* false ideas, and that was evidence of the citizen's insecurity, his lack of faith in his political system and in his own intelligence.

After twelve years of collecting the material, Commager brought out another source book in 1950, a two-volume work, *The Blue and the Gray: The Story of the Civil War as Told by Participants*, dedicated to his gallant forebears who had fought on opposite sides in the Civil War. Naturally there were omissions in the anthology: there was little sense of total war engulfing the two societies; there was little on the war behind the lines or on the war's impact on the development of capitalism or labor. With his editorial flair Commager succeeded in assembling from participants' accounts a vivid portrait of Americans on both sides: ordinary Americans hated war, but they would not turn away from it;

they were resourceful at meeting emergencies, generous to their foes, and generally went about their grim tasks with humor and sportsmanship. Laughter was the medicine to make palatable the unendurable. Douglas Southall Freeman praised the book as a "long-desired collection" by a man whose knowledge of the literature was unexcelled and whose penetrating judgment in selection was just.

Commager noted that the Civil War had left the deepest impression of any of America's wars. From it came the mythic creations of the nation's greatest national hero, Lincoln, and greatest sectional and military hero, Lee. From figures such as these, the standards for patriotism and courage were transmitted through songs, novels, and Hollywood. In his introductory comments, Commager noted ideas that have since become commonplace: that the war did not end either emotionally or psychologically in 1865; that it was the last of the old wars and the first of the modern wars; that both sides were *Americans* who displayed common characteristics; that both Blue and Gray were practical, experimental, intelligent, self-reliant, careless, amateurish, sentimental, moral, humorous, and generous. Similar ideas were found in Bell Wiley's books on the common soldiers of the war and later in Bruce Catton's studies, but *The Blue and the Gray* was unique in presenting participants' own words in a format which made those ideas come vividly to life. These two volumes exhibit two of Commager's principle goals in writing: to provide original sources to allow the lay reader to reach judgments on his own and to generalize from particulars and to arrive at a list which describes the character of Americans.

Also published in 1950 was Commager's single most influential interpretative book, *The American Mind: An Interpretation of American Thought and Character Since the 1880's*, which represented the fruition of his perspectives gained in lecturing and working abroad for the Office of War Information. He left the historian's safe ground of documents and facts and launched into the highly subjective and treacherous field of sketching an "American character." In Commager's view this character was forged in a crucial intellectual struggle between a brutal social Darwinism and a socially minded pragmatism. The former preached the sanctity of laissez-faire economics and the status quo; the latter protested the socioeconomic ravages engendered by accepting this frowning doctrine and affirmed government as an agent of social welfare. Within

this framework Commager's concern was with the ideas that have directed American intellectual and social traffic for sixty years, and he sprinted through the vast areas that interested him: literature, journalism, philosophy, religion, sociology, economics, law, and architecture.

Commager accepted the 1890s as a watershed of American history, but he argued that the American character had remained essentially the same before and after that crucial decade. He found the nineteenth-century American optimistic, materialistic, prone to quantitative and experimental thinking, amiable, and convinced of both the dignity of the individual and the superiority of "God's country" to the rest of the world. Between 1890 and 1950 dramatic changes occurred, especially in the shift in paradigms from Newton to Darwin. The first half of the book dealt with the disintegration of the Newtonian orthodoxy and the second half with reintegration through the affirmative responses of Americans to the challenge of the new Darwinian universe. The good men Commager described could not really put the universe back together; they could only devise techniques for living precariously among the ruins. It was not difficult to discern Commager's favorites among those dedicated to accomplishing this task. He was always, like V. L. Parrington, a Jeffersonian liberal, putting his trust in the people, so his favorites in *The American Mind* were Justice Oliver Wendell Holmes and Franklin D. Roosevelt, who both shaped law and government in the service of man.

Accompanying this change in paradigms were changes from rural to urban, from faith to doubt, from security to insecurity, and from isolationism to internationalism. Yet the differences in the American character were quantitative and material, not qualitative or moral. Commager found that his nineteenth-century generalizations could be applied to the mid-twentieth century, albeit with some qualifications: the optimism of Americans was tempered; conformity was much more important; there was intolerance of political dissent; and the past was of more concern than the future. *The American Mind* ended in ambiguity: the nation in 1950 was urban, but not urbane; it possessed leisure but was hurried; technology had largely freed women of drudgery, but one-quarter of American marriages ended in divorce; there was mass education, but this had not raised the level of knowledge; there was anxiety in the midst of complacency. Commager perceived the central problem as a struggle to prevent a centralized economic system from homogenizing all the ideas and values and freedoms that gave life meaning. *The American Mind* is an overview of the moral and intellectual resources with which the American people met this problem.

The great virtues of *The American Mind* are rich style and breadth of interest, but the effect is often a blur rather than a pattern. Nevertheless, Commager provokes the reader to probe several questions: In the realm of ideas, should the historian look for vertical eminence or horizontal spread? Which should be stressed, the thinker or his popularized thought? In what sense does a nation have a "mind" or a "character"?

During the 1950s Commager constantly attacked conformity and argued that the vitality of society depends on open discussion and on cherishing the right of dissent. Efforts to restrict thought would inevitably lead to an absence of thought and thereafter the death of society. The politicians who thundered their fears of an alien ideology were simply admitting that they had failed, or refused, to remove the social evils which communism could exploit, the theme of Commager's 1951 Swarthmore lecture published in *Civil Liberties Under Attack* and the theme of *Freedom, Loyalty, Dissent* (1954), a collection of essays written between 1947 and 1953. Commager touched on legal and natural rights arguments for freedom of expression, but he contended that we paid lip service to each but actually ignored both. He lamented that, "uncertain of principles, we fall back on emotion, unfamiliar with the past we guess at the future." Despairing of convincing Americans of the 1950s that their heritage demanded freedom of inquiry, Commager argued from the "practical necessity for freedom" and showed that choking dissent would drive the best minds away from research and soon jeopardize America's preeminence in technology and science. *Civil Liberties Under Attack* contains Commager's famous comment, "The great danger that threatens us is neither heterodox thought nor orthodox thought, but the absence of thought."

The dread sterility of the absence of thought was the price demanded by such pied pipers as the honorable junior senator from Wisconsin. Commager put McCarthyism in some historical perspective when he argued that only the antebellum South compared to the McCarthyite 1950s for the suppression of free speech and a generalized attack on nonconformity. Commager anticipated the coroners of American Viet Nam policy of the 1960s by attacking the McCarthyites of the 1950s for making diplomats afraid to tender unpopular

advice and blasted guilt by association by reminding us that the nation was founded by voluntary associations and that the nation retained its unique vitality because of them. He ended his argument by elevating McCarthyism to global significance—Western civilization rested on America's preserving a free society, which in turn required a proper regard for dissent and free inquiry.

Critics of Commager, such as Sidney Hook, argued that he warned of the dangers of stupid reactions to current problems, but that he did not offer any solution to such problems as preventing Communists from infiltrating sensitive agencies. Commager was accused of not realizing that there even *was* a security problem and that the very act of joining the Communist party was a conscious act on behalf of a hostile foreign power and therefore a punishable crime. To his critics Commager failed to live up to his own standards: he lauded pragmatists and their concern with concrete problems, but that was precisely what his woolly paeans to abstract rights failed to grapple with. Hook argued that there *was* a problem on American campuses with Communist professors under orders to indoctrinate students, and there *was* danger from fellow-traveler government officials. "Naive" was the damning epithet used to dismiss Commager's plea for civil liberties. The *Saturday Review* and other defenders of Commager countered the "naive" charge by declaring that he was not "just another egghead," that he had served his government in wartime, that he possessed unimpeachable loyalty, and that he was no "academic word-mincer." The tone of these defenses reveals the climate of opinion against which Commager aimed in his fight for free speech.

Whether or not he ever consciously reacted to the "naive" criticism, in his 1966 *Freedom and Order: A Commentary on the Political Scene*, Commager struggled to preserve his twin labels as "liberal and realist." For thirty years he had been consistent in both his theme and in his reasoning: both national security and a free society depended on preserving free inquiry. There were valid abstract arguments to demonstrate this, but Commager preferred to present practical reasons why this free inquiry was vital. When he returned to Viet Nam, Commager demanded that the government explain its blatant contradictions and abrupt policy shifts because lack of accurate information, a prerequisite to free inquiry, was itself a threat to national security. Freedom of inquiry was the only method of avoiding error, and to keep from wading deeper into the morass of Viet Nam, straight talk by policymakers was essential. Commager noted the pernicious habit of the government of equating hostility to the Viet Nam War with disloyalty or of dismissing dissent with the epitaph of "Communist dupe."

In his 1967 *The Search for a Usable Past*, Commager offered a collection of pieces written during the previous thirty years. As always, his style was limpid, simple, straightforward, and assertive as he explored the thesis that the United States was thrust into nationhood without any history and described how it proceeded to create a usable past. The primary ideas were that one could learn from history, that reason will eventually prevail over error, and that it was worthwhile to search for an American character. It is not now fashionable to talk in terms of a "national character." Such efforts are perceived as being woolly and not subject to quantification, but Commager thought the search for the national character was desirable, and he used the device well as a tool to shed light on what was distinctive in the American experience and what in our history was applicable to current predicaments.

Commager was not interested only in helping Americans interpret their nation for themselves. Since 1945 the Institute of International Education had published a survey, *Meet the U.S.A.*, which included a "Practical Guide for Academic Visitors." Commager did the 1970 edition, which met a real need since foreign academic visitors had increased from 7,500 in 1945 to 147,600 in 1969. He covered the main elements of American life and dwelt on his view of the American character. His was a successful effort because he had periodically studied and taught abroad since the 1920s, and he understood what struck foreigners as peculiar in America; and he had the happy facility of being able to explain these peculiarities to strangers.

Commager swept foreign visitors through the political, economic, and social development of the nation, admonishing them to remember unique features of the country: the size and emptiness of the bountiful domain in 1600; that the United States was the only nation whose whole history took place within the era of the Industrial Revolution; that the United States was the nineteenth century's greatest colonizer, but kept all her emigrants because the colonies became states; that Americans have a longer experience with self-government than anyone except the Swiss and Icelanders; that for 350 years Americans have been the most politically creative people on earth—they did put something new under the sun: a continental federal system. He reminded visitors, distressed to see all the unrest in America in 1970, that the idealism of the

1960s was a reassertion, not a repudiation, of our Revolutionary ideals of liberty and equality.

In *Meet the U.S.A.* Commager explained how he reconciled his admiration for Jefferson with his devotion to New Deal liberalism. Major social concerns, such as education, pollution, justice, health, and transportation, could no longer be the simple local affairs they had been in 1800. The states had made little effort to solve social problems and possessed little ability to cope with the problems of an integrated, continental economy. The result was that the national government had to step in to fill the voids and provide the greatest possible freedom and bounty for the individual.

In the mid-1970s, Commager's optimism faltered a trifle as he lamented in several forums that Americans no longer felt a sense of commitment to posterity. He argued that Americans had preserved the Founding Fathers' institutions but had betrayed their principles—government's just power was derived from the consent of the governed; the people could alter or abolish their government; there were constitutional limits on all power; the civil was always superior to the military; government's purpose was to establish justice and to secure life, liberty, and the pursuit of happiness.

For Commager the problem was that we no longer practice these principles because we no longer really believe them. We have lost the Revolutionary generation's sense that the happiness of future generations depends on us. We plunder our natural resources, pile up a national debt, and flirt with atomic war. To our minds progress is simply material, and we fear innovation in the political arena. Commager laid responsibility for this betrayal on the threat of nuclear war, because of which we have no genuine conviction that there will even be any posterity, and therefore we feel that there is no pressing need to plan for the future. He was afraid that this prophecy might be self-fulfilling.

In *Jefferson, Nationalism and the Enlightenment* (1975) Commager elaborated on his notions about Jeffersonianism and argued that our third president was "a man for the 1970s" because he believed man could determine his own destiny, man could triumph over history, and human nature could change in such a favorable environment as America. After a decade of racial turmoil, war, and Watergate, Commager felt that America needed a reminder that our national intellectual heritage included an optimist such as Thomas Jefferson who demanded that ordinary people be given—and exercise—responsibility over their own fates.

Commager realized there were two Jeffersons: one was the Jefferson of the Declaration, the Statute of Religious Freedom, and the Kentucky Resolutions. That Jefferson was an inspiration to resist unjust wars, to decry invasions of privacy, to root out discrimination, and to champion a free press. But there was another Jefferson: the Jefferson who was ambivalent on slavery, who spent profligately at Monticello, who at the University of Virginia censored textbooks and selected professors for their political opinions, who as governor required loyalty oaths and built detention camps for dissidents, who as president persecuted Aaron Burr on flimsy evidence, who fought an undeclared war, and who used the army to enforce his Embargo. Commager was aware of this Jefferson, but he did not really confront the contradictions.

In *Jefferson, Nationalism and the Enlightenment* Commager worried over how we came from Independence Hall to Watergate, from Yorktown to the Ia Drang Valley, from George Washington to Richard Nixon. He really did not answer these questions but devoted much of his energy to writing a hymn of praise to the Founding Fathers, whom he thought had done a remarkable job. He explored the relationship of America to the Enlightenment: Europe invented the Enlightenment, but America institutionalized it. In Europe philosophers tried to convert kings; in America philosophers were elected to power. The political genius of a generation forged institutions which allowed America to exploit its natural wealth and to disperse it on a wide scale and also to show that a far-flung democracy could work. Though Americans had lived off this political capital for 200 years, Commager was optimistic that the country could continue to flourish, if only it remained true to the ideals of this remarkable founding generation and lived up to their standards of responsible participatory democracy.

Commager continued his optimistic analysis of the acts of the Founding Fathers in *The Empire of Reason: How Europe Imagined and America Realized the Enlightenment* (1978), which J. H. Plumb said was almost "a prose hymn to the Republic." It is true that Commager passed over lightly such blights as bigotry, corruption, and plunder of the Indians, but his perspective was basically right: the Founding Fathers did create a world of hope that man had never before experienced and a nation that, for whites at least, was more equitable, prosperous, just, and free than any society before it. Commager was sufficiently wise to acknowledge that slavery bred doubt about this optimism, but he refused to remain skeptical of a society that achieved more sociopolitical democracy, more constitutional order, more

limits on government, more religious and press freedom, more popular education, and more abundance than any other society in human history.

For more than fifty years Commager argued in books, lectures, and articles that a historian's task was not to judge but to understand, recalling Justice Holmes's statement that "*I* prefer champagne to ditch water, but I see no reason to suppose the cosmos does." Commager argued that it displayed an intellectual arrogance to impose our moral standards on the past. The historian's task was to make the past vibrant and germane to the present. Commager wanted the reader to judge for himself; he believed that if people were given accurate information, they could be trusted to make their own decisions. There were vital, pragmatic missions for historians: their task was to explain and interpret, but Commager also realized that "doing" history was great fun and had aesthetic purposes. He argued that the study of history added perspective, that it allowed one to live vicariously through great events, to travel to new lands, and to gain new companions. History was also basically a humbling experience because its devotees were constantly faced with their own ignorance. For Commager, a historian was much like a lawyer: both reconstructed the past, both were confronted with evidentiary gaps, both made judgments on character, both tested their evidence and arguments by precedent, and neither could hope to arrive at ultimate truth, only its reasonable approximation. Any reader of his works would suspect, however, that Commager thought historians had much more fun than lawyers.

In addition to having fun, the historian had a definite function to perform for society. History was the collective memory of mankind, and the past was a model for the present. Jefferson had seemed to believe that America was unique, outside history, and therefore immune from its lessons, but on that point Commager parted with Jefferson. America's history was definitely a usable past for citizens of the United States, and this history was also a living proof to all the people of the world that such "good things" as continental self-government and socioeconomic mobility were possible. America's great accomplishment was that she had hardened the ideals of Europe's Enlightenment into two centuries of reality and accomplishment. This heterogeneous, ambivalent, and maddeningly contradictory American society had many flaws, but it disappointed the world precisely because American history and example showed the world it could expect so much from the nation. For Commager, the key to transcending that disappointment was to study America's heritage and remain true to the ideals and practical experience which constituted its history; surmounting that disappointment was not just an elite's task, it was everybody's task, and every person was capable of fulfilling that challenge, if only he were provided with sufficient information. Commager thought the philosophical and practical epitome of these challenges was Thomas Jefferson, and in 1967 he summed up his favorite American with words that might be applied to himself: "Vigor, breadth, energy, simplicity, ruggedness, homeliness, enthusiasm characterized his thought rather than depth, subtlety, refinement, or serenity."

Other:

Documents of American History, edited by Commager (New York: Crofts, 1934);

The Heritage of America, edited by Commager and Allan Nevins (Boston: Little, Brown, 1939);

The Story of the Second World War, edited by Commager (Boston: Little, Brown, 1945);

America in Perspective: The United States Through Foreign Eyes, edited by Commager (New York: Random House, 1947);

St. Nicholas Anthology, edited by Commager (New York: Random House, 1948);

Selections from "The Federalist", edited by Commager (New York: Appleton, 1949);

Second St. Nicholas Anthology, edited by Commager (New York: Random House, 1950);

The Blue and the Gray: The Story of the Civil War as Told by Participants, two volumes, edited by Commager (Indianapolis: Bobbs-Merrill, 1950);

William Dean Howells, *Selected Writings*, edited by Commager (New York: Random House, 1950);

Living Ideas in America, edited by Commager (New York: Harper, 1951);

The Spirit of 'Seventy-Six: The Story of the American Revolution as Told by the Participants, two volumes, edited by Commager and Richard B. Morris (Indianapolis: Bobbs-Merrill, 1958);

The Era of Reform, 1830-1860, edited by Commager (Princeton, N. J.: Van Nostrand, 1960);

James Bryce, *Reflections on American Institutions: Selections from "The American Commonwealth,"* edited by Commager (Greenwich, Conn.: Fawcett, 1961);

Immigration and American History: Essays in Honor of Theodore C. Bleger, edited by Commager (Minneapolis: University of Minnesota Press, 1961);

Chester Bowles, *The Conscience of a Liberal*, edited by Commager (New York: Harper & Row, 1962);

Winston Churchill, *History of the English-Speaking Peoples*, abridged and edited by Commager (New York: Bantam, 1963);

Noah Webster's American Spelling Book, edited by Commager (New York: Teachers College Press, 1963);

The Defeat of the Confederacy: A Documentary Survey, edited by Commager (Princeton, N. J.: Van Nostrand, 1964);

Fifty Basic Civil War Documents, edited by Commager (Princeton, N. J.: Van Nostrand, 1965);

Lester Ward and the Welfare State, edited by Commager (Indianapolis: Bobbs-Merrill, 1966);

The Struggle for Racial Equality: A Documentary Record, edited by Commager (New York: Harper & Row, 1967);

Winston Churchill, *Marlborough: His Life and Times*, edited by Commager (New York: Scribners, 1968);

Britain Through American Eyes, edited by Commager (New York: McGraw-Hill, 1973; London: Bodley Head, 1974);

Edward M. Kennedy, *This Day and Generation*, edited by Commager (New York: Simon & Schuster, 1979).

Interview:

John A. Garraty, "Henry Steele Commager: American Nationalism," in his *Interpreting American History: Conversations with Historians* (New York: Macmillan, 1970; London: Collier-Macmillan, 1970), I, pp. 93-115.

Avery Craven

(12 August 1885-21 January 1980)

John David Smith
North Carolina State University

SELECTED BOOKS: *Soil Exhaustion as a Factor in the Agricultural History of Virginia and Maryland, 1606-1860* (Urbana: University of Illinois Studies in the Social Sciences, 1926);

Edmund Ruffin, Southerner: A Study in Secession (New York: Appleton, 1932);

The Repressible Conflict, 1830-1861 (Baton Rouge: Louisiana State University Press, 1939);

Democracy in American Life, A Historical View (Chicago: University of Chicago Press, 1941);

The Coming of the Civil War (New York: Scribners, 1942);

The Growth of Southern Nationalism, 1848-1861 (Baton Rouge: Louisiana State University Press, 1953);

Civil War in the Making, 1815-1860 (Baton Rouge: Louisiana State University Press, 1959);

An Historian and the Civil War (Chicago: University of Chicago Press, 1964);

Reconstruction: The Ending of the Civil War (New York: Holt, Rinehart & Winston, 1969);

Rachel of Old Louisiana (Baton Rouge: Louisiana State University Press, 1975).

Avery Odelle Craven, historian of the American South, of agriculture, and of the causes of the Civil War, is best known for his "revisionist" interpretations of these subjects. "Revisionist" aptly describes Craven, for his most influential writings appeared during a vital transitionary period of American historiography. Such past masters as Edward Channing, William E. Dodd, Albert Bushnell Hart, Frederick Jackson Turner, and Ulrich Bonnell Phillips influenced Craven greatly. By the late 1930s, however, he increasingly came to challenge their views. This, Craven often explained, was not only natural, but mandatory. While his mentors also wrote during times of social change, Craven was profoundly influenced by dramatically different forces—the Great Depression, the New Deal, World War II, and the Cold War.

Craven was born in Lincoln Township, near Ackworth, Iowa, the son of Oliver Craven, a farmer, and Mary Elizabeth Pennington Craven. For years historians wrongly assumed that Craven was a North Carolinian and that his apparent Southern sympathies stemmed from his Southern background. Although his father was born in North Carolina, the Cravens were Quakers who left the South, the historian explained, "because of slavery and all other Southern values." Settling in south central Iowa, Craven's family established a Quaker community consisting of a school, church, and academy. "I am not a Southerner with plantation prejudice and anti-abolition attitudes," wrote Craven in 1970. "My whole Quaker background denies the charges. The fact that my father and mother went back to North Carolina in the mid 1880's for several months . . . and that I was there only a total of three weeks as a baby certainly does not justify the approach so often taken to my work, as that of a biased Southerner and a defender of slavery, a critic of abolitionists."

Avery Craven

Craven earned his A.B. degree (1908) in geology at Simpson College in Indianola, Iowa. He returned to the local academy to teach (1908-1911) and there was asked to teach American history as well as earth science. Totally unqualified in American history (he had taken only one college history course, and that in European history), Craven immersed himself in the volumes of *The American Nation* series. It was thus that Craven prepared himself for graduate school and, in the process, first became familiar with the works of Channing and Turner of Harvard University. After he had saved enough money to finance graduate work, Craven embarked for Cambridge. The young Midwesterner was eager to study under Channing but, as he recalled years later, was woefully unprepared. And upon arriving unannounced at Harvard, Craven committed an egregious faux pas—failing to ask Channing to accept him formally as a seminar student. After an initial rebuff from the professor, Craven again sought admission to the seminar. "You are a persistent cuss, aren't you?," asked Channing. "Yes sir," Craven replied, as Channing signed his course registration card. Because of his unpretentious academic credentials and his obscure Midwestern background, Channing inaccurately dubbed the graduate student "Craven from Oshkosh."

Harvard opened new vistas for Craven. He entered graduate school with neither special interest nor background in Southern history. His seminar work for Channing required extensive primary research in documents not only in Cambridge but in Washington and New York as well. "There was many a week," Craven recalled, "when I did not go to bed. I would work until four o'clock . . . throw myself down on the bed for a brief nap . . . go to an eight o'clock class." Such a routine that first semester resulted in Craven's eventual hospitalization.

In another course at Harvard, Professor Edward Gay's economic history class, Craven stumbled upon what eventually became both his dissertation topic and the subject of his first book. It was "ignorance and curiosity," he explained years later, which led him to study the depletion of New England soil, 1790-1900. So impressed was Gay with Craven's paper that he shared it with Turner. Following Turner's advice, Craven applied the research methods which he had utilized for New England to old Virginia and Maryland. He received his A.M. from Harvard in 1914. In the same year Craven married Grace Greenwood, who died in 1936. They had one daughter, Jean Greenwood Craven. In 1938 Craven married Georgia D. Watson, one of his former graduate students and granddaughter of

Georgia Populist and vice presidential candidate Thomas Watson.

Craven did not return to graduate school until after World War I. His reasons for leaving Harvard remain cloudy. One former student recalls that Craven was unhappy there. Another recollects that his mentor left Harvard for financial reasons. Craven himself explained that Turner urged him to transfer to the University of Chicago, where William E. Dodd specialized in Southern history. In any case, Craven received his Ph.D. from Chicago in 1924. Marcus W. Jernegan directed his doctoral dissertation on the topic which Turner had suggested years before.

While a graduate student Craven taught at the College of Emporia (1920-1923). He later held appointments at Michigan State College (1924-1925) and the University of Illinois (1925-1927). Craven returned to Chicago to teach in 1927, where he remained for almost five decades. According to a former student, Craven's seminar there was "extremely fine and useful. . . . He had a gift for phrase, a rather tart manner—witty and ironical—and of course knew the sources down to the very last document." Professor Elbert B. Smith remembers Craven's classes as "masterpieces of organization and interest, and [that] he was an extraordinarily brilliant as well as entertaining lecturer." Like Turner, in the classroom Craven focused on large general concepts and "never at any time asked his students to agree with him on anything as long as they were honest in using and interpreting the facts. . . . He let us do as we pleased," recalls Smith, "and usually corrected us only when we ignored facts or failed to write with style." A stimulating graduate professor, "Ideas flew off him like sparks, . . . he was constantly leaving untied strings flapping loose." All agree that Craven's boundless energy and complete enrapture with history made him a magnificent teacher. He demanded excellence, not conformity, from his many students.

While Turner no doubt influenced Craven's teaching style, he also imparted to his student a love for research—discovering "the hows and whys of things." But it was at Chicago, under Dodd and Jernegan, that Craven learned Southern history. His dissertation, "Soil Exhaustion as an Historical Factor in Virginia and Maryland, 1608-1860," was a pioneer study in Southern agricultural history. Published in 1926, the work argued that planters in seventeenth- and eighteenth-century Virginia and Maryland were the victims of staple-crop agriculture. Extensive tobacco cultivation not only rapidly exhausted the soil but created a monolithic market system that inhibited crop diversification and encouraged soil exhaustion. The result, Craven explained, was that planters abandoned their depleted lands and moved westward. "Expansion was the only escape, and expansion from the small to the large unit and from the older to the newer regions became a normal part of life." As expansion became more and more difficult, standards of living fell, social lines hardened, and conflict ultimately developed.

Craven blamed soil depletion not only on the single-crop system but on other factors as well. Insufficient plowing and shallow cultivation, he said, all but invited erosion. The constant replanting of tobacco in the same soils depleted the available plant-food materials and encouraged soil toxicity and the growth of harmful soil organisms. All the while planters failed to add organic matter or artificial fertilizers which might have promoted recovery and halted soil degradation. Although "ignorance and habit" were partly to blame, Craven concluded that exploitative, single-crop agriculture was typical of frontier areas in general and was not necessarily peculiar to the South. Such conditions were "normal" where land was more plentiful than capital or labor.

In his monograph Craven was careful not to single out the South for unusually backward agricultural practices. As a matter of fact, he gave the South in general, and Virginian Edmund Ruffin in particular, high marks in the cause of agricultural reform. In his second book, *Edmund Ruffin, Southerner: A Study in Secession* (1932), Craven expanded this theme. He viewed Ruffin "more as a type than as an individual." A lesser radical among Southern fire-eaters, Ruffin eventually became one of the most determined Southern nationalists. To a striking degree Ruffin's life mirrored that of the rise and fall of the Old South. After all, it was Ruffin who fired the first shot at Fort Sumter and, four years later, ended his own life rather than live under Yankee rule.

Craven probed Ruffin's character and personality with the deft hand of a seasoned biographer. Drawing upon his graduate training in the history of Southern agriculture, Craven carefully sketched Ruffin's valuable contributions to scientific farming. According to the Virginian, the application of marl, calcareous matter, to soils would neutralize vegetable acids and thereby increase fertility. Ruffin also was an early advocate of the wider production and use of barnyard manures, crop rotation, the building of covered drains, the growing of clover and cowpeas, and better plowing. But de-

spite fame and prestige as a progressive farmer, Ruffin lived in a cloud of bitterness, self-doubt, and disillusionment. In Southern nationalism, Craven explained, Ruffin found an outlet for his personal frustrations. He "transferred his 'feelings' to Yankees and found in them a substitute for enemies who had vanished at home."

While Craven ably penetrated Ruffin's psyche, some thought he exhibited a sectional bias which was strikingly similar to his subject's. In spite of these sentiments, *Edmund Ruffin, Southerner* garnered considerable praise. From Ulrich Bonnell Phillips, who recommended its publication, Craven received perhaps his highest compliment. "I envy you the authorship of this book," wrote Phillips. Craven's biography of Ruffin remains his most important work.

By the late 1930s Craven shifted the focus of his research. Less interested in narrow monographic studies, he now sought to place Southern nationalism, slavery, and the coming of the Civil War into a broad interpretive framework. In an article in 1936 in the *Journal of Southern History*, Craven laid the groundwork for many of his future publications. He tackled head-on the "irrepressible conflict" explanation for the start of the Civil War. Economic, social, and political differences between North and South, he said, were routine and never serious enough to lead to a bloody internecine struggle. The conflict resulted instead from "emotions, cultivated hostilities, and ultimately of hatred between sections. Bloodshed was 'necessary' because men associated their rivals with disliked and dishonorable symbols and crowned their own interests with moral sanctions. Differences were but the materials with which passions worked. . . . The conflict was the work of politicians and pious cranks!" Writing in the midst of the Depression, observing the ominous war clouds in Europe and Asia, Craven found solace in realism. The Civil War erupted, in his opinion, because men became obsessed with "mythical devils" and shunned realities.

Craven expanded this argument in his Walter L. Fleming lectures presented at Louisiana State University in 1938. They were published the following year as *The Repressible Conflict, 1830-1861*. Contrary to most conventional interpretations, when untangling the causes of the Civil War, Craven stressed intersectional similarities and intrasectional dissimilarities. The respective sections never were monoliths, he said. During the secession crisis, for example, Southerners lacked cohesiveness. It took the war itself to bring a sense of unity to the region. In contrast, years of living together had provided Northerners and Southerners with a surprisingly strong base from which to solve their problems. But emotion, not reason, prevailed. "It is no violation of the best historical judgments," wrote Craven, "to assert that any kind of sane policy in Washington in 1860 might have saved the day for nationalism."

In Craven's analysis, abnormal, largely psychological forces in both sections brought on war. Fear, suspicion, passion, propaganda, distortion—all paved the way for a national debacle. Emotion gained the upper hand, he explained, because self-serving, irresponsible leaders, North *and* South, allowed the country to drift toward war. "Men fought because they had come to fear and hate—because they had at last accepted a distorted picture of both themselves and the peoples in other sections." For more than three decades thereafter Craven portrayed over and again this self-destructive pattern as the "breakdown of the democratic process." It was "a national tragedy," he wrote repeatedly, one which reaped few benefits for North or South. When the smoke had cleared, the war had transformed the warp and woof of the American democracy. It represented, Craven explained in 1941, "the triumph of industry over agriculture; of centralization over local democracy; of one section over another; of the Republican party, representing bourgeois acquisitiveness, over its Democratic rival, representing an older agrarian ideal. Industrial capitalism was in the saddle and the urban world was to set the patterns for a new America." Much as with the Nashville Agrarians, these changes did not sit well with Craven. Despite them all, he said, the race question remained unsolved. In his judgment the nation had regressed, not progressed, since Appomattox.

These themes formed the interpretive framework for *The Coming of the Civil War*, Craven's most popular book, which appeared in 1942. Written from what some critics considered a pro-Southern slant, it traced the growing sectional tangle over slavery from 1815 to 1861 with immense knowledge of the period and artistically constructed portrayals. Here was a broadly conceived portrait of antebellum America—its expansion, its culture, its stresses and strains. Again, Craven blamed the senseless Civil War on human failings, North and South, on a "generation of well-meaning Americans, who, busy with the task of getting ahead, permitted their short-sighted politicians, their over-zealous editors, and their pious reformers to emotionalize real and potential differences and to conjure up distorted impressions of those who

dwelt in other parts of the nation. For more than two decades, these molders of public opinion steadily created the fiction of two distinct peoples contending for the right to preserve and expand their sacred cultures." While Craven found leadership wanting on both sides of Mason and Dixon's line, he sympathized more with Southern leaders than with the abolitionists. According to reviewer George M. Stephenson, Craven tended "to exaggerate the less intelligent antislavery propaganda," to uncover "flaws in the personal lives of the [Northern] propagandists and to slight levelheaded men like William Ellery Channing." The critic found Craven "argumentative," "militant," but unconvincing in what amounted to a defense of the South. Had not, he asked Craven, the South fired the first shot? In his opinion the breakup of the Union was "irrepressible," notwithstanding Craven's "revisionist" arguments.

Reviewer Fred A. Shannon attacked Craven even more severely. Not only did Craven defend slavery, claimed Shannon, but "he largely ignores all causes of the war except uncalled-for attacks on slavery." Shannon then lashed into Craven's apparent pro-Southern bias: "he seems rather naive in his defense of the beginning of slavery on the hoary arguments that the South could be developed in no other way; that the Negro benefited through Christianization and civilization; and that the Negro could thrive under climatic and labor conditions that would kill white men." He even questioned Craven's knowledge of recent research in soil science.

Craven, who according to Walter Johnson "was overly sensitive to criticism and . . . could explode," responded to Shannon with a broadside of his own. He ascribed Shannon's hostile review to a prior motive—a grudge over a critical review Craven had written in 1942. Defending *The Coming of the Civil War* from Shannon's assault, Craven wrote: "My book is not greatly concerned with the causes of the war or with war guilt. It is an attempt to show *how* the democratic procedure broke down under an unusual strain. . . . I believe the war to have resulted from the unfortunate tangling of the three great movements of the middle period—expansion, sectionalism, and a great humanitarian-democratic impulse. . . . I did not set out to defend slavery. I do not attempt to do so; I do not even believe that it can be defended. I simply attempted to explain a section's institution in terms of its own day and to present both its advantages and disadvantages as a labor system."

Today most historians identify Craven, like his

friend James G. Randall, with the "revisionist" interpretation of the Civil War. While Craven recognized full well that he was revising a previous generation's belief in the inevitability of the Civil War, he rejected the "revisionist" label. Writing in 1957, Craven defended his writings on the Civil War in general and *The Coming of the Civil War* in particular. Critics, he explained, misunderstood his work. "All kinds of interpretations, for which the book gave no foundations, were ascribed to it, until it is questionable whether many of the historians who write glibly about it know what the book actually says." To set the record straight, Craven insisted that he had never written categorically that the war was a "needless war"—a term in fact which he consistently avoided. As Mark E. Neely, Jr., has correctly noted, Civil War "revisionism" is an "unfortunately ambiguous term . . . —unfortunate because it has itself been much revised."

Craven thought long and hard on the nature of revisionism. By 1970, after he had published four more books (yet another would appear in 1975), he addressed himself to the general topic of revisionism. Just as he objected to those who blindly identified Turner with the "frontier thesis," Craven objected to the general misuse of the term "revisionist." And after four decades as a historian he felt obliged—at long last—to set the record straight.

Craven believed that every historian was (or should be) in an important sense a revisionist. His own writings, like those of every other historian, were destined to be revised. "There seems to be no final or ultimate history," he explained, "only history written in the sand." For him the one constant in historical scholarship was "the absence of anything constant and enduring." Impressed by the necessity of historical relativism, Craven argued that historians were culture-bound. Their writing about the past always was shaped by the conditions of their own day. Put another way, historians rewrite history to fit the needs of each new generation. While he admitted that revisionism was normal, Craven cautioned that "the more harsh and certain the revisionist is, the more ridiculous he himself will be in the eyes of those who write history in the next generation." According to Elbert B. Smith, late in his career Craven surprised even his most ardent critics. "Often, people on programs with him would go armed to contest the Craven of the 1930's, only to find that the Craven of the 1960's was quite different. His final book of any size—that on Reconstruction [1969]—is essentially revisionist, and one of his final essays indicates that he finally decided that

perhaps uncontrollable forces made the Civil War inevitable after all."

It was characteristic of Craven to be thinking ahead of what future revisionists would write. Having been a practicing historian during the major crises of the twentieth century, he had witnessed chaos and confusion, dislocation and war. "The historian's job," Craven once wrote, "is to find order in a disorderly world. He must seek out threads, whether they exist or not, which tie events together in a somewhat meaningful way. He must show that there is some sense in what has occurred."

Craven's most important works appeared in the interwar years, a period he later wrote, "when explaining *war* was the significant thing—not social matters as of today." Craven looked for solutions to contemporary crises in lessons learned from the Civil War. During the era of the New Deal and World War II, he pondered the nature of democracy. How, he asked, would a democratic society fare under the pressures of economic disaster at home and totalitarianism abroad? As a Quaker, he shunned violence and advanced peaceful solutions to problems whenever possible. Reared amidst Populism, he later became enamored with Wilsonian liberalism.

Conscious that "historical truth" was always elusive at best, Craven nevertheless tried to interpret the past with one eye on the present. In doing so he underestimated the complex forces which led to the outbreak of the Civil War. Craven never fully came to grips with the reasons why Northern and Southern leaders resorted to sectional propaganda. Moreover, he fell short of explaining why the people accepted it so blindly. And whether writing about the South before the Civil War or during Reconstruction, Craven tended to sympathize with the region. All the same, Craven's works remain important. They underscore the value of moderation, the folly of war, and the hope for life in a rational universe. He raised salient questions and offered alternative, albeit often controversial, historical explanations.

Periodical Publications:
"The Agricultural Reformers of the Ante-Bellum South," *American Historical Review*, 33 (January 1928): 302-314;
"The South in American History," *Historical Outlook*, 21 (March 1930): 105-109;
"Coming of the War Between the States: An Interpretation," *Journal of Southern History*, 2 (August 1936): 1-20;

"The 'Turner Theories' and the South," *Journal of Southern History*, 5 (August 1939): 291-314;

"Communications," by Craven and Fred A. Shannon, *American Historical Review*, 49 (October 1943): 195-198;

"The Civil War and the Democratic Process," *Abraham Lincoln Quarterly*, 4 (June 1947): 269-292;

"The 1840's and the Democratic Process," *Journal of Southern History*, 16 (May 1950): 137-147;

"The Price of Union," *Journal of Southern History*, 18 (February 1952): 3-19;

"Some Historians I Have Known," *Maryland Historian*, 1 (Spring 1970): 1-11.

Papers:

Simpson College, Indianola, Iowa, holds many of Craven's manuscripts and notes and much of his correspondence.

Merle E. Curti

(15 September 1897-   )

David L. Carlton

SELECTED BOOKS: *Austria and the United States, 1848-1852*, Smith College Studies in History, no. 11 (Northampton, Mass.: Department of History of Smith College, 1926);

The American Peace Crusade, 1815-1860 (Durham: Duke University Press, 1929);

Bryan and World Peace, Smith College Studies in History, no. 16 (Northampton, Mass.: Department of History of Smith College, 1931);

The Social Ideas of American Educators (New York: Scribners, 1935; revised edition, New York: Pageant Books, 1959);

Peace or War: The American Struggle, 1636-1936 (New York: Norton, 1936);

The Growth of American Thought (New York & London: Harper, 1943; revised, 1951, 1964);

The Roots of American Loyalty (New York: Columbia University Press, 1946);

The University of Wisconsin: A History, 1848-1925, 2 volumes, by Curti and Vernon Carstensen (Madison: University of Wisconsin Press, 1949);

Prelude to Point Four: American Technical Missions Overseas, 1838-1938, by Curti and Kendall Birr (Madison: University of Wisconsin Press, 1954);

Probing Our Past (New York: Harper, 1955);

American Paradox: The Conflict of Thought and Action (New Brunswick: Rutgers University Press, 1956);

The Making of an American Community (Stanford: Stanford University Press, 1959);

American Philanthropy Abroad: A History (New

Brunswick: Rutgers University Press, 1963);

Philanthropy in the Shaping of American Higher Education, by Curti and Roderick Nash (New

Merle E. Curti

Brunswick: Rutgers University Press, 1965);
Human Nature in American Historical Thought, Paul
Anthony Brick Lectures, seventh series (Co-
lumbia: University of Missouri Press, 1968);
Human Nature in American Thought: A History (Madi-
son: University of Wisconsin Press, 1980).

The importance of Merle Curti to American
historiography is both immense and elusive. Although possessed of a powerful and wide-ranging
mind, he has spent his career working within the
intellectual structure created by the "progressive
historians" of the early twentieth century. As their
disciple, Curti's principal role has been one of preservation and completion; his task has been to flesh
out the progressive synthesis and to pass it on to the
post-World War II generation. While Curti's most
monumental work has lost its central position in the
historical canon, its influence remains strong. More
important, his commitment to extending the pur-
view of history to include the lives and culture of
ordinary folk makes him a father both of the
American Studies movement and of the "new social
history."

Merle Eugene Curti was born on 15 September 1897 in Papillion, Nebraska, near Omaha,
the son of John Eugene Curti, a Swiss immigrant
businessman, and his wife, Alice Hunt Curti. His
origins had much to do with his historical proclivi-
ties; as a Midwesterner, he tended to regard the
American heartland as the source of American virtue and to view the East, especially Wall Street, as
the great enemy of the American dream. He was
confirmed and strengthened in his faith as a student
at Harvard; there he came under the influence of
Frederick Jackson Turner and eagerly imbibed
Turner's doctrine that American democracy was
rooted in the frontier experience. After receiving
his A.B. degree in 1920 and his A.M. in 1921, he
served for a year as an instructor at Beloit College in
Wisconsin before pursuing further graduate
studies at Harvard and the Sorbonne; he received
his Ph.D. from Harvard in 1927. During his stay in
Paris in 1925, he married his first wife, Margaret
Wooster Curti, a psychologist whose allegiance to
scientific method would be a major influence on her
husband's work; she died in 1961. Also in 1925 he
joined the faculty of Smith College, where he taught
until moving to Teachers' College, Columbia University, in 1937. In 1942 he became professor of
history at the University of Wisconsin, where he
remained until his retirement in 1968. In the year of
his retirement he married the former Frances

Becker, who died in 1978.

From the outset, Curti's scholarship has been
concerned with the relationship of ideas to social
action. Sympathetic to reform movements, Curti
began his career with a dissertation on the American peace movement, an interest which generated
three of his first five books. His treatment of
pacifism and its enemies conformed in large part to
progressive conventions. He regarded antiwar beliefs as self-evident truths and their adherents as
saints. Despite their idealism, though, the pacifists
were repeatedly defeated by the advocates of war
and militarism, a failure which Curti ascribed not to
the intellectual force of militarist arguments but to
their appeal to the "real world" of material interests,
above all, the capitalist drive for profits. Here Curti,
like such fellow "progressives" as Charles Beard,
used the role of ideas in society to reveal the self-
serving nature of the "eternal laws" invoked by his
philosophical adversaries in a historical manifestation of what Morton White called "the revolt against
formalism." Curti was no hack polemicist, though;
while applauding the ideals of his heroes, he was no
more sparing of them than of their opponents.
Much of the blame for the failure of the peace
movement, he asserted, lay in the complicity of
middle-class reformers in the very social order
which scorned their dream. Cleaving to a sentimental faith in moral suasion, they failed to understand that war could not be abolished in a world of
rampant self-interest and injustice; that world itself
would have to be changed.

Curti was similarly critical of another reform
movement of much greater importance in American history—the drive to expand public education.
In *The Social Ideas of American Educators* (1935), he
undertook an early revision of the self-congratulatory tradition in education historiography. Contrary to the claims of American schoolmen to have
strengthened democracy, he argued, they had in
fact been little more than servants of the established
order. Even their efforts to promote equality were
fatally compromised by their acceptance of American individualism, which led them to discounte-
nance the use of collective action to further social
change; by encouraging individual ambition, they
actually increased the imbalance of economic
power. Among major educators, only John Dewey
seemed to recognize the incompatibility of democracy and individualism, and the effectiveness of his
ideas was vitiated in practice.

Curti's work on reform movements was but
one aspect of his larger concern with the fate of

ideas and ideals in the United States. His most comprehensive effort to deal with these issues appeared in 1943 with *The Growth of American Thought*, a massive survey of American intellectual history that stands as one of the monuments of the progressive synthesis. As in Curti's earlier work, *The Growth of American Thought* is relentlessly environmental in its treatment of ideas; indeed, he described it as a "social history of American thought." In keeping with the progressive suspicion of "formalism," the role of logic and intellectual tradition—what Curti called the "interiors" of ideas—in shaping American thinking is slighted in favor of the environmental approach, which views ideas as reflective of the social and material world. In this respect Curti followed his mentor Turner, especially in rooting American values in the frontier experience.

In so doing, however, Curti was confronted with the same dilemma that other progressives faced; if ideas are specific to their social context, can they survive when the context changes? The problem was acute for the progressives because, their "relativism" notwithstanding, they owed their principal allegiance to an abstract ideal which Curti called "democracy." In his estimation, "democracy" involved far more than mere universal suffrage; it included mass political participation, multiple leadership, and, above all, an equable distribution of social and economic power. The ideal presupposed a social base consisting largely of independent farmers, artisans, and small businessmen, as in the idealized West of the nineteenth century. However, the story of America was one in which that base was steadily eroded by increasing concentrations of economic power centralized in the East. Worse, the trend was abetted by one of the bedrock values of American democracy, individualism. Although individualism arose as a prop to democracy, the closing of the frontier turned it into an antidemocratic force by encouraging men to seek power over their fellows while discouraging collective social change. Later historians would find a bleak beauty in the irony; to Curti it was intolerable.

Curti and the other progressives found the answer to their dilemma in the idea from which they took their label, the idea of progress. True, ideas were shaped by their environment; but intellectual history was a chronicle of man's increasing understanding of, and hence mastery over, his environment. *The Growth of American Thought* devotes considerable space to discussing the development of American science, which is depicted as inexorably liberating men from the formalistic "eternal ver-

ities," religious and secular, that bound man to accept his fate as dictated by divine or natural law. With the rise of modern psychology, human nature itself lost its fixity and became amenable to improvement. If the deadening hand of individualism could be removed from American society, Curti and the other progressives believed, the sort of social-engineering outlook exemplified by John Dewey could yet point the way to an ultimate realization of the democratic ideal.

Thanks to its sheer vastness as well as its summation of the dominant tradition in American historiography, *The Growth of American Thought* was regarded in the 1940s and early 1950s as the single most important historical work of the age; it won its author the Pulitzer Prize in 1944. Already, however, the synthesis on which it rested was beginning to crumble. The environmentalist, instrumentalist approach to intellectual history that Curti championed was increasingly challenged by an opposing school—led by Samuel Eliot Morison, Perry Miller, and Ralph Henry Gabriel—that emphasized the importance of intellectual structures in shaping man's relations with his environment and thus reasserted the autonomy of ideas. To a contemptuous Miller, *The Growth of American Thought* was "a seed catalogue," displaying and classifying a vast number of ideas but failing to analyze any. Curti himself admitted the partial justice of the criticism in succeeding editions of the book. He was criticized for glossing over the complexities and ironies of reform thought and for failing to deal with conservative thought on its own terms; his admiration for the achievements of science often entailed a subtle denigration of religious "supernaturalism." Finally, the totalitarian tendencies of the twentieth century suggested that the optimistic hopes placed by progressives in man's increasing mastery over nature were badly misplaced, that the tools of science could as easily be used to destroy democracy as to sustain it. Conservatives such as Morison, indeed, attacked the progressives for undermining faith in democracy as an autonomous value with their "relativism." Curti justifiably responded that the progressives had, if anything, affirmed democratic values more strongly than had conservative purveyors of "eternal verities"; but the failure of the environmentalist method to give empirical support to the progressive faith was all too evident. *The Growth of American Thought* remains a basic work in American intellectual history, but its modern influence owes less to its guiding themes than to its encyclopedic scope.

His magnum opus behind him, Curti's scholarship came to be dominated by his lifelong interest in the development of historical method. Given his concern with democracy, he had always defined intellectual history broadly enough to include popular culture as well as formal thought; folklore, ballads, almanacs, and dime novels appeared in the footnotes of *The Growth of American Thought* alongside the writings of theologians, philosophers, and statesmen. His interest in popular culture shaped his *The Roots of American Loyalty* (1946), a survey of patriotic sentiments that in typical progressive fashion traced the complex links between devotion to self-interest and devotion to the nation while at the same time insisting on the existence of a transcendent patriotism grounded in the democratic ideal, a patriotism which stands apart from, and even criticizes, the narrower impulses of chauvinism.

Curti's desire to penetrate the world of the common man and to establish its links to the grand themes of progressive history led him not only to the study of humbler documents but beyond documentary evidence altogether. The problems of evaluating documents, involving as they did the flawed perceptions of both their creators and the historian, had been at the heart of the controversy over historical relativism in the 1930s and 1940s. As chairman of the Committee on Historiography of the Social Science Research Council, Curti helped prepare its famous Bulletin No. 54, *Theory and Practice in Historical Study* (1946), which both summed up the "relativist" position on the limits of traditional historical method and called for historians to seek ways of transcending them. Thanks in part to the influence of his wife, an expert statistician, Curti was increasingly attracted to the use of quantitative evidence as a means of avoiding the problems imposed by biased, impressionistic documents. Quantification held special promise for establishing the links between the frontier experience and democratic values that Curti, after his mentor Turner, regarded as crucial to understanding American history. To test the "frontier thesis," Curti and several young associates undertook an extensive examination of the socioeconomic development of Trempealeau County, Wisconsin, on the mid-nineteenth-century frontier, combining census, tax, and voting data with documentary evidence. The resulting book, *The Making of an American Community* (1959), is perhaps Curti's most enduring work. He and his associates found Trempealeau to be the democratic bulwark they had anticipated; indeed, they found economic equality increasing over time

up to 1880. The frontier, according to their analysis, promoted independence, mutual aid, the tolerance of differing religious and ethnic groups, and political vitality. To be sure, their statistical methods were crude, and their interpretation of the results frequently let impressionism in by the back door. Furthermore, given the dearth of comparable studies, it was impossible at the time either to assess the representativeness of Trempealeau's experience or to compare it with nonfrontier or non-Midwestern locales. However valid its conclusion, *The Making of an American Community* is chiefly important for its immense methodological suggestiveness and the respectability it lent to the "new social history." Both the use of quantification, especially in studying social mobility and the distribution of wealth, and the device of studying ordinary people through their communities owe much of their common currency to Curti's pioneering efforts.

Since 1959 Curti has chiefly been engaged in exploring avenues of research suggested by his earlier work. Identifying philanthropy as one of the crucial links between the material world and the world of ideas, he helped organize a History of Philanthropy Project at the University of Wisconsin, and produced two surveys, *American Philanthropy Abroad: A History* (1963) and, with Roderick Nash, *Philanthropy in the Shaping of American Higher Education* (1965). He also turned to a more detailed examination of one of the major implicit themes of his work in American intellectual history, the evolution of ideas about human nature; in his early eighties he brought forth *Human Nature in American Thought: A History* (1980). While reviewers have generally been deferential, *Human Nature in American Thought* has been received primarily as a survey of the available materials, encyclopedic in scope but lacking a strong conceptual framework, a criticism also made of *The Growth of American Thought*. Its comprehensive quality notwithstanding, serious lacunae have been noted; in particular, Curti's old interest in the triumph of science over religion causes the book to neglect the continuing vitality in the twentieth century of religious conceptions of man. Despite its limits, though, *Human Nature in American Thought* is an enormously informative introduction to a previously unexplored subject and stands as testimony to the continued intellectual vitality of its author.

Other:

Theory and Practice in Historical Study: A Report of the Committee on Historiography, foreword by Curti

(New York: Social Science Research Council, 1946).

References:

E. David Cronon, "Merle Curti: Appraisal and Bibliography of His Writings," *Wisconsin Magazine of History*, 54 (Winter 1970-1971): 119-135;

R. A. Skotheim, *American Intellectual Histories and Historians* (Princeton, N.J.: Princeton University Press, 1966);

Skotheim, "The Writing of American Histories of Ideas: Two Traditions in the Twentieth Century," *Journal of the History of Ideas*, 25 (1964): 257-278.

William E. Dodd

(21 October 1869-9 February 1940)

Wayne Mixon
Mercer University

BOOKS: *Thomas Jefferson's Rückkehr zur Politik, 1796* (Leipzig: Grübel & Sommerlatte, 1899);

The Life of Nathaniel Macon (Raleigh, N.C.: Edwards & Broughton, 1903);

Jefferson Davis (Philadelphia: G. W. Jacobs, 1907);

Statesmen of the Old South: Or, from Radicalism to Conservative Revolt (New York: Macmillan, 1911);

Expansion and Conflict, volume 3 of *The Riverside History of the United States* (Boston & New York: Houghton Mifflin, 1915);

The Cotton Kingdom: A Chronicle of the Old South (New Haven: Yale University Press, 1919);

Woodrow Wilson and His Work (Garden City: Doubleday, Page, 1920);

Lincoln or Lee; Comparison and Contrast of the Two Greatest Leaders in the War Between the States. The Narrow and Accidental Margins of Success (New York & London: Century, 1928);

The Growth of a Nation, the United States of America, by Dodd, Eugene C. Barker, and Walter P. Webb (New York: Row, Peterson, 1928);

The Story of Our Nation, the United States of America, by Dodd, Barker, and Webb (New York: Row, Peterson, 1929);

Our Nation Begins, by Dodd, Barker, and Webb (New York: Row, Peterson, 1933);

Our Nation Grows Up, by Dodd, Barker, and Webb (New York: Row, Peterson, 1933);

Our Nation's Development, by Dodd, Barker, and Henry Steele Commager (New York: Row, Peterson, 1934);

The Old South: Struggles for Democracy (New York: Macmillan, 1937; London: Macmillan, 1938);

Ambassador Dodd's Diary, 1933-1938, edited by Wil-

William E. Dodd

liam E. Dodd, Jr., and Martha Dodd (New York: Harcourt, Brace, 1941; London: Gollancz, 1941).

A pioneer in the critical study of the Old South, William Edward Dodd, despite more than thirty years' residence in the urban North and abroad, remained throughout his life a son in spirit of the rural South into which he was born, and his reputation as a historian rests upon his writings that treat the region. His view of the South in its relationship with other sections informed his interpretation of the nation's past.

Dodd's perspective on regional and national history owed much to the circumstances of his youth. He was born in 1869 in Clayton, North Carolina, a farming community of some 300 families located near Raleigh, to John Daniel and Eveline Creech Dodd. After the Civil War, the lot of Southern yeoman farmers like the Dodds was a hard one. Dodd's grandfather had been prosperous enough to own a few slaves, but his father was hard put to make ends meet.

Steady work in the fields failed to keep Dodd from his studies, at which he excelled. Schooling at Clayton was succeeded by secondary education at a military institute in North Carolina during 1889-1890. In January 1891, having failed to secure appointment to the U.S. Military Academy, Dodd enrolled at the Virginia Agricultural and Mechanical College (after 1896, Virginia Polytechnic Institute). His interest in writing was soon apparent as he helped revive the college's defunct literary magazine, serving for a time as an editor and contributing essays on various topics, including the plight of the depressed South. By his senior year, a career in journalism seemed attractive, but a lack of job offers encouraged him to pursue a graduate degree after he received the bachelor of science. For the next two years, 1895-1897, Dodd studied literature and taught history at VPI.

With the master of science degree in hand and with money borrowed from an uncle, Dodd in June 1897 sailed for Germany to study at the University of Leipzig. By this time matriculation in German universities by young American scholars was no longer as common as it once had been. At Leipzig, Dodd came under the influence of Karl Lamprecht and Erich Marcks. Although Lamprecht's focus upon cultural history caught Dodd's interest, the impact of Marcks, who stressed the importance of the individual in history and the close relationship between history and biography, was greater.

Marcks's influence, together with Dodd's own background in the yeoman South, encouraged the young scholar to write a doctoral thesis that dealt with Thomas Jefferson. *Thomas Jefferson's Rückkehr zur Politik, 1796* (1899), published in a run of 100 copies by Grübel and Sommerlatte, a Leipzig house,

was slight in size (eighty-eight pages) and in immediate significance, for not more than 3 copies were circulated in the United States. Nevertheless, Dodd's assessment of Jefferson's role in organizing the political party that took his name has been supported by scholars working since the 1950s.

Having completed his dissertation, Dodd returned home in November 1899. The following fall, having been awarded the Ph.D. in the meantime, he accepted a post as professor of history at the men's campus of Randolph-Macon College, a small Methodist institution in Ashland, Virginia, near Richmond. Because of his appearance—he was short, lean, and plainly dressed—and his habits—he worked constantly and seemed to have no diversions—he was nicknamed "Monk." College folk and townspeople alike hardly knew what to make of the young professor whose sense of propriety, unlike that of anyone else on the faculty, made him refuse the privilege of a railroad pass for trips to Richmond.

Within two years of his arrival at Randolph-Macon, Dodd had settled into a busy yet pleasant routine: teaching, editing, writing, and cultivating his large garden at home, where he lived with his wife, Martha Johns Dodd, whom he had married on Christmas Eve, 1901. His writing eventually began to absorb more and more of his attention. When Dodd began writing American history, the authors who dominated the field viewed the country's past from the Northeastern-Federalist-Whig perspective. Dodd was determined to rectify that bias and write history from the Southern and Western, Jeffersonian and Jacksonian persuasion.

In 1903 a small publishing house in Raleigh, North Carolina, brought out in an edition of 1,000 copies Dodd's *The Life of Nathaniel Macon*, 300 copies of which had been subscribed for in advance. Dodd's concern to describe the times in which Macon lived caused the protagonist occasionally to get lost in the setting. Nevertheless, enough focus was kept upon Macon to show the author's admiration for the North Carolina congressman, who, Dodd believed, represented faithfully throughout his long career the interests of his Democratic constituents during the Age of Jefferson. This early work contained shortcomings that to varying degrees would plague all of Dodd's writings: imprecision, minor errors of fact, and grammatical weaknesses. Even so, *The Life of Nathaniel Macon* is a sound work that is still the standard biography of a major Jeffersonian figure eighty years after its publication.

Favorable reviews by prominent historians brought Dodd recognition both from outside the South and from outside scholarly ranks. The *New York Times* asked Dodd to write review-essays based upon historical works. Within five years of *The Life of Nathaniel Macon*, he had had published more than twenty such pieces, each ranging from 2,000-3,000 words, in that newspaper. In those essays he attacked the scientific school of historiography that was dominant among American scholars late in the nineteenth century. Unwilling to say anything that could not be documented, the "scientific" historian, Dodd charged, was often unable to address the question of *why* things had happened the way they had. Rather than be so bound, the historian should supplement a familiarity with the known facts with the use of imagination and intuition to render the past in its fullness. Such a rendering, Dodd reasoned, would broaden the study of the past to include social, economic, and intellectual as well as political history, would draw parallels between the past and the present, and would therefore make history useful for the conduct of current affairs. Along with Dodd, other scholars of his generation, such as Frederick Jackson Turner, Charles A. Beard, and Vernon Louis Parrington, subscribed to the New History, as this way of viewing the past was called. For a half-century, their work and ideas would dominate American historiography.

In addition to the review-essays Dodd was writing for the *New York Times*, he was contributing articles to the *Nation*, the *South Atlantic Quarterly*, and the *American Historical Review*. Many of these pieces dealt with the deplorable condition of higher education in the South and especially with the wretched state of historical scholarship there. The study of the region's past, he charged, was the preserve of professional Southerners instead, as it should be, of professional historians. As for himself, he declared he would continue to examine Southern history critically.

Dodd's next book, *Jefferson Davis* (1907), showed that he was as good as his word. Neither Northerners nor Southerners still fighting the Civil War would find ammunition in this biography, Dodd announced in the preface. Because of his commitment to the truth, the book, which took a good portion of four years to write, is an even-handed treatment of the Confederate president. Dodd contended that Davis's inability to compromise and his mistaken loyalty to incompetent friends sometimes served the Confederacy poorly but concluded that Davis was a man of honor who

served his people courageously and who was considerably more solicitous of their liberties than Abraham Lincoln was of the rights of his countrymen.

Although subsequent biographies of Davis have superseded Dodd's and although errors mar the book—for example, Dodd misdates both John Brown's raid on Harper's Ferry and the Hampton Roads Conference, confuses Joseph E. Johnston with Jubal A. Early, and calls Andrew Johnson a shoemaker—the work is nevertheless valuable, largely because of Dodd's development of the thesis that Confederate defeat was more the result of internal strife than of Davis's actions or of losses on the battlefield. That conclusion helped spark a discussion of Confederate leadership that still continues. One amateur historian was so impressed that he invited Dodd to lunch—at the White House. There Theodore Roosevelt commended the young scholar for his judicious appraisal of the Confederate president.

Dodd's writings had caught the eye of professional historians, too, and in 1908 the University of Chicago offered him a trial appointment as professor of history. The next year, Dodd in the meantime having rejected an offer of employment by the University of California at Berkeley, the appointment was made permanent. At Chicago, where he worked for twenty-five years, Dodd taught less and earned more than he had at Randolph-Macon. Moreover, he had the opportunity to exchange ideas with other members of an excellent department, to instruct graduate students in his specialty, Southern history, and to use the university's well-stocked library for his research. Over the next ten years he would do his most significant writing, much of it at his retreat in Virginia's Blue Ridge to which he repaired between terms after 1912.

At the same time that he accepted permanent appointment to Chicago's faculty, Dodd began the eighteen-months' work that resulted in his next book, *Statesmen of the Old South* (1911). Examining the ideas and the acts of Thomas Jefferson, John C. Calhoun, and Jefferson Davis, Dodd concluded that regional politics had evolved from a radical democracy of Jeffersonian yeomen to a revolutionary conservatism of wealthy planters. This change had occurred, Dodd argued, because of a diminution in the influence of frontier egalitarianism. The Southwest of Jefferson Davis that was dominated by slaveholding planters was, he maintained, a far cry from the first American frontier that was Thomas Jefferson's South. Evident in Dodd's interpretation is his debt to Frederick Jackson Turner's thesis that the impact of the frontier made American development unique. One of the first writers to apply the frontier thesis to the South, Dodd intimated that the hegemony of conservative planters was an aberration from the original course of antebellum Southern history. The region's democratic heritage had been subverted by propertied interests.

Dodd's theme that the conservatism of wealthy planters had subverted the South's democratic heritage had considerable impact upon later historians. *Statesmen of the Old South* exerted influence in other ways, too. Although the chapter on Davis was largely a condensation of Dodd's earlier biography, the assessments of Jefferson and Calhoun were fresh. The piece on Jefferson helped usher in a revival of interest in his life. The argument that Calhoun remained throughout his life a nationalist at heart who wanted the South to dominate the Union rather than to leave it has been echoed and elaborated on down to the present. If laudatory reviews of *Statesmen of the Old South* by scholars gratified Dodd, popular response disappointed him. After a year on the market, the book had sold fewer than 500 copies, a circumstance that its author attributed to the publisher's failure to advertise the volume properly.

In the year following the appearance of *Statesmen of the Old South*, Dodd contracted with a different publisher, Houghton Mifflin, for his next book. *Expansion and Conflict* (1915) was the third volume of a four-volume series, *The Riverside History of the United States*, which Dodd edited. Like Dodd, the other contributors—Carl L. Becker, Allen Johnson, and Frederic L. Paxson—were advocates of the New History determined to ascertain the "real" forces at work in the past. Dodd described his method in the preface to *Expansion and Conflict*: "long-winded speeches or tortuous decisions of courts have not been studied so closely as the statistics of the cotton or tobacco crops, the reports of manufacturers, and the conditions of the frontier, which determined more of the votes of members of Congress than the most eloquent persuasion of great orators."

Covering the years from Andrew Jackson's election as president to the end of the Civil War, *Expansion and Conflict* emphasizes sectional controversy in which the West was the pivotal region, courted by North and South alike. That the North won the West's hand in 1860 was the result not of moral abhorrence of slavery but of economic factors, particularly the expansion of a railroad network that connected the Northeast with the Mid-

west. Despite Dodd's high regard for Abraham Lincoln, he views the North's success as unfortunate insofar as it placed the country for years to come under the control of the Republican party, which he saw as the representative of property rather than of the people. Although Dodd laments what he perceived to be the South's abandonment of the democracy of Jefferson and Jackson for the autocracy of Calhoun and Davis, throughout the book he compares the industrial North unfavorably with the agrarian South and West. The chattel slavery of the South, he suggests, was hardly as pernicious as the wage slavery of the North. Moreover, he characterizes the abolitionists as irresponsible agitators motivated primarily by envy of Southern power in national affairs.

The volumes in the *Riverside History of the United States* were designed to be selective rather than exhaustive in their treatment of the periods covered. Even so, *Expansion and Conflict* skirts important topics that merited more attention: slavery as an institution, the ideology of nullification and secession, and aspects of each side's strategy during the war. Yet, despite the book's flaws, *Expansion and Conflict* is a worthy contribution to American historiography. Dodd helped to raise the discussion over the coming of the Civil War above the level of sectional chauvinism, and he contributed to a deeper understanding of the complexity of the disagreement between the sections. For a scholarly study, the book sold well. Forty years after publication, Houghton Mifflin reported that more than 25,000 copies had been purchased.

Significant as *Expansion and Conflict* was, it failed to equal the impact of Dodd's next book, *The Cotton Kingdom: A Chronicle of the Old South* (1919). A small volume of only 30,000 words written in a period of six weeks for the popularly oriented *Yale Chronicles of America* series, *The Cotton Kingdom*, although it lacks documentary notes, was the culmination of a lifetime of study and reflection. The research dated back to Dodd's childhood when he had made notes of stories that his mother told him. An examination of the culture of the Deep South in the decade before the Civil War, the volume contains chapters on the general state of the region in 1850, the economy, the planters' social philosophy, literature, religion and education, and politics. The lower South of the 1850s, Dodd contended, was a society dominated in all aspects by cotton planters who were democratic in manner—they knew that their poorer neighbors could vote—and reactionary in philosophy—they believed that all men are not created equal. The change in ideology from the radicalism of the Jeffersonian era to the conservatism of 1860 was the result, Dodd claimed, of various forces: the popularity of conservative statesmen such as John Marshall and John Randolph; the impact both of conservative thinkers such as the Virginians Thomas R. Dew and George Fitzhugh and the Scotsman Thomas Carlyle and of the romantic novelist Sir Walter Scott; and the profitability of slavery. Good government, these planters believed, should represent property and privilege.

Despite the prestige of the cotton planters, by and large they were, Dodd averred, an unpretentious lot who lived plainly and who commanded the allegiance of the lower whites. The presence of millions of black slaves made the white South a social unit in which the beau ideal was not to undercut the position of the planters but to become a planter oneself. As for the lives of the slaves, Dodd's picture is generally a benign, though hardly a maudlin, one. What is most striking in his account of that topic is an attractive reticence to characterize how the slaves themselves felt about their condition. That little was known of that subject in 1919 failed to deter many other writers from forming the image of the "happy darky."

Of particular note in *The Cotton Kingdom* is the chapter on Southern literature, written at a time when serious study of that subject was in its infancy. Dodd rightly recognized the considerable talent of William Gilmore Simms and Henry Timrod, although his praise of Paul Hamilton Hayne was excessive. More important than those conventional writers, Dodd believed, were the more original Southwestern humorists such as Augustus Baldwin Longstreet, Johnson Jones Hooper, and Joseph Glover Baldwin, whose work presaged Mark Twain's. In addition to Dodd's sound literary criticism, he made perceptive observations elsewhere in the book on the importance of evangelical Protestantism and of higher education in the cotton South.

Praised when published, *The Cotton Kingdom* has been greatly influential ever since. In the 1920s, before surveys of Southern history appeared, it was sometimes used as a textbook. Its interpretations have been incorporated into widely read texts on American history. According to an authority on American historiography, Michael Kraus, *The Cotton Kingdom* "contained enough ideas for a shelffull of books." And many have been written, some challenging Dodd's interpretations, more confirming and expanding them. Fifty years after the book's appearance, the standard text on the era of the Civil

War—J. G. Randall and David Donald's *The Civil War and Reconstruction* (1969)—adjudged the work to be "brilliant."

If *The Cotton Kingdom* is Dodd's best book, his next, *Woodrow Wilson and His Work* (1920), is his worst. In the latter, Dodd the partisan overwhelmed Dodd the historian. For twenty years, Dodd had wanted not only to write history but also to make it. At Randolph-Macon, he had fought with reform forces in a losing battle against Virginia's Democratic machine. By 1918, he had come to believe that elements of reaction were poised to gain control of the country. To resist them and to advance Wilson's domestic and diplomatic policies he would write a biography of the president. The result was hardly a full-scale "life," as Wilson's first fifty-five years were treated in less than one-fifth of the book. Nor was the assessment of Wilson's presidency, which occupied the bulk of the book, evenhanded. To Dodd, Wilson was a "modern St. George" locked in deadly combat with the dragon of plutocracy and parochialism. Seldom were the president's foes, primarily the minions of Northeastern industry, motivated by anything other than resentment of the achievements of a son of the democratic, agrarian South.

Disappointed by the reception given *Woodrow Wilson and His Work*—only 5,000 copies were bought within two years of publication and few periodicals ran reviews—Dodd nevertheless continued to show interest in studying the former president. As a result, shortly after Wilson's death, Dodd collaborated with the journalist Ray Stannard Baker to edit *The Public Papers of Woodrow Wilson* (six volumes, 1925-1927), a work that the foremost Wilson scholar, Arthur S. Link, would later call "an indispensable tool."

As Dodd was editing Wilson's papers, he was also writing popular articles for periodicals such as the *New York Times*, *Century*, and H. L. Mencken's *American Mercury*. The composition of these essays, which ranged widely over America's past, evinced Dodd's continuing concern that history, if it is to be broadly useful, must be taken to the people. Long on description and short on analysis, the pieces, three of which were published in book form as *Lincoln or Lee* (1928), were written in a style that sometimes treated the rules of English composition cavalierly but that was, withal, a lively and effective one praised by such literary craftsmen as Carl Becker, Carl Sandburg, and Allen Tate.

Pleased as Dodd was with these works of popular history, he complained of his inability to complete a scholarly history of the Old South that he had been planning for more than ten years. The work would run to three or four volumes and would be the capstone of his career. But his time was absorbed not only with taking history to the people through the popular press but also with teaching his classes, participating in Democratic politics, and cowriting a textbook for collegians, *The Growth of a Nation* (1928), that subsequently was revised and published under different titles for secondary and primary students. The decade ended with his having done little of the interpretative scholarly writing that had made his reputation.

The 1930s were little different. Appointment as American ambassador to Germany in 1933 seriously diminished the opportunity to write history. Nevertheless, in the odd moments when he was not performing official duties—all the while warning the Roosevelt administration of the menace of Nazism and keeping a diary that his son and daughter would edit and have published after his death—the ambassador worked to complete the first volume of a projected history of the Old South. Published in 1937, during Dodd's last year in Berlin, *The Old South: Struggles for Democracy* treats the Southern colonies in the seventeenth century. The book's subtitle reveals its theme, the efforts of the settlers of Virginia, Maryland, and Carolina to establish representative government, religious freedom, and economic opportunity. Ultimately, the work is unsatisfactory, for Dodd simply did not know enough about the colonial South to write about it with authority. He portrayed the early Southern colonists as greater democrats than they were.

Dodd projected three more volumes in his comprehensive history of the Old South. In the preface to *The Old South: Struggles for Democracy*, he set forth the outline of volume two. To be entitled "The First American Social Order," the second volume would deal with the changes occurring between 1690 and 1754, emphasizing Negro slavery and its effects on the region. Dodd assumed that he could move rapidly to finish *The Old South* now that he had completed the first volume and had, early in 1938, relinquished his ambassadorship and returned home. Yet throughout that year, except for the time he spent recovering from the shock of his wife's sudden death in May, he traveled about the country lecturing by invitation, warning his audiences of Adolf Hitler's evil designs on world peace. The following year, ill health rendered him unable to lecture or to work on "The First American Social Order." By fall he was failing rapidly, and on 9 February 1940 he died at his Blue Ridge farm.

The next day the *New York Times* declared that Dodd had been the "world's foremost authority on the history of the American South." That judgment was not excessive; Dodd's achievement was indeed impressive. Nine books by his own hand, six written or edited with others, and scores of articles and reviews composed a substantial body of work. *Expansion and Conflict*, *The Cotton Kingdom*, and *Woodrow Wilson and His Work* were all published in editions other than the first shortly after their original issue. Forty years after Dodd's death, five of his books are in print in reprint editions. Over the years much of Dodd's work has been superseded by the writings of other historians. Dodd would have thought that only proper. Each generation, he always believed, must write its own history because, as he himself once wrote, "history must have some bearing on the present."

As important as what Dodd wrote is the way in which he wrote it. Seldom dull, seldom obtuse, his writing is almost always brisk and clear, though occasionally it is clouded by too many long sentences and absolute constructions. The ability to condense, to summarize, to render the essence of an event or an issue highlight his style. At times his powers of description approach those of a good novelist, as in his portrait of Jefferson upon his matriculation at William and Mary in *Statesmen of the Old South*: "With a thorough training in the rudiments of Latin and Greek and an even more thorough knowledge of the strong men of the backwoods, young Jefferson was . . . sent, at the age of seventeen, to the College of William and Mary, then the best seat of learning in America. He was very tall, very awkward, timid by nature, uncomfortable in the presence of greatness and exceedingly homely. He had the distinction of being the homeliest youth in school—his eyes were gray-blue and restless, his cheek bones were high and his thin freckled skin covered no superfluous flesh, while his hands and feet were large and bony."

Other vivid examples of Dodd's literary power appear in his description of the fall of Richmond in *Expansion and Conflict* and of how the Southern coast appeared to the first settlers as recounted in the opening pages of *The Old South: Struggles for Democracy*. Dodd's best writing has that rare quality of capturing the reader's memory.

If Dodd's reputation as a historian were to rest only upon his writings, it would be substantial enough. Yet his impact on American historiography was enhanced by his superior ability as a teacher and by his encouragement of nonacademic historians. Into his classes at Chicago he drew able graduate students who subsequently made significant contributions to the writing of American history: Henry Steele Commager, Avery O. Craven, H. C. Nixon, Frank Lawrence Owsley, and James G. Randall, to name but a few of the fifty doctoral candidates whose work he directed. His desire to take history to the people, his belief that good history should have literary merit, and his kindly nature caused him to give counsel to non-academic historians such as Albert J. Beveridge, Lloyd Lewis, George Fort Milton, Carl Sandburg, and Allen Tate. People who read American history and who have never read Dodd have very likely encountered his ideas.

As a writer of history, Dodd's achievement was as a path-breaking analyst who helped guide the study of the Southern past beyond apologetics to critical examination. For much of the twentieth century, historians of the South have paid tribute to his writing. Not a meticulous scholar, Dodd was an imaginative one who, according to one of his students, Henry Steele Commager, "understood more than he knew and . . . knew more than he could prove." His pioneering work in regional history has deepened our understanding of the national past.

Other:

The Public Papers of Woodrow Wilson, 6 volumes, edited by Dodd and Ray Stannard Baker (New York: Harper, 1925-1927).

Periodical Publications:

"The Fight for the Northwest in 1860," *American Historical Review*, 16 (July 1911): 774-788;

"Social Philosophy of the Old South," *American Journal of Sociology*, 24 (May 1918): 735-746;

"Andrew Jackson and His Enemies, and the Great Noise They Made in the World," *Century*, 111 (April 1926): 734-745.

References:

Robert Dallek, *Democrat and Diplomat: The Life of William E. Dodd* (New York: Oxford University Press, 1968);

Wendell Holmes Stephenson, *The South Lives in History: Southern Historians and Their Legacy* (Baton Rouge: Louisiana State University Press, 1955);

Lowry Price Ware, "The Academic Career of William E. Dodd," Ph.D. dissertation, University of South Carolina, 1956;

Jack K. Williams, "A Bibliography of the Printed Writings of William Edward Dodd," *North Carolina Historical Review*, 30 (January 1953): 72-85.

Papers:

Dodd's papers are in the Library of Congress.

David H. Donald

(1 October 1920-   )

John McCardell
Middlebury College

SELECTED BOOKS: *Lincoln's Herndon* (New York: Knopf, 1948);

Divided We Fought: A Pictorial History of the War, 1861-1865 (New York: Macmillan, 1952);

Lincoln Reconsidered: Essays on the Civil War Era (New York: Knopf, 1956; revised edition, New York: Vintage, 1962);

Charles Sumner and the Coming of the Civil War (New York: Knopf, 1960);

The Civil War and Reconstruction, by Donald and J. G. Randall (Boston: D.C. Heath, 1961; revised, 1969);

The Divided Union, by Donald and Randall (Boston: Little, Brown, 1961);

The Politics of Reconstruction, 1863-1867 (Baton Rouge: Louisiana State University Press, 1965);

Charles Sumner and the Rights of Man (New York: Knopf, 1970);

The Great Republic: A History of the American People, by Donald and others (Lexington, Mass.: D. C. Heath, 1977);

Liberty and Union (Boston: Little, Brown, 1978).

David Herbert Donald has devoted a distinguished career to the study of nineteenth-century America. Both a superior teacher and an influential scholar, Donald ranks as one of America's leading

David Donald

authorities on the Civil War era.

Donald was born on a plantation in rural Goodman, Mississippi. The family of his father, Ira Unger Donald, had lived in the South for 300 years. His mother, Sue Ella Belford Donald, however, was the daughter of John Belford, a Vermont cavalry officer during the Civil War, who had moved to Mississippi during Reconstruction to operate a school for freedmen. Donald attended Holmes County Agricultural High School, Holmes County Junior College, and graduated summa cum laude with a B.A. degree in history from Millsaps College in 1941. Growing up in Mississippi shaped Donald's attitudes and outlook. From an early age he was, by his own admission, sensitive to what would later become a central theme in his writings, the conflict between majority rule and minority rights. "I grew up a white Southerner," he recalls, "in a state where the dominant white majority gave not the least attention to the rights of the numerous black minority." Later, as an adult living in the North, Donald became acutely aware of his Southern origins. "I have been part of the Southern minority in the

United States that has, whether willingly or under duress, been obliged to accept drastic social changes decreed by the national majority."

This "dual experience," as Donald calls it, has influenced his thinking on the causes, conduct, and consequences of the Civil War, the subject to which he has devoted his scholarly life. Often Donald has taken a deliberately provocative stance in order to stimulate a reconsideration of conventional historical wisdom. Virtually all of his writings reflect a desire to see his country steadily and whole. His best work is characterized by an uncommon willingness neither to praise nor to condemn but rather to understand.

Such also were the traits of the noted Lincoln scholar James G. Randall, under whose direction Donald began graduate study at the University of Illinois in 1941. In the lexicon of historiography, Randall has been labeled a "revisionist" for his interpretations of, among other subjects, the "blundering generation" of political leaders in the 1850s who were responsible for provoking a "needless" war. Randall, like all great teachers, imparted at least a portion of himself to his young graduate student. A paper prepared for a graduate seminar became Donald's first publication. Appearing in 1944 in the *Journal of Southern History*, "The Scalawag in Mississippi Reconstruction" was an auspicious shadow of things to come. The young Mississippian challenged a long-prevalent view by suggesting that the vilified "scalawags" were in fact former members of the Whig party who hoped, after the Civil War, to reconstitute an opposition against the states'-rights Democrats. They were not simply opportunistic, corrupt whites. Allen Trelease later called this pioneering revisionist article, written by a graduate student in his early twenties, "one of the freshest breezes to sweep this landscape in many years."

After earning his M.A. degree in 1942, Donald spent a year at the University of North Carolina, where he served as a teaching fellow, before returning to Illinois to commence work toward his Ph.D., which he received in 1946. With the strong encouragement of Randall, Donald wrote as his dissertation a biography of Abraham Lincoln's law partner and biographer, William Henry Herndon. The work of the colorful Herndon had largely been responsible for many inaccuracies concerning Lincoln's personal and public lives. For instance, it was Herndon who perpetrated the falsehood that Lincoln's broken romance with Ann Rutledge had shattered him emotionally, and it was Herndon who had made allegations concerning

Lincoln's legitimacy. Imaginatively retracing Herndon's steps and reexamining his sources, Donald produced not only a useful corrective but also an artistic triumph. In later years Donald always admonished his graduate students that a good dissertation should also make a good book. His own experience set the example, for *Lincoln's Herndon*, which appeared in 1948 with an introduction by Carl Sandburg, was, according to the *New York Herald Tribune*, "a masterful achievement of sound scholarship, enlightened exposition, and absorbing interest."

Reviewers were particularly impressed by Donald's vivid writing style, which would become a hallmark of his work and of which the following passage from *Lincoln's Herndon* is an example: "there was much that Herndon could tell. His memory was crowded to overflowing, like a ragbag. Here were the bright red patches of a victorious law suit, the blue scraps of philosophical discussions in the office, the flaming orange bits of a speech on the hustings. Here too were soiled edgings and rough wool tatters not so pleasant to remember. Endlessly, without apparent order, he evoked memories of the past and laid them before his hearer. And when they were all spread out together, there was the pattern of a man, contradictory and confusing, as beautiful and as ugly as life itself."

In 1947 Donald joined the faculty of Columbia University, where, but for a two-year sojourn at Smith College and Amherst College (1949-1951), he remained until 1959. In 1955 he married Aida DiPace, historian with whom he would later collaborate editorially and to whom he repeatedly expressed acknowledgment for her critical acumen. During this period he edited the Civil War diaries of Salmon P. Chase, the Confederate memoirs of George Cary Eggleston, and wrote the text for a pictorial history of the Civil War, *Divided We Fought* (1952). At the same time he began directing graduate students. A member of Donald's first Columbia seminar recalled the experience twenty years later. "He was a taskmaster who wrote more on the margin and back of seminar papers than his students wrote on the front," remembered Grady McWhiney. "He terrified us all. Each time we turned in a paper we feared that it would be our last. But his teaching techniques worked with us. A little fear stimulated our desire to improve and probably was just what most of us needed. He always mixed encouragement and sometimes even praise with devastating criticism." More important, "he would give his time without stint. He was accessible to his students and concerned with their welfare."

McWhiney's experience was not unique. The acknowledgments in a score of books that began as Donald-directed dissertations, volumes Donald proudly calls his "grandchildren" and prominently displays on his coffee table, attest to a special relationship between the teacher and his students.

But not all of Donald's prodigious energy was expended on editing and teaching. In 1956 he had published a collection of essays, *Lincoln Reconsidered*, which explored with insight and good humor the many sides of the sixteenth president and his times. Many of the topics treated grew out of Donald's research on Herndon. Indeed, one may read the epilogue of *Lincoln's Herndon* as a prospectus for *Lincoln Reconsidered*. For example, in the earlier work Donald repeated an admonition made in an article published in 1947, "The Folklore Lincoln," that the historian who employs the methods of the folklorist may glean new understandings of his subject. In 1951 he had published in *Harper's* the amusing "Getting Right With Lincoln," which extended the study of the legendary Lincoln. Both essays were reprinted in *Lincoln Reconsidered*.

By 1956 Donald was aware that, on the subject of the Civil War era, research had been quite thorough and writing equally extensive and brilliant. "Unless historiography degenerates into antiquarianism, with more and more biographies being written about less and less significant minor characters," he warned in the preface to *Lincoln Reconsidered*, "we must turn to fresh problems, and to fresh solutions of old problems, not accessible to the ordinary techniques of the historian." He proposed that historians might learn much from the work of cultural anthropologists, sociologists, and psychologists.

Following his own advice, Donald included in the volume an essay that has remained a point of controversy, "Toward a Reconsideration of Abolitionists," which examines the early leaders of the abolition movement. After identifying the "hard core of active antislavery leadership in the 1830s," a total of 106 individuals, Donald drew a composite portrait of abolitionist leadership that stunned many readers. He argued, on the basis of close analysis of his group, that, "descended from old and socially dominant Northeastern families, reared in a faith of aggressive piety and moral endeavor, educated for conservative leadership, these young men and women who reached maturity in the 1830s faced a strange and hostile world. They were an elite without a function, a displaced class in American society." And, in order to reestablish a sense of leadership and purpose in rapidly changing nineteenth-century America, they seized upon the cause of abolition.

Like a fire bell in the night, "Toward a Reconsideration of Abolitionists" quickly stirred other historians to respond. Their consciences pricked by Donald's findings, many historians confused Donald's explanation of motives with his evaluation of the worthiness of the abolitionists' cause. Like his Columbia colleague Richard Hofstadter, whose prizewinning *The Age of Reform* had offered a similarly revisionist explanation of the origins of the Progressive movement, Donald found himself beset by critics ranging from overeager graduate students to senior historians. The debate was heightened as time went on by the excitement of the civil rights movement, and contemporary affairs seemed to many of Donald's critics startlingly relevant to the political battles of the nineteenth century. The better part of a large anthology, *The Antislavery Vanguard*, published in 1965, was devoted to examining, mostly negatively, what had become the "Donald thesis." If Donald's intention in writing "Toward a Reconsideration of Abolitionists" had been to provoke reconsideration, he had succeeded.

The approach taken by Donald in reconsidering the abolitionists portended the contours of a larger study then in progress, a biography of Charles Sumner, one of the most radical of all New England antislavery men. Applying the same thoroughness of research and the same innovativeness of method that had distinguished his earlier works, Donald had published *Charles Sumner and the Coming of the Civil War*, which he dedicated to the memory of his New England-born maternal grandfather, John Belford, in 1960. Subtly interweaving social and psychological insights with a crisply written narrative, Donald graphically depicted a man of many facets who achieved national political prominence despite, rather than because of, his personal traits. In his preface to the volume, Donald revealed his sensitivity to the still-smoldering debate initiated by his 1956 essay on the abolitionists. "In trying to explain the motives underlying Sumner's actions," he wrote, "I am not making even an implicit judgment on the causes for which he fought. In particular, I hope that no one will accuse me of sympathizing with Negro slavery because I have not interjected a little moral discourse after each of Sumner's orations to the effect that he was on the side of the angels. Surely in the middle of the twentieth century there are some things that do not need to be said." More important than ladling out praise and blame, Donald thought, was trying to understand one of the most complex figures in American his-

tory. "My purpose," he wrote, "has been to understand Sumner and his motives, not to hale him for trial before the bar of history."

Reviewers generally agreed that Donald succeeded. "Donald has a remarkable talent for discerning and disclosing what lies behind the distortions of human personality," commented David M. Potter in the *American Historical Review*. "He achieves his result not by flashy psychographic passages, but by telling his story with a fullness and a depth that unfolds its own meaning. If [the book] does not make Sumner attractive, it certainly makes him understandable."

Meanwhile, in 1959-1960, Donald was occupying the prestigious Harmsworth Chair of American History at Oxford University. His inaugural lecture, "An Excess of Democracy," offered an important new interpretation of the causes of the Civil War. Challenging both those who viewed the war as an "irrepressible conflict" and those who deemed it a "needless war," Donald described a disorganized society incapable of devising a "conservative solution" to problems because it lacked institutional restraints upon the exercise of majority rule. "At a stage when the United States was least capable of enduring shock, the nation was obliged to undergo a series of crises, largely triggered by the physical expansion of the country," he stated. "These crises were not in themselves calamitous experiences. They were, however, the chisel strokes which revealed the fundamental flaws in the block of marble, flaws which stemmed from an excess of democracy."

Donald returned from Oxford to take up new duties as a member of the faculty of Princeton University in 1960. In the spring of 1961, he was awarded the Pulitzer Prize in biography for his Sumner volume. That same year he had published a major revision of Randall's standard textbook, the classic *The Civil War and Reconstruction*. Though still containing much of Randall's revisionist skepticism about the war's causes, the new edition also contained a significant reworking and updating of the sections on the war and Reconstruction. Not only did the book reflect the latest scholarship, it also provided an extensive and invaluable bibliography, further updated in 1969, which remains a departure point for anyone interested in studying the Civil War era. Also in 1961, Donald was named editor of *The Making of America* series, a six-volume project aimed at the intelligent general reader, who was, Donald believed, so often forgotten by the writers of unnecessarily dry academic tomes. Combining professional scholarship with a readable style, the series soon became an important contribution to public knowledge.

In 1962 Donald left Princeton for Johns Hopkins University. In 1964 he was named Harry C. Black Professor, and in 1966 he established the Institute of Southern History, which he directed until 1973. The institute, founded to restore Hopkins's prominence in the field of Southern history, brought together distinguished scholars from various disciplines whose only link was an interest in the South: political scientists, sociologists, teachers of literature, as well as historians. For the first time since the days of Herbert Baxter Adams, Hopkins was a center for the study of Southern history.

Meanwhile, Donald's scholarly activity proceeded apace. Five more edited volumes appeared, as well as *The Politics of Reconstruction, 1863-1867* (1965), a book which began as the Walter Lynwood Fleming lectures at Louisiana State University. Once more Donald presented a new look at a seemingly well-worked field. Employing the technique of roll call analysis, Donald discovered that a congressman's position on Reconstruction legislation was related to how "safe" his district was. Congressmen with "safe" seats could take firmer positions on controversial questions than those who faced determined opposition back home. A study more suggestive than conclusive, *The Politics of Reconstruction* was yet another imaginative methodological exercise that raised new questions for future historians.

In 1970 Donald had published the second volume of his Sumner biography, *Charles Sumner and the Rights of Man*, which portrayed Sumner as a man of ideas who tried to operate successfully in the world of politics; it examined how a man like Sumner managed to be so influential during the years of war and Reconstruction as a guardian of the rights of freedmen and as a shaper, as chairman of the Senate Committee on Foreign Relations, of foreign policy. Balancing political forces with careful calculation, Sumner was able to extend his political career long after most of his radical colleagues had disappeared from the scene. "Between the age of Thomas Jefferson and that of Woodrow Wilson," Donald concluded, "Sumner was the one American who had equal claim for distinction in the world of the intellect and the world of politics." And, though discussion of this portion of Sumner's life posed organizational and interpretative obstacles, reviewers generally praised Donald's ability to encompass in a volume so complex a man and a period. In particular they noted Donald's attempt to interrelate politics, diplomacy, economics, and social changes instead of viewing each of these areas separately.

While seeing the Sumner volume through the press, Donald also served, during 1969-1970, as president of the Southern Historical Association. At that organization's annual meeting in 1970, he delivered the presidential address, "The Proslavery Argument Reconsidered," a vintage Donald performance. Why, he asked, did so many Southerners whose personal and hereditary stake in the South's peculiar institution was apparently so slight become its ardent defenders? There was little, after all, in the backgrounds of such men as James Henry Hammond, William Gilmore Simms, or George Fitzhugh to warrant their tenacious adherence to slavery. Then, applying the same techniques he had used in analyzing abolitionist leadership, Donald suggested an explanation. These men, like their Northern counterparts, were disturbed by the rapid pace of change going on around them. Having achieved success in their professions, they expected the deference and respect that might have been, in earlier times, accorded them. But in nineteenth-century America such a hierarchical world had disappeared. Accordingly, these men grasped the proslavery argument as a means of restoring order and purpose to their lives by exercising leadership in a cause they had little objective reason to support so vocally.

Clearly, by the early 1970s Donald was working out a comprehensive view of Northern and Southern society. In 1973 he was named Charles Warren Professor of American History at Harvard University and shortly thereafter began work on a collaborative textbook with Bernard Bailyn, David Brion Davis, John L. Thomas, Robert H. Wiebe, and Gordon S. Wood. In his section of *The Great Republic*, published in 1977, Donald treated the period 1860-1890. Provocatively, he argued the essential similarity of the North and South by outlining the parallel paths taken by the Union and Confederate governments toward the solution of strikingly common problems. Both the North and the South experienced, necessarily, centralization and consolidation in most areas as a result of wartime pressures and demands. After the war, brakes were applied, in the form of economic localism, constitutionalism, racism, and party politics, so that the steps toward nationality taken between 1861 and 1865 by a United States emerging as a truly modern nation were halted during Reconstruction by a resurgence of local, parochial interests—in the North as well as in the South.

In 1978 Donald had published separately,

under the title *Liberty and Union*, the chapters he had written for *The Great Republic* along with an introductory section tracing developments from 1845 to 1860. He explained his decision to add to the huge assortment of works on the period by noting that historians have been unwilling to look at the period 1845-1890 as a whole. Usually the era is compartmentalized into the antebellum, the Civil War, and the Reconstruction periods, with the result that historians lose sight of the period as a whole. Donald urged his readers to reconsider this traditional approach and offered an alternative framework. "I have become convinced," he wrote, "that these important economic, social, and ideological conflicts can best be understood as special instances of a more general problem that nineteenth century Americans confronted," the conflict between majority rule and minority rights.

This conflict was one Donald had probed repeatedly in his career, whether in explaining the misunderstood scalawag, analyzing the impact of change on the attackers and defenders of slavery, tracing the career of the leading spokesman for the nineteenth century's equivalent of the Moral Majority, Charles Sumner, or evaluating the politics of Reconstruction. In *Liberty and Union* the conflict between majority rule and minority rights received not only definitive treatment but also an autobiographical introduction. "I am an unabashed American nationalist, proud of my country, and happy that it was able to maintain its unity," he wrote in the preface. "As a nationalist, I am not much impressed by the importance of sectional, or ethnic, or racial, or religious differences in the United States." But, he hastened to add, "I am not subscribing to a saccharine 'consensus' view that there have been no real conflicts in American history. We have quarreled among ourselves vigorously and at times viciously; but I insist that our quarrels have been family quarrels." He went on to identify himself as a "conservative" who has "little faith in legislated solutions or constitutional mechanisms to solve a nation's problems." Finally, Donald noted that the issue of majority rule and minority rights remained vital: "I have not much faith in those who claim they possess magic formulas that will protect minorities, and I have even less faith in those who assert that the will of the majority is in all cases to prevail." Forty years of studying nineteenth-century America had convinced him that "compromise is better than conflict, that pragmatic adjustments are more lasting than programmatic solutions, and that the power of an individual, a group, or even a generation to

effect drastic changes in the course of history is minuscule."

Such judgments might have signaled the premature end of a scholarly career, summed up by a typically provocative yet comprehensive publication. Indeed, one might have assumed that *Liberty and Union* was Donald's valedictory, particularly in light of a deeply pessimistic essay contributed by him at almost the same time to the "Op-Ed" page of the *New York Times*. In "Our Irrelevant History," Donald questioned the wisdom of presenting to undergraduates in 1977 what for so long had been the major topics in American history. "The bleakness of the new era we are entering," he wrote, and the fact that "the age of abundance has ended" suggest that "the 'lessons' taught by the American past are today not merely irrelevant but dangerous." What, then, should the teacher of history do? "Perhaps my most useful function would be to disenthrall [students] from the spell of history, to help them see the irrelevance of the past."

One might read "Our Irrelevant History" as simply the bitter musings of a veteran historian for whom the present seemed to hold little promise. Christopher Lasch in *The Culture of Narcissism* wrote that Donald's essay demonstrated the utter demoralization of humanistic study, indeed, of liberal culture. But to give the essay such a reading would be to misinterpret the purpose of the writer, who has devoted his career to challenging the complacent and prodding the comfortable. Instead, one should read "Our Irrelevant History" as simply the latest volley from a historian who has provoked a generation of readers with his willingness to seek "fresh solutions to old problems."

By the late 1970s Donald was hard at work on a project that marked a departure from the field he had cultivated so long and so well. Having summed up his thinking on the Civil War era in *Liberty and Union*, Donald decided to break new ground as he set to work on a biography of the twentieth-century novelist Thomas Wolfe. Wolfe was an appropriate subject: like Donald, he was born in the South but lived most of his adult life in the North; like Donald, he was a master at delineating character traits; like Donald, he chose as his subject America.

Indeed, Donald's still active career can be summarized by describing his influence upon readers and students in much the same way that the novelist William Styron summarized the impact of Thomas Wolfe. Wolfe, wrote Styron, conveyed "a sense of America as a glorious abstraction—a vast and brooding continent whose untold bounties were awaiting every young man's discovery. It was as if for the first time my whole being had been thrown open to the sheer tactile and sensory vividness of the American scene through which, until then, I was walking numb and blind, and it caused me a thrill of discovery that was quite unutterable."

Other:

Inside Lincoln's Cabinet: The Civil War Diaries of Salmon P. Chase, edited by Donald (New York: Longmans, Green, 1954);

George Cary Eggleston, *A Rebel's Recollections*, edited by Donald (Bloomington: Indiana University Press, 1959);

"Lincoln as Politician," in *Abraham Lincoln: A New Portrait*, edited by Henry B. Kranz (New York: Putnam, 1959), pp. 48-54;

"Abraham Lincoln: Whig in the White House," in *The Enduring Lincoln*, edited by Norman A. Graebner (Urbana: University of Illinois Press, 1959), pp. 47-66;

Why the North Won the Civil War, edited by Donald (Baton Rouge: Louisiana State University Press, 1961);

The Making of America, 6 volumes, edited by Donald (New York: Hill & Wang, 1961-1967);

"Lincoln Bibliography," in *The American Plutarch*, edited by Edward T. James (New York: Scribners, 1964), pp. 276-281;

Diary of Charles Francis Adams, 2 volumes, edited by Donald and Aida DiPace Donald (Cambridge: Harvard University Press, 1964);

"Devils Facing Zionwards," in *Grant, Lee, Lincoln and the Radicals*, edited by Grady McWhiney, (Evanston, Ill.: Northwestern University Press, 1964), pp. 72-91;

William A. Dunning, *Essays on the Civil War and Reconstruction*, edited by Donald (New York: Harper & Row, 1965);

Gone for a Soldier: The Civil War Memoirs of Private Alfred Bellard, edited by Donald (Boston: Little, Brown, 1975).

Periodical Publications:

"The Scalawag in Mississippi Reconstruction," *Journal of Southern History*, 10 (1944): 447-460;

"Why They Impeached Andrew Johnson," *American Heritage*, 8 (December 1956): 20-25;

"The Confederate as a Fighting Man," *Journal of Southern History*, 25 (1959): 178-193;

"American Historians and the Causes of the Civil War," *South Atlantic Quarterly*, 59 (1960): 351-355;

"The Quest for Motives," *Western Review*, 3 (1966): 55-60;

"The Grand Theme in American Historical Writing," *Journal of Historical Studies*, 2 (1969): 186-201;

"Black History," *Commentary*, 49 (1970): 85-88;

"The Proslavery Argument Reconsidered," *Journal of Southern History*, 37 (1971): 3-18;

"Between Science and Art," *American Historical Review*, 77 (1972): 445-452;

"Writing About the Past," *Commentary*, 54 (1972): 96-99;

"Promised Land or Paradise Lost: The South Beheld," *Georgia Review*, 29 (1975): 184-187;

"The Southernization of America," *New York Times*, 30 August 1976, p. 23;

"Our Irrelevant History," *New York Times*, 8 September 1977, p. 37.

William A. Dunning

(12 May 1857-25 August 1922)

Anne W. Chapman
College of William and Mary

BOOKS: *The Constitution of the United States in Civil
War and Reconstruction: 1860-1867* (New York:
J. F. Pearson, 1885);

*Essays on the Civil War and Reconstruction and Related
Topics* (New York: Macmillan, 1898; London:
Macmillan, 1898; revised edition, New York:
Macmillan, 1904; London: Macmillan, 1904);

A History of Political Theories: Ancient and Medieval,
volume 1 of *Political Theories* (New York:
Macmillan, 1902; London: Macmillan, 1902);

*A History of Political Theories from Luther to Montes-
quieu*, volume 2 of *Political Theories* (New York:
Macmillan, 1905; London: Macmillan, 1905);

Reconstruction, Political and Economic: 1865-1877,
volume 22 of *The American Nation: A History*
(New York: Harper, 1907; London: Harper,
1907);

The British Empire and the United States (New York:
Scribners, 1914);

A History of Political Theories from Rousseau to Spencer,
volume 3 of *Political Theories* (New York:
Macmillan, 1920);

*Truth in History and Other Essays by William A. Dun-
ning*, edited by J. G. de Roulhac Hamilton
(New York: Columbia University Press, 1937).

William Archibald Dunning, historian, political scientist, teacher, and editor of scholarly journals, was a major figure among the first generation
of professionally trained American historians.
While a professor at Columbia University from
1886 until his death in 1922, Dunning exerted,
through his own work and that of his many students, a lasting influence on historical scholarship in
the United States. Although his most ambitious
work was an epic study of political philosophy,
Dunning's interpretation of the Reconstruction
period following the American Civil War was his
most enduring contribution to historical knowledge
and dominated public and scholarly views of the
Reconstruction era for more than half a century.

Dunning, son of John H. and Catherine D.
Trelease Dunning, was born in Plainfield, New Jersey, four years prior to the outbreak of the American Civil War. John Dunning, a carriage manufacturer, amateur painter, and art critic, was a man of

William A. Dunning

wide intellectual interests, which he passed on to his
son. The elder Dunning was especially interested in,
and critical of, the process by which the Southern
states were restored to the Union; years later his son
would dedicate his major work on Reconstruction to
his father, "by whom I was first inspired with interest in the problems of Reconstruction."

While in high school Dunning grew especially
fond of one of his teachers, an alumnus of
Dartmouth College, and planned to enter
Dartmouth himself in the fall of 1875. When his
father suffered serious financial losses in the Panic
of 1873, Dunning was forced to delay his college
career for two years, during which time he worked
as a newspaper reporter in New York City. Finally
entering Dartmouth in 1877, he stayed there only a

few months before he was expelled for "a reprisal raid on certain sophomores," an escapade that later would delight his own undergraduate students at Columbia. Dunning himself must have been delighted when in 1916 Dartmouth awarded him an honorary doctor of laws degree.

Dunning continued his collegiate work at Columbia, an institution with which he would be associated as student or faculty member for nearly forty-five years. He earned an A.B. in 1881, an A.M. in 1884, and was awarded the Ph.D. in 1885 for his dissertation, *The Constitution of the United States in Civil War and Reconstruction: 1860-1867*, which was published the same year. In the 1880s the new American graduate schools, which would produce the first professional historians in the United States, were effecting major changes in the study, writing, and teaching of history through encouragement of the "scientific method" transplanted from German universities and the introduction of the graduate seminar. Columbia University was a pioneer in this new methodology. Dunning's own work and career were heavily influenced by his mentor, John W. Burgess, a German-trained historian who had inaugurated the graduate seminar in history and political science at Columbia and who encouraged his students to seek an ideal of objectivity through solid research in primary sources and the scientific testing of hypotheses. This method, Dunning learned, would expose history "as it really happened." During his period of graduate study, Dunning was himself for a short time at the University of Berlin, where he grew further to admire the German style of scholarship.

In 1886 Dunning joined the faculty at Columbia as a fellow. He passed rapidly through the ranks of lecturer and instructor to become a professor in 1891, and in 1913 Columbia awarded him the Francis Lieber professorship, established in honor of Columbia's first great teacher of politics. On 18 April 1888 Dunning married Charlotte E. Loomis of Brooklyn. She died 13 June 1917. The couple had no children.

A judicious assessment of Dunning's work requires understanding of the social and intellectual climate in which it was produced. In the decades surrounding the turn of the century, almost all white Americans shared an assumption that the Anglo-Saxon human type was innately superior to all others, a view which received sanction and respectability through scientific studies and the doctrine of Social Darwinism. Many Americans feared for the preservation of the dominant culture, and this fear was reflected in anti-immigration organizations which sought to prevent the admission of "inferior" peoples from Southern and Eastern Europe and in scholarly and popular works which pointed out the threat to the "superior" Anglo-Saxon character of the United States. The imperialism and expansionism that became a central feature of American foreign policy in the 1890s was also overlaid with this assumption of Anglo-Saxon superiority. The poverty and deterioration in the position of Negroes in the United States in the 1880s and early 1890s, as they were deprived of the few political and civil rights they had gained during Reconstruction, seemed to prove their innate inferiority. In this atmosphere Anglo-Saxonism and Aryanism became basic concepts in the writing of history, and Dunning's studies naturally reflect this cultural heritage. He shared the almost pervasive anti-Negro bias of white Americans of his day, and, as an anti-imperialist, he believed the nation's disastrous experience with imperialism demonstrated the rightness of views alleging nonwhite inferiority. However, many historians, in assessing Dunning's work, have tended to stress this feature while ignoring the solid contribution his studies made to historical knowledge.

Dunning believed, like most of his colleagues, that the study of history (Dunning considered history and political science to be one discipline) could best be served by an objective, impersonal, and "realistic" approach, one in which the historian stood apart from his subject lest he distort the truth. The scholar's task was to accurately and thoroughly amass the facts of past events, avoiding both romantic subjectivity and the imposition upon his studies of any overriding philosophy. Although Dunning spent much of his energy on a study of political theory, he finally came to believe that analysis of political events and of the development of institutions provided the key to the past. Dunning's works contain a wealth of information and set a high standard for content and thoroughness. He was highly critical of his own work and wrote slowly and deliberately, seldom revising his first efforts. His attention to detail has become legend. Upon discovering, after many hours of painstaking comparison of handwriting, that George Bancroft had written President Andrew Johnson's first message to Congress, Dunning wrote his wife: "I don't believe you can form any idea of the pleasure it gives me to have discovered this little historical fact."

Dunning's major studies are written with confidence but display definite caution and restraint. In marked contrast his articles, reviews, and personal letters reveal a caustic wit and a more relaxed style. Berating one author for the inclusion of extraneous material in his book, Dunning observed that even the intrusion of an unnecessary comma could wreak havoc with the sense of a sentence. Suppose, he wrote, that "a comma crept into position after the pronoun in the command, 'Saddle me the ass.' " When a former student wrote to thank him for "cheering up a gloomy day" with this review, Dunning replied: "If I did anything to cheer you up on a gloomy day I am glad of it. I should be glad to cheer you up on a brilliant day. I am entirely indifferent about the quality of the day on which I cheer you up."

On a trip to Rome in the fall of 1898, Dunning began work on the first volume of his three-volume study of political theory, a work which would claim a major part of his scholarly energies until 1920. *A History of Political Theories: Ancient and Medieval* (1902), volume one of the trilogy, reveals the strong influence of John W. Burgess and is dedicated to him. Dunning sought to evaluate the doctrines of the more important political writers from Plato to Machiavelli as they applied to the origins and development of the state. He limited the scope of his study to the Aryan peoples of Europe as "the only peoples to whom the term political may be properly applied" and excluded "the whole mass of primitive political theory" as not political at all but purely "sociological" on the grounds that "primitive communities do not . . . manifest the political consciousness." Even in this realm of ideas Dunning clung to his belief in the importance of studying institutions. "The history of political theory . . . is to be kept always in touch with the history of political fact because [political thought] is determined primarily by the institutions amid which it developed."

In 1905 *A History of Political Theories from Luther to Montesquieu*, volume two of Dunning's trilogy, appeared and carried to the mid-eighteenth century the work begun in volume one. Not until fifteen years later did Dunning complete the series with *A History of Political Theories from Rousseau to Spencer*, which carried his analysis to 1880. All three volumes were reprinted many times, and the work as a whole brought Dunning recognition as a leading American scholar in the field of political theory. The trilogy has not, however, proved as enduring as his studies of Reconstruction and is little known today. The volumes are repetitious, and a modern critic has called them "dull" and "magisterial." When the final volume went to press after nearly twenty years of study and writing, during which time his health declined rapidly, Dunning was dis-

couraged and pessimistic about the influence and development of systematic political philosophy. In a letter to a former student he wrote that "the silly mass of political theory that I have been engaged in precipitating on a defenseless public has now passed out of my hands into those of Macmillan. . . . My interest in it has dwindled to the vanishing point." In the final paragraph of *A History of Political Theories from Rousseau to Spencer*, Dunning declared that "in twenty-three centuries the movement of thought has but swung full circle. Such is the general lesson of the history of political theory." Dunning had come to believe the historian should remain a chronicler of events and always treat theory as a reflection of the environment from which it evolved.

Although the *Political Theories* trilogy claimed a lion's share of Dunning's scholarly effort, his real love was the history of the Civil War era and especially of the process of Reconstruction. The writing of American history at the turn of the century tended to subordinate the South and West to the East, and it distressed Dunning greatly "that at least 90 percent of the respectable historical literature about the United States had originated in New England and bore unmistakable marks of its origin." There were at least two sides to the story of the war and of the Reconstruction period, and, Dunning believed, such a sectional bias in historical writing tended to threaten scientific standards and objectivity. Thus the South found in Dunning a spokesman—one with its own sectional bias.

In 1898 Dunning had published *Essays on the Civil War and Reconstruction and Related Topics*, a collection of essays previously published in scholarly journals and considerably revised for this edition, in which he first brought together an interpretation of Reconstruction that continues to bear his name. The book focuses on the constitutional issues and the "profound problems of statecraft" involved in restoration of the Southern states to the Union. Although marred for the modern reader by Dunning's obvious championship of Southern white leadership and his antipathy to Negro suffrage, the collection is a clear, balanced, and closely argued statement of the controversy over interpretation of the Constitution with regard to the meaning of sovereignty, the exercise of war powers, and the status of the former Confederate states. Several selections present, for each of the Southern states, a good summary of the Reconstruction process from both a factual and constitutional viewpoint. While favoring neither the purposes nor the effects of Radical Reconstruction,

Dunning nonetheless found its efficiency, in an unprecedented situation, admirable. "The mechanism by which the end was achieved must command an appreciation on its merits." In the end, Dunning believed, war had resulted in a better union and Reconstruction had proved the soundness of the American system.

Dunning's other major work on the postwar period, *Reconstruction, Political and Economic: 1865-1877*, appeared in 1907 as volume twenty-two in *The American Nation: A History* series. Dunning brought together the results of his own earlier works and that of many of his students. He also acknowledged a large debt to the last two volumes of John Ford Rhodes's *History of the United States from the Compromise of 1850 to the Final Restoration of Home Rule at the South in 1877* (seven volumes), which appeared in 1906. Today Dunning's *Reconstruction, Political and Economic: 1865-1877* is remembered principally for its lack of sympathy for Negro aspirations to equality and political participation, while the balance he struck in discussing political and economic conditions in the North and West as well as the South is overlooked. Dunning regarded both the lawless tactics of Southerners and misgovernment in the North as a national tragedy, but in the end he celebrated Reconstruction as a triumph for constitutional authority and order. David Herbert Donald, a more recent student of the Reconstruction period, praised the book as "a comprehensive survey by a master historian" in which "Dunning's biases in favor of the South and against the Negro are muted . . . as he places Reconstruction in a national setting."

As Dunning's work corrected, or overcorrected, the Northeastern bias of Reconstruction historiography, it established his reputation as the foremost authority on that subject. But the impact of his scholarship on the writing of American history was perhaps secondary to his influence as a teacher. Throughout his long career at Columbia University Dunning taught a full complement of undergraduate courses, and his students remembered him as a stimulating lecturer who used wit and characterization to advantage. But he preferred his graduate seminars, and it was here that he excelled as a teacher. Graduate students, mostly from the South and drawn by Dunning's Southern bias, flocked to Columbia to study with him. Until Herbert Baxter Adams's death in 1901, his seminars at Johns Hopkins University had served as a kind of national center for Southern studies. When Dunning declined a position as Adams's successor at Johns Hopkins, the center of Southern activity

shifted to New York, and Columbia claimed first place as trainer of Southern scholars in history for the first two decades of the twentieth century. The many dissertations on the Civil War and Reconstruction completed there under Dunning's direction are commonly referred to collectively as the "Dunning School" of historiography. Many of Dunning's students returned to the South to pass the torch on to their own students and to greatly expand the teaching of Southern history in Southern institutions.

In his seminars Dunning taught historical method rigorously and aroused in his students a sustained enthusiasm for research and the writing of "scientific" history. He exhibited a warm personal interest in his students' work but never pampered them, leaving them on their own to locate sources and conduct their research, and examining their efforts only when in essentially complete form. Dunning, whom his students called "Old Chief," had sharp blue eyes which he could turn on an indolent student with an effect almost as devastating as the sharp blue pencil he favored for criticizing student essays and dissertations. He was never unkind or sarcastic, but his humor, logic, and quickness to spot deficiencies was disconcerting to many students. One student remembered that Dunning had written on the margin of a preliminary draft of his dissertation, "This is the worst sentence that was ever written." Despite his sometimes fearsome classroom demeanor, students remembered best his social charm and ready wit. When the wife of a former student, upon meeting Dunning for the first time, professed that she felt she already knew him from her husband's admiring description of him as a man, scholar, and teacher, Dunning replied, "Except that I do not admit your premises and your conclusion is wrong, your judgment is sound."

"Dunning's Men," as his students were often called, supplemented his own work and his influence on the writing of history in America with eight studies of Reconstruction in as many states, ten studies dealing with various phases of the Civil War and Reconstruction period, several works—including those of Ulrich Bonnell Phillips—on other topics in Southern history, and several studies in the field of political theory. These studies, especially those dealing with Reconstruction, reflect Dunning's biases and are informed by racist assumptions, but most are factually accurate, elaborately detailed, and based on extensive research in previously unexplored primary sources. Despite these similarities, the works of the Dunning school vary greatly in tone, emphasis, and quality. Some carried Dunning's biases to the extreme while others are more moderate. Many contain valuable political narratives as well as judicious treatments of social and economic issues. One student, J. G. de Roulhac Hamilton, whose *Reconstruction in North Carolina* is an extreme indictment of everything Northern, made a major contribution to the study of Southern history when he undertook the building up of the Southern Historical Collection of manuscripts at the University of North Carolina as his life work.

A scholarly synthesis of the process of Reconstruction based on the studies of Dunning and his students dominated high-school and college textbooks as well as the historical literature for at least fifty years. The Dunning school was not the first to investigate Reconstruction or to suggest the interpretation commonly attributed to it. Its members did, however, lend academic credibility and expert documentation to an already familiar story. In general the picture of the postwar period that emerged from these studies was one that accepted Negro inferiority, gave scarce notice to the achievements of former slaves, and sympathized with the attitudes of Southern white supremacists toward the introduction of the Negro into the civil and political life of the South. President Lincoln's plan for reunion was seen as a wise one, and Andrew Johnson was credited with a courageous attempt to carry it through. Johnson's stubbornness, however, alienated many in the North and eroded his support. The scene was thus set for congressional Reconstruction destined to be controlled by a handful of scheming and dishonest Radical Republicans. These politicians used ignorant Negroes to impose on the white South a self-interested policy designed to insure their own political and economic dominance. The nucleus of the Radical plan was Negro suffrage, and on this aspect of Reconstruction the Dunningites bestowed their harshest criticism. A period of corruption and fraud followed the establishment of Republican and Negro-dominated governments in most of the Southern states. In desperation Southern whites, wishing to reestablish a normal state of affairs and encouraged by a decline in support for Radical Reconstruction in the North, united to overthrow these governments and effect a return to white rule. Finally, in the disputed election of 1876, a deal between Northern and Southern politicians gave enough electoral votes to Republican Rutherford B. Hayes to assure his election in exchange for a return to home rule.

The Dunning school view of the Reconstruction era received scattered attacks during Dunning's lifetime, notably from Negro leader W. E. B. DuBois and from Dunning's sometime colleague at Columbia, Charles E. Beard, but the portraits of the Radicals, the freedmen, and Southern whites as painted by the Dunning school proved remarkably persistent. Vernon L. Wharton, a more recent historian of the Reconstruction years and a critic of the Dunning approach, has written that the endurance of the Dunning thesis "may be attributed to the fact that it was compatible with the practices, principles, beliefs, and prejudices that justified domination of the world by people whose origins were in northern and western Europe." Not until after World War II was there widespread or drastic revision in the story of Reconstruction as told by the Dunning school. Recent studies have shown a new concern for the contribution of the Negro to American life and a refurbishing of the image of the Radicals, whose motives are seen as more idealistic and less partisan. Dunning's work has suffered in reputation as his villains—congressional Radicals, carpetbaggers, scalawags, and Negroes—have become heroes, and his heroes—President Johnson and native Southern political leaders—have become villains. Dunning and his students, however, performed much of the primary research which provided the factual basis for subsequent studies. The essential differences between more modern, and usually more balanced, studies and those of the Dunning school are largely over points of interpretation. Modern criticism of Dunning's interpretation has perhaps been influenced as much by more popular and less restrained restatement of his thesis in such works as Claude G. Bowers's *The Tragic Era* and Walter Lynwood Fleming's *The Sequel to Appomattox* as by his own work.

Dunning's position as a major figure among American historians is a result not only of his influence as a scholar and teacher but also of his efforts on behalf of professional associations. He was an original member of the American Historical Association, founded in 1884, and a member of its governing council from 1899 until 1902. In 1907 Dunning accepted the chairmanship of the publications committee and was a frequent contributor to the *American Historical Review*, organ of the American Historical Association. His work on behalf of the AHA helped create a congenial reception for historians of the South in an organization generally dominated by the Northeast. In 1903 Dunning was instrumental in finally persuading the AHA to abandon Washington for its annual meeting in favor of New Orleans and in arranging a session there on "The Study and Teaching of History in the South." At the annual meeting in 1913 at Charleston, South Carolina, Dunning assumed the presidency of the AHA. Many of his former students attended to celebrate his success and to announce plans for a festschrift in honor of his presidency. Published in 1914, *Studies in Southern History and Politics* was edited by James W. Garner and contained contributions from sixteen of Dunning's students.

Dunning was also a founder of the American Political Science Association and its president from 1921 until his death in 1922. Many of his best articles appeared in the *Political Science Quarterly*, for which he served as managing editor from 1894-1903. His careful editing helped make the journal a major publication in the field of political theory. In 1924 thirteen of Dunning's former students contributed to a memorial festschrift in honor of his presidency of the American Political Science Association. Edited by Charles E. Merriam and Harry Elmer Barnes, the volume is entitled *A History of Political Theories, Recent Times*. While most professional historians admiringly acknowledged Dunning's contributions and dedication to historical knowledge and publication, a few disenchanted contemporaries spoke of the domination of professional organizations by Dunning and a small group of his acquaintances as a "history ring."

During the first two decades of the twentieth century, while Dunning served as mentor at Columbia for a coterie of graduate students, American society experienced a strong impulse for "progressive" reform. Many of Dunning's fellow professors at Columbia, especially Charles A. Beard, were active supporters of reform enterprises. Although intellectually committed to reform, Dunning tenaciously avoided political involvement. Hoping to demonstrate his dedication to objectivity, he strived never to allow his political affiliations or opinions to be known to his students. He displayed no such reticence, however, at the Century Club in New York, where he spent most of his leisure hours. There Dunning was a major participant in the intellectual sparring over current events so relished by the literati of New York.

In 1914 Dunning had temporarily abandoned work on the third volume of *Political Theories* to write and have published *The British Empire and the United States*, a survey of Anglo-American relations from 1814-1914 commissioned by the committees in charge of the celebration of 100 years of peace between the two nations following the Treaty of Ghent. Perhaps the least known of Dunning's major

publications, *The British Empire and the United States* reflects the "imperial" approach to Anglo-American history so favored in the early twentieth century by historians of the colonial era. Just as Charles McLean Andrews, Herbert Levi Osgood, and George Louis Beer looked at events in the American colonial period against a background of British policy and politics, Dunning attempted to assess relations between Britain and the United States in terms of the prevailing political climates in each nation. In line with his avowed purpose to correct the "overemphasis on the evidence of ill-feeling," Dunning revealed a century marked by much dissension but in which cooperation and peace were dominant themes. In conclusion he attributed the lasting peace to a consciousness on the part of both peoples that "some special fiat of God and nature enjoins enduring peace among those whose blood or language or institutions or traditions . . . go back historically to the snug little island of Britain."

Fifteen years after Dunning's death *Truth in History and Other Essays* (1937) was published with funds bequeathed by Dunning to Columbia University for the encouragement of historical studies. A collection of previously published essays, articles, and reviews, the volume is perhaps the best example of Dunning's versatility and the scope of his interests. The selections, which cover a wide range of topics and historical events, display less restraint and considerably more wit than his longer works. Dunning's presidential address to the American Historical Association, delivered at Charleston in December 1913, serves as the lead essay and is also entitled "Truth in History." In "Truth in History" Dunning set forth clearly his philosophy of history in an eloquent plea for historians to avoid presentism and condescension and judge the events of the past on their own terms. "The crying need in the study of history today is humility. . . . Contempt for those who lacked our light is the worst of equipments for understanding their deeds." Dunning entreated historians to remember that what contemporaries of past events believed to be true is a more accurate view of the past than interpretations produced by later researchers who could not know firsthand of the climate, thought, and action that produced these events.

William Archibald Dunning was one of the most influential American historians of his generation and one of those whose work heralded a new era of historical scholarship dominated by academically trained historians. A former student wrote that Dunning "seemed to fear nothing so much as to be considered prejudiced, unbalanced, immature in judgment [or] reckless in conclusion." His work on Reconstruction has been called all of these things, but judged as Dunning himself would have had it, in terms of its own time, his work and that of his students made a permanent contribution to Reconstruction historiography. His impact on historical scholarship in the South and on research and writing about the South can scarcely be overestimated. As scholar, teacher, and editor, Dunning helped set professional standards for a whole generation of American historians and political scientists.

Other:
"A Sketch of Carl Schurz's Political Career," by Dunning and Frederick Bancroft, in *The Reminiscences of Carl Schurz*, volume 3 (New York: McClure, 1908), pp. 315-455.

Bibliography:
A Bibliography of the Faculty of Political Science of Co- *lumbia University, 1880-1930* (New York: Columbia University Press, 1931).

References:
J. G. de Roulhac Hamilton, Introduction to *Truth in History and Other Essays by William A. Dunning*, edited by Hamilton (New York: Columbia University Press, 1937), pp. xi-xxviii;
Alan D. Harper, "William A. Dunning: The Historian as Nemesis," *Civil War History*, 10 (1964): 54-66;
Charles E. Merriam, "William Archibald Dunning," in *American Masters of Social Science*, edited by Howard W. Odum (New York: Holt, 1927), pp. 131-145.

Papers:
Dunning's papers, a collection of letters, manuscripts, clippings, and journals are at Columbia University's Butler Library.

Shelby Foote
(17 November 1916-   )

Clyde N. Wilson
University of South Carolina

See also the Foote entry in *DLB 2, American Novelists Since World War II*.

SELECTED BOOKS: *The Civil War: A Narrative: Fort Sumter to Perryville* (New York: Random House, 1958);
The Civil War: A Narrative: Fredericksburg to Meridian (New York: Random House, 1963);
The Civil War: A Narrative: Red River to Appomattox (New York: Random House, 1974).

Shelby Foote's *The Civil War: A Narrative* occupies an unusual place in twentieth-century American historical literature. George Garrett, poet and novelist, has referred to it as "the largest and most ambitious single piece of work attempted and completed by any American novelist in this century." Critic Louis D. Rubin has written: "In objectivity, in range, in mastery of detail, in beauty of language and feeling for the people involved, this work surpasses anything on the subject. Written in the tradition of the great historian-artists, . . . it stands alongside the works of the best of them."

On the other hand, academic historians have been more restrained in their evaluation and, on the whole, have given as yet rather little attention to the work, perhaps because, as C. Vann Woodward observed in a review of Foote's third volume, "The gradual withering of the narrative impulse in favor of the analytical urge among professional academic historians has resulted in a virtual abdication of the oldest and most honored role of the historian, that of storyteller."

Shelby Foote was born into a well-connected Mississippi family and grew up in the Delta city of Greenville. He attended the University of North Carolina from 1935 through 1937 without graduating and saw both army and Marine Corps service in Europe during World War II. He was in his late thirties and had published five critically successful novels when, at his home in Memphis, he began work on his history of the Civil War, the research and writing of which occupied him for the twenty years ending in 1974. Two of his novels and a collection he edited were also related to the great American struggle of 1861-1865.

Published in three successive volumes appearing in 1958, 1963, and 1974, Foote's history is, as its subtitle implies, first and foremost a narrative, and chiefly a military narrative. It begins with Jefferson Davis's resignation from the Senate early in 1861 and ends with Davis's death in 1889. As a narrative, its virtues are many. Perhaps no work has ever given a more justly proportional treatment to the different theaters of the war—the Eastern, the Western, and the Trans-Mississippi. As storytelling, it reflects great artistry. It is possible to argue that no accounts of the great battles have ever equaled Foote's in their portrayal of relevant events and in their balance between the viewpoint and experiences of commanders and common soldiers. Another virtue is the writer's way of carrying the reader with him to well-known events, such as the Battle of Gettysburg. The reader does not so much think to himself that he is going to read about a battle as he is gradually, with a sense of surprise, swept into the event, just as the participants must have been. In no other modern military history is the reader so unconscious of the technique of presentation.

Shelby Foote

Another strength of the work is in the characterizations. Foote's novelist's eye for the revealing incident and trait has allowed him to construct portraits of the great figures of the war, Lincoln, Grant, Sherman, Lee, Davis, and his favorite, Forrest, that are both true to fact and carry psychological conviction beyond fact. This treatment has been accorded not only the most important characters but also many scores of lesser figures and in most cases can be considered as definitive and unsurpassed in any other of the vast literature on the war.

The Civil War: A Narrative has achieved considerable attention from general readers and from literary observers. The published commentary of academic historians on the work as a whole, however, is not yet sufficient to summarize confidently their judgment and the reasons for it, though it is possible to suggest several lines of criticism. One doubt revolves around Foote's research methods. *The Civil War: A Narrative* appears without footnotes. The main guide to the writer's sources and procedures appears in short essays appended to the end of each volume. His sources are chiefly the *Official Records of the War of the Rebellion* (a massive late nineteenth-century compilation of documents), the published histories and memoirs of participants, and his own examination of battlefields.

An objection that Foote has not fulfilled the historian's obligation to use primary rather than secondary sources, however, is not quite on target. The *Official Records of the War of the Rebellion* and many other of his sources, although they have been printed, are primary documents in nature. In constructing his narrative the sources have been exhaustively absorbed, dismantled, and recombined in a manner that would be almost impossible to footnote point by point but the reliability of which lies more in responsible use of necessary license such as narrative historians have always employed than in point-by-point documentation. Even among academic historians, point-by-point footnoting has fallen into disuse in recent years, partly as a result of the pressure of printing costs, and has been replaced by long notes that sweepingly support whole passages.

Foote himself, in his afterwords and in an article in the *Mississippi Quarterly* in 1964, has at some length considered the methodological question and has defended himself as using the novelist's method without his license, the historian's standards without the historian's paraphernalia. The *"honest"* novelist and the honest historian are both seeking the same thing, he declares: "the truth—not a different truth; the same truth." Both "want to tell us *how it was*: to recreate it, by their separate methods, and to make it live again in the world around them." The two methods of seeking truth, he adds, "are not hermetically sealed off from one another."

Another possible line of objection to *The Civil War: A Narrative* lies in Foote's conception of the project, which, as Woodward points out, runs athwart the analytical urge of academic historians. Foote is simply not very interested in such important aspects of the war as industrialization, diplomacy, or sanitation, and it is hard to see how he could carry out his central purpose of historical narrative in the great and traditional sense had he become too involved in such matters.

Still another ground for academic distrust in Foote, it may be suspected, is political. He began work on his history in the same year that the U.S. Supreme Court handed down its most important desegregation decision. The appearance of the work thus has coincided almost exactly in time with the "Civil Rights Revolution." During that period the predominant interpretive framework for viewing the Civil War has been what might be termed neoabolitionist or neo-Radical Republican, an affirmation of the wickedness of the Confederacy and of the righteousness of the Union cause, especially in its more politically revolutionary aspects. While it would be inaccurate to say that Foote is indifferent to the larger political implications of the war, he is foremost an artist. As such he is interested equally in both sides and in personalities and events, not issues. His "interpretation" of the Civil War operates on a level, therefore, that transcends the various familiar categories of allegiance in American historiography. It is possible that, with the passage of time and with the replacement of present issues by others, the rating of Foote's work as historical literature will rise.

There is no question that *The Civil War: A Narrative* is history as literature and not history as social science. Certainly a talented novelist's devotion of twenty years to historical writing should not be underrated. (As Garrett has pointed out, Foote's total published work is longer than that of either Proust or Gibbon.) It is just possible that his effort to restore the broken bridge between history and literature (of which there are other contemporary manifestations—Aleksandr Solzhenitsyn, for instance) will be perceived eventually as a decisive contribution. With the completion of his history, meanwhile, Foote has turned back to novel writing with the twentieth-century as his scene.

The Civil War is the period in U.S. history that contains more dramatic events, unforgettable personalities, and crucial issues than any other. No other part of the American experience has occurred on so vast and complex a scale and has been so significant for national self-understanding. Walt Whitman predicted that the war must inevitably produce its epic, and Foote himself, in one of his afterwords, has referred to the product of his twenty-year labor as "this iliad." It is, at this time, at least possible to argue that he is right, that *The Civil War: A Narrative* is the promised epic. Most certainly, in the grandeur of its conception and in the deceptive simplicity of its execution, it has succeeded in casting great events into the timeless form of great literature.

Other:
"The Novelist's View of History," *Mississippi Quarterly*, 17 (Fall 1964): 219-225.

References:
George Garrett, "Foote's *The Civil War*: The Version for Posterity?," *Mississippi Quarterly*, 28 (Winter 1974-1975): 83-92;

Louis D. Rubin, "Old-Style History," *New Republic*, 171 (30 November 1974): 44-45;

Wirt Williams, "Shelby Foote's *Civil War*: The Novelist as Humanistic Historian," *Mississippi Quarterly*, 24 (Fall 1971): 429-436;

C. Vann Woodward, "The Great American Butchery," *New York Review of Books*, 22 (3 March 1975): 12.

Douglas Southall Freeman

John L. Gignilliat
Agnes Scott College

BIRTH: Lynchburg, Virginia, 16 May 1886, to Walker Burford and Bettie Allen Hamner Freeman.

EDUCATION: A.B., Richmond College (later the University of Richmond), 1904; Ph.D., Johns Hopkins University, 1908.

MARRIAGE: 5 February 1914 to Inez Virginia Goddin; children: Mary Tyler, Anne Ballard, James Douglas.

AWARDS AND HONORS: Pulitzer Prize for *R. E. Lee*, 1935; Franklin Medal of American Philosophical Society, 1947; Pulitzer Prize for *George Washington*, 1958; twenty-five honorary degrees.

DEATH: Richmond, Virginia, 13 June 1953.

BOOKS: *R. E. Lee*, 4 volumes (New York: Scribners 1934-1935);
The South to Posterity: An Introduction to the Writing of Confederate History (New York: Scribners, 1939);
Manassas to Malvern Hill, volume 1 of *Lee's Lieutenants: A Study in Command* (New York: Scribners, 1942);
Cedar Mountain to Chancellorsville, volume 2 of *Lee's Lieutenants: A Study in Command* (New York: Scribners, 1943);
Gettysburg to Appomattox, volume 3 of *Lee's Lieutenants: A Study in Command* (New York: Scribners, 1944);
Young Washington, volumes 1 and 2 of *George Washington* (New York: Scribners, 1948);
Planter and Patriot, volume 3 of *George Washington* (New York: Scribners, 1951);
Leader of the Revolution, volume 4 of *George Washington* (New York: Scribners, 1951);
Victory with the Help of France, volume 5 of *George Washington* (New York: Scribners, 1952);
Patriot and President, volume 6 of *George Washington* (New York: Scribners, 1954);
First in Peace, by John Alexander Carroll and Mary Wells Ashworth, based on Freeman's research, volume 7 of *George Washington* (New York: Scribners, 1957).

Douglas Southall Freeman

Douglas Southall Freeman, Virginian and biographer of Virginians, achieved recognition during his lifetime as the preeminent authority on Confederate military history, a judgment accorded both by the academic community and by the popular press. The compelling sweep and controlled mastery of detail of *R. E. Lee* and *Lee's Lieutenants* caused them to be hailed as literary classics. Long a notable public figure in his native state as editor of an important Richmond newspaper, Freeman attained real national celebrity as a historian in the last twenty years of his life. He was unquestionably one of the best-known American historians of his time. His final work, *George Washington*, does not claim the authoritative place in historical literature occupied by his studies of the Army of Northern Virginia, but it is one of the monumental American biographies, and it buttresses his position among the leading American biographers of this century.

That he was born in 1886 in Lynchburg, Virginia, mattered less in Freeman's development than the fact that his family moved to Richmond, the old capital of the Confederacy, when he was five. Richmond was to be his home for the rest of his life, and no inducement ever sufficed to make him leave it. His scholarship can only be understood as an individualized response to youthful experiences he could have encountered nowhere else, for Richmond at the turn of the century stood at the center of the South's commemorative movement, its ceremonial remembrance of the Confederate past. Reunions of veterans, dedications of monuments, mock battles, and military funerals of Confederate leaders provided the most vivid experiences of Freeman's boyhood. He early acquired a passionate interest in all particulars of the war.

The enthusiasm of the boy's response to these events bore a direct relationship to the values of his family as exemplified by his admired father, a veteran of the Army of Northern Virginia and a loyal participant in all activities of Richmond's R. E. Lee Camp, United Confederate Veterans. Walker Burford Freeman supported his family as the Virginia agent of a national insurance company, but Douglas saw him primarily as the heroic survivor of war and economic dislocation. Firm in the faith of his Baptist forebears, the elder Freeman had a personal ethic that stressed fortitude and the acceptance of God's will. It had sustained him through four years of service in the ranks until he stacked arms at Appomattox and had carried him through twenty lean postwar years while he searched for economic security. He indulged in no regrets. He valued his Confederate service as evidence of his proper duty to his country, but he did not lament for the past. He acknowledged the defeat of the Confederacy as the result of a fair fight, and he professed himself glad that slavery had ended as one incident of the war's outcome. He remained a tireless worker and an indomitable optimist, confident of the future for those who did their best as they understood it.

Without doubt Walker Freeman became Douglas's primary model, a fact constantly affirmed by the son throughout his life. As the youngest of four boys Douglas felt a particular closeness to his father. He accepted his father's values and worked with an industry that would later become famous to get the most out of his studies and make the most of his time. Even as a student at Richmond College he ordered his activities carefully and gradually shortened the hours he devoted to sleep. By the time Douglas was a graduate student at Johns Hopkins University the rigor of his labors caused his father

some concern, but the son was confident that work suited his constitution much better than play. And that would prove to be the pattern of his life.

Walker Freeman's influence on his son's historical orientation was direct and continuing. Douglas went to Johns Hopkins in 1904 with the specific and ambitious aim of preparing himself to write a complete history of the Civil War. He formed that purpose, he later stated, after a trip with his father in 1903 to a Confederate reunion in nearby Petersburg that featured a reenactment of the famous Battle of the Crater. The veterans that day were aging but game; to the seventeen-year-old Douglas it was obvious that their lives were drawing to a close. He determined then that they should not be cheated of their place in history. He would tell their story, which was also his father's story. When the elder Freeman became national commander-in-chief of the United Confederate Veterans in 1925, Douglas wrote his address for the occasion, which contained a ringing affirmation that the sons of Confederate fathers would remain "faithful" to the memory of their cause. In a sense Freeman's books on the Army of Northern Virginia mark the fulfillment of that promise, a fact he himself deliberately underlined by his diary entry on Memorial Day, 1944: "At 6:05 in the presence of dear friends, I finished *Lee's Lieutenants* and concluded twenty-nine years of work to preserve the record of our fathers of the Army of Northern Virginia."

Two other vocations considered by Freeman in his youth reveal traits that were to endure. His mother, Bettie Allen Hamner Freeman, wished him to become a minister, an idea that had recurrent appeal to him as late as the Johns Hopkins years. To prepare himself for that possibility he learned Greek, which remained a lifelong enthusiasm. The other possibility was more novel: in his second year at college after considerable success on the boards, Freeman decided to become a professional actor. To an older brother Douglas revealed his plans to leave school and become a member of a traveling theatrical stock company that an acquaintance was organizing. The troupe failed to materialize, much to the relief of his brother, who never doubted Douglas's determination. Though he soon thereafter went with his father to the Petersburg reunion and formed another ambition, the germ of his later accomplishments as a historian, he took with him into maturity a sensibility that always carried weighty moral and dramatic components.

Freeman's stint at Johns Hopkins, a notably successful one, produced honors and fellowships and a doctorate in history in 1908 when he was just twenty-two. There he learned much about historical technique and method. He tempered a fervent prose style and came to regard history as a "science," a concept that reflected the general influence of German scholarship and the self-conscious professionalism that Johns Hopkins had done so much to transplant to American shores. In a decade when proponents of the "New History," such as James Harvey Robinson and Charles Beard, were urging historians to study the social sciences in order to interpret the past, Freeman took a minor in economics and decided that the fundamental cause of the Civil War was the clash between the South's economic system and that of the rest of the nation.

Yet the impact of Johns Hopkins was limited. Freeman encountered there no mentor to whom he felt personally drawn, and he did not alter his fixed purpose to write a history of the war. If he accepted the importance of economic causation in history, he certainly never accepted the total prescription of the "New History," which urged both scientific method and a detachment from judgments based on nationalism or morality. To have bought the second half of this formula would have denied the essence of his enthusiasm for the war. This Freeman never did; in his beliefs about the significance of the war he showed himself always his father's son. His letters from Johns Hopkins differ little in their views from his later statements on the subject, which were usually contained in private correspondence. A strong nationalist, Freeman felt that national good emerged from the trauma of the Civil War, in that it produced a united nation rather than a mere confederation. He acknowledged that the war could have been avoided and that both sides bore responsibility for recourse to arms. Yet each side had its honest imperatives, and the failure to reconcile them produced a "mighty sight," two valorous foes submitting themselves to the test of combat.

Freeman's interpretation was consistent with an inherited philosophy that accepted the inevitability of struggle in life. "Man proposes and God disposes," as he wrote his father. Fortitude, in his view, was a prime moral necessity. A people who did the best of which they were capable could accept the outcome, even if adverse, with pride. Their failure against great odds might even constitute moral victory, a useful legacy of heroism for all Americans. Freeman never doubted that the essential element in the story he would tell would be heroism. In order to write it, he was willing to contemplate heroic labors. "Twenty years," he confided to his father, "is but a trifle for so great a work." There is

an element of prophecy in those words, for he was to begin work on *R. E. Lee* exactly twenty years before publication of its final volumes. In time he abandoned his grand design to write a total history of the war, but he never gave up his ambition to create a lasting monument to its heroism, particularly that demonstrated by the army of his father.

Freeman always cited the circumstances that led him to write *R. E. Lee* as proof of the efficacy of one of his basic precepts: small opportunities lead to larger ones. In the summer of 1906 he worked on his dissertation in the archives of the Virginia State Library in Richmond. When the reference librarian there took a vacation, Freeman was asked to serve as her substitute. His work so pleased her that she soon offered him a more important task. She was a prominent member of the Confederate Memorial Literary Society, an organization that had collected documents, pamphlets, and books of the war years, and she now wished to issue a descriptive calendar of their holdings. Freeman leaped at this editorial opportunity and spent most of the summer of 1907 annotating *A Calendar of Confederate Papers* (1908), his first published work, completed even before he received his degree.

The chain of opportunity continued. The most valuable collection in the Confederate Memorial Literary Society had come as a gift from a family in Savannah, Georgia. One day in 1911 Freeman, then earning his living as the secretary of the state tax commission, received an unexpected call from a member of the Savannah family, a man who admired Freeman's work on *A Calendar of Confederate Papers* and wished him to examine some documents. To Freeman's amazement he found himself holding two morocco-bound volumes that contained the confidential wartime correspondence from Robert E. Lee to Jefferson Davis, missing and unaccounted for since the evacuation of Richmond in 1865. The visitor explained only that he had purchased the letters from "a well-known Southern writer." Would Freeman be interested in editing them for publication? Freeman asked no questions as he eagerly assented, for he recognized this as a veritable coup. And so it proved to be. He could devote only part of his time to the work, but when *Lee's Dispatches to Jefferson Davis, 1862-1865* finally appeared in 1915, the *New York Times* devoted the front page of its Sunday book section to a review. That in turn triggered another query from the publishing house of Charles Scribner's Sons: would Freeman undertake a brief biography of Lee for the firm's "American Crisis Series"? From Freeman's assent *R. E. Lee* ultimately resulted—no brief biography, to be sure, but the direct outcome of the contract with Scribners and the indirect outcome of a chain of events emanating from a stint of two weeks as substitute librarian in the summer of 1906. The biography of Lee directed Freeman's efforts to that part of the war in which he had the keenest interest and to the one leader for whom he had, even then, the highest regard.

It is undoubtedly significant that Freeman's first published works dealt with the war itself rather than with its causes or preliminaries or results. There were other books he promised to write in the years immediately after he left Johns Hopkins that he somehow never got around to writing. He was drawn ineluctably to the war, and when opportunities arose in that direction, he followed through. His editorial performance on *A Calendar of Confederate Papers* and on *Lee's Dispatches to Jefferson Davis* demonstrated his early precision on matters relating to Confederate lore and his equal insistence on using original documentation whenever possible. *A Calendar of Confederate Papers* describes secondary materials and 5,000 miscellaneous documents ranging from papers of the Confederate Medical Department to legal exhibits prepared for the postwar trial of Jefferson Davis. Footnotes identify all places and people mentioned in the documents, no small achievement considering the variety of the material and the fact that Freeman was twenty-one when he did the job. *Lee's Dispatches to Jefferson Davis* shows an even more accomplished scholarship, for here Freeman used footnotes to compose a short narrative of that part of the war covered by the messages. The footnotes can stand alone as a condensed history of Lee's active command, and in almost every case the information therein came directly from documents published in the *Official Records of the War*. The preface to *Lee's Dispatches to Jefferson Davis* allowed Freeman his first, albeit brief, published verdict on the commander: he was, his future biographer concluded, a great soldier and an even greater Christian. "The sufferings he endured," Freeman stated, "were worth all they cost him in the example they gave the South of fortitude in disaster and courage in defeat." From the first Freeman saw in Lee the personification of his personal ideal.

In 1914 Freeman was married to Inez Virginia Goddin, a Richmonder who was herself the daughter of a Confederate veteran. In the years ahead he never failed to pay tribute to his wife's contributions to his career, which were, in fact, considerable. Her name heads the list of his lengthy acknowledgments at the end of each of his books. She accepted his

schedule and conducted household arrangements for their three children so that he could work at home undisturbed. Above all, she had complete faith in his ability to accomplish what he set out to do. He had that in mind when he wrote the dedication to *R. E. Lee*: "To IGF, who never doubted."

Delay in the completion of *R. E. Lee* came in part from its author's perfectionism, but even more from the circumstance that history remained a secondary concern with him for some years. At Johns Hopkins he had definitely rejected the teaching of history as a profession. He sought a wider influence than he could exert in the classroom, and what time he could give to history he wanted to devote entirely to research. It must therefore be an avocation; he must earn his living elsewhere. He did teach history for a few sessions at a school for girls immediately after his return to Richmond in 1908, but that was merely one of several jobs he used to support himself until he could find a vocation of suitable scope. In this period he also worked for several agencies of the state of Virginia, but it was in journalism that he ultimately found his métier. Starting as an occasional editorial writer in 1909, he became editor of the *Richmond News Leader* in 1915, the year of the contract with Scribners. Then and later the newspaper took first priority. Freeman acquired a stock interest in the paper in 1923, by which time it enjoyed a strong lead in circulation over any other daily in the state. To be sure, he never abandoned the biography, but it proceeded slowly and only as other activities permitted. Perhaps spurred by his fortieth birthday, he determined in 1926 to assign himself a definite allotment of fourteen hours each week for the book. He kept a careful record and never henceforth failed to meet his quota, though he often exceeded it. *R. E. Lee* progressed more steadily thereafter.

Meanwhile, Freeman was engaged in an extended tug-of-war with Scribners over the nature of the biography. The contract called for a book of 75,000 words, and the firm initially resisted any suggestion that its scope might be expanded. Once engaged on the project Freeman wished to use original sources and hung back from the superficial treatment a short book would entail. The impasse ended only with the appointment in 1923 of a discerning new editor at Scribners, Maxwell E. Perkins, who consented to a longer biography that would incorporate all known important material. The tug-of-war between importunate editor and reluctant historian then resumed on a different level. Perkins imposed no limit on length and never discouraged the incorporation of additional material; he sensed that Freeman must control, must do it his way. He did offer encouragement and tactfully urge expedition. Freeman repeatedly delayed in order to investigate additional documentary collections and trace hundreds of privately held letters and memoirs. In the spring of 1928 he sent Perkins the first completed portion of the manuscript, which dealt with Lee's postwar career at Washington College. The editor pronounced himself pleased but admitted its length at first alarmed him; at that point he estimated the total length of the work as 500,000 words. When Freeman in 1930 completed the part of the manuscript that covered Lee's prewar career, Perkins urged its immediate publication as a separate volume, but the author vetoed that idea because he feared the uneventfulness of Lee's early life might mislead the reader to expect a lack of excitement in the book as a whole. Finally, on 19 January 1933, Lee's birthday, Freeman wired Perkins that he had completed the text. Literary revision was completed on 10 December. The manuscript in final form totaled one million words; without complaint Perkins decided to issue it in four volumes. As for Freeman, he calculated that he spent 6,100 hours on *R. E. Lee*—Lee's habitual signature was chosen as the title—since that day in 1926 when he began his schedule of fourteen hours weekly. He was forty-eight when he saw the book through to completion.

R. E. Lee arrived to the accompaniment of general acclaim. Freeman ought to be awarded "at least ten" Pulitzer prizes, declared the poet Stephen Vincent Benét, and then the historian should be kept at his desk another twenty years and compelled to write a biography of Washington. (That suggestion, incidentally, was to serve as another link in Freeman's connected chain of opportunities.) After a laudatory public review, Henry Steele Commager privately informed Freeman that he regarded *R. E. Lee* as the greatest of all American biographies. Gen. Douglas MacArthur was unequivocal in his verdict: "I congratulate you on the production of a masterpiece," he wrote. Even the *New Yorker* took humorous note. A Helen Hokinson cartoon depicted a matron returning two weighty volumes to a bookshop with the comment, "I guess I bit off more *Robert E. Lee* than I could chew." The awarding of the Pulitzer Prize in biography in 1935 fulfilled at least a part of Benét's directive. By 1963, ten years after Freeman's death, 87,735 purchasers had placed four-volume sets of *R. E. Lee* on their bookshelves, and 72,786 more had bought single volumes.

The national mood was right for the reception of the biography. Freeman's prodigious research made it a scholarly tour de force, and its dramatic subject matter gave it a natural appeal; but its popularity gained much from the mood of national reaffirmation that characterized the years of the Great Depression. If the intellectual climate of the 1920s had been critical and cynical, Alfred Kazin later noted, that of the 1930s eagerly sought to know how Americans in the past had survived the crises of their times. Seeking historical reassurance, the nation now valued irreverent wit much less than a detailed account of a Civil War battle. The times could not have been more propitious for the reception of a book that was the product of a mind and a general intention formed years before.

The central figure of *R. E. Lee* is the same moral victor foreshadowed in the preface of *Lee's Dispatches*, only in infinitely expanded illustration. Lee "met the supreme tests of life in that he accepted fame without vanity and defeat without repining." The explanation for his calm self-control lay in a deep religious faith that could not be called fatalistic, because he felt a strong duty to do the best of which he was capable. Having done that, he could accept the outcome with equanimity. "Believing that God was Infinite Wisdom and Eternal Love, he subjected himself to seeming ill-fortune in the confidence that God's will would work out for man's good."

Contained in its final chapter, these are the conclusions in the only extended description of Lee the man in the whole book, but there is amply documented evidence throughout the four volumes on which to base the verdict. Freeman specifically disavowed any intention to "interpret" a man he considered "his own clear interpreter." The biographer's job, he said, was to report the facts fully as they occurred in the course of the life. Permissible summation at the end should merely organize, in extended form, generalizations justified and even made obvious by the earlier recountal of fact. Above all, no biographer should try to read his subject's mind; that would be unscientific. And so Freeman felt justified in concluding: "Beneath that untroubled exterior, they said, deep storms must rage; his dignity, his reserve and his few words concealed sombre thoughts, repressed ambitions, livid resentments. They were mistaken. Robert Lee was one of the small company of great men in whom there is no inconsistency to be explained, no enigma to be solved. What he seemed, he was—a wholly human gentleman, the essential elements of whose positive character were two and only two, simplicity and spirituality."

The narrative portions of *R. E. Lee* recount only those facts known to Lee at the time; the reader becomes acquainted with new circumstances only as Lee learns of them. This technique, dubbed the "fog of war" in the context of battle descriptions, Freeman considered more scientific because it was truer to actual circumstances. In that it heightens the suspense inherent in the uncertainties of the historical situation, it is also more dramatic, as he was aware. Footnotes, endnotes, and, in the case of major military engagements, retrospective analyses in the body of the text supply some supplemental information. The fog of war has its limitations as a technique for conveying complete understanding of the hectic confusion of military action, but for Freeman it provided great advantage for his particular biographical intention.

In his assessment of Lee's military performance Freeman deliberately avoided panegyric, with which he was all too familiar in the overheated atmosphere that had characterized military discussions during his boyhood. He also avoided controversy. In Richmond in the 1890s responsibility for Confederate defeat at Gettysburg, for example, had been at times quite literally a fighting matter. Freeman brought dispassion to his analysis. He refused to compare Lee's prowess to that of other generals; "military circumstance," he remarked, "is incommensurable." He acknowledged some flaws in the commander—only peripheral flaws in the case of Gettysburg, but more serious ones in his strategy during the Seven Days, in his occasional overestimation of his men's endurance or of an individual officer's potential for leadership, and especially in his general courteous deference to his subordinates.

On balance, though, Freeman declared the credit to Lee's military performance "clear and absolute." Even the famous deference he defended as sometimes helpful in a revolutionary situation involving notorious individualists in a volunteer army, many of them strangers to conventional military discipline. The general's calm tact in dealing with the civilian leadership of the government was an indispensable advantage for the Confederacy. His consideration for his men in the ranks, joined with his ability to bring them victories, created an army of superb morale. The infinite care he gave to administrative detail contributed as much to his army's effectiveness as his strategic audacity and logistical precision. In Freeman's judgment, the population of the South was sustained in its will to fight during the final year of the war primarily by its perception of Lee's character. In

R. E. Lee the military hero blends inextricably with the moral hero.

In the period after the publication of *R. E. Lee* Freeman did not turn immediately to another full-scale historical project. His life became busier than ever. Though he continued as editor of the *News Leader*, he accepted in 1934 a professorship in the School of Journalism at Columbia University, professional duality that entailed two nights each week on a Pullman commuting to New York, where he fulfilled his academic obligations in one full day. He held the position at Columbia until 1941. He became chairman of the board of trustees at his alma mater, by then the University of Richmond, in 1934. Though he had relinquished the Bible class he taught in the 1920s at Richmond's Second Baptist Church, he still delivered a religious lecture each Sunday by radio, as well as two daily newscasts. He continued to teach a weekly current events class of Richmond business and professional men. Long the accustomed orator for historical observances in Virginia, he spoke more widely at educational institutions throughout the nation after the publication of *R. E. Lee*, becoming, in addition, a regular lecturer at staff schools of the armed forces. In what was perhaps his busiest year for speaking, 1937, he calculated that he delivered eighty-three lectures.

In addition to the necessity for adjusting to his expanded activities, he felt some uncertainty as to what historical enterprise he should undertake next. Stephen Benét's suggestion of a biography of Washington fell on a receptive mind. If he could only write lives of Washington and Woodrow Wilson, Freeman informed Maxwell Perkins, he would have paid his tribute to all three of his special Virginia heroes. Perkins favored Washington, a natural choice in view of Freeman's military expertise, and the biographer actually made preliminary investigations of the Washington material before setting it aside in June 1936 to begin *Lee's Lieutenants*.

The most praised of Freeman's works, his own acknowledged favorite, *Lee's Lieutenants*, seems to have evolved almost as an afterthought. He later explained that he feared he had slighted Lee's subordinates in keeping the focus so strongly on their commander. He had unused material accumulated for *R. E. Lee*, and Perkins was enthusiastic about the commercial possibilities of the project. The familiar tug-of-war resumed. Perkins at first planned on a one-volume work for publication in the fall of 1937. Delays and expansion inevitably followed as Freeman found new material. He took time out in 1939 to write *The South to Posterity*, a personal and

Dust jackets for Freeman's 1942-1944 trilogy, his personal favorite among his works

informal survey of Confederate memoirs and reminiscences. The first of the three volumes of *Lee's Lieutenants*, subtitled *A Study in Command*, finally appeared in October 1942, the second in April 1943, and the last in October 1944. This time Freeman kept time accounts from the first: the total work consumed 7,121 hours of his time.

Published during the combat-conscious years of World War II, *Lee's Lieutenants* proved even more popular than *R. E. Lee*, in terms of single volumes sold. By 1963 the reading public had purchased 172,712 single volumes and 47,127 three-volume sets. *Lee's Lieutenants* also placed Freeman near the top of the nation's historical guild. In 1949 Henry Steele Commager, always an admirer, hailed the seven-volume shelf of Confederate biography as "the highwater mark of American literature since Parkman." Even T. Harry Williams, who was critical, later acknowledged Freeman's paramount reputation as a Civil War historian. "He sat in Richmond," Williams wrote, "surrounded by a vast admiration without parallel in modern historiography."

The nation's high command during World War II ranked among the most avid readers of *Lee's Lieutenants*. They seemed to take real comfort, amidst their own difficulties, in reading of the greater troubles of the Army of Northern Virginia. That was the specific reaction of Adm. Chester Nimitz, commander of the Pacific Fleet, and of Army Chief of Staff George C. Marshall. Adm. Ernest King, the naval commander in chief, became so engrossed in the second volume as bedtime reading that he told a staff member he found it difficult to make himself put it down and go to bed. Gen. Omar Bradley spent much of his leisure time before the invasion of Normandy reading the first two volumes. Many of the military leaders expressed an interest in the possibility that Freeman might undertake a history of the military command of *their* war. General MacArthur was especially enthusiastic over this prospect and offered to conduct the historian on a personal tour that would retrace his own campaigns in the Pacific. Though Freeman ultimately decided such a history should wait until all documents became available, at the end of hostilities he did accompany a party led by John J. McCloy, then assistant secretary of war, on an extended tour that spanned the globe to visit major military headquarters in all theaters of the war. The opportunity to meet the commanders and to examine some of the documents of the recent conflict was a high point in Freeman's life, and he gave advice thereafter to several of them as they wrote their memoirs.

In one case the advice seems to have been political, for General Eisenhower later acknowledged Freeman's influence on his decision to seek the presidency.

With the completion of *Lee's Lieutenants* and the end of World War II, Freeman entered a period of real national celebrity that came in good part from publicity about his disciplined use of time. "Time alone is irreplaceable," admonished the placard over his desk. "Waste it not." In following that injunction Freeman gradually evolved a definite schedule that allotted minutes to each task of the day. By 1948 he rose each morning at 2:30 and arrived at the newspaper office an hour later. He shaved and dressed in twelve minutes and drove to town from his suburban home in seventeen, invariably saluting the equestrian statue of Lee as he passed it on Monument Avenue on his way to work. After completing his editorial duties and two newscasts, he returned home at 1:00 P.M. for lunch, a short nap, and an afternoon devoted to history. Thanks largely to the Luce publications, whose *Time* and *Life* furnished the details of this controlled routine, Freeman became something of a national persona in the 1940s, recognized as a memorable personality even by many who never read his books.

Lee's Lieutenants is not a technical study of command or strategy. Rather, its genre is highly personal military biography. The focus remains consistently on the individual officers, and the unifying theme is the procurement of able commanders as the principals are winnowed by failure or casualty. There is no attempt to portray the complete lives of the lieutenants; essentially the reader encounters them on the field of battle, with a summary paragraph or two to explain their pasts. Supporting characters, such as families or friends who play an active part, enter the picture at the appropriate time. Employed in a narrative of multiple biography, the fog-of-war technique requires continual shifting of focus from one leader to another as the kaleidoscope of combat moves along. Freeman's smooth handling of the transitions in narrative demonstrated an impressive control over his material. Characteristically, he cited the difficulty of organizing the material as his principal reason for regarding *Lee's Lieutenants* as his best work; he always enjoyed a challenge.

On one important military judgment, responsibility for Confederate defeat at Gettysburg, Freeman completely changed his mind in *Lee's Lieutenants*. In *R. E. Lee* he placed the heaviest blame on James Longstreet, primarily because of the general's delay in attack on the morning of

2 July. Freeman believed the increase of Union forces along Cemetery Ridge during the delay determined the failure of the Confederate assault, but an irate protest of that verdict from an amateur critic and authority on the battle caused him to reconsider the evidence. Subsequently he concluded that the *Official Records of the War of the Rebellion* did indeed indicate sufficient troops of the Army of the Potomac in place early on the morning of 2 July to repulse the earliest attack a more cooperative Longstreet might have mounted. *Lee's Lieutenants* registers the altered judgment.

Freeman's change of opinion on Gettysburg throws considerable light on his historical orientation. When one critic taxed him for ignoring evidence in the *Official Records of the War of the Rebellion*, he also chided him for overreliance on the papers of the Southern Historical Society, a Richmond-based organization with which Freeman had been intimately involved in some fashion since his boyhood. Headed in its first years by the combative Gen. Jubal A. Early, the society had tended to favor Lee at the expense of Longstreet in its publications, which ran heavily to after-the-fact narratives by participants. Freeman knew Early's foibles and bias, as he demonstrated in comments in *The South to Posterity*. Yet he was predisposed to accord the society's publications weight, because they were an integral part of his introduction to the war. They were, so to speak, the literary arm of the veterans' groups for which he had such enthusiasm. He read the society's publications avidly in his youth and actually became the organization's last president in 1926. When, therefore, he changed his mind on Gettysburg and admitted a deficiency in some of the papers of the Southern Historical Society, his renunciation carried a special weight. It was both a sign of the fairness of his intentions and of the difficulties posed by his Richmond upbringing.

Historians who have been critical of Freeman as a historian of the Civil War have usually also been critical of Lee as a general. That is inevitable, given the affinity between the subject and his biographer. From Basil Liddell Hart to T. Harry Williams to Thomas L. Connelly the line of criticism runs fairly straight. Williams, the most careful of the group, stated it directly: "The problem of Freeman cannot be separated from the problem of Lee." Freeman, like Lee, adhered to the tournament concept of war. Like Lee, he attached too much importance to Virginia to the exclusion of the western theater of the war. Like Lee, he hesitated to wound in his recountal of fact. "He was a Virginia gentleman writing about a Virginia gentleman." Williams particu-

larly objected to the fog of war, in that it produced drama at the expense of clear understanding. And he was exasperated by Freeman's failure to link developments in warfare with what preceded and what followed the Civil War. He wanted historical context: "It is as though Lee and the Army of Northern Virginia are wrenched out of the context of military history to be presented brilliantly in a kind of historical void." Some of Williams's comments represent an almost classic clash of cultural assumptions—Midwestern versus Virginian. His statements about the fog of war and the lack of context, on the other hand, indicate an understandable lack of comprehension of Freeman's deepest intention—understandable because Freeman himself never publicly explained it. Technically speaking, that intention was more dramatic and literary than factual and historical.

The critics who came closest to understanding his intention, or at least recognized its effect, were not historians per se but students of literature with an interest in history. Their insights drew upon some shrewd guesses about the nature of the historian himself. Louis D. Rubin, Jr., a literary scholar whose Richmond upbringing gave him some knowledge of Freeman as a public figure, perceived the essential clue in the fact that the historian was a hero worshiper. Rubin suspected that Freeman found a refuge for his values in history that was not available to him in the largely unheroic activities he discussed daily as a newspaper editor. And Allen Tate, poet and critic, concluded that Freeman had "something of the sensibility of a poet" and used poetic technique to evoke a compelling mood of heroic assertion. Noting that Freeman's fog of war almost completely omitted two factors that most historians would feel they must deal with—the enemy and the South, or even the people of Virginia—Tate recognized in the lack of historical context a time-honored literary convention: "Lee's army is here cut off forever in a kind of 'cold pastoral' not only from the time of its action but from all history: it has been assimilated to a very great poetic convention, that of the Golden Age, in which we may all, North and South and men everywhere, participate, a Platonic world in which historical men achieve a Homeric stature. . . ."

While Freeman was always critical of those who resorted to war needlessly, he saw war as the ultimate test of fortitude, the heroic trait he most admired. In the fog of war he found a technique of presentation that maximized the drama of the testing. Though he wanted his facts to form a permanent record of the Army of Northern Virginia and showed enormous concern for details about the army, in his narrative he sought less an understanding of the total military situation than dramatic impact. Whether he was aware that he was following poetic convention is doubtful, but he was well aware of the mood he wished to evoke, and at times he sought rather direct poetic example. When he came to write the chapter on the surrender at Appomattox in *R. E. Lee*, Freeman wanted to create an atmosphere of high tragedy that would not lapse into sentimental excess. Remembering that Sophocles and Euripides, in moments of direst tragedy, resorted to the simplest language, he read Greek drama for three weeks before undertaking the chapter. The language of "The Ninth of April" is terse; the admiring readers who wrote Freeman about it did not find it lacking in dramatic impact.

Freeman recommended an eclectic approach to the writing of biography, and clearly he practiced it. That there might ever be any conflict between science and his desire to dramatize the heroic fortitude he perceived in the Army of Northern Virginia seems never to have occurred to him, but occasionally the two elements of his mixture did clash. They clashed more strongly in *R. E. Lee* than in *Lee's Lieutenants*.

Lee was unquestionably Freeman's greatest hero, and Freeman believed in the emulation of exemplars. It confuses the issue to state, as did T. Harry Williams, that Freeman and Lee were too much alike. They lived in different times, had different minds, played different roles, faced different problems and opportunities. What matters is that Freeman had such intense regard for Lee that he lacked a certain critical distance and became protective of his subject. The truism that all biography is in part autobiography would seem to have force in this case, in that Freeman accentuated qualities in Lee that represented his own highest values. Despite his intention to avoid overt interpretation, interpretation is always implicit in the very process of selectivity of evidence, a matter of proportion and emphasis. Not every reader agreed, even after compassing *R. E. Lee's* impressive array of evidence, that Lee was so lacking in complexity as Freeman insisted: Freeman's own brother, a physician who was probably his closest lifelong friend, disagreed on the probability of that analysis. Freeman steadfastly held to it, as if complexity would weaken his portrait of fortitude. The biographer recognized that Lee had his moments of discouragement, and he noted them, but he treated such incidents less fully than he would have had he seen them as more significant. In at least one case, involving an episode

on a Canadian boundary survey in Lee's youth, Freeman's protectiveness of Lee's moral reputation led him to misjudge altogether a document that surfaced after the publication of the biography. Because his admiration of and perhaps identification with his subject was so great, it is reasonable to assume there might have been other evidence he misjudged or other evidence he discounted as unimportant that not everyone would so regard. If he was most protective of Lee's moral heroism, he also seemed inclined at times to accept Lee's military judgment as the court of last appeal. Even when he admitted military error in Lee, as in his reconsidered account of Gettysburg in *Lee's Lieutenants*, he did not devote to it the same thorough analysis that he usually gave to the mistakes of others. His critiques of Lee always seem inhibited.

Freeman's *R. E. Lee* remains the most convincing biography of Lee extant, an American classic of heroism. While the heroic traits cannot be denied, it is no insult either to subject or to biographer to say that another case could be made, another emphasis argued. Freeman recognized the importance of viewpoint, which was why he sometimes stated that he wanted the first full-length biography of Lee to be written by a Southerner, by an appreciative author. Freeman assumed a certain universality in mankind, but he knew that values changed: witness his later statement, while engaged in writing *George Washington*, that the twentieth century was in many ways more like the eighteenth century than like the nineteenth. His own values, like those he admired in Lee, were more common in the nineteenth century than in the twentieth. While he placed considerable credence in medical information, his trust in genetics as a biographical tool seems associated less with science in the twentieth century than with the social attitudes of the nineteenth—and nineteenth-century Virginia to boot. Freeman's certainty in ascribing each of Lee's balanced traits to his fortunate inheritance from a specific ancestor—a certainty possible, he felt, because so much was known of those forebears— seems simplistic to a later age. Surprisingly for a historian, he thought blood counted more than ideas. He was skeptical of psychological interpretation and downright hostile to its Freudian component. If, seeing the extremes to which an over-reliance on psychology can sometimes lead, many historians in the last half of the twentieth century feel a like skepticism, they cannot altogether ignore a psychoanalytical awareness that is deep in the modern temper. The possibility for another life of Lee from another angle of vision does exist. From whatever angle it comes, it cannot afford to ignore *R. E. Lee*, and any historian who investigates the minutiae of battles fought by the Army of Northern Virginia will profit from the fact that Freeman traveled the same route.

Lee's Lieutenants, the by-product of *R. E. Lee*, shows more critical candor than the earlier book. Though the figure of Lee serves as the moral linchpin of the narrative, entering to make decisions, smooth quarrels, and offer commendation, the action belongs to his subordinates, a diverse and very

Freeman delivered two daily newscasts and a Sunday lecture for a Richmond radio station for more than twenty years.

human crew. Some of them bicker with each other repeatedly, and many more exhibit jealous competition for rank. The egotistical self-seeking of a few destroys their effectiveness; by transfer or retirement they disappear. Others who seem promising fail for some reason to realize their full potential as commanders. What the best of them have is bravery, boldness, and wholehearted commitment. All of them are tested repeatedly by the changing circumstances of battle, where a lost opportunity can change almost immediately into disaster.

The concept of testing is employed throughout the book. "He met the test" is the author's high-

est accolade. Not all of the lieutenants are judged to have met each specific test, but despite flaws and mistakes most of them exhibit a courage under fire that becomes more impressive as their numbers dwindle under the inexorable toll of battle. Their tests continue relentlessly until many face the "last enemy," death itself. In the case of the ablest of the lieutenants, "Stonewall" Jackson, the narrative follows the general through the excitement of his great success at Chancellorsville to his wounding, his sickroom, his death scene. Jackson is not the only commander who meets his end with composure. The survivors fight on indomitably, though each successive action confirms the likelihood that the decimated, exhausted army cannot replace its progressive loss of leadership. Even at Appomattox some of them quit the field before the surrender so that they can fight on.

"The story is Homeric in its tragedy," Freeman wrote Maxwell Perkins in 1936 as he began its telling; the completed volumes make that point. The collective portrait of quite human heroism in *Lee's Lieutenants* is Freeman's most successful memorial to the Army of Northern Virginia, a balanced blend of his science and his celebration of fortitude—and a mirror of significant aspects of an age.

The biographer's own philosophy was nowhere better demonstrated than in his decision in 1944 to quit the field of Confederate history and undertake the writing of *George Washington*, a formidable task for a man of his age and obligations. He was fifty-eight when he began it, still the editor of the *News Leader*, and he was planning even then a biography of his friend John Stewart Bryan, publisher of the newspaper. (He completed this biography, which was not published, in 1947.) His local activities continued unabated; outside Virginia they included service on the boards of charitable and business institutions as diverse as the Rockefeller Foundation and the Equitable Life Assurance Society. Though he made fewer speeches than he had in the past, he was still traveling about 20,000 miles a year. The goal he proposed for himself, a spacious life and times of Washington utilizing all important documentary sources, would require an expenditure of time comparable to that spent on his Confederate books, on which he had worked for a total of twenty-nine years. And a biography of Washington would take its author into an age to which he had had no previous scholarly exposure. Nevertheless, he went, heeding quite literally the words from Tennyson's "Ulysses" that he framed and placed on his desk at about this time: "something ere the end / Some work of noble note may yet be done, / Not unbecoming men that strove with Gods."

Several commentators were to suggest that Freeman also possessed a quality he found in young Washington, "the quenchless ambition of an ordered mind." Certainly his mind had both ambition and order. He wanted to write the book; friends, particularly Raymond B. Fosdick of the Rockefeller Foundation, urged it; the Carnegie Corporation, later joined by the John Simon Guggenheim Foundation, stood ready with funds to support a research and secretarial staff; the documents existed in accessible form, along with technology for copying them in the form of photostats and microfilm. Freeman assessed all the probabilities of the situation and went ahead. After the publication of the first two volumes, in order to have more time for the task, he resigned from the *News Leader* in 1949; his service there had just exceeded a full generation. He lived to complete six volumes of *George Washington* and to cover all but six years of his subject's life, expending some 15,693 hours in the process.

With the aid of the staff and his own organizational skills, Freeman proceeded rapidly. After the material was gathered, he arranged his notes so that he could find any information he wanted within moments. His numbered note cards of varying colors in chronological order were cross-referenced to longer notes uniformly sized and filed in ring binders. He outlined each chapter so thoroughly in advance that he knew precisely which numbered card would be used in what order in the writing. He sometimes wrote footnotes in advance of the textual composition. His order resulted in expedition, and the first two volumes of the book appeared in 1948, volumes three and four in 1951, volume five in 1952, and volume six, posthumously, in 1954. After Freeman's historical associates, Mary Wells Ashworth and John A. Carroll, wrote volume seven, the completed *George Washington* received the Pulitzer Prize in biography in 1958.

Publication of the first two volumes of the book in 1948 was the occasion for a cover story in *Time* featuring Freeman and his conclusions about young Washington; the biographer was probably at the peak of his national fame. Yet *George Washington* never elicited the same popular response that had greeted the Confederate books. Sales were impressive for a book of such scale—13,543 six-volume sets, 112,373 single volumes, for a total of 193,631 volumes by 1963. Comparable figures, however, are a total of 423,726 volumes for *R. E. Lee* and 314,093 for *Lee's Lieutenants*.

Nor were the professional critics uniformly warm in their praise. Though they expressed respect, sometimes awe, for Freeman's industry in assessing the vast documentary evidence, and though they granted the real detachment of his judgment, they questioned his sense of historical proportion. Some felt he devoted too much detail to unimportant matters while slighting others of real import. Several reviewers chided him for ignoring insights available from the scholarship of secondary sources. The critical consensus admired Freeman's battle descriptions and military judgment but found *George Washington* lacking in social, intellectual, and political context.

Freeman's critical distance from Washington could have been an advantage to him in writing the book; he never admired Washington as he did Lee. His portrait of Washington at the age of twenty-seven reveals a rather calculating young man whose ambition is balanced, in moral terms, only by a determination to accept responsibility and to deal fairly with his fellows, and even those qualities seem motivated by a desire for public "honor." The biographer found young Washington's lack of affection for his mother and his indifference to religion less than attractive. Those traits he noted again in his assessment of his subject at the end of the Revolution. Though he judged the mature man's administrative care and his self-control admirable and more responsible than military acumen for the success of his army, Freeman's summation is restrained: "He was a patriot of conscious integrity and unassailable conduct who had given himself completely to the revolutionary cause and desired for himself the satisfaction of having done his utmost and of having won the approval of those whose esteem he put above every other reward." Though Freeman was denied the final assessment that he intended in his last unwritten volume, it is clear that his personal approval of Washington fell far short of that he felt for Lee.

But if he was not inhibited by an overregard for his subject, certain parts of Freeman's historical experience and technique, other than his lack of background in the epoch, presented special difficulties in a life of Washington. Except for a short service in the Mexican War, Lee led a quiet life, carefully avoiding politics, until the Civil War propelled him onto center stage. Even then, the drama of his life occurred mostly in battle. Washington, on the other hand, from the time of his military participation on the frontier through the two terms of his presidency, had significant involvement in events of wide consequence involving politics and diplomacy as much as war. Though Freeman did not uniformly adhere only to Washington's point of view and included, for instance, a long descriptive chapter on Virginia in Washington's youth, he did tend to fall back repeatedly on the technique of viewing events through his subject's eyes. That technique, somewhat limiting in a biography of Lee, faced almost insuperable difficulties in a biography of Washington. It worked best on a narrative of dramatic action. It could be exciting, as when employed in recounting Benedict Arnold's desertion to the British, but it could not suffice to explain the clash of political personalities in a wider arena. That required an assessment of ideas, interests, and trends. Even if Freeman had had time to gain the same masterful grasp of factual matter that he had with his Confederate books, it is difficult to see how this technique, if he had adhered to it, could have produced fully satisfactory results. *George Washington* is a monument to its author's indefatigable industry, an invaluable source book for the period, a detailed record of Washington's concerns at each juncture of his life. It illuminated the character and personality of Washington and gave a solid footing for subsequent scholarship, but it did not achieve an authoritative synthesis.

In the last years of his life Freeman occasionally expressed regret that he had devoted so much time and effort to his public career rather than to scholarship. Newspaper writing, he concluded, was "writing in the sand." His sentiments at this period, though genuine, probably were not altogether realistic. If his life contained many compartments, each one met some personal need. Freeman needed his public involvements, needed to feel that he could influence the events of his time. Historical scholarship of itself would never have satisfied that need. He had become, as a journalistic colleague said of him, "a Virginia institution." It is significant that even after his retirement from the editorship of the *Richmond News Leader* he continued his daily radio broadcasts from his home, though he sometimes professed contempt for radio as a medium.

His regret over not having written more history does indicate his awareness that his greatest achievement lay in the historical field. His biographical volumes do in fact represent his most lasting contribution to American life, and all three of his major works are still in print.

Other:

A Calendar of Confederate Papers, edited by Freeman (Richmond: The Confederate Museum, 1908);

Lee's Dispatches to Jefferson Davis, 1862-1865, edited by Freeman (New York: Putnam's, 1915).

References:

Mary Tyler Freeman Cheek, "Douglas Southall Freeman: My Father as a Writer," *Richmond Literature and History Quarterly*, 1 (Spring 1979): 33-41;

Thomas L. Connelly, *The Marble Man: Robert E. Lee and His Image in American Society* (New York: Knopf, 1977);

John L. Gignilliat, "A Historian's Dilemma: A Posthumous Footnote for Freeman's *R. E. Lee*," *Journal of Southern History*, 43 (May 1977): 217-236;

Joseph H. Harrison, Jr., "Harry Williams, Critic of Freeman: A Demurrer," *Virginia Magazine of History and Biography*, 64 (January 1956): 70-77;

Dumas Malone, "The Pen of Douglas Southall Freeman," in *Patriot and President*, volume 6 of *George Washington* (New York: Scribners, 1954), pp. ix-xxxi;

Louis D. Rubin, Jr., *Richmond as a Literary Capital* (Richmond: Friends of the Richmond Public Library, 1966);

Time, "The Virginians," 52 (18 October 1948): 108-110;

T. Harry Williams, "Freeman, Historian of the Civil War: An Appraisal," *Journal of Southern History*, 21 (February 1955): 91-100.

Papers:

Freeman's papers are at the Library of Congress.

John A. Garraty

(4 July 1920-   )

Justus D. Doenecke
New College of the University of South Florida

SELECTED BOOKS: *Silas Wright* (New York: Columbia University Press, 1949);

Henry Cabot Lodge: A Biography (New York: Knopf, 1953);

Woodrow Wilson: A Great Life in Brief (New York: Knopf, 1956);

The Nature of Biography (New York: Knopf, 1957; London: Cape, 1958);

From Main Street to the Left Bank: Students and Scholars Abroad, by Garraty and Walter Adams (East Lansing: Michigan State University Press, 1959);

Is The World Our Campus?, by Garraty and Adams (East Lansing: Michigan State University Press, 1960);

Right-Hand Man: The Life of George W. Perkins (New York: Harper, 1960);

The American Nation: A History of the United States (New York: Harper & Row, 1966);

Theodore Roosevelt: The Strenuous Life, by Garraty and the editors of *American Heritage* (New York: American Heritage, 1967);

The New Commonwealth, 1877-1890 (New York: Harper & Row, 1968);

Interpreting American History: Conversations with Historians (New York: Macmillan, 1970; London: Collier-Macmillan, 1970);

Unemployment in History: Economic Thought and Public Policy (New York: Harper & Row, 1978).

John Arthur Garraty has long been one of America's leading historians. His contributions have been particularly strong in economic history, biography, the Gilded Age, and the Progressive era. Combining an able prose style with balanced judgments, he has produced volumes almost universally respected by historians, and because of his textbooks and biographical projects, he has long had a lay audience as well.

Born in Brooklyn, New York, Garraty received a bachelor of arts degree from Brooklyn College in 1941 and masters and doctoral degrees from Columbia University in 1942 and 1949, respectively. From 1942 to 1945, he was in the U.S. Navy, from which he was discharged as petty of-

ficer, first class. From 1947 to 1959, he was a member of the faculty at Michigan State University, and from 1959 on, he has been on the faculty of Columbia University. Garraty has received numerous honors: he was a Ford fellow (1953-1954), Social Science Research Council fellow (1954-1957), Guggenheim fellow (1955-1956), and fellow of the Center for Advanced Study in the Behavioral Sciences (1962-1963). From 1969 to 1971, he was president of the Society of American Historians, the organization that publishes *American Heritage*, and he has long played a leading role both in the society and its journal.

Garraty wryly notes that his interest in history began in the eighth grade, when his teachers encouraged him to make clay models of maps and

John A. Garraty

battle scenes. His first book, *Silas Wright*, was published in 1949 and was the product of a doctoral dissertation directed by John A. Kraut. Upon reading Arthur M. Schlesinger, Jr.'s *The Age of Jackson* (1945), Garraty learned that there was no serious biography of Silas Wright, the prominent Jacksonian leader of New York State, and he promptly attempted to fill that gap. Wright was a leader of the Albany Regency, the Democratic-Republican organization headed by Martin Van Buren. From 1824 until his death in 1847, Wright was usually in office, first holding local posts in Canton, New York, then the positions of state senator, congressman, state comptroller, U.S. senator, and governor of New York. Garraty portrayed Wright as a Jacksonian's Jacksonian, a man who always kept a wary eye on banks and internal improvements and who adhered steadfastly to hard money. Garraty went on to note that as the leading Jackson man on the Senate Committee on Finance, Wright played a major role in Old Hickory's war against the Bank of the United States. Wright did all he could to quiet the stir over slavery, and like his mentor Van Buren, he risked his political fortunes by opposing the annexation of Texas. Garraty stressed that Wright's run for the governorship in 1844 helped assure James K. Polk's capture of New York State and with it the presidency. However, as governor Wright refused to pardon convicted Antirenters and hence failed to be reelected in 1846.

For the most part, Garraty's biography downplayed interpretation and stressed narrative. In noting Wright's dedication to the eradication of debt and financial speculation, Garraty saw his subject as a forerunner of Grangers, Populists, Wilsonians, and New Dealers. Observing Wright's rigidity as governor, Garraty criticized him for failing to use party machinery, the symbol of man's foibles and baser elements, to promote the common benefit.

Garraty's next major project, *Henry Cabot Lodge: A Biography* (1953), was more interpretative than the Wright volume. Elected six terms to the Senate, Lodge was one of the most powerful members of that body. He was long a member of the Senate Foreign Relations Committee, and few Americans had a more sustained impact on foreign policy in the first quarter of the twentieth century. Garraty, who had written his master's thesis on Lodge, was quick to take advantage of the opening of the Lodge papers at the Massachusetts Historical Society.

Garraty began by claiming that he sought, above all, to show his subject's point of view, for such

a task, he believed, was the proper function of biography. He succeeded admirably in his goal—in his words—to avoid "the twin perils of the whitewash and the tar barrel." The previous, uncritical biographies of Lodge by Bishop William Lawrence and Charles S. Groves (both published in 1925) and the hostile treatment by Karl Schriftgiesser in 1944 pale by comparison. No other volume has so effectively captured such things as Lodge's aloof personality, patrician background, Harvard training, friendship with Henry Adams, and role in the Senate.

Given the negative picture of Lodge that has been carried down through much of the popular culture, Garraty's treatment was revisionist. Unlike Lodge's Brahmin contemporaries, who assailed him in 1884 for supporting the presidential candidacy of James G. Blaine, Garraty admitted that a politician must at times compromise his principles. Furthermore, Blaine was not as evil as the Mugwumps maintained. Conceding there might be some basis to reformers' charges that Lodge was a sordid politician, Garraty also found some justice in the claim that patrician idealism was most impractical.

Turning to foreign policy, Garraty asserted that such imperialists as Lodge and Theodore Roosevelt possessed an exaggerated sense of national honor, disregarded the means used to expand American influence, and cavalierly accepted war. However, Garraty also claimed that foes of expansion ignored certain realities of nineteenth-century life—the competition among European powers for raw materials, markets, and prestige; revolutionary developments in transportation, communication, and the science of warfare; and the growing interdependence of the world's economic structure. Hence, anti-imperialists were unable to face up to the implications of their own righteousness in the midst of universal sin. To Garraty, Lodge's opposition to unrestricted immigration had some rationale, for at the turn of the century it was by no means clear that the American melting pot could effectively dissolve the cultures of eastern and southern Europe. In discussing the Mexican and European crises of Wilson's presidency, Garraty went so far as to declare that had Wilson followed Lodge's advice, both conflicts would have been concluded more quickly and with less loss of blood and money.

Garraty went still further in finding some of Lodge's activities meritorious. He noted that Lodge's history of colonial America (1881) contained excellent sketches of life in 1765. He also saw Lodge's account of the League of Nations battle (1925) in many ways as quite candid and, given the depth of the senator's feeling, remarkably fair. (Garraty was less generous toward Lodge's books on Hamilton, Washington, and Webster. He also claimed that Lodge's editing of Alexander Hamilton's papers was sloppy and that his editing of his own long correspondence with Theodore Roosevelt contained gross doctoring.) In many ways, Garraty argued, Lodge was a good congressman, devoting much time to constituents and attending sessions regularly. Lodge spoke with logic and stuck to points at issue. As Garraty noted, he worked for black suffrage and civil service reform. Furthermore, Lodge believed in bimetallism, not in a pure gold standard, although Garraty said that Lodge's opposition to the Sherman Silver Purchase Act was wise. No mossback, Lodge was nonetheless suspicious of the new class of industrialists, and he supported such measures as the Hepburn Act, the eight-hour day, and the prosecution of the Northern Securities Company.

Garraty did not find Lodge entirely admirable. Lodge lacked warmth; his mien was haughty, his manner abrasive. In short, he was a selfish, stubborn man. Despite his intelligence, he was totally partisan and, as such, incapable of seeing the position of an opponent. Lodge's stance on the tariff was expedient. When control of the Panama Canal was at stake, he risked confrontation with Britain, doing so in defiance of international law. Garraty claimed that Lodge's reservations to the League of Nations Covenant centered on a genuine desire to define the obligations of the U.S. more clearly. However, Lodge's effort to advance China's status during the League debates was indefensible, particularly in light of the fact that the Lansing-Ishii agreements of 1917 recognized Japan's special interests in China.

In an article written for *American Heritage* in 1955, Garraty offered an even more revisionist picture of Lodge. The Massachusetts senator, Garraty stressed, was no isolationist, for he did not think that America could exist apart from Europe and Asia. Nor was he a reactionary, for he embraced almost in toto the domestic policies of Theodore Roosevelt. True, Lodge was sarcastic, aloof, and vain. Yet he was a serious scholar, had a genuine love of literature, and was scrupulously honest. Most important, "He loved his country and sought to serve its interests. He was often wrong, but never evil."

Garraty became even more interpretative in *Woodrow Wilson: A Great Life in Brief* (1956) and in an article on Wilson written a year later for the *South Atlantic Quarterly*. Here, in a book revealing a more psychological approach than his previous works,

Garraty sought to discover in Wilson's complex personality some explanation for the vicissitudes of his career. Garraty was appreciative of much about the man—his scholarship, intellect, eloquence, determination, self-confidence. Wilson, wrote Garraty, was "a brilliant political leader and a high-minded statesman." As president, Wilson saw clearly what reforms were needed and knew exactly how to achieve them. Although much criticized, the president's desire to tie the League of Nations to the Versailles treaty was wise, for this arrangement expedited overall work on the treaty itself. Indeed, according to Garraty, Wilson returned from Europe to America in 1919 "with a better treaty than many intelligent men had ever expected to see."

Yet Garraty's biography was quite critical. Garraty found Wilson a failure at understanding people, uncompromising when compromise was necessary, overdemanding in his friendships. An inner insecurity literally drove him from his fellows. Living within himself and drawing reassurance from moral absolutes, Wilson set standards for himself that were impossible to keep. Rather than face up to his inadequacies, he engaged in pitiful self-deception. By 1914, Wilson's domestic leadership was faltering, as shown by his unwillingness to antagonize business. His Latin American diplomacy was curiously ethnocentric and unrealistic. Wilson stupidly attempted to fashion an "uneducated, poverty-stricken, dictator-ridden" people into "the image of middle-class New Jersey progressivism and Nebraska farmers."

As far as World War I was concerned, Garraty saw Wilson foolishly balking at preparedness while treating Germany and Britain with a double standard. These actions, taken together, were sure to encourage German responses that would force the U.S. into the fight. During the war, Wilson naively believed that the Kaiser's government did not represent the will of the German people, and he thought, with equal naiveté, that the Allies were as ready as America for a just peace. He announced overambitious peace aims, while presiding over "a frenzied witch-hunt" at home. According to Garraty, Wilson surrendered much of the idealism of his Fourteen Points without a fight, perhaps without even realizing what he was doing. And, to Garraty, Wilson's conduct at Versailles and at home showed even more folly. The president attended the peace conference in person, failed to include influential Republicans in the negotiating team, and would not trust Allied leaders. His refusal to be conciliatory to moderate critics of the League showed that Wilson "was actually in search of martyrdom."

In 1956, Garraty edited the correspondence of the prominent historian James Ford Rhodes and a black Republican leader from Cleveland, George A. Myers. Before they appeared in book form, the letters had been published in four successive issues of the *Ohio Historical Quarterly*. Garraty found this collection "one of the most revealing and intimate correspondences between a white man and a Negro in existence." The correspondence shed light on a number of matters: Ohio politics at the turn of the century; issues of Reconstruction; the position of black Americans; various prominent politicians, including Mark Hanna; organized labor; tariff reform; and debates over World War I, the League, and Prohibition.

The next year, with three biographies behind him, Garraty wrote *The Nature of Biography*. In 1952, he had received a fellowship, bestowed by the Fund for the Advancement of Education, to study psychology. As he examined the psychoanalytical approach to human personality, he became more intrigued by biography. Further encouragement came from the Social Science Research Council, which gave him a three-year grant. *The Nature of Biography* traced the development of biography over time and presents a manual on biography as a literary and historical form. At the outset, Garraty noted that successful biography must be imaginative and artistic as well as scientific. Sympathy and sensitivity, he claimed, are essential to sound scholarship.

The first half of the book outlined the history of biography from the poet Ion of Chios, whose memoirs date from the fifth century before Christ, to such contemporaries of Garraty's as Allan Nevins. Along the way, Garraty commented on a score of prominent biographers: Plutarch, still unexcelled in "the masterly handling of anecdotal material"; Suetonius, who "had little to offer aside from sensationalism"; Samuel Johnson, who believed that "anybody's story, properly told, would be interesting"; Sigmund Freud, who, in reality, showed that "man was so complex that no simple determinism could explain him"; and Lytton Strachey, "more concerned with form than with substance." The second half of the book focused on method. Here Garraty delved into such topics as choosing a subject, the materials of biography, the problem of personality, and writing procedures. He showed genuine interest in psychological techniques, and he suggested possible aid to biographers in content analysis and the study of handwriting.

Garraty's next project was quite different. In 1959, together with economist Walter Adams, he wrote a major report on foreign study, *From Main Street to the Left Bank: Students and Scholars Abroad*. It was sponsored by Michigan State University and financed by the Carnegie Foundation. Garraty and his colleagues spent nine months on the European continent, and they interviewed about 400 people. The report covered a variety of matters: motives for foreign study; the differences between European and American higher education; diverse student orientations; problems of administration, learning, and making friends; the American professor overseas; and the impact of American education abroad. While strongly favoring foreign study, the authors called for more directed programs for undergraduates, thorough language preparation before arrival, and the reduction of academic regulations and restrictions. American students, they maintained, were being pampered far too much. The main impact of educational exchange, the authors stressed, was invariably upon the visiting scholars and not upon the host culture. During the following year, Garraty and Adams wrote another book on foreign study, *Is the World Our Campus?*, and in a further effort to aid students, Garraty has edited a guide to study overseas, one that is updated every few years.

Soon, however, Garraty was back to biography, and his next subject was George W. Perkins, a prominent Wall Street figure who had been, at the same time, a leading reformer. In *Right-Hand Man*, published in 1960, Garraty skillfully shows how Perkins's managerial skills enabled him to rise from office boy to first vice-president of New York Life Insurance Company. In 1919, Perkins became a partner of J. P. Morgan and organized such financial giants as International Harvester, International Merchant Marine, Northern Securities, and the United States Steel Corporation. Because of Perkins's belief in cooperation and combination, something he learned in business, he strongly fought the Sherman Antitrust Act and equally strongly advocated the New Nationalism of his close friend Theodore Roosevelt. Leaving Morgan in 1910, he joined the Progressive party as chairman of its finance committee. A philanthropist, Perkins fostered the establishment of Palisades Interstate Park and aided in directing the work of the Young Men's Christian Association in World War I.

Garraty was able to uncover Perkins's papers, and he used them skillfully. Showing himself very much at home in economic history, he offered one of the first scholarly studies of a new type of businessman—the organization builder and manager. He noted Perkins's innovations in life insurance, which included retirement pensions, profit sharing, and a new sales organization. Garraty also offered much material on investment banking and, in particular, on Morgan's role in the Panic of 1907. He demonstrated something that the Justice Department was never able to prove, that International Harvester was primarily formed in order to eliminate competition between two fierce rivals. He also described the telephone conversations in 1916 between Roosevelt at Oyster Bay and Perkins at the Progressive and Republican national conventions in Chicago and, in so doing, showed that Roosevelt very much wanted the Republican presidential nomination.

Perkins's career, Garraty noted, contained more tragedy than it appeared to. In business, he was a great success. Furthermore, wrote Garraty, "His basic political idea about the relation of government and big business, if still challenged, comes every year closer to acceptance in the modern world." Yet, when Perkins entered the House of Morgan, he turned from an activity at least nominally concerned with public service, the work closest to his heart, to one openly dedicated to sheer money-making. Such "service to the American symbol of wealth and privilege" limited "his future usefulness to society."

In a series on three Progressives written for *American Heritage* in 1961 and 1962, Garraty returned to Perkins. He found the Morgan banking partner to be a man too dictatorial ever to succeed in politics. In fact, according to Garraty, "the real nature of political democracy escaped him." In the same series, Garraty offered a revisionist treatment of William Jennings Bryan, whom he saw as a man unfairly ridiculed by many contemporaries. The Great Commoner, Garraty pointed out, devoted many years to reform and was surprisingly well-informed on certain matters. His tragedy lay in the fact that success came to him too early and too easily, thereby relieving him of the need to grapple with new ideas. Garraty was iconoclastic in his discussion of Robert M. La Follette, Sr. He conceded that the Wisconsin senator possessed certain outstanding qualities. La Follette was an able speaker; he had superb political skill; he could dramatize controversial questions; and he fought long and hard for depressed groups. Yet, as Garraty noted, he had certain grave personal weaknesses that greatly limited his effectiveness. A ruthless and suspicious man, La Follette oversimplified complex problems and refused to acknowledge the sincerity of his op-

ponents. Hence, he embodied a "promise unfulfilled."

The year 1966 saw the first edition of Garraty's college survey textbook, *The American Nation: A History of the United States*. The book has been extremely popular, and it is undoubtedly the most widely read of all his works. A fifth edition was published in 1982, and Harper and Row has several times published condensed versions. *The American Nation* presents Garraty's views on a host of matters. His interpretations are often original, always lively, and usually middle-of-the-road, as befits a successful text.

Harper and Row came out in 1968 with *The New Commonwealth, 1877-1890*, a volume in its New American Nation series. In it, Garraty produced a coherent synthesis of one of the most amorphous periods in American history. Garraty has also edited two anthologies on the era, one a general collection of primary sources from the years 1870 to 1890, the other selected portions of testimony before the 1883 Senate Committee upon the Relations between Labor and Capital. In *The New Commonwealth, 1877-1890* he was offering a more detailed perspective on the so-called Gilded Age of American history, a period that lacked any unifying personality, war, or political movement. Garraty took the historical actors on their own terms and by so doing avoided much of the mindless muckraking with which the period is so often treated. In short, the book was marked by its balance. To Garraty, the traditional picture of the years after the Civil War was not so much false as it was myopic. Industrialism, he maintained, did not really encourage selfish individualism; rather it forced Americans to cooperate, and his book in some ways was the story of that cooperation.

In a particularly perceptive introductory chapter, certain observations stand out: the Homestead Act had serious inadequacies; the average cowboy was as crude as the typical miner; it was hard to devise any intelligent solution to the Indian problem, for knowledge of anthropology was far too limited; many so-called robber barons were "intelligent, energetic, and creative"; businessmen were often scapegoats, not villains; many industrialists and financiers possessed genuine misgivings about government honesty and efficiency as well as about the techniques needed to manipulate the economy intelligently; the period was marked both by appreciation for all the highest forms of art and unprecedented advances in mass education.

Drawing upon the fresh research of others as well as his own, Garraty told why many persons saw the Greenback controversy in moral terms, why no single group could dominate the Senate, why increased silver coinage was actually deflationary, and why civil service reformers faced justifiable criticism. However, Garraty portrayed a new order emerging, one characterized by the corporatization of American life. He showed how this process operated in such realms as agriculture, industry, labor, and the city. Almost in passing, he noted the speculative side of farming, the erratic and competitive nature of the economy, the positive value of trusts, and the rise in real wages for workers. Garraty did not gloss over exploitation and poverty but put them in a broader economic context, one that of necessity lacked the kind of moralism historians have so often applied to the period.

Garraty found the presidents in the 1877-1890 period vigorous, intelligent, capable, and public-spirited. They all, however, lacked the personal qualities of leadership that a president must have. Contrary to myth, the moral standards of Congress improved with Grant's retirement, and in general the Congress was not an undistinguished or ineffective body. Parties were factionalized, noted Garraty, and they were based more on personal rivalries and emotional clashes than on issues. Neither party could cope with the radical changes that the country was undergoing, and all too often Republicans and Democrats ignored or straddled meaningful questions. Garraty wrote that the public looked upon politics as a kind of national game or spectacle, something like baseball, with the statesmen the players and the voters the fans in the bleachers.

In 1970, Macmillan published *Interpreting American History: Conversations with Historians*, twenty-nine interviews that Garraty had conducted with leading American historians. Garraty hoped to show how historians have evaluated their work—in his words, to reveal their "complex attempts to order many facts in such a way as to form consistent and persuasive explanations of some segment of the past." In addition, he hoped to discover what historians thought about the impact of their work on other scholars and to obtain current judgments on their own writing and careers. Garraty sent each subject a series of questions. Then he and the interviewee spent a day of free-ranging discussion in the presence of a tape recorder. From the discussion resulted a digested typescript that the historian being interviewed could review.

Garraty sought an outstanding scholar in each of many varied fields, though he readily conceded that any such selection forced one to eliminate many

distinguished historians. He noted that most of the men interviewed, being either middle-aged or elderly and holding chairs in the best universities, represented "the present-day historical establishment." Undoubtedly, claimed Garraty, the fact that most of his subjects had done the bulk of their work in the second third of this century placed them within the "consensus school," a school that—as he put it—tended "to minimize the past conflicts in the American experience and to stress the shared values the great majority of Americans have held." To have included New Left or Beardian scholars, he said, would have sacrificed consistency of approach and have greatly lengthened the work. Among those selected were Bernard Bailyn on the American Revolution, T. Harry Williams on the Civil War, David Donald on Reconstruction, Arthur S. Link on World War I, and Arthur M. Schlesinger, Jr., on the domestic politics of the past thirty years.

Two years after the interviews were published, Garraty and Peter Gay edited *The Columbia History of the World*. More than 1,200 pages long and weighing close to four pounds, it had contributions by more than 100 specialists and was five years in the making. The idea originated with Garraty, who insisted that the work should be one unified narrative, not an assemblage of unconnected scholarly articles. One model was H. G. Wells's *Outline of History*. Almost all of the contributors were either Columbia faculty or alumni, and although it was not an official publication of Columbia, the university authorized the use of its name. Contributors included Fritz Stern, Jacques Barzun, Shepard Clough, Immanuel Wallerstein, Lewis Hanke, Richard Hofstadter, and René Albrecht-Carrié.

In the preface, the two editors claimed that most world histories are culture-bound, displaying a distinctly Western perspective. That is, these works discussed other civilizations only as, and when, they interacted with the West. Garraty hoped that his work would look at each civilization in its own context, as it might be studied by a visitor from outer space. He did acknowledge that the closer the account came to the present, the more detailed it became, and that more space was devoted to the West than to other civilizations. Because the book was aimed at the general reader, it stressed the meaning of events and their broad influences, often doing so at the expense of dates and names. If the book was crowded with facts, said Garraty, it was because the facts were chosen to explicate the whole, not because the facts were ends in themselves.

In September 1973, Garraty became editor for

future supplements to the *Dictionary of American Biography*. At that time, the *DAB* had published more than 18,000 articles written by some 3,000 specialists. When his appointment was announced, Garraty jestingly referred to growing up in the Flatbush section of Brooklyn and said, "There are several Brooklyn Dodger players whom I'm going to get into the D.A.B." On a more serious note, he claimed that future supplements would include more women, members of minority groups, and figures outside the American establishment. In 1974, Garraty wrote a brief but lively history of the *DAB* for *American Heritage*.

Garraty's involvement in biographical projects did not stop with the *DAB*. In 1974, he coedited *The Encyclopedia of American Biography*, with Jerome L. Sternstein. The book covered more than 1,000 figures, with the editors selecting entries more on the basis of a person's influence than on achievement or fame. Hence, at times, Garraty and Sternstein chose relatively obscure individuals whose lives had changed American culture, while omitting more famous people whose careers reflected, rather than influenced, various changes in the nation's life. Unlike the *DAB*, living men as well as dead were included in *The Encyclopedia of American Biography*. So too were important women and members of minorities. The editors were careful, however, to reject any idea of applying different and lower standards to such people. "An encyclopedia," they wrote, "should be a record, not a device for righting ancient wrongs." Each entry was divided into two parts: the first presented the biographical facts concerning the subject's life and was usually written by graduate students at Columbia. The second part involved an evaluation of a person's career, and it included an attempt to capture a bit of the individual's personality. This part was written by a noted biographer or authority on the subject's field or profession.

Garraty's 1978 *Unemployment in History: Economic Thought and Public Policy* might well be his greatest tour de force. It was less a survey of the conditions of the unemployed than of the concept itself. As such, it is really an enterprise in intellectual history, one not tied to any time, place, or school of thought but crossing all of Western history. After tackling the problem of definition, Garraty moved quickly to the ancient and medieval world, where he found unemployment was relatively insignificant. Society always had drifters, beggars, and seasonally unemployed casual labor. In the sixteenth century, vagrancy laws and workhouses were in vogue throughout Western Europe, although such efforts

to create full employment almost always proved ineffective. It was, however, only with the industrial revolution that began late in the eighteenth century that the modern problem began, for now masses of people could suddenly become idle. Furthermore, it was only in the second half of the nineteenth century that unemployment was "discovered" and only in 1894 that it became a burning issue.

Although Garraty noted that every scheme to improve the lot of the unemployed was debated as far back as the sixteenth century, he assailed the leading classical economists for their ignorance. For example, in writing of David Ricardo, he said that "everyday reality had small significance in his intellectual system." To Garraty, Thomas Malthus's "reliance on the frail reed of moral restraint was an indication of his desperate search for a way to avoid his own conclusions." True, Karl Marx realized that unemployment was a normal aspect of capitalism; however, his "reserve army" thesis did not really confront its elimination. Indeed, Garraty claimed, debates about how to prevent unemployment, much less how to deal with its victims, proved inconclusive until the Keynesian revolution of the 1930s. In *The General Theory of Employment, Interest, and Money* (1936), Keynes was able to suggest how a free economy could better maximize and stabilize output, and thus eliminate both cyclical fluctuations and unemployment. "After Keynes," Garraty wrote, "full employment seemed a realizable goal of public policy; apparently the industrial reserve army of Malthus and Marx could be permanently demobilized."

Keynes's utopia of full employment, however, was not to last, and by the middle of the 1960s the West saw what Garraty called "the end of the golden age." There began chronic and massive unemployment with no end in sight. Garraty noted that unemployment insurance had alleviated much material distress, and workers went so far as to see it "as a right derived from their participation in a complex, manipulative political system." At the same time, however, it fostered the "element in human nature that prefers leisure to labor, an element that requires relatively little encouragement to assert itself." Make-work schemes, such as those introduced by the New Deal, have the difficulty of fitting the people who need work into the kinds of jobs that these projects provide. Garraty wrote, "Unemployed assembly-line workers do not ordinarily make adequate bricklayers nor are laid-off bricklayers likely to make capable (or willing) ditch-diggers." Moreover, the high investment involved can only lead to more inflation.

In the 1970s, Garraty was not simply concerned with theories concerning unemployment. He went into the effect of unemployment upon the labor force, and here he drew upon extensive research on the Great Depression. In *Unemployment in History* and in a series of articles for such journals as *Labor History*, Garraty offered some surprising information. Workers touched seriously by the Depression remained a minority. In fact, as prices fell faster than wages, many workers actively benefited from the hard times. Garraty went so far as to claim that probably more than half the world's wage earners actually improved their standard of living. Trade unions were primarily concerned with protecting those workers with jobs and usually rejected work-sharing as a means of coping with unemployment. The Depression did not markedly affect public health nor did it slow down the long-range trend toward increased longevity characteristic of industrial nations. Workers tended to become less militant politically, not more; they lost pride, avoided social contacts, and in general suffered burdens passively.

In a seminal essay published in the *American Historical Review* in 1973, Garraty compared the economic policies of Adolf Hitler and Franklin D. Roosevelt. Garraty argued that the Nazis were the more successful in curing the economic ills of the decade, for they reduced unemployment and stimulated industrial production faster than did the New Deal. In addition, they handled monetary and trade problems more successfully. Both governments not only used many of the same economic devices but also employed the latest technologies to influence public opinion. Although the Depression was over for Germany by 1936, neither regime—according to Garraty—solved the problem of maintaining prosperity without war.

As is true of many prominent historians, Garraty has edited several anthologies. Aside from those already mentioned, these include sixty radio sketches of "unforgettable" Americans, notable articles from *American Heritage*, and a documentary collection for survey courses. The documentary collection has gone through several editions and was coedited with Richard N. Current. One collection, *Quarrels That Have Shaped the Constitution* (1964) was serialized in *American Heritage*. It gave prominent scholars a chance to examine selected Supreme Court cases. Garraty's own essay dealt with *Marbury* v. *Madison* and was entitled "The Case of the 'Missing' Commissions." Garraty also wrote one book for younger readers, *Theodore Roosevelt: The Strenuous Life* (1967). The biography was no

blanket eulogy, for Garraty was quick to portray Roosevelt's arrogant and belligerent personality. Garraty's many book reviews have appeared in popular as well as professional journals, including the *New York Times Book Review* and the *Saturday Review of Literature*. Occasionally an essay appears in such journals as *TV Guide*, *Nation's Business*, and *Newsday*.

With a degree of unanimity unusual among historians, Garraty's books have been praised by his colleagues. Thoroughness of research, balanced judgments, and readable style have been pointed to by critics again and again. Occasionally critics have found him too hostile toward Wilson, or too reliant on certain collections (such as the Lodge or Perkins papers), or not always possessing a firm grasp of European intellectual history, or—in the case of the Wright and Perkins biographies—offering more description than evaluation. Yet there is no doubt that Garraty has received nearly unmatched respect from his peers.

It is easy to understand why Garraty has received such prominence. He has moved freely between various historical periods, from the time of Jackson to the Progressive era to the Gilded Age. He has not been afraid to ask "the big questions," be they on "the nature of biography" or "unemployment in history." He has written different types of history—biography, specialized study of an era, topics that transcend centuries and cultures, general syntheses for the layman. He has avoided polemic and thereby has not been involved in the feuding that has marred so much professional historical literature. At the same time, he has not been averse to making judgments. Garraty has exemplified professionalism in its finest sense, displaying an expertise that combines accuracy, balance, and craftsmanship, and ties them all to an obligation to educate the wider American public.

Other:

The Barber and the Historian: The Correspondence of George A. Myers and James F. Rhodes, 1910-1923, edited by Garraty (Columbus: Ohio Historical Society, 1956);

The Unforgettable Americans, edited by Garraty (New York: Channel, 1960);

Words That Made American History, edited by Garraty and Richard N. Current (Boston: Little, Brown, 1962);

Quarrels That Have Shaped the Constitution, edited by Garraty (New York: Harper & Row, 1964);

Labor and Capital in the Gilded Age: Testimony Taken by the Senate Committee upon the Relations between

Labor and Capital, edited by Garraty (Boston: Little, Brown, 1968);

The Transformation of American Society, 1870-1890, edited by Garraty (New York: Harper & Row, 1969);

Historical Viewpoints: Notable Articles from American Heritage, 2 volumes, edited by Garraty (New York: American Heritage Publishing Company, 1970);

"Radicalism in the Great Depression," in *Essays on Radicalism in Contemporary America*, edited by Leon Borden Blair (Austin: University of Texas Press, 1972);

The Columbia History of the World, edited by Garraty and Peter Gay (New York: Harper & Row, 1972);

Dictionary of American Biography, supplements 4-6, edited by Garraty (New York: Scribners, 1974-1980);

The Encyclopedia of American Biography, edited by Garraty and Jerome L. Sternstein (New York: Harper & Row, 1974).

Periodical Publications:
"Spoiled Child of American Politics," *American Heritage*, 4 (August 1955): 55-59;

"Bryan," *American Heritage*, 13 (December 1961): 4-11, 108-115;

"The Millionaire Reformer," *American Heritage*, 13 (February 1962): 40-43, 86-89;

"La Follette: The Promise Unfulfilled," *American Heritage*, 13 (April 1962): 76-79, 84-88;

"The New Deal, National Socialism, and the Great Depression," *American Historical Review*, 78 (October 1973): 907-944;

"Reading, Writing, and History: Distinguished Americans from A to Z," *American Heritage*, 25 (August 1975): 96-101;

"Unemployment During the Great Depression," *Labor History*, 17 (Spring 1976): 133-159.

Eugene D. Genovese
(10 May 1930-   )

Michael Bordelon
St. Thomas Episcopal School, Houston

BOOKS: *The Political Economy of Slavery: Studies in the Economy and Society of the Slave South* (New York: Pantheon, 1965; London: MacGibbon & Kee, 1966);

The World the Slaveholders Made: Two Essays in Interpretation (New York: Pantheon, 1969);

In Red and Black: Marxian Explorations in Southern and Afro-American History (New York: Pantheon, 1971);

Roll, Jordan, Roll: The World the Slaves Made (New York: Pantheon, 1974);

From Rebellion to Revolution: Afro-American Slave Revolts in the Modern World (Baton Rouge: Louisiana State University Press, 1979);

The American People, by Genovese, Forrest McDonald, and David Burner (New York: Revisionary Press, 1980);

The Fruits of Merchant Capital: Slavery and Bourgeois Property in the Rise and Expansion of Capitalism, by Genovese and Elizabeth Fox-Genovese (New York: Oxford University Press, 1983).

Eugene D. Genovese

In his book *In Red and Black* (1971), Eugene Genovese writes, "All Marxian history may, from one point of view, be judged good or poor by the extent to which it contributes to our understanding of class." Judged by this standard, Genovese is a successful historian. An avowed Marxist with a high-powered writing style and an early reputation as an activist, he has emerged as an influential historian of the slave South, his accounts of which intriguingly blend class struggle and an appreciation for such traditional aspects of culture as religion and honor. Not dogmatic, but not inclined to compromise in order to court popular favor, Genovese has been colorful and controversial.

Eugene Dominick Genovese was born and raised in proletarian Brooklyn, the son of Dominick F. and Lena Chimenti Genovese. Upon graduating from high school, he attended Brooklyn College, from which he received his B.A. degree in 1953. At Columbia University he received his M.A. (1955) and his Ph.D. (1959) degrees, studying both United States and Latin American history. For five years he taught at the Polytechnic Institute of Brooklyn before accepting a position on the faculty of Rutgers University in New Jersey in 1963. At Rutgers he quickly became a controversial figure as he demonstrated that his Marxist allegiance was more than academic; in various public ways he expressed opposition to the war in Vietnam and even admitted that he "welcomed a victory" by the Vietcong in their struggle against the American intruders. Reaction became so intense that his tenure at Rutgers grew into a campaign issue in New Jersey's 1965 gubernatorial campaign, during which Richard Nixon called three times for Genovese's removal from Rutgers. In 1967 Genovese left voluntarily, an action which was, as he later said, "to the great relief of all concerned."

Such personal matters might seem irrelevant to a consideration of the merits of his scholarship, except that the episode attests to the strength of his convictions as a Marxist. His departure from Rutgers did his career no lasting damage, however, since he immediately accepted a position as professor at Sir George Williams University (1967-1969) in Montreal, and he has since become a member of the executive council of the American Historical Association (1970-1975), president of the Organization of American Historians (1978-1979), and a fellow of the American Academy of Arts and Sciences.

Since 1969 Genovese has been permanently associated with the University of Rochester as pro-

fessor of history, except for brief visiting professorships at Yale and at Cambridge University. With the exceptions mentioned, his life has been spent solely in the states of New York and New Jersey. He has never lived in the South, and his lack of firsthand acquaintance with the region that has occupied so much of his scholarly attention has left him at times vulnerable to attack for having only a bookish knowledge of his subject matter.

Despite the manifold distractions of the 1960s, Genovese managed during the decade to write several dozen articles and reviews, many of which were published in such left-wing, relatively obscure, journals as *Science and Society* and *Studies on the Left*. The subject matter of these essays generally falls into three main categories: (1) works stemming from his graduate studies analyzing and comparing slave systems throughout the Western Hemisphere, (2) articles and reviews considering the character of slavery in the Old South, and (3) essays pertaining to the Black Power movement and the New Left radicalism of the 1960s.

Two essays in the last group are "Black Studies: Trouble Ahead" and "Class and Nationality in Black America." In the first article Genovese admits the propriety of black studies provided that they not be sentimental, divisive, or cheap academic substitutes for more serious and more difficult alternatives. In the second essay Genovese expresses some sympathy for the aspirations of the Black Power movement but warns that "total integration or complete separation of the races appear equally utopian." Both of these essays were reprinted in his book *In Red and Black*, which consists of about twenty loosely connected articles written during the last half of the 1960s. In these as well as in his other "relevant" pieces, Genovese's procedure is remarkably consistent: he uses a nice blending of common sense and penetrating insight to indicate sympathy for the radical activist movements of the decade without compromising himself into supporting their more extreme and foolish demands.

In Red and Black also contains strictly academic efforts, including several articles analyzing and comparing slavery systems in the New World. One particularly fine essay that explores the difficulties of comparing slave systems is appropriately entitled "The Treatment of Slaves in Different Countries: Problems in the Applications of the Comparative Method." Part one of Genovese's two-part book, *The World the Slaveholders Made* (1969), also deals comparatively with slavery in the Western Hemisphere. Entitled "The American Slave Systems in World

Perspective," this section's general thesis is that the development of the various slave systems (in the South, in Brazil, and in the British West Indies, for example) cannot be understood apart from each other and from the parent European cultures which sponsored them.

The work for which Genovese is best known and admired by scholars and lay readers alike, however, is not comparative, but is his deep and original investigation of slavery in the Old South. In the early 1960s he began to demonstrate his academic competence by publishing various minor essays, six of which were reprinted in his first book, *The Political Economy of Slavery* (1965). The book is actually a collection of ten related essays that apply Marxist principles and rhetoric to the study of various features of life in the Old South, including soil exhaustion, slavery expansionism, and the utility of slave labor in Southern factories. The treatment of these topics is rigidly Marxist and the unifying theme is that the use of slave labor was damaging to the Southern economy. Genovese himself later referred to the volume as "sometimes mechanistic."

By 1969, however, his work was clearly becoming less doctrinaire, at least in tone if not in content, and he was able to depict the master class with much greater detachment in part two of *The World the Slaveholders Made*, a section subtitled "The Logical Outcome of the Slaveholders' Philosophy: An Exposition, Interpretation, and Critique of the Social Thought of George Fitzhugh of Port Royal, Virginia." Somewhat surprisingly, Genovese readily concedes his respect and "affection" for the eloquent slaveholder Fitzhugh, a regard quite evident in the analysis. In part, the esteem expressed by Genovese for Fitzhugh is explained by the fact that he admires the Southerner's integrity, an admiration in keeping with Genovese's own character. He has always placed a premium on honesty wherever it is to be found, whether on the right or on the left, among his allies or his enemies.

Nonetheless, Genovese's regard for Fitzhugh is not altogether disinterested since the Virginian's candor makes him especially useful for the historian's purposes. Genovese writes, "Fitzhugh was the most consistent exponent of the slaveholders' world view . . . and he alone saw the necessary last step in the argument, which was that slavery could not survive without the utter destruction of capitalism as a world system." Such an argument is tailor-made for a Marxist historian who sees the meaning of history in class struggle. Furthermore, both the Marxist historian and the Virginian planter clearly admit hostility toward unbridled capitalism. It may well be

that the fairness with which Genovese has considered the slaveholders is traceable to this common bond—a similar perception of the human misery industrial capitalism has caused by its tendency to reduce human relations to the cash nexus.

As *The World the Slaveholders Made* indicates, by the late 1960s Genovese's works on antebellum slavery began to assume a more moderate character. Several essays included in *In Red and Black* suggest a maturing of Genovese as scholar and clearly foreshadow his 1974 masterpiece. The general theme emerging from these preliminary publications is that, under the yoke of slavery, blacks had managed to salvage for themselves a considerable degree of dignity and independence by developing a complicated set of quite human relationships with the master class. In two of these essays, "Rebelliousness and Dignity in the Negro Slave: A Critique of the Elkins Thesis," and "The Legacy of Slavery and the Roots of Black Nationalism," Genovese seeks to defend the dignity of black slaves against the charge of Stanley Elkins that the concentration-camp atmosphere of antebellum slavery tended to "infantalize" the blacks and make them incapable of independent action. In a related essay, "American Slaves and their History," Genovese defends the character of the slaves as basically decent and understandably human when they sought to adjust to their situations without engaging in open rebellion. Also reprinted in the same volume are two short works written with "ungrudging admiration" for the Southern historian of slavery, U. B. Phillips. In these pieces, as in the essay on Fitzhugh, Genovese candidly admits his respect, even admiration, for the integrity and perceptiveness of Phillips without necessarily accepting his overall perspective.

Besides conveying increased understanding of the master class, Genovese's writings on the Old South began to show maturity in other respects as well. In "On Being Socialist and a Historian," the introductory essay of *In Red and Black*, he goes so far as to reprove his fellow Marxists for insisting that the scholar also be an activist: "Being a historian is full-time work. . . . Those who think that they can make a contribution to society generally and to the Movement in particular by becoming political organizers have the duty as well as the privilege of doing so, and no one could reasonably insist that such a calling was inferior to that of the academic intellectual. But the reverse is also true—Socialist historians are not the last word in social necessity, but they do have important work to do—as socialists who work at history." To Genovese's Marxist/Socialist colleagues these words came hard. Since leaving Rutgers, he had become more dedicated to scholarship and less abrasively activist, had revealed a high regard for many members of the slaveholder class as well as for some of their defenders, had shown little sentimental concern over the plight of blacks either during or after slavery, and then had gone so far as to recommend that the scholar be a scholar rather than an activist. Coming in the late 1960s when political activism and academic concerns were mixed as never before in America, his admonition seemed to many far-leftists to be a sellout.

Predictably enough, Genovese's changing attitudes increased his difficulties with more doctrinaire Marxists who doubted the authenticity of his Marxist credentials. Both in print and in person he was obliged to contend with left-wing radicals over matters of doctrine and theory. Moreover, because Genovese's Marxism had always been a more sophisticated brand than that espoused by many of his colleagues, he had frequently chided them for their simplemindedness and dogmatism, for what he has often called "vulgar Marxism." Furthermore, Genovese's insistence that Marxism as class analysis should not be diverted by racial allegiances was not what some so-called Marxists had wanted to hear. His refusal to wax sentimental over the past or present plight of American blacks was even at times interpreted as a lack of interest in racial problems. The criticism was unjustified: the discerning reader of various Genovese works will be able to find a number of unequivocally sharp denunciations of white mistreatment of blacks. Still, the critics in the early 1970s were not satisfied. Genovese was clearly more interested in analysis than in polemic, and thus he lost some support from strident left-wingers. At the same time, however, he gained considerable admiration from the majority of the reading public, academic and nonacademic alike.

Indeed, there is good reason to question the conventionality of Genovese's Marxism. He has repeatedly, for instance, renounced any belief in "economic determinism"—the argument that the economic system of a society determines its every feature. In fact, so strongly has he emphasized general cultural influences that a reader could at times quite easily forget that Genovese is a Marxist. He has also contemptuously rejected the use of Marxism as an infallible tool for prediction, a task he says should be left to the astrologers. Time and again he has refused to assert any belief in the inevitability of the socialist victory so characteristically associated with conventional Marxism but dismissed by Genovese himself as "fatalism." Nor does Genovese

dogmatically categorize all religion as "quackery" or label all men of the Southern master class as primarily selfish and thus lacking in intelligence and virtue. While praising the "enemy," he has even chosen to criticize his mentor, Karl Marx himself, saying that at times the master was unworthy of his own thought, as when he showed a poor understanding of the character of the antebellum and wartime South. Moreover, Genovese has not proved to be especially soft on the Soviet Union. Finally, the historian has admitted that the Christian concept of original sin has exerted a powerful influence on traditional thought in Western civilization *and* on his own thinking as well. Because all his works are marked by a consistent observation that human beings are generally self-serving, Genovese never writes sentimentally or idealistically about even the lower classes.

The rationale for Genovese's treatment of race relations in "slavery times" is well defined in the following passage from part two of *The World the Slaveholders Made*: "If I do not dwell on the evils of slavery and the hypocrisy of its world view, it is for two reasons, the first being an assumption that all ruling-class ideologies are self-serving and that it is enough to point out the worst examples along the way, and the second being that few people any longer seem in need of sermons on the subject. The race question remains with us and properly stirs passions, but the struggle for racial equality needs a cool assessment of the past and of its legacy and does not need the inverted romanticism of the neo-abolitionist viewpoint."

Genovese's requirement for a "cool assessment of the past" was brilliantly realized in *Roll, Jordan, Roll: The World the Slaves Made* (1974), which paradoxically enough was the result of a well-controlled passion. "I started studying the masters," he admitted, "and decided I could not understand much about them unless I studied the slaves closely. Once I started, they became an obsession." The result was a masterpiece. Published in 1974, *Roll, Jordan, Roll* won instant acclaim. It received several major awards, including the Bancroft Prize in 1975, and was designated one of the year's ten best books by the *New York Times Book Review*. Its praises have been sung by academicians and nonacademicians from across the political spectrum.

Perhaps the main reason for *Roll, Jordan, Roll*'s popularity is that it is ruthlessly honest. More than eight hundred pages long, it contains so much material so candidly presented that virtually anyone can find something of interest in it. Accurately subtitled *The World the Slaves Made*, Genovese's epic does indeed describe in great detail the world fashioned by and for the slaves; it is also very much about the masters who helped the slaves fashion that world. Filled with anecdotes (a factor no doubt accounting for some of the book's popularity), *Roll, Jordan, Roll* is also heavily interpretative; scarcely any aspect of slavery in the Old South goes unnoticed. Among the many subjects canvassed are the names, the foods, and the clothes of the slaves, their religious practices and beliefs, their sexual and marital habits, their punishments received, and their forms of entertainment; practices and forms of behavior pertaining to every facet of slave life are all candidly discussed without either glorifying or apologizing for black conduct under slave conditions. While making it clear that he finds slavery abhorrent, Genovese provides an abundance of evidence which puts slavery in the Old South in a much more human light than is generally recognized in recent literature. Never does he seem vulnerable to the charge of representing the unusual or rare occurrence as typical or commonplace. His frequent analyses reveal him to be a master in handling generalization; he often uses such qualifiers as "some," "many," "few," "not many," "most," "occasionally," and "rarely," terms which permit the reader to understand the routine qualities and practices of slavery but which do not attempt to conceal incidents which deviate from the norm. *Roll, Jordan, Roll* is the perfect example of the precision in language that should mark all conventional scholarship; in fact, it rivals the precision of the statistical compilations that are the hallmark of econometrics, the parvenu of antebellum studies. In some ways *Roll, Jordan, Roll* is even the literary equivalent of the quantitative analysis found in *Time on the Cross*, Robert Fogel and Stanley Engerman's investigation-through-computer of slavery in the antebellum South, which was published the same year as *Roll, Jordan, Roll*. Put simply, both works emphasize the dignity of blacks under the burdens of slavery.

Although Fogel and Engerman are mentioned prominently in the acknowledgments and three times thereafter, Genovese's use of source material in *Roll, Jordan, Roll* is for the most part conventional. Strongly documented, the work has 123 pages of footnotes in which a lavish number of both primary and secondary sources are cited, including, of course, many references to such leading authorities as Stanley Elkins, Kenneth Stampp, David Brion Davis, and John Hope Franklin. Genovese also includes some unexpected references to various European authors such as Nietzsche, Hegel, Max Weber, Johan Huizinga, G. G. Coulton, R. H. Tawney, and Karl Kautsky. Surprisingly, Marx and Engels are mentioned only twice each.

The relative absence of ideologically oriented source material, the frequent use of conventional primary and secondary source material, the careful choice of language, and the detached reasonableness of his arguments, all serve to instill in the reader a confidence that the book has been written by an author in relentless search of the truth. Rarely does the reader feel that Genovese has merely recounted whatever information supports his presuppositions, while sweeping under the rug any evidence that might make him uncomfortable. Nor does the book seem marred by any heavy-handed ideological orientation. Virtually absent are the stock figures of most Marxist or Communist morality plays: the proletariat, the bourgeoisie, and the lumpen-proletariat receive only bit roles in Genovese's epic production. Nor do "mode of production," "alienation," and other key Marxian terminology constitute much of the book's vocabulary, largely because Genovese generally lets his characters speak for themselves. In fact, many may well read the work without suspecting its Marxist orientation.

But the reader should not be deceived. While the work is not grossly ideological, it is a decidedly Marxist effort. Scarcely any grand personages or events in history receive close scrutiny. No president, no election, no battles are given detailed attention; only passing references are made to such giants as Lincoln, Calhoun, and Washington, and hardly any of the events that we know as "political history" are analyzed intently. Good Marxist that he is, Genovese recognizes that the masses, not the giants, the commonplace, not the dramatic, form history's working materials.

The result is a work of uncommon insight. In Genovese's hands Marxism is a tool for analysis, not polemic or propaganda. His work is subtle, perceptive, even-handed, and persuasive. There are no grand pronouncements about the dictatorship of the proletariat and the inevitability of revolution, or tiresome recitals of the alienation, misery, and exploitation of the black masses. Rather Genovese's Marxism resides in two main tenets. First, he insists, as he did in *The World the Slaveholders Made*, that the problems of slavery should be regarded more as a class than as a race question, although he certainly perceives the interrelationship of the two. The results stemming from such a distinction are at times profoundly significant, all the more so when the implications are applied to contemporary black problems.

A second and more important Marxist feature of *Roll, Jordan, Roll* is the handling of the base-superstructure theme, that is, the Marxist theorem that the economic foundation of a nation (the mode of production) serves as a substructure supporting all of the nation's less significant features (including, for example, its language, customs, and traditions), which together constitute the "superstructure." In "Marxian Interpretations of the Slave South," an important essay included in *In Red and Black*, Genovese has succinctly formulated Marx's understanding but has added to it another observation by Marx which is much less commonly understood: "Marx and Engels tell us that ideas grow out of social existence, but have a life of their own. A particular base (mode of production) will generate a corresponding superstructure (political system, complex of ideologies, culture, etc.), but that superstructure will develop according to its own logic as well as in response to the development of the base." Thus, Genovese is, again, subtle rather than dogmatically reductive in his application of Marxist theory.

The subtlety with which Genovese analyzes substructure/superstructure relations in the plantation South can be illustrated by the following discussion of the frequency with which slaves deceived their masters: "The slaves' necessary resort to put-ons and lies had other ramifications, which might even fall under the rubric of ruling-class control. The masters often knew they were being deceived. Sometimes they fretted; sometimes they chuckled, as if delighted by the cleverness of their mischievous children. In either case, they took their slaves' behavior as confirmation of their own superiority. . . the whites as a matter of ideological control, welcomed—although with some fear—their slaves' prevarication and dissembling, and . . . tried to strengthen their own claims to being men of honor."

The advantages of such a calm assessment of the actions of men living in "slavery times" are obvious. First, Genovese does not indulge in the "romanticism," which he has found objectionable in many other historians, of denying that slaves in the Old South frequently lied to or deceived their masters. Second, the intelligence of the masters is not deprecated or understated. Third, the account does not credit either slaves or masters with extraordinary virtue and thus portrays members of both classes as quite believably human, so much so that the reader can easily imagine himself a participant

in either side of the relationship. And, finally, but certainly not least for Genovese's purposes, the example affords a fine opportunity to apply both conventional Marxism—base affecting superstructure—and his own point of emphasis, that ideas, once introduced, have "a life of their own" (in this case, that the masters "took their slaves' behavior as confirmation of their own superiority").

Genovese masterfully explores every facet of the various relationships of plantation times and cites instance after instance of master/slave connection showing how the masters attempted to maintain their economic dominance through subtle pressures and persuasions connected with superstructure categories. Thus, "the masters understood the strength of the marital and family ties among their slaves well enough to see in them a powerful means of social control" and accordingly encouraged their slaves to marry. The threat of the dissolution of a slave marriage through sale of one spouse or the other could easily become a powerful force a master might hold over his married slaves. In a matter of less gravity but in the same vein, Genovese observes "the whites' interest in the Christmas holidays as a means of social control"; that is, the masters could threaten to deny the holiday to unruly slaves. Typically, however, Genovese tempers his observations by admitting that "evidence that slaveholders in fact withheld these [holiday] 'privileges' cannot easily be found. To have withheld them in any except the most extreme instances of general insubordination would have invited the deepest resentment, sulking, disorder, and breakdown of morale and productivity. The slaves here as elsewhere had seized 'rights.'" In other words, the general celebration by the slaves of such holidays as Christmas and the Fourth of July came to have a life of its own, apart from its relationship to the mode of production, slavery itself. Similarly, the "Mammies" and the slave drivers developed multifaceted relationships with other members of the community, white and black, and these relationships cannot be exhausted by a narrowly economic analysis alone.

The interesting manner in which Genovese canvasses the tremendous variety of human interrelationships in the plantation South reveals much about the widespread appeal of his use of Marxism in *Roll, Jordan, Roll*. The reader gets an overall view of most of the antebellum South, comprehending the quality of life on the great majority of slave plantations; he simultaneously becomes a silent, invisible witness to intimate relationships of every kind, including those between master and house slaves, between mistresses and maidservants, between masters and overseers and drivers, between mammies and masters and mistresses. The attraction of Marxism, so powerfully revealed in *Roll, Jordan, Roll*, stems from the desire to know all and see all from the perspective of both distance and intimacy, aided in this case forcefully but not dogmatically by the special knowledge of Marxism that class struggle is the root meaning of history. By such a path is the reader led to perceive that history is the cumulative product of the lives and actions of the masses.

Impressive as is *Roll, Jordan, Roll*, the book is not without its weaknesses. The perhaps inevitable result of a focus on the master class and its charges is the loss of any attention to the routine lives of the smaller slaveholders (although Genovese admits there were many of them) and their slaves. Lost also is any serious attempt to accord the yeomanry a significant place in the social order of the Old South. One has the feeling from reading *Roll, Jordan, Roll* that the antebellum South consisted of one vast network of large and medium-sized plantations, stretching from region to region and state to state without any significant variations. Thus, to mention the observations of just one critic, Bennett Wall has accorded the book extravagant praise but has still roundly criticized it for its failure to take into account the particularities of antebellum plantation life which distinguished the various estates one from the other. Lacking also in the book (curious for a Marxist work) is any sense of the movement of time and history: the very generality of Genovese's observations tends to mislead the reader into thinking that life in the Old South was uniform from century to century, decade to decade, region to region, plantation to plantation.

Such criticisms, while worthwhile, are relatively minor. Genovese himself makes no claims to have analyzed all classes. Nor does he reveal any ignorance of the impact of certain events (such as Nat Turner's rebellion) on the quality of life experienced subsequently by the slaves. Nor does Genovese fail to make at least the larger distinctions between such regions as the Upper South and the Lower South. Yet because his book's subtitle is *The World the Slaves Made*, his work is carefully structured to suit his announced object, "to tell the story of slave life as carefully and accurately as possible." This he has done supremely well. His complex Marxism has informed his analysis to such a degree that he has surpassed the efforts of more established historians who have sometimes played favorites and tended to idealize various participants of

the era. Genovese thus has given us a description which reveals truth on many levels.

To some degree the deeper levels of meaning in *Roll, Jordan, Roll* are contained in its structure. *Roll, Jordan, Roll* is divided into four large "books," each introduced by either an Old or New Testament passage. Books one, two, and three, for example, are entitled "God is not Mocked," "The Rock and the Church," and "The Valley of the Shadow," and are concerned, respectively, with Southern "paternalism," the character of the slaves' religious practices and beliefs, and the routine lives of the slaves. Taken together these three books, along with their introductory passages and the volume's title, suggest the familiar analogy of the plight of the slaves and bondage of the children of Israel. Thus on several occasions Genovese refers to the "nationhood" of the black people being formed as they went through the soul-shaping experience of servitude, and we are reminded, implicitly at least, of Israel's experience under the pharaohs. Deliberately or not, the book is itself a testimony to the argument that Marxism's resemblance to religion is at least as great as to economics. *Roll, Jordan, Roll*'s parables, exemplified by the Egypt-Desert-Promised-Land motif, are more reminiscent of biblical narrative than of anything to be found in economics texts.

Fittingly for a Marxist history, the argument of *Roll, Jordan, Roll* progresses from paternalism and its manifestations through "The Valley of the Shadow" to revolution and resistance. Book four, "Whom God Hath Hedged In," therefore discusses the various ways in which slaves refused to submit to the system, a resistance discussed in chapters entitled "The Slave Revolts," "Standing Up to the Man," and "The Runaways." Both the tone and the character of the entire last book remain in keeping with the rest of the volume—honest, fair, and calm: Genovese candidly concedes that the slaves established no revolutionary tradition during their servitude. There are no suggestions that blacks today should engage in violence as retaliation for past exploitation nor are there hints that whites should feel guilty at having perpetrated such exploitation on the blacks. Because his tone is not vindictive and self-righteous, Genovese cannot be labeled a "neo-abolitionist."

His detached manner of dealing with his explosive subject matter in *Roll, Jordan, Roll* gained Genovese many admirers but lost him the enthusiastic support of his more zealous left-wing colleagues. His next book, however, *From Rebellion to Revolution: Afro-American Slave Revolts in the Modern*

World (1979), proved to be more satisfying to the zealots. Although the book has a thesis, it seems less important than the work's overall tone and its choice of subject matter, the slave rebellions in the New World. The thesis, clearly argued but not convincingly demonstrated, is that slave revolts in the New World assumed a different character after the French and American Revolutions: "By the end of the eighteenth century, the historical content of the slave revolts shifted decisively from attempts to secure freedom from slavery to attempts to overthrow slavery as a social system. The great black revolution in Saint-Domingue [Haiti] marked the turning point." Furthermore, the book is marred by a peculiarly un-Genovese-like quality—passion. The work is far more belligerent, rigid, and aggressive than his earlier efforts. As Genovese later observed in a letter, "A lot of Marxists who never have liked my work . . . seem to like *From Rebellion to Revolution*." Significantly, the celebration of violence absent from Genovese's more detached efforts makes a comeback in *From Rebellion to Revolution*. The tone is at times defiantly inflammatory, as when he unabashedly defends the Zimbabwe rebels of the late 1970s for having forced their own people to participate in revolution. For obvious reasons, *From Rebellion to Revolution* strengthens Genovese's credentials as a conventional Marxist but reduces to some degree his stature as a historian.

Although it was originally intended to be a portion of *Roll, Jordan, Roll*, *From Rebellion to Revolution* is for several reasons much less persuasive than *Roll, Jordan, Roll*. For one thing the book is short. The reader misses that feeling, so vividly experienced in *Roll, Jordan, Roll*, that he is privy to the secret thoughts and actions of the participants in the drama of revolution. Furthermore, although Genovese does supply an extensive concluding bibliographic essay, *From Rebellion to Revolution* lacks footnotes. Genovese's integrity is well-established, but his thesis cannot be properly examined by his peers unless they are in a position to consider his use of source material. Considering his many admirable critiques of the works of others and the respect he has displayed for all those who have done their homework, it is surprising that he has not made it easier for his colleagues to assess his work. This shortcoming is all the more evident since he himself admits that there are numerous exceptions and qualifications to his thesis.

The belligerent tone of *From Rebellion to Revolution* has been repeated in a recent publication entitled "Academic Freedom Today" (1980). In that essay Genovese flashes a reminder of his old activist tendencies by indicating a measure of sympathy for Castro's Cuba, describing it as "a small country with an apparently implacable super-power for an enemy." He also has some kind words for Stalinist Russia, speculating that "the Soviet Union may have been justified in suppressing freedom during its forced-march industrialization and long period of encirclement by hostile capitalist powers." Such comments help Genovese maintain his Marxist credentials by confirming him as a consistent enemy of the status quo; throughout his career—in his Herbert Aptheker piece, in the first essay in *The World the Slaveholders Made*, in *From Rebellion to Revolution*, and in a large portion of "Academic Freedom Today,"—a righteously indignant Genovese lashes out at the establishment and all non-Marxist ruling classes in general.

In 1969, a full decade before the appearance of *From Rebellion to Revolution*, Genovese wrote that "the special strength of Marxism resides in its usefulness as an explanation of transitions from one social system to another." Nonetheless, in many of Genovese's more topical works, the reader senses that the professor is still attempting to contribute to the movements of history, although in a more respectable and refined fashion than in his days of activism at Rutgers. Several of these works rather obviously suggest that he wants not only to "explain the transitions" but to encourage them as well—to give history a boost. "Without making nickel-and-dime prophecies," he prophesies, "or asserting some grand design of dialectical inevitability in which I do not believe, may I suggest that the probabilities heavily favor a worldwide transition to socialism in some form or more likely many forms."

"Academic Freedom Today" clearly reveals that Genovese is capable of being simultaneously doctrinaire and temperate. There are, in fact and by his own admission, two Eugene Genoveses, characterized—in his favorite dictum—by "Pessimism of the intellect; optimism of the will." Informed by his intellect, Genovese concedes the self-serving character of all classes, denies historical inevitability, admits the cruelties of Stalinism, and genuinely fears the loss of the valuable legacies of Western civilization. In fact, Genovese's intellect has so inclined him toward "social pessimism" that he has admitted to accepting "a commitment to the idea of original sin, which has passed into my Marxism." In various ways he has consistently expressed his awareness that perfection is not to be expected in this world. The Genovese of the intellect knows that "all ruling classes' ideologies are self-serving," that the Marxist has no special powers of prediction, and that socialist experiments thus far have often been disappointments.

The Genovese of the will is, in contrast, the Genovese who in his younger days berates Herbert Aptheker for his pacifism and who welcomes a victory by the Vietcong, the same but older Genovese who sympathizes with Castro's Cuba, justifies the terror tactics of the Zimbabwe rebels, celebrates violent nineteenth-century slave revolts in the Caribbean, and even suggests that Stalin's repressions may have had a certain logic to them. This Genovese wills the world to be changed and is clearly prepared to accept as necessary violence designed to effect deeply revolutionary transformations all over the globe. Yet given his "pessimism of the intellect," his common sense, and his perceptive knowledge of history itself, he must set aside his critical faculties and exert an act of the will in order to trust that the eventual triumph of socialism or Communism will bring the dawning of a new and better age.

Nonetheless, it would be unfair to label Genovese a bloodthirsty revolutionary. He is more clearly deserving of the title radical democrat, although he may be more radical than democratic. There is no suggestion in his works that he feels revolution in America would be justified, and yet there can be no doubt that he would like to see extreme measures taken on behalf of the "masses." As a confirmed Marxist, he has accepted devotion to the masses as his guiding light, and he accordingly feels that concentration on politics or political history alone is no way to understand or solve a nation's past or present problems. He has studiously eschewed any consideration of narrow political history, candidly admitting that to him the study of America in terms of a "Jefferson-Jackson-Roosevelt liberal tradition" is nothing more than a "parlor game." Genovese prefers to look at history's deeper currents, understanding the ebb and flow of America's sea changes in terms of mass movements.

Although Genovese is best known for his writings on slavery in the New World, he has also maintained a steady interest in the events of recent decades. Throughout his career he has written essays which have been ventures in political analysis rather than history, and he has not resisted the temptation to examine and support radical developments in the present day. In "Academic Freedom Today," for instance, he forthrightly stated his preference for "Eurocommunism" among the various socialist alternatives. Eurocommunism is not conventional Communism. It is itself diluted by its concessions to democratic processes, individual liberties, and mixed economics to pass for legitimate Marxism/Leninism. The Marxist has become respectable and is no longer a shocking personality. Although Genovese has repudiated the Stalinism which represents communism's most violent and extreme form ("ghastly," he has called it), he has not been bashful about expressing sympathy for various revolutionary movements. Brilliant as he is, he too is one of the many pawns of history, moved by the twentieth-century spirit.

Other:

Ulrich B. Phillips, *American Negro Slavery*, foreword by Genovese (Baton Rouge: Louisiana State University Press, 1969);

The Slave Economy of the Old South: The Selected Social and Economic Essays of Ulrich Bonnell Phillips, edited, with an introduction, by Genovese (Baton Rouge: Louisiana State University Press, 1969);

Slavery and Race: Quantitative Studies, edited by Genovese and Stanley Engerman (Princeton: Princeton University Press, 1975);

" 'Rather be a Nigger than a Poor White Man': Slave Perceptions of Southern Yeomen and Poor Whites," in *Toward a New View of America*, edited by Hans L. Trefousse (New York: Burt Franklin, 1977), pp. 79-96.

Periodical Publications:

"Recent Contributions to the Economic Historiography of the Slave South," *Science and Society*, 24 (Winter 1961): 53-66;

"Problems in the Study of Nineteenth-Century American History," *Science and Society*, 25 (Winter 1961): 38-53;

"Dr. Herbert Aptheker's Retreat from Marxism," *Science and Society*, 27 (Spring 1963): 212-226;

"On Southern History and Its Historians," *Civil War History*, 13 (June 1967): 170-182;

"Academic Freedom Today," *South Atlantic Quarterly*, 79 (Spring 1980): 125-140.

Reference:

Bennett H. Wall, "An Epitaph for Slavery," *Louisiana History*, 16 (Summer 1975): 229-256.

Lawrence Henry Gipson

(7 December 1880-26 September 1971)

J. Barton Starr
Hong Kong Baptist College

SELECTED BOOKS: *Jared Ingersoll: A Study of American Loyalism in Relation to British Colonial Government* (New Haven: Yale University Press, 1920; London: Oxford University Press, 1920);

The British Empire Before the American Revolution, volumes 1-3 (Caldwell, Idaho: Caxton Printers, 1936); volumes 4-15 (New York: Knopf, 1939-1970);

Lewis Evans . . . To Which is Added Evans' "A Brief Account of Pennsylvania" . . . (Philadelphia: Historical Society of Pennsylvania, 1939);

"Some Reflections Upon the American Revolution" and Other Essays in American Colonial History (Bethlehem, Penn.: Lehigh University, 1942);

"The American Revolution as an Aftermath of the Great War for the Empire, 1754-1763," and Other Essays in American Colonial History: Second Series of Essays (Bethlehem, Penn.: Lehigh University, 1950);

The British Empire in the Eighteenth Century: Its Strengths and Its Weakness (Oxford: Oxford University Press, 1952);

The Coming of the Revolution, 1763-1775 (New York: Harper, 1954; London: Hamilton, 1954).

Lawrence Henry Gipson—author of more than 150 books, articles, and reviews—ranks as one of the leading historians of colonial and revolutionary America. His fifteen-volume *The British Empire Before the American Revolution* (1936-1970) is characterized by reviewers as "history on a grand scale," "monumental," "magisterial," and "definitive." One reviewer expressed the conviction that the work would "be consulted for a hundred years."

The immersion for a half-century in the intricacies of the eighteenth-century British empire could hardly have been predicted for Gipson. He was born on 7 December 1880 to Albert Eugene and Lina Maria Gipson in Greeley, Colorado, but his family soon moved to Caldwell, Idaho, where young Gipson grew up. His father was a newspaper editor, and Gipson also planned a career in journalism. In his "Reflections," however, Gipson related his early interest in reading history. He recalled having cried at the age of eleven when his sister got a larger American history book than he did. He attended high school in Caldwell as well as the Academy of the College of Idaho there before enrolling at the University of Idaho, from which he received the A.B. degree in 1903.

The first group of Rhodes Scholars to go to Oxford University in 1904 included the former stagecoach driver, long-distance runner, and part-time journalist from Idaho Lawrence Henry Gipson. While Gipson was at Oxford, an event occurred which changed the direction of his life. He recalled that he was leaning toward pursuing further work in medieval history when he was asked in his first year to debate the subject "Resolved, That it would be to the best interests of Great Britain were the other members of the British Empire to become

Lawrence Henry Gipson

independent States." Sensing that the subject was a delicate one for an American, he unsuccessfully tried to decline. Thus, on a warm spring evening he presented his position, only to be greeted by silence. After a moment's pause, however, he was verbally assaulted by virtually every person in the audience. He recorded that he found himself "too ignorant of salient facts. . . ." But the incident was a turning point in Gipson's life: "I began to study with a degree of intensity that I had never shown for any other aspect of the past, the history of the British Empire, especially its early history." The last sixty-five years of Gipson's life were devoted to that study.

He received his B.A. from Oxford in 1907 and returned to the United States, where he taught at the College of Idaho for three years. In 1909 he married Jeannette Reed. He continued his studies at Yale University as a Farnham fellow in history. He was appointed to the history faculty of Wabash College in Crawfordsville, Indiana, in 1910 and remained until 1924. In 1917 he returned to Yale as a Bulkley fellow and received his Ph.D. degree in 1918.

While at Yale, his doctoral work was under the direction of Charles McLean Andrews. Andrews's influence on Gipson was profound as the latter pursued the "Imperial School" of interpretation of the Revolution espoused by Andrews. Gipson later dedicated volume ten of his magnum opus "to the Memory of a great historian, Charles McLean Andrews," whom he called "perhaps the greatest colonial historian." But Gipson was no blind follower as is evidenced by his decision to write his dissertation on the American Loyalist Jared Ingersoll despite the objections of Andrews, who directed his students toward "institutional" history.

While there is some dissent, it is generally agreed that Gipson was the last great "Imperial" historian of the American Revolution. Gipson wrote that "the imperial approach . . . views English colonization of the New World simply as part of the history of the rise and decline of the British Empire. In this approach London, the capital of the Empire, is always the nerve center." Throughout his career Gipson continued to observe American colonial history through British eyes, occasionally to the extent of ignoring the American point of view completely. But to label Gipson solely an Imperial historian is a gross oversimplification. In the introduction to volume six of *The British Empire Before the American Revolution*, Gipson expressed his philosophy of history, which goes beyond writing from an appropriate point of view: "The supreme mis-

sion of the historian is to determine the truth of the past—in so far as this is humanly possible—and to do so with detachment. Behind this mission stands the assumption that in so far as tradition has turned its back upon reality, upon historical truth, it cannot be wholly good—and may be wholly bad." History, however, cannot be totally objective, he asserted: It "is subjective to a degree not always clearly appreciated by the reading public. Historians like all other writers are creations of the age in which they live and thus heirs to certain preconceptions. . . . Hence the enquiring reader . . . must be aware that no one historian or school of historians can possibly be definitive and must recognize that each really serious effort to evoke the past usually contains valuable insights as well as blind spots."

While Gipson had written ten scattered articles by 1920, it was not until the appearance in that year of his *Jared Ingersoll: A Study of American Loyalism in Relation to British Colonial Government* that he came to the attention of the historical profession. His biography of this prominent Connecticut Loyalist was received with generally favorable reviews and was awarded the MacFarland Prize, the John Addison Porter Prize, and the Justin Winsor Prize.

It was after the publication of *Jared Ingersoll* that Gipson decided "to attempt to describe the whole Empire in some detail during the critical years before the outbreak of the War for American Independence. . . ." He realized, however, that to complete such a monumental task and to continue to teach full-time would be impossible. It was at this point that Lehigh University offered him a position as head of the department of history and government. He accepted and assumed the post in 1924 with the clear understanding that he would be given the opportunity to pursue his history of the British empire. He continued as head of the department until 1946, when he was appointed research professor. In 1952 he was appointed research professor emeritus, and Lehigh continued to support him in his work.

Gipson arrived at Lehigh with an outline to write a twelve-volume history divided into four books. For the next ten years he worked on the first three volumes of his British empire series. Having failed to find a New York publisher, Gipson turned to his brother, James H. Gipson, who was president of Caxton Printers of Caldwell, Idaho. Finally, the first three volumes appeared from Caxton Printers in 1936 under the title *The British Empire Before the American Revolution: Provincial Characteristics and Sectional Tendencies in the Era Preceding the American*

Crisis. The volumes were well received by reviewers for their thorough documentation. While there were some reservations because of typographical mistakes, a pedestrian style, and a somewhat partisan slant (one British reviewer said "Gipson is one of those historians who do almost too much justice to the English government and its attempts to organise an Empire"), it was obvious that a new major study of colonial America had begun.

At the age of fifty-six, Gipson in 1936 undertook the massive research and disciplined writing for the rest of the British empire series, which was to establish permanently his position among the elite of historians. Over the next thirty-four years he brought out twelve more volumes at the rate of one about every three years. Alfred A. Knopf picked up the publication of the series with volume four and also brought out a new edition of the first three volumes in 1958 and 1960.

In these fifteen volumes Gipson described the British empire in the mid-eighteenth century as he viewed it. He concentrated on economic, political, and military factors almost to the total exclusion of social and intellectual currents. He asserted that the British empire was a good place to live, that the system functioned fairly well, and that the "Great War for the Empire" (French and Indian War) "settled nothing less than the incomparably vital question of what civilization . . . would arise in the great Mississippi Basin and the valleys of the rivers draining it, a civilization, whatever it may be, surely destined to expand to the Pacific seaboard and finally to dominate the North American continent. The determination of this crucial issue is perhaps the most momentous event in the life of the English-speaking people in the New World and quite overshadows in importance both the Revolutionary War and the later Civil War, events which, it is quite clear, were each contingent upon the outcome of the earlier crisis."

He concluded, however, that after the Great War for the Empire was won, it was necessary for the British to maintain troops in America to protect the colonists. Given the undertaxation of the Americans, the British were justified in asking the colonists to help pay for the support of those troops. While not ignoring the constitutional issues, Gipson argued a legalistic position which essentially shows ungrateful children revolting against the mother country. In his preface to volume eleven, Gipson wrote that he wished he could change the title of the series to "The British Empire Before the American Declaration of Independence," for "I have long been convinced, along with John Adams, that the

Revolution was completed before the outbreak of what should properly be called the War for American Independence." Yet Gipson concluded his series by wondering if the Revolution was inevitable and—after fifteen volumes and two million words—essentially said he did not know. Upon completion of the series in 1970, he sighed, "Oh, my! What an education I have given myself."

Gipson worked on his series with unswerving energy and enthusiasm. Only rarely did he permit himself to take time away from *The British Empire Before the American Revolution* for other projects. In 1939 he published a beautiful volume on Lewis Evans, an eighteenth-century Pennsylvania mapmaker. There were no more major interruptions until 1951, when he accepted the Harmsworth Chair in American History at Oxford. Realizing that age was a factor in his race to finish his series, Gipson allowed only one other diversion, *The Coming of the Revolution, 1763-1775*, his contribution to the New American Nation series in 1954. Restating the same basic themes as *The British Empire Before the American Revolution*, this volume received mixed reviews, but it clearly was inferior to his leisurely multivolume series. As he strove for conciseness he tended to overstate his case, and the shrillness of his argument made it less convincing.

That Gipson's work is important is clearly attested by the awards he received for various volumes of *The British Empire Before the American Revolution*, including the Loubat First Prize in 1948 for the first six volumes, a Bancroft Prize in 1950 for *The Great War for the Empire: The Victorious Years, 1758-1760*, the seventh volume, and the 1962 Pulitzer Prize in history for *The Triumphant Empire: Thunder-Clouds Gather in the West, 1763-1766*, volume ten of the series. But an analysis of Gipson's work is difficult. He has been widely praised and compared favorably with Francis Parkman, Thomas Babington Macaulay, Edward Gibbon, and other great historians. His work has been described as "beautifully written," "lively and fascinating," and "easy reading." On the other hand, Gipson has been criticized for rewriting American history from a Tory point of view and for a turgid style. A balanced appraisal would lie somewhere between the two extremes. Certainly, the research involved in Gipson's works is massive and thorough. Few historians could compare with him in depth of understanding of colonial America. He was, however, no stylist. *The British Empire Before the American Revolution* is a collection of essays rather than a coherent whole with smooth transitions. He had a penchant for long sentences full of commas and semicolons.

While on occasion it could rise to the poetic, basically Gipson's writing was straightforward and undramatic.

Lawrence Henry Gipson, who was a "warmhearted, generous human being," who was "personally as modest as his work is ambitious," died in his sleep on 26 September 1971. He was a man with a mission who in the early 1920s projected a history of eighteenth-century America on a grand scale. With few deviations he devoted the rest of his life to the realization of that dream. Bernard Bailyn perhaps best summarized Gipson's contribution in 1966: "Gipson has fulfilled in grand style, with absolute integrity, a tradition of history that greatly deepened and broadened our understanding of American origins."

Other:

"The Imperial Approach to Early American History," in *The Reinterpretation of Early American History*, edited by R. A. Billington (San Marino, Cal.: The Huntington Library, 1966), pp. 185-199.

Periodical Publications:

"Charles McLean Andrews and the Re-Orientation of the Study of American Colonial History," *Pennsylvania Magazine of History and Biography*, 61 (July 1935): 209-222;

"Some Reflections Upon the American Revolution," *Pennsylvania History*, 9 (January 1942): 3-21;

"The American Revolution: A Symposium," *Canadian Historical Review*, 23 (March 1942): 34-41;

"A French Project for Victory Short of a Declaration of War, 1755," *Canadian Historical Review*, 26 (December 1945): 361-371;

"British Diplomacy in the Light of Anglo-Spanish New World Issues, 1750-1757," *American Historical Review*, 51 (July 1946): 627-648;

"Thomas Hutchinson and the Framing of the Albany Plan of Union, 1754," *Pennsylvania Magazine of History and Biography*, 74 (January 1950): 5-35;

"The American Revolution as an Aftermath of the Great War for the Empire, 1754-1763," *Political Science Quarterly*, 65 (March 1950): 86-104;

"Reflections," *Pennsylvania History*, 36 (January 1969): 10-15.

References:

Jackson Turner Main, "Lawrence Henry Gipson, Historian," *Pennsylvania History*, 36 (January 1969): 22-48;

Richard B. Morris, "The Spacious Empire of Lawrence Henry Gipson," *William and Mary Quarterly*, 3rd series, 24 (April 1967): 169-189.

Papers:

The Lawrence Henry Gipson Institute for Eighteenth-Century Studies at Lehigh University holds a large collection of Gipson's papers, including personal and family correspondence, photographs, research notes and materials, personal library, and materials related to the annual Gipson Symposium.

Oscar Handlin

(29 September 1915-   )

Arnold Shankman
Winthrop College

SELECTED BOOKS: *Boston's Immigrants, 1790-1865: A Study in Acculturation* (Cambridge: Harvard University Press, 1941; revised and expanded, 1959);

Commonwealth: A Study of the Role of Government in the American Economy: Massachusetts, 1774-1861, by Handlin and Mary Flug Handlin (New York: New York University Press, 1947; revised, Cambridge: Harvard University Press, 1969);

The Uprooted (Boston: Little, Brown, 1951; expanded, 1973);

Adventure in Freedom: Three Hundred Years of Jewish Life in America (New York: McGraw-Hill, 1954);

The American People in the Twentieth Century (Cambridge: Harvard University Press, 1954);

Chance or Destiny: Turning Points in American History (Boston: Little, Brown, 1955);

Race and Nationality in American Life (Boston: Little, Brown, 1957);

Al Smith and His America (Boston: Little, Brown, 1958);

John Dewey's Challenge to Education: Historical Perspectives on the Cultural Context (New York: Harper, 1959);

The Newcomers: Negroes and Puerto Ricans in a Changing Metropolis (Cambridge: Harvard University Press, 1959);

American Principles and Issues: The National Purpose (New York: Holt, Rinehart & Winston, 1961);

The Dimensions of Liberty, by Handlin and Mary Flug Handlin (Cambridge: Harvard University Press, 1961);

The Americans: A New History of the People of the United States (Boston: Little, Brown, 1963);

Fire Bell in the Night: The Crisis in Civil Rights (Boston: Little, Brown, 1964);

A Continuing Task: The American Jewish Joint Distribution Committee (New York: Random House, 1965);

The History of the United States (New York: Holt, Rinehart & Winston, 1967);

The American College and American Culture, by Handlin and Mary Flug Handlin (New York: McGraw-Hill, 1970);

Facing Life: Youth and the Family in American History, by Handlin and Mary Flug Handlin (Boston: Little, Brown, 1971);

Statue of Liberty, volume 3 of the Wonders of Man series (New York: Newsweek Books, 1971);

A Pictorial History of Immigration (New York: Crown, 1972);

The Wealth of the American People: A History of American Affluence, by Handlin and Mary Flug Handlin (New York: McGraw-Hill, 1975);

Occasions for Love (N.p.: Published by the author, 1977);

Truth in History (Cambridge: Harvard University Press, 1979);

Abraham Lincoln and the Union, by Handlin and Lilian Bombach Handlin (Boston: Little, Brown, 1980);

Oscar Handlin

The Distortion of America (Boston: Little, Brown, 1981);

A Restless People: Americans in Rebellion, by Handlin and Lilian Bombach Handlin (Garden City: Anchor/Doubleday, 1982).

Oscar Handlin, Harvard University historian and librarian, ranks as one of the most prolific and influential American historians of the twentieth century. Ethnic history, social history, and urban history are among the fields in which he has made pioneering contributions. Equally adept at writing history aimed at scholars and at the public, Handlin is one of a handful of professional historians whose works are popular with general readers. Oscar Handlin is also known for training many of America's leading historians, including Bernard Bailyn, Anne Firor Scott, Moses Rischin, Martin Duberman, Arthur Mann, David Rothman, Neil Harris, Nathan Huggins, Stephan Thernstrom, and Sam Bass Warner.

Born in New York City, Handlin was the oldest of three children of Jewish immigrants. His mother, the former Ida Yanowitz, had come to the United States from Russia in 1904 and worked in the garment industry. His father, Joseph Handlin, had attended a commercial college in the Ukraine prior to his arrival in America in 1913. At various times Joseph Handlin ran a grocery store, operated a steam laundry, and sold real estate.

Although Oscar Handlin was more than once expelled from school for being an enfant terrible, he excelled in academics. Active in athletics and talented in music, he participated in a wide variety of extracurricular activities. At age eight he resolved to become a historian and became a voracious reader who could often be seen reading books as he delivered groceries for his father. In 1931 he graduated from Brooklyn's New Utrecht High School. He then entered Brooklyn College, where he majored in history and was influenced by Jesse Clarkson, a specialist in Russian history. Within three years Handlin earned his bachelor's degree and was accepted for graduate work at Harvard University.

That Handlin became an American historian was accidental. He had intended to study medieval history with Charles H. Haskins at Harvard, but upon his arrival at the university he discovered that Haskins had retired. Because Handlin believed that the historian under whom he studied was more important than the field of history in which he specialized, he decided to write his dissertation for Arthur M. Schlesinger, Sr. Schlesinger suggested

that Handlin study Boston's immigrants in the late eighteenth and early nineteenth centuries, a subject that another doctoral candidate had abandoned. Handlin agreed to the topic and did his research in Boston, Washington, Dublin, and London. In 1940 he received his doctoral degree. One year later his dissertation, *Boston's Immigrants, 1790-1865: A Study in Acculturation* (1941), was published. The book was acclaimed as a model study, and Handlin was praised for creatively making use of census data and other government documents, for his familiarity with sociological concepts to explain assimilation and acculturation, and for his imaginative use of the immigrant press, a hitherto neglected source. The only major criticism of the book was that it lacked a systematic discussion of the family. In 1942, *Boston's Immigrants*, which is still frequently used as a required reading in college courses, won for Handlin the prestigious Dunning Prize of the American Historical Association for being the outstanding historical work published by a young scholar in 1941. In 1959 a revised and expanded edition of the book was published which took the story of Boston's immigrants to 1880.

While working on his dissertation Handlin taught for one year at Brooklyn College. In 1939 he joined the Harvard faculty. Although for several years he taught courses in the social relations department, eventually he became a full-time member of the history department. In 1962, eight years after he was promoted to the rank of full professor and five years after he organized Harvard's Center for the History of Liberty in America, he was named Winthrop Professor of History. During 1965 he became Charles Warren Professor of American History and director of the Warren Center for Studies in American History. Handlin was designated Carl Pforzheimer University Professor in 1973, and during the 1972-1973 academic year he was honored with the Harmsworth Visiting Professorship at Oxford University. In 1979 he was named director of the Harvard University Library.

During the 1940s Handlin quickly proved that he was not a one-book historian. In collaboration with his first wife, the former Mary Flug (1913-1976), whom he had married in 1937, he turned his attention to the way public attitudes toward government and its role in economic life had changed during the early nineteenth century. Out of their research came *Commonwealth: A Study of the Role of Government in the American Economy: Massachusetts, 1774-1861* (1947). *Commonwealth*, like *Boston's Immigrants*, creatively used primary sources. Although some critics thought that the Handlins gave insufficient attention in the book to the attitudes of laborers, most admitted that *Commonwealth* was a model monograph. The book showed how the government of Massachusetts, which had originally limited corporate charters to publicly useful businesses, gradually became more democratic and started to issue charters to nearly all who requested them. Meanwhile the Commonwealth of Massachusetts began more closely to regulate the lives of its citizens, taking a much greater role in public education, treatment of the poor and insane, and care of the criminal. As was true of *Boston's Immigrants*, *Commonwealth* pictured Massachusetts society in the 1790s as relatively stable contrasted to the heterogeneous and fragmented society in the 1850s.

Two years later Handlin published *This Was America: True Accounts of People, Places, Manners and Customs, As Recorded by European Travelers to the Western Shore in the Eighteenth, Nineteenth and Twentieth Centuries* (1949), an anthology of writings by visitors to the United States. While he was editing *This Was America*, Handlin was also at work on what would become his most famous book, *The Uprooted* (1951), which won a Pulitzer Prize in 1952. *The Uprooted*, the epic story of the more than thirty million immigrants who had come to America since 1820, opened with the now famous lines: "Once I thought to write a history of the immigrants in America. Then I discovered that the immigrants *were* American history." The theme of the book was that emigration was the "central experience of millions" of newcomers to America. Handlin was concerned with studying the nature and consequences of the alienation experienced by these immigrants. The book showed how peasants leaving European villages where they enjoyed a sense of community became increasingly helpless as they made their way to the United States and had to adjust to a radically different culture. Even the church, the only institution successfully transported to the New World, had to modify itself to thrive in the United States. The stress of learning how to fit into a new society was considerable and was greatly augmented with the birth of children who knew nothing firsthand of the Old World. *The Uprooted* contrasted sharply with most previous studies of immigrants which tended to be filiopietistic and concerned mainly with those newcomers who had become rich or famous. *The Uprooted* demonstrated Handlin's familiarity not only with the traditional sources for history and the literature of other social sciences but also with folklore, novels, and newspapers.

Initial reaction to *The Uprooted* was generally favorable. Its poetic quality and lucid prose were pleasant changes from the turgid style of previous works on immigration. Scholars, however, were not unanimous in their praise. Some who considered the book unduly gloomy declared that many emigrants left sophisticated, industrial towns rather than pastoral villages. Others, such as Rudolph Vecoli, claimed that Handlin's conclusions were invalid for Italian immigrants who settled in Chicago, peasants who experienced relatively little alienation. Vecoli also maintained that religion was less important to Sicilian immigrants than to the immigrants Handlin described. In addition, Andrew Rolle maintained that immigrants to the western United States did not fit into the bittersweet picture Handlin described of immigrant life in the cities. Still others were upset with *The Uprooted* because of its lack of documentation.

In a second, enlarged edition of *The Uprooted* published in 1973 Handlin answered his critics. He stated that the presence of footnotes in his book could show that he had accurately copied his sources but could not thereby prove or disprove his thesis. To some extent he had indicated the types of sources he considered important in a documentary collection, *Immigration as a Factor in American History*, which he had edited in 1959, and in *A Pictorial History of Immigration*, which he had published in 1972. Handlin agreed that some specifics in *The Uprooted* merited reconsideration. On the whole, however, he still believed that ethnic differences were outweighed by the common experiences of immigrants transplanted into an unstable, new environment and required to modify traits developed in other cultures.

Adventure in Freedom: Three Hundred Years of Jewish Life in America (1954) also generated some controversy. For several years Handlin had been writing on aspects of American Jewish history; this book was written for the general reader on the three hundredth anniversary of Jewish settlement in the United States. *Adventure in Freedom* showed why Jews found it advantageous to modify their cultural and religious institutions in America and how Jews acquired more political and civil rights and more security in the United States than in Europe. Like *The Uprooted* the book lacked footnotes, and this omission distressed some critics. Others thought that Handlin underestimated political handicaps suffered by Jews and ignored the presence of anti-Semitism in the Federalist era, during the Civil War, and in the Gilded Age. Most of the controversy concerned Handlin's chapter on anti-Semitism from 1890-1941. An expanded version of an essay he had written in 1951, the chapter asserted that anti-Semitism in the United States dated back only to the 1890s rather than to the 1860s or 1870s. It was in the 1890s, Handlin thought, that the stereotype of Jews as hook-nosed foreigners preoccupied with the acquisition of money first became popularized. The Jew was seen as an urban, parasitical businessman who got wealthy but produced nothing and who lived in crowded cities which rural dwellers viewed with suspicion and distaste. Handlin thus was among the first to see elements of anti-Semitism in the Populist movement, a subject that was later more fully considered by Richard Hofstadter. John Higham, Handlin doctoral student Frederick Cople Jahrer, and especially Norman Pollack challenged Handlin, questioning his use of sources and arguing that the Populists were not particularly anti-Semitic. Handlin, surprised at the volume and vehemence of the attacks upon him, later stated that some of his critics, notably Pollack, found it "necessary to ascribe to me views I did not express, so that they could be refuted."

The increasingly prolific Handlin also published two other books in 1954. One, *The Harvard Guide to American History*, for which he was the chief editor, was quickly recognized as one of the most authoritative bibliographical tools in the field of American history. The other, *The American People in the Twentieth Century*, was, in actuality, a history of American ethnic groups. The book traced the growth of racist thought in the early part of the 1900s and showed how after World War II prejudiced thinking was discredited; thus, white immigrants—but not black or native Indian Americans—were allowed to participate more fully in American society. Handlin stated that in the United States merit rather than ethnic origin increasingly determined one's economic and political opportunities.

Chance or Destiny: Turning Points in American History (1955), Handlin's next book, was based on a series of essays, several of which had been written for *The Atlantic Monthly*. Aimed at a popular audience, the book showed how chance determined the outcome of several key episodes in American history. Critics declared that Handlin sometimes oversimplified events, an allegation with a measure of validity, but these reviewers also missed the main purpose of the book. Handlin sought to show that history was "a line made up of a succession of points, with every point a turning point." Nothing was in-

evitable, he asserted, and "at the numerous turning points of the past [man] has been capable of acting freely, for good or ill, upon the opportunities the situation afforded."

Two years later, in 1957, Handlin published another series of essays, *Race and Nationality in American Life*. This book demonstrated the range of Handlin's interest in ethnicity. One particularly perceptive essay, "Old Immigrants and New," convincingly showed how the Dillingham Commission deliberately distorted data it collected on emigrants to promote immigrant restriction. The most controversial essay in the book was "Origins of Negro Slavery," coauthored with Mary Flug Handlin and published originally in 1950 under a slightly different title. Its thesis was that blacks were not initially treated very differently from white indentured servants. Slavery emerged gradually, the Handlins declared, "from the adjustment to America and conditions of traditional European institutions." Not until around 1660 did Negroes became permanent chattels: "Color then emerged as the token of slave status." The implication that racism was a by-product of and not the reason for slavery interested historians. Carl Degler, disputing the Handlins' view, maintained that the first colonists were prejudiced against blacks and gave Negroes inferior status shortly after the arrival of blacks in Virginia in 1619. Winthrop Jordan believed that slavery and racial prejudice emerged simultaneously. Peter Wood, on the other hand, studying colonial South Carolina in his book *Black Majority*, uncovered some data that was compatible with the Handlins' thesis on Virginia.

Biography was another subject that interested Oscar Handlin. As he wrote in *Truth in History* (1979), the "proper subject of biography . . . is not the complete person or the complete society, but the point at which the two interact. There the situation and the individual illuminate one another." As editor of the popular Library of American Biography, Handlin contributed introductions to each of the volumes and wrote biographies of Al Smith and Abraham Lincoln. *Al Smith and His America* (1958), which won a Christopher Award, was a spritely sketch of the New York governor and presidential hopeful. Written just two years before John Kennedy became the first Roman Catholic president, the book was seen by some as blaming Smith's presidential defeat in 1928 on religious bigotry. In truth, although Handlin did emphasize the role of anti-Catholic sentiment in the election, he was very careful to point out that there was no single cause for the defeat. Many reviewers also ignored Handlin's perceptive treatment of Smith's career after 1928 and of the complex reasons behind the rift between Smith and Franklin Roosevelt. In 1980, twenty-two years after the publication of this book, Handlin and his second wife, Lilian Bombach Handlin, whom he married in 1977, a year after Mary Flug Handlin's death, wrote another biography, *Abraham Lincoln and the Union*. Uncovering no new or startling information about the sixteenth president, the Handlins' short but engaging work emphasized Lincoln's early years, his family life, and the anguish he endured while president.

By the late 1950s Handlin was publishing nearly a book a year. Few aspects of American history escaped his gaze. Civil rights, ethnicity, urban history, the history of education, and foreign affairs all caught his attention. Some of his books, such as *A Continuing Task: The American Jewish Joint Distribution Committee* (1965), engendered little criticism. Such others as *The Historian and the City* (1963), which he edited with John Burchard, were considered major contributions to emerging fields of American history. A few books, however, not only significantly added to existing literature but also sparked controversy. Nowhere was this more evident than when Handlin dealt with contemporary issues. *The Newcomers: Negroes and Puerto Ricans in a Changing Metropolis*, published in 1959 as one of the volumes of the New York Metropolitan Region study, challenged the beliefs that these two groups were radically different from previous immigrants to New York. Handlin saw that blacks and Puerto Ricans shared many common features with earlier groups but also recognized that skin color caused complications for members of these groups. The book disputed the view that blacks and Puerto Ricans were necessarily more prone to criminal activities than other ethnic groups and expressed the belief that the development of communal institutions and better educational facilities would ease the social disorder experienced by the newcomers. Some critics disagreed with certain of Handlin's conclusions, but most recognized that his book, strongly based upon the history of New York, was one of the first scholarly studies of the topic.

Even more controversial was *Fire Bell in the Night: The Crisis in Civil Rights* (1964). The essays in this brief book surveyed the status of blacks and their civil rights in 1964. Handlin criticized separatists, segregationists, and suburban liberals, arguing that "we can be equal and different." Sympathetic to the aims of blacks and aware that the gains Negroes had made caused them to be more aware of the gaps that still existed, Handlin favored better educational opportunities as a way of improving the status of Afro-Americans. He disapproved of quotas, school busing, and affirmative action. "Preferential treatment," Handlin wrote, "demands a departure from the ideal which judges individuals by their own merits rather than by their affiliations." As might be expected, some reviewers found the book provocative and some blacks were incensed, but Handlin did not retreat from his views.

During the 1960s Handlin dealt with a wide variety of other topics. *The Dimensions of Liberty* (1961), coauthored with Mary Flug Handlin, sought to study the characteristics of liberty, to examine the natures of voluntary and restrictive associations, and to provide a framework for others who would later study aspects of these subjects in greater detail. The Handlins found that liberty was bound in with the complete development of the nation, not dependent upon a solitary phenomenon. Rather, liberty came about "as the way of life of a people who wished so to order their institutions that they would be able themselves to make decisions important to them." Not only liberty but also migration interested Oscar Handlin, and this subject was explored in *The Americans: A New History of the People of the United States* (1963). The book, aimed at a popular audience, de-emphasized the role of great men in shaping American culture and focused instead on the evolution of American political, economic, and social institutions. Handlin stressed the importance of mobility, ethnic diversity, and internal migration in fostering America's dynamic economic growth. European institutions, he noted, had to be modified in America to meet the needs of a different environment and a rapidly expanding landmass. Wealth in the United States, he observed, was mainly attained because of personal merit and achievement rather than because of status or inherited money. Handlin's conclusion was that America had "the best environment for freedom men had yet enjoyed."

A later book, *The Wealth of the American People: A History of American Affluence* (1975), coauthored with Mary Flug Handlin, reinforced many of these conclusions. This latter work sought to provide a historical explanation for American affluence. It linked productivity with freedom and noted that the government best assisted business by creating conditions that encouraged all to engage in commerce with confidence rather than by offering special privileges to some. The book had harsh words for the children of America's affluent society who systematically denigrated their country and its achievements.

Handlin's interest in the connection between the American educational system and upward mobility was revealed in three books. *John Dewey's Challenge to Education: Historical Perspectives on the Cultural Context* (1959) demonstrated how Dewey sought to rid schools of their rigidity and of conditions that stifled the learning process. *The American College and American Culture* (1970), written with Mary Flug Handlin, provided a social history showing that the growth of colleges came about in part because they offered training parents could not or would not directly impart and because they were seen as places where students could get preparation for careers and learn an ethical code of behavior. In *Facing Life: Youth and the Family in American History* (1971), the Handlins wrote a history of adolescence. In early American history youth were compelled to leave home and strike out on their own in their teens. In more recent decades, the Handlins noted, the American educational system dramatically changed employment practices. High school diplomas came to be required for even the most menial of jobs. Moreover, not only undergraduate diplomas but also professional and graduate degrees came to be needed for entry into the most specialized jobs. Therefore, many discovered that the age when one becomes financially independent of one's parents was pushed back from one's teenage years to his late twenties. The book concluded with a sharp critique of the student revolutions of the 1970s. The Handlins had little sympathy for the suburban spoiled brat who denounced materialism but was addicted to the luxuries it produced. "Tear it down; burn it; blow it up": These slogans, the Handlins declared, "were cheap for those who never felt want." Radicals purposefully made unreasonable demands to promote violent confrontations. Even worse, the Handlins continued, in many cases universities capitulated to these demands by establishing quotas, diluting standards for admission and requirements for graduation, and hiring faculty on the basis of color rather than on personal merit.

The turmoil of the 1960s and 1970s noted in *Facing Life* made Oscar Handlin wonder whether the American environment for freedom were being perverted to advance the forces of anarchy. Distress at the course of events in recent American history was evident in two of his late books, *Truth in History*

(1979) and *The Distortion of America* (1981). *Truth in History* contained brief monographic essays, rebuttals of criticisms directed at some of Handlin's books and articles, and the author's advice for historians. In the book Handlin expressed his displeasure that the 1930s and 1940s community of historians eager to search for truth and to assist one another had been replaced by a present-day, increasingly politicized band of men and women interested in using history and historical associations for their partisan purposes. Hiring quotas, the scheduling of conventions only in states that had ratified the Equal Rights Amendment, faddishness, overspecialization and fragmentation in fields of history, and deficiencies in graduate training all met with Handlin's disapproval. New Left historians were especially distasteful to Handlin, for he argued that they deliberately distorted facts to fit their preconceived interpretations. In so doing, Handlin felt, they mocked the craftsmanship expected of historians, for when intuition replaced evidence, the discipline was betrayed.

In several essays of this important book Handlin offered his view of the obligations of the historian and of the value of history. The historian, Handlin wrote, had an obligation to avoid seeking to solve the world's immediate problems. Rather, he needed to realize that the value of history is its capacity to advance and discover truth. Truth, Handlin stated, is absolute and does not exist to fit the preconceptions of the individual: "History is the distillation of evidence surviving from the past. Where there is no evidence, there is no history." The historian's job, Handlin concluded, was to provide the long view, to encourage reflection and reasoning from analogy.

The pessimism found in *Truth in History* was even more evident in *The Distortion of America*. Handlin conceded that this book was "polemical and passionate" because of "a sense of urgency and . . . a commitment to freedom, which is everywhere in danger." The "danger" was that America's coherent foreign policy of the 1940s and 1950s had disintegrated. No longer were there guidelines for a world experiencing an unending nightmare. Fervently anti-Communist, Handlin insisted that neutrals seeking to find positive aspects of Russian society were gullible. Communists, Handlin maintained, advocated a "militant doctrine of totalitarianism"; therefore, the free world had an obligation to point out the difference between freedom and communism. Critical of those who opposed the Vietnam War, Handlin insisted that dissenters had to accept the consequences of their activities and to recognize the right of the state to punish them. If freedom were to continue, the public had to "summon up the will to defend values from the past that are still valid for the future."

In addition to his writing monographs, articles, and even a book of poetry titled *Occasions for Love* (1977), and to his teaching classes at Harvard, Oscar Handlin has undertaken a variety of activities. These have ranged from helping manage a commercial television station in Boston to having written for several years a book column for the *Atlantic Monthly*. From 1962-1965 he was vice chairman and from 1965-1966 chairman of the United States Board of Foreign Scholarships, which oversees the awarding of Fulbright Scholarships. Since 1973 he has been a trustee of the American Academy of Arts and Sciences. Colby College, Hebrew Union College, Northern Michigan University, Oakland University, Seton Hall, Brooklyn College, and Boston College have awarded him honorary degrees. Perhaps his greatest honor came in 1979, however, when several of his former students published a festschrift, *Uprooted Americans: Essays to Honor Oscar Handlin*, a book praised for the craftsmanship of its essays and for the testimony it provided of Handlin's influence on the historical profession.

As his most recent books plainly prove, Handlin has not sought to shun controversy. For more than thirty years his views on the origins of slavery, the nature of immigration to America, the work of New Left historians, and the obligations of the student of history have sparked debates and caused the publication of countless articles. Some have rebuked him for aiming much of his work at popular audiences and for therefore oversimplifying his arguments to retain the attention of lay readers. But even his most severe critics have not denied that Oscar Handlin has made lasting contributions as a teacher and scholar. His students populate the history departments of the most prestigious American universities. There is, however, no Handlin school of history, nor was there ever any effort on the historian's part to form such a school. Although he has written on almost every aspect of American history, Oscar Handlin will probably be most remembered for his landmark contributions in American social history, especially for his writings on the importance of immigration and its role in the history of the United States.

Other:

This Was America: True Accounts of People, Places, Manners and Customs, As Recorded by European Travelers to the Western Shore in the Eighteenth, Nineteenth and Twentieth Centuries, edited by Handlin (Cambridge: Harvard University Press, 1949);

The Harvard Guide to American History, edited by Handlin and others (Cambridge: Harvard University Press, 1954);

Immigration as a Factor in American History, edited by Handlin (Englewood Cliffs, N.J.: Prentice-Hall, 1959);

Journey to Pennsylvania by Gottlieb Mittelberger, edited by Handlin and John Clive (Cambridge: Harvard University Press, 1962);

The Historian and the City, edited by Handlin and John Burchard (Cambridge: Massachusetts Institute of Technology Press, 1963);

Children of the Uprooted, edited by Handlin (New York: Braziller, 1966);

The Popular Sources of Political Authority: Documents on the Massachusetts Constitution of 1780, edited by Handlin and Mary Flug Handlin (Cambridge: Harvard University Press, 1966).

References:

Maldwyn A. Jones, "Oscar Handlin," in *Pastmasters: Some Essays on American Historians*, edited by Marcus Cunliffe and Robin W. Winks (New York: Harper & Row, 1969), pp. 239-277, 451-456;

Barbara Solomon Miller, "A Portrait of Oscar Handlin," in *Uprooted Americans: Essays to Honor Oscar Handlin*, edited by Richard L. Bushman and others (Boston: Little, Brown, 1979), pp. 3-8;

Bruce Stave, "A Conversation with Oscar Handlin," in *The Making of Urban History*, edited by Bruce Stave (Beverly Hills: Sage Publications, 1977), pp. 145-156;

Stephen J. Whitfield, "Handlin's History," *American Jewish History*, 70 (December 1980): 226-237.

Albert Bushnell Hart

(1 July 1854-16 June 1943)

Shirley A. Hickson
North Greenville College

SELECTED BOOKS: *The Coercive Powers of the Government of the United States of America* (Eisenach, East Germany: Druckder, 1885);

History 13: Outline of the Course in Constitutional and Political History of the United States, 1789-1861 (Boston: F. Wood, 1885-1886);

The Work of Students in the Course of History of the United States (Cambridge: W. H. Wheeler, 1887);

Introduction to the Study of Federal Government (Boston: Ginn, 1891);

Formation of the Union, 1750-1829, volume 2 of Epochs of American History series (New York & London: Longmans, Green, 1892);

Practical Essays on American Government (New York: Longmans, Green, 1893);

Studies in American Education (New York & London: Longmans, Green, 1895);

Guide to the Study of American History, by Hart and Edward Channing (Boston & London: Ginn, 1896);

Salmon Portland Chase, volume 28 of American Statesmen series (Boston & New York: Houghton, Mifflin, 1899);

Foundations of American Foreign Policy, With a Working Bibliography (New York & London: Macmillan, 1901);

Actual Government as Applied Under American Conditions (New York, London, & Bombay: Longmans, Green, 1903);

Essentials in American History (From Discovery to the Present Day), volume 4 of Essentials of History series (New York & Cincinnati: American Book, 1905);

Slavery and Abolition, 1831-1841, volume 16 of *The American Nation: A History* (New York & London: Harper, 1906);

National Ideals Historically Traced, 1607-1907, volume 26 of *The American Nation: A History* (New York & London: Harper, 1907);

Manual of American History, Diplomacy, and Government for Class Use (Cambridge: Harvard University Press, 1908);

The Southern South (New York & London: Appleton, 1910);

The Obvious Orient (New York & London: Appleton, 1911);

The Monroe Doctrine: An Interpretation (Boston: Little, Brown, 1915; London: Duckworth, 1916);

The War in Europe: Its Causes and Results (New York & London: Appleton, 1915);

New American History (New York & Cincinnati: American Book, 1917);

School History of the United States (New York & Cincinnati: American Book, 1918).

Albert Bushnell Hart

Albert Bushnell Hart, professor of American history and government at Harvard University, was, in his own words, "one of a group of young men who made history and government vital subjects for college and graduate school." He was a teacher, organizer, and promoter of American history who was also a prolific writer. His works, which ranged from informal newspaper articles to scholarly monographs and reference books, communicated history and the methodology of history to Americans of all ages and all walks of life during the half-century between 1885 and 1935.

Born to Albert Gaillard and Mary Crosby Hornell Hart in Clarksville (now Clark), Pennsylvania, and reared in the Western Reserve section of Ohio, A. B. Hart was clearly a product of his heritage and his environment. His energetic devotion to the protestant work ethic and his ethical and moral uprightness were evidence of the strong New England Congregationalist influence that existed in his family and in the communities where he grew up. However, Hart was also a Westerner with the Westerner's love for democracy and appreciation for the practical. His father, a physician, was an abolitionist whose interest in antislavery was deep enough to carry him to the 1848 Free Soil Party Convention in Buffalo. Albert G. Hart passed on his interests in politics, blacks, and community affairs to his son. The Civil War was another major influence in A. B. Hart's life. He later recalled realizing, as he watched soldiers march away to war, that they were going to fight for his country. He read the letters from his soldier-father and as a ten year old looked into the open coffin of the assassinated president when the Lincoln funeral train stopped in Cleveland on its way to Springfield. These experiences produced the fervent patriotism that characterized Hart for the remainder of his life.

By the time that Albert Bushnell Hart was a teenager, his family had moved to Cleveland, and in 1871 Hart graduated from that city's West High School. He was valedictorian of his class, and his speech, "American Progress," gave evidence of his developing interest in United States history. In his address Hart argued that post-Civil War materialism had robbed the nation of some of the qualities that had previously made it great. However, he saw the developing antiliquor crusade as an indication of the return of some of the prewar spirit. In closing Hart expressed the hope that the nation would be able to harmonize spiritual and material progress.

In spite of high school honors and a father with three college degrees, young A. B. Hart followed the example of his older brother, Hastings H. Hart, and soon after his graduation from high school, he took a job as a bookkeeper at the Cleveland firm of House and Davidson. However, his work did not prevent Hart from taking time for what was to become his favorite hobby, travel. In 1873-1874 Hart and a friend journeyed to the East. This trip provided Hart with his first publication, a newspaper article entitled "Two Cleveland Boys Go Travelling," which was published in the *Cleveland Leader* on 29 October 1874. It also provided some impressions of Harvard that caused Hart to con-

sider an academic career. With the encouragement of his minister and several former teachers, Hart sought special tutoring and then took the Harvard entrance examination. He passed with honors and entered the 1876 freshman class at the age of twenty-two.

Hart was one of only five Ohio boys in his class, but he liked Harvard and was successful as a student. After spending two years on classical studies, geology, and mathematics, Hart had time as a junior to concentrate on historical studies. That year he enrolled in Prof. Charles Eliot Norton's course on the history of fine arts. Norton, whose use of current events in the classroom was to influence his protégé to do likewise, was the professor at Harvard who had the most influence on Hart. Norton was so impressed with Hart's course thesis, "Guilds of Florence," that he encouraged the young man to seek publication for it and to make history his profession.

Prevented from becoming involved in campus athletics by health problems and from entering the top social clubs by a lack of proper connections, Hart became active in political activities and in doing so met an equally ardent Republican classmate named Theodore Roosevelt. The two became lifelong friends. In addition, Hart was tapped for membership in Phi Beta Kappa and joined the Signet Literary Society, the Finance Club, and the Rifle Club. He regularly contributed to Harvard's literary journal, the *Advocate*, and at one time was president of its board of editors. Hart was chosen by his classmates to give the Ivy Oration and in doing so humorously commented, "Summer comes but no *Summa Cums*." He almost fulfilled his own prophecy when, after getting caught lighting a bonfire of doormats in the Harvard Yard, he found himself in disciplinary trouble at commencement time. However, the matter was settled in time for Hart to graduate summa cum laude in the class of 1880.

Not only did Hart graduate with highest honors but he also received a three-year fellowship to study modern constitutional history. This award allowed him to spend one additional year at Harvard and two years in Europe. While in Europe he studied at the University of Berlin and L'Ecole Libre des Sciences Politiques in Paris, but he spent most of his time at the University of Freiburg. There he completed a doctorate under Professor Hermann Eduard von Holst, then the most famous living teacher and writer of United States history. Hart's dissertation, *The Coercive Powers of the Government of the United States of America* (1885), showed that he had narrowed his interest to American constitutional and political history. Although time would see Hart broaden his scope somewhat, he remained convinced that political history was the most important part of United States history because it was in the area of government that the United States had made its great contribution to the world.

In 1883, Dr. Albert Bushnell Hart returned to the United States to accept a position at his alma mater as instructor of the university's only American-history course. President Charles W. Eliot was looking for a good scholar who could organize, teach, and write American history. He was impressed with Hart's energy, breezy manner, and German Ph.D. and chose him over Edward Channing, holder of a Harvard Ph.D. and an applicant for the position. Channing had to be satisfied with teaching European history until the teaching load was large enough to merit his assistance. That time was not long in coming, and the two professors shared both undergraduate and graduate teaching loads, as well as several joint literary endeavors, during their many years as colleagues on the Harvard faculty.

Like many of his contemporaries of similar background and training, Hart saw history as a science. He believed that society and its institutions had an origin and a method of development and that it was the duty of the historian to find this origin and trace the development. Hart also believed that history was scientific in method. Since the historian generalized from an accumulation of data, he had to be concerned that he acquired the necessary materials and used them properly in drawing and verifying conclusions. Hart saw judgment as the key to this process. Judgment made generalization possible and could be used to deal with a limitless number of historical, current, and even future situations. Hence, history was of practical value because it taught a skill that could be used throughout life.

Hart set out to put his theories into practice in his course, History 13—The Constitutional and Political History of the United States, and he put them on paper in "Methods of Teaching American History," an essay published in the second edition of Stanley Hall's *Methods of Teaching History* (1885). In his essay, Hart deplored the ignorance of and misinformation about history that typified Americans. He denounced the old methods of teaching history by rote and recitation and called for an emphasis on judgment rather than memorization. He insisted that American history should focus upon groups of

people trying to solve their problems rather than upon lists of facts to be memorized. His course soon became one of the most popular in the Harvard curriculum, and his essay won the applause of Herbert Baxter Adams, the dean of American historians.

While Hart was writing about how to teach history, he was also continuing to pursue his own studies in constitutional history. He expanded his dissertation into a book, *Introduction to the Study of Federal Government* (1891), and organized a new course by the same name. The book was little more than a summary of his earlier work. Almost half of it dealt with background materials such as the theory of federal government and historical sketches of such governments. The remainder of the book was a conspectus of the constitutions of Canada, Germany, Switzerland, and the United States built around such points of comparison as relationships of states with the union and of states with states, powers of the states, and forms of state government. Hart concluded that the United States had made the federal plan of government work by combining the opportunities of a new land with the Teutonic love for personal freedom and respect for the law. Although *Introduction to the Study of Federal Government* was read mostly by the students who took Hart's course, it did attract some attention. A review rated it a good introductory work and praised its bibliography. Hart thus had published his first book-length work to appear in the United States; he had also suggested another basic tenet of his historical faith.

Hart believed that primary sources were vital to the proper study of history even at the undergraduate level, but he soon realized that the paucity of these materials and their locations would make such study impossible for most of the nation's college students. With his colleague, Edward Channing, Hart set about to solve this problem by editing the American History Leaflets. Between 1891 and 1902, the two professors published some three-dozen leaflets. Each leaflet treated a separate important episode in American history and contained a brief introduction written by the editors, a short bibliography of supplemental reading suggestions, and the contents of one or more important primary sources. Priced at ten cents each, these leaflets allowed undergraduates at Harvard and across the country inexpensive, convenient access to documents of American history.

When Hart began teaching, his choice of textbooks for History 13 was limited to Richard

Hildreth's aging six volume *History of the United States* (1849-1852) and Hermann E. von Holst's dull *Constitutional and Political History of the United States* (1876-1892). Unhappy with both, Hart taught the course without a textbook for a time. Instead of a text he developed a series of outlines which he had printed throughout the last part of the 1880s for use by his students. He added references for reading, advice on studying and taking notes, and eventually outlines for his other classes. The outlines became the basis for a series of manuals which were published for twenty years and served as guides for teachers at other institutions long after Hart's students had stopped using them.

Because of his concept of history as a progression of developments, Hart felt that students should begin their work by getting a brief overview of the period to be studied so that they could identify its main themes. With the main themes in mind, they could then work with the details to produce a comprehensive picture based on impressions rather than on memorized facts. Since there was no published text for such an overview that Hart could use in his classes, he at first resorted to the outlines, but as soon as possible, he took action to fill the need by editing the Epochs of American History series (1892-1926). The three small volumes of the initial edition of this series were individually written by Reuben Gold Thwaites of the Wisconsin State Historical Society, by Woodrow Wilson of Princeton University, and by Hart. Covering United States history from the colonial period through the last years of the nineteenth century, the volumes traced the development of the nation's most important ideas and institutions epoch by epoch.

The second volume of the Epochs of American History series was Hart's *Formation of the Union, 1750-1829* (1892). In it Hart traced the development of the national government beginning with the colonial conflict with Great Britain and continuing through the Revolution, Confederation, Constitution, early national period, and expansion of democracy in the 1820s. Not only did he provide the overview which traced the formation of the union but he also provided maps, supplemental reading suggestions, and helpful hints for teachers and students. Although his book was a new style of college text, it got a good reception. Reviewers praised its organization, its readability, and its approach to history. The public and the professors evidently agreed because Hart's volume and the entire series became textbook classics. Hart revised his volume in 1926 and got John Spencer Bassett to

add a fourth volume in order to bring the series up to date. Remaining in print for over forty years, Epochs of American History sold several hundred thousand copies.

Never an ivory-tower scholar, Hart from the beginning wrote for the general public as well as for the academic community. During his career he wrote nearly one thousand articles for periodicals. They ranged from short, informal newspaper articles to long, scholarly journal articles. Hart seemed impelled to communicate his ideas through the printed word, and often the ideas which shaped his larger works were first expressed in articles. Occasionally he simply had republished some of these works in books of essays on various subjects.

The first such book of essays was *Practical Essays on American Government* (1893). Ten of the eleven essays in the book had been published previously as separate articles. They varied greatly in both length and content. "The Speaker as Premier" was a short discussion of the power and influence of the Speaker of the United States House of Representatives, a subject which clearly related to the book's title. "Why the South Was Defeated in the Civil War," which was much longer than any of the other essays, had only the most indirect connection with the title. In it Hart argued that slavery so weakened Southerners that both they and the slavery system fell together. Yet Hart felt that these and the other essays were connected in that all dealt with the practical workings of government. This theme of practical versus theoretical would continue to be important to him as a teacher and a writer.

All six essays in *Studies in American Education* (1895) had previously been published as articles. In them Hart addressed various professional and methodological issues from the elementary level to the university. Essay titles included "Has the Teacher a Profession?," "How to Study History," and "The Status of Athletics in American Colleges." Hart saw all education as part of a single process, and he hoped to call attention to that idea with this group of essays. Because he believed that many methods could be used with equal effectiveness at all levels, he tried to encourage teachers from the various levels to learn from each other. He also sought to practice what he preached by serving for many years as a member of the Cambridge school committee.

In April 1895, Hart met with twenty-five other members of the American Historical Association to plan the *American Historical Review*. Hart had been a member of the association since shortly after it had been organized, and he had been actively working for the establishment of a scholarly journal for historians since 1892. Elected the first secretary-treasurer of the *American Historical Review*'s editorial board, he worked very hard to get the journal organized. He continued to serve on the editorial board during the first twelve years of the journal's existence and had much to do with formulating the high literary standards by which it operated.

By the 1890s the combined experience of Hart and his colleague Edward Channing had produced a virtual storehouse of ideas and materials for use in the teaching and studying of American history. The original idea to put these materials together into a reference book that would smooth the way for other teachers and scholars seems to have been Hart's, but beginning in 1893 the two professors collaborated on the project as equals. American history's first one-volume general reference book, *Guide to the Study of American History* (1896), was the result of their work. They filled the first two parts of their book with discussions about the nature of history, the value of the study of history, and the methods of teaching and research of history. Into the third part they put a well-organized, selected, but detailed, bibliography which covered the whole field of American history period by period. Then, they closed their work with a forty-three page double-column index to make it easy to use.

Publication of the *Guide to the Study of American History* brought praise for the editors and recognition for Harvard as the center for the study of American history. An unsigned review in the *American Historical Review*, which was probably written by J. Franklin Jameson, said, "it would be difficult to devise a book combining in itself more of the elements of practical utility." The first edition sold almost 9,000 copies, and the second edition, with Frederick Jackson Turner as an additional editor, sold another 7,000 copies. Eventually the *Guide* received new editors and the new title *Harvard Guide to American History* and as such continues to be known to every serious student of American history.

Hart often repeated the advice given to students by one of his German professors: "1) Read; 2) Read widely; 3) Read very widely." In *American History Told by Contemporaries* (1897-1929), he provided an anthology of letters, journals, speeches, poems, and autobiographical sketches to aid the student with his reading. Hart used a variety of materials that illustrated social, political, and economic conditions, showed how ordinary people lived, and gave more than one side of controversial issues. His

purpose was to provide his readers a "more real and more human" view of the past. These selections were intended for reading rather than research and reflected Hart's growing concern that students should view history as more than the political and military acts of a few great men. The original four-volume set of *American History Told by Contemporaries* was still in print when Hart retired in 1926. He added a fifth volume in 1929 to update the set. Looking back at the work of his mentor, Samuel Eliot Morison said in the mid-1940s that there had never been a better set of history readers than this one.

Although the first decade and one-half of his professional career had been filled with publications, most of Hart's work had had more to do with teaching and learning history than with the actual content of the subject. However, Hart did not completely forsake scholarly research, and the first book-length evidence of his work was *Salmon Portland Chase* (1899), which became the twenty-eighth volume of the American Statesmen series. Rather than writing a traditional, narrowly focused biography, Hart presented Chase as the central figure in three major historical developments. Therefore, he spent as much time describing the western antislavery movement, Civil War finances, and the Reconstruction-period Supreme Court as he did discussing Chase. Nevertheless, Chase did not suffer. Hart had carefully researched his subject using thousands of items from three collections of Chase's papers from which he appropriately quoted in his book. When he did choose to deal with Chase the man, Hart did so with an affinity that brought this difficult and complex figure to life without ignoring his many glaring faults. Hart ranked Chase as second only to Lincoln among the leaders of the Civil War era, but he also made it clear that he considered the gap between the two men to have been a wide one. This assessment of his subject raised eyebrows among Hart's reviewers; however, most agreed that his book was good and well-written history. Although Hart's book was the fourth biography of Chase to be written, it was popular with readers. It went through three editions, remained in print for over twenty years, and in the 1970s was reprinted as a part of three different series.

By the end of the century, Hart had every mark of the successful historian. American history was thriving at Harvard. His classes were well organized and well taught. His students were carrying his philosophy of history out into a world that was increasingly being influenced by Hart's thinking at both the academic and popular levels through his various publications. Harvard had recognized his achievements and given him the proper promotions, so that, in 1897, he received the rank of full professor. His private life was happy, too. His wife, Mary Hurd Putnam Hart, whom he had married in 1889, was an ideal professor's wife. In 1897, they adopted the twin sons who were their only children.

Because the end of the century was a time of change for the nation as it tried to determine its proper role on the world stage, Hart found much use for his theory that history was a valuable tool in understanding the present and making decisions about the future. There was considerable demand for what he had to say about such issues as isolationism, expansion, the Monroe Doctrine, and colonization, and, as always, Hart had plenty to say. He wrote a number of articles and eventually brought the best of them together into *Foundations of American Foreign Policy* (1901). Although he spoke as the voice of history, many of his points were very controversial. For example, he insisted that the nation's isolationist past had been greatly exaggerated, and he marshalled an impressive array of facts to support his conclusion. He also opposed imperialism, which he saw as a perversion of the spirit of democracy that had been the central theme of American history. One reviewer thanked him for providing some sane perspective, while another accused him of exaggerating history for his own purposes and in a scathing review criticized even the book's title as being far too big for a volume that was "merely a bunch of magazine articles." *Foundations of American Foreign Policy* may have been controversial in 1901, but it was important enough to be among Hart's books to be reprinted in the 1970s.

Although Hart broadened his interests, he never lost his belief that the most important part of United States history was the study of government. However, his focus was primarily on the practical workings of the government rather than on the principles of political science. He believed that there was great value in studying government from the bottom up rather than from the top down. Calling his concept "actual government," he wrote a college-level textbook to be used for such a study. *Actual Government as Applied Under American Conditions* (1903) brought to many their first realization that government could be studied as an everyday operation. Walter Wheeler Cook, who attempted to use Hart's book at the University of Nebraska, was very disappointed in it since he felt that theory had been too much subordinated and the book too carelessly written. However, not everyone agreed with Cook because the volume went through four editions and

remained a popular textbook for over twenty years.

At the same time that Hart was working on *Actual Government as Applied Under American Conditions*, he was also editing a series of high school textbooks. He included volumes on ancient, medieval, and modern English and United States history in the series, and he also wrote the volume on United States history. Entitled *Essentials in American History (From Discovery to the Present Day)* and published in 1905, this book applied Hart's philosophy of history to the high school level of the educational process. He emphasized political history but also included some social, economic, and diplomatic materials. Unlike many of his contemporaries, he gave very limited attention to military history, yet his tone was deeply patriotic, leaving no doubts that he was asking his readers to study the greatest nation on earth.

However, textbooks were only a small part of Hart's literary output during the early years of the twentieth century. In 1902, he announced the creation of a new series, *The American Nation: A History*, and requested that the Massachusetts Historical Society appoint a five-man committee to serve as consultants for this monumental cooperative enterprise. He planned twenty-five volumes to be arranged in chronological order, with each volume to be written by a professional historian with a special interest in the period about which he was writing. Hart's goal was a short definitive work on each period of United States history written from original sources and containing an extensive bibliography. Reserving the volume on slavery and abolition for himself, he chose twenty-four of the nation's best-known professional historians to write the other volumes, but he himself painstakingly planned the topics to be covered in each. Hart was generally a patient and good-natured man, but he was a very strict editor whose blue pencil worked overtime correcting, cutting, and consolidating the material sent to him so that it would produce the uniform volumes that he envisioned. He had no qualms about enforcing deadlines, and the result was that by 1908 the series, which eventually ran to twenty-eight volumes, was virtually complete. Hart even managed to get a completed book from the notorious procrastinator, Frederick Jackson Turner, but he had to resort to sending the famed Western historian a series of collect telegrams in order to accomplish the feat.

The American Nation: A History was promptly labeled the American Nation series, and among its volumes was Hart's own *Slavery and Abolition, 1831-1841* (1906). In planning the series Hart had decided that the great controversy over slavery deserved an entire volume, and he made room for it between William MacDonald's volume on the Jacksonian era and George Pierce Garrison's volume on western expansion, even at the expense of proper chronology. Although the subject matter was not his major area of interest, he decided to write the volume himself. He began the writing of the book with three chapters on the intellectual, social, and economic climate of the 1820s and used this information as the backdrop against which to discuss slavery in the South and abolition in the North. Most of Hart's work was descriptive, but the dearth of available sources in the South, which caused him to depend far too much on Frederick Law Olmsted, made writing difficult. Yet he managed to do the most extensive description of the workings of the slavery system that had been done up to that time. In the North there were many sources, and they made Hart all too well aware of the complexities of abolition. By using the tenets of scientific history to steer him through the emotionalism that still surrounded both sides of his subject, Hart was able to arrive at some reasonably dispassionate conclusions. He determined that the primary evil of slavery was in the system rather than the practice of the system and that the South's great mistake was in hanging on to this outdated institution. So far as the abolitionists were concerned, Hart concluded that the real strength of the movement lay in the conservative western fragment and that the abolitionists had been successful primarily because they had been able to exploit the weaknesses of the slave system and successfully ride the wave of history. Hart had ironically illustrated his own part in the wave of history by doing a book that would soon be outdated because of the developing interest of historians in the two subjects upon which he wrote.

National Ideals Historically Traced, 1607-1907 (1907) was Hart's other contribution to the American Nation series. This was the concluding volume, except for the index, until a book covering the 1907-1917 period was added in 1918. Unlike the other volumes of the series, *National Ideals Historically Traced* was a topical study, a sort of national philosophy of life, written from the perspective of 1907. Hart defined what he perceived to be the national ideals or leading tendencies of American life and thought and then traced their development across the span of American history. Although his analysis was strongest in the area of government, he also dealt with geographical, social, economic, and diplomatic developments. Some of his former students saw shades of History 13 in the book. No

doubt it was, at least in part, an orderly explanation of the points that Hart had tried to communicate in the classroom, but more than anything else it was a statement of an era's philosophy of American history. One reviewer compared Hart to Alexis de Tocqueville.

The years following the publication of the American Nation series were busy ones for Hart. His career had reached its apex. To have been his student was often sufficient reference for a former graduate student to secure a university teaching position. In 1909, Hart was elected president of the American Historical Association. Always a joiner, he was active in an increasingly large number of organizations and willingly lent his name to numerous good causes. With so much publicity he was in great demand as a public speaker, and if there were anything that he enjoyed more than writing American history, it was talking about the subject. He was a large man with a sonorous voice and impressive diction. His flowing beard and moustaches, which caused him to be labeled "Bushy Hart" on campus, added a dramatic quality to his appearance as a platform guest, and his speeches with their patriotic emphasis were certain to draw applause. Hart thoroughly enjoyed his contacts with the American public and increasingly popularized even his writings.

The Southern South (1910) was as much a sociological study as a historical one. Hart had long been interested in the section of the United States which one of his pupils, Franklin D. Roosevelt, would soon be labeling the nation's number-one problem, and he used the materials gleaned from years of travel and research to make a study of Southern distinctiveness. He examined the geography, economy, educational system, customs, and people of the South and compared them with those of the North in a series of statistical tables that would have been at home in the appendix of a more recent book. His conclusion was that the key element making the South distinctive was race. Like many of his contemporaries, Hart considered the Negro inferior. Hence, he saw the Southern dilemma of two races living together in an environment where one had a monopoly on the advantages of life while the other had all the disadvantages. Yet he could recommend only patience and education as solutions. Nevertheless, Hart's book attracted great attention and was the most widely reviewed work that he had written up to that point. Often the reviews said more about their writers' sectionalism than they did about Hart's book, but most of them agreed that Hart had handled a difficult subject well. Continued interest in the volume has resulted in three reprints during the last fifteen years, and the 1969 reprint was reviewed in the *Georgia Historical Quarterly* in 1970.

While spending a 1908-1909 sabbatical leave on a trip around the world, Hart used his observations and experiences as the basis for *The Obvious Orient* (1911). In the book he assessed the power and potential of each of the oriental countries which he visited. He also shocked many of his readers by classing the United States as an oriental power. He concluded that both Japan and China possessed the ingredients for leadership but did not see either as a serious immediate threat to the United States. *The Obvious Orient* was not intended to be exhaustive or scholarly but simply the observations of a traveler whose experiences had equipped him to see things often unseen by others. Yet the interest in the Orient at that time and Hart's reputation as a scholar caused the book to get more attention than it deserved. Reviews were mixed. Some praised its readable, entertaining commentary, while others who tried to judge it as a scholarly work decried its superficiality.

In 1910, when the American history and American government departments at Harvard were separated, Hart was named Eaton Professor of the Science of Government and chairman of the government department. He took his courses in diplomatic history and federal systems with him into the government division but continued to teach History 13 in the history department until 1915-1916 when the course was reorganized and renumbered. Once again Hart found himself in the role of organizer and promoter for a new department, but he was never as effective in government as he had been in history. The department grew under his leadership, and in 1912 he was elected president of the American Political Science Association, but he remained much more a political historian than a political scientist.

Hart's major contribution to the field of government during his years as department chairman at Harvard was his work on *The Cyclopedia of American Government* (1914), which he jointly edited with Andrew C. McLaughlin, professor of history at the University of Chicago. The two men worked for four years compiling this three-volume reference work. It contained 2,890 entries written by 245 contributors, with Hart's contributions numbering 212. Because the editors defined the term "government" very broadly, they included much history and biography in the volumes. Reviewers complained of mistakes and careless errors. While im-

portant, *The Cyclopedia of American Government* never gained the stature in political science of Hart's reference books in history.

During 1913, Hart had traveled in the Balkans and had written a series of articles for the *New York Times*; thus when war broke out in that part of the world during the summer of 1914, Hart drew from his knowledge of the area to write *The War in Europe: Its Causes and Results* (1915). Not intended as a definitive work, this little book was simply a popular effort to explain to the American public what he knew about the causes of the war and its possible effects on the United States.

Appearing in the same year was *The Monroe Doctrine: An Interpretation* (1915), Hart's last scholarly monograph and the most analytical of his works. Because he believed that Americans misunderstood the Monroe Doctrine, he set out to show them that this basic element in United States foreign policy was "not a term but a treatise; not a statement but a literature; not an event but an historic development." He maintained that the most consistent principle in United States foreign relations was the principle of self-interest. He showed how various presidents and secretaries of state had modified the Monroe Doctrine to fit their perceptions of the nation's best interests, gradually shaping what he called the "Paramount Interest Doctrine." Although the book was basically a historical study, Hart did not stop with history. He went on to discuss the pros and cons of the nation's current policy toward Latin America and Europe and to recommend another modification which he labeled the "Permanent Interest Policy." His tightly reasoned, highly organized discussion of this controversial current issue drew a great deal of attention. There were numerous reviews in both popular and scholarly journals. Most reviewers were impressed with Hart's ideas, and all were impressed with the quality of his writing.

During World War I, Hart continued to teach, to present public lectures, and to write. Now often referred to as the "Grand Old Man of American History," his name was synonymous with love of country based on a knowledge of its past. Yet in 1918, when a Senate subcommittee released to the press a German agent's mailing list which contained Hart's name, newspapers insinuated that he was pro-German. Incensed, Hart demanded a hearing. He told the subcommittee that he had written 100 articles about the war, every one of them either neutral or anti-German. With the vigorous assistance of Theodore Roosevelt, Hart publicly cleared his name.

During the war years, Hart wrote two more high school history textbooks. Both were surveys aimed at describing the events and people who had led the nation to greatness. *New American History* (1917) was unique in that one-third of its chapters dealt with the post-Civil War period. *School History of the United States* (1918) combined social with political history and included chapters on such topics as "How People Lived a Century Ago" and "New Business Methods, 1829-1860." It was well illustrated and contained fifteen maps. Both books were very popular and were widely used in high schools for twenty years.

Although he did not produce any more monographs, Hart continued his literary efforts well into old age. He wrote numerous articles, forewords, and encyclopedia entries. Furthermore, with the assistance of David Maydole Matteson, Hart turned the wall maps which he had earlier edited with Herbert Bolton into American history's first historical atlas, *American History Atlas* (1918), and also wrote a teacher's manual to go with the wall maps. In addition, he edited *The American Yearbook* for fifteen years and revised several of his earlier works. In the late 1920s he put together a five-volume history of the state of Massachusetts, *The Commonwealth History of Massachusetts* (1927-1930). In this cooperative venture each chapter was written by a different author, and Hart, as editor, had major problems with overlap and quality. However, the finished work was hailed as a model to emulate in the writing of state history. Unfortunately, the company that printed the books went out of business before they were widely distributed, and the work was not reprinted until 1967. Hart's last project was the *Theodore Roosevelt Cyclopedia* (1941). This tribute to his friend was a collection of Roosevelt quotes about everything from the Abbey Theatre to the Young Men's Christian Association. The volume was edited with the assistance of Herbert R. Ferlerger.

Although he kept busy, Hart's last years were often sad and lonely. His wife died in 1924, and his sons, with whom his relationships had never been good, neglected him. He retired in 1926 and was named professor emeritus, but many of his younger colleagues treated him with what he called "supercilious superiority." However, as the historian on the George Washington Bicentennial Commission, Hart worked very hard during the 1926-1932 period. He also continued to travel widely and even made a trip to Russia in 1929. Furthermore, he continued to give his views freely. In an interview with the *Harvard Crimson*, he explained, "I am not setting myself up as a sage. I am an old man, I have taught perhaps 10,000 students, I have traveled much of the world and I believe I know the men and ways of nations." Hart died on 16 June 1943, just short of his eighty-ninth birthday.

His work from "Two Cleveland Boys Go Travelling" to the *Theodore Roosevelt Cyclopedia* represented sixty-seven years of literary endeavor for Albert Bushnell Hart. Through these writings Hart tried to teach his generation how to learn American history, gave them tools with which to learn it, and provided examples of its value by using it himself to throw light on important current issues. His well-organized, simply written, and often quietly humorous works were very well received by his generation. The scientific history was his creed, and he used it to deal with a past to which his generation was still so close that only its methods could provide any hope of objective study. Yet Hart was not a slave to "scientific" history. In his presidential address to the American Historical Association, he told his fellow historians, "there is much in history which cannot be measured like atomic weights, or averaged like insurance losses." He went on to call for the use of the right kind of "imagination" in the study and writing of history and to employ it himself in a massive effort to teach Americans love of their country based upon an understanding of its past.

Although Hart's works were generally well received by both the scholarly and popular communities of his day, during the last years of his life many historians were beginning to question his methods and to criticize his style. Yet even in the middle years of the twentieth century when historians saw his work as superficial and simplistic, they generally recognized the value of the American Nation series and of the *Guide to the Study of American History* as important historiographical developments. In the 1970s there was enough interest to produce reprints of most of Hart's scholarly works. Furthermore, as American historians become increasingly involved in the study of historiography, they will undoubtedly come increasingly to agree with one of their colleagues who at the time of Hart's death called him "the most useful historical worker of his generation."

Other:

"Methods of Teaching American History," in *Methods of Teaching History*, edited by Stanley Hall (Boston: D. C. Heath, 1885);
American History Leaflets, edited by Hart and Edward Channing (New York: Lovell, 1891-1902);

Epochs of American History series, 4 volumes, edited by Hart (New York & London: Longmans, Green, 1892-1926);

American History Told By Contemporaries, 5 volumes, edited by Hart (New York & London: Macmillan, 1897-1929);

The American Nation: A History, 28 volumes, edited by Hart (New York & London: Harper, 1904-1928);

Essentials in History series, 4 volumes, edited by Hart (New York & Cincinnati: American Book, 1905);

The Cyclopedia of American Government, 3 volumes, edited by Hart and Andrew C. McLaughlin (New York & London: Appleton, 1914);

American History Atlas, edited by Hart, David Maydole Matteson, and Herbert Bolton (Chicago: Denoyer-Geppert, 1918);

Commonwealth History of Massachusetts, 5 volumes, edited by Hart (New York: States History Company, 1927-1930);

Theodore Roosevelt Cyclopedia, edited by Hart and Herbert R. Ferlerger (New York: Roosevelt Memorial Association, 1941).

References:
Carol F. Baird, "Albert Bushnell Hart: The Rise of

the Professional Historian," in Social Sciences at Harvard, 1860-1920: From Inculcation to the Open Mind, edited by Paul H. Buck (Cambridge: Harvard University Press, 1965), pp. 129-174;

Lester J. Cappon, "Channing and Hart: Partners in Bibliography," New England Quarterly, 29 (September 1956): 319-340;

"Historical News," American Historical Review, 49 (October 1943): 192-194;

Samuel Eliot Morison, "Albert Bushnell Hart, 1889-1939," Proceedings of the Massachusetts Historical Society, 65 (October 1936-May 1941): 435-438;

Morison, "A Memoir and Estimate of Albert Bushnell Hart," Proceedings of the Massachusetts Historical Society, 72 (1965): 28-52;

Clifford K. Shipton, "Albert Bushnell Hart," American Antiquarian Society Proceedings, 53 (20 October 1943): 120-125;

B. F. Wright, A. M. Schlesinger, Sr., and C. H. McIlwain, "Albert Bushnell Hart," Harvard Gazette, 39 (18 December 1943): 103-104.

Papers:
Some of Hart's papers are in the Harvard University Archives.

Robert Selph Henry
(20 October 1889 - 18 August 1970)

Thomas Fleming
College of Charleston

BOOKS: The Story of the Confederacy (Indianapolis: Bobbs-Merrill, 1931); revised edition, with foreword by Douglas S. Freeman (New York: Grosset & Dunlap 1936);

Trains (Indianapolis: Bobbs-Merrill, 1934);

The Story of Reconstruction (Indianapolis & New York: Bobbs-Merrill, 1938);

This Fascinating Railroad Business (Indianapolis & New York: Bobbs-Merrill, 1942);

"First with the Most" Forrest (Indianapolis & New York: Bobbs-Merrill, 1944);

The Story of the Mexican War (Indianapolis & New York: Bobbs-Merrill, 1950).

Robert Selph Henry was a Southern historian of the War Between the States who constructed in

separate works taken together a unified narrative of the period from the Mexican War to the end of Reconstruction, a period which Henry saw as the crucible out of which emerged the American nation. His books, based on a solid foundation of original research and careful thought, were written in a popular dramatic style that captured a wide readership for three decades. This very popularity, combined with his amateur standing, has caused Henry's name almost to disappear from notice in recent years. Yet Robert Selph Henry was the best sort of amateur historian. His active career as newspaperman, lawyer, railroad executive, and soldier gave him a wider perspective on men and events than is granted to most professionals.

Henry, the son of Robert Allison and Emily

James Selph Henry, was born in Clifton, Tennessee. On his father's side, his family had lived in the South since the early eighteenth century. He attended public school and Wallace's University School in Nashville before going on to Vanderbilt, where he received an L.L.B. in 1910 and an A.B. with Phi Beta Kappa honors in 1911. After World War I he spent a year at Queen's College, Cambridge. He did not further pursue an advanced degree, but in 1950 Henry received an honorary doctorate from the University of Chattanooga.

While a student at Vanderbilt, Henry went to work as a reporter for the *Nashville Tennessean*. After graduation he continued his reporting, both at the *Tennessean* and at the *Nashville Banner*, until 1913. Between 1913 and 1915 Henry was employed as private secretary to the governor of Tennessee, Ben W. Hooper, and between 1915 and 1921 he

practiced law. His legal career was briefly curtailed when Henry joined the U.S. Army in 1917 and soon found himself in France, a captain in the Field Artillery. He remained in the Army Reserve, in which he attained the rank of lieutenant colonel, until his formal retirement in 1952.

The major part of Henry's career was devoted to railroads. He served as assistant to the vice-president of the Nashville, Chattanooga, and St. Louis Railroad from 1921 to 1934 and as assistant to the president and vice-president of the Association of American Railroads from 1934 to 1958. Henry's primary service to the American railroad lay in education and public relations. He was indefatigable in promoting railroads: arranging special studies, organizing a film library and photographic file, producing radio programs, and distributing educational materials to the schools. Henry's enthusiasm for the American railroad was not confined to promotion. Between 1934 and 1945 he wrote numerous articles and two books—*Trains* (1934) and *This Fascinating Railroad Business* (1942)—on railroading.

Henry's connections with trains served him well when he wrote his first serious work of history, *The Story of the Confederacy* (1931). As Douglas Southall Freeman observed in the foreword to Henry's revised 1936 edition, the Southern rail systems "meant more than mountain ranges and scarcely less than the great rivers in determining the lines of attack and defense." No Civil War historian before Henry had paid quite so much attention to logistical problems of supply, transportation, and artillery technology, and no one after him could afford to neglect them.

If Henry seemed devoted to the portrayal of combat, it was not because he viewed war as a matter of glory. "There is no wisdom in war," he wrote in the preface to his revised 1936 edition of *The Story of the Confederacy*; "the thing itself is the negation of reason." Henry's experience in World War I had taught him that expectation of profit could no longer be regarded as a primary cause of war, since "there is no profit in war, win or lose. . . . no net in the venture." In Henry's view it was pride, Northern as well as Southern, that made war between the sections inevitable. At stake was the Federal Constitution itself, the definition of the states in their relation to the nation. The Southern states' attempt to exercise the right of a state to leave the Union was an abstract right in collision with "the concrete forces of economics and the inevitable trend of history." Thus Henry regarded the War Between the States as the central event of American history: "To crush 'the rebellion,' the North wrought a revolution" in which the states "have contentedly sunk from the sovereignty they so jealously maintained in 1787 to become little more than convenient administrative subdivisions of government."

Although Henry was not unconcerned with issues and ideas, the story of the Confederacy was, for him, the story of a war. As a result, the chief actors were warriors and not politicians. It was Lee, Jackson, and Forrest—above all Forrest—who occupied his attention. Henry was also particularly drawn to ingenious and less-known men of action who, out of the paltriest of materials, could rig together a brilliant success—men like "Prince John" Magruder, with his convincing "demonstrations" of nonexistent strength, and Isaac N. Brown, who constructed and commanded his own homemade ironclad, the *Arkansas*. As a result of this preoccupation with military affairs, the great political leaders and issues, on both sides, dwindled in significance. President Davis and his cabinet remained mere shadows, since Henry, like most Southerners, regarded Davis as great only in defeat. Even Lincoln was reduced to merely human proportions. Henry's Tennessee background may have given him a healthy skepticism for Lincoln's conduct of the war.

Henry's strong suit was his forceful, journalistic style combined with a clear vision of the events he was relating. A careful reader was rarely in doubt over such matters as geography, troop disposition and movements, or the significance of terrain and logistics. It was as if the historian felt it necessary to visualize an entire sequence of events before making any attempt to describe them. The result was a narrative clarity unusual among twentieth-century historians. Henry so valued clarity that he was willing to sacrifice drama in the interest of a lucid exposition. Some readers might even be disconcerted by the advance summaries prefixing the accounts of nearly every major battle or campaign.

In all his historical works, Henry not only sacrificed drama for clarity but also grappled honestly with sources. When, as sometimes happened, he was unable to reconcile conflicting sources in a coherent narrative, he resorted to the honest methods of Herodotus: he gave both sides. This quality was especially evident in his biography, *"First with the Most" Forrest* (1944), arguably his best work, both as a portrait of the title figure and as a useful introduction to the war's campaigns. In Forrest, a fellow Tennessean, Henry had found his subject. If *The Story of the Confederacy*, especially in the eyes of academic historians, suffered from its lack of footnotes and bibliography, the defect was to a great extent made up in the Forrest biography which contained a three-page bibliography of major sources as well as over sixty-five pages of notes.

The Bedford Forrest who emerged from Henry's painstaking and affectionate account was a three-dimensional figure saved from those admirers—as well as critics—who saw in him the archetypal poor white. Although Forrest proverbially outlined strategy as "To git thar fustest with the mostest men," Henry convincingly argued that Forrest actually said, "First with the most"; thus his title reflected the historian's efforts to take the true measure of his subject. The fairness of Henry's portrait was further revealed in his treatment of Forrest as a military leader. The general emerged as prudent and almost tenderly solicitous for his men, not as reckless and violent. Forrest, who did possess a temper, was enraged by nothing so much as the needless sacrifice of life. After the pointless and suicidal attack on Dover in 1863, for example, he refused ever to serve under Joe Wheeler again, a refusal that Wheeler was wise enough to honor. In actual combat, Forrest was by all accounts a fierce warrior scattering Yankees with his sharpened saber and his revolver and outrunning his own men in a charge; however, the greater part of his genius lay in his ability to think and to bluff. Like any sensible commander, Forrest always preferred to attain his objectives with the fewest possible risks.

If Bedford Forrest was no *beau sabreur* of the school of Jeb Stuart, he was in most respects a gentleman whose courtliness toward women of all ages was well established. Henry delightedly recounted Forrest's courtship of Mary Ann Montgomery and his gallantry to young Emma Samson. These episodes, along with his depiction of Forrest's behavior after the war, went a long way toward filling in the details of a complex character; tough, determined, and tempestuous, Henry's Forrest proved equally prudent, compassionate, and—in the end—religious, although his piety did not put an end to his cussing. Yet, however fascinating the general was as a subject, Forrest's own contribution to the effort was set firmly in the context of the wider strategies of Grant, Buell, and Sherman as well as of Johnson, Bragg, and Hood.

The Story of Reconstruction (1938), which was written before the Forrest book but which treated events following those in *"First with the Most" Forrest*, focused not on military matters but instead on the less congenial subject of politics, although Henry did view the period as a generally unarmed continuation of the struggle between the two regions. "The hardest part of war is not the fighting, but the cleaning up afterwards" might serve as the emblem of his Reconstruction history, since the years from 1865 to 1876 constituted a period of disorder, animosity, and adversity unparalleled in the nation's history.

Any general treatment of Reconstruction must be the history of the reconstructions of eleven states, each with its own political feuds, unique problems, and dominant personalities. Apart from introductory chapters and those on general themes, Henry sensibly approached the subject on a state-by-state basis. Such an approach, of course, tended to produce a statehouse history—all local politics with insufficient reference to national political issues, much less to economic and social forces that were helping to shape the United States in that critical period. Henry did devote chapters to education, Congressional activities, elections, and the impeachment of Andrew Johnson. Still, *The Story of Reconstruction* seemed more a mosaic than a continuous exposition. Despite the book's deficiencies and limitations, a reviewer in *The American Historical Review* described *The Story of Reconstruction* as "the best one volume work on the subject for the general reader." The same reviewer found Henry "uncommonly accurate" and "fair to both races." Remarkably evenhanded in his treatment of racial politics, Henry found good things to say about many black legislators in the Reconstruction governments while at the same time offering a defense of the activities of the Ku Klux Klan. It is doubtful that any historian writing today could risk such impartiality.

The last book in what could be called a Civil War chronicle was *The Story of the Mexican War* (1950), a work which Henry apparently regarded as a kind of preface to his earlier volumes. He quite rightly regarded the Mexican War as a kind of dress rehearsal for the Civil War. The Mexican War was also one of the causes of the Civil War, since the 1846-1848 conflict raised the question of the extension of slavery to the central position in the North/South political debate. Consistent with his vision of the Mexican War as a precursor of the Civil War, Henry was careful, whenever possible, to relate the role played by American officers in the Mexican conflict to their later activities in the Civil War.

In the great vexed issues of the Mexican War—the comparative worth of Generals Scott and Taylor, the claims and fighting ability of the Mexicans—Henry pursued a neutral course. His fairness to the Mexicans was unusual even so recently as 1950. Furthermore, as in his earlier histories, Henry stuck to the narrative. He was able to

make use of a great deal of research on the Mexican War and appeared to have done little of his own. Yet without offering either original research or new interpretations, Henry did succeed in sorting through the evidence and controversies to produce a lucid and consistent account. Debated issues or even critical judgments interrupted the flow of the story even more rarely than in previous works. The tale was the thing, and a good job was done in the telling. However, despite the adherence of the text to narrative, an underlying revisionist theme was made evident in Henry's preface: "Prevailing impressions of the Mexican War have been derived . . . from the writings of those who seem to have regarded the westward push of American population north of the Missouri Compromise line as a mission to civilize a continent, while looking upon the like westward push of population south of 36 degrees 30 minutes of North latitude as due to the machinations of the 'slave power.' "

In 1957 Robert Selph Henry became president of the Southern Historical Association, one of the few nonacademic historians to receive that distinction before or since. The required presidential address afforded Henry an opportunity to reflect on the South's part in the great affairs of U.S. history in a way that related to the theme that has been mentioned in *The Story of the Mexican War*. His theme was "West by South," a resumé of the predominant role played by Southerners in America's westward expansion. From the Virginian George Rogers Clark's activities at Vincennes to Jefferson's purchase of Louisiana to Andrew Jackson's victory at New Orleans (a battle which Henry insists saved Louisiana for the United States) to Sam Houston's endeavors in Texas—the westward expansion was led and carried out by Southern men. The movement climaxed in the campaign to annex Texas under Presidents Tyler (Virginia) and Polk (Tennessee) and in the Mexican War conducted by Generals Scott (Virginia) and Taylor (Louisiana).

Henry had grown up in Tennessee at a time when sectional animosities and jealousies were still lively to the point of bitterness. In World War I he apparently learned, as so many other Americans learned, that the Civil War was over and that the future belonged to the *United* States. If he remained keenly interested in his region's honor, it was not because he wished to be divisive. In Henry's eyes, the South's glories belonged to the nation. His literary efforts attempted to heal the old wounds and to make Northerners and Southerners proud of belonging to the same nation. *The Story of the Confederacy* appeared almost twenty years before Bruce

Catton's first volume and was a more serious and less journalistic kind of popular history than became predominant later. Douglas Southall Freeman, testifying to the popularity and respect accorded to Henry's history, said: "I regard *The Story of the Confederacy* . . . as . . . at present the book with which to begin one's study of the period it covers and the book to which to return when everything else on the subject has been read."

Other:

Headlights and Markers: An Anthology of Railroad Stories, edited by Henry and Frank P. Donovan

(New York: Creative Age Press, 1946);

As They Saw Forrest: Some Recollections and Comments of Contemporaries, edited by Henry (Jackson, Tenn.: McCowat-Mercer, 1956);

"West by South," in *The Pursuit of Southern History: Presidential Addresses of the Southern Historical Association, 1935–1963*, edited by George B. Tindall (Baton Rouge: Louisiana State University Press, 1964).

Papers:

Some Henry manuscripts are located in the Tennessee State Library.

Richard Hofstadter

Paula S. Fass
University of California, Berkeley

BIRTH: Buffalo, New York, 6 August 1916, to Emil A. and Katherine Hill Hofstadter.

EDUCATION: B.A., University of Buffalo, 1937; M.A., 1938, Ph.D., 1942, Columbia University.

MARRIAGES: 5 October 1936 to Felice Swados; child: Dan. 13 January 1947 to Beatrice Kevitt; child: Sarah Katherine.

AWARDS AND HONORS: Albert J. Beveridge Memorial Fund Award for "Social Darwinism in American Thought, 1860-1915," 1942; Pulitzer Prize for *The Age of Reform*, 1956; Emerson Award of Phi Beta Kappa for *Anti-Intellectualism in American Life*, 1963; Sidney Hillman Award for *Anti-Intellectualism in American Life*, 1963; Pulitzer Prize for *Anti-Intellectualism in American Life*, 1964.

DEATH: New York, New York, 24 October 1970.

BOOKS: *Social Darwinism in American Thought, 1860-1915* (Philadelphia: University of Pennsylvania Press, 1944; London: Oxford University Press, 1944); revised as *Social Darwinism in American Thought* (Boston: Beacon Press, 1955);

The American Political Tradition and the Men Who Made It (New York: Knopf, 1948; London: Cape, 1962);

Richard Hofstadter

The Development and Scope of Higher Education in the United States, by Hofstadter and C. DeWitt Hardy (New York: Columbia University Press, 1952);

The Development of Academic Freedom in the United States, part one by Hofstadter, part two by Walter P. Metzger (New York: Columbia University Press, 1955); part one republished separately as *Academic Freedom in the Age of the College* (New York: Columbia University Press, 1961);

The Age of Reform: From Bryan to F.D.R. (New York: Knopf, 1955; London: Cape, 1962);

The Constitution, by Joseph N. Welch, with Hofstadter and the Staff of Omnibus (Boston: Houghton Mifflin, 1956);

The United States: The History of A Republic, by Hofstadter, Daniel Aaron, and William Miller (Englewood Cliffs, N.J.: Prentice-Hall, 1957);

The American Republic, by Hofstadter, Aaron, and Miller, 2 volumes (Englewood Cliffs, N.J.: Prentice-Hall, 1959);

Anti-Intellectualism in American Life (New York: Knopf, 1963; London: Cape, 1964);

The Structure of American History, by Hofstadter, Miller, and Aaron (Englewood Cliffs, N.J.: Prentice-Hall, 1964);

The Paranoid Style in American Politics and Other Essays (New York: Knopf, 1965; London: Cape, 1966);

The Progressive Historians: Turner, Beard, Parrington (New York: Knopf, 1968; London: Cape, 1969);

The Idea of A Party System: The Rise of Legitimate Opposition in the United States, 1780-1840 (Berkeley, California: University of California Press, 1969);

America at 1750: A Social Portrait (New York: Knopf, 1971; London: Cape, 1972).

The most influential and one of the most distinguished American historians of the period between World War II and the Vietnam War, Richard Hofstadter epitomized the cosmopolitan, intellectual culture of the New York of his time. A vigorous exponent of cultural pluralism, internationalism, and secular modernism, Hofstadter's historical writing helped to define the mood and commitments of an era. His history, which often had a cutting edge, spoke to a wide audience and cast light on contemporary concerns while it sharply recast historians' views of the American past. A man of strong commitments, acerbic wit, and remarkable critical intelligence, Richard Hofstadter was also

one of the gentlest of men. Admired by friends, colleagues, and students for his personal civility and unpretentious charm, Hofstadter attained in his maturity an intellectual poise, personal integrity, and literary grace that reflected a lifetime of disciplined thought.

Hofstadter's scholarship was remarkable in its scope and penetration, but it was always very personal and written with an exploratory tone. Although the subjects of his writings ranged from the Puritans to the events of the 1960s, he never proposed a grandiose design or a single unifying vision of the past. Indeed, from the beginning of his career, he sought ways to dispute the single causal explanations of his intellectual mentors, especially Charles Beard, with whose simple materialist views Hofstadter wrestled intellectually throughout his career and whose interpretations he did much to replace. This work often classed Hofstadter among those described as "consensus historians," but that categorization obscures far more than it reveals about his thought and his work's significance. Hofstadter was neither a member nor a founder of a school of history. He was an independent who rejected the universal explanatory power of social science, just as he rejected all attempts to reduce the multiplicity of human experience found in history to any single cause, influence, or rigid constellation of factors. His temperament and talents sought out the unexpected, the previously unconsidered, often the apparently marginal aspects of events. In exploring their historical significance, he always added to the complexity of historical analysis and understanding.

In the quest for complexity, Hofstadter used whatever insights and concepts he could appropriate from among the social sciences, from psychology, and from literary criticism. Although he thereby enriched the resources available to historians in their search for explanations, Hofstadter's greatest contribution to history writing and thought probably lay less in his specific theses (although these were often shrewd and suggestive) than in the lucid style of his inquiry and his refusal to be satisfied by static answers. His work thus reflected as it proclaimed the nondogmatic values he lived by. Unlike his mentor Beard, he was never dismayed by historical relativism. He simply took it for granted and worked within its confines. In rejecting the sufficiency of large schemes and in abhorring the arrogance of all human pretensions to mastery—political totalitarianism, cultural imperialism, intellectual dogmatism, Hofstadter in his final years took comfort in the tragic endurance which for him was history's final message to its students.

Hofstadter's skepticism about simple answers and final truths and his commitment to secular, cosmopolitan values may have reflected the ambiguous pattern of his childhood and youth. The older of two children, he was born in Buffalo, New York, to Emil A. Hofstadter, a Polish-born Jewish immigrant, and Katherine Hill Hofstadter, an American-born Episcopalian of German background. Hofstadter thus grew up in a household that suggested some of the complexity of American culture. Although his mother died when he was ten, he was raised as a Protestant. Hofstadter later rejected both the church and the social and cultural affiliation to which it entitled him. He never subsequently saw religion as an important form of personal expression or as a significant resource. Nevertheless, he tended to define himself in terms of his father's Jewish and international roots. This self-perception, which enhanced his social marginality and probably his intellectual distance from the culture which he spent a lifetime studying, was thus, in part, freely chosen. It was augmented by his marriage in 1936 to Felice Swados, who was of Jewish descent and whom Hofstadter met as an undergraduate at the University of Buffalo.

Hofstadter's undergraduate years at Buffalo (1933-1936), where he studied history and philosophy, were significant also because they introduced him to the activist left-wing politics which engaged so many of America's intellectuals in the 1930s and inspired smart and rebellious college students of the period. At Buffalo, as elsewhere, Jewish students were especially prominent in politics, and Hofstadter's involvement with this group probably enhanced his identification with his Jewish father. At the same time, radical politics fed young Hofstadter's rebellion against authority and father figures of all kinds. This ambivalence, which required that he at once reject and identify with the same object, continued to define Hofstadter's extraordinarily subtle historical posture during his later career as a critic from *inside* the liberal tradition; the same ambivalence underlay the precarious balance he tried to maintain as a detached historical observer and an engaged social critic. It was also reflected, early and late, in his bold but loving battles with his predecessors, the Progressive historians. Politics provided Hofstadter with a fulcrum for that rebelliousness, indeed for the testing out of that alienation, which he saw as essential to the truly interesting and vigorous mind. Unlike William Jennings Bryan, whom he described in *The American Political Tradition and the Men Who Made It* (1948) as "Intellectually . . . a

boy who never left home" and as a figure whose "torpor of mind" came from a lack of "a sense of alienation," Hofstadter left home early and decisively. In helping him to identify as a marginal Jew, a political leftist, and a determined intellectual, Hofstadter's undergraduate years separated him from that commonplace, lower-middle-class, Protestant respectability that he at least partially glimpsed as the potential of his Buffalo childhood. At the same time, his college experience prepared him for New York.

Hofstadter arrived in New York at just the point in his life and in the life of the city that would prove extraordinarily fertile for each. In 1936, Hofstadter was a young man who had recently married and was about to begin preparation for the vocation to which he would commit the rest of his life. Just then, New York was becoming the center of a dynamic international culture, which was newly enlivened by a large, intellectual refugee immigration from Hitler's Europe, intensely excited by the prevailing Marxist dialectics of the time as well as the more immediate issues of Franklin Roosevelt's presidency, and engrossed in the growing international tensions soon to explode into war and genocide. Hofstadter was aroused by the intellectual and political whirlpools of this milieu and yet almost preternaturally able to distance himself from them. Alfred Kazin has described him at this time as "a natural conservative in a radical period, with a melancholy knowledge of the shoals and traps of human nature." He was already adept at the skeptical humor and talented mimicry that delighted his friends for the rest of his life and that were a means for him at once to empathize with and to create distance between himself and the objects of his observation. Despite his wife's deep and continued commitment to radical politics, Hofstadter began early to separate himself from its seductions. By the time of the Hitler-Stalin Pact of 1939, Hofstadter had already broken from the dominant Stalinism of New York's radical left. Unlike many New York intellectuals, he never found it necessary to defend and rationalize the actions of the Soviet Union internationally or domestically. In this, as in so much of his subsequent behavior, he was ever the independent. Years later, Hofstadter remarked that even in the heady atmosphere of the 1930s he had been engaged in studying "the formation and development of ideologies" which were "far more interesting for their extraordinary appeal to various types of individuals than they were for their rational and philosophical content." Politics had been a liberating force for the young Hofstadter. While he took politics seriously throughout his life, identifying himself even years later as a "radical liberal," politics had provided him with stimulating questions rather than certain answers and with a posture for obtaining the detachment he needed for study and for reflection.

In 1937, Hofstadter began his graduate studies at Columbia, the university with which he was affiliated for all but four years during the rest of his life and to which, despite tempting offers from other institutions, he would remain deeply loyal and attached. Hofstadter had scarcely commenced his studies when he began those exercises in writing history that would make him one of the most productive historians of his generation. His first article, "The Tariff Issue on the Eve of the Civil War," published in the *American Historical Review* in 1938, was a sparse, densely argued brief disputing the exaggerated role the Beards assigned to the tariff in the causation of the Civil War. In the essay Hofstadter wasted no time getting down to the empirical evidence, and although the exercise was a not undistinguished first appearance by a historian, it hardly foreshadowed the rich interpretive talents upon which his reputation would be based. It did, however, introduce a young man who boldly took on the big problems as well as the important historians, and it became the first scuffle of a lifelong contention with Charles Beard. From the beginning to the end of his life, Beard loomed not only as the intellectual father to be overthrown but as the master historian whose scholarship and example as an independent thinker were alone worthy of rebellious imitation.

At Columbia Hofstadter earned his M.A. in 1938 and his Ph.D. in 1942. While still a student, he published several articles in addition to his tariff paper, including one critical of another admired and inspiring mentor, Vernon L. Parrington, and he produced as well a steady stream of reviews. He also taught at Brooklyn College and the City College of New York. Most significantly, he completed work in 1942 on the dissertation that would shortly bring him recognition, "Social Darwinism in American Thought." That same year, Hofstadter was appointed assistant professor at the University of Maryland, where he remained until 1946. In 1944, Hofstadter's dissertation was published under the auspices of the American Historical Association by the University of Pennsylvania Press. With its appearance, Hofstadter's professional career began.

Social Darwinism in American Thought, 1860-1915 (1944) was not only an impressive book by a young historian but also an important contribution to American historiography. In the *New York Times Sunday Book Review*, Howard Mumford Jones described it as "compact, lucid, informed, vigorous," anticipating the adjectives which would thereafter define Hofstadter's intellectual style. More significantly, reviewers noted that the young historian had taken ideas seriously as "weapons of change and implements of action" and that he had undertaken the important task of describing the complex relationship between ideas and social change. Ray Billington called *Social Darwinism* an "important book" and "a rich contribution" to the "history of ideas."

The significance of Hofstadter's first book can be gauged by the fact that it was republished in a revised edition in 1955 and that his study probably more than any other introduced the idea and phrase "social Darwinism" into the fund of generally accepted intellectual concepts. At the same time, the book was modest and unpretentious. Hofstadter did not demonstrate the significance of Darwinism as an animating cultural vision during the Gilded Age as a whole. Despite a chapter entitled the "Vogue of Spencer" that examined the currency of such phrases as "survival of the fittest" and "struggle for existence" among American capitalists, *Social Darwinism* was primarily an analysis of the application of Darwinist and Spencerian ideas by social scientists in the period between the Civil War and World War I. *Social Darwinism* is less about the role of evolutionary ideas in action than about the evolution of an idea among thinkers who had very marked opinions about their society and how it should operate. Ideas became modes of action only indirectly as social Darwinism was transformed from the rationalization of a quiescent laissez-faire philosophy in a thinker such as William Graham Sumner to an activist pragmatism legitimizing Progressive reform in a philosopher like John Dewey. "There is nothing in Darwinism that inevitably made it an apology for competition or force," Hofstadter concluded. According to Hofstadter, ideas did have an important operational force, they mattered in human affairs, but the direction of their operation and their impact on society depended on human, often moral, choices not on their internal logic or any intrinsic scientific "truth."

While Hofstadter's first book was modest and brief, it was already marked by some of the qualities that characterized his later work. It was lucidly argued, and while the prose was still somewhat overblown and lacked the historian's later elegance, rhythm, and felicity of expression, it was forceful, expressive, and clear. The book was remarkably compact for a study which successfully took on an array of difficult and often abstruse thinkers, and it managed, in Ray Billington's phrase, to reduce "complex theories to crystal clarity." Billington added that Hofstadter's "intelligent organization allows him to develop his successive points so logically that his book has something of the fascination of a well-knit detective story." The book was throughout marked by a strong personal voice which made independent judgments. It had political implications since it suggested that change was possible and could be implemented through determined human intervention. Finally, in a work of fewer than two hundred pages, Hofstadter had managed to question the simple materialism that defined ideas as mere rationalizations and that still dominated the historiography of the period; moreover, he had convincingly demonstrated that ideas were significant subjects for historical analysis. "Ideas," Hofstadter noted, "have effects as well as causes."

Hofstadter's accomplishments with *Social Darwinism* helped to bring him further success in an appointment as assistant professor at Columbia University in 1946. But the significance and pleasure of his rapid professional ascent was marred by the death of his wife, Felice, in 1945, only one and one-half years after the birth of their son, Dan. Hofstadter's achievements were frequently shadowed by personal trials often associated with health problems, a pattern which haunted him until his own early death. According to Alfred Kazin, who knew the young Hofstadters well in New York, Richard Hofstadter "began to write *The American Political Tradition* on a pad in her darkened sickroom; he could not see the first words, but he finished the book." The experience darkly foreshadowed his struggles to write his final book, *America at 1750: A Social Portrait* (1971), as he lay dying in 1970. Hofstadter's painful awareness of the tragedy just beneath the surface of life's joys, tragedy seemingly linked with personal ambition, deepened and often saddened his most moving historical interpretations, like his portrait of Abraham Lincoln in *The American Political Tradition and the Men Who Made It* (1948) or of Vernon Parrington in *The Progressive Historians: Turner, Beard, Parrington* (1968). It is certainly not too much to suggest that his young wife's death, itself an echo of the earlier loss of his mother, underwrote the profound sense of humility Hofstadter brought to his analysis of human experience and of historical knowledge. It surely confirmed his abhorrence of pettiness, for which there was insufficient time in life, and his

hatred of arrogance, for which vulnerable men had no warrant.

Personal tragedy did not, however, impede Hofstader's labors and his zeal for life. In 1948, Hofstadter produced, with the assistance of an Alfred A. Knopf Fellowship awarded in 1945, *The American Political Tradition and the Men Who Made It*, the book that made him famous and that marked the beginning of his long, profitable association with the distinguished publishing house. The year before he had married Beatrice Kevitt and thus had forged another happy association that, like his relationship with Knopf, provided crucial support for the rest of his life. Hofstadter acknowledged his wife's assistance in each of his subsequent books as an indispensable companion to his thoughts and as an invaluable editor. As Alfred Kazin observed in an obituary notice, Hofstadter "was, among other distinctions, the most cherished of husbands," a not inconsiderable asset in the rigorous work to which he had committed himself. The Hofstadters had one daughter, Sarah, born on 22 July 1952.

The American Political Tradition has become a classic of American historiography. It is one of those volumes that generations of students can be expected to read with profit and delight and that for young historians of the 1950s and 1960s provided the kind of inspiration that came to Hofstadter's generation from reading Charles and Mary Beard's *The Rise of American Civilization* (1927). A determinedly personal statement, *The American Political Tradition* signaled Hofstadter's self-awareness as a thinker and social critic as well as an historian. Unlike *Social Darwinism*, both in its choice of political history as a subject and in its breathless interpretive range, it was also marked by an invigorating iconoclasm that came from newfound confidence in his ideas and in his prose. Hofstadter frequently noted that his mind was torn between two loves, the history of ideas and political history. In the two books which define the early stage of his career, he developed styles for both. If *Social Darwinism* demonstrated his devotion to the history of ideas and his careful attention to the requirements of disciplined exposition, *The American Political Tradition* showed a bold contentiousness resonant of his youthful political rebellions. Where *Social Darwinism* was scholarly and detached, the *American Political Tradition* was journalistic, acerbic, and frequently funny. Together *Social Darwinism* and *The American Political Tradition* marked the emergence of an historian of wide talents, acute intelligence, and extraordinary sensitivity to the varieties of historical experience.

Moving from the era of the founding fathers

through that of Franklin Roosevelt, *The American Political Tradition* consisted of twelve essay-portraits that evoked the substance and texture of a continuous political culture. The majority of essays were about presidents, but three, Wendell Phillips, John C. Calhoun, and William Jennings Bryan, concerned other influential figures—an agitator, a political theorist, and a losing, but important, presidential contender. Two others, on the founding fathers and the spoilsmen, were more attuned to the sense of an era than to the beliefs and assumptions of a single politician as representative individual. Many of the portraits contained deft analyses of personal psychology and its relationship to behavior and values. Above all, the essays showed a young historian making original sense of his country's history and doing so with critical and even breathtaking insight. *The American Political Tradition* was critical of much of the American tradition which, according to Hofstadter, overwhelmingly supported exploitative individualism and a rapacious entrepreneurial capitalism. For Hofstadter, even such presumptive heroes of a supposedly opposing democratic tradition as Jefferson, Jackson, and Wilson were exponents of its creed.

Thus, Hofstadter attempted and at least partially succeeded in questioning the Progressive view of American history as a continuing battle between two forces, the conservative interests and a liberal democracy, a view most cogently put forth by Charles Beard but also implicit in the work of many other historians from the 1920s through the 1940s. Hofstadter was not suggesting that the sources of the American political tradition were not securely lodged in material forces. On the contrary, here and in all subsequent studies, he always anchored the essential dynamic of historical change in a solid material base. What he challenged was the implication, in Beard and others, that only the forces of conservatism were so bound and the equally prevalent view that a materialist basis for history required that everything else be reducible to a simple economic explanation. Hofstadter had rejected this latter belief in *Social Darwinism*. In *The American Political Tradition* he undermined the belief further by showing that American political traditions and American ideologies had themselves become forces in history, and that, indeed, they often impeded necessary adjustment to changes in the material environment. Hofstadter was proposing that ideologies could be dysfunctional as well as functional and that, in fact, a single ideology could be both at different points in a nation's development. The historian was liberating ideas from a static determinism and

making them dynamic ingredients of a complex historical process. Thus, according to Hofstadter, William Jennings Bryan espoused an outdated Jefferson-Jacksonian philosophy of equal opportunity that, however realistic in early nineteenth-century terms, was simplistic and inhibiting in the urban-industrial context emerging at the end of the century. "After one hundred years of change in society the Jeffersonian-Jacksonian philosophy was intact. To those who accept that philosophy, this will appear as steadfastness of faith; to those who reject it, as inflexibility of mind." Hofstadter clearly rejected the philosophy as no longer appropriate. Its inappropriateness was nowhere better illustrated than in the essay on Herbert Hoover, for whom the ideology had become a noose; Franklin Roosevelt, in contrast, was able to break from that tradition. But while Hofstadter demonstrated a grudging respect for Roosevelt's challenge to Jeffersonian-Jacksonian ideals, there was little admiration in his portrait of the "hero" of the New Deal. In discarding the dominant political tradition, FDR replaced it with little more than opportune makeshifts, Hofstadter felt. The nation needed and still lacked a revised and revitalized democratic philosophy.

Years later, in a preface to the Hebrew language edition of *The American Political Tradition*, Hofstadter contended that it was the brief and hurried six-page introduction to *The American Political Tradition*, appended as an afterthought at the request of his publisher (who also supplied the title), that "probably made as much trouble for me as any other passage of comparable length" by identifying the thesis of his book with the emerging school of "consensus history." The historians of this group, including Daniel Boorstin and Louis Hartz, were in the 1950s to minimize the degree of actual conflict in American history and often to applaud its absence. Certainly, several passages from the introduction to *The American Political Tradition* have been quoted more often than any other. Among these were the statements that "However much at odds on specific issues, the major political traditions have shared a belief in the rights of property, the philosophy of economic individualism, the value of competition; they have accepted the economic virtues of capitalist culture as necessary qualities of man" and "Above and beyond temporary and local conflicts there has been a common ground, a unity of cultural and political tradition, upon which American civilization has stood." Of the so-called liberal tradition, Hofstadter also noted that "American traditions . . . show a strong bias in favor of equalitarian democracy, but it has been a democracy in cupidity rather than a democracy of fraternity." It is significant that Hofstadter usually wrote "political traditions" in the plural, implying opposing forces which shared some ground.

Nevertheless, Hofstadter did not need to add these six pages to make his point. Although the book offered no claim for the frictionless history sometimes identified as "consensus history," *The American Political Tradition* clearly tried to revise and to balance the progressive historical model defined by continuing dramatic conflict between conservative spokesmen protecting property and liberal spokesmen representing "the people." The book was above all an attempt to correct the myths constructed by progressives and Progressive historians who had themselves once tried to destroy unthinking homilies to the American past. Hofstadter was doing no more, and no less, than Beard had done in challenging reverence for the Constitution. However, Hofstadter now questioned the reverence for small-scale entrepreneurial capitalism and democratic opportunity so deeply part of progressive values. And like Beard, Hofstadter did his work from the left, to reform or to eliminate those features of the tradition of democratic thought which had become as rigid and pious as reverence for the Constitution and the founding fathers had once been.

The American Political Tradition was reviewed by several of the future notables of the postwar generation of historians, among them Arthur Schlesinger, Jr., C. Vann Woodward, Arthur Mann, and Daniel Aaron. Each, despite disagreements over details of the book, was impressed by its imaginative breadth and innovative view. Certainly *The American Political Tradition* would influence these and others of the emerging generation, and many of its original insights, as, for example, the entrepreneurial sources of Jacksonian Democracy, would serve as bases for several full-length studies. In fact, the book was full of brilliant throwaway ideas which would engage a full generation in exercises of proof and counterproof. Some of these ideas, like the contention about Theodore Roosevelt's basic conservatism or the notion that Lincoln's political ambitions led him to inconsistent positions on slavery, were not exactly new, but they had never before been presented in such a lively and boldly challenging way. Written with verve, style, and skeptical humor, the book was filled with quotable aphorisms. Hofstadter was able, often in a couple of sentences, to produce a sharp summary of an individual. Of Lincoln, Hofstadter noted, "Success of this sort eases and fattens smaller men; for more

restless souls it is a form of poison." Of Calhoun, Hofstadter observed, "Here surely is a man who lived by abstractions; it is amazing, and a little pathetic, that he sought to make his business the management of human affairs." Theodore Roosevelt served a "psychological function" by relieving the nation's accumulated "anxieties with a burst of hectic action. . . . he was the master therapist of the middle classes," and Thomas Jefferson was best summed up by the chapter title "The Aristocrat as Democrat." The book, which was reviewed on the front page of the *New York Times Book Review*, put Hofstadter before a wide public and at the dynamic center of a new generation of American historians. *The American Political Tradition* would become Hofstadter's most popular book with sales exceeding one million copies.

By 1948, Richard Hofstadter had completed the first stage of his intellectual odyssey and career. He had remarried, taken up his appointment at Columbia, and commenced his other lasting commitments to New York and to Knopf. His two books had brought him professional acclaim and public attention. Most significantly, however, he had charted his own path as a historian with a view of the dynamic role of ideas in the historical process and of the essential continuities of America's political development, a view which challenged the dominant Progressive interpretation. He had taken on his intellectual mentors, and if he had not yet integrated his divided loyalties to political history and to the history of ideas, he had at least shown his abilities at each and developed a subtle interpretive style which was adept at both explication and synthesis. He was only thirty-two years old, but he was about to enter the period of his greatest influence as a historian and as a social commentator.

During the next two decades, from 1948 to 1968, Hofstadter's work brought him national acclaim and an international reputation as an extraordinarily creative historian. His insights into the American past, his inventive use of the concepts of other disciplines, the subtle brilliance of his prose made him probably the most influential American historian of the 1950s and early 1960s and certainly one of the most imaginative practitioners of the historian's art. At this stage of his career, his influence extended well beyond the narrow confines of the historical profession or of the academy generally. Hofstadter's work in this period reflected his intellectual engagement in the wider political and cultural milieu. Just as he used issues of the present to reopen those of the past, so did he employ the detached, reasonable perspective of the historian to confront modern difficulties. Hofstadter's scholarly historical interests were throughout the period catalyzed by contemporary issues, particularly the cold war politics of the Eisenhower presidency and the domestic repressions of the McCarthy era, and his work as a historian in turn gave him standing as a commentator on those events. "What started me off as an historian," Hofstadter noted in 1960, "was a sense of engagement with contemporary problems. . . . I still write history out of my engagement with the present."

In this period, Hofstadter sought to use all means to achieve a more complex understanding of American experience. This striving for complexity often had mixed results which rendered his work at once extremely subtle and vulnerable to misunderstanding. If it thereby exposed him to sometimes biting criticism, Hofstadter's writings were always richly suggestive and fulfilled his own criterion for effectiveness in historical scholarship by adding to "the speculative richness of history." As Hofstadter noted in his essay "History and the Social Sciences," "The result may be that his [the historian's] conclusions become more tenuous and tentative, but this is a result to be welcomed. The [more fully the] historian comes, with whatever aids, to the full texture of historical reality, the more deeply is he engulfed in a complex web of relationships which he can hope to understand only in a limited and partial way. . . . His work has not greater certainty, but greater range and depth."

Although the range of Hofstadter's work in this period was too broad for any simple categorization, it can be profitably divided into three related areas. First, his interest in the role of ideas in history led him increasingly to an exploration of ideology and values. He became less concerned with ideas as fully fleshed examples of logical thought than in those systems of beliefs and constellations of values which underlay culture, especially political culture. Second, Hofstadter's interest in the enrichment of the range of historical understanding led him to appropriate the concepts provided by other disciplines, especially sociology and psychology; for example, he frequently examined ways in which anxiety, psychological projection, and concerns about status affected political stances and movements. Finally, Hofstadter became deeply concerned about the life of the mind and about the role and uncertain fate of the intellectual in America. All of Hofstadter's work during this period incorporated these three interests, but each can be best explored through a close examination of one of his books.

The Age of Reform: From Bryan to F.D.R. (1955), which won the Pulitzer Prize for history in 1956, was one of Hofstadter's best books. It was also the most controversial. The controversy it generated among historians on a variety of issues continues to stimulate and enliven American historical writing and will no doubt do so for a long time to come. In *The Age of Reform*, Hofstadter, for the first time, brought together his interests in political history and the history of ideas, and he brought them together by shifting his attention from ideas to ideology and by exploring not the political views of presidents and statesmen but instead the political values and assumptions of large segments of the population. In that double shift, Hofstadter brought his investigation not quite to the level of the inarticulate masses that would become the vogue in the late 1960s and the 1970s but certainly a long way toward the study of that social and cultural matrix which structures popular experience. In this sense, *The Age of Reform* was a social history, although it pretended neither to incorporate all groups in the population nor to investigate the daily and ordinary experiences of the people. Instead, *The Age of Reform* discussed the dynamic political force of the period from the 1890s through the New Deal—the impulse to reform—and related this activity to the fundamental social changes of the period as these were filtered through the lens of traditional American political values. While much attention and criticism focused on some of its more obvious and provocative theses—that populism was tainted by illiberalism and the parochial repressions of a resentful folk mentality, that progressivism was generated from middle-class anxieties about status, that the New Deal broke decisively from earlier types of liberal reforms—its underlying conception was the book's most profound contribution.

The Age of Reform was first of all about the tenacity of values and the influence of traditional ideology on how people behave and perceive of themselves. The book thus continued the central contention of *The American Political Tradition*. It described how the American belief in free enterprise, individualism, and equality of opportunity defined and circumscribed reform strategies even when this constellation of ideas was no longer either appropriate or effective. America's liberal tradition, Hofstadter asserted, was, in effect, also a conservative tradition, and American efforts at change were full of nostalgia for the presumed superiorities of an earlier day. Reform in America was ambiguous because "the United States was the only country in the world that began with perfection and aspired to progress." This was true both for urban middle-class Progressives whose sights were set on a small-town America in which they had respect and influence and for Populists inspired by the sylvan fantasies of preindustrial America in which the farmer was God's chosen instrument of virtue. Populist and Progressive views and reforms were class biased, since each group hoped to return America to conditions that assured its dominance. Hofstadter defined class interests not simply in terms of material conditions but also as values and myths, indeed as a whole cultural constellation by which class interests were expressed and enforced. In a brief final segment of the book, Hofstadter described the New Deal as different from populism and progressivism. Emerging in a context of almost complete economic collapse, the New Deal was unconstrained by nostalgia and able to operate in a pragmatic fashion. It was also the first reform enterprise whose values drew upon an urban-centered coalition of interests and classes.

The Age of Reform substituted a complex view of human motivation for the simple economic calculus espoused by the Progressive historians. Although Hofstadter repeatedly described the material changes underlying the reform events of this period—and in the case of the Populists the real economic hardships which forced them to seek relief, his emphasis was elsewhere. He was intent on defining and exploring a broad range of sources for behavior: myths and values, social class and social status, the roles of anxiety and of guilt. It would be a mistake to see any one of these sources for behavior as *the* Hofstadter thesis, although he emphasized one source or another in each of the exploratory essays composing the book. Rather, Hofstadter proposed that individuals live and act in a complex world defined by an interplay of history (traditions and myths), interests (class related values, status considerations, and the desire for material welfare), and personal psychology (anxieties, guilt, fantasies, and projections). In *The Age of Reform*, self-perception thus became as important as the reasoned calculation of profit and loss. And while any of its specific contentions (for example, the influence of status anxiety in generating Progressive reform or the role of the agrarian myth in Populist resentment) might be disputed—and, indeed, already have stimulated a large revisionist literature, Hofstadter's sensitivity to the manifold layers of historical reality and his rejection of monocausality in history will surely remain a lasting contribution to historical understanding.

Aside from its historiographical contribution,

The Age of Reform generated and continues to generate controversy about its political implications. In his introduction, Hofstadter asserted that he was writing from within the liberal-progressive tradition in which he was "reared and upon which my political sentiments were formed." Nevertheless, he found himself critical of that tradition in reexamining it "from the perspective of our own time," because he discovered much in that tradition that was illiberal, "retrograde and elusive, a little that was vicious, and a good deal that was comic." In being so clear and direct about the present perspective in which his analysis was rooted and by emphasizing the less savory aspects of the Progressive heritage, Hofstadter did more than enrich the historiography of reform. He was consciously and purposefully defining its limits as a vital and continuing political resource. Hofstadter did so from what he believed was the perspective of the left. But his critics, among them William Appleman Williams, Norman Pollack, and Michael Rogin, saw ample grounds for accusing him of giving comfort to the "new conservatives" of the post-Korean War period whose distrust of the people and democratic institutions could draw upon Hofstadter's picture of irrational and fanatical Populists and comical guilt-ridden Progressives to indict reform in general. This accusation was unfair to Hofstadter's intentions. As a highly self-conscious historian, Hofstadter was, however, fully aware of the role of history and of its mythmaking function in contemporary politics. "Men," Hofstadter was to observe some years later in *The Progressive Historians*, "who have achieved any civic existence at all must, to sustain it, have some kind of history, though it may be history that is partly mythological or simply untrue." In *The Age of Reform*, Hofstadter may have sought to destroy the whiggish Progressive myth of reform in order to free Americans to a more adequate and equitable adaptation to modern economic and social conditions and thus to stimulate them to find new means toward a more just society. Certainly his newly appreciative assessment of the New Deal and of Roosevelt's pragmatism gave substance to this position. But, to his critics, Hofstadter had provided no substantial alternative to the myths he exploded. He had instead denuded history of just those radical precedents by which each generation legitimizes its own goals for political change. In this context, Hofstadter's unsympathetic picture of the Populists who had traditionally served as America's indigenous radicals was far more disturbing than his portrait of the Progressives whose middle-class origins and respectable property values provided less inspiration to an emerging group of historians intent on a renewed appreciation of America's radical heritage. To his critics, Hofstadter had reduced a once sympathetic portrait of homegrown critics of monopoly capital, industrial exploitation, banks, and Eastern elites to a caricature of country bumpkins. Furthermore, he had made the Populists mean as well as provincial. As he portrayed them, they could appear as muddleheaded petty entrepreneurs disappointed by their speculative misadventures and as avaricious as they were intolerant.

Yet Hofstadter's portrait of the Populists was considerably more nuanced than this description suggests; he wrote sympathetically of their real hardships during a period of declining prices and international competition and of their creative reform proposals. Still, there can be little question that Hofstadter was less than enamored of the simple "folk" which served some historians as the carriers of historical progress. "Intellectuals," Hofstadter noted in his introduction, "readily succumb to a tendency to sentimentalize the folk. Hence they periodically exaggerate the measure of agreement that exists between movements of popular reform and the considered principles of political liberalism. They remake the image of popular rebellion closer to their heart's desire. They choose to ignore the elements of illiberalism that frequently seem to be an indissoluable part of popular movements." Hofstadter's attitude toward the folk was, however, more than just a counterbalance for intellectual sentimentality. It was also more than the posture of an urban intellectual repelled by the provincial simplicities of the rural and uneducated mind. Although Hofstadter retained all his life some of H. L. Mencken's contempt for country yahoos ("I soaked up everything of Mencken's when I was an undergraduate at the University of Buffalo," he observed in 1960), his criticism of the folk mentality and popular movements had far more serious roots.

Like many other intellectuals who experienced the 1930s and 1940s, Hofstadter had absorbed the lessons of Hitler's mass following and Stalin's popularity. In each case "the people" had been all too easily led, even into acts of unimaginable atrocity; their simplicities thus became anything but innocent, their actions not at all democratic. These experiences were followed in the United States by the demagogic successes of Joseph McCarthy (and before him of Huey Long and Father Coughlin). Taken together, contemporary events suggested the horrible potentials of an uninformed and intolerant populace vulnerable to easy answers and simple salvations. In this sense, Hofstadter's name has been correctly linked to those intellectuals of the 1950s and 1960s who rejected all ideologies as the weapons of powerful manipulators of the twentieth-century masses. Many of them, like Hofstadter—second-generation immigrants, urban centered, dedicated to cultural modernism, and often associated with the New York-based *Partisan Review*—had begun in the 1930s from the perspective of the left to challenge a sentimental populism. In addition, the intellectuals who had fled Nazi Germany were developing significant theories which informed Hofstadter's viewpoint. The psychological portraits developed by Theodore Adorno in *The Authoritarian Personality* (1950) and the theories about the special vulnerability of mass society to wholly new forms of totalitarianism proposed by Hannah Arendt (1951) were readily absorbed by Hofstadter who now sought to apply the lessons of history and social science to exploring and exposing the irrational underside of popular movements of the American past. For example, in describing Ignatius Donnelly's *Caesar's Column* (1891), which Hofstadter read as a document of the Populist mind, he noted, "It is perhaps a childish book, but in the middle of the twentieth century it seems anything but laughable; it affords a frightening glimpse into the ugly potential of frustrated popular revolt." Hofstadter added that, compared to the sinister potential of modern "authoritarian movements," populism existed in a "more innocent and more fortunate age." Still, sensitive to contemporary events and alert to the ideas of social science, Hofstadter in the mid-1950s shadowed his liberal political sentiments with increasing suspicion of the people.

This tendency in Hofstadter's thought was already evident in some of the ambiguities explored in the *Age of Reform*, but that book remained a much more balanced portrait than some of his critics contended, and it was throughout characterized by a degree of sympathy for his still largely "innocent" characters. Hofstadter's experimentation with social science and psychology and his increasing uneasiness with the sinister potentials of modern mass politics and ideologies were more fully expressed in the essays he wrote in the 1950s and early 1960s and collected in *The Paranoid Style in American Politics and Other Essays* (1965). Furthermore, his growing sense of the gap separating untutored popular sentiments and civilized, tolerant culture emerged most starkly in the personal essays of his book *Anti-Intellectualism in American Life* (1963). In both books, Hofstadter's normally skeptical and witty balance between personal engagement and scholarly detachment approached an uncomfortable sharpness toward—and even alienation from—the popular traditions and resources of American democratic culture.

The Paranoid Style in American Politics was divided into two parts. The first section collected Hofstadter's essays and reflections on contemporary politics, specifically the politics of the right from McCarthy through Goldwater. The second part included three historical essays written between 1952 and 1963, each essay about a distinct problem in late nineteenth- and early twentieth-century politics and each dealing with some popular enthusiasm—imperialism, the antitrust movement, and free silver. These three essays demonstrated Hofstadter's growing subtlety as a historian, his ability to weave narrative, analysis, and textual explication to shed new light on old problems. Each was an exercise in creative synthesis rather than original research and each also incorporated a psychological perspective to enrich the reader's sense of the historical episode. The essays demonstrated the range of Hofstadter's knowledge and interests; from foreign policy to Congressional politics and economics, his interpretations were always fully based in the most reliable secondary literature and were highly sophisticated in their grasp of the issues involved.

In the longest essay, "Free Silver and the Mind of 'Coin' Harvey," written in 1963, Hofstadter continued his explorations of the rural, folk mentality by examining the most popular prosilver tract of the Populist era, *Coin's Financial School* (1894). Hofstadter's essay was remarkable for the seriousness with which it explicated a tract of dubious intellectual value, thus elevating Harvey's work to a place of real worth as a historical document. The essay also demonstrated Hofstadter's sure grasp of underlying economic issues, which he presented simply and briefly but neither simplified nor dismissed. While examining the mind of "Coin" Harvey, Hofstadter not only retained an economic explanation of the free silver movement but also recreated the emotional attachments and associations to silver (and to gold, too, for that matter) which made free silver such a hot issue at the time. Hofstadter recreated the felt experience of the silver advocates, and if this technique made their behavior seem less rational, it also made their actions seem far more understandable. At the same time, Hofstadter's own stance as an historian, at some critical distance from the emotion-packed issues, exposed the crudities of the tract's ersatz economics. Ironically, Hofstadter's essay at one and

the same time took popular beliefs seriously as worthy of the historian's attention but did so at the expense of ridiculing the public which held those ideas. The essay consequently seemed contemptuous of popular thought. "Free Silver and the Mind of 'Coin' Harvey" illustrated some of the difficulty Hofstadter as historian was encountering as a critic writing from inside the democratic tradition. In choosing popular mentalities as his subject and in approaching them as an intellectual and a social critic, Hofstadter was becoming more and more alienated from those beliefs and from the people who held them.

Some of the richness of speculation demonstrated in these historical essays, as well as Hofstadter's increasing difficulties with the popular mind, was revealed in the essays that compose the first section of *The Paranoid Style in American Politics*. Critical to understanding Hofstadter's development during this period of his career, the essays defined the two factors most significant in catalyzing his choice of historical subject and the form of his analysis: The essays were about contemporary politics, and they relied heavily on the findings of sociology and social psychology.

As an intellectual Hofstadter was fascinated and often alarmed by the events of his own time. Since his undergraduate days at Buffalo and his early experiences in New York during the 1930s, Hofstadter had found the stimulants for his historical inquiries in contemporary issues. While radical politics may have been the original tonic of his historical imagination, the experience of totalitarianism in Europe and the repressions surrounding the Korean War in the United States were of greatest significance to his scholarship during his most influential years as a historian in the 1950s and early 1960s. During that period, Hofstadter's interests frequently coincided with the interests of other intellectuals and scholars. In the 1950s especially, the questions Hofstadter posed as a historian became very like those being posed by social scientists about contemporary events. In 1954, Hofstadter attended a Columbia University faculty seminar on McCarthyism; this extremely fruitful exchange of ideas among social scientists resulted in the publication of a 1955 collection, *The New American Right* (revised and republished in 1963 as *The Radical Right*), to which Hofstadter contributed an important theoretical essay.

Hofstadter's contribution to that volume, "The Pseudo-Conservative Revolt," became the first of a series of essays he wrote on contemporary right-wing politics. Of this essay, Hofstadter noted in 1965, "I have written nothing of comparable brevity that aroused more attention or drew more requests for quotation or reprinting." The essay, which helped to make its author an influential social commentator, contained several hypotheses about contemporary right-wing politics, hypotheses that Hofstadter was also beginning to use in his historical investigation. The first of these involved the distinction that he, like sociologist Seymour Martin Lipset, drew between interest politics and status politics. Interest politics, according to Hofstadter, was a politics which tended to prevail in the United States during hard times when Americans voted according to their clearly understood pocketbook interests. Status politics predominated during periods of prosperity. At such times Americans were less concerned with specific programs and remedies than with values and thus voiced their resentment against racial and ethnic minorities who seemed to threaten their social standing and cultural control. In a heterogeneous culture that espoused an ideology of equality, it was difficult to define who and what was truly American. As a result, some groups sought to define themselves and their values as American at the expense of other groups. "Old" Americans who needed to emphasize their dominance and "new" Americans who sought to affirm their allegiance were particularly vulnerable to status politics. Status politics reflected the insecurity created in a society where all were supposed to be equal but everyone sought priority of place. Hofstadter's emphasis on status was, in many ways, a continuation of Alexis de Tocqueville's insight into the jockeying for position that prevailed in a society defined by an ideology of equality.

A second hypothesis in the essay was the suggestion that so-called conservative politics in the 1950s was, in fact, a radical politics of the right. Its practitioners were less interested in conserving than in destroying, Hofstadter believed, and its proposals were based not on a subtle appreciation of slow and thoughtful change but on anger and resentment whose roots were psychological. The radical right, according to Hofstadter, was composed of dangerous and destructive fanatics. He drew up a portrait of the pseudoconservative which relied heavily on Theodor W. Adorno's *The Authoritarian Personality* (1950) profile in which "violence, anarchic impulses, and chaotic destructiveness" were the governing passions and which located the followers for this politics among "the less-educated members of the middle class." This psychological type, Hofstadter contended, became important within the context of status politics. In this and other essays

of this genre, Hofstadter was primarily concerned to locate and describe Senator McCarthy's public, the members of the John Birch Society, and the followers of Senator Barry Goldwater. But he was also beginning to construct a composite picture of the political fanatic and of the irrational components in all deeply felt politics that could be applied historically: the fanatic was ill-educated, provincial, insecure; his commitments were based on emotion rather than reason; he was closer to the folk than to the elite; he espoused an equalitarian philosophy and was a great hater of distinctions and of his superiors; and he was extremely dangerous in the mass. That fanatic who in the 1950s baited intellectuals and was suspicious of all excellence thus began to loom larger and larger as an American type in Hofstadter's historical imagination, and in the context of the growing distance Hofstadter felt from both the resources of the American democratic tradition and from the "folk," his portrait of the right-wing fanatic became Hofstadter's most extreme expression of his alienation as a critic and as an American.

Anti-Intellectualism in American Life (1963) did not appear on the surface to be as heavily influenced by social science as his essays on contemporary politics. Indeed it seemed less obviously a product of his reading in sociology and psychology than did *The Age of Reform*, published in 1955. Yet the composite portrait of the resentful fanatic that Hofstadter assembled from those readings was significant to the book, for it was the culture sustaining the fanatic which became, in *Anti-Intellectualism in American Life*, the main threat to the life of the mind in America. The book's contemporary roots were obvious since Hofstadter noted that it "was conceived in response to the political and intellectual conditions of the 1950s." *Anti-Intellectualism in American Life* won the Pulitzer Prize for nonfiction in 1964, as well as the Emerson Award of Phi Beta Kappa and the Sidney Hillman Award. Although occasionally brilliant, elegantly written, and always interesting, the book was not really successful as history or as social commentary. Full of only partially assimilated obiter dicta, it lacks the compelling historical richness of Hofstadter's other work.

Hofstadter had written before about the life and institutions of intellect in America. In *Academic Freedom in the Age of the College*, first published as part one of *The Development of Academic Freedom in the United States* (1955) by Hofstadter and Walter Metzger, Hofstadter explored the trials of American colleges for two hundred years from the founding of Harvard College to the emergence of

Dust jacket for Hofstadter's award-winning 1963 book, which examines American colleges over a period of 200 years from the founding of Harvard College in 1636

the American university system after the Civil War. During that time the professoriat had been starved, snubbed, and subordinated to administrative control. Yet he had written about these early years with a deep historical sense of the complex environment within which the colleges survived and of the often ambiguous route which increased freedom of intellectual expression had taken. While the questions which generated the study were clearly contemporary, Hofstadter never fell into the trap of searching for contemporary answers. The book studied the period without forcing direct connections to issues of academic freedom in the twentieth century. Hofstadter worked hard to find materials even marginally related to his concerns, but he never abused the complex historical record either to make his point or to draw a moral lesson. He handled his cases of academic freedom deftly and often with humor. Similarly, in *The Development and Scope of Higher Education in the United States*, coauthored with C. DeWitt Hardy and published in 1952, Hofstadter wrote three historical essays on various phases in

the institutional development of higher education—"The Age of the College," "The Age of the University," and "The Higher Learning in America"—which were often critical of the lack of material support and intellectual freedom available to scholars and frequently impatient with the vulgar demands made on intellect in America. The essays were nevertheless rooted in a careful assessment of the historical evolution and limitations of the institutions themselves. In *Anti-Intellectualism in American Life*, however, Hofstadter located the threats to intellectual life not in the specific limitations of the American academy but in the culture as a whole and more specifically in a continuous tradition of hostility to creative thought which Hofstadter linked to the culture's most democratic allegiances. Indeed, the complex appreciation, in *Academic Freedom in the Age of the College*, of how freedom often came as a by-product of ambiguous historical circumstances gave way, in *Anti-Intellectualism in American Life*, to an almost unrelieved indictment of a democratic tradition of hostility to the life and requirements of the mind. *Anti-Intellectualism in American Life* was structured to elicit from the past only what the book set out to find, and this tendentious quality made the work both unlike Hofstadter's other studies, which always gave the sense of fresh discovery, and contrary to the intellectual values the book supposedly espoused.

In four loosely connected sections, Hofstadter concentrated on different aspects of American culture—religion, politics, business, and education. In each case, with the possible exception of the section on business, Hofstadter concentrated on that aspect of his subject normally associated with greater democracy or at least with challenges to elite control—evangelicism in religion, the emergence of democratic politics in the Jacksonian period, and Progressive education. In each case, however, the complex, balanced assessment characteristic of *The Age of Reform* was missing. Instead Hofstadter wrote of his subjects with a single intent—to expose their contributions to a tradition of anti-intellectualism. Hofstadter recognized that "anti-intellectualism is usually the incidental consequence of some other intention, often some justifiable intention," but the book was structured in ways which captured only the incidental and therefore flattened the historical record. Certainly, Hofstadter was suggesting, once again, that the American liberal tradition had an ugly underside, but in *Anti-Intellectualism in American Life*, only the underside was visible, with few of the often more historically significant features of the story in view. Here Hofstadter's suspicions of the conforming masses, indeed of the mob lurking within the masses, came out most clearly.

Anti-Intellectualism in American Life seemed to demonstrate all the faults critics on the left had attributed to the *Age of Reform*. It was clearly hostile to the strategic components of America's liberal tradition, it was often unfair to a much more complex historical record, and it seemed to subordinate the historian's tools to a presentist political animus. The book was much too obviously a tract for its time. Ironically it came out at a point when intellectuals had gained stature, confidence, and political patronage. If it was in some ways a culmination of Hofstadter's intellectual and political commitments in the 1950s and 1960s, it also pointed up many of the difficulties involved in a historian's choice to be a social critic. The book provided a lesson Hofstadter would absorb and a choice he would not repeat.

Despite its shortcomings as history, *Anti-Intellectualism in American Life* was a passionate expression of Hofstadter's personal commitment to the pursuit of the intellectual life and the social and civic conditions necessary to its survival. The intellectual, Hofstadter believed, was defined by certain qualities—"disinterested intelligence, generalizing power, free speculation, fresh observation, creative novelty, radical criticism." He was unafraid (and must not be made afraid) to speak forthrightly and independently. His mind had the peculiar poise that came from a balance between "piety and playfulness." By "piety," Hofstadter did not mean a solemn reverence for his subject but instead an attitude toward the process of inquiry itself; this attitude assured the integrity of product and the commitment to the process of truth-seeking that sustained a lifetime's vocation and gave to intellectual life "a kind of primary moral significance." By "playfulness," Hofstadter meant to convey the sense of delight in submitting to the charms of untrammeled curiosity that all of the best intellectual work contained. The pursuit of truth was the "heart of the intellectual's business," but where the "pursuit is itself gratifying," the consummation might be "elusive." Indeed, he noted, "truth captured loses its glamour; truths long known and widely believed have a way of turning false with time; easy truths are a bore, and too many of them become half-truths." The remarkably epigrammatic quality of this statement ought not to obscure the degree to which it served as Hofstadter's creed. For him, truth was always elusive and complex, and while it might reveal itself in bits and pieces during the process of inquiry, it never existed as a final product.

Hofstadter's best work had this quality of a truth that emerged not in a final or static thesis but in the snatches of sensitive insight whose essence was not transferable but remained always part of the continuing search of a brilliant and restless mind in action.

Since truth was tentative and fragile, the conditions conducive to continuous inquiry, Hofstadter believed, must be boldly and unremittingly protected. The lessons of *Anti-Intellectualism in American Life*, like the lessons he drew from his studies of the academy, made Hofstadter a vigorous advocate of the modern university where, with all its problems and shortcomings, intellect had the best chance of surviving in a normally hostile world. That world rarely understood what the life of the mind was about and, when it did, frequently saw intellectual pursuits as threats to the more specific "truths" the world required in daily operation. When in 1968 Columbia University became the object of a massive student revolt and of an ugly, violent contest between students and administration that challenged the future of the institution, Richard Hofstadter, unlike most of his colleagues, was not surprised. The crisis seemed but one more illustration of the vulnerability of even the most seemingly safe intellectual sanctuaries to the worldly realities of politics and society. Indeed, Hofstadter's poise during the crisis was remarkable. Throughout he maintained a posture of genuine concern and active interest which impressed even some of the most hostile student critics of the institution and of its faculty. At the same time he stood firm on his commitments to academic freedom and against the threat that forced closings and student strikes posed. It was, therefore, appropriate that, in an effort to calm the situation, Richard Hofstadter was asked to give that year's commencement address, the first time in the institution's 214-year history that a faculty member, rather than the president, was so honored. Nor was it surprising that Hofstadter accepted.

The address delivered on 4 June 1968 opened with a poignant personal statement of the role that Columbia had played in Hofstadter's life. It went on to define the university as "committed to certain basic values of freedom, rationality, inquiry, discussion" and to observe that "the very possibility of civilized human discourse rests upon the willingness of people to consider that they may be mistaken." Hofstadter concluded by returning to the specific situation at Columbia. He acknowledged the need for reform but insisted that reforms could not "be carried out under duress." The address was short, unambiguous, and soft spoken.

Ironically, although the address was probably Hofstadter's most public occasion, it concluded the period of Hofstadter's most active influence. The Columbia crisis must have made Hofstadter painfully aware of the contradictions and anomalies of an intellectual too deeply committed to a solution of current problems. Politics had been brought deep within the walls of the academy and now seemed to threaten the values of intellectual life itself. The always precarious balance that Hofstadter had tried to maintain between his roles as a detached intellectual and as a political participant was now revealed as potentially costly to his integrity as a scholar. Hofstadter had always believed that people acted in self-interested ways. He had defined interests broadly and acknowledged that those interests were often only dimly understood, perceived through a haze of ideologies, myths, and the distortions produced by personal psychology. At the same time, the scholar, although not free of either self-interest or the distorting lenses of perception, could, at times, grasp fleeting truths. Above all, there was a kind of primal truthfulness in the commitment to inquiry which had to be preserved. By 1968, Hofstadter's identification with his craft and with the truth-seeking defined by that commitment had taken on an urgency that was in part the result of a clarification of purpose, in part the growing awareness of mortality.

Hofstadter's Columbia commencement address was a fitting consummation for the most public stage of his career. The 1950s and early 1960s had been full of official honors, awards, and recognitions. Among other distinctions, Hofstadter had received two Pulitzer Prizes and prestigious guest lectureships at Berkeley (1966), Harvard (1968), and other American universities; he also had served as Pitt Professor at Cambridge (1958-1959) and as a visiting Senior Fellow at Princeton (1962-1963). He had filled important appointments to advisory committees on education and on domestic affairs, and he was for eleven years the holder of the coveted De Witt Clinton Chair of American History at Columbia. These had been the decades of his most obvious concern about the political issues of his day and of his greatest influence as a critic of American life. After 1968 his influence would decline. As a historian, however, Hofstadter in 1968 was at the height of his powers, and while less than three years remained in his life, these were witness to an extraordinary productivity, a fertile rethinking of issues with which he had long been concerned, and a continued commitment to that sustained work which had been his life's most intimate companion.

Hofstadter had always worked with a committed discipline which impressed and sometimes amused other historians. "He was not always an easy man to vacation with," C. Vann Woodward observed after his death. "The beaches tended to be strewn with bibliographical disputation, and langorous tropical mornings tended to be disturbed by the clatter of a typewriter. He gave us all an inferiority complex." But never had he worked with the intensity that marked the last five or six years of his life. Between 1968 and his death in 1970, he published two books, *The Progressive Historians: Turner, Beard, Parrington* (begun around 1965 and published in 1968) and *The Idea of A Party System: The Rise of Legitimate Opposition in the United States, 1780-1840* (1969), and several chapters of a long-term project, published posthumously as *America at 1750: A Social Portrait* (1971). This last work was part of what he once described as "Hofstadter's folly," a proposed three-volume social history of the United States, each volume focusing at the midpoint of a century to explore the dynamic elements of American culture and society.

These three books, which make up the brief last stage of Hofstadter's career, were the most mature, considered, and refined expressions of his work as an historian. In many ways, they brought him back to the interests which animated his early career; in others they reflected his reassessment of the craft of history and of the role of the historian. They were clearly the integrated expression of a lifetime of reflection, and while they were no longer packed full of new social science concepts, they were informed throughout with a sensitivity which had absorbed what other disciplines had to offer but which returned finally to methods which were uniquely historical. The skeptical irony of his earlier work was replaced by a sad and often lyrical empathy with the men and women who had suffered the past, which, as Hofstadter once had written in an intensely personal estimation of the relation between history and social science, was the historian's real task. The social sciences, Hofstadter wrote in 1956, were important insofar as they stimulated the historian's imagination. "As soon as the historian's span of attention becomes sufficiently enlarged to take in more than a tiny segment of the historic past, he confronts the precariousness of human efforts, sees the passing not only of great states and powerful institutions but of militant faiths and, most pertinent for him, of the very historical perspectives that are identified with them. At this point he is persuaded to accept the imaginative as well as the cognitive side of his work, to think of history as being not only the analysis but the expression of human experience." Hofstadter had always rejected specialization and the monograph as depriving the historian of this breadth of vision and understanding. In his last three books, Hofstadter, who had never limited himself to any one period, subject, or single method, displayed the full vigor of his approaches.

The sense of the precariousness of all human enterprises and of all forms of interpretation defined *The Progressive Historians*. Hofstadter's study of Turner, Beard, and Parrington could be read on many levels: as his final conscious attempt to come to terms with his intellectual predecessors; as a reflection of his recognition of the compromises that historians make as soon as they become political and social figures as he himself had become; or as simply a final attempt to expose the inadequate vision of historical process contained in the Progressives' work. This last subject had occupied Hofstadter's early years as a scholar when he wrote a series of articles carefully showing the errors of their various arguments. Hofstadter's books, especially *The American Political Tradition* and *The Age of Reform*, had been implicit refutations of the simple materialism of Beard especially but also of the liberal-progressive alliance with which the three historians had been identified. Hofstadter had, in fact, spent a large part of his career replacing the Progressive's vision of reality with a denser, more balanced, and more up-to-date version.

Certainly, *The Progressive Historians* contained ample evidence for all of these interpretations. Hofstadter called it "a patricidal foray.... A reprise of that perennial battle we wage with our elders, particularly with our adopted intellectual fathers." He also noted how these historians' perspectives had become obsolete for "those of us who grew up during the Great Depression and the Second World War and who could no longer share the simple faith of the Progressive writers in the sufficiency of American liberalism. And the book, especially the long section on Beard, was shot through with an awareness of how political activism bruised the historian's vision. *The Progressive Historians* was at once sympathetic to Turner, Beard, and Parrington because they felt issues deeply and were unafraid to take bold stands, and sharply aware of the limitations and distortions this "political" involvement introduced into their work. In this sense, *The Progressive Historians* was also a personal assessment of Hofstadter's own contemporary engagements as a historian, as well as the story of his predecessors. Above and beyond these elements of a deeply personal book, *The Progressive Historians* was a loving portrait of limited but creative and admirable human beings. It was also a story about the historicity of all perspectives on human events and therefore the most philosophical statement by an extremely self-aware historian who normally stayed away from theories about history.

Even in his youthful essays where Hofstadter was most iconoclastic, he had never savaged Beard or any of his other mentors. In "Beard and the Constitution: The History of an Idea" Hofstadter wrote appreciatively about Beard's innovative methodology while disputing his findings. In Hofstadter's final statement on the subject in 1968, Beard still remained a figure treated with respect and affection. The portrait of Beard, who by the time of his death had become provincial, cranky, and something of a one-idea man—characteristics Hofstadter despised—concluded with the following words: "One longs to restore the earlier Beard, who is still remembered as a man of extraordinary kindliness, courage and honor. . . . One prefers to think of him in this way—as a productive scholar who was also an intrepid public spirit, as the patron and guide of younger colleagues, the distinguished and embattled defender of civil and academic liberties, the scourge of Hearst, the spokesman of native decencies—and one remembers that the life of a man does not end as a series of propositions that can simply be assessed and found true or false, but as a set of lingering resonances that for our own sake we must be attuned to hear." The book was a final tribute and a kind of memento mori.

Hofstadter always had a talent for weaving biography and analysis, for relating the personal to the political, social, or ideological. That talent had been hinted at in *Social Darwinism* and prominent in *The American Political Tradition*. In *The Progressive Historians* this ability came to fruition. The book was about three men and their ideas and only incidentally about Progressive historiography. The book was criticized by Robert Wiebe when it was published for failing to substitute a "grand, sustained synthesis" for the integrated visions of the Progressives. But this criticism wholly missed the point Hofstadter made and ignored the book's methodology and intentions. Hofstadter was interested less in demonstrating that Turner, Beard, and Parrington were wrong than in showing how each man's ideas were the delicate and transient products of his life and his times. In the end, Hofstadter made clear that all systems of thought were limited as the men who created them were limited. Historians, Hofstadter said, are caught in their times, and after a while they cease "to be the leading interpreters of our past and become simply a part of it." The last chapter of the book brought this lesson up to the present day. Here Hofstadter examined the ideas and faults of "consensus history," with which he had been identified. He saw this school too as transitory, already obviously limited, never more than partially correct anyway, and certain to be replaced by yet another partial, limited, transitory version of history. The best practitioners of the historical arts, Hofstadter noted, "have gone to the past with some passionate concern for the future," but this very passion which made them interesting also assured that they would be superseded. Nevertheless, by forcing the recognition of "continuous defeat and failure," the study of history, unlike the other social disciplines which were being driven toward "narrow positivistic inquiry," would "remain the most humanizing among the arts." *The Progressive Historians* was not only about the limitations of three eminent historians but also about the limits of history writing. For Hofstadter to have proposed a single, unifying historical vision to replace the Progressive view would have undermined the meaning of his inquiry and indeed canceled what he had learned as a historian.

While *The Progressive Historians* ultimately treated the big questions in history, *The Idea of A Party System* illustrated a historian's art practiced on a small but brilliant scale. Based on the Jefferson Memorial lectures delivered at the University of California at Berkeley in 1966, this book returned to the two loves with which Hofstadter began his career, political history and the history of ideas. He brought the subjects together, not as he had done in *The Age of Reform* through a study of popular ideology and political culture, but instead, by a consideration of the evolution of a political idea. In the book, Hofstadter demonstrated his mature insights into the nature of historical process. The party system, so essential to the maintenance of free political institutions, was, according to Hofstadter, a stepchild of the political culture of the eighteenth century. Unwelcomed, unplanned for, and often despised, it was several times nearly destroyed but finally permitted to grow from the realistic responses of American leaders to a dynamic political milieu. Neither the Federalists nor the Republicans of the 1790s welcomed opposition to their control of the government, and each identified loyalty to their policies and leaders with loyalty to the state. Neither side could easily distinguish between truth contained in the system of government defined by the

Constitution and their own specific versions of how the system could be best implemented. Like others, the founding fathers were limited men committed to their personal visions of truth and their own interests and beliefs. *The Idea of A Party System* was about the uncertain process by which Americans developed one of the most subtle, difficult, and significant of modern political conceptions—belief in the institutional process by which changes in government could occur peacefully. That concept rested on the recognition that the repression of opposition was more dangerous than the possibility of permitting others to make temporary mistakes. *The Idea of A Party System* was, therefore, at least in part, the story of the development of a political method resting "upon the willingness of people to consider that they may be mistaken," an idea that Hofstadter had proposed as the epitome of civilized discourse in his Columbia commencement address. By the 1830s and 1840s, party loyalty and respect for the idea of an organized opposition had become an honorable, indeed an obligatory belief. Hofstadter located the sources for this change in the emergence of a new political generation best represented by men like Martin Van Buren, men who were political bureaucrats and organizers rather than thinkers. They, rather than the more high-minded founding generation, created the theoretical rationalization of that party system which made democracy possible. Hofstadter's appreciation of men like Van Buren was in line with his increasing respect for Franklin Roosevelt as a cunning politician whose freedom from dogma permitted him to act in innovative ways. Hofstadter had come a long way from the view implicit in *The American Political Tradition*, that none of America's political leaders had a thought worthy of the name, to a view in which important ideas often came from unexpected sources and usually as a by-product of practical experience.

This idea was at least partly the animating force in Hofstadter's last work. But that work, the partial results of which were published in *America at 1750*, was remarkable less for any specific idea than for its overwhelming sadness and its extraordinarily sensitive portrayal of the human trials of settlement. David Donald called it "the most subtle and pessimistic of Hofstadter's books." *America at 1750* was, unfortunately, only a fragment of a much more grandly conceived project. Written urgently and hastily during a period of debilitating illness, it reflected the mind of a consummate historian contemplating an American society being formed from its human materials. The book was about the formation of institutions, the course of ideas, and the nature of culture in the American colonies of the eighteenth century when political and religious institutions and a tolerant pluralistic culture were beginning to take shape. But it was above all about people—black slaves, white indentured servants, small yeoman farmers, and aspiring artisans—whose struggles for life and for meaning were frequently ground down by the hardships of colonial existence. The contrast between a vigorous society clearly moving toward an expansive future and the heavy human costs of this development provided the dynamic tension of the book. The story of colonial development was portrayed, in fact, as full of moral ambiguity: the pursuit of profit resulting on the one hand in the slave trade, on the other in the establishment of the Pennsylvanian colony for the practice of religious liberty; the dark thunder of evangelicalism providing some with a healing vision while it led others to suicide; the religious intolerance by both sides during the Great Awakening leading to greater religious liberty. And always there was the irony that those who came to America came not full of hopes for their future in a land of golden opportunity but usually in anger or in shackles. As Hofstadter wrote, "The nobles, the wealthy, the established and the contented, stayed at home; it was the aggrieved middle classes and the impoverished who found themselves, voluntarily or involuntarily, becoming Americans." Most of them had few illusions. *America at 1750* showed Hofstadter in a new role, not as a social critic but as a tragic philosopher for whom history was less a model for future behavior than an illustration of the human condition. The book was filled with a profound sense of the sadness that is part of all human experience. It showed Hofstadter once more drawing close to the people, but it never demeaned the people it portrayed by sentimentalizing them. It was a stoic not a romantic vision and contained some of Hofstadter's most effective prose.

Like almost all of Hofstadter's other studies, the volumes of which *America at 1750* was to be part were intended as a synthesis. Because he had never been a scholar active in the exploration and development of primary source materials, Hofstadter's work had been repeatedly criticized on these grounds. "If one were to compare the proportion of time given to expression with that given to research," he once noted about himself, "my emphasis is on the first." The synthesis on which Hofstadter was working was more expansively conceived than any of his other studies. Indeed, he projected a work of a million and one-half words to Alfred A.

Knopf in 1969. It was perhaps to be his final answer to Charles Beard, whose *Rise of American Civilization* had been such an inspiration and bold challenge to him as a student and scholar. It was perhaps to be a response to critics like Robert Wiebe who assailed him for failing to propose a comparably coherent and vital alternative vision. Most likely, it would have taken the form of those subtly connected essays of which Hofstadter was a master. Certainly, it would have spoken with soft accents, sensitively evoking the complex and ambiguous in human history, rather than in arrogant tones and sweeping generalizations. The book would surely have provoked substantial interest befitting a major historian, but it would not have produced the controversy that greeted Hofstadter's earlier work, the absence of which already had troubled him on the appearance of *The Progressive Historians*. In many ways, Hofstadter by 1968, and certainly by 1970, had become a kind of institution, a figure fully honored but no longer central to the dynamic impulses of the craft now seeking out other methods such as quantification, increasingly devoted to monographic studies, and whose younger practitioners expressed their own deep commitments to the subjects of inquiry (the working class, women, blacks). Hofstadter had foreseen the transience of his own influence in *The Progressive Historians*. It would have saddened but not surprised him.

Richard Hofstadter died on 24 October 1970. He had worked on his final book until almost the very end, and friends and colleagues who visited him in his room at New York's Mt. Sinai Hospital found him still reflecting on aspects of American history about which he was changing his mind: slavery and black culture, evangelical religion, the nature of the American consensus. He left behind ten books, two of these major turning points in American historiography; several important collections of documents; a popular textbook on American history; more than thirty articles; a long roster of reviews; and a reputation for being civilized, brilliant, and humane.

Other:

"Manifest Destiny and the Philippines," in *America in Crisis*, edited by Daniel Aaron (New York: Knopf, 1952), pp. 173-200;

"Charles Beard and the Constitution," in *Charles A. Beard: An Appraisal*, edited by Howard K. Beale (Lexington: University of Kentucky Press, 1954), pp. 75-92;

"The Pseudo-Conservative Revolt," in *The New*

American Right, edited by Daniel Bell (New York: Criterion Books, 1955), pp. 33-55; revised as *The Radical Right* (Garden City: Doubleday, 1963), pp. 75-95;

The Great Issues in American Politics, edited by Hofstadter (New York: Fund for Adult Education, 1956); republished as *Ten Major Issues in American Politics* (New York: Oxford University Press, 1968);

"History and the Social Sciences," in *The Varieties of History*, edited by Fritz Stern (New York: Meridian Books, 1956), pp. 359-370;

Great Issues in American History: A Documentary Record, 2 volumes, edited by Hofstadter (New York: Vintage, 1958);

American Higher Education: A Documentary History, 2 volumes, edited by Hofstadter and Wilson Smith (Chicago: University of Chicago Press, 1961);

The Progressive Movement, 1900-1915, edited by Hofstadter (Englewood Cliffs, N.J.: Prentice-Hall, 1963);

W. H. Harvey, *Coin's Financial School*, edited, with an introduction, by Hofstadter (Cambridge, Mass.: Harvard University Press, 1963);

"The Revolution in Higher Education," in *Paths of American Thought*, edited by Arthur M. Schlesinger, Jr., and Morton White (Boston: Houghton Mifflin, 1963), pp. 269-290;

"Pseudo-Conservatism Revisited: A Postscript," in *The Radical Right*, edited by Daniel Bell (Garden City: Doubleday, 1963), pp. 97-103;

"What Happened to the Antitrust Movement? Notes on the Evolution of an American Creed," in *The Business Establishment*, edited by Earl Cheit (New York: Wiley, 1964), pp. 113-151;

"Alexis de Tocqueville," in *Atlantic Brief Lives: A Biographical Companion to the Arts*, edited by Louis Kronenberger (Boston: Little, Brown, 1965), pp. 795-798;

Sociology and History: Methods, edited by Hofstadter and Seymour Martin Lipset, Sociology of American History Series (New York: Basic Books, 1968);

"History and Sociology in the United States," in *Sociology and History: Methods*, edited by Hofstadter and Lipset (New York: Basic Books, 1968), pp. 3-19;

Turner and the Sociology of the Frontier, edited by Hofstadter and Lipset (New York: Basic Books, 1968);

"Political Parties," in *The Comparative Approach to American History*, edited by C. Vann Wood-

ward (New York: Basic Books, 1968), pp. 206-219;

Great Issues in American History, 3 volumes: *From Settlement to Revolution, 1584-1776*, edited by Hofstadter and Clarence L. Ver Steeg; *From the Revolution to the Civil War, 1765-1865*, edited by Hofstadter; *From Reconstruction to the Present Day, 1864-1969*, edited by Hofstadter (New York: Vintage, 1969);

American Violence: A Documentary History, edited by Hofstadter and Michael Wallace (New York: Knopf, 1970).

Periodical Publications:

"The Tariff Issue on the Eve of the Civil War," *American Historical Review*, 44 (October 1938): 50-55;

"Parrington and the Jeffersonian Tradition," *Journal of the History of Ideas*, 2 (October 1941): 391-400;

"U. B. Phillips and the Plantation Legend," *Journal of Negro History*, 39 (April 1944): 109-124;

"From Calhoun to the Dixiecrats," *Social Research*, 16 (June 1949): 135-150;

"Turner and the Frontier Myth," *American Scholar*, 18 (October 1949): 433-443;

"Winston Churchill: A Study in the Popular Novel," by Hofstadter and Beatrice K. Hofstadter, *American Quarterly*, 2 (Spring 1950): 12-28;

"Beard and the Constitution: The History of an Idea," *American Quarterly*, 2 (Fall 1950): 195-213;

"The Pseudo-Conservative Revolt," *American Scholar*, 24 (Winter 1954-1955): 9-27; also in *Perspectives USA*, 12 (1955): 10-29;

"Could a Protestant Have Beaten Hoover in 1928?," *Reporter*, 22 (17 March 1960): 31-33;

"A Note on Intellect and Power," *American Scholar*, 30 (Autumn 1961): 588-598;

"The Child and the World," *Daedalus*, 91 (Summer 1962): 501-525;

"The Paranoid Style in American Politics," *Harper's Magazine*, 229 (November 1964): 77-86;

"Fundamentalism and Status Politics on the Right," *Columbia University Forum*, 8 (Fall 1965): 18-24;

"The 214th Columbia University Commencement Address," *American Scholar*, 37 (Autumn 1968): 583-589;

"A Constitution Against Parties: Madisonian Pluralism and the Anti-party Tradition," *Government and Opposition*, 4 (Summer 1969): 345-366;

"The Importance of Comity in American History,"

Columbia University Forum, 13 (Winter 1970): 9-13.

Interviews:
David Hawke, "Interview: Richard Hofstadter," *History III* (New York: Meridian Books, 1960), pp. 135-141;

John A. Garraty, "Richard Hofstadter: The Development of Political Parties," *Interpreting American History: Conversations with Historians* (New York: Macmillan, 1970; London: Collier-Macmillan, 1970), I: 143-160.

References:
Lawrence A. Cremin, "Richard Hofstadter (1916-1970)," *Proceedings of the National Academy of Education*, 1 (1965-1974): 156-174;

Stanley Elkins and Eric McKitrick, "Richard Hofstadter: A Progress," in *The Hofstadter Aegis: A Memorial*, edited by Stanley Elkins and Eric McKitrick (New York: Knopf, 1974), pp. 300-367;

Paula S. Fass, "The Writings of Richard Hofstadter: A Bibliography," in *The Hofstadter Aegis: A Memorial*, edited by Stanley Elkins and Eric

McKittrick (New York: Alfred A. Knopf, 1974), pp. 368-381;

Peter Gay, "Richard Hofstadter," Biographical Supplement, *International Encyclopedia of the Social Sciences* (New York: Free Press, 1979), pp. 310-312;

Daniel Walker Howe and Peter Elliott Finn, "Richard Hofstadter: The Ironies of an American Historian," *Pacific Historical Review*, 43 (1974): 1-23;

Alfred Kazin, "Richard Hofstadter, 1916-1970," *American Scholar*, 40 (Summer 1971): 397-401;

Christopher Lasch, Foreword to the twenty-fifth anniversary edition of *The American Political Tradition and the Men Who Made It* (New York: Knopf, 1973);

Arthur M. Schlesinger, Jr., "Richard Hofstadter," in *Pastmasters: Some Essays on American Historians*, edited by Marcus Cunliffe and Robin W. Winks (New York: Harper & Row, 1969), pp. 278-315, 456-464.

Papers:
Richard Hofstadter's papers are at Columbia University, New York.

J. Franklin Jameson
(19 September 1859-28 September 1937)

Richard A. Shrader
Southern Historical Collection
University of North Carolina Library

BOOKS: *William Usselinx, Founder of the Dutch and Swedish West India Companies* (New York & London: Putnam's, 1887);

The History of Historical Writing in America (Boston & New York: Houghton Mifflin, 1891);

Dictionary of United States History, 1492-1894 (Boston: Puritan Publishing Company, 1894);

The American Revolution Considered as a Social Movement (Princeton: Princeton University Press, 1926).

J. Franklin Jameson, historian, teacher, editor, organizer, and collector, stood at the forefront of his profession in promoting sound historical scholarship. While he never produced a magnum opus, Jameson's career dramatically reflected a

change, in the late nineteenth-century writers of history, from the predominance of gifted amateurs possessing wealth and leisure to the emergence of seminar-trained college professors viewing history as a science. Unlike his predecessors, who selected subjects for intrinsic dramatic and literary possibilities and who expected their works to achieve permanence, Jameson prided himself on tracing the evolution of American institutions and fully expected his works to be superseded. Using occasional flashes of dry humor, Jameson possessed a refined prose style, somewhat severe in its simplicity but always clear in conveying his thoughts. Jameson's highly developed critical judgment was revealed in a wide variety of writings: books about American colonial and revolutionary history and about

American historiography; introductions to collections of documents and to other works he edited; articles, reports, and lectures about constitutional, political, and social history and about biographical subjects; and historical and textual criticisms of archival and other historical records. However, it was not Jameson's literary achievements but rather his provision of source materials and inspiration to other historical writers which gained for him an exalted place among fellow-historians.

John Franklin Jameson was born to John and Mariette Thompson Jameson in Somerville, Massachusetts, and reared under the strict discipline of his father, a master of the Boylston School in nearby Boston. J. Franklin, as he preferred to be called, attended local public school and prepared for college at Roxbury Latin School. With a memory of extraordinary retentiveness, an orderly mind, and a constructive imagination, he was admitted to Harvard University in 1874. Believing the fifteen year old too young to withstand the rigors of academic life, J. Franklin's father delayed the youth's college education for a year and sent him instead to stay on the farm of his maternal grandparents near

Woburn. In this rural western Massachusetts community, young Jameson, while searching town records and cemetery markers to compile a genealogy for his grandparents, first became interested in exploring his past.

Much against J. Franklin Jameson's wishes, his father moved the family in 1875 to Amherst, Massachusetts, and enrolled his son in Amherst College. Recovering from the disappointment of not going to Harvard, the youth entered fully into the life of the college. During his freshman year Jameson decided to devote his academic career to the study of history and began to read many classical histories including those of Thomas Macaulay and Edward Gibbon. So great was Jameson's zest for reading that once, when the library was closed to students, he climbed through a window to continue his favorite pastime. Jameson's academic courses provided ample opportunities to improve his writing skills, but he sought additional experience as an editor of the college newspaper. Interested in the activities of the school, Jameson also wrote a history of his class of 1879, in which he graduated as valedictorian.

After an unsuccessful year of teaching in high school, where his inordinate shyness prevented him from maintaining discipline in the classroom, Jameson enrolled in 1880 in the recently founded history graduate program at Johns Hopkins University. Because of an interest in his own family heritage and of his recent stimulation by the celebration of the American Revolution centennial, Jameson changed his focus from world history to American history.

Refining his research and writing skills in the German-inspired seminar of Professor Herbert Baxter Adams, Jameson explored various topics from current troubles in Barbados to the early history of New York City. Like a laboratory which carefully tests mineralogical specimens, Adams's seminar taught Jameson to examine rigorously historical data and to organize carefully his findings before writing about them. Jameson reflected this "scientific" approach to history in a widely researched and well-organized essay, "The Origins and Development of the Municipal Government of New York City," published in the *Magazine of American History* in 1882. That year he also finished his dissertation, "Montauk and the Common Lands of East Hampton," which appeared later in the same magazine. Jameson's lifelong modesty regarding his works is typified by his consideration of these two studies as mere exercises in research and writing rather than as contributions to the knowledge of these subjects.

J. Franklin Jameson

After receiving in 1882 the first Ph.D. in historical studies awarded by Johns Hopkins University, Jameson remained there for six more years serving both as assistant and associate professor. During this time he helped develop further Adams's seminar and offered a new graduate course on the principles and processes of historical criticism. Although Jameson was appreciative of the opportunity to improve his teaching and research skills at Johns Hopkins, he also was mindful of certain pressures felt by his colleagues, as revealed in the following stanza of a humorous poem he wrote for an alumni reunion program: "How doth the little Hopkins man / Improve the shining hour? / He toils to please the twelve trustees, / Olympians, clothed with power."

In 1884 Jameson was among the small group of scholars who founded the American Historical Association at a meeting in Saratoga, New York. Three years later he published his first substantial piece of historical research, *William Usselinx, Founder of the Dutch and Swedish West India Companies* (1887). As a graduate student Jameson had become familiar with the large role the two trading companies had played in the early development of New York. In his study he expanded this interest to incorporate a biography of the companies' founder. At home in four languages, Jameson had little trouble mastering the available foreign-language materials, but his publication received little notice despite the new material uncovered and the clarity of his writing.

At the age of twenty-eight Jameson left Johns Hopkins University in 1888 for an appointment as full professor at Brown University. Not long after arriving at Brown, he published two works. To encourage more interest in constitutional history, Jameson in 1889 produced his first edited work, *Essays in the Constitutional History of the United States in the Formative Period, 1775-1789*, a collection of articles written by graduates and former members of Johns Hopkins University; it included his own essay "The Predecessors of the Supreme Court." From public lectures first delivered at Johns Hopkins and later repeated at Brown, Jameson also wrote a thoughtful little book, *The History of Historical Writing in America* (1891). Comparing historical writers and writings in four different time periods, Jameson displayed broad knowledge of American historiography. Viewing the development of American historical writings as still being in its adolescence, he challenged fellow-historians to bring maturity to their profession by exploring new avenues of research and writing.

Jameson's life took on new meaning in 1893 with his marriage to Sara Elizabeth Elwell which produced two children, Francis C. and Katrina, and over forty years of companionship. Although marriage brought change to the life of the thirty-three-year-old bachelor, it did not diminish his professional activities.

To provide history students with a needed reference book Jameson published in 1894 the *Dictionary of United States History, 1492-1894*. This volume included over 700 pages of alphabetically arranged descriptions of principal events, persons, places, and problems in American history. Since no other volume contained as much helpful historical information, it long remained a much consulted work in most college and university libraries.

Jameson's ability as an editor was recognized by his fellow-historians in 1895 when, in addition to fulfilling his teaching responsibilities, he was asked to become the chairman of the American Historical Association's newly created Historical Manuscripts Commission and the managing editor of the recently established *American Historical Review*. As chairman of the commission for seven years, Jameson inventoried and collected historical manuscripts for the association and served as general editor in publishing selected documents for its *Annual Reports*. One of Jameson's most impressive editorial efforts, appearing in the *Annual Report for 1899*, was the *Correspondence of John C. Calhoun*. Containing over 500 letters to and from the South Carolina statesman, letters which covered all periods of his career, this work received praise as an important contribution to political history. As a model for historical editors to follow, Jameson neither suppressed passages which would favor a particular school of political thought nor omitted words for the benefit of Calhoun's reputation. Despite favorable attention given to the standard-setting work, Jameson viewed his publication as a meager effort to provide source material for others to use in writing political histories or biographies of Calhoun.

Except for a period between 1901 and 1905, Jameson served as managing editor of the *American Historical Review* from its inception until 1928. He not only determined its policies but also edited copy, suggested and solicited articles, selected books and book reviewers, and edited manuscripts for its documents section. His guidelines for reviewing books maintained such high standards that they were later adopted by the editors of the *Mississippi*

Valley Historical Review and reprinted in the *Harvard Guide to American History* (1954). Jameson also kept his *Review* afloat during its early years of limited operating funds, broadened the historical interests of its readers, and discovered and encouraged its young, talented writers.

Leaving Brown University in 1901, Jameson accepted a position to head the history department of the University of Chicago. No longer managing editor of the *American Historical Review* but saddled with many administrative duties at Chicago, he found little time for writing. However, while at Chicago he was able to complete one short work, "Studies in the History of the Federal Convention of 1787," appearing in the Association's *Annual Report for 1902*. This publication laid the foundation for Max Farrand's later authoritative work, *The Records of the Federal Convention of 1787* (1911).

With a massive store of knowledge, a precision of expression, a penetrating understanding of human motives, and a subtle sense of relationships, Jameson possessed many qualities of gifted historical writers. However, while at Chicago and still in his early forties, he decided to give up any ideas of writing an important book. Perhaps the decision was the result of a low estimation of himself as a historical writer or of a belief that he lived in a time unconducive to great literary achievements. Whatever the reason, however, Jameson now appeared happy when working vigorously behind the scenes and became content "to make bricks for others to use."

Jameson never felt at home in the midwestern city of Chicago; therefore, when he was offered a position in 1905 as director of the Carnegie Institution's Bureau (later Department) of Historical Research in Washington, D.C., he readily accepted. Even more exciting than the move back to the East was the challenge in directing the newly established branches of the bureau's work, which included exploration of foreign repositories for materials about American history, publication of documentary material, editorial duties for the *American Historical Review*, and maintenance of a clearinghouse of information for historical researchers.

Not long after assuming the new job, Jameson sent a staff of scholars to major archives in Europe and elsewhere to locate and describe materials relating to American history. As a result the bureau published or subsidized the publication of twenty-two useful guides to sources of American history in locations from the West Indies to Russia.

Under Jameson's planning and supervision

the bureau also produced during the 1920s and 1930s important documentary publications, including *Letters of Members of the Continental Congress*; *Proceedings and Debates of the British Parliament Respecting North America, 1452-1727*; *Correspondence of Andrew Jackson*; and *Atlas of Historical Geography*. Although Jameson's name did not appear on any of these volumes, he did handle all of the difficult administrative problems, and he smoothed the way for others in foreign archives or with private manuscript owners.

In addition to resuming duties as managing editor of the *American Historical Review*, Jameson also assumed responsibilities as general editor of the multivolume series, *Original Narratives of Early American History*, sponsored by the American Historical Association. From 1906 to 1917 Jameson supervised the publication of its nineteen volumes, which included travel accounts, explorations, chronicles, contemporary history, and literature. In 1909 and 1910 Jameson himself edited two of the volumes, *Narratives of New Netherland* and *Johnson's 'Wonder-Working Providence.'* His series proved to be one of the most useful sources of published information for writers of colonial American history.

The bureau under Jameson performed invaluable service as a clearinghouse of data for historical writers. Conveniently located in Washington, Jameson and his staff were besieged by calls, especially from young scholars with questions related to history. Jameson never turned a deaf ear to any sincere inquirer, nor did he lose patience with the constant demands of outsiders on his time and talents.

Jameson's position at the Bureau of Historical Research allowed him to play a more important role in organizing professional historical activities than any person before or since. After the well-known Jameson was elected president of the American Historical Association in 1907, he began an active and prolonged campaign for the construction of a national archives building to house the growing accumulation of historical documents and for the creation of an administrative establishment to supervise its operation. From 1907, when President Theodore Roosevelt called for an estimate of space requirements for an archives building, to 1934, when President Franklin Roosevelt approved the National Archives Act, Jameson led archives supporters in the long battle by writing numerous letters to government officials, sending circulars to historical societies, speaking to various professional and civic organizations, and obtaining newspaper and periodical publicity for the successful quest. Today a bronze plaque hangs in the lobby of the National Archives Building as a tribute to Jameson's prominent role in making this valuable documents repository a reality.

Overshadowed by his struggle to establish the National Archives was Jameson's campaign to create a national commission for the publication of important records and papers. In 1906, as an active member of the Historical Manuscripts Commission, Jameson lamented the small amount of money America had spent on document publication in an *American Historical Review* article entitled "Gaps in the Published Records of the United States." While president of the American Historical Association, he appointed a special committee to review the needs of historical document publication and to propose a plan for dealing with the deficiency. With committee recommendations he helped write a legislative bill for the creation of a national publication commission, but the bill lay in limbo in congressional files until 1934 when it passed as companion legislation to the National Archives Act. Unfortunately, Jameson did not live to see the fruits of his work. The National Historical Publication Commission accomplished very little until after its reorganization in 1950 and its subsequent sponsoring of important letterpress and microfilm document projects.

As Jameson had used his membership in the American Historical Association for the benefit of historical writers, he likewise employed his affiliation with the American Council of Learned Societies to the same end. Taking part in organizing the council in 1919, Jameson accepted the invitation five years later to serve as chairman of its committee considering the publication of the *Dictionary of American Biography*. Lacking the necessary funds to begin the multivolume work, Jameson traveled to New York, where he successfully secured the financial support from Adolph Ochs of the *New York Times*. Jameson not only recommended the publication's first editor, Allen Johnson, but also served on its committee of management and offered advice about policy when needed. In the last of the twenty volumes planned, Jameson collaborated with Dumas Malone, second editor of the *Dictionary of American Biography*, in writing a history of the multivolume project.

Although busy with many long-term projects throughout the 1920s, Jameson followed the advice he had offered fellow historians over thirty years before and explored new avenues of research and writing. Seeking to provide little-known information about the early maritime history of America, Jameson edited a work entitled, *Privateering and Piracy in the Colonial Period* (1923). It contained documents ranging from a brief decree by a judge of the vice-admiralty court to a long and detailed account of the career of the pirate William Kidd. Critics praised Jameson's selections not only for being representative but also for providing exciting and dramatic material for scores of novels. As usual, the book contained a storehouse of reliable and illuminating annotations about its subjects and rarely failed to leave items unexplained.

In 1926 Jameson produced his most popular and most influential book, *The American Revolution Considered as a Social Movement*. Believing that the political struggle accompanying the war had set free many economic desires and social aspirations among the colonists, Jameson saw these changes as releasing forces which profoundly altered such aspects of colonial society as the relations of social classes to each other, the institution of slavery, the system of landholding, the course of business, and the direction of intellectual and religious life.

Considering that Jameson's small volume was published by a university press with limited advertising resources, the sale of almost a thousand copies was most impressive. The positive reaction by many young historians to Jameson's almost radical economic and social interpretation of the American Revolution reflected a broad conception of history that was emerging very rapidly in the late 1920s. The general reading public also was delighted that a well-known historian at last had considered the everyday affairs of people. His intention being only to challenge American historians by suggesting new directions for future research, Jameson laid no claim to having written a classical study. Yet in a poll taken during the 1950s among American historians to name the best historical work published between 1920 and 1935, *The American Revolution Considered as a Social Movement* was voted one of the top fifteen books and had the best vote-getting record per word of all listed books.

While subsequent studies of the American Revolution have suggested that the war was less revolutionary in changing the status of people than Jameson supposed and that there was less distribution of land than he believed, the "Jameson thesis" is still considered sound and useful. Because of his emphasis on the importance of the interrelations among human activities, he is considered by many scholars as one of the founders of American cultural and social history.

When a chair in American history was created

at the Library of Congress in 1928, Jameson was invited to be its first recipient and also to serve as chief of the Manuscripts Division of the library. Having learned that the Carnegie Institution planned to terminate appropriations for future historical research and to ask for Jameson's retirement in 1929 when he would be seventy years old, he readily accepted the library's offer. From then until his death in 1937, Jameson supervised the completion of such projects as the editing of the final volume of the *Journals of the Continental Congress* and of the two concluding volumes of the *Records of the Virginia Company* and the photocopying of manuscripts from European archives related to American history. Having important contacts with American manuscript dealers and collectors as well as with major American historical societies and archives, Jameson also was allowed to photostat their valuable holdings. Subsequently he built up a great collection of domestic papers at the Library of Congress and created an eminent research center for historical writers.

On a sunny March afternoon in 1937, Jameson stepped from the curb in front of the Library of Congress's main entrance and was struck by an automobile. Spending an entire summer in Maine to allow his broken leg to heal, Jameson looked forward to returning to his job. However, before he was able to undertake full-time work, he suffered a heart attack, contracted pneumonia, and died at his Washington home several days after his seventy-eighth birthday. Jameson was buried in Oak Hill Cemetery in the Georgetown section of the capital city.

While organizing professional activities, editing documentary material, managing a notable historical journal, and counseling young scholars, Jameson devoted much of his life to the collection and preservation of important American documents for use by historical writers. Jameson also produced a variety of useful and suggestive writings. However, without hope of ever completing a monumental book himself, Jameson put an enormous amount of energy into the creation of significant multivolume works for others to use in writing their masterpieces. Jameson never considered himself to be a historian in the strictest sense, but he was regarded by both his contemporaries and successors as a historian's historian.

Other:

Essays in the Constitutional History of the United States in the Formative Period, 1775-1789, edited by Jameson (Boston: Houghton Mifflin, 1889);

Correspondence of John C. Calhoun, volume 2 of American Historical Association *Annual Report for 1899*, edited by Jameson (Washington, D.C.: U. S. Government Printing Office, 1900);

Original Narratives of Early American History, volumes 1-19, edited by Jameson (New York: Scribners, 1906-1917);

Privateering and Piracy in the Colonial Period, edited by Jameson (New York: Macmillan, 1923).

Periodical Publications:

"Gaps in the Published Records of the United States," *American Historical Review*, 11 (July 1906): 817-831;

"The American Historical Association, 1884-1909," *American Historical Review*, 15 (October 1909): 1-20;

"The Need of a National Archive Building," *Bulletin of the American Library Association*, 8 (July 1914): 130-140.

Letters:

Elizabeth Donnan and Leo F. Stock, eds., *An Historian's World: Selections from Correspondence of John Franklin Jameson* (Philadelphia: American Philosophical Society, 1956);

References:

John Walton Caughey, "Historians' Choice: Results of a Poll on Recently Published American History and Biography," *Mississippi Valley Historical Review*, 39 (September 1952): 289-302;

Ruth Anna Fisher and William L. Fox, *J. Franklin Jameson: A Tribute* (Washington, D.C.: Catholic University of America Press, 1965);

Victor Gondos, Jr., *J. Franklin Jameson and the Birth of the National Archives, 1906-1926* (Philadelphia: University of Pennsylvania Press, 1981);

Donald R. McCoy, *The National Archives, America's Ministry of Documents, 1934-1968* (Chapel Hill: University of North Carolina Press, 1978);

Frederick B. Tolles, "The American Revolution Considered as a Social Movement: A Re-Evaluation," *American Historical Review*, 60 (October 1954): 1-12;

David D. Van Tassel, "John Franklin Jameson," *Keepers of the Past*, edited by Clifford L. Lord (Chapel Hill: University of North Carolina Press, 1965), pp. 81-96.

Papers:

Jameson's papers are at the Manuscripts Division, Library of Congress.

Merrill Jensen

(16 July 1905-30 January 1980)

Michael E. Stevens

South Carolina Department of Archives and History

BOOKS: *The Articles of Confederation: An Interpreta-
tion of the Social-Constitutional History of the
American Revolution, 1774-1781* (Madison:
University of Wisconsin Press, 1940);
*The New Nation: A History of the United States During
the Confederation, 1781-1789* (New York:
Knopf, 1950);
The Making of the American Constitution (New York:
Van Nostrand Reinhold, 1964);
*The Founding of a Nation: A History of the American
Revolution, 1763-1776* (New York: Oxford
University Press, 1968);
The American Revolution Within America (New York:
New York University Press, 1974).

Merrill Jensen

Merrill Jensen has often been characterized as
the last of the Progressive historians. Although he
looked upon that label with amusement, his works,
following those of Charles Beard and Carl Becker,
helped to delineate the conflicts that marked
American political life between 1763 and 1789.
Writing bold, iconoclastic histories, Jensen ably defended his view that the period had been marked by
an internal revolution, followed by a counter-
revolutionary Constitution.

Merrill Monroe Jensen was born to John M.
and Julia Seymour Jensen near the town of Elk
Horn, Iowa. He spent his youth on farms there and
in South Dakota. After attending high school, he
taught in a one-room school in Woonsocket, South
Dakota, before heading west to Seattle, Washington. He enrolled at the University of Washington,
where he received a bachelor's degree in 1929 and
where one of his teachers, Edward McMahon, recognized Jensen's talents and encouraged him to
continue his study of history. First, Jensen went
back to South Dakota to marry Genevieve Privet in
December 1929, and then he returned with her to
Washington, where they both attended the university. Jensen received a master's degree in 1931 and
enrolled in the doctoral program at McMahon's
alma mater, the University of Wisconsin.

The Depression years spent in Madison were
financially difficult. Jensen worked at the State
Historical Society of Wisconsin on the project of
calendaring (that is, arranging and describing) the
vast nineteenth-century collection of Lyman C.
Draper papers. He worked also at the university as a
teaching assistant. When Jensen received his Ph.D.
in 1934, academic jobs were scarce, and he failed at
first to locate a position. In the following year, however, Jensen received an appointment as an instructor at the University of Washington, where his
duties included a five-day teaching schedule plus
the managing editorship of the *Washington Historical
Quarterly*. With Genevieve Jensen's help, between
1935 and 1942 he edited the journal, which he gave
the new title *Pacific Northwest Quarterly*. Although

these early years at Washington were marked by illness for both Jensens, the period was also a productive one. In addition to his teaching and editing, Jensen revised his dissertation for publication and wrote several articles in which he presented themes that he would more fully develop in later works.

Jensen's first article, "The Cession of the Old Northwest," which appeared in the *Mississippi Valley Historical Review* in 1936, is a solid piece of research outlining the maneuvering of opposing land speculators during the creation of the national domain. Jensen attacked the accepted view that Maryland had virtuously blocked ratification of the Articles of Confederation until Virginia ceded its western lands to Congress. Instead, he argued that the causes for the establishment of the national domain "lay less in patriotic abstraction and national vision" than in the interests of practical politicians who were influenced by economic motives. Here Jensen exhibited a willingness to cut through political rhetoric in searching for causes, an outlook that also characterized his future work.

In the following year, the *Pacific Historical Review* published "The Articles of Confederation: A Re-interpretation." In this essay Jensen criticized the prevailing view, popularized by John Fiske, which held that the Confederation era between the end of the Revolution and the adoption of the Constitution was a period of chaos. Jensen argued that this interpretation was a result of skillful Federalist propaganda. Instead, he asserted, the Articles of Confederation should be seen as a product of the "social-political turmoil" that marked the Revolution. Jensen insisted that the prewar divisions between radicals and conservatives in American society continued during and after the Revolution. Once independence became inevitable, conservatives sought a centralized government that could regulate trade, control local governments, dispose of western lands, and quiet internal dissent. While they failed to achieve their aims in the Articles of Confederation, the conservatives succeeded in attaining their goals with the adoption of the federal Constitution. Jensen's categories for defining radicals and conservatives were somewhat simplistic and sketchy, yet he was successful in outlining themes that he would later refine.

In 1939, the *Mississippi Valley Historical Review* printed Jensen's "The Creation of the National Domain, 1781-1784," a continuation of his 1936 article, which told the story of congressional acceptance of Virginia's land cession and stressed the importance of economic interests in national politics. The essay also hinted at a theme later to be developed in *The New Nation* (1950)—that "the Confederation Congress showed both vigor and originality" and that it should be credited for initiating an effective federal land policy.

Jensen's first book, *The Articles of Confederation: An Interpretation of the Social-Constitutional History of the American Revolution, 1774-1781* (1940), established his reputation as a leading historian of the Revolution. In this work, which by 1981 had gone through eight printings and had sold 38,000 copies, Jensen described a revolution "fought out on grounds that were material rather than nonmaterial, internal rather than international" and led by practical men who "knew precisely what the issues were." He argued that the Revolution "was essentially, though relatively, a democratic movement within the thirteen American colonies, and that its significance for the political and constitutional history of the United States lay in its tendency to elevate the political and economic status of the majority of the people. The Articles of Confederation were the constitutional expression of this movement and the embodiment in governmental form of the philosophy of the Declaration of Independence." Jensen also discussed the conflicts between radicals and conservatives in Congress and outlined the problems they faced in drafting the articles. The fight between the two factions culminated a decade later in the Constitution which, according to Jensen, was "a conservative counterrevolution." In later years, Jensen stated that he wished he could modify some parts of his book. For instance, he believed that his choice of words had created problems. On later reflection he would call the radicals "popular leaders" and would distinguish between factions within that group. He would also qualify ideas that he had stated too boldly. Nonetheless, he stood firmly behind the book's main theses about the nature of the Revolution.

During World War II, Jensen's heart problems kept him out of the military, although he briefly worked as a historian for the Army Air Force in 1944. In that same year, he left the University of Washington to accept an appointment as an associate professor at the University of Wisconsin. He was promoted to the rank of professor in 1946 and served on the faculty until his retirement in 1976. As a teacher, Jensen was an imposing figure. In his undergraduate classes, although he was usually tied to his notes, he lectured forcefully and dramatically. His well-developed physique, a product of hard work during summers in the forests of Washington state, created a sense of awe. In his graduate classes, he gained respect for his bibliographic knowledge and high academic standards. Jensen saw forty-four of his graduate students at Wisconsin receive the Ph.D., including many who later established themselves as prominent historians in their own rights.

Jensen's second book, *The New Nation: A History of the United States During the Confederation, 1781-1789*, was published in 1950. Broader in scope than *The Articles of Confederation*, this volume covered the political, social, economic, and cultural history of the period, although the work seemed most thorough in its discussion of politics. According to Jensen, there was a "continuity of conflict" between the true "federalists" who wanted to preserve the Confederation and the nationalists who wanted a central government with coercive powers. Jensen argued that there were two important results of the Revolution—the unleashing of democracy, which found expression in revolutionary state constitutions, and the elimination of an imperial central government. Thus, it was the true "federalists," frequently misnamed Antifederalists, who worked to continue the essence of the Revolution. Throughout the volume, Jensen stressed the achievements of the Confederation government and tried to dispel the notion that the era was a period of political and economic chaos.

In the 1950s and early 1960s, Jensen's time was primarily occupied by teaching, editing, and promoting historical studies. He edited *Regionalism in America* (1951), as well as a lengthy volume, *American Colonial Documents to 1776* (1955), for the English Historical Documents series. Jensen also served from 1961 to 1964 as chairman of the University of Wisconsin's history department, a task that he relinquished after leading the department through a period of remarkable growth. In addition, he promoted the study of American history in Europe and Asia during these years. For the 1949-1950 academic term, he was Harmsworth Professor at Oxford, where he found little interest in American history. On his return to the United States, he reported that "American history in England is a subject that may have a future. It certainly has very little past." In 1955 he led a seminar at the University of Tokyo, and in 1960 he taught American colonial history at the University of Ghent in Belgium. He returned to Japan in 1961 to give seminars at Kyoto University. Making seven more trips to Japan, Jensen became one of the leaders in developing American studies programs in that country. A whole generation of Japanese students thus was influenced both by his curriculum development and by his published works, some of which appeared in Japanese editions. His students, many of

whom are now leading academics in Japan, referred to him affectionately as "Grandpa Jensen" and subsequently sent their students to study at the University of Wisconsin.

Jensen's international experiences perhaps helped him to avoid the parochialism that affected some Americans in the 1950s. In an essay that appeared in 1958, he warned that those who try to export American political institutions too often "seem to have little comprehension of the complexities of political societies." Nations cannot escape their history, Jensen declared, and while revolutions may disturb the surface, "any alteration of fundamental attitudes takes generations, not decades."

Appointed Vilas Research Professor at Wisconsin in 1964, a position that lightened his teaching load and provided him with research assistance, Jensen became a highly productive writer and editor. Between 1964 and 1978, eight books as well as a number of articles appeared under his name. *The Making of the American Constitution*, a book that he believed was among the best things that he had written, appeared in 1964. In this brief work, Jensen outlined the background leading to the Constitutional Convention and analyzed the issues faced by the delegates. Noting the compromises and bargains that made the Constitution possible, he argued that the convention succeeded, where the British had failed, in centralizing American government.

During the 1960s and 1970s, as dissent and violence arose on college campuses, Jensen's belief in a conflict-filled American past seemed to make more sense than the "consensus history" of the 1950s, and his early work therefore gained acceptance. For instance, *The Articles of Confederation*, which had sold fewer than 2,000 copies between 1940 and 1959, was reissued in paperback and sold about 36,000 copies during the next twenty years. Jensen defended his earlier work with new vigor while also disseminating the findings of his recent research. In 1966 his essay "Historians and the Nature of the American Revolution" appeared in a volume edited by Ray Billington. In his essay Jensen outlined the historiography of the Revolution from writers of the period itself to those of the present and used his outline as a vehicle to blast neoconservative historians who had tried to refute the work of Becker, Beard, and himself. He also edited a volume entitled *Tracts of the American Revolution, 1763-1776*, which appeared in 1967. For this volume, Jensen selected seventeen significant pamphlets and newspaper articles and, in a lengthy introduction, set them in their historical context.

In the following year, he published his classic *The Founding of a Nation: A History of the American Revolution, 1763-1776*. This volume, *The Articles of Confederation*, and *The New Nation* constituted an informal trilogy containing Jensen's thoughts and findings on the period from 1763-1789. Unlike the two earlier volumes in which he specifically argued a thesis, here Jensen subtly incorporated his interpretation into the text. As might be expected, he outlined the bitter struggles between different factions in the colonies, stressed American disunity, and noted the rise of new popular leaders. In its 704 pages of flowing narrative, Jensen set forth the complex history of the times.

President of the Organization of American Historians in 1969-1970, Jensen in his April 1970 presidential address before the group reaffirmed his work of the previous thirty-five years. He took some portions of his speech from *The Founding of the Nation* but added new material as well. Asserting that the War for Independence was also a "people's revolution," Jensen emphasized its creation of new attitudes about society. He noted that the Revolution brought about a new role for the people, a decline in prestige for the leadership, and growing attacks on property.

In the late 1960s, Jensen took on new responsibilities as an editor. He had previously edited two volumes of documents, a volume of essays, and a scholarly journal, but he was now asked to take on a more massive task. In 1966 he was appointed editor of *The Documentary History of the First Federal Elections, 1788-1790*, a projected three-volume series that gathered documents on the formative elections following the adoption of the Constitution; one volume of the series was completed under Jensen's supervision. Three years later, he also assumed editorship of *The Documentary History of the Ratification of the Constitution and the Bill of Rights*. This project would eventually gather approximately 55,000 documents from hundreds of repositories in the United States and Europe. Jensen planned to publish this material on the adoption of the Constitution and the Bill of Rights in nineteen volumes and numerous microfiche supplements. The project had begun in 1958 under the editorship of Robert E. Cushman. When Cushman died in 1969, Jensen was asked to replace him, and the project's files were moved from Washington, D.C., to Wisconsin in 1970. Jensen scrapped Cushman's galleys for the first volume and redesigned the series. Over the following ten years he was assisted by a staff of young scholars, most of whom had studied under

him, in gathering and editing this material. The first three volumes appeared under his direction.

Jensen delivered the Anson G. Phelps lectures at New York University in 1973, and in the following year they were published as *The American Revolution Within America*. The book focused on the internal politics of the Revolution and again emphasized themes of social conflict and political continuity. Also in 1974, the United States Congress honored Jensen by inviting him to address the body on the occasion of the two-hundredth anniversary of the Continental Congress.

Jensen formally retired from the University of Wisconsin in 1976, the bicentennial year of American independence. The university marked his retirement with a symposium on the Revolution conducted by leading scholars, and his former students honored him with a volume of essays entitled *The Human Dimensions of Nation Making* (1976). In that same year, the first two volumes in the ratification series and the first volume in the federal elections project appeared. Volume one of the ratification series, entitled *Constitutional Documents and Records, 1776-1787*, illustrated the continuity of constitutional development. The second volume, called *Ratification of the Constitution by the States: Pennsylvania*, revealed the bitter fight over the Constitution in that state. The first volume of *The Documentary History of the First Federal Elections*, coedited with Robert A. Becker, included documents dealing with the Confederation Congress, and with Massachusetts, New Hampshire, Pennsylvania, and South Carolina. In a brief introduction, Jensen noted that the struggle over the ratification of the Constitution carried over into the first federal elections.

In the years after 1976, Jensen continued his involvement with the ratification and elections projects, although he was able to spend less time in the projects' offices because of eye surgery and other health problems. However, volume three of the ratification series, entitled *Ratification of the Constitution by the States: Delaware, New Jersey, Georgia, Connecticut*, appeared in 1978. In this volume, Jensen included the usual editorial apparatus and also added a long essay on Connecticut politics in the Confederation era. It was to prove his last extended work. On 30 January 1980, after a lingering illness, he died in Madison, Wisconsin.

As a historian, Jensen wrote clear, crisp prose. He also had a good sense of irony and a knack for finding the exact quote needed to make his point. For instance, to illustrate wartime profiteering, he quoted a letter from Revolutionary leader Carter Braxton who urged merchants to keep their profits down to three-hundred percent for the sake of the cause. Jensen resisted attempts to categorize him, stating that once labels are pasted on historians, "mental rigor mortis sets in." Yet it is still possible to determine the influences that affected him without losing sight of his complexity and individuality. His rural background predisposed him to examine the outlook and interests of farmers. E. James Ferguson, one of Jensen's former students, described his philosophy as "vaguely Populist, combining a sympathy for the common man with a realistic sense of human motives and a hardheaded recognition of how the loaves and fishes are divided." Thus, while his research was thorough and sound, Jensen always made it clear where his sympathies lay. He believed that history was complex, but he also realized that it was the historian's job to express that complexity in a clear, orderly fashion. He therefore had little use for timid historians who refused to stake out their positions. Merrill Jensen best expressed his view of how history should be written when in the 1959 printing of *The Articles of Confederation* he declared, "Conceivably one could write a book on the Revolution with one line of generalization at the top of each page, with the rest of the page consisting of footnotes pointing to the exceptions, qualifications, and contradictions. It might be history, but I doubt it."

Other:

Regionalism in America, edited by Jensen (Madison: University of Wisconsin Press, 1951);

American Colonial Documents to 1776, edited by Jensen, volume 9 of the English Historical Documents series, (New York: Oxford University Press, 1955; London: Eyre & Spottiswoode, 1955);

"A Note to the Reader" and "Commentary," in *Political Ideas of the American Revolution: Britannic-American Contributions to the Problem of Imperial Organization, 1765-1775*, by Randolph G. Adams (New York: Barnes & Noble, 1958), pp. 1-31;

"Historians and the Nature of the American Revolution," in *The Reinterpretation of Early American History: Essays in Honor of John Edwin Pomfret*, edited by Ray Allen Billington (San Marino, Cal.: Huntington Library, 1966), pp. 101-127;

Tracts of the American Revolution, 1763-1776, edited by Jensen (Indianapolis: Bobbs-Merrill, 1967);

"The Colonial Phase," in *The Comparative Approach to American History*, edited by C. Vann Woodward (New York: Basic Books, 1968), pp. 18-33;

Joseph Galloway, *Historical and Political Reflections on the Rise and Progress of the American Rebellion*, introduction by Jensen (New York & London: Johnson Reprint Corporation, 1972);

"The Articles of Confederation," in *Fundamental Testaments of the American Revolution* (Washington, D.C.: Library of Congress, 1973), pp. 49-81;

"The Bicentennial and Afterwards," in *The Publication of American Historical Manuscripts*, edited by Leslie W. Dunlap and Fred Shelley (Iowa City: University of Iowa Libraries, 1976), pp. 47-55;

The Documentary History of the First Federal Elections, 1788-1790, volume 1, edited by Jensen and Robert A. Becker (Madison: University of Wisconsin Press, 1976);

The Documentary History of the Ratification of the Constitution and the Bill of Rights, volumes 1-3, edited by Jensen (Madison: State Historical Society of Wisconsin, 1976-1978);

"The Sovereign States: Their Antagonisms and Rivalries and Some Consequences," in *Sovereign States in an Age of Uncertainty*, edited by Ronald Hoffman and Peter J. Albert (Charlottesville: University Press of Virginia for the United States Capitol Historical Society, 1981), pp. 226-250.

Periodical Publications:

"The Cession of the Old Northwest," *Mississippi Valley Historical Review*, 23 (June 1936): 27-48;

"The Articles of Confederation: A Re-Interpretation," *Pacific Historical Review*, 6 (June 1937): 120-142;

"The Creation of the National Domain, 1781-1784," *Mississippi Valley Historical Review*, 26 (December 1939): 323-342;

"The Idea of a National Government During the American Revolution," *Political Science Quarterly*, 58 (September 1943): 356-379;

"Democracy and the American Revolution," *Huntington Library Quarterly*, 20 (August 1957): 321-341;

"The American Revolution and American Agriculture," *Agricultural History*, 43 (January 1969): 107-124;

"The American People and the American Revolution," *Journal of American History*, 57 (June 1970): 5-35.

Reference:

E. James Ferguson, "Merrill Jensen: A Personal Comment," and James Kirby Martin, "The Human Dimensions of Nation Making: Merrill Jensen's Scholarship and the American Revolution," in *The Human Dimensions of Nation Making: Essays on Colonial and Revolutionary America*, edited by Martin (Madison: State Historical Society of Wisconsin, 1976), pp. 3-22.

Arthur S. Link
(8 August 1920-   )

Marcia G. Synnott
University of South Carolina

BOOKS: *Wilson: The Road to the White House* (Princeton: Princeton University Press, 1947);

Woodrow Wilson and the Progressive Era, 1910-1917, The New American Nation Series, edited by Henry Steele Commager and Richard B. Morris (New York: Harper, 1954);

American Epoch: A History of the United States Since the 1890s, by Link and William B. Catton (New York: Knopf, 1955); republished in 2 volumes as *American Epoch: A History of the United States Since 1900* (New York: Knopf, 1980);

Lectures and Seminars at the University of Chicago, January 30-February 3, 1956, in Celebration of the Centennial of Woodrow Wilson (Chicago: University of Chicago Press, 1956);

Wilson: The New Freedom (Princeton: Princeton University Press, 1956);

Wilson the Diplomatist: A Look at His Major Foreign Policies, The Albert Shaw Lectures on Diplomatic History, 1956 (Baltimore: Johns Hopkins Press, 1957);

President Wilson and His English Critics; an Inaugural Lecture Delivered before the University of Oxford on 13 May 1959 (Oxford: Clarendon Press, 1959);

La política de los Estados Unidos en América Latina, 1913-1916, Traducción de Fernando Rosenzweig (Mexico: Fondo de Cultura Económica, 1960);

Wilson: The Struggle for Neutrality, 1914-1915 (Princeton: Princeton University Press, 1960);

Our American Republic, by Link and David Saville Muzzey (Boston: Ginn, 1963);

Woodrow Wilson: A Brief Biography (Cleveland: World, 1963);

Arthur S. Link

Our Country's History, by Link and Muzzey (Boston: Ginn, 1964);

Wilson: Confusions and Crises, 1915-1916 (Princeton: Princeton University Press, 1964);

*Wilson: Campaigns for Progressivism and Peace, 1916-
    1917* (Princeton: Princeton University Press,
    1965);

*The Growth of American Democracy: An Interpretive
    History* (Boston: Ginn, 1967);

The Democratic Heritage: A History of the United States,
    by Link and Stanley Coben, 2 volumes (Wal-
    tham, Mass.: Ginn, 1971);

*The Higher Realism of Woodrow Wilson and Other
    Essays* (Nashville: Vanderbilt University Press,
    1971);

Crucial American Elections, by Link and others,
    Memoirs Series, volume 99 (Philadelphia:
    American Philosophical Society, 1973);

Woodrow Wilson: Revolution, War, and Peace (Ar-
    lington Heights, Ill.: AHM, 1979);

The American People: A History, by Link, Coben,
    Robert V. Remini, Douglas Greenberg, and
    Robert C. McMath, Jr. (Arlington Heights,
    Ill.: AHM, 1981).

Arthur S. Link, biographer, editor, and director of the comprehensive project to publish the
letters and papers of Woodrow Wilson, has no rival
as the foremost historian of the twenty-eighth
president. His interpretation of Wilson's character
and leadership has evolved over almost four decades of extensive research. He communicates his
ongoing evaluation in a vigorous, concise style that
holds the attention not only of scholars but also of
undergraduates and nonstudents beginning seriously to read twentieth-century United States history.

Arthur Stanley Link was born to John William
and Helen Link Link in the Shenandoah Valley
town of New Market, Virginia, almost forty miles
north of Staunton, where Wilson himself had been
born on 28 December 1856. Like Wilson, Link grew
up in and attended school in the South. Wilson had
enrolled for one year at Davidson College near
Charlotte, although he later attended and graduated from Princeton in 1879. After Princeton, Wilson had spent one and one-half years studying law
at the University of Virginia and about one year
practicing law in Atlanta before entering the doctoral program at Johns Hopkins University. There
he had studied history, economics, and government
and received his Ph.D. in 1886. Link matriculated at
the University of North Carolina, where he received
his bachelor's degree with highest honors in 1941,
his M.A. in 1942, and his Ph.D. three years later. He
also studied under Henry Steele Commager at Columbia University during the 1944-1945 academic
term. Both Wilson and Link taught at Princeton:

Wilson had become professor of jurisprudence and
political economy in 1890; Link was appointed an
instructor of history in 1945 and was promoted to
assistant professor in 1948. He then went to Northwestern University as an associate professor in
1949, and after nine years there, with promotion to
full professor in 1954, Link was appointed director
of the editorial project for the Wilson papers sponsored by the Woodrow Wilson Foundation. In 1960,
he rejoined the Princeton faculty. Distinguished
professorships followed: he was Edwards Professor
of American History from 1965 to 1976, and since
1976, he has been George Henry Davis '86 Professor of American History.

Although Link remained the scholar whereas
Wilson had gone on to become president of
Princeton, governor of New Jersey, and then president of the United States, they shared the view that
history taught moral values. Influenced by the religious teachings of their fathers, who were ministers, both men were devout Presbyterians although
neither was rigid in his faith. Wilson, Link wrote
with understanding, was "a man committed very
deeply to fundamental Christian affirmations about
moral law, but also enormously flexible about details and methods, so long as they did not violate
what he thought was right." Link himself was a lay
leader in the United Presbyterian Church and,
from 1963 to 1966, a vice-president of the National
Council of Churches. Religious values thus per-
meated both men's sense of history: Wilson believed
that God had created the United States to fulfill a
special mission of serving mankind, and in a 1981
textbook, *The American People: A History,* Link and
his coauthors stated unequivocally, "We also deeply
believe that history is a profoundly moral discipline
and teaches moral lessons." That statement was one
with which Woodrow Wilson would have assuredly
agreed.

In preparation for his later works on Woodrow Wilson, Link studied his own region in his doctoral dissertation, "The South and the Democratic
Campaign of 1910-1912." This work provided him
with the background that would enable him subsequently to analyze the evolution of the Democratic party from 1908 to 1916. Link's thinking
about Southern history was influenced by his professors at the University of North Carolina, particularly by his dissertation director Fletcher M.
Green, who was Kenan Professor, chairman of the
history department, and author of a book on constitutional development in Southern states. In 1966,
Link, as coeditor, and other former students produced *Writing Southern History: Essays in Historiog-*

raphy in Honor of Fletcher M. Green. Link himself was remembered at Chapel Hill not only by his professors but also by fellow students who commented on "his incredible drive and prodigious memory." From his intensive research on the nature of Progressive reform in the South and its relationship to the national Democratic party came a number of articles, the most important of which were reprinted in a collection entitled *The Higher Realism of Woodrow Wilson and Other Essays* (1971).

Through his study of Southern history and his own ties to the South, Link was in a position to understand the regional influences that shaped Wilson. Although both men lived outside the South during most of their adult lives, they maintained contacts with the region through family and attachment to place. Wilson returned periodically to South Carolina and Georgia to visit relatives and the grave sites of his parents and sister in Columbia; Link has spent part of each summer in Montreat, North Carolina. It was therefore appropriate that, in his October 1969 presidential address to the Southern Historical Association, Professor Link discussed "Woodrow Wilson: The American as Southerner." Because President Wilson was a nationalist in his thinking while identifying himself as a Southerner, he was able, Link contended, to bring the South ("the only place in the world, where nothing has to be explained to me") into the American political mainstream.

A combination of factors undoubtedly led Link to embark on his ambitious project to write a multivolume life of Woodrow Wilson, an undertaking that would unite the personal perspective of the biographer with the analytical and narrative skills of the historian. In a 1948 review essay on recent biographical contributions, Link maintained that "the biographer assumes the greatest obligations and responsibilities of all writers of history" because of his "opportunity to reach a large reading public in a way that the monographist or even the general historian never can." Because readers lacked the detailed knowledge and critical training to detect distorted interpretations, the biographer "can easily become a historical demagogue," overstating his subject's contributions while minimizing his defects. Consequently, Link committed himself to becoming a historical biographer who placed his subject squarely within the context of the political, economic, and social developments of the figure's own times.

In his 1948 survey of the biographical studies written on Wilson, Link found few with any enduring merit. He did, however, praise Ray Stannard

Baker's multivolume works, *Woodrow Wilson: Life and Letters* (1927-1939) and *Woodrow Wilson and the World Settlement* (1922), as "still our most authoritative sources for the entire Wilson period." Baker had served other scholars and biographers by collecting so much source material on Wilson. Yet it was, wrote Link, "no derogation" of Baker to point out that his authorized study was "only the beginning of the Wilson biography and not the end"; the definitive Wilson biography still needed to be written. Indeed, even before he had finished his doctoral dissertation, Link "had audaciously announced," as Dewey W. Grantham recounted in his foreword to *The Higher Realism of Woodrow Wilson and Other Essays*, "that he was beginning a new multivolume biography of Woodrow Wilson, a work which he confidently expected to supersede" Baker's substantial contribution.

In his first articles and books, published between the mid-1940s and the late 1950s, Link was rather critical of Wilson. For example, in a 1956 article entitled "A Portrait of Woodrow Wison," which he wrote for the *Virginia Quarterly Review*'s issue commemorating the centennial of Wilson's birth, Link described his subject as "so contradictory, so baffling, so enigmatic." While acknowledging that Wilson possessed "many admirable qualities" that enabled him to attain the "heights of personal and political greatness," Link found it difficult to "explain the curious contradictions in Woodrow Wilson—his craving for affection and his refusal to give friendship on equal terms, or the bigness of his political visions and the pettiness of his prejudices." In his essay Link concluded that "probably only a psychiatrist could give an authoritative answer" in regard to the contradictions in Wilson's personality.

His questions about Wilson's personality and leadership were not entirely answered in the first volumes of his biography. But as he delved more deeply into the documentary evidence, he began to reevaluate his earlier interpretations. Indeed, over the thirty-two years during which he has become intimately acquainted with Wilson, Link has moved, in the words of reviewers, from being "coldly and detachedly critical" in his biography's first volume, *Wilson: The Road to the White House* (1947), to being "overly generous" in judging his subject by a "neo-Wilsonian yardstick" in his recent *Woodrow Wilson: Revolution, War, and Peace* (1979). Whatever his final evaluation of Wilson may be, Link should be commended for modifying earlier interpretations as his understanding of Wilson has grown.

Because of thorough, multiarchival research,

his earlier works are still useful. For example, the notable contribution of *Wilson: The Road to the White House* was its detailed examination of the years 1910-1912, from the time Wilson ran for the governorship of New Jersey until his election to the presidency of the United States. This first volume also provided a summary of Wilson's presidency of Princeton and defined the controversies which developed over his proposals to democratize university life by housing undergraduates in residential quadrangles and by locating the graduate college in the middle of the campus.

In the light of subsequent research by himself and others, however, Link recently concluded that his earlier interpretation of the graduate-college controversy was "inadequate and unbalanced." In a 1978 article appearing in the *Political Science Quarterly*, which Link wrote with Edwin A. Weinstein and James William Anderson, the authors fully recognized that Wilson fought for his concept of the graduate college not simply because he wanted to get rid of its dean, Andrew Fleming West, but because he realized that the crucial issue was the future educational mission of Princeton University. Wilson envisioned an intellectually invigorating and more democratic Princeton; West wanted to make the graduate college into a snobbish club. The stroke Wilson suffered in 1906, which caused almost complete blindness in his left eye and a weakness in his right arm, affected his behavior by paradoxically contributing to his overconfidence and stubbornness, to his failure to prepare carefully the groundwork for his proposed quadrangle plan and then for his conception of the graduate college, and to his overly personalized reaction to alumni and faculty opposition. Link's understanding of Wilson's health problem and its relation to the defeat of his plans at Princeton was greatly helped by the research and analysis of Dr. Edwin A. Weinstein, whose essay "Woodrow Wilson's Neurological Illness" appeared in the September 1970 issue of the *Journal of American History*, and whose book *Woodrow Wilson: A Medical and Psychological Biography* was published in 1981 by Princeton University Press as a supplementary volume to *The Papers of Woodrow Wilson*. Link, Weinstein, and Anderson disagreed strongly with two books that had endeavored to psychoanalyze Wilson and to find the causes for his defeats at Princeton and later in the White House in unresolved childhood conflicts. The study *Thomas Woodrow Wilson*, written by Sigmund Freud and William C. Bullitt but not published until 1967, was, according to Link, Weinstein, and Anderson, "a biased application of a simplistic and distorted version of psychoanalytic theory" based on "wildly inaccurate and at times even fabricated" evidence.

The other book, Alexander L. and Juliette L. George's *Woodrow Wilson and Colonel House: A Personality Study* (1956), was, Link, Weinstein, and Anderson contended, an equally inaccurate portrayal of Wilson, despite its initial wide acclaim. Not only did the Georges fail to explore all the available documents but they also manipulated evidence to suit their theory while ignoring Wilson's neurological illness and its effect on his behavior. They tried to argue that Dean West was opposed by Wilson because he felt repressed hostility toward his own father. His unresolved conflict with a father figure would reappear, they alleged, during Wilson's fight with Sen. Henry Cabot Lodge over ratification of the Treaty of Versailles. However, Link showed conclusively through letters and other documents that Wilson, in fact, enjoyed a warm, mutually supportive relationship with his father. Furthermore, although Wilson suffered intermittently for almost thirty years from cerebral vascular disease, he had periods of remission during his governorship of New Jersey and his first presidential administration. Before his health deteriorated almost completely after his stroke in 1919, he showed flexibility and a capacity to develop expertise in dealing with domestic and foreign problems. One of Link's significant contributions, then, has been to help bury the poorly conceived and misinformed psychological interpretations of Wilson's conduct.

Link's second major book, *Woodrow Wilson and the Progressive Era, 1910-1917* (1954), like his first, has also become dated in some of its interpretations, especially in regard to Wilson's handling of foreign policy. Published as the first book to appear in the New American Nation Series edited by Henry Steele Commager and Richard B. Morris, the work was "in the nature of an outline" of the research that Link had done for the first three volumes of his Wilson biography. In the early 1950s, Link shared some of the views of the so-called "realist" school (as exemplified by George F. Kennan and Hans J. Morgenthau) in regard to Wilson's "missionary diplomacy" in Mexico. Wilson was viewed as a moralist who justified extensive United States intervention into Latin American internal affairs on the grounds that he knew what was best for these countries, even if his course of action aroused opposition from Latin American leaders and people. In the second volume of his biography, *Wilson: The New Freedom* (1956), Link showed a similar critical attitude toward the president's diplomacy, although in later books the historian would cast Wilson's actions in the positive light of defending the Mexican Revolution against the intervention of European countries and of American investors. On the other hand, Link's analysis of the president's New Freedom program (the passage of the Underwood Tariff and the Federal Reserve Acts) and of his movement toward the adoption of Theodore Roosevelt's New Nationalist program (trust regulation by a Federal Trade Commission) broke new ground and remains valid today. Moreover, he portrayed Wilson as a strong leader, one whose "expansion and perfection of the powers of the presidency" promised to be his most enduring legacy. Link's well-documented scholarship deservedly won the Bancroft Prize for biography in 1957.

Volume three, *Wilson: The Struggle for Neutrality, 1914-1915* (1960), also earned the Bancroft Prize in 1961. The book described Wilson's efforts to keep the United States neutral after the outbreak of World War I in Europe. Drawing upon extensive research in British, French, German, and American archives, Link analyzed Wilson's diplomacy in terms of the complex international situation involving European powers. During the early 1960s, he began to reevaluate the nature of Wilsonian idealism. In his October 1962 Founder's Day address to the Presbyterian Historical Society in Philadelphia, Link spoke eloquently on "The Higher Realism of Woodrow Wilson." He took issue with English, French, and German historians who still considered Wilson to have been "a well-intentioned idealist, a man good by ordinary Christian standards, but essentially a destructive force in modern history because he was visionary, unrealistic, provincial, and ignorant of European problems." Their negative view of Wilson was shared by those American scholars who called themselves "realists." While Link acknowledged that Wilson might be best described as "*primarily* a Christian idealist" and as "a crusading idealist," he argued that "among all the major statesmen and thoughtful critics of his age, President Wilson was in fact the supreme realist." He was not, Link now insisted, "fundamentally, a moralist, as he so often seemed to be, but a man who lived in faith, trying to be guided by the Holy Spirit in meeting the complex problems of a changing nation and world." Wilson saw beyond the short-term "realities" of power politics to the long-term moral issues and thus advocated "a peace of reconciliation" as the only settlement that would endure.

By 1917, Link argued, Wilson had become a skilled diplomat; he had learned from the mistakes made during his first two years in office. His development was expertly described in the fourth and fifth volumes of the Wilson biography: *Confusions and Crises, 1915-1916* (1964) and *Campaigns for Progressivism and Peace, 1916-1917* (1965). These works primarily concerned Wilson's adoption of advanced progressive reforms (rural credits, child labor legislation, and an eight-hour day for railroad workers), his reelection in November 1916, and his momentous decision to bring the United States into the war against Germany the following April. In the preface to the 1965 volume, Link summarized the documentary record in regard to Wilson's policies toward the European war from 1914 to 1917: (1) Wilson dominated American foreign policy and often acted against the advice of William Jennings Bryan, Robert Lansing, and Col. Edward M. House; (2) Wilson never followed an unyielding policy toward Germany but rather sought compromises that would allow Americans to travel on passenger ships without denying Germany the use of its submarines; (3) Wilson tried to adopt strictly neutral policies toward the Entente Allies; (4) by the middle of 1916, Wilson vigorously sought to mediate a negotiated peace; and (5) Wilson went to war because it was the only way "to protect American national rights and shipping on the high seas in the face of repeated German assaults" and because the U.S. entry would bring a quicker end to the conflict. Not only had Link's evaluation of Wilsonian foreign policy significantly evolved but also the author himself, reviewers noted, had begun to express his judgments unequivocally, instead of letting the facts speak for themselves, as in earlier volumes.

Even though no additional volumes of his Wilson biography have appeared since 1965, Link is still ranked, in the estimate of a present-day critic Robert D. Accinelli, as "the premier historian of Wilson's foreign policy." Link's preeminence has been due in part to the influential Albert Shaw Lectures on Diplomatic History that he presented at Johns Hopkins University, 3-7 December 1956. Published the following year as *Wilson the Diplomatist: A Look at His Major Foreign Policies*, this book was widely read because it covered all eight years of Wilson's presidency. This important work was reprinted in 1969 and 1974 and then rewritten as "a new book with new themes" in 1979. Entitled *Woodrow Wilson: Revolution, War, and Peace*, it was eminently suitable, at 128 pages and in paperback, for college classes or for interested adult readers. The author distilled into this pithy book the essential points of his interpretation of Wilson's foreign policy. Link now argued that Wilson was not naive; on the contrary, he had "better training for the conduct of foreign affairs than any Chief Executive since John Quincy Adams." While he occasionally oversimplified complicated problems, Wilson was "never visionary, incapable of facing reality; on the contrary, he was keenly intelligent and often shrewd," Link contended. Although Wilson faced greater challenges than any president had confronted since the early 1800s, his responses were determined by consistently held principles that derived from his "general thinking about God, ethics, the nature and ends of government, and the role of the United States in advancing democracy and the cause of human rights throughout the world." He therefore applied himself with a "driving force, relentless energy, and striving for definitive solutions." Although he failed to achieve many of his goals in the postwar settlement, Wilson is now honored for his failures. The world, said Link, "remembers the heroic and often lonely figure standing foursquare at Paris against forces of hatred, greed, and imperialism." Link's portrayal of Wilson was persuasive, but critics contended that he glossed over the president's shortcomings in pursuing a totally realistic foreign policy in war and peace.

Whatever the extent to which other scholars might disagree with Link, they would find it very difficult to equal his mastery of the documentary evidence. Since 1958, when he was appointed editor-in-chief of the Wilson project, he has devoted the major portion of his time to directing the publication of "all important letters, articles, speeches, interviews, and public papers by Woodrow Wilson." An outgrowth of the Wilson Centennial in 1956, the project was funded by the Woodrow Wilson Foundation; Princeton University became a cosponsor in 1959 and agreed to provide offices for The Papers of Woodrow Wilson. Together with associate editors Johns Wells Davidson and David W. Hirst, Arthur Link undertook the enormous task of locating documents, photocopying some 250,000 items, and then selecting from among them for publication those that were "essential to understanding his thought and activity." Initially, about forty volumes were projected, which, commented Frank Freidel in the *American Historical Review*, was five times as many as *The Letters of Theodore Roosevelt* and four times as many as *The Public Papers and Addresses of Franklin D. Roosevelt*. The first volume—which opened with entries in the family Bible and extended to early 1881 with Wilson's decision to withdraw from the University of Virginia Law School because of ill health—marked "the beginnings of an enterprise of massive dimensions and commensurate scholarly value," Freidel continued. Since then the projected number of volumes has

been increased to some sixty. Published in 1982, *Volume 40: November 20, 1916-January 23, 1917*, documents the two months from Wilson's successful reelection on a platform of advanced progressive reform to his unsuccessful effort to secure peace by appealing to the people of all countries. Evidently, the remaining twenty volumes will cover the period from Wilson's reluctant decision for war in the wake of Germany's fateful blunder of resuming unrestricted submarine warfare (volume 41), through his heroic though ultimately doomed efforts to achieve a just peace acceptable to both the European allies and the United States Senate, to his stroke and the last years of his life.

In their general introduction to volume 1, the editors of *The Papers of Woodrow Wilson* carefully outlined their principles or objectives for publication as well as their editorial methods. They felt it necessary, however, to give readers a new statement in volume 27, the first of the presidential volumes. In order to "achieve [their] supreme objective—the presentation of as complete a record as possible of the development of Wilson's significant thought and activities in all their varied aspects," they could no longer follow the conventional definition that limited an individual's papers to "documents written or received by him or her." They would also print other relevant documents: a brief outline of a speech, a news report, or even memoranda, diaries, and letters to third parties written by friends and associates.

To control the amount of material selected for publication, the editors made an essential distinction between papers that illuminated some aspect of Wilson the person and the leader (whether they were documents which he wrote, which he personally saw, or which had been written about him) and other papers that pertained to the era rather than directly to him. To other scholars, the editors left the task of compiling a documentary study of the era. Furthermore, in keeping with their goal of printing reliable texts, they strictly followed the policy of word for word transcription, including spelling and typographical errors, although they deleted passages of insignificant interest. As in past volumes, the editors provided explanatory notes only when it was necessary to identify individuals who were not well known or to discuss developments that were not already adequately covered in published sources.

The editors also listed the major papers and records examined for the presidential period. While the major source continued to be The Papers of Woodrow Wilson in the Library of Congress, other collections in that repository contained important information: The Papers of Edith Bolling Galt Wilson, The Papers of Robert Lansing, The Diary of Josephus Daniels, and The Papers of William Jennings Bryan, whose Library of Congress collection was supplemented by a second collection in the National Archives. Also in the National Archives were State Department files and Wilson's letters to departmental and agency heads. In addition, Princeton University Library had a significant collection of Woodrow Wilson letters and papers and all of the shorthand notebooks of Charles L. Swem, who recorded Wilson's speeches, press conferences, and public statements as well as much of his correspondence from 1913 to 1921. The Yale University Library had three collections essential for understanding Wilson's conduct of foreign affairs: The Papers of Colonel House, The Diary of Colonel House (which the project editors called "the single most important document of the Wilson era," although they readily acknowledged that its reliability was questionable in places due to House's egotism), and The Papers of Sir William Wiseman, the president's liaison with the British government. In addition to these extensive collections, the editors explored the diplomatic materials in foreign archives and read through a wide range of newspapers and periodicals.

The sixty-volume edition of *The Papers of Woodrow Wilson* may well become Link's richest legacy to other scholars, aspiring students, and the interested reading public. It will be the definitive source from which all future major studies on Woodrow Wilson must come, whether they deal with his role as an educator, as a domestic leader, or as a world statesman. Calling Link's earlier five-volume work on Wilson "biography in the grand manner" and "his most impressive achievement" to date, historian Dewey Grantham asserts that *The Papers of Woodrow Wilson* "may eventually equal or surpass his contribution in writing the biography."

Link has also sought an audience wider than the scholarly community by writing books to meet the needs of college students and of nonstudent readers. These books, which have drawn upon his wealth of knowledge, are of four kinds: collections of documents, edited and containing introductory notes, to illuminate particular crises or developments; a brief biography of Wilson; several textbooks for survey and upper-level undergraduate courses; and a bibliography for the Progressive Era and World War I. Of his edited books of thematically organized documents, probably the most widely used has been the survey *Problems in*

American History, coedited with Richard Leopold in 1952; a two-volume revision, edited by Link, Leopold, and Stanley Coben, was published in 1972. Both his edited book *Woodrow Wilson: A Profile* (1968) and his *Woodrow Wilson: A Brief Biography* (1963) were compact enough to be assigned to undergraduates, although *Woodrow Wilson: Revolution, War, and Peace* has now superseded those earlier books because of its excellent discussion of foreign policy. Professor Link has also coauthored several textbooks, including surveys of American history from colonial times to the present and a comprehensive narrative of the twentieth century. His most recently published textbook, *The American People: A History* (1981) promised an honest survey of the national past with these words: "We can be set free to deal with the problems of the present and future only if we confront the truth that our nation has been guilty of genocide, slavery, continuing racism and sexism, aggression, persecution, and other violations of our own best historic ideals." In 1980, *American Epoch*, which Link coauthored with William B. Catton, appeared in its fifth edition twenty-five years after it was first published. Available in two conveniently divided paperback volumes—*An Era of Economic Change, Reform, and World Wars 1900-1945* and *An Era of Total War and Uncertain Peace 1938-1980*—*The American Epoch* is, in the opinion of many professors who have assigned it to upper-level undergraduate classes, the best available textbook on the twentieth century. This concise and vigorously written text gives students the necessary background for independent research. Also of great use to students of the Wilson era is the bibliography compiled by Link and William M. Leary, Jr., and entitled *The Progressive Era and the Great War, 1896-1920* (1969). In the revised 1978 edition published as one of the Goldentree Bibliographies, the compilers stated that they had selected books, articles, and dissertations for their continuing usefulness and "without bias in favor of any particular historiographical school."

In addition to his many publications, Link has been in demand as a lecturer. In celebration of the centennial of Woodrow Wilson's birth, he led a 1956 seminar session at the University of Chicago. The same year, he delivered the Albert Shaw Lectures on Diplomatic History at Johns Hopkins University. As Harmsworth Professor of American History at Oxford University during 1958-59, Link delivered his inaugural lecture entitled "President Wilson and his English Critics." At Freiburg University, he presented, as the final lecture in a series on American civilization, "The Idealistic Realism of Woodrow

Wilson." Ten years later, he reassessed Wilson's conduct of foreign affairs in a Harvard University address, " 'Wilson the Diplomatist' in Retrospect." In 1973, he participated in an international symposium on Wilson, and in 1977 he again went to England as Commonwealth Fund lecturer at the University of London. His reputation as the foremost scholar of Woodrow Wilson was established on both shores of the Atlantic Ocean.

Professor Link has also advanced the purposes of the historical profession by membership and service in numerous organizations. Most notably, he was a member of the National Historical Publications Commission from 1968 to 1972, and from 1959 to 1962 he was a member of the executive committee of the Organization of American Historians, for which he also served on the editorial board of its *Journal of American History* from 1967 to 1970, and as vice-president-elect, 1982-1983. In the Southern Historical Association, he was a member of the board of editors of its *Journal of Southern History* from 1955 to 1958 and from 1963 to 1966, vice-president from 1967 to 1968, president from 1968 to 1969, and a member of the executive council from 1969 to 1972. In 1983 Link was elected president of the American Historical Association.

Because of his impressive scholarly achievement, Link has received numerous awards and honors. He has held Rosenwald, Guggenheim, and Rockefeller fellowships and has been a member of the Institute for Advanced Study at Princeton. Two volumes of his Wilson biography have won the Bancroft Prize. In addition to an M.A. from Oxford University in 1958, Link has received several honorary degrees, including the Doctor of Letters from Bucknell University (1961), the University of North Carolina (1962), and Washington and Lee University (1965); the Doctor of Humane Letters from Washington College (1962); and the Doctor of Humanities from Davidson College (1965).

In spite of his extremely demanding career (in which Margaret Douglas Link, whom he married in 1945, has shared as critic and editor), Professor Link has found time for family life and three children. Among his avocations are music and the reading of nineteenth- and twentieth-century novels.

Arthur S. Link's interpretation of Woodrow Wilson has evolved over almost forty years of research, and the portrait is not yet finished. Link's audience awaits the completion of his multivolume biography, which, in turn, may be delayed until most of the remaining volumes of *The Papers of Woodrow Wilson* are published. His standing in the scholarly community is secure; critics take issue with him over differences of emphasis rather than over matters of substance. Consequently, his reception among students and interested adult readers may be expected to grow. Like Woodrow Wilson, Professor Link has labored as much for future generations as for his own time.

Other:

Problems in American History, edited by Link and Richard Leopold (New York: Prentice-Hall, 1952; revised in 2 volumes, edited by Link, Leopold, and Stanley Coben (Englewood Cliffs, N.J.: Prentice-Hall, 1972);

"The Progressive," in *The Greatness of Woodrow Wilson*, edited by Em Bowles Alsop (New York & Toronto: Rinehart, 1956), pp. 137-150;

"The Cotton Crisis, the South, and Anglo-American Diplomacy, 1914-1915," in *Studies in Southern History in Memory of Albert Ray Newsome, 1894-1951*, edited by J. Carlyle Sitterson (Chapel Hill: University of North Carolina Press, 1957), pp. 122-138;

"Woodrow Wilson: The Philosophy, Methods, and Impact of Leadership," in *Woodrow Wilson and the World of Today; Essays by Arthur S. Link, William L. Langer, Eric Goldman*, edited by Arthur P. Dudden (Philadelphia: University of Pennsylvania Press, 1957; London, Bombay & Karachi: Oxford University Press, 1957), pp. 1-21;

Writing Southern History: Essays in Historiography in Honor of Fletcher M. Green, edited by Link and Rembert W. Patrick (Baton Rouge: Louisiana State University Press, 1966);

The Papers of Woodrow Wilson, 41 volumes to date, edited by Link and others (Princeton: Princeton University Press, 1966-   );

The First Presbyterian Church of Princeton: Two Centuries of History, edited by Link (Princeton: First Presbyterian Church, 1967);

Woodrow Wilson: A Profile, edited by Link (New York: Hill & Wang, 1968);

The Impact of World War I, edited by Link (New York: Harper & Row, 1969);

The Progressive Era and the Great War, 1896-1920, compiled by Link and William M. Leary, Jr. (New York: Appleton-Century-Crofts, 1969);

"Woodrow Wilson and His Presbyterian Inheritance," in *Essays in Scotch-Irish History*, edited by E. R. R. Green (London: Routledge & Kegan Paul, 1969; New York: Humanities Press, 1969), pp. 1-17;

The Diplomacy of World Power: The United States

1889-1920, edited by Link and Leary, Jr., Documents of Modern History Series (London: Arnold, 1970; New York: St. Martin's, 1970);

Wilson's Diplomacy: An International Symposium, by Link, Jean-Baptiste Duroselle, Ernest Fraenkel, and H. G. Nicholas (Cambridge, Mass.: Schenkman Publishing Company, 1973);

Woodrow Wilson and a Revolutionary World, 1913-1921, edited by Link (Chapel Hill: University of North Carolina Press, 1983)—supplementary volume to *The Papers of Woodrow Wilson*.

Periodical Publications:

"The Underwood Presidential Movement of 1912," *Journal of Southern History*, 11 (May 1945): 230-245;

"The Baltimore Convention of 1912," *American Historical Review*, 50 (July 1945): 691-731;

"The Progressive Movement in the South, 1870-1914," *North Carolina Historical Review*, 23 (April 1946): 1-24;

"The Negro as a Factor in the Campaign of 1912," *Journal of Negro History*, 32 (January 1947): 81-99;

"The Enigma of Woodrow Wilson," *American Mercury*, 65 (September 1947): 303-313;

"A Decade of Biographical Contributions to Recent American History," *Mississippi Valley Historical Review*, 34 (March 1948): 637-652;

"The South and the 'New Freedom': An Interpretation," *American Scholar*, 20 (Summer 1951): 314-324;

"Woodrow Wilson and the Democratic Party," *Review of Politics*, 18 (April 1956): 146-156;

"A Portrait of Woodrow Wilson," *Virginia Quarterly Review*, 32 (Autumn 1956): 524-540;

"What Happened to the Progressive Movement in the 1920s?," *American Historical Review*, 64 (July 1959): 833-851;

"The Higher Realism of Woodrow Wilson," *Journal of Presbyterian History*, 41 (March 1963): 1-13;

"The Case for Woodrow Wilson," *Harper's Magazine*, 234 (April 1967): 85-93;

"Woodrow Wilson and the Study of Administration," *Proceedings of the American Philosophical Society*, 112 (December 1968): 431-433;

"Woodrow Wilson: The American as Southerner," *Journal of Southern History*, 36 (February 1970): 3-17;

"Woodrow Wilson's Political Personality: A Reappraisal," by Link, Edwin A. Weinstein, and James William Anderson, *Political Science Quarterly*, 93 (Winter 1978): 585-598.

References:

Robert D. Accinelli, "Link's Case for Wilson the Diplomatist," in "Confronting the Modern World: Woodrow Wilson and Harry S Truman," *Reviews in American History*, 9 (September 1981): 285-294;

Dewey W. Grantham, Foreword to *The Higher Realism of Woodrow Wilson and Other Essays* (Nashville: Vanderbilt University Press, 1971), pp. xi-xxii;

Daniel M. Smith, "National Interest and American Intervention, 1917: An Historiographical Appraisal," *Journal of American History*, 52 (June 1965): 5-24;

Richard L. Watson, Jr., "Woodrow Wilson and His Interpreters, 1947-1957," *Mississippi Valley Historical Review*, 44 (September 1957): 207-236;

Samuel F. Wells, Jr., "New Perspectives on Wilsonian Diplomacy: The Secular Evangelism of American Political Economy, A Review Essay," *Perspectives in American History*, 6 (1972): 389-419.

Dumas Malone

(10 January 1892 -   )

Paul A. Horne, Jr.
University of South Carolina

SELECTED BOOKS: *The Public Life of Thomas Cooper, 1783-1839* (New Haven: Yale University Press, 1926; London: Oxford University Press, 1926);

Saints in Action (New York: Abingdon Press, 1939);

Edwin A. Alderman: A Biography (New York: Doubleday, Doran, 1940);

Jefferson the Virginian, volume 1 of *Jefferson and His Time* (Boston: Little, Brown, 1948; London: Eyre & Spottiswoode, 1949);

Jefferson and the Rights of Man, volume 2 of *Jefferson and His Time* (Boston: Little, Brown, 1951);

The Story of the Declaration of Independence, narrative by Malone, pictures by Hirst Milhollen and Milton Kaplan (New York: Oxford University Press, 1954; London: Oxford University Press, 1954);

Empire for Liberty: The Genesis and Growth of the United States of America, by Malone and Basil Rauch (New York: Appleton-Century-Crofts, 1960);

Jefferson and the Ordeal of Liberty, volume 3 of *Jefferson and His Time* (Boston: Little, Brown, 1962);

Thomas Jefferson as Political Leader (Berkeley: University of California Press, 1963; London: Cambridge University Press, 1963);

Jefferson the President: First Term 1801-1805, volume 4 of *Jefferson and His Time* (Boston: Little, Brown, 1970);

Jefferson the President: Second Term 1805-1809, volume 5 of *Jefferson and His Time* (Boston: Little, Brown, 1974);

The Sage of Monticello, volume 6 of *Jefferson and His Time* (Boston: Little, Brown, 1981).

Dumas Malone is an educator, historian, and editor who excels in the biographical method of writing history. His first concern is to get the facts straight. His second is to report events in the context of their own time. His third is always to be honest and fair-minded about his subjects, never the prosecutor or defender of them. By utilizing these principles, he has set a high standard for twentieth-century biographical writing.

Dumas Malone was born to John W. and Lillian Kemp Malone in the small northwestern Mississippi town of Coldwater. He spent the first ten years of his life in Mississippi before his father moved the family to Cuthbert, Georgia. There John Malone, a Methodist minister, assumed the presidency of Andrew College, a small school for women.

Education and religion played key roles in the Malone household. Lillian Malone taught her children at home, and the educational aspirations of Malone's parents were high: his father prided himself on having managed to send all seven of his children to college, and one of the stories told about Malone's mother was that she wanted every one of her children to take a Ph.D. All three of her sons earned that degree, and five of the seven Malone children were involved with the field of education for most of their lives. Kemp Malone, Dumas Malone's older brother, was an English professor for many years at Johns Hopkins University. Miles Malone, the youngest of the three brothers, taught history at Phillips Academy in Andover, Massachusetts, for a quarter of a century. One sister

Dumas Malone

>>Missing: v. 17? 48 62

Check on v. 13 — June 2 pt 2's

O=MARION

Vol. ?? 1-2?

33201

BREVARD CC/COCOA

V.1 1: CALL NUMBER: [REF] PS221 .D5 -- Ref Book -- Available   *000 234 646*
V.2 2: CALL NUMBER: [REF] PS221 .D5 -- Ref Book -- Available)   *000 348 628*
     3: CALL NUMBER: [Ref] PS 221 .D5 -- Vol. 125 -- Ref Book -- Available
     4: CALL NUMBER: [Ref] -- Vol.3 -- Ref Book -- Available
     5: CALL NUMBER: [Ref] -- Vol.4 -- Ref Book -- Available
     6: CALL NUMBER: [Ref] -- Vol.5 -- Ref Book -- Available
     7: CALL NUMBER: [Ref] PS221 .D5 -- vol.126 -- Ref Book -- Available
     8: CALL NUMBER: [Ref] PS221 .D5 -- vol.127 -- Ref Book -- Available
     9: CALL NUMBER: [Ref] PS221 .D5 -- vol.130 -- Ref Book -- Available
    10: CALL NUMBER: [Ref] PS221 .D5 -- v.130 -- Ref Book -- Available
    11: CALL NUMBER: [Ref] PS221 .D5 -- v.129 -- Ref Book -- Available
    12: CALL NUMBER: [Ref] PS221 .D5 -- v.132 -- Ref Book -- Available
    13: CALL NUMBER: [Ref] PS221 .D5 -- v.131 -- Ref Book -- Available
    14: CALL NUMBER: [Ref] PS221 .D5 -- vol.133 -- Ref Book -- Available

spent her life as a teacher, and another was married to a college professor.

John and Lillian Malone's household was, in addition, distinctly religious. However, the religion taught by his parents was, Malone recalled, highly tolerant. The atmosphere of independent thinking that prevailed was perhaps most dramatically characterized by Lillian Malone's advocacy of woman's suffrage, an idea that was advanced for her time and locality.

Traveling only 150 miles from home, Dumas Malone chose Emory College as his place of higher learning. He graduated with an A.B. degree in 1910 at the age of eighteen, and his first job after graduation was teaching in high school. The desire to teach on the college level welled within him, but he could not decide on a subject. Finally, after studying religion and receiving a bachelor of divinity degree from Yale in 1916, he chose history. He wanted to concentrate on the history of his native region and on the historical experiences of Southerners, but before he could pursue his graduate degree, World War I intervened. During the conflict he served for eighteen months as a second lieutenant in the Marine Corps.

After his discharge from the marines, Malone entered Yale University as a graduate student in history. He was also an instructor of history while he studied, and he earned a master's degree in 1921 and a doctorate in 1923. At Yale he worked under Allen Johnson, the man who steered him toward the biographical approach to history. Malone's doctoral dissertation, "The Public Life of Thomas Cooper, 1783-1839," won the John Addison Porter Prize at Yale in 1923.

The strong points of Malone's future work were all foreshadowed in his dissertation, which was published as a book in 1926. He concentrated in this study on the public life of Cooper because that was the area for which records existed. Many of the records concerning the childhood and early life of Cooper had been destroyed by fire during the Civil War, and Malone felt it would be wrong to attempt to describe events or people about which he had no documentary evidence. This approach Malone has never abandoned; instead, he has always worked exhaustively with recorded information and refused to speculate without concrete data.

The Public Life of Thomas Cooper, 1783-1839 bore evidence of Malone's background and interests. Cooper, a supporter of the Jeffersonian opposition to the Federalists, was involved in "many important political, economic and intellectual movements," and Malone skillfully described his subject's actions within the movements as well as the movements themselves. The work was an impartial appraisal of Cooper's life and contributions to humanity. Malone never criticized Cooper for his liberal religious attitudes or controversial political ideas but instead emphasized his close association with education. A professor of chemistry and president of South Carolina College, Cooper was also associated with Thomas Jefferson, a future subject of Malone's. Besides presenting a balanced appraisal of his subject's public life, Malone utilized his most important contribution to the art of biography, that of depicting the subject within his own time period and not judging him by present-day standards or beliefs. Throughout all of Malone's works this approach has stood out, but he was unable to employ it on his most challenging subject, Thomas Jefferson, until much later.

Malone was involved in many projects after he received his doctorate. He moved from Yale to the University of Virginia as a professor in 1923. He married Elisabeth Gifford in 1925, and they remained in Virginia until 1929. That year Malone joined his mentor, Allen Johnson, as an editor of the monumental *Dictionary of American Biography*. For two years he worked closely with Johnson to produce a multivolume work that provided short, definitive biographies of important Americans who had died before 1928. He became editor-in-chief of the project upon the death of Johnson in 1931. No other effort has done as much to promote biography, and Malone worked on it with fervor until it was completed in 1936. Maintaining high scholarly standards for the entries, he wrote no fewer than seventeen sketches himself, the most important one being on Thomas Jefferson. The *Dictionary of American Biography* stands as one of the most important historical works of the twentieth century, and Malone deserves much of the credit for its scholarly style, completeness of coverage, and ease of use.

Upon completion of the *Dictionary of American Biography*, Malone became director and chairman of the board of syndics of Harvard University Press. The position prohibited him from carrying out his most loved activity, teaching, but it did allow him time for writing. Three years after assuming the directorship, he released *Saints in Action* (1939).

Saints in Action was a book of lectures delivered at Drew University in 1939. Through the lectures, Malone sought to emphasize the importance of religion in American history. The lectures were biographies of people Malone felt had achieved an aura of saintliness, either by their religious accomplishments or by their contributions to society and mankind. A tolerant religious background was evident in this work. Malone did not challenge his figures' beliefs but instead honored their influences and accomplishments.

Malone's next work appeared in 1940 and exemplified again his interest in education and its place in history. The work, *Edwin A. Alderman: A Biography*, focused on this man's contributions to higher education. At heart a teacher, Malone clearly admired Alderman's work in the field of education. Alderman believed that the educational process should be democratic in nature; he wanted everyone to have the chance for an education. Malone concentrated on Alderman's public life as he had done with Thomas Cooper, but this time for different reasons. The biographer believed that knowledge of an individual's personal life was important to the reader only if it were essential to the understanding of the person as a whole. Malone saw that Alderman had centered much of his personal life around education, especially since his first wife had died early and he had had no children. Thus, because education was really Alderman's whole life, it became Malone's focus in the work.

The biography of Alderman also gave Malone a chance to work in the field of history which most interested him—the history of the South. A Southerner born in North Carolina, Alderman remained in the South throughout his life. He championed the cause of public education in North Carolina as director of teacher learning and as president of the University of North Carolina at Chapel Hill. Alderman also carried his qualities to other parts of the South as president of Tulane University and of the University of Virginia. Having served on the faculty at Virginia under Alderman, Malone had great respect for the man as a person. But the admiration he held for Alderman was primarily for the man's contributions to education, especially in the South.

Malone remained at Harvard University Press until 1943. That year he began *Jefferson and His Time*, the first multivolume work on the third president since Henry S. Randall's *Life of Thomas Jefferson*, issued shortly before the Civil War. From 1943 to 1945 Malone, financed by a grant from the Rockefeller Foundation, concentrated on research for the series. He also returned to teaching in 1945 as professor of history at Columbia University, and even though teaching prohibited full-time concentration on the Jefferson biography, Malone still worked diligently on the project. He snatched time at night, on weekends, and during the summers and

applied it toward writing. Malone described those summers as "marvelous" because he was able to write every day.

His labor began to show its fruits in 1948 when the first volume of *Jefferson and His Time* was published. Entitled *Jefferson the Virginian*, the book covered the initial forty-one years of Thomas Jefferson's life and traced his personal development. The first half of the work was concerned with Jefferson's growing up, going to school, becoming a lawyer, and learning the ways of a planter in his home state of Virginia. This was the time that formed Jefferson's character and determined his actions for the rest of his life. The second half of the volume traced young Jefferson's rise to prominence through the Declaration of Independence, the American Revolution, and his governorship of Virginia. These were trying years when Jefferson saw some of his ideas come of age but saw others ignored, challenged, and rejected.

The first volume of *Jefferson and His Time* established the standards that Malone maintained throughout the series. First and foremost, Jefferson was examined within his own age. He was not compared with men of or judged by ideals of the twentieth century. Because Jefferson's participation in the American Revolution was an outgrowth of his upbringing in the eighteenth century, his actions must be understood in relation to his time. According to Malone, present-day beliefs and issues had to be avoided in writing history, especially biography.

But Malone's virtues in this work did not end there. Researching his subject thoroughly, he consulted all available sources and let them speak through his writing; there was very restrained authorial interpretation of the information. Furthermore, Malone wrote in a readable style that could appeal to all; one did not need to be a scholar to understand the historian's prose. The detail was endless, but the style of writing and the topic itself encouraged the reader to continue.

Malone predicted in the preface of the first volume that his series on Jefferson would encompass four volumes. An arduous task for a fifty-six-year-old man to undertake, the project became even more difficult than anticipated. While working on volume two of the series, Malone discovered that the wealth of material on the era 1784-1801 necessitated the section be divided into two parts. Thus, the original volume two became volumes two and three. While working on this section of *Jefferson and His Time*, Malone also became an editor for the History Book Club.

But even though Malone was working simultaneously as a teacher at Columbia University, as an editor for the book club, and as writer of the Jefferson biography, he was able to complete volume two, *Jefferson and the Rights of Man*, in 1951; with it the story of Jefferson's life was completed through the year 1792. Because the sources for this period of Jefferson's life were rich, Malone expanded his work to include every possible detail of importance. The period of 1784-1792 found Jefferson in a wider world than Williamsburg and Monticello afforded. He spent months at a time in Paris and Versailles, London, New York, and Philadelphia. The events of the period were extremely complicated, but Malone's writing portrayed them clearly.

The biographer traced Jefferson's role in the international scene and in the beginnings of the new government at home. Malone felt that his portrait of Jefferson's diplomatic career in France was somewhat disappointing because that career had proved unrewarding and unsuccessful to Jefferson himself. But Malone remained loyal to his own biographical standards and told the story as it had happened. Once again the man was portrayed in his own setting and the research was exhaustive. The style remained flowing, clear, and graceful. Malone worked occasional pauses, designed to appraise the evidence presented, into his narrative. Yet in pointing out Jefferson's mistakes and successes, he continued to be as impartial as possible, thus adding further value to the work as a whole.

The popularity of Malone's first volume was evident when 1952 sales figures revealed that the book had sold over 13,583 copies by that year; furthermore, the *Mississippi Valley Historical Review* placed it fifth on the preferred list of American biography. The only works which eclipsed it in popularity on its fourth birthday were Douglas S. Freeman's *R. E. Lee* (1934-1935), Samuel Eliot Morison's *Admiral of the Ocean Sea: A Life of Christopher Columbus* (1942), James G. Randall's three-volume *Lincoln the President* (1945-1952), and Henry F. Pringle's *Theodore Roosevelt* (1931).

The popularity of Malone's biography of Jefferson could have inspired him to complete the series quickly, but he refused to lower quality for speed. Instead, he turned to research for his third volume which, unfortunately, proceeded slowly because of his numerous activities. During the academic year 1951-1952, he was a Guggenheim fellow, and he used much of this time for research. However, he was not too busy to speak at the University of South Carolina at the celebration of its sesquicentennial. He was chosen for two obvious reasons: his reputation as a historian and his knowl-

edge of Thomas Cooper, who had been president of the university in its early years. Malone's address at the celebration urged the university to remain, as South Carolina College had been earlier, a bulwark of conservatism in the field of education, but not of obstructive conservatism. Malone urged the university to preserve freedom in study and high quality in education. He also encouraged the university to remember the importance of its own history. Malone's speech at the University of South Carolina presented two of his main beliefs: that education enriches people's lives and that history should be the story of all aspects of a civilization, not just of its wars and political events. Biography, the speaker declared, reports the history of a people through the life of an individual.

Malone continued to work on his biography of Jefferson after 1951, but he also spent much time on other activities. From 1953 to 1959 he was managing editor of *Political Science Quarterly*. While editor of this journal, he released *The Story of the Declaration of Independence* (1954), a pictorial history of the events that led to the signing of the Declaration in 1776. Providing a brief biography of each of the signers of the document and a concise account of the Declaration as seen in 1776 and after, the book was oriented to the popular reader, not designed to break new ground in history. It was, instead, a layman's handbook to the Declaration of Independence.

Malone continued his interest in history for the people by writing a textbook with Basil Rauch, a colleague at Columbia University. This two-volume work was entitled *Empire for Liberty: The Genesis and Growth of the United States of America* (1960). The title came from a letter Thomas Jefferson had written to James Madison in 1809, asserting that the United States was "an Empire for Liberty as She [the world] has never surveyed since the Creation." The narrative of American history by Malone and Rauch attempted to do justice to all the important aspects of history—political, economic, constitutional, diplomatic, social, religious, artistic, and intellectual. Two topics were followed by the authors throughout, international relations and the importance of ideas.

According to Malone and Rauch, the work had no special thesis, except for that contained in the title—the United States had been an Empire for Liberty, with occasional exceptions, throughout its history. Gracefully written, the book attempted to interpret the meaning of the American experience. Malone and Rauch were positive in their reporting of American history, but not to the extent of claiming that America had done no wrong in the past. The work is now dated, but at the time it was published it provided a good narrative of American history in the Jeffersonian tradition. The book was an outgrowth of its time, and Malone would later request that it be judged on that basis, not on the events of the 1970s or 1980s.

Empire for Liberty was published one year after Malone left Columbia University. His last move was a return to the hallowed grounds of Thomas Jefferson and the University of Virginia. Malone occupied the position of Jefferson Foundation Professor of History at the school from 1959 until his retirement in 1962. He had returned to the area of Virginia that Jefferson had loved, and it is only fitting that he wrote the last four volumes of his great work on Jefferson there.

In 1962, volume three of *Jefferson and His Time* was released. Entitled *Jefferson and the Ordeal of Liberty*, the book concerned the years 1793-1801. These were years of controversy for Jefferson, and no other volume of Malone's biography created as much furor, especially among historians sympathetic to Alexander Hamilton. Jefferson was embroiled in a conflict with the political faction led by Hamilton, and Malone gave much space to his discussion of the key year 1793. That year Jefferson retired from his position as secretary of state and returned to Virginia. However, he did not leave national politics but continued to watch events in Washington that affected him extensively. Jefferson would have been happiest if he could have remained in retirement in Virginia, but two events forced him back into politics. The first was George Washington's denunciation of republican societies, which caused Jefferson to feel Washington had become a party man. The second was the adoption of the Jay Treaty, which Jefferson felt surrendered national independence to Great Britain and departed from the policy of neutrality. Jefferson returned to politics in 1796 because he felt that party politics was a necessity, and he would emerge as leader of the opposition after Madison's retirement in 1797.

Malone was sympathetic to Jefferson in the volume, but unlike the historians who had favored Jefferson earlier, he was also sympathetic to John Adams. Malone believed that the differences between Adams and Jefferson were not fundamental. The historian felt that Adams was not really a High Federalist, a member of the group with which Jefferson fought long and hard. Instead, Malone suggested, Adams did not support the Alien and Sedition Acts, the High Federalists' supreme efforts

to circumvent the American liberty so valued by Jefferson. Even though Malone was generally sympathetic to Jefferson in the third volume, as throughout the series, his treatment of Adams was equally balanced. The historian continued to evaluate these figures by the criteria of their own age, not by twentieth-century standards.

Malone's next work was a by-product of his third volume on Jefferson. It was *Thomas Jefferson as Political Leader* (1963), a series of lectures delivered at the University of California at Berkeley. Addressed to the general public, the book examined how Jefferson emerged as the national leader of the Republican party. Malone evaluated Jefferson between 1790 and 1800 and found faults in his actions, especially in his private outbursts against John Adams. Malone emphasized that Jefferson was mortal and capable of error but that he was also the champion of liberty who wanted to preserve the 1776 revolution and prevent any return of tyranny. Malone thus once again stressed that *any* historical character must be judged within his own setting and time. The lectures provided a good summary of Jefferson's emergence as a political leader prior to his presidency.

With the publication of *Thomas Jefferson as Political Leader*, Malone had written nine books, three being volumes of *Jefferson and His Time*. He had retired from active teaching in 1962 and had become resident biographer at the University of Virginia. Seventy years of his life had passed, the last nineteen having been concentrated on Jefferson. Malone did not slow down in his drive to complete his biography but instead continued to research Jefferson and his presidency. While he was working on volume four of *Jefferson and His Time*, he served as president of the Southern Historical Association during the academic year 1967-1968. He was also awarded the Thomas Jefferson Award at the University of Virginia in 1964 for his contributions to scholarship.

The long-awaited fourth volume of *Jefferson and His Time* was published in 1970. Although he finally could concentrate most of his time on the biography, Malone chose to delay releasing the work until he had nearly finished his research on the fifth volume. Volumes four and five were originally supposed to have been volume three, but Malone's thoroughness and the abundance of his sources necessitated that he divide the materials of the period into two books.

Volume four of Malone's comprehensive study, *Jefferson the President: First Term 1801-1805*, concentrated on the decisions Jefferson faced while presiding over the infant republic. During this time, Malone showed, Jefferson never forgot the revolution of 1776, and he strove to ensure its permanence. He urged Congress to repeal the "midnight appointments" created by the Federalist Judiciary Act of 1801. Many other republican ideas also were realized during his first term through his good relations with the legislative branch, and even the Supreme Court backed away from open controversy when John Marshall denied jurisdiction to the court in the case of *Marbury* v. *Madison*.

Malone found that Jefferson's first administration, as a whole, did not deviate from his earlier public conduct and his previously expressed convictions. Even the purchase of Louisiana was not a change in policy, as Jefferson had advocated the acquisition of the area when he was secretary of state. Jefferson showed great forethought in obtaining this area, Malone felt, for the president knew that the allegiance of the occupants of the trans-Appalachian region to the United States could never be guaranteed until the free navigation of the Mississippi River was secured. Jefferson was thus preserving the revolution of 1776 by capturing the allegiance of the inhabitants of the trans-Allegheny region.

Malone's love for education and those associated with its advancement came out again in volume four. Jefferson was portrayed as forever interested in science and learning in general and as urging Virginia to establish a state university. Malone concentrated one full chapter on this aspect of Jefferson's first term, a time when he was recognized as America's leading patron of learning.

Malone's fifth volume, *Jefferson the President: Second Term 1805-1809* (1974), took Jefferson through the sixty-sixth year of his life. During Jefferson's second term, Lewis and Clark made their famous journey, the United States fought a successful naval "war" with the Barbary Pirates, former U. S. Vice President Aaron Burr was tried for treason, and Jefferson attempted to impose an embargo on exports in reaction to the impressment of American seamen by foreign powers. The volume ends with an account of Jefferson's return to his beloved Monticello at the close of his political career.

Although some historians believed that Jefferson had dominated the entire government of the United States during his presidency, Malone contradicted this point of view. He argued that Jefferson advocated and practiced a government based on the doctrine of separation of powers; he exerted very little control over members of the other two branches of government, even though he obviously was the leader of the nation. Jefferson's wishes or desires, therefore, were not always met. He was unable to secure an embargo for exports without a struggle, and Aaron Burr was not convicted of treason as Jefferson felt he should have been. Always balanced in his judgment, Malone chided Jefferson for his actions during the Burr trial.

Malone believed that Jefferson had been a good president for his time period and that his actions must be interpreted within the framework of that era. However, in an interview given after volume five had been published, the historian expressed his opinion that Jefferson would not be the leader today that he was in his own time. Malone contended that Jefferson would be displeased with the extent of governmental interference into business and the private lives of the nation's citizens and that he probably would be unable to run a government as large as today's. But Jefferson cannot be president now, the point made in Malone's study: Jefferson was right for his age and he strove to protect the liberties the men in 1776 had fought to secure for Americans.

The fifth volume of *Jefferson and His Time* received a Pulitzer Prize in 1975. This was not the only award bestowed on Malone. In 1972, he had been given the John F. Kennedy Medal by the Massachusetts Historical Society and the Wilbur L. Cross Medal by Yale University.

Malone's comprehensive biography of Thomas Jefferson had taken him to this point thirty-one years to write. Scholars and laymen interested in history agonized over whether Malone would be able to complete the series with a volume on Jefferson's last seventeen years. They were rewarded with *The Sage of Monticello*, the final volume in the Jefferson biography. Malone, even though he was nearly blind and required the help of two assistants and a machine to write, finished the work in 1981. The work was not disappointing. Even though Malone was eighty-nine years of age, he had retained the standards of exhaustive research and of a graceful style he had set for himself in volume one.

The Sage of Monticello, the fulfillment of thirty-eight years of study, reported the last seventeen years of Jefferson's life, all spent at his home Monticello. Jefferson's final years were complicated. He was constantly plagued by financial difficulties, increased by the depletion of Virginia farmlands and by the bankruptcy of his son-in-law. Jefferson also was faced with numerous family problems—he had to support his daughter's large family and one of his granddaughters married an alcoholic. His private life was filled with sorrow. What kept Jefferson going in his final years was his desire for a public university in Virginia. Even though the former president was unable to achieve a complete system of public education at all levels, the state did provide for the university during his lifetime. The university was Jefferson's great escape, and Malone compared his own work on Jefferson to it: the study of Jefferson was Malone's great escape.

Jefferson also was able to mend his personal break with John Adams during his retirement, and it is only fitting that the two men died on the same day, 4 July 1826. Volume six of Jefferson's biography was published on 4 July 1981, also a fitting memorial to a great leader and to a great work.

While each volume of *Jefferson and His Time* can stand on its own merits, the true contribution of Malone is the work as a whole. In his acclaimed series, Malone portrayed Jefferson for the historian and the layman in an immensely thorough but readable way. He explained how Jefferson's early childhood and life in Virginia influenced his later life. Jefferson's entire public life was centered around one central issue, the securing of the liberties of the American people. He first helped secure these liberties through the Declaration of Independence and the American Revolution. When in later years he felt the liberties were being threatened by the action of the Federalists, he returned to public life and became president, all to preserve the liberties he had seen purchased by the blood of soldiers in the American Revolution. Jefferson continually advocated a free economy, championed free education, and was responsible for the growth of the American nation. He believed in freedom and enlightenment, as did many eighteenth-century men.

In his comprehensive and detailed treatment of Jefferson, Malone utilized the four principles that he believed necessary for any biography. First and foremost, Malone treated Jefferson fairly. The historian viewed his subject within his own time period and did not judge him by twentieth-century standards. Second, the purpose of the biography was to tell the complete story of Jefferson's life. Before any value judgments were made, Malone presented the events as thoroughly and fairly as possible in an easy-flowing narrative. Third, after Malone told the story, he made sound value judgments about Jefferson, but they were not based on personal biases. Finally, Malone utilized all available resources for his study. He exhausted all manuscript material but did not let the arduous task

dampen his enthusiasm for Jefferson nor keep him from finishing the work. The biography took thirty-eight years to complete, but it suffered no unevenness because of the long time span.

After volume six had gone to the publisher in 1981, Malone was asked by an interviewer which part of the Jefferson biography was the hardest to write. His answer was volume three. That volume treated the events of 1793, and Malone recalled that he felt he would never finish writing about that year. Yet the book which resulted proved very complex, critically important, and vastly documented. Malone stated that perhaps he had written more on that year than he should have but that he felt it all needed to be said.

Malone viewed himself first as a teacher, a result of his mother's influence on him, but he also always liked to write. He, however, found writing more difficult, not less, with the passing years as he became more demanding and as his eyesight failed him. Yet, he did not give up when others might have quit. Instead, he chose to finish the work which always will be viewed as a model biography.

Malone's contribution to historical writing has been extensive. He has combined excellent scholarship with a readable style. He has left no source untouched in his desire to learn all about his subjects, whether Thomas Jefferson, Thomas Cooper, or Edwin A. Alderman. His editing of the *Dictionary of American Biography* with Allen Johnson established the methods and standards for short, definitive biography. The multivolume work, *Jefferson and His Time*, will be definitive for a long time; in fact, it is hard to see any better work ever being written on Jefferson. Whether or not he produces further works, Dumas Malone's contributions to historical writing will be enduring.

Other:
Correspondence between Thomas Jefferson and Pierre Samuel duPont de Nemours, 1789-1817, edited by Malone (Boston: Houghton Mifflin, 1930);
Dictionary of American Biography, volumes 2-4, edited by Malone and Allen Johnson; volumes 5-20, edited by Malone (New York: Scribners, 1930-1936);
"Biography and History," in *The Interpretation of History*, edited by Joseph R. Strayer (New York: Peter Smith, 1950), pp. 119-149;
Autobiography of Thomas Jefferson, introduction by Malone (New York: Putnam's, 1959).

Periodical Publications:
"The Threatened Prosecution of Alexander

Hamilton under the Sedition Act by Thomas Cooper," *American Historical Review*, 29 (October 1923): 76-81;

"Mr. Jefferson and the Traditions of Virginia," *Virginia Magazine of History and Biography*, 75 (April 1967): 131-142;

"Presidential Leadership and National Unity: The Jeffersonian Example," *Journal of Southern History*, 35 (February 1969): 3-17;

"Mr. Jefferson's Private Life," *American Antiquarian Society Proceedings*, new series 84 (April 1974): 65-74.

Reference:

Jeffrey Smith, "In the Autumn of His Years, Dumas Malone Reaps a Rich Harvest," *Emory Magazine*, 58 (December 1981): 8-12.

Forrest McDonald
(7 January 1927-)

Justus D. Doenecke
New College of the University of South Florida

BOOKS: *Let There Be Light: The Electric Utilities Industry in Wisconsin, 1881-1955* (Madison: American History Research Center, 1957);

We the People: The Economic Origins of the Constitution (Chicago: University of Chicago Press, 1958);

Insull (Chicago: University of Chicago Press, 1962);

E Pluribus Unum: The Formation of the American Republic, 1776-1790 (Boston: Houghton Mifflin, 1965);

The Torch is Passed: The United States in the Twentieth Century (Reading, Mass.: Addison-Wesley, 1968);

Enough Wise Men: The Story of Our Constitution (New York: Putnam's, 1970);

The Boys Were Men: The American Navy in the Age of Fighting Sail (New York: Putnam's, 1971);

The Last Best Hope: A History of the United States, by McDonald, Leslie Decker, and Thomas P. Govan (Reading, Mass.: Addison-Wesley, 1972);

The Presidency of George Washington (Lawrence: University Press of Kansas, 1974);

The Phaeton Ride: The Crisis of American Success (Garden City: Doubleday, 1974);

The Presidency of Thomas Jefferson (Lawrence: University Press of Kansas, 1976);

Alexander Hamilton: A Biography (New York: Norton, 1979);

The American People, by McDonald, David Burner, and Eugene D. Genovese (New York: Revisionary Press, 1980);

A Constitutional History of the United States (New York: Franklin Watts, 1982).

Forrest McDonald

Few contemporary historians have been as prolific as Forrest McDonald, and few have created so much debate within the discipline. From 1957, when his account of the Wisconsin utilities industry was published, to today, when he is investigating Southern ethnicity, McDonald's career has been one long exercise in demythologizing. Unlike so many of his colleagues, he has not been known politically as either a liberal or a radical. Rather, he has long been unabashedly a conservative, one who in 1964 served as state chairman of the Goldwater for President Committee of Rhode Island and who since 1978 has been listed on the masthead of *National Review*.

McDonald's major works have challenged stereotypes of predatory and indifferent industrialists, have replaced Charles A. Beard's simplistic economic interpretation of the Constitution with a far more intricate one of his own, and have juxtaposed a rather stupid George Washington and a rather destructive Thomas Jefferson to an extremely able Alexander Hamilton. Yet, despite the impassioned discussion he has so often engendered, he has shown so much mastery in his two fields of expertise—the early national period and general business history—that no serious scholar can write in these areas without confronting his conclusions. McDonald, in short, has helped to change our way of looking at certain segments of American history, and it is this capacity, more than the accumulation of new data, that is the mark of a truly able historian.

McDonald was born to Forrest and Myra McGill McDonald in Orange, Texas. Too short and light to play football in high school, he opted for baseball, and it was athletic aspirations that led him to enroll at the University of Texas. He interrupted his college career to join the navy, where he was trained as a combat aircrewman. Because World War II ended just as McDonald completed his training, he returned to the University of Texas. The need to support a wife and several children led him to work over forty hours a week, mainly as waiter, janitor, and newspaper carrier. Yet, by continually overloading his schedule, he was able to jump from second semester freshman to a master's degree in less than three years. Hoping to write the Great American Novel, he took his B.A. in English in 1949. He then switched to history, where he received the M.A. the same year and the Ph.D. in 1955. Major intellectual influences on his career included University of Texas historians Eugene Campbell Barker (whom he called "the grand old man of Texas history"), Walter Prescott Webb ("a masterful generalizer"), and Fulmer Mood ("the

range and depth of his factual knowledge were genuinely awesome").

Beginning his career as a teaching fellow at the University of Texas in 1950-1951, McDonald then moved to the State Historical Society of Wisconsin, where from 1953 to 1956 he was utilities research director, and from 1957 to 1958 he was executive secretary of the American History Research Center. He has held faculty positions at Brown University (1958-1967), Wayne State University (1967-1976), and the University of Alabama (1976-present), where he is currently professor of history and distinguished senior fellow of the Center for the Study of Southern History and Culture. McDonald has received numerous awards and fellowships, including ones bestowed by the John Simon Guggenheim Memorial Foundation, the Social Science Research Council, the American Council of Learned Societies, the Volker Fund, and the Relm Foundation.

McDonald's earliest writings were in business history, and from the beginning of his career he was involved in controversy. In 1956, McDonald wrote two articles concerning battles waged at the turn of the century between the city of Milwaukee and the city's electric streetcar company. McDonald found that the company's opponents were not the noble reformers of legend but were instead antibusiness demagogues who cared little about decent service and low rates. A year later came McDonald's first book, *Let There Be Light: The Electric Utilities Industry in Wisconsin, 1881-1955*. Historians, so McDonald claimed at the beginning of his study, had been so preoccupied with politics that they had failed to examine crucial economic changes. When it came to the electrical industry, textbooks might offer a sentence or so on Thomas Edison's invention of the incandescent lamp, but they inevitably paid most attention to the so-called evils of public utility holding companies and to the rectification of these evils by New Deal reformers. Hence, the more significant facts had been forgotten: for the first time in recorded history man had an abundance of cheap power at his disposal; this power gave the United States enough energy to perform any task it chose; this power also resulted in such a marked increase in living standards that the nation, to borrow a line from Will Rogers, "was the first nation in history to occupy a poor house equipped with a radio, electric lights, a washing machine, and a refrigerator." Indeed, McDonald contended, the growth of the power industry was the linchpin in a technological revolution "of a magnitude that mankind never before witnessed and may never witness again."

The book was divided into four parts, with each part covering seventy-five years and suggesting a theme: the "pioneers" were followed by "promoters," who were followed by "giants," who were followed by "institutions." McDonald stressed the advantages of the central power station and the transmission line over independent supply by individual users. In one of the more controversial sections of the book, he defended holding companies for making it possible to accumulate the capital needed to develop large modern utility services and for doing so at low cost. McDonald asserted, in fact, that the Rural Electrification Administration retarded rural electrification in Wisconsin for as much as five years. In addition, REA charged high rates and wasted its generous government subsidies.

McDonald's study was financed by the Wisconsin Utilities Association through a grant to the State Historical Society of Wisconsin. A historical committee, consisting of representatives of nine power companies, helped him gain records and interviews. In his preface, McDonald acknowledged that he was presenting his findings from the viewpoint of the men who developed and managed the state's utilities industry. To use any other method, he continued, was to bring "a preconceived value system" into the study and was therefore ahistorical. Critics differed with McDonald, claiming that even if partisanship were inadvertent, it was nonetheless there. Defenders countered that the Historical Society had had three "hostile" historians, including William B. Hesseltine and Paul W. Gates, examine McDonald's manuscript before publication.

Even more iconoclastic was *Insull* (1962), McDonald's life of the Chicago utilities magnate. Samuel Insull had been widely revered in the 1920s as a great industrial statesman. Yet his reputation never recovered from his indictment during the early 1930s for mail fraud, for violating federal bankruptcy laws, and for embezzlement. McDonald wrote, "Whether you like him or not, when you get to know him, is a matter of total indifference to me." However, McDonald's work was as laudatory as it was revisionist. It was Insull, McDonald asserted, who made electric power cheap and abundant to millions. Indeed, Insull made possible centralized electric power, worked out a model of nationwide distribution copied by virtually all American industry, and innovated in mass production. Moreover, Insull was, McDonald showed, the father of government regulation of public utilities, a progenitor of rural electrification, a promoter of welfare capitalism and trade unions, and a pioneer in public

relations. There was still more, for Insull devised a system for marketing securities that made certain great corporations possible. There was little wonder that at the height of his power Insull presided over a group of properties worth two to three billion dollars and had over four million people dependent upon him for utilities and transportation. McDonald's book was drawn from Insull's own papers and from the manuscripts of major midwestern utility companies.

The historian traced Insull's career from the time he was a fourteen-year-old office boy, working in London on a weekly salary of five shillings, to his death in 1938. McDonald noted Insull's roles as Edison's private secretary, as builder of the Edison Machine Works in Schenectady, and as animating spirit behind the General Electric Company. Insull also founded the Commonwealth Edison Company of Chicago, the greatest single producer of electricity on the globe. Before 1912 he had introduced such technical innovations as the rotary converter, the rural electrification grid, and the giant steam turbogenerator. Such achievements were rooted, McDonald showed, in enormous energy, quick analytic thought, a good grasp of human nature, and an ability to pick superior subordinates.

Unable to resist a bit of psychologizing, McDonald accounted for Insull's decision to create a vast financial empire and to enter the gas and traction business, by the claim that his wife had refused him sexual privileges. McDonald also blamed the fall of the Insull empire in 1932 on New York bankers. Led by the House of Morgan, these bankers composed a "club" of "buccaneers" that, moving "sharklike" for the kill, conspired to prevent Insull from borrowing a paltry sum needed to keep his empire alive. Though Insull's stockholders enthusiastically stood by him, an unwise loan from a subsidiary company smacked of fraud. He was subsequently acquitted of a host of charges, but his career and reputation were ruined. At the point of crisis, he could not bring himself to commit the single immoral act that might have saved him—to sell Commonwealth Edison short.

The book was criticized on a number of grounds, particularly for exaggerating the innovative nature of Insull's accomplishments, identifying too closely with its subject, disposing too easily of Insull's critics, and not giving full play to the jerry-built structure of utility holding companies. It was, however, a rare reviewer who did not praise McDonald's exhaustive research, grasp of the electric industry, and able prose style. A reviewer in the *Economist* said that it read like "a true thriller." To many professional historians, McDonald proved his fundamental case: that Insull was an able businessman who made major contributions to the American economy and who deserved better treatment from his countrymen and from posterity.

McDonald has done other work in business history, including sketches of such utilities magnates as Insull, Floyd Leslie Carlisle, Harvey Crowley Couch, and Matthew Scott Sloan for the *Dictionary of American Biography* and of John Pierpont Morgan and Jacob Henry Schiff for *The Encyclopedia of American Biography*. In a 1970 review written for *Business History Review*, he opposed what he called the "liberal" view of history, which, in his words, "viewed business as bad guys (the bigger the badder)" and which saw "the coming of regulation as the gradual triumph of persistent reform politicians." He claimed, however, that his fellow business historians had all too often "merely reversed the demonology—making businessmen good and reformers bad, viewing regulation as a form of unmerited punishment, and suggesting that everybody would have been better off if businessmen in their great wisdom had just been left alone."

In 1974, Doubleday published a series of McDonald's lectures that traced the entire course of American business and that combined sweeping historical interpretation with Cassandra-like warnings. McDonald began *The Phaeton Ride: The Crisis of American Success* by describing the economic crisis of 1973 when, he said, the West was approaching the limits of its potential. As its cultural system was incredibly wasteful and the planet's resources finite, it could never reach the millenium. "Man has been hungry, cold, and at the mercy of the elements throughout most of his history, and so will most of humanity remain," he wrote. Prices, taxes, waste, and unemployment would inevitably increase, and shortages would grow. Their effect would be minimized, however, if the United States returned to coal as its primary source of power, shifted toward electrically powered mass transportation, phased out trucking except for short hauls, and abandoned the automobile as it has been known.

McDonald, in this history, claimed that although the rise of giant business brought prosperity to millions, noncorporate portions of the society could only survive by devising institutional innovations of comparable quality and scale. The problem was compounded by an anticommercial ideology first propounded by the eighteenth-century philosopher Henry St. John, Viscount Bolingbroke, and then carried down through the Jeffersonian and Jacksonian movements. McDonald wrote,

"Even as we applaud and encourage and boast about our material progress, we castigate the agents of that progress, the businessmen who have been its prime movers." Because such individuals as Alexander Hamilton, Nicholas Biddle, Jay Cooke, and Samuel Insull were so creative, they had to be destroyed. Yet, once big business realized how strong the anticommercial tradition was, it was able to turn the tradition to business's own ends, doing so by manipulating progressive reform in the interests of rationalization and efficiency. Also at work was what McDonald called "the Brer Rabbit technique," whereby "politicians gave businessmen what they wanted, while each believed that punishment was inflicted by one upon the other."

Turning to the development of welfare capitalism, or what he called "The Corporation as Father," McDonald noted how such corporate giants as General Electric and the Insull empire promoted profit-sharing, free medical benefits, and retirement plans. When Franklin D. Roosevelt became president, the government, in a sense, nationalized and politicized this paternalism by acting as "godfather" to the population of an entire nation. Outright subsidies benefited some groups, including labor, agriculture, the South as a section, and selected corporations, such as Kaiser steel and Reynolds aluminum. Federal procurements demanded by World War II and then the cold war seemed to insure that the government-sponsored bonanza would last forever and that the United States at last had a "no-fail economy." Indeed, McDonald declared, the economy could even sustain a wave of consumerism and environmentalism, headed by such "Luddites and Barnburners" as Ralph Nader.

The seeds of destruction, however, were already deeply implanted, McDonald continued. Government eventually lost the ability to regulate. While it remained vital as a consumer and redistributor of income, it was locked into destructive policies that it could not undo. True, McDonald wrote, much of the defense budget was allocated to support soldiers not trained to fight and to procure weapons often no better than existing ones. Yet to dismantle the defense establishment would entail social costs the nation simply could not afford, and the same dilemma applied to welfare and other subsidies.

McDonald's second set of contributions lay in the era of the American Revolution and that time following it, which some historians, such as John Fiske, have called "the critical period." His very first venture was an essay entitled "The Relation of the

French Peasant Veterans of the American Revolution to the Fall of Feudalism in France, 1789-1792," which was published in *Agricultural History* in 1951. Here he argued that French participants in the American conflict had formed the dynamic element in the later fall of feudalism in France. Although within five years his claim was challenged by the French historian Jacques Godeshot, it did help promote a reexamination of the relationship between the two great revolutions.

In 1958, McDonald's *We the People: The Economic Origins of the Constitution* was published. The book so strongly attacked Charles A. Beard's classic on the subject, *An Economic Interpretation of the Constitution of the United States* (1913), that hardly one conclusion of the earlier work remained intact. Beard had claimed that the Constitution was an economic document created by a consolidated group whose interests were truly national, that the struggle for ratification revealed a split between financial and commercial interests on the one hand and small farming and debtor elements on the other, and that public security holders played a considerable role in effecting eventual adoption. It was the economic interests of the framers, Beard went on, that led them to produce a document giving the government power to tax, to control commerce, and to dispose of western lands.

Admittedly, Beard at several points used the language of hypothesis, confessed that his work was "frankly fragmentary," and indicated the incompleteness of his own research. And admittedly, many historians had long been suspicious of Beard's arguments, although none had taken him on comprehensively until Robert E. Brown wrote his *Charles A. Beard and the Constitution: A Critical Analysis of "An Economic Interpretation of the Constitution"* (1956). But it was McDonald who, in the words of Arthur M. Schlesinger, Jr., bestowed "the *coup de grace* to the Beard thesis"; such historians as Edmund Morgan, Richard P. McCormick, and James B. Hedges concurred. David M. Potter called *We the People* "one of the most smashing analyses ever mounted in the literature of historical criticism."

McDonald had become strongly suspicious of Beard's arguments while listening to Eugene Campbell Barker's lectures at the University of Texas. In a master's thesis of well over 300 pages, McDonald set out to prove Barker correct and Beard wrong. He later said of his challenging so distinguished a scholar as Beard: "When I enter into any aspect of it [history], I do so on the assumption that the territory is unexplored, that nothing anyone has written is likely to be sound. I chart my

own way as I go along." Fulmer Mood convinced McDonald to explore thoroughly the years 1763 to 1790. The Social Science Research Council gave him a two-year grant, during which he travelled the equivalent of three times around the globe in search of records. He worked through so many primary sources that he compiled about ten thousand pages of notes, what he has since called his "lifetime capital fund." His doctoral dissertation, directed by Mood and serving as the basis for *We the People*, was drawn from a small fragment of these notes.

In a brief introductory section of his book, McDonald summarized the central points that Beard advanced, described the internal structure of Beard's analysis, and exposed the logical and methodological assumptions upon which Beard made his investigation. (In a separate essay on Beard written in 1969, McDonald claimed that Beard confused his role as teacher, in which capacity one advances controversial hypotheses, with his role as historian, where accuracy counts above all.) McDonald then brought together data on the political and economic backgrounds of the fifty-five delegates to the Philadelphia Convention. He outlined the principal geographical areas, the leading political factions in each state, the economic interests of the participants, and the voting behavior of each member. In so doing, McDonald denied that there was any united front of merchants and security holders against farmers and debtors. Indeed, the members of the Constitutional Convention were not a cohesive group. Unmoved by any identity of economic concern, they did not vote their economic interests. Fully one quarter of the delegates had, in state legislatures, supported paper money or debtor relief laws, the very kind of legislation that Beard claimed the delegates had sought to suppress. Another one-fourth of the delegates had important economic interests that were adversely affected, directly or indirectly, by the Constitution that they had helped to write.

Next on McDonald's agenda were the state ratifying conventions. Here again, he listed the delegates, showing their occupations and economic interests to the degree that he could trace them. He noted that two states ratified the Constitution easily: Georgia, because of an exposed frontier, and New Jersey, because it had no port of its own. In these two states, and in Delaware, Connecticut, and Maryland as well, farmers and adherents of paper money supported ratification. Other states—including New York, Virginia, North Carolina, and Rhode Island—at first opposed the Constitution, for they saw themselves as self-sufficient. Still other states were divided over the Constitution. Among these were Pennsylvania, Massachusetts, South Carolina, and New Hampshire, basically strong states that ratified the document only because "they had certain characteristics that sapped their strength or gave them the illusion they were weak." As in the case of the Constitutional Convention, many creditors and security holders opposed ratification. Moreover, and again contrary to Beard's assessment, agrarian rather than fiscal property was by far the greatest source of wealth for the majority, both at Philadelphia and in the state conventions. Beard's claim of a "consolidated economic interest" simply did not hold up. Indeed, if anything, Antifederalists actually owned more property and possessed a higher social status than did those who supported the Constitution.

In the final section of *We the People*, McDonald evaluated his data. Here he explored the validity of the Beard thesis, the role of economic interests in framing and adopting the Constitution, and the fruitfulness of economic analysis as a tool in investigating the document. McDonald conceded that economic forces played a vital role in ratification, but he found economic life far more pluralistic than Beard had maintained. Economic interests, he went on, were related to the economic conditions and aspirations of each occupational group within a state, and they did not follow any broad pattern. Furthermore, these groups were so diverse that it was not possible, even theoretically, to ascribe economic self-interest as the principal motive behind ratification.

Despite the many endorsements noted above, *We the People* was criticized on several grounds. Robert Schuyler said that McDonald should have evaluated the size of, not merely counted, security holdings in the state conventions. Holders of securities in excess of a thousand dollars tended by over two to one to favor ratification. Conceding that McDonald had "substantially increased our knowledge" and had done "some excellent research," Jackson Turner Main claimed that *We the People* minimized the property held by Federalists while exaggerating that held by Antifederalists. McDonald offered a rebuttal to Main's challenge.

McDonald's next study of the "critical period" was a wider one. In *E Pluribus Unum: The Formation of the American Republic, 1776-1790* (1965), he focused on the events that led up to the Federal Convention. He began his narrative by comparing two groups: the "hard-shelled republicans," such as Thomas Jefferson and John Adams, who "believed in the natural rights of man and the possibility of a

clean rational break with the past," and the "nationalists," such as Alexander Hamilton and John Dickinson, who stressed the experience of history over abstract logic and who saw men's motives as containing evil as well as good. To the nationalists, whom McDonald much admired, one filled public office not only out of esteem for a public trust but also out of desire for personal gain. Yet such gain, if it served to give individuals a stake in the new nation, could be of real benefit to the entire commonwealth. During the period of the Articles of Confederation, the republicans had triumphed, and as a result a destructive anarchy developed, McDonald contended. By the early spring of 1787, "the very life of the Republic was on trial," for "the freest people in the world had ceased to care whether the Republic lived or died." The question was a simple one: "Would this politically be one nation, or would it not?"

McDonald covered the Middle states, the South, and the East and offered much detail on factions within each state. In regard to the 1787 Constitutional Convention in Philadelphia, McDonald sought to overturn several accepted interpretations. To him, the Mount Vernon Conference of 1785 was not a forerunner of the Philadelphia Convention, and the Annapolis Convention of 1786 was composed more of "visionaries" than of "men of great vision." Furthermore, perhaps the most important feature of the Constitution, the system of checks and balances, was adopted during the 1787 Convention almost by accident. The contract clause was "audaciously" inserted by Gouverneur Morris after it had been rejected by the convention delegates. The crucial bargain was not between large and small states but was rather a private deal between John Rutledge and Robert Sherman concerning jurisdiction over land disputes, the slave trade, and federal taxation of exports. McDonald's book ended with a paean to those "giants in the earth," whose labor doomed the American people, despite themselves, "forever to be free." Sinners themselves, the Founding Fathers took the doctrine of original sin into their reckoning and hence in 1787 created a work that survived treason and fratricidal war.

E Pluribus Unum saw McDonald at his most iconoclastic. In his discussion of the South, he found the region's supposed unity a myth, denied that Virginia was aristocratic, and asserted that North Carolina was populated with "a lot of rednecks and a few Second Families of Virginia." As for South Carolina, it was ruled by planters who possessed a "callous disregard for human life and suffering . . .

probably unmatched anywhere west of the Dnieper." Turning to personalities, McDonald said that George Washington "could have added little to the intellectual average of any convention," and James Madison sounded "for all the world like a man with a flexible brain, whereas at base he was a brittle doctrinaire theorist." Debunking did not end here. When spring came to New Hampshire, McDonald declared, "all men save the most industrious got fiercely drunk and made other men's wives pregnant." Furthermore, McDonald asserted, Robert Morris's famous tobacco contract did not ruin Virginia planters; on the contrary, it stimulated a rise in the price of tobacco. The *Federalist Papers* were "monumental propaganda pieces," and Shay's rebellion was more rooted in the blind rage of an aspiring politician, Benjamin Austin, Jr., than in the economic distress of the Massachusetts farmers.

As with many of his other books, *E Pluribus Unum* created sharp debate. Most reviewers praised McDonald's wit, memorable vignettes, and mastery of complicated financial matters. Yet one critic found him too much of an economic determinist, while another argued that McDonald had neglected class and sectional conflicts. Still a third saw him as too bound by Beard's categories, even in trying to refute them. To some historians, McDonald placed inordinate stress upon the Rutledge-Sherman deal, misunderstood the New Jersey and Virginia Plans, and oversimplified human motivation by juxtaposing shrewd double-dealers to inert, unimaginative masses. In a preface to the second edition, which he wrote in 1978, McDonald asserted that had he been writing the book again, he would have been more cautious in describing the Rutledge-Sherman deal and would have been more appreciative of Hamilton and Madison.

McDonald has contributed other work on the Founding Fathers. Lively sketches of Gouverneur Morris, Roger Sherman, John Dickinson, and Alexander Hamilton appear in *The Encyclopedia of American Biography*. In an article on the Antifederalists, published in 1963, McDonald stressed the cupidity of such leaders as Governor George Clinton of New York. One of his most creative works has been a 1978 essay on the libraries of the Founders. Here McDonald stressed the beliefs many of them had in the "natural" goodness of people, the evils of coercion, and the virtue of real property as opposed to personal property. He also edited and wrote an introduction to *Empire and Nation: Letters from a Farmer in Pennsylvania by John Dickinson and Letters from the Federal Farmer by Richard Henry Lee* (1962),

letters written, respectively, in 1767 and 1787. McDonald juxtaposed the pragmatism of Dickinson, who helped draft the Constitution, to the rigidity of Lee, who "opposed national government founded on any principles." With his wife, Ellen Shapiro McDonald, McDonald also edited *Confederation and Constitution, 1781-1789* (1968), an anthology of primary sources on "the critical years." Even in a book entitled *Enough Wise Men: The Story of Our Constitution* (1970), a volume for younger readers, McDonald offered a fresh approach. He described how British and American combat differed, praised the generalship of Nathanael Greene and Benedict Arnold, and found Washington's Fabian tactics most wise. He also reiterated his claim that the Constitutional Convention ended chaos in the nation, and he stressed the importance of the agreement that Sherman made with Rutledge.

McDonald's third major activity has consisted of studies of the early national period, and here the focus has been upon three figures: Washington, Jefferson, and Hamilton. In *The Presidency of George Washington* (1974), McDonald downplayed Washington's role. "The Father of his Country," McDonald wrote, "was not, except in a symbolic sense, particularly efficacious in establishing the permanence of his country, or even of the executive branch of his country's government." Washington had nothing to do with Hamilton's financial system, except in resisting a temptation to veto the charter of the Bank of the United States. He watered down his neutrality proclamation, was far too permissive toward "Citizen" Edmund Genét, and at first opposed Jay's Treaty. He deserved no credit, McDonald wrote, for Pinckney's Treaty, which was simply dumped into his lap by the Ministry of Spain. Furthermore, the president first appointed an incompetent general, Arthur St. Clair, to remove the British and the Indians from the Northwest. When Washington's next appointment, "Mad Anthony" Wayne, succeeded in this task, he did so because he totally ignored Washington's instructions. Yet McDonald gave Washington great credit, particularly for serving as "the means by which Americans accommodated the change from monarchy to republicanism." In fact, Americans so feared executive authority that, had it not been for Washington, the office of president might well have not existed. Fortunately, Washington was "a myth that happened to be true," in the sense that he possessed the stature that any chief executive must have.

To McDonald, it was not Washington but Hamilton, "the most brilliant bastard in American history," who was at the center of the story, for it was

Hamilton's financial system that held the new nation together. Far less of McDonald's admiration went to the Virginia Republicans, a ruling class that, he said, intrigued with the French, was hypocritical concerning agrarian values and used ideology as a mere cosmetic for greed. McDonald hypothesized that Madison's political alliance with Jefferson resulted from an epileptic seizure revealed to Jefferson during the famous "botanical expedition" of 1791. Yet Madison is given credit for imparting needed vigor to the government in 1789 through the first tax law, the Bill of Rights, and the creation of the executive departments. John Adams was hardly taken seriously: most of his time was spent in the Senate, where he conducted himself so pompously that he acted as if he were Polonius debating a Greek chorus!

Critics claimed that McDonald underestimated Washington's role, possessed an anti-Jeffersonian bias, and—in the words of Richard E. Ellis—showed "a perverse desire to be clever and to shock." Yet almost every reviewer praised McDonald's treatment of complicated economic issues as well as his style. One passage, describing Hamilton's fiscal system, shows how succinct McDonald could be. "The strength of the system," he wrote, "lay not so much (as historians have been wont to suggest) in binding the interests of the wealthy and more influential members of society to the fate of the national government," as it did in "making national government *convenient* to the society it served and the absence of such government indescribably inconvenient" (emphasis his).

In 1976, McDonald's book *The Presidency of Thomas Jefferson* appeared. The historian began by tracing Republican ideology to the writings of Viscount Bolingbroke, of Thomas Gordon, of John Trenchard, and of the English Oppositionists who fought the financial revolution of the 1720s and 1730s. Believing that virtue and the good society rested upon a society of gentry, yeomen, and craftsmen, they opposed a modern capitalistic system based upon public debt, bank notes, stock, and credit. The Jeffersonian Republicans, according to McDonald, not only "swallowed the Oppositionists' ideas and ideology whole" they also grafted upon them a few beliefs of their own, such as states rights, absolute separation of powers, territorial expansion, and the preservation of slavery.

McDonald found the first three years of Jefferson's presidency successful. For all practical purposes, the chief executive presided over a revolution, one that "made a more profound turn toward what a majority of its people desired than had

almost any other government, ancient or modern." As president, Jefferson accomplished much: he abolished practically all internal taxes; went far toward liquidating debt; drastically reduced the military establishment; and repealed the Alien and Sedition Acts. True, he violated his own principles of morality by proposing the seizure of West Florida. He also set aside his aversion to high debts and a strict construction of the Constitution in acquiring the Louisiana Territory, although in so doing he doubled the size of the nation. In other ways, however, he remained ideologically rigid, most destructively so in his commercial warfare against the British when accommodation was necessary. In fact, had the United States cooperated with Britain, the U.S. economy, McDonald claimed, would have remained healthy and prosperous. Yet, by enforcing the embargo, Jefferson so trampled on the rights of his own people that whole towns were declared treasonous, pitched battles frequently erupted, and some Americans were killed. Wrote McDonald, "Verily, in its effort to avoid war with Europe, the Republican government of the United States was levying war against its own citizens." Furthermore, the embargo resulted in the starvation of tens of thousands of black slaves in the West Indies, the one area dependent upon the United States for food. As far as the issue of impressment was concerned, McDonald stressed one fact: the number of Americans forced into the British naval service was several times smaller than the number of Britons recruited to the American merchant fleet.

To McDonald, Jefferson was destructive in other ways as well. Manifesting a contempt for due process of law, indeed for law itself, Jefferson sought to emasculate the judiciary. He encouraged Aaron Burr to provoke a war with Spain so that the United States might seize West Florida and Mexico. However, once the usefulness of a war against Spain evaporated, Jefferson readily sacrificed Burr. By slashing military and naval appropriations to the bone, he rendered his nation incapable of defending itself. (McDonald had already made this indictment of Jefferson's presidency, and of Madison's as well, in *The Boys Were Men: The American Navy in the Age of Fighting Sail*, 1971, a lively and highly readable history of the American navy for younger readers. By reducing the army and navy to mere shadows, McDonald wrote, both presidents permitted America to suffer insult and injury from Britain and France, and the United States went to war in 1812 woefully unprepared.)

Despite his power, Jefferson could not break the Hamiltonian system. "On the broader scale," wrote McDonald concerning the Jeffersonians, "they failed, and failed calamitously—not because of their shortcomings, but because their system was incompatible with the immediate current of events, with the broad sweep of history, and with the nature of man and society." McDonald concluded, "He [Jefferson] and his followers set out to deflect the course of History, and History ended up devouring them and turning even their memory to its own purposes."

This study, like McDonald's others, received many laudatory reviews. Occasional dissent was registered concerning the role of Oppositionist ideology and Jefferson's supposed rigidity in financial matters. In the same year, 1976, that the Jefferson book was published, McDonald also wrote an article for *Commentary* magazine in which he blamed the third president for destroying George Washington's executive system. Washington, he noted, had divided the functions of the presidency between the chief executive, who was a symbolic and beloved figure, and such cabinet figures as Hamilton, who proposed and supervised the passage of legislation. The Jeffersonians destroyed this split system and erected no viable alternative in its place, thereby leaving a problem that "has plagued us throughout the nation's history," McDonald claimed.

In his masterful *Alexander Hamilton: A Biography* (1979), McDonald portrayed Washington's secretary of the treasury as the man most responsible for launching a powerful nation. Steeped in *The Papers of Alexander Hamilton* (1961-1975, edited by Harold C. Syrett and others), the successive volumes of which McDonald had reviewed for the *William and Mary Quarterly*, he challenged the traditional picture at every turn. He denied the accepted conclusion that Hamilton, while in the cabinet, acted improperly in conversing with Britain's minister to the United States. Nor did Hamilton seek to dump John Adams in 1796 or to attempt to dominate the Adams administration afterward. Furthermore, Hamilton in 1798 favored no reactionary policy of repression. If anything, he wanted to make government more popular.

McDonald attempted to put more myths concerning Hamilton to rest. Hamilton, McDonald showed, never owned slaves, nor did he commit adultery with his wife's beautiful sister. Far from making money while secretary of the treasury, he ended his term deeply in debt. McDonald claimed that Hamilton was right in seeking suppression of the Whiskey Rebellion; the insurrection was no uprising of oppressed yeomen but defiance of author-

ity by a lazy, brutal, and unruly mob. If Hamilton was a pessimist, believing that people were governed by "passion and prejudice," he continually appealed to the intelligence and virtue of his fellow citizens. Indeed, he never sought to build a power base in Congress and deplored the very idea of party. Moreover, McDonald asserted, it was Hamilton, not Jefferson, who was responsible for a genuinely free press.

As McDonald made a point of reading every thinker who influenced Hamilton, he was able to discuss thoroughly his subject's political philosophy. The reader learned that Hamilton wrote revolutionary tracts just as sophisticated as, and far more radical than, those of Jefferson or Adams. Contrary to what was said in numerous textbooks, McDonald wrote, Hamilton never advocated government by the rich and well born. Rather, he wanted all officials to be chosen by the people, or by a process of election originating with the people. No monarchist, Hamilton found it particularly vital that the national government be republican. The lower house, he hoped, would be chosen by universal male suffrage, but the Constitutional Convention found his proposal too radical. In McDonald's words, Hamilton sought a meritocracy wherein "contrary to the biblical order, the race went to the swift, bread to the wise, favor to men of skill." Such views were bound to draw the enmity of the Virginia oligarchy, those Jeffersonian slaveholders to whom virtue lay in owning and tilling land and to whom "paper money"—and all business based upon it—was immoral and effeminate. (McDonald elaborated on Hamilton's thought in two essays, one published in *National Review* in 1980 and the other in *Modern Age* the following year.)

McDonald's indictment of Jefferson went further, however. He saw the Sage of Monticello as no sage at all but as a pretentious elitist. Jefferson, he noted, had first endorsed much of Hamilton's fiscal program and a loose construction of the Constitution (as did Madison), only balking when he realized that Hamilton threatened his favorite class, the landed aristocracy. Not only did Jefferson covertly assist Citizen Genét, thereby violating American neutrality; his pro-French policy risked war with England in 1791. Jefferson subsidized the vicious slanders of Philip Freneau and paid an editor to call Washington a traitor. Even the Louisiana Purchase, when hidden costs were added, was no bargain; Hamilton's plan to seize the area and then to negotiate would have been far cheaper, McDonald claimed.

As with McDonald's other works, the life of

Hamilton was strongly debated. Few critics failed to praise the clear explanation of complicated financial matters. Also receiving strong approval was the exposition of Hamilton's thought, which made those sections of the book a tour de force in intellectual history. Some reviewers, however, claimed that McDonald underplayed Hamilton's role in undermining the Adams presidency; they saw McDonald as far too hostile to Jefferson and Adams and too uncritical concerning such actions as Hamilton's involvements with Britain and schemes to "liberate" South America. Although McDonald did not reply, his admiration of Hamilton remained firm. In his final review of the *The Papers of Alexander Hamilton*, appearing in the *William and Mary Quarterly* in 1980, McDonald wrote, "The charges and slurs of his critics and enemies will not stand up in the light of the record; and though I confess to ambiguity in my feelings about the quality of the world that Hamilton, above all others, brought into existence, I cannot with reason fault him for anything he ever said or did."

For the past several years, McDonald has been engaged in examining the ethnic roots of the American South. With Grady McWhiney, often his coauthor and collaborator on this topic, McDonald established the Center for the Study of Southern History and Culture at the University of Alabama. Both authors have promised a major work on Southern origins. In the meantime, they have written a series of articles that have shown the fruits of their preliminary research.

In May 1975, McDonald and McWhiney wrote an essay on Southern herdsmen for the *Journal of Southern History*. Here McDonald pointed to the crucial role that livestock played in the South, an area that raised two-thirds of the nation's hogs. "In most of the Old South," he wrote, "the hog was king." The authors challenged such historians as Ulrich B. Phillips, Frederick Jackson Turner, and Frank L. Owsley, all of whom—they claimed— "considered livestock as primitive, passing, and inferior to the superior and more permanent plant growers." Yet far from displacing such herdsmen or ranking above them, many farmers depended upon drovers as their principal market. Indeed, in Mississippi, North Carolina, and Tennessee, more than half the cultivated acreage was devoted not to cotton but to corn. Such herdsmen came from the Celtic areas of Great Britain, that is, from the southwestern, western, and northern parts of England, the Scottish Lowlands and Highlands, and particularly "the Scotch-Irish" plantations of Lowland Scots in Ulster. The Scotch-Irish, whose migration to

America took place between 1715 and 1837, first went to Philadelphia, then to various valleys from Maryland to Georgia, and finally to Texas.

As McDonald developed his explorations into ethnic history, he claimed that the culture of the South, unlike that of the rest of the nation, has always been dominated by persons of Celtic extraction. Arguing against Turner's idea that the frontier served to homogenize immigration, McDonald asserted that the frontier made it possible for the Celtic Southerner to retain his folkways and thereby to preserve the ways of his ancestors long after the old country began to be Anglicized. Such folkways included laziness, boisterous behavior, fierce local loyalties, a stress on personal religious salvation, a penchant toward rebellion, and the seeking of justice in powerful paternal figures rather than in the law. At one point, McDonald and McWhiney argued that Julius Caesar's accounts of the ancient Gauls sounded like a caricature of contemporary rural Alabama. Moreover, the similarity was not accidental. In a review-essay published in 1977, both authors claimed that "The wild, primitive, pristine southerner was fighting 'civilized' people before Alexander the Great—and had been resisting enculturization by outsiders ever since."

In 1980, the *William and Mary Quarterly* published an essay that McDonald wrote in collaboration with his wife, Ellen Shapiro McDonald. In "The Ethnic Origins of the American People, 1790," the McDonalds claimed that the Celtic base of America's early population had been greatly underestimated. New England was the closest to being purely English, having been populated by English dissenters in the seventeenth century. The middle states were polyglot. The South, however, had long possessed a strong Celtic base.

During that same year, 1980, McDonald— again with McWhiney—inferred that, as Celts and Englishmen had been perpetually at war for at least a millennium, the roots of the American Civil War were cultural. Moreover, both authors claimed in *History Today* that the Celtic South, with its "leisure ethic," was still attempting to hold out against the depersonalization and regimentation associated with bureaucratic industrial society. "Perhaps," they mused, "it is better to go hunting and fishing than to work nine-to-five in an office or factory."

The arguments of both authors received professional attention and debate in the December 1980 issue of the *American Historical Review*. Here McDonald and McWhiney reiterated several themes, including the Southern contempt for work, the lavish self-sufficiency provided by the livestock system, the Celtic basis of Southern society. They then went on to claim that the Civil War proved ruinous to the white "plain folk." The South's post-bellum landlords had found it more advantageous to import foodstuffs than to buy locally, and they had fenced the grazing areas where pigs could run free and thereby thrive. Little wonder that many white Southerners fell victim to tenant farming, share-cropping, and factory labor. "And thus," concluded the historians, "the gigantic trap slowly, steadily, inexorably closed upon them, until almost no one in the South remained free."

Rowland Berthoff challenged the McDonalds' "Celtic interpretation" in the *William and Mary Quarterly* soon after their article appeared, and to the *American Historical Review* essay several other responses were made. Thomas B. Alexander questioned "Celtic" as an adequate designation of a single cultural group. Stanley L. Engerman said that McDonald and McWhiney were projecting the behavior of one component group in the South—the upland small farmers—upon the region as a whole. Edward Pessen accused the authors of operating on "the bizarre assumption" that gathering massive quantitative data on "what they call Celts" best explained "the behavior of the South and North, if not all of American history." Yet all the participants in the debate, which took the form of an *American Historical Review* "Forum," praised McDonald and McWhiney for the detail and scope of their research, and in particular for bringing a neglected aspect of Southern life to the fore.

Like a good many other prominent historians, McDonald has also written textbooks. In 1968, he wrote *The Torch is Passed*, a book covering twentieth-century American history. Much of the book then was incorporated into a wider survey of the nation's past. This survey, *The Last Best Hope* (1972), listed Leslie Decker and Thomas P. Govan as McDonald's coauthors.

The writing in both texts was sprightly, often elliptical, and never dull. The reader immediately discovered that Christendom was "one of the most primitive and least potent of the world's great cultures." Such figures as Al Capone were treated as part of the history of entrepreneurship. One chapter title read, "Wherein An Entire Nation Blew Its Cool; and Partially Regained It, 1963-1972." Descriptions were often pithy. James Otis was given to "insane ravings"; John Hancock used liberty "as a synonym for wanton greed"; Charles Townshend was "a sport, a wit, and in some ways a half-wit"; Walt Whitman was a "middle-aged flower child"; General Nathan Bedford Forrest was "a mean red-neck if ever one lived"; Thaddeus Stevens possessed "the fierce hyperthyroid eyes of a fanatic"; Harry S. Truman entered office as "a pipsqueak, a minor leaguer"; and Lyndon B. Johnson, unable to comprehend a wider world, was "superman in a vacuum."

The authors also offered a general schema of American history, which—in capsulized form—reads as follows: The British Empire was an efficient, orderly, and manageable organization with some administrators, such as Sir Edmund Andros, being both shrewd and enlightened. Yet this well-planned empire was destroyed, at least in part, by men of base, sordid, and petty motives. Fortunately, amid the chaos of the American Revolution, nationalists triumphed over priggish and narrow republicans. Landgrubbing Jeffersonians and anarchistic Jacksonians, however, created such chaos that bloody fratricide was the inevitable result. The industrialization that took place after the Civil War eventually turned the nation into a "surrealistic nightmare," for Americans discovered that they could neither live with the corporation nor live without it. Some reform proposals, such as those advocated by the Populists, could only ruin the nation. Finally, order was imposed by such farsighted businessmen as J. P. Morgan and by such enlightened administrators as Lyman Gage, William McKinley's secretary of the treasury. With the Panic of 1907, a hitherto constructive Progressivism took a destructive turn, one culminating in the dangerous moralism of Woodrow Wilson. The authors continued in this vein, tolerating the administrations of the 1920s, praising the interventionism of Franklin D. Roosevelt and his successors, and hailing Richard Nixon for supposedly cooling national passions and turning over the conduct of the war in Southeast Asia to the Vietnamese.

Within this schema, there was much demythologizing. African black kingdoms "evolved a culture quite comparable to Europe's own." The Townshend Acts, which so aroused the Revolutionists' ire, were quite painless. The Alien and Sedition Acts were harmless in themselves; the enforcement act for Jefferson's embargo was far more destructive of civil liberties. England was the world's last outpost of freedom against Bonaparte, who wanted to rule the globe. Moving to the nineteenth century, the authors stressed the benefits received by supposedly impoverished farmers, and they stressed as well the business origins of such regulatory legislation as the Elkins, Hepburn, and meat-inspection acts. The book portrayed Henry Cabot Lodge as a greater realist than Woodrow Wilson, for Lodge supposedly recognized the role of power in international relations. Wilson's domestic witch-hunting claimed hundreds of times more victims than McCarthyism. The New Deal did little for the poorest of Americans.

McDonald also used concepts of cultural anthropology to describe the workings of American politics. He asserted that periodic political campaigns had, since the time of Jackson, displayed a ritualized and ceremonial effect. Indeed, the public actually benefited, for through these rituals it could release its emotions and resort to impassioned rhetoric without committing wanton destruction. Furthermore, the structure of the American government itself, with its complexities of "checks and balances" on many levels, enabled the country continually to avoid fundamental problems. Moreover, the early British use of "pacification" and "search and destroy" against the Indians, the adoption by American revolutionaries of the Indian tactics of guerrilla warfare, and Jefferson's efforts to turn war itself into a moral crusade found contemporary counterparts in the often useless "strategic bombing" of World War II and of the My Lai massacre. Vietnam was described as "not war at all . . . but wholesale murder on both sides."

In 1980, McDonald, David Burner, and Eugene D. Genovese wrote another text, *The American People*. The first two chapters, those dealing with America up to 1763, were McDonald's. After that, his contribution took the form of "debates" with Genovese, a prominent socialist and revisionist. McDonald emphasized the conservative nature of the American War of Independence. The Revolution, he wrote, "was not for the sake of winning a bearable life against a brutal monarch, but aimed at preserving a life of abundance." When the new government was launched, it was committed to the premise that "the desire for private profit could in fact be the wellspring of great public good"; indeed, McDonald went on, "the free interchange of goods for private profit can better serve the material needs of society than can government planning, community spirit, prayer, and love of mankind." Such a Valhalla was not to last forever, McDonald wrote. The Jeffersonians and the Jacksonians were soon charging that winners in the capitalist race were public enemies. At the same time, the Jeffersonians and Jacksonians so weakened national authority that the split between the North and South could not be bridged.

When he came to the Gilded Age, McDonald praised the corporation, that unique device that, in his words, "*created* talent, capital, jobs, raw mate-rials, and markets" and that by the turn of the century had also created a material progress of nearly miraculous proportions. By 1930, the average worker put in one-sixth fewer hours (the equivalent of one day per week) than in 1890, but he was bringing home three times as much in wages. But as the country grew richer, so McDonald claimed, destructive elements among its leadership became ever more powerful. First was Theodore Roosevelt, a man who did many favors for business but whose rhetoric "kept alive an obsolete anti-corporate and anti-business tradition in a civilization that was increasingly dependent upon corporate enterprise." Second was Woodrow Wilson, who forgot that the function of government was to make the world safe not for democracy but for its citizens. McDonald argued that Wilson did irreparable harm: he linked government and business in numerous destructive ways, created an international power vacuum into which both Nazism and communism moved, and paved the way for the world economic collapse of the 1930s. The Great Crash was caused, McDonald claimed, by the Federal Reserve, which channeled an excessive flow of money into capital accumulation.

McDonald conceded that the New Deal sought to save capitalism from its own failings, but he denied that it revived the economy. There was, he asserted, too much contradiction in its programs for it to operate effectively. Some New Deal measures, such as the Securities and Exchange Commission and the Federal Deposit Insurance Corporation, benefited the nation. Others, however, did as much harm as good, and here McDonald noted the Holding Company Act and the Communications Act. Still others, including the National Recovery Administration, were counterproductive.

If McDonald took little issue with United States intervention in World War II, he offered major critiques of postwar America. He attacked the messianism of the cold war mentality but on different grounds from most revisionists. Their fear that Americans were possessed by "the bogey of international communist conspiracy," he wrote, "obscured from them the real and potential danger of Soviet Russian Imperialism." In response to this bonafide threat, American leaders showed panic in the 1950s by erecting shaky regional pacts and displayed arrogance in the 1960s by taking upon themselves "the role of liberator and Lord Protector to the Third World—of which they were ignorant and in which they were unwelcome." By the 1970s, the United States had "lost its nerve and lost its wits in the bargain." The Carter era, in particular,

McDonald found a guilt-ridden one in that a country, which had less to be ashamed of than any other nation on earth, sought pathetically to be loved.

McDonald was, if anything, even more critical of American domestic policy. He wrote: "Men are not angels, and they therefore need government to protect them in their lives, their liberty, and their property, and they need government to provide for the common defense and promote the general welfare. Liberalism has destroyed the capacity of government to perform to its legitimate and necessary functions. When the Federal Register required 60,000 pages of small print just to list the new federal regulations promulgated in a single year; when the Department of Health, Education, and Welfare spent a third of a trillion dollars annually and in the doing hastened the decline of the nation's health, education, and welfare; when the Interstate Commerce Commission issued its trillionth regulation; when federal judges ordered that black children be integrated with white children by busing them 100 miles a day to attend schools that whites had long since abandoned; then any resemblance to government, good or bad, theoretical or historical, has ceased to exist."

Such conservatism is reflected in another field of endeavor, American constitutional history. In a work published in 1982, *A Constitutional History of the United States*, McDonald combined his reverence for the Constitution with a strong critique of today's Supreme Court. The book is really an extended essay, for McDonald sought more to offer fresh generalizations than to provide encyclopedic coverage.

Beginning with the evolution of constitutional theory, McDonald focused on the concept of "mixed government," which had theoretically formed the basis of both the English and colonial systems. Once the United States declared its independence, however, the new state governments abandoned this system. Indeed they abused their powers to such a degree that "Americans were less secure in their lives, liberty, and property than they had been under royal authority." Fortunately, the Constitution restored a mixed system and added the entity of federalism to it. Hence the new nation possessed "the finest system of government that had ever been devised."

Moving to what he deemed the crucial question of the early republic, who determines constitutionality, McDonald noted that until late in the nineteenth century, much authority was shared. In this sense, the often cited *Marbury* v. *Madison* (1803) was misleading. McDonald then turned to the bud-

ding capitalist economic order, and here he showed how the free market theory of contracts replaced equity theory. In covering antebellum federal-state relations, he claimed that the Taney court was so permissive that state governments were actually swallowing the national government. The Civil War temporarily expanded the powers of this national government beyond all precedent, but by 1876 states rights (and the accompanying racial segregation) were again in the ascendency. The Supreme Court was able to liberate large-scale interstate corporations from the restraining hand of state government, a move that resulted in prosperity for big business and for the rest of the country as well. Incidentally, so McDonald asserted, the justices of the Gilded Age were not rewriting the Constitution in order to bring it into line with laissez-faire philosophy. The Court did not even seek to curtail government power but rather to keep it lawful, "and that is what constitutional government is all about."

Trouble began in 1890 with the drafting of the Sherman Antitrust Act, for, if the words "conspiracy in restraint of trade" were taken literally, the legislation outlawed virtually any form of economic activity. Furthermore, as new heavy industries required huge amounts of capital and predictable markets, either monopoly or oligarchy was necessary. The Supreme Court added to the chaos by permitting, in *Muller* v. *Oregon* (1908), sociological evidence. Such criteria as the "rule of reason" (in antitrust cases) and "clear and present danger" (in civil liberties cases) caused infinite difficulties. When the Court offered sweeping decisions in defense of New Deal legislation, it had "all but abolished the constitutional limitations on the powers of Congress."

From 1937 to 1957, the United States was involved in a constitutional revolution, one not always to McDonald's liking. The Supreme Court arrogantly ruled that a company had no right to make a profit (*Federal Power Commission* v. *Hope Natural Gas Company*, 1944), abolished the distinction between inter- and intrastate commerce (*Wickard* v. *Filburn*, 1942), and claimed that thousands of innocent citizens could be held behind barbed wire (*Korematsu* v. *U.S.*, 1944). In addition, it declared that if an evil were potentially great enough, the courts could imprison people irrespective of the likelihood of this evil ever occuring (*Dennis* v. *U.S.*, 1951). Only in cases of Negro rights did McDonald praise Court efforts, and even here he could be most critical. For example, McDonald claimed that the 1954 school desegregation ruling was "a monumental step toward the ideal of social justice." However, by wording the ruling the way the Court did, Chief Justice Earl Warren was substituting social science for the Constitution, casting judicial restraint to the winds, and implying that—in a peculiarly racist perspective—it was not disadvantageous for whites to be in a classroom lacking blacks.

By the time McDonald reached his last chapter, the book was becoming a jeremiad. The Kennedy administration, by giving freedom riders the protection of federal marshals, had allowed a situation when, for the first time in American history, "the chief law-enforcement officers in the land employed the power of the federal government to support groups that engaged in overt violations of state and local laws and made calculated attacks upon peace and order." Legislation of the 1960s and 1970s embodied a host of follies: Congress and regulatory agencies created lower meat standards, increased fuel consumption while adding to pollution, and taxed Americans for greater sums than they were spending on food, clothing, and shelter combined. Because of foolish laws, federalism was eroded, checks and balances were destroyed, and "the Constitution ceased to be a fundamental law governing government." In the process, race again became a factor in education and employment, abortion was declared a constitutional right, and Congress was deprived of its constitutional power to determine the qualifications of its own members. In fact, if current trends were not reversed, "the United States would have forfeited the legitimate reason for its own existence."

McDonald's activities do not stop with his books and his scholarly articles, for more of his ideas can be found in his many book reviews. As a critic, McDonald can be either benign or biting. He strongly endorsed Cecil Currey's *Code Number 72: Benjamin Franklin, Patriot or Spy?* (1972), in which Currey argued that Franklin served as a double agent during the American Revolution. However, McDonald found Page Smith's bicentennial history of the American Revolution, entitled *A New Age Now Begins: A People's History of the American Revolution* (1976), so bad that it came within the Supreme Court definition of obscenity: "offensive to ordinary standards of decency and contains no redeeming social value." Commenting on Gabriel Kolko's *Main Currents in Modern American History* (1976), a book that portrayed capitalism as predatory and reform as a sham, McDonald saw the work as an exercise in demonology. "The Mathers," he said, "made a far more plausible case."

Yet McDonald has been quick to express his gratitude to other scholars. He once said that as he could not repay those people from whom he learned, he did the next best thing; "write and publish what I learn, so scholars in the future can draw upon what I have done. Thereby one contributes to the fashioning of an endless chain of scholarship—and, one hopes, adds one's bit to the sum total of human knowledge."

Years from now, people will probably remember several things about McDonald's work: that one does not have to support the Jeffersonians or even favor the American Revolution to appreciate the Founding Fathers; that the Founders bestowed a much richer and more complex heritage than had been thought; that philosophical conservatives like Alexander Hamilton and John Dickinson often played a more constructive role than democrats like Thomas Jefferson and Richard Henry Lee. Future readers will gain also a renewed appreciation of an approach to economic history that bases judgments concerning the wisdom and folly of business leaders on a working knowledge of the industry involved. They will have a model for investigating a new area within ethnic studies, one using a detailed study of the British Isles to understand a segment of the white, Anglo-Saxon "majority" in America. McDonald is as likely to be remembered as much for his methodological innovations as for his revisionist conclusions. In his case, innovation is done with such felicity of expression that we not only have a rigorous historian and a spirited debater but a genuine man of letters as well.

Other:

Empire and Nation: Letters from a Farmer in Pennsylvania by John Dickinson and Letters from the Federal Farmer by Richard Henry Lee, edited by McDonald (Englewood Cliffs, N.J.: Prentice-Hall, 1962);

Confederation and Constitution, 1781-1789, edited by McDonald and Ellen Shapiro McDonald (New York: Harper & Row, 1968);

"Charles A. Beard," in *Pastmasters: Some Essays on American Historians*, edited by Marcus Cunliffe and Robin W. Winks (New York: Harper & Row, 1969), pp. 110-141;

"Floyd Leslie Carlisle," "Harvey Crawley Crouch," and "Matthew Scott Sloan," in *Dictionary of American Biography, Supplement III* (New York: Scribners, 1973), pp. 137-138, 191-193, 715-716;

"John Dickinson," "Alexander Hamilton," "Gouverneur Morris," "Roger Sherman," "Samuel Insull," "John Pierpont Morgan," and "Jacob

Henry Schiff," in *The Encyclopedia of American Biography*, edited by John A. Garraty and Jerome L. Sternstein (New York: Harper & Row, 1974).

Periodical Publications:

"The Relation of the French Peasant Veterans of the American Revolution to the Fall of Feudalism in France, 1789-1792," *Agricultural History*, 25 (October 1951): 151-161;

"Street Cars and Politics in Milwaukee, 1896-1901," *Wisconsin Magazine of History*, 39 (Spring 1956): 166-170, 206-212; 39 (Summer 1956): 253-257, 271-273;

"Rebuttal to Jackson T. Main, 'Charles A. Beard and the Constitution: A Critical Review of Forrest McDonald's *We the People*,'" *William and Mary Quarterly*, 17 (January 1960): 102-110;

"The Anti-Federalists, 1781-1789," *Wisconsin Magazine of History*, 46 (Spring 1963): 206-214;

Reviews of *The Papers of Alexander Hamilton*, volumes 1-4, in *William and Mary Quarterly*, 20 (January 1963): 280-283; volumes 5-8, 26 (January 1969): 114-119; volumes 14-17, 31 (October 1974): 678-680; volumes 20-22, 33 (October 1976): 677-681; volumes 23-24, 34 (October 1977): 670-671; volumes 25-27, 37 (April 1980): 330-333;

"The Antebellum Southern Herdsman: A Reinterpretation," by McDonald and Grady McWhiney, *Journal of Southern History*, 41 (May 1975): 147-166;

"A New Age Begins: History as Bunk," *Virginia Quarterly Review*, 52 (Autumn 1976): 701-706;

"A Mirror for Presidents," *Commentary*, 62 (December 1976): 34-41;

"A Founding Father's Library," *The Literature of Liberty*, 1 (January-March 1978): 4-15;

"The Ethnic Factor in Alabama History: A Neglected Dimension," *Alabama Review*, 31 (October 1978): 256-265;

"The Ethnic Origins of the American People, 1790," by McDonald and Ellen Shapiro McDonald, *William and Mary Quarterly*, 37 (April 1980): 179-703;

"The Celtic South," by McDonald and McWhiney, *History Today*, 30 (July 1980): 11-15;

"Understanding Alexander Hamilton," *National Review*, 32 (11 July 1980): 827-833;

"The South from Self-Sufficiency to Peonage: An Interpretation," by McDonald and McWhiney, *American Historical Review*, 85 (December 1980): 1095-1118, 1160-1163;

"The Rhetoric of Alexander Hamilton," *Modern Age*, 25 (Spring 1981): 114-124.

References:

"AHR Forum—Antebellum North and South in Comparative Perspective: A Discussion," *American Historical Review*, 85 (December 1980), remarks by Thomas B. Alexander, pp. 1150-1154; Stanley L. Engerman, pp. 1154-1160; Edward Pessen, pp. 1163-1166; Communications by McDonald, Grady McWhiney, and Pessen, *American Historical Review*, 86 (February 1981): 243-245;

Morton Borden, "A Neo-Federalist View of the Jeffersonians," *Reviews in American History*, 5 (June 1977): 196-202;

Peter J. Coleman, "Beard, McDonald, and Economic Determinism in American Historiography," *Business History Review*, 34 (Spring 1960): 113-121;

James F. Doster, "The *Tertium Quid* in Historical Interpretation: Another View of McDonald's Theory," *Wisconsin Magazine of History*, 42 (Autumn 1958): 50-51;

James Ferguson, Review of *E Pluribus Unum*, *William and Mary Quarterly*, 23 (January 1966): 148-155;

Roy N. Lokken, "McDonald's Theory of History: A Critique," *Wisconsin Magazine of History*, 41 (Summer 1958): 264-269;

Jackson Turner Main, "Charles A. Beard and the Constitution: A Critical Review of Forrest McDonald's *We the People*," *William and Mary Quarterly*, 17 (January 1960): 86-102;

Jackson Turner Main, "The Prosecuting Historian," *Nation*, 188 (13 June 1959): 538-539;

Robert Livingston Schuyler, "Notes and Documents: Forrest McDonald's Critique of the Beard Thesis," *Journal of Southern History*, 27 (February 1961): 73-80.

Perry Miller

Robert M. Calhoon
*University of North Carolina
at Greensboro*

BIRTH: Chicago, Illinois, 25 February 1905, to Dr. Eben Perry Miller, M.D., and Gertrude Eddy Miller.

EDUCATION: Ph.B., 1928, Ph.D., 1931, University of Chicago.

MARRIAGE: September 1930 to Elizabeth Williams.

AWARDS AND HONORS: American Council of Learned Societies Distinguished Scholarship in the Humanities Award; Guest Professor, University of Leiden, 1949-1950; Guest Professor, Tokyo University, 1952; Institute of Advanced Study, 1953-1954, 1962-1963; D. Litt., Gonzaga University, 1955; D. Litt., Grinnell College, 1957; D. Litt., Northwestern University, 1958; D. H. L., Syracuse University, 1957; Powell M. Cabot Professor of American Literature, Harvard University, 1960-1963; D. Litt., Boston College, 1962; Pulitzer Prize for *The Life of the Mind in America*, 1966.

DEATH: 9 December 1963.

BOOKS: *Orthodoxy in Massachusetts, 1630-1650: A Genetic Study* (Cambridge: Harvard University Press, 1933);
The New England Mind: The Seventeenth Century (New York: Macmillan, 1939);
Jonathan Edwards (New York: Sloane, 1949; London: Mayflower, 1959);
Society and Literature in America (Leiden: University of Leiden Press, 1949);
The New England Mind: From Colony to Province (Cambridge: Harvard University Press, 1953);
Roger Williams: His Contribution to the American Tradition (Indianapolis: Bobbs-Merrill, 1953);
Errand Into the Wilderness (Cambridge: Harvard University Press, 1956; London: Oxford University Press, 1956);
The Raven and the Whale: The War of Words and Wits in the Era of Poe and Melville (New York: Harcourt, Brace, 1956);
The Life of the Mind in America: From the Revolution to

Perry Miller

the Civil War (New York: Harcourt, Brace, & World, 1965; London: Gollancz, 1966);
Nature's Nation (Cambridge: Harvard University Press, 1967; London: Oxford University Press, 1967);
The Responsibility of Mind in a Civilization of Machines: Essays, edited by John Crowell and Stanford J. Searl, Jr. (Amherst: University of Massachusetts Press, 1979);
Sources for The New England Mind: The Seventeenth Century, edited by James Hoopes (Williamsburg: Institute of Early American History and Culture, 1981).

Perry Gilbert Eddy Miller was born and raised in Chicago, received his undergraduate and graduate education at the University of Chicago, taught for his entire academic career at Harvard

272

University, and produced at least six major books, three volumes of essays, and sixteen volumes of edited texts. Yet this academic vita scarcely does justice to Miller's explosive impact on scholarship and ideas. By training and academic appointment he was a student of literature, yet his greatest influence was on the interpretation of history. An agnostic, he took Calvinist theology more seriously than any American intellectual since Jonathan Edwards. An earthy, profane, hard-drinking, immensely convivial figure, he reserved his most passionate energies for textual analysis. One of his Harvard colleagues noted that, because of his parents' New England roots, "all through the years when Miller was growing up he thought of himself as a transplanted Yankee who would never be truly at home in the Middle West. Yet when he finally settled in New England, he steadfastly retained many qualities that the world thinks of as Chicagoan, including a hearty, informal manner, a lusty humor, a stupendous capacity for hard work, and, above all, a refusal to take the East at its word."

Restless and disappointed to have missed the adventure of World War I, Miller dropped out of the University of Chicago at the end of his freshman year in 1923 and, during three years of nomadic roaming, wandered, first to Colorado; then to the New York City area, where he tried his hand as a Shakespearean actor; and finally to Mexico, the Mediterranean, and the west coast of Africa as a merchant seaman. "At Matadi, on the banks of the Congo," he later recalled, "while supervising in that barbaric tropic, the unloading of drums of case oil flowing out of the inexhaustible wilderness of America," he asked himself what it must have meant for Europeans to enter the American wilderness—as forbidding to them as was the African jungle to Miller—for the first time. So it was that he returned to Chicago in 1926 and over the next four years completed his undergraduate and most of his graduate education. His selection of early Massachusetts Puritan thought as a dissertation topic prompted warnings from his teachers that Puritanism was a barren field of study. However, Professor Percy Holmes Boynton, perhaps sharing his colleagues' doubts but also believing (in his student's words) "that a boy should be allowed to do what a boy genuinely, even if misguidedly, is convinced should be done," encouraged Miller to persevere in his research on Puritanism.

In 1930 Miller and his bride, a fellow graduate student, Elizabeth Williams Miller, went to Cambridge, Massachusetts, to complete the research for his dissertation and to broaden his knowledge of colonial New England by studying under Samuel Eliot Morison and Kenneth B. Murdock. In 1931 he became a tutor in history and literature at Harvard and in 1938 associate professor of American literature. Harvard University Press published his dissertation under the title of *Orthodoxy in Massachusetts, 1630-1650: A Genetic Study* in 1933. A systematic rebuttal of the then standard interpretation of Puritan New England as a rigid theocracy and an "intellectual glacier," *Orthodoxy in Massachusetts* was a witty, pugnacious introduction to the writings and thought of scores of English and New England Puritans.

The first four chapters placed Puritanism in the context of the English Reformation struggle to form a satisfactory church polity and described the efforts of Anglicans, separatists, and non-separatists to reconcile the need for religious uniformity with swirling currents of conscientious pluralism. By the time Miller took up "Non-separatist Congregationalism" in chapter four, his prose was flashing with theatricalities—amazement, irony, hyperbole—recalling his brief passion for the stage seven years earlier. "By the exercise of a superlative genius for casuistry," he wrote, the non-separatist party of moderate Puritans "did make out its case, . . . did find ways to reconcile irreconcilables." The halfway position of these people—their insistence on the need to purify the Church of England but their refusal to strike that posture from outside the Anglican Church, as did the separatists—struck Miller as almost comic, were it not for the high moral and intellectual stakes in the debate. Their position, he wrote, "may seem to us utterly fantastic; we may with difficulty believe that any men, much less sincerely religious men, ever told so thin a story and then stuck so doggedly to it."

This hyperbole set up Miller's prose for a characteristic thrust at the raw, emotive human energies which, he felt, underlay the Puritans' thought and belief: "to understand the operation of their minds, we must realize what they conceived was at stake, what tremendous urgencies drove them to such desperate shifts." The separatists had defied reason and tradition by denying the need for uniformity; "they not merely attacked certain vested interests, but by rending the seamless garment of the Church they opened up a whole prospect of social disorganization." The fear and abhorrence this spectre raised in non-separatist Puritan minds, Miller concluded, was sufficient explanation for their incredible scheme of erecting autonomous, Calvinist congregations within the hierarchical, Arminian Church of England: "Their plea might be a cobweb of sophistry, their conduct might amount to virtual schism, but that did not matter if by their own rationalization they could write for themselves a clean bill of political health." In the phrases "by their own rationalization" and "write for themselves" appear the beginnings of Miller's original historical sense of ideas as immediate manifestations of human impulses, fears, and consciousness.

The movement of a small number of these fantastic casuists to Massachusetts Bay—carrying the charter of their joint stock company with them—not only created a New World colony, it also rendered their strange notions of church government suddenly workable. In the New England wilderness autonomous churches provided the institutional nucleus of towns: the token, theoretical tie with the Church of England provided the Puritans with a reminder of who they were in a world of hostile nations and from whence their worldly support and succor came. Thus, instead of crediting Massachusetts's notions of self-government to the example of the separatist Pilgrims at Plymouth, as historians of New England had always done, Miller argued that the ecclesiastical theory of the non-separatists in England provided the genius of Puritan politics. "We do not go to New England as separatists from the Church of England, though we separate ourselves from the corruptions in it," Miller quoted Francis Higginson, "but we go to practice the positive part of church reformation and propagate the gospel in America." Here was an entirely different orientation toward England from that held by the purists at Plymouth; the non-separatists realized that human societies must be constructed from available materials, corruptible and flawed though they be.

The remaining half of *Orthodoxy in Massachusetts* then narrated what was in 1933 a strange new story and has since become almost a commonplace of American history—the careful distinction the Massachusetts Puritans drew between church and state in which the former had moral authority and the latter political responsibility, the unsuccessful attempt by the early Massachusetts leaders to impose their authority on the settlers and the remarkable democratization which occurred with the right of freemen to elect their own representatives, and the way in which the curtailment of Roger Williams's individual freedom in the interests of cohesion and survival led by 1648 to the imposition of doctrinal and ecclesiastical uniformity on the churches of the province through the Cambridge Platform.

Orthodoxy in Massachusetts launched Miller into the wider study of Puritanism which would culminate years later in two volumes on *The New England Mind*. En route to that magisterial work came numerous shorter studies, three of which illuminate his development as a scholar. The first, a lengthy article entitled "Thomas Hooker and the Democracy of Early Connecticut," written as a seminar paper for Morison and published in the *New England Quarterly*, challenged Vernon L. Parrington's treatment of Hooker as an early democrat. Acknowledging some tentative democratic innovations in Hooker's Connecticut, Miller nonetheless insisted that both Connecticut and Massachusetts framed their governments on the basis of a social covenant, inspired by the divine covenant, in which rulers were responsible to God and to the people who elected them. Critics of the article, Miller recalled years later, "blandly asserted that the truth lay somewhere in the 'middle,' between Parrington and me. On this matter there is no middle. Parrington simply did not know what he was talking about."

The next article was an ambitious outline of the argument of *The New England Mind: The Seventeenth Century* (1939), a study entitled "The Marrow of Puritan Divinity" and published in 1935 in the *Publications* of the Colonial Society of Massachusetts. Here Miller identified the central place which the Dutch Christian humanist Petrus Ramus played in the formation of Puritan theology, a discovery he announced with a brashness which others at first imitated with what Miller later regarded as disastrous results: "The history of the reception of this paper is, on a minor level, an instructive lesson in the vagaries of American scholarship. At first ignored (since not many persons outside the Colonial Society of Massachusetts pant for its *Publications*), it rather suddenly enlisted an almost universal, not to say embarrassing, acceptance. . . . Friends of the delicate proposition so freely embraced it that they presented it to a world not generally skilled in theological discrimination as a solid block of historical fact. They published the glad tidings, in my name, that Puritans were not and never had been Calvinists. Consequently, what was intended to be an investigation into the subtleties of human development has been vulgarized into a platitude obstructive both to living appreciation and to further analysis."

In 1938 Miller and Thomas H. Johnson edited *The Puritans*, a two volume anthology of Puritan writings. In the general introduction and the introductions to each section of the book, Miller sketched in the boldest terms the place of the Puritans in

American history. "Puritanism," he argued in a typically shocking fusion of Calvin and Freud, "would make every man an expert psychologist, to detect all makeshift 'rationalizations,' to shatter without pity the sweet dreams of self-enhancement in which the ego takes refuge from reality."

Published in 1939, the product of nearly a decade of research into Puritan theology, imagination, philosophy, and morality—indeed a distillation of much of what Puritan writers said about their faith and mission in the world—*The New England Mind: The Seventeenth Century* was an entirely new kind of intellectual history. The rehabilitation of the Puritans by Morison, Murdock, and others had been going on for some fifteen years, but never before had any scholar placed Puritan ideas and beliefs in so spacious a setting. "He who undertakes to narrate any chapter in the history of the Reformation," Miller declared as he opened chapter 7, "The Uses of Reason," "must have an appetite for paradox and an appreciation of the ironic. . . . Perhaps the most highly paradoxical and ironic of the doctrines [of the Reformation] was that of total depravity, for it contained in the face of it a view of life that seems to make all endeavor useless, yet in effect it aroused Protestants to fervent action. . . . The more theologians denounced the depravity of man, the more vividly they were obliged to describe the eminence from which he had fallen, so that while in their sermons they painted the horrors of unregenerate existence in the most lurid colors, by their implications they were continually etching a fine portrait of the original grandeur."

Miller was charting in this book the unexpectedly spacious dimensions of Puritan intellectuality. Puritanism was a force in human affairs because it dealt in an intellectually powerful way with human intention, desire, motivation, and capacity at a moment of great flux in the study of these issues. By their attachment to the neo-Platonic philosophy of Ramus, the Puritans gained access to the rich humanistic appreciation of man that arose in the Renaissance; by their identification with the first generation of Protestant reformers—Calvin, Miller insisted, was only one of the founders of the Reformed tradition acknowledged by the Puritans— they acquired militancy and elan. Both of these great traditions in European religious thought enabled the Puritans to take reason seriously, seeing it as the one gift of God that human beings could comprehend and that served therefore as a link with the infinite and also as a practical tool for dealing with everyday life. Where the Puritan Samuel Willard wrote that "it is impossible for us to know or understand things but by some rule or reason" and that "we know nothing of God but by putting some logical notion upon him," Miller found an indication of the enormity of the task Puritans undertook. Faith proceeded from rational thought but it also transcended that thought. "Religion," Willard serenely declared, "is the wisdom of God which cannot cross itself, and reason lisps out something to faith, though this entertains more than reason is able to express." For Miller, this passage "vibrate[d]" with implications for understanding the intensity and complexity of Puritanism—the holding together of conflicting but interdependent beliefs about faith and reason in a system of architectural tension and grandeur.

At the heart of *The New England Mind: The Seventeenth Century* was Miller's conviction that Puritanism was a vital center of psychological security and intellectual certainty. This sort of inner strength derived, in Miller's view, not only from the perilous times and conditions in which the New England Puritans lived or from their religious faith but also, more fundamentally, from their cultural and intellectual grounding in the best of Renaissance and Reformation thought. The relationship of these two traditions was complex, and Miller skirted it by simply emphasizing the way in which the Neoplatonist, Ramus, injected into Puritan thought a richly humanistic view of man and nature and thereby modified the influence of Calvinism.

For Miller, a prime example of Ramus's influence was the notion of "technologia" in which God placed concrete phenomena in the world to serve divine purposes and in which humans could comprehend the divine plan by managing the world according to God's apparent intentions. Quoting from Alexander Richardson, an English Puritan widely read in Massachusetts, Miller brought the operation of technologia into vivid focus: "the genesis of everything is God's and man must see the rules of art . . . from singulars by analysis and know them by his senses' observation, induction, and experience. . . . This teacheth man . . . that he is to seek out and find the wisdom of God in the world and not be idle, for the world and the creatures in it are like a book wherein God's wisdom is written and there we must seek it out." For Miller this passage was the finest statement in all of Puritan theology illustrating "the dialectic of Ramus . . . blended perfectly with the theology of Augustine and Calvin." By regarding nature and creation as guides to conduct; by specifying watchful, pious, observant involvement as a moral imperative and as the proper end and purpose of life; and by claiming that knowledge so obtained was only a fragmentary glimpse of divine truth, Puritanism fused desire and self-consciousness into a dialectical view of reality. "Art," wrote a Harvard student in 1670, "is a reflex apparition of divine light resplendent in intellectual night." For Miller and his readers, this statement became a suggestive and haunting image.

The Puritan creation which best expressed this lodging of the divine in material and visible phenomena was the sermon, the homiletics which Miller called "The Plain Style." Unlike the Anglican sermon which exhorted the listener to righteous intention and raced toward a dramatic conclusion with accelerating tempo, the Puritan sermon sought laconic understatement, simplicity, and directness in order to communicate the essential meaning of the text. The task of the preacher was to draw from numerous pools of insight—from Biblical "metaphors, metonymies, allegories, and similitudes," as one Puritan textbook put it—axioms of God's will in unembellished, unrhetorical prose.

Miller had treated piety and thought in book 1 under the title "Religion and Learning" and had grouped his chapters on reason and nature in book 2 under the heading "Cosmology." "The Plain Style" brought to a conclusion book 3, "Anthropology." Thus the section headings of *The New England Mind: The Seventeenth Century* commenced with traditional historical terms and then became increasingly unconventional. For after "Anthropology" came book 4, "Sociology." One is, at first, tempted to regard these terms simply as Miller's jesting poke at modern behavioral science. But these terms conveyed a more serious intention. In the preface to the book's second printing in 1953 Miller spoke of "the modern ethos" which "emerged out of . . . Puritan scholasticism." In the most important way, the chapters of book 4 on covenant theology, the social covenant, church government, and the Puritan concept of history were an integrated and schematic science of collective human behavior, in a word, a sociology.

While Puritans justifiably gloried in their traditionalism and lack of innovation in historical Christian belief and while Miller agreed that apart from rhetoric and argumentation Puritanism largely partook of older Christian forms and thought, he insisted that the notion of the covenant in Puritanism was a profoundly original and far-reaching conception. Intended to avoid unintentional heresy through restricted definitions of God, "the theory of the Covenant resulted from the Puritan effort . . . to find . . . the submerged grounds for moral obedience and for an assurance of any man's salvation," Miller declared. The covenant was the visualization of salvation as a free gift

by one party (God) to another totally undeserving party (mankind) as a unilateral act of grace. Because everyone, from the most urbane merchant to the simplest laborer, knew what a covenant or contract was, this concept enabled all to understand the divine plan; through covenant theology the mystery of the awesome love of the creator became adjusted to human understanding and thus a fit object of rational thought.

The implications of covenant theology were enormous; the saint's response to discovery of the covenant and his subsequent dedication to a disciplined and obedient life filled him with purpose and gratification, and yet nothing a person did as a saint added, completed, or ratified the divine initiative. On the basis of this theory, the Puritans built their ethics, their notions of civic duty, their theory of church and state, their ecclesiastical structure, and their rich meditational life—all the elements of their experience in New England which Miller subsumed under the heading "Sociology."

In a magnificent coda, the last chapter of book 4 entitled "God's Controversy with New England," Miller pulled all the strands of his book together with a consideration of the Puritan conception of history. Viewing history as cyclical, as involving periods of corruption and then reform, they were certain that one such impulse toward reform had begun with the first stirrings of religious liberalism and humanism during the Middle Ages and early Renaissance; 'Dantes, Marcillium, Potavinus, Ocham, Gregorius, Ariminius, Petrarchus, Wickliffe,' Miller quoted one Latinized honor roll, and the list included as well Hus, Savonarola, and Luther. Yet once the Puritans had brought the covenant to New England and had built their "city upon a hill," they believed they had stepped outside of history and formed a society which did not need to subside back into sin and spiritual stupor. If they kept the covenant, the Puritans could expect God to protect them from sin, from historic cycles of decline and rejuvenation, forever. They admittedly remained, as good Calvinists, sinful, but as long as they made penitence and piety the central civic experiences in their culture, they would retain the privilege of refreshment from the covenant, they believed. God's goading of their consciences, therefore, was what they called his "controversy with New England."

"The academic world," Edmund S. Morgan observed, "received *The New England Mind* with cautious, bewildered plaudits," and not until after Miller's death did critics identify fundamental critical weaknesses in the volume on the seventeenth century. George M. Marsden and David D. Hall complained that Miller stressed the Ramean and humanist qualities of the Puritan intellect at the cost of acknowledging its Calvinist and Biblical content. And in a scathing examination of Miller's documentation—Miller deposited his notes, which were too extensive to be published in the book, in the Harvard library, and they were published separately, edited with an introduction by James Hoopes; in 1981—George Selement castigated Miller for ignoring the separatists, Baptists, and other New Englanders who did not conform to the non-separatist, congregationalist, covenant-theology mold.

To a degree, Miller anticipated these criticisms. His conception of the mind of a society was normative rather than representative, and the dominant, vital center of Puritan orthodoxy had a social and psychological coherence which dissenting, peripheral religious thought lacked; furthermore, because Miller's concept of the intellect traced the quest for human consciousness and autonomy, his celebration of Ramus, rationality, and covenantal concepts overshadowed his treatment of Puritan striving for piety and spirituality. In Marsden's words, "When we remember, as Miller demonstrated, that the Puritans were tough-minded men of the Renaissance, let us also recall that they were uncompromising Christians and (in the twentieth-century view) bigoted Calvinists. As for the thesis that the covenant of grace represented a revision of Calvinism, Miller has created a myth that has been so elegantly presented and widely repeated that it will be difficult to destroy." But Miller's failure to deal convincingly with splinter groups or with the influences of traditional Calvinist piety as well as his polemicism about intellectual history invited such charges and raised the questions about his historical craftsmanship which would surround discussion of the sequel volume of *The New England Mind*, subtitled *From Colony to Province* and published in 1953.

The sequel was Miller's most ambitious book and his most misunderstood. He intended it to chart the decay of Puritanism from the 1650s to 1730s in America and to suggest the influences of that decline on American culture. His own words from the preface came as close as any he wrote to locating his work historiographically: "the fascination of this region [New England] . . . is that it affords the historian an ideal laboratory. It was relatively isolated, the people were relatively homogeneous, and the forces of history played upon it ways that can more satisfactorily be traced than in more complex

societies. . . . What I would most like to claim for this study is that it amounts to a sort of working model for American history." The phrase "a sort of working model" was prophetic. A decade before the appearance of Thomas S. Kuhn's *The Structure of Scientific Revolutions* (1962), which formulated and popularized the notion that scholarly knowledge is organized into provisional, hypothetical clusters of assumptions, findings, implications, and internal connections, Miller saw the possibility of using Puritanism as the organizing principle for a wholly new kind of American history—one which was apparently concerned with the history of ideas but at a deeper level was infused with a sense of irony and tragedy.

From Colony to Province charted the journey from the well-defined sense of mission of English Puritans in the 1650s to their anxious recognition by the 1730s that New England was a new land in which wilderness conditions and peculiarly American experiences had indelibly altered the traditional values which Winthrop's generation had brought from England. In the course of this journey, which can now be regarded as a transition from youth to maturity, the Puritans perceived that the second and third generations of New England settlers had fallen away from the high goals and standards of the founders. Using a Puritan term, Miller called this process "declension," and it took on a life of its own, as Miller identified a literary form—the jeremiad or sermon about moral decline—which gave expression to a strong sense of human failing.

Like its predecessor, *From Colony to Province* was divided into four "books." book 1, on "Declension," achieved its highest drama in a chapter on "The Expanding Limits of Natural Ability." While Puritans believed with all Protestants in salvation by faith alone, their unique concept of a *covenant*, or contract, between God and man meant that the covenant's terms had to be made known to men before the process of sainthood and regeneration began. By preparing themselves for the disciplined life of the saint, the people known as the elect sought to make their profession of faith so pure, so unfettered, so forceful that they would leave no impediment in the way of the Creator as He worked the miracle of redemption and regeneration. This expansion of man's natural ability to behave morally smacked theologically of Arminianism—the view, heretical to Calvinists, that good works play an integral part in salvation. But for the Puritans, the doctrine of preparation was a call to the very sort of heroic exertion which would be necessary for Puritanism to endure at the center of New England's culture for a century.

By insisting on the primacy of the covenant in Puritan thought and by insisting even more staunchly that a logical corollary of this "federal theology" was a period of scrupulous negotiation between God and man, Miller built logical constructs within logical contructs. His resulting paradoxes prompted such critics as David H. Fischer and Robert Middlekauff to accuse Miller of draining Puritan intellectuality of passion and emotion. Yet Miller was not guilty of this charge. Instead, he showed that the second and third generation divines gave all of their emotional energy to the task of holding these paradoxical beliefs together because they had invested their strongest aspirations and fears in living out the terms of the covenant. " 'As your conviction is, such your faith is,' " Miller quoted the Puritan writer Samuel Mather; " 'as is the preparation work, such is the closing with Christ. . . , and there is more preparation needful than many think of.' " Miller's achievement was to restore to statements like Mather's their lost resonance.

With this highly intellectual reading of Puritan morality and covenant theology, Miller was most vulnerable to criticism and, at the same time, most compelling. Norman Pettit, in *The Heart Prepared* (1966), challenged Miller on the subject of Puritan preparation. In an argument which was more plausible than Miller's and more consistent with recent scholarship on Reformation theology, Pettit considered preparation "as part of a growing consciousness in Puritanism of the entire range of biblical prescription, as part of an ongoing examination of the facts of regeneration as the Puritans experienced it." His emphasis on the Bible recalling Marsden's criticism of the neglect of scripture in *The New England Mind: The Seventeenth Century*, Pettit's focus on a process of regeneration modified Miller's account of the dramatic encounter between God and man into a more protracted devotional experience.

Yet because he wrote from within the tradition of Puritan scholarship which Miller had created, Pettit enriched that field of study even as he called into question one of the major grounds for Miller's enthusiasm about Puritan originality. Furthermore, critics clearly perceived the philosophical basis for Miller's art. David A. Hollinger, in "Perry Miller and Philosophical History," (probably the best serious critical study of Miller) concludes that the historian "was primarily an artist not because he wrote with resonance and verbal richness, but because his organization, architecture, and intricacy of concep-

tion reveal an intensely purposive and creative activity. . . . Distressed that America had chosen to follow the optimistic, rationalistic line of Benjamin Franklin and William Dean Howells, that it had been generally uncomfortable with paradox and impatient with mystery, Miller assiduously sought out the minority that shared the insight he valued; he effected a kind of scholarly epiphany whenever he found an American who had faced paradox." The Puritan theologians who wrote in such clinical terms about preparation were men who had walked through a testing fire of doubt about the capacity of covenantal theology to hold a society and a culture together. In Hollinger's—and Miller's—terms, they were heroes who had confronted paradox and the terror of the unknown with every bit of their emotional and mental stamina.

Yet as "Confusion" and "The Splintering of Society," books 2 and 3 of *From Colony to Province*, showed, conditions for the Puritans became much more difficult. The jeremiads of moral and spiritual decline grew darker and more despairing as the century wound down. In events of the 1680s, Miller found rich and bitter irony. King James II's imposition in 1685 of the Dominion of New England, a repressive consolidation of the New England colonies, destroyed the charter of 1628 and thus imperiled the Congregational system of church government. As Miller saw it, however, the real culprits were the so-called "Moderate party" who had opposed the most vocal spokesmen of the Puritan theocracy, the Mathers, and who had paraded themselves as religious liberals. "They were anything but libertarians," Miller snorted; "they were authoritarians ready to give up the charter because, in their experience, it supported elected officers and rampaging persons who could not keep the populace in order." One such "moderate" was Gershom Bulkeley of Connecticut who served in the regime of Sir Edmund Andros, governor of the Dominion of New England, until he was overthrown in 1689. Upon being turned out of office, Bulkeley wrote a brilliant but reactionary vindication of authoritarian government—"the first explicitly anti-democratic utterance in our literature," Miller called it. Once more the historian built constructs within constructs: the jeremiads were the work of despairing clerics living in an increasingly brittle culture and flailing helplessly as New England departed farther and farther from the ideal of harmonious piety; yet the critics of the jeremiads, the so-called "moderates" who seemed to be more interested in practical solutions to problems than in vindication of doctrine were themselves the most doctrinaire, pompous, and deluded of men. Here, in Miller's hands, was history without heroes or villains and moral implications without moral lessons.

Amid this moral confusion arose the witch trials of Salem, and Miller's treatment of the famous witchcraft frenzy of 1692 stands as one of the most penetrating and arresting passages in all of his historical writing. Of course, as the great rehabilitator of the reputation of Puritanism as a coherent and intellectually respectable point of view, Miller was forced to refute the shibboleth that the Puritans burned witches with the same hypocritical and fanatical zeal that they did everything else. But his chapter "The Judgment of the Witches" is highly complex and charged with irony.

The key figure in the witchcraft frenzy was Cotton Mather who became, from this point on, the central figure in the book but not as fomentor of the frenzy. Miller exonerated Mather on that score, as had other recent scholars, but he nonetheless found the Puritan leader's conduct in the frenzy, to quote Edmund S. Morgan's review of *From Colony to Province*, "completely reprehensible because he employed the doctrine of the covenant . . . in order to vindicate the judicial murders committed by the witch court." Thus, although he did not instigate the witch trials, he did attempt to justify them. Determined to write a book which would account for witchcraft, Mather had arranged for the chief judge in the Salem trials to send him a written account of the evidence against the accused. With this material, Mather felt certain he could demonstrate that the frenzy was the work of the devil and not evidence of any flaw in Congregationalist theology or polity. When the promised package of evidence (notes taken by Stephen Sewall, brother of the clerk of the Salem court) did not arrive, Mather went ahead with the book on the assumption that the facts would support his case. "He ransacked his library for stories of apparition," Miller wrote, "hoping that they might substantiate what he was about to receive." The manuscript was already a fat one when Sewall's notes did arrive; Mather hastily summarized five of the twenty cases and sent the "monstrous collection to a printer."

Miller's conclusion about Mather and the frenzy went to the heart of what he regarded as the New England mind: the power of the covenant and the jeremiad to control human imagination and will. Mather, Miller explained, "suffered from a monstrous lust for publication, that much is certain; but the fuller explanation, accounting for the discharge of his conscious and unconscious motiva-

tions, is the compelling force of the jeremiad. He had to find a rationale for his country's ordeal and at the same time a modicum of peace with himself; he did both by forcing this wretched business into the traditional scheme of sin and retribution, which was the only form that would give conceivable significance either to New England's tragedy or to his own comprehension of it."

Book 3, "The Splintering of Society," which treated the fragmentation of community in New England during the first three decades of the eighteenth century, was the least successful portion of Miller's major volumes on New England. Ranging widely across economics, medicine, political theory, and colonial-imperial relations, this section sought to use the Puritan ideas still orthodox in New England as keys to the interpretation of society itself. Having to piece together a neglected period from other historians and from his own reading, Miller, as Bernard Bailyn explains, had "to run far ahead of his interference, . . . to extemporize . . . a social history far subtler than any yet written." In debates over the money supply, for example, Miller found the first explicit Puritan appeal to self-interest a valid guide to behavior. Moreover, as New England society became more heterogeneous, it produced increasingly shrill Puritan jeremiads against rampant gambling and idleness in settlements which had become "the very brothel houses of Satan." Furthermore, Cotton Mather's controversial attempt to immunize Bostonians against small pox in 1731 took the form of a bizarre struggle for moral and intellectual preeminence between Mather and his anticlerical opponents. Vivid but opinionated, these chapters exposed the dangerous vagueness of Miller's definition of the "mind" as everything "said and done publicly"; here the "mind" was not set within a framework defining the larger social context and the flow of increasingly non-Puritan ideas.

What book 3 lost in cohesion, book 4, "The Socialization of Piety," regained. For here Miller led his readers through a series of incredibly bitter fights in which inherited religious values and new social circumstances clashed to produce an ugly contagion of acrimony and suspicion—the very sort of tight framework missing in book 3. He described the Puritan acceptance of experimental science, the rise of Anglicanism in New England, Cotton Mather's project to institutionalize piety in his "do-good" essays, and finally the Puritan struggle to keep Anglicans off the Harvard College Board of Overseers. For Miller, there was still much to admire in Puritan thought, but the central creative intellectual energy of the society was now turned inward to prepare defenses against new ideas. "It was a parched land," he wrote, "crying for deliverance from the hold of ideas that had served their purpose and died."

In the closing pages of the work's last chapter, "Polity as a Form of Patriotism," Miller used Cotton Mather's last major book, *Ratio Discipline Fratrum Nov* [sic] *Anglorum* (1726), a defense of Congregationalist control of Harvard, as the occasion for a summing up. "In a hundred respects," he wrote, "Mather is the most intransigent and impervious mind of his period, not to say the most nauseous human being, yet in others he is the most sensitive and perceptive, the clearest and most resolute." The *Ratio* may have been a bombastic assault on Anglican intellectuality and ambition; it may have been hypocritical, considering the nonseparatist origins of New England Congregationalism. "But in one respect, it is the most honest thing Cotton Mather ever wrote: it says, by forthright implication, that these are a peculiar people, no longer pretending to be a model for Europe, but fully conscious of how they came to be what they are, resolved henceforth to be just that."

The fourteen year gap between the two volumes of *The New England Mind* was the result not only of Miller's service in the Office of Strategic Services in World War II but also of his realization that Jonathan Edwards was the most important figure in all of early American intellectual history and that the first century of New England Puritanism could in one sense be understood as a prelude to Edwards's achievement. Thus, in the mid-1940s, before completing *Colony to Province*, he wrote *Jonathan Edwards*, an intellectual biography published in 1949.

He divided the book into separate chapters treating either "external biography" or philosophical concepts. Very little of Edwards's daily life and ministry concerned Miller; it was Edwards's fixation with abstract ideas which made him, the historian thought, a great man, although Miller also believed that in Edwards's case philosophical inquiry was intimately related to everyday life: "No writer ever emerged more directly out of the passions, the feuds, and the anxieties of his society; his peculiar kind of objectivity must, in fact, be interpreted, not as insensitivity to his surroundings, but as an effort to protect himself against their clutch." The major original argument of the book was that Edwards owed an enormous intellectual debt to the seventeenth-century philosopher John Locke, an interpretation systematically refuted in Norman

Fiering's *Jonathan Edwards's Moral Thought and Its British Context* (1981). The book's rhetorical strategy, on the other hand, was to kindle in the reader's consciousness the exquisite tension at the core of religious experience. No sooner had Miller described the omnipotence of God and the terror of the helpless sinner in Edwards's revivalism than he confronted his audience with the climactic drama of preaching: "In the moment of triumph, Edwards threw off disguises and exposed the secret long nurtured; the last remnant of scholasticism was discarded, and God was no longer bound by any promise, whether of metaphysics or of law. Edwards brought mankind, as Protestantism must always bring them, without mitigation, protection, or indulgence, face to face with a cosmos fundamentally inhuman."

Even more influential than this book, however, were three articles which Miller had published in 1940, 1950, and 1952. These articles were collected and made widely available in the first volume of his essays, *Errand into the Wilderness*, which was published by Harvard University Press in 1956. Arranged in *Errand* by the logic of their subject matter, the first of these, "Jonathan Edwards and the Great Awakening," was written as a lecture to be delivered at Bennington College in 1949 as part of a series on the American response to crisis; the lectures in the series were then published as essays in 1952 as *America in Crisis*, edited by Daniel Aaron. In "Jonathan Edwards and the Great Awakening," Miller considered the political implications of Edwards's attack on intellectual and moral complacency in New England Congregationalism, a "theme . . . with which Edwards dealt only by indirection." In fewer than six pages Miller summarized the polity of Puritan churches from 1630 to 1740. It was a brilliant compression of nearly all of his previous work, and in a moment of stylistic drama he concluded that "the greatness of Jonathan Edwards is that he understood what had happened." He saw that the social and spiritual aspects of the covenant in New England no longer coincided. The clergy's use of rationalist and plain style homiletics no longer made any sense to the mass of the population. Only through the use of the sensual imagery of Lockean psychology, Edwards declared, could preaching once again foster social and spiritual unity.

This revolutionary cultural change became the theme of "The Rhetoric of Sensation," an essay first published in 1950 and reprinted in *Errand*. Here Miller reconstructed Locke's theory regarding the relationship between sensory perception and learning, the essence of which was that "language, like government, is artificial; it rests upon contract." Edwards, Miller declared, "became a revolutionary artist because he took with painful seriousness Locke's theory that words are separable from all reality." Words, therefore, had to be so charged with experiential implication that they exploded within the consciousness of the hearer, not the routine words of the marketplace, perhaps, but assuredly words about sin and the human condition. " 'To have an actual idea of a thought,' " Miller quoted Edwards, " 'is to have that thought . . . in our minds. To have an actual idea of any pleasure or delight, there must be excited a degree of that delight.' " Here Miller found a "dramatic refashioning of the theory of sensational rhetoric," as well as a key to the Great Awakening.

The concluding essay in this trilogy, "From Edwards to Emerson," was actually the first written, an article published in the *New England Quarterly* in 1940. Here Miller sought to puncture the liberal myth that Emerson was a free spirit while Edwards was caged in theological dogma. "The real difference" between the two men, he explained in a prefatory headnote in *Errand*, was "that Edwards went to nature, in all passionate love, convinced that man could receive from it impressions which he must then try to interpret, whereas Emerson went to Nature, no less in love with it, convinced that in man there was a spontaneous correlation with the received impressions."

Indeed the headnotes in *Errand* and the preface to the volume are among the most self-revelatory of Miller's writings and perhaps the best introduction to his work. The preface contained the story of his seeing a vision of his life's work while unloading American oil at the edge of the African jungle, and the headnotes placed each piece of writing in the context of the "mission, . . . thrust upon me, . . . of expounding what I took to be the innermost propulsion of the United States." Years later his friend Father Walter Ong recalled that "Perry was given to epiphanies. . . . He had enough of the Protestant search for conversion in him to look for things that could suddenly change his life. It was the kind of thing he liked to remember."

In addition to the three essays on Edwards and the two previously published studies, "The Marrow of Puritan Divinity" and "Thomas Hooker," *Errand* contained a long, two-part article, which had appeared in the *William and Mary Quarterly* in 1948 and 1949, on the religious vision of the early Virginia settlers; an early example of Miller's treatment of romanticism, "Nature and the National Ego"; a

haunting comment on American apocalyptic thought occasioned by the *United States Bombing Survey* on Hiroshima; and the title "piece," as he liked to designate the selections in the book, a lecture given at a 1952 John Carter Brown Library exhibition of books, one of which was an election sermon entitled *A Brief Recognition of New England's Errand into the Wilderness*.

The completion of his five major works on Puritanism, which traced the development of the Puritan mind from the early seventeenth to the mid-eighteenth century, brought to a close exactly twenty-five years of scholarly work. Henceforth Miller would devote himself to his next major task, carrying the story of the American mind from the middle of the eighteenth century to the eve of the Civil War. As a member of the Harvard English department, his major teaching interest was American Romanticism. Bringing that golden age of American literature, centered as it was in New England, into proper relationship with its Puritan beginnings therefore became the consuming ambition of his later career.

Miller's work on the late eighteenth and early nineteenth centuries deserves the same intricate analysis that critics have given to his Puritan writings. There is ample material for such a study, "From Edwards to Emerson" and "Nature and the National Ego" in *Errand*, for two examples, and a curiously anecdotal book, *The Raven and the Whale: The War of Words and Wits in the Era of Poe and Melville* (1956) for yet another. In 1961 Miller produced a breathtaking reevaluation of religion from the 1770s to the 1830s; entitled "From Covenant to Revival," the essay appeared in a multi-volume study, *Religion in American Life*, edited by James W. Smith and A. L. Jamison and published by Princeton University Press. Furthermore, seven of the sixteen volumes of texts that he edited were literary works or historical sources from the early to mid-nineteenth century, among them *America* (1961) by Philip Schaff, the nineteenth-century German Reformed theologian and commentator on American religion and culture; *The American Transcendentalists: Their Prose and Poetry* (1956); *Consciousness at Concord: the Texts of Thoreau's Hitherto 'Lost Journal' (1840-1841) Together with Notes and a Commentary* (1958); *The Golden Age of American Literature* (1959); *The Legal Mind in America: From Independence to the Civil War* (1962); *Margaret Fuller: American Romantic* (1963); and *The Transcendentalists: an Anthology* (1950). Just as *Errand* brought into sharper focus Miller's work on Puritanism, another anthology, *Nature's Nation* (1967), which was published after his death, contained ten essays treating the period from the Revolution to the Civil War; two others, "The Shaping of American Character" and "The Insecurity of Nature," spanned the whole of American history. (*Nature's Nation* also reprinted two early treatments of subjects central to *From Colony to Province*, long essays on "Declension" and "Preparation" originally published in 1941 and 1943.) Finally, there is the fragment of the great work toward which all these editions and writings were leading, *The Life of the Mind in America: From the Revolution to the Civil War*, published posthumously in 1965.

In *The Life of the Mind* were two completed "books" and the beginnings of a third. Book 1 was entitled "The Evangelical Basis" and book 2, "The Legal Mentality"; book 3, "Tension: Technology and Science" contained one chapter and extensive notes for six others. Successive projected books were to deal with education, political economy and association, philosophy, theology, nature, and "the self."

It is impossible to say where all of this material and insight would have led Miller had he lived long enough to finish the intellectual history of the nation from the Revolution to the Civil War and to give it the same grand scale he had achieved in his earlier work on Puritanism and the Great Awakening. What he did accomplish in the late 1950s and early 1960s was a series of arresting propositions which might well have formed the beginnings of a new framework of interpretation for the historical study of late eighteenth-and early nineteenth-century America.

The most striking of these ideas appeared in the *Religion in American Life* essay, "From Covenant to Revival," where Miller noted the central place of covenant theology in the public pronouncements of the American Revolution. By calling for penitence as a necessary precondition for divine intervention, the Continental Congress in 1775 brought into play a fundamental quality of American character—the sense of belonging to God as a people and of being guaranteed his protection and his judgment through the humanly understandable instrument, the covenant. The essay then argued for the pervasiveness of this covenantal theology in the sermons and oratory of the War for Independence, a view recently corroborated by Charles Royster in *A Revolutionary People at War* (1979). By feeding the revolutionaries' sense of being the children of God, the War for Independence, in unpredictable ways, intensified the yearning for union with the sublime which lay behind preaching and exhortation. The victory over the British, therefore, had revolu-

tionary religious consequences. As Miller explained, "There was no place in the theology of the covenant for a people to congratulate themselves." Thus, the success of American arms and the growing idea that individual as well as national prosperity was the proper consequence of American independence rendered the covenant irrelevant to the celebration of American nationalism. Therein, Miller suggested, lay the theological seeds of the Second Great Awakening and the triumph of a new, more optimistic, increasingly flamboyant American culture in the early nineteenth century.

The discovery that the covenant was both a cause and a victim of the Revolution was closely related to another of Miller's original ideas about the late eighteenth century, his view that religious liberty was an accident. In one of his earliest essays, "The Contribution of the Protestant Churches to the Religious Liberty in Colonial America" (1935), as well as in a later treatment, "The Location of American Religious Freedom" (1954), and in a chapter entitled "Separation of Church and State" in *The Life of the Mind*, Miller probed the complex cultural and psychological roots of the First Amendment. In 1935 he argued that American Protestants "did not contribute to religious liberty; they stumbled into it; they were compelled into it; they accepted it at last because they had to, or because they saw its strategic value." In 1954 he repeated the phrase, "stumbled into" religious freedom; American culture, he insisted, was located between opposite poles of Nature and Biblicism, each of which made supreme claims of authority on individuals, and pluralism in religious belief and practice accommodated, as no other arrangement could have, those powerful forces. These insights enabled Miller in *The Life of the Mind* to anticipate William G. McLoughlin's later finding that separation of church and state was intended by most of its advocates to guarantee the triumph of Protestant Christianity in the United States rather than the creation of a secular state.

The striving of Americans in the early national period to create a Christian commonwealth therefore emerged as Miller's central concern as he began writing *The Life of the Mind*. In book 1, "The Evangelical Basis," he constructed a richly textured and highly suggestive analysis of the religious spirit at the core of American culture from the age of Jefferson to that of Jackson. However, he never discovered the "marrow" of evangelicalism, as he had of Puritanism, and his depiction of revivalism consequently groped for language to communicate the core of evangelical belief and experience. He called it a "cauldron," a "dynamic force in the society," a "spasm among the populace, a violent explosion of emotions which for long had been seeking release, an overwhelming portent for the future of the continent."

In the process of organizing the often controversial outpourings about revivalism, however, Miller found a novel point of entry into the interior of evangelical experience. He was fascinated by three critics of revivalism: the Scottish Presbyterian Robert Baird, the German Reformed theologians John Nevin and Philip Schaff, who attempted to interpret American religion to British and continental readers. In the writings of these three men Miller found a diagnosis of American culture that he regarded as vastly superior to that of Alexis de Tocqueville, who, overlooking evangelicalism, saw only nervous energy, anxiety, and amoral individualism as the impetus of democracy. Schaff, an outsider, could marvel at the social energy unleashed by a voluntary system of religious discipleship; Nevin, a former Presbyterian, focused on the external methods of revivalism as a way of rallying antirevivalist, confessional Protestantism; and Baird created what Miller called "the finest philosophical statement" explaining the dynamic impact of voluntary, individualistic Christianity on American life.

What these and other critics of revivalism stumbled upon was the evangelical ambition of devising, through "human ingenuity," prescribed rules for the ordering, purifying, or redirecting of the life of the whole "community." All of the revivalists' talk about personal conversion experience, in Miller's view, was simply an indirect way of advocating the revitalization of the community. And buried within these appeals was the assumption that America was locked into a pattern of religious declension and then revival, a pattern which could be regulated by human intervention; the periods of declensions could be shortened and softened by protracted revivalism while the revivals themselves could reach, in the institutionalized form of missionary activity, ever further across the landscape and into human consciousness.

What the human mind and spirit had to confront in nineteenth-century America, Miller suspected, was not so much sin or even excesses of national pride as it was the curse of machinery and technology. Miller's fragmentary section on "Science—Theoretical and Applied" will probably have more influence on future students of history than his completed book 2, "The Legal Mentality"—which was an elegant treatise on

emerging professionalism written without reference to the development of legal history as a subdiscipline in its own right. Miller's single completed chapter on science argued that, in Jefferson's time, the Enlightenment provided an elaborate system for connecting theory and practice, knowledge and inquiry, American uniqueness and scientific curiosity. The notes for the unwritten chapters sketched the breakdown of this synthesis. Discussions of agriculture, geology, physiology, scientific theory, and technology, and the proper use of the bequest for a Smithsonian Institution all led toward Miller's concluding notation: "The forlorn hope: that technology, by binding the continent into a unit of railroads and telegraphs and steamboats, will prevent any split. . . . Hence [the] ironic effect of the Civil War, the real result of the conflict is not so much the humbling of the South and abolition of slavery, but a tremendous impetus given to accelerated subjection of [the] natural continent to the mechanisms of technology."

Closely related to this concern with the application of science to an increasingly uncontrolled technology was one of Miller's most audacious essays, "The Responsibility of Mind in a Civilization of Machines," the title essay in the final volume of his collected writings. Prepared for a conference in 1961, "Toward a Community of Learning," and originally published in the *American Scholar*, "The Responsibility of Mind" challenged the surrender to a materially oriented, machine-powered culture by modern Americans who surreptitiously yearned to join Thoreau at Walden Pond: "Why do I discover when addressing a classroom loaded with the heirs of industry and with future vice presidents that the mordant aphorisms of Thoreau are greeted with an appreciative recognition? . . . Millions of Americans . . . have only vague notions, barely restive worries, as to the existence of any . . . enmity [between technology and humane learning]. The terrible fact is that they have no slightest sense of responsibility for any bifurcation of which they cannot conceive. They dwell in a fog of perpetual neutralism."

The Responsibility of Mind contained, in addition, six other essays on modern education, five previously unpublished lectures on Puritan topics, and three on later and wider historical themes. Several of these pieces of work, as well as Miller's outpouring of book reviews (the Kinnamon bibliography lists more than 180 of them), clearly reveal Miller's extraordinary role in American intellectual life, one which transcended the academic fields of history and literature. Miller was one of the handful of intellectuals—Hannah Arendt, Reinhold Niebuhr, and Richard Hofstadter were others—who mastered their craft in the 1930s and then, addressing a wide audience after World War II, reintroduced philosophical rigor and coherence into the humanities in America, brought to their work an awareness of the complexity of and tragedy in human nature, and appreciated the importance of form in the expression of thought.

There is no evidence that Miller sensed an affinity between his work and Arendt's, though both wrote posthumously published works entitled *The Life of the Mind*. Central to both writers, however, was a concern with the nature of freedom as an urgent issue in contemporary discourse. In his study *Roger Williams: His Contribution to the American Tradition*, published in book form in 1953, Miller praised Williams as one "who knew that the meaning of life lies not on the surface but somewhere underneath and that it must be perpetually sought. He attacked the political pedant and the textual literalist, not because they were evil men or their motives not admirable, but because they did not recognize the true nature of freedom. They lose the essential in the circumstantial, and so deceive themselves into making of their virtue an instrument of tyranny."

Niebuhr and Miller, in contrast, were close friends and had over many years a fruitful dialogue about the nature of Christianity and the responsibility of intellect, a dialogue sharpened by Niebuhr's belief in neo-orthodox Protestantism and Miller's agnosticism. "Miller," declared Niebuhr, "was . . . a believing unbeliever, . . . believing in the sense that he regarded Jonathan Edwards as a superior guide to the labyrinths of the human heart." A colleague of Miller's agreed: "when Miller proclaimed himself an unbeliever, or derided various believers as men of shallow faith, he did so with a profane gusto which concealed a sacred rage."

Furthermore, Miller astutely saw Richard Hofstadter's historical tract, *The American Political Tradition* (1948), as the harbinger of a new kind of history, the work of writers "trained in the methods of scholarship but capable of working within the structure, and above all [within] the dynamic tendency, of ideas. . . . They understand what ideas mean . . . because they have taken ideas into their own consciousness." Miller surely included himself in that company.

Taking ideas into his own consciousness in order to write history was for Perry Miller an excruciating, exhilarating discipline. "More and more his nervous energies sought the relaxation of al-

cohol," wrote his friend, Harry Levin. "People almost seemed to hope that he was drinking himself to stupefaction," Edmund Morgan recalled, "so that his relentless creativity would not continue to chide." He died in his study in Leverett House at Harvard University on 9 December 1963.

Other:

The Puritans, 2 volumes, edited by Miller and Thomas H. Johnson (New York: American Book Company, 1938; revised edition, New York: Harper & Row, 1963);

The Transcendentalists: An Anthology, edited by Miller (Cambridge: Harvard University Press, 1950);

The American Puritans: Their Prose and Poetry, edited by Miller (Garden City: Doubleday, 1956);

The American Transcendentalists: Their Prose and Poetry, edited by Miller (Garden City: Doubleday, 1957);

Consciousness at Concord: The Text of Thoreau's Hitherto 'Lost Journal' (1840-1841) Together with Notes and a Commentary, edited by Miller (Boston: Houghton Mifflin, 1958);

The Golden Age of American Literature, edited by Miller (New York: Braziller, 1959);

Philip Schaff, *America*, edited by Miller (Cambridge: Harvard University Press, 1961);

The Legal Mind in America: From Independence to the Civil War, edited by Miller (Garden City: Doubleday, 1962);

The Complete Writings of Roger Williams, volume 7, edited by Miller (New York: Russell & Russell, 1963);

Margaret Fuller: American Romantic, edited by Miller (Garden City: Doubleday, 1963);

The Great Awakening: Documents Illustrating the Crisis and Its Consequences, edited by Miller and Alan Heimert (Indianapolis: Bobbs-Merrill, 1967).

Bibliographies:

Kenneth Kinnamon, "A Bibliography of Perry Miller," *Bulletin of Bibliography and Magazine Notes*, 26 (1969): 45-51;

John C. Crowell, "Perry Miller as Historian: A Bibliography of Evaluations," *Bulletin of Bibliography and Magazine Notes*, 34 (1977): 77-85.

References:

Francis T. Butts, "The Myth of Perry Miller," *American Historical Review*, 87 (1982): 665-694;

John Crowell and Stanford J. Searl, Jr., Introduction to *The Responsibility of Mind in a Civilization of Machines: Essays*, edited by Crowell and Searl (Amherst: University of Massachusetts Press, 1979), pp. 1-7;

Ann Douglas, "The Mind of Perry Miller," *New Republic*, 186 (3 February 1982): 26-30;

Donald Fleming, "Perry Miller and Esoteric History"; Alan Heimert, "Perry Miller: An Appreciation"; Reinhold Niebuhr, "Perry Miller and Our Embarrassment"; and Edmund S. Morgan, "Perry Miller and the Historians"; *Harvard Review*, 2 (1964): 25-59;

David D. Hall, Introduction to *Orthodoxy in Massachusetts* (New York: Harper & Row, 1970);

David A. Hollinger, "Perry Miller and Philosophical History," *History and Theory*, 7 (1968): 189-202;

Harry Levin, "Perry (Gilbert Eddy) Miller (1905-1963)," *Year Book of the American Philosophical Society* (1964), pp, 136-140;

Kenneth Lynn, et al., "Perry Miller," *Harvard University Gazette*, 60 (16 January 1965): 107-108;

Karen Anne Lystra, "Perry Miller and American Puritan Studies: A Case Study in a Scholarly Community," Ph.D. dissertation, Case-Western Reserve University, 1973;

George M. Marsden, "Perry Miller's Rehabilitation of the Puritans: a Critique," *Church History*, 39 (1970): 91-105;

Michael McGiffert, "Puritan Studies in the 1960s," *William and Mary Quarterly*, 27 (1970): 36-67;

Robert Middlekauff, "Perry Miller," in *Pastmasters: Some Essays on American Historians*, edited by Marcus Cunliffe and Robin W. Winks (New York: Harper & Row, 1969), pp. 167-190;

Kenneth B. Murdock, Introduction to *Nature's Nation* (London: Gollancz, 1966; Cambridge: Harvard University Press, 1967), pp. ix-xvi;

Richard Reinitz, *Irony and Consciousness: American Historiography and Reinhold Niebuhr's Vision* (Lewisburg, Pa: Bucknell University Press, 1980);

George Selement, "Perry Miller: A Note on his Sources in *The New England Mind: The Seventeenth Century*," *William and Mary Quarterly*, 31 (1974): 453-464;

Robert Skotheim, *American Intellectual Histories and Historians* (Princeton: Princeton University Press, 1966), pp. 186-212;

Gene Wise, *American Historical Explanations: a Strategy for Grounded Inquiry* (Homewood, Ill.: Dorsey Press, 1973), pp. 134-139, 315-343;

Wise, "Implicit Irony in Perry Miller's *New England Mind*," *Journal of the History of Ideas*, 29 (1968): 579-600.

Papers:

Harvard University Archives has a collection of Miller's papers.

Edmund S. Morgan

(17 January 1916-   )

William D. Liddle
Southwest Texas State University

SELECTED BOOKS: *The Puritan Family: Religion and Domestic Relations in Seventeenth-Century New England* (Boston: Boston Public Library, 1944; revised and enlarged edition, New York & London: Harper & Row, 1966);

Virginians at Home: Family Life in the Eighteenth Century (Williamsburg, Va.: Colonial Williamsburg, 1952);

The Stamp Act Crisis: Prologue to Revolution, by Morgan and Helen M. Morgan (Chapel Hill: University of North Carolina Press, 1953; London: Oxford University Press, 1953);

The Birth of the Republic, 1763-1789 (Chicago: University of Chicago Press, 1956; London: Cambridge University Press, 1957);

The American Revolution: A Review of Changing Interpretations (Washington, D.C.: Service Center for Teachers of History and the American Historical Association, 1958);

The Puritan Dilemma: The Story of John Winthrop (Boston: Little, Brown, 1958);

The Gentle Puritan: A Life of Ezra Stiles, 1727-1795 (Chapel Hill: University of North Carolina Press, 1962; New Haven & London: Yale University Press, 1962);

The National Experience: A History of the United States,

by Morgan and others (New York: Harcourt,
Brace & World, 1963);

Visible Saints: The History of a Puritan Idea (New York:
New York University Press, 1963; London:
Oxford University Press, 1965);

Roger Williams: The Church and the State (New York:
Harcourt, Brace & World, 1967);

So What About History? (New York: Atheneum,
1969);

*American Slavery, American Freedom: The Ordeal of
Colonial Virginia* (New York: Norton, 1975);

*The Meaning of Independence: John Adams, George
Washington and Thomas Jefferson* (Charlottesville: University Press of Virginia, 1976);

The Challenge of the American Revolution (New York:
Norton, 1976);

The Genius of George Washington (New York: Norton,
1980).

It would be interesting to know how many
young people of the last quarter century first encountered a piece of the American past, outside the
normally dreary confines of textbook accounts, in
Edmund S. Morgan's skillfully drawn portrait of
the first governor of the Massachusetts Bay Colony.
The most successful volume in Little, Brown's "Library of American Biography," *The Puritan Dilemma:
The Story of John Winthrop* (1958), frequently appears
on reading lists for U.S. history courses in American
colleges and universities, and the book is entirely
suitable for use in advanced classes in secondary
schools. A beautifully written volume, *The Puritan
Dilemma* introduces the reader to the social and
economic life, the evolving political institutions, and
the religious experience of early America by tracing
John Winthrop's life from youth to maturity, when
he decided to emigrate from England, and through
the two decades in which he played a leading role in
the affairs of Massachusetts Bay. The result is an
illuminating treatment of "the central Puritan dilemma, the problem of doing right in a world that
does wrong," and of the many subordinate dilem-
mas which plagued and enhanced the lives of
seventeenth-century New Englanders.

The Puritan Dilemma is not Edmund S. Morgan's favorite, best, or most influential book, but it
may be his most widely read work, one that reveals
his talents as a scholar and writer of American history. Perhaps the book's most conspicuous and
characteristic feature is the human touch with
which its author treats complex beliefs and ideas.
Morgan's writings generally exhibit an affinity for
people, a preoccupation with the details of their
daily lives, and a concern for even the most mun-

Edmund S. Morgan

dane events and experiences when they touch
upon things human. Attracted to the concrete and
averse to abstractions, Morgan traces the history of ideas in their specific settings. He thus uses
Winthrop's life primarily as a vehicle for exploring
the ideas of the New England Puritans. While the
reader of *The Puritan Dilemma* encounters conceptions as abstruse as the "Covenant Theology" or
"Arminianism" and disputes as recondite as Congregationalism versus Presbyterianism or "preparation for salvation" versus "immediate revelation," he discovers these ideas and conceptual controversies in the particular context of John Winthrop's experiences.

The son of Edmund Morris and Elsie Smith
Morgan, Edmund Sears Morgan was born in Minneapolis, Minnesota. His father was then a member
of the law school faculty at the University of Minnesota, but the family moved three times during the
decade following the younger Morgan's birth. First,
his father accepted a position as an assistant to the
judge-advocate general of the United States during
World War I and took his family to Washington.

After the war, he joined the faculty of the Yale Law School from which he moved in 1925 to Harvard Law School. Except for occasional trips back to the Midwest, where other members of the family operated a summer resort at Isle Royal on Lake Superior, and periodic excursions to Texas, where his father taught during summer sessions, Edmund S. Morgan spent his developing years in the environs of Cambridge, Massachusetts. After graduation from the Belmont Hill School in 1933, he entered Harvard University, receiving his A.B. degree in 1937. In that same year, on the recommendation of Felix Frankfurter, he began his graduate training at the London School of Economics. Family finances dictated that he return to Harvard University in 1938 when that institution offered him a fellowship. There he completed his graduate studies. In addition, on 7 June 1939, he married Helen Theresa Mayer. By the time he finished his doctoral dissertation in 1942, the first of their two daughters was on the way—and the whole world was engulfed in the flames ignited by Adolf Hitler.

Morgan harbored no illusions about the evils of fascism, but he had opposed war in principle. The Wehrmacht's stunning victories in the spring of 1940 obliged him to reconsider his convictions. Increasingly persuaded that American intervention in the European war was both likely and proper, he withdrew his application for status as a conscientious objector before the year ended. When he finished his dissertation in 1942, he enrolled in an intensive, three-month course in machine work and then found a job as a machinist in the radiation laboratory at the Massachusetts Institute of Technology, where he spent the war years. He never resented the war's intrusion into his life and academic career. On the contrary, he found gratification in becoming skilled at a trade, and he has maintained a high regard for the independence gained in the acquisition of such a skill. He, in fact, still keeps a workshop, including a modest drill press, at home.

It would be a mistake to assume that the demands imposed by work in the radiation lab removed Morgan entirely from the world of scholarship. His dissertation, a study of the family in Puritan New England, began to appear piecemeal in *More Books*, a publication of the Boston Public Library, in 1942 and 1943. The pieces were reunited in book form, *The Puritan Family: Religion and Domestic Relations in Seventeenth-Century New England*, in 1944. Morgan's research for the dissertation also yielded other results, most notably an essay, "The Puritans and Sex," which appeared as the lead article in the December 1942 issue of the *New England Quarterly*. Rarely have the Puritans emerged from modern scholarship as more human figures than in these writings. Concerned with the way in which people actually related to each other as individuals and as exemplars of their various social roles, Morgan surveyed an extensive body of homiletic literature, diaries and other personal writings, court proceedings, and town records in order to discover how the family functioned in the daily lives of seventeenth-century New Englanders. The result was a charming portrait of the "human side" of Puritanism. Morgan's research revealed how a people who "were a much earthier lot than their modern critics have imagined" dealt with matters such as love and marriage, child rearing and education, and managing servants and surviving servitude.

Morgan accepted a position as instructor in the social sciences at the University of Chicago in 1945, and, two years later, he moved to Brown University. His scholarship prospered with his teaching. He made further contributions to Puritan studies by editing "The Diary of Michael Wigglesworth 1653-1657: The Conscience of a Puritan" (1951) and to the history of the American family, by writing a small volume, *Virginians at Home: Family Life in the Eighteenth Century* (1952). In Michael Wigglesworth, Morgan confronted a coldly orthodox Puritan figure who challenged the modern, revisionist image of the Puritans as more "hearty, warm-hearted creatures" than past mythologies would allow. Much of the format of *Virginians at Home* resembled that of *The Puritan Family*, as it dealt with the topics of childhood, marriage, managing servants and slaves, and the houses and holidays of eighteenth-century Virginia. Significantly, this volume was addressed to the general reader rather than the academic specialist. An account of daily life in eighteenth-century Virginia, the book has been called "deceptive" in its "simplicity."

The ideal of the teaching scholar is to a remarkable degree realized in Edmund S. Morgan. By all accounts, his lectures are models of exposition, combining depth of research and analysis with cogency and clarity. He spends an inordinate amount of time on his professional duties both in and out of the classroom. His teaching also has provided a stimulus for important scholarly work, as chapters of books have been initially worked out as lectures for his courses. In particular, his long and productive inquiry into the meaning of the American Revolution originated in his use of documents to illustrate, for his students, the evolution of colonial ideas about the extent of Parliament's authority. His sources suggested that the information he "had been taught about the progression of colonial arguments might conceivably not be so." His research indicated that Americans opposed "Parliamentary taxation without differentiation between internal and external taxation" from the outset of the imperial controversy "until the 1770's when they advanced to the more radical position of denying the authority of Parliament to legislate as well as to tax." This discovery led ultimately to the publication of a major book.

The Stamp Act Crisis: Prologue to Revolution (1953) stands as one of the early monuments of modern scholarship on the American Revolution. The book's significance was twofold. First, it offered a powerful argument that the most important consequence of the Stamp Act controversy was "the emergence, not of leaders and methods and organizations, but of well-defined constitutional principles." The British government had attempted to tighten up the administration of its overseas empire and to raise a portion of the funds needed to maintain that empire through taxes imposed on the colonists by acts of Parliament. These British measures provoked colonists, Morgan wrote, to resort to "those magic words, 'the Rights of Englishmen,' which more than once had measured the tread of marching feet." Colonial actions in turn provoked British spokesmen to assert "the authority of Parliament." Britons and colonists thus found themselves taking positions which could not be reconciled so long as each was rigidly maintained. Despite the fact that repeal of the Stamp Act temporarily relieved the crisis, Britons had been "encouraged to believe that the Americans were seeking independence in easy stages and the Americans to think that the English were trying to enslave them by slow and insensible degrees."

Besides advancing an important set of ideas, *The Stamp Act Crisis* was also well structured. As a topic for exposition and analysis, the Stamp Act controversy posed troublesome problems of organization. Morgan avoided the "wallpaper effect" of a colony-by-colony survey by choosing "to see general issues so far as possible through the eyes of particular men," especially as these perceptions could be described in biographical sketches of six of the more important players in the drama. These short biographies are the most charming and, in some ways, the most instructive portions of the book. Combined with vignettes of other major figures scattered throughout the narrative, they reveal the variegated details that made up the mosaic of the colonial experience during the mid-1760s. The technique has been described as seeking "historical objectivity through cumulative partiality." In Morgan's hands, it produced history with a profoundly human countenance and with a "resonance" (to use his own favorite term) that "goes beyond the statements about the past themselves and speaks to the common and everyday experience of man."

One additional feature of *The Stamp Act Crisis* distinguishes it from Morgan's other writings: Helen M. Morgan is listed as coauthor. Yet Mrs. Morgan's contribution to her husband's scholarship has extended well beyond the pages of this single book. Although the focus of her formal education was in the sciences, she became skilled in historical research while working with her husband. Under his direction, they carry on research together. He then writes draft after draft. When a manuscript begins to take shape, she critiques his work, returning the final and finished draft only after careful review. This working relationship reflects a broader world of common interests and concerns. As one example, a delight in walking together led to a mutual enthusiasm for bird-watching, a pastime from which they draw great pleasure. The partnership they developed over the years is a significant part of Edmund S. Morgan's professional as well as private life.

Following *The Stamp Act Crisis* Morgan expanded the scope of his work on the American Revolution by writing a volume for The Chicago History of American Civilization series. *The Birth of the Republic, 1763-1789* (1956) filled a void in historical literature when it appeared and, after twenty-five years, it has remained the best available short survey of the Revolutionary era. The elegant prose in the book smoothly conveyed the wealth of information, the depth of understanding, and the sophistication of analysis offered between its covers. Combining narrative with explanation, Morgan asserted his particular construction of the Revolutionary period, carefully identified important points of clashing interpretation among modern historians, and dealt with the issues involved in historical controversy, where appropriate, all without breaking the essential flow of his narrative.

Morgan saw the Revolutionary era as a time distinguished by "the Americans' search for principles." The quest began when Britain decided that colonists should bear a portion of the burden imposed by recent enlargement of the empire. Colonists perceived the resulting Parliamentary measures as threats to the security of their property, and, for them, "property was not merely a possession to be hoarded and admired; it was the source of life and liberty." Americans thus issued formal statements that began "to survey the bounds and map out, in however crude and tentative a fashion, the area of human freedom." As the controversy intensified and events compelled colonists either to pursue further or to drop their claims, it became increasingly clear that "there was no room in the existing British empire for a people who wanted the rights that Americans demanded." In the process of finding their way out of that empire, the colonists unearthed "the principle of human equality," an idea "that would turn the course of history in a new direction." Not all the implications of that idea surfaced at once, but its ferment began to work in the lives and in the institutions of the former colonies even as Americans carried on the war that secured their independence. They also found something else—nationhood. Despite the centrifugal forces at work in American life, "the union of three million cantankerous colonists into a new nation" was achieved with remarkable ease and permanence. The American nationality that originated in independence both advanced and regressed during the "Critical Period," Morgan believed. The Constitution of 1787, although ratified "by methods that cannot be defended," represented a logical culmination of the Revolutionary movement. For "if the Revolution was a struggle to make property secure, the Constitution was the final fulfillment of that struggle."

The Birth of the Republic rested squarely on the assumption that the ideas espoused by Americans of the Revolutionary era should be taken seriously. Morgan also discounted class conflict as a significant theme in Revolutionary America. These features of his book, particularly the latter, led some readers to identify him with a consensus-oriented "Neo-Whig" school of conservative historians that emerged after World War II. In fact, this identification reflects a misreading of *The Birth of the Republic*. Morgan actually thought colonial ideas had "progressive" if not radical implications for the future. He saw the Revolution as a transforming experience, changing as well as preserving much in American life and promising to change even more.

There is no "Morgan thesis" on the American Revolution or on any other subject, and there is no "Morgan school" either. As he never became a disciple, so he never sought disciples. His own research and writings span more than two centuries of early American history and have touched upon a variety of topics, most involving the study of ideas. As a

teaching scholar at Brown and, after 1955, at Yale (where in 1965 he became Sterling Professor) he has supervised dissertations for nearly fifty doctoral candidates, some choosing topics associated with the American Revolution, some investigating problems in the history of Puritanism, and some selecting subjects connected with other areas of study altogether. These students used different methodologies in their research, approached their diverse topics differently, and reflect a variety of ideological persuasions in their work.

By the time Morgan finished *The Birth of the Republic*, scholarship on the American Revolution had reached a kind of watershed. For more than a half-century, the "Whig" interpretation associated with the great Anglo-American writers of the nineteenth century had been under siege. The most important revisionists were associated with the imperial school of colonial history, with a group of Progressive historians, and with Sir Lewis Namier in England. None of these scholars put much stock in the notion that a colonial "search for principles" played a significant role in the Revolutionary era. Historians of the imperial school suggested that the Revolution resulted from organic processes, as distinctive American institutions matured within the protective framework of a benevolently administered British empire. Progressives found the dynamic force at work in eighteenth-century America to be internal conflict, particularly socioeconomic class conflict. Preoccupied with structural analysis of British Parliamentary and ministerial politics, Namierist scholarship was in fact profoundly hostile to the study of ideas. Morgan's own research indicated that even as these revisionists corrected oversimplifications, they produced new distortions in the story of the American Revolution. Although he was not alone in finding "that for one brought up on a diet of professional history, the original sources were full of surprises," it was Edmund S. Morgan who first called for a general and searching reappraisal of the history of the American Revolution.

Morgan critiqued twentieth-century scholarship in "The American Revolution: Revisions in Need of Revising," a paper presented at the 1956 meeting of the Mississippi Valley Historical Association. He thought that imperial historians failed to explain how a British empire that governed with "beneficence and farsightedness" had so alienated responsible colonists as to provoke them to rebellion. He found the work of Progressive historians even more deficient, primarily because so much of it hinged on "the assumption that a conflict between property rights and human rights has been the persistent theme of American history." He believed that Namier and his disciples at least made sense of the movement for independence by showing that British politicians "were too dominated by local interests to run an empire." Even so, Morgan felt that Namier's work left unanswered important questions about George III and that it unjustly presumed "a consistent hypocrisy or delusion on the part of the Whig opposition." He ended with remarks intimating "that the Whig interpretation of the American Revolution may not be as dead as some historians would have us believe." Comments on the paper indicated that Morgan touched a tender nerve here and a responsive chord there.

In *The American Revolution: A Review of Changing Interpretations* (1958), Morgan offered a balanced and thorough assessment of individual historians and their works as well as of schools of interpretation. His analysis suggested that while each generation, each broad interpretive perspective, and each scholar extended and deepened our understanding of the Revolution, the subject remained fertile ground for further research and for new insights. "We must continue to ask, for we still do not fully know, what the Revolution was," he wrote. No better guide to the historical literature of the American Revolution from the nineteenth century to the mid-1950s existed. Later historiographical analyses of the period supplement this essay.

Morgan's works pointed out an important direction new research should take. He suggested that the colonists' language should be thoroughly explored, for their conceptions and language would certainly illuminate events and their responses to events in their world. Other scholars began to take colonial rhetoric seriously, to accept the prospect that the use of terms such as "corruption" and "slavery" might represent more than mere propaganda or needless hysteria. These historians thus discovered the "ideology" of the Revolution and began to delineate a classical, humanistic, and republican tradition, which was distinct from either the Puritan heritage or the liberal philosophy acquired primarily from recently enlightened Englishmen and which constituted a significant element in the mentality of eighteenth-century America. The intellectual history of the American Revolutionary era was rewritten by scholars who followed the path marked out by Edmund S. Morgan.

In his own writings on the American Revolution, Morgan frequently and productively used the papers of Ezra Stiles. Those documents revealed much about Stiles that was attractive: he was an intellectual, a spectator by inclination who nevertheless became involved in the affairs of his world, and a good if not great man. A biography appeared almost inevitable, but Morgan did not entirely relish the project of writing it. As he has stated, the challenge of writing resides in turning a mass of information extracted from sources into a "book," in bringing "order" out of "chaos"; yet biography ordinarily structures itself, as its author is stuck with a beginning and an end with assorted developments occurring in predetermined sequence in between. Fortunately, such authorial reservations did not deprive readers of *The Gentle Puritan: A Life of Ezra Stiles, 1727-1795* (1962). Though less widely read than *The Puritan Dilemma*, *The Gentle Puritan* is, if anything, a more substantial work of scholarship.

Morgan never let his growing interest in the American Revolution suppress his earlier attachment to the study of Puritanism, and he believed that the history of Puritanism intersected with the history of the Revolution at critical points. Perhaps it was only coincidental that during the years in which the great Puritan scholar Perry Miller passed from a state of deteriorating health to eventual death, Morgan turned again to the seventeenth century, to the people who settled New England, and to Puritan ideas. Miller, who had been Morgan's tutor during his sophomore and junior years at Harvard and who later supervised his dissertation, received the dedication to *Visible Saints: The History of a Puritan Idea* (1963), which appeared just before Miller's death. The book revealed the extent of Morgan's debt to Miller, but it also illustrated well the distinctive method, approach, and style that made up Morgan's way of dealing with the Puritans. Those who casually consigned *Visible Saints* to a "Miller school" (or, to a "Harvard school") of Puritan studies missed the mark. *Visible Saints* examined "the origins and history" of a single if central Puritan conception, "the idea of membership in the church." Of course, related notions inevitably intruded on the analysis of this issue. The close relationship between Puritan ideas about the experience of regeneration and their concept of what the church should be necessitated a carefully controlled explanation of the Puritan "morphology of conversion." This disciplined approach made the "human touch" so characteristic of Morgan's writings less plainly evident than in other works, though it remained present and decisive. *Visible Saints* traced the passage of a specific idea through the minds and words of particular Puritans over an extended period of time. Morgan's exposition of how those individuals and groups handled the problem of church membership revised the history of Puritanism, including Perry Miller's.

Visible Saints represented Morgan's most substantial contribution to Puritan studies; it is justly regarded by some as his best book. Four new publications on Puritanism followed in short order. In *The Founding of Massachusetts: Historians and the Sources* (1964), Morgan gathered together samples from earlier historians' accounts of early New England and linked them with complete texts of "most of the surviving materials written in Massachusetts Bay before 1634, as well as a number of pertinent ones written in England before 1630." *Puritan Political Ideas, 1558-1794*, published in 1965, included selections from Puritans of both old and New England, from Christopher Goodman's justification of resistance to tyrannical rulers, written during the reign of Queen Mary, and from Ezra Stiles's defense of regicide, written amidst the trauma of the French Revolution. The introduction to these excerpts from the documents was a modest but provocative essay on the course and the central tenets of Puritan political thought. The durability of Morgan's attraction to this topic showed up again in "The Puritan Ethic and the American Revolution," a 1967 article published in the *William and Mary Quarterly*, and in a new book about an old Puritan maverick.

Few characters in the American past have caused historians more trouble than Roger Williams. At one moment, he seems the prophet of modern democracy; in the next, he reappears as a spiritual pilgrim enveloped in nostalgia. He came off rather poorly, compared with John Winthrop, in *The Puritan Dilemma*. Yet after "consecutively and systematically" working through a new edition of Williams's writings, Morgan decided that he had "misunderstood and misjudged the man" and promptly set the matter right. *Roger Williams: The Church and the State* (1967) revealed this man to possess a restless and "original mind" and the courage to pursue his "ideas through their implications to conclusions that his contemporaries would not accept." His relentless application of essentially orthodox doctrines and conventional interpretations of Scripture to the problem of the church and the problem of the state led him to creative conclusions which astonished and alienated others of his time.

Even as he put the finishing touches on *Visible Saints* in the early 1960s, Morgan began to consider the way in which the connection between Puritan thought and economic developments seemed to be one of those "critical points" at which the religious heritage of seventeenth-century New England touched the American Revolutionary experience. His judgment of the potential significance of that link was based on the discovery of an "unexpected theme" in literature associated with colonial nonimportation efforts of the 1760s and 1770s. Morgan found that "the authors praised austerity for its own sake or for the sake of the virtue and good character that austerity would foster. Doing without British imports, it seemed, would be good for the soul, whatever Parliament did." From colonists' words, it appeared that "the Revolution was shaped by forces that reached well beyond the immediate quarrel over Parliamentary taxation." "The Puritan Ethic and the American Revolution," Morgan's most important contribution to periodical literature, thus traced the influence of the Puritan concept of austerity on the American Revolution and on the life of the new nation born out of the struggle for independence.

An important part of Morgan's genius has been his ability to write compelling prose at different levels for specifically different audiences. He quite successfully reached beyond the community of professional scholars in *Virginians at Home*, in his introductions to exhibits at the John Carter Brown Library, and in his introduction to *Paul Revere's Three Accounts of His Famous Ride* (1961), among other writings. His address to the 1959-1960 freshman class of Yale University was yet another example of this talent. He urged those young people to catch the contagion of curiosity, to be discontent with how little was known about subjects that interested them, and to commit themselves to "the search for truth" for its own sake. He also warned them against an unhappy academic vice: "A scholar at his worst sometimes seems to be simply a man who cannot make up his mind. . . . 'There are two schools of thought on this question, and the truth probably lies halfway between them.' When you hear this sentence repeated, or when you are tempted to repeat it yourself, remember that the truth may lie between two extremes, but it assuredly does not lie halfway between right and wrong." The complement to curiosity, Morgan continued, was the "compulsion to communicate," especially in writing: "Many people suppose that they know something if they can stammer out an approximation of what they mean in speech. They are mistaken. It is extremely unlikely that you have thought clearly if you cannot express yourself clearly, especially in writing. Writing is more than an instrument of communication. It is an instrument of thought."

In Morgan's view, the historian's obligation to reach out to a larger world was not discharged by establishing discourse with only the university educated. Also concerned with the status of history in the public schools, he agreed to serve as a consultant for a project, beginning in 1964, to propose innovative programs in social studies. Disillusioned with the slow pace of this enterprise, he set out on his own to write a book for junior-high students describing the nature of history. Although he required only about a week to compose the text of *So What About History?* (1969), he took two years to gather the seventy-four photographs, prints, and drawings used for illustrations. The result of this labor was a sparkling analysis of the debris from the past that men have encountered and used, the ways ideas have survived and influenced men, how ideas have changed over time and thus have affected the ways men act and think, and how revolutions have come about while retaining much of the past. The book tells plainly and engagingly why history is worth studying. *So What About History?* is a unique introduction to the discipline, not merely for adolescents but also for undergraduates and even for professionals who occasionally need to refresh their spirits.

Morgan believes that history is by its very nature a discipline which cannot be restricted to "the aristocracy of intellect." Unlike the sciences, history is not a body of knowledge set apart to be applied only by specialists. Neither does history filter down to the average man, as the sciences currently do in the form of advanced technology or in the fantasy literature of science fiction. History must be transmitted directly from the scholar to the "consumer," and it therefore behooves the historian to communicate his findings and his ideas in language chosen to reach the widest possible audience. Morgan, better than most historians of this century, has reached that wide reading public as well as the professionals he must satisfy. He has done so primarily by writing in language distinguished by simplicity, precision, grace, and wry humor. To achieve clarity and resonance he assumes that his audience is brighter than he is but completely ignorant of his subject and therefore dependent on the information he makes available. With Morgan, this is a formula for writing remarkable history.

The history he writes is intended to be "a creative ordering of past events." His sensitivity to the ambiguous relationship between the historian and his sources has been evident in all his works and made explicit in some. In his introduction to *Prologue to Revolution*, he warns of "the welter of complexities and contradictions that may lie behind the simplest statement of fact" in any history book. He comments at greater length on this difficulty in *The Founding of Massachusetts* (1964). Acknowledging that the historian's distance from past events grants him more objectivity than participants could hope to have, he also notes that the historian "is subject to a similar tendency to see events as he wants to see them, to see things happening as he thinks they ought to have happened." For this reason, "serious historians and teachers of history always insist on the need for continual recurrence to the sources." They and their students should be acutely aware "that what happened, what the sources say happened, and what historians say happened are not necessarily the same thing," Morgan declares. The importance of remaining alive to unanticipated possibilities in the records of the past cannot be overemphasized. Good historians expand our understanding of the past by seeing things they expected to find in the sources; great historians change our thinking about the past by finding things they never expected to see in the sources.

When Morgan turned to examine the founding of Virginia, the natural beginning point for a larger history "of American attitudes toward work" and their implications, he found first a problem and then a paradox. The attempt to establish an outpost where the "good Indians" of Virginia might be brought under "the gentle government of the English" and where the dispossessed of overpopulated England might build a society blessed with "peace and prosperity" resulted in a "fiasco." Instead of creating a model community of Englishmen living in easy harmony with their Indian neighbors, James Town's settlers passed from truculent dependence on trade with the natives to progressively escalating warfare with them. Instead of becoming "a haven for England's suffering poor," Virginia became "a death trap for most who went there," a colony which existed in a state of almost continuous crisis during its first two decades. Most explanations of that disastrous record refer to the idle disposition or the laziness of the colony's inhabitants. Evidently, the wrong Englishmen with the wrong expectations had been sent to Virginia, and the settlement had been organized under the wrong kind of arrangements. What the colony needed was a healthy dose of free enterprise, or, at least until the colony got its feet on the ground, the so-called "stern discipline" of a Captain John Smith to shake the laggards up. For generations, historians have gone to Smith's description of his reordering of life in James Town: "the company [being] divided into tennes, fifteenes, or as the business required, 4 hours each day spent in worke, the rest in pastimes and merry exercise." By his own account, those words brought Morgan up short. Four hours' labor a day amounted to "stern discipline"? What manner of work ethic was this? Where were the traces of any version of a "Puritan Ethic" to be found? Morgan determined that such traces could not be found, that he faced a different problem altogether, and that its dimensions were enormous. His first thoughts on the problem appeared in the 1971 essays, "The Labor Problem at Jamestown, 1607-1618" and "The First American Boom: Virginia 1618 to 1630." He disclosed the broad outlines of his thesis in his presidential address to the Organization of American Historians in April 1972 and finally brought his treatment of the problem to conclusion in *American Slavery, American Freedom: The Ordeal of Colonial Virginia* (1975). This is, arguably, Morgan's most important book; it is unquestionably his most controversial work.

His analysis of how African slavery became the dominant element in Virginia's labor system and of how the small group of freemen who so frightened the big planters during Bacon's Rebellion of 1676 came to be their reliable allies a half-century later is rich in complexity and irony. Morgan insisted that "slave labor, in spite of its seeming superiority, was actually not as advantageous as indentured labor during the first half of the seventeenth century." Only when conditions changed did planters buy slaves instead of servants, but by the end of the century they were buying them in such numbers as to transform the plantation system. That slaves never passed from servitude to discontented freedom and thus never threatened the peace of the colony and the property of the prosperous as indentured servants had done was an incidental byproduct of change. Yet Morgan found nothing incidental about the coming of racism to Virginia. The men who "learned their first lessons in racial hatred by putting down the Indians" did not, he argued, transfer their loathing naturally and automatically to the blacks. Instead, the planter elite systematically promoted racism in order "to separate dangerous free whites from dangerous slave blacks by a screen of racial contempt."

In the ultimate paradox of *American Slavery, American Freedom*, Morgan suggested that the close connection between the growth of "liberty and equality" and "the rise of slavery" in Virginia constituted a "marriage" of the two developments. When Virginians became remarkably eloquent about the threat of "slavery" and the danger to their "liberties" in new British measures of the 1760s and 1770s, Morgan saw in their rhetoric a vital link between the very real freedom they enjoyed, the bondage they imposed on others, and "a conglomeration of republican ideas" from which the ideology of the Revolution was drawn. The concept of "independence" was central. The very existence of republicanism required a large body of free, independent citizens. Because dependent, men only nominally free men were a menace to a republic. Several British authorities actually recommended enslavement or something very like it for the indigent poor, Morgan learned. Virginians thus solved the social question most troublesome to republicanism by building "a society in which most of the poor were enslaved." They could embrace republican liberty and republican equality because slavery, compounded with the racism it acquired in America, dispelled "the fear and contempt that men in England . . . felt for the inarticulate lower classes." This solution, for Morgan, raised unanswered final questions: "Was the vision of a nation of equals flawed at the source by contempt for both the poor and the black? Is America still colonial Virginia writ large?"

American Slavery, American Freedom surely seemed paradoxical for some of Morgan's readers. Anyone persisting in the notion that the writer fit comfortably into the conservative, "Neo-Whig" school of Revolutionary history must have been at least puzzled by this book. Morgan had earlier tried to disclaim that label in "Conflict and Consensus in the American Revolution." Again disputing the existence of class conflict in Revolutionary America, he insisted that conflict, especially sectional conflict, had been an important part of that world. On the other hand, controversy with England "tended to suppress or encompass social conflicts" within America. Yet American Revolutionaries achieved "not a static consensus but one . . . that invited conflicts and still invites them." For the Bicentennial, he gathered together this and other articles, including one previously unpublished piece, in a collection called *The Challenge of the American Revolution* (1976). The new essay, "Challenge and Response: Reflections on the Bicentennial," suggested that the crux of the Revolution was the movement's success in enabling men to "realize that things they had taken for granted were not necessarily so." The Revolutionary experience led Americans to discard or alter three important, long-standing assumptions. First was the belief that American diversity defied the creation of a union, for Americans achieved union within a remarkably short piece of time. Second was the judgment that geographic and demographic conditions would forever "make manufacturing an unprofitable, uneconomical, and unwise activity for Americans"; adapting the country to manufacturing took longer, but the change came no less surely. Last, Morgan saw in the Revolution "a challenge to think whether society might not do better to leave men the way God created them, namely equal, rather than piling the weight of the extravagant few on the shoulders of the many, in the hierarchy of social dignity that men had hitherto taken for granted." If this be Whiggery, or Neo-Whiggery, it is of the order which shakes foundations.

The Bicentennial also offered Morgan the chance to reflect, in *The Meaning of Independence* (1976), on the beliefs of John Adams, George Washington, and Thomas Jefferson. All were men of substance and drive, yet in Morgan's opinion, only Jefferson "would have attained a large stature in any century or in any country," and none of them might have risen beyond modest provincial prominence had the first British Empire continued undisturbed. In a sense, the American Revolution created Adams, Washington, and Jefferson, as we know them, and Morgan offered provocative suggestions about how it did so. All three were ambitious, hardworking men, but, in all three, ambition and exertion extended beyond mere self-gratification. Each also had his vanities, frailties, aspects of personality and character that rendered him less than a god, which is to say human. Adams's provinciality, constriction of mind, and tactlessness intruded upon every endeavor. Washington sometimes manifested "an unabashed concern for his own economic interest in his correspondence" that still makes the reader gasp. Jefferson, the most cosmopolitan of the three, viewed cities and city people parochially, and his "attitudes toward blacks and toward women" were almost antediluvian. Yet each man achieved greatness in the world the Revolution made, Morgan declared. Given the chance to act and to think in a Continental sphere, Adams outgrew many of his limitations. Washington turned what were in other circumstances unlovely traits "into national assets." And Jefferson, for all the flaws, "in most questions relating to human dignity, and especially in devising ways to protect and nourish human dignity . . . *was* ahead of his time and ahead of ours."

Morgan is presently working on a study of the great "political fictions" which prevailed in Anglo-American culture between the seventeenth and the early nineteenth centuries. His research is built on the premise that every "government, of course, rests on fictions, whether we call them that or self-evident truths." Some qualities can be anticipated in the finished work. It will be written, of course, in sparkling prose. Furthermore, Morgan's fascination with the paradoxical, the ironic aspects of the predicaments men confronted in the past, will no doubt continue. His alertness to the possibility that the sources will suggest things about the past he never expected to find will also prevail, as will his sensitivity to the subtle nuances of the human experience in whatever time and place. Moreover, his treatment of people and events of the past will feature, whenever possible, his characteristic dry wit. Nothing less is possible, from the man who returned from a 1968-1969 stint as Johnson Research Professor at the University of Wisconsin to report delightedly to his friends in New Haven that he had discovered a popular rock band in Madison, Wisconsin, calling itself The Puritan Dilemma.

Other:

"The American Indian: Incorrigible Individualist," introduction to *The Mirror of the Indian: An Exhibition of books and other source materials by Spanish, French, and English historians and colonists of North America from the 16th throughout the 18th century* (Providence: Associates of the John Carter Brown Library, 1958), pp. 5-19;

Prologue to Revolution: Sources and Documents on the Stamp Act Crisis, 1764-1766, edited by Morgan (Chapel Hill: University of North Carolina, 1959; London: Oxford University Press, 1960);

"The Making of Paul Revere," introduction to *Paul Revere's Three Accounts of His Famous Ride* (Boston: Massachusetts Historical Society, 1961);

"The American Revolution Considered as an Intellectual Movement," in *Paths of American Thought*, edited by Arthur M. Schlesinger, Jr., and Morton White (Boston: Houghton Mifflin, 1963), pp. 11-33;

The Founding of Massachusetts: Historians and the Sources, edited by Morgan (Indianapolis: Bobbs-Merrill, 1964);

Puritan Political Ideas, 1558-1794, edited by Morgan (Indianapolis: Bobbs-Merrill, 1965);

The American Revolution: Two Centuries of Interpretation, edited by Morgan (Englewood Cliffs, N. J.: Prentice-Hall, 1965; Lytham St. Annes, U. K.: Spectrum Books, 1966);

"The Historians of Early New England," in *The Reinterpretation of Early American History*, edited by Ray Allen Billington (San Marino, Cal.:

Huntington Library, 1966), pp. 41-63;
"Conflict and Consensus in the American Revolution," in *Essays on the American Revolution*, edited by Stephen G. Kurtz and James H. Hutson (Chapel Hill: University of North Carolina, 1973), pp. 289-309.

Periodical Publications:

"The Case Against Anne Hutchinson," *New England Quarterly*, 10 (December 1937): 635-649;

"Light on the Puritans from John Hull's Notebooks," *New England Quarterly*, 15 (March 1942): 95-101;

"The Puritans and Sex," *New England Quarterly*, 15 (December 1942): 591-607;

"Colonial Ideas of Parliamentary Power, 1764-1766," *William and Mary Quarterly*, 5 (July 1948): 311-341;

"Thomas Hutchinson and the Stamp Act," *New England Quarterly*, 21 (December 1948): 459-492;

"The Puritan's Marriage with God," *South Atlantic Quarterly*, 38 (January 1949): 107-112;

"The Postponement of the Stamp Act," *William and Mary Quarterly*, 7 (July 1950): 353-392;

Michael Wigglesworth, "The Diary of Michael Wigglesworth, 1653-1657: The Conscience of a Puritan," edited by Morgan, in *Transactions, 1942-1946*, Publications of The Colonial Society of Massachusetts, 35 (1951): 311-444; republished in book form as *The Diary of Michael Wigglesworth, 1653-1657: The Conscience of a Puritan* (New York: Harper & Row, 1965; London: Harper & Row, 1966);

"The Colonial Scene," introduction by Morgan, in *Proceedings* of the American Antiquarian Society, 60 (April 1951): 54-71;

"Edmund Pendleton on the Virginia Resolves," *Maryland Historical Magazine*, 46 (June 1951): 71-77;

"The American Revolution: Revisions in Need of Revising," *William and Mary Quarterly*, 14 (January 1957): 3-15;

"John White and the Sarsaparilla," *William and Mary Quarterly*, 14 (July 1957): 414-417;

"What Every Yale Freshman Should Know," *Saturday Review*, 43 (23 January 1960): 13-14;

"New England Puritanism: Another Approach," *William and Mary Quarterly*, 18 (April 1961): 236-242;

"John Adams and the Puritan Tradition," *New England Quarterly*, 34 (December 1961): 512-529;

"Perry Miller and the Historians," *Proceedings* of the American Antiquarian Society, 73 (April 1964): 11-18;

"Miller's Williams," *New England Quarterly*, 38 (December 1965): 513-523;

"The Political Establishments of the United States 1784," edited by Morgan, in *William and Mary Quarterly*, 23 (April 1966): 286-308;

"The Puritan Ethic and the American Revolution," *William and Mary Quarterly*, 24 (January 1967): 3-43;

"The First American Boom: Virginia 1618 to 1630," *William and Mary Quarterly*, 28 (April 1971): 169-198;

"The Labor Problem in Jamestown, 1607-1618," *American Historical Review*, 76 (June 1971): 595-611;

"Slavery and Freedom: The American Paradox," *Journal of American History*, 59 (June 1972): 5-29;

"The Great Political Fiction," *New York Review of Books*, 25 (9 March 1978): 13-18.

References:

Jack P. Greene, "The Flight from Determinism: A Review of Recent Literature on the Coming of the American Revolution," *South Atlantic Quarterly*, 61 (Spring 1962): 235-259;

Greene, ed., *The Reinterpretation of the American Revolution: 1763-1789* (New York: Harper & Row, 1968), pp. 2-72;

John Higham, "Beyond Consensus: The Historian as Moral Critic," *American Historical Review*, 67 (April 1962): 609-625;

Darret B. Rutman, "God's Bridge Falling Down: 'Another Approach' to New England Puritanism Assayed," *William and Mary Quarterly*, 19 (July 1962): 408-421;

Page Smith, "David Ramsay and the Causes of the American Revolution," *William and Mary Quarterly*, 17 (January 1960): 51-77;

Gordon S. Wood, "Rhetoric and Reality in the American Revolution," *William and Mary Quarterly*, 23 (January 1966): 3-32;

C. Vann Woodward, "The Southern Ethic in a Puritan World," *William and Mary Quarterly*, 25 (July 1968): 343-370.

Samuel Eliot Morison

B. D. Bargar
University of South Carolina

BIRTH: Boston, Massachusetts, 9 July 1887, to John Holmes and Emily Marshall Eliot Morison.

EDUCATION: A.B., Harvard College, 1908; Ecole des Sciences Politiques, Paris, 1908-1909; Ph.D., Harvard University, 1912.

MARRIAGES: 28 May 1910 to Elizabeth Shaw Greene; children: Elizabeth Gray, Emily Marshall, Peter Greene, and Catharine; 29 December 1949 to Priscilla Barton.

AWARDS AND HONORS: Pulitzer Prize for *Admiral of the Ocean Sea: A Life of Christopher Columbus*, 1943; Columbia University Bancroft Prize for *The Rising Sun in the Pacific* (volume 3, *History of United States Naval Operations in World War II*), 1949; Theodore Roosevelt Distinguished Service Medal, 1956; Edison Foundation Award, 1957; Pulitzer Prize for *John Paul Jones: A Sailor's Biography*, 1960; Mahan Award of the Navy League, 1961; Balzan Foundation Award for History, 1963; Presidential Medal of Freedom, 1964; Bancroft Prize for *The European Discovery of America: The Northern Voyages*, 1972; eleven honorary doctorates.

DEATH: Boston, Massachusetts, 15 May 1976.

BOOKS: *The Life and Letters of Harrison Gray Otis, Federalist, 1765-1848*, 2 volumes (Boston & New York: Houghton Mifflin, 1913);
The Maritime History of Massachusetts, 1783-1860 (Boston & New York: Houghton Mifflin, 1921; London: Heinemann, 1923);
The Oxford History of the United States, 1783-1917, 2 volumes (London: Oxford University Press, 1927);
The Growth of the American Republic, by Morison and Henry Steele Commager (New York & London: Oxford University Press, 1930); revised in 2 volumes, by Morison, Commager, and William E. Leuchtenburg (New York & London: Oxford University Press, 1969);
Builders of the Bay Colony (Boston & New York: Houghton Mifflin, 1930; London: Oxford University Press, 1930);

The Tercentennial History of Harvard University, 3 volumes (Cambridge: Harvard University Press, 1929-1936);
The Puritan Pronaos: Studies in the Intellectual Life of New England in the Seventeenth Century (New York: New York University Press, 1936; London: Oxford University Press, 1936); revised as *The Intellectual Life of Colonial New England* (New York: New York University Press, 1956);
Three Centuries of Harvard, 1636-1936 (Cambridge: Harvard University Press, 1936);
The Second Voyage of Columbus: From Cadiz to Hispaniola and the Discovery of the Lesser Antilles (Oxford: Clarendon Press, 1939);
Portuguese Voyages to America in the Fifteenth Century (Cambridge: Harvard University Press, 1940);
Admiral of the Ocean Sea: A Life of Christopher Columbus, 2 volumes (Boston: Little, Brown, 1942); abridged as *Christopher Columbus, Mariner*, 1 volume (Boston: Atlantic/Little, Brown, 1955; London: Faber & Faber, 1956);
Fullness of Life: A Memoir of Elizabeth Shaw Morison, 1886-1945 (Boston: Merrymount Press, 1945);
History of United States Naval Operations in World War II, 15 volumes (Boston: Atlantic/Little, Brown, 1947-1962; London: Oxford University Press, 1948-1962);
History as a Literary Art: An Appeal to Young Historians (Boston: Old South Leaflets, Series 2, no. 1, 1949?);
The Ropemakers of Plymouth: A History of the Plymouth Cordage Company, 1824-1949 (Boston: Houghton Mifflin, 1950);
By Land and By Sea: Essays and Addresses (New York: Knopf, 1953);
Freedom in Contemporary Society (Boston: Little, Brown, 1956; London: Oxford University Press, 1956);
The Story of the "Old Colony" of New Plymouth, 1620-1692 (New York: Knopf, 1956);
Strategy and Compromise (Boston: Atlantic/Little, Brown, 1958); republished as *American Contributions to Strategy of World War II* (London: Faber & Faber, 1958);
John Paul Jones: A Sailor's Biography (Boston: Little,

Samuel Eliot Morison in the study at his Boston home

Brown, 1959; London: Faber & Faber, 1960);

The Story of Mount Desert Island (Boston: Little, Brown, 1960);

The Scholar in America (New York: Oxford University Press, 1961);

One Boy's Boston, 1887-1901 (Boston: Houghton Mifflin, 1962);

The Two-Ocean War: A Short History of the United States Navy in the Second World War (Boston: Little, Brown, 1963);

The Caribbean As Columbus Saw It, by Morison and Mauricio Obregón (Boston: Little, Brown, 1964);

Vistas of History (New York: Knopf, 1964);

Spring Tides (Boston: Houghton Mifflin, 1965);

The Oxford History of the American People (New York &

London: Oxford University Press, 1965);

"Old Bruin": Commodore Matthew C. Perry, 1794-1858
(Boston: Little, Brown, 1967; London: Oxford University Press, 1968);

Harrison Gray Otis, 1765-1848: The Urbane Federalist
(Boston: Houghton Mifflin, 1969);

Dissent in Three American Wars, by Morison, Frederick Merk, and Frank Freidel (Cambridge: Harvard University Press, 1970; London: Oxford University Press, 1970);

The European Discovery of America: The Northern Voyages, A.D. 500-1600 (New York: Oxford University Press, 1971);

Samuel de Champlain: Father of New France (Boston: Little, Brown, 1972);

The European Discovery of America: The Southern Voyages, A.D. 1492-1616 (New York: Oxford University Press, 1974);

Vita Nuova: A Memoir of Priscilla Barton Morison
(Northeast Harbor, Maine: Privately printed, 1975);

A Concise History of the American Republic, by Morison, Commager, and Leuchtenburg (New York: Oxford University Press, 1977);

Sailor Historian: A Samuel Eliot Morison Reader, edited by Emily Morison Beck (Boston: Houghton Mifflin, 1977).

Samuel Eliot Morison, the eminent Harvard historian, followed in the footsteps of many earlier historians who believed that history should be well written as well as accurate prose. Practicing this dictum, he produced more than forty volumes of widely read biographies and other historical narratives of unusually high literary value, as well as more than two hundred articles for learned journals and historical publications. His career was filled with many surprising contrasts. His long lifetime included elements of both stability and mobility: he resided in the same house in Boston for most of his eighty-eight years, but he also traveled extensively, visiting Britain, Spain, Greece, Morocco, Mexico, the South Pacific, Japan, and the coasts of North and South America from Labrador to the Straits of Magellan. His writing and historical research required him to spend a great deal of time in academic cloisters, but he also led a very active life outside the university; he served his country in both war and peace. During World War I he briefly wore an army uniform before acting as a consultant to the American delegation to the Paris Peace Conference in 1919. In World War II he received a commission in the United States Navy and participated in many of the sea battles he was later to describe so vividly.

This son of New England was very proud of his Puritan heritage, and yet his own life was quite ecumenical. If there was one thing that his Puritan ancestors detested more than Satan himself, it was episcopacy, yet this scion of several of New England's oldest families preferred to take communion in the Episcopal church. By contrast with the antipapist attitude of his ancestors, Morison gladly accepted nearly one-third of his honorary doctorates from Roman Catholic colleges; he even journeyed to Rome in order to receive the prestigious Balzan Award in the company of fellow-recipient, Pope John XXIII.

History, as far as Morison was concerned, was primarily literature. He continued in his own career the tradition established by George Bancroft, John L. Motley, William H. Prescott, and especially Francis Parkman. In so doing, Morison ignored or avoided several contemporary trends such as economic determinism and psychohistory. The stories that he fashioned out of historical data were usually inspired by one or more recurrent themes. First, his love for his own family directed his attention as an historian to his ancestors and the New England region, especially the colonial period. Second, a boyhood interest in sailing developed into a lifelong love of the sea; historically, this meant sailors, navigators and their problems, explorations, and the whole vast canvas called "the expansion of Europe." Maritime commerce and the story of great naval engagements also are part of this theme. Finally, Morison admired great leaders who lived during his own time as well as in the past. Intrepid explorers, discoverers of new coastlines, and great naval heroes from John Paul Jones to admirals in World War II fascinated him and therefore recur time and again in his historical writings.

Born in his grandfather's house, the Boston dwelling which he would eventually acquire as his own home, Morison was surrounded by history. His grandfather could recall once having been held on the lap of the Marquis de Lafayette when the great revolutionary leader visited Boston in the early nineteenth century. His schooling included a basic classical curriculum at St. Paul's in preparation for his entrance to Harvard College in 1904. Although he first thought that he would become a mathematician, some negative experiences with calculus combined with strong, positive influences from distinguished historians turned him in the direction of history. As an undergraduate, he knew and worked closely with Albert Bushnell Hart, Edward Channing, and Frederick Jackson Turner. He assisted Hart, often returning to Harvard with graded papers for Hart's classes in his horse's saddlebags, and he eventually took over Channing's colonial history class. His graduate studies culminated in the Ph.D. degree in 1912. After a brief interval teaching in California, he joined the Harvard faculty, where he remained for forty years. Morison retired from his teaching duties in 1955 as the Jonathan Trumbull Professor of American History, emeritus.

While spending his early years in his grandfather's house, Morison became aware that some important papers, which had belonged to one of his ancestors, were stored in the wine cellar. Those manuscripts became the principal data for Morison's doctoral dissertation and his first book, *The Life and Letters of Harrison Gray Otis, Federalist, 1765-1848* (1913). His great-great-grandfather, Harrison Gray Otis, had been an important leader of the New England Federalists. Morison amply considered the political side of his ancestor's accomplishments; in fact, he devoted six chapters to a discussion of the Hartford Convention during which New Englanders seriously considered seceding from the Union. But to a political narrative, Morison added innumerable details concerning the social life of Otis's times, an innovation not entirely approved by his peers and critics. An aspect of Morison's style was already apparent in this first publication—an influence no doubt of his classical education—the use of antithesis: Otis was "Sociable without dissipation, . . . brilliant without hypocrisy," according to his young descendant. Even in this first book, the reader became aware that the author was a man of decided opinions forcefully stated when supported by the historical facts.

Morison was very familiar with Frederick Jackson Turner's thesis concerning the influence of the frontier upon American historical development. He also admired the contributions of the English historian R. H. Tawney in the relatively new area of socioeconomic history. Most of all, he admired the writings of Francis Parkman and the evocative way in which he had described the wilderness. Morison decided to combine these various influences and apply them to the sea. His regional loyalties and his hobby of sailing admirably suited him to compose his second book, *The Maritime History of Massachusetts, 1783-1860*, published in 1921. The author delighted in describing the lives of both sea captains and common sailors. He lovingly painted word pictures of the great clipper ships used in the China trade. In fact, Morison regarded these beautiful sailing vessels as America's contribution to art and technology worthy of comparison to the Parthenon of ancient Greece or the Gothic cathedrals of medieval France.

In 1922, Morison accepted the invitation of Oxford University to become the first Harmsworth Professor of American History. This post was unique at the time since English universities regarded the history of the United States as too young a subject for serious study. During his three years at Oxford, Morison compiled an introductory textbook, *The Oxford History of the United States, 1783-1917*, published in 1927. With English students very much in mind, he included a great deal of material which would not be generally familiar to non-American readers. The preparation of such a book for American college students was the logical next step. Thus, in collaboration with Henry Steele Commager, Morison published a text, familiar to generations of undergraduates, *The Growth of the American Republic*. First published in 1930, this popular survey underwent six editions and is still available. Some students, however, find it difficult to share their instructors' enthusiasm for this textbook. In the first edition, Morison contributed all the chapters dealing with the colonial period and national history up to the Civil War. In more recent editions, he also wrote some of the World War II material.

The 1930s found Morison turning his attention increasingly to the seventeenth century in New England. He was living in an atmosphere in which it was popular to be anti-Puritan. Such disasters as Prohibition and book banning were blamed upon "Puritanism," which was wrongly identified as a direct inheritance from early New England. Morison may have felt that his ancestors and his region were being maligned, but he also decried the kind of history which he classified as "debunking." He strove to demonstrate in his writing the many constructive features of colonial Puritans. In *Builders of the Bay Colony* (1930), for example, he emphasized their many intellectual contributions. Morison did not agree with the narrow theology of the Puritans nor with their obsession with sin, but it was a Puritan, after all, Henry Dunster, who founded Harvard College. Thus, Puritanism did not consist entirely of arid sermons and acrimonious disputes.

As Morison's alma mater approached her three-hundredth birthday, he announced his intention to write a history of the institution. The president of Harvard, A. Lawrence Lowell, endorsed the idea, and *The Founding of Harvard College* rapidly appeared, followed by a two-volume study, *Harvard College in the Seventeenth Century*. This trilogy, collectively known as *The Tercentennial History of Harvard University* (1929-1936), was eventually followed by a fourth volume entitled *Three Centuries of Harvard, 1636-1936* (1936). This procedure illustrates a technique which Morison was to use on an even grander scale when he wrote about World War II: the first several volumes contained his story in great detail; the last volume encapsulated and summarized the whole narrative in a relatively few pages. *Three Centuries of Harvard* was obviously intended for a wider audience than professional historians, especially among alumni. Its subject matter ranged from student games and pranks to presidential inaugurations and other official ceremonies. *The Tercentennial History of Harvard University* shows Morison's ability to blend three different types of history: official, academic, and popular. It was official because the institution endorsed the project; it was academic because it was based upon deep and accurate research; it was popular because the author had already developed an engaging style which could appeal to any educated reader.

It was typical of Morison's working habits that he often had more than one project in progress at the same time. He once said that he liked to have a minor effort going while he was engaged in a major work. While seeing his Harvard volumes through the presses, he also published *The Puritan Pronaos* in 1936. Although scarcely a "minor work," it contained within the covers of a single volume several *Studies in the Intellectual Life of New England in the Seventeenth Century*, to cite the subtitle. Twenty years later, a second editon of this book appeared, without the rather mystifying Greek word in the title, as *The Intellectual Life of Colonial New England* (1956). Providing yet further evidence of intellectual activity among the Puritans of the colonial period, Morison ardently disputed the contention of Charles Francis Adams in 1893 that this was a "glacial period" in American history.

While it was fashionable for the "debunkers" to point to feet of clay, Morison strongly believed that people needed their heroes. He agreed with earlier attitudes, such as Thomas Carlyle's, that Great Men are significant in history. One did not need a Parson Weems to fabricate the story of George Washington and the cherry tree, but the truth about outstanding leaders and their constructive contributions should be the stuff of history. While the multivolume *Dictionary of American Biography* was in the process of publication, Morison contributed more than two dozen biographical sketches to the collection. Thus, he was able to practice what he preached in writing short, constructive accounts of many leaders of colonial America.

Two of the major influences in Morison's life,

his love of the sea and his interest in biography, combined to lead him into the preparation of one of his most entertaining books, *Admiral of the Ocean Sea: A Life of Christopher Columbus* (1942). The first two volumes of this biography of Christopher Columbus contain ample critical apparatus in the form of footnotes and documentation; a one-volume popular edition for the general reader omitted the footnotes and concentrated upon the telling of a good but factually accurate story. Eventually, a paperback version, *Christopher Columbus, Mariner*, appeared in 1955, greatly reducing the bulk without jeopardizing the substance of Morison's yarn.

The preparation of these volumes dealing with the life of Columbus constituted a unique contribution to historical methodology and literature. Like Parkman, Morison believed in visiting the scene of historical events, but Columbus had spent most of his life at sea. Of course Morison consulted the available published and manuscript material in Spain, but it was his tracing of the sea routes and land falls of Columbus's four voyages to the New World that gave this biography its special flavor. For this purpose Morison organized the Harvard Columbus Expedition in 1939, using a modern sailing vessel approximately the size of the *Santa Maria* to cross the ocean. With a copy of the Admiral's *Journal* at hand, the navigator followed the historic path from the Canary Islands to the West Indies. Since many of the names on modern charts had been changed since Columbus's day, this method made it possible for the first time in the twentieth century to know precisely which headland or island Columbus discovered, named, and claimed for Castile in the 1490s. These transatlantic voyages he supplemented with several shorter visits to the Caribbean. The result is to give this biography a quality of immediacy which had been missing in all previous studies of the Admiral's life. In addition, Morison's style had developed to the point where the narrative flowed along with the ease of works of fiction. The reader could readily recapture the feelings and experiences known to those who actually sailed with Columbus. The Pulitzer Prize committee chose well when they awarded the prize for biography to this book in 1943.

Previous biographies of Columbus had been written by the type of authors whom Morison described as "armchair navigators." On the other hand, he contributed to historical knowledge the identification of more than thirty New World landfalls recorded in Columbus's *Journal*. Morison's firsthand observation was indispensable in this effort. Retracing the comings and goings of the Admiral, especially among the islands of the Caribbean, caused the historian to admire his hero's navigational ability. The book also contained some exceptionally fine descriptions of the sea, the sky, and the clouds. Some recent scholars have felt that Morison was too uncritical of Columbus, that he was "pro-Columbus," in other words. Morison, however, acknowledged certain defects of character which made Columbus a poor administrator but gave high praise to the Admiral's seamanship where such praise was due. Admittedly, Columbus's biography is filled with controversies and historical arguments. The simple question of where the man was born, for example, has several possible answers. Morison used two methods of dealing with these arguments: sometimes he stated both sides of the debate and allowed the reader to choose his own preferred position; more characteristically, however, he dismissed all possible answers but one. Some critics have found this approach a bit arrogant, but the result is a masterful interpretation, which the reader is tempted to share rather than to wallow in ambiguity. The question of birthplace, for example: European writers tended to speculate that the great explorer was born in Portugal, Castile, Catalonia, the Balearics, or France, the exact location usually depending upon the nationality of the author. Morison simply swept these theories to one side and accepted with the confidence of common sense and his own research the conclusion that Columbus had been born in Genoa.

If there is one single thread that appears early and recurs frequently throughout Morison's long and distinguished career, it is the "Columbus Theme." After completing three years at Oxford in the Harmsworth professorship, he, the first Mrs. Morison, and their children returned to the United States by way of Spain. Thus, it was as early as 1925 that he first saw archival material dealing with Columbus. In 1939 he had published a monograph entitled *The Second Voyage of Columbus: From Cadiz to Hispaniola and the Discovery of the Lesser Antilles* and the following year, *Portuguese Voyages to America in the Fifteenth Century*. These two works served as preliminary essays in the field and paved the way for the great work, *Admiral of the Ocean Sea*, in its various two-volume and one-volume manifestations. After World War II, Morison returned to the Columbus question, this time assisted by Mauricio Obregón. Together they flew over the many islands in the Caribbean discovered by Columbus and prepared an illustrated book, *The Caribbean as Columbus Saw It* (1964). Thus for a period of approximately forty years Morison was concerned with Columbus and

had, as early as the Pulitzer Prize year (1943), proven himself to be a qualified authority on the subject.

During World War II Morison thought that he could make a valuable contribution to the war effort by applying his "Columbus technique" to a history of the United States Navy in combat. When he suggested such a project to Franklin D. Roosevelt, the president concurred. Morison received a commission as lieutenant commander in the Naval Reserve and a very unusual assignment. The resulting works were quite different from the official histories produced by the other branches of the armed forces in that Morison secured an agreement which freed him from any censorship or board of review. By consenting to publish nothing until after the war, the writer was enabled to undertake genuine history untainted by propaganda. In his own mind he would follow the example of the great Greek historian Thucydides and write objectively about a war in which he was actually participating. Many of the officers with whom he served had already read *Admiral of the Ocean Sea* and were prepared to cooperate with him, in spite of (as he later wrote) "the Navy's congenital suspicion of officers who write books."

In preparing his material for later publication, Morison crossed the Atlantic several times, especially in connection with antisubmarine warfare. Most notably, he traveled over the Pacific and gained a firsthand view of naval campaigns against the Japanese. While the other services entrusted their respective histories to committees, Morison worked with a very small staff. Some of his former students, now ensigns, supplied information about operations where he could not be present. Only two clerical and two professional assistants helped him to produce the fifteen-volume *History of United States Naval Operations in World War II* at the rate of about one volume per year between 1947 and 1962.

The agreement to delay publication until after hostilities had ceased gave Morison distinct advantages: he was able to consult captured enemy documents, and he was also enabled to visit in peacetime various beachheads and other important sites like Tokyo Harbor. This procedure helped him to write a balanced and objective account. To cite one example: He once thought he witnessed two Japanese vessels set afire during a night battle. Japanese records later revealed, however, that only one ship had been lost at the time; it had broken in half after an explosion and looked like two ships afire. Such painstaking questing for accuracy was a hallmark of Morison's method, and yet his style made the fifteen volumes very exciting to read. Some of the same sense of immediacy was easily recaptured in the television series "Victory at Sea." In this series, one of Morison's staff assistants, Henry Solomon, Jr., applied the historian's "Columbus technique" to the war on the oceans, supplementing vivid word pictures with old newsreels and other visual documents.

There is a sharp contrast between Morison's history of the navy and the accounts produced by the other services. The army, for example, eventually published more than sixty volumes; the air force and the marines also had their multivolume series. Prepared by groups of historians working under "official" supervision, none of them approaches Morison's work either for popularity or readability.

Yet not everyone who read the work agreed with the author's interpretations. In 1948, for example, when volume three, *The Rising Sun in the Pacific*, appeared, the influential *Chicago Tribune* took umbrage with Morison's account of the Japanese attack on Pearl Harbor. The newspaper had always alleged that President Roosevelt himself was largely responsible for American entrance into World War II. Morison's presentation of the story differed so radically from theirs that the *Tribune* published an editorial in which they branded him "A Hired Liar." The argument also extended into the ranks of professional historians, with the venerable Charles A. Beard taking strong issue with Morison's interpretation. Greatly resenting the appellation "Court Historian," Morison insisted that he wrote from a historian's viewpoint and not from an official navy line. It was true that he had known FDR when they were both students at Harvard and that they had conversed in later years, but the historian insisted that the president had not attempted to influence his presentation of naval history. Detractors could argue that Morison was already so sympathetic with the administration that no pressure was necessary.

Still this naval history is no dryasdust, "objective" account. Morison was present at much of the action about which he wrote. He therefore infused his account with a sense of involvement, a quality of immediacy that makes the history live. The reader feels strong empathy not only with the commanders on the bridge but also with the ordinary seamen. The author made no attempt to disguise his admiration for certain heroes, Admirals Ernest King and Chester Nimitz, while he also recognized the abilities of enemies like Doenitz and Yamamoto.

As remarkable as this multivolume work is, it is all the more impressive for being the work of one man. True, he had the assistance of a small staff, but he verified all the research and composed the text in all fifteen volumes himself. The style remains consistent throughout; it is clearly not the work of a committee.

In accordance with his usual working methods, Morison was not satisfied with fifteen volumes replete with detail. He soon turned his attention to the preparation of a condensed one-volume account, *The Two-Ocean War: A Short History of the United States Navy in the Second World War*, which appeared in 1963. The scholarship entailed in the magnum opus thus became available to a wider audience. It was also typical of Morison's methods that during the years in which the naval history was his major project, he should write or edit eight other volumes.

Morison's philosophy of history is perhaps best comprehended by reading his books where he told "the story." But there were several occasions on which he felt compelled to articulate his attitude toward his craft. For example, when peers recognized his contributions to history by electing him president of the American Historical Association for 1950, he delivered an address entitled "Faith of an Historian," later incorporated in *By Land and By Sea: Essays and Addresses* (1953). Another of his essays containing similar sentiments, "The Experiences and Principles of an Historian," appeared in a subsequent collection, *Vistas of History* (1964). As outlined in these essays, Morison's view of history was based largely upon the lessons taught by Thucydides and Leopold von Ranke. The great Athenian defined history as the "true picture of events." The nineteenth-century German historian aspired to write of the past "exactly as it happened" (*wie es eigentlich gewesen*). In subscribing to these views, Morison believed that every historian should avoid presenting preconceived conclusions on the one hand and on the other that he should avoid romantic fiction.

Current in his own lifetime was a contrary view about the purpose of history espoused most notably by Charles A. Beard and Carl L. Becker. This school, the New History, advocated the use of history as a tool for social progress. Morison agreed with these progressive historians only to the extent of denying that complete, scientific objectivity was impossible. (History, Morison would agree, is not a science, not even a social science.) But, he continued, it is the duty of every historian to present the facts and not slant them in favor of a particular view of "progress." Morison, for example, believed that

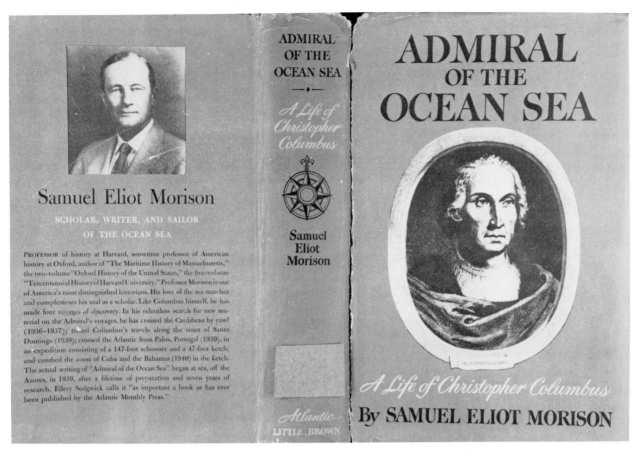

Dust jacket for Morison's 1942 book, in preparation for which he organized the Harvard Columbus Expedition to trace Columbus's routes in a modern sailing ship approximately the size of the Santa Maria

many of his contemporaries had allowed the horrors of World War I to drive them away from the study of war as a fact of history. Because of their concern with peace—and even with outright pacifism, in some cases—these historians had failed to prepare their students for the coming of World War II. In fact, historians as a group were losing influence which they had formerly possessed with the reading public, Morison believed, and he blamed "debunkers" for this trend. Depriving people of their heroes reduced their desire to read history. Furthermore, Morison was convinced that Marxism had also had a deleterious influence upon the writing of history. Ascribing historical motivation to impersonal forces, such as economics and dialectical materialism, gave the reader the impression that people had no control over their own lives. Needless to say, Morison also had little use for Freudian interpretations or psychohistory.

Believing very strongly that polished literary style was essential for the writing of history, Morison in the 1940s prepared an essay, *History as a Literary Art*, for his graduate students. This essay

was subsequently published by the Old South Association for general distribution in their pamphlet series; still later it was incorporated into the *Harvard Guide to American History*. Morison emphasized that history is literature; thus, style, clarity, and objectivity are all important. He denied that facts could speak for themselves but insisted instead that the historian must select and present the fruits of his research in an interesting and impartial manner. Because the best teachers of this approach were the classics, students who could not read Greek and Latin should read great literary historians, such as Parkman, Prescott, and John Fiske, who modeled their English composition upon classical stylists. Such recommendations were advanced in a period when Freudianism and the educational philosophy of John Dewey were very popular. Morison rejected both of these schools as proper guides for his students—or, indeed, for anyone who would write history.

In contrast to Morison's own interest in creating historical pictures painted upon broad canvases, he also advocated the study of local history as a pursuit for young historians. He had a curiously practical purpose in mind, for he believed that the aspiring historian who involved himself in local projects would avoid becoming "just another professor." Setting an example for his students to follow, Morison produced three works of essentially local history: *The Ropemakers of Plymouth: A History of the Plymouth Cordage Company, 1824-1949* (1950); *The Story of Mount Desert Island* (1960); and *One Boy's Boston, 1887-1901* (1962).

Also during the 1950s and 1960s, Morison edited for publication the works of several older historians, making it easier for modern readers to become acquainted with their ideas and their styles. *The Parkman Reader* (1955), for example, contains some of the best examples of that admired historian's writings about the struggle between England and France for the domination of North America. In a similar vein, a new edition of Prescott's *History of the Conquest of Peru* (1957) gives the reader a convenient glimpse of that historian's fascinating story of the Spanish in South America. Morison's *Journals and Other Documents on the Life and Voyages of Christopher Columbus* followed in 1963. But probably the most important contribution which Morison made in this aspect of his work was the editing of Governor William Bradford's *Of Plymouth Plantation* (1952). The original manuscript contained quaint spellings and odd usages which were characteristic of the early seventeenth century but were distracting and discouraging for many modern readers. Morison's version was easy to read because he modernized the text without depriving the reader of any of the flavor of Bradford's style. The story of the Pilgrims and of the beginnings of their settlement in New England was clearly and ably recounted by a contemporary who served as governor of the colony and thus participated in its ordeals and triumphs.

Morison, like any historian dealing with the Pilgrim Fathers, had to confront the legend of "Plymouth Rock." Everyone has seen a piece of calendar art, showing the first settlers, men and women, stepping ashore in a group. The good ship *Mayflower* lies at anchor in the background, while everyone steps onto the famous rock. Morison dealt with this legend more than once: Bradford and a small party of explorers in a ship's boat chose the actual site, while the *Mayflower* was anchored many miles away. Later, the settlers disembarked, probably without benefit of any rock. Yet, in his *The Ropemakers of Plymouth*, Morison quite uncharacteristically conceded, "We shall leave the Plymouth Rock tradition unchallenged." Perhaps even more typical of his adventuresomeness in historical writ-

ing was his statement in Bradford's *Of Plymouth Plantation* that Dorothy Bradford had committed suicide. The only evidence for this statement was Bradford's comment in a letter that he had returned from the reconnaissance to the ship where he learned that his wife had fallen overboard and "was drowned in the harbor." Later, in his history *Of Plymouth Plantation*, the governor failed to mention his wife's death at all. For Morison to conclude that Dorothy took her own life is a very bold argument based upon negative evidence, but he may have been right.

The sea was always a major theme in Morison's mind. From time to time he wrote essays about diverse subjects ranging from modern yacht design to Aeschylus's account of the Battle of Salamis. Eventually, he published a collection of these essays as a book, *Spring Tides* (1965). The sea and its tides provide a unifying theme throughout the small volume. Toward the end of his life, Morison helped his daughter Emily Morison Beck edit a representative selection of his writings, *Sailor Historian* (1977). The introduction to the penultimate essay eloquently depicts Morison's own view of the sea: "To ply, unhurried, the blue deeps, . . . communing with the element whence life sprang, hearing no other sound but the plash of oar, the flap of sail, the whistling of wind in the rigging, . . . revives one's strength and refreshes one's spirit."

Long after his official retirement from his Harvard classroom in 1955, Professor Morison was still dedicated to the art of biography; even longer after his retirement from the navy, Admiral Morison was devoted to the lives of naval heroes. In fact, in less than a decade he produced studies of the lives and careers of two distinctly different personalities: *John Paul Jones: A Sailor's Biography* (1959) and *"Old Bruin": Commodore Matthew C. Perry, 1794-1858* (1967). Typically, he had visited many of the scenes of the former's naval victories off the coasts of Scotland and England; he had also familiarized himself with Tokyo Bay before recounting the life of Perry, the man who "opened Japan." Not so characteristically, for an author who insisted upon classical standards in composition, Morison lapsed into unadulterated slang on many occasions. For example, he contrasted Perry's great dignity in diplomacy to "Biddle's palsy-walsy approach"; he described the Bakufu, or Council of the Shogunate, as being "really on the spot"; and a few pages later, he stated that the Japanese officials displayed "standoffishness." Some of his critics, especially in Great Britain, found these Americanisms a bit "off-putting." And yet, the Pulitzer Prize committee found the Jones biography worthy of an award in 1960.

Considering his own advice to young historians not to become "just another professor" and his own personal involvement with two world wars and with the controversy over FDR's responsibility for Pearl Harbor, Morison had surprisingly little to say about the major crisis of his later lifespan, the war in Vietnam. At a time when campuses and faculties were taking sides, sometimes with violence, the historian who had criticized his colleagues for pacifism in the 1920s and 1930s was virtually silent. He did, however, participate as one of the joint authors of a volume entitled *Dissent in Three American Wars* (1970). Morison's contribution naturally dealt with the War of 1812, which New Englanders insisted at the time was "Mr. Madison's War." This conflict was so unpopular that the region even considered secession. But, as Morison pointed out, dissent is not the same thing as treason, which may serve as a clue to his feelings about those who opposed American involvement in Southeast Asia.

In his mid-seventies, Morison wrote a single-volume summary of three centuries of American history published by the Oxford University Press and entitled *The Oxford History of the American People* (1965). The work was at the same time a triumph and a disappointment. In it, the author embodied the distillation of many decades of teaching and writing about historical problems. It was basically political history, but Morison typically included a great amount of social history as well. His emphasis was continuity rather than change; fundamental American institutions have survived great stresses, such as the Civil War. Some critics were disappointed that Morison had infused so little philosophy into the account, but he had always been more interested in the role of great leaders and in the development of human institutions. It is thus perfectly consistent with his prolific publications of the past that he should minimize impersonal forces: this book does not predict an inevitable Marxist utopia, nor an irresistible decline of Western civilization. The victory of the United States and her allies in World War II was less the work of Providence, according to Morison, than of the leadership of really able men. The best result of this kind of human leadership is the preservation of our classical heritage from Greece and Rome. By contrast, all forms of totalitarianism, including communism, clearly contradict ancient humanistic ideals. This is the extent of the "philosophy" set forth by this brilliantly narrated history of three hundred years of the American experience.

Long after retiring from teaching and at an age when another man would have been content to rest upon his laurels, Morison continued to write significant and consistently interesting books. In preparing his two volumes *The European Discovery of America: The Northern Voyages, A.D. 500-1600* (1971) and *The European Discovery of America: The Southern Voyages, A.D. 1492-1616* (1974), he varied his "Columbus technique" slightly. Since it was patently impossible for him to visit the entire coastline of two continents in a small sailboat, he supplemented his research with light airplanes. In visiting the many, occasionally controversial, landfalls of the first European explorers, the author flew over coastlines between Labrador and the Straits of Magellan. Making his observations from low-altitude flights, Morison once again succeeded in describing the early voyages of exploration with the sense of immediacy and with the attention to detail that can come only from personal experience.

One possible criticism of this valuable account is its ethnocentrism. Morison was convinced that Western civilization, with its classical heritage, was far superior to the culture of any American Indian group. Viewed from this perspective, Spain's "gift" to the native Americans, including Christianity, was incomparably greater than any loss they may have suffered. The facts that the conquistadores often acted in very uncivilized ways, that they used hunting dogs to terrorize the "savages," that they introduced the Inquisition, slavery, and epidemic diseases such as smallpox were easy to overlook. The "blessings" of Western civilization are, at best, mixed.

Characteristically, in the two volumes of *The European Discovery*, the historian calmly confronted controversial questions such as where in "New Albion" did Sir Francis Drake careen his ship the *Golden Hind*? Admiral Morison was able to use a United States Coast Guard cutter to visit the several places which Californians contended were the true landing site. Morison confidently rejected the Golden Gate and San Francisco Bay in favor of a beach just north of that area. This was "Drake's Bay," said the expert, and the reader feels compelled to agree.

In undertaking this vast research project, Morison encountered (not for the first time, of course) another hero, Samuel de Champlain. Departing slightly from the format adopted for *The Northern Voyages*, Morison produced a biography, *Samuel de Champlain: Father of New France* (1972), which paid tribute to the French explorer who deserves his title "Father of Canada." Again, the author supplemented his archival research with overflights in a small aircraft from which he viewed many of the areas discovered by Champlain. This bird's-eye view did not deprive the reader of any of the pleasure of traveling vicariously in Champlain's canoe. Occasionally, however, Morison's special sense of timeliness was misdirected. For example, in describing the promiscuity of the Huron adolescents, he wrote, "Every evening the boys and girls ran from lodge to lodge, copulating as they pleased (as if in a 1972-style college dormitory)."

Morison originally planned to write a three-volume study of the European discovery of America. This would have been an ambitious project for even a young historian. For a man in his eighties, unfortunately, it was impossible to complete. *The Southern Voyages*, intended as the second volume in a trilogy, proved to be Morison's last work.

His many admirers regarded Morison as a gentleman and a scholar. Other observers considered his aristocratic manner and yacht-club wardrobe as signs of arrogance. He could haughtily dismiss the opinions of "armchair navigators" as not worth listening to. His disdain for American historians who were ignorant of Greek, Latin, or even modern European languages was well known. But he could converse with elderly Boston ladies, Down East fishermen, presidents of the United States, and common seamen with equal ease.

The writing of history was for Morison clearly literary art. Most of his more than twoscore titles were very popular. Many of them were published in later editions, revisions, and foreign translations, facts which testify to their wide readership. Ironically, it was the so-called "court-historian" and not the relativists of the New Left who produced the books which were widely read—for both enjoyment and instruction.

As a disciple of Herodotus, Morison traveled widely and told good stories; as an admirer of Parkman, he added a new dimension, the sea, to his explorations of the historical past. Only someone intimately acquainted with maritime life could have penned these lyrical lines: "Every few hours the square sails changed color: golden gossamer when the last quarter of the moon rose, polished silver just before dawn, ruddy at sunrise, and cream-white at high noon." Whatever volume of Morison's work a reader chooses to consult, he will put the book down with the distinct feeling that the author knew what he was talking about. The qualities of immediacy and authority are characteristic of everything he wrote. He once identified the three qualities which he believed contributed to the success of Francis Parkman's histories: research, evaluation, and pre-

sentation, or literary style. These qualities made Parkman's writing great literature. The same is certainly true of Morison's.

Other:

The Key of Libberty [sic], *Written in the Year 1798 by William Manning*, edited by Morison (Billerica, Mass.: Manning Association, 1922); reprinted in *William and Mary Quarterly*, 13 (1956): 202-254;

Sources and Documents Illustrating the American Revolution and Formation of the Federal Constitution, edited by Morison (Oxford: Clarendon Press, 1923);

The Development of Harvard University, 1869-1929, edited by Morison (Cambridge: Harvard University Press, 1929);

Harold R. Shurtleff, *The Log Cabin Myth, a Study of the Early Dwellings of the English Colonists in North America*, edited by Morison (Cambridge: Harvard University Press, 1939);

William Bradford, *Of Plymouth Plantation*, edited by Morison (New York: Knopf, 1952); parts republished in *Major Writers of America*, edited by Perry Miller (New York: Harcourt, Brace & World, 1963);

The Parkman Reader, edited by Morison (Boston: Atlantic-Little, Brown, 1955); republished as *France and England in North America* (London: Faber & Faber, 1955);

William H. Prescott, *History of the Conquest of Peru*, edited by Morison (New York: Limited Editions Club, 1957; New York: Heritage Press, 1957);

Journals and Other Documents on the Life and Voyages of Christopher Columbus, edited by Morison (New York: Limited Editions Club, 1963; New York: Heritage Press, 1964).

Bibliography:

K. Jack Bauer, "Bibliography of Writings of Samuel Eliot Morison," *North American Society for Oceanic History Newsletter* (December 1977).

References:

"Admiral and his mission," *Newsweek*, 56 (18 July 1960): 89-90;

Carl N. Degler, "History Without a Beard," *Tri-Quarterly*, 6 (Spring 1966): 144-150;

David Herold, "Samuel Eliot Morison, 1887-1976," *American Writers: A Collection of Literary Biographies: 1979 Supplement*, edited by Leonard

Unger (New York: Scribners, 1979), pp. 479-500;

Herold, "Samuel Eliot Morison and the Ocean Sea," *Dalhousie Review*, 54 (Winter 1974-75): 741-748;

L. Nichols, "When history was being made, the historian was there," *New York Times Book Review*, 5 June 1960, p. 6.

Papers:
Morison's papers are in the Harvard Archives and his personal library in the Harvard Library.

Richard B. Morris
(24 July 1904-   )

Peter A. Coclanis
Columbia University

SELECTED BOOKS: *A Guide to the Principal Sources for Early American History (1600-1800) in the City of New York*, by Morris and Evarts B. Greene (New York: Columbia University Press, 1929);

Studies in the History of American Law, with Special Reference to the Seventeenth and Eighteenth Centuries (New York: Columbia University Press, 1930; London: King, 1930);

Government and Labor in Early America (New York: Columbia University Press, 1946);

Fair Trial; Fourteen Who Stood Accused, from Anne Hutchinson to Alger Hiss (New York: Knopf, 1952; London: Macdonald, 1953);

The American Revolution, A Short History (New York: Van Nostrand, 1955; London: Watts, 1971);

The Peacemakers: The Great Powers and American Independence (New York: Harper & Row, 1965);

The American Revolution Reconsidered (New York: Harper & Row, 1967);

John Jay, the Nation, and the Court (Boston: Boston University Press, 1967);

The Emerging Nations and the American Revolution (New York & London: Harper & Row, 1970);

Seven Who Shaped Our Destiny; The Founding Fathers as Revolutionaries (New York: Harper & Row, 1973).

Richard B. Morris, renowned professor of history first at the City College of New York and later at Columbia University, ranks among the most versatile and prolific scholars of the twentieth century. Though perhaps best known for his work in early American legal and economic history, Morris's research interests have ranged from Jewish history to juvenile literature, from the diplomatic history of the American Revolution to the presidency of

Richard B. Morris

Franklin Roosevelt. As author or editor of literally hundreds of works over a sixty-year period, Morris has brought the message of history to two generations of readers, to both the scholarly community and the general public alike.

Richard Brandon Morris, son of Jacob and Tillie Rosenberg Morris, was born in New York City. He grew up in the borough of the Bronx, but because of his obvious academic potential attended high school in Manhattan at Townsend Harris Hall, a preparatory school associated with the City College of New York. While at this school Morris developed a keen interest in American history, and under the influence of two of his teachers, Herman Gray, later a professor of law at New York University Law School, and Austin Baxter Keep, he decided to become a historian. In 1920 Morris, at the age of fifteen, published his first article, a piece entitled "Alexander Hamilton as a Hebraist" in *The American Hebrew*. With this short study, an amazingly productive academic career had begun.

Upon his graduation from Townsend Harris Hall, he continued his education at CCNY, from which institution he was graduated cum laude with a major in history in 1924. He published a number of articles in Jewish history while still an undergraduate, and his overall performance at City College was so advanced that he was largely responsible for the inception of the school's honors program, a program which nurtured a great number of eminent young intellectuals during the school's heyday in the 1930s and 1940s. At CCNY Morris was particularly influenced by two historians, Nelson P. Mead and J. Salwyn Schapiro, and by the legal philosopher Morris Raphael Cohen. He later claimed that his contact with these three scholars inspired him to direct his attention to the early history of American law, a subject for which Morris would later become famous.

Morris continued his intellectual trek in the fall of 1924 when he ventured down Amsterdam Avenue to begin his graduate training in history at Columbia University. He was awarded an M.A. from that university in 1925 and continued on to receive a Ph.D. from Columbia in 1930. Morris did well in his course work throughout his graduate career and, in addition, published a book and several articles, including an important piece in the *American Historical Review* in 1926 on the legal history of early Massachusetts. The young scholar, who was twenty-one years old when that article appeared, somehow found the time to teach at the college level as well. In 1927 he became an instructor at CCNY and continued to teach there through the rest of his years in graduate school. Indeed, he did not end his formal association with CCNY until 1949.

In his graduate years at Columbia, Morris was heavily influenced by the English constitutional historian Robert L. Schuyler, by Richard Powell, a professor of real property at Columbia Law School, and by Evarts B. Greene, the Harvard-trained colonial historian who had come to Columbia from the University of Illinois in 1923. Greene, a distinguished constitutional and institutional historian, directed Morris's dissertation and, in addition, coauthored a reference guide with his young student in 1929. This work, *A Guide to the Principal Sources for Early American History (1600-1800) in the City of New York*, is, in revised form, still used widely today.

Morris completed his dissertation *Studies in the History of American Law, with Special Reference to the Seventeenth and Eighteenth Centuries* in 1930, and Columbia University Press published the work under the same title later that year. The young scholar attempted in this study to outline in a sociological manner the evolution of American law in the thirteen British colonies on the mainland of North America. Through an analysis of colonial laws and legal practices regarding land distribution and alienation, the rights of women, and liability for tortious acts, Morris concluded that in these areas at least the legal systems in the various colonies differed sufficiently from that of the mother country to justify the use of the term "American law" as an analytical tool. He argued that social and environmental conditions in early America rendered much of the English common law useless and at the same time forced the colonists to create a legal system more attuned to their needs. The system which ultimately evolved—a complex amalgam of English common and borough law, biblical precepts, and practical concessions to the American environment—adequately met the needs of the colonial population and, furthermore, formed the foundation upon which the modern American legal system was erected.

One finds in *Studies in the History of American Law* the intellectual independence, the prodigious research, and the clear prose that have become identified with Morris's work over the past half century. That Morris, a native New Yorker working at Columbia University under a distinguished institutional historian, should produce a study with a distinct neo-Turnerian flavor typifies the free-thinking which would inform the scholar's writing throughout his long career.

Studies in the History of American Law was well received by scholarly reviewers who found the work a thoughtful and, at times, brilliant attempt to create an analytical framework within which to view the evolution of American law. Reviewers agreed, however, that the book represented a preliminary rather than definitive treatment of the subject. Morris won a $1,000 prize awarded jointly by the Colonial Dames of America and the National Society of Colonial Dames for the book, and *Studies in the History of American Law* is, after two reprintings, still required reading for legal historians.

Morris continued his research in early American legal history while teaching at CCNY during the 1930s, publishing several major articles in the field and editing two important collections of legal proceedings over the course of the decade. As he matured as a scholar in this period, his conception of legal history evolved as well. While Morris, like Frederic William Maitland, whom he greatly admired, had always viewed the law and legal history within a broad context, he gradually shifted the emphasis of his own legal research during the decade of the 1930s. Whereas *Studies in the History of American Law* was a broadly conceived interpretation of the evolution of American legal institutions, Morris increasingly in the 1930s used his legal research to help address larger economic and social questions. The role of the law in society as a whole rather than the development of a society's legal institutions became paramount to the young professor. This approach, which prefigured the "external approach" to legal history popular today, was eloquently described by Morris in a 1934 *West Virginia Law Quarterly* article entitled "The Sources of Early American Law: Colonial Period." Though the first fruit of Morris's research reorientation appeared in the late 1930s, not until the decade of the 1940s did the harvest really begin in earnest.

Change also marked Morris's professional and personal life in the 1930s. The young historian advanced steadily up the academic ladder at CCNY, becoming an assistant professor by 1932, then rising to the associate level in 1937. His rise had not gone unnoticed; he served as regional director for New York of the WPA's Survey of Federal Archives in 1936-1937 and, in addition, was appointed secretary of the Committee on Legal Research of the American Historical Association. Finally, and perhaps most importantly, Morris's life had changed when he married Berenice Robinson on 12 June 1932. The marriage produced two sons in the course of time, Jeffrey Brandon, who later followed his father on the faculty at CCNY, and Donald Robinson.

During World War II, Professor Morris, remaining in New York, served both as director of the Civilian Defense Council at CCNY and as a member of the regional War Labor Board. When time per-

mitted he continued to do research and to write, publishing several pieces over the course of the war. In 1946 Morris's magisterial work, *Government and Labor in Early America*, was published by Columbia University Press. The huge study, upon which Morris had himself labored for a full decade, outlined in excruciating detail the various forms of governmental intervention in the economy, particularly the state's attempts to regulate labor, from the founding of Jamestown to the early nineteenth century. With the notable exception of slave labor, upon which Morris merely touched because of the availability of numerous other works on the subject, *Government and Labor in Early America* provided an unparalleled look at the American labor force—both bound and free, skilled and unskilled—and the relations of the government with the same. The book, based largely on legal records, including an analysis of some 20,000 unpublished cases from the inferior courts of the American colonies, contained an incredible amount of data on such topics as wages, labor combinations, indentured servitude, impressment, and imprisonment for debt. Though the size and scope of the work had been reduced considerably by the paper restrictions introduced during the late war, Morris had brought together in *Government and Labor in Early America* more material both on the government's role in the early American economy and on the American worker than anyone had done before him.

The scholarly community immediately recognized the importance of the book. While a few critics wrote that Morris would have done well to have included more analysis in the work and some averred that they felt enervated after reading the massive tome, all of them concluded that the study was an incredible research achievement and a major contribution to the literature. Indeed, in a poll conducted among professional historians several years later to determine the best historical works of the 1936-1950 period, *Government and Labor in Early America* received a considerable number of votes. The study, which catapulted Morris to the very top of the historical profession, remains the standard work on the subject and is still in print today.

Though formally still on the faculty at CCNY until 1949, Morris's growing reputation and the concomitant demand for his services after the publication of *Government and Labor in Early America* led to a period of rapid change in his professional life. Between 1946 when the book appeared and 1949 when he accepted a full professorship in history at Columbia University, Morris won a Guggenheim Fellowship, was a fellow at the Institute for Advanced Study, and was a visiting professor at both Princeton and Columbia. While Morris was to teach and lecture at a number of other universities as a visiting professor in the years after 1949, Columbia's Morningside Heights campus was to serve as his academic home for the remainder of his career.

Morris continued his research in economic and labor history in the years immediately after the appearance of *Government and Labor in Early America*. In an important 1949 article in the *American Historical Review*, for example, Morris challenged on three counts Arthur M. Schlesinger, Jr.'s celebrated Jacksonian "wage-earner" thesis. First, Morris argued that Jackson was no great friend of labor as Schlesinger had contended. Indeed, the seventh president's policies toward the eastern industrial laborer were, according to Morris, neutral at best. Secondly, Morris argued that eastern industrial workers did not constitute the most solid part of Jackson's political support as Schlesinger had claimed but were instead ambivalent about Jackson, often supporting other candidates. Finally, Morris denied Schlesinger's assertion that one could trace the linear progression of American liberalism directly from Old Hickory to FDR. Professor Morris's article, along with the work of his colleague Joseph Dorfman and the studies of a number of graduate students—Edward Pessen among them—in one of Morris's seminars at Columbia, did considerable damage to Schlesinger's thesis and helped in the construction of a more sophisticated interpretation of Jacksonian political economy.

Pursuing another line of inquiry in a series of articles between 1948 and 1954 on white labor in the antebellum South, Morris argued that tighter controls existed on poor whites in the region than historians had hitherto appreciated and that white laborers could, and sometimes did, fall into a state of "quasi-bondage." In his classic 1965 study, *The Political Economy of Slavery*, the eminent Marxist historian Eugene D. Genovese, a Morris student, wrote that these articles contained perspectives and material on the antebellum South that other scholars had missed. It is indeed unfortunate that these articles remain relatively obscure even today.

In addition to his research and scholarly writing in the fields of labor, economic, and legal history, Morris began in the late 1940s and early 1950s to devote more attention to works for the general public. Morris became a frequent contributor in this period, for example, to *Saturday Review*, and his articles began to appear in *American Heritage* as well. He has continued to write on historical matters for

popular magazines ever since. Writing on topics ranging from the French Revolution to the American eagle, from the trial of Whittaker Chambers to the humor of our presidents, Morris has both entertained and enlightened the general reader in dozens of pieces over the years in *U. S. News & World Report*, *The New York Times Magazine*, *The Smithsonian*, and *Nation's Business*, as well as in the two other magazines mentioned above.

Morris's writings for the general public, however, were not limited to relatively short magazine pieces. In his lively 1952 work, *Fair Trial; Fourteen Who Stood Accused, from Anne Hutchinson to Alger Hiss*, for example, Morris, writing for a broad audience, detailed fourteen notable criminal cases from the American past, providing his readers first with the pertinent facts of each case, then challenging them to decide whether or not the various defendants had received fair trials. Though one could read the book as a work in the "court-room drama" subgenre of detective fiction, Morris brought up important questions about the American judicial system throughout *Fair Trial*. By pointing out problems in the conduct of each trial and by comparing the American judicial process with that of England, Morris provided his readers with numerous insights about the meaning of justice in the United States and the manner in which that meaning has changed over time. Yet, Morris's writings for the general public were not restricted to that part of this market that had reached adulthood. Indeed, he wrote a half dozen historical works in the F. Watts First Books series for children during the 1950s and early 1960s.

Despite all of these interests and activities, Morris at the same time began to increase his commitment to both historical editing projects and to the systematic study of American history during the Revolutionary era, that is, between about 1760 and 1800. These two commitments, while often dovetailing, continue to occupy most of the scholar's attention.

One of the most significant of these editing projects, Morris's invaluable reference guide, the *Encyclopedia of American History*, appeared in print for the first time in 1953. This compendium of facts, statistics, and short interpretive sketches has proved both reliable and extremely successful over the years. That it has gone through four more editions since its original publication attests to its popularity among students and scholars alike.

The New American Nation series, coedited by Morris and his Columbia colleague and longtime friend Henry Steele Commager, has proved similarly successful in the years following the publication in 1954 of the first volume in the series, Arthur S. Link's *Woodrow Wilson and the Progressive Era, 1910-1917*. This multivolume series, the goal of which is to provide a comprehensive survey of the American past, consists today of thirty-odd volumes by various scholars, each detailing a particular period or important theme in American history. Conceived originally to replace a similar series edited by Albert Bushnell Hart early in the twentieth century, *The New American Nation* series, under the stewardship of Morris and Commager, has provided a generation of readers with useful, if somewhat uneven, syntheses of various aspects of America's past.

Morris's work on the Revolutionary era and its leading statesmen began to appear in print in the mid-1950s. Indeed, in three essays published between 1955 and 1957, Morris laid out many of the themes that would recur time and again in his subsequent publications. His basic interpretation of the American Revolution was outlined in 1955 in an eighty-page essay that Morris wrote to supplement a collection of documents in a volume entitled *The American Revolution, A Short History*. While the bulk of this essay was narrative history detailing the main events of the period, Morris made two important interpretive points in the piece, points upon which he would elaborate in later articles and especially in the 1967 work *The American Revolution Reconsidered*. First, Morris argued that the American Revolution was no narrow conservative movement, the sole purpose for which was political independence, but a broad movement that sought not only political independence but ongoing, essentially liberal social reform as well. Secondly, he contended that the Revolution was not a class struggle, as the Progressive historians had claimed, but rather one in which upper-, middle-, and lower-class elements appeared in substantial numbers on each side.

Morris broadened and extended in time his critique of Progressive and neo-Progressive notions about the Revolutionary era in a historiographical essay on the Confederation period, which appeared in the *William and Mary Quarterly* in 1956. Arguing that the Beard-Jensen view of the 1780s as a period of gradual economic expansion, increasing political stability, and basically democratic government was conceptually simplistic and factually wrong, Morris sided with those writers of the "national" tradition that saw the period rather as one fraught with serious, if not critical, problems, problems that could be solved only with the adoption of a stronger central government. This nationalist interpretation was emphasized in a brief but very suggestive essay which Morris wrote in 1957 to introduce a collection of papers entitled *Alexander Hamilton and the Founding of the Nation*. In defending Hamilton and the broad Hamiltonian conception of the Constitution in this skillfully edited work, Morris tied together, albeit loosely, his views on the entire Revolutionary era. For Morris believed in 1957, and has continued to believe ever since, that the Constitution, broadly conceived, was the institutional fulfillment of the Revolutionary dream. The strength and purpose inherent in this frame of government, according to Morris, allowed and at times hastened the far-reaching social reforms that have proved the legacy of the American Revolution, reforms that the Whiggish founders of our nation may never have intended but would have understood.

The historiographical independence which Morris displayed in these essays on the Revolutionary era is striking even today. Setting himself apart not only from the Progressive historians but also from the Consensus historians then coming to the fore, Morris settled into an intermediate position between these two groups and in so doing helped recast the liberal interpretation of this period into a mold which corresponded more faithfully to the liberalism of the urban, Northeastern, ethnic world to which he was born.

With the exception of 1957 when he spent part of the year at the University of Hawaii as a visiting professor, Morris taught at Columbia throughout the decade of the 1950s. Indeed, his sixth-floor office at the top of Fayerweather Hall was both the figurative and literal center of Morris's ever expanding intellectual universe during these busy years. His extraordinary contributions to Columbia as both scholar and teacher were rewarded in 1959 when that university appointed him Gouverneur Morris Professor of History. In that same year, Morris's alma mater, CCNY, honored him with its highest award, the Townsend Harris Medal, for his accomplishments over the course of his distinguished academic career. Morris received a number of other honors in this period as well. He was appointed to the Council of the Institute of Early American History and Culture at Williamsburg, Virginia, in 1959 and was in the following year named chairman of the editorial board for the journal *Labor History*. While his appointment to the former post was for three years only, he was to serve as chairman of the editorial board at *Labor History* until 1976. During the 1961-1962 academic year, Morris taught at the Sorbonne as a Fulbright research scholar and, in addition, was named a

Guggenheim fellow for the second time in his career. In 1963 he received an honorary doctorate from Hebrew Union College, the first of three honorary doctorates he was to receive in his career.

Morris continued to work on his various research and writing projects in the early 1960s, paying particular attention to the Revolutionary era as he had for the past decade. While he published several important articles in this period, his efforts were not to be fully rewarded for a number of years. Indeed, it was only after he published five major books in the nine years between 1965 and 1973 that it became apparent how fruitful Morris's research in the early 1960s had been.

The first book to appear in this extraordinarily productive period was Morris's 1965 work, *The Peacemakers: The Great Powers and American Independence*, a study of the negotiations between 1779 and 1783 that ultimately ended the Revolutionary War. Based on manuscript research in the archives of ten countries, *The Peacemakers* was by far the most comprehensive account of these negotiations ever to appear in print. Morris, writing in his usual vigorous style, brought life to the labyrinthine peacemaking process and to both the prominent statesmen and shadowy figures that had participated in it. In revising, confirming, or debunking numerous assumptions about both the negotiations and the negotiators themselves, Morris made significant contributions not only to diplomatic history but to the historiography of the American Revolution as well.

The Peacemakers won immediate scholarly acclaim. Reviewers were almost unanimous in their praise of Morris's cogent and thoughtful study and of the vast research upon which the study rested. A few critics, it is true, thought the book's detail excessive, and one felt that Morris's treatment of the European negotiators was overly harsh. Even those critics, however, tempered their criticism with praise. In 1966 Morris won a coveted Bancroft Prize for *The Peacemakers*. This prize, offered annually by Columbia University to the authors of the two best books in American history or diplomacy, is considered one of the historical profession's highest honors.

Morris published two books in 1967, both of which were based on lecture series he had recently delivered. *John Jay, the Nation, and the Court* consists of three interpretive essays originally presented at Boston University in 1965 as the Gaspar G. Bacon Lectures on the Constitution of the United States. In these essays Morris, who had been assembling and editing Jay's unpublished papers for a number of years, attempted to rehabilitate the reputation of the first chief justice, a task he had begun earlier in *The Peacemakers*. He argued that Jay was both an effective statesman and a very creative republican thinker whose intense nationalism and tight legalism were influential in the development of an American constitutional tradition. Scholars, by and large, have accepted Morris's reassessment, and Jay has grown steadily in stature over the years.

In *The American Revolution Reconsidered*, a collection of four essays prepared in 1966 for the Anson G. Phelps Lectures on Early American History at New York University, Morris provided a summary statement of his ideas on the whole Revolutionary era. The essays treat the historiography of the American Revolution, its diplomatic history, the similarities and differences between the American and French revolutions, and the nature of the relationship between the American Revolution and the Constitution. While he offered some new insights in the essays, particularly in the one comparing the French and American revolutions, Morris basically elaborated upon themes discussed in his earlier works. In arguing, for example, that the American Revolution had both immediate political and long-term social dimensions and that the Constitution fulfilled rather than compromised the Spirit of '76, Morris was simply reiterating views with which he had been associated for the past decade. Similarly, much of the material on the diplomacy of the Revolution could be found in *The Peacemakers* as well. To say, however, that there was little new in the way of interpretation in *The American Revolution Reconsidered* is not to denigrate Morris's engagingly written book. For in this case interpretive consistency reflected the soundness and sophistication of his earlier positions rather than an unwillingness to change his views as new research came to light. Thus, *The American Revolution Reconsidered*, perceived as the summation of a senior historian, received uniformly favorable reviews.

Morris's 1970 book, *The Emerging Nations and the American Revolution*, won considerably less acclaim. The Columbia professor attempted in this work both to point out that similarities existed between the American Revolution and liberation movements in the emerging nations today and to prove that the American Revolution has been in the past—and ought to remain in the future—the preferred "model" for would-be revolutionaries. Moreover, he reminded both Americans and the world that the United States was born of revolution, is by tradition and character a revolutionary nation, and with some notable exceptions has generally supported the liberation of other peoples from colonial rule. Critics, with some justification, alleged that the work was a defense rather than a dispassionate analysis of the historical role of the United States in world affairs and, in addition, attacked Morris for his incomplete, at times simplistic, statements about the emerging nations and the ostensible influence of the American Revolution upon them. *The Emerging Nations and the American Revolution*, written in a defensive tone at the height of the war in Vietnam, seems in retrospect an unsuccessful, if understandable, liberal affirmation of America and its history, a response to the country's critics in an increasingly skeptical world.

In 1973, the year of his official retirement from Columbia, Morris published *Seven Who Shaped Our Destiny; The Founding Fathers as Revolutionaries*, an entertaining and informative set of biographical sketches on Franklin, Washington, John Adams, Jefferson, Jay, Madison, and Hamilton. Each of these men came to life on the pages of the book, for Morris treated them as normal human beings, not as mythopoeic heroes. While Morris's own nationalist bent was evident in the essays, he was fair to each man, to Jefferson and Jay alike. He argued in any case that their similarities outweighed their differences, that nationalism and republicanism in some admixture informed the life of each. Morris, writing in the wake of the governmental excesses of the Johnson and Nixon years, was especially concerned in these essays with the question of leadership. The seven men profiled in the book, the only public figures of the Revolutionary era to pass his triple test of charismatic leadership, staying power, and constructive statesmanship, constituted, according to Morris, the finest group of leaders America has ever produced. He ended the book on a gloomy note, however, suggesting that the thoughtful and deliberative nature of these men would have proved unpopular in the glib, media-oriented wasteland we call politics today.

Seven Who Shaped Our Destiny, unlike Morris's previous book, received very favorable reviews. Critics praised the historian for his thorough research, his fresh opinions on the Founding Fathers, and for his sparkling writing style. Clearly, Professor Morris, on the eve of "retirement," was back in form.

That Morris would remain active after his passage to emeritus status at Columbia in September 1973 was in little doubt. For even between 1965 and 1973, a period in which he had written five books, Morris had found time to publish a number of articles, work on various editing projects, serve as

chairman of the editorial board of a major journal, and fulfill his teaching obligations. He had, as indicated earlier, delivered distinguished lectures at both Boston University and New York University in that period and had held visiting professorships at the Free University of Berlin in 1969 and at the Hebrew University of Jerusalem in 1969 and 1970. Morris had, in addition, lectured under the auspices of the United States Information Service in Yugoslavia, Iran, Afghanistan, and the USSR, had served as chairman of New York Mayor John Lindsay's Task Force on Municipal Archives, and had even testified in March 1972 at U.S. Senate hearings over the Javits-Stennis bill.

Morris kept up this hectic pace after his alleged retirement. He continued to teach for several years, first as a special lecturer at Columbia between 1973 and 1976, then, later in 1976, as the John A. Burns Professor of History at the University of Hawaii at Manoa. He has served on the editorial boards of *New York History* and the *American Journal of Legal History* and, as stated previously, was chairman of the editorial board of *Labor History* until 1976. Morris was a delegate between 1973 and 1975 on the U.S.-Mexico Joint Commission on Cultural Cooperation and during the American Revolution's bicentennial celebration served on a wide variety of public panels and committees on both the state and national levels. He was also from 1974 to 1976 a historical consultant both for the CBS Bicentennial Minute television series and for the American Film Institute's American Revolution series. Since 1977 he has served as president of the Board of Trustees of the John Jay Homestead.

Morris has also continued to write and edit. He has in recent years produced a number of lectures originally prepared for the bicentennial as well as the first two volumes of the John Jay papers. Each of the volumes of Jay papers, which appeared in 1975 and 1980 respectively, received glowing reviews.

Morris's regal academic career, which was crowned in 1976 when his colleagues elected him president of the American Historical Association, has not yet come to an end. He is currently preparing for publication the last two volumes of the Jay papers and is coordinating, along with James MacGregor Burns, Project '87, a rigorous ten-year program designed to encourage and stimulate a reexamination of the American Constitution. The project, jointly sponsored by the American Historical Association and the American Political Science Association, includes both scholarly and public activities and will culminate in 1987, the Constitution's bicentennial year.

Richard Brandon Morris's numerous contributions to American history defy easy classification. Like Sir Isaiah Berlin's fox, Morris knows many things and, indeed, has written about most of them. It is fair to say, however, that Morris has directed most of his attention over the course of his long career to the study of early American history, that is, to the period from the founding of Jamestown through the presidency of Andrew Jackson. Working mainly within these temporal limits, he has produced scores of important studies in a half dozen different areas. Moreover, he has at various times produced them for scholars, laymen, and children alike. In so doing, he has become a titan of twentieth-century American historiography, a scholar whose versatility, prodigious research and output, interpretive independence, and engaging style will not soon be forgotten.

Other:

Select Cases of the Mayor's Court of New York City, 1674-1784, edited by Morris (Washington, D.C.: American Historical Association, 1935);

The Era of the American Revolution; Studies Inscribed to Evarts Boutell Greene, edited by Morris (New York: Columbia University Press, 1939);

Encyclopedia of American History, edited by Morris (New York: Harper, 1953);

The New American Nation series, edited by Morris and Henry Steele Commager (New York: Harper, 1954-);

Alexander Hamilton and the Founding of the Nation, edited by Morris (New York: Dial, 1957);

The American Revolution, 1763-1783; A Bicentennial Collection, edited by Morris (Columbia: University of South Carolina Press, 1970);

Basic Documents on the Confederation and Constitution, edited by Morris (New York: Van Nostrand Reinhold, 1970);

Harper Encyclopedia of the Modern World; A Concise Reference History from 1760 to the Present, edited by Morris and Graham W. Irwin (New York: Harper & Row, 1970); republished as *An Encyclopaedia of the Modern World: A Concise Reference History from 1760 to the Present* (London:

Weidenfeld & Nicolson, 1970);

The Unpublished Papers of John Jay, 2 volumes to date, edited by Morris (New York: Harper & Row, 1975-);

The U.S. Department of Labor Bicentennial History of the American Worker, edited by Morris (Washington, D.C.: U.S. Government Printing Office, 1976).

Periodical Publications:

"Massachusetts and the Common Law: The Declaration of 1646," *American Historical Review*, 31 (April 1926): 443-453;

"The Sources of Early American Law: Colonial Period," *West Virginia Law Quarterly*, 40 (April 1934): 212-223;

"Andrew Jackson, Strikebreaker," *American Historical Review*, 55 (October 1949): 54-68;

"The Measure of Bondage in the Slave States," *Mississippi Valley Historical Review*, 41 (September 1954): 219-240;

"The Confederation Period and the American Historian," *William and Mary Quarterly*, 13 (April 1956): 139-156;

"Class Struggle and the American Revolution," *William and Mary Quarterly*, 19 (January 1962): 3-29;

"The Spacious Empire of Lawrence Henry Gipson," *William and Mary Quarterly*, 24 (April 1967): 169-189;

" 'We the People of the United States': The Bicentennial of a People's Revolution," *American Historical Review*, 82 (February 1977): 1-19.

Reference:

Perspectives on Early American History: Essays in Honor of Richard B. Morris, edited by Alden T. Vaughan and George Athan Billias (New York: Harper & Row, 1973).

Papers:

Morris's papers are housed at the Rare Book and Manuscript Library of Columbia University. They will not, however, be available for examination until 1987.

Allan Nevins

Richard M. McMurry
North Carolina State University

BIRTH: Camp Point, Illinois, 20 May 1890, to Joseph A. and Emma Stahl Nevins.

EDUCATION: A.B., 1912, A.M., 1913, University of Illinois.

MARRIAGE: 30 December 1916 to Mary Fleming Richardson; children: Anne Elizabeth, Meredith.

AWARDS AND HONORS: Pulitzer Prize for *Grover Cleveland*, 1933; Pulitzer Prize for *Hamilton Fish*, 1937; Bancroft Prize for *Ordeal of the Union*, 1947; Scribner's Centenary Prize for *Ordeal of the Union*, 1947.

DEATH: Menlo Park, California, 5 March 1971.

SELECTED BOOKS: *Ponteach; or, The Savages of America; a Tragedy by Robert Rogers; with an Introduction and a Biography of the Author by Allan Nevins* (Chicago: Caxton Club, 1914);
Illinois (New York: Oxford University Press, 1917);
The Evening Post: A Century of Journalism (New York: Boni & Liveright, 1922);
The American States During and After the Revolution, 1775-1789 (New York: Macmillan, 1924);
The Emergence of Modern America, 1865-1878 (New York: Macmillan, 1927);
Frémont, the West's Greatest Adventurer (New York: Harper, 1928); revised as *Frémont, Pathmarker of the West* (New York & London: Appleton-Century, 1939);
Henry White: Thirty Years of Diplomacy (New York & London: Harper, 1930);
Grover Cleveland: A Study in Courage (New York: Dodd, Mead, 1932);
Abram S. Hewitt: With Some Account of Peter Cooper (New York & London: Harper, 1935);
Hamilton Fish: The Inner History of the Grant Administration (New York: Dodd, Mead, 1936);
The Gateway to History (Boston & New York: Heath, 1938; revised edition, Garden City: Doubleday, 1962);
John D. Rockefeller: The Heroic Age of American Enterprise (New York: Scribners, 1940); revised as *Study in Power: John D. Rockefeller, Industrialist and Philanthropist* (New York: Scribners, 1953);

Allan Nevins

America in World Affairs (New York: Oxford University Press, 1942);
The Making of Modern Britain, A Short History, by Nevins and John Bartlet Brebner (New York: Norton, 1943);
A Century of Political Cartoons: Caricature in the United States from 1800-1900, by Nevins and Frank Weitenkampf (New York: Scribners, 1944);
The Ordeal of the Union (New York & London: Scribners, 1947-1971)—includes *The Ordeal of the Union: 1. Fruits of Manifest Destiny, 1847-1852* (1947); 2. *A House Dividing, 1852-1857* (1947); *The Emergence of Lincoln: 1. Douglas, Buchanan and Party Chaos, 1857-1859* (1950); 2. *Prologue to Civil War, 1859-1861* (1950); *The War for the Union: 1. The Improvised War, 1861-1862* (1959); 2. *War Becomes Revolution, 1862-1863* (1960); 3. *The Organized War, 1863-1864* (1971); 4. *The Organized War to Victory, 1864-1865* (1971);

The World of Eli Whitney, by Nevins and Jeannette
Mirsky (New York: Macmillan, 1952);
Ford, by Nevins and Frank Ernest Hill (New York:
Scribners, 1954-1963)—includes *The Times, the
Man, the Company* (1954); *Expansion and Chal-
lenge, 1915-1933* (1957); *Decline and Rebirth,
1933-1962* (1963);
Herbert Lehman and His Era (New York: Scribners,
1963);
James Truslow Adams: Historian of the American Dream
(Urbana: University of Illinois Press, 1968).

Joseph Allan Nevins was one of the most versatile, probably the greatest, and certainly the most
prolific of twentieth-century American historians.
In a long career as journalist, teacher, speaker, and
writer, Nevins authored over a score of significant
books, wrote about fifty others of lesser importance,
edited a large number of useful works, wrote an
unknown number of articles (perhaps a thousand
by one estimate), reshaped historians' understandings of some major topics in American history, acted
as a catalyst for several historical projects, trained
hundreds of masters and doctoral students, and
made the only major effort since World War II to
provide Americans with a full-scale, balanced reinterpretation of their Civil War-Reconstruction era.

Nevins was not, however, an ivory tower
academician. He worked for almost two decades as a
journalist and did not enter academe until he was
nearly forty. He maintained a healthy lifelong
interest and involvement in the world beyond the
university, especially in literature and politics. He
served briefly in the United States Army in World
War I until he was discharged for medical reasons,
and in World War II, when he was in his fifties, he
broke a leg running an obstacle course with some
Australian troops while he was in the South Pacific
as a special representative of the Office of War
Information.

Because Nevins was passionately committed to
the belief that history should be a major part of
every citizen's life, he labored unceasingly to make it
so. He organized a society and a magazine to bring
history to the general public, and he spoke to lay
and professional audiences as diverse as the group
in Santa Ana, California, celebrating National Library Week in its public library, the Society of
American Archivists, the American Petroleum Institute's Division of Refining, the Committee on
History of the Association for Education in Journalism, the Manuscript Society, and the Vermont
Historical Society. In most of these addresses he
hammered away at one of his favorite themes: his-

tory needs the public and the public needs history.

The education of Allan Nevins began on his
parents' 220-acre farm near Camp Point, Illinois,
close to the Mississippi River, where he was born to
Joseph Allan and Emma Stahl Nevins, and continued throughout his life. Camp Point (population: 1,200) was blessed with what was, for the time
and place, a remarkable respect for letters. There
were several libraries in the town, and the mail
brought current issues of such magazines as *Youth's
Companion, McClure's, Century,* and *Harper's.* The
Nevins family possessed some five hundred books
and belonged to a group of families that exchanged
among themselves the magazines to which they subscribed. Allan Nevins, not surprisingly, began at an
early age to read works of literature, history, theology, and economics. By the time he was twelve, he
had read William H. Prescott's *Conquest of Mexico*
and several volumes of Francis Parkman's long account of the struggle between Britain and France
for mastery of the New World. Selling rabbits and
apples to earn money, Nevins spent a large portion
of his funds to buy books from the Montgomery
Ward mail order catalog.

Omnivorous reading, a lifelong habit for
Nevins, furnished the thousands of quotations and
examples with which he sprinkled most of his writings. A cursory examination of any of his essays on
history will show that he had read extensively in
literature, philosophy, economics, and other fields
as well as in his own discipline. In the opening
half-dozen pages of *The Gateway to History* (1938)
Nevins quoted Daniel Webster, Lucian, Henry
Adams, Chancellor Kent, Thomas Jefferson, and
Charles Sumner. He used incidents from the lives
of Theodore Roosevelt, Alfred Thayer Mahan,
Willa Cather, George Washington, Alexander
Hamilton, Woodrow Wilson, Harry Truman, and
John Kennedy to illustrate his points; and he
made reference to, among others, Thucydides,
Livy, Tacitus, Hume, and Voltaire. He was, one
historian has written, "the only real genius I have
ever known. . . . [He] had immeasurable knowledge
about so many things."

Nevins's boyhood was full of valuable experiences. The farm was largely self-sufficient, and the
closely knit family was reasonably prosperous. The
house had a telephone and acetylene lighting. His
parents (his father was a Scot; his mother, a German) were Presbyterians who labored conscientiously to raise their three sons and two daughters.
The children were expected to help with the pigs,
wheat, corn, and other animals and crops, but they
were also encouraged to develop their minds. It was

assumed that the boys would go to college and that the girls would receive the equivalent of a college education. "Above all," Nevins remembered of his parents when he was in his seventies, "they believed in work."

Like many a bright rural youngster, Nevins found farm life monotonous, and from a very early age he was determined to pursue a career that would enable him to live in a city. By the time he finished high school in 1908, he had decided upon journalism. In September of that year he arrived in Urbana to enroll at the University of Illinois as an English major. On the basis of a competitive examination, he had won a scholarship that paid his tuition, ninety-six dollars, for over four years. He was then, to use his own words, "countrified, homely, shy, and had no money to spare." These handicaps, Nevins later recalled, combined with the five-to-one male-female ratio at the university meant that he "had nothing to offer any of the young women, and kept quite clear of them all my four years."

The University of Illinois was then rapidly developing into a fine school, and Nevins profited greatly from the years he spent there. He came to know several faculty members very well. He was on friendly terms with many other students and participated in picnics, excursions, and football games. Nevins proved an excellent student, and his work in an advanced composition class drew high praise from his professor and his classmates. He continued to read avidly—Thorstein Veblen, Graham Wallas, Herbert Croly—as well as works of literature.

Ironically, he did not relish the study of American history. Years later he remembered, "I was then callow enough to regard American history in particular as a limited and dull subject, which held little of the richness and inspiration of English literature." One class, taught by Evarts B. Greene, promised to be an exception. When Greene was absent, however, the class was taught by another historian, and Nevins's worst opinion was confirmed. The replacement proved to be "a precisionist, a disciplinarian, and a pedant, utterly lacking in imagination."

In the summer of 1910 Nevins worked as a reporter for the *Illinois State Register* in Springfield. It was a miserable experience for the aspiring journalist despite his six-dollar weekly salary. The weather was unusually hot, he knew no one in Springfield, and he, a staunch Democrat, was working for a paper that was solidly Republican.

In his senior year at the university (1911-1912), Nevins was a reporter for the "ambitious student newspaper, the *Illini*," and he wrote a sixty-one page bachelor's thesis entitled "The Relationship of William Hazlitt to Jean Jacques Rousseau." Hazlitt was, Nevins once remarked, "one of the authors for whom I felt a special enthusiasm." A half century after writing the thesis, the words of the English essayist remained vivid in Nevins's mind, and he cited Hazlitt in his presidential address to the American Historical Association.

Nevins spent the summer after his 1912 graduation traveling in Europe with two friends from the university. The trio visited Germany, Switzerland, France, and then Great Britain. Nevins, in 1963, recalled his dismay at the manifestations of militarism and nationalism that he had witnessed in Europe and confessed that the Illinois farm boy had been "horrified" by the open vice on the streets of Germany and France. Britain, however, was different. Nevins described his feelings when he arrived: "All around me people were speaking English, and I had an intoxicating realization that I was home, back in my own civilization, surrounded by my own folk. From that moment dates much of the militant Anglophile feeling that I have always retained."

In 1912-1913 Nevins was a graduate student at Illinois supporting himself by working as a teaching assistant in the English department. While in England he had done research at the Public Records Office for his master's thesis. The thesis topic, "Introduction to Rogers' 'Ponteach,'" had been suggested by Clarence W. Alvord, a member of the history department. Although written for the English department, the thesis luckily united history—in which Nevins had become interested despite his bad experiences—with literature. *Ponteach* was a play that had been published anonymously in London in 1766. Nevins had done a great deal of research to find information on the life of Robert Rogers, the Massachusetts-born frontiersman and military hero, who was probably its author. In 1914 the thesis became Nevins's first book: *Ponteach; or, The Savages of America; a Tragedy by Robert Rogers, with an Introduction and a Biography of the Author by Allan Nevins.* Nevins never bothered to get a doctoral degree; he had no need of one.

While a reporter for the *Illini*, Nevins had covered a lecture given in Urbana by Paul Elmer More, editor of the *Nation*. More was impressed by the young journalist's work, and, thanks to the intervention of mutual friends, he promised Nevins a trial as an editorial reporter for the *Nation* when his work at Illinois was completed.

In the fall of 1913, therefore, Nevins began a fifteen-year career as a journalist in New York. He was on the staff of *Nation* (1913-1928) and of its sister publication, the *Evening Post* (1913-1924), writing editorials and literary articles. His home was near Columbia University in a neighborhood inhabited by many people connected with the academic world. He chose the location both because several of his friends from Illinois lived there and also because it offered him easy access to the Columbia library where he could do the research for his writing.

Nevins became literary editor of the *New York Sun* in 1924. In the following year Walter Lippmann lured him to the *New York World* where he remained until 1927. His journalistic work brought Nevins into contact with many prominent figures in literary and intellectual life—Hilaire Belloc, Ernest Boyd, Ellen Glasgow, James Truslow Adams, and William Allen White, among others. He got to know the Russian exile Aleksandr Kerenski, and the popular amateur historian Claude Bowers was a colleague at the *New York World*. Nevins played an editorial role in such causes as civil liberties, assistance for farmers, and support for labor unions. He was caught up in the intellectual currents and cosmopolitanism of the city that was the publishing and financial center of the nation.

"Most metropolitan newspapermen," Nevins observed in 1963, "have an ambition to produce books." Accordingly, while a journalist, Nevins devoted most of his spare time to research and writing. His interests came to focus increasingly on history. This growing interest in the discipline he had once abhorred might have resulted from the natural partnership between that discipline and journalism. Perhaps it was a respite from his daily grind of work as a literary editor; perhaps it was merely the natural outgrowth of combining literature and history in his master's thesis. One certain influence in turning Nevins to history, however, was *Evening Post* editor Oswald Garrison Villard, grandson of William Lloyd Garrison and author of a biography of the abolitionist fanatic John Brown. Nevins had not been at the *Evening Post* for many months before he and Villard were planning to write a history of the Civil War naval blockade, although nothing ever came of the project.

Nevins's fate was probably sealed when Oxford University Press sought an author for the volume on Illinois in its "Great American Universities" series. The editor of the series, an English professor at Columbia, was advised by friends in Urbana that Nevins would be an excellent choice to do the volume on their school. Nevins undertook the task, and his history of the University of Illinois was published in 1917. Other historical studies grew logi-

Allan Nevins

cally from his newspaper work. *The Evening Post: A Century of Journalism* (1922) was first published as a series of articles in the paper. After Nevins wrote an editorial on Englishmen in America, a publisher who read it suggested that he compile a volume on the subject. The result was an edited work, *American Social History as Recorded by British Travelers* (1923).

Whatever the reason for his interest in history, Nevins devoted more and more time to it. When his day's work at the paper was finished, Nevins, often joined by his friend Bowers, dashed from the office to the New York Public Library. There he labored until closing time when he emerged with an armload of books to carry home and work with late into the night.

The most important of Nevins's early historical works was *The American States During and After the Revolution, 1775-1789*. As early as 1914 Nevins had realized that the histories of the thirteen colonies had been studied in detail up to the beginning of the War for Independence in 1775 but that there was a great gap in state histories of the period after the war began. At first he envisioned an ambitious series of books that would cover the histories of the states throughout the nineteenth century, but, because a lack of funds and the pressure of other tasks delayed the project, it was published in 1924 as a work of much smaller scale covering only the states' internal conflicts generated by the political and social changes that accompanied the war and its immediate aftermath. Nevins dealt with such problems as taxes, paper money, debtor laws, tariff legislation, and treatment of the Loyalists.

Except for *Ponteach*, which was criticized for poor style and inaccurate quotations, Nevins's early ventures into the writing of history were generally well received. One reviewer called *The Evening Post* the best of the recent histories of newspapers and praised the author's "good judgment in arrangement and emphasis [and] . . . clear and easy style." Another reviewer found the volume on British travelers "a valuable tool for the history teacher as well as an interesting and thought-stimulating book for the general reader." Samuel Eliot Morison, although critical of some aspects of *The American States During and After the Revolution* (especially Nevins' treatment of Massachusetts), noted that the book "is a valuable one, crammed full of useful facts that were not readily available heretofore."

The American States During and After the Revolution was highly regarded by the committee that awarded the Pulitzer Prize. The prize, however, went to another, more readable work. Nevins concurred with the decision. "My book is altogether too labored and dull," he commented, "simply because it is a tired piece of historical writing. I was tired when I wrote it late at night; I was tired when I brought it out; and it has a tired air about it." Perhaps this experience helped lead Nevins to place great stress on the quality of the writing in his subsequent works.

By the late 1920s Nevins's "little body of books" had attracted the attention of historians and publishers, and he began to receive offers to write and edit other volumes. Even more attractive was an opportunity to lecture at Cornell University in Ithaca, New York. The lectures were followed in 1927 by the offer of an assistant professorship in the history department of that institution. Nevins had long thought about college teaching. Ten years earlier he had observed, "it is amazing what a lot of unwritten history of interest and importance I am digging up. The one difficulty is that I have so little time. With the pressure of a newspaper office so constant, I sometimes heartily wish I could get a University post with a decent salary, where I could have my long vacation and better winter facilities for research."

Nevins spent a year at Cornell, lecturing on American political history from the time of the War for Independence to World War I. He was not happy away from New York City, and he frequently returned to his old urban haunts on the weekends. In 1928, largely through the intervention of his friend Lippmann, he was able to work out an arrangement to teach at Columbia while he continued to write for the *New York World*. Gradually, however, he made the changeover from journalist to professional historian.

In 1931 Nevins became De Witt Clinton Professor of History at Columbia, a post he held until 1958 when he reached the school's mandatory retirement age. He was happy at the university. "I always felt a sense of greatness at Columbia," he recalled five years after he retired. The school's long history, its lengthy list of distinguished alumni and its sense of important and large matters rather than "the narrow and pedantic" all appealed to Nevins. At Columbia he could indulge the "passion for American history" that he had developed.

Ray Allen Billington, who was a close friend of Nevins, pointed out that three major interests ran through Nevins's long teaching career. One of these was the era of the American Civil War which became increasingly the focus of Nevins's research and writing. The second was an effort to bring into his courses material on the very recent past. History, Nevins once argued, "lies this side the horizon, and indeed all around us," not just in remote periods and distant places. At a time when most historians shunned the decades immediately preceding their own day, Nevins taught such courses as Studies in American Political History, 1865-1925, which became in 1933 American Political History, 1865-1932.

The third area of Nevins's teaching interest was graduate instruction in historiography and methodology. In those courses Nevins lectured on "The Great Literature of American History" and stressed the necessity of the historian's developing his literary talents as well as his research abilities. The historian who wrote well would reach a wider audience and perform a greater public service than would the "dryasdust" scholar who plodded along grinding out dull prose and reaching few readers.

Nevins was a demanding instructor. "I work," he told a class in 1931; "so will you." "And," a former student recalled with awe a half century later, "we did." His teaching, however, provoked quite different reactions among the students. Even his friends admitted that he was not a dynamic performer in the classroom, especially in his early professorial years, and lazy and indifferent students dreaded his courses. Even some good students found his classes hard to appreciate. "A dull lecturer," one of them recalls, "practically running across the campus to get to or from the library." Nevins wrote out and read in his "gravelly" voice his lectures, which one admiring former student remembers as "rich, stimulating, full of factual detail, marvelously crafted and sprinkled with an engaging wit."

As Nevins's reputation grew, many students came to Columbia hoping that he would agree to direct their work. One year he walked into a room filled with graduate students and brusquely announced that he would accept the two women in the room as his students; the men whose work he directed were to be chosen on the basis of their grade point averages. "That way," one of the ladies recalled, "he got us and the cream of the crop." She added that "he was an excellent [dissertation] director, allowing his students free rein to explore their sources critically. Students were independent and intelligent. They were expected to know their way around their sources with little help from their director unless, of course, they ran into some special problem. . . . In the end he was marvelous, scrutinizing the final draft with a critical eye, correcting prose, spelling, everything, and often writing marginal comments like 'too much fluff.' None of his students had any reason to complain that he did not address himself thoroughly to their work."

Nevins and his wife, Mary, held occasional dinner parties for his students in his home near Bronxville, parties that one student still remembers "with great warmth." Yet a detractor writes, "I was told that he never joined guests in his home for cocktails, appeared just before dinner, and then excused himself to return to his writing immediately after dinner."

Nevins's work with his students often continued after their graduation. He frequently read and criticized the manuscripts of their books and wrote forewords for them. He was also willing to take the time to help others who were writing (or trying to write) historical studies. A now distinguished historian, while a graduate student in the 1960s, wrote Nevins seeking information about the subject of his dissertation, a Southern author who had known Nevins. Somehow, the historian squeezed the time from his busy schedule to send a long and informative reply. Nevins even read and criticized a work which, in the words of his friend Billington, was "an antiquarian study of monumental insignificance. . . . [a] deadly tome." Nevins prepared a careful evaluation of the work, praising those parts he thought worthy of praise and encouraging the author, a retired librarian, to undertake revisions calculated to occupy the remaining years of her life. The author, naturally, was pleased at the attention she received from the great historian.

Although he carried a very heavy teaching and research load at Columbia, Nevins continued his accustomed involvement in nonacademic pursuits. "The New Deal," he once stated, "had no more ardent adherent than myself," and he wrote for newspapers and popular magazines in support of many of Franklin Roosevelt's programs. When World War II broke out Nevins became active with William Allen White's Committee to Defend America by Aiding the Allies. He produced many articles to combat the isolationists and to assist the peoples who were then fighting the Germans in a war which, Nevins believed, would inevitably involve the United States.

As his reputation grew, Nevins was often away from the Columbia campus to lecture or to serve as a visiting professor. He was chosen Harmsworth Professor of American History at Oxford University for 1940-1941, a post that he held again in 1964-1965. After a roundabout trip via Portugal, he arrived in war-torn Britain to find that he had ample opportunity to indulge his "militant Anglophile" sentiments. He lectured all over the country, seeking to encourage the British with his belief that the United States would enter the war. Nevins later admitted that he had "had no right to hold out such a hope to them" and that his belief was based only on his own judgment. He taught at Birmingham University, where he came under German bombing. He also wrote for the *Times* of London, and he made broadcasts for the BBC. When danger of a German invasion seemed great, he joined the Oxfordshire Home Guards, and, with those sturdy soldiers, he drilled and participated in target shooting and mock bayonet fights.

After the United States entered the war, Nevins offered to serve in any capacity where he could be useful. The Office of War Information sent him to Australia and New Zealand to help inform the people of those countries about the American role in the war. Only medical problems prevented his going to South Africa on a similar mission. Furthermore, for three summers after the war he served as the chief public affairs officer at the United States Embassy in London.

Following his 1958 retirement from Columbia, Nevins moved to California, where he was a senior research fellow at the Huntington Library in

San Marino. In October 1961, he was appointed to the Civil War Centennial Commission, and in December of that year he was elected the organization's chairman. Nevins worked during the centennial to ensure that the Civil War would be commemorated in a manner befitting the nation and the people who had suffered so much during the 1860s. "We shall use our energies and influence to help make the national commemoration of the Civil War both instructive and constructive," he proclaimed in 1962. "To this end we shall discourage observations that are cheap and tawdry, or that are divisive in temper, or that in any other respect fall short of expressing the magnanimity of the spirit shown by Lincoln and Lee, that fall short of honoring the heroism of the 600,000 men who gave their lives. We shall encourage observations which will assist the American people to understand the mingled tragedy and exaltation of the war and to draw from it lessons both practical and moral commensurate with its importance."

Under Nevins's leadership the commission sponsored a fitting commemoration. He insisted, for example, that full recognition be given to the history of black Americans in the war. "A host of white southerners died for what they believed a just cause; a host of white northerners died for what they held a sacred duty; a host of Negroes died, many in the uniform of the United States, for the achievement of freedom and human equality," he said. "We must honor them all. When we finally reach the commemoration of Appomattox, we shall treat it not as victory or defeat, but as a beginning—the beginning of a century of increasing concord, mutual understanding, and fraternal affection among all sections and social groups of the republic." Choosing to stress history, education, and the large moral significance of the war, the commission sponsored booklets, bibliographies, and symposia at which both professional and lay historians presented papers on various aspects of the 1860s.

Nevins spent most of his last years in San Marino, California. He suffered the first of a series of strokes in 1967, but he continued to write, trying to complete a massive history of the Civil War era before he died. His death occurred on 5 March 1971.

Unlike many twentieth-century historians, Nevins devoted a great deal of time and thought to his discipline's essential nature and to its place in human society. The result of this cogitation—while not a traditional philosophy of history, a mode that Nevins distrusted—was a small collection of litera-ture setting forth what might be called the Nevins creed of history.

History, he maintained, was too important to the individual, to the nation, and to the species to be left to the historians. Clio's discipline, he believed, was useful as a "guide for men in their daily round." It shaped human dreams and ambitions, it helped improve the quality of life, it was a "womb or matrix of nations," the basis for the "complex character and enduring strength of any human organization," "a maker of nations . . . [and] their inspirer," he declared in *The Gateway to History* (1938). The discipline fortified higher human resolves, teaching that "In the larger accomplishments of the [human] race we feel we have a share." History was "a bridge connecting the past with the present, and pointing the road to the future."

The discipline, however, could be perverted, as the Nazis had done in Germany and the Bolsheviks had done in the Soviet Union. Both groups had followed a "crude policy of deforming history to suit an ideological purpose and . . . [had used] the weapons of totalitarian compulsion to enforce an arbitrary view of the past." Only history produced with a high intention, "an earnest effort to ascertain the truth objectively," could "truly nourish, inspire, and guide a people over a long period of time," Nevins believed. History as the "servant of truth cannot be slave of party or nation." True history, therefore, operates to free men and nations, but it must be constantly and jealously guarded.

Good history is essential to democracy, Nevins believed. It provides guidance for social and political leaders, it affords instruction in general citizenship for the average man, and it contributes to the creation of an overall climate of public opinion. In the late 1940s Nevins, while with the embassy in London, argued that an accurate knowledge of American industrial and labor history would help the British public to understand the United States and would therefore lead to better Anglo-American relations. Good history is usable history that people need and, Nevins believed, want. "History," he argued in 1939, "is defeated and worthless if it does not gain a popular following."

In his 1959 presidential address to the American Historical Association, Nevins spelled out the criteria by which good history could be recognized. Such history is characterized by "a broad catholicity" so that it is available in many forms to every person (variety, he once noted, is also good for history). Good history is written with "gusto" and "delight." The writing of history, Nevins opined in 1962, "ought to be kept a reasonably free and joyous pursuit." A great part of good history must be "assimilable to current needs" and therefore usable to "the democratic public [that] lives in the present and future." Finally, "the cardinal requirement" is that it must not be dehumanized; it should be narrated "in terms of living men and women seen as individuals, groups, or communities." "Journalism," he once said, "teaches an observant man that to understand history he must understand human nature."

Good history, Nevins argued, must be based the scientific method—the careful, systematic collection, observation, and organization of information; inductive logic; and the use of hypotheses to reach conclusions. As he goes about his work, the true historian, like the scientist, "casts off, so far as possible, the prejudices of race, nationality, class, and faction." He constantly seeks new techniques, such as statistics, demography, and psychology, to help him reach a better understanding of the past.

Good history, however, is only based in science. It becomes, in its final form, literary art. Nevins, who had great admiration for the "literary historians" of the nineteenth century—Prescott, Motley, Bancroft, Parkman, Hallam, Macaulay, Napier, Carlyle—deplored the ascendancy that the "scientific school" had gained over the discipline. Such "scientific" historians as Buckle, Renan, and Burckhardt, with their mechanistic theories borrowed from the natural sciences, had produced a "colder . . . more austere" and depersonalized history than had their predecessors. In so doing, these "scientific" writers had separated historians from the public. With their appearance history had ceased to be literature, Nevins asserted, and its influence on the American people had begun to decline.

Nevins maintained that the historian owed the public four things: the fullest possible research, strict care to avoid factual errors, his best powers of insight and judgment, and imagination. Too many professional historians had overvalued the first two and ignored the last two. This distorted sense of values had lowered the literary quality of history and was, Nevins held, largely responsible for the fact that in the twentieth century history was virtually excluded from the realm of American letters.

As an art rather than a science, history would be attractive to the average citizen, Nevins believed. Without abandoning the accuracy of the scientific school, historians should seek to restore literary grace and excitement to their prose. Success at this task would regain for history a wide popular following. Such a following would both restore history to its traditional place as a major factor in public life

and letters and enhance the quality of American democracy, Nevins contended.

With these ideas he fought his battles against the "dryasdust" historical writers, the "academic glossologists," the "school of pedants," who "write dull books and abuse good ones," who corrupt novice historians into their ways with "petty monograph subjects" and for whom factual accuracy was the purpose of research. Such historians delighted in the public neglect of history because they believed that their discipline should be "the possession of a Germanic-minded few, a little knot of *Gelehrten* squeezing out monographs and counting footnotes," Nevins wrote. These "dryasdusts" controlled many university history departments, most of the historical associations, and most of the research funds. Their "deadly ponderosity" was a burden that history could not carry. They must be driven "back to the cobwebs" whence they came.

Although he expended much energy attacking pedants, Nevins criticized also those whose sole purpose was popularity. In his menagerie there were three major groups of historians. One was the sound scholar who was a bad writer and therefore either virtually useless because no one read the truth he discovered or even dangerous because his wearying prose frightened the reader away from good history. A second undesirable type was the incompetent researcher, often not a professional historian, who was an able writer and was thus dangerous because he attracted readers to his false view of the past and hence of the present and the future. Last and best was Nevins's ideal—the competent historian who wrote well. "The best history," Nevins asserted in 1939, "is neither mere pedestrian fact accumulation on the one side, nor mere pleasant writing on the other, but represents a fusion of facts, ideas, and literary grace in a single whole." Nevins, who described himself in 1962 as "an amateur of history," railed against the first two types of historians and sought to encourage the third through both exhortation and example.

His years as a journalist, Nevins always maintained, had given him valuable training for his work as an historian. Specifically, he believed, journalism had taught him to get to work to meet deadlines and to go rapidly through a large mass of evidence. Unlike many professors, he once observed, he did not waste time puttering around. Journalism also emphasized the importance of the human factor in history. Perhaps most important, journalism taught him to write better, to put his prose in as exciting a form as possible, and he consequently often rewrote his pages three or four times in an attempt to better the style and heighten the sense of drama.

Books flowed from Nevins's pen in a stream that ended only with his death. So vast was this oeuvre that only a few of the volumes that Nevins wrote can be considered here. Many of his works, it should be noted, were written with the assistance of others. Graduate students were expected to help with his research (for which they were paid), and many of his later books were produced with massive assistance from two competent historians, Frank Ernest Hill and E. B. (Pete) Long.

Probably the most far-reaching of all Nevins's writings were those in which he forced historians to reexamine their ideas about industrial development in the United States. Historians had long viewed industrialization from the social, political, and economic perspectives of the Progressive reformers of the early twentieth century. Industrialization, such Progressive historians as Charles A. Beard had believed, had produced great misery for the average American and spawned the "robber barons" whose avariciousness had despoiled the environment, corrupted the government, ruined genteel society, and generally enriched the few at the expense of the many.

Nevins's rethinking of this subject had begun with his *The Emergence of Modern America, 1865-1878* (1927), a volume in the History of American Life series. It continued when he wrote *Abram S. Hewitt: With Some Account of Peter Cooper* (1935), a biography of industrialists who had played a major role in developing the iron and steel industry in the nineteenth century and who had also been active in philanthropy, education, civic reform, and politics. Cooper, in fact, had been the agrarian-based Greenback party's presidential candidate in 1876. The two men simply did not fit the Progressives' stereotype of the greedy, grasping, corrupt, rapacious, boorish American businessman.

The book on Hewitt and Cooper attracted the attention of the Rockefeller family, and Nevins was asked to write a biography of John D. Rockefeller, Sr., founder of the Standard Oil Company, builder of the petroleum industry, and philanthropist. Research in Rockefeller business and family records for the biography, initially entitled *John D. Rockefeller: The Heroic Age of American Enterprise* (1940), gave Nevins new insight into industrialization. He had much the same experience in writing *Ford* (1954-1963), a three-volume biography of Henry Ford, the automobile manufacturer, and in composing *The World of Eli Whitney* (1952), a study of the inventor of the cotton gin and the man who introduced the concept of interchangeable parts that led to mass production.

From these investigations Nevins developed the thesis that historians should take a less jaundiced view of the men who had created industrial America. The basis of American progress since at least 1800, he concluded, had been business and industry, and the actions for which the industrialists had been so roundly condemned had not been crimes in their own day. Industrialization in the United States, in fact, had been accomplished with far less human suffering than had accompanied the transformation in other nations. Industrialization, Nevins argued, had raised the American standard of living and lowered the cost of manufactured goods. The conduct of big businesses had often been more ethical and less dishonest than that of their smaller competitors who had been so beloved by earlier historians. Most important, Nevins maintained, the businessmen had forged a great industrial power from an agricultural republic just in time to insure victory over Germany in World War I and World War II.

Nevins also wrote several important political biographies. His *Frémont, the West's Greatest Adventurer* (1928), an account of John Charles Frémont, the "Pathfinder of the West" and the 1856 Republican presidential candidate, was widely praised for its excellent style as well as for its historical significance. In addition, Nevins was asked by his friend John Campbell White to write a biography of his diplomat father. *Henry White: Thirty Years of Diplomacy*, appeared in 1930 to general acclaim. One reviewer called it the "most important and valuable historical production of the year." "The only sour note," Nevins once remarked about *Henry White*, "was struck by a jaundiced creature . . . who wrote an unreasonably caustic paragraph in the *American Historical Review*. What ailed the pedant I never found out, for he happily died a few months after penning this acid effusion; probably from an excess of bile."

Nevins had noticed that the earlier American Statesmen series of biographies had virtually ceased after producing volumes on political leaders prominent before 1865, and he persuaded the publishing firm of Dodd, Mead and Company to launch the American Political Leaders series to cover more recent politicians. Nevins edited the series and wrote for it *Grover Cleveland: A Study in Courage* (1932), which won a Pulitzer Prize in 1933. Offering a new look at Cleveland's role in labor and foreign affairs, Nevins placed great emphasis on Cleveland's moral courage, common sense, and honesty during a period of generally low morality in public life. In another excellent biography for the series, *Hamilton Fish: The Inner History of the Grant Administration* (1936), Nevins clarified many of the political and diplomatic problems of the 1860s and 1870s. *Hamilton Fish* received a Pulitzer Prize in 1937.

In all of his biographies Nevins sought by thorough research to develop in detail the personalities and characters of his subjects, to evaluate them fairly against the broad background of their times, and to combine scholarship, interpretation, and good literary style. He was occasionally criticized for writing what were, in some cases, family-sponsored biographies and for often aligning himself with his subjects, especially with capital against labor. Nevins, however, was not blind to the shortcomings of those whose lives he studied, and his books were reasonably balanced accounts. The praise and awards that the books received attested to Nevins's success as a biographer.

In the mid-1940s, during intervals in his war work, Nevins began what would become his magnum opus, a general history of what he called "the greatest of the world's civil wars." When he was a young man, Nevins had read the volumes of James Ford Rhodes and James Schouler that described the dramatic events of the Civil War era. Perhaps, as Nevins himself once suggested, his own Illinois background was the real beginning of his interest in that period of American history. Illinois was the state of Abraham Lincoln, Stephen A. Douglas, and Ulysses S. Grant. Camp Point and surrounding Adams County were in west-central Illinois on the Mississippi River and in Nevins's early years had had a population that included many Southerners. As a boy and a young man Nevins had known many veterans of the great conflict.

Whatever the ultimate origins of the dream, Nevins, as soon as he became interested in history, wanted to write a complete account of the United States from the Mexican War through Reconstruction, an account that would be written, he said, "after the style, if I may be so bold as to name much greater examplars, of Macaulay and George Macaulay Trevelyan." It would also, he hoped, be a balanced and fair work.

Nevins planned *The Ordeal of the Union* as a ten-volume work. Each volume would be complete and stand by itself, but the whole would form a comprehensive history that would not only be balanced between the contending sections but would also redress what Nevins saw as the unfortunate preponderance of military subjects in histories of the period. Ninety-nine percent of the writing on the Civil War, he complained in 1961, had focused on the military aspects of the struggle.

The first two volumes of Nevins's history appeared in 1947; the third and fourth in 1950. These works opened with the surrender of Mexico City to the United States Army in 1847 and closed with the inauguration of Abraham Lincoln on 4 March 1861. The early years of the war were covered in the fifth and sixth volumes, published in 1959 and 1960 respectively. The seventh and eighth volumes, which dealt with the last years of the conflict, appeared in 1971. Death kept the historian from writing the planned two volumes on Reconstruction. The 1971 volumes, in fact, were completed and seen through publication by E. B. (Pete) Long, Mary Nevins, and Allan Nevins's secretary Lillian Bean.

True to his pledge, Nevins emphasized political, social, administrative, cultural, and economic history. His early volumes contained chapters on social and economic reform, slavery, railroads, industrialization, immigration, and the "Contrast of Cultures" between North and South. In the later volumes Nevins stressed the way in which the struggle evolved from the "improvised war" of 1861-1862 through a "revolution" in 1862-1863 into the "organized war" of 1863-1865. He was especially interested in describing how the changes wrought by the conflict acted as a catalyst to prepare the nation for its industrial future. "The old individualism," he wrote, "yielded in a hundred ways to [the] disciplined association" that was characteristic of the modern industrial state.

The two most controversial issues raised by the first four volumes were Nevins's treatment of slavery and his interpretation of the causes of the war. These matters must be understood in terms of both the writer's own experiences and of the more or less orthodox interpretations at the time he wrote. Most older historians had experienced a great shock at the horrors of World War I which they saw as an aberration in the natural, peaceful evolution of human society toward progress. These historians ("the revisionists") deplored war and disparaged those whose refusal to compromise led to armed struggles. War, they thought, was needless and in itself produced few, if any, beneficial results but many that were undesirable. North and South, the revisionists believed, had had no fundamental differences nor was there any moral issue involved in the struggle of the 1850s and 1860s. The Civil War was, therefore, the unfortunate result of fanaticism, especially on the part of the uncompromising Northern abolitionists. It produced no good results (slavery would have ended without the war) and many that were bad, such as the rise of the greedy industrialists.

Nevins, although almost as old as some of the revisionists, had experienced World War II first-hand and, like many younger historians, had come to a different conclusion about human conflict. War, he agreed, was terrible, but it was sometimes necessary and could sometimes produce good results that outweighed the suffering and death it caused. North and South, he concluded, had had fundamental differences. Put simply, their visions for the future of the American nation were incompatible. The poor quality of political leadership in the 1850s had made it impossible to work out a compromise that would both preserve the Union and end slavery. Similarly, the world wars had been necessary to preserve the civilization of the English-speaking peoples and to eradicate the evil of nazism. Furthermore, Southern resistance to racial equality in the 1940s and 1950s indicated how deep anti-Negro prejudice was and raised serious questions about whether the Southerners of the 1840s and 1850s would ever willingly have abandoned their peculiar institution. Slavery, Nevins stressed, was only a part of the larger problem of race adjustment that seemed so intractable in his own day. Given the poor political leadership and the fierce Southern opposition to changing the status of blacks, the Civil War had been, Nevins concluded, both inevitable and necessary. In no other way could slavery have been removed from American society. The war, he argued, had ended slavery and preserved the Union. It therefore was worth what it cost.

The historian devoted two chapters of his first volume to a discussion of slavery. In trying to show "a strong and equal sympathy for both slave and slaveholder; not emotional bias, but the sympathy which leads to understanding," Nevins "strongly emphasized that the evils of slavery appertained to the institution, and not to any special traits of the Southern people." Individual slaves might be decently fed and housed and reasonably content with their lot, but "Slavery was the greatest misery, the greatest wrong, the greatest curse to white and black alike that America has ever known."

Reviewers pounced on Nevins. Southerners such as Fletcher Green, Charles E. Cauthen, and Robert H. Woody criticized him for showing a Northern bias. They contended that he, like the abolitionists, was blinded by his moral values and therefore unable to judge fairly the antebellum South. Such Northerners as Oscar Handlin and Arthur M. Schlesinger, Jr., criticized Nevins for being too harsh in his comments about the abolitionists and for being too vague in his moral condemnation of slavery. As the remarks of his reviewers showed, Nevins achieved the balance he sought.

In volumes five through eight Nevins continued to emphasize the social and political history of the period. These works were less controversial than the earlier volumes had been. The historian's descriptions of the war years were well done and involved issues that were of less immediate concern in the lives of his reviewers. In addition, many of Nevins's interpretations of the 1860s had been adumbrated in some of his earlier writings. Reviewers praised the thoroughness of his research, the breadth of his coverage, and his literary grace and pointed out that in almost every chapter he had been able to increase historians' knowledge of the period. Some critics, however, faulted him for being mostly a synthesizer, for his slight treatment of the South (which Nevins had justified on the grounds that the South had already been thoroughly studied), and for not giving due credit to other historians whose work he had probably consulted. One must remember, however, that Nevins himself had done so much research that he may have developed independently the same ideas that other historians had formulated. A more serious criticism was that Nevins, although acknowledging its existence, underestimated the extent of Northern anti-Negro prejudice. He therefore, like many of his contemporaries, tended to see mid-nineteenth (as well as mid-twentieth) century racism as more exclusively a Southern than a national problem.

In addition to teaching and writing, Nevins also involved himself in several projects designed to benefit historical study in the United States. Two of these projects deserve special mention. Sometime in his early years at Columbia Nevins realized that history needed "a new adjunct in carrying the results of its researches to the public, for history can never be healthy without public interest and support." By the late 1930s he was advocating a magazine to "present historical events, developments, and personalities in a colorful, vigorous, yet authentic way to the great body of people who, I knew, were hungry for such fare."

Nevins first tried to interest the American Historical Association in publishing such a journal, but that "learned, hidebound and then [late 1930s] essentially pedantic organization [of] rather narrow-minded Ph.D.'s" voted down his proposal. Undaunted, Nevins and some of his friends organized the Society of American Historians to publish a popular magazine of history and to encourage and reward literary excellence in historical writing. Eventually Nevins, working with "a gifted group of young men trained on *Time* and *Life*, and in Western journalism," helped launch *American Heritage*. Nevins watched proudly as its circulation grew to well over 300,000 before his death. Bruce Catton, like Nevins a journalist turned historian, also played a major role in the success of the magazine.

Nevins's experiences as a journalist, teacher, and writer also led him to the second major project. His work as a newspaperman and his interest in late nineteenth- and early twentieth-century history brought him into contact with individuals who had made the history that he lectured and wrote about. As a newspaperman he had interviewed people and realized that the testimony he was hearing from them would not be available to future researchers. Later, Nevins had talked with Mrs. Grover Cleveland and with some of the people who had known John D. Rockefeller, Sr., in conjunction with the research for his biographies of those men.

The practice of interviewing people to obtain information about the historical events in which they had participated was not new; Hubert H. Bancroft had done extensive interviewing of old pioneers in the West. However, Nevins advocated an organized effort to gather information from living people for use by future historians. Papers and other documents would continue to be important, but Nevins realized that much modern communication was by telephone or other means that left no trace. To counter this threat to the historical record, he began in 1948 the Oral History Project at Columbia.

Many historians were indifferent to the project or skeptical that it would have either value or success, but Nevins persisted. He raised money; he conducted interviews; he organized the Oral History Association. Gradually information was gathered, transcribed, and organized. Scholars after several years discovered the richness of the resources in the Oral History Collection at Columbia, and the value of Nevins's concept was fully demonstrated. Similar projects have been launched by other universities and even by private businesses. One of the businesses which created its own oral history program, Nevins liked to point out in his later years, was a bank that had refused his request for financial aid when the Columbia project was getting underway.

Nevins's enormous contributions to history were made possible, in large part, by his wife, Mary, whom he married in 1916 when he was on the staff of the *Evening Post* and she a student at Columbia. Mrs. Nevins devoted herself to handling day-to-day family matters so that her husband would be as free of distractions as possible.

Nevins's productivity was also attributable to his own characteristics—incredible energy, good health, iron discipline, and the ability to concentrate on his writing to the momentary exclusion of everything else. Because he was a workaholic who "could never sit back and do nothing," his efforts to devote every possible minute to his historical work have spawned numerous anecdotes. Nevins read galley proofs as he walked between his office and the library at Columbia. When the historian once went to an upstate New York university to lecture, his host arranged a cocktail party and dinner in his honor. Guests who arrived early heard a furious pounding on a typewriter behind the closed door of the host's study. At exactly 7:30 P.M., when the party was to begin, the typing stopped and Nevins emerged to join the guests for a "delightful" evening. On yet another occasion Nevins went to Atlanta in 1964 for a meeting of the Civil War Centennial Commission. The airline having lost part of his luggage, a telephone call sent friends at Emory University scrambling madly to round up a portable typewriter to be rushed to the motel so that Nevins could work during the times he was not attending to the business of the commission. Furthermore, he normally ran up the stairs at the Huntington because the elevator was so slow that it wasted valuable time that could be devoted to writing. On one occasion, while showing two guests around his house, Nevins reached the room which served as his study. "This," he announced, "is where I work." He then sat down and began to type, forgetting the visitors.

One historian remembers that "during the [Civil War] Centennial I was his house guest. . . . I stood awe-struck at his office door at home and watched him move from one typewriter to another as he worked on three projects simultaneously." C. Vann Woodward called Nevins "a one-man history-book industry, a phenomenon of American productivity without parallel in the field."

Allan Nevins's history, like all history, was the result of its author's experiences as well as of his research. Nevins was clearly the product of the United States' traditional, British-oriented culture, and he was a middle-class "liberal," as that imprecise term was used in the middle of the twentieth century. Many of his interpretations of history can be explained by these factors. His views toward war and the absolute necessity of defeating Nazi Germany, his attitude toward the American industrial giant that made German defeat certain, and his obvious sympathy for black Americans in their struggle for equality all affected his history.

Allan Nevins's most enduring monuments will be *American Heritage* and the Oral History Project. Most of his historical writings will eventually be superseded, and his reputation will rise or fall as the prejudices of later historians become similar to or different from his own. American letters in general and American history in particular, however, will always be fuller, richer, and better because of Allan Nevins and the "history of interest and importance" that he discovered and about which he wrote so much and so well.

Other:

American Social History as Recorded by British Travellers, edited by Nevins (New York: Holt, 1923); revised as *America Through British Eyes* (New York: Oxford University Press, 1948);

The Diary of Philip Hone, 1828-1851, edited by Nevins (New York: Dodd, Mead, 1927);

American Press Opinion, Washington to Coolidge: A Documentary Record of Editorial Leadership and Criticism, 1785-1927, edited by Nevins (Boston: Heath, 1928);

The Diary of John Quincy Adams, 1794-1845: American Political, Social, and Intellectual Life from Washington to Polk, edited by Nevins (New York: Longmans, Green, 1928);

Polk: The Diary of a President, 1845-1849, edited by Nevins (New York: Longmans, Green, 1929);

Letters of Grover Cleveland, 1850-1908, edited by Nevins (Boston: Houghton Mifflin, 1933);

The Letters and Journals of Brand Whitlock, edited by Nevins (New York: Appleton-Century, 1936);

Selected Writings of Abram S. Hewitt, edited by Nevins (New York: Columbia University Press, 1937);

Forever Freedom: Being an Anthology in Prose and Verse from England and America, edited by Nevins and Josiah C. Wedgwood (Harmondsworth & New York: Penguin, 1940);

George Templeton Strong, *Diary*, edited by Nevins (New York: Macmillan, 1952);

A Diary of Battle: The Personal Journals of Colonel Charles S. Wainwright, 1861-1865, edited by Nevins (New York: Harcourt, Brace & World, 1962);

Civil War Books: A Critical Bibliography, compiled by Nevins and others (Baton Rouge: Louisiana State University Press, 1967-1969).

References:

Ray Allen Billington, "Allan Nevins, Historian: A Personal Reminiscence," in *Allan Nevins on History*, edited by Billington (New York: Scribners, 1975);

Lucille Marie Magnon, "Allan Nevins' Evaluation of Public Speakers as an Influence in American Culture, 1847-1861," M.A. thesis, University of Illinois, 1951;

Robert J. Terry, "The Social and Intellectual Ideas of Allan Nevins," M.A. thesis, Western Reserve University, 1958;

Harvey Wish, "Allan Nevins and Recent Historiography," in *The American Historian: A Social-Intellectual History of the Writing of the American Past* (New York: Oxford University Press, 1960).

Papers:

Major collections of Nevins's papers are in the Butler Library at Columbia University and at the Huntington Library. The Oral History Collection at Columbia has his reminiscences. The library at the University of Illinois, Urbana-Champaign, has a few of his letters.

Roy F. Nichols

(3 March 1896-12 January 1973)

Carol Reardon
University of Kentucky

BOOKS: *The Democratic Machine, 1850-1854* (New York: Columbia University Press, 1923);

Franklin Pierce: Young Hickory of the Granite Hills (Philadelphia: University of Pennsylvania Press, 1931; London: Oxford University Press, 1958; revised edition, Philadelphia: University of Pennsylvania Press, 1969);

The Growth of American Democracy, by Nichols and Jeannette P. Nichols (New York: Appleton-Century, 1939);

The Republic of the United States, by Nichols and Jeannette P. Nichols (New York: Appleton-Century, 1942);

A Short History of American Democracy, by Nichols and Jeannette P. Nichols (New York: Appleton-Century, 1943);

The Disruption of American Democracy (New York: Macmillan, 1948; London: Collier-Macmillan, 1967);

The Historical Study of Anglo-American Democracy (Cambridge: Cambridge University Press, 1949);

Advance Agents of American Destiny (Philadelphia: University of Pennsylvania Press, 1956; London: Oxford University Press, 1957);

Religion and American Democracy (Baton Rouge: Louisiana State University Press, 1959);

The Stakes of Power, 1845-1877 (New York: Hill & Wang, 1961; London: Macmillan, 1965);

Blueprints for Leviathan: American Style (New York: Atheneum, 1963); republished as *American Leviathan* (New York: Harper & Row, 1966);

The Invention of the American Political Parties (New York: Macmillan, 1967; London: Collier-Macmillan, 1967);

The Pennsylvania Historical and Museum Commission: A History (Harrisburg: Pennsylvania Historical and Museum Commission, 1967);

A Historian's Progress (New York: Knopf, 1968).

Roy Franklin Nichols, longtime professor of history and dean of the graduate school at the University of Pennsylvania, stands high among major interpreters of nineteenth-century American political history. His detailed investigations into the dis-

Roy F. Nichols

integration of the Democratic party during the 1850s won him his greatest acclaim. However, Nichols was also among the first to attempt an explanation of political events in their cultural contexts. As early as the 1930s, he borrowed heavily from psychology, sociology, and the natural and physical sciences to support traditional narrative political history with humanistic insights from the emerging field of social history.

Professor Nichols was born in Newark, New Jersey, to Franklin Coriell and Annie Cairns Nichols. He enjoyed a comfortable, even pampered, childhood as an only child; two older brothers had died before he was born. He reflected much later in life that he had inherited his love for learning and the drive to succeed from his parents. His early attraction to books of all sorts, his avid

328

interest in local Republican politics, his curiosity about his family history, and the celebrations surrounding the centennials of Lee's and Lincoln's birthdays and semicentennial of the Civil War all influenced Nichols's choice of career. By the age of fourteen, he had already decided to become a teacher of history. Nichols later recalled that his career began very inauspiciously, when at a grade school open-house program he confidently announced that the Pilgrims had settled Jamestown.

Nichols's formal historical training began in earnest when he enrolled at Rutgers in 1914. Four years later, after the acceptance of his thesis, "Personal Influence in United States Politics," a topic which had interested him since his boyhood involvement in Newark party battles, Nichols received his bachelor's degree. He remained at Rutgers for his masters degree, which he received in June 1919.

For his doctoral studies, Nichols attended Columbia University. There he studied under a number of the most distinguished historians of the early twentieth century, including William A. Dunning, Nathaniel W. Stephenson, Dixon Ryan Fox, and Benjamin B. Kendrick. When he wrote his professional autobiography, *A Historian's Progress* (1968), Nichols reflected nostalgically on his days at Columbia. That institution, he idealistically recalled, had been "designed to insure *his* intellectual nurture. It was *his* home and *he* was a central figure in it."

Nichols first worked under the direction of Dunning, who substantially influenced his career. It was Dunning who suggested that Nichols exploit his interest in personal influence in politics by analyzing the dissolution of the Democratic party during the 1850s, a course of events usually overshadowed by the rise of the Republicans. Despite initial misgivings and his own Republican leanings, Nichols undertook the project; thereafter, the political history of the 1850s remained his primary professional interest.

In Dunning's seminar Nichols met Jeannette Paddock, a fellow doctoral student from Wisconsin. They were married on 27 May 1920. While their professional interests only rarely coincided, they shared research trips and endured long separations to further their careers independently. At the same time, Nichols always happily noted, they remained each other's best friend and most severe critic. Both received their doctorates from Columbia in June 1923, the first married couple to do so from the same department on the same day in the university's history.

The accepted styles of historical writing in the 1920s naturally influenced Nichols's earliest works. However, when his dissertation was published as a book, *The Democratic Machine, 1850-1854* (1923), narrative political history that recounted events with little original research or analysis was already fading in popularity. Consequently, while Nichols was not deterred from his study of Democratic politics, he felt no need to adhere to traditional methods of presentation. Instead, he investigated the political behavior of individual candidates and other major figures during the presidential campaign of 1852 and the subsequent formation of Franklin Pierce's cabinet. Nichols was not so much interested in chronological events as in how and why a little-known New Hampshire man could be elevated to the presidency. He sought to explain the phenomenon in terms of politicans' personal struggles to rise to power, or to maintain it, in the rapidly growing and restive nation of the 1850s.

Biography as a historical tool also enjoyed some popularity as Nichols began his career. Before he had completed his doctoral dissertation, his mentor Dunning died, and the direction of his work fell to Nathaniel W. Stephenson whose biography of Lincoln had attracted much notice and popular acclaim. Stephenson's method of using biography not only to portray the life and times of his subject but also to explore individual motivation and behavior—truly a personal history—appealed to Nichols's interest in private influence in American politics. After considering Salmon P. Chase, Nichols chose as his subject the often misunderstood and maligned fourteenth president who had figured so largely in his dissertation, Franklin Pierce.

Nichols sought to recreate Pierce's life and the environment which had shaped his values. He spent much time in the New Hampshire capital at Concord where Pierce had practiced law. He read widely in contemporary local newspapers. He ferreted out previously undiscovered manuscript resources from descendants of persons influential in Pierce's political development. By his own admission, Nichols tried "to place Pierce in his habitat." *Franklin Pierce: Young Hickory of the Granite Hills* (1931) still stands as the definitive biography of New Hampshire's only president.

Nichols concluded that Pierce, like most of his contemporaries, simply did not understand the complexities attendant to national growth. His ideals remained those of a simpler, more pastoral age. The president failed to understand the depths of sectional hostility or the potentially divisive effects of a shift of political power accompanying urbanization, industrialization, and immigration.

Pierce chose to see political instability as mere party ploys rather than as manifestations of deeper social change. Compromise, which resolved nothing and satisfied few, became the president's favorite political tactic. But, Nichols concluded, Pierce was not alone in his confusion; the problems he failed to solve were handled no better by his contemporaries, nor were they resolved by the Civil War.

Nichols's deepest investigation into the political history of the 1850s was his most widely acclaimed work, *The Disruption of American Democracy* (1948). In this volume he established his growing reliance on a broad spectrum of social sciences. He described the United States not only as a political federalism, but more importantly, as a cultural federalism. Five divisive culture influences—metropolitanism, New Englandism, antislaveryism, territorialism, and Southernism—developed rapidly and unevenly, creating confusion and stirring agitation across the country, Nichols contended. Factionalism was inevitable. Unenlightened self-interest temporarily took precedence over statesmanship. The failure of Democratic politicians to appreciate the complexities of cultural federalism splintered the party and helped to foment an emotional struggle among representatives of various sectional interests to maintain power. "Hyperemotionalism" had sought its release through conventional political channels. When these efforts failed, North and South resorted to confrontation on the battlefield. Still, Nichols believed, along with Avery O. Craven, James G. Randall and others who rejected the idea of an irrepressible conflict, that war was not inevitable. The Civil War, Nichols felt, resulted from "the processes of human behavior," especially when competitive behavior overrode the urge for cooperation. While it followed that strife was inevitable, Nichols's behavioral concept suggested that war was only the most extreme alternative available to resolve the nation's emotional turmoil, not its sole choice.

The Disruption of American Democracy won the Pulitzer Prize for history in 1949. Despite such recognition, some reviewers for historical journals received the book with only guarded praise. Historians described the volume both as a monument to thorough research and as a mind-boggling mass of details that even lively writing could not save from boring its reader. Striking metaphors and incisive characterizations had not made a complicated story more comprehensible. Reviewers did acknowledge that the volume was more than a political history of the prewar years. Less apparent, however, was that the social and economic forces Nichols described were not mere addenda to his explanations of political events but an attempt to blend a host of factors that contributed to the nation's mass hysteria. Nichols explored not only what caused the war but also why war broke out at all and why it erupted when it did.

The Disruption of American Democracy was perhaps Nichols's first major effort to approach his subject from what he termed the "cultural" perspective. He had begun to use this technique when he explored the motivations and personal feelings of Franklin Pierce and his cabinet members and other associates, but now, employing in part the language of the social sciences, Nichols tried to explain how an entire national institution, the Democratic party, failed "to cope under stress." As his career progressed, he welcomed the use of increasingly more sophisticated analytical tools borrowed from sister disciplines. In his last major exploration of Civil War-era politics, *The Stakes of Power, 1845-1877* (1961), Nichols summarized a mass of precentennial historical writing, including pioneering quantitative studies and works which gave some insight into the feelings of the masses rather than focusing on the leaders.

But Nichols's research interests were not limited to the events of the 1850s. He also studied widely in diverse fields. His interest, for instance, in the application of the laws of the physical and natural sciences to the social processes he sought to explain led him to exchange ideas with Albert Einstein and Loren Eiseley. His activities with the Social Science Research Council stimulated Nichols's interest in the responsibilities of historianship, and he developed his own philosophy of the role of the professional historian.

Nichols was concerned with several specific barriers that he felt unnecessarily restricted the scope of historical inquiry. He especially deplored obsessive nationalistic biases and what he termed "an unrealistic attitude toward time." His own attempts to overcome these traps were apparent in a number of his works. His efforts to avoid these restrictions in part explain the wide range of topics Nichols chose to address and the manner in which he approached them.

Excessive nationalism had marked much American historical writing, a characteristic partly traceable to the example provided by popular nineteenth-century historians like George Bancroft. One result of this obsession, Nichols believed, was a tendency to describe only what appeared to make the American experience unique and to ignore that which linked this nation to others. He sought to escape this trap in two ways.

First, Nichols traced the European roots—especially the English roots—of American political institutions. A Pitt Professorship at Cambridge University in 1948-1949 provided him with an opportunity to use English libraries and archives. From his research he determined that many American institutions, including the two-party system, could be detected in some form as far back as the tenth-century invasions. This subject he explored in depth in *The Invention of the American Political Parties* (1967). Moreover, in *Religion and American Democracy* (1959), two lectures delivered at Rice University, Nichols traced American Christianity to its roots in the Middle Ages. Further, he paid attention to the role of the Catholic church in those areas of the nation settled by Spanish or French colonists, a break with traditional works on early American history which stressed only the various Protestant sects along the eastern seaboard.

Second, Nichols countered the tendency toward excessive nationalism by delving into the smaller sectors of society which made up the United States. He thus became an avid supporter of state and local history. After serving on the Pennsylvania Historical Commission for many years, he wrote *The Pennsylvania Historical and Museum Commission: A History* (1967), the story of the expanded organization which had developed with his help. Nichols also took an intense interest in genealogy and served as president of the Genealogical Society of Pennsylvania. Writing numerous articles for Middle-States historical journals, he bemoaned the fact that the important New York-New Jersey-Pennsylvania area had been lost between the colorful images of "New England" and "the South." By looking beyond national borders and within the component parts of the United States, Nichols challenged an entire school of American historical writing that assumed the uniqueness and uniformity of the nation's experience.

Nichols also abhorred attempts to split American history into short epochs, a common practice he found too artificial and confining to be useful. In *Advance Agents of American Destiny* (1956), for instance, he investigated some neglected and therefore obscure individuals who had influenced the course of the nation's foreign policy long before the establishment of formal diplomatic ties and of ministries abroad. Curiosity or the search for personal gain—not the service of the state—led pioneering traders, sailors, and merchants like William Shaler to far corners of the world, Nichols wrote. The connections they made, even the feath-

ers they ruffled, all ultimately influenced the course of United States foreign relations with the Orient, the Pacific Islands, North Africa, and South America.

Nichols also deplored historians' increasing tendency toward specialization since he feared that this impulse would stifle the capacity to synthesize and to understand the evolution of wide ranges of human behaviors and institutions. A particularly imaginative volume, *Blueprints for Leviathan: American Style* (1963), exemplified Nichols's penchant for stretching his own intellectual horizons and adapting the concepts of sister disciplines. In order to explain the historical development of self-government in the U.S., he borrowed Thomas Hobbes's biomechanical concept of the Leviathan, "an 'artificiall' organism or engine with 'artificiall' life." The American Constitution and the institutions created by it were the Leviathan. Though artificially designed, the Leviathan was capable, once launched, of growth, development, and adaptation to changing conditions. Usually the adaptations worked, as in the case of the Bill of Rights. Only once could the breakdown of the Leviathan not be prevented, and the nation plunged into civil war.

The new Southern Confederacy created its own Leviathan, curiously similar to the one from which it had seceded. It failed because the new country's own ambivalence toward its goals could not sufficiently motivate the new "engine." Was it really independence the South wanted, Nichols queried, or would simple readjustment of the existing Leviathan have satisfied its demands as well? Yet the process of reaching a consensus, so important to keeping the American Leviathan running, had not been incorporated into the Southern Leviathan, and thus the South's ambivalence was fatal.

Despite Nichols's unusual approaches to American history, his volumes generally received the acclaim of academic reviewers. His works were invariably well written and thoroughly researched. His ability to synthesize, to explain events, and to suggest new questions was unchallenged. Still, his intellectual boldness bothered some of his colleagues. Some historians questioned his use of phrases like "the dynamics of moral indignation," and others decried the loss of personal identity under a barrage of social science models. Reviewers often disagreed with Nichols's underlying assumptions. Generally, however, he received the respect, if not always the praise, of his peers for his imaginative observations and succinct syntheses.

In addition to his varied research interests,

Nichols maintained a lifelong interest in teaching history and improving graduate education. Early in his professional career, among his first teaching assignments at Columbia University, he became part of a team-taught, interdisciplinary course called The Civilization of Western Man. Impressed with the unified whole resulting when the viewpoints of anthropologists, sociologists, psychologists, and other social scientists were merged with the historian's usual chronological and factual approach, Nichols and colleagues John A. Krout, Witt Bowden, and later, Julian P. Boyd, published several course outlines to encourage this mode of teaching the background of American civilization.

During World War II, Nichols and his wife coauthored *The Growth of American Democracy* (1939), *The Republic of the United States* (1942), and *A Short History of American Democracy* (1943), three textbooks on American history for officer candidates. Borrowing heavily from the experiences in his interdisciplinary college courses, they prepared imaginative texts, combining political events with the social and economic environment. Further, they paid attention to the generally overlooked contributions of the Spanish, the French, and the Indians to American cultural patterns. They offered, perhaps for the first time, an American history textbook that was not primarily Eastern and Anglophilic. Florida, Texas, and the Pacific Northwest now could feel that they too were part of the American mainstream rather than subordinate, if colorful, adjuncts to the nation's Anglo-Saxon heritage.

In 1953 Nichols became dean and later assistant provost at the University of Pennsylvania, where he had served in the history department as a professor since 1925. During his tenure as an administrator, he served as president of the Association of Graduate Schools. He and his wife traveled widely, including a two-month whirlwind trip around the world in 1962 which incorporated a number of lectures in India and Japan under the auspices of the U.S. State Department.

Nichols also remained active in professional activities. From 1949 to 1953 he served as chairman of the Social Science Research Council, of which he had been a member for twenty-two years. He also served on numerous Middle States and Pennsylvania local history associations. In 1966, at the close of his academic career at the University of Pennsylvania, he was elected president of the American Historical Association. Despite all these organizational commitments, however, his first priority remained his own research and writing. It was totally consistent for him to have required guarantees that he could continue his personal research projects before accepting administrative positions he feared might interfere with his work.

Roy Franklin Nichols died in Philadelphia on 12 January 1973. Labeled by a colleague as one of the last "gentleman scholars," Nichols liked to point out that he had seen an entire historiographical cycle pass during his career. Entering his profession as a political historian, he had not surrendered his major interest while social and economic history eclipsed it in popularity during the 1920s and 1930s. When political history regained its stature in the 1950s and 1960s, complete with the methodological refinements supplied from many disciplines, Nichols had moved gracefully through the transition. Few men possessed the persistence or the intellectual stamina not only to welcome such changes but even to encourage them as a prime responsibility of professional growth.

Interview:

John A. Garraty, "Roy F. Nichols: The Causes of the Civil War," in his *Interpreting American History: Conversations with Historians* (New York: Macmillan, 1970; London: Collier-Macmillan, 1970), I: 277-291.

Papers:

The University of Pennsylvania Archives holds a large collection of the papers of Roy F. Nichols and of his wife, Jeannette Paddock Nichols. The collection includes personal and professional correspondence, diaries, speeches and classroom lectures, and other material.

Reinhold Niebuhr

(21 June 1892 - 1 June 1971)

David L. Carlton

SELECTED BOOKS: *Faith and History* (New York: Scribners, 1949; London: Nisbet, 1949);

The Irony of American History (New York: Scribners, 1952; London: Nisbet, 1952);

Pious and Secular America (New York: Scribners, 1958);

A Nation So Conceived, by Niebuhr and Alan Heimert (New York: Scribners, 1963; London: Faber & Faber, 1964);

The Democratic Experience: Past and Prospects, by Niebuhr and Paul E. Sigmund (New York: Praeger, 1969; London: Pall Mall, 1969).

Reinhold Niebuhr was not, strictly speaking, a historian. While most of his writings after World War II make extensive use of historical illustration and are informed by his elaborate philosophy of history, they are less works of scholarship than tracts for the times, topical books using historical examples to bolster an argument about the direction of public policy. For that reason his works have dated quickly and have generally stood apart from the mainstream of postwar American historiography. His major historical contributions are embodied in two books, one a study of the philosophy of history which expresses in systematic form the moral quandaries of intellectuals in the late 1940s and early 1950s, the other an influential application of that philosophy to a problem in American history.

Reinhold Niebuhr was born in 1892 in Wright City, Missouri, and grew up in a succession of small Midwestern towns where his father, a German-born Evangelical minister, held pastorates. Admiration for his father led Niebuhr into the ministry; after graduation from Elmhurst College in Illinois, seminary training at Eden Theological Seminary in St. Louis, and postgraduate study at the Yale Divinity School, he took a pastorate at the Bethel Evangelical Church in Detroit in 1915. During the next thirteen years, he built the small congregation into a large and influential church and became a leading member of the community; at the same time, he was building a national reputation through numerous articles written primarily for the social gospel press. Thus from the beginning of his career he was both an intellectual and an active participant in the community, energetically involved with the problem of reconciling Christian ideals with the requirements of effective action in the world. In 1928 he left Detroit for a position on the faculty of Union Theological Seminary in New York, which served as his home base until his retirement in 1960.

A committed liberal Christian, Niebuhr's disillusionment with Woodrow Wilson's moralistic diplomacy, and his observations of Detroit in the heyday of Henry Ford, made him increasingly skeptical of traditional liberal idealism with its faith in progress through education and moral suasion. The "children of light," he thought, were generally ignored or used by the true wielders of power, the "children of darkness." In this mood he became attracted to Marxism, especially after the Crash of 1929. For all their flaws, the Marxists recognized

Reinhold Niebuhr

333

that the core of the social problem resided in the disparity of power between man and man, power which was essentially self-justifying. The Christian ideal of self-denying love, while valid as an ultimate standard of judgment, was hardly an adequate guide to solving this problem, which required the sort of moral calculation explicitly rejected by an ethic of self-abnegation. That rejection, according to Niebuhr, was itself sinful, because by turning its back upon the world it gave the forces of evil greater scope in which to operate. Power could not be ignored, nor could it be reasoned with; it could only be checked by setting power against it. To wield power against power was, of course, to join the powerful in their sin; but sin was unavoidable in any case, and the responsible Christian had to be willing to soil his hands if he wished to be effective in the world. Throughout most of the 1930s Neibuhr identified this need for action with the need for a socialist revolution, though never without concern that victory would make the revolutionaries more corrupt, because more powerful, than their predecessors. Toward the end of the decade, however, forces far worse than American capitalism were loose in the world, and Niebuhr became increasingly impressed with the success of the New Deal, in its ad hoc, deviously political way, in creating a system of countervailing power which avoided the dangers of revolutionary self-righteousness and postrevolutionary monopolization of power. He was even more impressed with the achievement of Franklin Roosevelt in "beguiling" a nation loath to become involved in corrupt international power struggles into alignment with the forces ranged against the far more corrupt powers of fascism.

In the meantime Niebuhr was elaborating his general theological outlook, a process culminating in the publication of *The Nature and Destiny of Man* in 1941 and 1943. A portion of his system was a philosophy of history, which he elaborated in 1949 in *Faith and History*. Like most of Niebuhr's work, *Faith and History* has a polemical purpose; its target is what Niebuhr labeled the "modern conception of history." Simply put, the "modern conception" is the idea of progress, the notion that man, as he moves through history, will ultimately become perfectly virtuous and create a perfectly just society. In modern times this view has taken two forms: a liberal evolutionary form which sees man triumphing over his animal nature through reason, and a radical revolutionary form which sees man bursting the institutional chains holding him down. Niebuhr rejects them both; the root of evil in human history is neither irrationality nor social institutions but is

within man himself. If the standard of perfection in behavior is that of Christ on the cross, laying down his life for his friends, man's persistent efforts at self-preservation and self-justification are intrinsically sinful. Worse, the very virtue of man, his ability to transcend his animal nature, is the source of his sin. His ability to recognize his own limits, above all his mortality, causes anxiety, which he tries to resolve either through a cynical concentration on his own self-interest or an effort to transcend his limits by creating something which will outlast him. This latter urge, especially, is the propulsive force of history, but it does not propel in the direction of virtue. For, while man can convince himself that he has broken his own bounds, he can never actually do so; he is thus doomed to be forever masking his self-interest behind a stance of idealism. The ultimate examples of this fatal human flaw appear among the Communists. In their idealism, and their limited vision, they mistake an immediate cause of injustice (private property) for its root; when they succeed in abolishing property, they establish a worse tyranny, for there is no longer any external power to impede their own corrupted will. A similar flaw appears among liberal social planners and conservative free-market theoreticians, all of whom also use transcendent ideals to justify potentially oppressive distributions of power. Due to this tendency for virtue and vice to inhere in the same historical act, any given historical event can have both good and evil consequences. Thus, "progress" in history, while potentially good, creates new evils as it goes, and will until the end of time; this, to Niebuhr, is the "irony" at the core of history. To stress the "irony" of history, though, is not to be quietistic or to deny the potential for meaningful action. The appropriate behavior for man is one of struggle against injustice but coupled with humility and tolerance based on recognition of his own corruption. It follows that the best society (*not* the ideal society) is one in which the inexorable tendencies of man to oppress man are restrained by a system of checks and balances, placing no one in charge while keeping everyone under control.

Niebuhr's philosophy of history was enormously influential among postwar intellectuals, especially those concerned both with understanding the past and shaping the future. His stress on humility, tolerance, and countervailing and dispersed power as the hallmarks of liberal democracy gave such men as Arthur Schlesinger, Jr., a justification for a faith to replace the hope of human progress destroyed by the revelations of totalitarianism and war. His concern with the hidden defects of moralists also attracted the foreign policy "realists," notably George Kennan and Hans Morgenthau, who argued that the projection of "ideals" onto the international stage wrought far more havoc than did a frank but circumspect focus on "the national interest" as the chief end of policy. Niebuhr himself joined the ranks of the realists with his most important effort to apply his philosophy to the actual writing of history, *The Irony of American History* (1952). This brief work was concerned not with a single irony but with a whole system of ironies, set forth in a style so compressed as to be frequently confusing. Simply put (if possible), Niebuhr argues that the United States was established by "children of light," who believed that they had created here a uniquely pure and virtuous society which, clear of the corruptions of old Europe, could move unencumbered toward perfection. It was to these ideological origins, drawn from New England Calvinism and Enlightenment rationalism and reinforced by economic abundance and continental security, that Niebuhr attributed the American national character as he read it. While Niebuhr found the American obsession with individual liberty salutary both in itself and in its stimulation of economic growth, he was chiefly interested in the way in which the American ideology generated qualities which undercut its own intentions. Domestically, it led, on the one hand, to a rigid and complacent idolatry of the free market which ignored the oppressive power of large concentrations of privately held wealth, and, on the other, to a potentially oppressive faith in perfection through social planning. In world affairs it led alternately to isolationist efforts to keep virtuous America unsullied by foreign corruption and to disastrous crusades to impose those virtues on others. Fortunately, said Niebuhr, American success at balancing the forces of capital with those of government and labor showed both that we were "wiser than our creed" and wiser than the Soviet "children of light," who solved the same problem by creating a far greater one. Americans had now to learn a similar lesson in foreign affairs. Our power, and the need to counterbalance Soviet power, required us to surrender our ostentatious geopolitical piety; we had henceforth to act as a responsible great power but to do so in the recognition that our ideals were neither universally applicable nor necessarily unalloyed with self-regard.

As perhaps the most accessible of Niebuhr's major postwar works, *The Irony of American History* attracted considerable attention upon publication. While many, including some historians, found it impressive, its criticism of social planning and the giddier hopes placed in such devices as the United Nations, and its general skepticism about human progress, drew considerable fire, especially from liberals of a Deweyan stripe who resented being termed "unrealistic." The book's long-term influence is far more difficult to gauge. C. Vann Woodward modeled his celebrated essay "The Irony of Southern History" explicitly on *The Irony of American History*, and certain of its themes echoed through various studies of the "national character" produced in the 1950s and early 1960s. Many of these themes, however, were already present in the secondary works on which Niebuhr had largely relied in constructing his argument. For the most part, his book seems to have had little lasting impact. Its principal limitation lies in its polemical intent, which distorts its argument and dates its conclusions. Pursuing his quarrel with liberal rationalists, Niebuhr read their optimistic view of man and their progressive view of history as dating back to the Founding Fathers, whose views of man and of history were probably closer to Neibuhr's own than they were to John Dewey's. Nor did American prosperity and security from invasion and war apply prior to 1815 at the earliest. Niebuhr is undoubtedly guilty of caricaturing the liberal frame of mind, ignoring the "realistic" elements in thinkers from Locke to Dewey. The principal flaw of *The Irony of American History*, though, is its implicit tendency to justify the status quo of the early 1950s. Here, to paraphrase C. Vann Woodward, the irony caught up with the ironist. Niebuhr's belief that in our domestic life we were "wiser than our creed," a fact which he thought should teach us to be wary of pretension, became in other hands a new source of American self-congratulation, a validation of "can-do" pragmatism. The United States heeded his call to take up its world burdens but readily forgot his warning to be circumspect in its use. When the "ironic refutation" of American pretensions came in Vietnam, a new generation of moralists accused Niebuhr of having helped foster the new illusions. Christopher Lasch dismissed him as a cheerleader for America; the Christian socialist William Appleman Williams branded him a "heretic" for rejecting the millennial tradition in Christian thought. Niebuhr himself was little help; his health failed in 1952, and his subsequent work in history seemed tired, pallid, and derivative. *Pious and Secular America* (1958), a collection of essays, dealt with some specialized topics, notably the race question, anti-Semitism, and the role of religion in American life. *A Nation So Conceived* (1963), written with Alan Heimert, and *The*

Democratic Experience: Past and Prospects (1969), written with Paul E. Sigmund, mainly repeated familiar themes with lessened power.

Niebuhr's history, then, came to be viewed as an artifact of early postwar America, of little importance to later generations of historians. While true, that assessment is nonetheless unfortunate, for while Niebuhr's history is dated, his way of viewing history is not. His insistence on the ambiguity and irony of historical acts can provide a needed corrective to the melodramatic excesses of many of America's best younger historians, including some of Niebuhr's harsher critics. Niebuhr was, like most of them, committed to social change but, unlike many of them, had a far deeper understanding of the crucial force in history, the human psyche. It is this, a sense of the wholeness of man in both his aspirations and his depravity and as both creator and creature of history, that comprises Reinhold Niebuhr's most lasting contribution to our historical understanding.

Bibliography:

D. B. Robertson, *Reinhold Niebuhr's Works: A Bibliography* (Boston: G. K. Hall, 1979).

References:

June Bingham, *Courage to Change: An Introduction to the Life and Thought of Reinhold Niebuhr* (New York: Scribners, 1961);

Charles Frankel, *The Case for Modern Man* (New York: Harper, 1955);

Charles W. Kegley and Robert W. Bretall, eds., *Reinhold Niebuhr: His Religious, Social, and Political Thought*, volume 2 of Library of Living Theology (New York: Macmillan, 1956);

Henry F. May, "A Meditation on an Unfashionable Book," essay on *The Irony of American History, Christianity and Crisis*, 28 (27 May 1968): 120-122;

Arthur M. Schlesinger, Jr., "Prophet For a Secular Age," *Reporter*, 55 (24 January 1972): 11-14;

Nathan A. Scott, Jr., ed., *The Legacy of Reinhold Niebuhr* (Chicago: University of Chicago Press, 1975);

Scott, *Reinhold Niebuhr*, University of Minnesota Pamphlets on American Writers, no. 31 (Minneapolis: University of Minnesota Press, 1963);

Ronald H. Stone, *Reinhold Niebuhr: Prophet to Politicians* (Nashville, Tenn.: Abingdon Press, 1972);

Morton White, *Social Thought in America: The Revolt Against Formalism* (Boston: Beacon Press, 1957).

Papers:

Niebuhr's private papers are in the Library of Congress. Other Niebuhr material is on deposit with the Columbia University Oral History Project.

Frank L. Owsley
(20 January 1890-21 October 1956)

M. E. Bradford
University of Dallas

BOOKS: *State Rights in the Confederacy* (Chicago: University of Chicago Press, 1925);

King Cotton Diplomacy: Foreign Relations of the Confederate States of America (Chicago: University of Chicago Press, 1931); revised edition, edited by Harriet Chappell Owsley (Chicago: University of Chicago Press, 1959);

A Short History of the American People, volume 1, by Owsley and Oliver Perry Chitwood (New York & Princeton: Van Nostrand, 1945; revised, 1955);

A Short History of the American People, volume 2, by Owsley, Chitwood, and H. C. Nixon (New York & Princeton: Van Nostrand, 1948);

The United States From Colony to World Power, by Owsley, Chitwood, and Nixon (New York & Princeton: Van Nostrand, 1949; revised, 1954);

Plain Folk of the Old South (Baton Rouge: Louisiana State University Press, 1949);

Know Alabama: An Elementary History, 1890-1956, by Owsley, John Craig Stewart, and Gordon Thomas Chappell (Birmingham: Colonial Press, 1957);

Frank L. Owsley

The South: Old and New Frontiers. Selected Essays of Frank Lawrence Owsley, edited by Harriet Chappell Owsley (Athens: University of Georgia Press, 1969).

As Samuel Eliot Morison was of Massachusetts, Bruce Catton of Michigan, and Walter Prescott Webb of Texas, so was Frank Lawrence Owsley *of* Alabama. There was a connection in each of these cases between the vocation of the historian and the place of origin, a link which bound native identity to the choice of subject for scholarly research. Frank Owsley came to the discipline of history out of the desire to correct and replace fashionable but abusive misunderstanding of the past of his own people. As he wrote to his friend Allen Tate, "The purpose of my life is to undermine by 'careful' and 'detached,' 'well documented,' 'objective' writing, the entire Northern myth from 1820 to 1876." Though always careful to observe the distinction between scholarship and apologetics, he wrote Southern history as an "interested party," as one conscious of the role of nationalist and sectionally motivated Northern historiography in that great intellectual sequel to the War Between the States, the "conquest of the Southern mind." Owsley was thus both the historian of the South and the Southerner as historian. He found no conflict between the roles from the time, as a student of George Petrie at Auburn, he discovered in historical research and teaching an activity which could engage all his faculties and command his enthusiasm over the course of a lifetime.

Frank Owsley was born to Lawrence Monroe and Annie Scott McGehee Owsley in Montgomery County, Alabama, on a portion of the plantation inherited from his pioneer ancestor, Abner McGehee. His people had been among the first settlers of the state. Earlier ancestors had belonged to Clan MacGregor and to other intrepid and fiercely independent stock. Owsley grew up inside the postbellum South and was in his youth surrounded by the stories of old times not forgotten. What he knew of the Old South, its character and its rationale, came from acquaintance with people who had lived through its ordeal and had no apology for the decisions they and their families had made.

Owsley's earliest schooling was in the neighborhood of his father's holdings and was followed from 1906 to 1909 by further education at the Fifth District Agricultural School at Wetumpka, Alabama. From Wetumpka, Owsley went to Auburn (at that time Alabama Polytechnic Institute), from which he was graduated in 1911; from the same school he was in 1912 awarded the master of science with honors in history. What he learned at Auburn, under Professor Petrie, was that the study and teaching of history could be a profession, that there were techniques of writing and research in the discipline, and that what Americans from other regions of the country had written concerning the South did injustice to his people. The significance of Owsley's career is his success in correcting such calumny.

From 1912 to 1914, Frank Owsley taught history and Latin at the Fifth District Agricultural School, where he had originally prepared to be a farm demonstration agent. In 1914-1915 he was an instructor in history at Alabama Polytechnic. The following year he farmed, ran an agricultural experiment station, and read a little law. Then, having made a final decision for a career as a historian, he resumed his graduate studies at the University of Chicago, where he was a protégé of the Southern scholar and diplomat William E. Dodd. Owsley studied at Chicago from 1916 to 1919 with a brief interruption for military service. He taught at Birmingham-Southern the year following the completion of his course work at Chicago. Once back in Alabama, he met and married Harriet Chappell, who was to collaborate in much of his future research. They had two children, Frank Lawrence, Jr., and Margaret Chappell.

In 1920 Owsley accepted an appointment as assistant professor of history at Vanderbilt University in Nashville, Tennessee. Upon the completion of his doctorate in 1924, he was promoted to associate professor. In the following year his dissertation was published as *State Rights in the Confederacy*. He then began his study of Confederate diplomacy and, with Dean Walter Lynwood Fleming, made plans for the development of a Ph.D. program in history at Vanderbilt.

State Rights in the Confederacy is like Owsley's later books in its audacity, its overturning of received opinions. Evidence of resistance to the national government in Richmond by state authorities in Georgia, North Carolina, and other member commonwealths supports Owsley's argument that the Confederate States of America were undone from within, by an abstract passion for state sovereignty and not by the force of Northern arms. In his own words, "If a monument is ever erected as a symbolical gravestone over 'the lost cause,' it should have engraved upon it these words: 'Died of State Rights.' " Some Southern governors, Owsley shows, ignored requests for troops and supplies coming from President Jefferson Davis, preferring instead to protect their own territory—as if to imagine that the survival of state authority within the Confederacy was not predicated upon the independence of the entire region, as maintained on the field of battle by a *national* army. Of this peculiar and self-defeating behavior as practiced by Joseph E. Brown and Zebulon B. Vance, Robert Toombs and Alexander H. Stephens, Andrew Lytle has observed that "the principle of State Rights extended limited and specific powers to unlimited and selfish ends on the part of the states, and more narrowly, to the private wills of governors and various politicians." Readers are reminded of St. Paul's parable (I Corinthians 12: 12-27) of the rebellion of the limbs of the body against themselves. The point which Owsley makes says much about the political character of Americans in general in their relation to authority, of which the Southern version is only an exaggeration.

Owsley's second book, *King Cotton Diplomacy: Foreign Relations of the Confederate States of America* (1931), was the product of a year's research in the French and English diplomatic archives with a 1927-1928 Guggenheim Fellowship. The burden of this massive work is that the Confederacy in its foreign policy made a mistake in assuming that the material interests of the European powers, their need for cotton, would force them to break the Federal blockade of Southern ports and recognize the new nation. Owsley's analysis of the motives of European statesmen who made a policy with respect

to the South undercuts the theory that they were motivated by their own or their countrymen's profound hostility to the institution of slavery. The concluding chapter of the book, "Why Europe Did Not Intervene," is a scholarly classic, and it is still the authoritative treatment of the subject. According to Owsley, Great Britain always believed that the South would defend its independence with success. Moreover, for political and military reasons, it hoped to see the United States permanently weakened by its division into two republics. England was also making a lot of money out of the war by selling arms to both sides. Furthermore, were it to take sides with the South, Great Britain risked the loss of its merchant marine, of Canada, and of its wheat supply. Southern leaders miscalculated because they did not understand the English economy. However, Charles Francis Adams, Lincoln's minister to Great Britain, did.

Between 1930 and 1948 Owsley concentrated much of his effort in building a graduate program in history at Vanderbilt. In these years he directed over forty doctoral dissertations, plus innumerable master's theses. At the same time he joined with a number of his friends and colleagues, most of them with some connection to the Vanderbilt English department, in producing the memorable *I'll Take My Stand: The South and the Agrarian Tradition, by Twelve Southerners* (1930), a classic expression of Southern social and political thought and of resistance to the idea of culture "poured in from the top." As one of the original twelve Southerners who made the manifesto of what came to be called the Nashville Agrarians, Frank Owsley wrote many essays of opinion concerning the needs and grievances of his region. In a sense the Agrarian essays are an application of what he had learned from his study of history that had relevance to the situation of the South as a near colony while yet a component part of modern America. However, they also owe much to Owsley's piety, his devotion to the long continuity of life that had produced in the South a distinctive civilization: a devotion to the South *as a whole*. The most famous of these personal statements is "The Irrepressible Conflict" in *I'll Take My Stand*, a performance which, according to Thomas J. Pressly, left Owsley "in a position analogous to [that of] the Southern 'fire-eaters' " of the 1850s. Owsley's critics have attempted to denigrate the rest of his work by equating it with his partisan defense of his region. It is a great mistake, however, to confuse Owsley's objective historical scholarship with his statements on public policy and politics, for they differ in form and purpose and observe different decorums. But the public man who speaks in these topical exercises is also the historian who has discovered the link between distortions of the Southern past—the nationalist and Puritan version of the American identity—and the problems of the contemporary South in preserving its integrity as a traditional agrarian province of a modern industrial state.

As an Agrarian Frank Owsley wrote "Scottsboro, the Third Crusade: The Sequel to Abolition and Reconstruction" (1933) and "The Pillars of Agrarianism" (1935). He also contributed "Foundations of Democracy" to the second Agrarian symposium, *Who Owns America? A New Declaration of Independence* (1936), and wrote a number of book reviews from an openly Agrarian perspective. The spirit animating these works was that of the old-fashioned Southern Democracy, Jeffersonian, and committed to the notion that a healthy society is not overgoverned by Washington or dominated by giant corporations and big trade unions; that society is also not constituted by an urban proletarian majority whose members hold no real property and enjoy none of the principled independence which accompanies such possession. The Agrarian commitment to the kind of order which they hoped (while it still existed) to see preserved was rooted in their respect for its human product—the freedom and dignity of landed men living inside such a regime—and for its ability to restrain the endless hunger for power that characterized modern industrial civilization.

In a retrospect upon the Agrarian enterprise printed in the summer 1952 issue of *Shenandoah*, Owsley made it clear that most of his associates in that cause had in mind nothing more extreme than a balance between agriculture and industry, insofar as they spoke of political economy per se. Agrarian society embodied a modest approach toward the providentially "given" elements in the human situation, not a Faustian aggression against nature, Owsley suggested. Civility and the arts, religion and family could "not be expected to flourish" within a context established by ontological impiety. The other common denominator uniting the group was a shared devotion not to a pastoral myth but to a real South. This devotion reflected a fierce sectionalism which fostered hostility to most characteristics of modernity, a protest "not just against industrialism but against the brazen and contemptuous treatment of the rural South as a colony and a conquered province." When functioning as historian, Owsley was temperate in his approach, argued from evidence, and considered alternative interpretations. But he was also a trained rhetorician, a stylist who,

when writing in the character of citizen (which is logically prior to the role of historian), knew how to argue, to be (in his own words) "deliberately provocative," and how to persuade—when the survival of his world, as subsumed in the survival of its memory of itself, was at stake. There was no division of sensibility at the heart of his career.

The most important work either directed or conducted by Frank Owsley during his twenty-nine years at Vanderbilt concerned the collection and interpretation of evidence proving that a rural middle class existed in the antebellum South. This class was a freeholding yeomanry which made up a clear majority of the white residents of every Southern state, a majority that owned few if any slaves and that coexisted without class tension with a supposedly dominant minority of great planters who provided the region with most of its political leadership. As Owsley discovered, most of the "plain folk" either had relatives among the gentry or hope of advancing into that select company, on their own or through ambitious children and grandchildren. And the planters, in a society where jealous pride in personal dignity, backed up by a readiness to answer a challenge, was a basic presumption of all manners, were aware that deference on their part was a precondition of the deference they hoped to receive and, indeed, did receive, as Jefferson had expected.

Owsley, as a disciple of the "revisionist" historians, had no commerce with the simplistic and self-congratulatory readings of the American past propounded by the leaders of the nationalist school. He saw as nothing more than a mask for power politics the argument that the War Between the States had been fought over the future of Negro slavery. His explanation of the conflict, as developed in his November 1940 presidential address to the Southern Historical Association, was "egocentric sectionalism," a struggle between intellectual styles and religions, political theories and economic interests. That the nation, as Lincoln demanded, should be forced to become "*all* one thing, or *all* the other" would require moralistic bullying and some kind of conquest. From 1787 the states had existed in a federal union on the condition that such extreme rhetoric as appeared in the 1850s would not be a part of the ordinary exchange of political opinion between the sections. For the Southern yeomanry, the plain folk who had no economic stake in preserving slavery, the abolitionist attack on their region was nonetheless an affront and a threat to their identity. For if the South, on the basis of the moral sentiment (as opposed to Constitutional scruples) of its critics, could be isolated or dragooned with reference to its peculiar institution, then it might, on the basis of the same kind of enthusiasm, be subjugated "in all cases whatsoever." Moreover, slavery was a system of social control important even for those who owned no slaves. No Southerner welcomed the idea of his community being regulated by an administration put in power by a Northern sectional majority. The social and economic security of his region was dependent upon its right to self-government in the sphere of its domestic concerns. And finally there was the matter of honor, tribal loyalty, the *Gemeinschaft*. A traditional society was bound to make some kind of manly response to so much "hateful talk." In deciding for secession, even if their votes meant war, the plain people of the Old South chose to defend the kind of liberty for which their ancestors had fought the American Revolution, the kind of liberty which they embodied in the self-sufficiency of their day-to-day existence.

The labor of unearthing and documenting the freeholding middle class majority of a democratic antebellum Southern society involved not only Frank and Harriet Owsley but also a large number of Professor Owsley's students, whose monographs on the plain people in specific states constituted an impressive series. Critics of this research, such as Fabian Linden and Rupert Vance, who have quibbled with Owsley's statistical method, his definitions, and his political gloss upon the evidence, have done nothing to undermine his demonstration that the majority of the white inhabitants of the Old South were yeoman freeholders. Owsley found his plain people in the unpublished census records, in tax books, and in the diaries, letters, and newspapers of local history; he found them because he *knew* they were there, buried under the myth of "the Slavocracy." *Plain Folk of the Old South* (1949), first given as the Walter Lynwood Fleming lectures at Louisiana State University in 1948, is a landmark of American history. It is a model of exposition and Owsley's greatest achievement. It continues to have a major influence on the understanding of the South, particularly as reinforced by recent research by Forrest McDonald and Grady McWhiney on the cattle business in the Old South.

In the years of his research on the rural middle class in the antebellum South, Owsley also wrote, with Oliver Perry Chitwood and H. C. Nixon, the two-volume *A Short History of the American People* (1945, 1948). This text was reprinted repeatedly, and was, from the late 1940s through the 1960s, a widely adopted survey of American history. During the 1940s Owsley also played a major role in the development of the Southern Historical Association, which was to be important in disseminating the results of revisionist scholarship. It in fact became the most influential of the regional organizations. Owsley, in addition, served on the editorial board of the *Journal of Southern History* and on the executive committee of the Mississippi Valley Historical Association. When his mentor, Professor Dodd, was president of the American Historical Association, Owsley contributed "America and the Freedom of the Seas, 1861-1865" to *Essays in Honor of William E. Dodd* (1935). He also was a visiting professor at Columbia, the University of Illinois, Duke, and several other institutions. His reputation grew.

In 1949 he left Vanderbilt to accept an endowed chair as Friedman Professor of American History at the University of Alabama. Owsley had been frustrated by the lack of basic research materials in the Vanderbilt collection, and there had been some talk of deemphasizing regional history by a new administration at the Tennessee school. Moreover, the circle of friends so important to the middle years of his career had been dispersed from Nashville. Back in Alabama, he served for a time as chairman of his department and focused on locating source materials in Alabama history. He coauthored a textbook in state history, *Know Alabama: An Elementary History, 1890-1956* (1957), to which John Craig Stewart and Gordon Thomas Chappell (Owsley's brother-in-law) also contributed. In addition, he helped to inaugurate a new graduate program in history and directed many theses and dissertations on Alabama history.

Frank Owsley flourished in Tuscaloosa. He resumed work on an enlarged study of American foreign policy during the Civil War, a survey in which he planned to include an examination of the diplomatic records of Lincoln's government. This survey he intended to incorporate in a new and revised edition of *King Cotton Diplomacy*, which had gone out of print in 1954. At the University of Kentucky he also delivered the Blazer lecture for 1955, "Democracy Unlimited," a fierce attack on the alien character of egalitarianism when considered in the context of traditional American thought, a comment on the judicial activism of the Warren Court. He then attended a meeting of some of his old comrades in Agrarianism at Vanderbilt in May of 1956. For the fall of 1956 Owsley was given a Fulbright grant, which provided the opportunity for research in England but also involved an appointment as lecturer in St. John's College, Cambridge University. This work he had barely begun when he died suddenly at Winchester, England, on 21 October 1956. Harriet Owsley received a Fulbright grant to continue with the project, which in 1959 resulted in the publication of a revised edition of *King Cotton Diplomacy*. In 1969 Mrs. Owsley also brought out a posthumous collection, *The South: Old and New Frontiers. Selected Essays of Frank Lawrence Owsley*, which made generally available a wide sampling of her husband's articles and essays.

Frank Owsley had a powerful impact on the study of American history and on the teaching of the subject in the South, where his students are widely distributed. Many of them hold positions of importance at the present time. In some respects, Owsley was the center of an informal circle of Southern historians. He was genial, avuncular, devoted to animated exchange and argument, and a gifted raconteur. By all the members of this fraternity, Owsley was recognized as a special person, one of the "memory-keepers."

A community is bound together by Memory—Mnemosyne, "the mother of the Muses." Memory, of course, lives primarily outside the confines of written history. Her rites are celebrated in the hearts of a group of individuals linked together by struggle, blood, and fortune, by individuals who share a past. The English historian J. H. Plumb argues that this kind of bond in and through a common history, a past with authority, will soon disappear because it is in the way of unfolding perfections which none of us will agree to do without. Owsley as historian, though he was a master of the methods of modern historical scholarship, eschewed the mindless worship of facts qua facts, mere "social science." The admonitory past, the past as prescript, was to him not a dead but a comforting, friendly hand. In particular, he feared what would happen to the South if that hand were withdrawn and that memory destroyed. In such a case Southerners would forfeit an ingredient in their identity, and much of their liberty along with it. Bigness and concentration of power were always the adversaries for Owsley, even when in the 1930s he suggested a temporary intervention in the economy by state or federal authorities in order to encourage a wide distribution of property ownership, and the corporate liberty was always an object of his proprietary concern. He was an Agrarian who knew what it was to farm (owning and operating a farm during many of the years when he was teaching); a democrat who valued the leadership of gentlemen (as shown in his Plutarchian essay on Lee, "The Soldier Who Walked with God"); a chronicler who recovered a truth about his people by imaginatively living *into*

their experience and by submitting to the evidence all around him (and in his bones). Southerners, Owsley declared, were, in their various rebellions, "revolting not just against but for something," as much from love as from hate. No scholar of his time has had a greater influence on the interpretation of Southern history.

Other:
"The Irrepressible Conflict," in *I'll Take My Stand: The South and the Agrarian Tradition, by Twelve Southerners* (New York & London: Harper, 1930), pp. 61-91;

"America and the Freedom of the Seas, 1861-1865," in *Essays in Honor of William E. Dodd*, edited by Avery Craven (Chicago: University of Chicago Press, 1935), pp. 194-256;

"Foundations of Democracy," in *Who Owns America? A New Declaration of Independence*, edited by Herbert Agar and Allen Tate (Boston: Houghton Mifflin, 1936), pp. 52-67.

Periodical Publications:
"Defeatism in the Confederacy," *North Carolina Historical Review*, 3 (July 1926): 446-456;

"Scottsboro, the Third Crusade: The Sequel to Abolition and Reconstruction," *American Review*, 1 (Summer 1933): 257-285;

"The Soldier Who Walked with God," *American Review*, 4 (February 1935): 435-459; 5 (April 1935): 62-74;

"The Pillars of Agrarianism," *American Review*, 4 (March 1935): 529-547;

"The Historical Philosophy of Frederick Jackson Turner," *American Review*, 5 (Summer 1935): 368-375;

"A Key to Southern Liberalism," *Southern Review*, 3 (Summer 1937): 28-38;

"Mr. Daniels Discovers the South," *Southern Review*, 4 (Spring 1939): 665-675;

"The Economic Basis of Society in the Late Ante-Bellum South," by Owsley and Harriet Chappell Owsley, *Journal of Southern History*, 6 (February 1940): 24-25;

"The Origin of the Civil War," *Southern Review*, 5 (Spring 1940): 609-626;

"The Economic Structure of Rural Tennessee, 1850-1860," by Owsley and Harriet Chappell Owsley, *Journal of Southern History*, 8 (May 1942): 161-182;

"The Agrarians Today," *Shenandoah*, 3 (Summer 1952): 22-28;

"Democracy Unlimited," *Georgia Review*, 15 (Summer 1961): 129-143.

Bibliography:

Harriet Chappell Owsley, "Frank Lawrence Owsley: A Bibliography, 1925-1962," in *The South: Old and New Frontiers. Selected Essays of Frank Lawrence Owsley*, edited by Harriet Chappell Owsley (Athens: University of Georgia Press, 1969), pp. 259-269.

References:

William C. Binkley, "Frank Lawrence Owsley, 1890-1956: A Memorial Foreword," in Owsley's *King Cotton Diplomacy: Foreign Relations of the Confederate States of America*, revised and edited by Harriet Chappell Owsley (Chicago: University of Chicago Press, 1959);

M. E. Bradford, "What We Can Know for Certain: Frank Owsley and the Recovery of Southern History," *Sewanee Review*, 78 (October-December 1970): 664-669;

Bernarr Cresap, "Frank L. Owsley and *King Cotton Diplomacy*," *Alabama Review*, 26 (October 1973): 235-251;

Fabian Linden, "Economic Democracy in the Slave South: A Reappraisal of Some Recent Views," *Journal of Negro History*, 31 (April 1946): 140-189;

Andrew Lytle, Foreword to *The South: Old and New Frontiers. Selected Essays of Frank Lawrence Owsley*, edited by Harriet Chappell Owsley (Athens: University of Georgia Press, 1969), pp. ix-xiv;

Michael O'Brien, *The Idea of the American South, 1920-1941* (Baltimore: Johns Hopkins University Press, 1979), pp. 162-184;

Edward Shapiro, "Frank L. Owsley and the Defense of the Southern Identity," *Tennessee Historical Quarterly*, 36 (Spring 1977): 75-94.

Papers:

Owsley's papers are at Vanderbilt University.

Vernon L. Parrington

Michael O'Brien
University of Arkansas

BIRTH: Aurora, Illinois, 3 August 1871, to John William and Louise McClellan Parrington.

EDUCATION: B.A., Harvard University, 1893; M.A., College of Emporia, 1895.

MARRIAGE: 31 July 1901 to Julia Rochester Williams; children: Elizabeth, Louise Wrathal, Vernon Louis.

AWARDS AND HONORS: Pulitzer Prize for *Main Currents in American Thought* (volumes 1 and 2), 1928.

DEATH: Winchcomb, Gloucestershire, England, 16 June 1929.

BOOKS: *The Colonial Mind, 1620-1800*, volume 1 of *Main Currents in American Thought: An Interpretation of American Literature From the Beginnings to 1920* (New York: Harcourt, Brace, 1927; London: Hart-Davis, 1963);

The Romantic Revolution in America, 1800-1860, volume 2 of *Main Currents in American Thought* (New York: Harcourt, Brace, 1927; London: Hart-Davis, 1963);

The Beginnings of Critical Realism in America, 1860-1920, volume 3 of *Main Currents of American Thought* (New York: Harcourt, Brace, 1930).

Vernon Louis Parrington, whose *Main Currents in American Thought* has been the most influential Jeffersonian statement of American intellectual history in the twentieth century, must be numbered among the Progressive school of historians. Unlike Charles Beard and Frederick Jackson Turner, however, his contribution came late and rested upon a single uncompleted work. Few historians have been so obscure as Parrington, so suddenly famous, so latterly unread. Like the agrarian revolts he celebrated, he came from the American hinterland, touched the centers of power, and then retreated without explanation, leaving only the text of his magnum opus as graceful testimony of the disturbance.

Parrington was born in Aurora, Illinois, in 1871. His grandfather, John Parrington, had immigrated from Yorkshire in the 1820s, a fugitive from English industrial change and unrest, an enthusiast for the radicalism of Tom Paine. His father, John William Parrington, had been born in Maine and had moved in the 1850s to Illinois where he had married Louise McClellan, the daughter of an abolitionist and former Baptist minister. During the Civil War Parrington's father served in the Union army as a captain and after 1866 became a lawyer, a minor Republican party official, and, at the time of his second son's birth, clerk of Kane County. In 1877 the family moved to a farm near Americus, Kansas, where John William Parrington prospered to the possession of three farms, a stand of timber, and a town lot in Americus. His son was to remember the bleakness and severity of the climate and the ugliness of their home, a house that "even the softening touch of years could not beautify or render other than bleak and inhospitable"; he thus found especial evocation in Hamlin Garland's descriptions of the Middle Border. But Parrington's father was no struggling Scandinavian farmer and no farmer at all after 1884 when he was elected judge of probate for Lyon County and the Parringtons moved to Emporia. So Parrington, though he was to write with sympathetic passion of the agrarian dispossessed of the West, was for only seven years a farm boy, though these were years of impressionability. In spirit, however, Vernon Parrington was a small-town boy, a lover of carefully fashioned things, of rigorous and thoughtful architecture, of disciplined gardens, of fastidious dress.

The younger Parrington attended the College of Emporia, a Presbyterian school, though without absorbing too much of that pessimistic creed. An oration, "God in History," delivered in his junior year before the Kansas Intercollegiate Oratorical Association, is notable for a millenarian enthusiasm subsequently scotched by reading Herbert Spencer.

In 1891 he went for the final two years of his college education to Harvard. It was not a happy choice, for he seems to have been lonely in a snobbish institution disposed to regard the westerner as a yahoo, made few or no friends, and received only intermittent illumination from his teachers. His greatest achievement and satisfaction was to play for the 1893 college baseball team. Much later, Harvard was to grow in his remembrance as a place of stunting claustrophobia, though it is probable that, as the insecure provincial, he had at the time placed the responsibility for his discontent upon himself, not upon the enveloping majesty of Cambridge. In 1918, more self-confident and focused, he wrote to his classmates disparagingly: "The past five years I have spent in study and writing, up to my ears in the economic interpretation of American history and literature, getting the last lingering Harvard prejudices out of my system. I become more radical with

every year, and more impatient with the smug Tory culture which we were fed on as undergraduates. I haven't been in Cambridge since July, 1893. Harvard is only a dim memory to me. Very likely I am wrong in my judgment, yet from what little information comes through to me I have set the school down as a liability rather than an asset to the cause of democracy. It seems to me the apologist and advocate of capitalistic exploitation—as witness the sweetsmelling list of nominees sent out yearly for the Board of Overseers." He refused to permit his own son to attend Harvard.

In 1893 he returned to teach English and French at the College of Emporia, from which he also received an M.A. in 1895. By his own confession, he had drifted into teaching with no vocation. He did introduce mild reforms into the curriculum, not unreminiscent of Harvard, and brought football with ubiquitous energy to the campus; he was simultaneously coach, trainer, captain, and quarterback. More importantly he drifted from his father's staunch Republicanism into a sympathy for populism. In 1896 he voted for William Jennings Bryan over the objections of William Allen White, a friend. In 1897 he led a delegation from his home ward to a Kansas Populist convention and wrote occasional pieces for his college newspaper to indict industrial oligarchy and to recommend the social thought of John Ruskin and William Morris. And he ran unsuccessfully for the local school board upon the "Citizen's" ticket, though this was not obviously a Populist vehicle.

But the distinguishing characteristic of Parrington's early years at Emporia and then at the University of Oklahoma, where he moved in 1897, was apparently inconsequential drift. He wrote very little: a few poems for himself and local newspapers, the beginnings of a novel later destroyed by fire, pieces for the college periodical. He became the university's first football coach, a matter that today in Norman justifies the christening of a "Parrington Oval" as much as, if not more than, his later intellectual achievement. (He was, it seems, among the roll of Oklahoma football coaches, one of the most successful.) Mostly he seemed to be settling into that convivial existence frequently characteristic of the provincial American college. He gardened, he married, he supported the football and baseball teams, he hunted, and he became known for the idiosyncrasy of his teaching. Socratically he would cross-examine his students in lectures, taking a pleasure in the bemusement of the dim-witted or the energy of the intellectually excitable. To take a course with Parrington became a tradition. And there were

many and various classes to take. The English department at Norman was then very small, having just three faculty members in 1906, and so Parrington's responsibilities were legion: courses upon English literature from Spenser to Pope, from Johnson to William Morris, upon Shakespeare, upon Tennyson and Browning, upon Ruskin and Morris, upon the eighteenth-century novel, upon the nineteenth-century novel, upon the French Revolution and English poetry, upon—often and inevitably—the brute niceties of English composition for freshmen. He did not much like Norman. "Crude and bare and vulgar," he called it. But it gave him a modest living, enough to marry Julia Williams in 1901, enough to take him (though not her) on an extended visit to Europe in 1903 and 1904 where he studied gardens and buildings and read in the Bibliotheque Nationale and the British Museum, enough to design and build partly by his own labor a house of Elizabethan temperament. He would doubtless have pleasantly doodled away the rest of his life.

Fortunately he was fired, quite abruptly, in 1908. Oklahoma had become a state in 1907. Its new governor was a Bryanite, a Democrat, and reliant upon the Methodist church that held the faculty at

Norman in horror as infidels, Easterners, dancers, drinkers, cigarette smokers, card players, competing avatars of youth's corruption. Parrington, smoker and Harvard man, qualified for extirpation, though he did not drink, like to dance, play cards, or hold his Harvard credentials in high esteem. With and before him went the president of the university and thirteen other professors. It was a famous purge that placed Parrington suddenly into unemployment and almost as quickly into a new job at the University of Washington in Seattle, about as far from Norman and Harvard as it was possible to go without departing the continental United States. It was his saving.

In Seattle he was to find the pleasant, even beautiful, physical environment that he had always craved and almost never had, a few intelligent friends interested in ideas, and, eventually, a clarified aesthetic and political philosophy. From a dabbler, he became—not a serious scholar, attentive to detail—a serious writer. He started to teach American, as opposed to English, literature. He became aware of the great outburst of Progressive writing, economic and presentist. At Norman, he later wrote, "the economic interpretation of history had not yet risen for me, but it lay just below the horizon and was soon to become the chief luminary of my intellectual sky. My new interest in American literature opened a fresh field for me and in that field I applied the economic interpretation more and more rigidly." In 1913 he began in earnest a volume initially entitled *The Democratic Spirit in American Literature: 1620-1870*, later upon his publisher's advice altered to *Main Currents in American Thought*. It was written away from public attention, away from the gaze of most of his colleagues, written by a man lonely and absorbed, obscure and increasingly distant from a progressive movement intense in 1913 but tapering by 1927. For it did not prove easy to find a publisher, a search Parrington undertook after 1917. A university press accepted it in 1924 but asked for a $500 subsidy. B. W. Huebsch took it but reneged for reasons of financial difficulty. Then Van Wyck Brooks, Huebsch's reader for the manuscript, solicited Harcourt, Brace, who finally accepted it in 1925, two years before the final publication of the first two volumes, *The Colonial Mind* and *The Romantic Revolution in America*. The frustrating delay could not have lightened Parrington's sense of remoteness, of the distance between the American hinterland and the centers of power.

But the delay was fortunate. *Main Currents in American Thought* was a book somewhat after its time, the Progressive era, and so became a book somewhat before its time, the New Deal that authorized a Washington monument to Thomas Jefferson. *Main Currents in American Thought* had to be quickly appreciated, or it was lost. For, as Lionel Trilling was to observe, only a little unkindly, in 1940, "Parrington was not a great mind; he was not a precise thinker or, except when measured by the low eminences that were about him, an impressive one. Separate Parrington from his informing idea of the economic and social determination of thought and what is left is a simple intelligence, notable for its generosity and enthusiasm but certainly not for its accuracy or originality." Great minds can with some confidence hope for vindication from posterity; lesser minds must be timely so that the posterity that judges is committed to assessment.

American literary history was largely unwritten, even by 1927. American scholars had been absorbed by English literature and philology, by Beowulf, Tennyson, and the *ing* ending in Middle High German. The English department of Harvard had, as Richard Hofstadter has pointed out, accepted just three doctoral dissertations upon American literature by 1926. There were no scholarly journals devoted to American literature exclusively and little research. Constantly Parrington was hindered by the absence of adequate texts and biographies. Such literary history as did exist—such as that of Barrett Wendell, who had taught Parrington at Harvard—was genteel in philosophy, New England in emphasis, conservative in tone. Parrington was conscious of writing a synthesis before the materials for a synthesis existed and thus was apologetic. He was pleased and disarmingly candid, however, about his presentist liberal politics. "The point of view from which I have endeavored to evaluate the materials," he wrote upon his first page, "is liberal rather than conservative, Jeffersonian rather than Federalistic; and very likely in my search I have found what I went forth to find, as others have discovered what they were seeking. Unfortunately the *mens aequa et clara* is the rarest of attributes, and dead partisanships have a disconcerting way of coming to life again in the pages of their historians. That the vigorous passions and prejudices of the times I have dealt with may have found an echo in my judgments is, perhaps, to be expected; whether they have distorted my interpretation and vitiated my analysis is not for me to determine." His motto, taken from Carl Becker, read, "The business of history is to arouse an intelligent discontent, to foster a fruitful radicalism."

Parrington's was a lonely but not uninfluenced achievement. In Seattle he had befriended J. Allen Smith, whose writings upon economics and the Constitution as a reactionary class document had impressed Parrington (just as they did Charles Beard) and to whom *Main Currents in American Thought* was dedicated. Hippolyte Taine's history of English literature had suggested to Parrington a sociological model for American literature as well as a narrative technique, the biographical-critical portrait. William Morris's radical revolt against the industrial city succored the aesthetic imagination of Parrington, architectural student and lover of form. The American would have been flattered to think that his considered prose might have merited an edition upon the Kelmscott Press founded by Morris. And lastly, though less often observed, Parrington was an enthusiast of the Augustan wits, notably Alexander Pope and Charles Churchill, an admirer of their conciseness, balance, trenchancy, and partisanship upon matters of literature and society. The great ladies who, in Pope's heyday, affixed a patch upon one cheek if Tory, and upon another if Whig, anticipated neatly the engaged spirit of Vernon Parrington. It will be observed that several of these influences are not American, which can be explained by the precedence of Parrington the student of European literature over Parrington the author upon American themes. Indeed his own mind was a microcosm of what he saw in the history of American thought, the interaction of European intellectual traditions with the forces of American society.

The form and technique of *Main Currents in American Thought* can be quickly summarized, for it is not complex. The volumes proceed by a series of brief biographical sketches of American authors, political thinkers, and politicians. Each sketch characterizes, judges, and slots each figure into the essential dichotomy of American thought, the struggle between liberalism and conservatism, Jeffersonianism and Federalism. Interspersed are chapters that explain the socioeconomic context. As such, it was not a study of American literature so much as of American political thought refracted through literature. Chronologically it divides American hisory into three phases: the colonial period, which lasted until the election of Jefferson to the presidency in 1800; the romantic revolution from 1800 to the Civil War; the "beginnings of critical realism," from 1865 until 1920. These eras correspond to the three volumes of the work, although the last was published posthumously and was unfinished, indeed badly mangled. Spatially

Main Currents in American Thought divides American culture into sections: New England, the Middle States, the South, and the West. This pattern is strongest after 1800, for the first volume is almost entirely a study of New England, with the exception of portraits of Benjamin Franklin, John Dickinson, Francis Hopkinson, Alexander Hamilton, Tom Paine, Thomas Jefferson, and Hugh Henry Brackenridge. It is a study of heroes and villains, winners and losers, those in favor of the times and those against them. Thus it is a classic piece of Whig history, even to the point of seeing Luther as the instigator of tolerant liberty. But it is Whig history long past the prime of Victorian confidence, and Parrington's distaste for the corrosive centralization of industrialism gave to a crescent history a depressed faltering, an alternating bitterness at the surrender of Jefferson's America to plutocracy and uncertain hope that "critical realism" might retrieve the debacle.

The main currents of American thought, according to Parrington, spring chiefly from Europe. Varying systems of the European imagination—"English Independency and Whiggery, French romantic theory, the laissez faire ideas that rose with modern industry and commerce, nineteenth-century science as it affected social and literary thought, the various strains of Continental utopianism or collectivism," to use Hofstadter's paraphrase—collide in America, the issue being decided by the energies of individual idealists, the resistance of moneyed conservatives, and the exigency of the American economic environment. In the colonial period a rigid Puritan theocracy was challenged by a tolerant liberalism, bolstered by a yeoman class possessed of an abundance of free land, and by an acquisitive merchant gentry. The American Revolution was a displacement of sensibility toward egalitarianism but achieved by a coalition of merchants, planters, and frontier liberals. The merchants provided a reactionary Constitution; the frontier, after a schooling in the freedom of French Physiocratic and romantic theory, produced the triumph of Thomas Jefferson. The nineteenth century early saw a struggle of romanticisms: of the upper class in the South and of the middle class in the Middle States and New England. The West provided a Jacksonianism that impelled political democracy but lost the realistic economics of Jefferson. The Civil War released the energies of an acquisitive middle class compounded by an aggressive capitalism. The late nineteenth century was a "Great Barbecue," in which the richest fare fell to the East and the middle class, the poorest to the

farmer for whom populism was a losing and final fling. Only in the dawning critical sensibility of intellectual rebels was there a countervailing force and hope.

Parrington's narrative technique embodied his vision of continuing struggle. Conservative was set against liberal: John Winthrop against Roger Williams, Thomas Hutchinson against Benjamin Franklin, Alexander Hamilton against Thomas Jefferson, Fisher Ames against Ralph Waldo Emerson, John C. Calhoun against William Lloyd Garrison, Jay Cooke against Henry George, Thomas Bailey Aldrich against Edward Bellamy. As Kermit Vanderbilt has shown, the main currents of American thought were liberal in Parrington's descriptive language, the impediments were conservative. Thus Emerson "understood quite clearly how the waves of humanitarian aspiration broke on the reefs of property rights." Thus Daniel Webster was "launched between tides on a stormy sea and his stately bark foundered in the squall of Abolitionism." Thus John Marshall ignored "the turbid waters of frontier leveling and states-rights democracy [that] washed fiercely about him." Those that disdained the currents were, in turn, condemned to cloistered sterility. Increase Mather "closed the windows of his mind against the winds of new doctrine." The mind of James Russell Lowell withered in "the stagnant atmosphere of [his] . . . Elmwood study." But the creative liberals were open to the free and open winds and tides. Roger Williams was "an adventurous pioneer, surveying the new fields of thought laid open by the Reformation." Thomas Jefferson ensured that "the man of affairs kept a watchful eye on the philosopher in the study."

This vision was essentially ahistorical. In Parrington's view, only the forms of history change, never the essential struggle. That which came later in American history is always intimated, that which came earlier is always surviving. There are seventeenth-century Tories and liberals, twentieth-century Federalists and Jeffersonians. The Federalist is invariably an anachronism, the Jeffersonian always the guardian of the future. Classes rise and fall in Parrington, never quite reaching apogee, never quite disappearing. Everything is tenacious.

Two criticisms have been consistently leveled against Parrington: he misread the nature of European intellectual influence, and he was insensitive to apolitical aesthetic values. On the first matter, he grossly overestimated the role of French thought in the American imagination. He placed it too early, by making Rousseau an influence upon the liberal elements of the American Revolution. He made it too pervasive, by making Jeffersonian and Jacksonian frontiersmen the students of Physiocracy. In this he was eager to evade English intellectual responsibility for American democratic liberalism. This mild Anglophobia, as Hofstadter has written, "disposed him to accept readily enough the English ancestry of ideas he disliked but caused him to minimize or even deny the English ancestry of ideas he approved. This feeling is charmingly laid bare near the end of his third volume where, discussing the importance of the Progressive attack on the Constitution, he remarks that the myths that had gathered about it were dispelled by the work of J. Allen Smith and Beard, and that 'the document was revealed as English rather than French'—as though this were indeed a revelation, and also the last word in condemnation." Equally troubling in Parrington was the vagueness of his Europe. His references to important European thinkers are usually more sonorous than precise. Very few are quoted directly, and most are just names. One can infer occasionally that he had read in original European sources, notably in Harrington, Locke, Quesnay, and Rousseau. But his bibliographies and text—the latter usually devoid of annotation— suggest a reliance upon secondary sources, like William Archibald Dunning's *History of Political Theories* (1902) and Harold J. Laski's *Political Thought from Locke to Bentham* (1920). Indeed the imprecision of Parrington, the chief proponent in his generation of the centrality of European thought to the American mind, helped to put that vision into a disrepute from which it recovered only in the 1960s; Bernard Bailyn upon the ideological origins of the American Revolution is Parrington with intellectual genealogies corrected.

Parrington was self-consciously disdainful of the merely "belletristic." The political imagination was highest in his hierarchy of intellectual endeavors, so Parrington was notoriously weak upon writers uninterested in politics or absorbed by the texture of human relationships or fascinated with the delicate potentialities of words. Parrington figuratively clumped up to Edgar Allan Poe, enquired what the *Tales of Mystery and Imagination* had to say about frontier Physiocracy, and, receiving nothing but a startled and slurred response, went on his way. Poe was dismissed in just two pages as "quite outside the main current of American thought," a problem to be "left with the psychologist and the belletrist with whom it belongs." This dismissal was the more striking because Parrington was

aware that Poe was "the first of our artists and the first of our critics, . . . a rebel in the cause of beauty, discovering in consequence a finer romanticism than was before known in America." Equally, Parrington wrote of Hawthorne's "intellectual poverty"; he was "an artist for reason that only through the mastery of a refined technic could his scanty stock of ideas make any show at all." Henry James was dispatched as promptly as Poe, as oversubtle and emigré, inferior to the robust American materiality of Sherwood Anderson. For Parrington, technique was evasion, not substance. Seeing with clarity, he wished to see only clarity, not introspective doubt. In the fragmentary preface to the third volume of *Main Currents in American Thought*, written after the reviews of the first two, Parrington defended himself: "It ought not to be necessary to add that in these volumes I have not essayed to write a history of American literature—that rather difficult task for which no scholar is as yet equipped. But I have suffered so many gentle reproofs for failing to do what I did not set out to do that it may be well to repeat what I said in the Foreword to Volume I, that I have been concerned in the present study with the total pattern of American thought—the broad drift of major ideas—and not with vagrant currents or casual variations. . . . After due consideration I see no cause to apologize for my treatment of Poe. . . ." Parrington was persuaded that cultures have common denominators that provide the basis of critical judgment; cultures are not the aggregates of idiosyncrasy and generality.

One can see in his portraits of the "belletristic" the source of Parrington's unease with a Poe or Hawthorne. The sketches are not, in fact, entirely without sympathy or insight. To observe of Poe that "he suffered much from his aloofness, but he gained much also" is shrewd. Parrington was probably so insistent upon censure of those who told little or wrongly about the stern realities of American development because he himself had been "belletristic." He had doodled verses. He had taken many years to understand the "reality" of America. Had he not therefore earned the right, the duty, to castigate those who had lacked the moral vision to make the same pilgrimage? Would not too cozy a tone toward such authors bring him uncomfortably close to the footling pedants and Tennysonians with whom Parrington had spent too many uninspiring years? "Is there a stouter conservatism than the conservatism of scholarship, unless indeed it be the conservatism of religion?" he had asked in 1917, mostly of his own colleagues. "The economist has long been knocking at the gates of literary criticism, but the porter is in no haste to open to him. The critics will disagree heartily enough among themselves, but they all turn the cold shoulder to this newcomer. Classicist, philologist, humanist listen impatiently to his apologies and explanations, regarding him as an upstart intruder in the haunts of gentlemen. Who is he with his rude materialism to set himself up for a judge of colours and perfumes, a connoisseur of fragile and elusive beauty?" This is not quite the same Parrington who had observed to the president of the University of Oklahoma in 1906, before their respective annihilations, of campus building: "I feel that we talk too much about a big university and too little about a beautiful university. To prefer the utilitarian and to assume that the utilitarian must necessarily be ugly, and conversely that the beautiful is useless and therefore effeminate is one of our national heresies." This transformation Parrington perhaps had in mind when he composed a poem, entitled "Apologia Pro Vita Mea," which has the lines, "What life has taught me with the years, / That I have counted gain— / What, open-hearted, I have learned, / That I have taught again." Parrington was a miniaturist who drove himself into responsibility for the grand mural, a fox determined to be a hedgehog and thus wary of the company of other foxes lest he backslide. This tendency is well illustrated in his writing habits. He wished always to work outward from the phrase. A friend recalled: "He habitually began with his thesis—a phrase, a sentence, or a revealing figure. This was examined and stripped of its implications as one would peel an onion layer by layer. So imperious was the habit of this procedure that his ability to write would be blocked until he had in mind a perfectly crystallized concept expressible at the maximum in one sentence. An example of this occurred shortly before he left on his trip to England. He had been working on the period that Mark Twain had labeled the 'Gilded Age,' but found the title inadequate to his idea and, as a result, his writing did not get on. Another day some weeks later there was an obvious satisfaction expressed in his bearing and an exceptionally pronounced twinkle in his eye. 'I have found the phrase,' he said; 'I will call it The Great Barbecue.' Similarly, the three volumes of this work began in a single paragraph which by progressive unfoldings he expanded to its present scope."

An affection for the disregarded and obscure pervades *Main Currents in American Thought*. Though many of its heroes, like Jefferson, were already celebrated, many were sought out by Parrington, dusted down, and sweetly evoked. He was,

for instance, notably sensitive to the Southern mind, and his account of the antebellum generation of Southern intellectuals remains, to this day, one of the few that grants them standing not as political curiosities but as thinkers of intrinsic note. Parrington had the talent of going to an original text unread for generations by historians and seeing it with refreshed eye. Not the least of his gifts to his readers was the feeling, absent from a historian like Barrett Wendell, that American intellectual history had a fresh agenda ripe for reconsideration. This was a greater gift than the ideological straitjacket of his Jeffersonianism. Yet his taste was not always prophetic. His last volume is full of the obscure who have remained obscure: Theodore Woolsey and H. H. Boyesen are not resonant names. And his enthusiasm for the "incomparable" James Branch Cabell has not been emulated, except by Edmund Wilson, though subsequent generations may here be as improperly denigrating as Parrington was overecstatic.

Upon its publication in 1927, *Main Currents in American Thought* was an immediate success. Historical journals, taking note of its subtitle, did not review it. But Charles Beard was enthusiastic in print and in private. Parrington's Seattle colleagues were astonished and uncertainly pleased by the prodigy. As a friend remembered, "They were not so much surprised that he could write it as surprised that he had written it. There had been such an absence of antecedent pother. Of course it was known that Parrington—like everybody else—was writing a book. He would probably go on writing his book—like everybody else—and it might come out sometime. . . . But none save those who had read the manuscript was prepared for the event. The book made a stir, took a prize, brought a shower of flattering offers of academic appointment." The prize was the Pulitzer, sweet recompense.

With swiftness *Main Currents in American Thought* became a fixed monument on the American intellectual landscape, a standard item on college reading lists. By modern paperback standards its sales were not astonishing: 3,500 sets in its first two years, annually some 600 sets during the 1930s, its heyday. Later paperback editions brought the sales, by 1967, to 304,000 volumes. Its influence became unquestionable. Parrington was obscure before its issuance, and he died in the summer of 1929 before completing the third volume. He was not to be catapulted to visibility or obliged to justify and explain. *Main Currents in American Thought* was just there, take it or leave it. That most people took it would, one fancies, have disappointed him. He had wished to foment controversy. He had thought himself daring, a challenger to the seats of power. But he was so acceptable that he might have lived to regret the decision to replace throughout his original manuscript the word *radical* with *liberal*. He would certainly have been pained to read Lionel Trilling's regrettably just observation: "Parrington's ideas are the more firmly established because they do not have to be imposed—the teacher or the critic who presents them is likely to find that his task is merely to make articulate for his audience what it has always believed, for Parrington formulated in a classic way the suppositions about our culture which are held by the American middle class so far as that class is at all liberal in its social thought and so far as it begins to understand that literature has anything to do with society." For in Parrington's lexicon no phrase had been damned as sweepingly as "middle class," unless it had been "Tory."

Suspended in intellectual strategy between politics and literary criticism, *Main Currents in American Thought* was after 1940 to be outflanked. Politics lost touch with the old dichotomies of Jeffersonianism and Federalism. Literary criticism, transformed by the "New Critics," abjured context and burrowed deeper into the nuances of text. The darkly ironic side of Parrington, so evident in *The Beginnings of Critical Realism in America*, was to find little place in his reputation, perhaps because his third volume was truncated and less read. By 1967 Richard Hofstadter could speak with confidence of Parrington's "abrupt decline" and pen an assessment that was obituary. Of the luminaries of the Progressive school of history, only perhaps James Harvey Robinson underwent so final a dismissal. There are still Turnerians, still Beardians, but of a Parringtonian no sighting has been reliably reported for several decades.

Other:
"The Puritan Divines, 1620-1720," in *The Cambridge History of American Literature*, edited by W. P. Trent and others (New York: Putnam's, 1917; Cambridge: Cambridge University Press, 1917), I: 31-56;

The Connecticut Wits, edited by Parrington (New York: Harcourt, Brace, 1926);

"The Development of Realism," in *The Reinterpretation of American Literature*, edited by Norman Foerster (New York: Harcourt, Brace, 1928), pp. 139-159;

Ole Rölvaag, *Giants in the Earth*, introduction by Parrington (New York & London: Harper, 1929);

"American Literature to the End of the Nineteenth Century" and "Nathaniel Hawthorne," in *Encyclopaedia Britannica*, 14th edition (Chicago: Encyclopaedia Britannica, 1929);

"Brook Farm," in *Encyclopedia of the Social Sciences*, edited by E. R. A. Seligman and A. Johnson (New York & London: Macmillan, 1930), III: 13-14;

Introduction to *The Growth and Decadence of Constitutional Government*, by J. Allen Smith (New York: Holt, 1930; London: Williams & Norgate, 1930).

Periodical Publications:
"The Incomparable Mr. Cabell," *Pacific Review*, 2 (December 1921): 353-366; reprinted in *The Beginnings of Critical Realism in America*, pp. 335-345;

"On the Lack of Privacy in American Village Homes," *House Beautiful*, 13 (January 1930): 109-112;

"Economics and Criticism," (circa 1917), edited by Vernon Parrington, Jr., *Pacific Northwest Quarterly*, 44 (July 1953): 97-105.

References:
James L. Colwell, "The Populist Image of Vernon Parrington," *Mississippi Valley Historical Review*, 49 (June 1962): 52-66;

Arthur A. Ekirch, Jr., "Parrington and the Decline of American Liberalism," *American Quarterly*, 3 (Winter 1951): 295-308;

Joseph B. Harrison, *Vernon Louis Parrington: American Scholar* (Seattle: University of Washington Book Store, 1929);

Richard Hofstadter, *The Progressive Historians: Turner, Beard, Parrington* (New York: Knopf, 1968), pp. 349-439, 486-494;

Merrill D. Peterson, "Parrington and American Liberalism," *Virginia Quarterly Review*, 30 (Winter 1954): 35-49;

Richard Reinitz, "Vernon Louis Parrington as Historical Ironist," *Pacific Northwest Quarterly*, 68 (July 1977): 113-119;

Robert Allen Skotheim, *American Intellectual Histories and Historians* (Princeton: Princeton University Press, 1966), pp. 124-148;

Lionel Trilling, "Reality in America," in his *The Liberal Imagination: Essays on Literature and Society* (New York: Viking, 1950), pp. 1-19;

William T. Utter, "Vernon Louis Parrington," in *The Marcus W. Jernegan Essays in American His-*

toriography, edited by William T. Hutchinson (Chicago: University of Chicago Press, 1937), pp. 394-408.

Papers:

Parrington's papers are now in the possession of his family but are destined for the Archives of the University of Washington in Seattle.

Ulrich B. Phillips

Kirk Wood
University of South Carolina

BIRTH: LaGrange, Georgia, 4 November 1877, to Alonzo R. and Jessie Young Phillips.

EDUCATION: B.A., 1897, M.A., 1899, University of Georgia; Ph.D., Columbia University, 1902.

MARRIAGE: 22 February 1911 to Lucie Mayo Smith; children: Ulrich Bonnell, Jr., Mabel Elizabeth, Worthington Webster.

AWARDS AND HONORS: Justin Winsor Prize of the American Historical Association for "Georgia and State Rights," 1902; fellow, Carnegie Institution of Washington, D.C., 1904; Little, Brown and Company Award for the best unpublished work of American history for *Life and Labor in the Old South*, 1929; honorary degrees, Columbia and Yale, 1929; Albert Kahn Foundation fellowship, 1929; fellow, Royal Historical Society.

DEATH: New Haven, Connecticut, 21 January 1934.

BOOKS: *A History of Transportation in the Eastern Cotton Belt to 1860* (New York: Columbia University Press, 1908);
The Life of Robert Toombs (New York: Macmillan, 1913);
American Negro Slavery: A Survey of the Supply, Employment and Control of Negro Labor as Determined by the Plantation Regime (New York: Appleton, 1918);
Life and Labor in the Old South (Boston: Little, Brown, 1929);
The Course of the South to Secession, edited by E. Merton Coulter (New York: Appleton, 1939).

The name Ulrich Bonnell Phillips is indelibly

Ulrich B. Phillips

imprinted in the annals of American and Southern history. Not only was he the author or editor of nine major historical works but he also contributed numerous articles to professional journals, biographical-encyclopedic collections, and multi-volume histories. It would not be incorrect to state that Phillips deserves to be considered as the founding father of modern Southern history by virtue of his pioneering researches into such subjects as politics, transportation, and slavery and of his herculean efforts to uncover primary source materials and to bring them to light in the form of documentary publications.

In his own lifetime Phillips came to be regarded as the preeminent authority on the Old South, particularly with respect to slavery and the plantation system. Although a few scholars voiced early criticisms of his works, most notably Carter G. Woodson, W. E. B. Du Bois, and Frederic Bancroft, it was only after his death that Phillips's reputation declined. After World War II a new wave of critics, led by Kenneth M. Stampp, began to raise questions about Phillips's research and perspective on the Old South. In addition to limiting his research to upland Georgia and South Carolina, they argued, Phillips was selective in his use of evidence, citing some sources incompletely while ignoring others altogether. As a native Southerner, moreover, he took too kind a view of slave-owning planters, whom he described as benevolent patriarchs. Above all, however, there was his belief in the inherent inferiority of the Negro, which prevented any real understanding of the slaves' adjustment to and life under the "peculiar institution." In short, subjective influences and methodological shortcomings had seriously compromised his portrayal of slavery in the South.

At the heart of this critical assault on Phillips, and the real reason for his decline, was the emergence of a newer attitude toward blacks that coincided with the civil rights movement of the 1950s and 1960s and that brought with it a different perspective on the slave experience under the plantation system. Thus, where Phillips and other Southern writers had portrayed the slaves' successful adaptation to slavery, thanks in part to the paternalism of their masters, scholars such as Stampp and Stanley Elkins took an entirely opposite view. Not only was slavery inherently cruel and exploitative but the slaves themselves had resisted at every turn. In effect, what newer scholars in the field were doing was tracing the origins of the civil rights movement to the antebellum era and the heroic struggles of blacks to preserve their own personalities and to maintain some semblance of family life and self-respect under slavery. In short, blacks had a history, too, and the central theme uniting these two widely separated eras was their common struggle to overcome adversity and hardship. As Eugene D. Genovese explained this

reversal in opinion regarding Phillips: "Times have changed. Racism and a patronizing attitude toward the Negro have gone out of style since they began to embarrass United States foreign policy. What could be more natural than that Ulrich Phillips, a Georgian who loved the Old South and never could take the Negro seriously, should have gone out of style too?"

Although Phillips's works are little read today (they are considered to be out-of-date, too indulgent toward the planter, and antiblack), they nevertheless command respect both for the research that went into them and for the many valuable insights they provide into antebellum society. According to Genovese, Phillips's most important latter-day enthusiast, "his work, taken as a whole, remains the best and most subtle introduction to ante-bellum Southern history and especially to the problems posed by race and class." "Much of what Phillips wrote," declared C. Vann Woodward, "has not been superseded or seriously challenged and remains indispensable." In the words of Bennett H. Wall, "it was Phillips who was the real pioneer and formative scholar." In this sense, if his works are not the last words on their subjects, they are certainly "the indispensable first."

Phillips's interest in Southern history and his "sympathetic understanding of plantation conditions" were the natural by-product of his background and upbringing. He grew up in the cotton-belt town of LaGrange, Troup County, Georgia, where he spent his early youth and attended public schools. As Phillips would later recall in *Life and Labor in the Old South* (1929): "In happy childhood I played hide-and-seek among the cotton bales with sable companions; I heard the serenade of the katydids while tossing on a hot pillow, somewhat reconciled to the night's heat because it was fine for the cotton crop. . . . Later I followed the pointers and setters for quail in the broom-sedge, the curs for 'possums and 'coons in the woods, and the hounds on the trail of the fox." As a boy, too, Phillips "had picked cotton for short periods as a diversion" and occasionally attended camp meetings. He no doubt also heard many war stories of surviving Confederate veterans, an experience that would surely fire the imagination of an impressionable youth.

At about the age of twelve, Phillips moved with his family to Milledgeville, Georgia. The occasion for the relocation was a new business enterprise into which the elder Phillips had entered and which, according to Wood Gray, was "ultimately unsuccessful." Despite this financial setback, however,

Phillips's parents were still able to send Ulysses (Phillips's actual first name) to Tulane University Preparatory School in New Orleans. At about this time, he changed his name from Ulysses to Ulrich after discovering that the original appellation was a "damnyankee" name. Ulrich, apparently chosen at random, at least preserved the original initial.

As for Phillips's parents, not much is known about his father except that he was "a yeoman of lower-middle class stock" and that Phillips did not mention him in his letters. His mother, on the other hand, "was related to such leaders in secession and the Confederacy as William L. Yancey and Joseph E. Brown and connected with the plantation gentry from the Old Dominion to the Gulf Coast"; her family had, in fact, owned 1,500 acres and twenty-five slaves before the Civil War. She was also an educated woman, having taught at a girls' school in Milledgeville and later at the Industrial College in Greensboro, North Carolina. In Phillips's words, she was "a boon companion" and was sorely missed after her death in 1906.

In 1893, Phillips enrolled in the University of Georgia to pursue a baccalaureate degree in history. At that time, the total number of students enrolled in the university was only 1,500. The faculty numbered 34, including the school's chancellor William Ellison Boggs. Library holdings consisted of about 20,000 volumes, a number that increased to 30,000 by the time Phillips left Athens in 1900. The program in history, quite standard for its time, included a freshman course in general history, a sophomore course in English political and constitutional history, a junior course in United States history, and, for seniors, a class in political economy "with principles applied to American economic history."

Wendell Holmes Stephenson, who has studied Phillips's career closely, states that "a perusal of Phillips's undergraduate record leaves the impression that the student was as good as he wanted to be. His grades varied from 75 to 100, with eight of the former offset by seven of 95 or higher." He did manage to make the Blue List in history twice, once as a freshman and again as a junior. Considering that Phillips never enjoyed the best of health and had to withdraw from the university for one semester because of eyestrain, his B average is perhaps all the more remarkable.

The head of the history department at the University of Georgia while Phillips was there was Dr. John H. T. McPherson. A native of Baltimore, McPherson earned undergraduate and graduate degrees from Johns Hopkins University, at the time

the leading graduate school in America, in addition to studying at the University of Berlin and at the Sorbonne. After completing the Ph.D. in 1890 (his dissertation was a "History of Liberia"), he served one year as instructor at the University of Michigan before coming to Georgia in 1891. Not surprisingly, the method and course of instruction that McPherson adopted was patterned closely after that at Johns Hopkins, with a heavy emphasis upon political history, a genre Phillips would later reject in favor of a broader social-cultural approach.

With McPherson's encouragement and guidance, Phillips continued at the University of Georgia as a master's student, taking courses in English constitutional history, historiography, and federal-state relations as well as in French and German in preparation for the Ph.D. For his thesis topic, Phillips selected local political parties in Georgia, a subject he would later expand into his doctoral dissertation at Columbia University, "Georgia and State Rights." To gain teaching experience, he also served as a tutor in the history department, teaching the sophomore course in English history and sharing with McPherson the duties of instructing freshmen in general history. Upon attaining the M.A. degree in 1899, Phillips served both as a tutor in history and as assistant librarian.

Having decided upon a career as a teacher and professional historian, Phillips, in 1900, enrolled in the Ph.D. program at Columbia University. Columbia was a natural choice given the presence of Professor William A. Dunning, whose "seminars in southern history had already won wide recognition," and the contingent of Southern students who were already studying there. Dunning, an acknowledged expert in the field of the Civil War and Reconstruction, had become interested in that era while a graduate student of John W. Burgess at Columbia University. Breaking tradition with previous Northern scholars, Dunning made "a conscientious effort to understand the southern viewpoint," and his *Reconstruction, Political and Economic* (1907) won wide praise both for its impartial tone and the author's "mastery of the subject and its literature."

If one can single out a decisive factor influencing Phillips's desire to pursue a professional historical career, it was his own growing conviction that the history of his native region had yet to be treated fairly or fully by the prejudiced Northern historians whose works dominated discussion of the subject. "Apart from mere surface politics," he wrote in 1905, "the antebellum South is largely an unknown country to American historians." "The

South," he later complained in "Plantation and Frontier," "has already suffered grievously from the conjectures of hit-or-miss writers; and it is partly to reduce the acceptance of such harmful conjectures that this work is intended." Phillips, for example, had read the early volumes of James Ford Rhodes and John Bach McMaster as an undergraduate and found them deficient at least in some respects. According to Wendell Holmes Stephenson, Rhodes's chapter on slavery in the first volume of his *History of the United States from the Compromise of 1850* (1893-1906) "was a strange medley of truth, half-truth, and error." McMaster's view "differed only in degree."

In Phillips's own mind, the true history of the South could only be written by Southerners who had inherited Southern traditions and knew regional customs and manners. Indeed, "a correct picture could not be presented, Phillips believed, until Southerners, trained in scientific method, delved into the records and made the truth available." Unfortunately, the South had not done much to make its historical records available. In Phillips's words: "From the South itself they [Northern investigators] have received little assistance; for, before the war Southerners were content, as a rule, to transmit traditions without writing books and since the war they have been too seriously engrossed in adapting themselves to new conditions to feel any strong impulse towards a scientific reconstruction of the former environment."

In the final analysis, then, it was this desire to set the record straight that directed Phillips toward the study of history and drove him to write: "Southern History is almost a virgin field, and one of the richest in the world for results. The history of the United States has been written by Boston, and largely written wrong. It must be written anew before it reaches its final form of truth. And for that work . . . the South must do its part in preparation. New England has already overdone its part. There have been antiquarians and chroniclers at work in the Southern field, but few historians—few thinkers—and thought is the all-essential. I have only begun to dabble in the edge of it; but the results are quite surprising. A study of the conditions of the Old South from the inside readily shows an immense number of errors of interpretation by the old school of historians." Indeed, he added, "my lectures on the history of slavery. . . ; on the plantation system; and on political parties and doctrines in the South, are received as little short of revelations by men who have thought that they knew American history."

While Phillips would have preferred to remain in the South to accomplish his great work, he nevertheless realized that he would have to leave his native region to have any great impact upon the writing and interpretation of Southern history. Not only did Northern schools have more money and better resources but the publishing houses were all concentrated in the North. Hence his decision, first, to attend Columbia University and, later, his preference for Northern colleges and universities over those in the South. With the exception of a brief stint at Tulane University from 1908 to 1911 and occasional research forays southward, Phillips's career was spent at a succession of Northern schools—Wisconsin, Michigan, and finally Yale.

Phillips's choice of schools was by no means accidental. Each one was calculated to advance his professional career if not his fortunes. For this reason, he had selected Wisconsin as his first college teaching assignment in 1902. In 1907, Phillips was offered $2,000 ($600 more than he earned at Wisconsin) to accept the history department chairmanship at the University of North Carolina, but he turned it down in favor of a similar position at Tulane University. Besides paying more money, the Tulane appointment also provided the opportunity to edit the newly discovered manuscript letters of the antebellum Georgia leaders Howell Cobb, Alexander H. Stephens, and Robert Toombs. (As he wrote to his friend Professor Yates Snowden of South Carolina College in 1909: "You will be interested to know that since I left your State I have unexpectedly come into control of a perfectly stunning collection of several hundred Ms. letters written to Alex. H. Stephens by Toombs, Howell Cobb, Joe E. Brown and other contemporaries. I now expect to publish a collection of the 'Correspondence of the Georgia Secession and War Time Leaders' in addition to my Life of Toombs.") His later and final move to Yale from the University of Michigan was based on a reduced "four-hour teaching schedule" that allowed him "much more time than heretofore for authorship."

In the end, Phillips's decision to remain in the North paid off as he soon rose to the top of his chosen profession. In 1902, his dissertation, "Georgia and State Rights: A Study of the Political History of Georgia from the Revolution to the Civil War, with Particular Regard to Federal Relations," was awarded the Justin Winsor Prize by the American Historical Association and published in its *Annual Report*. In 1904, he was appointed a research fellow with the Carnegie Institution of Washington, D.C., which was preparing a full-scale history of transportation in the U.S. before 1860. Soon after joining the faculty at the University of Michigan, he became a member of the Executive Council of the American Historical Association in 1915, "itself a measure of [his] high standing among [his] peers." In 1929, "the zenith of his career," Phillips was chosen a second time as a member of the AHA Executive Council and as chairman of the Albert J. Beveridge Memorial Fund. During the same year, Little, Brown and Company "awarded a substantial prize" of $2,500 for his *Life and Labor in the Old South* manuscript; the Albert Kahn Foundation "granted him a choice fellowship for a year of foreign study of the plantation and the Negro"; and Yale and Columbia awarded him honorary degrees.

In large measure, Phillips's reputation was based on his publishing record, not his teaching skills. Teaching, after all, was simply a means to the end of writing books, then, as now, the more important and better rewarded function. Although "Phillips performed his classroom duties enthusiastically," at least early in his career (McPherson gave him high marks for his classroom manner and presence), teaching became something of a chore "after he attained recognition as a scholar." Many of his students, recalls Wendell Holmes Stephenson, "enrolled for easy credit rather than a burning desire for knowledge." Phillips made class attendance "more or less optional" and gave "few grades less than the 'Gentleman's C.'"

As for his actual manner of conducting class, it is apparent that he "gave little thought to preparation." For the most part, he would bring index cards from his research files and read them "for the whole period, sometimes with an interspersal of comment." On other occasions, he "would lay his notes aside and just talk about the South" or sing "southern ballads and Negro spirituals." Whatever his teaching methods, the students he taught apparently thought highly of him. Not only was he remembered for "many courtesies" but he was also appreciated for dramatizing the subject of Southern history. One of Phillips's students, Albert R. Newsome, was impressed with his "grasp and interpretation of history" and ability to make him "understand the real causes and effects of movements and events." Perhaps the best tribute to Phillips came from a class of eighty-two students he taught during a summer session at the University of Southern California in 1922; they collectively expressed esteem "for the treasures in subject matter, the grasp of purpose in studying history and the inspiration that [his] presence has been to us."

As a writer, however, there is no question that

"he was extraordinarily productive." Over the course of his career, "there came from his pen five books, four volumes of edited documents, some fifty-five articles, and nearly fifty book reviews." Whether judged by quantity or quality, writes Wendell Holmes Stephenson, "Phillips's productive record was impressive" and "serves as a monument to his industry." Indeed, Phillips's record of achievement was based on sheer hard work and a little luck. In the first place, he was an indefatigable researcher, always on the lookout for new source materials. "Whether at Madison, Ann Arbor, or New Haven . . . Phillips made frequent foraging expeditions into the South to press his quest for plantation diaries, journals, account books, correspondence, and a medley of miscellany." "Zest as a researcher," moreover, "did not wane as Phillips accumulated thousands of note cards and acquired stature as a historian." By the time of his death in 1934, he had assembled one of the largest extant collections of historical materials on the South, which he bequeathed to Yale University.

To help pay for these research trips, Phillips often "solicited lecture engagements." Writing to Yates Snowden in 1907, for example, Phillips stated that Snowden's letter had reached him at Ann Arbor, where "I have recently been giving a few lectures on Southern history to the Univ. of Michigan students." In a later letter to Snowden, Phillips said that he was "at Columbia where I'm to earn a few shekels." During his years at Michigan, he frequently traveled to New York City to teach summer classes at Columbia University and later accepted visiting professorships at the University of Southern California (1922) and the University of California (1924).

If Phillips spent countless free hours on the road in search of new source materials, he also took extra care to revise his manuscripts and perfect the literary style that makes his works enjoyable to read and which won acclaim from his contemporaries. "It was his habit," notes Wood Gray, "to keep at hand a dictionary of several volumes to which he constantly referred in search of variety and precision for his vocabulary. He also took careful note, too, of felicities in style and uncommon usages in the works of others." Not surprisingly, Phillips required the same exacting standards of his graduate students and often returned reports or theses that "were submitted with faulty method or fuzzy style. . . . Students might flounder, and many of them fell by the wayside, but those who profited from his counsel learned research and writing."

While there is certainly no doubt about Phillips's industry, he was also fortunate in his professional associations and acquaintances and in the opportunities they provided for significant research and publication. Soon after his appointment at Wisconsin, for instance, Phillips was able to secure a research fellowship with the Carnegie Institution of Washington, D.C., an assignment that contributed to the publication of *A History of Transportation in the Eastern Cotton Belt to 1860* (1908). (Phillips was one of several authors commissioned to write essays on antebellum transportation for *A History of Transportation in the United States before 1860*, which study was published by the Carnegie Institution in 1917.) While he was at Wisconsin, Richard T. Ely inaugurated the American Bureau of Industrial Research and its ambitious undertaking of publishing *A Documentary History of American Industrial Society* in ten volumes. The first two volumes of this series, *Plantation and Frontier Documents*, (1909) were edited by Phillips. As director of research for the "southern field," moreover, he was able to travel extensively, "visiting personally the libraries of Richmond, Charleston, Columbia, Atlanta, Savannah, Louisville, Nashville, New Or-

leans, and other minor points." His teaching assignments in California, finally, provided the basis for his 1925 article, "Plantations with Slave Labor and Free," in which Phillips compared large-scale agriculture there with the Southern plantation system.

Equally valuable were personal friends who gave Phillips access to heretofore unpublished manuscripts or rare documents. First and foremost in this respect was Wymberley Jones DeRenne of Wormsloe, Isle of Hope, Georgia, the noted collector of Georgiana who opened his extensive library to Phillips, not to mention his "ancestral cellar of sherries and madeiras." Another key source was the Porcher family of Pinopolis, South Carolina. ("I have long esteemed it one of my pieces of great good fortune, bringing both profit and delight," he wrote in 1907, "to have acquired the Porchers as such good warm friends.") Yet another valuable associate and friend was Yates Snowden, professor of history at South Carolina College, who regularly provided Phillips with antebellum pamphlets that he was busy collecting in Columbia, South Carolina. Writing in 1906, Phillips expressed his "great plea-

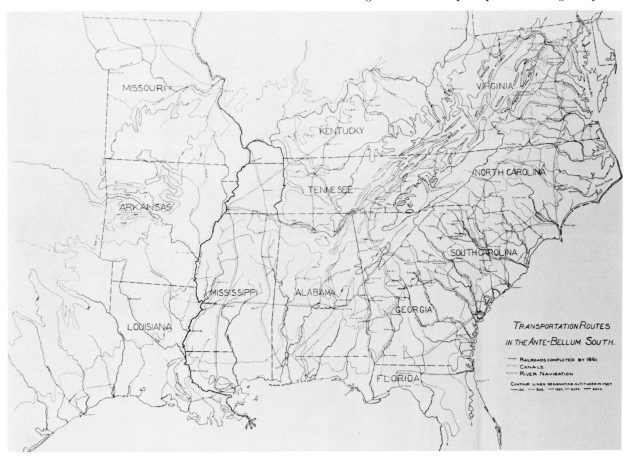

Phillips's map for A History of Transportation in the Eastern Cotton Belt to 1860

sure at learning of your purpose to collect plantation documents." "For God's sake," he added, "keep 'em in a fire-proof vault." In another letter, undated, he thanked Snowden for a copy of *Sherwood's Gazetteer* and commented that "you send me valuable gifts faster than I can acknowledge them!"

Many of Phillips's published works in fact resulted from his uncovering of new source materials. Both *The Life of Robert Toombs* (1913) and "The Correspondence of Robert Toombs, Alexander H. Stephens, and Howell Cobb" (1913) followed the discovery of letters in the possession of Mrs. A. S. Erwin of Athens, Georgia, and Col. John C. Reed and Mr. Burgess Smith of Atlanta. A biography of Toombs had been originally contemplated by Colonel Reed, who had "assembled a mass of his hero's correspondence." Although he and Phillips had agreed on joint authorship, failing health forced Reed to turn the project over to the professional historian for completion. In similar fashion, Phillips's *Florida Plantation Records from the Papers of George Noble Jones* (1927, a volume coedited with James David Glunt) was based on a collection of materials from the papers of George Noble Jones. Other examples include Phillips's articles on plantation life in Jamaica and Antigua. In the former case, Phillips used the plantation book kept by Rose Price, Esq., manager of the Worthy Park plantation, which he purchased at an auction in New York. In the latter case, the historian was directed by Dr. Worthington C. Ford to the manuscript account books of Shute Shrimpton Yeamans.

Actually, there was more method than madness to this seemingly haphazard publication record. Phillips, it appears, did have an overall plan and a broader view in mind. As he explained in 1905: "For the present I am concerning myself with industrial society and transportation. When I shall have obtained a sufficient grasp of economic developments I shall turn again to politics [as in "Georgia and State Rights"] and try to work out the bearings of questions of industry, commerce and society upon political policy with special regard to sectionalism." True to his goal, Phillips directed his attention first to transportation, then to his study of "Plantation and Frontier." The political theme was further developed in his biography of Toombs, while *American Negro Slavery: A Survey of the Supply, Employment and Control of Negro Labor as Determined by the Plantation Regime* (1918) represented the culmination of his work on Southern industrial life— slavery and the plantation system. As for the larger questions of political policy and sectionalism, Phillips planned to treat them in a series of interpreta-

tive works beginning with *Life and Labor in the Old South* (1929), the best and perhaps most famous of his works. "The present volume," he penned in 1929, is one "in a group which is planned as a history of the South. The second will trace the course of public policy to 1861, and a third may bring the consolidated social and political themes onward from that epochal year." Unfortunately, his death on 21 January 1934, at age fifty-six, cut short this projected series with the result that Phillips completed only *Life and Labor in the Old South* and part of another volume, *The Course of the South to Secession* (1939), published posthumously with the editorial assistance of E. Merton Coulter.

A casual perusal of Phillips's career suggests the obvious: he was more than a historian of slavery, at least as defined in terms of plantation life and conditions only. His interest was much broader than that and extended to all subjects that were related to and affected by the pervasive influence of the "peculiar institution." His field of interest, in other words, was nothing less than the whole South in all of its aspects, a fact often overlooked by his critics. As Phillips expressed it in the preface to *A History of Transportation in the Eastern Cotton Belt to 1860*: "To me the *ante-bellum* South is the most interesting theme in the history of this continent. I seek to understand the history of the South, and hope to explain it. The economic and social aspects seem to offer the best line of approach to the general problem, and hence my attention to the present subject along with others parallel, such as the plantation system. Migration, industry, commerce, politics, society, and even race relations are all inter-related with the transportation development."

In this sense, Phillips was very much influenced by Frederick Jackson Turner. Although Dunning was his mentor at Columbia University and fondly remembered by him (he was "the most cordial and suggestive man there"), Phillips did not share Dunning's interest in the era of Reconstruction but avoided the subject altogether throughout his career. Phillips even declined "to adopt the suggestion of several gentlemen . . . to add the period of Civil War and Reconstruction" to his narrative of Georgia State politics. Nor was he attracted to Dunning's emphasis upon politics and constitutional developments. There was, Phillips thought, more to the study of history than abstract ideas or mere political chronology. For his own part, he sought "the causes of things" and preferred to follow developments to their conclusion over a wide time frame. "A broad treatment," he stated in 1905, "will possess features of value which more concentrated study could not develop."

Phillips had first encountered Turner in the summer of 1898 at the University of Chicago, where the latter was temporarily a member of the faculty. In addition to attending Turner's seminar on American colonial institutions, Phillips also had the occasion to hear Turner lecture on the history of the West and the influence of sectionalism on American history in general. The lecture, as Wood Gray wrote, "was his light on the road to Damascus" and "furnished him with the key to the subject with which he had been struggling in his dissertation." More important, it suggested "a direction for his further undertakings," and in this regard Phillips acknowledged his debt to Turner to the end of his life. An early expression of Phillips's deep gratitude can be found in the introduction to *Plantation and Frontier Documents*: "A deepening appreciation of the historical significance of the plantation and of the preceding frontier regimes I owe to Dr. Frederick Jackson Turner of the University of Wisconsin, whose constant disciple I have been since 1898."

Turner was a practitioner of what would become known as the New History. Taking exception to the old view that history was nothing more than past politics with events being singly determined by political developments, Turner "emphasized the importance of a broad, interdisciplinary approach to historical study." Historical events, he believed, had multiple causes and the diligent inquirer had to concern himself with a combination of factors— economic, political, social, geographical, even psychological—to understand fully past events and developments. At the same time, the study of history had a more practical value, namely, to demonstrate the mistakes of the past and thus to point the way to a better future. The end of historical study, Turner declared in "The Significance of History," should be "to let the community see itself in the light of the past, to give it new thoughts and feelings, new aspirations and energies." In a word, history was relevant to the present.

Turner's influence upon Phillips is readily evident in all of the latter's works, from the first to the last. Just as Turner made extensive use of maps and charts, many of his own making, Phillips also made and used similar pictorial illustrations to depict voting behavior and trends, class composition, the size of slaveholdings, cotton prices, and transportation patterns. His "Georgia and State Rights," for example, contains no less than twelve maps of Georgia, illustrating, among other things, voter preferences in selected gubernatorial and presidential elections from 1796 to 1860, the vote on

secession, the Georgia frontier of 1780, Indian cessions, and products of the state of Georgia in 1835. Other notable examples of maps and charts can be found in *A History of Transportation in the Eastern Cotton Belt to 1860* and *Life and Labor in the Old South*. Like Turner, too, Phillips emphasized the influence of geography and climate upon historical developments in the South as the following quotes demonstrate: "In the coast region in the neighborhood of Charleston and Savannah the influence of physiography upon social, industrial, and commercial history can hardly be overestimated." "The influence of physiography on the social, industrial, and commercial development of the coast region in the neighborhood of Charleston and Savannah is unmistakable. Coast configuration, soil, and climate have been determining factors." "The lie of the land directed the currents of transportation and commerce; for those currents followed the lines of least resistance. . . . The particular channels through which the volume of commerce should flow were chosen and developed by the activity of the people under the general conditions of their environment."

Phillips's interpretation of the history of the Old South, for that matter, was really nothing more than a Southern version of the frontier thesis, albeit with a major difference. The South, of course, was originally a frontier, and its history, like that of the West, was largely the story of the occupation and settlement of the available land and the resulting adaptation of men and women to their new environment. The history of industrial society in the South, "like all social history," Phillips wrote in *Plantation and Frontier Documents,* "is in one great aspect the record of the adjustment of men to their environment." Beginning with the first phase, the initial settlement of the land, a dynamic process was created that led ultimately to the establishment of higher civilization or culture and industry. As in the West, too, "the frontier [in the South] had a lasting influence . . . in its giving a stamp of self-reliance and aggressiveness to the character of men." Unlike the West, however, the frontier in the South did not lead to the same desired results. Instead of producing urbanization and industrialization, the frontier intensified the production of staple crops and the system of plantation slavery. Instead of democracy, it fostered only an aristocracy of slave owners who controlled the wealth and politics of the region. Instead of nationalism, it engendered a sense of separateness and local allegiance. Ultimately, it gave rise to secessionism as Southerners endeavored to preserve their "peculiar institution."

The explanation for this difference in development between North and South, according to Phillips, was the emergence within the Southern frontier of the plantation system. While "the frontier influence was the more widely extended" and "affected nearly all the country, North and South," the impact of the plantation system "was more local and lasting": "The system gave a tone of authority and paternalism to the master class, and of obedience to the servants. The plantation problems, further, affected the whole community; for after the close of the seventeenth century the plantation problem was mainly the negro problem, and that was of vital concern to all members of both races in all districts where the negroes were numerous. The wilderness and the Indians were transient; the staples and the negroes were permanent, and their influence upon the prevailing philosophy became intensified with the lapse of years. It eventually overshadowed the whole South, and forced the great mass of the people to subordinate all other considerations to policies in this one relation."

Indeed, Phillips concluded, once the slave plantation system was established, it dominated the entire social-political-economic fabric of the antebellum South, all for the worse. "The great fault of the antebellum system of plantations," Phillips complained, "lay in its exclusive devotion to the staple crops, and in its discouragement of manufacturing and other forms of industry." "Over-dependence upon the staples" and the consequent "over-production of tobacco and cotton," he added, "prevented the economic independence of the South." "In virtually every phase, after the industrial occupation of each area had been accomplished," he wrote in *American Negro Slavery*, "the maintenance of the system was a clog upon material progress."

As one illustration of this general failure of the South to develop economically and industrially like the North, Phillips pointed to the antebellum Southern rail network. Although "the South had come to be equipped with at least the skeleton of a well-planned railway system" by 1860, "in the larger aspect, that system was a source of weakness and a failure." Besides being inferior in terms of construction and being unsystematic (there was really no planned system of rails, just a collection of different railroads), "the building of railroads led to little else but the extension and the intensifying of the plantation system and the increase of the staple output." "In contrast with the North, the cotton belt railroads did not greatly increase the local productive resources; nor . . . did they vastly increase the

volume of commerce. . . . The railroads, in a word, under the existing circumstances, proved less to be trade makers than trade catchers."

The reason for this failure, and for the South's general lackluster record in industrial and urban development, was the "institution of slavery" that with its "investment of wealth in slave labor . . . tended strongly against the presence of floating capital." The presence of Negroes, moreover, "reduced the number of European immigrants" and created "a singular dearth of floating labor." Finally, "the plantation system, dominating the whole industrial life of the South, attracted nearly all the men of capacity into agricultural development, and caused a shortage of efficient promoters and managers in other industries." Put another way, "the slaveholding regime kept money scarce, population sparse, and land values accordingly low; it restricted the opportunities of many men of both races, and it kept many of the natural resources of the Southern country neglected."

If slavery inhibited the economic development of the South, it also dictated the course of the South to secession. The real issues here, of course, were race and "a common resolve indomitably maintained—that it [the South] shall be and remain a white man's country." Phillips emphasized this point: "Negro slavery was established in the South as elsewhere, because the white people were seeking their own welfare and comfort. It was maintained for the same economic reason, and also because it was thought to be essential for safety. As soon as the negroes were on hand in large numbers, the problem was to keep their savage instincts from breaking forth and to utilize them in civilized industry." Given this resolve to guarantee white supremacy, not to mention Southern fears of "the possibility of social death from negro upheaval," which the "community had always in contemplation," it was only natural that the South would react vigorously and vehemently when slavery was attacked. From such responses came the first group of Southern "fire-eaters" in the 1820s and, in the period 1830-1860, their successors who fought the abolitionists over the gag rule, Texas annexation, and the Wilmot Proviso. Despite a temporary surcease in anti-slavery agitation with the Compromise of 1850, the whole slavery issue was refueled with the "fateful Kansas-Nebraska bill." Confronting the increased abolitionist activity in the mid-1850s, and the horror of John Brown's raid in 1859, Southerners became increasingly alarmed at the trend of events. The turning point came with the election of 1860 and with it the triumph of the Republican party. Now convinced that there was no hope in the Union for the protection of slavery, in view of "congressional mathematics" and Northern intransigence on the slavery issue, the South opted for separate independence before the strength and resolve of the North could grow stronger "and be consolidated for crushing purposes." The alternative, quite simply, was "separate nationality or the Africanization of the South."

Here, then, was the central theme of Southern history and of Phillips's works as well: the all-pervasive and totally negative impact of slavery upon the ideas, institutions, and economic development of the South. (As much as Phillips couched his studies in the trappings of "scientific history," it is not true that he eschewed generalization.) All of his studies, in one form or other, are concerned with this larger theme of enervation, including his later and more famous studies of slavery. *American Negro Slavery* and *Life and Labor in the Old South* were undertaken, in fact, not to portray a "moonlight and magnolias" view of slavery replete with happy slaves and kindly masters but rather to present a more detailed account of the process by which slavery impeded the progress of the Old South. That Phillips emphasized the paternalism of planters and the civilizing influence of the plantation system was only natural since they were retardant features themselves, the first because it lessened the inherent capitalistic tendencies of planters, who "showed strong progressive spirit," and the second because of the time and effort required to train "the available low-grade labor to serviceable ends."

For a supposed pro-Southern advocate, Phillips had very little positive to say about the Old South. Not only was he critical of the institution of slavery, because of its adverse economic impact, but he stood opposed to the states' rights tradition and the whole course of Southern politics from 1830 to 1860, which he characterized in terms of a "Great Reaction." For that matter, he viewed secession as a "crisis of fear" in which Southerners, faced with the prospect of a racial war, fled the Union rather than submit to abolitionism. As for the resulting war itself, it was the product of misguided zeal and blundering, truly a "needless" conflict rather than an "irrepressible" one. In short, Phillips was not really a defender of the Old South. Although Southern-born, he looked not to the past but to the future. As far as he was concerned, the days of slavery were gone forever, and all for the better.

If anything, Phillips more properly belongs to the New South school of historians, which included Woodrow Wilson, William P. Trent, William E. Dodd, John Spencer Bassett, and William Garrott Brown, all of whom were highly critical of the antebellum experience for basically the same reasons. Like Phillips, the New South school focused upon the institution of slavery and blamed it for the ills of the South. Slavery, they argued, kept the South feudal and thus prevented the growth of industries and cities as had occurred in the North. Slavery, moreover, also caused Southerners to embrace the patently false theory of states' rights as a subterfuge to protect their "peculiar institution." In sum, because of slavery the South became "entangled in wrong policies" and as a consequence suffered poverty, frustration, and defeat. However, the war "prepared the way for a new and better South by removing slavery and the type of sectionalism represented by secession." Out of the ashes of the old, a new and revitalized region would emerge.

In common with other liberal Southern historians of the postbellum era, too, Phillips's basic purpose in writing about the South was to demonstrate that, notwithstanding the antebellum past and its dismal record of economic underachievement and political reaction, there was nevertheless a basis both for reform and reunification after the Civil War. Indeed, overcoming the burden of Southern history was an important first step in the creation of a New South mentality and toward that end Phillips literally reconstructed a South that never really existed and which embodied "traditional Yankee virtues." In effect, the Old South in Phillips's analysis became the New South of his own day and time. No longer was there to be a "Cavalier myth" of gracious, indolent planters who were opposed to progress and to the cash-nexus basis of society or even a "Lost Cause" that upheld states' rights and slavery at the expense of more modern ideas.

Phillips's solution to this problem of discontinuity, quite simply, was to reconstruct Southern history. To establish that continuity which was so crucial to his vision of a New South, Phillips first turned the Old South into a liberal-progressive society. On the other hand, and to explain the course of the South to secession as well as its failure to urbanize and industrialize, Phillips placed the blame not upon Southerners personally but on the institution of slavery. As Phillips elaborated this theme in "Conservatism and Progress in the Cotton Belt" (1904), "the statesmen of the South. . . have been as a rule far from retrogressive, except in certain instances where slavery was concerned." Indeed, "in promoting sentiment leading to the Declaration of Independence, the formation of the

Union, and the declaration of war in 1812, men of the South were among the most progressive and powerful leaders." As further proof of this assertion that Southerners were really liberals (and nascent capitalists as well), Phillips pointed to the Southern frontiersmen who "accomplished the conquest of the trans-Allegheny wilderness, opened the Southwest for cotton production" and in the process "called the Northwest into being" to supply it food products. The South also "set a mighty precedent in educational lines" by establishing public state universities and for years "led New England and the Middle States in railway development (a forgotten fact but true)." "In all of these matters," he added, "the governing class in the South showed strong and progressive spirit. But that spirit was hampered and its work partly vitiated by two great adverse institutions—the institution of slavery and over-dependence upon the agricultural staples." In like fashion, "its strenuous efforts for the development of manufactures were defeated only by the institution of slavery and the superior attractiveness of cotton production."

The assumption here was that the South really wanted to develop like the North but because of slavery was unable to do so. More important, once the "peculiar institution" was removed, the way would be prepared for the real entrepreneurial talent of the South to emerge and lead the way to a newer and more progressive society: "In the great system of Southern industry and commerce, working with seeming smoothness, the negro laborers were inefficient in spite of discipline, and slavery was an obstacle to all progress. The system may be likened to an engine, with slavery as its great fly-wheel—a fly-wheel indispensable for safe running at first, perhaps, but later rendered less useful by improvements in the machinery, and finally becoming a burden instead of a benefit. Yet it was retained, because it was still considered essential in securing the adjustment and regular working of the complex mechanism. This great rigid wheel of slavery was so awkward and burdensome that it absorbed the momentum and retarded the movement of the whole machine without rendering any service of great value. The capitalization of labor and the export of earnings in exchange for more workmen [slaves], always of a low degree of efficiency, together with the extreme lack of versatility, deprived the South of the natural advantage which the cotton monopoly should have given. To be rid of the capitalization of labor as a part of the slaveholding system was a great requisite for the material progress of the South." As Phillips commented in *A*

History of Transportation in the Eastern Cotton Belt to 1860, only "in *post-bellum* times, after the waste of several decades in a chaotic transition, [did] the railroads furnish a large part of the equipment by which, as a result of the freeing of capital from its bondage to the slavery system, the cotton belt is developing widely diversified industry and is beginning to enjoy a prosperity unexampled in its past."

Phillips's efforts at reconstructing the antebellum past can also be seen in his interpretation of secession and of the Civil War, which he blamed not on the majority of people of either section but on minority extremists ("abolitionists" and "fire-eaters") who inflamed public opinion and otherwise exaggerated sectional differences where there were really none. ("The South, as a conscious entity," he observed in *The Course of the South to Secession*, "was emergent only now and then, here and there. It had no prior coherence, no constitutional status, and seemingly no cogent occasion to procure specific establishment.") What Phillips was doing here, in effect, was not upholding but denying the traditional Confederate view of the war as the inevitable result of a long-standing conflict between two fundamentally different and hostile societies. To admit that there were significant differences—economic, cultural, political, constitutional—or that public opinion generally supported secession was to reduce the possibilities for reform and reunification after the war. Hence Phillips emphasized the more immediate origins of the Civil War (the events of 1854 and after), interpreted secession as a "crisis of fear," and believed that the war was not "irrepressible."

In his desire to make Southern history relevant (following Turner's philosophy of history) and to place the South in "the vanguard of progress," however, Phillips conveniently overlooked aspects of the antebellum past that conflicted with his larger theme of continuity. Phillips, for example, paid little attention to Southern "individualism and conservatism," which he admitted had as debilitating an impact upon the economic development of the region as did the political theory of states' rights. (Referring to transportation in the South and especially to the idea of a national system of internal improvements, Phillips stated that "the South, being mainly a stronghold of strict construction, furnished little advocacy of such a system.") He also neglected Southerners' attachment to the land and their agrarian outlook which formed an integral part of their inheritance of republicanism from the Revolutionary generation. Moreover, Phillips gave short shrift to the critique of capitalism, industrialism, and urbanism that was inherent in the proslavery argument itself, not to mention discounting entirely the Southern "Lost Cause" apologia that not only gave further expression to the South's hostility to the *isms* of the day but emphasized the constitutional aspects of the long North-South conflict. Indeed, had Phillips conducted more extensive research, he would have discovered both in the press of the day and in private opinion a widespread sentiment against "Yankeeism" and its attendant notions of democracy, nationalism, and capitalism. (As Avery Craven recognized years ago, "the South lacked some things in the Northern pattern because her ideals and values had been taken from rural England. Southerners did not always want a diversified economic life or a public school system or a great number of cities. The South often deliberately chose rural backwardness.") Phillips would have also realized that secession and the "right of revolution" were part and parcel of America's and the South's republican heritage and the Southerners, in seeking such remedies, were only expressing fundamental Whig principles of 1776 in their "revolution of '61."

There is, in fact, a fundamental and debilitating contradiction in Phillips's analysis of the Old South. On the one hand, he believed that the South really represented a different civilization from that of the North. "The conditions, the life, the spirit of its people were so different from those which prevailed and still prevail in the North . . . that it is difficult for Northern investigators to interpret correctly the facts which they are able to find." Yet, on the other hand, he assumed that the South should have developed like the North and even faulted it for not doing so. "Slavery as an inseparable element of the plantation," he remarked, "tended to devote the great bulk of negro labor incessantly to the production of staple crops. This fixed the community in a rut and deprived it of the great benefits of industrial diversification." Although towns developed in the South, he added, they "numbered barely three score" and "counted their population by hundreds rather than by thousands; and in the wide intervals between there was nothing but farms, plantations and thinly scattered villages."

Ironically, for one who wanted to correct past myths about the Old South, Phillips ended up obscuring as much as he revealed about the antebellum past. He did so because of his own New South-progressive persuasion and his desire to "prove the Old South a capitalistic society." Phillips's great achievement, writes Daniel Singal, was to

show "that the antebellum period could be interpreted within the framework of New South values." In his view, the antebellum planter, "far from being an idle aristocrat," was "a veritable captain of industry, a man whose primary claim to distinction rested not on his pedigree but on his remarkable skill as a manager." "In this way," Singal concludes, "Phillips became the first major southern intellectual to challenge the Cavalier myth. . . . Phillips may well have done his best to continue the plantation legend, as Hofstadter contends, but the net effect of his work in the long run was to help undermine it."

In effect, Phillips was guilty here of reading history backwards and judging the past by the present. While this accomplishment certainly made Southern history more understandable to Phillips and many others by its continuity, it has nevertheless presented problems to later interpreters who have yet to reach any consensus regarding the economy, society, and politics of the Old South. Was the "central theme" of Southern history racism, romanticism, or agrarianism? Was the Southern economy capitalistic, feudal, or a combination of both (a "dual economy")? Were planters really capitalists or not? Was secession a movement rooted in fear, or was it based upon principle? Was the Civil War the end result of a long-standing controversy between fundamentally different civilizations and therefore "irrepressible," or was it "repressible" in the sense that there were no real differences except for agitators who exaggerated the issues and otherwise led unwilling people to war?

In this sense, Phillips's works must be viewed for what they really are, not scientifically objective analyses of their subjects but highly interpretative accounts that present Phillips's view of what the history of the Old South should have been, not what it actually was. Nor can it be said that he conducted exhaustive research in view of the many issues he failed to address. Phillips, it appears, was not so reluctant to generalize after all.

Many of these aspects of Phillips's life and works have been generally neglected by scholars, especially by his critics, who have been, for their own reasons, interested only in his later studies of slavery and particularly in his role in the creation of a "plantation legend." Indeed, eager to promote their own more liberal views about slavery in the South, historians such as Richard Hofstadter, Kenneth Stampp, and Stanley Elkins have emphasized those things that prove what they want Phillips to be, namely, a pro-Southern and antiblack scholar. Hence they focus on his Southern roots and his racism. Hence, too, they prove primarily interested in *American Negro Slavery* and *Life and Labor in the Old South* and neglect his other works.

The end results of this preoccupation with Phillips's studies of slavery have been a necessarily one-sided view of Phillips as a historian of slavery and a defender of the Old South and a failure to appreciate other influences on his life, such as his New South origins and progressive beliefs that point to a different conclusion altogether. Phillips's formative years, after all, coincided with the emergence of a New South (the year of his birth, 1877, marked the traditional end of Reconstruction in the South). Phillips also advocated such progressive reforms as improved education, a better rail network, diversification in agriculture to rid the South of the evil of staple-crop specialization, and the introduction of manufacturing to provide the South with an industrial base as well as a better market for its agricultural products. Phillips, it is often overlooked, also spent much of his life outside the South and in the company of such scholars as Richard Ely, John R. Commons, and Frederick Jackson Turner, who were progressives themselves.

In summation, "Phillips's interpretation of the Old South was informed by his vision of a New South in a Progressive America." As Eugene Genovese reminds us, "the most serious error committed by his detractors has been their oft-repeated and widely accepted charge that he looked back nostalgically to a romantic age of moonlight and magnolias." In Genovese's view, however, "he did not pine away over the loss of the golden age of slavery, much less desire in the slightest its restoration. Phillips accepted without hesitation the industrial-commercial civilization of the United States and sought actively, as a journalistic reformer as well as a historian, to ease the South toward it." To this extent, "his sympathetic and appreciative portrayal of the plantation regime of the Old South . . . must be understood not as a defense of slavery but as an appeal for the incorporation of the more humane and rational values of prebourgeois culture into modern industrial life."

Other:

"Georgia and State Rights: A Study of the Political History of Georgia from the Revolution to the Civil War," in the *Annual Report of the American Historical Association for the Year 1901* (Washington, D.C.: U.S. Government Printing Office, 1902), pp. 3-220;

"The Public Archives of Georgia," in the *American Historical Association Annual Report for the Year 1903* (Washington, D.C.: U.S. Government Printing Office, 1904): I: 439-474;

"Georgia Local Archives," in the *American Historical Association Annual Report for the Year 1904* (Washington, D.C.: U.S. Government Printing Office, 1905), pp. 555-596;

"Documentary Collections and Publications in the Older States of the South," in the *American Historical Association Annual Report for the Year 1905* (Washington, D.C.: U.S. Government Printing Office, 1906), pp. 200-204;

Plantation and Frontier Documents: 1649-1863, illustrative of industrial history in the Colonial and Antebellum South; collected from MSS and other rare sources, edited by Phillips, volumes 1 and 2 of *A Documentary History of American Industrial Society,* edited by John R. Commons and others (Cleveland: A. H. Clark, 1909-1911);

"The Southern Whigs, 1834-1854," in *Essays in American History dedicated to Frederick Jackson Turner,* edited by Guy S. Ford (New York: Holt, 1910), pp. 203-229;

"The Correspondence of Robert Toombs, Alexander H. Stephens, and Howell Cobb," in the *American Historical Association Annual Report for the Year 1911* (Washington, D.C.: U.S. Government Printing Office, 1913), II: 7-743;

"The Literary Movement for Secession," in *Studies in Southern History and Politics: Inscribed to William Archibald Dunning . . . by his former pupils, the authors,* edited by James W. Garner (New York: Columbia University Press, 1914), pp. 33-60;

"Roads, Canals, and Waterways in the South" and "Railroads in the South" in *A History of Transportation in the United States before 1860,* edited by Caroline E. MacGill (Washington, D.C.: Carnegie Institution, 1917), pp. 249-279, 414-486;

Florida Plantation Records from the Papers of George Noble Jones, edited by Phillips and James David Glunt (St. Louis: Missouri Historical Society, 1927).

Periodical Publications:

"The Economics of the Plantation," *South Atlantic Quarterly,* 2 (July 1903): 231-236;

"Historical Notes of Milledgeville, Ga.," *Gulf States Historical Magazine,* 2 (November 1903): 161-171;

"Conservatism and Progress in the Cotton Belt," *South Atlantic Quarterly,* 3 (January 1904): 1-10;

"The Plantation as a Civilizing Factor," *Sewanee Re-*

view, 12 (July 1904): 257-267;

"Transportation in the Antebellum South: An Economic Analysis," *Quarterly Journal of Economics*, 19 (May 1905): 434-451;

"The Economic Cost of Slaveholding in the Cotton Belt," *Political Science Quarterly*, 20 (June 1905): 257-275;

"The Origin and Growth of the Southern Black Belts," *American Historical Review*, 11 (July 1906): 798-816;

"The Slave Labor Problem in the Charleston District," *Political Science Quarterly*, 22 (September 1907): 416-439;

"The Decadence of the Plantation System," *Annals of the American Academy of Political and Social Science*, 25 (January 1910): 37-41;

"A Jamaica Slave Plantation," *American Historical Review*, 19 (April 1914): 543-558;

"The Plantation Product of Men," *Proceedings of the Second Annual Session of the Georgia Historical Association* (1918): 14-15;

"Plantations with Slave Labor and Free," *American Historical Review*, 30 (July 1925): 738-753;

"An Antigua Plantation, 1769-1818," *North Carolina Historical Review*, 3 (July 1926): 439-445;

"The Central Theme of Southern History," *American Historical Reivew*, 24 (October 1928): 30-43.

Biographies:

Wood Gray, "Ulrich Bonnell Phillips," in *The Marcus W. Jernegan Essays in American Historiography*, edited by William T. Hutchinson (Chicago: University of Chicago Press, 1937), pp. 357-374;

Wendell Holmes Stephenson, *The South Lives in History: Southern Historians and Their Legacy* (Baton Rouge: Louisiana State University Press, 1955), pp. 58-94;

Stephenson, *Southern History in the Making: Pioneer Historians of the South* (Baton Rouge: Louisiana State University Press, 1964), pp. 165-183;

John H. Roper, "A Case of Forgotten Identity: Ulrich B. Phillips as a Young Progressive," *Georgia Historical Quarterly*, 60 (Summer 1975): 165-175.

References:

Robert W. Fogel and Stanley Engerman, *Time on the Cross: The Economics of American Negro Slavery*, 2 volumes (Boston: Little, Brown, 1974);

Eugene D. Genovese, *In Red and Black: Marxian Explorations in Southern and Afro-American History* (New York: Pantheon, 1971);

Genovese, ed., *Ulrich Bonnell Phillips: The Slave Economy of the Old South: Selected Essays in Economic and Social History* (Baton Rouge: Louisiana State University Press, 1968);

Richard Hofstadter, "U. B. Phillips and the Plantation Legend," *Journal of Negro History*, 29 (April 1944): 109-124;

Ruben Kugler, "U. B. Phillips' Use of Sources," *Journal of Negro History*, 47 (July 1962): 368-380;

Fred Landon, "Ulrich Bonnell Phillips: Historian of the South," *Journal of Southern History*, 5 (August 1939): 364-371;

Philip C. Newman, "Ulrich Bonnell Phillips—The South's Foremost Historian," *Georgia Historical Quarterly*, 25 (September 1941): 244-261;

Sam E. Salem, "U. B. Phillips and the Scientific Tradition," *Georgia Historical Quarterly*, 44 (1960): 172-185;

Robert E. Shalhope, "Race, Class, Slavery, and the Antebellum Southern Mind," *Journal of Southern History*, 38 (November 1971): 557-574;

Daniel Singal, "Ulrich B. Phillips: The Old South As The New," *Journal of American History*, 63 (March 1977): 871-891;

John David Smith, "Historical or Personal Criticism? Frederic Bancroft vs. Ulrich B. Phillips," *Washington State University Research Studies*, 49 (June 1981): 73-86;

Smith, "The Historiographic Rise, Fall, and Resurrection of Ulrich Bonnell Phillips," *Georgia Historical Quarterly*, 65 (Summer 1981): 138-153;

Kenneth M. Stampp, "The Historian and Negro Slavery," *American Historical Review*, 57 (April 1962): 613-624;

William L. Van DeBurg, "Progress and the Conservative Historian," *Georgia Historical Quarterly*, 55 (Fall 1971): 406-416;

Allan M. Winkler, "Ulrich Bonnell Phillips: A Reappraisal," *South Atlantic Quarterly*, 71 (Spring 1972): 234-245;

W. K. Wood, "U. B. Phillips, Unscientific Historian: A Further Note on His Methodology and Use of Sources," *Southern Studies*, 21 (Summer 1982).

Papers:

Phillips's papers are at the Sterling Memorial Library, Yale University. Other Phillips letters can be found in the Southern Historical Collection, University of North Carolina; the South Caroliniana Library at the University of South Carolina (the

Yates Snowden Collection); the Frederic Bancroft Letters at Columbia University; the Frederick Jackson Turner Papers, Huntington Library, San Marino, California; and the American Historical Association Papers, Editorial Correspondence, Library of Congress, Washington, D.C.

David M. Potter

Mark T. Carleton
Louisiana State University

BIRTH: Augusta, Georgia, 6 December 1910, to David Morris and Katie Brown Potter.

EDUCATION: A.B., Emory University, 1932; M.A., Yale University, 1933; Ph.D., Yale University, 1940.

MARRIAGES: 1939 to Ethelyn Elmer Henry, divorced. 18 July 1948 to Dilys Mary Roberts; daughter: Catherine Mary.

AWARDS AND HONORS: Dinkelspiel Award from Stanford University, 1968; fellow of American Academy of Arts and Sciences; member of American Philosophical Society, Phi Beta Kappa, and Omicron Delta Kappa; awarded senior fellowship, National Endowment for the Humanities, 1968-1969; president, American Historical Association, 1970-1971, and Organization of American Historians, 1970-1971; Pulitzer Prize for *The Impending Crisis, 1848-1861*, 1977; three honorary degrees.

DEATH: Palo Alto, California, 18 February 1971.

BOOKS: *Lincoln and His Party in the Secession Crisis* (New Haven: Yale University Press, 1942; London: Oxford University Press, 1942);
The Lincoln Theme and American National Historiography: An Inaugural Lecture Delivered Before the University of Oxford on 19 November 1947 (Oxford: Clarendon Press, 1948);
People of Plenty: Economic Abundance and the American Character (Chicago: University of Chicago Press, 1954);
The South and the Sectional Conflict (Baton Rouge: Louisiana State University Press, 1968);
The South and the Concurrent Majority, edited by Don E. Fehrenbacher and Carl N. Degler (Baton Rouge: Louisiana State University Press, 1972);

David M. Potter

Division and the Stresses of Reunion, 1845-1876, volume 4 of the Scott, Foresman American History Series (Glenview, Ill.: Scott, Foresman, 1973);
History and American Society: Essays of David M. Potter, edited by Fehrenbacher (New York: Oxford University Press, 1973);
Freedom and Its Limitations in American Life, edited by Fehrenbacher (Stanford: Stanford University Press, 1976);

The Impending Crisis, 1848-1861, completed and edited by Fehrenbacher (New York: Harper & Row, 1976).

When David Morris Potter died in 1971, he was president of both the American Historical Association and the Organization of American Historians, the two largest associations of professional historians in the United States. His comprehensively researched and exceptionally penetrating books, articles, and lectures on the South, the causes of the Civil War, the American character, the writing of history, and other subjects convinced many of Potter's colleagues that he may have been the greatest American historian of the mid-twentieth century.

Even though much of his work was conceptual in nature, Potter's style of writing was precise and clear. He always defined his terms with great care, rarely used words in excess of three syllables, was neither condescending nor bombastic, and never sought refuge in jargon, although he did utilize some of the terminology of behavioral science. Potter's prose was also refreshingly economical. Many respectable historians would consume a page or more to communicate what Potter could have said in a paragraph or less.

These attributes of the superbly gifted writer make his work comprehensible to any intelligent reader. Nonetheless, Potter remains largely unknown to the reading public. Unlike more popular historians, Potter did not concentrate on describing "what happened"; rather, he sought to *interpret* the causes and results of what happened. Potter was above all an "idea man," a "historian's historian" whose insights inspired the reconsideration of several traditional interpretations and methodologies. He never summarized in detail any Civil War battles, for example, but he did author two masterful accounts of why the nation had dissolved by 1861 and why armed conflict between North and South was not avoided. In each case Potter scrupulously reexamined the known evidence, critiqued previous scholarly accounts, and put forth his own measured assessment. As a writer and interpreter of history, Potter, in a figurative sense, was much more the Haydn or Beethoven of his profession than its Cole Porter or John Lennon.

A scholar whose work was more analytical and interpretative than descriptive and narrative, Potter presented his findings chiefly through the media of professional gatherings, scholarly journals, and university presses. He thus further isolated his work from the general reader and ensured that his audi-

ence would consist principally of colleagues and students within an academic community which included Potter himself as a major figure for most of his adult life.

Among members of that community, Potter's influence was profound and durable, especially among his fellow historians. The conclusions he reached, while substantially persuasive and brilliantly argued, will likely be surpassed by the memory of his consistently superior performance as a professional craftsman who demonstrated mastery of the relevant literature, rigorous honesty and objectivity in assessing source material, a creative but disciplined historical imagination, and avoidance of ideological preconceptions. Potter did not use history as a vehicle for proving or disproving anything; instead, he insisted that history itself should be rationally and dispassionately *understood*. Potter's lifelong commitment to that ideal may be his most important professional legacy.

Little is known of Potter's early life or childhood memories; he rarely spoke of those experiences and apparently never wrote about them, except in the preface to a collection of his essays on the South published in 1968, long after he had ceased to reside in Georgia or in the South, and only three years prior to his death: "In one of her incomparable sketches, Frances Gray Patton once observed that no one born in the South later than World War I could remember the Civil War personally. I found this statement most arresting, because though I was born in Georgia in 1910, I have always had a feeling that in an indirect, nonsensory way I could remember what was still called 'The War'—as if there had been no other. If I did not see the men in gray march off to battle, I saw great numbers of them march in parades on a Memorial Day which did not fall on the same day that was observed in the North. If I did not experience the rigors of life 'behind the lines in the Southern Confederacy,' I lived in the long backwash of the war in a land that remembered the past very vividly and somewhat inaccurately, because the present had nothing exciting to offer, and accuracy about either the past or the present was psychologically not very rewarding. . . . But on balance I have lived longer outside of the South than in it, and hopefully have learned to view it with detachment, though not without fondness. Certainly no longer a Southerner, I am not yet completely denatured."

In the process of becoming a denatured Southerner, if indeed he ever did, Potter contributed as much as any historian to understanding the past experience of his native region, its distinctive characteristics, and its relation to the rest of the nation. Throughout his career, the South remained Potter's ongoing focus of scholarly investigation and reflection.

After attending local Augusta schools, Potter enrolled in Atlanta's Emory University, graduating, Phi Beta Kappa, with an A.B. degree in 1932. (In 1957 Emory bestowed the honorary doctor of letters degree upon Potter, by then an internationally recognized scholar.) From Emory Potter went directly to Yale University to pursue graduate study under the guidance of Ulrich B. Phillips, the foremost historian of the South at that time.

Potter received his M.A. degree from Yale in 1933; after three further years of graduate study, Potter commenced his teaching career, in which he also excelled, as an instructor at the University of Mississippi in Oxford. Two years later, in 1938, Potter became an instructor at Rice Institute (subsequently Rice University) in Houston, Texas, where he remained until 1942. In the meantime, Yale had awarded him a doctorate in 1940. Potter returned to his graduate alma mater as an assistant professor in 1942, the same year in which his dissertation, an excellent piece of revisionist scholarship, was published as *Lincoln and His Party in the Secession Crisis*.

Completing his dissertation, refining it for publication, and satisfying the demands of teaching absorbed most of Potter's time and attention between 1936 and 1942. His only publications prior to 1942 were two articles, two book reviews, and a bibliography of the published works of Phillips, who had died in 1934. Following his return to Yale, however, the thirty-two-year-old Potter (already a respected authority on Lincoln, the South, and the Civil War) embarked upon one of the busiest, most productive, and most significant academic careers in recent decades.

During his nineteen years at Yale (1942-1961), Potter rose rapidly from assistant professor to William Robertson Coe Professor of American History (1950-1961), served as Harmsworth Professor of American History at Oxford University (1947-1948), edited the *Yale Review* (1949-1951), and delivered at the University of Chicago the 1950 Walgreen Lectures, which evolved into his second major book, the unique and multidimensional *People of Plenty: Economic Abundance and the American Character* (1954).

Somehow Potter found time to compose a "wise, balanced and brilliant" introduction to the diary of a federal officer who had served in the South during Reconstruction and to write an introduction to the overland journal of a Gold Rush expedition which was "as interesting and scholarly an essay on the mass movement West in 1849 as one will find anywhere." These were only two examples of what soon became Potter's forte—the concise but fully developed article or essay, always lucidly written and embodying the author's customarily original and memorable interpretation.

It was also no later than Potter's early Yale period that omnivorous reading began to expand his knowledge to encyclopedic dimensions and that persistent critical reflection raised his naturally keen intellect to maturity. (Many years later a reviewer stated that it was "often difficult to perceive and analyze Potter's growth and development, for he has been a wise historian for almost three decades.")

In 1961 Potter left Yale for Stanford University, where he also held the chair of Coe Professor of American History until his death ten years later. While on the Stanford faculty Potter delivered at University College, London, the 1963 Commonwealth Fund Lectures (posthumously published in 1976 as *Freedom and Its Limitations in American Life*) and at Louisiana State University the 1968 Walter Lynwood Fleming Lectures in Southern History (posthumously published in 1972 as *The South and the Concurrent Majority*). Articles and book reviews continued to appear frequently, most of the outstanding ones dating from Potter's Stanford period.

In 1968 the Louisiana State University Press published a selection of Potter's essays on the South entitled *The South and the Sectional Conflict*. A posthumous collection of other articles, edited by Potter's Stanford colleague Don E. Fehrenbacher, was published in 1973 as *History and American Society: Essays of David M. Potter*. Potter's most ambitious project, a comprehensive analysis of the breakup of the Union prior to the Civil War, on which he had labored since 1954, remained unfinished when he died. Fehrenbacher completed the two concluding chapters and edited the work, which appeared in 1976 as *The Impending Crisis, 1848-1861*.

It would be impossible within the confines of this essay to comment extensively on all or even most of Potter's writings; there are simply too many of them. A worthwhile selection, however, would have to include the three major scholarly works, one each from Potter's early, middle, and later years—*Lincoln and His Party in the Secession Crisis*, *People of Plenty*, and the *Impending Crisis, 1848-1861*. The two collections of Potter's essays also deserve inclusion, as do the published versions of his Commonwealth Fund and Fleming Lectures.

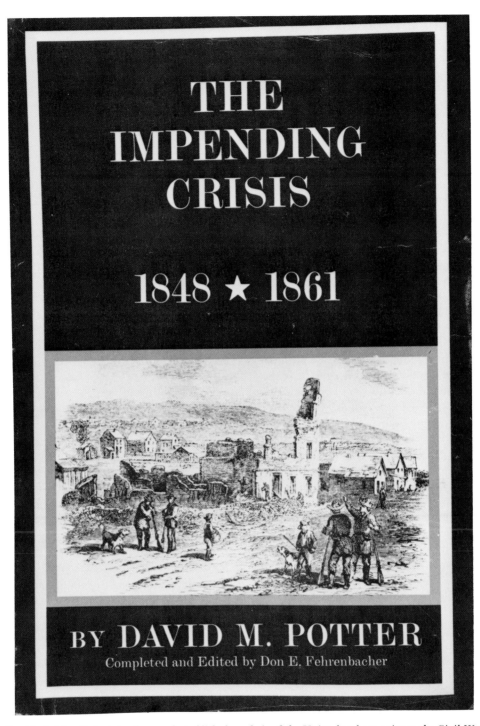

Dust jacket for Potter's posthumously published analysis of the Union break-up prior to the Civil War

Potter's first major scholarly publication was *Lincoln and His Party in the Secession Crisis*, a refinement of his Yale doctoral dissertation, published in 1942. *Lincoln and His Party in the Secession Crisis* was a

revisionist account of developments between the election of Lincoln as president in November 1860 and the bombardment of Fort Sumter on 12 April 1861, which started the Civil War. Historically speaking, a "revisionist" study reexamines what is known according to new evidence and/or new perspectives; Potter's objective, therefore, was not simply to narrate a sequence of familiar events but to offer a new interpretation of what motivated, and resulted from, those events.

Incorporated in Potter's treatment was a subtle, but nonetheless forceful, assault upon hindsight, which persuades most laymen (and some historians) to conclude that what happened was "inevitable" or it would not have happened. What Potter did in *Lincoln and His Party in the Secession Crisis* was to assess the problems of 1860-1861 as the participants themselves faced them along the way, a technique precluding foreknowledge of what the final result—civil war—would be.

Potter discovered that by 1860 Southern threats to secede were no longer taken seriously by Lincoln and most of his fellow Republicans since similar threats had been uttered many times before and had not materialized. Even after the lower South did leave the Union during the waning months of Democrat James Buchanan's administration, Lincoln persisted in believing that the secessionists were an ephemeral minority of Southerners and that refusing to give the secessionists what they demanded (admission of slavery into the territories) would soon discredit them while simultaneously strengthening the Southern Unionists, whom Lincoln confidently expected would regain the initiative in the departed states and restore them to the Union. Besides, conceding slavery in the territories would be politically suicidal for Lincoln and his party associates. In 1860 the Republicans were themselves a national minority—closer, indeed, to a faction than a party—made up of ex-Whigs, antislavery Democrats, and office-seekers that as a group had never held power before. Thus, to concede slavery in the territories would repudiate the platform and disrupt the fragile organization of his own party, as Lincoln saw it. Late in the crisis, Lincoln attempted to retain Fort Sumter because he could not as president allow a final erosion of federal authority by giving up the vulnerable but inescapably symbolic installation in Charleston Harbor.

Lincoln did not, therefore, see war as the "inevitable" consequence of his no-compromise/no-concession policy until "it came" with the attack on Fort Sumter. Nor did Potter find any convincing evidence to support a conclusion by earlier historians that Lincoln had intentionally manipulated the South into firing the "first shot" of an inevitable conflict. Lincoln's principal "blunder" had been to underestimate the position of the secessionists while

expecting too much from Southern Unionists. Rather than villains or heroes, Potter's analysis revealed fallible human beings on both sides trapped by a series of choices whose ultimate consequences could not have been foreseen in the beginning. As the able British historian of the United States, Sir Denis Brogan, put it, Potter demonstrated in *Lincoln and His Party in the Secession Crisis* that "one must consider the possibilities that did not materialize before one can understand what did happen."

One reviewer praised Potter's "careful research," "high degree of objectivity," and "keen historical imagination." Another described *Lincoln and His Party in the Secession Crisis* as "the authoritative work on the subject." Although criticizing Potter's choice of original sources and questioning some of his conclusions, a third reviewer conceded that *Lincoln and His Party in the Secession Crisis* "will be the last word." Reprinted in paperback by the Yale University Press on the twentieth anniversary of its original appearance, *Lincoln and His Party in the Secession Crisis* is still regarded as one of the most illuminating accounts of political history written by an American.

Twelve years after publication of *Lincoln and His Party*, Potter's second major scholarly study appeared. As its title suggests, *People of Plenty: Economic Abundance and the American Character* had nothing to do with Potter's previous interests. Yet he had by no means abandoned the South, sectionalism, or Lincoln but had simply followed his curiosity to other fields of investigation in which he quickly and characteristically became an expert. Reviews of *People of Plenty* were (with one striking exception) enthusiastic, and the impact of Potter's second book upon historians and social scientists as well has been even more far-reaching than the durable *Lincoln and His Party in the Secession Crisis*.

A sense of the originality and unconventionality of *People of Plenty* as a book written by a historian can be gained from the titles of its components: "History, the Behavioral Studies, and the Science of Man," "The Study of National Character," and "Abundance and the Shaping of American Character." Potter began the book with a review of separate paths taken in the study of national character by, on the one hand, behavioral scientists (cultural anthropologists, psychologists, and sociologists) and, on the other, historians. He concluded the initial section of the book by suggesting that the conceptual insights of behavioral science should be constructively interwoven with the empirical methodology of history to produce a clearer and more useful assessment of national character.

In the final section of *People of Plenty*, Potter analyzed the entire American historical experience as having derived from economic abundance. Sixty years earlier, Frederick Jackson Turner had declared that the central factor in the American experience had been an open frontier of free and accessible land. Potter broadened Turner's definition to include not only land but also natural and mineral resources, together with the "nation's system of production and distribution," in effect, with the totality of America's socioeconomic way of life.

Among the by-products of his thesis that Potter perceptively discussed were the historical relationships between abundance, mobility, and status in the United States; the effects of abundance upon foreign policy and upon foreign views of the United States; and the function of advertising in a modern society of abundance—essentially to transform peripheral wants into conscious needs ("Wouldn't you really rather have a Buick?") so that mass consumption would keep pace with increasing production.

Was this history? One of the nation's traditionally-oriented historians, Fred A. Shannon, believed not and gave vigorous vent to his feelings in a debunking review of *People of Plenty*: "To me, the sad part of it all is that for many years I have been blissfully reading about what happened, how it happened, why it happened and the consequence thereof, all written according to the best ability of the historian, and have never bothered my foolish head about the American character. In my benighted condition, even after reading this book, I can envision 162,000,000 American characters, perhaps divisible into 327 categories with wide divergencies in each, but I still cannot see an American character. . . . As philosophy, the book makes intriguing reading in spite of the occasional jawbreaking words and involved rhetoric. If it is history, then a great number of us old codgers have lived entirely too long."

Other reactions to *People of Plenty* were decidedly positive. Boyd C. Shafer believed that Potter's volume would "rank among the significant books that have influenced historical interpretation in the United States," while Karl W. Deutsch praised *People of Plenty* as an "important book which lifts the whole problem [of national character] to a new level of analysis and understanding." *People of Plenty* reappeared in paperback in 1958 and by 1969 was available in Japanese, Spanish, French, and Korean translations. Its themes remain provocative and deserving of continued study and reflection, especially in an age of declining abun-

dance, which Potter did not live to witness or comment upon. *People of Plenty* will also continue to serve as a model for synthesizing the conceptual approaches of behavioral and social sciences with the field of historical investigation.

In the same year (1954) that produced *People of Plenty*, Potter agreed to write a volume on the coming of the Civil War for Harper's New American Nation Series. For the remainder of his life Potter struggled to complete the project, devouring the literature on the subject and working on a manuscript when not distracted by numerous other responsibilities and undertakings. He died leaving the last two chapters unfinished and previous chapters in readable, though not publishable, form. Completed and edited by Don E. Fehrenbacher, Potter's posthumous magnum opus appeared in 1976 as *The Impending Crisis, 1848-1861*.

Potter's longest, most comprehensive, and best written work was a sequel, in reverse, to *Lincoln and His Party in the Secession Crisis*. Instead of going forward, past the Sumter affair into the Civil War itself and beyond, *The Impending Crisis* went back in time through the discordant 1850s to the roots of national dissolution—the Mexican War and the controversy concerning admission of slavery to territories acquired as a result of that conflict. Just as he had assessed the behavior of Lincoln and his contemporaries between the 1860 election and the commencement of hostilities between North and South, so Potter again applied the same technique to the broader and vastly more complex thirteen-year period preceding the Civil War; he approached the sequence of events from the participants' viewpoints rather than from the biased ex post facto perspective of hindsight.

The scope of *The Impending Crisis* was both familiar and immense—from the Compromise of 1850, through the demise of the Whig party, the Kansas-Nebraska Act, the birth of the Republican party, the Dred Scott case, "Bleeding Kansas," the ineffective and tragic Buchanan regime, the pivotal 1860 election, and the final breakup of the Union. But the work was not "a mere narrative of well-known historical facts." In the established pattern of Potter's writing, *The Impending Crisis* was "a fascinating and sophisticated analysis of a wide range of alternatives that might have led the nation onto different paths." As reviewer Thomas H. O'Connor continued, "Drawing upon the wisdom of a lifetime of scholarship, Potter takes no outcome for granted and sees nothing as absolutely inevitable."

Typically cautious, Potter refrained from placing all his apples in any single basket. One of his most notable characteristics was a mature and realistic appreciation of the nuances and indefinables of the human past that make it risky for historians to say with certainty that "X definitely resulted from Y in terms of Z." Thus, while it is apparent from reading *The Impending Crisis* that Potter, like other historians of the period, was convinced that slavery lay at the heart of the sectional controversy, one will not find categorical statements proving how slavery was "the" cause of secession or of the Civil War.

In a short, laudatory review Holman Hamilton's concluding tribute to Potter proved to be prophetic: "Even more than the felicitous style, his distinctively faithful recreation of an era and his mature assessment of it make *The Impending Crisis* of Pulitzer and Bancroft Prize quality." In 1977, one year after its publication, *The Impending Crisis* in fact received the Pulitzer Prize for history.

While he was alive only two book-length works of original scholarship were published under Potter's name—*Lincoln and His Party in the Secession Crisis* and *People of Plenty*. That both were exceptional was lost sight of by some who knew that many of Potter's contemporaries had published several more books than he during comparable periods of time and who may have felt that Potter's scholarly reputation was overrated. Yet no such reservations troubled those who attentively followed Potter's production roster, which included 43 quality articles or essays and 102 published reviews of 133 different books.

Each of these many shorter pieces received the same meticulous preparation and embodied the consistently original insights and clarity of expression found in Potter's major projects. Even if he had written no books at all, Potter's other (rather than lesser) writings would have secured his reputation as a formidable historian. Originally published in professional journals, Potter's articles, essays, and reviews initially enlightened only colleagues and graduate students. However, a number of the more outstanding pieces were subsequently offered to a potentially larger readership in two selected collections, one by Potter himself in 1968 as *The South and the Sectional Conflict* and the other by Don E. Fehrenbacher in 1973 as *History and American Society: Essays of David M. Potter*.

In his review of *The South and the Sectional Conflict*, Martin Duberman expressed a widely held view that "David Potter may be the greatest living historian of the United States" and concluded that "to read him is to become aware of a truth that only the greatest historians have been able to show us:

that the chief lesson to be derived from a study of the past is that it holds no simple lesson, and that the historian's main responsibility is to prevent anyone from claiming that it does."

Because *History and American Society* appeared two years after the author's death, colleagues who reviewed the second collection of essays may have been even more inclined to praise Potter's work, saddened by the realization that they would see little more of it. George B. Tindall found the volume "an invaluable and thought-provoking book . . . from which the general reader as well as the historian can profit." The essays revealed Potter's "consistent dedication to rational judgment, to live issues, and to a simple felicity of style happily free from polemics and jargon." Ray Allen Billington assessed *History and American Society* as "a volume that will prick the conscience of the profession and benefit the writing of history for generations to come. . . . Potter, more than any other historian of his generation acted as a bell wether leading the rest of us into rich pastures for historical grazing." Echoing a consensus that the tight structure of Potter's style prevented any of his work from being effectively skimmed, John A. Garraty advised that the essays "must be read whole to be appreciated and when read they are truly gripping." Earlier in his review Garraty had labeled Potter as "one of the outstanding historians of our time."

Included in *The South and the Sectional Conflict*, with the year of original publication, were "The Enigma of the South" (1961), "On Understanding the South" (1964), "The Historian's Use of Nationalism and Vice Versa"—considered by some as the absolute best of Potter's writings—(1963), "The Literature on the Background of the Civil War" (1961), "The Lincoln Theme and American National Historiography" (1948), "Depletion and Renewal in Southern History" (1967), "John Brown and the Paradox of Leadership Among American Negroes" (not previously published), "Horace Greeley and Peaceable Secession" (1941), "Why the Republicans Rejected Both Compromise and Secession" (1965), "Jefferson Davis and the Political Factors in Confederate Defeat" (1960), and "The Civil War in the History of the Modern World: A Comparative View" (1968).

Much more varied were the selections reprinted in *History and American Society*: "Is America a Civilization?" (1958), "The Quest for the National Character" (1962), "American Women and the American Character" (1962), "Explicit Data and Implicit Assumptions in Historical Study" (1963), "American Individualism in the Twentieth Century" (1963), "The Roots of American Alienation" (1963), "C. Vann Woodward" (1969), "Changing Patterns of Social Cohesion and the Crisis of Law Under a System of Government by Consent" (1971), "Roy F. Nichols and the Rehabilitation of American Political History" (1971), and a review of Richard Hofstadter's *The Progressive Historians: Turner, Beard, Parrington* (1968). Included in both volumes was "The Historian's Use of Nationalism and Vice Versa." Almost all of the topics raised in these and other articles that Potter wrote could have inspired book-length treatments by other scholars. But one of Potter's talents was the ability to present a complete analysis of a complex theme within a concise format. His interests also ranged widely and solidly, from John Brown to women in American culture, alienation in America, and pitfalls to avoid in writing history. As the study of history suffers from ongoing overspecialization, Potter's stature will grow larger as one of the last "Renaissance men" within his discipline.

Among the several prestigious lectures Potter delivered were the Commonwealth Fund Lectures at University College, London, in 1963, and the Walter Lynwood Fleming Lectures at Louisiana State University in 1968. The former were eventually published as *Freedom and Its Limitations in American Life* (1976) and the latter as *The South and the Concurrent Majority* (1972). Persons who have read none of Potter's writings might introduce themselves to his work with these short but rewarding reflections.

In *Freedom and Its Limitations in American Life*, Potter suggested that Americans may not in fact be as free as they themselves or others assume them to be, that the freedom Americans possess has not evolved without its imperceptible costs and qualifications. Drawing upon earlier assessments by the astute foreign observers Alexis de Tocqueville, Michael Chevalier, and Lord Bryce, Potter concluded that while Americans since 1783 have maintained freedom from the overt coercion of kings and ruling classes, in their mobile and classless society "freedom meant equality of opportunity, which meant a society without fixed status, which meant that there were not persons sufficiently elite to defy authority, which meant that the individual would comply with the expectations of the majority. One began with freedom and ended with conformity."

In the last of four essays, "Noncoercive Control," Potter carried his analysis into the modern era as he described mass media advertising's use of "power without coercion" to persuade Americans

how to conform desirably as consumers rather than as citizens. After some sobering passages on the manipulative and sometimes exploitative messages projected by commercial television, Potter concluded with a warning: "Perhaps what all this means is that freedom for the modern American depends less than ever before on resistance to the controls exerted by others and more than ever on his own willpower and self-control. Eternal vigilance remains the price of liberty, but the first person to watch is oneself."

The South and the Concurrent Majority began with a summary of the devices John C. Calhoun advocated to constitute a "negative power" or "concurrent majority" by which the antebellum slaveowning South might protect itself from the faster growing, numerically superior North: nullification or state "interposition"; a dual presidency, with the Northern and Southern coexecutives each having a veto over congressional action; and, as a last resort in defense of state sovereignty, secession. Nullification was attempted by South Carolina alone in 1831-1832 and failed. The dual presidency was never created, and secession also failed with the South's defeat in the Civil War.

Ironically, it was *after* the Civil War and Reconstruction that a real "concurrent majority" took shape and in the form previously shunned by Calhoun himself as unworkable: Southern dominance of the congressional seniority system and Southern control of the congressional Democratic caucus. By 1900 the habitual reelection of Democratic senators and congressmen from the one-party South (in which almost all blacks had been disfranchised) gave Southerners seniority among Democratic committee members and numerical ascendancy in the Democratic caucus of each chamber. When the Democratic party controlled Congress, as in the Wilson and Franklin Roosevelt administrations, Southerners chaired most committees and thus controlled the legislative process. When the Democratic party was not in the national majority, which was most of the time between 1877 and 1933, well-organized filibusters by Southerners in the Senate could still thwart passage of unwanted legislation such as measures to prohibit poll taxes and lynching. National policy on almost all occasions, therefore, had to take Southern wishes and interests into account.

But this later "concurrent majority" operated securely only so long as the South remained a "majority within the minority party." Franklin Roosevelt's New Deal coalition was national, however, and from 1933 onward the South was forced increasingly on the defensive as a "minority within the majority party." A Congress top-heavy with Northern and Eastern liberals during the Kennedy-Johnson era ended the "concurrent majority" by changing rules so as to make filibustering and other obstructionist tactics more difficult and by passing the Voting Rights Act of 1965 which, in restoring the franchise to Southern blacks, broke the conservative grip on Southern politics both in Washington and at home. Nonetheless, as Potter concluded: "Insofar as it is true that, for a century of our national history, power was seldom exercised by a numerical majority without restraint, and that it could usually be exercised only by the joint consent of two separate concentrations of power, this truth might be regarded as a matter of prime significance not only for the history of the South but also for the history of the nation. In this sense it would perhaps not be pushing simplification too far to say that one important way of understanding the period between the middle of the nineteenth century and the middle of the twentieth, is to recognize that, in one of its aspects, it was the Century of the Concurrent Majority."

Although Potter's writings have been the specified theme of this essay, the words he left on paper comprise only part of his professional contributions and reveal little of Potter the person. As Carl N. Degler recalled in a worthy and moving obituary, "Potter's influence in the profession derived from more than his scholarly work, important as it is; it flowed from the man himself. Few people—students or professional colleagues—who came into contact with him remained unaffected by the experience." A "man of uncommon mind and personal dignity," Potter was nonetheless "a natural wit from whom hilarious stories, clever turns of phrase, and piquant historical facts came in an unfailing stream."

The largest group of people to come into personal contact with Potter was his students. He must have lectured to thousands of them and interacted with hundreds, graduate and undergraduate alike. If some academicians place exclusive priority on research and publication while paying only lip service to excellent teaching, Potter was an impressive quality on both sides of the academic scale. As a colleague recalls, "A Potter lecture was usually a little masterpiece. Clearly organized, authoritative, broad in scope, penetrating in its analysis, and admirably fair in the treatment of controversial points, it was delivered in a characteristically intimate and reflective tone, which invited his auditors to share with him the pleasures and perplexities of studying

the past." Another colleague remembered that "the iron logic of his thought, the originality of his ideas, and the precision of his diction could hold a hall of three hundred students in unwonted quiet." Highly regarded by serious students wherever he encountered them, Potter in 1968 received one of academia's most treasured honors for exceptional teaching, Stanford University's Dinkelspiel Award.

Potter was also an academic statesman of the first rank. Not only did he contribute time to administrative service at Yale and Stanford but "in times of crisis and passion, his was often the voice of accommodation and always of reason. He was an inspiring and at the same time a stabilizing influence. There are others of us who will join Edmund S. Morgan in saying: 'He was the wisest man I ever knew.'"

A man of Potter's reputation and accomplishments could easily have succumbed to pomposity, obsession with the preeminence of his own projects, and disdain toward others. Potter chose instead to be friendly, genuinely interested in the work of others, and unceasingly helpful, regardless of the pressures and preoccupations with which he may have been coping at the time.

Stress, frustration, and tragedy marred Potter's personal life. The high regard in which he was held brought numerous requests for books or articles dealing with subjects on which he had become an authority. Invitations to lecture and to serve on various boards and committees came in steadily. Because Potter turned down few of these requests, they painfully overburdened even his considerable energies and talents. A first marriage ended in divorce after six years; the second Mrs. Potter took her own life, and less than two years later Potter himself died of cancer in his sixty-first year, leaving several major projects unfinished. Yet through all of this personal difficulty, Potter continued to do his best at what he always did best with remarkable serenity until the end.

In words of tribute to Potter written by three of his closest associates, "Those who knew him with some intimacy will remember not only David Potter's sterling intellectual qualities but his unfailing courtesy and considerateness, his integrity, his bright wit, and his quiet fortitude in the presence of personal tragedy. They mourn the passing of a gifted scholar and teacher, but even more poignant is the untimely loss of a good companion and noble spirit."

Other:

Trail to California: The Overland Journey of Vincent

Geiger and Wakeman Bryarly, edited by Potter (New Haven: Yale University Press, 1945);

John William De Forest, *A Union Officer in the Reconstruction*, edited by Potter and James H. Croushore (New Haven: Yale University Press, 1948);

Nationalism and Sectionalism in America, 1775-1877: Select Problems in Historical Interpretation, edited by Potter and Thomas G. Manning (New York: Holt, 1949);

Government and the American Economy: 1870 to the Present: Select Problems in Historical Interpretation, edited by Potter and Manning (New York: Holt, 1950).

Bibliography:

George Harmon Knoles, "Bibliography of the Published Works of David M. Potter," in *Freedom and Its Limitations in American Life*, by Potter,

edited by Don E. Fehrenbacher (Stanford: Stanford University Press, 1976), pp. 65-89.

References:

Sir Denis Brogan, "David M. Potter," in *Pastmasters: Some Essays on American Historians*, edited by Marcus Cunliffe and Robin W. Winks (New York: Harper & Row, 1969), pp. 316-344;

Carl N. Degler, "David M. Potter," *American Historical Review*, 76 (October 1971): 1273-1275;

Don E. Fehrenbacher, Howard R. Lamar, and Otis A. Pease, "David M. Potter: A Memorial Resolution," *Journal of American History*, 58 (September 1971): 307-310.

Papers:

Potter's papers are in the Stanford University Archives and are closed to use until 1991.

James G. Randall
(24 June 1881-20 February 1953)

John David Smith
North Carolina State University

SELECTED BOOKS: *The Confiscation of Property During the Civil War* (Indianapolis: Mutual Printing, 1913);

Constitutional Problems Under Lincoln (New York & London: Appleton, 1926);

The Civil War and Reconstruction (Boston & New York: Heath, 1937; revised by David Donald, 1961);

Lincoln, the President, 4 volumes; volume 4, by Randall and Richard N. Current (New York: Dodd, Mead, 1945-1955; London: Eyre & Spottiswoode, 1945-1956);

Lincoln and the South (Baton Rouge: Louisiana State University Press, 1946);

Lincoln, the Liberal Statesman (New York: Dodd, Mead, 1947; London: Eyre & Spottiswoode, 1947).

James Garfield Randall, biographer of Abraham Lincoln and historian of the Civil War, helped to establish these fields as major subjects of inquiry for professional historians. Before the appearance of his writings, books dealing with Lincoln and the

Civil War largely were the province of amateurs—clergymen, military figures, politicians, and journalists. Professional historians, graduate-school-trained scholars who earned their livelihoods from studying history, tended to avoid examining the middle period. For them the decades surrounding the Civil War were too controversial, too laden with sectional polemics to satisfy the rigors of "scientific" historical scholarship. But Randall disagreed. Exhaustive research, he insisted, coupled with a dedication to objectivity, would allow the historian to untangle the myths and misunderstandings surrounding Lincoln and his age. Masterful analysis of the administrative and constitutional questions of the Civil War period became Randall's trademark and, ultimately, his foremost contribution to American historiography.

Randall was born in Indianapolis, Indiana, the son of a businessman, Horace Randall, and of Ellen Amanda Kregelo Randall. While a student in public schools in Indianapolis, Randall exhibited unusual artistic talent and an early fascination with Abraham Lincoln. He loved to draw Lincoln's rugged

James G. Randall

but sensitive face and, at age twelve, painted his idol's portrait in oils. Shortly before graduating from high school, Randall spoke on Lincoln before his church. After receiving his A.B. degree from Butler College in 1903, Randall entered the University of Chicago. Earning his own way through graduate school, he received his A.M. and Ph.D. degrees in 1904 and 1911, respectively. In the latter year Randall married Edith Laura Abbott, his childhood sweetheart and classmate at Butler, who died in 1913. The Randalls had no children.

Randall's doctoral dissertation, *The Confiscation of Property During the Civil War*, combined his lifelong interests in Lincoln, the Civil War, and constitutional history. Under the direction of professors Claude H. Van Tyne and Andrew C. McLaughlin, Randall focused on the bearing of federal confiscation policies on larger constitutional and legal questions. In his dissertation he classified data gleaned from court records and outlined the legal problems facing Lincoln's administration as it dealt with the complex question of property rights. Although he devoted little attention to economic

and social matters, virtually ignoring the sequestration and emancipation of slaves, Randall's dissertation was a model monograph for its day. The *American Historical Review* published portions of it in 1912 and 1913.

Randall left graduate school determined to teach and write history at a large university. Unfortunately, university positions were scarce. He thus taught at Roanoke College (1912-1918), was appointed Harrison Research Fellow at the University of Pennsylvania (1916-1917), and served as historian for the U.S. Shipping Board (1918-1919). After World War I he joined the faculty of Richmond College (1919-1920). In 1920 Randall was invited to join the faculty at the University of Illinois. At last he had found a school with the library resources and academic environment necessary to support his research.

Randall and his second wife, Ruth Elaine Painter, whom he married in 1917, thoroughly enjoyed life in Urbana. It was here that Randall established himself as a Lincoln and Civil War scholar, and he remained at Illinois until his retirement in 1949. During almost three decades of teaching at that university, he published thirteen books and more than fifty articles. Graduate students flocked to Illinois to study with him. They encountered a quiet, warm, supportive, open-minded professor who was eager to grasp what students thought and who therefore encouraged students to express themselves. "There is too much woodenness in the ordinary relation of teacher & student," wrote Randall at the time of his first coming to Illinois. His graduate students recall fondly the Sunday night suppers and good fellowship at the Randalls' apartment. Few professors had a better rapport with and understanding of their students than did Randall. Generous with his time, he directed twenty-six doctoral dissertations and fifty-five master's theses.

Randall's first book, *Constitutional Problems Under Lincoln*, appeared in 1926. This was no rehash of his doctoral dissertation. Instead, Randall wrote a fresh, broadly based analysis of the relation of Civil War constitutional questions to the era's social motives and forces. This time he sidestepped none of the intricate questions that he had excluded from his dissertation. Exhaustive research had prepared him to treat not just confiscation but also military rule, arbitrary arrests, and emancipation. In Randall's opinion, Lincoln unquestionably usurped "more arbitrary power than perhaps any other President has seized. Probably no President has carried the power of proclamation and executive order (independently of Congress) so far as did Lincoln." The historian went on to list the extreme wartime measures initiated by Lincoln: enlarging the army and navy beyond limits fixed by law, freeing the slaves by emancipation, reorganizing state governments, suspending the writ of habeas corpus, proclaiming martial law, and spending public monies without congressional appropriation. In doing so, Lincoln both enlarged the powers of the executive and seized legislative and judicial functions.

But there was another side of the picture, explained Randall. Neither the U.S. Congress nor the Supreme Court exerted strong restraints on Lincoln. This was "an eccentric period," added Randall, "a time when constitutional restraints did not fully operate and when the 'rule of law' largely broke down." Anticipating his later writings on Lincoln, the historian argued that the president's personal qualities went a long way toward explaining why arbitrary rule never reigned: "His humane sympathy, his humor, his lawyerlike caution, his common sense, his fairness toward opponents, his dislike of arbitrary rule, his willingness to take the people into his confidence and to set forth patiently the reasons for unusual measures—all these elements of his character operated to modify and soften the acts of overzealous subordinates and to lessen the effect of harsh measures upon individuals. He was criticized for leniency as often as for severity."

Randall's judicious untangling of Civil War constitutional questions did not go unnoticed. In 1929 he was commissioned by editor Allen Johnson to write the lengthy sketch of Lincoln for the prestigious *Dictionary of American Biography*. Randall's essay, published in 1933, remains one of the best introductions to Lincoln's life. The success of this article sparked him to more extensive research on the sixteenth president. In 1933 Randall also edited the two-volume *Diary of Orville Hickman Browning* for the Illinois State Historical Library. In order to grasp Browning's role in Andrew Johnson's cabinet, Randall scoured the archives of the secretary of the interior's office. The historian gained from Browning "a sense of revolution, of social unrest and of threatening anarchy" during Reconstruction. Randall clearly sympathized with Johnson, not with the radical Republicans. He praised Browning's diary for its accuracy and, always alert to important primary sources, noted its "interesting touches for the social historian."

Although Randall had planned next to write a constitutional history of the United States, instead he devoted the early 1930s to the writing of *The Civil War and Reconstruction*, which appeared in 1937. This assignment came via the invitation of historian Allan Nevins and Heath and Company. From its first publication, Randall's work became not only the most popular textbook in the field for college students but a basic reference tool as well. According to David Donald, who revised it in 1961, Randall's was "a remarkable book, notable for its accuracy, its comprehensiveness, and its readability." Based largely on previously unused manuscript collections, the textbook offered strikingly new material on border-state complications, intellectual life during the war, and other nonmilitary aspects of the conflict. *The Civil War and Reconstruction* contained several of the themes most often associated with Randall: a pro-Southern cast, a belief in the repressibility of the war itself, an emphasis on the importance of institutional as well as military history, and a belief in the fundamental tragedy of war in general and of the Civil War in particular. While Randall admitted weaknesses in the section on Reconstruction, his book remains one of the most important contributions to the historiographical synthesis of the Civil War.

Even while working on his Civil War text, Lincoln's image loomed large in Randall's mind. In 1929 he noted in his diary that writers had yet to salvage Lincoln's "personality from the myth & fiction with which it is encrusted." He developed this argument further in "Has the Lincoln Theme Been Exhausted?," which was published in the *American Historical Review* in 1936. Randall responded to his own question with a decisive "no." In addition to suggesting various subjects and strategies for future research, he urged Lincoln scholars to mine vast amounts of source materials still untouched, to authenticate facts, and to approach their subject with a new sense of commitment and professionalism. The Lincoln field was wide open, Randall argued, and he challenged students to respond.

Randall led the way in answering his call. He spent seven years researching and writing the first two volumes of his magnum opus, *Lincoln, the President*, which appeared in 1945. The historian published the third volume seven years later and began work on a final volume shortly before his death. It was completed from his notes in 1955 by colleague Richard N. Current.

Lincoln, the President stands as the fullest and most accurate account of Lincoln's White House years. The study established Randall as the "dean of Lincoln scholars." The volumes received enthusiastic reviews and were awarded both the Bancroft and

Loubat prizes. They thrust Randall into national prominence. In November 1945 his portrait joined that of Lincoln's on the cover of the *Saturday Review of Literature*. Two years later he was among the experts invited to attend the formal opening of Lincoln's presidential papers at the Library of Congress. In July 1947, Randall, along with Carl Sandburg, Jay Monaghan, and Paul Angle, gave a national radio broadcast on Lincoln.

Randall's most salient contributions to Lincoln scholarship are found in *Lincoln, the President* and in a collection of his essays, *Lincoln, the Liberal Statesman* (1947). He had little patience for such nagging apparent fictions as the story of Lincoln's love for Ann Rutledge. According to Randall, there was no reliable evidence to support William Herndon's famous, but erroneous, claim. Randall also defended Lincoln from charges that he purposely tricked the Confederates to fire on Fort Sumter. And the biographer admitted that Lincoln was not the great emancipator of popular legend but instead preferred a compensated emancipation scheme with the colonization of the freedmen somewhere beyond the United States. In short, Randall rejected all simplistic appraisals of Lincoln. He cautioned researchers to beware of the exceedingly complex Railsplitter: "In approaching the subject of Lincoln and the Civil War one is reminded of Saxe's poem in which six blind men of Indostan—all very learned—investigate the elephant. One by one, after feeling the side, the trunk, the tusks, and so on, each came through with his verdict. The animal was like a wall to the one who touched the side, like a spear to the one who felt the tusk. The third blind man was sure with the squirming trunk in his hands that he was dealing with a snake. The leg convinced the fourth that the creature was like a tree, the ear suggested a fan to the fifth, and the sixth, grasping the tail, knew positively that the elephant was like a rope." Much like the blind men and the elephant, warned Randall, historians all too often had distorted Lincoln's motives and methods.

In the biographer's opinion, the key to understanding Lincoln was not expediency, wartime abnormality, or a lust for presidential power. Rather, Lincoln could best be described "in terms of courageous and undaunted liberalism." Responding to the crises around him "with a kind of Jeffersonian liberalism," Lincoln, "a tough-minded liberal realist," was no rigid ideologue. He focused instead on realities and refused always "to surrender to the cynicism of reaction." But Lincoln's pragmatism lessened neither his sensitivity for the aesthetic nor his appreciation for the humorous side of life. "He could reason," wrote Randall, "but his mind was no mere machine; he could also feel, and at times his feeling was clothed in language of high eloquence and rare beauty. So in the art of government: he could chart an administrative course, but not without the personal touch or the tactful gesture. The quieting of quarrels, the studious avoidance of offense, and the soothing of hurt feelings are factors that run continually through his writings in the presidential period. No man in the whole roster of Presidents gave more constant attention to the human element."

Randall did much to boost, if not to canonize, Lincoln's towering image in the American mind. He credited the sixteenth president with a long list of positive qualities. Lincoln was more worldly and better traveled than most of his debunkers would admit. Lincoln was a devoted family man, an indulgent husband and father. As a politician Lincoln was an anomaly. He combined standards of unusual propriety with the adroit skills of a seasoned ward operative. According to Randall, Lincoln approached the Sumter crisis with a definite plan, one designed to prevent, not cause, the outbreak of war. If war were to come, reasoned the president, the South would have to be the aggressor. Finally, Randall preferred Lincoln's moderate plans for Reconstruction over those of the vindictive, intriguing radical Republicans. In the historian's opinion, the radicals used abolition as a ploy to mask their goals of economic and sectional dominance.

On the negative side, Randall openly criticized Lincoln's handling of the secession crisis. The historian believed that the president should have been more conciliatory in order to keep the middle slave states in the Union. He also faulted Lincoln's dealings with Congress and his treatment of Gen. George B. McClellan. Contrary to most historians, Randall defended McClellan and charged Lincoln with replacing him in order to placate radicals within his party. Recognizing that Lincoln, like any other historical figure, had to be judged objectively, Randall wrote, "It is not necessary to argue that Lincoln was perfect, for he was very human; but because we think of him as a symbol, however unique he was in person, it is of value to become informed in some detail as to the historical validity of the symbolism."

When writing about Lincoln and the secession crisis, Randall addressed squarely the question of the causation of the Civil War. Historians must, he cautioned in 1940, cast off the romanticized view of war in favor "of the sophisticated and unsentimental searchlight of reality." Again, realism was Randall's watchword. He deplored war, referring to it at various times as "organized murder," "human slaughterhouse," and "stupendous fraud." It had an "irrational relation to human interests and destiny." Lincoln's biographer was distressed on the eve of America's entrance into World War II. The mere thought of his graduate students serving in a war sickened him. "It is more than one can endure to think of such young men becoming cannon fodder," recorded Randall in his diary.

Just like this twentieth-century war, Randall found the Civil War a senseless waste. It was a repressible, needless, escapable conflict that resulted in few benefits to Americans, North or South. Looking back to the mid-nineteenth century from the vantage point of the 1940s, Randall questioned whether the issues of the 1850s and 1860s merited war at all. The alleged "causes" of the war, he declared, were inaccurate. The war was sparked by "emotional unreason," "fanaticism," and "bogus leadership," *not* insurmountable sectional differences. The historian blamed the war on the rhetoric of extremists like the abolitionists who exploited and distorted sectional differences to the point of bloody civil war. Randall, like fellow "revisionist" Avery O. Craven, lamented the fact that the "blundering generation" of the 1850s and 1860s rejected moderation in favor of extremism.

Yet the historian's abhorrence of war was based neither on isolationism nor on disillusionment with American foreign policy. "Rather," writes David Donald, "it was the result of Randall's temperamental aversion to any deterministic interpretation of history . . . and it reflected his ingrained distrust of public figures who assumed rigid ideological positions." His faith in reason and realism served as his historical credo. Possessing the same pragmatism that he identified in Lincoln, Randall reminded readers that "a cautious historian may well choose to record the event, not indeed without interpretation, but without committing himself to a particular formula of determinism, or, indeed to any hypothesis." Late in 1952 Randall summarized those qualities which he deemed vital for the "ideal historian." This individual possesses, he wrote, "reasonableness, loyalty, conviction, appreciation of human values. He has a training that sharpens his perceptions. From tested evidence he strives to recreate a past episode. In addition to all the craftsmanship that pertains to evidence, he rec-

ognizes the many-sidedness of historical interpretation. He has understanding that guards against unenlightened or partisan argument."

These words came from Randall's December 1952 presidential address delivered, though he was absent, before the American Historical Association. Too sick to attend, the historian died of leukemia two months later. But his pathbreaking work remained, and for decades it dominated the literature on Lincoln and the Civil War. Today Randall's writings still receive praise, even from those who suggest that he misunderstood the nature of nineteenth-century party allegiance. He clearly left a vital legacy to American historiography. Faith in democracy, patience, good sense, restraint, humor—these were qualities Randall identified in Lincoln. They are also qualities historians have come to associate with Randall.

Other:
The Diary of Orville Hickman Browning, 2 volumes, volume 1 edited by Randall and Theodore C. Pease, volume 2 edited by Randall (Springfield: Illinois State Historical Library, 1927-1933).

Periodical Publications:
"Has the Lincoln Theme Been Exhausted?," *American Historical Review*, 41 (January 1936): 270-294;
"The Blundering Generation," *Mississippi Valley Historical Review*, 27 (June 1940): 3-28;
"Historianship," *American Historical Review*, 63 (January 1953): 249-264.

References:
Mark E. Neely, Jr., "The Lincoln Theme Since Randall's Call: The Promises and Perils of Professionalism," *Papers of the Abraham Lincoln Association*, 1 (1979): 10-70;
Harry E. Pratt, "James Garfield Randall," *Journal of the Illinois State Historical Society*, 46 (Summer 1953): 119-131;
Ruth Painter Randall, *I Ruth: Autobiography of a Marriage* (Boston: Little, Brown, 1968).

Papers:
The University of Illinois holds 7 boxes of Randall's papers. The Library of Congress holds 102 boxes of the papers of James G. and Ruth P. Randall.

Carl Sandburg

(6 January 1878-22 July 1967)

Mark E. Neely, Jr.
Louis A. Warren Lincoln
Library and Museum

SELECTED BOOKS: *Abraham Lincoln: The Prairie Years*, 2 volumes (New York: Harcourt, Brace, 1926; London: Cape, 1926);

Abe Lincoln Grows Up (New York: Harcourt, Brace, 1928);

Mary Lincoln: Wife and Widow, by Sandburg and Paul M. Angle (New York: Harcourt, Brace, 1932);

Abraham Lincoln: The War Years, 4 volumes (New York: Harcourt, Brace, 1939);

Storm over the Land (New York: Harcourt, Brace, 1942; London: Cape, 1943);

The Photographs of Abraham Lincoln, by Sandburg and Frederick Hill Meserve (New York: Harcourt, Brace, 1944);

Lincoln Collector: The Story of Oliver R. Barrett's Great Private Lincoln Collection (New York: Harcourt, Brace, 1949);

A Lincoln Preface (New York: Harcourt, Brace, 1953).

Carl Sandburg

The historical writings of Carl Sandburg were the most important twentieth-century factor in Abraham Lincoln's continuing popularity. Sandburg's massive Lincoln biography was an immediate sensation, and today's bookstores are likely to carry Sandburg's volumes on their shelves even if they contain no other book on Lincoln.

Sandburg, the son of Swedish immigrants August and Clara Mathilda Anderson Sandburg, was born and raised in Galesburg, Illinois. There Civil War veterans, old associates of Lincoln, and memorials to the Lincoln-Douglas debate which took place at Galesburg's Knox College, piqued Sandburg's interest in the sixteenth president. The youth left school after the eighth grade, took rough odd jobs, and rode boxcars. Service with the Sixth Infantry Regiment, Illinois Volunteers, in the Spanish-American War apparently gave him a taste for soldiering, for he was appointed to West Point. However, failing the military academy's entrance examination, he decided to go back to school and in 1899 enrolled in Galesburg's Lombard College, which he left in 1902 before graduating.

Experience as editor-in-chief of the *Lombard*

Review led to a career in journalism and in writing poetry. His first essay on Lincoln, "The Average Man," which was produced in 1906 or 1907, to some degree reflected his interest in socialism. A member of the Social Democratic party, Sandburg campaigned with Socialist presidential candidate Eugene V. Debs in Wisconsin in 1908 and then became the private secretary of Milwaukee's Socialist mayor in 1910.

Moving to Chicago in 1914, Sandburg commenced a period of great poetic output that extended to 1923. All the while, he was gathering information on Lincoln for a juvenile biography. By 1923 he realized that his work would be more than a book for boys. He first submitted his Lincoln manuscript to Harcourt, Brace in 1924, but extensive revisions delayed publication of his two-volume *Abraham Lincoln: The Prairie Years* until 1926.

Sandburg had thought that the book would "be a sort of History and Old Testament of the United States," as he told his publisher Alfred Harcourt in 1923, "a joke almanac, prayer collect, and compendium of essential facts." Even before he finished his own work or saw Albert Beveridge's scholarly *Abraham Lincoln: A Biography* (1928), Sandburg conceived of his book as a contrast to the "Arrow Collar biography" that the handsome former senator was, in Sandburg's thinking, bound to produce. *The Prairie Years* covered Lincoln's life to 1861, and its nature was well summed up both by its writer's description for Harcourt and by one of the titles Sandburg suggested for the book: "Lincoln the Western American." This Lincoln was decidedly folksy and bucolic and was widely praised as the "real" Lincoln rather than a cold statue or a Sunday-school model for aspiring youths. The historian wrote lyrically and relied upon the accumulation of a mass of details of frontier life and anecdotes about Lincoln to provide the biographical strand in the books.

Sandburg owed his principal historiographical debt to Ida Minerva Tarbell's popular works on Lincoln published about the time Sandburg reached maturity. In the 1890s Miss Tarbell had made a trend-setting contribution to Lincoln biography by arguing that the sixteenth president grew to greatness because of and not in spite of the hardscrabble frontier environment of his youth. "In the short and simple annals of the poor," Sandburg wrote, "it seems there are people who breathe with the earth and take into their lungs and blood some of the hard and dark strength of its mystery. During six and seven months each year in the twelve fiercest formative years of his life, Abraham Lincoln had the pads of his foot-soles bare against the clay of the earth. It may be the earth told him in her own tough gypsy slang one or two knacks of living worth keeping." The books were immensely popular, but critic Edmund Wilson was to dismiss them as pure corn, feeling "that the cruellest thing that has happened to Lincoln since he was shot by Booth has been to fall into the hands of Carl Sandburg."

Sandburg realized that dealing with President Lincoln would be an altogether different enterprise from writing about the frontier lawyer in Illinois, and for a time he had his doubts about the subject's suitability to his folklore style. He started to dismiss the rest of Lincoln's life after 1861 in a summary chapter, published years later as *A Lincoln Preface*

(1953), but he liked Lincoln and America's middle period so much that he decided by 1928 to write a sequel to *The Prairie Years* on the war years. The project occupied the next eleven years of his life, interrupted by his writing other shorter works and by his undertaking cross-country tours on which he lectured, read poetry, and strummed folk songs on a guitar. The two principal influences on his treatment of the war years were his journalistic experience and his changed political views. Having worked for various magazines and Chicago newspapers, Sandburg tended to see historical events as a newspaperman, as an endless stream of daily dispatches, news stories unconnected by historical threads and measured by their daily impact rather than by their significance in retrospect. By the 1930s his socialism was replaced by an ardent fondness for Franklin Delano Roosevelt and the New Deal. The Depression era's sense of chaos and crisis led Sandburg to vaunt Lincoln's worldwide reputation as the best statesman that a modern democracy could produce, and as early as 1933 he told New Dealer Raymond Moley that he saw "many striking parallels between Lincoln and Franklin Roosevelt in political method, in decision amid chaos, in reading trends, in development of policy so as to gather momentum, in resilience and acknowledgment of hazards—and much else." At the end of the long process of writing his huge opus on Lincoln's presidency, Sandburg saw Lincoln as "the pivotal figure in the national ordeal and agony from which came the living and amalgamated Union of States which today faces the world with a solidarity beyond price . . . and as the one American figure cherished by the human family the earth over as the foremost incarnation or patriot saint of democracy."

Abraham Lincoln: The War Years appeared in 1939. Most reviewers were staggered by its sheer bulk, more words than the collected works of either Lincoln or Shakespeare. Once again Sandburg relied on a massive accumulation of details, but *The War Years* was less lyrical than *The Prairie Years*. It was less folksy too, because Sandburg's myriad of quotations from Lincoln's contemporaries now came from the greatest politicians in Lincoln's era and not from the old settlers' reminiscences on which he had relied for his portrait of Lincoln's early life. The books had no single theme and appeared to most reviewers to give almost a journalistic chronicle of the developing Lincoln administration. Sandburg again presented the president as a human being, a beleaguered man facing a crisis of immense proportions. Lincoln's vilification in the contemporary press and on the hustings received heavy emphasis, especially that dished out by the radicals of his own party. Sandburg managed to depict Lincoln as both a stern war leader and a personally forgiving man—an amalgam perhaps most easily seen by a man like Sandburg who had been both a soldier and a kindly socialist.

The War Years was widely acclaimed as a literary masterpiece, though it was less markedly literary than *The Prairie Years*. Professional historians, customarily grudging in their praise of amateurs, also commended the books. James G. Randall, soon to be the dean of scholarly Lincoln biographers, said in 1942 that Sandburg's made all other Lincoln books "dull or stupid by comparison." He and Sandburg became friends, and Randall gained a reputation in later years as one of the few academic defenders of Sandburg's work.

At the time of its appearance, however, other professional historians commended *The War Years* for more than style. This praise was all the more remarkable because of Sandburg's unfortunate position in the 1928 literary scandal that ever after functioned as the line of demarcation between professional and amateur students of Lincoln. When in that year the prestigious *Atlantic Monthly* published Wilma Frances Minor's clumsy forgeries of letters purportedly documenting the Lincoln-Ann Rutledge romance, Sandburg was among those who defended their authenticity for a time. Nevertheless, just four years after the unfortunate Minor affair, Paul M. Angle, the principal architect of the criticism which demolished the forgeries, joined Sandburg in publishing *Mary Lincoln: Wife and Widow* (1932), a book meant to resurrect Mrs. Lincoln's reputation. Angle and historian Milo M. Quaife praised *The War Years*, though they admitted that the books were too loosely constructed to be considered biography. Charles Beard liked the books too, despite their being "more like a diary or saga" than systematic history.

Sandburg's overtly literary style was not enough, of course, to fool the professionals into praise of a work without real historical merit. The books did have merit. What won the historians over was Sandburg's thorough immersion in the printed sources. In these leisurely paced, discursive, overlong books, his readings of obscure speeches, newspapers, and ephemeral campaign literature were piled one on top of another, often in such a way that one could completely reshuffle the paragraphs without damaging the point or narrative drive. In fact, *The War Years* decidedly lacked both point and narrative drive, but the impressively abundant daily reports on the Lincoln administration, which

Sandburg had noted on slips crammed in numerous cigar boxes, were there. And they were useful as long as one checked their sources—a difficult task since Sandburg eschewed footnotes or any other scholarly apparatus.

The War Years also gained friends among professionals and Civil War buffs alike because it fit the political and social spirit of the 1930s and 1940s. Sandburg's Lincoln was middle western and liberal. In 1941 the writer said that he had studied Lincoln "in the hope of getting a better understanding of this man who the Republican party and the G.A.R. and the preachers magnified until he was too big to see." He found Lincoln's picture in the offices of politicians and big businessmen who "do not understand him and probably would not approve of him if they did." Skirting Lincoln's Whiggish economic views, Sandburg portrayed him as an embodiment of democracy, a man with a secret bond to "The People." The writer liked the Lincoln his poetic predecessor had liked: "For [Walt] Whitman," Sandburg said, "Lincoln was a great voice and a sublime doer in the field of democracy. He regarded both Lincoln and himself as foretellers of a New Time for the common man and woman." Sandburg frequently compared Lincoln to President Roosevelt and told the president himself in 1935, "you are the best light of democracy that has occupied the White House since Lincoln." This parallel gave the books a long life because World War II made the subject of *The War Years* particularly apt. In fact, the 1942 publication of *Storm over the Land*, a one-volume synthesis of material from *The War Years*, was a result of the timeliness of a study of an American president at war.

Sandburg's work on Lincoln was substantially complete in 1939. His *The Photographs of Abraham Lincoln* (1944), written in conjunction with the first great collector of Lincoln photographs, Frederick Hill Meserve, merely indulged a Sandburg hobby. Interested in photography because he had sold stereo photographs as a youth and because in 1908 he had married Lillian Paula Steichen, the sister of photographer Edward Steichen, Sandburg also wrote for moving pictures. Among his other less important Lincoln works was *Lincoln Collector: The Story of Oliver R. Barrett's Great Private Lincoln Collection* (1949), Sandburg's homage to the Chicago collector who allowed him to use his fabulous collection of manuscripts and fugitive Lincoln materials to great effect. (Only Barrett and Miss Tarbell had been allowed to read *The Prairie Years* before publication.) *Lincoln Collector* was, however, so rambling and diffuse as to be almost unreadable and marked a sharp decline from the vigorous writing of *The War Years*.

For the most part, Sandburg gathered laurels. For *The War Years* he won the Pulitzer Prize for history in 1940. He published *Abraham Lincoln: The Prairie Years and The War Years, One-Volume Edition*, a condensed version of the six volumes, in 1954. This edition added greatly to his fame both by making his work available to those intimidated by the immense size of the original books and by correcting or eliminating many of the errors in the originals. The pinnacle of his success came with the sesquicentennial of Lincoln's birth. On 12 February 1959, Sandburg delivered a Lincoln Day address before a joint session of Congress attended by the Supreme Court, the cabinet, and the diplomatic corps. Sandburg began the speech with words that many who were present can still recall: "Not often in the story of mankind does a man arrive on earth who is both steel and velvet, who is as hard as rock and soft as drifting fog, who holds in his heart and mind the paradox of terrible storm and peace unspeakable and perfect."

The growing gulf between professional historians and popular history, however, was steadily undermining Sandburg's influence. His books were filled with maddening errors from wrong first names and erroneous middle initials to more notorious examples of gullibility, like his emphasis in *The Prairie Years* on the Ann Rutledge romance. Sandburg's criterion for evidence, especially early on, was more poetical than historical; he liked good stories. He soft-pedaled Lincoln's racial views and failed to comprehend the significance of his long adherence to the Whig party. The party of respectable bankers and businessmen (as the Whigs were interpreted in Sandburg's day at least) never really fit the writer's rumpled and homespun son of the prairie, modeled in part on Sandburg's view of himself. "Like him," the poet-turned-Lincoln-biographer said, "I am a son of the prairie, a poor boy who wandered over the land to find himself and his mission in life."

Sandburg "wanted to take Lincoln away from the religious bigots and the professional politicians and restore him to the common people," and he therefore never came to grips with the importance of political parties and organized religion in Lincoln's America. The biographer accumulated masses of fascinating details, but he never felt it necessary to organize them, to impose systematic historical understanding on them, or even to sort out the important from the trivial. His long passages from the president's critics in the awful summer of

1864, for example, merely cite instance after gripping instance and fail even to organize them into criticisms from the left and from the right. His fascination with what seemed to constitute "a handbook and manual of defamation" blinded him to the root of that phenomenon in the subsidization of nineteenth-century newspapers by political parties.

At times, Sandburg confused good scholarship with bourgeois respectability, something he always delighted in outraging. His sure grasp of what had popular appeal sometimes shaded off into contempt for the more tedious sources of political history. He did not worry that his magnum opus would have to be written without the benefit of the Robert Todd Lincoln Collection of the Papers of Abraham Lincoln at the Library of Congress. Sandburg had "an impression that it is a very restricted circle that gives any thought to the R.T.L. papers in the Lib of Cong." This circle, he believed, had "no slightest flash that will compare with what our friend [Emanuel] Hertz . . . dug up and presented in 'The Hidden Lincoln,' " a book based on William H. Herndon's interviews with old settlers who had known Lincoln.

To be sure, Sandburg's more distinguished defenders, like Roy P. Basler, always said that his understanding of the public man was weak and praised him for his portrait of the private Lincoln. Yet even here, Sandburg's claim has lost adherents. Many early reviewers mistook Western earthiness for a realism which separated Sandburg's Lincoln from the patriotic pieties of Lincoln Day rhetoric. Edmund Wilson more shrewdly objected that Lincoln's writings "do not give the impression of a folksy and jocular countryman swapping yarns at the village store or making his way to the White House by uncertain and awkward steps or presiding like a father, with a tear in his eye, over the tragedy of the Civil War."

Despite the impressive shelf life of Sandburg's biography, one suspects that it is less read today than revered. Much of its appeal was time-bound. It was a tonic for the Depression-ridden and war-weary America of the 1930s and 1940s. As Stephen Vincent Benet noted in the December 1939 *Atlantic Monthly*, *The War Years* was a "good purge for our own troubled time and for its more wild-eyed fears." Such was clearly Sandburg's point, as he said in *The War Years*: Around Lincoln "gathered some of the hope that a democracy can choose a man, set him up high with power and honor, and the very act does something to the man himself, raises up new gifts, modulations, controls, outlooks, wisdoms, inside the man, so that he is something else again than he was before they sifted him out and anointed him to take an oath and solemnly sign himself for the hard and terrible, eye-filling and center-staged, role of Head of the Nation." In his time, nevertheless, Sandburg greatly broadened the audience for books on Lincoln. His secret, as Henry Steele Commager noted in a 1940 issue of *The Yale Review*, was that he "realized that Lincoln belongs to the people, not to the historians."

Letters:
Herbert Mitgang, ed., *The Letters of Carl Sandburg* (New York: Harcourt, Brace & World, 1968).

References:
Alfred Haworth Jones, *Roosevelt's Image Brokers: Poets, Playwrights, and the Use of the Lincoln Symbol* (Port Washington, N.Y.: Kennikat Press, 1974);
Edmund Wilson, *Patriotic Gore: Studies in the Literature of the American Civil War* (New York: Oxford University Press, 1962).

Papers:
Sandburg sold his papers and library to the University of Illinois for $30,000 in 1956.

Arthur M. Schlesinger, Jr.
(15 October 1917-)

Edwin A. Miles
University of Houston

SELECTED BOOKS: *Orestes A. Brownson: A Pilgrim's Progress* (Boston: Little, Brown, 1939); republished as *A Pilgrim's Progress: Orestes A. Brownson* (Boston: Little, Brown, 1966);
The Age of Jackson (Boston: Little, Brown, 1945; London: Eyre & Spottiswoode, 1946);
The Vital Center: The Politics of Freedom (Boston: Houghton Mifflin, 1949); republished as *The Politics of Freedom* (London: Heinemann, 1950);
The General and the President and the Future of American Foreign Policy, by Schlesinger and Richard H. Rovere (New York: Farrar, Straus & Young, 1951; London: Heinemann, 1952); revised as *The MacArthur Controversy and American Foreign Policy* (New York: Farrar, Straus & Giroux, 1965);
The Crisis of the Old Order, 1919-1933, volume 1 of *The Age of Roosevelt* (Boston: Houghton Mifflin, 1957);
The Coming of the New Deal, volume 2 of *The Age of Roosevelt* (Boston: Houghton Mifflin, 1959);
The Politics of Upheaval, volume 3 of *The Age of Roosevelt* (Boston: Houghton Mifflin, 1960);
Kennedy or Nixon: Does It Make Any Difference? (New York: Macmillan, 1960);
The Politics of Hope (Boston: Houghton Mifflin, 1963);
A Thousand Days: John F. Kennedy in the White House (Boston: Houghton Mifflin, 1965; London: Deutsch, 1965);
The Bitter Heritage: Vietnam and American Democracy, 1941-1966 (Boston: Houghton Mifflin, 1967);
The Crisis of Confidence: Ideas, Power, and Violence in America (Boston: Houghton Mifflin, 1969; London: Deutsch, 1969);
The Imperial Presidency (Boston: Houghton Mifflin, 1973; London: Deutsch, 1974);
Robert Kennedy and His Times (Boston: Houghton Mifflin, 1978; London: Deutsch, 1978).

Since World War II, Arthur Meier Schlesinger, Jr., has been perhaps the nation's most widely known and controversial historian. He has won two Pulitzer Prizes and two National Book Awards, and several of his books have generated high sales and attracted considerable attention. He has also gained a wide audience by writing for popular magazines and newspapers. As a testimony to his status as a celebrity, he has been the subject of a *Playboy* interview, and his face has appeared on the cover of *Time*.

Schlesinger's fame and the controversies surrounding him, of course, have derived as much from his political activities as from his best-selling historical writings. He has conscientiously acted in accordance with his often-expressed conviction that the intellectual has a serious responsibility to participate in and influence political life. A founder of the Americans for Democratic Action in the late 1940s, he later served as a speech writer for Democratic presidential candidate Adlai E. Stevenson in the 1950s and as a close associate of John F. and Robert F. Kennedy in the 1960s. Called by Henry Fairlie "the most representative figure of mid-twentieth century liberalism," he has on numerous occasions expounded what he considered to be the appropriate political agenda for democratic liberals in the "vital center" of American politics. As a result of his vigorous articulation of this centrist position, he has elicited spirited attacks from conservatives and radicals alike. In 1966 *Playboy* referred to him as "one of the stormiest political petrels in American public life."

The son of Arthur Meier and Elizabeth Bancroft Schlesinger, "Young Arthur," as he was commonly referred to in his early career, owed much to

his parents for his interest in American history and politics. His father, a member of the Harvard University history department for thirty years, gained distinction as an innovative social and cultural historian. (He served in 1942 as president of the American Historical Association, an honor which has thus far eluded his more famous son.) Elizabeth Schlesinger, a collateral descendant of noted nineteenth-century Massachusetts historian and prominent Jacksonian Democrat George Bancroft, was a pioneer in the study of women's history. "One of the great pleasures recalled from my childhood," Schlesinger reminisced in 1979, "was my mother reading to me. She was a splendid reader-aloud, spirited and expressive." But she was also an "astute skipper." When her young auditor discovered that she was leaving out "static descriptive passages" in *Ivanhoe* and the footnotes in Francis Parkman's *History of the Conspiracy of Pontiac*, he "objected and

Arthur M. Schlesinger, Jr., working for Adlai Stevenson's 1956 presidential campaign

insisted on the unexpurgated text."

Both of his parents were political activists—his father "in a quiet way" and his mother as a more outspoken champion of feminist and other liberal causes. (In her eighties she marched with her granddaughters to protest the Vietnam War.) Temperamentally more akin to his mother, Arthur wrote in 1968 that "I was always less detached and judicious than my father, more eager for commitment and combat. I think this from time to time disconcerted him, but . . . he always backed me in everything, no matter how misguided he may privately have thought my activities to be." Like his father, Arthur championed liberalism and regarded the Democratic party as its proper home. His father's "skepticism about extreme views" and "dislike of absolutisms" also strongly influenced in another important respect the shaping of his political views. As a youth, while many intellectuals of his generation were attracted to Marxism as the answer to the weaknesses and inequities of the American capitalistic system, Arthur already regarded himself as a decided anti-Communist.

Arthur Schlesinger, Jr., was born in Columbus, Ohio, while his father taught at Ohio State University. Originally named Arthur Bancroft Schlesinger, he requested while a teenager that his middle name be changed to that of his father. "In retrospect," he wrote Marcus Cunliffe in 1968, "I sometimes wish I had stuck to 'Bancroft' since I do feel a sort of intellectual and political kinship with old George." But when the alteration was made he very much "wanted to be Arthur Schlesinger, *Jr.*"

Arthur Schlesinger, Sr., moved his family to Iowa City in 1919 when he accepted an appointment at the University of Iowa, and to Cambridge, Massachusetts in 1924 when he joined the Harvard faculty. Firm believers in the American system of popular education, Arthur's parents at first sent him and later his younger brother, Tom, to local Cambridge public schools, but they ultimately despaired of the poor quality of instruction their sons received in comparison with the education available in New England private schools. (On one occasion Arthur's public-school history teacher stated that the inhabitants of Albania were called Albinos because of their white hair and pink eyes.) Thus the Schlesinger boys, like most children of Harvard faculty, were eventually enrolled in private schools. "This sacrifice of principle did not come easily," Arthur Schlesinger, Sr., wrote later, "but appeared unavoidable if the boys were to have proper intellectual advantages." After two years in the Cambridge Latin School, Arthur transferred to Phillips

Exeter Academy, where he graduated in 1933 before his sixteenth birthday. Shortly thereafter he accompanied his parents and brother on a year's trip around the world, visiting Hawaii, Japan, China, the Philippines, Indochina, Siam, Burma, India, Egypt, Greece, Italy, France, and Great Britain before returning to the United States.

Moving into a campus dormitory, Arthur entered Harvard in the fall of 1934. He specialized in the study of history and literature; F. O. Matthiessen was his tutor for one year and Perry Miller for two. His undergraduate career clearly foreshadowed his later scholarly success. As a freshman, his historical essay, one of 613 submitted, was awarded the LeBaron Russell Briggs Prize. He was elected to Phi Beta Kappa in his junior year. For his senior honors thesis, he took his father's suggestion to undertake a study of Orestes A. Brownson. Through his investigation, he became fascinated with Brownson, a comparatively neglected New England literary figure of the Jacksonian era, who vigorously championed a number of the political and religious movements of the day only to abandon them for other positions that he espoused with equal enthusiasm. Once a defender of Andrew Jackson, Martin Van Buren, and the laboring classes, he ultimately became a conservative admirer of John C. Calhoun; at various times a Presbyterian, Universalist, Free Thinker, and Unitarian, he died the foremost American Catholic layman of his time. To Schlesinger he symbolized "the intellectual restlessness and vitality" of the period, and for the young undergraduate, a study of Brownson's career offered an exciting approach to intellectual history and Jacksonian America.

Graduating summa cum laude in 1938, Schlesinger, with the encouragement of his father, hastened to revise his study of Brownson for publication. That summer he did additional research, particularly in the Brownson Papers in the Notre Dame University Library, and he prepared a revised manuscript that Little, Brown agreed to publish. That fall he set out for England where, despite the ominous international situation, he spent a "most fascinating year" as a Henry Fellow at Cambridge. By the time he returned in the summer of 1939, *Orestes A. Brownson: A Pilgrim's Progress* had already been published.

The reviews of Schlesinger's first book were remarkably favorable—particularly in view of the fact that the manuscript was originally an undergraduate thesis completed before the author's twenty-first birthday, a fact apparently not known to most reviewers. Many took notice of his excellent style and the rapid pace with which the narrative moved. Odell Shepard in the *Saturday Review* detected "the hand of the young master." Writing in the *New York Times Book Review*, Henry Steele Commager was even more lavish in his praise: "Mr. Schlesinger's study of Brownson is a masterly one. It has technical brilliance—a sure control of materials, an effective handling of background, a skillful use of colors and a certain bravura of execution. It has, in addition, sincerity and integrity, sympathetic understanding, and an astonishing maturity. . . . It not only rescues from undeserved oblivion a striking and authentic figure in our history, but announces a new and distinguished talent in the field of historical portraiture."

Upon his return from England, Schlesinger accepted a three-year appointment to Harvard's Society of Fellows, an organization designed to aid in the development of young scholars who had already demonstrated "promise of notable contribution to knowledge and thought." This appointment permitted him to continue his study of history while avoiding the "PhD mill," as he later expressed it. In 1940 he married Marian Cannon, who was a daughter of a Harvard physiologist and a writer of children's books as well as an illustrator and portrait painter. In the meantime he continued to probe the intellectual background of the Jacksonian period. At one time he intended to write a biography of George Bancroft but soon decided upon a broader study when invited to deliver a series of lectures at Boston's Lowell Institute. He chose for the title of his series "A Reinterpretation of Jacksonian Democracy," and the lectures he gave in the fall of 1941 formed the basis for *The Age of Jackson*.

By mid-1942 Schlesinger, writing with his accustomed swiftness, had finished a rough draft of his contemplated work, but the exigencies of World War II delayed its completion. That year he moved to Washington, D.C., to serve first with the Office of War Information and later with the Office of Strategic Services. ("I gained more insight into history from being in the war and working for the Government than I did from my academic training," he would later write.) While in Washington, he worked nights and on weekends to complete his Jackson project, and in June 1944, as he was awaiting a transfer to a new OSS assignment with the army in Europe, he signed a contract with Little, Brown for the publication of his completed manuscript. As in the case of his earlier book, he was out of the country when *The Age of Jackson* was published in September 1945. While he was serving as a corporal in the army, his wife and father did "the

dirty work of seeing the book through the press."

The Age of Jackson stands as a significant landmark in the writing of the nation's history, and reviewers immediately recognized it as such. Richard Hofstadter regarded it as "a major contribution to American historiography," while Merle Curti called it "a triumph of historical scholarship, analysis, and interpretation." Its literary craftsmanship was of the highest order: the author's sense of drama, his colorful style, and his crisply written narrative produced a highly readable book. Writing in the *American Historical Review*, Russel B. Nye hailed it as "the most stimulating historical writing of the past decade."

Schlesinger's book set off a historiographical debate regarding the meaning of Jacksonian America that has continued ever since. Rejecting Frederick Jackson Turner's view that Jacksonianism was primarily a frontier phenomenon, he argued that Jacksonian Democracy should be regarded "as a problem not of sections but of classes" and that it represented a crucial phase in the history of American liberalism, which "has been ordinarily the movement on the part of other sections of society to restrain the power of the business community." Emphasizing the importance of the war against the Bank of the United States, he maintained that the workingmen of the East provided the main impetus for the Jacksonian political program. Jacksonian Democracy differed significantly from Jeffersonian Democracy in its willingness to use Hamiltonian means to achieve Jeffersonian ends.

The time was ripe in 1945 for such an interpretation of Jacksonian America. For years other historians had been raising questions concerning the validity of the Turnerian approach to the American past. As Schlesinger had written six years earlier in the opening lines of his Brownson study, "The measure of what is historically important is set by the generation that writes the history, not by the one that makes it." That his strong sympathy for Franklin D. Roosevelt and his administration influenced Schlesinger's interpretation of Jacksonian Democracy is undeniable. (In *Time*, Whittaker Chambers called his book "a brilliant justification of the New Deal disguised as a history of the age of Jackson.") His last chapter, "Traditions of Democracy," presented reflections upon the history of liberalism in America, a theme that he would elaborate upon on many occasions in the years to come.

Attacks upon *The Age of Jackson* were not long in coming. Despite the generally favorable reception accorded the book, some reviewers criticized the author's decided pro-Jackson bias and his "unwillingness to discipline personal enthusiasms." The most vigorous dissenting voice was that of Bray Hammond, whose review in the *Journal of Economic History* pointed to the direction that revisionists of the Schlesinger thesis would take. In Hammond's view, Schlesinger overlooked the entrepreneurial impulse behind the Jacksonian assault upon the Bank of the United States. To Hammond the age was one of "triumphant exploitation" rather than of "triumphant liberalism," and he argued that *The Age of Jackson* "thickens the myths around a political leader who had more capacity for action than for accomplishment." In 1957 Hammond, longtime staff member of the Federal Reserve Board, refined and expanded his argument in *Banks and Politics in America from the Revolution to the Civil War*, in which he accused both Jackson and Schlesinger of colossal ignorance concerning the central banking functions of the Bank of the United States. Several scholars associated with Columbia University, including Richard Hofstadter, Joseph Dorfman, Harold C. Syrett, Richard B. Morris, and some of their students, reinforced the Hammond entrepreneurial interpretation; they also questioned Jackson's sympathy for labor, the support given him by the laboring classes, and the assumption that the workingmen's parties of the 1830s were genuine labor parties.

By the late 1950s, with the dominance of the consensus interpretation of the nation's history, the Schlesinger view of sharp class and ideological differences between Democrats and Whigs fell into disfavor; historians of the Eisenhower era tended to minimize the points of differences and emphasize the commonality of views held by Americans in the past. Then, in 1961, in his *The Concept of Jacksonian Democracy: New York as a Test Case*, Lee Benson emphasized the ethnocultural basis of the politics of early-to-mid-nineteenth-century America. He denied a class basis for the Democrat-Whig rivalry in the Empire State, he disputed the view that the Jacksonians with their negative liberal state ideology could be regarded as embryonic New Dealers, and indeed he challenged the notion that Jackson's party supported what would later be known as the concept of Jacksonian Democracy. In 1967 Edward Pessen's *Jacksonian America* likewise challenged the Old Hero's claims as the leader of a liberal democratic movement. But Schlesinger has had his defenders too, most notably Robert V. Remini, who maintained in 1977 that "although some particulars of his thesis have been modified," *The Age of Jackson* "remains an important and valid interpretation of

the pre-Civil War period."

In one of his own rare allusions to the debate about his controversial book, Schlesinger told an interviewer in 1966 that it was "very much a young man's work and had some of the advantages and some of the defects of that, by which I mean that it was probably more of a partisan work." He also conceded that at the time he "knew almost nothing about economics." He spoke vaguely of a plan some day to write *The Age of Jackson Re-visited*, which will be a series of essays and reflections twenty-five years later, on issues raised in the earlier book." Such a sequel has remained unwritten. For the most part, once his study of the Jackson period appeared, Schlesinger chose not to involve himself in the historiographical controversy that its publication sparked. Instead he turned his attention to work on his next major undertaking—and one that has yet to be completed—the history of the age of Franklin D. Roosevelt, a later saga in the annals of American liberalism.

The Age of Jackson established overnight Schlesinger's reputation as a major American historian. The book sold 90,000 copies during its first year and was virtually conceded the 1946 Pulitzer Prize in history long before the announcement confirmed its selection. The Guggenheim Foundation awarded him a fellowship to launch his study of the Roosevelt years, and in the spring of 1946 Harvard granted him an associate professorship in the same department with his father—no mean accomplishment, observed *Time*, for a young scholar who "was only 28, had neither master's nor doctor's degree, and little teaching experience." His name became increasingly better known outside of academic circles. In 1946 and 1947 he wrote articles on various historical and contemporary subjects for a host of magazines, including *American Mercury*, *Atlantic Monthly*, *Collier's*, *Fortune*, *Life*, *New Republic*, *New York Times Magazine*, and *Saturday Evening Post*. He reviewed books frequently, particularly for *Nation* and *New York Times Book Review*. The United States Junior Chamber of Commerce named him an "outstanding young man" of 1946.

In addition, Schlesinger participated actively in liberal Democratic politics. He became a charter member and a vice president of the Americans for Democratic Action (ADA), established in 1947 to promote policies consistent with New Deal liberalism. Toward Harry S. Truman Schlesinger entertained—then and later—mixed feelings. "President Truman appears to have little instinct for liberalism," he lamented in early 1948. Seeking a more suitable candidate in the upcoming election, he and other prominent members of the ADA launched a much publicized but abortive movement to draft Dwight D. Eisenhower as the Democratic candidate. ("That was the greatest mistake I ever made," he recalled twenty years later.) In retrospect Schlesinger wrote that Truman's surprising victory over Thomas E. Dewey "reinforced one's belief in the prospects of liberal democracy." But at the time his reservations about the Missourian persisted; a month after the election he predicted that Truman "will continue to blow hot and cold for the liberal movement."

Schlesinger nevertheless vigorously supported Truman's foreign policy, particularly his moves to contain the expansion of Soviet influence in the early days of the cold war. For a brief period in 1948 Schlesinger served as a special assistant to Averell Harriman during the implementation of the Marshall Plan. Upon his return from Western Europe, "still filled with the excitement engendered" by that "brilliant" and "generous" undertaking, he began writing *The Vital Center: The Politics of Freedom*, whose publication in 1949 established him as a major spokesman for postwar American liberalism.

Schlesinger's new book would subsequently be referred to as "something of an ideological handbook for the anti-Communist liberal." It was in part an expansion of ideas expressed in the last chapter of *The Age of Jackson*, in which he had called upon modern-day liberals to engage in "an earnest, tough-minded, pragmatic attempt to wrestle with new problems as they come, without being enslaved by a theory of the past, or by a theory of the future." Schlesinger's nonideological liberalism had been reinforced by his attraction to the writings of theologian Reinhold Niebuhr, with whom he had become acquainted as a cofounder of the ADA. Once a Socialist, Niebuhr had by the 1940s rejected political absolutism. Recognizing that man's sinful nature made the millennium unattainable, he still urged the need for piecemeal step-by-step practical reform measures. The following passage in *The Vital Center* clearly demonstrated Niebuhr's influence: "Problems will always torment us, because all important problems are insoluble; that is why they are important. The good comes from the continuing struggle to try and solve them, not from the vain hope of their solution."

Schlesinger rejected both rightist and leftist alternatives to his brand of undoctrinaire liberalism. In America the only conservative opposition historically came from the business community, which in his opinion had never demonstrated its capacity to govern. He showed greater concern for the threat from the left. Indeed, one of the most distinctive features of *The Vital Center* was its militant anticommunism, which he had demonstrated as early as July 1946 in a lengthy article for *Life* on the American Communist party. His most withering fire was directed toward those leftists who cooperated with Communists—for example, the "doughface Progressives" who had backed Henry A. Wallace's presidential candidacy in 1948. Within a few years Schlesinger himself would be roundly criticized by Sen. Joseph R. McCarthy for being "soft" on communism. (In reply, he maintained that he was "tired of these Joe-come-latelys in the fight against communism.") On the other hand, Carey McWilliams of the *Nation*, whom Schlesinger had singled out as one of the "Typhoid Marys of the left, bearing the germs of infection even if not suffering obviously from the disease [of communism]," accused the "Communist-obsessed Schlesinger" of speaking "the language of McCarthy with a Harvard accent."

Before its publication, Schlesinger wrote Justice Felix Frankfurter that *The Vital Center* was "a political tract, designed to get my private views out of my system so they won't get in my way when I write the New Deal book." The "New Deal book"—which turned out to be a multivolume series—was still many years away from publication. While pursuing research into his main project, he produced frequent articles and book reviews for national magazines and for several years wrote a "History of the Week" column for the *New York Post*. Perhaps his most significant and widely publicized article of this period was "The Causes of the Civil War," which appeared in the *Partisan Review* in 1949. Schlesinger vigorously attacked the revisionist interpretation which represented the Civil War as a "needless" conflict that a "blundering generation" could have and should have avoided. Denouncing the revisionists as sentimentalists who believed in the inevitability of progress and ignored the moral dimensions of the slavery controversy, he challenged the view, then generally held, that the nation's "peculiar institution" could have been abolished without the war.

On political matters Schlesinger continued to air his "private views." After Sen. Robert A. Taft charged that President Truman "had no authority whatever to commit American troops to Korea without consulting Congress and without Congressional approval," Schlesinger cited numerous historical precedents to denounce the accusation as "demonstrably irresponsible." (Some twenty years later, after subsequent presidents had committed hundreds of thousands of American troops to Indochina, he would regret the vehemence of his attack upon Taft's position.) He collaborated with Richard H. Rovere in writing *The General and the President and the Future of American Foreign Policy*, published less than six months following Truman's dismissal of Gen. Douglas MacArthur from his command in Korea. Rovere and Schlesinger undertook to dissect the "MacArthur legend" and to offer a spirited defense of the Truman East Asian policy. For a few months in late 1951 and early 1952 Schlesinger went to Europe again for the administration as an aide to Harriman, now administrator of the Mutual Security Agency.

In 1952 and 1956 Schlesinger took leaves of absence from Harvard to serve as a speech writer in the presidential campaigns of Democratic candidate Adlai E. Stevenson. John Kenneth Galbraith, his close friend and fellow "researcher" on Stevenson's staff, recalled in 1981 that "Alone among all I've ever observed in this craft he could remove his coat, address his typewriter and without resort to reference books, documents or pause for thought produce an entire speech at one sitting. Within weeks he had achieved a perfect mastery of Stevenson's balanced sentences and could play perfectly to his delight in antonyms and his frequent willingness to subordinate meaning to euphony." According to Galbraith, Schlesinger's participation in the Stevenson campaigns was "psychologically therapeutic"; his family noted that "he was always unnaturally agreeable when writing speeches for Adlai Stevenson."

But Schlesinger was keenly disappointed by Stevenson's failure to win the presidency. As a result, he pondered much during the 1950s about the future of American liberalism. He took some comfort—but it was small indeed—in his belief that "the New Deal and Fair Deal were victims of success," that their various programs had not only resolved the nation's most serious economic problems but had also won at least grudging acceptance from most conservatives, thus making them no longer live political issues. With the electorate's memory of the Great Depression fading, Schlesinger called for a shift from a quantitative to a qualitative liberalism, one that would no longer emphasize economic concerns but rather would promote programs to better the quality of people's lives and broaden opportunities for all Americans. He also found consolation in his faith in the future applicability of a cyclical thesis propounded years earlier by his father.

The elder Schlesinger had pointed out that American political history had been regularly characterized by alternating periods of progressive activity and conservative inertia. Just as surely as the administration of President Dwight D. Eisenhower had ushered in a period of quietude and complacency, so too, his son reasoned, there must inevitably come a new period of dynamic action once national problems accumulated to the point that they demanded public attention.

For Schlesinger the political activist, the national mood of the Eisenhower era was disappointingly lethargic; for Schlesinger the historian, the latter half of that period witnessed the most productive years of his career: the inauguration of *The Age of Roosevelt* series. In 1957 Houghton Mifflin Company brought out *The Crisis of the Old Order, 1919-1933*, followed two years later by *The Coming of the New Deal* and in 1960 by *The Politics of Upheaval*. Many historians consider *The Age of Roosevelt* Schlesinger's most distinguished contribution in the field. The volumes attest to his superb style, felicity of phrase, keen sense of drama, and successful blending of narrative and analytical history. Writing in 1979, Stephen B. Oates maintained that *The Crisis of the Old Order* might well be "the most perfectly sculptured work of historical art in this country, a book distinguished for its novelistic use of time, its symphonic organization, its vivid scenes and graphic vignettes, its telling quotations and dramatic narrative sweep." It won both the Francis Parkman Award of the Society of American Historians and the Frederic Bancroft Prize granted by Columbia University. All three volumes were Book-of-the-Month Club selections.

The Crisis of the Old Order set the stage for the era dominated by Franklin D. Roosevelt, who was introduced briefly in the "Prologue" but then was relegated to the background for almost two-thirds of the book. Following a sympathetic appraisal of the legacies of Theodore Roosevelt's New Nationalism and Woodrow Wilson's New Freedom—both of which influenced his protagonist—Schlesinger, turning next to the New Era of the 1920s and the early years of the Great Depression, severely indicted the nation's business and political leadership of that period. Emphasizing the Depression's profound psychological impact upon the generation it confounded, he suggested that the nation stood on the brink of a possible revolution in 1933. Turning finally to Roosevelt himself, Schlesinger traced his subject's early career, stressing the conservative influences upon his political and social outlook as well as his willingness to experiment in search of solutions to new problems.

In *The Coming of the New Deal*, Schlesinger treated the period from Roosevelt's inaugural to the midterm elections of 1934. The emphasis was upon the Hundred Days congressional session of 1933 and the implementation of the spate of legislation that it enacted. To Schlesinger, the New Deal signified no radical departure in American politics; instead, he cited important precedents for its measures in the programs of Populism, the New Nationalism, the New Freedom, the social welfare movement, and legislation earlier passed in the more progressive states. Refusing to accept the conventional interpretation of Roosevelt as a poor administrator, he argued that the president's practice of ignoring traditional lines of authority assured that innovative ideas were brought to his attention. Schlesinger also maintained that Roosevelt's tendency to give overlapping authority to different administrators created a healthy spirit of competition that led to more productive activity on the part of eager-to-please subordinates.

The Politics of Upheaval, perhaps the liveliest volume of *The Age of Roosevelt*, focused upon the last two years of FDR's administration. Accepting the concept of the "two New Deals," Schlesinger maintained that after 1935 the administration reflected more the imprint of the heirs of Woodrow Wilson's New Freedom whereas before that year legatees of Theodore Roosevelt's New Nationalism had shaped the most significant New Deal programs. This change resulted in part from the declining importance of Roosevelt's original Brain Trust from Columbia University and the ascendancy of Harvard Law School advisors whose views had been influenced by Prof. Felix Frankfurter and Justice Louis D. Brandeis (who had helped devise Wilson's original New Freedom program in 1912). Schlesinger also dealt with the threats to the New Deal from the right and the left and the emergence of a new coalition that produced the landslide victory in 1936.

The three published volumes of *The Age of Roosevelt* voted emphatically for FDR and the New Deal. On occasion Schlesinger mildly criticized his champion; for example, he deplored his handling of the London Economic Conference of 1933. But such an adverse judgment was rare indeed. He even found much to praise in the often abused National Recovery Administration, struck down in 1935 by a unanimous Supreme Court decision considered by many historians otherwise sympathetic to the New

Deal as a mercy killing. To Schlesinger, Roosevelt personified the ideal leader of a political movement located in the "vital center" between the rigid doctrinaires of the right and left. Once again in American history a liberal administration had prevented the capitalists from destroying the capitalistic system while at the same time resisting the pressures from leftist ideologues. He viewed Roosevelt and his coworkers as pragmatists who possessed the "instinctive contempt of practical, energetic and compassionate people for dogmatic absolutes. Refusing to be intimidated by abstractions or to be overawed by ideology, the New Dealers responded by doing things."

Such an outspoken defense of the New Deal naturally exposed Schlesinger to criticism. Some reviewers regretted his tendency to view the political struggles of the era almost exclusively in terms of a contest between "good (liberal, Democratic) men against bad (conservative, Republican) men." ("For an avowed Niebuhrian," observed William E. Leuchtenberg, "he is curiously Manichean.") Conservatives who regretted the changes that occurred during the age of Roosevelt accused Schlesinger of writing hagiography under the guise of history, while radicals deplored his vindication of a New Deal that failed to make fundamental changes in the structure of American society. Leftist critics particularly took exception to his characterization of the New Deal as pragmatic. "Experimentalism is impossible from the vital center," Jacob Cohen wrote in 1961. "It has no over-all sense of the society upon which it is experimenting, and, more important, its implicit view of history conveys the suggestion that history is likely to resist experimentation."

The Politics of Upheaval appeared less than two months before the presidential election of 1960, in which campaign Schlesinger became deeply involved as a member of the staff of Sen. John F. Kennedy. While many liberals had hoped that Stevenson would once again be the candidate, the former standard bearer's reluctance to contend for the nomination as well as a growing belief that he would probably lose to Vice President Richard M. Nixon led Schlesinger, John Kenneth Galbraith, and some other former supporters to endorse Kennedy as offering the Democrats' best chance for victory. "I'm nostalgically for Stevenson, ideologically for [Hubert] Humphrey, and realistically for Kennedy," Schlesinger told James Reston in March 1960, adding that he "would work gladly for any two-legged liberal mammal who might beat Nixon." When he announced his decision for Kennedy, his family was badly divided on the presidential issue. His father helped organize Massachusetts Volunteers for Humphrey, while his mother and wife refused to abandon Stevenson. ("Can't you control your own wife—or are you like me?," asked Robert F. Kennedy after Marian Schlesinger made public her position.) During the campaign Schlesinger wrote a brief campaign tract, *Kennedy or Nixon: Does It Make Any Difference?* (1960), which answered the question raised in the decided affirmative. Conceding that both men were ambitious, he argued that Nixon was merely interested in selling himself and sought the presidency merely for "private gratification," while Kennedy wanted to win because only that office "would give him the power to fulfill purposes which have long lain in his mind and heart."

Kennedy's victory afforded Schlesinger an opportunity to become a part of the new administration when shortly after the election he was offered the post of special assistant to the president. Tired of "being upstairs writing the speeches while the political decisions were being taken elsewhere," Schlesinger took a leave of absence from Harvard to accept the position. Although Galbraith initially found him "unhappy and uncertain" concerning his ill-defined assignment, he soon found the assistantship challenging and rewarding; and when his leave of absence expired in 1962, he resigned from the Harvard faculty to remain in Washington. On the White House staff, Schlesinger acted as liaison to the United States mission to the United Nations, headed by his old friend Ambassador Adlai E. Stevenson, and as a policy adviser on Latin American relations. More informally, he became the administration's contact with liberals and the intellectual and cultural communities. In addition, according to presidential counsel Theodore Sorensen, he served "as a source of innovation, ideas, and occasional speeches on all topics, and incidentally as a lightning rod to attract Republican attacks away from the rest of us." On one occasion, when conservative criticism of him mounted, he suggested that he should resign, but Kennedy curtly dismissed the idea. "Don't worry about it," the president said. "All they are doing is shooting at me through you."

Schlesinger developed a profound admiration for Kennedy, with whom he had much in common. About the same age, the two men were both residents of Massachusetts, Harvard graduates (with published senior honors theses), Pulitzer Prize winners in history, and attuned to the world of ideas. Schlesinger viewed Kennedy's election, despite the razor-thin margin of victory, as fulfilling a

prophecy he had voiced in *Esquire* a few months earlier that a "new mood" in American politics dictated that "the present period of passivity and acquiescence in our national life" be replaced by an era of innovation and creativity. Though Schlesinger's White House assignment greatly limited his contributions to popular magazines, he did write a few articles in support of Kennedy's policies, much to the annoyance of administration critics who raised objections to such moonlighting on the part of a presidential assistant. In 1963 Houghton Mifflin published *The Politics of Hope*, a collection of twenty previously published essays by Schlesinger for the most part expressing his liberal philosophy. "My father and I," he wrote in the introduction, "are both indebted to John F. Kennedy for vindicating the cyclical theory of American politics." A remarkable transformation had taken place within a very short period. "We no longer seem an old nation, tired, complacent and self-righteous," he wrote. "Our national leadership is young, vigorous, intelligent, civilized, and experimental." Then, remembering the lessons he had learned from Reinhold Niebuhr, he cautioned his readers that it would be "premature to suppose that we are approaching the millennium" or that "mankind will behold a new heaven and a new earth." But for the immediate future his tone was euphoric rather than Niebuhrian: "We are Sons of Liberty once again; or, at least, we admit this as a legitimate ambition. We have awakened as from a trance; and we have awakened so quickly and sharply that we can hardly remember what it was like when we slumbered."

And then it ended so abruptly that November day in 1963 when the president was in Dallas en route to the Trade Mart to deliver a luncheon address and Schlesinger was dining with Galbraith and Katharine Graham in *Newsweek*'s executive dining room in New York City. Returning to Washington following Kennedy's assassination, Schlesinger agreed to new President Lyndon B. Johnson's entreaties that he remain on the White House staff, but the position of special assistant to the president no longer held the attraction it had had under the previous incumbent. "The exhilaration came from working with Kennedy," he said at the time of his resignation in January 1964. "With Kennedy gone, it was no longer exhilarating." Rejecting offers to return to the academic world, he remained in the nation's capital to begin work on what he would later call "a personal memoir by one who served in the White House during the Kennedy years."

When Kennedy had appointed Schlesinger to

the White House staff in 1961, *Time* suggested that perhaps the new special assistant would become "the author of the yet to be written *Age of Kennedy*." (The same newsmagazine also later related the story—doubtless apocryphal—of the time when the president approached Schlesinger who was busily engaged on his typewriter. "Now Arthur, cut it out," he allegedly quipped. "When the time comes, I'll write *The Age of Kennedy*.") Schlesinger later insisted that it had not been his original intention to write an account of the Kennedy years. Early in his presidency, Kennedy, aware of how words "tossed off gaily or irritably in conversation" made quite an unfavorable impression in print, requested his aides not to keep journals relating to their discussions with him; he wanted "no restraint on his own freedom of expression." But after the Bay of Pigs affair, he asked Schlesinger if he had kept a record of the events leading up to that fiasco, only to be reminded of his earlier wishes. The president then instructed him to keep a journal: "You can be damn sure that the CIA has its record and the Joint Chiefs theirs. We'd better make sure we have a record over here. So you go ahead." By the time of Kennedy's death, Schlesinger's journal numbered some 500 single-spaced typed pages. He intended that it would be useful to the president in writing his memoirs. After the tragic end to the Kennedy administration, members of the late president's family urged Schlesinger to prepare his own account of the Kennedy presidency.

Renting an office in downtown Washington, Schlesinger set out in earnest to begin research on the book that he would entitle *A Thousand Days: John F. Kennedy in the White House*. Even for such a well-known prodigious worker, the speed at which he worked was amazing; according to one account when he reached the writing stage he turned out 420 manuscript pages during one period of a single month. There was reason for haste, at least insofar as Houghton Mifflin, his publisher, and *Life*, which had the prepublication serial rights, were concerned, for it was well known that Theodore Sorensen, Kennedy's aide and intimate friend, was nearing completion of a similar volume for Harper & Row and *Look*. Although Sorenson's *Kennedy* (1965) was published in book form two months before *A Thousand Days*, *Life* won the earlier race between the magazines. On 16 July 1965 it began publishing *A Thousand Days* in serial form, over two weeks before *Look* began printing excerpts from the Sorensen book.

The serialization of *A Thousand Days* elicited more controversy than anything Schlesinger has ever written. Attracting the most attention was the author's revelation in the third installment of Kennedy's disenchantment with Secretary of State Dean Rusk, who continued to serve in that same capacity in the Johnson administration. By the autumn of 1963, according to Schlesinger, Kennedy had become so exasperated with Rusk's inability to manage the State Department and his banal approach to and conduct of foreign policy that he had decided to replace him after the 1964 presidential election. Accusing Schlesinger of weakening Rusk's position, congressmen, columnists, and editorial writers denounced him as a "White House tattler," "peephole historian," and worse. Rep. William B. Widnall, a Republican from New Jersey, calling the account "instant history, untempered by time," proposed that limitations be placed on what former White House personnel could make known regarding "privileged conversations and the background of key decisions." Schlesinger's remarks about Rusk led President Johnson to reaffirm his own support for "one of the most able and most competent and most dedicated men I have ever known"; Vice President Humphrey, an old friend of Schlesinger, called his remarks "harmful" and "mischievous"; and even Robert F. Kennedy, while declining to comment on the reported plan to replace Rusk, said that his brother had "great confidence" in his secretary of state. Also causing considerable attention was Schlesinger's disclosure that neither John nor Robert Kennedy actually wanted Johnson as Kennedy's running mate in 1960; they had been taken aback at the alacrity with which the Texan had accepted the vice presidency, an offer that they had anticipated would be turned down. To his critics Schlesinger expressed amazement "that the people who attack me never ask the first question that a historian would ask: Is it true?" And on several occasions he quoted the remark of Sir Walter Raleigh: "Whosoever, in writing a modern history, shall follow truth too near the heels, it may haply strike out his teeth."

Serialization of Schlesinger's account of the Kennedy presidency whetted the reading public's appetite for its publication in book form. Written in his usual graceful style and with his rare gift of making his characters come alive, *A Thousand Days* became a Book-of-the-Month Club selection, and it moved rapidly to the top of the best-sellers lists. James MacGregor Burns, writing for the *New York Times Book Review*, called it "Arthur Schlesinger's best book"; it subsequently won in 1966 the Pulitzer Prize for biography and the National Book Award for history and biography.

Despite the national mood that insured a generally favorable reception for *A Thousand Days*—it was published almost exactly two years to the day after Kennedy's assassination—there were some reservations. As Marcus Cunliffe has observed, Schlesinger's unabashed partisanship appeared to damage his professional standing, at least for a while. He represented Kennedy as a pragmatic liberal much in the tradition of Franklin D. Roosevelt and emphasized his efforts after the Cuban missile crisis to seek a détente with the Soviet Union, as exemplified by the nuclear test ban treaty ratified shortly before his death. Some liberals, who questioned the late president's credentials as one of them, believed that Schlesinger glossed over certain aspects of Kennedy's career—for example, his refusal to oppose Sen. Joseph R. McCarthy in the 1950s and his appointment of staunch segregationists to the federal judiciary in the Southern states. Believing that there had been more style than substance to the New Frontier, many questioned Schlesinger's judgment that Kennedy "had accomplished so much" in such a short time. On the other hand, New Left historians, their voices becoming louder in the late 1960s, tended to view Kennedy as an unregenerate Cold Warrior whose buildup of American forces in Vietnam led to even more massive intervention under his successor.

Following the publication of *A Thousand Days*, Schlesinger announced that he intended to resume work on *The Age of Roosevelt*, and for that purpose he accepted a four-months residency in early 1966 as a visiting fellow at the Institute for Advanced Study in Princeton. That fall he joined the faculty of the City University of New York (CUNY) as one of the newly created and widely publicized state-supported Albert Schweitzer professors of humanities. (The professorship initially provided for a salary of $30,000, but an even greater enticement to Schlesinger was a minimal teaching load and an additional $70,000 annual outlay for staff, research, conferences, and other expenses.) He chose the CUNY offer, he later told Mitchell Ross, "partly because the Schweitzer chair offered me more opportunity for my own research and writing and partly, I guess, because I had already lived nearly forty years of my life in Cambridge and felt that the time had come for a change." While his wife Marian continued living in Washington, Schlesinger quickly adapted to the New York scene where he was instantly recognized as a celebrity whose opinions were constantly solicited on a variety of subjects. He served as a movie critic for *Vogue* from 1966 to 1972 (and later for *Saturday Review* from 1977 to 1980). Because he was

frequently seen at discotheques and other night spots, *Time* referred to him in 1967 as a "swinging soothsayer."

Schlesinger's New York residence made him a constituent of Sen. Robert F. Kennedy, with whom he formed an even closer relationship than he had earlier enjoyed with the late president. Kennedy often consulted with Schlesinger, who made no secret of the fact that he hoped someday to see the senator become president of the United States. (Indeed, according to William Manchester, within twenty-four hours of John F. Kennedy's death Schlesinger discussed with friends the possibility of nominating Robert Kennedy instead of Lyndon Johnson as the Democratic candidate in 1964.) Although he approved of Johnson's Great Society programs, Schlesinger resented the encomiums heaped upon the new president by those who praised him as more effective than his predecessor in obtaining the passage of a legislative program. Pointing out that Kennedy had placed most of the Great Society measures on the nation's political agenda, he maintained that their passage had resulted largely from the national sense of grief following his death that had given President Johnson large congressional majorities in the election of 1964.

While conceding Johnson's domestic accomplishments, Schlesinger became increasingly critical of his conduct of foreign policy. He publicly opposed the dispatch of American troops in 1965 to intervene in a civil war in the Dominican Republic. Aware of the ambiguous legacy that the Kennedy administration had left in regard to Indochina, he at first supported Johnson's announced peace objectives in that area; in fact, as late as May 1965 he was listed as an administration supporter at a Vietnam teach-in in Washington. But he soon became increasingly concerned about the growing "Americanization" of the conflict as a result of the dispatch of hundreds of thousands of American troops to Southeast Asia and the bombing of targets in North Vietnam.

In 1967 Schlesinger brought out *The Bitter Heritage: Vietnam and American Democracy, 1941-1966*, a series of previously published essays on the war and its impact on the United States. Arguing that American intervention in Vietnam had sprung from "a series of small decisions," he regarded the American policy there as representing "a triumph of the politics of inadvertence." (He implied that if John F. Kennedy had lived, things would have turned out differently—a notion, as Irving Howe pointed out, "both impossible to refute and difficult to accept.") Unfortunately, according to Schlesinger, each step by the United States to widen the war had "led only to the next, until we find ourselves entrapped today in that nightmare of American strategists, a land war in Asia." Fearful that the Vietnam controversy might lead to a revival of McCarthyism in the United States, he urged all concerned in the debate to refrain from "explosions of political irrationality." Yet Schlesinger himself could not always restrain his own contempt for Lyndon Johnson. "The President of the United States," he said at one point, "can hardly understand the eastern seaboard of his own country; why in the world does he think he can understand the eastern seaboard of Asia?"

As befitted one accustomed to the "vital center," Schlesinger urged a "middle course" between those who wanted to commit additional resources and men in an effort to bring about a military victory in Vietnam and those who wanted an immediate American withdrawal from that country. To him, the former course of action was illusory, while the latter step would have "ominous effects" in that area of the globe. Instead he advocated a lessening of U.S. military action and a halt to the bombing of North Vietnam as a means of making possible a negotiated settlement. As might have been expected, neither "hawks" nor "doves" found his proposal entirely satisfactory.

Although as the war in Vietnam dragged on Schlesinger came more and more to share the view of those who regarded American involvement there as a foolish policy, he vehemently took issue with those critics of the war who maintained that the nation's policy in Indochina was a logical legacy of the militant anticommunism advocated following World War II by such liberals as himself. The controversy over Vietnam thus inevitably led to a reexamination of postwar diplomatic relations between the United States and the Soviet Union, in which debate New Left historians rejected the orthodox American view that the cold war was simply "the brave and essential response of free men to communist aggression." In an article for *Foreign Affairs*, Schlesinger disputed those cold war revisionists who blamed the United States for bringing about postwar tensions between the Communist and non-Communist world. Because of the Leninist view of an inevitable conflict between capitalism and communism, the totalitarian nature of the Soviet government under Stalin, and the "madness" of Stalin himself, Schlesinger contended that only an abject surrender to all Russian demands after the war would have prevented the development of an

intractable foreign policy by the Soviet Union. In his view, the revisionists had been misled by the divisions within the Communist world since the 1940s, the less menacing demeanor of post-Stalin leaders, and the failure of communism as a worldwide revolutionary movement. None of these developments, he argued, altered the fact that the "responsible" anti-Communist—or anti-Stalinist—stance of American liberals of the late 1940s and early 1950s had been entirely justified.

Convinced that the Johnson administration had not pursued a negotiated settlement in Vietnam with even a fraction of the "zeal, ingenuity and perseverance" with which it had sought a military victory, Schlesinger determined to support in 1968 a presidential candidate with a more flexible stand on war. Thus in February he joined with a majority of the board members of the Americans for Democratic Action in endorsing Minnesota senator Eugene McCarthy's challenge to the renomination of Lyndon Johnson. But after McCarthy's strong showing in the New Hampshire primary, Schlesinger and other advisers of Robert F. Kennedy persuaded the New York senator to enter the race. Accordingly, Schlesinger switched his support to Kennedy, believing that he would make a better president than McCarthy. (His "Why I am for Kennedy" article in the *New Republic* was republished in full in the *New York Times* as an advertisement by the New York State Citizens for Kennedy Committee.) After Kennedy's assassination in June 1968, Schlesinger did not return to his earlier support of McCarthy because he believed that the Minnesotan, whom he regarded as "a somewhat indolent and frivolous man," favored the emasculation of the presidency; instead, he supported the effort to rally the Kennedy delegates behind the belated candidacy of South Dakota senator George McGovern. After the Democratic convention nominated Vice President Hubert Humphrey (backed by President Johnson after his surprise withdrawal from the race), Schlesinger pointedly made no endorsement in the presidential contest between Humphrey and Republican candidate Richard M. Nixon until late in the campaign. Then, after a conversation with Humphrey, he supported the Democratic candidate on the grounds that he would be more likely than Nixon to reverse the Johnson policy in Vietnam.

In many ways the death of Robert Kennedy affected Schlesinger even more deeply than that of his brother. The closeness of their association, the cumulative impact of the assassination following those of John Kennedy and Martin Luther King, the national malaise resulting from social disorders at home and an unpopular war abroad, and Schlesinger's view that the senator was badly misunderstood by his detractors—all contributed to the intensity of his reaction to the tragedy in Los Angeles. When he learned the sorrowful news, he was preparing to give a speech the next day at the commencement exercises of the City University of New York. Discarding his prepared text, he substituted an address on "The Politics of Violence," in which he labeled Americans as "the most frightening people on earth." In view of the circumstances, the extremity of his expression was understandable; he subsequently revised the speech for publication in *Harper's* and still later for a new volume of essays, *The Crisis of Confidence: Ideas, Power, and Violence in America*, published in 1969.

The state of feeling exhibited in *The Crisis of Confidence* bore no resemblance whatever to that of *The Politics of Hope*, published just six years earlier. Contrasting the mood of present-day America with that of the late nineteenth century, he observed that "we are a good deal less buoyant today about ourselves and our future. Events seem to have slipped beyond our control; we have lost our immunity to history." Schlesinger's liberalism, which had been viewed as at least temporarily victorious over conservatism in *The Politics of Hope*, now faced a more serious challange, this time from the left rather than from the right. Continuing his debate with the New Left begun in his *Foreign Affairs* article (republished in *The Crisis of Confidence*), he sharply attacked two of their gurus, Herbert Marcuse and Noam Chomsky, who "when they get to public policy, . . . don't know what they are talking about." He took issue with those radicals who insisted that intellectuals should not assume positions of influence in politics lest they become seduced by the intoxicating allure of power. Perhaps the least satisfying portion of the book was that devoted to the theme of violence, since he conceded that such a course of action could be justified "when the recourses of reason are demonstrably exhausted and when the application of force remains the only way of achieving rational ends." And, as one reviewer noted, he was equivocal about the role of violence in the American past. "It is not clear," wrote Marcus Cunliffe, "whether Schlesinger believes that America is still essentially sound, whether the nation was once sound but is now corrupt, or whether it was always menaced by interior weaknesses."

One phase of Schlesinger's personal life ended in November 1970 when Marian Cannon Schlesinger, who had returned to Cambridge, divorced him after thirty years of marriage. Then in the following July he married Alexandra Emmet Allan in a Manhattan ceremony witnessed only by close family members of the bride and groom. Among those in attendance were his sons, Stephen Cannon and Andrew Bancroft; his daughters, Katharine Schlesinger Kinderman and Christina Schlesinger; and his mother. In 1972 Schlesinger and his wife became the parents of a son, Robert Emmet Kennedy Schlesinger, named for Robert Kennedy and also for Robert Emmet, the Irish patriot who was a collateral ancestor of Alexandra Schlesinger.

In the meantime Schlesinger no longer gave high priority to the rapid completion of *The Age of Roosevelt* project. In the early 1970s he served as principal editor of four multivolume series published by Chelsea House: the four-volume *History of American Presidential Elections, 1789-1968* (1971); the four-volume *History of U.S. Political Parties* (1973); the five-volume *The Dynamics of World Power: A Documentary History of United States Foreign Policy, 1945-1973* (1973); and the five-volume *Congress Investigates: A Documentary History, 1792-1974* (1975). The last series, designed to capitalize upon public interest in a current political controversy, concluded with a section on the role of Congress in probing the Watergate scandals that led to the resignation of President Richard M. Nixon.

Schlesinger had viewed Nixon's accession to the presidency in 1969 with grave misgivings, though as late as 1972 he conceded that Nixon had not "been the utter disaster some had predicted." He noted, however, that those Nixon actions he tended to approve—the new China policy and the use of price controls, for example—had been taken by the president "at the expense of his long-proclaimed principles." If Schlesinger's apprehensions that Nixon would seek a wholesale dismantling of domestic social programs proved unwarranted, he found much to criticize in the new president's foreign policy, particularly the extension of the Vietnam War into Cambodia.

In 1972 Schlesinger, who served as a New York delegate to the Democratic convention in Miami, enthusiastically supported George McGovern in his bid to defeat Nixon's reelection. His article "How McGovern Will Win" for the *New York Times Magazine* was predicated upon the assumption—erroneous, so it later appeared—that Americans wanted "a change from the system and men who have got the nation into deep trouble at home and abroad." Although Schlesinger emphasized McGovern's personal qualifications for the presidency rather than those projected programs that earned the candidate a reputation for radicalism, his participation in the McGovern campaign has been termed "highly ironic." "He who had taught the left its Niebuhrian lessons, who had so assiduously instructed liberals over the years in the evils of sentimentality and self-righteousness," James A. Neuchterlein wrote in 1977, "found himself involved in the most revivalistic campaign of any major candidate in recent history."

The American involvement in the Indochina War during the Johnson and Nixon administrations induced Schlesinger to reconsider his views on the power of the presidency. The White House protagonists of his major works—Andrew Jackson, Franklin D. Roosevelt, and John F. Kennedy—had been practitioners of strong executive leadership, and Schlesinger had written approvingly of their expansion of presidential powers. He had particularly endorsed the concept of the liberal exercise of executive power in foreign affairs. (In reply to Schlesinger's defense of Truman's commitment of troops to Korea without congressional approval, Edward S. Corwin had accused him of ascribing to the presidency a "truly royal prerogative in the field of foreign relations.") As late as 1968 Schlesinger criticized Eugene McCarthy for proposing "to cut back the powers of the Presidency at precisely the time when only a strong President will be able to hold the nation together in dealing with our most urgent and difficult national problems."

But Johnson's "Americanization" of the Vietnam War and Nixon's widening of that conflict—involving actions taken by the two presidents without the explicit endorsement of Congress and in some cases even without its knowledge—deeply troubled Schlesinger. At first, his concern regarding the growth of executive power related almost exclusively to the area of foreign affairs. But while he was preparing a book-length manuscript on the subject, new revelations about the abuse of executive powers in domestic matters caused him to widen his discussion of the dangerous expansion of presidential authority. If the Vietnam War inspired the writing of his new book, the public spotlight on the Watergate scandals of the Nixon administration assured that it would attract wide attention. A Book-of-the-Month Club selection, *The Imperial Presidency*, published by Houghton Mifflin in November 1973, became yet another Schlesinger best-seller.

Freely conceding his own contributions to the "rise of the presidential mystique," Schlesinger traced the aggrandizement of the presidency largely to America's new role in international affairs since the outbreak of World War II. In dealing with modern presidents, he tended to exculpate his favorite occupants of the White House, as several reviewers pointed out. According to Schlesinger, Franklin D. Roosevelt, in working out his controversial destroyers-naval bases deal with Britain, "paid due respect to the written checks of the Constitution and displayed an unusual concern for the unwritten checks on presidential initiative." John F. Kennedy "superbly handled" the Cuban missile crisis, and it "could not have been handled so well in any other way." But, he admitted, "one of its legacies was the imperial conception of the Presidency that brought the republic so low in Vietnam."

Other recent presidents were treated less gently. As a result of his dispatch of troops to Korea without seeking congressional approval, Harry S. Truman "dramatically and dangerously enlarged the power of future Presidents to take the nation into major war." Eisenhower made the Central Intelligence Agency "the primary instrument of American intervention in other countries," and, despite his supposedly Whig concept of presidency, he espoused the new doctrine of executive privilege, making "the most absolute assertion of presidential right to withhold information from Congress ever uttered to that day." But his most severe criticism was reserved for Lyndon B. Johnson and Richard M. Nixon. As a result of their prosecution of the war in Indochina, the belief that foreign affairs could be safely trusted to the president "went down in flames in Vietnam."

The aggrandizement of the presidency reached its fullest development under Nixon, though Schlesinger noted that his enlargement of executive authority "was not an aberration but a culmination." What distinguished the Nixon administration from those of his predecessors was the bold effort to make the presidency all-powerful in dealing with matters at home as well as abroad. Citing the impoundment of funds appropriated by Congress, the selective enforcement of the laws, the unprecedented claims of "executive privilege" and "national security" to withhold information, the efforts to intimidate the news media, and ultimately "the use of the White House itself as a base for espionage and sabotage directed against the political opposition," Schlesinger argued that the Nixon administration "signified the extension of the imperial Presidency from foreign to domestic affairs." Nixon, despite his "conventional exterior, was a man with revolutionary dreams," who "aimed at reducing the power of Congress at every point along the line and moving toward rule by presidential decree." Then, of course, "retribution came, and its name was Watergate."

Watergate served a very useful purpose, Schlesinger declared. It stopped "the revolutionary Presidency in its tracks. It blew away the mystique of the mandate and reinvigorated the constitutional separation of powers." But Schlesinger once again sought a middle course—this time between the advocates of strong presidential powers and those who would exalt Congress at the expense of the White House. "The answer to the runaway Presidency," he wrote, "is not the messenger-boy Presidency. The American democracy must discover a middle ground between making the President a czar and making him a puppet." He hoped for the reestablishment of congressional "comity" with the president rather than any fundamental constitutional changes, because "we need a strong Presidency— but a strong Presidency within the Constitution." As for Nixon (though written in the autumn of 1973, *The Imperial Presidency* always spoke of him in the past tense as if anticipating that his days were numbered), Schlesinger suggested, without explicitly endorsing, impeachment and removal from office as the proper way to deal with the tarnished incumbent. After publication of his book, he soon abandoned any ambivalence on the subject, as evidenced by his article, "What If We Don't Impeach Him?," published in the May 1974 issue of *Harper's*.

Before writing *The Imperial Presidency*, Schlesinger had already begun work on a biography of Robert F. Kennedy, a project undertaken with the encouragement of the late senator's family. "A sort of sequel" to *A Thousand Days*, his new study took much longer to write than Schlesinger had foreseen. (In December 1973 he anticipated its completion "about a year from now," but it was not published until September 1978.) The delay was due in no small measure to the abundance of sources available to the author. He relied heavily upon Kennedy's voluminous papers, to which he had been given exclusive and unrestricted access, but he also utilized numerous oral history interviews in the John F. Kennedy Library. A mammoth book (916 pages of text), *Robert Kennedy and His Times* won for him in 1979 a second National Book Award. "Some day," he said, "I'm going to conquer the art of writing short books."

Although Schlesinger's new book made the best-sellers' charts, it met a mixed reception from reviewers, many of whom did not share the author's admittedly sympathetic view of his subject. "I was a great admirer and devoted friend of Robert Ken-

nedy," he warned in the preface. "Association with him over the last decade of his life was one of the joys of my own life." As a result, one critic noted, "this is a biography with passion"—a quality much more pronounced in *Robert Kennedy and His Times* than in his earlier works on Brownson, Jackson, and Roosevelt, and even in his treatment of John F. Kennedy in *A Thousand Days*. Many reviewers believed that Schlesinger ignored or glossed over aspects of Robert Kennedy's career that led to the frequent charge that he was both ruthless and opportunistic. One of them called the book "a 916-page promotional pamphlet of exculpation and eulogy."

While conceding that there were some unattractive phases in Kennedy's early public life, Schlesinger emphasized his subject's capacity for change and intellectual growth. At first, his interest in black Americans was mainly political, but as attorney general he became an open advocate of the movement to attain their full civil and political rights. Toward the end of his life, he became the "tribune of the underclass" who deeply empathized with and championed the causes of other powerless groups as well—Chicanos, Indians, the poor of Appalachia, and the victims of urban blight. In the cases of both John and Robert Kennedy, Schlesinger observed, there had been sharp contrasts between the public image and the real man: "John Kennedy was a realist disguised as a romantic; Robert Kennedy, a romantic stubbornly disguised as a realist." At the time of his tragic death, Robert Kennedy was "the most creative man in American public life." In Schlesinger's view, "he possessed to an exceptional degree what T. S. Eliot called an 'experiencing nature.' History changed him, and had time permitted, he might have changed history."

Throughout the 1970s Schlesinger continued to give vent to his opinions on current political matters, mainly through articles in magazines and editorial-page essays—about one a month—for the *Wall Street Journal*. (He became a member of that paper's Board of Contributors in 1973.) Except for the departure of Richard Nixon from active public life, Schlesinger found little else to his liking in the political developments of the decade. He supported Morris Udall for the presidency in 1976 and was keenly disappointed when Jimmy Carter captured the Democratic nomination. He disliked Carter's vagueness on the issues, his appeals to conservatives, his "Trust me" campaign, and, above all, his moralizing tone. He took almost proprietary offense at Carter's claim that his political philosophy had been greatly influenced by the writings of Reinhold Niebuhr. (Citing Niebuhr's warnings about the irrelevance of Christianity to the problem of justice in modern society, Schlesinger doubted that Carter comprehended the theologian's message. "The fact is," he wrote, "that Niebuhr's whole argument was directed against the notion that the problems of secular society would respond to simple moral preachments.") Although he detected little difference between Carter and the incumbent Gerald R. Ford on most issues, he applauded the Georgian's stand on behalf of racial justice and shared his concern about the dangers of nuclear war. Finally he unenthusiastically endorsed the Democratic candidate, though adding, "I sometimes feel that I am buying a peanut in the poke." On the eve of the election he wrote that "one prefers the risk of Mr. Carter to the hopeless certainty of Mr. Ford. But what an abysmal, demeaning, offensive, empty campaign on both their parts. What a hell of a way to celebrate the Bicentennial!"

Schlesinger soon regretted his reluctant choice. Though he approved of some Carter actions in foreign affairs—such as the Panama Canal treaty, the normalization of diplomatic relations with the People's Republic of China, and the SALT-II agreement—he believed that a Ford administration would have taken essentially the same positions "and had an easier time with them." Admitting that Carter was an intelligent man, he pointed out that his intelligence was that of an engineer, a backhanded compliment that led to the observation that Herbert Hoover bore the same distinction. In domestic matters the Carter administration lacked coherence; furthermore, it lacked competence. ("Lacking any unifying vision, displaying no interest in the way specific policies relate to each other, he ad hocs it all over the place, while the country sinks ever deeper into the morass.") Labeling Carter a "crypto-Republican," Schlesinger called him the most conservative Democratic president since Grover Cleveland and pronounced his administration the most incompetent since that of Warren G. Harding.

In the summer of 1979 Schlesinger urged his fellow ADA members to support a liberal for the Democratic nomination in 1980—if Sen. Edward M. Kennedy would not run, then someone else who would be willing to challenge the incumbent. Toward the end of the Carter presidency, Schlesinger stepped up his criticism of the administration's record in foreign affairs, especially its handling of the Iranian hostage crisis and its alleged overreaction to the Soviet occupation of Afghanistan. When faced

with a presidential campaign which pitted Carter against the Republican candidate Ronald Reagan, he chose neither major party nominee. "Who can really know what the difference would be," he asked, "between this demonstrably poor President and this speculatively hopeless aspirant. 'Sir,' said Dr. Johnson, 'there is no settling the point of precedency between a louse and a flea.'" Although finding it difficult to forsake "lifetime habits of Democratic regularity," he voted for independent candidate John Anderson as "the only way to rebuke the major parties for offering us Mr. Carter and Mr. Reagan."

With the completion of *Robert Kennedy and His Times*, Schlesinger announced that he was turning once again to the long-deferred *Age of Roosevelt* project. Because it had been eighteen years since the latest volume of that series had been published, some had come to wonder if his intervening involvement in national politics might make it difficult for him to regain his former interest in the Roosevelt administration. "Alas," mused one reviewer of his book on Robert Kennedy, "perhaps the fascination with FDR has worn thin in the 'age of Carter.'" In his *The Literary Politicians* (1978), Mitchell Ross expressed the hope that Schlesinger "stay far enough away from politics to write books of enduring value in his final years," yet he noted that "he must stay close enough to politics to give his books their peculiar, partisan edge."

Indeed, Schlesinger's political activism more than anything else has distinguished him from other prominent historians of his generation, and his "vital center" perspective has significantly shaped his interpretation of American history. On the whole, he has maintained a considerable degree of consistency both in the utterance of his liberal philosophy and in his treatment of the American past. From time to time, of course, he has modified his views. Obviously influenced by the consensus mood of the 1950s, he has downplayed in subsequent works the theme of class conflict so prominent in *The Age of Jackson*. He has softened his earlier criticism of the political competence of businessmen, though on occasion he has reverted to his previously expressed opinion on that subject. (Commenting on the costly transition team of the incoming Reagan administration in January 1981, he observed that "sending business leaders to cure the evils of bureaucracy is like sending Typhoid Mary to stop an epidemic.") While altering his view on the role of the presidency in foreign policy, he has consistently supported the need for an activist president and an energetic federal government to promote liberal domestic programs. While conceding that New Left historians made a valid point in stressing Soviet concern for security after World War II, he has yielded little else to them in the debate over the origins of the cold war.

Schlesinger's commitment to his own distinctive brand of liberalism and his active participation in politics have assured him a host of critics within and outside the historical profession. He has been aptly described as "an embattled figure among intellectuals—with cannon to the left of him, cannon to the right of him, while he tried valiantly to defend the vital center." Radicals (whether Old Leftists like Herbert Aptheker or New Leftists like Jesse Lemisch) tend to see little difference between his liberalism and the conservatism of a Daniel Boorstin, while conservatives like William F. Buckley, Jr., and Clare Booth Luce regard him as a closet socialist. For his part, Schlesinger has always been more comfortable in debating with conservatives, for he believes that they have a legitimate, if somewhat misguided, role in American politics. But his cyclical view of the United States as a nation that inevitably alternates between periods of conservative quiescence and liberal resurgence has no place for a radicalism that would fundamentally alter the system.

Nor is Schlesinger universally admired by all who regard themselves as liberals. Some, for example, do not subscribe to the Niebuhrian pessimism upon which his political philosophy is grounded, nor do all share his contempt for ideology. Still others, citing his switch from Adlai Stevenson to John Kennedy in 1960 and his abandonment of Eugene McCarthy for Robert Kennedy in 1968, regard him as an opportunist in search of power and influence. (McCarthy compared him to "mistletoe in a birch tree," adding "You know mistletoe is the ultimate parasite.") Some of Schlesinger's critics believe that he indulges too much in hero-worship, and that his modern-day Democratic heroes have been those who possessed "style"—politicians like the Kennedys, Franklin D. Roosevelt, or Averell Harriman, all from wealthy Eastern backgrounds. (In view of Schlesinger's indictment of Lyndon Johnson for failing to understand "the eastern seaboard of his own country," it is interesting to note that his least favorite Democratic politicians of recent years—Truman, Johnson, Rusk, and Carter—have all come from the hinterlands.)

Schlesinger has spiritedly defended himself from those historians who take the position that a scholar should not accept an active role in the management of government lest he become "corrupted by partisanship and power." To one such critic of his involvement in the Kennedy White House he replied: "Does he really wish the management of affairs to be handed over exclusively to lawyers, bankers, businessmen and generals? He must be kidding." In 1965 he was widely criticized when it was revealed that he had given the *New York Times* a cover story misrepresenting the size and the nature of the Bay of Pigs landing force, an action of his that he defended as being "in the national interest." (One wonders if Schlesinger had this deception of the press in mind when as special assistant to the president he told an audience of the American Historical Association in 1962 that he considered newspaper and magazine accounts "sometimes worse than useless" in revealing the inner workings of government. He added: "I have too often seen the most conscientious reporters attribute to government officials the exact opposite of which the officials are advocating within the government to make it possible for me to take the testimony of journalism in such matters seriously again." At the time Schlesinger's remarks were interpreted as blaming the press, not government officials, for such misrepresentations.)

In 1977 the revelation of a newly declassified memorandum from Schlesinger to Kennedy reopened the controversy concerning the special assistant's role in the Bay of Pigs affair. On 10 April 1961 he had suggested to the president how to handle possible press conference questions to give the impression that the upcoming landing was strictly a Cuban affair with no involvement by the United States government. Insisting that the memorandum "was not an attempt to persuade a President to lie," Schlesinger defended the propriety of his course of action. "Compromise is involved in every activity of life, not in government alone," he said. "It is entirely possible to deal with practical realities without yielding inner convictions; it is entirely possible to compromise in program and action without compromising in ideals and values." Such an explanation failed to satisfy some of Schlesinger's critics. According to New Left historian William Appleman Williams, the White House aide, in the Bay of Pigs episode, "valued his future influence more than his present morality."

Schlesinger has not only defended the right of scholars to take an active role in the management of government, but he has also maintained that such participation is valuable experience for a political historian. Involvement should bring him "to a proper humility before the welter of the past"; it should "prompt him to ask new questions which open up fertile new possibilities for the profession to explore"; and, above all, it should give him knowledge and insight into the way in which government operates. Historians who have been "immersed in the confusion of events" should also be "less inclined to impose an exaggerated rational order on the contingency and obscurity of reality." "Nothing in my own recent experience," he wrote while serving in the White House, "has been more chastening than the attempt to penetrate into the process of decision. I shudder a little when I think how confidently I have analyzed decisions in the ages of Jackson and Roosevelt, traced influences, assigned motives, evaluated roles, allocated responsibilities and, in short, transformed a dishevelled and murky evolution into a tidy and ordered transaction."

There are dangers too in such involvement, as Schlesinger has recognized: "To act is, in many cases, to give hostages—to parties, to policies, to persons. Participation spins a web of commitments which may imprison the chronicler in invisible fetters." Some critics believe that in his books about the Kennedys Schlesinger was too much influenced by a desire to present his protagonists—and himself—in the most favorable light. In *A Thousand Days*, for example, he labels as "curious" Dean Rusk's suggestion that "someone other than the President make the final decision [regarding the Bay of Pigs operation] and do so in his absence—someone who could be sacrificed if things went wrong." He did not state, as his 10 April 1961 memorandum to Kennedy clearly reveals, that at the time he saw "merit" in Rusk's proposal. Because of his desire to protect the "character and repute" of the president, "one of our greatest national resources," he was intrigued by the suggestion that there should be someone "whose head can later be placed on the block if things go terribly wrong." Kennedy, however, rejected the idea and assumed full responsibility for the abortive operation.

Schlesinger holds no brief for those historians who have questioned the professional propriety of his books about the Kennedys. (He has always carefully distinguished between the character of the two works—*A Thousand Days* being a personal memoir and *Robert Kennedy and His Times* a formal biography.) Books such as the former are valuable if only for the use made of them by later historians. "I have no question," he said in 1966, "that by writing *A Thousand Days* the year after President Kennedy's death, I was able to suggest something about the mood and relationships of the Kennedy years which

no future historian could ever get on the basis of the documents—indeed, which I myself could not have reproduced, with the fading of memory, the knowledge of consequences, and the introduction of new preoccupations and perspectives, had I tried to write the book ten or twenty years later." He has also defended his qualifications to write a life of Robert Kennedy despite his close attachment to the memory of his good friend. ("If it is necessary for a biographer of Robert Kennedy to regard him as evil," he said in the preface, "then I am not qualified to be his biographer.") But in Schlesinger's view, "sympathy may illumine as well as distort." Elsewhere he has argued that "far from historical truth being unattainable in contemporary history, it may almost be argued that in a sense truth is *only* attainable in contemporary history. For contemporary history means the writing of history under the eye of the only people who can offer contradiction, that is, the witnesses."

Schlesinger maintains that "history has values of its own, and that we degrade history when we use it merely as a weapon in political struggles." But at the same time he argues that "a belief in history for its own sake need imply no withdrawal from political and social activism," though it should "make us conscious of the differences between being historians and being activists; it should make us determined to keep the two things separate." (His critics question how successful he has been in maintaining that distinction.) What lies ahead for Schlesinger the activist? Buoyed by his faith in the cyclical theory of American politics, he remains confident that liberalism in America is not, as its critics assert, "used up, finished, a burnt-out case." According to his vision, once again—"sometime in the 1980s"—the nation will be forced to "confront the urgent problems of the domestic community." Inflation and energy are likely to be the "detonating issues" that will assure a return to liberalism, for the quest for solutions to those problems makes "affirmative government a technical imperative, a functional necessity, in the years ahead." If Schlesinger is right, perhaps his influence in the Democratic party—at an all-time low following his bolt from the ranks in 1980—will once again be felt.

As for Schlesinger the historian, his permanent place in American historiography will probably rest largely upon *The Age of Roosevelt* series—the three volumes published between 1957 and 1960 and those that are still to come. Concerning his willingness to be diverted from this project by other attractions, he once said, "I am consoled by the memory of my remote ancestor George Bancroft who published the first volume of his *History of the United States* in the 1830s and the last volume in the 1880s." (If he maintains Bancroft's pace, *The Age of Roosevelt* will be completed when he is about ninety years old. Bancroft fortunately lived to that age, but just barely.) The remaining volumes will be increasingly addressed to readers with only dim or nonexistent memories of Franklin D. Roosevelt, the New Deal, and World War II. These volumes will undoubtedly be—as Arthur Mann described the earlier ones—"narrative history in the grand style, written from the inside, with life, color, passion, drama and conviction." If so, they, as well as *The Crisis of the Old Order*, *The Coming of the New Deal*, and *The Politics of Upheaval*, will be read for generations to come, for historical works that survive from one age to another, so Schlesinger has written, "do so in the main less as history than as art."

Other:

Paths of American Thought, edited by Schlesinger and Morton White (Boston: Houghton Mifflin, 1963);

History of American Presidential Elections, 1789-1968, 4 volumes, edited by Schlesinger, Fred L. Israel, and William P. Hansen (New York: Chelsea House, 1971);

History of U.S. Political Parties, 4 volumes, edited by Schlesinger (New York: Chelsea House, 1973);

The Dynamics of World Power: A Documentary History of United States Foreign Policy, 1945-1973, 5 volumes, edited by Schlesinger (New York: Chelsea House, 1973);

Congress Investigates: A Documentary History, 1792-1974, 5 volumes, edited by Schlesinger and Roger Bruns (New York: Chelsea House, 1975).

Periodical Publications:

"The Need for a Cultural Comprehension of Political Behavior," *Pennsylvania Magazine of History and Biography*, 72 (April 1948): 180-198;

"The Humanist Looks at Empirical Social Research," *American Sociological Review*, 27 (December 1962): 768-771;

"The Historian and History," *Foreign Affairs*, 41 (April 1963): 491-497;

"The Historian as Artist," *Atlantic*, 212 (July 1963): 35-41;

"On the Inscrutability of History," *Encounter*, 27 (November 1966): 10-17;

"On the Writing of Contemporary History," *Atlantic*, 219 (March 1967): 69-74;

"Nationalism and History," *Journal of Negro History*, 54 (January 1969): 19-31;

"The Historian as Participant," *Daedalus*, 100 (Spring 1971): 339-358.

Interviews:

Henry Brandon, "On Writing History: A Conversation with Professor Arthur Schlesinger, Jr.," *Conversations with Henry Brandon* (London: Deutsch, 1966), pp. 40-54;

"Playboy Interview: Arthur Schlesinger, Jr.," *Playboy*, 13 (May 1966): 75+;

John A. Garraty, "Arthur M. Schlesinger, Jr.: Political and Social Change: 1941-1968," *Interpreting American History: Conversations with Historians* (New York: Macmillan, 1970; London: Collier-Macmillan, 1970), II: 265-288;

Lynn A. Bonfield, "Conversation with Arthur M. Schlesinger, Jr.: The Use of Oral History," *American Archivist*, 13 (Fall 1980): 461-472.

References:

"The Combative Chronicler," *Time*, 86 (17 December 1965): 54-60;

Marcus Cunliffe, "Arthur M. Schlesinger, Jr.," in *Pastmasters: Some Essays on American Historians*, edited by Cunliffe and Robin W. Winks (New York: Harper & Row, 1969), pp. 345-372;

James A. Neuchterlein, "Arthur M. Schlesinger, Jr., and the Discontents of Postwar American Liberalism," *Review of Politics*, 39 (January 1977): 3-40;

Ronald Radosh, "Historian in the Service of Power," *Nation*, 225 (6 August 1977): 104-109; reply with rejoinder, *Nation*, 225 (20 August 1977): 147-148;

Mitchell S. Ross, "Arthur M. Schlesinger, Jr.," in *The Literary Politicians* (Garden City: Doubleday, 1978), pp. 56-110;

Arthur Meier Schlesinger [Sr.], *In Retrospect: The History of a Historian* (New York: Harcourt, Brace, 1963);

John Taft, "The Once and Future Mandarin," *New Republic*, 171 (26 November 1977): 16-19.

Papers:

Schlesinger's White House staff papers are in the John F. Kennedy Library, Boston, Massachusetts.

Kenneth M. Stampp

(12 July 1912-   )

John G. Sproat
University of South Carolina

SELECTED BOOKS: *Indiana Politics During the Civil War* (Indianapolis: Indiana Historical Bureau, 1949; Bloomington & London: Indiana University Press, 1978;

And the War Came: The North and the Secession Crisis, 1860-1861 (Baton Rouge: Louisiana State University Press, 1950);

The Peculiar Institution: Slavery in the Ante-Bellum South (New York: Knopf, 1956; London: Eyre & Spottiswoode, 1964);

The National Experience: A History of the United States, by Stampp, John M. Blum, and others (New York: Harcourt, Brace & World, 1963);

The Era of Reconstruction, 1865-1877 (New York: Knopf, 1965);

The Imperiled Union: Essays on the Background of the Civil War (New York & Oxford: Oxford University Press, 1980).

Born in Milwaukee, Wisconsin, in 1912, Kenneth M. Stampp is of the generation of historians that came into the profession in the age of the Great Depression. It was a time when liberalism completed its metamorphosis from the classical laissez-faire formulation of the nineteenth century to its modern predication of the state as the guarantor of social welfare as well as of individual liberty. Although strongly influenced by the socialist-pacifist traditions of the German-American community in which he grew up, Stampp developed his early perceptions of the American past in the climate of opinion provided by New Deal liberalism. In his long and distinguished career as a social and political historian, Stampp has always concerned himself with the democratic experience, especially in its humanistic and ethnic dimensions. His major works deal with the collapse of the democratic process in the sectional conflict, the harsh realities of chattel slavery in the antebellum South, and the convergence of idealism and self-interest in the era of Reconstruction. If his professional interests have centered on mid-nineteenth century America, his works deal as well with the functioning of democratic society in general.

Stampp's attachment to Clio dates from his elementary school years in Milwaukee and perhaps

Kenneth M. Stampp

especially from the day he announced to his fellow fifth-graders that he intended one day to be a history teacher. He majored in his favorite subject as an undergraduate, first at Milwaukee State Teacher's College, then at the University of Wisconsin in Madison, where he earned his bachelor's degree in 1935. After a brief stint of high-school teaching, he entered into graduate study at Madison with a teaching assistantship in the history department. Historians were not notably in demand during the Depression years, and for a time he considered transferring to law school. But as his contacts with some of Wisconsin's leading scholars deepened, so did his commitment to history. Curtis Nettels taught him colonial history and sharpened his awareness of economic factors in the American past. As an undergraduate, Stampp had minored in philosophy. In graduate school, he turned to labor economics as his secondary field, studying it with its master, Selig Perlman. A speculative scholar with a wide-ranging knowledge of history, Perlman approached the study of American labor with a fine sensitivity to the unique historical experience of working people in this country. His scholarship was something of a corrective to the indiscriminate economic determinism then fashionable among young historians, to whom Charles A. Beard was a prophet. Stampp, too, was a great admirer of Beard, and his doctoral dissertation on Indiana politics during the Civil War was written from the perspective of economic determinism. But he was too independent a thinker ever to attach himself to any single "school" of history, and early in his career he tempered his predilection for an economic interpretation of history with growing appreciation of the roles cultural and psychological elements play in the human drama.

The most interesting and dynamic scholar Stampp encountered at Wisconsin was William Best Hesseltine, historian of the sectional conflict and the South. Brilliant, brash, and hugely opinionated, Hesseltine had at once a formative and provocative influence on Stampp. Relations between mentor and student were often stormy and sometimes downright bitter. But their association had its positive side, as well, for Hesseltine kindled Stampp's interest in Southern history and provided him with a model of dynamic teaching. Moreover, the two men worked together well enough to enable Stampp to write his dissertation under Hesseltine's direction and thus to receive his doctorate in 1941.

After teaching for a year at the University of Arkansas, Stampp joined the faculty at the University of Maryland in 1942 as an assistant professor of history. Among his friends and colleagues during his four years there were such other promising young scholars as Richard Hofstadter and Frank Freidel in history and the sociologist C. Wright Mills. Stampp took excellent advantage of his proximity to the Library of Congress, a repository whose manuscript and newspaper collections he worked extensively in preparation for the book he planned to write on the secession crisis. Then in 1946 came his appointment as assistant professor at the University of California in Berkeley, where he quickly became a mainstay in a history department that developed, over the next several decades, into one of the most prestigious in the profession. In

1957 he became Morrison Professor of American History.

World War II and the vicissitudes of the Indiana Historical Bureau delayed the publication of Stampp's revised dissertation until 1949, when it appeared as *Indiana Politics During the Civil War*. Based upon an exhaustive survey of newspapers and manuscripts in the Indianapolis archives, the book was revisionist history in the sense that it emphasized economic factors as the stimulant of political controversy in the state during the war and sought to reestablish the reputations of Indiana Democrats, whose role earlier historians had discredited. In his preface to a second edition that appeared in 1978, Stampp acknowledged that the economic perspective of the book, while still of value in explaining the social tensions in the state during the war, now impressed him as somewhat too narrow and simplistic. He also conceded that he had passed over too lightly the racism that infused political rhetoric in the Northern states, especially among the "Peace Democrats," a fault some earlier critics had noted. The experience of reexamining in the 1970s the work he had done as a young scholar was a sobering experience for Stampp, one that fed his skepticism that "even the best methodology will ever transcend our limitations of vision and produce definitive historical works." What had changed in some thirty years was not the evidence but instead the world around him and his own conceptions of what was important. Whereas economic issues had seemed of overriding importance to him in the Depression years, by the 1970s the problem of racism had come to be a major conditioner of his thinking. Whatever its shortcomings in this regard, *Indiana Politics* impressed reviewers in 1949 as an effective rejoinder to earlier versions of the state's complex political history, especially in its penetrating analysis of Republican leaders and their motives.

A year later his second book, *And the War Came: The North and the Secession Crisis, 1860-1861* (1950), appeared. Although Stampp emphatically disclaimed any intention to undertake the "fruitless and impossible" task of proving or disproving that the Civil War was inevitable, the very nature of his inquiry into the question of *why* war came made him a participant in the larger debate. Still, the book was more exposition than argumentation, and its political realism made it one of the most dispassionate examinations of the secession crisis ever to appear. To Stampp, it was all but self-evident that the war had deep and fundamental causes that the superficial compromise proposals of the time simply could not reach. History itself had generated the crisis, in the sense that a long series of developments over the years had widened the gap between sections to the point where the existing political system became incapable of bridging it. As long as chattel slavery survived, as long as Northern politicians insisted on advancing their own special interests at the expense of the South, what possible basis for sectional harmony could exist by 1860?

Much of the book was a close examination of Northern public opinion, and Stampp concluded that by the secession winter a consensus had developed in favor of "the Union as it was." Just why such a notion of "perpetual Union" should have taken hold so firmly was a question he would pursue again later in his career. In the secession crisis, he observed, Lincoln fused his own and his party's commitment to the Union with the interests of the nation as a whole, thereby giving legitimacy to his own unhappy conclusion that while peace was preferable, war was acceptable if necessary to preserve the Union. As the acts of secession and the reality of disunion dispelled his hopes for peace, Lincoln developed his "strategy of defense," a simple device to throw the initiative for war to the secessionists. The strategy "worked"—and the war came.

Stampp's tone of realism persisted throughout the book, and in the final paragraph he noted the ironic contrast between noble purposes and sordid results. Yankees went to war motivated by the highest ideals of the nineteenth-century middle classes, he observed, but what they achieved was a triumph of middle-class vices: "The most striking products of their crusade were the shoddy aristocracy of the North and the ragged children of the South. Among the masses of Americans there were no victors, only the vanquished."

And the War Came established Stampp's reputation nationally as an authority on the sectional conflict. But even as it appeared, its author was already immersed in research for the book that would elevate him to the first rank of twentieth-century American historians and touch off a historiographical revolution in the study of slavery. Published in 1956, just two years after the Supreme Court's momentous decision on racial segregation in the schools, *The Peculiar Institution: Slavery in the Ante-Bellum South* was a book whose time had come. The prevailing word on slavery in the antebellum South, uttered in 1918 by U. B. Phillips, was that the institution basically had been a benevolent one, sustained by high-minded masters at an economic

loss to themselves in the interests of social stability. Despite mounting dissatisfaction with this interpretation, especially after World War II, no historian had yet confronted it head-on. To be sure, a few scholars had considered aspects of slavery in ways that foreshadowed a major historical reinterpretation, among them W. E. B. Du Bois, Carter G. Woodson, John Hope Franklin, Richard Hofstadter, and Herbert Aptheker. But it remained for Stampp to provide the long-awaited direct counterweight to Phillips.

Reflecting the racial views of his time, Phillips had assumed throughout his studies of the South that blacks were inherently inferior to whites. As white economic history, his work still commands respect and provides insight into the role of the master class. But it contributes almost nothing to an understanding of slavery as it affected the slaves or of how black people managed to survive the ordeal of bondage. Writing in the *American Historical Review* in 1952, Stampp laid the foundations for a reassessment of slavery by subjecting Phillips's work to a searching critique. Far from displaying animus toward black people, he noted, Phillips had simply ignored them as major participants in the dynamics of slavery. In *The Peculiar Institution*, Stampp opened his own inquiry into the subject with the assertion that "innately Negroes *are*, after all, only white men with black skins, nothing more, nothing less." Some critics read into that statement a patronizing racism of Stampp's own; but in the context of the challenge he raised to Phillips, he meant only that he had found no evidence of significant differences between blacks and whites in their emotional traits and intellectual capabilities. The point was to acknowledge the humanity of black people and to study the institution of slavery within that perspective, to view slavery through the eyes of the slave as well as through the eyes of the slaveholder.

Gathering evidence from an impressive array of plantation records, census reports, writings of ex-slaves, and papers of slaveholding families, Stampp presented a comprehensive account of slave life. Work routines, maintenance, family life, spiritual care, resistance, discipline and punishment, slave trading, and slave codes all underwent careful scrutiny. Challenging Phillips's contention that slavery "educated" blacks to the Christian religion and Anglo-European institutions, he countered that it "took away from the African his native culture and gave him, in exchange, little more than vocational training." He also demolished a host of myths about the master-slave relationship to reveal a chronic condition on most plantations of social tension in wary coexistence with pragmatic accommodation. As for the economics of slavery, Stampp was unequivocal in rejecting Phillips's insistence that the institution was unprofitable. Most owners earned a reasonably satisfactory return from their investments, he claimed, while only the most hopelessly inefficient masters failed to profit from owning slaves. Moreover, he found no evidence to indicate that slavery was on the way to "natural extinction" at the time war brought it to an abrupt end.

Within a remarkably few years of its appearance, *The Peculiar Institution* became the generally accepted account of slavery, and the paperback edition found its way into classrooms throughout the nation, even the Deep South. Doubtless, its success derived in part from its literary craftsmanship: it was history written in clear, crisp prose, restrained in tone on matters of emotional controversy, and imaginative and energetic in its challenges to conventional wisdom. But the book also was in complete accord with the changing temper of the times on questions of race and civil rights, and it is fair to assume that it played a significant part in shaping the racial perceptions of a generation of young Americans. No reader could doubt that Stampp considered slavery a baneful institution, or that he viewed its demise with satisfaction, or that he deplored the tragic legacies it left to all Americans, and especially to black people. Nor did Stampp deny that the book reflected a discernible bias, and he was more amused than discomfited that some critics labeled him a "neoabolitionist" for his views. He had no illusions about being a product of his times and environment, but he was also a meticulous scholar who let his conclusions evolve from the preponderance of evidence he found in his research. From his study of the historiography of the subject, he believed that any history of slavery had to make generalizations that were significantly unproved and perhaps unprovable and that derived essentially from the conscientious perceptions of the investigator. "To understand fully the perceptions of each historian on these highly subjective questions," he reflected, "one must understand the historian himself, for each of his impressionistic generalizations is a segment of a broader conceptualization that he has imposed on fragmentary evidence."

In the years since Stampp first called for new inquiries into slavery, a prodigious outpouring of scholarship has extended, modified, qualified, and occasionally supplanted his findings. As a general account of slavery, however, *The Peculiar Institution*

remains the place from which to begin. It has been challenged, but not superseded. As early as 1959, Stanley Elkins questioned Stampp's assumptions about how slaves perceived themselves, theorizing that slaves internalized roles prescribed by their masters and thus developed personalities akin to childlike, obedient Sambos. Stampp responded that the Sambo image was simply one of many masks slaves donned for whites and noted that slave personality was a complex matter that deserved further careful investigation. Approaching the subject from a Marxist perspective, Eugene D. Genovese rejected Stampp's economics in favor of Phillips's and set forth in several important studies a view of slavery as an almost perfect model of preindustrial paternalism. Over the years a running debate between Stampp and Genovese produced intellectual sparks and likely attracted a number of bright young historians to the study of slavery, but it could not reconcile differences that had ideological roots.

Doubtless the most serious—and dubious—challenge came in 1974 from Robert M. Fogel and Stanley L. Engerman, two Cliometricians who not only faulted Stampp's scholarship and rejected his conclusions but also went on to claim "scientific" infallibility for their own statistical study of slavery. That conceit alone was enough to insure a vigorous reponse from Stampp. While gladly accepting the adjunct evidence provided by Cliometricians and other computer-oriented scholars, he contended that Fogel and Engerman had dehumanized the slaves by reducing their existence to statistical abstractions and ignoring the "untidy world of reality" in which, as human beings, they must have lived. For Stampp, nothing could be *less* definitive than history drawn from impersonal statistics alone, if only because all historical sources, like life itself, were replete with ambiguities and contradictions. His rejoinder was both a reaffirmation of the humanistic tradition in historical scholarship and an evenhanded effort to bridge the methodological gap that often isolated humanists from social scientists to the detriment of both.

By the time Stampp's next major book, *The Era of Reconstruction, 1865-1877*, appeared in 1965, the many hundreds of students at Berkeley who, over the years, had taken his course on "Reconstruction and the New Nation" were at least vaguely familiar with its contents. For as he stated in the book's preface, his views on Reconstruction had evolved gradually as he accumulated material for his classroom lectures. A brief political history of one of the most troubled periods in the American past, the book was not "original" scholarship in the conventional sense of the term. Rather, it was a synthesis of work other scholars had been doing for some years, an effort to give "general currency" to their findings. As such, it was an extraordinary success (one leading Southern scholar called it "the best book ever published on the Reconstruction period" for the general reader). It won for its author an extended review-article in *Time*, a magazine not ordinarily given to publicizing the work of professional historians. But even the popular press understood that this particular history of Reconstruction had a great deal to tell the American people about why they were just then in the throes of a civil rights revolution.

Stampp began with an unsparing review of the "tragic legend" of Reconstruction that underlay, in both North and South, the general public's perception of events following the Civil War. Grounded in the historical studies of William A. Dunning and his followers, the legend had worked its way into public consciousness in the early twentieth century through a rash of romantic novels and motion pictures and through Claude G. Bowers's immensely succesful "popular history" *The Tragic Era: The Revolution After Lincoln* (1929). In outline, the legend depicted the South as prostrate in defeat before a ruthless, vindictive conqueror, who plundered its land, corrupted its institutions, and, worst of all, turned its society upside down by handing over political control to the ignorant, half-civilized former slaves. After suffering years of brutal military occupation and corrupt rule, righteous white leaders drove the blacks and their carpetbagger/scalawag allies from power and restored honest, virtuous government to the "redeemed" Southern states. The legend posited two overriding lessons from the ordeal: first, that blacks were incapable of coexisting with whites on anything approaching equality; and second, that racial discord would never have developed in America if only the white South had been left alone to reconstruct itself.

As Stampp observed, the legend had grave consequences beyond its misrepresentation of historical facts. Equally serious, it "has exerted a powerful influence upon the political behavior of many white men, North and South." In systematically dismantling the legend, Stampp scrutinized the policies of Presidents Lincoln and Johnson, the motives and behavior of radical leaders in Washington and elsewhere, the actual operations of radical governments in the South (including, especially, the role of blacks), and the dynamics of the overthrow of Reconstruction. An eloquent summation of revisionist scholarship on Reconstruction, Stampp's

succinct account refuted the Dunning interpretation at almost every point. Reviewers commended its judicious and fair-minded handling of matters that were still, in the 1960s, highly charged with emotion and misunderstanding. There were no clear-cut heroes or villains in his history, only mortal men, who were struggling with unfamiliar problems in unprecedented circumstances, were pushed along by indeterminate combinations of idealism and self-interest, and were never entirely sure of their directions or ultimate goals. Events in the postwar years did not take place in a moral or historical vacuum, Stampp reminded his readers in his suggestion that Radical Reconstruction ought to be seen in part as "the last great crusade of nineteenth-century romantic reformers."

As with his study of slavery, there was no mistaking the perspective in which Stampp viewed the era of Reconstruction. He acknowledged frankly that the Fourteenth and Fifteenth Amendments could only have been adopted under the conditions of Radical Reconstruction but asserted too that they made even the more tragic blunders of the time "dwindle into insignificance." If it had been worth four years of war to save the Union, he observed, "it was worth a few years of radical reconstruction to give the American Negro the ultimate promise of equal civil and political rights." Considering that most textbooks and conventional accounts had, for years, relegated the Radical Republicans of the North and the scalawags and carpetbaggers of the South to a gallery of monsters, his success in bringing these crucial participants in the drama into rational focus was a major contribution to historical common sense. So was his temperate, but uncompromising, confutation of Dunningite racism. In these and other departures from conventional wisdom, Stampp was not simply adjusting his views to a changing climate of opinion. More to the point, his work incorporated source materials that had been unavailable to earlier scholars, new methodologies, and the recent findings of sociologists, psychologists, and other social scientists, all of which provided intellectual reinforcement to a changing view of the past.

The Imperiled Union: Essays on the Background of the Civil War (1980) addressed topics Stampp had probed off and on throughout his career. Several essays extended his thoughts on slavery. Others returned to the politics of the sectional conflict to put new emphasis on the pervasiveness of racism in the debates, either as an open topic or a haunting specter. In "The Concept of a Perpetual Union," which was also his presidential address before the

Organization of American Historians in 1978, Stampp pondered again the question of how a full and systematic argument to uphold the perpetuity of the Union had evolved. He concluded that for nationalists, at least, the Union had become an absolute by 1833, for by then, "the time had passed when the people of a state might resort to the remedy of secession without confronting the coercive authority of the federal government." But he also noted that the case for state sovereignty (and secession) had flourished far longer, especially in the South, and that the ambiguities of the Constitution weakened the argument for perpetual Union. In the showdown of 1861, the consensus for Union remained largely confined to the North, and the question of federalism was thereupon decided on the battlefield. In a related essay, Stampp took sharp issue with those historians who disparaged the view that slavery was a root cause of the Civil War and charged that they failed to assign sufficient importance to the fundamental forces in nineteenth-century civilization that had made slavery a profound problem and antislavery an inevitable response to it. In both essays, it was evident that Stampp considered the Civil War to have been an "irrepressible conflict."

Doubtless, the most controversial and provocative of Stampp's essays was "The Southern Road to Appomattox" (first published in 1969), in which he developed his hypothesis that many Southerners had inward doubts about the Confederate cause and welcomed its defeat, albeit unconsciously. The evidence he proffered to support this challenging notion was empirical or circumstantial in nature, and his case obviously was an unprovable one. Still, the questions he raised about the anomalous behavior of Confederate leaders and other Southerners during the war remain unanswered. At the least, the essay was further evidence of his willingness to test the validity of assumptions long held and inadequately verified.

As a teacher of American history, Stampp's achievements match those as a scholar and writer. In addition to his long service in the classroom at Berkeley, he has lectured at scores of colleges and universities in this country and abroad and has been visiting professor at Harvard and Colgate. In 1960 he was Commonwealth Lecturer at the University of London; a year later he held the Harmsworth Chair at Oxford. On several occasions he has been Fulbright Lecturer at the University of Munich. Many of the qualities of mind and temperament that account for his excellence as a scholar inform his teaching as well. Whether lecturing before hundreds of restless academic novices in a cavernous auditorium or to upper division students in his courses on the sectional conflict, or supervising a dozen separate inquiries in his seminars, his presentations uniformly reflect his deep respect for the discipline of history and his delight in teaching. Like his writings, his lectures are superbly organized, composed with a sensible balance of generalizations and facts, and delivered with understated eloquence. Perhaps the professional historians he has trained over the years are too independent themselves ever to comprise a distinctive "Stampp school" of history. Yet most of them follow his lead in investigating controversial topics with a scholarship at once disciplined and imaginative, and many consciously emulate his classroom demeanor and share his regard for high standards of performance, in themselves and others.

In his distinguished studies of the sectional conflict, Kenneth M. Stampp has pushed aside musty curtains and opened sensitive topics to fresh inquiry. He has never deluded himself into believing that his work is "definitive," for his grasp of the human factors in the historical equation makes it apparent to him that other generations will write histories conditioned by their own perspectives. Yet, his contributions are not likely soon to be set aside and forgotten. For the most enduring quality of his work may well be his capacity to comprehend the essence of a historical situation, then to express it in terms that make it all but self-evident. Nowhere is this quality more apparent than in the closing lines of his classic study of slavery: "One can feel compassion for the antebellum southern white man; one can understand the moral dilemma in which he was trapped. But one must remember that the Negro, not the white man, was the slave, and the Negro gained the most from emancipation. When freedom came—even the quasi-freedom of 'second-class citizenship'—the Negro, in literal truth, lost nothing but his chains." It is difficult to conceive of an intellectual climate in America in which that truism could be refuted.

Other:

"The Republican National Convention of 1860," in *Antislavery and Disunion, 1858-1861: Studies in the Rhetoric of Compromise and Conflict*, edited by J. Jeffery Auer (New York & Evanston: Harper & Row, 1963);

The Causes of the Civil War, edited by Stampp (Englewood Cliffs, N.J.: Prentice-Hall, 1965; revised, 1974);

"Why the Republicans Rejected Both Compromise and Secession—Comments," in *The Crisis of the Union, 1860-1861*, edited by George H. Knowles (Baton Rouge: Louisiana State University Press, 1965);

Reconstruction: An Anthology of Revisionist Writings, edited by Stampp and Leon F. Litwack (Baton Rouge: Louisiana State University Press, 1969);

"Introduction: A Humanistic Perspective," in *Reckoning With Slavery: A Critical Study in the Quantitative History of American Negro Slavery*, edited by Paul A. David and others (New York: Oxford University, 1976);

"Slavery—The Historian's Burden," in *Perspectives and Irony in American Slavery*, edited by Harry P. Owens (Oxford: University of Mississippi Press, 1976).

Frederick Jackson Turner

Odie B. Faulk
Northeastern Oklahoma University

BIRTH: Portage, Wisconsin, 14 November 1861, to Andrew Jackson and Mary Olivia Hanford Turner.

EDUCATION: A.B., 1884, M.A., 1888, University of Wisconsin; Ph.D., Johns Hopkins, 1890.

MARRIAGE: 16 November 1889 to Carolina Mae Sherwood; children: Dorothy Kinsey, Jackson Allen, and Mae Sherwood.

AWARDS AND HONORS: Pulitzer Prize for *The Significance of Sections in American History*, 1933.

DEATH: Pasadena, California, 14 March 1932.

BOOKS: *The Character and Influence of the Indian Trade in Wisconsin, A Study of the Trading Post as an Institution* (Baltimore: Johns Hopkins University Press, 1891);

Rise of the New West, 1819-1829, volume 14 of *The American Nation, A History*, edited by A. B. Hart (New York & London: Harper, 1906);

Guide to the Study and Reading of American History, by Turner, Edward Channing, and Hart (Boston & London: Ginn, 1912);

The Frontier in American History (New York: Holt, 1920);

The Significance of Sections in American History (New York: Holt, 1932);

The United States, 1830-1850: The Nation and Its Sections, edited by Avery O. Craven, Merrill H. Crissey, and Max Farrand (New York: Holt, 1935);

Frederick Jackson Turner's Legacy: Unpublished Writ-

Frederick Jackson Turner

ings in American History, edited by Wilbur R. Jacobs (San Marino: Huntington Library, 1965).

Frederick Jackson Turner is best known as the father of the "Frontier (or Turner) Thesis," but he also generated a "Sectional Thesis" which had a considerable impact on historians and historiography. In addition, although little-remembered for working in the field of diplomatic history, Turner edited a greater body of work in this area than in any other.

Freddie, as he was known as a child and as students later would laughingly call him among themselves, was born on 14 November 1861, the youngest child of Andrew Jackson Turner and Mary Olivia Hanford Turner. The ancestors of both parents were of New England Puritan stock, the Turners having arrived in Massachusetts in 1634 and the Hanfords in Connecticut in 1642. On both sides of the families, there were numerous preachers, and in the best tradition of the frontier thesis, both families gradually westered, Jack Turner meeting Mary Hanford at Portage, Wisconsin, in 1858. Two years later they married and settled down in Portage, where Jack worked as a typesetter for the *Portage Record*. Eventually he came to own the paper, and in it he chronicled the birth of his three children, Frederick Jackson, Rockwell Lafayette (Will) Turner, and Ellen Breese Turner.

Turner grew to adulthood in a time that others, in nostalgic retrospect, would characterize as ideal. School, church, hunting, fishing, swimming—all the sylvan pleasures of small-town, Midwestern life were available to him, even the Young Men's Lyceum, in which, at age fifteen, he delivered a "declamation" about the Civil War dead. From his father's personal store of 400 books and from a traveling library, Turner read widely, displaying a remarkable appetite for the classics as well as the contemporary. In school he was an excellent student, receiving special distinction when he graduated from Portage High School in 1878. In the final orations that were part of this ceremony, he won first prize and was awarded a set of Thomas B. Macaulay's *History of England* for his effort.

Years later, in recalling his boyhood and the influences this period had on his subsequent career, Turner noted that from his father he acquired a love of local history, an intimate acquaintance with local politics (his father was a totally dedicated Republican), and a lifelong passion for fishing. For the remainder of his life, Turner would neglect everything, even the most pressing publisher's deadline, to take rod and reel in hand and depart for some promising stream.

From Portage, he left in September of 1878 for nearby Madison and the University of Wisconsin, at that time numbering fewer than 500 students. His high-school training was so inadequate that he was enrolled as a subfreshman, and he spent his first year studying Greek and Latin, geometry

and trigonometry, botany, and oratory, completing the year with a 90.8 average.

His sophomore year was postponed by what was diagnosed as spinal meningitis, and he did not return until the spring term of 1881, graduating with distinction in 1884 and with an abiding interest in history. His original intent had been to pursue a career in journalism, but he had fallen under the spell of William Francis Allen, who had trained at Harvard and in Germany in the new "scientific" historical method.

In 1884, history seemed a poor choice for a profession unless one aimed at teaching in high school. Until 1881 no American university had a professorship in history, and three years later there were only fifteen professors and five assistant professors of history in the nation. For a time Turner turned to journalism to make his living, serving as a correspondent for the *Milwaukee Sentinel*, but in the spring of 1885 he was asked to fill in for Professor Allen, who was on leave of absence. This experience convinced Turner that his future lay in college teaching.

That fall, with Allen back on campus, Turner continued at the University of Wisconson and taught rhetoric and oratory along with a half-time load in a growing history department. When the university decided in 1886-1887 to begin awarding the master's degree, Fred J. Turner, as he then signed himself, was listed as a candidate. The only requirement was a thesis, and he undertook "The Character and Influence of the Fur Trade in Wisconsin." He received his master's degree in June of 1888, and subsequently his thesis was published by the State Historical Society of Wisconsin. He had taken three years to perform the task of writing a thesis not only because he first had to learn French but also because he dawdled endlessly. Fishing at nearby Lake Mendota was attractive, as were games of whist with friends and reading whatever came to hand. Gradually he came to realize that he worked only under the extreme pressures of a deadline. When at last he did begin, he could meet deadlines, and during the last year of his work on his master's degree he produced book reviews, an encyclopedia article on the history of Wisconsin, and a small pamphlet for the National Bureau of Unity Clubs, as well as completed his thesis.

The other incentive which spurred him to complete work was his engagement to Carolina Mae Sherwood of Chicago, whom he had met when her younger sister enrolled at the University of Wisconsin. In order to marry Mae Sherwood, Turner had to be able to earn a salary that would provide for them. In the fall of 1888 he enrolled at Johns Hopkins University to study for the new degree, the doctorate of philosophy in history, which he thought would get him a job as a university instructor.

In 1888 Johns Hopkins University was alive with the excitement of intellectualism for its own sake. Young faculty members, recently returned from Germany with doctorates and the so-called "scientific" method of research, were working with a corps of graduate students, all pooling their findings in seminars and classroom. Facts, statistics, and footnotes were the tools of a profession shaped by German historian Leopold von Ranke, and objectivity was their goal. Led by Herbert Baxter Adams and aided by Richard T. Ely, the department of history at Johns Hopkins was attracting a brilliant corps of graduate students: Woodrow Wilson, Charles Homer Haskins, Charles McLean Andrews, and Fred J. Turner.

The year that followed was difficult, both intellectually and financially. Turner had to pass examinations in both French and German, write long seminar papers, and rewrite his thesis into a dissertation that conformed to the "scientific" method demanded at Johns Hopkins. He returned to the University of Wisconsin in the fall of 1889 as an assistant professor of history at a salary of $1,500—and with so much of his work behind him at Johns Hopkins that the doctorate was assured at commencement exercises in 1890.

His ability to support a family attained, he and Mae married on 16 November 1889, and to them were born three children: Dorothy Kinsey Turner in 1890, Jackson Allen Turner in 1892, and Mae Sherwood Turner in 1894. Personal tragedy marred the family side of his life, however. Doting father that he was, he never fully recovered from the death of daughter Mae Sherwood in February of 1899 from diphtheria and then from the death of his son, Jackson, of a ruptured appendix in October that same year.

In his professional life, he advanced rapidly. The death of Professor Allen in December 1889 left young Turner the sole historian on the staff, and by teaching his own plus Allen's courses that year, in addition to completing his doctorate, he was able to win a coveted full professorship at Wisconsin as well as the chairmanship of the department of history, which was expanded to include Turner's friend Charles Homer Haskins as an instructor in European history. This advancement was aided in part by the assured publication, in the prestigious *Johns Hopkins University Studies in History and Political Science*, of his dissertation under the title *The Character and Influence of the Indian Trade in Wisconsin, A Study of the Trading Post as an Institution* (1891) and in part by glowing letters of recommendation from former professors and university associates.

The next several years were extremely busy ones for Turner. As with all professors, he served on numerous university committees, made endless speeches to civic and social clubs, prepared and gave lectures, graded papers, and lobbied for the expansion and upgrading of his department. With great delight he served as go-between for the University of Wisconsin and Richard T. Ely, who was lured to Wisconsin after a quarrel with Herbert Baxter Adams over control of the department of history at Johns Hopkins. In addition, because of pressing economic need, he had to teach summer and extension courses to make ends meet. Yet Turner always did more than was expected, neglecting the historical writing that would have spread his reputation and instead becoming an inspector of high schools in order to insure the improved teaching of history in the public schools. His training at Wisconsin and Johns Hopkins had instilled in him a sense of guildsmanship that saw him totally dedicated to the cause of history—of extending the excitement of history not only to his students at the university but also to students in the public schools and to a wider audience through the writing of articles for newspapers.

Turner actually believed in the value of history to an extent almost totally forgotten by his intellectual descendants. Especially did he believe in Western history, hating the snobbishness of Eastern professors and their ignorance of what he increasingly was coming to believe was the most essentially "American" part of the United States. Happily he spent long days grubbing in the dusty collections of the State Historical Society of Wisconsin, and for it he served as curator and helped design its new building, which opened in 1900. Local history, he thought, was where every practicing historian should do his best work.

At Wisconsin he also was willing to experiment to a degree largely unknown to his intellectual descendants. He became the first professor in the United States to offer a course on the American West, just as his department also would be the first to offer a course in diplomatic history. For him there was no objection to teaching something never before taught. So long as the content seemed to offer insights into the process of history, he felt it legitimate.

His teaching during these years was exciting

only to those totally dedicated to the field of history. When it came time to deliver a lecture, he reached into his files to find everything he had on whatever the topic happened to be. He then would arrive in class where he did not lecture but rather talked, pausing to search for an appropriate quote to prove whatever point he was trying to make. In short, he demonstrated to his classes the historical method at work. For anyone other than a history major, his pauses as he searched for some bit of material, which could stretch on into several minutes, were interminable. For the aspiring lawyer or engineer who happened into Turner's classes, his constant references to bibliographic materials were not opportunities for further reading but rather insurmountable tasks. His lectures were not structured so that anyone taking notes and then memorizing salient points could make a high mark. Rather he kept stressing the need for thought and research and organization—not the *what* but the *why* and the proof behind it. Needless to say, his classes, other than the basic required survey in American history, were small.

Gradually an idea began to form in his mind during these early years of drudgery: that the frontier was where democracy had been born in America and that a study of the frontier explained what made the United States different from Europe. Such an idea was not new with Turner. Michel de Crevecoeur, writing under the name J. Hector St. John, in 1782 published *Letters from an American Farmer*, in which he said that the immigrant recently arrived in the New World pushed out to the edge of the line of settlement. There he was forced to shed his European garb for the clothes of a frontiersman; there also he was forced to shed his European modes of thought and adopt those of the New World; there too he dropped his old prejudices and attitudes to form new ones. In short, the frontier transformed the immigrant from a Frenchman or German or Englishman into an American. Furthermore, Benjamin Franklin and Thomas Jefferson had talked about the West as a "safety valve" that siphoned off discontented and surplus laborers from the East and thereby held down the protest and unrest that plagued Europe. E. L. Godkin's 1865 "Aristocratic Opinions of Democracy" averred that 300 years of westering in the United States had produced a lack of appreciation for the arts and literature, a love of material things, a firm belief in democracy, and a contempt both for authority and for theory; westering, Godkin contended, had led to a respect for the practical.

Turner's studies gradually convinced him of the truth of all these ideas and led him even further. His dislike of the contempt with which professors in Eastern and Mid-Atlantic states held the West also caused him to disagree with their belief in the origin of most American institutions in the forests of Germany. In the 1890s the Teutonic Theory held full sway in most universities of the United States, an understandable phenomenon inasmuch as many professors of the time had studied in Germany and had come to idealize that nation. Thus New England villages, according to Herbert Baxter Adams, were imitations of medieval Germanic villages. Turner saw the frontier as the birthplace of American institutions, and in 1893 he was offered a forum from which to bespeak his beliefs.

That year the city of Chicago was holding the World's Columbian Exposition to mark the four hundredth anniversary of Christopher Columbus's epic voyage. There were to be not only displays of the marvels of the age and a mammoth midway but also a glittering galaxy of offerings from the world of literature and the arts, including a "World's Congress of Historians and Historical Students." Aiding in putting on this exhibition was the American Historical Association, whose secretary was Herbert Baxter Adams. In February 1893 Adams issued the invitations to speak, one of which went to his student Frederick J. Turner, who responded that he would read a paper entitled "The Significance of the Frontier in American History."

Subsequently Turner wrote to suggest that two of his own students, Orin Grant Libby and Albert Hart Sandford, be added to the list of speakers and, if room could not be found for them, that Libby be substituted for himself. Fortunately this request was ignored, and Turner arrived in Chicago for the august gathering, his paper, as usual, not completed. For the last several hours before he was to read, he stayed in his room furiously writing, the deadline of his speaking hour forcing him to complete the paper.

On 12 July his was the fourth of four papers to be read that afternoon. When at last he came to the podium he issued what Ray A. Billington later would call "a declaration of independence for American historiography." According to Turner, the frontier was *the* decisive factor in welding together an American nation and nationality distinct from other nations and nationalities as well as in producing distinctly American traits. The frontier, to Turner, was a state of mind as well as an area of sparse settlement where "savagery and civilization" came together. It was an area where the dominant traits were individualism, freedom, inquisitiveness, ingeniousness, materialism, strength, a laxness of business morals—and democracy.

On the frontier, according to Turner, most individuals were placed at a similar economic level, leading to a firm belief by these frontiersmen in equality and in political programs for the good of the common man. This belief implied governmental programs for social amelioration as well as for the encouragement of individualism, freedom of opportunity, and the acquisition of wealth. The frontier, moreover, was a "safety valve of abundant resources open to him who would take," Turner declared, meaning that the Westerner felt the natural resources of the nation should be exploited. In line with this thesis, frontiersmen wanted the public domain passed into private ownership as rapidly as possible so that it could be put to productive use.

These desires had resulted in an American nationalism that favored lenient land legislation, internal improvements at governmental expense, a protective tariff, and a strong central government, Turner contended. Yet, paradoxically, these currents also provoked a hearty dislike for authority, a belief in individual initiative, and an attraction to the free-enterprise concept. This new man, this American, became noted for getting things done. He excelled in the production of tangibles, and thus had little time for philosophizing. On the frontier, the man who painted a picture or composed a symphonic piece had no one to view it or to listen to the result, but if he cultivated his fields he had food on the table during the winter. He could see tangible results from his labor, but not from his philosophizing, Turner declared.

Yet according to the census of 1890, which Turner noted, the free land in the West was largely gone. No longer could young men seeking a new start or older men looking for a place to start over again find free or even inexpensive land on the frontier, or, as Turner phrased it, no longer would the frontier "furnish a new field of opportunity, a gate of escape from the bondage of the past." Americans would have to adjust to this fact in the future, but for historians, said Turner, a study of the succeeding wave of frontiers was the key to understanding America's past and present.

His listeners that day in Chicago, historians from across the nation, were monumentally unimpressed with Turner's speech. In summaries of what had transpired, few noted Turner's name among the speakers, and the sole Chicago newspaper that mentioned him did so on page three. The essay first was published in the *Proceedings of the State Historical Society of Wisconsin* and later in the *Annual Report of the American Historical Association*, neither of which would expose it to a wide readership.

Turner, however, did as much as possible to spread the new gospel. In lectures, which he increasingly was asked to give and which he increasingly accepted in order to profit from the fees paid, he preached the gospel of the frontier. He even undertook to spread his message through articles in newspapers and in magazines of mass circulation, such as the *Atlantic Monthly*. Sometimes in the heat of a speech, when he felt the audience responding, Turner was moved to make extravagant claims for the influence of the frontier, and later he would be ridiculed by revisionist historians of the 1930s and 1940s for these. However, in his academic writings, where he chose his words and his footnotes carefully, he never made such extravagant claims. Perhaps his best writing on the subject was for *Johnson's Universal Encyclopedia* in 1894. In this source he defined the frontier as "a belt of territory sparsely occupied by Indian traders, hunters, miners, ranchers, backwoodsmen, and adventurers of all sorts," and he claimed only that the frontier had brought about an "energetic and self-reliant spirit" among Americans who, as a result, had become a pragmatic and inventive people.

Turner's fame was spread more by his graduate students and his converts than by his writing and speaking. In the months, years, and decades that followed, a host of Turnerians spread across academic America to lecture the virtues of the frontier thesis and its author and to write learned books and articles based on the concept, until there gradually came a countermovement in the 1930s which sought to debunk everything written previously.

Thanks to the controversy generated, Frederick Jackson Turner, as he was coming to style himself, did earn a growing reputation among the top historians of his era. Increasingly he was asked to write book reviews for such major publications as the *Atlantic Monthly* and *The Nation* and to do articles for major newspapers and magazines. However, Turner proved himself rarely able to meet a deadline or to estimate how long a piece he had written would be in print. To Walter Hines Page of the *Atlantic Monthly* he confided in 1897 that writing was a painful process to be avoided if possible. And he was so honest in his book reviews that he alienated many of his friends, a situation leading him at last to swear he would never write another review.

Yet much as he disliked forcing himself to sit

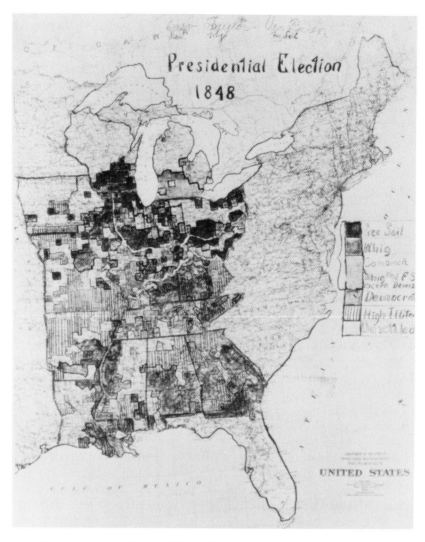

Turner's map correlating 1848 presidential election returns with illiteracy

down and write, much preferring fishing or hunting or reading or the pleasure of research as an end in itself, he found himself pursued by publishers as his reputation grew. And rarely was he able to resist the wooing of a publisher. Henry Holt, Macmillan, A. C. McClure and Houghton Mifflin publishing houses all offered contracts which he signed: for grammar-school, high-school, and college textbooks; for a volume on "The Old West"; for a biography of George Rogers Clark; and for a work on "Western State-Making." None of these works, however, reached print despite some advances paid, the promise of quite large royalties, and the embarrassment of years of letters asking when a manuscript might at last be delivered. Turner was long on promises, short on delivery. Ray A. Billington, his biographer, characterized Turner as "a

perfectionist by nature and a dawdler by inclination, unwilling to endure the sustained effort needed to produce a major volume and unwilling to place on record the imperfect account demanded by any broad subject." Most historians of a later age would imitate the master, but without generating a thesis that would perpetuate their names or without working so hard to popularize history.

Only one publisher, Harper, managed to force a volume from Turner's pen. In 1899 the American Historical Association conceived a multivolume work embodying the best of the "scientific school" of history, and Albert Bushnell Hart, chairman of the committee, persisted both in signing Turner to a contract and then in extracting a manuscript from a reluctant author. Eternally late with promised chapters, Turner eventually produced a manuscript much too long (Hart wrote that it would have to be reduced to "procrustean dimensions"), missed deadlines in the rewriting, produced a bibliography twice the length allotted for it, and then sat on galleys for interminable weeks as he tried to rewrite the entire work. Yet the labor proved worthwhile, appearing in 1906 under the title *Rise of the New West, 1819-1829*, and receiving a warm reception in the reviews.

During these same years while his reputation was growing and he was signing a multitude of unfulfilled publishing contracts, Turner also was showing himself to be adept in university politics. In 1897, he used an offer from the University of Pennsylvania as leverage at Wisconsin to get his salary raised. Then in 1900 came courtship by the University of Chicago, and he used that offer to pry from Wisconsin a separate department of history, a pay raise, and a year's sabbatical leave. This he used in 1900-1901 to take his wife on a tour of Europe, hoping both she and he could recover from the deaths of two of their three children.

There were many reasons for Turner's reluctance to write. One was his natural tendency to procrastination. Another was his love of fishing, which caused him ever to be ready to abandon academic pursuits for a lake. Yet another major factor was his love of research and his tendency to wander off on tangents that interested him but that had little relation to his area of greatest fame, the frontier. For example, the opening in 1896 of the fabulous Draper Collection at the State Historical Society of Wisconsin led Turner down the path of diplomatic history for several years.

Lyman C. Draper during his lifetime had collected more than 400 volumes of manuscript material, most dealing with the Trans-Appalachian frontier. Approached by J. Franklin Jameson, editor of the newly authorized *American Historical Review*, to submit an article for volume one, Turner reported that he would do something on "State Making in the West, 1772-1789" based on materials in the Draper Collection. In researching this article—for which he soon began begging an extension of the deadline and additional space in the quarterly—Turner gradually concluded that the story of the frontier could be told properly only after the European side was explored more fully. After completing the article, which ran not the allotted sixteen but thirty-five pages, he agreed to edit the original documents for publication by the National Historical Manuscripts Commission. These documents from the Draper Collection filled 200 pages in the *Annual Report of the American Historical*

Association for 1896. Turner's edited work was entitled *Selections from the Draper Collection in the Possession of the State Historical Society of Wisconsin, to Elucidate the Proposed French Expedition Under George Rogers Clark Against Louisiana, in the Years 1793-1794* (1897).

Research in French documents, supplied by a copyist in France, also led to a lengthy list of edited works dealing with the controversy surrounding Citizen Genêt and Nootka Sound. These works brought Turner a commission from Worthington C. Ford at the National Historical Manuscripts Commission to edit the papers of three French ministers to the United States between 1791 and 1797. Turner promised that the work would be finished within a year and would print out at 100 pages; when delivered a year late, the work *Correspondence of the French Ministers to the United States, 1791-1797* (1904) came to 1,100 pages in print. His interest in diplomatic history would continue for several years, until he began to formulate his second major thesis.

On almost all committees related to history, Turner was selected to represent the West. And as he read American history, he noted time and again how the history of the United States was one of sections pitted against each other: North against South, East against West. By the late 1890s he was so intrigued that he began a major effort through wide reading to educate himself about sectionalism in American history, even enlisting his graduate students in the effort. By 1899, when he was asked to revise his essay "The Significance of the Frontier in American History" for republication by the National Hebart Society, he stressed geography and sectionalism and compared each area to "nations of the old world." By the turn of the century, he was convinced that the United States was a federation of sections, each shaped by its geography, its pattern of immigration, and its economy, and that it was the interaction and consolidation of these sections that had made Americans a "composite" people. Each section had drawn its institutions from Europe but had modified these according to local conditions caused by the settlement of a new country; inasmuch as each part of the new country had a different geography, it followed that each section would have its differences. This thesis, in turn, led Turner to believe that historians, in order to understand sectionalism, needed to draw on scholars from other disciplines, such as geography, sociology, and literature.

After long years of study and research, he was ready to propound this thesis. The occasion he used was a session devoted to the topic at a meeting of the American Historical Association at Madison, Wisconsin, in December 1907. The result was disappointing, for his colleagues either dismissed geography as a causative factor in history or else simply yawned. He spent the remainder of his life preaching the gospel of sectionalism in understanding American history, but with no great result.

In February 1904 the Turners journeyed east as he taught one semester at Harvard for an absent faculty member, but his enrollment in a course on the American West was disappointing. This stint was followed that summer by teaching at the University of California at Berkeley, as he would again in the summer of 1906.

During the first decade of the twentieth century, Turner also was busy dabbling in university politics at Madison, leading a faction that secured and then later quarreled with Charles R. Van Hise as president. In addition, Turner sought to build a great department of history at Wisconsin filled with luminaries in each field. In this effort he was largely successful, only to find that when one of them fulfilled his early promise, he soon was lured east by greater prestige, better library facilities, and a larger salary.

And during this period he was attracting, training, and placing a long list of graduate students who would go on to win prominence for themselves and to spread word of Turner's greatness. Among his students were Carl Becker, Ulrich B. Phillips, Louise P. Kellogg, Lewis H. Haney, John L. Conger, Joseph Schafer, and William V. Pooley.

Turner during this period also fought for reforms in the offerings of the department by arguing that a major part of its responsibility was to train teachers during summer sessions and to pioneer in the offering of new courses. And leading a fight to clean up athletics, particularly football, at the university, he served as chairman of a seven-member committee, which took up endless hours of his time.

By 1910 Turner was at the height of his powers as a teacher of graduate students, as a member of the tight inner circle (called the "Nucleus Club") which ruled the American Historical Association, as the recipient of several honors, and as the father of the frontier thesis. By 1910 almost every author of American history textbooks, whether at the public-school or university level, had drafted or revised his work along the lines suggested by Turner in his frontier thesis. He was a hot academic property and was being widely courted to lure him away from Wisconsin. As offers came in, Turner continued to bargain with the university for two months off with

pay each year for research, for additional funds, for more graduate student stipends, for additional faculty members.

It was old friend and former colleague Charles Homer Haskins, now a distinguished medieval historian, who brought him to Harvard. Haskins had left Wisconsin years before for the Ivy League, and there he had risen to chairmanship of the department of history at Harvard. Learning that Turner was unhappy with the changing political climate in Wisconsin and that he was preparing to sign a contract with the University of California at Berkeley, Haskins wired to ask him to delay his decision. In October 1909, while at Harvard to accept an honorary degree and to attend the inauguration of a new president, Turner indicated his acceptance of a position at that institution. His salary was to be $5,000 annually, with the promise of a $500 raise in the near future. He arrived on the Harvard campus in September 1910 to begin full-time service there and to finish a twenty-five-page article for the *Encyclopaedia Britannica* on the United States since 1865; when at last he sent it off, it was 272 pages long and also included a bibliography that ran 1250 words more than stipulated—all for a fee of $500.

The years that followed were marked by an occasional encyclopedia article, undergraduate students more interested in their social standing and their "gentleman's C" than in scholarship, a stream of graduate students who would add luster to his name, and continuing financial struggles as he and Mae Turner tried to live within their income. Always there was the threat of bankruptcy, for Mrs. Turner had a lifelong love of good clothes, while his passions were books and fishing tackle. Never was he able to devise a sensible budget and stick with it.

As at Wisconsin, his students at Harvard were either mightily bored with him or else totally enthralled, for he was a demanding taskmaster; in his courses he required 120 pages of reading each week, tests every two weeks, a midterm and a final exam, and a term paper of twenty-five pages. His enrollments were never large.

There was joy in the marriage of the Turners' daughter, Dorothy, to John S. Main and in the birth of their grandson Jackson Turner Main, himself to become a distinguished historian. And there was a constant worry at Turner's declining health. Each summer he sought a change of climate by traveling to Maine, where he and his wife owned a summer cottage, or to Oregon or Montana or some other part of the Rocky Mountains, where he rested and readied himself for another bout of teaching each fall. There always was an invitation to lecture at

Berkeley or some other school on the West Coast, each carrying a small honorarium that helped defray expenses. Turner thus could delight in the camaraderie of the Bohemian Club, near San Francisco, or in packing into the Sierras to rough it or search for virgin trout streams. Then it was back to Boston's winters and students seeking only C's. His one academic delight was his seminar for graduate students where the excitement of historical research still caught him up in the glory of history, and with each class he shared the excitement of discovery. The students of this era were as distinguished as those produced at Wisconsin: Solon J. Buck, Edward E. Dale, James B. Hedge, Arthur P. Whitaker, Thomas P. Abernathy, Frederick Merk, Colin B. Goodykoontz, and Samuel F. Bemis.

Yet little flowed from his own pen, for there were always assignments for the American Historical Association, of which he became president in 1909 and on whose Board of Editors for the *American Historical Review* he served for twelve years. In 1914, however, he resigned from the executive committee in order, as he said, to have time to talk to young historians. That same year he became the spokesman of a group of reformers trying to wrest control of the American Historical Association from the two dozen or so professors at a few prestigious universities who had dominated it since its founding—and of which founding group Turner had been a member. However, he was not associated with the extremists in this movement, who sought to discredit all past leadership, including Turner's. Democratization of the association came, as Turner had hoped, without resorting to extremes.

In 1916-1917, Turner spent a sabbatical year researching at the Carnegie Institution, but he still loved research more than writing and little printed work thus resulted. Also while in Washington, after the outbreak of World War I, he agreed to serve on the nine-member National Board for Historical Services, a board neither totally impartial nor totally a channel for Allied propaganda.

Out of the war years came one great satisfaction to Turner, the publication of his scattered essays in one volume. Many of his essays were listed, in a bibliography compiled by the National Board for Historical Studies, as important in understanding the American character; this recommendation led to a considerable demand for these articles. Moreover, many professors, especially those teaching classes on the American West, wanted his articles available for their students. Edward N. Bristol, editor of Henry Holt and Company, which

for twenty years had been trying to get a manuscript from Turner, in 1920 submitted a contract to do a book consisting of some of his most significant essays. Turner accepted, somehow forcing himself to do little reworking of these articles, and *The Frontier in American History* appeared just four months later to almost unanimous praise, more for the author than the contents of the volume.

In the spring of 1918 Turner would expand on his thoughts about sectionalism in a series of eight lectures delivered to the Lowell Institute in Boston. In these lectures he asserted, "The frontier

Turner at the Huntington Library in San Marino, California, circa 1928

and the section lie at the foundation of what is distinctive in American history." It was in the conflict and compromise between the sections that Americanism was formed. Subsequently he refined his thoughts concerning sectionalism and delivered these first as a speech at the universities of Michigan and Chicago, then published these ideas in 1922 in *The Yale Review*. In this article he argued, "We in America are in reality a federation of sections rather than of states. State sovereignty was never influential except as a constitutional shield for the section." Yet Turner in his lectures and writings had raised more questions than he answered, and few major historians rushed forward to do the articles and books he felt were needed to prove his thesis. Sectionalism would continue to be a factor in the study of American history but not a revolutionary approach as had been his frontier thesis.

Turner understood that, in order to make his fellow historians take his new thesis seriously, he needed to write a book incorporating and synthesizing his ideas about the frontier and sectionalism, and in 1917 he had signed a contract with Holt and Company to deliver such a manuscript in just one year. Holt, which had been trying to get a manuscript from him since 1895, found this promise as empty as previous ones. Turner intended to write what he began calling "THE BOOK," but somehow he never could finish it. There were fish to be caught and endless research to be done. There were speeches to be delivered, for the fees were needed, and there were courses to teach, dissertations to be read and corrected, and students to be advised and counseled.

All his life Turner had been plagued by two major enemies, procrastination and an overpowering urge to do yet more research. As the 1920s began, a third enemy appeared and grew increasingly more menacing: ill health. Work on THE BOOK went slowly, and no sooner would a chapter and some maps be in Holt's vault than Turner would be asking to get these back to revise them in the light of new research findings.

By late 1923 it became obvious to Turner that his health was failing, and he decided that if he were ever to finish his book he would have to retire and devote all of his time to do it. Without great regret he left Harvard in June 1924 and moved back to Madison, Wisconsin, where he and Mrs. Turner built a modest home adjoining that of their daughter and her husband. After a lifetime of teaching, he had, as biographer Ray A. Billington noted, "a home worth less than $10,000, a cottage in Maine, stock in the Sullivan Machinery Company that paid $220 yearly, royalties of less than $200, and one $5000 life insurance policy."

In retirement, work on THE BOOK went slowly because of pressing financial necessity. He had to continue to accept lecturing assignments, which his fame caused to be numerous, for the fees offered. And the cold winters of Wisconsin left him miserably ill. Several months each year were spent huddled before the fire in his home suffering with a cold or other respiratory illnesses. Gradually he became depressed until his sister, Breese De Moe, offered him the money to winter in a warmer climate. Late in 1926 he and his wife went to Claremont, California, and there his health and spirits improved dramatically.

Max Farrand, an old friend from graduate school days, was director of the Huntington Library and Art Gallery in California, and he arranged for Turner to be named a senior research associate at the Huntington with an annual salary of $5,000. Happily he accepted and bought a home in Pasadena; during the next several years he advised the Huntington about its library and archival acquisitions, gave lectures, wrote endless letters on behalf of former doctoral students, advised them about their publications, and made painfully slow progress on THE BOOK despite the services of Merrill H. Crissey as a full-time secretary.

On 14 March 1932, Frederick Jackson Turner died of a clot in his heart, THE BOOK unfinished. Crissey and Avery O. Craven undertood the task of completing the work, and in 1935 Holt and Company finally was able to publish *The United States, 1830-1850: The Nation and Its Sections*. Turner's disciples were sufficiently numerous—and therefore sufficiently threatening to many other historians—that the book received some good reviews, but in total the reception would greatly have disappointed Turner. By the mid-1930s his ideas were extremely well known, not fresh, and the mood of the country had changed from what it had been in the 1890s. Because the nation was in the depth of a Depression, its mood was pessimistic. Moreover, there had been major strides in historiography, with increasing stress on social and intellectual interpretations of America's past. Thus the reviewers were not kind, some of them suggesting that Turner was out-of-date, an optimist writing about a more rustic time.

Turner's other posthumous publication was yet another gathering of his scattered essays. Some months before his death he had conceived the gathering of his articles on sectionalism into a volume similar to *The Frontier in American History*, even suggesting the appropriate eleven articles, the revisions to be made in them, and a title, *The Significance of Sections in American History*. Holt and Company agreed to publish the work, and the necessary permissions eventually were secured. Although the book received scant notice from reviewers, it was awarded the 1933 Pulitzer Prize in history.

For years after his death, Turner's major thesis, the significance of the frontier in American history, would continue to influence the way history was written and taught. During the revisionist era of the 1930s and 1940s, reputations could be made by attacking one or more points of the Turner thesis. During these years, however, there always was a cadre of believers. His students had risen to full professorships and were training their own host of graduate students, who then would be employed at institutions starting new doctoral programs and training yet more young Ph.D.'s in the doctrine according to Turner. This would result in an about-face during the 1970s as historians agreed that in large measure the Turner thesis had validity in regard to the American past.

Today few historians would quarrel with an assessment that Frederick Jackson Turner ranks as one of the five most influential American historians. He may have dawdled endlessly in trying to write books, but on at least two occasions he had original ideas which he managed to promulgate through essays and lectures, ideas that changed Americans' perception of themselves and their history.

Other:

Selections from the Draper Collection in the Possession of the State Historical Society of Wisconsin, to Elucidate the Proposed French Expedition Under George Rogers Clark Against Louisiana, in the Years 1793-1794, edited by Turner in *Annual Report of the American Historical Association for 1896* (Washington, D.C.: U.S. Government Printing Office, 1897);

Correspondence of the French Ministers to the United States, 1791-1797, edited by Turner in *Annual Report of the American Historical Association for 1903* (Washington, D.C.: U.S. Government Printing Office, 1904).

Letters:

"Dear Lady": The Letters of Frederick Jackson Turner and Alice Forbes Perkins Hooper, 1910-1932, edited by Ray A. Billington and Walter M. Whitehill (San Marino: Huntington Library, 1970).

Bibliography:

Everett E. Edwards, *The Early Writings of Frederick Jackson Turner* (Madison: University of Wisconsin Press, 1938).

Biography:

Ray A. Billington, *Frederick Jackson Turner: Historian, Scholar, Teacher* (New York & London: Oxford University Press, 1973).

References:

Carl L. Becker, "Frederick Jackson Turner," in *American Masters of Social Science*, edited by Howard W. Odum (New York: Holt, 1927), pp. 273-318;

Avery Craven, "Frederick Jackson Turner," in *The Marcus W. Jernegan Essays in American Historiography*, edited by William T. Hutchinson (Chicago: University of Chicago Press, 1937);

Wilbur R. Jacobs, ed., *The Historical World of Frederick Jackson Turner. With Selections from His Correspondence* (New Haven: Yale University Press, 1968);

Howard R. Lamar, "Frederick Jackson Turner," in *Pastmasters: Some Essays on American Historians*, edited by Marcus Cunliffe and Robin W. Winks (New York, Evanston & London: Harper & Row, 1969), pp. 74-109.

Papers:

Turner's letters, papers, and personal library were willed to the Huntington Library in San Marino, California. That collection has been subsequently added to by his daughter, students, and friends. Additional material can be found at Harvard, the State Historical Society of Wisconsin, and the University of Wisconsin.

Walter Prescott Webb
(3 April 1888-8 March 1963)

Thomas L. Connelly
University of South Carolina

SELECTED BOOKS: *The Story of Our Nation, the United States of America*, by Webb, Eugene C. Barker, and William E. Dodd (New York: Row, Peterson, 1929);

The Great Plains (Boston: Ginn, 1931);

The Texas Rangers: A Century of Frontier Defense (Boston: Houghton Mifflin, 1935); republished as *The Story of the Texas Rangers* (New York: Grosset & Dunlap, 1957);

Divided We Stand: The Crisis of a Frontierless Democracy (New York: Farrar & Rinehart, 1937; revised edition, Austin: Acorn Press, 1944);

The Great Frontier (Boston: Houghton Mifflin, 1952; London: Secker & Warburg, 1953); revised edition with introduction by Arnold J. Toynbee (Austin: University of Texas Press, 1964);

More Water for Texas: The Problem and the Plan (Austin: University of Texas Press, 1954);

An Honest Preface, and Other Essays (Boston: Houghton Mifflin, 1959);

Flat Top: A Story of Modern Ranching (El Paso: Hertzog, 1960);

History as High Adventure, edited and with an introduction by Eugene C. Barksdale (Austin: Pemberton Press, 1969).

After Walter Prescott Webb's death in 1963, Governor John Connally of Texas observed that Webb had been "the foremost interpreter of the State of Texas to the nation and to the world." Governor Connally noted that while Webb was renowned as a scholar and writer, he also lived as the embodiment of his beloved Great Plains, "tended cattle, drank coffee from a can with the Texas Rangers as he went on their manhunts, shot the rapids of Santa Elena Canyon to focus national attention on the natural wonders of Texas." After Webb had risen to prominence as a historian, interviewers would question him as to when he had begun research on his famous book *The Great Plains* (1931). "When I was four," Webb would reply.

The answer was not without elements of truth. In the 1880s, Casner Webb had brought his wife and small daughter from the cottonlands of Monroe County, Mississippi, into the Piney Woods locale of east Texas. Here Walter Prescott Webb was born

on 3 April 1888, the only one of four brothers to survive childhood. Young Webb and his family lived in the Piney Woods region—almost an extension of the Delta cotton belt—until the lad was nearly five years old. Then Casner Webb moved his family to Stephens County, Texas. Here was engendered Walter Webb's love for the culture of the Great Plains. The county lay within the western Cross Timbers on the very edge of the plains of Texas. The frontier by then was more memory than reality. The Plains Indians had been subdued, rail lines stretched across the Cross Timbers, and communities of Webb's boyhood, such as Cisco and Ranger, possessed schools, churches, tax systems, and other trappings of civilization.

Still, in two respects, the beauty and harshness of the Texas plains remained to stir Walter Webb's ever-growing imagination. There was a rich oral tradition passed along by elderly men who still carried revolvers as, if nothing more, status symbols. There was also the reality of the physical geography of the semiarid region. Expanses of open range remained. Pride in horsemanship was traditional. Fierce arctic storms called "Northers" blew in from the north, while sometimes cotton acreage was demolished by fiery gusts of warm, dry air which appeared from the south. There was a leathery nature to the life and the land, one which Walter Webb later displayed in his rugged, blunt mannerisms.

Casner Webb was more fortunate than some of his neighboring small farmers. Webb had acquired a reasonable amount of education, and his services were in demand constantly as a schoolmaster in several counties of the area. Years later, while an undergraduate at the University of Texas, Walter Prescott Webb penned an autobiographical essay titled "The Chain," which recounted his early love for books. Casner Webb appreciated the intellectual curiosity of his son, who obviously possessed special talents. Walter Webb was provided access to his father's small library and to the schoolhouse libraries nearby. In 1905 Casner Webb moved his family to nearby Ranger, Texas, in order that Walter might attend high school.

These times were critical ones for the later success of Walter Prescott Webb. Because of his father's itinerant status as a schoolmaster and the work demands on the family farm, Walter Prescott Webb's education thus far had been erratic. After a single year of high school, Webb in 1906 passed a qualifying examination which allowed him to teach the second grade of elementary school. His teaching career began that year in a one-room school at Center Point, Texas. At this time Webb actually possessed only four full years of formal education. The rigors of life on the edge of the Great Plains too often had required his labors on the farm.

In response to this situation, young Webb in 1904 already had taken a step which would influence his career decisively. He wrote a letter to the editor of an Atlanta publication entitled *The Sunny South*. In his letter, Webb expressed a desire to obtain a better education but explained that a lack of funds hampered his efforts. A New York businessman, William E. Hinds, read the youth's letter and was impressed by his determination. Thus began a relationship which lasted several years between Walter Webb and a benefactor whom he never saw. For several years Hinds sent Webb books,

magazine subscriptions, and letters of advice. He also provided financial support for Webb's college education.

In 1909, Walter Prescott Webb enrolled at the University of Texas. Although Hinds gave partial financial support by loans, Webb was required to earn part of his college support. Thus, between 1909 and his graduation from the university in 1916, he taught in rural Texas schools at Cisco, Beeville, Cuero, and San Marcos.

These were formative years for Webb's later abilities as a seminar teacher, in which he was characterized by wit, interest in his students, and an ability to stimulate intellectual curiosity. In his spare hours as a teacher in the rural Texas atmosphere, Webb acquired a deep love for the folklore of his region. In 1914, two years before his graduation from college, he wrote his first scholarly treatise, "Notes on Folk-lore of Texas," which was published the following year in the prestigious *Journal of American Folklore*.

Still, as his biographer Gregory Tobin has asserted, there was little evidence that Walter Webb at this time foresaw a career for himself as an academic historian or a specialist on the Southwestern frontier. After graduation Webb took a position as high-school teacher in Cuero, Texas, and from 1916-1918 taught in the public school system of San Antonio. During this time Webb made several forays into possible business careers as brokerage agent, salesman of toiletry articles, and bookkeeper. Finally, his future profession began to take shape when, in 1918, he was appointed an instructor in the department of history at the University of Texas.

So began a forty-year career at the university. Eventually, Webb would become a Distinguished Professor, probably the best-known academician in the state, an internationally famous author, and the trainer of dozens of scholars in Southwestern history. However, for the first decade or more at the university, Webb's career was on dubious ground. Not until 1932 would he receive a doctorate degree from the University of Texas. His first attempt to obtain the degree had ended in bitter failure. In 1922, at the age of thirty-four, Webb began graduate studies in the history department at the University of Chicago. Within a year he had returned to Texas, after an unhappy experience with his preliminary examinations.

Nor was Walter Webb's reputation as a writer of Southwestern history established quickly. During the decade 1920-1930, Webb did contribute articles to several scholarly and popular magazines. A 1928 contribution to the *West Texas Historical Association*

Yearbook discussed "The Land and Life of the Great Plains," while in 1922 the *Southwestern Historical Quarterly* published "The Last Treaty of the Republic of Texas." Meanwhile *Scribner's Magazine* in 1927 published his "The American Revolvers and the West," while *Holland's Magazine* printed "A Texas Buffalo Hunt." There were other periodical contributions during this era, and Webb in 1929 coauthored a textbook with William E. Dodd and Eugene C. Barker entitled *The Story of Our Nation*. Still, until 1931, almost fifteen years after his arrival at the history department of the University of Texas, Walter Prescott Webb had published nothing major of a scholarly nature.

The year 1931 marked the great turning point in Webb's fortunes with the publication of *The Great Plains*. The long years of yeoman service in the research and writing of magazine pieces came to fruition with the publication of this remarkable book, the culmination of long learning that stretched back to his youthful days on the cotton farm in the Cross Timbers and through his many hard years as a rural schoolteacher. Webb, a historian of his environment, believed strongly in the interrelationship of geography, history, economics, and regional characteristics.

The academic debate over Webb's thesis in *The Great Plains* had not ceased by the time of his death in 1963. Yet regardless of whether scholars agreed with Webb's ideas, there was little challenge to the fact that he had expounded an original thesis. His central concern in *The Great Plains* was to record what he considered a massive environmental change in the progress of westward expansion in the nineteenth century. To Webb, one could sever the cultural geography of the United States into two sections. East of the ninety-eighth meridian, Americans from the era of Jamestown to the years of the Missouri Compromise had learned to adjust to a woodland culture rich in water and wood. Ample transportation was available even in colonial days because of the dual watershed that ran west and east from the Appalachian slopes. The eastern woodland Indians, sedentary and agricultural, provided a far less difficult problem than their kinsmen on the plains.

Webb's thesis held that massive cultural and technological changes took place when the line of civilization approached the ninety-eighth meridian. Americans accustomed to a well-watered agricultural land now faced a subhumid climate where vast regions could offer less than twenty inches of rainfall yearly. The absence of forests also produced immense problems for Americans accustomed to a wealth of timber for buildings and fences.

There were other new problems of environment found west of the ninety-eighth meridian. Navigation was poor on rivers which rose on the slopes of the Rockies and meandered to the Mississippi Valley. The various tribal groups of the Great Plains Indians posed a serious obstacle to westward expansion. Unlike their kinsmen to the east, the tribes of the Great Plains were nomadic, dependent upon the buffalo. Such traits made them extremely difficult to defeat through methods of Indian warfare practiced since the seventeenth century. In addition, the various plains tribes, such as the Comanche and Cheyenne, were unusually adept in the techniques of war which involved skillful use of the bow and arrow and equally good horsemanship. In Webb's opinion, the Indian bow on the plains was more than a match for the single-shot, muzzle-loading rifle settlers carried across the Mississippi River in the first decades of the nineteenth century.

Webb chronicled other facets of what he considered to be a massive change in environment and therefore in culture. Thousands of square miles of open grassland were filled with strange, new types of animals such as the bison, antelope, and jackrabbit. There were also new patterns of weather turbulence—"Northers" that blew icy blasts from the Arctic region, "Chinooks" that brought hot, dry winds from the Gulf, and fierce blizzards.

So the line of American settlement drew back, Webb suggested, and remained for decades confused by the new problems of environment. For a time, the mainstream of westward expansion avoided the Great Plains or only traversed it to establish settlements in more desirable regions west of the Rocky Mountains. For many people the plains became until after the Civil War the "Great American Desert." Then the burgeoning technological revolution conquered the Great Plains—or at least made life possible in the region. Barbed wire solved the problem of a lack of wood for fencing. Railroads stretched for hundreds of miles along the channels of rivers unsuitable for navigation. The windmill, irrigation, and dry farming helped to diminish the problems created by lack of rainfall. Meanwhile, the fierce tribes of the Great Plains were also victims of technology. The development of the revolver reversed the weapons disadvantage suffered by frontiersmen.

After Walter Prescott Webb's death, a distinguished historian of the American West, Joe B. Frantz, wrote a poignant tribute to Webb in *The American West: Magazine of the Western History Association*. As Frantz observed, Walter Webb was an artist and thinker more than he was a conventional historian. If some criticized his *The Great Plains* for dealing in sweeping generalities, such was Webb's approach. To him, the culture he observed in the cotton farms of the Cross Timbers was the Idea, and the Idea provided a massive cultural synthesis of geography, history, sociology, and other disciplines centered upon his beloved plains environment.

There is no small irony in the fact that only a month before Webb's death, Professor Fred Shannon also died. In a historiographical vein, the situation resembled the almost simultaneous deaths of Thomas Jefferson and John Adams. Shannon, longtime professor at the University of Illinois, was a leading historian of American agriculture and was respected as well for his frank, scholarly appraisals of the work of other writers. Fred Shannon emerged as the leading critic of Webb's thesis of the Great Plains. In 1938, the Social Science Research Council inaugurated a policy of providing a scholarly appraisal of important writings in the humanities. Webb's study was among a half dozen chosen by the Council for Scholarly Review by a specialist. Fred Shannon was selected to examine *The Great Plains*.

Shannon's famous appraisal of Webb's study is well known in academic circles. It appeared in book form in 1940 as *Critiques of Research in the Social Sciences: III; An Appraisal of Walter Prescott Webb's The Great Plains: A Study in Institutions and Environment*. The lengthy, detailed critique assailed Webb chiefly on two fronts. Shannon believed that Webb had oversimplified the basic division of the American environment into two parts; indeed, Shannon observed, varieties of geographical difference were not new to Americans when they approached the ninety-eighth meridian. More important, Shannon drove home the argument that the concept of technological change wrought by a new environment was certainly nothing new. Vast changes were demanded, for example, as the frontier line crossed the Appalachian Mountain system in the eighteenth century.

For years historians would debate the fine points of Webb's original thesis. Many academics failed to appreciate the attempts at synthesis one finds in Webb's writings. In one important analysis of Webb's scholarly approach, Professor Joe Frantz quoted a comment by Southwestern writer J. Frank Dobie that Walter Webb never let facts stand in the way of truth.

This embracing of large truths rather than of discrete facts was the approach Webb took in most of his major work. Perhaps his view of the writing of history was best described in an editorial he wrote for a magazine entitled *Junior Historian*. Webb, always mindful of the value of inspiring young minds to develop historical imagination, had founded an organization known as the Junior Historians. In the group's magazine, he penned a brief essay entitled "The Function of History." Webb's view was that history's purpose was to make understandable the forces which have shaped the destiny of modern man. To the observer, Webb wrote, the same rules applied whether the topic discussed was global, national, state, or local history. Regardless of the locale or the limitations of the subject, history remained an artistic exercise whereby the researcher attempted to document how man acquired the "baggage" called civilization.

Most of Webb's major writings, such as *The Great Plains*, *Divided We Stand*, and *The Great Frontier* attempted to incorporate an interdisciplinary approach. The attempt to provide synthesis was present also in Webb's second book, *The Texas Rangers: A Century of Frontier Defense* (1935). Webb had begun research on this project not long after his appointment at the University of Texas. In fact, his study of the institutional background of the Texas Rangers was more than a conventional treatment of a rather limited topic. He again combined geography, history, politics, and other subjects in discussing the Rangers.

The same approach characterized Webb's third major book, *Divided We Stand: The Crisis of a Frontierless Democracy* (1937). Although he had little interest in the writing of Southern history, he came from east Texas, which in many respects extended the socioeconomic structure present in the family's Mississippi heritage. Thus, like other Southern authors of his generation, Webb shared that last memory of the Confederate generation. In an essay entitled "Walter Prescott Webb and the South," Frantz noted that despite his Southwestern orientation, Webb savored the tales of his father's Confederate boyhood in Mississippi, particularly those stories related to the Northern invasion, which became the central focus of Webb's third important book.

In many respects, *Divided We Stand* fit squarely within the regional literature engendered by the groundswell of the Southern Renaissance and might be compared to the manifesto of the Vanderbilt Agrarians, *I'll Take My Stand: The South and the Agrarian Tradition by Twelve Southerners* (1930). Actually, however, Webb's book was a more militant assertion of regionalism than was the volume by the twelve Southerners such as Robert Penn Warren, Donald Davidson and Frank L. Owsley. The literary focus of *I'll Take My Stand* asserted the importance of Southern values in an era where local traits were disappearing beneath a tide of national consensus. Webb's book was a far more strenuous assault upon the tide of nationalism. The writer divided the nation into three geoeconomic regions: the North, the West, and the South, which included Texas. Webb, in an approach which smacked of the regional divisions of Frederick Jackson Turner, maintained that the industrial and financial power of the North had reduced the other regions to the status of mere colonial appendages.

The book's subtitle, *The Crisis of a Frontierless Democracy*, perhaps indicated the course of Webb's thinking in his mature years as a historian. His last great effort, *The Great Frontier* (1952) was the climax of over thirty years of research and thought into the combined forces of history, geography, and economics that affected his region. In this work, as in *The Great Plains*, Webb demonstrated again that he was as much an artist as a historian, one who preferred the broad sweeping canvas of human events to the narrow confines of historical facts. Webb's thesis was that the entire cultural fabric of North America had been shaped by a 400-year boom. In the seventeenth century, the forces which eventually produced a dynamic capitalism had been stirred to action by the discovery of the New World. The barren treasurehouses of Europe, the excess of population in England and on the mainland, and the strictures of sparse land supporting a heavy population were affected profoundly by the discovery of abundant wealth in the Americas, coupled with the realities of endless acres of soil and a relatively nonexistent population. Here, Webb argued, was the mainstay of modern capitalistic enterprise—a commingling of great wealth, ample land, and a population small enough to function within the mode of a capitalistic enterprise. Always the thinker, Webb questioned here and later, what was to happen to the economic and social world that had been created by the Great Frontier when the frontier environment disappeared.

Webb, of course, did not live to provide the answer. His death in 1963 removed a controversial, individualistic thinker from the ranks of American historians. In the course of his long career, Webb was a prolific writer of textbooks and of academic and popular articles on both historical and current subjects. His productivity was stirred by a desire to transfer his passion for the American cultural landscape to others. His bibliography in *Texas Libraries* exceeds five pages; another listing of Webb writings occupies fourteen typescript pages.

Webb was no less active in professional historical activities. He served as editor of the *Southwestern Historical Quarterly* and labored many years as a director of the Texas State Historical Association. In 1954 he served as president of the Mississippi Valley Historical Association. Four years later, Webb became president of the nations's most prestigious historical group, the American Historical Association.

Webb's selection as president of the American Historical Association no doubt brought him immense satisfaction, if not a sense of vindication. He had been the poor Texas farm boy who failed in his efforts to obtain an advanced degree from the University of Chicago. For well over a decade Webb had labored in near obscurity until the publication of *The Great Plains*. Too, his presidency may have invoked feelings of regional vindication. Webb said as much in his presidential address, entitled "History as High Adventure." He noted that he was the only person ever elected as president of the American Historical Association who was teaching in a Southern institution. As well, he reminded the group that he was the only president elected while a teacher in an institution west of the Mississippi River. The title of Webb's speech serves to underscore another of his lasting contributions. Regarding history as "high adventure," Webb brought his own excitement about his subject into the classroom where he thus enlivened the imaginations of his students just as he continued to engage his nonstudent readers.

Other:

The Handbook of Texas, edited by Webb (Austin: Texas State Historical Association, 1952);

Washington Wife: From the Journal of Ellen Maury Slayden, edited by Webb (New York: Harper & Row, 1963).

Periodical Publications:

"The Last Treaty of the Republic of Texas," *Southwestern Historical Quarterly*, 25 (January 1922): 151-173;

"The American Revolvers and the West," *Scribner's Magazine*, 81 (February 1927): 171-178;

"The Land and Life of the Great Plains," *West Texas Historical Association Yearbook*, 4 (June 1928): 58-85;

"The Great Plains Block the Expansion of the South," *Panhandle-Plains Historical Review*, 2 (1929): 3-21;

"Some Vagaries of the Search for Water in the Great Plains," *Panhandle-Plains Historical Re-*

view, 3 (1930): 28-37;

"How the Republican Party Lost Its Future," *Southwest Review*, 34 (Autumn 1949): 392-437;

"Ended: Four Hundred Year Boom," *Harper's Magazine*, 203 (October 1951): 25-33;

"The Historical Seminar: Its Outer Shell and Its Spirit," *Mississippi Valley Historical Review*, 42 (June 1955): 3-23;

"The American West: Perpetual Mirage," *Harper's Magazine*, 214 (May 1957): 25-31;

"History as High Adventure," *American Historical Review*, 64 (January 1959): 278-281;

"Geographical-Historical Concepts in American History," *Annals of the Association of American Geographers*, 50 (June 1960): 85-93;

"The Search for William E. Hinds," *Harper's Magazine*, 223 (July 1961): 62-69.

Bibliography:

"Walter Prescott Webb, 1888-1963, a Bibliography," in *Essays on the American Civil War*, edited by William F. Holmes and Harold M. Hollingsworth (Austin: University of Texas Press, 1968), pp. 88-107.

References:

Joe B. Frantz and others, *Essays on Walter Prescott Webb* (Austin: University of Texas Press, 1976);

Frantz, "Walter Prescott Webb," *American West*, 1 (Winter 1964): 40-43;

Necah Stewart Furman, *Walter Prescott Webb: His Life and Impact* (Albuquerque: University of New Mexico Press, 1976);

Rupert N. Richardson, "Walter Prescott Webb: A Tribute," *Southwestern Historical Quarterly*, 67 (July 1963): 86-88;

Fred A. Shannon, *An Appraisal of Walter Prescott Webb's "The Great Plains"* (New York: Social Science Research Council, 1940);

Gregory M. Tobin, *The Making of a History: Walter Prescott Webb and the Great Plains* (Austin: University of Texas Press, 1976).

Papers:

Significant collections of Webb materials can be found at the Texas Archives, University of Texas at Austin; the Texas State Library, Austin; and at the University of Texas at Arlington.

Bell Irvin Wiley

(5 January 1906-4 April 1980)

John Barnwell
Vanderbilt University

SELECTED BOOKS: *Southern Negroes, 1861-1865* (New Haven: Yale University Press, 1938; London: Oxford University Press, 1938);

The Life of Johnny Reb, the Common Soldier of the Confederacy (Indianapolis & New York: Bobbs-Merrill, 1943);

The Plain People of the Confederacy (Baton Rouge: Louisiana State University Press, 1943);

The Life of Billy Yank, the Common Soldier of the Union (Indianapolis: Bobbs-Merrill, 1952);

The Road to Appomattox (Memphis: Memphis State College Press, 1956);

They Who Fought Here, text by Wiley, illustrations selected by Hirst D. Milhollen (New York: Macmillan, 1959);

Embattled Confederates, an Illustrated History of Southerners at War, text by Wiley, illustrations compiled by Milhollen (New York: Harper & Row, 1964);

Lincoln and Lee (Oxford: Clarendon Press, 1966);

Civil War Books, a Critical Bibliography, 2 volumes, by Wiley, Allan Nevins, and James I. Robertson, Jr. (Baton Rouge: Louisiana State University Press, 1967, 1969);

Confederate Women (Westport, Conn. & London: Greenwood Press, 1975).

Bell Wiley, one of the most prolific scholars of his generation, pioneered the social history of American soldiers. More broadly, he addressed himself to the "plain people—men and women, white and black—caught up in the maelstrom of civil war."

Born in the west Tennessee town of Halls, Bell

Irvin Wiley was the sixth child of Ewing Baxter and Anne Bass Wiley. The elder Wiley was a "minister-teacher-farmer"; his wife was also a teacher. During the summers the Wiley siblings stayed by turns with their maternal grandmother, Fredonia Abernathy Bass, widow of a Confederate veteran. In later years Wiley remembered her as a "splendid Christian woman" who "loved God and most of his children—Yankees excepted." He remembered, too, her tales of an invaded South, the ebb and flow of battle across Tennessee, and the deprivations visited on civilians by Union and Confederate troops.

The family often invited George Washington Bunker and Will Martin, both Civil War veterans, to Sunday dinner. Young Wiley would listen for hours as Bunker, a Northerner, and Martin, a Southerner, reminisced about their experiences. "Everything would go along amicably," the historian recalled, "until and unless the conversation happened to drift to the question of the comparative fighting abilities of the soldiers of the two armies. Then . . . my father would have to invoke his ministerial tact to restore harmonious relations." Thus when asked once by an interviewer why he had specialized in Civil War history, Wiley replied, "I grew up with the Civil War."

His family lived next door to the community church, and he was reared in an abstemious environment. Although he eventually became an Episcopalian, in his youth Wiley was profoundly influenced by fundamentalist Methodist Christianity. Colleagues frequently noted his religiousness. And a friend of forty years' standing saw "ever present" in Wiley a "streak of the proselytizing evangelical, extremely sensitive to wrongs, indignities and injustice." Like four of his older brothers and sisters, he enrolled in Asbury College, a Kentucky school with a strong Wesleyan tradition, and took his bachelor's degree there in 1928.

Wiley had intended to teach in public schools, but upon graduation he was offered a part-time position with the debating program at Asbury. He accepted the job and soon became assistant professor of history as well as the debating coach. After four decades Wiley still retained great fondness and respect for his own debate instructor at Asbury, Zachary T. Johnson, "because not only was he a very inspiring teacher, but also he took a great personal interest in his students. I am indebted to him," Wiley allowed, "more than to any other person, save my mother and father, for the things that have happened to me in my career." While teaching at Asbury, Wiley began graduate studies at the Uni-

Bell Irvin Wiley

versity of Kentucky. In 1931 he received his master's degree and turned northward to Yale for a doctorate.

Wiley's friends in New Haven remembered him as tall and "rangy, with a lot of dark hair," engaging manners, and a strong Southern accent. Extremely hardworking and diligent, he could rarely be tempted to forego work in favor of a party. A few of his Southern classmates, feeling rather defensive in a New England stronghold, took occasionally to wearing Confederate uniforms and giving Rebel yells. Although friendly with his fellow Southerners, Wiley did not participate in these displays.

At Yale he came under the tutelage of U. B. Phillips, who directed his dissertation. Wiley shared something of his mentor's fascination with black culture, and his later tendency to salt lectures with songs and stories drawn from folk life apparently owed much to Phillips's classroom technique. Wiley gratefully acknowledged his professor's "splendid example in thoroughness of research, and in writing readable prose." And if he never equaled Phillips's literary grace, he nevertheless became a careful and accomplished stylist.

Although their racial assumptions differed immensely, Phillips consistently encouraged Wiley as he pursued the history of blacks in the South during the Civil War. He completed his study and received his Ph.D. in 1933. With some changes and additions, his dissertation was shortly published under the title *Southern Negroes, 1861-1865* (1938). The second half of the book, dealing with federal supervision of blacks in the occupied South, lapsed at times into a catalog of minutiae. Wiley conceded that he had no flair for administrative history and considered it dull and difficult to write. The great strengths of his first book were meticulous primary research and evenhanded presentation of his findings—characteristics which also would mark Wiley's subsequent work.

When *Southern Negroes* was reprinted in the mid-1960s, C. Vann Woodward observed that it was still the best general treatment of the subject. The book unsparingly demolished the comfortable and diametrically opposing myths cherished by descendants of slaveholders and liberators. Wiley noted that planters, refugeeing from advancing federal troops, selected valuable slaves "for removal and left the old and decrepit ones behind for the 'Yankees.' " Not only the Southern legend of the eternally generous and kindly planter but also the caricature of the ever loyal and contented slave fell before Wiley's scrutiny. Self-serving myths that flourished in the North fared no better. The writer documented frequent exploitation of black laborers on plantations leased by the federal government to Northern operators. He also detailed shabby treatment of blacks in Union camps and the extent to which the Union victimized black soldiers in regard to pay, promotion, food, medical care, assignment, and duty. "The outbreak of the war and the coming of the 'Yankees' fired the hope and enthusiasm of the blacks throughout the South," he concluded. But the war years brought a train of unhappy experience, and "it must have been apparent to Southern Negroes when the triumph of the North in 1865 assured the final end of slavery that the fight for real freedom had just begun."

In 1934, with his newly acquired Ph.D., Wiley became professor of history and head of the department at Hattiesburg State Teachers College, soon to be Mississippi Southern College and later the University of Southern Mississippi. During the summers of 1935-1939, he taught at Peabody College. In 1937, breakfasting as usual in a Nashville drugstore, he met Mary Frances Harrison, a native

of Savannah, Tennessee, and a student at Peabody. The following spring she graduated Phi Beta Kappa, but "much of her senior year in college was occupied in . . . courtship with the young professor she had met in the drugstore." In December 1937 they were married. The couple had two sons, George Bell, born in November 1946, and John Francis, born in December 1954. Mary Frances was wife, mother, and partner in her husband's work. In prefacing *The Life of Johnny Reb*, Wiley wrote: "my wife contributed so vitally to the research and writing as to deserve a co-author's rating, and it is only her firm refusal that prevents this recognition."

In the summer of 1938, Wiley accepted a professorship at the University of Mississippi, and the family moved to Oxford. One of their neighbors was William Faulkner, who took a liking to the university's new professor "because young Bell didn't constantly bring up the great novelist's work." The two spent time together fishing, but if the novelist's creative insights influenced the historian's interpretations of the South and Southerners, Wiley left that influence unrecorded. At the University of Mississippi he began research for *The Life of Johnny Reb, the Common Soldier of the Confederacy* (1943), a book which would establish his reputation as a leading historian of the Civil War.

After Appomattox a veteran of the Army of Northern Virginia ruefully observed that historians "would hardly stop to tell how the hungry private fried his bacon, baked his biscuit, smoked his pipe." Until *Johnny Reb* appeared, that lament was accurate. The voluminous historical literature on the war had rehearsed campaigns and battles, bolstered or undermined the reputations of generals, and largely ignored the man in the "ranks, who after all," Wiley noted, "was the army." The enforced separations and the extraordinary circumstances produced by the Civil War prompted thousands of Southerners who seldom wrote (and who in many cases were barely literate) to record a wealth of detail about their lives. Mining letters and diaries in depositories and private hands throughout the South, Wiley made visible the lives of ordinary Confederate soldiers.

The single chapter of *Johnny Reb* devoted exclusively to the horror and exhilaration of battle is especially notable for frequent and effective use of the historical present. But the book is informed by the realization that "Soldiering can be a very dull job. . . . comparatively little time was occupied in actual fighting." Wiley examined and described a wide range of Johnny Reb's experiences in war: the mundane and the spiritual, the macabre and the humorous, the ridiculous and—very rarely—the sublime. The common soldier's hardships and afflictions were faithfully chronicled, from food so bad that "buzzards would not eat it at any season of the year" to makeshift uniforms that hung in tatters, from diarrhea and dysentery to syphilis and gonorrhea. The portrait of Johnny Reb was "not always flattering but ever solid and human." Wiley, a contemporary critic observed quite accurately, "has dared to write this straightforward book from a stronghold of the Confederacy, which is within itself a matter of historical significance."

Wiley always quoted extensively from his source materials, and *Johnny Reb*, especially, illustrated this characteristic. Wiley rated it the book he most enjoyed writing, and his appreciation for the rich, irreverent, and earthy humor of Confederate soldiers was apparent. Rollicking as this humor was, though, it never led him to romanticize the war. He hinted briefly at his revisionist belief that the fratricidal "struggle of the sixties was . . . in many respects a crazy and a needless war," but he did not exaggerate or sentimentalize episodes of fraternization between Union and Confederate troops: "Hatred and fighting far outweighed friendliness and intermingling." As a warrior Johnny Reb had a "streak of individuality and of irresponsibility that made him a trial to officers during periods of inactivity. But on the battlefield he rose to supreme heights of soldierhood. He was not immune to panic, nor even to cowardice, but few if any soldiers have had more than he of *élan* . . . and of the sheer courage which it takes to stand in the face of withering fire."

In 1943, the year that *Johnny Reb* appeared, Wiley gave the annual Walter Lynwood Fleming lectures at Louisiana State University. These were published as *The Plain People of the Confederacy* (1943). Two of his essays, "The Common Soldiers" and "The Colored Folk," drew heavily on *Johnny Reb* and *Southern Negroes*. The third was devoted to Confederate civilians, and in "The Folk at Home" he sounded a rare theme of class conflict. Beginning with the slightly touchy assertion that the "great majority" of the Confederacy's "humble white folk . . . compared favorably with the planter class in self-respect, in integrity, and in the other attributes of character and citizenship," Wiley contended that the morale of these plain people was destroyed less by extreme hardships than by the "conviction that they were being discriminated against by the privileged classes." He scored the Confederate government for failing to exempt from conscription nonslaveholding males "upon

whose labor the livelihood of wives and small children was vitally dependent" and for failing to take effective action against speculators and profiteers. Thus, he concluded, was the "doom of the Confederacy . . . sealed by the widespread defection of her humblest subjects."

In March 1943 Wiley was commissioned as first lieutenant and immediately became a staff historian for the United States Second Army. In August he was transferred from Memphis to Washington, where he served as assistant historical officer at the headquarters of Army Ground Forces. There he worked with Kent R. Greenfield and R. R. Palmer on *The Organization of Ground Combat Troops* (1947) and with Palmer and W. R. Keast on *The Procurement and Training of Ground Combat Troops* (1948). "I recall," he said in 1973, "that one of the monographs I wrote during World War II was 'The Activation and Training of Non-Divisional Units by Army Ground Forces.' That is so dull that I cannot endure looking back over it today." Still, he must have enjoyed some aspects of military life, for he received the Legion of Merit in 1945, and he left the army as a lieutenant colonel in August 1946. He remained in the reserves, was promoted to colonel in 1961, and retired in 1966.

In the fall of 1946 Wiley left Washington to take up his new duties as professor and head of the history department at Louisiana State University. Almost immediately he plunged into his next project: *The Life of Billy Yank, the Common Soldier of the Union* (1952). Securing a twelve-month leave from teaching, he pursued documents from Minnesota to Maine while traveling well over 20,000 miles in the course of his research. He based *The Life of Billy Yank*—like *The Life of Johnny Reb*— largely on the words of the soldiers themselves and consulted, he said, "some thirty thousand of their letters and more than a thousand of their diaries" in preparation for the companion volumes. Wiley undertook his study of the Union's ordinary soldiers "to get acquainted with the foes of *Johnny Reb*," and he feared initially that *Billy Yank* might elicit little sympathy or fairness from one "nurtured in the Confederate tradition." But as "I came to know the Northern soldier," he wrote, "I came to respect him, and as the acquaintance ripened I developed a genuine affection for him."

Wiley's focus in *Billy Yank*, as in *Johnny Reb*, was "social rather than military." His purpose was "to write a social history of men in arms," and he succeeded admirably. Many of the topics he examined in *Johnny Reb* and *Billy Yank* were necessarily the same: the soldiers' food and clothing, their reactions to discipline and army routine, their high jinks and diversions, and their appalling death rates from a variety of diseases. Once again Wiley quoted freely from his sources, so freely, remarked one scholarly reviewer, as to "add to the sale of the book by getting it banned" in Boston. Although the historian devoted relatively little space to battles, his chapter entitled "The Supreme Test" contained some of his best prose. With a deft and certain touch, he evoked the "awful, impenetrable, lonely silence" before battle, the fear and exhilaration of combat, and, in its aftermath, the sight of dead "rebels . . . laying over the field bloated up as big as a horse and as black as a negro."

Despite similarities between *Johnny Reb* and *Billy Yank*, the second book had a distinctive tone. Comparisons between the characteristics of soldiers in the Civil War and World War II—rare in *Johnny Reb*—were quite noticeable in *Billy Yank*. Influenced perhaps by the combination of his subject and his recent army experience, the author's nationalism reverberated from the pages of *Billy Yank* more strongly than from his previous books. Northern discipline was superior to the Southern variety. "Otherwise," Wiley observed, "the North would not have won the war. And despite the fact that a few Southerners have not yet 'surrendered,' the North *did* win." Historian Fred A. Shannon voiced the consensus of his colleagues when he wrote that "above everything else, Wiley is eminently fair in his treatment of the Union soldier."

Bruce Catton, reviewing *Billy Yank* while his own trilogy on the Army of the Potomac was in progress, wrote that he was "filled with admiration" for Wiley's book and wished "he had written it himself." Wiley must have relished that praise because he thought highly of Catton's work. But the journalist-cum-historian had a "feeling that there was somehow a little more zest and gusto in *Johnny Reb*." Did the rebel soldier, "perhaps, *ab initio*, gain Mr. Wiley's affection just a little more than Billy Yank did?," Catton asked.

Certainly Catton's Union soldiers differed from Wiley's, especially in motivation. Unlike Catton, Wiley found most volunteers in the North—and in the South for that matter—largely unconcerned with ideology. In Catton's portrayal Union soldiers slowly but firmly embraced the role of liberators; they became champions of oppressed humanity. Indeed, the righteousness of Catton's troopers seemed to increase as the civil rights struggle intensified during the 1950s and 1960s. Among the Union rank and file, Wiley, by contrast, found love of the Union to be continuously and vastly

more important than desire to end slavery or befriend blacks. "One who reads letters and diaries of Union soldiers encounters an enormous amount of antipathy toward Negroes." And Wiley concluded that "initial prejudices sometimes were softened by army experience but usually the reverse was true."

Righteousness, in Wiley's study of Civil War soldiers, was less a matter of social reform than of individual piety. His Methodist upbringing was apparent in "Besetting Sins" and "Evil and Goodness," chapters in which he recounted the frailties of Johnny Reb and Billy Yank. The soldiers strayed widely and often from the code of behavior demanded by the evangelical Protestant tradition in which, Wiley believed, most of them were nurtured. Profanity, gambling, drinking, stealing, obscenity, and "association with lewd women" were all too common in both armies, he concluded sadly. "Countless Yanks serving in widely scattered commands testified to the prevalency of evil and the degenerating influences of army life"—a judgment that held for Rebs as well.

Wiley's presidential address to the Southern Historical Association in 1955 celebrated his long association with the "plain Americans of the Civil War period—the Johnny Rebs and Billy Yanks who carried the muskets and their folk at home who labored in fields and factories and ran the households." While conceding the "shortcomings of the plain folk both individually and collectively," he chose on that occasion "to point up and dwell on their virtues." He admired their spontaneous humor and their sentimental, melancholy tunes that made sorrow more bearable by recognizing it as an inescapable part of life. In reading thousands of Civil War letters, he had found more than one gentle soldier "whose soul was attuned to beauty." He noted the devotion of "plain people of Civil War times" to home and family and observed that it was most often "pride in self and family [that] kept soldiers at their posts." Wiley praised, lastly, the courage of the soldiers in blue and gray—courage nourished by an acute sense of duty to "their associates in arms," courage that enabled them to face incredible casualty rates. "At Balaklava the Light Brigade, whose charge was immortalized by Tennyson, suffered a loss in killed and wounded of 36.7 per cent. But at Gettysburg the First Minnesota Regiment sustained a loss of 85.5 per cent, . . . the First Texas had 82.3 per cent of its officers and men killed or wounded at Antietam, and the total number of regiments on both sides suffering losses of more than 50 per cent in a single battle ran to well over one hundred."

Wiley joined those historians who opposed the Southern Historical Association's racial policies and, during his year as president, worked with James W. Silver and others toward desegregating the organization. "Bell Wiley," an Emory colleague confided, "was never backward in expressing his opinions and, in particular, in voicing his opposition to racial discrimination (it was 'illogical, contrary to common sense, and indefensible'). . . ." His opposition to segregation "cost him many friendships in his native South." Losing those friends was painful, but he held to his course. He freely acknowledged that Confederate soldiers fought to preserve white supremacy, but "I abhor it," he told a Georgia journalist, "when I see the symbols of the Confederacy used by racist groups. . . . I admire the heartihood and gallantry and the character and the endurance in adversity of [Confederate soldiers]. I consider it gross and utterly reprehensible for the Confederate flag to be used as an adornment in which despicable demagogues seek to wrap themselves to acquire respectability." When matters of principle or historical accuracy were at issue, Wiley always spoke his mind. And in his long career as a lecturer, he sometimes riled audiences—black as well as white—by his candor.

Wiley thought that teaching made him a better writer and that writing made him a better teacher. He found Emory University a congenial place to do both, and in 1960 he was rewarded with one of Emory's newly-created Charles H. Candler professorships. Asked why he "stayed in the South and at Emory," Wiley replied, "I like the people, I like the climate, I like the trees, the beauty of the countryside. . . . Another reason that I have stayed here is that I feel a sense of commitment to the South." He received a number of offers to go elsewhere and was particularly tempted once by a "distinguished professorship at the University of Chicago, but fortunately," he said, "Emory made an attractive counter-offer," and he therefore remained in Atlanta.

Wiley maintained an interest in his students that extended well beyond academic affairs. His graduate students characterized him as a demanding taskmaster who was relentless in criticism, especially of sloppy prose. "During my days at Emory, I supported my family by working in a local funeral home. Yet in four years," wrote one of Wiley's most successful proteges, "I never saw anything bloodier than one of my dissertation chapters after Dr. Wiley's red pencil had done its work." His consideration was also manifested in gentler ways, such as his calling an "anxious wife to announce that her hus-

band had passed his oral examinations." Grateful for Wiley's loyalty to them, his graduate students returned that feeling copiously. And in their testimony about him, a note of protectiveness mingles with admiration and pride.

Tall, slightly stooped, with his silver-grey locks worn in a "John C. Calhoun haircut," Wiley was a lecturer whose presence commanded attention. He spoke in a "rather soft" voice but had the knack of keeping even large classes quiet. He rarely strayed from carefully prepared material which paralleled the topical outlines complete with bibliographies that he distributed to students. Occasionally chuckling audibly, he loved to quote from letters and diaries, imparting to his students color and humor and the "increasing realization that history depended upon people, both the actors and the dramatists, as it were." Stories about the detailed knowledge required by Wiley's tests are legion. Students in at least one of his courses on the Old South formed a "Trivia Club to anticipate the killer question, and for several days before a test," remembers an Emory history major, "we would gather in Cox Hall to share the results of nitpicking." The award-winning item that term was the "contribution that in Alabama during the early 1800s, syphilis was attributed to eating too many green peppers."

During his tenure at Emory, Wiley's speaking and teaching engagements ranged far beyond the campus's bounds. He spoke often to Civil War Round Tables, and in the centennial year of Sherman's march to the sea, he delivered "A Southerner's View" of that campaign to the students of General Sherman Junior High School in Lancaster, Ohio. In the summers of 1964, 1965, and 1967, he taught at the Universities of Colorado, Alaska, and Hawaii. At intervals from October 1964 through July 1966, he journeyed to Great Britain, Denmark, Norway, France, Austria, Germany, Yugoslavia, and Italy as a Department of State American specialist lecturer. Under State Department auspices he later visited Korea, Australia, and New Zealand. He was also honored, for the 1965-1966 academic year, with the Harmsworth Professorship of American History at Queen's College, Oxford University.

During the 1960s awards in bunches descended on Wiley. He chaired the National Civil War Centennial Commission's executive committee and its committee on historical activities. By 1968 he had received five honorary doctorates. But in spite of this gratifying recognition, the latter part of the decade was a time of troubles for Wiley. Sometime after 1965 he began to suffer from depression. At intervals, without apparent cause, he would become so melancholy that colleagues occasionally had to take over his courses. Following these bouts of dejection, Wiley found himself suddenly and ironically under attack in 1969-1970 by a number of Emory students, especially black students. Their complaints originated in his objection to the "university's proposal to admit twenty blacks whose academic credentials were below current Emory standards." Defending his commitment to academic excellence and equal standards for all applicants, he wrote, "I do not want to be called a racist if I am unwilling to pass a student whom my better judgment tells me I should fail." Though his spirits sagged during the late 1960s, Wiley's zest for teaching eventually returned, and his scholarly productivity continued until his death.

After completing *Billy Yank*, Wiley began to delve increasingly into the affairs of the elite and the powerful. He turned occasionally to political history; he spoke and wrote more frequently about towering figures of the Civil War era—Davis, Lincoln, and Lee. In the J. P. Young lectures, delivered at Memphis State College and published as *The Road to Appomattox* (1956), Wiley considered the causes of Confederate defeat. The South's downfall, he emphasized, "was due as much, if not more, to its own failings as to the superior strength of the foe." His essay on Confederate morale was largely a reprise of themes developed in *The Plain People of the Confederacy*. However, his evaluation of Jefferson Davis's leadership and his interpretation of the Confederate nation's failures justified T. Harry Williams's opinion of the book as "one of the best analyses you can get of the Lost Cause and why it was lost."

The Confederate president had many personal virtues. Poised, proud, and scrupulously honest, Davis used his demeanor to advantage before the war. He was disciplined and logical as an orator, and he displayed considerable charm in private gatherings. All this Wiley acknowledged. Unfortunately for the Confederacy, he argued, Davis's charm was rarely used on the Confederacy's fractious legislators and generals. His stubborn pride too often diverted his energies into self-righteous, if logical defenses of his actions. He "tended to personalize opposition. Like Woodrow Wilson—and similarities between the two are both numerous and striking—he found it almost impossible to like people who disagreed with him, and antipathies born of opposing opinions often degenerated into bitter quarrels that weakened the administration and injured the Confederacy." As an administrator,

he spent an inordinate amount of time on details better left to cabinet officers or even clerks. Despite his complete devotion to the Confederacy, Davis could not articulate his vision of its cause, nor did he often make the attempt, Wiley declared. "He never developed among the masses that sense of intimacy or identity of interests that distinguishes the master politician." Davis, as a wartime leader, has recently found able defenders, most notably Frank Vandiver. But Wiley's indictment remains a trenchant one.

At the core of the Confederacy's failures, Wiley found "disharmony among its people." Squabbles between Davis and his generals, between Davis and the Confederate Congress, between the Richmond government and those in the states were endless. The "exaggerated individualism" nurtured in the Old South's gentry made them almost incapable of effective cooperation in wartime. Suffering from *"Big-man-me-ism,"* the Confederacy's leaders were distracted from the war effort by fierce internecine feuds. The Confederacy failed, too, Wiley suggested, because of the government's mistrust of ordinary citizens. "Neither Davis nor Congress ever seemed to realize the necessity of winning the hearts and minds of the people and making them full partners in the struggle by keeping them amply and promptly informed about what was going on."

The Road to Appomattox was not a pathbreaking book in terms of interpretive themes, many of which had been advanced before. Its excellence lay in thoughtful and lucid synthesis. Curiously, it was not widely reviewed in the major historical journals. But its importance and success were demonstrated when Atheneum reprinted it in 1968.

Wiley's interest in Lincoln and Lee culminated in his Harmsworth lecture by that title. Taking these men as the best of their age, he traced their "notable contrast" in background, personality, and political loyalties. Still, he opined, they had important virtues in common. "Lincoln and Lee were both generous and tolerant." They were alike in "their devotion to duty." Both men "demonstrated exceptional capacity for growth, . . . one of the most critical factors in greatness." In praising Lee's reconciliation with the Union and Lincoln's vision of its purpose, Wiley once again confessed his own nationalistic faith.

In 1974 Wiley retired from Emory, but he fulfilled his intention "to continue teaching on a year-to-year basis" at other institutions. He subsequently held visiting appointments at the University of South Carolina, Tulane University, Agnes Scott College, and the University of Kentucky. As he prepared to leave Emory, his scholarly curiosity—and his willingness to encourage the curiosity of others—remained strong. A University of North Carolina doctoral candidate, doing research on U. B. Phillips, found Wiley exceedingly helpful and still recalls "that engaging laugh and those big hands slapping one on the knees and . . . urging one on to his tasks."

During his last years at Emory, Wiley's research centered on Southern women during the Civil War. In December 1971 he gave a series of lectures at the University of Tennessee which were published four years later as *Confederate Women*. He decided to devote a chapter each to Mary Chesnut, Virginia Clay, and Varina Davis because they were members of the ruling gentry, they documented their experiences and opinions abundantly, and "they represented distinct types of Confederate womanhood: Mrs. Chesnut, the childless intellectual; Mrs. Clay, the inveterate Southern belle; and Mrs. Davis, First Lady, wife, and mother." In the last chapter of *Confederate Women*, he discussed the wartime roles of Southern women in general. Historians gave the book a mixed reception. While most reviewers conceded the thoroughness of his research, a number of specialists in women's history took Wiley to task for failing, in the words of one critic, "to place these women in their social context or to view their behavior within a pertinent conceptual framework." But some of these reviews had about them an air of petulance, as though the authors resented having an authority on the Civil War trenching on their preserve. However, Wiley's critics properly implied that a more appropriate title for his book might have been Confederate Ladies; the vignettes of Chesnut, Clay, and Davis were more impressive than the essay on "Women of the Lost Cause."

In *Confederate Women* Wiley showed perhaps the surest touch in dealing with Mary Boykin Chesnut. Unlike several recent authors, he did not seek to convert Chesnut's diary into a tract for the twentieth century by exaggerating her feminist and antislavery opinions. "She hated slavery," Wiley noted, "but she thoroughly enjoyed the conveniences and comforts that it afforded, such as breakfast in bed, anticipation and prompt filling of all her needs . . . and the satisfaction of having a faithful companion who would share all her woes, agree emphatically with whatever she said, and shower her with compliments when her ego needed replenishment." To be sure, Mary Chesnut resented the domination of Southern society by males—and the domination of wives, in many cases, by their less capable husbands.

But what "she loathed most about" the intertwined system of slavery and patriarchy "was its corrupting influence on the white men of the South." Male supremacy survived the Civil War, but the "war and Reconstruction did weaken the patriarchy. The Southern male, whose dominance both sexes accepted in antebellum times, lost caste by suffering defeat in the war he made and conducted."

In addition to the books he wrote, Wiley edited or coedited fifteen others. A number of these were republications of famous Civil War narratives, ranging from *"Co. Aytch," Maury Grays, First Tennessee Regiment, or a Side Show of the Big Show* (1953) by Sam R. Watkins to *A Southern Woman's Story: Life in Confederate Richmond* (1959) by Phoebe Yates Pember. Two of his editorial projects, *Slaves No More: Letters from Liberia, 1833-1869* (1980) and *Reminiscences of Confederate Service, 1861-1865* (1980) by Francis W. Dawson, were still in press when he died in 1980.

When he felt strongly about an issue, Wiley spoke out, but he was not by temperament a crusader. In the classroom and out, his manner was courtly. Dedicated to his profession, well aware and intensely proud of the number of books he had authored, Wiley gave himself wholeheartedly to research and writing. *Johnny Reb* and *Billy Yank* constituted his magnum opus; the books were several times reissued, both separately and together under the title *The Common Soldier in the Civil War*. "In my view," Wiley once said, "the essence of history is people, and in all of my writings I have tried to make human beings the focus or the center of my consideration."

Other:

Sam R. Watkins, *"Co. Aytch," Maury Grays, First Tennessee Regiment, or a Side Show of the Big Show*, edited by Wiley (Jackson, Tenn.: McCowat-Mercer, 1953);

W. W. Heartsill, *Fourteen Hundred and 91 Days in the Confederate Army*, edited by Wiley (Jackson, Tenn.: McCowat-Mercer, 1954);

W. A. Fletcher, *Rebel Private Front and Rear*, edited by Wiley (Austin: University of Texas Press, 1954);

The Confederate Letters of John W. Hagan, edited by Wiley (Athens: University of Georgia Press, 1954);

William N. Wood, *The Reminiscences of Big I*, edited by Wiley (Jackson, Tenn.: McCowat-Mercer, 1956);

George Dallas Musgrove, *Kentucky Cavaliers in Dixie: The Reminiscences of a Confederate Cavalryman*, edited by Wiley (Jackson, Tenn.: McCowat-Mercer, 1957);

G. Moxley Sorrel, *Recollections of a Confederate Staff Officer*, edited by Wiley (Jackson, Tenn.: McCowat-Mercer, 1958);

This Infernal War: The Confederate Letters of Sgt. Edwin H. Fay, edited by Wiley (Austin: University of Texas Press, 1958);

The Letters of Warren Akin, Confederate Congressman, edited by Wiley (Athens: University of Georgia Press, 1959);

Phoebe Yates Pember, *A Southern Woman's Story: Life in Confederate Richmond*, edited by Wiley (Jackson, Tenn.: McCowat-Mercer, 1959);

American Democracy: A Documentary Record, edited by Wiley and J. Rogers Hollingsworth (New York: Crowell, 1961);

James C. Nisbet, *Four Years on the Firing Line*, edited by Wiley (Jackson, Tenn.: McCowat-Mercer, 1963);

Slaves No More: Letters from Liberia, 1833-1869, edited by Wiley (Lexington: University of Kentucky Press, 1980);

Francis W. Dawson, *Reminiscences of Confederate Service, 1861-1865*, edited by Wiley (Baton Rouge: Louisiana State Univeristy Press, 1980).

Interview:
John Duncan, "An Interview with Bell Wiley," *Civil War Times Illustrated*, 12 (April 1973): 32-38.

Periodical Publication:
"A Time of Greatness," *Journal of Southern History*, 22 (February 1956): 1-35.

References:
John Porter Bloom, comp., "Bibliography of Bell Irvin Wiley," in *Rank and File. Civil War Essays in Honor of Bell Irvin Wiley*, edited by James I. Robertson, Jr., and Richard M. McMurry (San Rafael: Presidio Press, 1976), pp. 157-164;

Henry T. Malone, "Bell Irvin Wiley: Uncommon Soldier," in *Rank and File. Civil War Essays in Honor of Bell Irvin Wiley*;

Gene Moore, "Focus: Bell I. Wiley," *Georgia Magazine* (March 1973): 44ff.

Papers:
Wiley's papers are at Emory University.

T. Harry Williams

Joseph G. Dawson III
Texas A&M University at Galveston

BIRTH: Vinegar Hill, Illinois, 19 May 1909, to William Dwight and Emaline Louisa Collins Williams.

EDUCATION: B.Ed., Platteville State Teachers College (later Wisconsin State University at Platteville), 1931; Ph.M., 1932, Ph.D., 1937, University of Wisconsin.

MARRIAGES: 2 September 1937 to Helen M. Jenson, divorced; 26 December 1952 to Estelle Skolfield Lower; child: Mai Frances Doles.

AWARDS AND HONORS: Harry S. Truman Award for contributions, writings, and scholarship in the field of Civil War history, 1964; Pulitzer Prize for *Huey Long*, 1970; National Book Award for history and biography for *Huey Long*, 1970; Louisiana Literary Award for *Huey Long*, 1970.

DEATH: Baton Rouge, Louisiana, 6 July 1979.

BOOKS: *Lincoln and the Radicals* (Madison: University of Wisconsin Press, 1941);

Lincoln and His Generals (New York: Knopf, 1952; London: Hamilton, 1952);

P. G. T. Beauregard, Napoleon in Gray (Baton Rouge: Louisiana State University Press, 1955);

A History of the United States, by Williams, Richard N. Current, and Frank Freidel (New York: Knopf, 1959);

Americans at War (Baton Rouge: Louisiana State University Press, 1960);

Romance and Realism in Southern Politics (Athens: University of Georgia Press, 1961);

McClellan, Sherman, and Grant (New Brunswick:

T. Harry Williams, 1952

Rutgers University Press, 1962);
The Union Sundered, volume 5 of The Life History of the United States (New York: Time-Life Books, 1963);
The Union Restored, volume 6 of The Life History of the United States (New York: Time-Life Books, 1963);
Hayes of the Twenty-third: The Civil War Volunteer Officer (New York: Knopf, 1965);
Huey Long: A Biography (New York: Knopf, 1969);
The History of American Wars from 1745 to 1918 (New York: Knopf, 1981).

T. Harry Williams was a master of the written and spoken word. During his forty-year career, he wrote and edited significant books on important

subjects, concentrating on civilian and military leadership in the Civil War and culminating in an assessment of Huey Long, Louisiana's controversial governor and senator of the Great Depression era. Williams's books have had a wide audience among general readers as well as scholars because he believed that the best historians focus on and analyze the past's prominent figures, the great men who led armies, governed nations, or controlled states.

Studying the lives of commanding leaders, Williams reached conclusions that were sometimes controversial. But his conclusions and theses were well reasoned, well argued, and above all written to help the reader "see" the people of the past as they moved toward triumph or disaster. Williams carefully crafted his books, combining substance, analysis, and style. Customary research materials—correspondence, newspapers, diaries, official documents—provided the sources for his books on the Civil War, but he masterfully employed the untraditional techniques of oral history in writing *Huey Long: A Biography* (1969).

Vinegar Hill, Illinois, birthplace of Thomas Harry Williams, was as he often liked to relate, "just two axe handles and a twist of tobacco from Galena, home of Ulysses S. Grant." In 1911, before Williams was two years old, his mother died. His father, a former schoolteacher and lead miner of Welsh stock, took his only child to a small sheep farm near Hazel Green, a village of 600 persons in the lead-mining district of southwest Wisconsin. There affectionate relatives, including an uncle, "Big Harry" Williams, helped to raise the boy. As a youth, Williams read avidly and widely in history, historical fiction, the classics, and compendiums of speeches by famous orators. The father ardently followed the political fortunes of Robert LaFollette, and this midwest liberalism rubbed off on the son.

Graduating from high school in 1927, Williams thought that he would become a secondary-school teacher, and with his father's financial assistance, he matriculated at nearby Platteville State, a teacher's college that enrolled about 500 students. A professor at the college encouraged Williams to study history (reinforcing the hoary dictum that good teachers beget good teachers), and when he completed the requirements for the bachelor's degree in education, the Great Depression was nearing its nadir. Slight of build and standing about 5'8", the bespectacled neophyte schoolmaster could not find a job. Thinking that a teaching spot would open up in a few months, Williams's father encouraged him to apply for graduate study at the University of Wisconsin, recognized as the liberal seat of higher learning in the Midwest. Unsure as to exactly how to proceed once he arrived in Madison, Williams was told "to ask for Professor Carl Russel Fish." Although Williams did not know it at the time, Fish's specialty was the Civil War. In 1931 Fish directed Williams's master's thesis, a study of Benjamin F. Wade, Radical Republican from Ohio. Fish died the next year, but Williams was hooked on the Civil War.

Still unable to locate a high school teaching job, Williams resolved—again with the encouragement of his father—to continue graduate work and pursue his Ph.D. He was admitted into the university's doctoral program, and his new professor was William Best Hesseltine. Williams did not wither under Hesseltine's bantering wit and constructive but sometimes caustic criticism; on the contrary, the slender student thrived and matured intellectually in the academic atmosphere of the 8,000-student university and in his professor's formative graduate seminars. Hesseltine was only seven years older than Williams, the professor's first Ph.D. candidate at Wisconsin, and the two eventually developed into colleagues rather than having a more distant student-professor relationship. In graduate school Williams was something of a "cut-up," sometimes prone to clowning and making overemphatic actions and statements; Hesseltine himself was described as "bombastic," "dramatic," and a frequent user of hyperbole. In short, both professor and student were flamboyant. Hesseltine favored a pipe, and later Williams did too. The seminar director stressed that papers and theses must be cogent, written in well-fashioned English, and presented with flair if possible. He hammered home to his students that they must critically weigh the worth of documents and recommended that a healthy dollop of skepticism be served as a side dish with all historical evidence. Hesseltine was a great teacher, and from his seminar came several excellent historians, among them Richard N. Current and Frank Freidel. Other friends from Williams's graduate school days included semanticist S. I. Hayakawa and historian George E. Mowry.

In 1936, while finishing his dissertation, Williams for a time was a gypsy-scholar. Taking the road for the University of Wisconsin Extension Division, he drove 600 miles a week to teach American history to part-time college students. He earned his Ph.D. in 1937, taught the summer session at West Virginia University, and returned to the Extension Division for a few more months. He planned to revise his dissertation, conduct additional research, and look for a full-time college teaching position. He found one in Nebraska as instructor in history at the University of Omaha.

During his three years at Omaha, Williams completed his first book. Revising and adding to his doctoral dissertation, "The Committee on the Conduct of the War: A Study of Civil War Politics," he retitled it *Lincoln and the Radicals*. The University of Wisconsin Press printed 2,000 hardback copies of the book in 1941. (Twenty years later two paperback printings totaled more than 15,000 copies.) Paul M. Angle chose it as one of the fifty-eight best books to sit on the select *Shelf of Lincoln Books* (1946). *Lincoln and the Radicals* still commands the attention of students of the Civil War. It is written in a dramatic style and advances a controversial thesis. Williams postulated that President Abraham Lincoln—a pragmatic, cautious, and skillful politician—had a bitter and continuously stormy political relationship with the most radical members of his own Republican party, including Ben Wade, Thaddeus Stevens, Zachariah Chandler, and George Julian. As Williams described them, the radicals were marked by economic rather than social extremism, and they comprised a vindictive cabal which he likened to the Jacobins of the French Revolution. According to Williams, the radicals formed a cohesive and dedicated faction whose members doubted that Lincoln's modest abilities and cautious ways would both win the war and destroy the institution of slavery. The author highlighted the divisions within the Republican party by quoting many examples of the radicals' harsh criticisms of Lincoln and concluded that the Jacobins' strongly worded diatribes and fierce opposition to their president was an abnormal case in American politics. The principal vehicle the radicals used to badger and dominate the moderate president and criticize Union army commanders was the Committee on the Conduct of the War, a special congressional sounding board and investigative panel ruled by the Jacobins. As Williams subsequently emphasized, "the situation that created the war was not normal, the war itself was not normal, and the politics of the war could not have been normal." Years later historians of the so-called "consensus" school answered Williams's "conflict" approach to the Civil War. The consensus historians (which included David H. Donald and Hans L. Trefousse downplayed the fissures in the Republican party and portrayed Lincoln and the radicals harmoniously acting in concert on most issues. But by the time the historians of consensus responded to the conflict Williams described between Lincoln and the radicals, the book had influenced the image of the president and his party in the full-length biographies of Lincoln by Benjamin P. Thomas and James G. Randall that were published in the 1950s.

In *Lincoln and the Radicals* Williams's lively writing built a momentum that carried the reader along through the chronological story of the Civil War. In this first book he demonstrated several features characteristic of most of his later works. Usually a chapter opened with men in motion, leaders making decisions, or a speaker delivering an oration on a significant topic of the day. The opening of chapter one provides an example: "On a warm June night in 1862 an impassioned orator stood before a New York audience at Cooper Union, 'the nation's forum.' He was analyzing the radical and conservative factions in the Republican Party that were struggling for the mastery of the administration of Abraham Lincoln. Owen Lovejoy of Illinois belonged to the radical faith. Zealous, fiery, the Calvinist minister in politics, hating slavery since a mob had murdered his abolitionist brother twenty-five years before, he had prophesied in the House of Representatives long before the Civil War that the slaves would walk to emancipation as the children of Israel had journeyed to the Promised Land, 'through the *Red Sea.*'"

Similarly, a chapter usually concluded at a point when someone was about to act—to organize a caucus, to run for office, to fight a battle. Furthermore, in *Lincoln and the Radicals* Williams was already developing his use of the life-giving analytical descriptions of the major characters in his story; he summarized their lives, physical characteristics, and ideals in a few lines of pithy prose. For instance, he wrote of General John Pope: "If John Pope had possessed a coat of arms, it would have been bombast rampant upon an expansive field of incompetence." And he pictured Ulysses S. Grant as a "stumpy, bearded, taciturn, cigar-chewing, sloppily dressed general." A number of usually brief quotations from the speeches or letters of the main personalities helped to flesh out the story, to give it a flavor of the times. Williams rounded off his presentation with sparse footnotes which rarely took issue with another writer. The bibliography listed sources used, but it was not a platform for launching critical historiographical essays.

In later years Williams jokingly remarked that a young historian should never have an original or sharply pointed idea in his first book. Such a state-

ment indicated that the strong responses in the stream of articles and books written to refute all or part of his thesis in *Lincoln and the Radicals* had struck a nerve in Williams. To his critics he replied often, trading verbal and written salvos and upholding his line of argument. Williams's first book thus met with a generally favorable reception in the 1940s, and subsequently brought on a continuing and worthwhile debate among historians as to the nature of Lincoln's Republican party.

Lincoln and the Radicals was published after Williams had accepted a position as assistant professor at Louisiana State University. With the exception of special or occasional visiting professorships, he remained academically affiliated with L.S.U. for the rest of his life. Coming to Louisiana from the Midwest meant quite a change for him. From May through September the weather was virtually subtropical; the mixture of Anglo-American, Latin, Creole, and black cultures was fascinating; and the highly seasoned food could be found nowhere else in the United States. And politics, Williams found, was the avocation of nearly every adult Louisianian. He recalled later that he had "never seen a state where people follow politics so intensely." Founded in 1860 near Alexandria and later relocated to the beautiful tree-lined grounds of a former plantation near Baton Rouge, the L.S.U. campus had experienced unprecedented physical expansion and growth in enrollment between 1928 and 1935 under the aegis of Governor Huey Long. When Williams arrived in 1941, the number of registered students stood at more than 5,400, triple the registration of fourteen years before. In addition, the *Journal of Southern History*, which began publication in 1935, was headquartered on the campus.

At L.S.U., "T. Harry," as he soon became known to his students, taught introductory American history classes and later began offering a course on the Civil War. It was soon one of the most popular classes at the university. In presenting the Civil War, Williams gesticulated from and gyrated around the podium; he was always in motion, arms outstretched, then waving, hand pointing in distinctive fashion—forefinger touching thumb with the three other fingers flagging. The class centered on the actions and decisions of the great men on both sides—presidents, cabinet secretaries, generals—but also included descriptions of the Rebs and Yanks who had marched in the ranks and who figuratively marched again through Williams's vivid characterizations. He concentrated on the themes that the Civil War was the first modern war and the "central episode in our history." He presented the unorthodox view—or one that seemed unusual to many in his Southern audiences—that as a general Ulysses S. Grant had been superior to Robert E. Lee. Furthermore, Williams had come to the conclusion that Lincoln had been an unparalleled chief executive and a great war leader and had outstripped his counterpart, Jefferson Davis, in both of these regards. The professor had been studying the Civil War for fifteen years and highly respected the works of several British historians, including J. F. C. Fuller's *Grant and Lee: A Study in Personality and Generalship* (1933) and *Generalship of Ulysses S. Grant* (1929), Colin R. Ballard's *The Military Genius of Abraham Lincoln* (1926), and Sir Frederick Maurice's *Statesmen and Soldiers of the Civil War* (1926).

After having lived in Louisiana for a time, Williams naturally learned that there was no modern study of General P. G. T. Beauregard, Louisiana's highest ranking Confederate military officer. Recognizing that the Creole was an extraordinary character, Williams decided to write Beauregard's biography; he thus set out on the research trail and examined documents and papers in several archives. Part of this research he incorporated into two important essays on the Reconstruction era, essays that were published in the *Journal of Southern History*. Central to both of these articles was Williams's argument that economic factors played the most important role in deciding mens' courses of action during Reconstruction. Then he stopped to consider an unusual offer that had been extended to him, one that called for him to put the Beauregard book aside temporarily.

In 1947, upon the recommendation of Professor James G. Randall, the Alfred A. Knopf publishing firm invited Williams to write a book on Lincoln's relationship with his top-ranking generals. The historian readily agreed to write such a book, which he envisioned as "more general in nature than *Lincoln and the Radicals*" and to which he intended to bring "color and drama" as well as interpretation.

Thus Williams set to work on *Lincoln and His Generals* (1952). In a small frame house nestled on a tree-covered lot south of the university, he wrote at a folding card table. He was backed by shelves holding notecard boxes and books. As the writing progressed, he kept a thought in mind: history is familiar to historians, but they often lose sight of the fact that it is not so familiar to the "average reader," the educated layman who occasionally reads history or biography. Accordingly, Williams set his goals: to write his story in a style that would appeal to a

variety of readers, yet to offer meaty interpretations that other historians could chew on at length. In view of the difficulty of the goals, Williams succeeded remarkably well.

First of all, it was evident that Williams succeeded in authoring a well-written book about the most important leaders of the Civil War, the major event in America's history. This was just the kind of book to appeal to a mass audience, and the Book-of-the-Month Club chose *Lincoln and His Generals* as its selection for March 1952. Late in February, Williams and Lincoln shared the cover of the *Saturday Review of Literature*; inside the magazine Allan Nevins praised the book as "a full-bodied, swift paced narrative" and concluded that "the reader will gain as clear and shrewd an overall comprehension of the Northern effort from this volume as from any other in print." Another reviewer remarked that Williams "displays a craftsmanship that holds the reader in suspense even when he knows exactly how the incident ends." Again Williams provided incisive word-portraits of would-be Napoleons. For instance, he pictured General George B. McClellan as vain, headstrong, but personally captivating: "a brilliant administrator and a fine trainer of troops, he was at his best in getting an army ready to fight." By contrast, "Don Carlos Buell was a McClellan without charm or glamor." Readers could figure what kind of a field marshal Henry W. Halleck would be when he had command of a "hazardous desk." They also could expect the Army of the Potomac to march to disaster under Ambrose Burnside's leadership. Williams characterized him: "He was a good subordinate general. But he did not have the brains to command a large army. He had been right when he had twice before refused the command because he doubted his ability."

Incorporated into *Lincoln and His Generals* were the themes Williams had illustrated in his Civil War classes at L.S.U.—that the Civil War was the first modern war, that Lincoln was a great war leader, and that Grant was a better general than Lee. These themes stood out to readers of *Lincoln and His Generals*, but Williams sharpened some finer interpretive points aimed toward his fellow historians. These additional points included the assertion that Lincoln was "a great natural strategist, a better one than any of his generals"; that Lincoln supervised Grant closely even *after* he was promoted to general-in-chief; and, most challenging of all, that during the course of the Civil War the Union developed a military command system that was the precursor of the modern one instituted after the turn of the century. Altogether, Professor Williams had written a lively chronological history of the Civil War and had made interpretations sure to spark dissent.

Williams agreed with other historians, especially J. F. C. Fuller, that the "Civil War was the first of the modern total wars." Trying to win the epic struggle, both sides employed great numbers of soldiers using industrially produced weapons. Of supreme importance was the fact that each side came to fight for ideological reasons that would not be compromised: the North to preserve the Union and to destroy slavery; the South to obtain independence and to defend slavery.

Unquestionably, Williams saw Lincoln as a "power artist," a master of the politics of maneuver and compromise. The president had saved the Union. Never failing to meet any challenge, drawing from a deep well of political wisdom, astutely using patronage, Lincoln encouraged Democrats to join the war effort, formed a hardworking cabinet, and endured intense pressure from within his own party over matters such as confiscating Confederate property and emancipating the slaves. On these and other issues, Lincoln went as far and as fast as he believed was politically possible. Meanwhile, he exercised his extraordinary talents regarding military strategy. This is where some critics appeared to misread Williams's point: they could acknowledge that Lincoln was a great civilian leader, but they drew the line at giving the rail-splitter high marks as a *general*. Actually, Williams was arguing, along lines proposed by Colin Ballard, that Lincoln possessed a great natural ability to understand the fundamentals of grand strategy, the kind of understanding a war director or a general-in-chief definitely needs. Lincoln looked at a map, saw the scope of the conflict, and agreed to target high-level objectives such as blockading the Southern coast or cutting the Confederacy in two along the Mississippi River line. Furthermore, as Williams clearly showed, the President insisted that his generals make their objective the defeat of the enemy armies within each theater of war; he would not allow them to settle for winning hollow victories by taking abandoned towns or rail centers. Williams correctly concluded that several senior generals did not have the basic strategic sense that Lincoln had. But that did not mean Lincoln would have been a successful *battlefield* general. From Washington, however, Lincoln pressed even Grant, reminding him that Lee's army, not simply the Confederate capital of Richmond, was his main objective. Williams concluded, "It might be said that before Grant, Lincoln acted as commander in chief and frequently as general in chief and that after Grant he contented himself with the function of commander in chief. Consequently, as Grant assumed a larger role Lincoln took a smaller one—but he never left the stage entirely."

Seen in the light of World War II, the ultramodern global war, Grant's accomplishments stood apart from other nineteenth-century generals. A hard-bitten, professionally trained officer who rejected the plume-in-hat traditionalism flaunted by his Confederate opponents, Grant excelled at managing huge numbers of fighting men, cooperating with the navy, and balancing the intricate strategical, logistical, and organizational complexities of modern war that apparently were beyond Lee's grasp. In view of these facts, Grant was the war's top general. Williams, however, rated Lee as the other great general of the war. The iron-gray Southerner was eventually defeated, Williams contended, not by numbers alone. Lee had, with fewer soldiers, time and again outsmarted and outfought a succession of lesser Northern generals. Yet Grant, modern-minded and commanding a powerful and modernistic army, took hold of Lee and refused to let go. Grant had no inclination to pull back or regroup. He intended to bring Lee to a showdown battle and forced his will on the Southerner. Williams's summation was that "Lee was the last of the great old-fashioned generals, Grant the first of the great moderns."

Critics of *Lincoln and His Generals* agreed with Williams that the Union's command system contributed to the North's victory. This arrangement included Secretary of War Edwin Stanton (managing army bureaus and civilian resources), Chief of Staff Henry Halleck (providing "liaison between Grant and the generals commanding departments" and acting as military interpreter between Lincoln and Grant), General-in-Chief Ulysses Grant (formulating strategy, applying it to the theaters of war, and especially "directing" the Army of the Potomac against Lee), and Commander-in-Chief Abraham Lincoln (ultimately ruling on overall strategy). Reviewers of the book acknowledged that this system functioned satisfactorily for only a few months but pointed to the lack of a modern general staff as one of its deficiencies. Following the end of the war, with the pressures of disunion gone, the system was dismantled; some critics refused to see it as the homegrown institution that led directly in the early 1900s to the new command system, which depended on European models.

In spite of this criticism, *Lincoln and His Generals* was a tremendously popular book. It sold more than 175,000 copies in hardback within ten years and was still being offered by a military-history book club more than twenty years after its first publication. Over 65,000 paperback copies have been printed, and the book has had wide use in college history classes.

Lincoln and His Generals set the stage for the rest of Williams's career. It was on several "best books of the year" lists, including those of the *New York Times* and *Newsweek*. Williams had served on the program committees of the Southern Historical Association and the Mississippi Valley Historical Association and on the editorial board of the *Journal of Southern History*, but the book provided him with the national recognition that comes to a best-selling author. Williams's standing rose at L.S.U., in Louisiana, in the nation, and in academe. Readers from all across the country wrote praising letters and requested that he autograph their copies of the book. A few readers sent their criticisms, but many sent compliments; the one who wrote that Williams had "made history interesting and readable" represented the typical correspondent. In 1953 Williams was one of the first three persons at L.S.U. named Boyd Professor, a special professorship named in honor of early presidents of the university.

At this point in his life Williams married for the second time. He had first been married, toward the end of his graduate career, to Helen M. Jenson, a master's candidate studying under Hesseltine's direction. In fact, Williams had been introduced to her at the Hesseltines' house. He was intrigued by Jenson's obvious intelligence, her charm, wit and style. They had a joint interest in the study of American history, appreciated similar literature and films, and enjoyed sharing the hospitality of their mentor's home. After meeting in the fall of 1936, the couple got their graduate degrees—she a Ph.M., he a Ph.D.—and wed the next year. In 1939 they coauthored an article based on Jenson's master's thesis. When he taught for the Wisconsin Extension Division, she accompanied him often on his cross-country automobile jaunts. She vividly recalled the gigantic snowbanks obscuring the roadside in winter. Moving to Omaha, they lived in a "cockroach-infested apartment with a phone in the hall." She read his drafts of *Lincoln and the Radicals* and relocated their furniture and books to Baton Rouge when Williams took the job at Louisiana State University. There she began premedical studies while Williams plunged into his teaching and research. They were divorced in 1947.

Subsequently, Williams met Estelle S. Lower,

an instructor in the L.S.U. English Department. Williams saw in her many fine qualities. She was vivacious, had social grace, and possessed a keen mind. She was of Baton Rouge's old Skolfield family; she was of Louisiana, its traditions, its fabric. Harry and "Stell" were married in December 1952. Responding to the accolades of *Lincoln and His Generals* (he had dedicated the book to her), the newlyweds designed a spacious, comfortable house, which they dubbed Lincolnand. The wood-frame cottage they kept and made into Williams's study. Anchored and now a part of the place, surrounded by floor-to-ceiling bookshelves, he would write his other books. Mrs. Williams would become his research assistant, typist, and social director. They would entertain often—out-of-state visitors, faculty, graduate students—in a combination of the Hesseltine and Southern traditions. In the future, tempting offers would be extended from other universities, but Williams never seriously considered leaving Louisiana.

In 1955 Williams completed his biography of *P. G. T. Beauregard, Napoleon in Gray*, a volume in the Southern Biography Series published by Louisiana State University Press. (Williams served as editor of that series from 1947 to 1978.) Because the Creole had a "paradoxical personality" and a "dramatic life," Williams "was drawn to study him and to try to analyze him." In his preface, the author tantalizingly sketched the life of "the most colorful of all the Confederate generals." Williams wrote: "He was an ardent Southerner, and yet, as a Creole, he was in many ways an alien in the Anglo-Saxon Confederacy. Before a battle he was often visionary and impractical, but once in a fight he was a grim and purposeful soldier. He affected the manners of a cavalier of the Old South, but after the war he helped to destroy the old agrarian way to build the New—the industrial—South." Few generals could be ranked as "great," Williams cautioned, and Beauregard was not among them. He was a good general, but "with several caveats against him," especially his consistent neglect of the vital factor of logistics. Nevertheless, the Creole deserved a biography because he had held several important commands during the Civil War—in Charleston, South Carolina, when Fort Sumter was shelled; at First Manassas; at Shiloh; and in Charleston again and in Petersburg, Virginia, where he organized the defenses of those cities against federal attack. Moreover, Beauregard and President Jefferson Davis had serious disagreements over strategy. And finally, in contrast to several other high Confederate leaders, Beauregard had been politically unorthodox and financially successful after the war. In other words, he was exceptional.

In early 1861 Beauregard commanded Southern forces menacing Federal soldiers isolated in Fort Sumter; ironically, a few weeks before he had been superintendent of the United States Military Academy at West Point. Treated as a hero across the new Confederate nation in the victorious glow generated by Sumter and First Manassas, Beauregard's star declined after the Battle of Shiloh. Although the Confederates lost at Shiloh to Union forces led by Grant, Williams concluded that Beauregard then had the experience necessary to be a good army commander, despite his penchant for grandiose battle plans of Napoleonic design. However, Jefferson Davis removed Beauregard from field service when the general evacuated the railroad center at Corinth, Mississippi, without giving battle.

The Davis-Beauregard feud was just one of several that the Confederate president conducted during the war and after. Early in the war Davis rejected as too risky or too complicated three plans Beauregard offered for concentrating forces and conducting campaigns in the Virginia theater. Subsequently, a series of petty jealousies, minor misunderstandings, and carping criticisms of command decisions at Manassass and Shiloh led to mutual hatred between the two men. Williams judged that the Davis-Beauregard imbroglio was detrimental to the Confederacy's cause and to the careers of both leaders. Mixing oil and water would have been easier than unifying the efforts of the haughty Mississippian and the colorful Creole. In brief, Williams wrote, "they were born to clash." Despite this bitter rift between the president and the general, Beauregard went on to conduct the defenses of Charleston and Petersburg, thereby performing outstanding service to the Confederacy. Williams noted that Beauregard's contributions, while brilliantly conceived and executed, came late in the war while the general was on the defensive. In consequence he did not receive for these accomplishments the kind of lasting laurels George Pickett won in glorious defeat at Gettysburg. But according to Williams, Beauregard understood the situation at Petersburg better than Lee and probably saved the Confederate line. Thus Williams lowered Lee another notch.

Critical reception of *Beauregard* was favorable. For example, one reviewer judged that it was a "fine biographical achievement" and "written with literary skill." The book was selected by the Civil War Book Club. Eventually more than 9,000 hardback copies were printed, and a wide-selling paperback reprint later became available. Another critic in the *Saturday Review* wrote that "Williams has made a real and lasting contribution to the literature of the War Between the States." In 1981 the editors of *Civil War Times Illustrated* agreed, picking *Beauregard*, along with *Lincoln and His Generals*, to be classed with the 150 best books on the Civil War.

Williams's first venture into full-length biography was successful, but he had not tried to promote Louisiana's hero to the pinnacle of generalship. He neither bestowed undue praise on Beauregard nor gratuitously concluded that the general had been America's Napoleon unjustly denied a place in some mythical military pantheon. Instead Williams saw biography as a way "to explain the inner life of the subject." The writer believed that biography should not only place the subject in relation to his life and times, but fix him under study as a "type"—a political type, a military type, a social type. Of course, a biographer can be critical without condemning his subject and write the person's life without finding in his favor in every controversy. Furthermore, Williams found that writing biography was different from writing a monograph. A biography has to cover the subject's entire life, usually bridging several historical periods, whereas a monograph might cover five or ten or twenty years. Accordingly, biography, in Williams's view, should be "a full and balanced account and analysis of all aspects of a man's life." The biographer must take care not to let the subject "disappear" or be overshadowed by other figures; the subject has to maintain "center stage."

Beauregard held center stage in *Napoleon in Gray*; the Mexican War, the Civil War, and Reconstruction were seen from his "point of view," and Williams found that the general's postwar career was a continuing paradox. Beauregard endorsed the Louisiana Unification Movement, an unusual arrangement designed to bring blacks and whites together politically. White organizers of the movement, including Beauregard, were wealthy and mostly from south Louisiana. They hoped that unification would reduce taxes and unseat the Republicans; in exchange, whites would have to acknowledge basic rights for blacks. But the ship of unification broke up on the rocks of racism; white politicians and businessmen could not convince the mass of their fellows to support such an unorthodox alliance. Meanwhile, Beauregard made investments in a number of financial or industrial enterprises; some of them seemed out of character for a general who had served the Lost Cause. Particularly notable in that regard was Beauregard's employment with the shady Louisiana Lottery Company.

At his death, the Creole left a considerable estate and many mementos. The description of the general's possessions shows Williams's perception of character and is a prime example of his writing style. There were a few "faded and pathetic relics of the Old South"—a flag, a kepi, a sword. "There too, and more numerous and significant, were the stocks, the real estate, the promissory notes, the speculative investments—the glittering symbols of the New South. And so even to the last he was a paradox. Despite all that he seemed and all that he had fought for, he did not really look back to Contreras and the planting South and the mellow glories of the ancient regime, but forward to International House and the New Orleans industrial district and the bustling delta of tomorrow."

By this time in his career, Williams had written three books, made progress on several other projects, and developed a certain routine or writing regimen. Gone was the folding card table. A large desk and a library table were placed back to back in the center of his study or "studio," the original house on his wooded lot. He arranged his teaching schedule to permit blocks of time so that he could write fresh in the mornings. Usually he sat at the table, his note cards spread around a yellow legal tablet. To Williams the typewriter had never been a willing instrument, and he did not use one to write his books. Instead he picked up a sharpened pencil and usually started by looking closely at the last paragraph left from the previous day. Otherwise, he checked to make sure that the chapter was progressing in an orderly manner, and that the transitions led logically from topic to topic. Sometimes he erased quite a bit, reshaping a stubborn passage until he got it the way he wanted it; then he moved on. He erased every word he did not want, rather than lining out unsatisfactory words or paragraphs. From his tablet Mrs. Williams typed the draft. They both read the typescript and made necessary revisions. Occasionally he hit a snag. When that happened he took a break by puttering around his library, rearranging the titles, thinking, or he went for a walk. In earlier days it might have been a walk around the neighborhood; later he was usually content to tread through the trees and azaleas in the yard. Refreshed, Williams went back to the table, and his pencil started moving across the yellow page again while smoke curled out of a favorite briar from his pipe collection. In his writings he aimed "to create the impression of reality in the illusive past." To do that he liked to use common words—

"cowhiding" instead of whipping, "beat up" rather than defeated or exhausted. Understatement or irony also played a part: in *Beauregard*, he described a Confederate submarine that "demonstrated a technical defect. It sank but did not rise." General Beauregard was an inveterate letter writer, "a quality which many generals of both North and South shared. They wrote better than they fought." Williams tried, of course, to evoke the mood of the past. Some important events lay outside the focus of his story. Such an event was the assassination of Lincoln. Instead of spending several paragraphs describing the plotters and their conspiracy and the president's trip to Ford's theater, Williams brought *Lincoln and His Generals* to a close this way: "On April 8, a Saturday, Lincoln boarded the *River Queen* and started home. As the ship swung out from the pier, Lincoln stood a long time looking back at the land. He may have been thinking of the weary years of defeat—of McClellan, Burnside, Hooker—or of the hour of victory and Grant and Sherman. That day John Wilkes Booth registered at the National Hotel in Washington."

Few professors of history can bring to the classroom the combination of substance and anecdote, fact and drama equal to that which Williams possessed. Some part of this gift for generating educational excitement may have come from his mentor, William B. Hesseltine. According to most who knew Williams, however, it is evident that his own talent for teaching was vast. Thus "T. Harry" was a lecturer and visiting professor much in demand inside and outside Louisiana. Speaking before college commencements, civic clubs, community or student groups, he held forth, restraining his natural impulse to move away from the rostrum, captivating his audiences with descriptions and analyses of natural-strategist Lincoln, self-doubting McClellan, modern-minded Grant, grandiose-planner Beauregard. He was particularly skillful in addressing a varied audience that included undergraduate and graduate students, fellow professors, and members of the general public. But he regularly taught undergraduates throughout his career, and they may have been his most demanding and receptive audiences. He saw them on the consistent basis a college course demands, and in each class session they came to expect the nearly impossible feat of a presentation that was educational *and* entertaining. Somehow, Williams did the impossible in a variety of course topics, including sectional controversy, Reconstruction, military history, and, of course, the Civil War. His lecturing style was, he acknowledged, unorthodox; he spent as much time away from the lectern as in back of it. Professors of speech were hard put to classify or categorize Williams as a speaker, but they agreed that he was effective: those attending listened and learned. Williams introduced the leaders of the past by creating a physical and psychological word picture. He relished taking the stance of the historical figures under discussion, and somehow he changed personages with alterations in posture, voice and inflection. In fact, his voice surprised many listeners. It was an unexpectedly rich and deep voice that came from a short and spare frame. After one class, accommodating some of his students who gave him a present, he slipped on a genuine Union cavalryman's jacket, and for nearly thirty years thereafter the legend circulated that Williams annually wore a full uniform during one of his lectures. "History should be made as dramatic and interesting as possible without sacrificing its seriousness," he once told an interviewer. "It's a story, easy to make fascinating, because it's a story of human beings."

Following Hesseltine's example, Williams invested great amounts of time in his graduate students. Eventually, thirty-six persons earned their Ph.D. degrees under his supervision, and many others took his direction on their master's theses. There was no stereotype of a "Williams student"; they were a varied lot. But they demonstrated an élan, shared an esprit in the knowledge that they were studying under a great teacher. With several of his students Williams maintained a bantering, joking relationship, and observers saw a link to the Hesseltine-Williams affiliation dating back to the seminar days at Wisconsin. It was not just a matter of continuing tradition, however; this "mock-insulting" humor was as natural to Williams as breathing, and he enjoyed finding friends outside academia who specialized in repartee, the swift delivery of the barbed remark. In some ways it was difficult to study under Williams's direction. He looked for much from his students but did not press them; he expected a great deal of self-motivation. Not all of them could meet the expectations of the "Old Man"; the burdens of graduate study were not for everyone. But for those who kept to the task, and applied themselves rigorously, the rewards were many.

During his own graduate school days Williams enjoyed going to the movies, especially westerns and detective thrillers. In later years, Hollywood's product did not appeal to him as much as those Depression-era double features. In the evenings one of his major diversions was reading light fiction. He zipped through mystery yarns and later thrived

on the naval adventures of C. S. Forester's Hornblower and Alexander Kent's Bolitho. The characters of Edgar Rice Burroughs, Tarzan and the Men of Mars, provided many enjoyable escapes. Williams followed L.S.U. football, but his favorite sport was baseball, and the Boston Red Sox were his boys of summer. From 1963 to 1978 he spent the heated months at a summer cottage in Wisconsin and looked forward to the opportunity of watching major league games in Milwaukee. In the fall, back in Louisiana, he sometimes stepped out of a Civil War roundtable meeting to check on the score of a Red Sox game.

His loyalty to the Baton Rouge Civil War roundtable and his enthusiastic willingness to speak before other roundtables indicated how Williams always tried to encourage general audiences to study history. To this end he agreed to review books for the *Baton Rouge Advocate*. He reviewed more than 400 books for that newspaper over an eleven-year period (1956-1966). Although most of the books he reviewed—in twos and threes—were on the Civil War, Williams's columns in the *Advocate* were, as one of his colleagues put it, like "little history lectures" meant to be "instructive" to the average reader and to spark his interest in American history in general.

During the late 1950s and early 1960s Williams reached an ever-widening audience. His projects included editing Beauregard's Mexican War journal (1956), revising a brief collection of Lincoln's writings and speeches (1957), coauthoring a textbook, *A History of the United States* (1959), explaining the American wartime command systems in *Americans at War* (1960), surveying the *Romance and Realism in Southern Politics* (1961), editing E. P. Alexander's *Military Memoirs of a Confederate* (1962), analyzing the generalship of *McClellan, Sherman, and Grant* (1962), and writing the narrative for *The Union Sundered* and *The Union Restored*, two of the ten volumes in The Life History of the United States Series (1963). Meanwhile, he served on a number of state and national historical commissions, including the Civil War Centennial Commission, and was elected president of the Southern Historical Association (1959).

Williams's next major book came about through the encouragement of Watt P. Marchman, director of the Rutherford B. Hayes Library. As Williams recalled in his preface to *Hayes of the Twenty-third: The Civil War Volunteer Officer* (1965). "Mr. Marchman hoped that someday some writer would want to do a book on Hayes as a soldier, and his desire and my rising interest in unit history coincided." The Hayes Library provided research assistance, and Williams began his chronicle of the regimental infantry officer who would become president. Simultaneously, Williams edited parts of Hayes's diary, leading to the book *Hayes: The Diary of a President, 1875-1881, Covering the Disputed Election, the End of Reconstruction, and the Beginning of Civil Service* (1964).

In contrast to his previous books, the main character in Williams's study of the Twenty-third Ohio volunteers was not a dominating leader of the Civil War. Later in his life, Rutherford B. Hayes would be a congressman, three-time governor of Ohio, and then president. Williams concluded, "It is quite probable that without his military record he would never have been the President of the United States." During the war he rose in rank from major to major general of volunteers. Although he commanded brigades and divisions late in the war, Hayes spent most of the conflict leading the only Union regiment that had on its rolls two future presidents, the other being Major William McKinley.

Consequently, in *Hayes of the Twenty-third* Williams was writing about a different level of the Civil War, the unit level. The primary outfit, the building block of Civil War military organization, was the regiment. Ideally numbering 1,000 soldiers, few regiments had full complements. Typical regiments mustered 600 men or fewer. In an excellent introductory chapter, Williams explained the composition and operation of a typical Civil War regiment. Without enough regular officers to go around, civilians, like Hayes, turned into military officers and, Williams reminded readers, "not in an atmosphere of academic leisure but in the heat and haste of war itself." Appointed or elected, these colonels had "to learn about many new and strange things—military rules and regulations, military administration, and most puzzling of all, tactics." In order to solve the puzzle, many of the fresh army officers referred to Silas Casey's *Infantry Tactics* (1862). All of this preparation was to good purpose. Williams stressed that one of the most difficult jobs an officer has in any war is controlling his troops. In predawn darkness, smoke-filled woods, tree-strewn fields, or fog-shrouded evenings soldiers could lose their way, and officers could lose control of their men: thus the need for never-ending drill of the close order, elbow-to-elbow ranks an officer in the mid-nineteenth century had to use. Not having the benefit of electronic devices for conferences or for projecting voices across distance, officers shouted individual commands, and martial music produced by drums and bugles gave direction to units on the field, or at least tried to reduce the confusion inherently a part of battle.

In the early years of the war Hayes fought and marched in West Virginia, one of the backwaters of the conflict. There he learned soldiering and became competent at it. Williams expertly drew the reader through Hayes's different levels of command—regiment, brigade, division—to show how all of the units functioned in the larger scheme of maneuver and battle. These years prepared Hayes to participate in one of the climaxes of the war, General Philip H. Sheridan's Shenandoah Valley campaign against General Jubal Early in 1864.

Sheridan looms large in the last third of the book. From Williams's pen, "Little Phil" materializes: "Sheridan had that charismatic quality of leadership that could lift masses of men to seemingly impossible endeavors. The possessor of an awesome stock of profanity, he loosed it on anyone who pleaded that he could not make the last desperate effort that would bring victory. . . . No Union general had a more driving desire for victory, and none was more ruthless in employing officers and men in any way necessary to attain it. . . . Although he had commanded an infantry division in the West, his only experience in independent command had been with the cavalry; yet he would demonstrate real talent for handling an army of combined arms." In brief, Williams marked him as "a soldier who knew his business."

Under Sheridan's spurring, Hayes and his men fought well. The future president twice led decisive charges to break Early's line. Then the brunt of the Confederate counterstrike fell on him at Cedar Creek, the high point of the fighting. Using spirited descriptions, Williams took the reader through the quiet evening before the battle, the initial Confederate successes and Union setbacks, and Sheridan's ultimate triumph. Victorious at Cedar Creek, the Union army controlled the Shenandoah and aided Lincoln's reelection. The North appeared on the verge of winning the war, and Hayes was elected to Congress, his first political step toward the White House.

Hayes of the Twenty-third was a critical success, but it had a disappointing public reception, selling only 4,000 copies. One reviewer, Dee Brown, found much to compliment: it was a "first-rate Civil War narrative" containing "the excitement of battles and marches, much about Hayes the man," and written with "the verve and polished style that we have come to expect from its author." Another critic, Warren

Hassler, remarked on Williams's "dynamic mode of presentation." A third, Stephen Ambrose, concluded that "T. Harry Williams is one of the few historians who could take Hayes's Civil War career and make it exciting and significant." Undoubtedly Williams had hoped that more readers would have been interested in the volunteer unit commanders that Hayes appeared to typify. His objective was to show that the war had a middle level, that it could be viewed from a vantage other than that of presidents and army commanders or Billy Yank and Johnny Reb. However, as a colleague later pointed out, Hayes was not Lincoln. To most readers, despite Williams's efforts to single him out, Hayes's identity was hopelessly confused in the jumble of look-alike leaders in the Gilded Age.

Upon the publication of *Hayes of the Twenty-third* in 1965, Williams had completed an impressive body of literature on the Civil War, the pivotal event of America's past. He had viewed the war from Northern and Southern perspectives and from civilian and military angles. In addition, *Hayes of the Twenty-third*, his books on Lincoln, *Beauregard*, and numerous analytical essays measuring generalship suggest three major conclusions that Williams reached about the War Between the States.

The first conclusion, one that Williams often reiterated, was that the Civil War was the first modern war. In support of this contention Williams pointed out that both sides employed ironclad ships, multiple-shot firearms, military railroads and telegraph, mine warfare, complex trench systems, and mass armies. Moreover, these mass armies inflicted great damage to civilians and their property. Certainly the fact that each side waged war in an uncompromising fashion over ideological differences—Union or disunion, slavery or emancipation—modernized the conflict. Bruce Catton and David Donald joined Williams in naming the first modern war, and Joseph Harsh, writing in a 1973 issue of the journal *Civil War History*, dubbed the three historians the "modernists." Such a total war must have centralized civilian leadership, as did the later global wars. In his essay "Abraham Lincoln: Pragmatic Democrat," Williams concluded that Lincoln was the epitome of America and American leadership. Furthermore, Williams stressed that in a modern war generals no longer made war on other generals, that far-reaching decisions could not be made in a military vacuum. Generals, such as George McClellan, who could not accommodate themselves to these changes, were cast aside. A total war meant that policy and strategy would be formulated differently from limited wars

of the past. A nation's total energies would be marshaled for the duration. In other words, the American Civil War pitted society against society as never before. Conscription and mass armies, government contracts and purchases, new national currency and war taxes, among other things, indicated how much the Federal government intruded into citizens' lives. And the demands of the war, Williams found, made the North fight in a more revolutionary manner than the South. The Union government increased its power while the Confederacy was hamstrung by state limitations; Lincoln overstepped some legal bounds, enlarging the regular army, ordering arbitrary arrests, and issuing the Emancipation Proclamation; Generals William T. Sherman and Philip H. Sheridan ruthlessly laid waste to civilian lands, all in order to win the war. In response to Williams and the trend set by the other "modernists," Emory Thomas argued, in his book *The Confederacy as a Revolutionary Experience* (1971), that the South also took modern and extraordinary steps.

Second, Williams emphasized that the ideas of Baron Henri Jomini had greatly influenced generalship on both sides in the Civil War. Subject to diverse interpretations, Jomini's writings suggested to Williams that a military commander's "primary objectives in war were places rather than armies," especially such places as the enemy's capital. Jomini considered that the offensive was important, but implied that war could be fought with relatively little loss of life or destruction of property and that at heart war was a chivalric exercise among gentlemen, professionals who knew how the show was supposed to be run. Senior generals on both sides were Jominian, including McClellan, Halleck, Beauregard, and Lee, the most Jominian of the South's generals in Williams's estimation. McClellan in many ways typified a Jominian general: "With him the only question was when the professionals would be ready to start the game," Williams wrote. He inferred that the Federals' reliance on Jominian generals early in the war prolonged the conflict. According to Williams, Grant was not Jominian because he struck more at opposing armies, not simply at places, making him a natural proponent of the ideas of Prussian military thinker Karl von Clausewitz. (Grant, who was not a bookish soldier anyway, had not read Clausewitz, whose treatise *On War* was not available at the time in English translation.) On the other hand, the Confederates' continual dependence on Jominian principles contributed significantly to the South's defeat.

A third significant feature in Williams's writings concerned the factor of character or will in a general. In the perceptive book of essays *McClellan, Sherman, and Grant*, he analyzed "character," the singular quality with many facets possessed by all great commanders of any age. (In seminars he recommended C. S. Forester's *The General* as perhaps the best fictional study of generalship.) In his essay "Military Leadership of North and South," Williams cautioned that such factors as education, experience, and intelligence "may be highly meritorious and desirable, [but] are not sufficient in themselves to produce greatness." More than these, a great battle captain needs the "temperament" for war—"a mental strength and a moral power that enables him to dominate whatever event or crisis may emerge on the field of battle," or, in other words, "plain nerve," as Williams put it. Napoleon once remarked that a commander must keep a cool head no matter what happens, no matter how events turn, good or bad. McClellan's psychological quirks and his lack of a coolheaded ability to dominate the situation prevented him from exerting his will over his enemy or even over the inertia of his own army. (Clausewitz, whom Williams often quoted, pointed out basic features of effective generalship.) Sherman also had his psychological quirks, and strangely enough he was a captain who *avoided* battle, but he recognized the vital links between a nation's society and economy and its ability to make war. Grant was the war's greatest "generalissimo," as Williams once called him. Importantly, Grant comprehended the connection between war and politics. He accommodated newspaper reporters, put up with political appointees who wore general's stars, and refused to retreat in the Vicksburg campaign when "going by the book" called for regrouping at Memphis, a retrograde movement that would have hurt Northern morale. Moreover, Grant had an excellent grasp of logistics, put together an efficient staff, and saw the war's strategic "big picture." In contrast, according to Williams, Lee insufficiently organized his staff, inadequately coordinated logistics and railroads and, seemingly preoccupied with the war in Virginia, failed to see the strategic implications of the whole conflict. For Lee, war was still a professional exercise; he could not break the mold of traditionalism. Albert Castel, writing in a 1970 issue of *Civil War History*, noted that Williams had often approvingly quoted J. F. C. Fuller's criticisms of Lee and had added some of his own. Castel concluded that such a body of criticism could be called the "Fuller-Williams thesis."

In 1965, the same year that *Hayes of the Twenty-third* was published, Oxford University an-

nounced that T. Harry Williams would serve as Harmsworth Professor for the following academic year. Williams always ranked this appointment as one of the peaks in his career. The Oxford dons expected that the American historian would present a series of lectures on the Civil War era. Sojourning in England from the fall of 1966 to the spring of 1967, Williams did lecture on the Civil War, of course, but he also surprised his audiences on occasion by speaking on a subject that had become his consuming interest—the political career of Huey P. Long, Louisiana's premier politician.

Williams had begun research for Long's biography in 1956 after a "quick check of various sources" revealed that no other scholar had started such a project, "apparently because no significant collection of Long manuscripts was known to exist." Williams was naturally drawn to Huey Long, just as he had been attracted to Beauregard, despite the fact that the two Louisianians represented different historical eras. For researching Civil War history, writers depended upon collections of personal letters, diaries, and newspapers—traditional sources. However, in the twentieth century, especially since 1920, many conversations and personal exchanges of historical importance had been transmitted by telephone; although literally tons of state and national government documents had been printed, there appeared to be fewer letters and diaries, the stuff of history that permitted biographers to find the inner self of the subject. But the memories of the past were still there in the minds of participants or witnesses. Columbia University had already started collecting what would be for historians a major new research tool, the recorded interview. Thinking about the growing collection of interviews at Columbia, Williams realized that "someone should use the technique of oral history as basic research for a biography of Huey P. Long." Eventually Williams and his wife Estelle conducted nearly 300 interviews with men and women who recollected their memories of and observations on the Louisiana Kingfish and his political machine.

Williams revealed some of his preliminary findings to his colleagues at the Southern Historical Association convention in 1959: his presidential address was "The Gentleman from Louisiana: Demagogue or Democrat?" The research mounted; he worked through magazines and newspapers, state and federal documents. The interviewing continued, and it was so addictive that Williams did not want to stop. He recorded the words of Long's friends and relatives, rivals and enemies, staff members and bodyguards, legislators and judges, football coaches and players. When the interviewing was finished, Williams concluded "that the full and inside story of politics is not in *any* age committed to the documents." Simultaneously the historian was, metaphorically, taking his own journey back in time, to his graduate-school days during the Great Depression when he recalled hearing Long speak on the radio and when the subject of economics was one of more than simply academic interest.

Williams's formative years of study at the University of Wisconsin helped to shape his ideas on economics. In graduate school he had accepted some of the conclusions in *The Rise of American Civilization* (1927) by Charles and Mary Beard, who argued that the Civil War resulted from the clash of the sections' rival economic systems, the industrialism of the North and the agrarianism of the South. Industrial capitalism won. Williams cited favorably *The Critical Year: A Study of Andrew Johnson and Reconstruction* (1930) by Howard K. Beale, who extended the Beards' thesis into Reconstruction, when Northern industrial barons directed national policy. Economics and power had been important factors in *Lincoln and the Radicals*, but Williams admitted later that historians trained in the 1930s (presumably including himself) were inclined to "exaggerate the importance of the economic element in human motivation and to overlook or subordinate other motives." Certainly in his influential articles published in the *Journal of Southern History* (1945 and 1946), Williams stressed that both Republicans and Democrats (including Beauregard and the Unification Movement, for example) had acted out of economic motives, and he belittled the notion that idealism had driven the Radical Republicans. Accordingly, economics plays a significant part in Williams's interpretation of Huey Long's reign. The historian had to place economics in relation to power and racism in the South and did so in his essays collected in *Romance and Realism in Southern Politics*. In the South, the mythic Lost Cause and the ancient imperative of white supremacy regularly became entangled with economics in post-Civil War politics. Williams saw a pattern, from Reconstruction through the Populist revolt and into the Progressive era, of goateed gentlemen maintaining power in the old Confederate states by combining demagoguery with race baiting. This pattern prevailed until the election of Huey Long.

Huey Long: A Biography (1969) is a sterling example of narrative biography in which Williams fixed the subject as a political type, a "power artist" who would manipulate men and manage circumstances to his liking. As a type, then, Long was similar to Lincoln. Williams told Walter Clemons of the *New York Times* that he "started with a predilection for Huey, as a realistic operator who got things done that needed doing in a Southern state with a blind resistance to change." Williams then succeeded in cutting "through the myths that have grown up about [Long] . . . to see the real man." Warning readers that he had "certain concepts about Long and leaders like him," Williams went on to say that such leaders, "men of power, can influence the course of history. They appear in response to conditions, but they may alter the conditions, may give a new direction to history. In the process they may do great good or evil or both, but whatever the case they leave a different kind of world behind them . . . Huey Long was this kind of man."

"Huey," as Williams informally referred to him throughout the book, was born in Winn Parish in hilly north central Louisiana at a time when populism was rife. Williams found that Winn provided a home for Louisiana's political mavericks—opponents of secession, leaders of populism, proponents of socialism. Populism had an especially strong impact on the politics of the parish's inhabitants. Long's middle-class family gave him educational opportunity, but he never made the most of it; he read omnivorously on his own but neither finished high school nor obtained any college diplomas. Working as a traveling salesman who peddled a variety of goods, Long drove through Oklahoma and Texas as well as Louisiana. According to Williams, Huey Long became a specialist at meeting people, talking to them, taking their measure. In a day when an ambitious youth could still become a lawyer by simply passing the bar examination, Long studied law books and audited university courses. Taking the exam in a breeze, he practiced law for several years and often handled cases in which he became identified with the "little man"—the farmer or laborer. Then Long took the first of a series of political offices that he thought would ultimately lead to the presidency. Elected in 1918 to the Louisiana Railroad Commission (later renamed the Public Service Commission), Long became well known for battling giants like Standard Oil and the telephone company. Basing his campaign on the publicity obtained from these cases, Long ran for governor in 1924. He lost. Carefully preparing for the next election, he ran again and won in 1928. He had reached a position of power where he might institute reforms, help the majority of the state's citizens, and modernize Louisiana. Yet attempting such actions would bring him into conflict with Louisiana's archconservative businessmen and

Bourbon-like government leaders who were determined to defend their vested interests.

Early biographers and most historians had not been sympathetic to Long or his plans. These writers variously characterized him as a swamp-state buffoon from a poor family or an outsized sample of the South's many racist demagogues who were disruptive of reasonably good government and used evil and underhanded tactics. Perhaps he delivered a few more jobs and construction projects than most of his ilk, but his national image was that of "redneck messiah," a power-grabbing hillbilly

T. Harry Williams, 1970

spreading dangerous, half-baked ideas among the Depression era's vulnerable disaffected souls. Moreover, most historians agreed, Long took so much power that he eventually became dictator of Louisiana.

In contrast to these conclusions, from Williams's carefully researched biography emerged Huey Long the well-read, sharp-witted politician. He might put on an act for constituents, but he was an astute leader, not a bumpkin. He demonstrated this political acumen in his address before the Democratic National Convention of 1932. Furthermore, Williams argued that Long did not fit the demagogue stereotype. He seldom made racist re-

marks and based his campaigns neither on race-baiting nor glorified recollections of the Confederacy. Rather than making promises and not fulfilling them, Long made good on construction programs and social reforms that propelled Louisiana into the twentieth century. Long's accomplishments included paving hundreds of miles of roads, building more than one hundred bridges, constructing several state hospitals, laying out a new airport at New Orleans, erecting an ultramodern capitol in Baton Rouge, providing free school textbooks for children, establishing adult education classes, expanding Louisiana State University, and abolishing the poll tax. The gentlemanly Bourbonesque politicians, whose regime had lasted nearly five decades, were shocked witnesses to the destruction of their self-serving system. Williams contended that "government by goatee" had not changed Louisiana significantly since 1877. The conservatives had brutally stemmed the radical populist tide and had carefully taken most of the reform out of progressivism. There appeared to be no reason to suspect that wealthy businessmen, planters, and their political pawns would bring about meaningful improvements in the lot of the state's poor and neglected, whites as well as blacks. Through his programs, Huey had made those improvements. He then reached for higher office.

In 1930, Long took what he expected would be his next step toward the presidency. Elected to the U.S. Senate, he arranged for a puppet to occupy his governor's chair and laid plans to build a national constituency. Examining Long's Senate career closely, Williams looked beyond his subject's clowning to find a dissatisfied radical who supported and proposed substantial and important pieces of legislation and whose cogent speeches ranged over the Depression's major issues. Making the Senate his public platform, Long announced his "Share Our Wealth" plan. Williams judged that Share Our Wealth represented more than just the rantings of a "redneck messiah." Using radio broadcasts and publishing his own newspaper, Long described Share Our Wealth, which included such revolutionary features as a guaranteed annual income, a $5,000 family allotment or "homestead" (house, car, radio), old age pensions, free college education to qualified students, provisions to purchase and store agricultural surpluses, bonuses for veterans, and increased taxes on the wealthy. These concepts were more than the ramblings of a bayou baron; over 4.6 million persons enrolled in 27,000 Share Our Wealth Clubs across the nation. Others, such as Father Charles Coughlin and Dr.

Francis Townsend, criticized the New Deal and offered simplistic alternatives, but Williams concluded that Long's "plan differed from the others in being more complex and far-reaching." President Franklin D. Roosevelt, whom Long had supported for a time, took the Louisiana senator seriously, feared his rising influence, and pegged him as one of the two most dangerous men in the nation, the other being General Douglas MacArthur. Roosevelt acknowledged the influence of Long and his other critics by proposing such measures as the Wealth Tax of 1935 and the Social Security Act.

Rather than conceding that Long was a modernistic politician, most of his contemporaries, and many historians as well, called him a dictator. The exception once again, Williams demurred at labeling Long with a word that linked him with bona fide dictators in Europe. The term *dictator* should not be applied to Long, Williams argued, because the politician had not depended on religious or racial hatred to promote himself or his programs; he "was too American and too Southern ever to see himself in such a role." The historian kept Long "in an American context, in the milieu of parties and politics," employing "the traditional methods of the politician—cajolery, compromise, organization, and, when it was necessary, the slick deal." Rather than *dictator* Williams preferred the phrase *mass leader*, adopted by Eric Hoffer to characterize men with great followings, including (it is important to note) Abraham Lincoln, Franklin D. Roosevelt, Gandhi, Adolf Hitler, Benito Mussolini, and Joseph Stalin. Hoffer also said that such mass leaders could be classified as either "good" or "bad." Long seemed to be a borderline case; he manifested both qualities.

Williams acknowledged that Long added to his powers and wielded them in an extraordinary fashion. But before he became too powerful, his political and economic opponents had impeached him and tried to remove him from office. The opposition's use of this political gambit then seemed to change Long from an extremely energetic reformer to a single-minded leader who disregarded some of the "democratic means" of securing his objectives.

Accordingly, Long set out to stifle what Williams termed a "relentless opposition" and to ensure his own supremacy. For example, he kept on file signed but undated resignations from his appointees, exercised unusual control over the state police and units of the Louisiana National Guard, ramrodded laws through his pliant legislature, and deducted money from the paychecks of state employees for his discretionary use. In his last

months Long pulled all the levers of power within his reach, intending to undercut, ruin, suppress, and then crush individual rivals and opposing factions. He proposed to give the governor (his puppet) control over municipal police forces and the ability to fill vacancies in all state and local offices. It thus appeared that Long was moving to acquire dictatorial sway over Louisiana. Williams wrote that Long "wanted to do good, but to accomplish that he had to have power. So he took power and then to do more good seized still more power and finally the means and the end became so entwined in his mind that he could not distinguish between them, could not tell whether he wanted power as a method or for its own sake. . . . He could not tell, himself, whether he would ever have enough." But Williams concluded: "If [Long's] system had been perfected, and if it had endured—which is a bigger 'if'—it would have been the most daring and dangerous concentration of power ever established in American state government." Eventually the unnatural pressures of this system grew too great for one young man, the son-in-law of a political rival of Long's. The young man, a physician, shot Long on 8 September 1935. Long died two days later at the age of forty-two.

Critical reaction to *Huey Long*, although generally favorable, was diverse. However, most reviewers quickly complimented Williams for masterfully exploiting the recorded interview. One called the book a "triumphant demonstration of the value of oral history"; another termed it "methodologically pathbreaking"; a third recommended that "any scholar planning to use oral history ought to make this book required reading." Some reviewers called attention to Williams's unorthodox listing in his footnotes of "confidential communications" from living sources who did not want their names revealed. But the tapes or transcripts were under "time seal" in the L.S.U. Library, where researchers could investigate them at a future date. Most reviewers acknowledged that Williams had provided a needed corrective to Long's bayou-bumpkin image; indeed, the politician had accomplished much in his efforts to improve Louisiana. And some conceded that Long had been more important on the national scene than they heretofore had realized. Nevertheless, most reviewers concluded from Williams's evidence (the book was nearly 900 pages long) that Huey had been a dictator, the biographer's protestations to the contrary notwithstanding. Others countered that Williams had not given moderate reformers such as Governor John M. Parker enough credit; in time, this line of argument went, such moderates might have brought the state along gradually rather than rudely yanking it into the twentieth century. Some historians, even those summing up the whole book as a grand tour de force, agreed that Williams tended to be too sympathetic to Long and that some additional analysis was needed on selected points. Yet although there were a few dissenters, the majority of reviewers praised Williams's writing by calling it "gifted" and "brilliant" and by saying that the pages "radiate vitality." One concluded with high praise: the book, he declared, was "an unmistakable masterpiece of American biography."

Huey Long stirred the critics and was well received by the public. Unsure of the book's market, the publisher started off with a small first printing. It lasted one month. Second, third, and fourth printings followed in November 1969. The History Book Club made *Huey Long* one of its selections; the Book-of-the-Month Club did likewise. Fifth and sixth printings flowed off the presses in January and March 1970. Eventually, nearly 50,000 hardbacks were printed, and a mass-market paperback put more than 200,000 copies on the bookstands. (A second paperback version was printed in 1981.) The *New York Times* chose *Huey Long* as one of the top twelve books of 1969. It won the National Book Award for history and biography and then the crowning achievement—the Pulitzer Prize for biography. For good measure, *Huey Long* also won the Louisiana Literary Award. Obviously, when one historian concluded that *Huey Long* was "a work of great merit," he was sounding the consensus of opinion. In the future, whoever wrote about Long and his role in the politics of the Great Depression would have to contend with Williams's Huey.

Unquestionably, and deservedly, Williams enjoyed the acclaim and success of his prizewinning biography. The Organization of American Historians elected him its president, and in 1973 he delivered a spicy presidential address linking President Lyndon B. Johnson to Huey Long's tradition of Southern radicalism. An unexpected, though gratifying, recognition came when a New Orleans taxi driver recognized Williams's name after taking him aboard as a fare. The cabbie exclaimed, "Are you *the* 'T. Harry'?! I read your book on Huey Long!"

Naturally Williams, continuing to pursue his teaching, reviewing, and writing, maintained the steady pace of work that had yielded many books. When he died in 1979, he had several projects underway. He had started interviewing persons—using oral history again—for a biography of Lyn-

don Johnson. (Williams had pegged Johnson as a radical Southern politician in the Huey Long mold.) And he had written two-thirds of a volume on American military history.

The History of American Wars from 1745 to 1918 (1981), which was published in truncated form, covered the colonial wars to World War I. In this book Williams surveyed the growth of the military establishment and how it affected the nation. If a country wages war, then how does it raise armies, select officers, pick and produce weapons, and finance all of these martial matters? Responding to these rhetorical questions, Williams addressed other topics as well, including the development of the president as commander-in-chief, the making of strategy and policy during wartime, and the relationship between diplomacy and war. Clearly, in Williams's view, politics and military affairs were intertwined and had been since colonial times.

Of the many topics discussed in *The History of American Wars*, two can be emphasized. First, taking the opportunity to evaluate many generals, not just those in blue and gray, Williams picked up a thread that can be followed through all of his books on military history. Most generals, he observed, do not force themselves to look at their situation through their opponent's eyes. That is, commanders often take their adversary for granted and create a self-imposed mental picture of the campaign or battle as they want it to be. One example Williams cited occurred during the Mexican War. General Antonio Lopez de Santa Anna, defending his capital, left one flank virtually unprotected. Santa Anna apparently thought that the terrain near La Atalaya, a low hill outside Mexico City, would not permit the passage of troops. Williams captured Santa Anna's error: "In neglecting to fortify Atalaya, he was making a frequent mistake of generals in war: assuming that the enemy would attack the defenders' strongest point." Instead, General Winfield Scott sent soldiers through the supposedly impassable area and forced "the entire opposing line to collapse." Other instances of generals' miscalculating enemy capabilities included Grant's being caught unawares at Shiloh, Jubal Early's surprising Sheridan's idling troops at Cedar Creek, and Beauregard's drawing up defense plans at Manassas with only a Union attack on his center in mind. As Williams concluded in his interview with John A. Garraty, "War is not what is; it's what is in a general's mind, you see." Second, Williams reminded readers that wars, especially great wars, often produce unexpected consequences. In the Civil War, the destruction of slavery and the massive increase in the federal govern-

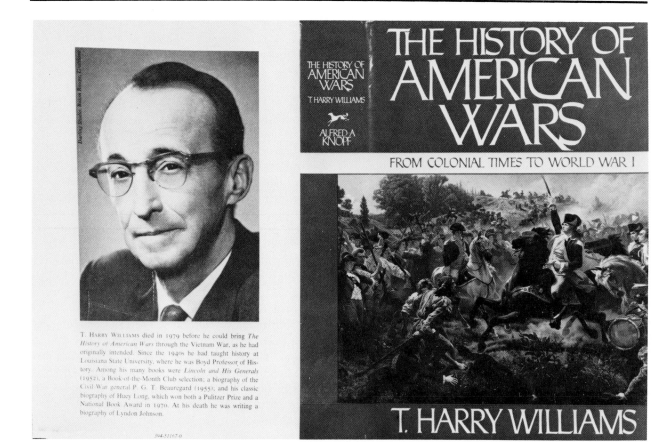

Dust jacket for Williams's posthumously published study of the interrelationship of American politics and military affairs

ment's power were but two examples. In World War I, unanticipated results included blacks' migrations from the South to the North, women's entrance into the labor force, and, again, the government's increase in power over railroads, propaganda, food production, and industrial output.

The critical response to *The History of American Wars* was respectful but subdued. In contrast to their reviews of Williams's previous books, critics did not add freewheeling asides or pinpointed barbs. Some reviewers may have been aware that the book had been originally planned years before with Otis A. Singletary as a multivolume work. But other projects had intervened, especially *Huey Long*. Even so, the History Book Club made *The History of American Wars* one of its selections, and a respectable run, more than 8,000 copies, was printed.

For many years Williams has been highly regarded by fellow historians and the general public as one of the leaders in the historical profession. His body of work on the Civil War will stand as a great collective achievement. And the Pulitzer Prize for *Huey Long* was a superlative individual distinction.

Writing for multiple audiences, Williams appealed to the broadest nonacademic readership possible without disregarding or dismissing historians. He made his books meaningful to both groups, a not inconsiderable accomplishment. His success at writing history placed him among a small circle of university professors whose books and names were recognized by readers across the nation.

Williams tied together his study of history by examining men of power, great men struggling against great odds. His central figures took power and used it—or misused it—in distinctive and fascinating ways. One of his great accomplishments was his ability to make readers "see" the people of the past—Lincoln and the Radical Republicans, Beauregard and McClellan and Grant, and the Kingfish of Louisiana. Through forty years of studying history, T. Harry Williams wrote books that helped the reader vividly perceive great figures from the American past.

Other:

With Beauregard in Mexico, edited by Williams (Baton

Rouge: Louisiana State University Press, 1956);

Abraham Lincoln: Selected Speeches, Messages, and Letters, edited by Williams (New York: Holt, Rinehart & Winston, 1957);

"Abraham Lincoln: Pragmatic Democrat," in *The Enduring Lincoln*, edited by Norman A. Graebner (Urbana: University of Illinois Press, 1959), pp. 23-46;

"Military Leadership of the North and South," in *Why the North Won the Civil War*, edited by David Donald (Baton Rouge: Louisiana State University Press, 1960), pp. 23-47;

"The American Civil War," in *The Zenith of European Power*, edited by J. P. T. Bury, volume 10 of *The New Cambridge Modern History* (Cambridge: Cambridge University Press, 1960), pp. 631-658;

E. Porter Alexander, *Military Memoirs of a Confederate*, edited by Williams (Bloomington: Indiana University Press, 1962);

"Disruption of the Union: The Secession Crisis, 1860-1861," in *Major Crises in American History*, edited by Leonard W. Levy and Merrill D. Peterson (New York: Harcourt, Brace & World, 1962), I: 465-472, 535;

"Lincoln and the Radicals: An Essay in Civil War History and Historiography," in *Grant, Lee, Lincoln and the Radicals*, edited by Grady McWhiney (Evanston: Northwestern University Press, 1964), pp. 92-116;

"Trends in Southern Politics," in *The Idea of the South*, edited by Frank E. Vandiver (Chicago: University of Chicago Press, 1964), pp. 57-65;

Huey P. Long, *Every Man a King*, edited by Williams (New York: Quadrangle Books, 1964);

Hayes: The Diary of a President, 1875-1881, Covering the Disputed Election, the End of Reconstruction, and the Beginning of Civil Service, edited by Williams (New York: McKay, 1964);

"Huey Long and the Politics of Realism," in *Essays on Recent Southern Politics*, edited by H. M. Hollingsworth (Austin: University of Texas Press, 1970), pp. 115-132;

"The Coming of the War," in *Shadows of the Storm*, volume 1 of *The Image of War: 1861-1865*, edited by William C. Davis (Garden City:

Doubleday, 1981), pp. 14-27.

Periodical Publications:

"Wisconsin Republicans and Reconstruction," by Williams and Helen J. Williams, *Wisconsin Magazine of History*, 23 (September 1939): 17-39;

"The Louisiana Unification Movement of 1873," *Journal of Southern History*, 11 (August 1945): 349-369;

"An Analysis of Some Reconstruction Attitudes," *Journal of Southern History*, 12 (November 1946): 469-486;

"Freeman, Historian of the Civil War: An Appraisal," *Journal of Southern History*, 21 (February 1955): 91-100;

"Beauregard at Shiloh," *Civil War History*, 1 (March 1955): 17-34;

"The Gentleman from Louisiana: Demagogue or Democrat?," *Journal of Southern History*, 26 (February 1960): 1-21;

"Politics of the Longs," *Georgia Review*, 15 (Spring 1961): 20-33;

"Huey, Lyndon, and Southern Radicalism," *Journal of American History*, 60 (September 1973): 267-293.

Interview:

John A. Garraty, "T. Harry Williams: The Civil War," in his *Interpreting American History: Conversations with Historians* (New York: Macmillan, 1970; London: Collier-Macmillan, 1970), I: 293-316.

References:

Walter Clemons, "T. Harry Williams, at Home Down South," *New York Times Book Review*, 2 November 1969, pp. 2, 42;

William B. Hesseltine, *Sections and Politics: Selected Essays*, edited by Richard N. Current (Madison: State Historical Society of Wisconsin, 1968).

Papers:

Williams's papers are in the Department of Archives and Manuscripts, Troy H. Middleton Library, Louisiana State University, Baton Rouge.

William Appleman Williams
(12 June 1921-   )

William Marina
Florida Atlantic University

SELECTED BOOKS: *American-Russian Relations, 1781-1947* (New York: Rinehart, 1952);

The Tragedy of American Diplomacy (Cleveland: World, 1959; revised edition, New York: Dell, 1962; revised again, 1972);

The Contours of American History (Cleveland: World, 1961; London: Cape, 1961; revised edition, Chicago: Quadrangle, 1966);

The United States, Cuba, and Castro: An Essay on the Dynamics of Revolution and the Dissolution of Empire (New York: Monthly Review Press, 1962);

The Great Evasion: An Essay on the Contemporary Relevance of Karl Marx and on the Wisdom of Admitting the Heretic into the Dialogue About America's Future (Chicago: Quadrangle, 1964);

The Roots of the Modern American Empire; A Study of the Growth and Shaping of a Social Consciousness in a Marketplace Society (New York: Random House, 1969; London: Blond, 1970);

Some Presidents: Wilson to Nixon (New York: New York Review, 1972);

History as a Way of Learning; Articles, Excerpts, and Essays (New York: New Viewpoints, 1974);

America Confronts a Revolutionary World: 1776-1976 (New York: Morrow, 1976);

Americans in a Changing World: A History of the United States in the Twentieth Century (New York: Harper & Row, 1978);

Empire as a Way of Life: An Essay on the Causes and Character of America's Present Predicament Along With a Few Thoughts About an Alternative (New York: Oxford University Press, 1980).

William Appleman Williams is perhaps the best known practitioner of what has been identified as a "New Left" approach to American history. His revisionist interpretation of the American past, which emphasizes the importance of what he has called "open door imperialism," has had considerable influence, especially among younger scholars. His career has been controversial, as was evident in the struggle surrounding his election to the presidency of the Organization of American Historians for 1981-1982.

Williams was born and grew up in rural Atlantic, Iowa. He has observed that among the circumstances helping to shape his later values were "an extended family . . ., working on a farm in the summers, suffering [through] a depression in its psychological as well as economic aspects, and being raised by people who had community values at the very center of their lives." Both his grandmothers "were liberated women, painters and singers," as was his mother.

On the basis of both grades and athletic ability, Williams was offered a basketball scholarship to Kemper Military School in Boonville, Missouri. Two years there taught him that "it was fun to do the best you could and accept the losses [and] defeats, along with the victories." He also learned about the business aspect of collegiate sports; giving up basketball to spend more time on academics and music was impossible because it would have meant the loss of the scholarship he needed in order to remain in school.

In 1941 Williams received a three-year appointment to the United States Naval Academy. During the first year and a half he took required science already covered at Kemper, and his free time allowed him to read novels, economics, and history. Williams enjoyed his "highpowered" classmates, the fact that the students were "taken very damned seriously," and the opportunity to learn about power. During the last fifteen months of World War II he served as an officer on a landing ship in the Pacific. At the end of the war, he was sent to Corpus Christi, Texas, to train as a naval pilot. While there Williams became involved with the National Association for the Advancement of Colored People's effort to extend voting rights and with attempts by some naval personnel to integrate workers on the flight line. These activities led to a controversy which eventually involved the King Ranch, General Motors, Catholic hierarchy, and the navy.

In the course of this struggle Williams was beaten up several times and offered the navy a three-page, single-spaced letter of resignation, which was refused as unacceptable. The navy then decided to transfer him to Bikini, the atom bomb test site, to see, as Williams put it, "if you could in fact hit a beach after you've bombarded it with nuclear weapons." But navy doctors decided that his various injuries made any such participation impossible. Williams was in and out of hospitals for thirteen months, over nine weeks of which were spent in a cast from the neck to the knees. He decided not to try a spinal-fusion operation when a roommate at the hospital returned from one paralyzed.

Upon resigning from the navy, he contemplated accepting an engineering offer from General Electric or another in aircraft design from Lockheed. What decided him on graduate school and a career in teaching was an opportunity to work with third-graders in his mother's class in Wisconsin. He chose the University of Wisconsin because he believed it had this country's best history department, filled not with famous names but instead with sound people who were actually in residence and teaching rather than off on leave.

Williams recalled that he chose history because, like many GI's, he wanted to find out "what the hell was going on," and "history was the best way to figure out the way the world ticked." He received his M.A. in 1948 with a thesis in Russian history but soon decided that lack of access to sources was too great a problem and switched from Russian history to the study of American foreign policy.

Before starting his doctoral studies, he went to Europe for five months to participate in seminars on socialist economics conducted by the Labour government in Great Britain, seminars in which cabinet ministers visited Leeds University to give tutorials. One session was directed by A.J. Brown, an economist, whom Williams has called "the shrewdest and toughest Liberal in the English tradition." As he recalls: "I think that I was certainly affected by the kinds of questions he would not let us evade. He said that if you come to power in a failing capitalism you face enormous problems and suggested thinking about decentralization as a partial response. That way the problems wouldn't interact at such a structural level that if one thing went wrong, everything would probably go wrong." Such an orientation obviously contributed to the development of Williams's ideas about the direction of American history.

Back in Wisconsin, Professor Howard K. Beale called Williams's attention to Raymond Robbins, whose career became the subject of Williams's dissertation. Robbins, who had been on a mission to Russia toward the end of World War I, experienced the revolution there and later became an advocate of U.S. recognition of the Soviet Union. After

William Appleman Williams

graduation in the summer of 1950, Williams expanded the biography into a study entitled *American-Russian Relations, 1781-1947*, which was published in 1952.

This first book contained themes found in Williams's later studies. An early-established American friendship with Russia, according to Williams, had deteriorated in the face of late nineteenth-century U.S. expansion into Asia. An important intellectual influence in this expansive policy was historian Brooks Adams. The Open Door notes provided the basic rationale for such expansionism. Raymond Robbins and Sen. William Borah of Idaho, expressing a minority view, failed in their efforts to persuade other American leaders that recognition of the Bolshevik regime was a surer way to moderate its behavior than was attempting to either ostracize or pressure it. The "tragedy of the thirties," Williams wrote, was that, even after official recognition of the regime in 1933, American attitudes prevented cooperation as advocated by Russian leaders such as Maxim Litvinov, cooperation which might have prevented later German and Japanese aggression. In the book's final chapter, which covered the years from 1940 to 1947, Williams argued that the containment policy, adopted on the recommendation of policymakers such as George F. Kennan and with Soviet awareness that the United States had a monopoly on the atomic bomb, was a mistake. This policy compounded the wartime error of postponing agreement with Russia over her interests in Eastern Europe, ignored the reality of Soviet military power in the area, and delayed economic aid badly needed as a result of the devastation of Russia.

Williams later discovered that his final chapter had been sent by the publisher—unbeknownst to him—to *Foreign Affairs*, unofficial journal of the American foreign policy establishment, which kept it a long time before writing him that the essay had been circulated, and had been read with great interest. It had stimulated considerable discussion, "but the decision had finally been that it was a bit too sharp personally." He was never certain what this statement meant but concluded that the "personally" reference was to Kennan.

From 1952 until 1957 Williams taught at the University of Oregon. In 1956 he edited *The Shaping of American Diplomacy; Readings and Documents in American Foreign Relations, 1750-1955*, a large volume in a historical series under the general editorship of his mentor, Fred Harvey Harrington; an extensive revision of the volume was done in 1970. Williams argued that foreign relations were influ-

enced by economics and ideology as well as by political or military considerations. He also stressed the extent to which foreign policy was a product of conflicts among interest groups within the United States. Yet while public opinion played a role in policy decisions, the public was seldom able to initiate alternatives. Control of information, therefore, became an important aspect of the power exercised by policymakers. Bureaucratic procedures and specialization had added to the complexity. The public usually had a chance only to give assent or disapprove of a foreign policy decision: "Very seldom do the people have an opportunity to choose between alternatives," Williams declared.

In 1957 Williams returned to the University of Wisconsin to teach. Two years later he produced the book for which he is best known, *The Tragedy of American Diplomacy*. The original essay was only 200 pages with 7 pages of bibliographical comment, but in 1962 a paperback edition expanded the essay to over 300 pages.

Tragedy was originally accepted by Braziller with an advance of about $2,500 and was to be a selection of Book Find Club. James Reston of the *New York Times* had agreed that a quotation of his which began the volume could be used on the jacket. At that point, Max Ascoli, editor of the *Reporter*, read the manuscript and "just went through the ceiling," threatening to terminate his friendship with the publisher, who then backed out of the contract, although Williams kept the advance.

The most important review of *Tragedy* was by Adolph Berle, former ambassador and assistant secretary of state, in the *New York Times*. Berle used it, according to Williams, as an opportunity "to begin to get off the containment bandwagon." After John F. Kennedy's election to the presidency in 1960, Berle was appointed to deal with Latin American Affairs and asked Williams to be his personal first assistant. Williams seriously considered the offer but in rereading the campaign material and concluding that Kennedy had "used" the issue of Cuba, he decided that "you can't trust the Kennedys" and declined the offer. In light of the Bay of Pigs, Williams later reflected, "Thank God! I would have had to resign before I'd even found an apartment to live in."

Tragedy was published at a time when the leading textbooks in American diplomatic history, such as those by Thomas A. Bailey or Samuel Flagg Bemis, gave very little attention to economic factors in American foreign policy. Bailey's light style and numerous reproduced cartoons stressed the role of public opinion, while Bemis's ponderous narrative emphasized the formal aspects of diplomatic negotiations. Both tended to suggest that, although America had flirted with imperialism at the turn of the century, public opinion and policymakers had retreated from such a program. This view was perhaps best summed up in Bemis's memorable phrase about empire as "the great aberration of 1898." Any exercise of American power since 1898 was viewed as an unavoidable but atypical response to fascist aggression or the spread of communism.

Tragedy challenged that outlook. To Williams the tragedy of American diplomacy grew out of a contradiction between American ideals with respect to social change and the way in which these ideals were reflected in actions. The United States had enormous power and a generous humanitarianism, coupled with a commitment to the idea of self-determination. Its leaders, however, found it difficult to accept revolutionary change unless the revolution conformed to American expectations.

In *The Shaping of American Diplomacy* and several early articles, Williams had emphasized expansion as a fundamental part of American experience. Others had noticed the importance of the 1890s as a "watershed" or had emphasized the "psychic crisis" of that decade. For Williams, to the contrary, the 1890s were best characterized as a period of economic crisis. He saw the debate which culminated in the declaration of war against Spain and the subsequent annexation of the Philippines, not as the traditional two-sided conflict of imperialist versus anti-imperialist, but rather as a three-sided one. There were advocates of colonialism such as Theodore Roosevelt and Sen. Henry Cabot Lodge. At the other extreme were opponents of empire totally opposed to colonialism. In the middle were reluctant colonialists who advocated a kind of "imperial anti-colonialism." Rejecting the spheres of interest used by other powers, American leaders chose the middle way, an Open Door policy, as a means of securing markets and areas for investment. In subsequent chapters of *The Shaping of American Diplomacy*, Williams sought to demonstrate how policymakers expanded this policy to a global scale in the years after 1898. But implementation of such a policy inevitably led to opposing revolutions, as in China and Mexico. Williams asserted that the parameters of this policy were already in place *before* the Bolsheviks took power in Russia. What emerged within the Open Door policy, in Williams's description, was an institutionalized arrangement between the business community, especially financial interests, and the government, so that "Tax monies collected from individual citizens came to be used to provide corporations with loans and other subsidies for overseas expansion, to create the power to protect those activities, and even to create reserve funds with which to make cash guarantees against losses."

In Williams's analysis, the American debate over the League of Nations in 1919 was essentially a renewal of the three-cornered debate of 1898 rather than of the two-sided isolationist vs. internationalist model that has dominated descriptions of twentieth-century American foreign policy. It thus was misleading to place Lodge and Borah together simply because they both criticized Woodrow Wilson and the League or to call that policy isolationism. While no longer defending outright colonialism per se, Lodge wanted the essentially unilateral use of American power in a revolutionary world. He thus opposed Wilson's view that stability could best be insured by the major "have" nations working together through the League, an arrangement in which the United States would have a very large role. Borah, on the other hand, simply did not believe that American power, acting either alone or in concert, could hold back social change or deny the idea of self-determination.

Williams argued that the notion that America had withdrawn from world affairs during the 1920s—"the legend of isolationism"—was simply incorrect. Failure to participate in the League had not precluded a strong unilateral American policy of armed interventions into China and into Nicaragua, for example. Williams suggested that the "Good Neighbor" policy was more the creation of Herbert Hoover than of Franklin D. Roosevelt. New Deal policymakers, however, were no less committed to maintaining the Open Door and expanding overseas trade, Williams declared, and they resurrected reciprocity as a tactical means of doing so. The Roosevelt administration increasingly perceived Japan and Germany as threats to the Open Door policy. Armament spending superseded the New Deal as a means of sustaining prosperity. When economic pressures failed to work, American policymakers in late 1941 moved toward what Williams called "the war for the American frontier." His analysis of the end of World War II and the onset of the cold war were an elaboration of his earlier study of American-Russian relations. He then ended with chapters on the stalemate brought about by "the Impotence of Nuclear Supremacy" and concluded that the United States must accept "the Wisdom of an Open Door for Revolution" that would allow self-determination and change rather than attempting to stifle them.

Berle's *New York Times Book Review* piece (15

February 1959) helped to draw attention to *Tragedy*, and the book gained in influence during the 1960s. But some scholars, even in the beginning, called the book an "argument rather than diplomatic history," declared that it "cannot be taken seriously as history," and described Williams as "a brilliant but perverse historian." The book was the forerunner of the New Left revisionism which flourished during the 1960s as part of the debate over the war in Vietnam. Many of the scholars involved were students of Williams and of what became known as the Wisconsin School. Except for Gabriel and Joyce Kolko, most revisionist historians have acknowledged an intellectual debt to Williams.

It was not until 1973 that a serious attack on *Tragedy* was developed by Robert James Maddox in *The New Left and the Origins of the Cold War*. Maddox's chapter on Williams was not a systematic challenge to Williams's interpretation but rather a detailed analysis of Williams's methodology, of the ways in which he had taken diverse quotations and put them together so as to provide the impression he desired. Maddox's book was featured by the *New York Times Book Review*, which also printed replies (17 June 1973) by Williams and other revisionists. Yet how little criticism has changed Williams's thinking is evident in his recent textbook on twentieth-century America, *Americans in a Changing World: A History of the United States in the Twentieth Century* (1978), which repeats virtually intact one of the passages in *Tragedy* questioned by Maddox.

"*Tragedy* obviously upset a lot of people," Williams later said, for as he was preparing his next book, *The Contours of American History* (1961), he was subpoenaed by the House Un-American Activities Committee. Friends at the law school at Wisconsin put Williams in touch with Paul Porter of Arnold, Fortas, and Porter. Porter took him "up and down and sideways and backways trying to figure out why they were after me. Because they were after me in a way they never went after anybody else. They subpoenaed the manuscript of *Contours*." Porter went over Williams's earlier activities in Texas. Had he joined the Communist party? He *had* written in various left-wing publications and received a grant from the Rabinowitz Foundation, "but obviously," according to Williams, "they were after me to stop the book." Porter decided not to surrender the manuscript unless the HUAC got an order from the Supreme Court, which he believed it never could do. Finally, lawyer Thurman Arnold worked out a deal. Williams appeared before the committee for ten minutes, and they agreed to drop the subpoena.

In *Contours* Williams departed the confines of diplomatic history for a far-ranging interpretation of American experience. He stressed the influence of ideas organized into a coherent world view and the ways in which such a Weltanschauung determined human action. He suggested that American history had experienced three shifts in such world views. First, the colonies were settled while England was developing a mercantilist outlook in which expansion played a crucial role. Though revolting from England, the Founding Fathers accepted this view and sought to develop an American variant. In the nineteenth century, however, the mercantilist world view was superseded by one of *laissez nous faire* that also stressed expansion but did so by emphasizing the role of the individual over that of society. Finally, emerging to dominance late in the nineteenth century, was the world view of corporate capitalism, or corporate syndicalism, as Williams often termed it. The historian described the rise, adaptation, acceptance, transformation and passing of each of these world views. In discussing how a commitment to expansion inevitably led to war and to a denial of self-determination, Williams argued that only an American socialism could break this vicious cycle and restore a sense of community. Very interesting was his sympathy for the South and for other conservative forces that had emphasized community over "possessive individualism."

Although a reviewer in the *Nation* found *Contours* beautifully reasoned, many critics in scholarly journals called it shallow and polemical. The most scathing review was by Oscar Handlin, who termed the book an absurd and "elaborate hoax" written in the literary style of an "unskilled freshman." After citing several factual errors, Handlin concluded, "There has never been anything like it before."

Yet *Contours* remains the fullest development of Williams's ideas. An essentially friendly critic, Christopher Lasch, recognized this fact in 1978 as he praised Williams's contributions to the historical profession despite the ridicule and ostracism he had faced. Lasch suggested, however, that in attempting to avoid economic determinism, Williams "sometimes seems to endow ideas with an autonomous directive force of their own." Further, an even "more serious criticism" was that "his thought remains embedded in the progressive tradition it challenges in so many ways." Lasch also contended that "because Williams pays so little attention to the conflicts out of which ruling class ideologies emerge, he finds it difficult to explain the transition from mercantilism to laissez faire and from laissez faire to corporate capitalism." For example, Williams failed to explain why expansion "failed to prevent a major upheaval—a great civil war." In the area of foreign policy he seemed "to rule out the possibility that American policy makers responded at any time to external threats to the capitalist system." But if that were so, why criticize them for turning to expansion? Finally, "Williams' critique of American expansionism seems to assume that alternatives to expansionism can be found within the terms of corporate capitalism." Lasch concluded that, on the contrary, "Twentieth-century capitalism forces us to choose between liberal imperialism and fascism, which in any case generates an imperialistic dynamic of its own."

In 1962, just as the Cuban missile crisis broke, Williams published *The United States, Cuba, and Castro: An Essay on the Dynamics of Revolution and the Dissolution of Empire*. He attempted to show how, since 1898, the United States had blocked any radical social change in Cuba. In the 1930s Fulgencio Batista had risen to power through advocating a New Deal-type corporate state. Fidel Castro's program was not hidden or obscure but had stressed democratic socialism and full implementation of the radical Cuban Constitution of 1940. According to Williams, American policymakers' stated objective of putting Castro "through the wringer" weakened the moderates in the revolutionary coalition and drove them toward seeking Soviet help to protect the revolution against outright American intervention. The Bay of Pigs failure and the missile crisis proved that imperial armed intervention was no longer so easily carried out and that any confrontation between the superpowers might lead to nuclear disaster.

Two years later Williams published *The Great Evasion: An Essay on the Contemporary Relevance of Karl Marx and on the Wisdom of Admitting the Heretic into the Dialogue About America's Future* (1964). By the Great Evasion he meant America's "manipulation of nature," the exploitation of the frontier "to avoid a confrontation with the human condition and with the challenge of building a true community." His subtitle hinted that many of Karl Marx's ideas were relevant to a "dialogue about America's future." Williams stressed the notion of alienation in a "market-place" economy, which led to a dominance relationship between the metropolis and the country. He argued that expansion had neither avoided conflict nor alleviated rising economic misery and increasing sociopsychological proletarianization. Williams concluded that "capitalism as possessive competitive individualism" could never resolve its contradictions. One variant that had been proposed was a "feudal socialism" advocated by some conser-

vative representatives of the American gentry. Another was "bourgeois socialism" of an urban or rural variety as represented by progressivism and populism, respectively. Finally, there was "corporate socialism" in which the base of ownership had been widened to increase capital without "providing such investors any significant share in making basic decisions." Without attention to details, Williams closed by urging a "restructuring and rebuilding of American society" along the lines of a regional, decentralized socialism. Critics were not kind to *Great Evasion*. One called it "vulgar, self-serving, imprecise and shallow," while another termed it of little use except for students of the sociology of religion "who could find it an interesting case study of Marxian theology of exegesis."

During 1966-1967, Williams took a sabbatical from Wisconsin, a leave which he spent on the Oregon coast while he worked on the manuscript of what was to become *The Roots of the Modern American Empire; A Study of the Growth and Shaping of a Social Consciousness in a Marketplace Society*. Although he participated in teach-ins on Vietnam and testified before Congress, his role in the protests was more intellectual than activist. Williams also attempted to work out an arrangement with Wisconsin to spend half of each year in Oregon. When this possibility did not develop, he moved to Oregon State University in Corvallis, where he still teaches.

The Roots of the Modern American Empire was published in 1969. Williams had expressed concern that unsympathetic reviewers had criticized some of his work for lack of footnote citation. His thoughts about such reviewers were addressed in the new foreword to the paperback issue of *Contours* (1966), entitled "Concerning Such Matters as Authors, Reviewers, Readers, and Even the Book Itself." *The Roots of the Modern American Empire* was a big volume with the kind of footnotes that, except for scholarly articles, Williams had not utilized since his first book.

The preface was more in the nature of an intellectual autobiography than anything Williams had previously written. In the book he sought to do two things. One was to show that the American expansionist policies of the turn of the century and after, about which he had written at length, had not been the initial creation of industrial leaders but rather of the agrarian sector's search for markets abroad after the Civil War. Certainly he offered an enormous amount of data demonstrating agrarian interest in foreign markets.

A second purpose was indicated by the subtitle "A Study of the Growth and Shaping of Social Consciousness in a Marketplace Society." In this endeavor he was much less successful, acknowledging later that even some of his otherwise perceptive admirers have failed to understand that the book was "only marginally about 'farmers.'" Several reviewers suggested that Williams had attempted to fit too much of American politics and foreign policy into this thesis and had produced an overly long study which was frequently "tedious" and "dull."

The most laudatory review was by diplomatic historian Richard W. Van Alstyne in the *Nation*. He concluded, however, that Williams's "pious hope at the end that the forces of history can be reversed seems the merest wishful thinking." Van Alstyne cited the somber verdict of John A. Hobson in his 1902 classic, *Imperialism*, that such a policy was "a depraved choice of national life, imposed by self-seeking interests which appeal to the lusts of quantitative acquisitiveness and of forceful domination. . . . It is the besetting sin of all successful States, and its penalty is unalterable in the order of nature."

In 1972 a number of Williams's book reviews from the *New York Review of Books* were reprinted under the title *Some Presidents: Wilson to Nixon*. The presidents discussed also included Hoover, Franklin Roosevelt, Eisenhower, Kennedy and Johnson. Williams's introduction was a succinct summary of the thesis of most of his work. Presidents, he argued, were the key figures in an effort to construct a corporate system that would function effectively and undercut the appeal of alternatives. Over the years this system had led to centralization, manipulation, secrecy, evasion, lies, and a loss of confidence. Williams's critique of the imperial presidency predated that post-Watergate discovery by such later writers as Arthur M. Schlesinger, Jr. As in earlier works, Williams's sympathy lay with those presidents who had sought to transcend interest group politics of empire such as Hoover, Eisenhower, and even Johnson in his domestic reform efforts.

In 1974 a volume containing eighteen short works was published as *History as a Way of Learning; Articles, Excerpts, and Essays*. Among these were pieces whose influence was indicated by the number of requests for reprints over the years, and included were two essays on Charles Beard, whose intellectual influence Williams had acknowledged. The volume concluded with an essay promoting a socialist community in which he argued against violent protest based on an assumption that America was ripe for revolution and in favor of a

"*sustained* deepening and focusing of radical consciousness."

For the Bicentennial, Williams wrote *America Confronts a Revolutionary World: 1776-1976* (1976). It repeated his theme that expansion and centralization into empire was an evasion of community and created more problems than it solved. Thus he had some good things to say about the Articles of Confederation and suggested that the North ought to have had the courage to honor its rhetoric about self-determination and to have let the South secede in 1861. "It is," Williams reflected, "a contradiction in terms to talk about being a citizen in an empire." He thus urged a "new federalism" that would focus sovereignty in a number of regional units. Some reviewers found the book less history than social prophecy, "eccentric" and even "bizarre."

In 1978 Williams produced a textbook, *Americans in a Changing World: A History of the United States in the Twentieth Century*. From the standpoint of interpretation it offered little not already presented elsewhere, but pedagogically Williams sought to employ methods he had used as a teacher to acquaint students with historical reality. One of his reasons for going to Oregon was a continued interest in teaching introductory history to undergraduates. This concern was evident in statements he made as president of the Organization of American Historians. History, he said, needed to be brought back in the secondary curriculum for "the consciousness of history in the public at large is weaker than it has been in many times."

Williams's most recent book is *Empire as a Way of Life: An Essay on the Causes and Character of America's Present Predicament Along With a Few Thoughts About an Alternative* (1980). It reiterates his earlier works in seeking to alert Americans to the corrosive effects of empire. In August 1980, a condensation of the book was published in the *Nation* magazine and distributed to delegates at the Democratic National Convention. Its editors described *Empire* as an "astonishing analysis." Critics, however, were not so kind. One, who thought it "the latest indication of Williams' intellectual and literary degeneration," pointed to chapter three, which was titled "A Psychologically Justifying and Economically Profitable Fairy Tale: The Myth of Empty Continents Dotted Here and There with the Mud Huts, the Lean-tos, and the Tepees of Unruly Children Playing at Culture," as an example of the "turgid and prolix style" of the political pamphleteer. Another mentioned that Williams's style was "vulgarian" and pedantic. The book contained errors, "which in former times would have debarred him from the lectern of any reputable institution of higher learning," and he declared that Williams's position as president of the OAH simply reflected "the present state of professional historianship in the United States."

In the face of such controversy, what can be said about Williams's work and its impact upon the historical profession? Much of the influence of his work derives from his commitment as a teacher and from the way in which his students and colleagues have carried forward his ideas. Whatever intellectual disagreements one might have with him, he has proved constantly willing to discuss ideas and generously acknowledges the help given him by his students and colleagues. He has often opened himself to attack by critics precisely because he has been personally candid to the point of vulnerability.

Despite the extent and influence of his interpretation of American history, no one thus far has offered a full-scale critique of Williams's work. Even if one concedes Williams's misuse of some documents and the colloquial prose of several of his later works, his still remains an enormous contribution to American history. Williams has been less than careful in some of his citations, erroneously recording such items as publication dates. He has even miscited some of his own writings, and in a recent vita had several such errors. Williams simply does not view such matters as important. In some ways he harks back to the economist John A. Hobson, who went to some lengths to stay out of scholarly directories.

Williams has always, in the tradition of Henry Adams, viewed the calling of the historian as a moral one. He was willing to write about the American empire and its economic-political underpinnings at a time when, in a cold war atmosphere, many other historians found it expedient to avoid doing so. It seems fair to say, however, that his recent work is to a great extent simply an elaboration of themes in *Contours* or *Tragedy*, yet it would have been difficult not to expand upon the broad landscape laid out in *Contours*. However, there are at least two areas where even essentially sympathetic critics can point to omissions in Williams's analyses. One of these involves defects in his description of the nature of empire, especially as to the nature of its causes; and the other has to do with the possibility of a decentralized socialist community.

Despite his often citing of the influence of Frederick Jackson Turner and Charles Beard, or even Marx, Williams has stressed of late the extent

to which his ideas draw upon a European tradition, including thinkers such as Dilthey, Mommsen, and Brown. In his early work Williams emphasized the role of economic interests in pushing imperialism, but in some of his later work it is possible to infer his belief that power considerations were paramount. This leads to a natural question—where can Williams be placed in the context of the debate over imperialism? Writers have discussed imperialism from the perspectives of three schools of thought, often called Leninist, Hobsonian and Schumpeterian.

What characterizes the Leninist approach is its view that imperialism is intrinsic to capitalism. There are passages in Williams's writings, especially in *The Great Evasion*, where his analysis seems close to this outlook. Hobson, in contrast, stressed factors other than the economic and argued, despite some of his more pessimistic statements, that an imperialist system could be reformed. Charles Beard made it clear in *America in Midpassage* (1938) that his outlook was essentially Hobsonian. Despite Williams's numerous comments on Beard, he has never mentioned that key insight into Beard's world view. The Schumpeterian interpretation of imperialism emphasizes power instead of any structural economic necessity and suggests that reactionary feudal groups being displaced by expanding market forces will seek to use imperial policies as a means of retaining control of the state. This is the view of libertarian critics whose advocacy of the free market places them seemingly at the extreme from Williams's fundamental criticism of capitalism. In 1971, Williams did an introduction to *The New Leviathan*, a collection of essays edited by Ronald Radosh, a former Wisconsinite radical, and by Murray N. Rothbard, a free market libertarian, but there is little evidence of any real dialogue between Williams and the libertarians, certainly not in his writings.

Marxist-Leninist theories of imperialism recently have had to acknowledge the possibility of the state as an independent variable in the imperial equation. Once that is accepted, however, what remains of the Leninist interpretation? Williams dismissed this debate over causation as a pseudoproblem in a notable, lengthy footnote in *Tragedy*, but his own writings offer a voluminous amount of data about the extent to which imperial actions were initiated at the insistence of political power interests whose existence derived from a growing state and not from market motives or needs.

Williams has not differentiated with any degree of clarity between such phenomena as a quest for foreign markets, expansion, colonialism, and imperialism. Carl Schurz and other anti-imperialists on whom, as a group, Williams was rather harsh in *Tragedy* for supposedly accepting economic imperialism, did attempt to differentiate. They certainly opposed formal spheres of interest. It is ironic, therefore, to hear Williams in a recent interview falling back toward Herbert Hoover's position (which alarmed his radical interviewer) that "maybe we can make it with the [western] hemisphere." Furthermore, Williams's alternative of a decentralized, socialist community has not been truly tested. Nowhere has he confronted theorists such as Robert Nisbet who demonstrated in *The Quest for Community* that socialism inevitably requires political and economic centralization, which is antithetical to community.

Some years ago, a sympathetic critic who had learned much from him urged Williams to explore these questions by writing what might jokingly be called "Son of Great Evasion." Williams acknowledged that in some ways this request was similar to his editor Ivan Dee's desire for further details about the socialist, decentralized community discussed at the end of *Great Evasion*. Perhaps it is time for him squarely to confront the role of the state in the process of empire and to explain how the centralization and state power seemingly inherent in the structure of socialism can be reconciled with a goal of a decentralized community.

Other:

The Shaping of American Diplomacy; Readings and Documents in American Foreign Relations, 1750-1955, edited by Williams (Chicago: Rand McNally, 1956; revised edition, updated to 1968, 1970);

America and the Middle East: Open Door Imperialism or Enlightened Leadership?, edited by Williams (New York: Rinehart, 1958).

Interview:

"An Interview with William Appleman Williams," *Radical History Review*, 22 (Winter 1979-1980): 65-91.

References:

Christopher Lasch, "William Appleman Williams on American History," *Marxist Perspectives*, 3 (Fall 1978): 118-126;

Edward S. Shapiro, "Revisionism R.I.P.," *Intercollegiate Review*, 17 (Fall/ Winter 1981): 55-60.

Carter G. Woodson
(19 December 1875-3 April 1950)

Edward L. Cox
University of South Carolina

SELECTED BOOKS: *The Education of the Negro Prior to 1861* (New York & London: Putnam's, 1915);

A Century of Negro Migration (Washington, D.C.: Association for the Study of Negro Life and History, 1918);

The History of the Negro Church (Washington, D.C.: Associated Publishers, 1921);

Early Negro Education in West Virginia (Institute, W. Va.: West Virginia College, 1921);

The Negro in Our History (Washington, D.C.: Associated Publishers, 1922); adapted for elementary-school students as *Negro Makers of History* (Washington, D.C.: Associated Publishers, 1928); adapted for high-school stu-

dents as *The Story of the Negro Retold* (Washington, D.C.: Associated Publishers, 1935);

African Myths, Together with Proverbs (Washington, D.C.: Associated Publishers, 1928);

The Negro as a Businessman, by Woodson, John H. Harmon, Jr., and Arnett C. Lindsay (Washington, D.C.: Association for the Study of Negro Life and History, 1929);

The Negro Wage Earner, by Woodson and Lorenzo J. Greene (Washington, D.C.: Association for the Study of Negro Life and History, 1930);

The Rural Negro (Washington, D.C.: Association for the Study of Negro Life and History, 1930);

The Mis-Education of the Negro (Washington, D.C.:

Associated Publishers, 1933);

The Negro Professional Man and the Community (Washington, D.C.: Association for the Study of Negro Life and History, 1934);

The African Background Outlined (Washington, D.C.: Association for the Study of Negro Life and History, 1936);

African Heroes and Heroines (Washington, D.C.: Associated Publishers, 1939).

Carter Godwin Woodson is generally regarded as the father of modern black history. In the early 1900s when racial discrimination and prejudice threatened to reach unprecedented heights in the United States, Woodson stimulated new interest in the contributions of blacks to the growth of the nation through both his scholarly publications and the pioneering work carried out by the Association for the Study of Negro Life and History, which he founded in 1915.

Born at New Canton in Buckingham County, Virginia, on 19 December 1875, Carter G. Woodson was one of nine children born to the former slaves James and Ann Eliza Woodson. Being of a large and

Carter G. Woodson

poor family, young Carter was unable to attend the local school during most of its five-month school year. His parents needed his assistance on the farm to improve eventually the economic and social circumstances of the entire family.

Rather than dampening his resolve, this situation merely inculcated in Carter Woodson a spirit of determination which was to serve him well throughout his life. For despite the obvious handicaps which he faced, by age seventeen Woodson had acquired, largely through self-instruction, a rudimentary education. With a view toward enlarging his horizons and improving his educational possibilities, he moved with his brother Robert Henry Woodson to Huntington, West Virginia. Plans to continue school immediately were shelved as Woodson found it necessary to work as a miner in the Fayette County coalfields in order to earn a living.

In 1895, when twenty years old, Woodson finally entered Douglass High School in Huntington, from which institution he earned a diploma in less than two years. Six years later, he received a teacher's high-school certificate for Huntington schools, and in 1903, after two years of study, earned the degree of Litt.B. from Berea College, Kentucky, one year before the laws of that state officially put an end to racial coeducation.

Thereafter, Woodson's career as an educator quickly mushroomed. Serving briefly as principal of the Douglass High School, he resigned this position in late 1903 and enrolled as a student at the University of Chicago. But the offer of a post as teacher of English in the Bureau of Education for the Philippine Islands proved too enticing for Woodson to refuse. With the prospect of an annual salary of $1,200, he arrived at Manila on or about 19 December 1903 and was assigned by the Civil Service Board to the town of San Isidro in the province of Nueva Ecija. Later, he was appointed as supervisor of schools in the towns of Agno and Bani, where his main duty was to train Filipino teachers, a position he held until ill health forced him to resign in February 1907, in order to return to the United States.

Woodson returned in time to enroll at the University of Chicago in the fall semester of 1907, from which institution he obtained his A.M. in August 1908. In the meantime, he had spent a year of travel and study in Asia and Europe, including a semester's enrollment as a special student of European history at the University of Paris. Having failed to receive a response to a request he had made, in June 1908, for reinstatement to his position in the Philippines, Woodson enrolled at Harvard University as a Ph.D. student in September of that year. There he successfully combined the roles of teacher and student. Woodson taught French, Spanish, English, and history in the high schools of Washington, D.C., his competency in the two former languages having been improved during his stay at Paris and the Philippines respectively. Through employment in Washington, Woodson found the holdings of the Library of Congress to be of much use in researching his doctoral dissertation, "The Disruption of Virginia." By the time he received the degree of Ph.D. from Harvard University in 1912, Woodson had clearly become convinced of the dire necessity of doing original research on Afro-Americans and of publishing monographs dealing with their history.

Specifically what pushed him in that direction is difficult to determine. Reportedly, the well-known historian Edward Channing had remarked in a class that blacks had no history. In response to the exception which Woodson took to that statement, Channing challenged him by suggesting that if blacks did have a history then Woodson should try to discover it. The professor's position reflected the sentiment of a wide cross section of contemporary American historiography. Most of the history books and courses in American institutions of higher learning either failed to mention blacks or did so in a most unfavorable light. Even Woodson's doctoral dissertation makes hardly any mention of blacks. To rectify this general situation, he initiated the twin processes of research and publication both to fill the existing hiatus and to create respect for blacks in the minds of Americans as a whole. Being convinced that racism was America's greatest problem, Woodson clearly hoped to utilize a racial chauvinism of sorts to correct this imbalance in the texts and promote self-awareness among blacks.

The initial vehicle for this movement was the Association for the Study of Negro Life and History, formed in Chicago in 1915 by Woodson and a few loyal supporters to investigate and disseminate information concerning blacks. One year later, the first issue of the association's quarterly, the *Journal of Negro History*, appeared, largely the result of Woodson's personal financial and editorial support. Nor was this an isolated phenomenon. During the first few years of the *Journal*'s existence, Woodson frequently utilized portions of his salary as a teacher at Armstrong High School in Washington, D.C., to help keep the *Journal* financially solvent.

As editor of the *Journal*, Woodson was instrumental in stimulating a number of junior and senior scholars to utilize the medium of publication both to increase knowledge and ultimately to further their own research. Individuals like Charles H. Wesley, Rayford W. Logan, W. E. B. DuBois, and Marcus W. Jernegan were among the early contributors of articles and reviews. Largely through Woodson's efforts both as editor and as frequent writer of articles, the *Journal* became invaluable to young scholars during the 1960s when black history was becoming increasingly fashionable. Not only was this publication a scholarly collection of articles and essays on blacks in Africa and the New World as a whole but it also contained a number of newly discovered primary documents of great importance to researchers.

While the *Journal*, with its focus on black history, was clearly enjoying an impressive success record by catering to the interests and needs of the academic community, Woodson early recognized the limitations of its utility not only to high school students and teachers but also to a broad cross section of the general literary public. To offset partially this obvious deficiency, he convinced members of Omega Psi Phi Fraternity, which had annually celebrated the literary achievements of blacks, to cosponsor this celebration with the Association for the Study of Negro Life and History. The result of this joint venture was the initiation of Negro History Week in 1926, an event which led to the popularizing of black literary accomplishments on a new, larger scale. The clarion call in support of the movement was taken up by ministers, businessmen, teachers, social workers, state departments of education, and practically all agencies and individuals with direct access to and impact on the black community. The monthly *Negro History Bulletin*, first published in 1937, catered especially to the needs of the general public, schoolteachers, and pupils for heavily illustrated literature and little-known facts about blacks the world over.

Through his impressive record as founder and leader of the Association for the Study of Negro Life and History, his successful tenure as editor of the *Journal of Negro History*, his contributions to the *Journal*, his initiation of Negro History Week, and the publication of the *Negro History Bulletin*, Carter G. Woodson demonstrated his immense commitment to revealing, to as wide an audience as possible, the achievements of blacks in the world as a whole. A prolific writer who sincerely believed in publishing the truth as the best means of offsetting a number of generally accepted myths about black inferiority, Woodson worked for long hours under generally adverse conditions toward the attainment of his goals. Yet he jealously guarded the organization against possible interference from others, including, at times, his own associates. The story is told that in 1945 Lorenzo J. Greene, Charles H. Wesley, and a number of his trusted associates asked Woodson what plans he was making for the continuation of the Association for the Study of Negro Life and History when he died. Woodson replied that he *was* the association, he had founded it, and he *would remain* the association until he died. Thus, only after his death in 1950 were official plans hastily developed to carry on the task.

Impressive though his record might be as founder of the association and as editor and regular contributor to the *Journal*, Woodson's literary fame rests squarely on his record as author of more than twenty scholarly monographs. He believed that research and scholarship were important largely because they were the means by which he developed a perspective to be applied to the political and socioeconomic problems of black Americans. In a real sense, then, the hallmark of his publications was the new political framework they provided without being essentially vehicles of propaganda.

Woodson's doctoral dissertation, "The Disruption of Virginia," was never published, apparently because Charles H. Ambler had published in 1910 his *Sectionalism in Virginia from 1776 to 1861*, which covered essentially the same period and subject. Woodson, therefore, concentrated his energies on unearthing the history of black Americans and in 1915 published *The Education of the Negro Prior to 1861*. Thus began a period of researching and writing on the historical background of, and opportunities available in education for, blacks in the United States. This book grew out of an effort Woodson had made to produce a small volume on the education of blacks up to 1915. Thinking that he would have to deal largely with the movement after the Civil War, he was surprised at the richness of material available for the antebellum period where records indicated that "the accounts of the successful strivings of Negroes for enlightenment read like beautiful romances of a people in an heroic age."

Woodson's work, the first major study of this important aspect of history, noted significant changes in the quality and nature of education afforded to blacks before and after 1835. Prior to 1835, educational instruction was given on a fairly large scale to slaves on the plantations; after 1835, in the wake of reaction to such insurrectionary activities as the Nat Turner and Denmark Vesey conspiracies, this patriarchal educational system disappeared because of the generally accepted view that education for blacks would lead to excessive self-

assertion. Slaves thereafter received only industrial educations.

The book was an immediate success because of its level of documentation, its exceptional standard of scholarship, and its author's lucidity of expression. One reviewer noted that the book was "a work of profound historical research, full of interesting data on a most important phase of race life which has heretofore remained unexplored and neglected." Another reviewer saw it as a "model of scholarship" in that the author had carefully collected and made available to the reader not only a beautifully written text but also a "painstaking index" and a "scholarly bibliography." Furthermore, Woodson had been careful to append a "valuable set of documents. . . , including many not hitherto laid open to the general public." The same reviewer, noting the objectivity of what others called "a thorough and intelligent study with just enough sympathetic spirit to humanize its array of well-ordered facts," pointed out, in what can perhaps be regarded as the finest tribute to Woodson's scholarship and restraint, that the book was written "with such an impersonal style that no one could tell by its perusal whether its author was white or black." By the time a second edition of this work appeared in 1919, Woodson had clearly established himself as a historian with impeccable credentials.

Woodson's second major work, *A Century of Negro Migration* (1918), built on his tradition as a meticulous scholar and writer. In this topical volume, published during the great migration of blacks in the World War I period, Woodson demonstrated that while there had been much black migration from rural to urban areas, from South to North, from East to West, during the war period, this movement should be perceived within the broader context of continuous migration of blacks promoted by the submarginal position which members of that group occupied within the United States. Though well-documented and written in clear style, the book contained few earth-shattering statements or positions with which one could take issue. In what was perhaps one of the most novel positions adopted at that time, Woodson described the breaking up of Northern black communities in the post-Civil War period when many of their members followed the Union armies and tried to take part in the reconstruction of the Confederate states. Yet this work elicited from a reviewer in the *Times Literary Supplement* the tart observation that it contained "no exuberance of statement, no fervid inaccuracy, no frothy declamation." All reviewers agreed, in fact, that Woodson's objectivity was first-class and his research thorough, a fact which would seem to rank this work with his earlier one as probably his most scholarly publications in terms of documentation and general objectivity.

By this time, Woodson's reputation was so well established that he was appointed in 1919 as Dean of the School of Liberal Arts at Howard University. The following year saw him accepting a similar position at West Virginia State College. But in addition to finding administration less exciting and gratifying than research and writing, Woodson quickly recognized the necessity of making his home permanently in Washington if he were to continue research and writing in the meaningful manner he envisaged. Thus, he eventually resigned his position at West Virginia and returned permanently to Washington and to writing. Yet by combining, however imperfectly, the roles of administrator and scholar, he had made optimum use of his proximity to Washington to bring out two other books, *The History of the Negro Church* (1921) and *The Negro in Our History* (1922).

Woodson was the first to admit the inadequacies of his *History of the Negro Church*, in which he sought to trace the evolution of this important black institution from the earliest times to the contemporary situation. These imperfections, he argued, arose from his inability to obtain much-needed information from a number of denominations which had failed to maintain systematic written records. Further, oral recollections of individuals affiliated with such denominations were difficult to obtain because of their indifference to the project he had undertaken. These difficulties do not by themselves explain, however, the lack of adequate documentation in the work and the absence of a bibliography. In a way, the difficult circumstances under which he wrote this book probably caused Woodson to be less careful than he would otherwise have been in distinguishing and evaluating the thoughts and beliefs of black church leaders on important political and economic issues over time. And yet Woodson praised the traditional conservatism of the church leaders on racial matters as being "fortunate," presumably a reflection of his nineteenth-century faith in the slow educational process as being the best way of eventually improving racial relations in America as a whole.

The Negro in Our History, intended as a work of general information about blacks for high-school and college students as well as for the general public, was repeatedly revised and enlarged after its 1922 publication in response to students' interests and needs. By 1928, the fifth edition had appeared, and while still in its ninth edition in 1950, more than 50,000 volumes had already been sold, a fact which clearly indicates the broad appeal of the book to its intended audience. Earl Thorpe has stated that the volume was "unquestionably the best textbook on the subject until the appearance in 1947 of John Hope Franklin's *From Slavery to Freedom*." According to the sociologist Alain Locke, this book, probably more than any other, "bore the brunt of the movement for the popularization of Negro History" insofar as it undoubtedly "remolded the attitude of the popular mind, especially among Negroes, as to the place and importance of the Negro in American History."

Yet Woodson remained especially temperate and objective in this book. Indeed, he brought an added amount of caution to this work, prompting Locke to remark that it was at once "essentially a compendium of facts" while at the same time it belonged "to that select class of books that have brought about a revolution of mind." Where interpretation was lacking, Woodson's obvious hope was that the facts would speak for themselves. As the book grew in size with subsequent editions, Woodson adapted it to a biographical version, *Negro Makers of History* (1928), for elementary-school students, and a shorter version, *The Story of the Negro Retold* (1935), for high-school students. Also published as a supplementary reader for public-school students was *African Myths, Together With Proverbs* (1928), which contained folktales from various parts of Africa.

All the above books were published by the Associated Publishers, which Woodson had astutely organized while at West Virginia State College. For by this time he had come to recognize how hesitant publishers were to give their seals of approval to studies which diverged from the traditionally accepted view of black inferiority, particularly if the author did not belong to the Southern Revisionist school of historians then firmly entrenched in academic circles even in New York and Boston. By the time of Woodson's death in 1950, the Associated Publishers had published more than fourteen books written or edited by him and upwards of fifty works by other authors.

Returning once more to his pet theme of education for blacks, Woodson published a small booklet, *Early Negro Education in West Virginia* (1921), and a larger work, *The Mis-Education of the Negro* (1933). The latter work found Woodson deploring the lack of adequate race pride among black Americans and condemning the quality of education given to members of that race. He saved some of his harshest words for the so-called "educated Negroes" who exhibited an "attitude of contempt toward their own people because in their own as well as in their mixed schools they are taught to admire the Hebrew, the Greek, the Latin and the Teuton and to despise the African." The philosophical basis of all of Woodson's activities over the years can be found in this volume where he argued quite persuasively for teaching the black "about his race and its history and such training of his special gifts as will restore in him both individual and racial self-respect." As far as Woodson was concerned, therefore, a revamping of the entire American educational system, especially of its curriculum, was essential if blacks were to make any meaningful progress in the United States.

Response to this book was extensive and generally favorable. One commentator noted that "the author does not take the position that everything in the world is wrong, but he does charge to the account of the so-called friends of the race its present plight, and he calls upon the Negro to free his mind from outside control." Essentially the same point was made in the *New York Times* of 26 February 1933 by a reviewer who added that "this is a challenging book."

But Woodson was more than a negative critic. To aid in the teaching of Afro-American history, he published *The African Background Outlined* (1936) as a syllabus which attempted to outline the African background of blacks in America. Essentially, it was a compilation of information on Afro-American life, culture, and history, supplemented by a topical study outline. One reviewer felt that the book was very "timely," though he noted that its chief weaknesses were "its repetitiousness and its conglomerate appearance." Rayford W. Logan, a contemporary of Woodson, declared that the syllabus was "one of the most useful and scholarly works" that Woodson produced.

In keeping with his avowed belief that difficultly obtained primary materials should be made accessible to scholars and students, Woodson published *Free Negro Owners of Slaves in the United States in 1830* (1924) and *Free Negro Heads of Families in the United States in 1830* (1925). Both of these were edited works which utilized the 1830 census reports to provide largely statistical compilations of a much neglected aspect of American history. Most of the basic research was actually conducted by employees of the association through a grant obtained in 1921 from the Laura Spellman Rockefeller Memorial. *Negro Orators and Their Orations* (1925) and *The Mind of the Negro as Reflected in Letters Written During the*

Crisis, 1800-1860 (1926) sought to present black speakers and writers in their own words rather than through the impressions of others. Both edited works were extremely useful and well received. Although a number of the letters included in *The Mind of the Negro as Reflected in Letters Written During the Crisis* had already appeared in issues of the *Journal of Negro History*, the *Catholic World* rightly concluded that the publication contained a "mine of information" for students.

The late 1920s and early 1930s witnessed the publication of two works in which Woodson collaborated with other scholars. *The Negro as a Businessman* (1929), coauthored with John H. Harmon, Jr., and Arnett C. Lindsay, was the offshoot of a project undertaken by the association on studies on the economic development of blacks since the Civil War. *The Negro Wage Earner* (1930) was coauthored with Lorenzo J. Greene, a young Ph.D. history graduate from Columbia University who became a longtime friend and colleague of Woodson.

These two works were evidence of a new focus by Woodson. Having apparently done as much as he possibly could to popularize the general achievements and contributions of blacks, he was shifting his emphasis to more specialized areas. *The Rural Negro* (1930), a treatment of the health, farming, industry, religion, and education of rural Southerners, continued this trend. Based largely on U.S. census reports and questionnaires sent out to rural families, the book was criticized by one reviewer as being little short of a tract against certain forms of exploitation and inadequately documented. Another reviewer, however, hailed the publication as "a first-hand piece of research," which was "well-documented."

As a companion to *The Negro Wage Earner*, *The Negro Professional Man and the Community* (1934) provided special emphasis on the professions of medicine and law, though not to the exclusion of other professions. Containing little documentation, this volume also obviously relied heavily on U.S. census reports and questionnaires. The *New York Times* regarded the study as a "valuable sociological contribution to knowledge" while Alain Locke, writing in the August 1934 issue of *Survey*, considered it "the best available appraisal of the important group leadership exercised by the Negro minister, teacher, lawyer, nurse, welfare worker, and artist."

A biographical account of famous Africans appeared under the title *African Heroes and Heroines* (1939). Intended mostly for junior-high and high-school students, the book highlighted the militancy and resistance of African groups and nations to European and Arabic invaders and included a survey of the geography and peoples in Africa. While one reviewer lamented the "strong note of militant vindication that rather mars the strictly expository portions of the book," even he had to admit that it filled "a gap in our fund of information."

Carter G. Woodson, then, clearly deserves to be ranked very high among the foremost of American historians of the twentieth century. Never married, he gave his life to the Association for the Study of Negro Life and History and to its endeavors to fill the tremendous hiatus which had existed in American historiography. His prolific writing knew no boundaries in furthering truth and in generally uplifting individuals of African descent. In Woodson's mind, this end could best be achieved through scientific studies on blacks in America and the dissemination of the knowledge gained. He openly questioned a number of prevailing racial assumptions that marred history books, and he sought to expose them for what they were worth. Somewhat reclusive, he was also terribly intolerant and strongwilled. Even some of his closest associates dreaded having to oppose any position he adopted. Yet he made an indelible impression on the minds of a whole generation of American historians and educators. The study, writing, and teaching of American history has not been the same since Woodson successfully countered the ignorance and misinformation that had surrounded the contributions of blacks to the building of the United States.

Like most pioneers, Woodson was somewhat ahead of his time. As the work of the association increased and his writing flourished, he incurred the hostility of a number of his erstwhile white supporters. In Woodson's own words, Thomas Jesse Jones, educational director of the Phelps-Stokes Fund, "conducted a campaign against the Association for the Study of Negro Life and History because the Director questioned the wisdom of Jones' African policy. By 1930 he succeeded in lopping off support of the Association from boards and foundations." This sort of attack was probably instrumental in Woodson's leaving behind a number of white liberals whose commitment to his cause he doubted. By 1930, his writings reflected an increasing bitterness toward the white establishment and a growing urgency for black solidarity.

Woodson's greatest regret was probably his inability to complete his most cherished project, the publication of an *Encyclopedia Africana*. Though he clearly had collected an adequate amount of material, the requisite financial support was lacking.

However, thanks to his revisionist writings and the material that he edited in the *Journal of Negro History*, serious students of Afro-American history cannot help but give him due credit. A number of treasured documents, which he gathered during a lifetime of scholarship, today constitute the Carter G. Woodson deposit in the Library of Congress.

Other:

Free Negro Owners of Slaves in the United States in 1830, edited by Woodson (Washington, D.C.: Association for the Study of Negro Life and History, 1924);

Free Negro Heads of Families in the United States in 1830, edited by Woodson (Washington, D.C.: Association for the Study of Negro Life and History, 1925);

Negro Orators and Their Orations, edited by Woodson (Washington, D.C.: Associated Publishers, 1925);

The Mind of the Negro as Reflected in Letters Written During the Crisis, 1800-1860, edited by Woodson (Washington, D.C.: Associated Publishers, 1926);

The Works of Francis J. Grimké, 4 volumes, edited by Woodson (Washington, D.C.: Associated Publishers, 1942).

Periodical Publications:

"The Negroes of Cincinnati Prior to the Civil War," *Journal of Negro History*, 1 (January 1916): 1-22;

"Freedom and Slavery in Appalachian America," *Journal of Negro History*, 1 (April 1916): 123-150;

"Anthony Benezet," *Journal of Negro History*, 2 (January 1917): 37-50;

"Beginnings of Miscegenation of the Whites and Blacks," *Journal of Negro History*, 3 (October 1918): 335-353;

"Negro Life and History in Our Schools," *Journal of Negro History*, 4 (July 1919): 273-280;

"The Relations of Negroes and Indians in Massachusetts," *Journal of Negro History*, 5 (January 1920): 45-57;

"Fifty Years of Negro Citizenship as Qualified by the United States Supreme Court," *Journal of Negro History*, 6 (January 1921): 1-53;

"Early Negro Education in West Virginia," *Journal of Negro History*, 7 (January 1922): 22-63;

"Ten Years of Collecting and Publishing the Records of the Negro," *Journal of Negro History*, 10 (October 1925): 598-606;

"Insurance Business Among Negroes," *Journal of*

Negro History, 14 (April 1929): 202-226;
"The Negro Washerwoman, a Vanishing Figure," *Journal of Negro History*, 15 (July 1930): 269-277;
"Some Attitudes in English Literature," *Journal of Negro History*, 20 (January 1935): 27-85;
"Attitudes of the Iberian Peninsula," *Journal of Negro History*, 20 (April 1935): 190-243;
"An Accounting for Twenty-Five Years," *Journal of Negro History*, 25 (October 1940): 422-431;
"Notes on the Bakongo," *Journal of Negro History*, 30 (October 1945): 421-431.

References:

Mary McLeod Bethune, "The Torch is Ours," *Journal of Negro History*, 36 (January 1951): 9-11;
William M. Brewer, "Anniversary of the *Journal of Negro History*," *Journal of Negro History*, 51 (April 1966): 75-97;
John Hope Franklin, "The New Negro History," *Journal of Negro History*, 42 (April 1957): 89-97;
Frank J. Klingberg, "Carter G. Woodson, Historian, and His Contribution to American Historiography," *Journal of Negro History*, 41 (January 1956): 66-68;
R. [ayford] W. L[ogan], "Carter Godwin Woodson," *Journal of Negro History*, 35 (1950): 344-348;
Negro History Bulletin, special Woodson issue, 13 (May 1950);
Earl E. Thorpe, *Black Historians: A Critique* (New York: Morrow, 1971);
Charles H. Wesley, "Carter G. Woodson as a Scholar," *Journal of Negro History*, 36 (January 1951): 12-24.

C. Vann Woodward

Elisabeth Muhlenfeld
Florida State University

BIRTH: Vanndale, Arkansas, 13 November 1908, to Hugh Allison and Bess Vann Woodward.

EDUCATION: B.Phil., Emory University, 1930; M.A., Columbia University, 1932; Ph.D., University of North Carolina, 1937.

MARRIAGE: 21 December 1937 to Glenn Boyd MacLeod; child: Peter.

AWARDS AND HONORS: Bancroft History Prize, for *Origins of the New South*, 1952; National Institute of Arts and Letters Award, 1954; Pulitzer Prize for *Mary Chesnut's Civil War*, 1982; numerous honorary degrees.

BOOKS: *Tom Watson, Agrarian Rebel* (New York: Macmillan, 1938; republished with an introduction, 1955; Oxford: Oxford University Press, 1963, 1975);
The Battle for Leyte Gulf (New York: Macmillan, 1947; London: Landborough, 1958);
Reunion and Reaction: The Compromise of 1877 and the End of Reconstruction (Boston: Little, Brown, 1951; revised, 1966);
Origins of the New South, 1877-1913, volume 9 of *A History of the South*, edited by W. H. Stephenson and E. M. Coulter (Baton Rouge: Louisiana State University Press, 1951; revised, 1971);
The Strange Career of Jim Crow (New York: Oxford University Press, 1955; revised with a new introduction, 1957; revised again, 1966; revised again, 1974);
The Burden of Southern History (Baton Rouge: Louisiana State University Press, 1960; revised, 1968);
The National Experience, by Woodward, John M. Blum, Edmund S. Morgan, Willie Lee Rose, Arthur Schlesinger, Jr., and Kenneth M. Stampp (New York: Harcourt, Brace & World, 1963);
American Counterpoint: Slavery and Racism in the North-South Dialogue (Boston: Little, Brown, 1971).

C. Vann Woodward's active career, now spanning nearly forty-five years as a historian of the American South, is remarkable both for its impact and for its durability. Since the publication of his masterful *Origins of the New South, 1877-1913*, in 1951, Woodward has been regarded by his col-

C. Vann Woodward

leagues, supporters and detractors alike, as preeminent in his field—the one historian whose works must be mastered and reckoned with by serious students of Southern history. And with *The Strange Career of Jim Crow* (1955), followed by essays and reviews of consistently high quality and readability in such periodicals as *Commentary*, *Harper's*, and the *New York Review of Books*, he has achieved a popular readership and public acclaim as well. In a profession in which—at least in the twentieth century—sweeping reinterpretations of historical periods rarely stand long without serious challenge, Woodward's reading of Southern history as discontinuous, his analysis of the nature of Southern identity, and his emphasis on the crucial importance of the interrelationships between races in the post-Reconstruction South are still regarded as authoritative.

Woodward, one of the first historians to recognize the importance of what has come to be called the Southern Literary renaissance, in fact deserves to be considered a part of that renaissance. Writing after the first great outpouring of Southern litera-

ture in the late 1920s, Woodward may fruitfully be discussed as a significant figure in what has sometimes been called the second generation of the Southern Renaissance: its historian, one of its finest essayists, and even to some degree its philosopher. Educated in the late 1920s and early 1930s, Woodward read widely in writers such as William Faulkner (whose early work at first disturbed him), Thomas Wolfe, Katherine Anne Porter, and the Nashville Agrarians, whose manifesto *I'll Take My Stand* was published in 1930. From them he learned much; in important ways these writers shaped his view of the South and of history and he, in turn, was throughout his career to provide historical underpinnings for major themes of the Southern Literary Renaissance.

In 1956, Woodward made a formal bow to Southern letters in a revealing essay entitled "The Historical Dimension," in which he discussed the ideological and moral relationships between the literature of the twentieth-century South and new directions in Southern historical scholarship. In that essay he discussed the work of contemporary Southern writers as literature "in which the historical imagination played a supreme part," in which past is always relevant to present—always, in fact, part and parcel of the present. But such literature, grounded firmly in the tradition of the great realists, had no axes to grind, no old myths to uphold. Instead, these writers, fully conscious of "the chaos and irony of history," wrote vividly, created complex worlds, and forced their readers to rethink old prejudices, to let loose outmoded mythologizing or treacle, and to abandon cynicism or self-destructive guilt. Further, Woodward found valuable for the historian the emphasis writers such as Faulkner, Robert Penn Warren, and Eudora Welty placed upon the individual, not as alienated, but as "an inextricable part of a living history and community, attached and determined in a thousand ways by other wills and destinies of people he has only heard about." Woodward closed his essay by acknowledging the shared tools and aims of the novelist and the historian—an acknowledgment that Henry James earlier had made in *The Art of Fiction* (1884) as he argued for the artistic merit of the novel. Woodward similarly called for historians to abandon "an old and false analogy with the natural sciences" and instead to admit that the historian "attempts to 'explain' history in the same way he explains events in ordinary life . . . with much the same language, moral and philosophical."

Woodward's insistence upon the close relationship between ordinary life and what he has often called the craft of history provides an important key to his career. He has consistently regarded history as a useful enterprise, and many of his books may be understood as efforts to teach us about the present, to explain where we are in light of where we have been. Focusing on the South, which he (like novelists and poets such as Faulkner and Warren) finds to be a fertile microcosm of the human experience, Woodward has forged a view of history as a complicated blend of mass and individual, economics and ideology, caste and class, mind and matter which has important implications for both present and future. His first book, *Tom Watson, Agrarian Rebel* (1938), a study of a Populist politician turned demagogue, clearly illustrated Woodward's remarkable insight into the relationship of the individual to society; furthermore, it gave notice that he would always be open to the ironic inconsistencies of human nature, both in the individual and in the aggregate.

Origins of the New South, 1877-1913 (1951) and its predecessor by several months, *Reunion and Reaction: The Compromise of 1877 and the End of Reconstruction* (1951), constituted an important revisionist view of a period in Southern history that, by the turn of the century, had in the main been labeled and then ignored. Both books suggested finally the degree to which regional pieties and political dogma could obscure reality; in both books Woodward continued the process he had begun in *Tom Watson, Agrarian Rebel*. He questioned the prevailing view of the "Solid South" in the period following Reconstruction, and he amassed a damning case for the economic exploitation of the South by its own rising industrial capitalist leaders acting in concert with Northern interests. Moreover, in *Tom Watson* and *Origins of the New South*, Woodward laid the groundwork for his lifelong study of race relations.

The results of that study reached Woodward's widest audience in 1955 with the publication of *The Strange Career of Jim Crow*, which asserted that the system of legal racial discrimination did not spring up full-blown immediately following Reconstruction but instead emerged as policy in the 1890s and evolved through the first decades of the twentieth century. *The Strange Career of Jim Crow*, published just as the civil rights movement was gaining strength in the mid-1950s, showed a historian plying his trade to teach an immediately relevant truth: far from having their roots in a distant, sacred past, such laws had grown up fairly recently in response to an interlocking network of economic and political expediencies. The obvious implication of Wood-

ward's study was that abolition of such laws would help to correct the exploitative political policies he had outlined. As such, the book not only constituted a work of historical scholarship but also a moral critique that offered a guide to political action.

Similarly, the essays collected in *The Burden of Southern History* (1960) and *American Counterpoint: Slavery and Racism in the North-South Dialogue* (1971) frequently combined Woodward's skill as a researcher, his interpretative power, and his ability to draw parallels between experiences in the history of the American South and political and social realities of the present. In "The Irony of Southern History," written in 1953 and collected in *The Burden of Southern History*, Woodward, for example, offered provocative parallels between the Southern white's certainty of the nobility and rightness of his "cause" in the 1850s and 1860s and the American belief in the country's invincibility during a period of McCarthyism and cold war. Several essays dealing with race relations in these books spoke to a mid-twentieth-century America embroiled in racial unrest and violence and always aimed to illuminate the reader's understanding and to liberate his sensibilities by removing the origins of American race relations from a fog of anecdote, myth, and magnolia-mongering. Woodward believed that Americans must use history to see clearly that the past is not the present but that studying it could help to clear away the illusions harbored about the nation.

As a moralist and a liberal, Woodward has never regarded the study of history as sufficient in itself; one bothers to explain the past in part with the hope that knowledge and understanding will effect change—or at the very least enable the reader to cope more effectively with the world in which he finds himself. But Woodward has never allowed either his concern for civil rights or his love of his native South to obscure unpleasant truths. As the body of his work attests, he has a mind that admits contradictions and indeed revels in them. His is a tragic view of history and of man, and he is carefully attuned to the ironies which such a view reveals. When Woodward looks at man en masse, he most often finds greed, self-aggrandizement, a voracious appetite for power, and the machinations and manipulations necessary to feed them. Thus Woodward delights in the painstaking detective work necessary to unveil elaborate conspiracies and cover-ups. However, when Woodward looks at the individual, he is most often drawn to the independent thinker, the outsider, the objective mind, the ironic voice; such individuals not only touch a responsive chord in him but also offer him the opportunity to examine historical events and whole periods from a fresh perspective.

Woodward's best work combines a view of whole societies with close examinations of individual men and women who observed and acted in those societies. He writes with a characteristically clean, metaphorical style in which lucid analysis is spiced with wit. A master of the essay form, Woodward well deserves to be called a man of letters, a close kinsman to the Southern writers he has read and admired throughout his career. Significantly, his most recent work, *Mary Chesnut's Civil War* (1981), awarded the 1982 Pulitzer Prize for history, is the definitive edition of a neglected Southern writer fascinated by politics. Mary Boykin Chesnut was a realist who called herself a "close observer . . . of men and manners" and whose salient characteristic was her ironic wit.

Born on 13 November 1908 in Vanndale, Arkansas, a small village named for a great-grandfather who had come to the area about 1850, Comer Vann Woodward was the son of Hugh Allison and Bess Vann Woodward. His father was from Tennessee, his mother from an English family which had settled in North Carolina before the Revolution. A grandfather, John Vann, as a boy had served four years in the Confederate army. Woodward spent much of his youth in Morrilton, near the center of the state, where his father was superintendent of the public schools.

Woodward's childhood and youth steeped him not only in the Southern culture and Klan-colored mores of Morrilton but also in a liberal tradition embraced by his parents, both devout Methodists. His father's role as an educator brought the young Vann into contact with outspoken Southern liberals, among them his uncle Comer M. Woodward, a professor of sociology at Southern Methodist University, and Rupert B. Vance, who was a friend and neighbor in Vann's childhood and who, by the time Woodward attended the University of North Carolina at Chapel Hill in the mid-1930s, was a renowned sociologist there. Howard W. Odum, also at the University of North Carolina when Woodward was enrolled, came to know the Woodward family about 1928, when Hugh Woodward accepted a post as dean of Emory University's junior college at Oxford, Georgia, where Odum's parents lived.

Woodward settled on a career in history almost by accident. After two years at Henderson Brown, a small Arkansas college, he transferred to Emory University in Atlanta, where his uncle was then teaching sociology and from which he graduated in 1930 with a bachelor of philosophy degree. The following year, he taught English at Georgia Institute of Technology and then attended Columbia, where, in 1932, he earned a master's degree in political science. That summer, eager to view firsthand what many of his fellow students regarded as the wave of the future, he traveled to France, Germany, and Russia. In Russia, half a world from home, he was impressed that criticism of America focused on the race relations of the American South—and, in particular, on the Scottsboro case. Returning to Atlanta, he again taught English at Georgia Institute of Technology.

During his years in Atlanta, Woodward made several important friendships that were to shape his future. He came to know a number of prominent blacks as well as Will W. Alexander of the Commission of Interracial Cooperation. Glenn Rainey, a graduate student and debate coach at Emory when Woodward attended, also became a good friend. Rainey, whose outspoken views on racial equality at one point earned him the official opprobrium of the Georgia legislature, served as an intellectual mentor, forcing Woodward to clarify his own thinking about race. When a young black Communist organizer, Angelo Herndon, was arrested in 1932 and charged with the capital crime of inciting insurrection, Woodward joined others on a committee formed to save Herndon, a committee Woodward chaired for a time. The Herndon case ended five years later when the U.S. Supreme Court in 1937 declared the insurrection law unconstitutional. Yet Woodward's involvement had been brief; he had left the committee disillusioned by internal bickering and by Communist manipulation of the case for propaganda purposes.

Ostensibly because of budgetary cutbacks but possibly because of his involvement in the Herndon case, Woodward lost his teaching job and returned for several months to Oxford, Georgia, where he worked briefly on a farm survey for the WPA. In Oxford he turned his attention to a project he had been planning: a book, tentatively entitled "Seven for Demos," which would sketch the lives of seven Southern radicals, "possibly Ben Tillman, certainly Tom Watson." However, during the months of WPA work, he abandoned the unwieldy project and focused instead on Watson, whose life proved to Woodward to be a mass of fascinating contradictions. Woodward discovered that Watson, who earned infamy among liberals between 1904 and his death in 1922 as the quintessential racist, had worked effectively in the 1880s and 1890s as a

Populist spokesman advocating social and economic reforms that included a coalition of small farmers both black and white. Furthermore, Watson had upon occasion placed his political future on the line to support black leaders. His career provided Woodward with clear evidence that the post-Reconstruction South had not unanimously supported rigid segregation. Here, for Woodward, was a tragic and ironic story of a courageous and able man who had gone against prevailing opinion and political custom in his young adulthood but who in maturity had bowed to political realities and turned all his energies and abilities to tearing down the very bonds between races he had once worked to establish.

What aroused Woodward's sympathies was not the Watson of the Great War years and early 1920s but the stirring Populist leader whose early career proved that there *had* been exceptions in the South. The historian was later to acknowledge the importance of this discovery to his career: "If there had indeed been no exceptions, no breaks, and things had always been the same," as the standard historical reading of the post-Reconstruction South stoutly maintained, "there was little hope of change." Having obtained the Watson family's permission to work with the politician's papers, Woodward secured a General Education Board fellowship through the aid of Howard Odum and began his doctoral studies at the University of North Carolina in 1934. He went to Chapel Hill because the Watson papers were there; he chose to study history simply because his was most logically a history project.

At Chapel Hill, as in Atlanta, the young Woodward often moved outside the formal academic community. There he met Gertrude Stein, playwright Paul Green, and the publisher William T. Couch. On a debate trip to Nashville with Couch, he met Andrew Nelson Lytle, Frank L. Owsley, Allen Tate, and Donald Davidson. Later he met Robert Penn Warren, with whom he was to form a lifelong friendship. More important to his scholarly career, however, was the intellectual climate of the university in the 1930s. Woodward worked under the direction of Howard K. Beale but also found much to interest him in the work of Rupert Vance and Odum, by now the region's leading sociologists. And it was also at Chapel Hill that Woodward met and married a young North Carolina woman, Glenn Boyd MacLeod, thus entering into a marriage which lasted until her death in 1982.

When his degree was granted in 1937, he accepted a position teaching social science and moved with his bride to the University of Florida in Gainesville. The following year, when he was twenty-nine, his dissertation was published as *Tom Watson, Agrarian Rebel* and was praised by Allan Nevins on the front page of the *New York Times Book Review*. Woodward's career as a historian of the American South was off to a fortuitous start.

Tom Watson, Agrarian Rebel, the first of four books recasting postbellum Southern history, made a major departure from prevailing interpretations. Southern historians had concentrated on the antebellum and Civil War periods and on a chamber-of-commerce view of the New South but had paid little attention to the period in between. With few exceptions, in the formal studies of the period it was axiomatic that the postwar political struggles were between a landed agrarian establishment and external capitalist forces controlled by the industrial Northeast. As David Potter has noted, it was this oversimplified agrarian/industrial dualism, a thesis held even by so clear-eyed a historian as Charles Beard and accepted by Woodward's teacher Howard Beale, that Woodward shrewdly questioned: "Woodward . . . perceived that there had always been Whiggish forces in the South, ready to embrace industrial goals, and that the defeat of the Confederacy had set the stage for these forces to take over. Therefore the real struggle was internal—within the South—rather than external."

Woodward saw that at the close of Reconstruction the "Redeemers" who came to power were not the old aristocracy but a rising class of industrial capitalists—in Georgia, men like John B. Gordon, Alfred H. Colquitt, and Joseph E. Brown, who obscured their real political interests through Stars-and-Bars rhetoric. These giants of Georgia politics (and, as Woodward would later show in *Origins of the New South*, their counterparts in other states) had generally been called "Bourbons"; Woodward preferred to call them by their 1872 slogan, "New Departure" Democrats. Operating largely through fear, "fear of the Negro menace, the scalawag menace, the Federal menace," they demanded—and received—unquestioning allegiance. Thus Watson, as an agrarian spokesman, found himself in direct and bitter conflict not only with an old patrician order but also with a Southern establishment dedicated to industrial development (symbolized by the railroad syndicates) at the expense of the small farmer.

As Woodward charted Tom Watson's role in the formation of a Southern Populist party challenge to conservative Democrats and to New South industrialists, he also carefully chronicled the plight of the black farmer entombed in a cycle of debt and severely handicapped by legal, social, and political discrimination. The assumptions that emancipation had, in the main, solved the Negro problem and that the end of Reconstruction left Southerners free to work out for themselves the best course for race relations were fallacious. So was the impression that white supremacy and opposition to black enfranchisement had sprung forward unchallenged after 1876. Rather, Democrats throughout the last decades of the nineteenth century frequently encouraged and controlled black votes to defeat political opponents, including Populists and just as frequently used the race issue to disguise their own economic interests.

Woodward's biography of Watson depicted a man of paradox, whose early career contrasted startlingly with his later stance. Woodward saw Watson in both phases of his life not as responsible for the bigotry he finally came to represent but instead as a product of an economic system and of a heritage of history, politics, and race relations to which he finally succumbed. Watson's tragedy was, in Woodward's private view expressed in his preface, "the tragedy of a class, and more especially the tragedy of a section."

Tom Watson, Agrarian Rebel, long since considered a classic and still in print, won immediate praise for its author. Allan Nevins recognized the book as an exhaustive study that probed "deep into the life and mind of the South," thus pointing to one of the book's most important assets: although *Tom Watson, Agrarian Rebel*, was the biography of one man, its painstaking scholarship, the deep and broad reading in primary sources that would distinguish all of Woodward's major work, revealed on every page his ability to understand and portray major social and political movements as well. Furthermore, Henry Steele Commager called the book a "model of its kind," a study written in a style "always vigorous and sometimes brilliant." *Tom Watson, Agrarian Rebel*'s reception was in large measure responsible for Woodward's appointment as visiting assistant professor of history at the University of Virginia in 1939 (his first academic post as a historian); the following year he moved to Scripps College as associate professor of American history and biography.

From 1943 to 1946, Woodward served as a lieutenant in the navy, in the Office of Navy Intelligence, and in the Naval Office of Public Information. While in the navy, he became involved in a study of operations in the Philippines, a study which resulted in his second book, *The Battle for Leyte Gulf* (1947), the only one of his books entirely outside the area of Southern history. Here his subject was not a single man, but thousands, of different ranks and opposing nationalities, all engaged in what he called "the greatest naval battle of the Second World War and the largest engagement ever fought on the high seas." Again Woodward, this time in a branch of history completely new to him and well known for its technical difficulty, impressed his reviewers with his command of his subject, his objective eye, and his ability to make history intensely readable for experts and lay readers alike. Here his emphasis was not on interpretation but sheer narrative. Reviewers called Woodward's achievement "authoritative." Fletcher Pratt, in the *New York Times*, found his picture of the entire series of naval engagements "so correct, so complete and so soundly documented that it is hard to see how anyone, ever, will be able to improve on Mr. Woodward's presentation of the facts in this case."

The Battle for Leyte Gulf, lying outside the main body of Woodward's work, would seem to shed little light on his career in Southern history. But in fact the book illustrated two important qualities. First, it showed Woodward quite at home in contemporary history: judiciously reserved about interpreting current events but comfortable and skilled at making sense of them. Second, *The Battle for Leyte Gulf* suggested a quick mastery of material, thus foreshadowing the magisterial *Origins of the New South*. By the time *The Battle for Leyte Gulf* was published, Woodward was already at work on *Origins of the New South*, had received a Guggenheim Fellowship, and had settled in Baltimore as associate professor of history at Johns Hopkins University, where he would remain for fourteen years.

The two books published by Woodward in 1951, *Reunion and Reaction: The Compromise of 1877 and the End of Reconstruction* and *Origins of the New South, 1877-1913*, may properly be considered together, and in fact *Reunion and Reaction* appeared in summary form as the second chapter in *Origins of the New South*. In beginning work on *Origins of the New South*, to be published as volume nine of the prestigious *A History of the South* series published by the Louisiana State University Press, Woodward had recognized the Compromise of 1877 as "an unsolved puzzle," and in the course of that work he uncovered clues which enabled him to piece together a solution. Thus, *Reunion and Reaction* was the result of what David Potter has called "the kind of detective work which historians dream about."

In his acknowledgments to *Reunion and Reac-*

tion, Woodward offered a tribute to Charles A. Beard as "the originator of the concept of the Civil War and Reconstruction as a revolution—the Second American Revolution," and this acknowledgment stands as a proper starting point for *Origins of the New South* as well. For the period following Reconstruction was, as Woodward saw it, equivalent to the Thermidor following the French Revolution. In the Compromise of 1877, generally credited with marking the end of Reconstruction, the North preserved the economic fruits of the Civil War while abandoning idealistic and humanitarian commitments, particularly commitments made to newly freed black citizens.

Far from being the dramatic outcome of last-minute secret meetings at the famous Wormley Conference, the Compromise of 1877 was, Woodward found, what today would be called a media event, a device used to provide convenient, simple explanations and acceptable rationales for a series of often sordid negotiations and bargains struck through preceding months between the Republicans and Southern Democrats. Until Woodward wrote, these bargains had remained concealed for nearly three quarters of a century—oddly so, since newspaper editors at the time had reported the implications of the political machinations that led to Rutherford B. Hayes's assumption of the presidency.

Woodward began his account of the so-called Bargain of 1877 by noting that, at the time it was made, Southerners had already committed themselves to the cause they supposedly adopted at the conference table and that Hayes had already agreed to conciliation of the South. In fact, a week before the negotiations of the Wormley Conference began, the Democratically controlled House of Representatives had refused to pass any military appropriations bill that did not include a clause in effect forbidding the use of federal troops to uphold Republican governments in the Southern states. Thus, Hayes's friends in the Bargain of 1877 gave up "something they no longer really possessed in exchange for something that had already been secured by other means," and Southerners "were solemnly accepting something that had been secured by other means in exchange for adherence to a course to which, by that time, they were already committed." "It was, on the whole," wrote Woodward, "one of the strangest bargains in the annals of horse swapping."

In *Reunion and Reaction*, Woodward showed that the importance of the Wormley Conference lay in its propaganda value; unlike the complicated negotiations which had preceded it, the conference "could be, and was, made to appeal to the chivalrous Southern heart as a knightly deed—the rescue of a distressed sister state [Louisiana] from the tyrannical heel of the Carpetbagger. . . . Such a chivalrous deed would excuse much—even voting with Republicans. And so the whole complicated arrangement could be explained in terms of one of its parts. And it was so explained, and has been ever since." Having carefully documented the power politics and economic interests of the redeemer governments, Woodward made clear the way in which such interests had obscured an earlier national commitment to the freedmen. In a final chapter, the writer discussed the outcome of the Compromise of 1877, which, instead of restoring an old order, instead of returning the South to economic and political parity with other sections, had delivered the South to "Redeemers" under whose conservative and "practical" control the region "became a bulwark instead of a menace to the new order" of the Gilded Age.

Reunion and Reaction may be seen as an extended prologue to *Origins of the New South*, which opens in 1877, the year of the end of Radical Reconstruction, and examines the South through the beginning of the Wilson years, which marked an apparent resurgence of Southern power in national politics. Had Woodward's career produced *Origins of the New South* alone, his distinction as a historian would be assured, for *Origins of the New South* is Woodward's masterpiece, elegantly written and dense with the documentation necessary to extend and support the theses he had set forth on a smaller scale in *Tom Watson, Agrarian Rebel*, and *Reunion and Reaction*. He began with a roll call of Redeemers throughout the former Confederate states, noting wryly how frequently their "extrapolitical" interests ran to railroads, iron, and coal, and how rarely their roots were firmly planted in the antebellum aristocracy. Thus, by the close of the first three chapters, he had once again blasted the cherished myth of redeemer governments restoring the old order. The immediate legacy of Reconstruction, as Woodward saw it, was a continuation of the gerrymandering, fraud, and repressive devices used to control votes by the radicals but now refined and employed to entrench the redeemer regimes. Virtually every succeeding chapter would, as well, lay another myth to rest. His subject was a dark and tragic period in Southern history, and throughout *Origins of the New South* he examined his period with a penetrating eye.

Perhaps the most striking assertion of *Origins*

of the New South was at the same time its most sweeping: Woodward avowed that the famed economic "recovery" of the New South was essentially nonexistent. As he examined statistical data in state after state, he painted a picture of a region mired in a poverty so deep and so far-reaching that it infected every dimension of Southern life. Woodward called the New South a "colonial economy," which even as late as 1919 (the first year reliable per capita income estimates were available), lagged forty percent behind the national average. In a chapter entitled "The Industrial Evolution," he found erroneous the prevailing belief in the South's entry into the industrial revolution in the 1880s. For instance, the textile industry and the cotton-mill town originated in the antebellum South, not in the 1880s, a decade which saw merely an acceleration of the profits that had grown steadily since 1865. In fact, new industrial activity in the South after 1880 was almost always a result of Northern exploitation of cheap labor pools, exploitation enthusiastically supported by Southern business and political interests anxious to "adjust," to "standardize," to conform to the progress of the industrial Northeast. And in an effort to make progress, to attract outside industry, a host of reprehensible practices grew up designed to insure a pool of cheap labor. One of the worst was the convict-lease system born of military governments immediately after the war, nurtured by carpetbaggers and given legitimacy by redeemer governments overwhelmed by increasing crime rates. Grasping at what seemed a profitable solution to an outmoded penitentiary system, the redeemer legislatures granted leases of ten to thirty years to Southern and Northern syndicates, mining corporations, and other large lessees whose profits came from subletting convicts.

Somewhat better off than the victims of the convict lease system were the farmers, now slaves to a lien system which, because it was "no respecter of race or class," sucked whites into debt cycles indistinguishable from those of the blacks. As the century drew to a close, farmers earned less and less for the same amount of work; they paid usurious interest rates, from thirty to seventy percent, to merchants; yet Woodward found no evidence to blame this system on the merchants who themselves paid outrageous rates to factors—all buckets "on an endless chain by which the agricultural well of a tributary region was drained of its flow."

By the early 1880s, the Southern farmer was ready to embrace the Populist movement that was gaining strength in the West and Midwest. In *Origins of the New South* Woodward carefully fleshed out the story he had outlined in *Tom Watson, Agrarian Rebel*. Again, what most appealed to Woodward about Southern Populists was their early effort to enlist black farmers in their cause. The early Southern Populists were realists, fully conscious of the political motives lying behind the increasingly rigid color line and aware that black and white farmers could be kept weak and be managed more easily if they were divided. Woodward established that Populist efforts had been on behalf of political and economic cooperation—never social equality—yet he was fully attuned to the tragic failure of those efforts because of white supremacy and to the ironic turnabout of the very reformers who had striven to combat entrenched racial discrimination.

In his detailed study of race relations and the progression of legislation to formalize discrimination and legislate white supremacy, Woodward charted new ground. Pointing out that some prominent Southern whites had advocated enfranchisement of the Negro in the years immediately following the war, he went on to trace the history of disenfranchisement, which shifted to high gear in Mississippi in 1890 and spread to other states over the next two decades. Supporters of disenfranchisement insisted that it was nothing more than a practical political reform. They argued that it would cut down on election fraud, which it did: Woodward noted that an "effective means of stopping the stealing of ballots, of course, is to stop the people from casting them." Furthermore, disenfranchisement would eliminate the "Negro Question" from politics, supporters asserted, thus enabling citizens to concentrate on "fundamental issues" and thereby to improve race relations.

But, Woodward demonstrated, behind the seemingly unified front that supported these laws lay a bitter struggle between various white interest groups, usually between whites in "Black Belt" counties and those from sections with small numbers of Negro voters. The very laws which successfully disenfranchised blacks performed the same function for poor whites unable to pass property or literacy tests or to pay poll taxes. Since, more often than not, whites who were disenfranchised under the new laws were the very men who had supported the Populist movement, it was white supremacy that finally united the Solid South—not the other way around. Thus the struggle to insure white supremacy could be seen as a class struggle in which the Negro was frequently all but forgotten.

Furthermore, race relations did not improve. Instead, disenfranchisement was followed by Jim Crow laws, widened the gulf between the races, and produced tension, suspicion, and mistrust. Woodward would more fully tell this story four years later in *The Strange Career of Jim Crow*, but with its fundamental point established and documented in *Origins of the New South*.

Almost unnoticed by commentators on *Origins of the New South* were two aspects of the book that foreshadowed work to which Woodward would turn after 1953. Both were closely related to themes being explored then by such writers as William Faulkner and Robert Penn Warren. The first was an examination of the way Southerners viewed themselves in the postbellum period. Because of his wide reading in both the literature and journalism of the era, Woodward perceived that "[o]ne of the most significant inventions of the New South was the 'Old South.'" The seed of the myth of the Old South was a romanticization of the Lost Cause; this began in the 1880s, grew with the fashion of Confederate reunions in the 1890s, and achieved an aura of religious fervor by 1895 with the organization of the United Daughters of the Confederacy. And from the Lost Cause, Southerners of all classes began to idealize a more distant past. They developed a consuming interest in genealogy and clamored for tales of moonlight on the veranda. Curiously, as Woodward showed, the impetus for this romanticizing often came from the "most active propagandists for the New Order." In Woodward's work, the sweet perfume of the Old South myth was overwhelmed by the stench of white supremacist demagoguery, which flowered by its side; but clearly the two "ideals" were closely linked in the psychology of the region—a subject which Woodward frequently skirted but rarely dealt with directly, preferring like Faulkner and Warren to teach by implication.

A second aspect of *Origins of the New South* rarely noted was Woodward's discussion of the cultural doldrums of the period. He observed the vogue of the historical novel, which relieved Southern authors of the necessity to face clearly their own time. Surveying art and architecture, he noted "[s]ome slight advantages derived from isolation. The South was too poor . . . to do much building in the period when architectural taste reached its lowest ebb." In addition, he examined interdenominational warfare among Protestants and provided a thoroughgoing analysis of education in the South after Reconstruction. Certainly his careful detailing of the intellectual poverty of higher education in the South in the last decades of the nineteenth century and his recounting of the beginnings of academic vigor at the turn of the century reflected his own deep belief in the importance of universities.

Writing more than twenty years after the publication of *Origins of the New South*, Michael O'Brien observed that "Seldom can a subject have been raised from such obscurity to such illumination at a single bound. Just as a piece of technique, an effort of research, it was a virtuoso performance." Furthermore, the vision of the book, its "fresh moral geography," was "maintained throughout the work with a tenacity whose coherence made it one of the few works of art that Southern historical literature has produced." Reviewers recognized the importance of *Origins of the New South* from the outset. Bell I. Wiley called it a "pioneer work" and stated categorically that thenceforth all students of the New South would have to master it. Dumas Malone, for whom the book illuminated a "disheartening" period in a "devastatingly honest" way, pronounced it a "work of real distinction and great importance," and asserted that "the general history of the United States between Reconstruction and Woodrow Wilson [would] have to be rewritten in certain important respects in the light of it."

Both reviewers were perceptive; Southern historiography in the three decades following its publication has built on Woodward's work, expanding, refining, occasionally disagreeing on one point or another, or proposing new emphases but not as yet offering a successful challenge to the larger outline of Woodward's portrait of the New South. *Origins of the New South* in effect defined a whole new area of historical study waiting to be done, and scholars writing subsequent to Woodward have profited by the starting point he provided, most importantly in the extensive bibliographical essay—itself the first in the field—with which he concluded his book. One indication of the importance of *Origins of the New South* was the mass of scholarship on the New South that followed it; a 1971 printing included an essay on scholarship after 1951 compiled by Charles B. Dew and three times as long as the original essay. In a 1972 essay on *Origins of the New South*, Sheldon Hackney examined challenges to Woodward's book, concluded that *Origins of the New South* had "survived relatively untarnished through twenty years of productive scholarship," and suggested that just possibly its author was "right about his period . . . despite the notorious elusiveness of historical truth."

Origins of the New South earned Woodward the Bancroft History Prize in 1952, the same year he assumed the presidency of the Southern Historical Association. Two years later, he received an award from the National Institute of Arts and Letters, served as Commonwealth Lecturer at the University of London and, in the fall of 1954, became James W. Richard Lecturer at the University of Virginia. While Woodward was filling the Harmsworth Professorship in American History at Oxford in 1955, the Richard lectures, which had been sparked by the 1954 Supreme Court decision in *Brown* v. *Board of Education of Topeka, Kansas*, were published as *The Strange Career of Jim Crow*. The book represented a significant new direction in Woodward's career, a movement outward to a far wider audience who, as citizens, had the potential to *use* the lessons of history Woodward presented but who had neither the background to place his lessons in context nor the ear to hear the careful qualifications of the responsible historian. Thus, *The Strange Career of Jim Crow*, the first of Woodward's books to achieve a mass readership (it has sold well over a half million copies), plunged him into controversy.

The thesis of *The Strange Career of Jim Crow* had been presented in brief in *Origins of the New South* but here took on urgency in light of the civil rights struggle of the mid-1950s. Woodward wrote, "The policies of proscription, segregation, and disfranchisement that are often described as the immutable 'folkways' of the South, impervious alike to legislative reform and armed intervention, are of a more recent origin [than Reconstruction]. The effort to justify them as a consequence of Reconstruction and a necessity of the times is embarrassed by the fact that they did not originate in those times. And the belief that they are immutable and unchangeable is not supported by history." In order to show that things had "not always been the same in the South," Woodward began by offering eyewitness reports suggesting that within the post-Reconstruction South blacks and whites mingled rather more freely prior to 1890 than had been previously supposed. Woodward then went on to show that three "forgotten alternatives"—all indigenously Southern—had enjoyed some attention prior to the rash of Jim Crow laws enacted after 1890. The first, a conservative, paternalistic philosophy, which held that Negroes should be subordinate because they were inferior but that they need not be ostracized, ultimately lost ground because of its class association with the old patrician order. The second, advocated for a time by Tom Watson and other Populists, fell to the political expediencies Woodward had thoroughly discussed in previous works. The third, a liberal view held by Cable and Lewis Harvey Blair—whose *A Southern Prophecy: Prosperity of the South Dependent upon the Elevation of the Negro* (1889) would be edited and republished by Woodward in 1964—urged full

equality for the Negro but failed to attract any following.

The South settled on a legal system of segregation only after a slow accretion of developments in deteriorating race relations over nearly thirty years. Prior to the Civil War, Woodward claimed, legal segregation as a regional policy did not exist, if only because it would have proved cumbersome in a plantation economy. During Reconstruction, blacks voluntarily withdrew from white churches sometimes over protest, whites insisted on segregated schools, and a new pattern of separation between the races evolved fairly gradually, not enjoying legal sanction until the last decade of the century. And in fact, the racist forces in the South might not have been so successful in enacting Jim Crow legislation had they not been buttressed by the United States's new imperialism at the turn of the century, an imperialism which brought some eight million members of "inferior races" in the Caribbean and the Pacific under American jurisdiction and which prompted a new outpouring of paternalism and racism in the country at large.

In his introduction, Woodward made clear that he was writing in the middle of the "Second Reconstruction," an era of change in Southern race relations the outcome of which no one could then know. Thus, for the first time, his discussion of the history of segregation was firmly placed in the context of the present, and he carried his account of racial tension well beyond the Woodrow Wilson years, up to 1955. In so doing, he gave *The Strange Career of Jim Crow* an immediacy which contributed to its impact. But its very immediacy—and the moral imperative which pervaded every chapter—led also to a host of misunderstandings. In the hands of a historiographically sophisticated reader, *The Strange Career of Jim Crow* provided a corrective to the notion that Jim Crow laws were as much a part of the South as mosquitoes and equally ancient. But because Woodward had deemphasized the social and cultural aspects of Southern racism, concentrating instead on the narrower question of legal discrimination, many readers interpreted him to be saying that prior to the 1890s, the South had experienced something close to racial harmony. Such a misreading was contrary to Woodward's intention; indeed he had, in his first chapter, labeled "preposterous" the idea that there had ever been a "golden age of race relations." However, by emphasizing the degree to which Jim Crow was a twentieth-century phenomenon, Woodward *had* intended to shock his readers out of the comfortable belief that racial discrimination was an immutable fact of life. (It was, of course, difficult to justify a system which had decreed in Atlanta as late as 1932 that whites and blacks could not play baseball within two blocks of each other or which, in Birmingham in 1930, made it illegal for members of the two races to play dominoes or checkers together.) As David Potter later pointed out in a perceptive analysis of the whole controversy, Woodward's own commitment to historical realism had to some degree yielded to his heartfelt desire to "find constructive meanings in the past for the affairs of the present."

Other scholars, among them Charles E. Wynes, Frenise A. Logan, Joel Williamson, and Richard C. Wade, quickly took up the challenge to test or correct Woodward's assertions, and in 1966, in the third edition of *The Strange Career of Jim Crow*, Woodward took note of this work and incorporated its findings into his revision. In the preface to this second revised edition, which included a final chapter dealing with the civil rights movement in the ten years since the book's first publication, he noted somewhat ruefully that his decision to write about current events—"the immediacy of lived experience"—involved many risks, among them a lack of perspective from which the first edition had "admittedly suffered." Nevertheless, he went on to defend his concentration on the legal aspects of discrimination, asserting that like "acts of intolerance, discourtesy, and inhumanity, acts of segregation acquire a new significance when they are endowed with . . . the majesty of law."

Although what he later called "The Strange Career of a Historical Controversy" caused Woodward some embarrassment, it in no way diminished his commitment to history as an important tool for the present. Nor did it deter him from becoming actively involved in the civil rights struggle, though he would never again take the kind of public role he had assumed in the Herndon case. Woodward had contributed his expertise to NAACP leaders as they prepared briefs in the 1954 Supreme Court argument, in 1965 he joined in the march to Selma, Alabama, of Dr. Martin Luther King, Jr., and he continued to write regularly about race relations, not only in scholarly journals but also in such magazines as *Harper's* and *Time*. But the experience surrounding *The Strange Career of Jim Crow* did induce him even more carefully to qualify his observations as he sought to disprove the unwarranted generalizations of others; moreover, the controversy forced him to examine the relationship between his liberal concerns and his role as historian. In a 1971 essay in *American Counterpoint*, he astutely and objectively summed up the problems

surrounding *The Strange Career of Jim Crow*; speaking of himself in the third person, Woodward noted that, "While he did take pains to say in so many words when he originally advanced his thesis that the 'new era of race relations was really a heritage of slavery times,' he probably did not sufficiently emphasize the paternalistic character of those relations. In neglecting to do this, he (unconsciously?) permitted the hopeful but unwary modern reader to identify such casualness and permissiveness as graced that remote Southern interlude of paternalism with the type of open, color-blind egalitarianism to which the modern liberal aspires. That was a mistake."

The mistake acknowledged here was primarily that of emphasis, but in another instance in his career, Woodward was led to change a position completely. Three years after *The Strange Career of Jim Crow*, at the 125th anniversary of the founding of Gettysburg College, he delivered a lecture entitled "Equality: The Deferred Commitment" and published later that year in the *American Scholar*. In his lecture, he noted that among the North's objectives during the Civil War, the first, the clear goal of preventing the secession of the Confederate states, was arrived at quickly; the second, a moral crusade for the emancipation of the slaves, did not crystallize until well into the second year of fighting. He

C. Vann Woodward

then went on to argue that a third war aim, equality, gained strength among radicals after the Emancipation Proclamation and that it slowly assumed the stature of a formal commitment in the Fourteenth and Fifteenth Amendments and in the Civil Rights acts of 1866 and 1875, a commitment which was broken, abandoned, and forgotten for nearly a century. After tracing the reasons why the commitment was broken, Woodward summed up his argument using an economic metaphor: "The Union fought the Civil War on borrowed moral capital. With their noble belief in their purpose and their extravagant faith in the future, the radicals ran up a staggering war debt, a moral debt that was soon found to be beyond the country's capacity to pay, given the undeveloped state of its moral resources at the time. After making a few token payments during Reconstruction, the United States defaulted on the debt and unilaterally declared a moratorium that lasted more than eight decades."

Once again, Woodward—here speaking in the very town in which Lincoln had eloquently rededicated the nation to the proposition that all men are created equal—sought to find sanction in history for his own belief in the urgent need for racial equality. Subsequent work by other scholars, particularly by W. R. Brock in *An American Crisis: Congress and Reconstruction, 1865-1876* (1963) and by G. Seldon Henry in a Yale dissertation entitled "Radical Republican Policy Toward the Negro During Reconstruction" (1963), demonstrated to Woodward's satisfaction that the Republicans had never in fact committed themselves to full equality and that the legislation on which Woodward had based his assumptions was intentionally evasive on such a politically explosive subject. By the time these studies appeared, Woodward had already included "Equality: The Deferred Commitment" in *The Burden of Southern History*, but in 1966 he recanted his earlier position in "Seeds of Failure in Radical Race Policy," published in the *Proceedings of the American Philosophical Society*, then in a volume edited by Harold M. Hyman, and finally in his own *American Counterpoint*.

If *The Strange Career of Jim Crow* was Woodward's most widely read book, the volume of essays which followed in 1960, *The Burden of Southern History*, was without question his most important contribution to the Southern Literary Renaissance. Of the eight essays it included (two more would be added to the revised edition in 1968), the first and last, both deeply thematic, provided a structural and conceptual context by which the South and its meaning could be approached. Written in rich and

moving prose, *The Burden of Southern History* sought to define the South and its relationship to the nation as a whole. Clearly such a broad attempt offered an ample target to critics eager to disprove Woodward's thesis that the distinctiveness of the South lay in the differences between its experience as a region and the experience of the non-Southern portions of the country. And such critics have appeared regularly in the more than twenty years since the book's publication, most of them charging that the historian who had, in his more formal works, consistently questioned Southern myths of unity and continuity was now relying on a consensus theory, thus contradicting himself in the most fundamental way. But such criticisms probably represent a misunderstanding of the book's intent and form. *The Burden of Southern History* might properly be read not as a series of scholarly historical essays but as a work in which Woodward used the tools at his command as a historian to shape something very close to a philosophical view of the South's role in the nation.

Woodward's tone in *The Burden of Southern History* was always that of the historian, writing in the past tense and from an objective perspective, and yet, as he suggested in his preface, the very nature of his enterprise was fraught with difficulties not usually encountered by the historian. The character of any people is a notoriously elusive quality, and the experience of the South was particularly complex. Yet he felt the effort worth making because, as he suggested in "The Irony of Southern History"—the last essay in the book although one of the first to be written—the experience and perspective of the South had the potential to teach Americans as a people some important lessons. In particular, the American faith in "unlimited progress, in the efficacy of material means, in the importance of mass and speed, the worship of success, and the belief in the invincibility of American arms" was one which the South could share only vicariously. Its own experience with frustration, failure, poverty, submission, and accommodation to conditions it had sworn never to accept, much more closely resembled that of nearly all Europe and Asia. Thus a thorough understanding of Southern history should help to sober our national self-image and might have a salutary effect toward a more realistic foreign policy.

The Burden of Southern History began with a 1958 essay, "The Search for Southern Identity," which noted that many easily identifiable features of the South were disappearing with great rapidity in the "Bulldozer Revolution" whose dominant symbol, the bulldozer, paved the way for massive changes in living patterns, primarily rural to urban, and propelled the South toward far more uniformity with national demographic, economic, and cultural norms. Virtually the only thing about the South impervious to change was its history, the "collective experience of the Southern people." While America as a whole had experienced wealth, abundance, and a living standard far in excess of most of its sister nations, the South had undergone "a long and quite un-American experience with poverty." While success and victory were "national habits of mind," the South had a distinctive heritage of failure and defeat. Nor was the South wholly able to participate in the nation's moral complacency, born of its conviction that America had successfully freed itself from the Old World evils of tyranny and oppression. However much the South might have mouthed the rhetoric of American innocence, its preoccupation was with guilt. For half its history, the South had "lived intimately with a great social evil and the other half with its aftermath," spending its intellectual capital in fruitless efforts to rationalize its peculiar institution. Woodward ended "The Search for Southern Identity" with a call to Southerners to be secure in their identity, not because, as the Agrarians had argued in *I'll Take My Stand*, the world of the Old South was more humane than its modern industrial counterpart but because the Southern heritage constituted "a dimension of historical experience that America very much needs, a heritage that is far more closely in line with the common lot of mankind than the national legends of opulence and success and innocence."

The same concern lay at the heart of "The Irony of Southern History," the major essay in the collection. Woodward took his title and his theme from Reinhold Niebuhr's *The Irony of American History*, an analysis of the American character emphasizing the ethical hypocrisy and indeed the danger inherent in an America that commands immense power in the world but that clings to national illusions of innocence and virtue. Adopting Niebuhr's ironic interpretation of history, Woodward sketched briefly the incongruities of America's role vis-à-vis her allies, the emerging Third World, and the Soviet Union (another nation convinced of its special virtue), and went on to suggest that the experience of the American South might well provide historians with a somewhat detached point of view from which to understand the "ironic plight" of modern America. To put it very simply, in a nation that still held to a dream of leadership in a perfectible world, the South had lived through the shattering of a similar dream and

had received a harsh education no other section of the country had experienced. Woodward was careful to note that such an education had by no means left individual Southerners "any wiser than their fellow countrymen," but it *had* left a record of experience from which twentieth-century American historians could profit.

For the social critic, for the ethicist, and above all, for the historian, the history of the South could offer a much needed corrective to a number of tendencies in twentieth-century American thought and practice that seemed to Woodward wrongheaded. As Southerners' experience had shown, Americans were by no means immune to the forces of history, despite their unbroken string of successes; by clinging to a self-image of virtuous innocence, they invited national and international crises born of blindness. In the eight years following the publication of *The Burden of Southern History*, racial and campus unrest throughout the nation and a frustrating involvement in Vietnam did much to confirm Woodward's warnings, and in a 1968 revision, he added an "extended postscript" entitled "A Second Look at the Theme of Irony." In it he argued that "history had caught up with America" and professed the now muted hope that the nation still might learn something from the South's ironic experience with history. The payment of our debts to our poor might well require revolutionary changes comparable to those the South underwent during Reconstruction. And as that region had learned, such changes could not be made without an accompanying "revolution in attitudes as well and a wholesale abandonment of myths—particularly those of moral complacency and innocence and those that hold equality and justice and virtue compatible with opulence."

At the urging of George Pierson, colleagues such as his former student Robin Winks, and an old friend, Robert Penn Warren, Woodward left Johns Hopkins University in 1961 to become Sterling Professor of History at Yale University. The move to New England meant a thorough displacement from his native South. Baltimore, the city he had once described as "at one and the same time the last refuge of the Confederate spirit in exile and a lying-in hospital for the birth of the New Order" in the South, had been a comfortable home for him, a kind of border between the Arkansas and Georgia of his youth and the great seats of intellectual activity in the Northeast. Yet the movement north intensified his interests in comparative history, both within the United States and among nations. One outgrowth of this increased emphasis on the comparative approach was Woodward's work in the late 1960s as editor of the Voice of America series of Forum Lectures on American history. Growing out of that series was *The Comparative Approach to American History* (1968), containing two brief essays by Woodward, who edited the volume, and contributions by twenty-two other historians.

His settling in New Haven also suggested to Woodward a more specific theme, the North and South as counterpoints in history. This contrast between the two regions, which grew out of the concerns expressed in *The Burden of Southern History*, would be explored in a number of Woodward essays during the 1960s, essays collected in *American Counterpoint: Slavery and Racism in the North-South Dialogue* (1971). The emphasis in this second collection of essays on the North-South dialogue revealed the ways in which North and South, focusing on slavery and race relations, have used one another throughout history to intensify their own distinctiveness.

The most interesting essay in *American Counterpoint* from the point of view of Woodward's own career dealt with W. J. Cash's exceedingly influential *The Mind of the South* (1941). "The Elusive Mind of the South," a slightly revised version of an essay in the *New York Review of Books*, called for a reassessment of a book that had, in large part because of its vigorous and lively prose, enjoyed an ever-increasing reputation in the 1940s, 1950s, and 1960s as the definitive work on the distinctiveness of the South. Woodward began by acknowledging the far-reaching prestige of *The Mind of the South*, a book that had been "quoted, paraphrased, and plagiarized so regularly as to have practically entered the public domain." Cash's book, Woodward declared, had few rivals in influence among professional historians and none at all among laymen. But, of course, Cash's principal rival was Woodward himself, and in this essay Woodward questioned in some detail the validity of Cash's view of the South, and at the same time reiterated, in broad terms, his own.

The central difficulty with Cash's *The Mind of the South* lay in its limited perspective, Woodward asserted. Cash had written not about the mind of the South as a whole but of the white South and, more particularly, of the yeoman white South of North Carolina and the Piedmont region. Further, Cash's book gave slight attention to historical background, brushing over the colonial period and concentrating so heavily on the twentieth century that it became a mass of historical relativism. Woodward identified two underlying theses in *The*

Mind of the South: the thesis of unity—the "spiritually solid South"—and the thesis of the continuity of Southern history. Although the South certainly had shared experience and cultural values, which it transmitted through generations and periods of history, Woodward noted that to insist on a South united in thought patterns and values with a history characterized by continuity was to ignore a great deal of evidence of lack of consensus in any specific period or between historical eras. Cash had, in other words, vastly oversimplified the Southern mind throughout its history by viewing it from the vantage point of the mid-twentieth century, and he had been "taken in by the very myth he sought to explode—by the fancy-dress charade the New South put on in the cast-off finery of the old order, the cult of the Lost Cause, the Plantation Legend and the rest." Woodward's discussion of Cash was an answer to those who had criticized Woodward for emphasizing, on the one hand, the diversity in Southern thought and the discontinuity of the Southern experience in *Origins of the New South* and, on the other, the distinctiveness of the South as a region in *The Burden of Southern History*. For in this essay Woodward made the point that what was at issue in the kind of discussion Cash was offering was "not the existence, but rather the character and degree of unity and continuity." Such questions were not absolute but relative, and the careful historian must make every effort to deal in a balanced way with the complexity and relativity of his subject.

American Counterpoint, a far more traditional collection of essays than *The Burden of Southern History*, aimed not only at exploring various aspects of the North-South dialogue but also at delineating the obligation of the historian to fully appreciate the complexity of the human experience and the ironies of history. Too, it suggested areas of historical experience worthy of further study. In a sense, then, Woodward mapped out in *American Counterpoint* directions which future historians might fruitfully explore. As such, the book reflected concerns in which Woodward had been interested for many years, the same concerns which underlay "The Irony of Southern History": what possibilities does the study of the past hold for the present; what responsibilities does the historian have toward society at large?

In 1959 Woodward delivered his most important statement about the future of historiography and about the role of the historian in interpreting the past to those who are shaping the future. This paper, "The Age of Reinterpretation," was first published in a 1960 issue of the *American*

Historical Review, then as a separate pamphlet by the American Historical Association Service Center for Teachers of History. In the essay, which David Potter characterized as "his most significant single piece of work and . . . one of the major contributions to the interpretation of American history," Woodward argued that the changes brought about by the discovery of nuclear power and shifting international power bases after World War II required a thorough reexamination and reinterpretation of large areas of history. These changes brought into sharp relief the "free security" which the United States had enjoyed from the close of the War of 1812 until World War II; physical security from attack or invasion resulted simply from the country's geographical location, which allowed it to maintain its security with only a token army or navy and to spend its resources instead on the remarkable economic expansion of the nineteenth century.

This free security, which America took for granted, had far-reaching effects beyond mere economic ones. It lessened the country's concern for a strong military posture and allowed the government to function for long periods of time without the concentrations of political power endemic to other nations for whom security was a first priority, not a natural right. It gave America the luxury of slowly working out our internal problems (during, for example, the Civil War) without concern for foreign intervention or occupation. And finally, the era of free security fostered in a significant way the American conviction of its innocence "in a wicked world"—a world which had to fight continually for something America received through grace.

American historians, then, *must* reinterpret past history in order that present policymakers can understand the anachronistic assumptions with which they have been dealing, Woodward declared. The natural belief in historical continuity, that the lessons of the past can offer guidance for the present, may be dangerously misleading in times of rapid change, but the historian can, by discovering discontinuity, help to comprehend and to interpret that change. Moreover, historians of the present generation have a unique opportunity: "They will be the only generation of historians in history who will be able to interpret the old order to the new order with the advantage and authority derived from firsthand knowledge of the two ages and participation in both." Not only can historians employ their unique opportunities, but the need is urgent that they do so.

Woodward's concern for the role of the historian and his thoughtful approaches to matters of

interest to historians as members of a guild earned him the presidency in 1969 of both the American Historical Association and the Organization of American Historians. His presidential addresses for both organizations were concerned with broad concepts in historiography. "Clio with Soul," delivered before the Organization of American Historians, discussed the demand for black history in American universities as the "moral storm center of American historiography." It offered historians an opportunity to eliminate the moral obtuseness that Woodward considered to characterize much historical literature, thus enabling historians to revise myths associated with European-centered history and contributing significantly to the self-image of American blacks by providing them with a past which had traditionally been ignored or obscured. On the other hand, both black and white historians should guard against lending support to any sort of new separatism and against the simple adaptation to black history of the myths and denials of the ironies of history that have distorted the history of whites. In "The Future of the Past," delivered before the American Historical Association, Woodward assessed the declining status of history both in academia and in the intellectual community-at-large and warned his colleagues that an increasing emphasis on specialization and a willingness to pander to popular tastes were undermining the stature of the discipline. Finally, he reiterated that to insist upon history as continuity, to deny the disjunctures of the modern world, was to doom the study of history to antiquarianism. On the contrary, the historian must learn to recognize anachronisms, "the peculiar concern of the historian," so that he can "serve as mediator between man's limitations and his aspirations, between his dreams of what ought to be and the limits of what, in the light of what has been, can be."

The decade of the 1970s began with sorrow for Woodward. Within a twelve-month period he lost his only child, Peter, to cancer, and two close friends, Richard Hofstadter and David Potter, succumbed to the same disease. Nevertheless, the decade was a fruitful one for the historian in his sixties. In addition to service on numerous national and international committees, he continued to publish essays and frequently contributed reviews to such periodicals as the *New York Review of Books*. In 1974, he edited *Responses of the Presidents to Charges of Misconduct*, a collaboration among fourteen historians assembled by Woodward at the behest of the government during the height of the Watergate controversy. As the possibility of impeachment ap-

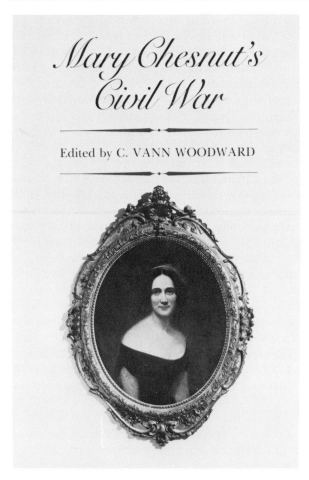

*Dust jacket for Woodward's 1981 Pulitzer Prize-winning
edition of a Southern woman's war diary*

peared imminent, Woodward was asked to prepare in short order a historical overview of analogous situations in earlier administrations. Although the impeachment did not take place, the book nevertheless represented a primer for those interested in the scandals of American government and the ways in which charges of misconduct had been handled over the course of history.

Woodward retired from teaching duties in 1977 but left the classroom with such a large stock of impending projects and professional obligations that he was heard to remark the following year to a friend that retirement "didn't take." He had learned how it ought to be done, though, he said, and was going to "try to get it right next time." After a celebratory cruise on the Aegean in a chartered boat with his wife and the Robert Penn Warrens, he settled into a retirement that involved daily trips to the university and steady work in a compact, downstairs study hidden away from the main floor

of the charming, gabled cottage he had shared with his wife, Glenn, since their arrival in New Haven.

In 1978, Woodward, delivering the seventh annual Jefferson Lecture on the Humanities at the Library of Congress, spoke on "The European Vision of America." Following the Jefferson Lecture, he turned his full attention to a project he had already been working on for several years: the Civil War journal of Mary Boykin Chesnut, a South Carolinian who had long been a favorite figure for him, and one he had quoted to good effect on several occasions throughout his career. Chesnut was a daughter of Stephen Decatur Miller (who served South Carolina as a congressman, governor, and U.S. senator) and the wife of James Chesnut, Jr., senator from South Carolina in the years immediately before the Civil War and a Confederate statesman and general. She had kept a diary throughout the Confederacy, a diary which she later revised so extensively that it became a work of serious literary merit. Her book revealed a remarkably intelligent woman blessed with a sharp eye for irony and an irreverent and original wit— all qualities which endeared her to Woodward. Chesnut was a woman of striking paradoxes, a thoroughgoing intellectual, and yet also the very essence of the patrician Southern Lady. Furthermore, her social skills, her knack for being in the right place at the right time, and her numerous friendships in high places (in particular her close relationship with the Jefferson Davises) made her book a treasure of inside information on Confederate life. Chesnut's revised journal had been published in two incomplete previous editions under the title *A Diary from Dixie* and had achieved a reputation as the best single firsthand account of the Confederacy. But neither existing edition made clear the fact that the "diary" was actually a revised and enlarged version written twenty years after the original journal.

When Woodward decided to edit the Chesnut journal, his first intention was to use as his copy text not the revision Chesnut made in the early 1880s but the diary she had actually kept during the war years. Such a choice was a natural one for a historian attuned to the "immediacy of lived experience" and skeptical of hindsight. But as he grew familiar with the whole body of Chesnut manuscripts, he gained an appreciation for the way Chesnut had revised and expanded her own diaries; and he came to acknowledge that the revised journal, which preserved the diary format, had the integrity of a literary work and was remarkably free of the biases which might have been expected to creep into the work of a woman who had lived through the experience of Reconstruction in South Carolina. Abandoning his original intention, Woodward determined to edit the entire revised journal but also to insert a few brief portions of the original diary where they provided insight lost or modified in revision.

The undertaking proved to be an enormous task, for the Chesnut manuscripts with which he worked also contained two interim revisions, the whole totaling three-quarters of a million words, and all written in a somewhat idiosyncratic hand. The text was replete with allusions and with the names of hundreds of unidentified people, each of whom required annotation. And most importantly, the project demanded a knowledge of the techniques of both historical and literary editing, specialized areas of scholarship outside the wide range of Woodward's skills and interests. Just as he had taught himself the intricacies of naval history in preparation for *The Battle for Leyte Gulf*, Woodward set himself to master a new specialization.

The result, *Mary Chesnut's Civil War*, published in 1981, was an impressive achievement. With its introductory material detailing the nature of the text and with its copious and yet admirably brief annotations, the work made clear Mary Boykin Chesnut's own achievement. Surely one of the happiest ironies associated with Woodward's own career was that the man who had rescued Chesnut from her relatively minor status as an important historical source and awarded her full honors as a writer—in fact, the most important Southern woman of letters in the immediate postbellum period—was not a literary scholar but the "dean of Southern historians." *Mary Chesnut's Civil War* earned Woodward the Pulitzer Prize for history in 1982, an award that also, by implication, took notice of the consistently high quality of the whole body of Woodward's work over a forty-five year period.

Now five years into "retirement," Woodward is presently involved in several important projects. Two of them illustrate major dimensions of his career. The first, his role as general editor of a new eleven-volume Oxford History of the United States, bespeaks his increasing interest after 1955 in national character and in the broad sweep of American history. The first volume of the Oxford History of the United States, *The Glorious Years* by Robert Middlekauff, was published in 1982 with a brief preface by Woodward, and subsequent volumes are scheduled to be published in the 1980s. The second project harks back to *Tom Watson, Agrarian Rebel* and Woodward's abiding interest in individual Southerners who both loved their region and lamented its faults. An outgrowth of his original intention in regard to the Chesnut manuscripts, the second project will be an edition of the source material for *Mary Chesnut's Civil War*, the actual diaries kept by Chesnut from 1861 to 1865. To be coedited with Chesnut's biographer, Elisabeth Muhlenfeld, the book is scheduled for publication in 1984.

Woodward's is a humane voice in a troubled world. His lifelong study of history has instilled in him a deep pessimism, a product of his realistic look at the foibles and failings of mankind. But it has not dimmed his hope that Americans will abandon their immature clinging to national myths of innocence (or, in the most recent decade, of collective guilt) and begin to see themselves clearly. Woodward has always been a liberal, but he remains, like the great Southern writers he admires, a conservative in the sense that he profoundly believes Americans must preserve the best that their heritage contains. Robert Coles, in a 1972 *New Yorker* review, admiringly called him an "old-fashioned historian." Coles meant that Woodward has never relied solely on "new" techniques of statistical analysis or sociological survey, although he has often spoken generously of their value to the historian. He has known from the beginning that the highest reward and value of his discipline is the illumination of what Faulkner once called "the problems of the human heart in conflict with itself."

Other:

George Fitzhugh, *Cannibals All! or, Slaves Without Masters* (1857), edited, with an introduction, by Woodward (Cambridge: Harvard University Press, 1960);

"The Case of the Louisiana Traveler: *Plessy* v. *Ferguson*, 163 U. S. 537," in *Quarrels that Have Shaped the Constitution*, edited by John A. Garraty (New York: Harper & Row, 1962), pp. 145-158;

Lewis H. Blair, *A Southern Prophecy: The Prosperity of the South Dependent upon the Elevation of the Negro* (1889), edited, with an introduction, by Woodward (Boston: Little, Brown, 1964);

Whitelaw Reid, *After the War: A Tour of the Southern States, 1865-1866* (1866), edited, with an introduction, by Woodward (New York: Harper & Row, 1965);

The Comparative Approach to American History, edited, with two essays, by Woodward (New York: Basic Books, 1968);

Responses of the Presidents to Charges of Misconduct,

edited by Woodward (Washington, D.C.: Delacorte, 1974);

"The Future of Southern History," in *The Future of History, Essays in the Vanderbilt University Centennial Symposium*, edited by Charles F. Delzell (Nashville: Vanderbilt University Press, 1977), pp. 135-149;

Mary Chesnut's Civil War, edited, with an introduction, by Woodward (New Haven: Yale University Press, 1981).

Periodical Publications:

"Tom Watson and the Negro in Agrarian Politics," *Journal of Southern History*, 4 (February 1938): 14-33;

"Bourbonism in Georgia," *North Carolina Historical Review*, 16 (January 1939): 23-35;

"The 'New Reconstruction' in the South: Desegregation in Historical Perspective," *Commentary*, 21 (June 1956): 501-508;

"The Age of Reinterpretation," *American Historical Review*, 66 (October 1960): 1-19;

"The Unreported Crisis in the Southern Colleges," *Harper's*, 225 (October 1962): 82-89;

"From the First Reconstruction to the Second," *Harper's*, special supplement (April 1965): 127-133; reprinted in *The South Today: 100 Years After Appomattox*, edited by Willie Morris (New York: Harper & Row, 1965);

"Clio with Soul," *Journal of American History*, 56 (June 1969): 5-20;

"The Future of the Past," *American Historical Review*, 75 (February 1970): 711-726;

"Yes, There Was a Compromise of 1877," *Journal of American History*, 60 (June 1973): 215-223;

"The Erosion of Academic Privileges and Immunities," *Daedalus*, 103 (Fall 1974): 33-37;

"Why the Southern Renaissance?," *Virginia Quarterly Review*, 51 (Spring 1975): 222-239;

"The Aging of America: A Bicentennial Essay," *American Historical Review*, 82 (June 1977): 583-594;

"The Fall of the American Adam," *Bulletin of the American Academy of Arts and Sciences*, 35 (November 1981): 26-34.

Interview:

John A. Garraty, "C. Vann Woodward," in his *Interpreting American History: Conversations with Historians* (New York: Macmillan, 1970), II: 43-68.

Bibliography:

Louis P. Masur, "The Published Writings of C. Vann Woodward: A Bibliography," in *Region, Race, and Reconstruction: Essays in Honor of C. Vann Woodward*, edited by J. Morgan Kousser and James M. McPherson (New York: Oxford University Press, 1982), pp. 451-463.

References:

Robert Coles, "In Black and White," *New Yorker* (15 April 1972): 141-146;

Eugene D. Genovese, "Potter and Woodward on the South," in his *In Red and Black* (New York: Pantheon, 1968), pp. 299-314;

Sheldon Hackney, "Origins of the New South in Retrospect," *Journal of Southern History*, 38 (May 1972): 191-216;

Richard H. King, *A Southern Renaissance: The Cultural Awakening of the American South, 1930-1955* (New York: Oxford University Press, 1980);

Michael O'Brien, "C. Vann Woodward and the Burden of Southern Liberalism," *American Historical Review*, 78 (June 1973): 589-604;

Patrick O'Sheel, "The Uses of Adversity," *Humanities*, 8 (April 1978): 1-6;

David M. Potter, "C. Vann Woodward," in *Pastmasters: Some Essays on American Historians*, edited by Marcus Cunliffe and Robin W. Winks (New York: Harper & Row, 1969): 375-407;

John H. Roper, "C. Vann Woodward's Early Career—The Historian as Dissident Youth," *Georgia Historical Quarterly*, 64 (Spring 1980): 7-21;

Robert B. Westbrook, "C. Vann Woodward: The Southerner as Liberal Realist," *South Atlantic Quarterly*, 77 (Winter 1978): 54-71.

Louis B. Wright
(1 March 1899-   )

Suzanne Krebsbach
University of South Carolina

SELECTED BOOKS: *Middle-Class Culture in Elizabethan England* (Chapel Hill: University of North Carolina Press, 1935; London: Oxford University Press, 1935);

Puritans in the South Seas, by Wright and Mary Isabel Frey (New York: Holt, 1936);

The First Gentlemen of Virginia (San Marino, Cal.: Huntington Library, 1940);

Religion and Empire: The Alliance Between Piety and Commerce in English Expansion, 1558-1625 (Chapel Hill: University of North Carolina Press, 1943);

The First Americans in North Africa (Princeton: Princeton University Press, 1945; London: Oxford University Press, 1954);

The Atlantic Frontier: Colonial American Civilization, 1607-1763 (New York: Knopf, 1947); republished as *Colonial Civilization of North America, 1607-1763* (London: Eyre & Spottiswoode, 1949);

The Colonial Search for a Southern Eden (University: University of Alabama Press, 1953);

The British Tradition in America (Birmingham: Rushton Foundation, 1954);

Culture on the Moving Frontier (Bloomington: Indiana University Press, 1955);

The Cultural Life of the American Colonies (New York: Harper, 1957; London: Hamilton, 1957);

Shakespeare for Everyman (New York: Washington Square Press, 1964);

Shakespeare's Engeland (The Hague: Gaade, 1965; London: Cassell, 1965);

The Dream of Prosperity in Colonial America (New York: New York University Press, 1965);

Everyday Life in Colonial America (New York: Putnam's, 1965; London: Batsford, 1965);

Everyday Life on the American Frontier (New York: Putnam's, 1968);

The Folger Library: Two Decades of Growth, An Informal History (New York: Washington Square Press, 1968; London: Oxford University Press, 1968);

Breve Historia de Los Estados Unidos de America (Mexico: Limusa-Wiley, 1969);

Gold, Glory, and the Gospel: The Adventurous Lives and Times of the Renaissance Explorers (New York: Atheneum, 1970);

The Renaissance: Maker of Modern Man (Washington, D.C.: National Geographic Society, 1970);

Everyday Life in the New Nation (New York: Putnam's, 1972);

Barefoot in Arcadia: Memories of a More Innocent Era (Columbia: University of South Carolina Press, 1974);

Tradition and the Founding Fathers (Charlottesville: University Press of Virginia, 1975);

South Carolina: A Bicentennial History (New York: Norton, 1976);

Of Books and Men (Columbia: University of South Carolina Press, 1976);

Magna Carta and the Tradition of Liberty (Washington, D.C.: U.S. Capitol Historical Society, 1976).

Louis Booker Wright, cultural historian of the

Louis B. Wright

English Renaissance and of colonial America, is not only a highly successful writer but also a builder of two major research centers. Wright was instrumental in developing the Huntington Library in San Marino, California, and the Folger Shakespeare Library in Washington, D.C. Molding rare book collections into active research centers has been a vital part of Wright's intellectual life, and his writing must be seen as part of that activity. Scholarship, he has said, ought to have genuine utility: "Intellectual research, research that seeks fresh information and fresh interpretation, vitalizes instruction."

Wright was born 1 March 1899, in Greenwood County, South Carolina, eldest of three surviving children of Thomas Fleming and Lena Booker Wright. The family came from Scottish, English, and French Huguenot stock. In his boyhood, Wright hunted and fished in nearby McCormick County, the so-called "Dark Corner" of the state, notorious for its isolation and primitive ways. He grew to maturity in the early decades of the twentieth century, and he remembers not so much the isolation as a rural social pattern of school, church, and work. The Up Country of South Carolina, contrasted to the Low Country as exemplified by Charleston, was settled by Scotch-Irish Presbyterian pioneers, his spiritual if not lineal ancestors. Wright, in several works, especially *The British Tradition in America* (1954), considered the Scotch-Irish the epitome of the American pioneer, hardworking, pious, and keenly interested in education.

Wright's father taught school in Phoenix, South Carolina, and elsewhere, and Wright, as a boy, spent summers with his maternal grandfather on a plantation nearby. The combined influences of a literate family and a rural environment were important to his early intellectual development. As he writes in *Barefoot in Arcadia: Memories of a More Innocent Era* (1974), his father allowed him free run of the bookshelves. Wright read indiscriminately, but his early favorites were G. A. Henty's historic tales for boys, the Roman historian Livy, and fairy tales. The elder Wright read the King James Bible aloud at the dinner table, and young Louis Wright remembered the measured phrases and sonorous passages, which are echoed in his own finely crafted and graceful prose.

Although well read and well educated as a youth, Wright felt that equally useful elements of his education came from sources other than books. He especially liked to ramble in the woods and fields and later insisted that he got a liberal education listening to sawmill hands, black and white. The cotton fields were also a source of folklore and information.

If literature was an intimate aspect of the Wright home, history was equally important. Wright's grandfathers, one originally from Virginia and one from South Carolina, were Confederate veterans. The two old soldiers, when they met at the Wright home, argued endlessly about the War Between the States, especially the Battle of Gettysburg. According to Wright, Grandfather Booker always ended the debate by pounding the table and declaring, "If you fellows under Longstreet hadn't been picking raspberries on the second day's battle, we would have won the war."

Wright's family life cultivated common sense, good humor, and good manners. From the rural, Protestant South of the early twentieth century, he acquired a keen eye for essential qualities of middle-class culture and came to understand the importance of religion in middle-class life, themes and sensibilities he was to utilize in his histories.

Louis Wright majored in chemistry at Wofford College in Spartanburg, South Carolina. When World War I interrupted his studies, Wright joined the army. He saw no action in Europe but did spend some time in Plattsburg, New York. After graduating from Wofford in 1920, Wright became a newspaperman for the *Spartanburg Herald*, then moved to the *Greenwood Index-Journal* for several years. The education he gained in journalism taught him much more than many years in a college or university would have done, he claimed. "Not to have worked on a country newspaper is to have missed a postgraduate instruction in contemporary history."

Despite the excitement of covering bootleggers, local murders, and the Ku Klux Klan, Wright decided in 1923 to leave journalism and begin graduate studies in literature at the University of North Carolina. Gradually he became more interested in what literature revealed about the social mores of an age and about the living people who had become the theme and substance of literary creation than in literature itself. What men and women had accomplished in an earlier time was important, he felt, for an understanding of man's current life. While his doctorate was earned in 1926 for "Vaudeville Elements in Elizabethan Drama," his studies soon were directed to social history.

A Guggenheim grant in 1928 allowed Wright to pursue research in London on his first major historical work, *Middle-Class Culture in Elizabethan England* (1935). Critical reception was positive; one historian declared that *Middle-Class Culture in Elizabethan England* was an important work for all students of Anglo-American cultural history. Wright dealt in this book with the mentality and aspirations of the English middle classes as reflected in the printed materials that they read. He was able to draw a literary portrait of Shakespeare's audiences with rare insight from histories, poems, and self-help books popular at the time.

Wright was a member of the English faculty at the University of North Carolina from 1926 to 1932. But in 1930 he was appointed a visiting scholar at the Huntington Library. His appointment was originally for one year. Wright proved so valuable to the burgeoning research establishment that he remained until 1948 as a key member of the library and editorial staff. On accepting the appointment at the Huntington, Wright rejected a position at the University of Michigan. It was a decision, he said, which he never regretted. He continued to teach in a variety of institutions on occasion, but Wright's rejection of a professorship meant that he was to have a career different from that of most professional historians of this century. He was to be a scholar-administrator rather than an academician.

A pioneer research center, the Huntington Library was one of the first libraries to shift its emphasis from being merely a repository of books and artifacts to being an institution dedicated to the active utilization of its materials. This remarkable library attracted and paid scholars to use its collections. One of Wright's early colleagues at the Huntington was Frederick Jackson Turner, and during the 1930s Wright worked with Robert Frost, Sir Hugh Walpole, Edwin F. Gay, Godfrey Davies, Dixon Wecter, and Robert Cleland—a spectrum of scholars and interests perhaps unequaled elsewhere.

The years in southern California in the stimulating atmosphere of the Huntington were fruitful for Wright. In addition to serving on the editorial boards of historical journals such as the *William and Mary Quarterly* (1944-1945) and the *Journal of the History of Ideas* (1940-1955) and being editor of the *Huntington Library Quarterly*, he engaged in extensive research on Anglo-American culture. *Puritans in the South Seas* (1936), with Mary Isabel Frey, was his first publication written entirely at the Huntington. It was followed by *The First Gentlemen of Virginia* (1940), an interpretation of the evolution of a ruling class. In the latter book Wright examined the intellectual qualities and cultural attributes of the group who became leaders of the Virginia colony during the first two or three generations of English settlement. He analyzed the books

collected in colonial Virginia gentlemen's libraries as well as letters written by leading men. He concluded that the Virginia gentry were very conservative in that they sought to reproduce the social structure of rural England with themselves as the squirearchy. Critical response was favorable. One critic, noting Wright's objective of dispelling the "moonlight and magnolia" myth, observed that his book was a sane and scholarly reexamination of a way of life that had received too much romanticization.

Religion and Empire: The Alliance Between Piety and Commerce in English Expansion, 1558-1625 followed in 1943. In this book Wright examined a wide variety of printed works—sermons, moral essays, travel narratives—and pointed out that religious literature constituted over half of all printed material in the early modern era. He thus concluded that the propaganda and other religious influences of Protestant clergymen were powerful factors in creating public sentiment during the first era of English expansion overseas. The clergy gave expression to some of the more advanced ideas of imperialism of the period. Critical response to *Religion and Empire* was, as usual, positive. One historian applauded Wright's valuable contribution to the social history of Christianity and commerce. Another admitted that his painstaking study of the sermons was useful as well as delightful.

The Atlantic Frontier: Colonial American Civilization, 1607-1763 also stems from this extremely fertile period. Published in the United States in 1947, the first British edition appeared in 1949 as *The Colonial Civilization of North America, 1607-1763*. Giving a brief account of the growth of culture in the colonies, Wright systematically examined the political, social, and intellectual development in the early history of each region. The author's lucid, graceful style, a feature of all of his works, complemented his thorough knowledge of the Elizabethan English society from which the early colonizers sprang. Reviewers praised this work as the scholarly, well-written production of a top-flight historian, although one quibbled that, whenever possible, Wright joined a generalized adjective with each noun.

In 1948 Wright left the Huntington to assume the directorship of the Folger Shakespeare Library, where he continued unabated his investigations of Anglo-American culture. The most succinct statements of his findings appeared in lectures during the early 1950s, published under the titles *The British Tradition in America* and *Culture on the Moving Frontier* (1955). In these works Wright again saw the colonists as conservative perpetuators of the British culture of the early modern era. The pattern of American society, which was established in the colonial period, continued during the nineteenth century as the nation expanded westward. The most significant cultural element in determining American history was the Anglo-Saxon tradition: English law, language, and literature, and British religion and customs. Historians greeted *The British Tradition in America* and *Culture on the Moving Frontier* with the, by now, familiar praise. Henry Steele Commager commented: "We are indebted to Mr. Wright for reminding us of the importance of the obvious."

Wright remained director of the Folger Library until his retirement in 1968. The scholarly reputation he achieved is indicated by his receipt of nearly thirty honorary degrees and by his chairmanship of the advisory board of the John Simon Guggenheim Foundation from 1950 to 1971. Since 1971 he has been historical consultant to the National Geographic Society.

A prominent aspect of Wright's career has been his extensive editorial work. In accord with his early interest in Virginia history, Wright edited important colonial documents, among them the *Letters of Robert Carter, 1720-1727* (1940), *The Secret Diary of William Byrd of Westover, 1709-1712* (1941), *The History and Present State of Virginia, 1705*, by Robert Beverley (1947), and two volumes, published in 1958 and 1966, of William Byrd's prose works and London diary. Wright's most ambitious editorial project by far, however, was *The Folger Library General Reader's Shakespeare* (1959-1969). In this series Wright and Virginia LaMar edited and published in paperback the complete works of Shakespeare. Each play and the sonnets and other poems were carefully prepared from authoritative texts at the Folger. The extremely popular series had sold over eight million copies by 1968. These volumes, along with Wright's readers' guide, *Shakespeare for Everyman* (1964), succeeded, as one historian approvingly noted, in bringing William Shakespeare home to man's business and man's bosom.

This attitude of making the scholarly and esoteric accessible and popular gained criticism for Wright from some historians and literati who preferred to reserve history for the initiated. Wright defended the General Reader's series, stating that it was good to make Shakespeare available for all, that Shakespeare the stimulant was far superior to Shakespeare the tranquilizer. In response to a pompous criticism, he wrote: "This edition, Col-

onel, is equipped with the complete and accurate text of each play, and the natives are busily spelling out the words. If the notes attempt to simplify the hard passages you will forgive us, Colonel, because the aborigines who live along the banks of the Tombigbee and the Chattahoochee have not had all the advantage of you who dwell on the Isis and the Cam. But they are making out, and they find Shakespeare right stimulating."

In the 1970s Wright, in addition to his editorial and consulting duties, produced several popular histories on exploration and the Renaissance. In *Gold, Glory, and the Gospel: The Adventurous Lives and Times of the Renaissance Explorers* (1970), he discussed the principal motivations that drove Spanish conquistadores to "perform miracles" of exploration and faith. He narrated the spectacular achievements of men who conquered unknown lands and seas in the fifteenth and sixteenth centuries. Although the stories were well known, Wright selected important and dramatic episodes to retell them in his own powerful style. This work received mixed reviews. Applauded for his consistently lucid writing by some, the author was criticized by others for presenting a rehash of well-worn themes peopled with cardboard characters.

In *Barefoot in Arcadia* Wright turned his eye and pen homeward. "As a historian," he observed, "I have spent most of my life trying to recreate social milieus of the past. Since my life in small towns and [in a part of] the country that I propose to describe is unknown to most moderns, perhaps it is worth recalling." Wright's extensive background in colonial history and recent experience in writing South Carolina reminiscences thus prompted the editors of the State and Nation series to urge him to write *South Carolina: A Bicentennial History* (1976). This work was "interpretative," as the editors noted, and Wright stated that he used few new sources in compiling his narrative. He dwelled on the earlier centuries of South Carolina's development because he saw the early colonial origins as critical to later patterns of behavior and regional differences. Although this work was intended as a personal interpretive history, Wright's emphasis on the colonial period drew criticism from historians who castigated him for neglecting the nineteenth and twentieth centuries.

Of Books and Men (1976) is a sequel to Wright's personal narrative of his earliest experiences in South Carolina, Chapel Hill, and London. In this work he discusses his intellectually stimulating decades at the Huntington and Folger and elaborates his philosophy of book collecting, librarianship, and scholarship in general. He concludes: "I am grateful to my ancestors for providing a persistent instinct for curiosity about the great world and a respect for diligence that permanently inoculated me against boredom."

Wright has never felt that history and literature are the preserve of the elite. On the contrary, his smoothly readable prose confirms the observation that good literature and good history are available to all who can read. Sound history does not need to be dull. Some critics have faulted Wright for his popular appeal and for making history so readable. He writes for and from the middle class. In his work, the history of the culture of the English-speaking middle class reaches a new level of sophistication that enriches all of American life.

It is a measure of Wright's easy, popular style that his work appears not only in English but also in Dutch and Spanish. The man who writes so fluently about the development of American culture should be, fittingly, one whom Latin Americans, Europeans, and all of the English-speaking world read.

Other:

Letters of Robert Carter, 1720-1727, edited by Wright (San Marino, Cal.: Huntington Library, 1940);

The Secret Diary of William Byrd of Westover, 1709-1712, edited by Wright and Marion Tinling (Richmond: Dietz Press, 1941);

The American Tradition, edited by Wright and H. T. Swedenberg, Jr. (New York: Crofts, 1941);

Quebec to Carolina in 1785-1786: Being the Travel Diary and Observations of Robert Hunter, Jr., a Young Merchant of London, edited by Wright and Tinling (San Marino, Cal.: Huntington Library, 1943);

An Essay Upon the Government of the English Plantations on the Continent of America, 1701, edited by Wright (San Marino, Cal.: Huntington Library, 1945);

Robert Beverley, *The History and Present State of Virginia, 1705*, edited by Wright (Charlottesville: Dominion Books, 1947);

The Historie of Travell Into Virginia Britania, 1612, by William Strachey, Gent., edited by Wright and Virginia Freund (London: Hakluyt Society, 1953);

American Heritage, An Anthology and Interpretive Survey of Our Literature, 2 volumes, edited by Wright, Leon Howard, and Carl Bode (New York: Washington Square Press, 1955);

William Byrd of Virginia, *The London Diary, 1717-1721, and Other Writings*, edited by Wright and Tinling (New York: Oxford University Press, 1958);

The Folger Library General Reader's Shakespeare, edited by Wright and Virginia LaMar (New York: Washington Square Press, 1959-1969);

Advice to a Son: Precepts of Lord Burghley, Sir Walter Raleigh, and Francis Osborne, edited by Wright (Ithaca: Cornell University Press, 1962);

Life and Letters in Tudor and Stuart England, edited by Wright (Ithaca: Cornell University Press, 1962);

Richard Eburne, *A Plain Pathway to Plantations, 1624*, edited by Wright (Ithaca: Cornell University Press, 1962);

Four Famous Tudor and Stuart Plays, edited by Wright (New York: Washington Square Press, 1963);

The Play's the Thing: Seventeen of Shakespeare's Greatest Dramas, edited by Wright (New York: Harper & Row, 1963);

Four Great Restoration Plays, edited by Wright (New York: Washington Square Press, 1964);

The Elizabethan's America: A Collection of Early Reports, edited by Wright (Cambridge: Harvard University Press, 1965; London: Cassell, 1965);

The Prose Works of William Byrd of Westover, edited by Wright (Cambridge: Harvard University Press, 1966);

The Arts in America: The Colonial Period, edited by Wright (New York: Scribners, 1966);

Shakespeare Celebrated; Anniversary Lectures Delivered at the Folger Library, edited by Wright (Ithaca: Cornell University Press, 1966);

The American Heritage History of the Thirteen Colonies, edited by Wright (New York: American Heritage, 1967);

English Colonization of North America; Documents of Modern History, edited by Wright and Elaine W. Fowler (London: Arnold, 1968);

The Folger Guide to Shakespeare, edited by Wright and LaMar (New York: Washington Square Press, 1969);

West and By North: North America Seen Through the Eyes of Its Seafaring Discoverers, edited by Wright and Fowler (New York: Delacorte, 1971);

Essays in Honor of David Lyall Patrick by Rene Jules Dubos, Germaine Bree, and Louis Booker Wright, edited by Wright (Tucson: University of Arizona Press, 1972);

The Moving Frontier: North America Seen Through the

Eyes of Its Pioneer Discoverers, edited by Wright
  and Fowler (New York: Delacorte, 1972);
*A New and Accurate Map of Virginia Wherein Most of the
  Counties are Laid Down From Actual Surveys by
  John Henry*, edited by Wright (Charlottesville:
University of Virginia Press, 1977).

Reference:
*Louis Booker Wright: A Bibliography and an Apprecia-
  tion* (Charlottesville: University of Virginia
  Press, 1968).

Supplementary Reading List

The following is a selective list for further reading on American historians and their works and on twentieth-century historians' methods and philosophies.

Barzun, Jacques, and Henry F. Graff. *The Modern Researcher*. New York: Harcourt Brace Jovanovich, 1970.

Bassett, John Spencer. *The Middle Group of American Historians*. New York: Macmillan, 1917.

Beard, Charles A. *The Discussion of Human Affairs*. New York: Macmillan, 1936.

Becker, Carl. *Everyman his Own Historian*. New York: Crofts, 1935.

Bellot, Hugh Hale. *American History and American Historians*. Norman: University of Oklahoma Press, 1952.

Benson, Lee. *Toward the Scientific Study of History. Selected Essays*. Philadelphia: Lippincott, 1972.

Bernstein, Barton J., ed. *Towards a New Past. Dissenting Essays in American History*. New York: Random House, 1968.

Bloch, Marc. *The Historian's Craft*. New York: Vintage, 1964.

Butterfield, Herbert. *Man on His Past. The Study of the History of Historical Scholarship*. Boston: Beacon, 1960.

Butterfield. *The Whig Interpretation of History*. London: Bell, 1931.

Carr, E. H. *What is History?* New York: Knopf, 1962.

Caughey, John W. "Historians' Choice: Results of a Poll on Recently Published American History and Biography," *Mississippi Valley Historical Review*, 39 (September 1952): 289-302.

Cochran, Thomas C., ed. *The Inner Revolution: Essays on the Social Sciences in History*. New York: Harper & Row, 1964.

Collingwood, R. G. *Essays in the Philosophy of History*. Austin: University of Texas Press, 1965.

Collingwood. *The Idea of History*. Oxford: Clarendon Press, 1946.

Cunliffe, Marcus, and Robin W. Winks. *Pastmasters. Some Essays on American Historians*. New York: Harper & Row, 1969.

Davis, Allen F., and Harold D. Woodman, eds. *Conflict or Consensus in American History?* Boston: Heath, 1966.

De Jouvenal, Bertrand. *The Art of Conjecture*. New York: Basic Books, 1967.

Durant, Will and Ariel. *The Lessons of History*. New York: Simon & Schuster, 1968.

Fischer, David Hackett. *Historians' Fallacies; Toward a Logic of Historical Thought*. New York: Harper & Row, 1970.

Francois, Michel, and Boyd C. Shafer, and others. *Historical Study in the West*. New York: Appleton-Century-Crofts, 1968.

Freeman, Edward A. *The Methods of Historical Study*. London: Macmillan, 1886.

Gardiner, Patrick. *The Nature of Historical Explanation*. London: Oxford University Press, 1965.

Garraty, John A. *Interpreting American History: Conversations with Historians*. New York: Macmillan, 1970.

Garraty. *The Nature of Biography*. New York: Knopf, 1957.

Gay, Peter. *Style in History*. New York: McGraw-Hill, 1974.

Gottschalk, Louis, ed. *Generalization in the Writing of History*. Chicago: University of Chicago Press, 1963.

Gottschalk. *Understanding History*. New York: Knopf, 1969.

Grob, Gerald N., and George A. Billias. *Interpretations of American History*. New York: Free Press, 1967.

Gustavson, Carl G. *The Mansion of History*. New York: McGraw-Hill, 1976.

Handlin, Oscar, and others, eds. *Harvard Guide to American History*. Cambridge, Mass.: Belknap Press, 1954, and subsequent editions.

Handlin. *Truth in History*. Cambridge: Harvard University Press, 1979.

Hexter, J. H. *Doing History*. Bloomington: Indiana University Press, 1971.

Hexter. *Reappraisals in History*. London: Longmans, Green, 1961.

Higham, John, ed. *The Reconstruction of American History*. London: Hutchinson, 1962.

Higham, Leonard Krieger, and Felix Gilbert. *History*. Englewood Cliffs, N.J.: Prentice-Hall, 1965.

Hofstadter, Richard. *The Progressive Historians: Turner, Beard, Parrington*. New York: Knopf, 1968.

Hutchinson, William T., ed. *The Marcus W. Jernegan Essays in American Historiography*. Chicago: University of Chicago Press, 1937.

Jameson, J. Franklin. *The History of Historical Writing in America*. Boston & New York: Houghton Mifflin, 1891.

Jones, H. G. *The Records of a Nation: Their Management, Preservation and Use*. New York: Atheneum, 1969.

Katz, Stanley N., and Stanley I. Kutler, eds. *New Perspectives on the American Past*. Boston: Little, Brown, 1969.

Kraus, Michael. *The Writing of American History*. Norman: University of Oklahoma Press, 1953.

Link, Arthur S., and Rembert W. Patrick, eds. *Writing Southern History: Essays in Historiography in Honor of Fletcher M. Green*. Baton Rouge: Louisiana State University Press, 1965.

Lukacs, John. *Historical Consciousness*. New York: Harper & Row, 1968.

Maddox, Robert J. *The New Left and the Origins of the Cold War*. Princeton: Princeton University Press, 1973.

Meyerhoff, Hans, ed. *The Philosophy of History in Our Time*. Garden City: Doubleday, 1959.

Morison, Samuel Eliot. *Vistas of History*. New York: Knopf, 1964.

Nevins, Allan. *The Gateway to History*. Boston: Heath, 1938.

Niebuhr, Reinhold. *The Irony of American History*. New York: Scribners, 1952.

Noble, David W. *Historians Against History*. Minneapolis: University of Minnesota Press, 1965.

Odum, Howard W., ed. *American Masters of Social Science*. New York: Holt, 1927.

O'Neill, Edward H. *A History of American Biography, 1800-1935*. New York: Barnes, 1961.

Perkins, Dexter, and others. *The Education of Historians in the United States*. New York: McGraw-Hill, 1962.

Pole, J. R. *Paths to the American Past*. New York: Oxford University Press, 1979.

Robinson, James Harvey. *The New History: Essays Illustrating the Modern Historical Outlook*. New York: Free Press, 1965.

Rundell, Walter. *In Pursuit of American History; Research and Training in the United States*. Norman: University of Oklahoma Press, 1970.

Saveth, Edward N., ed. *American History and the Social Sciences*. New York: Free Press of Glencoe, 1964.

Schlesinger, Arthur M., Sr. *New Viewpoints in American History*. New York: Macmillan, 1922.

Skotheim, Robert Allen. *American Intellectual Histories and Historians*. Princeton: Princeton University Press, 1966.

Smith, Page. *The Historian and History*. New York: Knopf, 1966.

Social Science Research Council. *Theory and Practice in Historical Study: A Report of the Committee on Historiography*. New York: Social Science Research Council, 1946.

Stephenson, Wendell Holmes. *The South Lives in History: Southern Historians and Their Legacy*. Baton Rouge: Louisiana State University Press, 1955.

Stern, Fritz. *The Varieties of History, From Voltaire to the Present*. New York: Meridian, 1956.

Strayer, Joseph R., ed. *The Interpretation of History*. Princeton: Princeton University Press, 1943.

Szasz, Ferenc M. "The Many Meanings of History," *History Teacher*, 7 (August & November 1974): 552-563; 8 (February 1975): 54-63, 208-227.

Tindall, George B., ed. *The Pursuit of Southern History; Presidential Addresses of the Southern Historical Association, 1935-1963*. Baton Rouge: Louisiana State University Press, 1964.

Webb, Walter Prescott. *History as High Adventure*. Austin, Tex.: Pemberton Press, 1969.

Wedgwood, C. V. *The Sense of the Past*. London: Cambridge University Press, 1957.

White, Morton. *Foundations of Historical Knowledge*. New York: Harper & Row, 1965.

Winks, Robin W., ed. *The Historian as Detective: Essays on Evidence*. New York: Harper & Row, 1969.

Wise, Gene. *American Historical Explanations. A Strategy for Grounded Inquiry*. Minneapolis: University of Minnesota Press, 1980.

Wish, Harvey. *The American Historian: A Social-Intellectual History of the Writing of the American Past*. New York: Oxford University Press, 1960.

Woodward, C. Vann, ed. *The Comparative Approach to American History*. New York: Basic Books, 1968.

Contributors

Frank Annunziata ....*Rochester Institute of Technology*
B. D. Bargar ....*University of South Carolina*
John Barnwell...*Vanderbilt University*
Michael Bordelon...*St. Thomas Episcopal School, Houston*
M. E. Bradford ....*University of Dallas*
John Braeman...*University of Nebraska-Lincoln*
Amy Bushnell...*Historic St. Augustine Preservation Board*
Robert M. Calhoon..*University of North Carolina at Greensboro*
Mark T. Carleton...*Louisiana State University*
David L. Carlton ....*Columbia, South Carolina*
Anne W. Chapman ....*College of William and Mary*
Allan D. Charles ....*University of South Carolina at Union*
Kendrick A. Clements..*University of South Carolina*
Lawrence Wells Cobb ....*Oklahoma City University*
Peter A. Coclanis ....*Columbia University*
Thomas L. Connelly ....*University of South Carolina*
Edward L. Cox ....*University of South Carolina*
Joseph G. Dawson III ....*Texas A&M University at Galveston*
Justus D. Doenecke ....*New College of the University of South Florida*
Herbert J. Doherty, Jr. ....*University of Florida*
Marion Edmonds.................*South Carolina Department of Parks, Recreation and Tourism*
A. Roger Ekirch....................................*Virginia Polytechnic Institute and State University*
Paula S. Fass ....*University of California, Berkeley*
Odie B. Faulk ....*Northeastern Oklahoma University*
Thomas Fleming...*College of Charleston*
Steven P. Gietschier ....*South Carolina Department of Archives and History*
John L. Gignilliat ....*Agnes Scott College*
Shirley A. Hickson ....*North Greenville College*
Paul A. Horne, Jr..*University of South Carolina*
Herbert A. Johnson ....*University of South Carolina*
Milton M. Klein ....*University of Tennessee*
Suzanne Krebsbach..*University of South Carolina*
Jessica Kross ....*University of South Carolina*
William D. Liddle..*Southwest Texas State University*
William Marina...*Florida Atlantic University*
John McCardell ....*Middlebury College*
Richard M. McMurry ....*North Carolina State University*
Edwin A. Miles ....*University of Houston*
Wayne Mixon ....*Mercer University*
Elisabeth Muhlenfeld ....*Florida State University*
Mark E. Neely, Jr. ....*Louis A. Warren Lincoln Library and Museum*
Michael O'Brien ....*University of Arkansas*
Carol Reardon...*University of Kentucky*
Arnold Shankman...*Winthrop College*
Richard A. Shrader...*University of North Carolina Library*
John David Smith ....*North Carolina State University*

John G. Sproat ....*University of South Carolina*
J. Barton Starr..*Hong Kong Baptist College*
Michael E. Stevens ....*South Carolina Department of Archives and History*
Marcia G. Synnott ....*University of South Carolina*
C. James Taylor..*University of South Carolina*
George D. Terry ....*University of South Carolina*
Clyde N. Wilson ....*University of South Carolina*
Kirk Wood..*University of South Carolina*

Cumulative Index

Dictionary of Literary Biography, Volumes 1-17
Dictionary of Literary Biography Yearbook, 1980, 1981
Dictionary of Literary Biography Documentary Series, Volumes 1-3

Cumulative Index

DLB before number: *Dictionary of Literary Biography*, Volumes 1-17
Y before number: *Dictionary of Literary Biography Yearbook*, 1980, 1981
DS before number: *Dictionary of Literary Biography Documentary Series*, Volumes 1-3

A

Abbott, Jacob 1803-1879 ....DLB1

Adamic, Louis 1898-1951 ....DLB9

Adams, Henry 1838-1918 ....DLB12

Adams, James Truslow 1878-1949 ....DLB17

Ade, George 1866-1944 ....DLB11

Adeler, Max (see Clark, Charles Heber)

Agassiz, Jean Louis Rodolphe 1807-1873
....DLB1

Agee, James 1909-1955 ....DLB2

Aiken, Conrad 1889-1973 ....DLB9

Albee, Edward 1928- DLB7

Alcott, Amos Bronson 1799-1888 ....DLB1

Alcott, Louisa May 1832-1888 ....DLB1

Alcott, William Andrus 1798-1859 ....DLB1

Aldiss, Brian W. 1925- DLB14

Algren, Nelson 1909-1981 ....DLB9; Y81

Alldritt, Keith 1935- DLB14

Allen, Hervey 1889-1949 ....DLB9

Josiah Allen's Wife (see Holly, Marietta)

Allston, Washington 1779-1843 ....DLB1

Alvarez, A. 1929- DLB14

Amis, Kingsley 1922- DLB15

Amis, Martin 1949- DLB14

Ammons, A. R. 1926- DLB5

Anderson, Margaret 1886-1973 ....DLB4

Anderson, Maxwell 1888-1959 ....DLB7

Anderson, Poul 1926- DLB8

Anderson, Robert 1917- DLB7

Anderson, Sherwood 1876-1941
....DLB4, 9; DS1

Andrews, Charles M. 1863-1943 ....DLB17

Anthony, Piers 1934- DLB8

Archer, William 1856-1924 ....DLB10

Arden, John 1930- DLB13

Arnow, Harriette Simpson 1908- DLB6

Arp, Bill (see Smith, Charles Henry)

Arthur, Timothy Shay 1809-1885 ....DLB3

Asch, Nathan 1902-1964 ....DLB4

Ashbery, John 1927- DLB5; Y81

Ashton, Winifred (see Dane, Clemence)

Asimov, Isaac 1920- DLB8

Atherton, Gertrude 1857-1948 ....DLB9

Auchincloss, Louis 1917- DLB2; Y80

Auden, W. H. 1907-1973 ....DLB10

Austin, Mary 1868-1934 ....DLB9

Ayckbourn, Alan 1939- DLB13

B

Bacon, Delia 1811-1859 ....DLB1

Bagnold, Enid 1889-1981 ....DLB13

Bailey, Paul 1937- DLB14

Bailyn, Bernard 1922- DLB17

Bainbridge, Beryl 1933- DLB14

Bald, Wambly 1902- DLB4

Baldwin, James 1924- DLB2, 7

Baldwin, Joseph Glover 1815-1864
....DLB3, 11

Ballard, J. G. 1930- DLB14

Bancroft, George 1800-1891 ....DLB1

Bangs, John Kendrick 1862-1922 ....DLB11

Banville, John 1945- DLB14

Baraka, Amiri 1934- DLB5, 7, 16

Barker, A. L. 1918- DLB14

Barker, Harley Granville 1877-1946
....DLB10

Barker, Howard 1946- DLB13

Barks, Coleman 1937- DLB5

Barnes, Djuna 1892-1982.........................DLB4, 9

Barnes, Margaret Ayer 1886-1967...............DLB9

Barnes, Peter 1931- DLB13

Barney, Natalie 1876-1972..........................DLB4

Barrie, James M. 1860-1937.......................DLB10

Barry, Philip 1896-1949 ....DLB7

Barstow, Stan 1928- DLB14

Barth, John 1930- DLB2

Barthelme, Donald 1931- DLB2; Y80

Bartlett, John 1820-1905.............................DLB1

Bartol, Cyrus Augustus 1813-1900.............DLB1

Bass, T. J. 1932- Y81

Bassett, John Spencer 1867-1928...............DLB17

Bassler, Thomas Joseph (see T. J. Bass)

Baumbach, Jonathan 1933- Y80

Bawden, Nina 1925- DLB14

Bax, Clifford 1886-1962.............................DLB10

Beach, Sylvia 1887-1962.............................DLB4

Beagle, Peter S. 1939- Y80

Beal, M. F. 1937- Y81

Beale, Howard K. 1899-1959.....................DLB17

Beard, Charles A. 1874-1948.....................DLB17

Becker, Carl 1873-1945..............................DLB17

Beckett, Samuel 1906- DLB13, 15

Beecher, Catharine Esther 1800-1878
....DLB1

Beecher, Henry Ward 1813-1887................DLB3

Behan, Brendan 1923-1964 ....DLB13

Behrman, S. N. 1893-1973..........................DLB7

Belasco, David 1853-1931...........................DLB7

Belitt, Ben 1911- DLB5

Bell, Marvin 1937- DLB5

Bellamy, Edward 1850-1898 ....DLB12

Bellow, Saul 1915- DLB2; DS3

Bemis, Samuel Flagg 1891-1973 ....DLB17

Benchley, Robert 1889-1945 ....DLB11

Benedictus, David 1938- DLB14

Benedikt, Michael 1935- DLB5

Benét, Stephen Vincent 1898-1943
....DLB4

Benjamin, Park 1809-1864 ....DLB3

Bennett, Arnold 1867-1931.......................DLB10

Berg, Stephen 1934- DLB5

Berger, John 1926- DLB14

Berger, Thomas 1924- DLB2; Y80

Berrigan, Daniel 1921- DLB5

Berrigan, Ted 1934- DLB5

Berry, Wendell 1934- DLB5, 6

Bester, Alfred 1913- DLB8

Beveridge, Albert J. 1862-1927.................DLB17

Bierce, Ambrose 1842-1914? DLB11, 12

Biggle, Lloyd, Jr. 1923- DLB8

Biglow, Hosea (see Lowell, James Russell)

Billings, Josh (see Shaw, Henry Wheeler)

Bird, William 1888-1963 ....DLB4

Bishop, Elizabeth 1911-1979.......................DLB5

Bishop, John Peale 1892-1944.................DLB4, 9

Blackburn, Paul 1926-1971..............Y81; DLB 16

Blackwood, Caroline 1931- DLB14

Bledsoe, Albert Taylor 1809-1877...............DLB3

Blish, James 1921-1975 ....DLB8

Bly, Robert 1926- DLB5

Bodenheim, Maxwell 1892-1954..................DLB9

Boer, Charles 1939- DLB5

Bogarde, Dirk 1921- DLB14

Bolt, Robert 1924- DLB13

Bolton, Herbert E. 1870-1953....................DLB17

Bond, Edward 1934- DLB13

Boorstin, Daniel J. 1914- DLB17

Botta, Anne C. Lynch 1815-1891 ....DLB3

Bottomley, Gordon 1874-1948....................DLB10

Boucher, Anthony 1911-1968......................DLB8

Bourjaily, Vance 1922- DLB2

Bova, Ben 1932- Y81

Bowen, Elizabeth 1899-1973 ....DLB15

Bowen, Francis 1811-1890 ....DLB1

Bowen, John 1924- DLB13

Bowers, Claude G. 1878-1958....................DLB17

Bowers, Edgar 1924- DLB5

Bowles, Paul 1910- DLB5, 6

Boyd, James 1888-1944................................DLB9

Boyd, John 1919- DLB8

Boyd, Thomas 1898-1935 ....DLB9

Boyesen, Hjalmar Hjorth 1848-1895..........DLB12

Boyle, Kay 1902- DLB4, 9

Brackett, Leigh 1915-1978 ....DLB8

Brackenridge, Hugh Henry 1748-1816

    ....DLB11

Bradbury, Malcolm 1932- DLB14

Bradbury, Ray 1920- DLB2, 8

Bradford, Gamaliel 1863-1932....................DLB17

Bradley, Marion Zimmer 1930- DLB8

Bradley, William Aspenwall 1878-1939

    ....DLB4

Bragg, Melvyn 1939- DLB14

Braine, John 1922-..................................DLB15

Brautigan, Richard 1935- DLB2, 5; Y80

Bremser, Bonnie 1939- DLB16

Bremser, Ray 1934- DLB16

Brenton, Howard 1942- DLB13

Bridie, James 1888-1951 ....DLB10

Briggs, Charles Frederick 1804-1877

    ....DLB3

Brighouse, Harold 1882-1958.....................DLB10

Brisbane, Albert 1809-1890.........................DLB3

Bromfield, Louis 1896-1956 ....DLB4, 9

Brooke-Rose, Christine 1926- DLB14

Brooks, Charles Timothy 1813-1883............DLB1

Brooks, Gwendolyn 1917- DLB5

Brooks, Jeremy 1926- DLB14

Brophy, Brigid 1929- DLB14

Brossard, Chandler 1922- DLB16

Brother Antoninus (see Everson, William)

Brougham, John 1810-1880,.....................DLB11

Broughton, James 1913- DLB5

Brown, Bob 1886-1959...............................DLB4

Brown, Christy 1932-1981..........................DLB14

Brown, Dee 1908- Y80

Brown, Fredric 1906-1972 ....DLB8

Brown, George Mackay 1921- DLB14

Brown, William Wells 1813-1884..................DLB3

Browne, Charles Farrar 1834-1867 ....DLB11

Browne, Wynyard 1911-1964.....................DLB13

Brownson, Orestes Augustus 1803-1876......DLB1

Bryant, William Cullen 1794-1878...............DLB3

Buck, Pearl S. 1892-1973 ....DLB9

Buckley, William F., Jr. 1925- Y80

Budrys, A. J. 1931- DLB8

Buechner, Frederick 1926- Y80

Bukowski, Charles 1920- DLB5

Bullins, Ed 1935- DLB7

Bumpus, Jerry 1937- Y81

Burgess, Anthony 1917- DLB14

Burgess, Gelett 1866-1951..........................DLB11

Burnett, W. R. 1899- DLB9

Burns, Alan 1929- DLB14

Burroughs, Edgar Rice 1875-1950 ....DLB8

Burroughs, William S., Jr. 1947-1981 ....DLB16

Burroughs, William Seward 1914-

    ....DLB2, 8, 16; Y81

Burroway, Janet 1936- DLB6

Busch, Frederick 1941- DLB6

Byatt, A. S. 1936- DLB14

Byrne, John Keyes (see Leonard, Hugh)

C

Cabell, James Branch 1879-1958 ....DLB9

Cable, George Washington 1844-1925
.....................DLB12

Cahan, Abraham 1860-1951 ....DLB9

Caldwell, Erskine 1903- DLB9

Calhoun, John C. 1782-1850.....................DLB3

Calisher, Hortense 1911- DLB2

Calmer, Edgar 1907- DLB4

Calvert, George Henry 1803-1889.................DLB1

Campbell, John W., Jr. 1910-1971...............DLB8

Cannan, Gilbert 1884-1955 ....DLB10

Cannell, Kathleen 1891-1974.....................DLB4

Cantwell, Robert 1908-1978.........................DLB9

Capote, Truman 1924- DLB2; Y80

Carroll, Gladys Hasty 1904- DLB9

Carroll, Paul 1927- DLB16

Carroll, Paul Vincent 1900-1968.................DLB10

Carruth, Hayden 1921- DLB5

Carter, Angela 1940- DLB14

Carter, Lin 1930- Y81

Caruthers, William Alexander 1802-1846
.....................DLB3

Cary, Joyce 1888-1957.....................DLB15

Casey, Juanita 1925- DLB14

Casey, Michael 1947- DLB5

Cassady, Carolyn 1923- DLB16

Cassady, Neal 1926-1968.....................DLB16

Cassill, R. V. 1919- DLB6

Cather, Willa 1873-1947.....................DLB9; DS1

Catton, Bruce 1899-1978.....................DLB17

Caute, David 1936- DLB14

Chambers, Charles Haddon 1860-1921
.....................DLB10

Channing, Edward 1856-1931 ....DLB17

Channing, Edward Tyrrell 1790-1856
.....................DLB1

Channing, William Ellery 1780-1842
.....................DLB1

Channing, William Ellery, II 1817-1901
.....................DLB1

Channing, William Henry 1810-1884
.....................DLB1

Chappell, Fred 1936- DLB6

Charles, Gerda 1914- DLB14

Chayefsky, Paddy 1923-1981 ....DLB7; Y81

Cheever, John 1912-1982.....................DLB2; Y80

Cheney, Ednah Dow (Littlehale) 1824-1904
.....................DLB1

Cherryh, C. J. 1942- Y80

Chesnutt, Charles Waddell 1858-1932
.....................DLB12

Chesterton, G. K. 1874-1936.....................DLB10

Child, Francis James 1825-1896.....................DLB1

Child, Lydia Maria 1802-1880 ....DLB1

Childress, Alice 1920- DLB7

Chivers, Thomas Holley 1809-1858
.....................DLB3

Chopin, Kate 1851-1904.....................DLB12

Christie, Agatha 1890-1976.....................DLB13

Churchill, Caryl 1938- DLB13

Ciardi, John 1916- DLB5

Clark, Charles Heber 1841-1915 ....DLB11

Clark, Eleanor 1913- DLB6

Clark, Lewis Gaylord 1808-1873.................DLB3

Clark, Walter Van Tilburg 1909-1971..........DLB9

Clarke, Austin 1896-1974.........................DLB10

Clarke, James Freeman 1810-1888
.....................DLB1

Clausen, Andy 1943- DLB16

Clemens, Samuel Langhorne 1835-1910
....DLB11, 12

Clement, Hal 1922- DLB8

Clifton, Lucille 1936- DLB5

Coates, Robert M. 1897-1973
....DLB4, 9

Cobb, Irvin S. 1876-1944 ....DLB11

Cochran, Thomas C. 1902- DLB17

Cole, Barry 1936- DLB14

Colegate, Isabel 1931- DLB14

Coleman, Emily Holmes 1899-1974
....DLB4

Colwin, Laurie 1944- Y80

Commager, Henry Steele 1902- DLB17

Connell, Evan S., Jr. 1924- DLB2; Y81

Connelly, Marc 1890- DLB7; Y80

Conrad, Joseph 1857-1924..................DLB10

Conroy, Jack 1899- Y81

Conroy, Pat 1945- DLB6

Conway, Moncure Daniel 1832-1907
....DLB1

Cooke, John Esten 1830-1886..................DLB3

Cooke, Philip Pendleton 1816-1850
....DLB3

Cooke, Rose Terry 1827-1892 ....DLB12

Cooper, Giles 1918-1966 ....DLB13

Cooper, James Fenimore 1789-1851
....DLB3

Coover, Robert 1932- DLB2; Y81

Corman, Cid 1924- DLB5

Corn, Alfred 1943- Y80

Corrington, John William 1932- DLB6

Corso, Gregory 1930- DLB5, 16

Costain, Thomas B. 1885-1965..................DLB9

Coward, Noel 1899-1973..................DLB10

Cowley, Malcolm 1898- DLB4; Y81

Coxe, Louis 1918- DLB5

Cozzens, James Gould 1903-1979
....DLB9; DS2

Craddock, Charles Egbert (see Murfree, Mary N.)

Cranch, Christopher Pearse 1813-1892
....DLB1

Crane, Hart 1899-1932..................DLB4

Crane, Stephen 1871-1900..................DLB12

Craven, Avery 1885-1980..................DLB17

Crayon, Geoffrey (see Irving, Washington)

Creeley, Robert 1926- DLB5, 16

Cregan, David 1931- DLB13

Crews, Harry 1935- DLB6

Crichton, Michael 1942- Y81

Cristofer, Michael 1946- DLB7

Crockett, David 1786-1836..................DLB3, 11

Crosby, Caresse 1892-1970 and Crosby,
Harry 1898-1929..................DLB4

Crothers, Rachel 1878-1958 ....DLB7

Crowley, Mart 1935- DLB7

Croy, Homer 1883-1965..................DLB4

Cullen, Countee 1903-1946..................DLB4

Cummings, E. E. 1894-1962..................DLB4

Cummings, Ray 1887-1957 ....DLB8

Cunningham, J. V. 1911- DLB5

Cuomo, George 1929- Y80

Cuppy, Will 1884-1949..................DLB11

Curti, Merle E. 1897- DLB17

Curtis, George William 1824-1892
....DLB1

D

Dall, Caroline Wells (Healey) 1822-1912
....DLB1

Daly, T. A. 1871-1948 ....DLB11

D'Alton, Louis 1900-1951..................DLB10

Dana, Charles A. 1819-1897 ....DLB3

Dana, Richard Henry, Jr. 1815-1882
....DLB1

Dane, Clemence 1887-1965..................DLB10

Davidson, Avram 1923- DLB8

Davidson, Lionel 1922- DLB14

Daviot, Gordon 1896-1952 ....DLB10

Davis, Charles A. 1795-1867 ....DLB11

Davis, Clyde Brion 1894-1962 ....DLB9

Davis, H. L. 1894-1960 ....DLB9

Davis, Margaret Thomson 1926- DLB14

Davis, Ossie 1917- DLB7

Davis, Richard Harding 1864-1916

....DLB12

Davison, Peter 1928- DLB5

Day, Clarence 1874-1935 ....DLB11

Day Lewis, C. 1904-1972 ....DLB15

Deal, Borden 1922- DLB6

De Bow, James D. B. 1820-1867 ....DLB3

de Camp, L. Sprague 1907- DLB8

De Forest, John William 1826-1906

....DLB12

de Graff, Robert 1895-1981 ....Y81

Delaney, Shelagh 1939- DLB13

Delany, Samuel R. 1942- DLB8

Delbanco, Nicholas 1942- DLB6

DeLillo, Don 1936- DLB6

Dell, Floyd 1887-1969 ....DLB9

del Rey, Lester 1915- DLB8

Dennis, Nigel 1912- DLB13, 15

Derby, George Horatio 1823-1861 ....DLB11

Derleth, August 1909-1971 ....DLB9

DeVoto, Bernard 1897-1955 ....DLB9

De Vries, Peter 1910- DLB6

Dick, Philip K. 1928- DLB8

Dickey, James 1923- DLB5

Dickey, William 1928- DLB5

Dickinson, Emily 1830-1886 ....DLB1

Dickson, Gordon R. 1923- DLB8

Didion, Joan 1934- DLB2; Y81

Di Donato, Pietro 1911- DLB9

Dillard, Annie 1945- Y80

Dillard, R. H. W. 1937- DLB5

Diogenes, Jr. (see Brougham, John)

DiPrima, Diane 1934- DLB5

Disch, Thomas M. 1940- DLB8

Dix, Dorothea Lynde 1802-1887 ....DLB1

Doctorow, E. L. 1931- DLB2; Y80

Dodd, William E. 1869-1940 ....DLB17

Doesticks, Q. K. Philander, P. B. (see Thomson, Mortimer)

Donald, David H. 1920- DLB17

Donnelly, Ignatius 1831-1901 ....DLB12

Donleavy, J. P. 1926- DLB6

Doolittle, Hilda 1886-1961 ....DLB4

Dorn, Edward 1929- DLB5

Dos Passos, John 1896-1970

..........................DLB4, 9; DS1

Douglass, Frederick 1817?-1895 ....DLB1

Downing, J., Major (See Davis, Charles A.)

Downing, Major Jack (see Smith, Seba)

Doyle, Kirby 1932- DLB16

Drabble, Margaret 1939- DLB14

Dreiser, Theodore 1871-1945

..........................DLB9, 12; DS1

Drinkwater, John 1882-1937 ....DLB10

Duffy, Maureen 1933- DLB14

Dugan, Alan 1923- DLB5

Dukes, Ashley 1885-1959 ....DLB10

Duncan, Robert 1919- DLB5, 16

Duncan, Ronald 1914-1982 ....DLB13

Dunne, Finley Peter 1867-1936 ....DLB11

Dunne, John Gregory 1932- Y80

Dunning, Ralph Cheever 1878-1930

....DLB4

Dunning, William A. 1857-1922 ....DLB17

Plunkett, Edward John Moreton Drax, Lord Dunsany 1878-1957 ....DLB10

Durrell, Lawrence 1912- DLB15

Duyckinck, Evert A. 1816-1878 ....DLB3

Duyckinck, George L. 1823-1863.................DLB3

Dwight, John Sullivan 1813-1893 ....DLB1

Dyer, Charles 1928- DLB13

Dylan, Bob 1941- DLB16

E

Eastlake, William 1917- DLB6

Edgar, David 1948- DLB13

Edmonds, Walter D. 1903- DLB9

Effinger, George Alec 1947- DLB8

Eggleston, Edward 1837-1902....................DLB12

Eigner, Larry 1927- DLB5

Elder, Lonne, III 1931- DLB7

Eliot, T. S. 1888-1965............................DLB7, 10

Elkin, Stanley 1930- DLB2; Y80

Elliott, Janice 1931- DLB14

Elliott, William 1788-1863.......................DLB3

Ellison, Harlan 1934- DLB8

Ellison, Ralph 1914- DLB2

Emerson, Ralph Waldo 1803-1882
....DLB1

Erskine, John 1879-1951 ....DLB9

Ervine, St. John Greer 1883-1971
....DLB10

Eshleman, Clayton 1935- DLB5

Everett, Edward 1794-1865.......................DLB1

Everson, William 1912- DLB5, 16

Exley, Frederick 1929- Y81

F

Farmer, Philip Jose 1918- DLB8

Farrell, J. G. 1935-1979...........................DLB14

Farrell, James T. 1904-1979
....DLB4, 9; DS2

Fast, Howard 1914- DLB9

Faulkner, William 1897-1962
....DLB9, 11; DS2

Faust, Irvin 1924- DLB2; Y80

Fearing, Kenneth 1902-1961......................DLB9

Federman, Raymond 1928- Y80

Feiffer, Jules 1929- DLB7

Feinstein, Elaine 1930- DLB14

Felton, Cornelius Conway 1807-1862
....DLB1

Ferber, Edna 1885-1968...........................DLB9

Ferlinghetti, Lawrence 1919- DLB5, 16

Field, Rachel 1894-1942 ....DLB9

Fields, James Thomas 1817-1881 ....DLB1

Figes, Eva 1932- DLB14

Finney, Jack 1911- DLB8

Finney, Walter Braden (see Finney, Jack)

Fisher, Dorothy Canfield 1879-1958
....DLB9

Fisher, Vardis 1895-1968 ....DLB9

Fitch, William Clyde 1865-1909
....DLB7

Fitzgerald, F. Scott 1896-1940
....................................DLB4, 9; Y81; DS1

Fitzgerald, Penelope 1916- DLB14

Fitzgerald, Robert 1910- Y80

Flanagan, Thomas 1923- Y80

Flanner, Janet 1892-1978..........................DLB4

Flavin, Martin 1883-1967 ....DLB9

Flecker, James Elroy 1884-1915
....DLB10

Fletcher, John Gould 1886-1950
....DLB4

Follen, Eliza Lee (Cabot) 1787-1860
....DLB1

Follett, Ken 1949- Y81

Foote, Shelby 1916- DLB2, 17

Forché, Carolyn 1950- DLB5

Ford, Charles Henri 1913- DLB4

Ford, Corey 1902-1969............................DLB11

Ford, Jesse Hill 1928- DLB6

Fornés, María Irene 1930- DLB7

Foster, Michael 1904-1956 ....DLB9

Fowles, John 1926- DLB14

Fox, John, Jr. 1862 or 1863-1919
....DLB9

Fox, William Price 1926- DLB2; Y81

Fraenkel, Michael 1896-1957 ....DLB4

France, Richard 1938- DLB7

Francis, Convers 1795-1863 ....DLB1

Frank, Waldo 1889-1967 ....DLB9

Frantz, Ralph Jules 1902- DLB4

Frayn, Michael 1933- DLB13, 14

Frederic, Harold 1856-1898 ....DLB12

Freeman, Douglas Southall 1886-1953 ....DLB17

Freeman, Mary Wilkins 1852-1930
....DLB12

Friedman, Bruce Jay 1930- DLB2

Friel, Brian 1929- DLB13

Friend, Krebs 1895?-1967? DLB4

Frothingham, Octavius Brooks 1822-1895
....DLB1

Fry, Christopher 1907- DLB13

Fuchs, Daniel 1909- DLB9

Fuller, Henry Blake 1857-1929 ....DLB12

Fuller, Roy 1912- DLB15

Fuller, Sarah Margaret, Marchesa
  D'Ossoli 1810-1850 ....DLB1

Furness, William Henry 1802-1896
....DLB1

G

Gaddis, William 1922- DLB2

Gaines, Ernest J. 1933- DLB2; Y80

Gale, Zona 1874-1938 ....DLB9

Gallico, Paul 1897-1976 ....DLB9

Galsworthy, John 1867-1933 ....DLB10

Galvin, Brendan 1938- DLB5

Gardam, Jane 1928- DLB14

Gardner, John 1933-1982 ....DLB2

Garland, Hamlin 1860-1940 ....DLB12

Garraty, John A. 1920- DLB17

Garrett, George 1929- DLB2, 5

Garrison, William Lloyd 1805-1879
....DLB1

Gass, William 1924- DLB2

Geddes, Virgil 1897- DLB4

Gelber, Jack 1932- DLB7

Gems, Pam 1925- DLB13

Genovese, Eugene D. 1930- DLB17

Gernsback, Hugo 1884-1967 ....DLB8

Gerrold, David 1944- DLB8

Geston, Mark S. 1946- DLB8

Gibson, William 1914- DLB7

Gillespie, A. Lincoln, Jr. 1895-1950
....DLB4

Gilliam, Florence DLB4

Gilliatt, Penelope 1932- DLB14

Gillott, Jacky 1939-1980 ....DLB14

Gilman, Caroline H. 1794-1888
....DLB3

Gilroy, Frank D. 1925- DLB7

Ginsberg, Allen 1926- DLB5, 16

Giovanni, Nikki 1943- DLB5

Gipson, Lawrence Henry 1880-1971 ....DLB17

Glanville, Brian 1931- DLB15

Glasgow, Ellen 1873-1945 ....DLB9, 12

Glaspell, Susan 1882-1948 ....DLB7, 9

Glass, Montague 1877-1934 ....DLB11

Glück, Louise 1943- DLB5

Godwin, Gail 1937- DLB6

Godwin, Parke 1816-1904 ....DLB3

Gogarty, Oliver St. John 1878-1957 ....DLB15

Gold, Herbert 1924- DLB2; Y81

Gold, Michael 1893-1967............DLB9

Goldberg, Dick 1947- DLB7

Golding, William 1911-............DLB15

Goodrich, Samuel Griswold 1793-1860
............DLB1

Gordon, Caroline 1895-1981
............DLB4, 9; Y81

Gordon, Giles 1940- DLB14

Gordon, Mary 1949- DLB6; Y81

Gordone, Charles 1925- DLB7

Goyen, William 1915- DLB2

Grau, Shirley Ann 1929- DLB2

Gray, Asa 1810-1888 ....DLB1

Gray, Simon 1936- DLB13

Grayson, William J. 1788-1863
............DLB3

Greeley, Horace 1811-1872............DLB3

Green, Henry 1905-1973............DLB15

Green, Julien 1900- DLB4

Green, Paul 1894-1981............DLB7, 9; Y81

Greene, Asa 1789-1838 ....DLB11

Greene, Graham 1904- DLB13, 15

Greenough, Horatio 1805-1852
............DLB1

Greenwood, Walter 1903-1974
............DLB10

Greer, Ben 1948- DLB6

Persse, Isabella Augusta,
    Lady Gregory 1852-1932............DLB10

Grey, Zane 1872-1939 ....DLB9

Griffiths, Trevor 1935- DLB13

Griswold, Rufus 1815-1857............DLB3

Gross, Milt 1895-1953............DLB11

Grubb, Davis 1919-1980............DLB6

Guare, John 1938- DLB7

Guest, Barbara 1920- DLB5

Guiterman, Arthur 1871-1943............DLB11

Gunn, James E. 1923- DLB8

Gunn, Neil M. 1891-1973............DLB15

Guthrie, A. B., Jr. 1901- DLB6

Guthrie, Ramon 1896-1973............DLB4

Gwynne, Erskine 1898-1948............DLB4

Gysin, Brion 1916- DLB16

H

H. D. (see Doolittle, Hilda)

Haines, John 1924- DLB5

Haldeman, Joe 1943- DLB8

Hale, Edward Everett 1822-1909
............DLB1

Hale, Nancy 1908- Y80

Hale, Sara Josepha (Buell) 1788-1879
............DLB1

Haliburton, Thomas Chandler 1796-1865
............DLB11

Hall, Donald 1928- DLB5

Halleck, Fitz-Greene 1790-1867
............DLB3

Halper, Albert 1904- DLB9

Hamilton, Cicely 1872-1952............DLB10

Hamilton, Edmond 1904-1977
............DLB8

Hamilton, Patrick 1904-1962............DLB10

Hamner, Earl 1923- DLB6

Hampton, Christopher 1946- DLB13

Handlin, Oscar 1915- DLB17

Hankin, St. John 1869-1909
............DLB10

Hanley, Clifford 1922- DLB14

Hannah, Barry 1942- DLB6

Hansberry, Lorraine 1930-1965
............DLB7

Hardwick, Elizabeth 1916- DLB6

Hare, David 1947- DLB13

Hargrove, Marion 1919- DLB11

Harness, Charles L. 1915- DLB8

Harris, George Washington 1814-1869
...................................DLB3, 11

Harris, Joel Chandler 1848-1908
....DLB11

Harris, Mark 1922- DLB2; Y80

Harrison, Harry 1925- DLB8

Hart, Albert Bushnell 1854-1943...............DLB17

Hart, Moss 1904-1961 ....DLB7

Harte, Bret 1836-1902............................DLB12

Hartley, L. P. 1895-1972 ....DLB15

Harwood, Ronald 1934- DLB13

Hawkes, John 1925- DLB2; Y80

Hawthorne, Nathaniel 1804-1864
....DLB1

Hay, John 1838-1905............................DLB12

Hayden, Robert 1913-1980 ....DLB5

Hayne, Paul Hamilton 1830-1886
....DLB3

Hearn, Lafcadio 1850-1904.......................DLB12

Heath, Catherine 1924- DLB14

Hecht, Anthony 1923- DLB5

Hecht, Ben 1894-1964............................DLB7, 9

Hecker, Isaac Thomas 1819-1888
....DLB1

Hedge, Frederic Henry 1805-1890
....DLB1

Heinlein, Robert A. 1907- DLB8

Heller, Joseph 1923- DLB2; Y80

Hellman, Lillian 1906- DLB7

Hemingway, Ernest 1899-1961
........................DLB4, 9; Y81; DS1

Henderson, Zenna 1917- DLB8

Henry, Robert Selph 1889-1970 ....DLB17

Hentz, Caroline Lee 1800-1856
....DLB3

Herbert, Alan Patrick 1890-1971
....DLB10

Herbert, Frank 1920- DLB8

Herbert, Henry William 1807-1858
....DLB3

Herbst, Josephine 1892-1969
....DLB9

Hergesheimer, Joseph 1880-1954
....DLB9

Herrick, Robert 1868-1938
....DLB9, 12

Herrmann, John 1900-1959
....DLB4

Hersey, John 1914- DLB6

Heyen, William 1940- DLB5

Heyward, Dorothy 1890-1961 and
     Heyward, DuBose 1885-1940..............DLB7

Heyward, DuBose 1885-1940
....DLB9

Higgins, Aidan 1927- DLB14

Higgins, George V. 1939- DLB2; Y81

Higginson, Thomas Wentworth 1822-1911
....DLB1

Hildreth, Richard 1807-1865 ....DLB1

Hill, Susan 1942- DLB14

Himes, Chester 1909- DLB2

Hoagland, Edward 1932- DLB6

Hochman, Sandra 1936- DLB5

Hodgman, Helen 1945- DLB14

Hoffenstein, Samuel 1890-1947
....DLB11

Hoffman, Charles Fenno 1806-1884
....DLB3

Hoffman, Daniel 1923- DLB5

Hofstadter, Richard 1916-1970.................DLB17

Hogan, Desmond 1950- DLB14

Holbrook, David 1923- DLB14

Hollander, John 1929- DLB5

Holley, Marietta 1836-1926.......................DLB11

Holmes, John Clellon 1926 ....DLB16

Holmes, Oliver Wendell 1809-1894
....DLB1

Home, William Douglas 1912- DLB13

Honig, Edwin 1919- DLB5

Hooper, Johnson Jones 1815-1862
....DLB3, 11

Horovitz, Israel 1939- DLB7

Hough, Emerson 1857-1923 ....DLB9

Houghton, Stanley 1881-1913....................DLB10

Housman, Laurence 1865-1959.................DLB10

Howard, Richard 1929- DLB5

Howard, Sidney 1891-1939.........................DLB7

Howe, E. W. 1853-1937.............................DLB12

Howe, Julia Ward 1819-1910......................DLB1

Howells, William Dean 1837-1920
....DLB12

Hoyem, Andrew 1935- DLB5

Hubbard, Kin 1868-1930 ....DLB11

Hughes, David 1930- DLB14

Hughes, Langston 1902-1967
....DLB4, 7

Hughes, Richard 1900-1976.......................DLB15

Hugo, Richard 1923-1982.............................DLB5

Humphrey, William 1924- DLB6

Humphreys, Emyr 1919- DLB15

Huncke, Herbert 1915- DLB16

Hunter, Jim 1939- DLB14

Hunter, N. C. 1908-1971..........................DLB10

I

Ignatow, David 1914- DLB5

Imbs, Bravig 1904-1946 ....DLB4

Inge, William 1913-1973 ....DLB7

Ingraham, Joseph Holt 1809-1860
....DLB3

Irving, John 1942- DLB6

Irving, Washington 1783-1859
....DLB3, 11

Isherwood, Christopher 1904- DLB15

J

Jackson, Shirley 1919-1965 ....DLB6

Jacob, Piers Anthony Dillingham (see Anthony, Piers)

Jacobson, Dan 1929- DLB14

James, Henry 1843-1916............................DLB12

Jameson, J. Franklin 1859-1937.................DLB17

Jellicoe, Ann 1927- DLB13

Jenkins, Robin 1912- DLB14

Jenkins, William Fitzgerald (see Leinster, Murray)

Jensen, Merrill 1905-1980......................DLB17

Jerome, Jerome K. 1859-1927
....DLB10

Jewett, Sarah Orne 1849-1909
....DLB12

Joans, Ted 1928- DLB16

Johnson, B. S. 1933-1973........................DLB14

Johnson, Diane 1934- Y80

Johnson, Pamela Hansford 1912- DLB15

Johnson, Samuel 1822-1882.........................DLB1

Johnston, Denis 1901- DLB10

Johnston, Jennifer 1930- DLB14

Johnston, Mary 1870-1936...........................DLB9

Jolas, Eugene 1894-1952 ....DLB4

Jones, Glyn 1905- DLB15

Jones, Gwyn 1907- DLB15

Jones, Henry Arthur 1851-1929
....DLB10

Jones, James 1921-1977............................DLB2

Jones, LeRoi (see Baraka, Amiri)

Jones, Lewis 1897-1939 ....DLB15

Jones, Major Joseph (see Thompson, William Tappan)

Jones, Preston 1936-1979..........................DLB7

Jong, Erica 1942- DLB2, 5

Josephson, Matthew 1899-1978

....DLB4

Josipovici, Gabriel 1940- DLB14

Joyce, James 1882-1941...........................DLB10

Judd, Sylvester 1813-1853........................DLB1

K

Kandel, Lenore 1932- DLB16

Kanin, Garson 1912- DLB7

Kantor, Mackinlay 1904-1977 ....DLB9

Kaufman, Bob 1925- DLB16

Kaufman, George S. 1889-1961 ....DLB7

Kavanagh, Patrick 1904-1967.....................DLB15

Keane, John B. 1928- DLB13

Keeffe, Barrie 1945- DLB13

Kelley, Edith Summers 1884-1956

....DLB9

Kelly, George 1887-1974............................DLB7

Kelly, Robert 1935- DLB5

Kennedy, John Pendleton 1795-1870

....DLB3

Kennedy, X. J. 1929- DLB5

Kerouac, Jack 1922-1969 ....DLB2, 16; DS3

Kerouac, Jan 1952- DLB16

Kerr, Orpheus C. (see Newell, Robert Henry)

Kesey, Ken 1935- DLB2, 16

Kiely, Benedict 1919- DLB15

Kiley, Jed 1889-1962 ....DLB4

King, Clarence 1842-1901 ....DLB12

King, Grace 1852-1932............................DLB12

King, Francis 1923- DLB15

King, Stephen 1947- Y80

Kingsley, Sidney 1906-...............................DLB7

Kingston, Maxine Hong 1940- Y80

Kinnell, Galway 1927- DLB5

Kirkland, Caroline 1801-1864......................DLB3

Kirkland, Joseph 1830-1893.......................DLB12

Kizer, Carolyn 1925- DLB5

Klappert, Peter 1942- DLB5

Klass, Philip (see Tenn, William)

Knickerbocker, Diedrick (see Irving, Washington)

Knight, Damon 1922- DLB8

Knoblock, Edward 1874-1945 ....DLB10

Knowles, John 1926- DLB6

Kober, Arthur 1900-1975...........................DLB11

Koch, Kenneth 1925- DLB5

Komroff, Manuel 1890-1974........................DLB4

Kopit, Arthur 1937- DLB7

Kops, Bernard 1926?................................DLB13

Kornbluth, C. M. 1923-1958 ....DLB8

Kosinski, Jerzy 1933- DLB2

Kraf, Elaine 1946- Y81

Kreymborg, Alfred 1883-1966.....................DLB4

Krim, Seymour 1922- DLB16

Kumin, Maxine 1925- DLB5

Kupferberg, Tuli 1923- DLB16

Kuttner, Henry 1915-1958..........................DLB8

Kyger, Joanne 1934- DLB16

L

La Farge, Oliver 1901-1963 ....DLB9

Lafferty, R. A. 1914- DLB8

Lamantia, Philip 1927-.............................DLB16

L'Amour, Louis 1908?- Y80

Landesman, Jay 1919-   and
      Landesman, Fran 1927- DLB16

Lane, Charles 1800-1870.............................DLB1

Laney, Al 1896- DLB4

Lanham, Edwin 1904-1979 ....DLB4

Lardner, Ring 1885-1933 ....DLB11

Laumer, Keith 1925- DLB8

Lavin, Mary 1912- DLB15

Lawrence, D. H. 1885-1930.................DLB10

Lea, Tom 1907- DLB6

Leary, Timothy 1920- DLB16

Lee, Don L. (see Haki R. Madhubuti)

Lee, Harper 1926- DLB6

Le Gallienne, Richard 1866-1947
................DLB4

Legare, Hugh Swinton 1797-1843
................DLB3

Legare, James M. 1823-1859.................DLB3

Le Guin, Ursula K. 1929- DLB8

Lehmann, Rosamond 1901- DLB15

Leiber, Fritz 1910- DLB8

Leinster, Murray 1896-1975.................DLB8

Leitch, Maurice 1933- DLB14

Leland, Charles G. 1824-1903.................DLB11

Leonard, Hugh 1926- DLB13

Lessing, Doris 1919- DLB15

Levertov, Denise 1923- DLB5

Levin, Meyer 1905-1981
................DLB9; Y81

Levine, Philip 1928- DLB5

Levy, Benn Wolfe 1900-1973
................Y81; DLB13

Lewis, C. Day (see Day Lewis, C.)

Lewis, C. S. 1898-1963.................DLB15

Lewis, Charles B. 1842-1924.................DLB11

Lewis, Henry Clay 1825-1850 ....DLB3

Lewis, Sinclair 1885-1951.................DLB9; DS1

Lewis, Wyndham 1882-1957.................DLB15

Lewisohn, Ludwig 1882-1955.................DLB4, 9

Liebling, A. J. 1904-1963.................DLB4

Linebarger, Paul Myron Anthony (see Smith, Cordwainer)

Link, Arthur S. 1920- DLB17

Lipton, Lawrence 1898-1975.................DLB16

Littlewood, Joan 1914- DLB13

Lively, Penelope 1933- DLB14

Livings, Henry 1929- DLB13

Llewellyn, Richard 1906- DLB15

Locke, David Ross 1833-1888 ....DLB11

Lockridge, Ross, Jr. 1914-1948 ....Y80

Lodge, David 1935- DLB14

Loeb, Harold 1891-1974 ....DLB4

Logan, John 1923- DLB5

London, Jack 1876-1916 ....DLB8, 12

Longfellow, Henry Wadsworth 1807-1882
................DLB1

Longfellow, Samuel 1819-1892
................DLB1

Longstreet, Augustus Baldwin 1790-1870
................DLB3, 11

Lonsdale, Frederick 1881-1954.................DLB10

Loos, Anita 1893-1981.................DLB11; Y81

Lopate, Phillip 1943- Y80

Lovingood, Sut (see Harris, George Washington)

Lowell, James Russell 1819-1891
................DLB1, 11

Lowell, Robert 1917-1977 ....DLB5

Lowenfels, Walter 1897-1976.................DLB4

Lowry, Malcolm 1909-1957 ....DLB15

Loy, Mina 1882-1966.................DLB4

Luke, Peter 1919- DLB13

Lurie, Alison 1926- DLB2

Lytle, Andrew 1902- DLB6

M

MacArthur, Charles 1895-1956.................DLB7

MacDonald, John D. 1916- DLB8

MacInnes, Colin 1914-1976.................DLB14

Macken, Walter 1915-1967.................DLB13

MacLean, Katherine Anne 1925- DLB8

MacLeish, Archibald 1892-1982 ....DLB4, 7

Macleod, Norman 1906- DLB4

MacNamara, Brinsley 1890-1963
....DLB10

MacNeice, Louis 1907-1963 ....DLB10

Madden, David 1933- DLB6

Madhubuti, Haki R. 1942- DLB5

Mailer, Norman 1923- DLB2, 16; Y80; DS3

Malamud, Bernard 1914- DLB2; Y80

Malone, Dumas 1892- DLB17

Malzberg, Barry N. 1939- DLB8

Mamet, David 1947- DLB7

Manfred, Frederick 1912- DLB6

Mangan, Sherry 1904-1961 ....DLB4

Mankowitz, Wolf 1924- DLB15

Mann, Horace 1796-1859............................DLB1

Mano, D. Keith 1942- DLB6

March, William 1893-1954 ....DLB9

Marcus, Frank 1928- DLB13

Markfield, Wallace 1926- DLB2

Marquand, John P. 1893-1960
....DLB9

Marquis, Don 1878-1937............................DLB11

Marsh, George Perkins 1801-1882
....DLB1

Marsh, James 1794-1842 ....DLB1

Marshall, Edward 1932- DLB16

Martin, Abe (see Hubbard, Kin)

Martyn, Edward 1859-1923........................DLB10

Masefield, John 1878-1967.........................DLB10

Matheson, Richard 1926- DLB8

Mathews, Cornelius 1817-1889 ....DLB3

Matthews, Jack 1925- DLB6

Matthews, William 1942- DLB5

Matthiessen, Peter 1927- DLB6

Maugham, W. Somerset 1874-1965
....DLB10

Mavor, Elizabeth 1927- DLB14

Mavor, Osborne Henry (see Bridie, James)

Maxwell, William 1908- Y80

Mayer, O. B. 1818-1891 ....DLB3

McAlmon, Robert 1896-1956 ....DLB4

McCaffrey, Anne 1926- DLB8

McCarthy, Cormac 1933- DLB6

McCarthy, Mary 1912- DLB2; Y81

McClure, Joanna 1930- DLB16

McClure, Michael 1932- DLB16

McCoy, Horace 1897-1955 ....DLB9

McCullers, Carson 1917-1967 ....DLB2, 7

McDonald, Forrest 1927- DLB17

McEwan, Ian 1948- DLB14

McGahern, John 1934- DLB14

McGinley, Phyllis 1905-1978 ....DLB11

McGuane, Thomas 1939- DLB2; Y80

McIlvanney, William 1936- DLB14

McKay, Claude 1889-1948 ....DLB4

McLaverty, Michael 1907- DLB15

McMurtry, Larry 1936- DLB2; Y80

McNally, Terrence 1939- DLB7

Mead, Taylor ?- DLB16

Medoff, Mark 1940- DLB7

Meek, Alexander Beaufort 1814-1865
....DLB3

Meinke, Peter 1932- DLB5

Meltzer, David 1937- DLB16

Melville, Herman 1819-1891 ....DLB3

Mencken, H. L. 1880-1956..........................DLB11

Mercer, David 1928-1980 ....DLB13

Meredith, William 1919- DLB5

Merrill, James 1926- DLB5

Merton, Thomas 1915-1968 ....Y81

Merwin, W. S. 1927- DLB5

Mewshaw, Michael 1943- Y80

Micheline, Jack 1929- DLB16

Michener, James A. 1907?- DLB6

Middleton, Stanley 1919- DLB14

Millar, Kenneth 1915- DLB2

Miller, Arthur 1915- DLB7

Miller, Caroline 1903- DLB9

Miller, Henry 1891-1980

....DLB4, 9; Y80

Miller, Jason 1939- DLB7

Miller, Perry 1905-1963...........................DLB17

Miller, Walter M., Jr. 1923- DLB8

Millhauser, Steven 1943- DLB2

Milne, A. A. 1882-1956 ....DLB10

Mitchell, Donald Grant 1822-1908

....DLB1

Mitchell, James Leslie 1901-1935..............DLB15

Mitchell, Julian 1935- DLB14

Mitchell, Langdon 1862-1935 ....DLB7

Mitchell, Margaret 1900-1949....................DLB9

Monkhouse, Allan 1858-1936 ....DLB10

Monsarrat, Nicholas 1910-1979 ....DLB15

Montgomery, John 1919- DLB16

Montgomery, Marion 1925- DLB6

Moody, William Vaughn 1869-1910

....DLB7

Moorcock, Michael 1939- DLB14

Moore, Catherine L. 1911- DLB8

Moore, George 1852-1933.........................DLB10

Moore, Ward 1903-1978 ....DLB8

Morgan, Berry 1919- DLB6

Morgan, Edmund S. 1916- DLB17

Morison, Samuel Eliot 1887-1976..............DLB17

Morley, Christopher 1890-1957

....DLB9

Morris, Richard B. 1904- DLB17

Morris, Willie 1934- Y80

Morris, Wright 1910- DLB2; Y81

Morrison, Toni 1931- DLB6; Y81

Mortimer, John 1923- DLB13

Mosley, Nicholas 1923- DLB14

Moss, Arthur 1889-1969............................DLB4

Moss, Howard 1922- DLB5

Motley, John Lothrop 1814-1877

....DLB1

Muir, Helen 1937- DLB14

Murdoch, Iris 1919- DLB14

Murfree, Mary N. 1850-1922....................DLB12

Murray, Gilbert 1866-1957........................DLB10

Myers, L. H. 1881-1944............................DLB15

N

Nabokov, Vladimir 1899-1977

....DLB2; Y80; DS3

Nasby, Petroleum Vesuvius (see Locke, David Ross)

Nash, Ogden 1902-1971............................DLB11

Nathan, Robert 1894- DLB9

Naughton, Bill 1910- DLB13

Neagoe, Peter 1881-1960 ....DLB4

Neal, John 1793-1876................................DLB1

Neal, Joseph C. 1807-1847.......................DLB11

Neihardt, John G. 1881-1973.....................DLB9

Nemerov, Howard 1920- DLB5, 6

Nevins, Allan 1890-1971 ....DLB17

Newby, P. H. 1918- DLB15

Newcomb, Charles King 1820-1894

....DLB1

Newell, Robert Henry 1836-1901

....DLB11

Newman, Frances 1883-1928 ....Y80

Nichols, Mary Sargeant (Neal)
Gove 1810-1884 ....DLB1

Nichols, Peter 1927- DLB13

Nichols, Roy F. 1896-1973 ....DLB17

Niebuhr, Reinhold 1892-1971....................DLB17

Niggli, Josefina 1910- Y80

Nims, John Frederick 1913- DLB5

Nin, Anaïs 1903-1977...............................DLB2, 4

Niven, Larry 1938- DLB8

Nolan, William F. 1928- DLB8

Noland, C. F. M. 1810?-1858.....................DLB11

Noone, John 1936- DLB14

Nordhoff, Charles 1887-1947

....DLB9

Norris, Charles G. 1881-1945 ....DLB9

Norris, Frank 1870-1902............................DLB12

Norse, Harold 1916- DLB16

Norton, Alice Mary (see Norton, Andre)

Norton, Andre 1912- DLB8

Norton, Andrews 1786-1853

....DLB1

Norton, Charles Eliot 1827-1908

....DLB1

Nourse, Alan E. 1928- DLB8

Nye, Bill 1850-1896 ....DLB11

Nye, Robert 1939- DLB14

O

Oates, Joyce Carol 1938- DLB2, 5; Y81

O'Brien, Edna 1932- DLB14

O'Brien, Kate 1897-1974............................DLB15

O'Brien, Tim 1946- Y80

O'Casey, Sean 1880-1964 ....DLB10

O'Connor, Flannery 1925-1964

....DLB2; Y80

Odets, Clifford 1906-1963............................DLB7

O'Faolain, Julia 1932- DLB14

O'Faolain, Sean 1900- DLB15

O'Hara, Frank 1926-1966 ....DLB5, 16

O'Hara, John 1905-1970.......................DLB9; DS2

O. Henry (see Porter, William S.)

Oliver, Chad 1928- DLB8

Oliver, Mary 1935- DLB5

Olsen, Tillie 1912 or 1913- Y80

Olson, Charles 1910-1970.......................DLB5, 16

O'Neill, Eugene 1888-1953 ....DLB7

Oppen, George 1908- DLB5

Oppenheimer, Joel 1930- DLB5

Orlovitz, Gil 1918-1973 ....DLB2, 5

Orlovsky, Peter 1933- DLB16

Orton, Joe 1933-1967 ....DLB13

Orwell, George 1903-1950 ....DLB15

Osborne, John 1929- DLB13

Owen, Guy 1925- DLB5

Owsley, Frank L. 1890-1956 ....DLB17

P

Pack, Robert 1929- DLB5

Padgett, Ron 1942- DLB5

Page, Thomas Nelson 1853-1922

....DLB12

Palfrey, John Gorham 1796-1881

....DLB1

Pangborn, Edgar 1909-1976 ....DLB8

Panshin, Alexei 1940- DLB8

Parker, Dorothy 1893-1967.......................DLB11

Parker, Theodore 1810-1860.......................DLB1

Parkman, Francis, Jr. 1823-1893

....DLB1

Parrington, Vernon L. 1871-1929 ....DLB17

Pastan, Linda 1932- DLB5

Patchen, Kenneth 1911-1972 ....DLB16

Patrick, John 1906- DLB7

Paul, Elliot 1891-1958.......................DLB4

Paulding, James Kirke 1778-1860

....DLB3

Peabody, Elizabeth Palmer 1804-1894

....DLB1

Peake, Mervyn.......................DLB15

Percy, Walker 1916- DLB2; Y80

Perelman, S. J. 1904-1979.......................DLB11

Perkoff, Stuart Z. 1930-1974.......................DLB16

Peterkin, Julia 1880-1961 ....DLB9

Phillips, David Graham 1867-1911
....DLB9, 12

Phillips, Jayne Anne 1952- Y80

Phillips, Stephen 1864-1915 ....DLB10

Phillips, Ulrich B. 1877-1934 ....DLB17

Phillpotts, Eden 1862-1960 ....DLB10

Phoenix, John (see Derby, George Horatio)

Pinckney, Josephine 1895-1957
....DLB6

Pinero, Arthur Wing 1855-1934
....DLB10

Pinter, Harold 1930- DLB13

Piper, H. Beam 1904-1964 ....DLB8

Plath, Sylvia 1932-1963 ....DLB5, 6

Plumly, Stanley 1939- DLB5

Plunkett, James 1920- DLB14

Plymell, Charles 1935- DLB16

Poe, Edgar Allan 1809-1849 ....DLB3

Pohl, Frederik 1919- DLB8

Poliakoff, Stephen 1952- DLB13

Poole, Ernest 1880-1950 ....DLB9

Porter, Eleanor H. 1868-1920
....DLB9

Porter, Katherine Anne 1890-1980
....DLB4, 9; Y80

Porter, William S. 1862-1910 ....DLB12

Porter, William T. 1809-1858 ....DLB3

Portis, Charles 1933- DLB6

Potter, David M. 1910-1971 ....DLB17

Pound, Ezra 1885-1972 ....DLB4

Powell, Anthony 1905- DLB15

Pownall, David 1938- DLB14

Powys, John Cowper 1872-1963 ....DLB15

Prescott, William Hickling 1796-1859
....DLB1

Price, Reynolds 1933- DLB2

Price, Richard 1949- Y81

Priest, Christopher 1943- DLB14

Priestley, J. B. 1894- DLB10

Pritchett, V. S. 1900- DLB15

Propper, Dan 1937- DLB16

Purdy, James 1923- DLB2

Putnam, George Palmer 1814-1872
....DLB3

Putnam, Samuel 1892-1950 ....DLB4

Puzo, Mario 1920- DLB6

Pym, Barbara 1913-1980 ....DLB14

Pynchon, Thomas 1937- DLB2

Q

Quad, M. (see Lewis, Charles B.)

Quin, Ann 1936-1973 ....DLB14

R

Rabe, David 1940- DLB7

Randall, James G. 1881-1953 ....DLB17

Raphael, Frederic 1931- DLB14

Rattigan, Terence 1911-1977 ....DLB13

Rawlings, Marjorie Kinnan 1896-1953
....DLB9

Ray, David 1932- DLB5

Read, Piers Paul 1941- DLB14

Reed, Ishmael 1938- DLB2, 5

Reed, Sampson 1800-1880 ....DLB1

Remington, Frederic 1861-1909 ....DLB12

Rexroth, Kenneth 1905-1982 ....DLB16

Reynolds, Mack 1917- DLB8

Rice, Elmer 1892-1967 ....DLB4, 7

Rich, Adrienne 1929- DLB5

Richardson, Jack 1935- DLB7

Richter, Conrad 1890-1968 ....DLB9

Riddell, John (see Ford, Corey)

Ripley, George 1802-1880.............................DLB1

Ritchie, Anna Mowatt 1819-1870
....DLB3

Robbins, Tom 1936- Y80

Roberts, Elizabeth Madox 1881-1941
....DLB9

Roberts, Kenneth 1885-1957.....................DLB9

Robinson, Lennox 1886-1958 ....DLB10

Roethke, Theodore 1908-1963 ....DLB5

Rogers, Will 1879-1935 ....DLB11

Roiphe, Anne 1935- Y80

Rölvaag, O. E. 1876-1931 ....DLB9

Root, Waverley 1903- DLB4

Rosenthal, M. L. 1917- DLB5

Ross, Leonard Q. (see Rosten, Leo)

Rossner, Judith 1935- DLB6

Rosten, Leo 1908- DLB11

Roth, Philip 1933- DLB2

Rothenberg, Jerome 1931- DLB5

Rubens, Bernice 1928- DLB14

Rudkin, David 1956- DLB13

Rumaker, Michael 1932- DLB16

Runyon, Damon 1880-1946 ....DLB11

Russ, Joanna 1937- DLB8

S

Saberhagen, Fred 1930- DLB8

Sackler, Howard 1929- DLB7

Sage, Robert 1899-1962............................DLB4

Salemson, Harold J. 1910- DLB4

Salinger, J. D. 1919- DLB2

Sanborn, Franklin Benjamin 1831-1917
....DLB1

Sandburg, Carl 1878-1967 ....DLB17

Sanders, Ed 1939- DLB16

Sandoz, Mari 1896-1966..............................DLB9

Sargent, Pamela 1948- DLB8

Saroyan, William 1908-1981
....DLB7, 9; Y81

Sarton, May 1912- Y81

Saunders, James 1925- DLB13

Sayers, Dorothy L. 1893-1957....................DLB10

Schlesinger, Arthur M., Jr. 1917- DLB17

Schmitz, James H. 1911- DLB8

Schulberg, Budd 1914- DLB6; Y81

Schuyler, James 1923- DLB5

Scott, Evelyn 1893-1963 ....DLB9

Scott, Paul 1920-1978 ....DLB14

Seabrook, William 1886-1945....................DLB4

Sedgwick, Catharine Maria 1789-1867
....DLB1

Selby, Hubert, Jr. 1928- DLB2

Settle, Mary Lee 1918- DLB6

Sexton, Anne 1928-1974 ....DLB5

Shaffer, Anthony 1926- DLB13

Shaffer, Peter 1926- DLB13

Shairp, Mordaunt 1887-1939......................DLB10

Sharpe, Tom 1928- DLB14

Shaw, Bernard 1856-1950.........................DLB10

Shaw, Henry Wheeler 1818-1885
....DLB11

Shaw, Irwin 1913- DLB6

Shaw, Robert 1927-1978 ....DLB13, 14

Sheckley, Robert 1928- DLB8

Sheed, Wilfred 1930- DLB6

Sheldon, Alice B. (see Tiptree, James, Jr.)

Sheldon, Edward 1886-1946 ....DLB7

Shepard, Sam 1943- DLB7

Sherriff, R. C. 1896-1975 ....DLB10

Sherwood, Robert 1896-1955....................DLB7

Shiels, George 1886-1949..........................DLB10

Shillaber, Benjamin Penhallow 1814-1890
....DLB1, 11

Shirer, William L. 1904- DLB4

Shulman, Max 1919- DLB11

Shute, Henry A. 1856-1943 ....DLB9

Shuttle, Penelope 1947- DLB14

Sigourney, Lydia Howard (Huntley) 1791-1865
....DLB1

Sillitoe, Alan 1928- DLB14

Silverberg, Robert 1935- DLB8

Simak, Clifford D. 1904- DLB8

Simms, William Gilmore 1806-1870
....DLB3

Simon, Neil 1927- DLB7

Simpson, Louis 1923- DLB5

Simpson, N. F. 1919- DLB13

Sinclair, Andrew 1935- DLB14

Sinclair, Upton 1878-1968.......................DLB9

Singer, Isaac Bashevis 1904- DLB6

Singmaster, Elsie 1879-1958.......................DLB9

Sissman, L. E. 1928-1976............................DLB5

Slavitt, David 1935- DLB5, 6

Slick, Sam (see Haliburton, Thomas Chandler)

Smith, Carol Sturm 1938- Y81

Smith, Charles Henry 1826-1903
....DLB11

Smith, Cordwainer 1913-1966 ....DLB8

Smith, Dave 1942- DLB5

Smith, Dodie 1896- DLB10

Smith, E. E. 1890-1965............................DLB8

Smith, Elizabeth Oakes (Prince) 1806-1893
....DLB1

Smith, George O. 1911- DLB8

Smith, H. Allen 1907-1976.......................DLB11

Smith, Seba 1792-1868............................DLB1, 11

Smith, William Jay 1918- DLB5

Snodgrass, W. D. 1926- DLB5

Snow, C. P. 1905-1980............................DLB15

Snyder, Gary 1930- DLB5, 16

Solano, Solita 1888-1975 ....DLB4

Solomon, Carl 1928- DLB16

Sontag, Susan 1933- DLB2

Sorrentino, Gilbert 1929- DLB5; Y80

Southern, Terry 1924- DLB2

Spark, Muriel 1918- DLB15

Sparks, Jared 1789-1866 ....DLB1

Spencer, Elizabeth 1921- DLB6

Spicer, Jack 1925-1965............................DLB5, 16

Spielberg, Peter 1929- Y81

Spinrad, Norman 1940- DLB8

Squibob (see Derby, George Horatio)

Stafford, Jean 1915-1979 ....DLB2

Stafford, William 1914- DLB5

Stallings, Laurence 1894-1968
....DLB7, 9

Stampp, Kenneth M. 1912- DLB17

Stanford, Ann 1916- DLB5

Stapledon, Olaf 1886-1950.......................DLB15

Starkweather, David 1935- DLB7

Steadman, Mark 1930- DLB6

Stearns, Harold E. 1891-1943....................DLB4

Steele, Max 1922- Y80

Stegner, Wallace 1909- DLB9

Stein, Gertrude 1874-1946.......................DLB4

Stein, Leo 1872-1947................................DLB4

Steinbeck, John 1902-1968
....DLB7, 9; DS2

Stephens, Ann 1813-1886 ....DLB3

Stewart, Donald Ogden 1894-1980
....DLB4, 11

Stewart, George R. 1895-1980 ....DLB8

Still, James 1906- DLB9

Stoddard, Richard Henry 1825-1903
....DLB3

Stoppard, Tom 1937- DLB13

Storey, Anthony 1928- DLB14

Storey, David 1933- DLB13, 14

Story, William Wetmore 1819-1895

....DLB1

Stowe, Harriet Beecher 1811-1896

....DLB1, 12

Strand, Mark 1934- DLB5

Streeter, Edward 1891-1976.................DLB11

Stribling, T. S. 1881-1965.................DLB9

Strother, David Hunter 1816-1888

....DLB3

Stuart, Jesse 1907- DLB9

Stubbs, Harry Clement (see Hal Clement)

Sturgeon, Theodore 1918- DLB8

Styron, William 1925- DLB2; Y80

Suckow, Ruth 1892-1960.....................DLB9

Suggs, Simon (see Hooper, Johnson Jones)

Sukenick, Ronald 1932- Y81

Sullivan, Frank 1892-1976..................DLB11

Summers, Hollis 1916- DLB6

Sutro, Alfred 1863-1933.....................DLB10

Swados, Harvey 1920-1972 ....DLB2

Swenson, May 1919- DLB5

Synge, John Millington 1871-1909

....DLB10

T

Tarkington, Booth 1869-1946.................DLB9

Tate, Allen 1896-1979........................DLB4

Tate, James 1943- DLB5

Taylor, Bayard 1825-1878....................DLB3

Taylor, Henry 1942- DLB5

Taylor, Peter 1917- Y81

Tenn, William 1919- DLB8

Tennant, Emma 1937- DLB14

Terhune, Albert Payson 1872-1942

....DLB9

Terry, Megan 1932-........................DLB7

Terson, Peter 1932- DLB13

Theroux, Paul 1941- DLB2

Thoma, Richard 1902- DLB4

Thomas, Dylan 1914-1953 ....DLB13

Thomas, Gwyn 1913-1981....................DLB15

Thomas, John 1900-1932....................DLB4

Thompson, John R. 1823-1873

....DLB3

Thompson, William Tappan 1812-1882

....DLB3, 11

Thomson, Mortimer 1831-1875

....DLB11

Thoreau, Henry David 1817-1862

....DLB1

Thorpe, Thomas Bangs 1815-1878

....DLB3, 11

Thurber, James 1894-1961 ....DLB4, 11

Ticknor, George 1791-1871 ....DLB1

Timrod, Henry 1828-1867 ....DLB3

Tiptree, James, Jr. 1915- DLB8

Titus, Edward William 1870-1952

....DLB4

Toklas, Alice B. 1877-1967 ....DLB4

Tolkien, J. R. R. 1892-1973..................DLB15

Tonks, Rosemary 1932- DLB14

Toole, John Kennedy 1937-1969

....Y81

Tracy, Honor 1913- DLB15

Traven, B. 1882? or 1890?-1969................DLB9

Travers, Ben 1886-1980 ....DLB10

Tremain, Rose 1943- DLB14

Trevor, William 1928- DLB14

Trocchi, Alexander 1925- DLB15

Troop, Elizabeth 1931- DLB14

Tucker, George 1775-1861 ....DLB3

Tucker, Nathaniel Beverley 1784-1851

....DLB3

Tuohy, Frank 1925- DLB14

Turner, Frederick Jackson 1861-1932........DLB17

Twain, Mark (see Clemens, Samuel Langhorne)

Tyler, Anne 1941- DLB6

U

Upchurch, Boyd B. (see Boyd, John)

Updike, John 1932- DLB2, 5; Y80; DS3

Upton, Charles 1948- DLB16

Ustinov, Peter 1921- DLB13

V

Vail, Laurence 1891-1968 ....DLB4

Vance, Jack 1916?- DLB8

van Druten, John 1901-1957......................DLB10

Van Duyn, Mona 1921- DLB5

van Itallie, Jean-Claude 1936- DLB7

Vane, Sutton 1888-1963 ....DLB10

Van Vechten, Carl 1880-1964
....DLB4, 9

van Vogt, A. E. 1912- DLB8

Varley, John 1947- Y81

Vega, Janine Pommy 1942- DLB16

Very, Jones 1813-1880 ....DLB1

Vidal, Gore 1925- DLB6

Viereck, Peter 1916- DLB5

Vonnegut, Kurt 1922-
.....................................DLB2, 8; Y80; DS3

W

Wagoner, David 1926- DLB5

Wain, John 1925- DLB15

Wakoski, Diane 1937- DLB5

Walcott, Derek 1930- Y81

Waldman, Anne 1945- DLB16

Walker, Alice 1944- DLB6

Wallant, Edward Lewis 1926-1962
....DLB2

Walsh, Ernest 1895-1926............................DLB4

Wambaugh, Joseph 1937- DLB6

Ward, Artemus (see Browne, Charles Farrar)

Ward, Douglas Turner 1930- DLB7

Ware, William 1797-1852............................DLB1

Warner, Rex 1905- DLB15

Warner, Susan B. 1819-1885 ....DLB3

Warren, Robert Penn 1905-
....DLB2; Y80

Wasson, David Atwood 1823-1887
....DLB1

Waterhouse, Keith 1929- DLB13

Watts, Alan 1915-1973 ....DLB16

Waugh, Auberon 1939- DLB14

Waugh, Evelyn 1903-1966..........................DLB15

Webb, Walter Prescott 1888-1963...............DLB17

Webster, Noah 1758-1843 ....DLB1

Weinbaum, Stanley Grauman 1902-1935
....DLB8

Weiss, John 1818-1879 ....DLB1

Weiss, Theodore 1916- DLB5

Welch, Lew 1926-1971?.............................DLB16

Weldon, Fay 1931- DLB14

Wells, Carolyn 1862-1942..........................DLB11

Welty, Eudora 1909- DLB2

Wescott, Glenway 1901- DLB4, 9

Wesker, Arnold 1932- DLB13

West, Anthony 1914- DLB15

West, Jessamyn 1902- DLB6

West, Nathanael 1903-1940
....DLB4, 9

West, Paul 1930- DLB14

Whalen, Philip 1923- DLB16

Wharton, Edith 1862-1937 ....DLB4, 9, 12

Wharton, William 1920s?- Y80

Wheeler, Charles Stearns 1816-1843
....DLB1

Wheeler, Monroe 1900- DLB4

Whetstone, Colonel Pete (see Noland, C. F. M.)

Whipple, Edwin Percy 1819-1886
....DLB1

Whitcher, Frances Miriam 1814-1852 ....DLB11

White, E. B. 1899- DLB11

White, William Allen 1868-1944
....DLB9

White, William Anthony Parker (see Boucher, Anthony)

Whitehead, James 1936- Y81

Whiting, John 1917-1963 ....DLB13

Whitlock, Brand 1869-1934 ....DLB12

Whitman, Sarah Helen (Power) 1803-1878
....DLB1

Whitman, Walt 1819-1892.........................DLB3

Whittemore, Reed 1919- DLB5

Whittier, John Greenleaf 1807-1892
....DLB1

Wieners, John 1934- DLB16

Wilbur, Richard 1921- DLB5

Wild, Peter 1940- DLB5

Wilde, Oscar 1854-1900 ....DLB10

Wilde, Richard Henry 1789-1847
....DLB3

Wilder, Thornton 1897-1975
....DLB4, 7, 9

Wiley, Bell Irvin 1906-1980 ....DLB17

Wilhelm, Kate 1928- DLB8

Willard, Nancy 1936- DLB5

Williams, C. K. 1936- DLB5

Williams, Emlyn 1905- DLB10

Williams, Heathcote 1941- DLB13

Williams, Joan 1928- DLB6

Williams, John A. 1925- DLB2

Williams, John E. 1922- DLB6

Williams, Jonathan 1929- DLB5

Williams, Raymond 1921- DLB14

Williams, T. Harry 1909-1979 ....DLB17

Williams, Tennessee 1911- DLB7

Williams, William Appleman 1921- DLB17

Williams, William Carlos 1883-1963
....DLB4, 16

Williams, Wirt 1921- DLB6

Williamson, Jack 1908- DLB8

Willingham, Calder, Jr. 1922- DLB2

Willis, Nathaniel Parker 1806-1867
....DLB3

Wilson, A. N. 1950- DLB14

Wilson, Angus 1913- DLB15

Wilson, Colin 1931- DLB14

Wilson, Harry Leon 1867-1939
....DLB9

Wilson, Lanford 1937- DLB7

Wilson, Margaret 1882-1973 ....DLB9

Windham, Donald 1920- DLB6

Wister, Owen 1860-1938 ....DLB9

Woiwode, Larry 1941- DLB6

Wolfe, Gene 1931- DLB8

Wolfe, Thomas 1900-1938
....DLB9; DS2

Wood, Charles 1932-1980 ....DLB13

Woodson, Carter G. 1875-1950 ....DLB17

Woodward, C. Vann 1908- DLB17

Woolson, Constance Fenimore 1840-1894
....DLB12

Worcester, Joseph Emerson 1784-1865
....DLB1

Wright, Harold Bell 1872-1944 ....DLB9

Wright, James 1927-1980 ....DLB5

Wright, Louis B. 1899- DLB17

Wright, Richard 1908-1960.........................DS2

Wylie, Elinor 1885-1928 ....DLB9

Wylie, Philip 1902-1971................................DLB9

Y

Yates, Richard 1926- DLB2; Y81

Yeats, William Butler 1865-1939 ....DLB10

Young, Stark 1881-1963................................DLB9

Z

Zangwill, Israel 1864-1926 ....DLB10

Zebrowski, George 1945- DLB8

Zelazny, Roger 1937- DLB8

Zimmer, Paul 1934- DLB5

Zindel, Paul 1936- DLB7

Zukofsky, Louis 1904-1978

    ....DLB5